D0142501

Relief

Meters	Feet
3,050	10,000
1,525	5,000
610	2,000
305	1,000
0	0
Below sea level	Below sea level

PACIFIC OCEAN

BROOKS RANGE
Mt. McKinley ▲
Fairbanks
Yukon River
Anchorage ◉
ALASKA RANGE
Kenai Peninsula
ALASKA
GULF OF ALASKA
Kodiak Island

CANAD

Cape Flattery
WASHINGTON
Seattle
Spokane
Olympia ◉
Tacoma
Mt. St. Helens ▲
▲ Mt. Rainier
Portland
CASCADE RANGE
Salem ◉
Eugene
OREGON

MONTANA
Great Falls
Helena ◉
Billings
WYOMING
IDAHO
Boise ◉
Idaho Falls
Snake River
Pocatello
Casper
North River

ROCKY MOUNTAINS

Cape Mendocino
CALIFORNIA
Reno
NEVADA
Carson City ◉
Lake Tahoe
Sacramento ◉
Great Salt Lake
Ogden
Salt Lake City ◉
Provo
Mt. Elbert ▲
UTAH
CO

DEATH VALLEY
Oakland
San Joachim R.
San Francisco
San Jose
Fresno
▲ Mt. Whitney
Las Vegas
Colorado River
Bakersfield
MOJAVE DESERT
Los Angeles
Anaheim
ARIZONA
Albuquerque
NEW
Long Beach
Santa Ana
San Diego
Phoenix ◉
Mesa
Gila River
La
Tucson
Rio

BAJA CALIFORNIA

HAWAII

KAUAI
OAHU
Honolulu ◉
MOLOKAI
LANAI
MAUI
PACIFIC OCEAN
Hilo ·
HAWAII

PUERTO RICO

San Juan
CARIBBEAN SEA

The African-American Odyssey

COMBINED VOLUME

Seventh Edition

The African-American Odyssey

Darlene Clark Hine
Northwestern University

William C. Hine
Formerly of South Carolina State University

Stanley Harrold
South Carolina State University

Pearson

330 Hudson Street, NY NY 10013

Portfolio Manager: Ed Parsons
Content Developers: Maggie Barbieri and John Reisbord
Content Developer Manager: Beth Jacobson
Portfolio Manager Assistant: Amandria Guadalupe
Content Producer: Rob DeGeorge
Field Marketer: Wendy Albert
Product Marketer: Nicholas Bolt
Content Producer Manager: Melissa Feimer
Digital Studio Course Producers: Heather Pagano
and Rich Barnes

Cover Credit: Jim West/Alamy
Cover Design: Lumina Datamatics, Inc.
Cartographer: International Mapping
Full Service Project Manager: Karen Berry/SPi Global
Compositor: SPi Global
Printer/Binder: LSC Harrisonburg
Cover Printer: LSC Harrisonburg

Library of Congress Cataloging-in-Publication Data

Names: Hine, Darlene Clark, author. | Hine, William C., author | Harrold, Stanley, author.
Title: The African-American Odyssey / Darlene Clark Hine (Northwestern University), William C. Hine (formerly of South Carolina State University), Stanley Harrold (South Carolina State University).
Description: Seventh edition. | Boston : Pearson, 2016. | Includes index.
Identifiers: LCCN 2016013318| ISBN 9780134483955 (combined volume) | ISBN 0134483952 (combined volume)
Subjects: LCSH: African Americans. | African Americans—History.
Classification: LCC E185 .H533 2016 | DDC 973/.0496073—dc23
LC record available at http://lccn.loc.gov/2016013318

2   18

Combined Volume:
ISBN 10: 0-13-449090-8
ISBN 13: 978-0-13-449090-8

Instructor's Review Copy,
Combined Volume:
ISBN 10: 0-13-448541-6
ISBN 13: 978-0-13-448541-6

Volume 1:
ISBN 10: 0-13-448951-9
ISBN 13: 978-0-13-448951-3

Instructor's Review Copy, Volume 1:
ISBN 10: 0-13-449095-9
ISBN 13: 978-0-13-449095-3

Volume 2:
ISBN 10: 0-13-449096-7
ISBN 13: 978-0-13-449096-0

Instructor's Review Copy, Volume 2:
ISBN 10: 0-13-449100-9
ISBN 13: 978-0-13-449100-4

Dedicated to
Charlyce Jones Owen

Brief Contents

Contents

17   African Americans and the 1920s, 1918–1929   481

Maps

Figures

Tables

Preface

"One ever feels his two-ness,—an American, a Negro; two souls, two thoughts, two unreconciled strivings; two warring ideals in one dark body." So wrote W. E. B. Du Bois in 1897. African-American history, Du Bois maintained, was the history of this double-consciousness. Black people have always been part of the American nation that they helped to build. But they have also been a nation unto themselves, with their own experiences, culture, and aspirations. African-American history cannot be understood except in the broader context of American history. Likewise, American history cannot be understood without African-American history.

Since Du Bois's time, our understanding of both African-American and American history has been complicated and enriched by a growing appreciation of the role of class and gender in shaping human societies. We are also increasingly aware of the complexity of racial experiences in American history. Even in times of great racial polarity, some white people have empathized with black people and some black people have identified with white interests.

It is in light of these insights that *The African-American Odyssey* tells the story of African Americans. That story begins in Africa, where the people who were to become African Americans began their long, turbulent, and difficult journey, a journey marked by sustained suffering as well as perseverance, bravery, and achievement. It includes the rich culture—at once splendidly distinctive and tightly intertwined with a broader American culture—that African Americans have nurtured throughout their history. And it includes the many-faceted quest for freedom in which African Americans have sought to counter white oppression and racism with the egalitarian spirit of the Declaration of Independence that American society professes to embody.

Nurtured by black historian Carter G. Woodson during the early decades of the twentieth century, African-American history has, since the 1950s, blossomed as a field of study. Books and articles have been written on almost every facet of black life. Yet *The African-American Odyssey* is the first comprehensive college textbook of the African-American experience. It draws on recent research to present black history in a clear and direct manner, within a broad social, cultural, and political framework. It also provides thorough coverage of African-American women as active shapers of that history.

The African-American Odyssey balances accounts of the actions of African-American leaders with investigations of the lives of ordinary men and women in black communities. This community focus makes this a history of a people rather than an account of a few extraordinary individuals. Yet the book does not neglect important political and religious leaders, entrepreneurs, and entertainers. It gives extensive coverage to African-American art, literature, and music.

Because African-American history starts in Africa, this book begins with an account of life on that continent to the sixteenth century when the forced migration of millions of Africans to the Americas began. The following two chapters present the struggle of black people to maintain their humanity during the slave trade and as slaves in North America during the long colonial period.

The coming of the American Revolution during the 1770s initiated a pattern of black struggle for racial justice in which periods of optimism alternated with times of repression. Several chapters analyze the building of black community institutions, the antislavery movement, the efforts of black people to make the Civil War a war for emancipation, their struggle for equal rights as citizens during Reconstruction, and the strong opposition to these efforts. There is also substantial coverage of African-American military service, from the War for Independence through American wars of the nineteenth, twentieth, and into the twenty-first centuries.

During the late nineteenth century and much of the twentieth century, racial segregation and racially motivated violence that relegated African Americans to second-class citizenship provoked despair, but also inspired resistance and commitment to change. Chapters on the late nineteenth and early twentieth centuries cover the Great Migration from the cotton fields of the South to the North and West, Black Nationalism, and the Harlem Renaissance. Chapters on the 1930s and 1940s—the beginning of a period of revolutionary change for African Americans—tell of the economic devastation and political turmoil caused by the Great Depression, the growing influence of black culture in America, the emergence of black internationalism, and the racial tensions caused by black participation in World War II.

The final chapters tell the story of African Americans in the closing decades of the twentieth century and the first decades of the twenty-first century. They portray the freedom struggles and legislative successes of the civil rights movement at its peak during the 1950s and 1960s and the electoral political victories of the Black Power movement during the more conservative 1970s and 1980s. Finally, there are discussions of black life during the past 15 years, with focus on the election, reelection, and achievements of Barack Obama, the first African-American president of the United States. The last chapter focuses on the national and international impact of contemporary black culture produced by the hip-hop generation as it wrestles with issues of social justice, economic opportunity, and human rights.

In all, *The African-American Odyssey* tells a compelling story of survival, struggle, and triumph over adversity. It will leave readers with an appreciation of the central place of black people and black culture in this country and a better understanding of both African-American and American history.

About *The African-American Odyssey, 7e*

The many special features and pedagogical tools integrated within *The African-American Odyssey* are designed to make the text accessible to students. They include a variety of tools to reinforce the narrative and help students grasp key issues.

Part-opening timelines thematically organize events in African-American history and provide a reference to the many noteworthy individuals discussed in the chapters.

Chronologies are included throughout the chapters to provide students with a snapshot of the temporal relationship among significant events.

Voices boxes provide students with first-person perspectives on key events in African-American history. Brief introductions and study questions help students analyze these primary source documents and relate them to the text.

Profile boxes provide biographical sketches that highlight the contributions and personalities of both prominent individuals and ordinary people, illuminating common experiences among African Americans at various times and places.

Connecting the Past essays examine important milestones of the African-American experience over time: evolution of the black church, the emergence of black autobiography, black migration, desegregation of the military, and black culture.

Marginal glossary terms throughout the chapter guide the student to key terms for review.

Key Supplements and Customer Support

Supplements for Instructors

Instructor's Resource Center. www.pearsonhighered.com/irc. This website provides instructors with additional text-specific resources that can be downloaded for classroom use. Resources include the Instructor's Manual, PowerPoint presentations, and the Test Bank. Register online for access to the resources for *The African-American Odyssey.*

Instructor's Manual. Available at the Instructor's Resource Center for download, www.pearsonhighered.com/irc, the Instructor's Manual contains detailed chapter overviews, including Revel interactive content in each chapter, activities, resources, and discussion questions.

Test Bank. Available at the Instructor's Resource Center for download, www.pearsonhighered.com/irc, the Test Bank contains more than 2,000 multiple choice, true-false, and essay test questions.

PowerPoint Presentations. Strong PowerPoint presentations make lectures more engaging for students. Available at the Instructor's Resource Center for download, www. pearsonhighered.com/irc, the PowerPoints contain chapter outlines and full-color images of maps and art.

MyTest Test Bank. Available at www.pearsonmytest.com, MyTest is a powerful assessment generation program that helps instructors easily create and print quizzes and exams. Questions and tests can be authored online, allowing instructors ultimate flexibility and the ability to efficiently manage assessments anytime, anywhere! Instructors can easily access existing questions and edit, create, and store using simple drag-and-drop and Word-like controls.

Chapter Revision Highlights

What's New in the Seventh Edition

Each chapter in the seventh edition of *The African-American Odyssey* has been revised and improved with updated scholarship.

Chapter 1

Several points in the "Birthplace of Humanity" and "West Africa" sections have been clarified. The bibliography has been updated.

Chapter 2

The "Slave Trade in Africa" and the "Origins of the Atlantic Slave Trade" sections have been combined. "The Ending of the Atlantic Slave Trade" section has been revised and expanded. The bibliography has been updated.

Chapter 3

The "Race and the Origins of Black Slavery" and "Bacon's Rebellion and American Slavery" sections have been revised to provide greater clarity. The Anthony Johnson profile has been revised and expanded. The bibliography has been updated.

Chapter 4

"The Impact of the Enlightenment" section has been revised to provide greater clarity. The Bibliography has been updated.

Chapter 5

The "First Black Schools," "Slave Uprisings," and "Missouri Compromise" sections have been revised to provide greater clarity. The bibliography has been updated.

Chapter 6

"The Character of Slavery and Slaves" section has been revised to provide greater clarity. The bibliography has been updated.

Chapter 7

The introductory section, which deals with demographics, has been expanded. The "Free African Americans in the Upper South" section has been revised to provide greater clarity. The bibliography has been updated.

Chapter 8

The "From Gabriel to Denmark Vesey "and "Slavery and Politics" sections have been revised to provide greater clarity. The bibliography has been updated.

Chapter 9

The bibliography has been updated.

Chapter 10

The section on the African American response to the 1850 Fugitive Slave Law has been revised. There is a new section on slaves who ran away and settled in communities and rural areas in Canada.

Chapter 11

A new section on the Louisiana Native Guards and their black and white officers has been added.

Chapter 12

There is additional information on class and status among African Americans after the Civil War. The section on the Black Codes has been revised and enhanced. There is a new "Voices" that features Jourdan Anderson's 1865 letter to his former master.

Chapter 13

The essay on voting rights and politics in the *Connecting the Past* section that follows the chapter has new a commentary on the importance of voting and President Barack Obama's 2015 statements on the Voting Rights Act.

Chapter 14

The section on convict leasing has been enhanced and new information on black women in the convict lease system has been included.

Chapter 15

There is a new section on the emergence of gospel music. There is also a new discussion on African American men and their role in the development and growth of horse racing.

Chapter 16

There is added information on W. E. B. Du Bois and *The Souls of Black Folk*.

Chapter 17

The discussion of scientific racism has been revised and expanded. There is a new section on Amy Jacques Garvey, the wife of Marcus Garvey, and a new section on Harlem radical and intellectual Hubert Harrison.

Chapter 18

The discussion of the Tuskegee Syphilis Experiment was revised. New books have been added to the bibliography. The timelines have been revised.

Chapter 19

The discussion of black culture and cultural leaders was expanded and updated. A profile of Duke Ellington was added, as was an expanded discussion of Paul Robeson. The chapter includes revised and updated timelines, with the insertion of more individuals. An updated discussion of Jesse Owens is also included.

Chapter 20

A new discussion of President Truman's Executive Order 9981 has been added. The discussion of Black women in the military during World War II was expanded. A longer discussion of the post–World War II violence that returning black servicemen encountered, especially in the South, has been added.

Part VI

The chapter includes a significantly updated timeline that covers The Black Revolution to the present.

Chapter 21

A new profile of Oklahoma activist Clara Luper has been added along with more discussion of the civil rights movement in Oklahoma. A discussion of twenty-first century efforts to reduce black voting has been added. The discussion of the Little Rock Nine has been expanded to include President Eisenhower's support for the parents and children, as well as the subsequent careers of the graduates, including Ernest Green.

Chapter 22

Updated discussion of the Nation of Islam and Malcolm X and Black Nationalism and the Black Panther Party is included. Additional coverage of Lorraine Hansberry and an updated bibliography are also included in this chapter.

Chapter 23

The order and presentation of Chapters 23 and 24 have been switched in this edition to keep the chronological flow of information about African-American history. This chapter includes an added discussion of President Obama's second-term election and several of the most consequential recent accomplishments of his presidency, including normalization of relations with Cuba and the Iran nuclear agreement on the international front. Details about the national epidemic of mass murders combined with the police shootings that inspired the formation of the Black Lives Matter Movement during the closing years of the Obama presidency have been provided. Additional analysis of recent USSC decision on education discrimination has been included. A new table on African American Participants in U.S. Presidential Inaugurations has been included.

Chapter 24

This chapter includes updated statistical charts relating to mass incarceration, black family composition, changes in the number of children living with single mothers, and health care statistics. Expanded discussion of cultural changes focuses on the lives and contribution of cultural activists from the civil rights movement era to the contemporary hip-hop era. Discussion of past and present women and men in the STEM professions has also been expanded. In addition, the chapter provides updated tables on HIV/AIDS health care crisis. A map on black unemployment rate is also now included.

Revel™

Educational technology designed for the way today's students read, think, and learn

When students are engaged deeply, they learn more effectively and perform better in their courses. This simple fact inspired the creation of Revel: an immersive learning experience designed for the way today's students read, think, and learn. Built in collaboration with educators and students nationwide, Revel is the newest, fully digital way to deliver respected Pearson content.

Revel enlivens course content with media interactives and assessments—integrated directly within the authors' narrative—that provide opportunities for students to read about and practice course material in tandem. This immersive educational technology boosts student engagement, which leads to better understanding of concepts and improved performance throughout the course.

Learn more about Revel
http://www.pearsonhighered.com/revel/

The African-American Odyssey, 7e, features many of the dynamic interactive elements that make Revel unique. In addition to the rich narrative content, *The African-American Odyssey* includes the following:

- Key Term Definitions: Key Terms appear in bold and include pop-up definitions inline that allow students to see the meaning of a word or phrase while reading the text, providing context.
- Photos with "Hotspots": Selected photos in the text include "hotspots" that students can click on to learn more about specific, important details related to the image.
- Interactive Maps: Interactive maps throughout the text include a pan/zoom feature and an additional feature that allows students to toggle on and off map details.

- Assessments: Multiple-choice end-of-module and end-of-chapter quizzes test student's knowledge of the chapter content, including dates, concepts, and major events.
- Additional Resources: This section includes Retracing the Odyssey, Recommended Reading and an Additional Bibliography, all of which are designed to assist students in further research of a particular topic covered in the chapter.
- Chapter Review: The Chapter Review—which contains a timeline, Key Term flashcards, an image gallery, video gallery and review questions—is laid out using interactive features that allow students to click on specific topics to learn more or test their knowledge about concepts covered in the chapter.
- Source Collections: An end-of-chapter source collection includes three to five documents relevant to the chapter content. Each document includes header notes, questions, and audio. Students can highlight and make notes on the documents.
- Journal Prompts: Revel is rich in opportunities for writing about topics and concepts and the Journal Prompts included are one way in which students can explore themes presented in the chapter. The ungraded Journal Prompts are included inline with content and can be shared with instructors.
- Shared Writing Prompts: These prompts provide peer-to-peer feedback in a discussion board, developing critical thinking skills and fostering collaboration among a specific class. These prompts appear between modules.
- Essay Prompts: These prompts appear in Pearson's Writing Space and can be assigned and graded by instructors.

Documents Available in Revel™

The following documents are available in the Revel version of *The African-American Odyssey*, Seventh Edition.

Chapter 1: Africa, CA. 6000 BCE–CA. 1600 CE
- Al-Umari Describes Mansa Musa of Mali (c. 1330)
- An Egyptian Hymn to the Nile (ca. 1350–1100 BCE)
- Leo Africanus Describes Timbuktu (c. 1500)

Chapter 2: Middle Passage, CA. 1450–1809
- Willem Bosman, from *A New and Accurate Description of the Coast of Guinea Divided into the Gold, the Slave, and the Ivory Coasts* (1705)
- Alexander Falconbridge, *A Slave Ship Surgeon Writes About the Slave Trade* (1788)
- Olaudah Equiano, The Middle Passage, 1788
- Venture Smith, A Slave Tells of His Capture in Africa in 1798
- Bryan Edwards Describes the "Maroon Negroes of the Island of Jamaica" (1807)
- A Defense of the Slave Trade

Chapter 3: Black People in Colonial North America, 1526–1763
- The Colony of Virginia Defines Slavery (1661–1705)
- Maryland Addresses the Status of Slaves, 1664
- William Berkeley, Declaration against the Proceedings of Nathaniel Bacon, 1676
- Runaway Notices From the *South Carolina Gazette* (1732 and 1737)
- James Oglethorpe, The Stono Rebellion, 1739
- Venture Smith, from *A Narrative of the Life and Adventures of Venture* (1798)
- An Architect Describes African American Music and Instruments in 1818

Chapter 4: Rising Expectations: African Americans and the Struggle for Independence, 1763–1783
- John Woolman, An Early Abolitionist Speaks Out Against Slavery, 1757
- Phillis Wheatley Publishes Her Poems, 1773
- Slaves Petition the Governor of Massachusetts to End Slavery (1774)
- Proclamation of Lord Dunmore (1775)
- Jefferson's "Original Rough Draft" of the Declaration of Independence (1776)
- Prince Hall, A Free African-American Petitions the Government for Emancipation of All Slaves, 1777
- Benjamin Banneker, *Letter to Thomas Jefferson* (1791)

Chapter 5: African Americans in the New Nation, 1783–1820
- John Wesley, "Thoughts Upon Slavery" (1774)
- Prince Hall, A Free African-American Petitions the Government for Emancipation of All Slaves, 1777

- Two Slaves Call on Connecticut to End Slavery (1779)
- Preamble of the Free African Society (1787)
- Congress Prohibits the Importation of Slaves (1807)
- Absalom Jones Delivers a Sermon on the Occasion of the Abolition of the International Slave Trade, 1808
- Missouri Enabling Act (March 1820)
- Thomas Jefferson, Thomas Jefferson Reacts to the "Missouri Question," 1820
- Richard Allen, "Address to the Free People of Colour of these United States" (1830)

Chapter 6: Life in the Cotton Kingdom, 1793–1861
- Thomas R. Dew's Defense of Slavery, 1832
- An Englishman Describes a Washington, D.C., Slave Pen (1835)
- Farm Journal Reports on the Care and Feeding of Slaves, (1836)
- Charles C. Jones, *The Religious Instruction of the Negroes in the United States* (1842)
- Henry Watson, A Slave Tells of His Sale at Auction, 1848
- Reverend A. T. Holmes, *The Duties of Christian Masters* (1851)
- A Catechism for Slaves (1854)
- Frederick Law Olmsted, from *A Journey in the Seaboard States* (1856)

Chapter 7: Free Black People in Antebellum America, 1820–1861
- Sarah Mapps Douglass Describes Her Encounter with Northern Racism (1837)
- Journal of Charlotte Forten, Free Woman of Color (Selections from 1854)
- John Gloucester, *The Founder of the First African Presbyterian Church of Philadelphia* (1857)
- Harriet Wilson, From *Our Nig; or, Sketches from the Life of a Free Black* (1859)

Chapter 8: Opposition to Slavery, 1730–1833
- Ben Woolfolk, *A Virginia Slave Explains Gabriel's Conspiracy* (1800)
- An Account of the Late Intended Insurrection Among a Portion of the Blacks of this City (1822)
- David Walker, *Walker's Appeal* (1829)
- Nat Turner, *The Confessions of Nat Turner*, 1831
- William Lloyd Garrison Demands an Immediate End to Slavery, 1831
- The American Anti-Slavery Society Declares Its Sentiments, 1833
- Runaway Slave Advertisements, 1838–1839

Chapter 9: Let Your Motto Be Resistance, 1833–1850
- Levi Coffin's Underground Railroad Station, 1826–1827
- An Abolitionist Lecturer's Instructions (1834)

Acknowledgments

In preparing *The African-American Odyssey*, we have benefited from the work of many scholars and the help of colleagues, librarians, friends, and family.

Special thanks are due to the following scholars for their substantial contributions to the development of this textbook: Hilary Mac Austin, *Chicago, Illinois*; Pero Dagbovie, *Michigan State University*; Brian W. Dippie, *University of Victoria*; Thomas Doughton, *Holy Cross College*; Jack Dodds, formerly of *Harper College*; W. Marvin Dulaney, *University of Texas at Arlington* ; Sherry DuPree, *Rosewood Heritage Foundation*; Peter Banner-Haley, *Colgate University*; Robert L. Harris, Jr., formerly of *Cornell University*; Wanda Hendricks, *University of South Carolina*; Rickey Hill, *Jackson State University*; William B. Hixson, formerly *Michigan State University*; Barbara Williams Jenkins, formerly of *South Carolina State University*; Earnestine Jenkins, *University of Memphis*; Hannibal Johnson, *Tulsa, Oklahoma*; Wilma King, *University of Missouri, Columbia*; Karen Kossie-Chernyshev, *Texas Southern University*; Frank C. Martin, *South Carolina State University*; Jacqueline McLeod, *Metropolitan State University of Denver*; Freddie Parker, *North Carolina Central University*; Christopher R. Reed, *Roosevelt University*; Linda Reed, *University of Houston*; Mark Stegmaier, *Cameron University*; Marshanda Smith, *Northwestern University*; Robert Stewart, *Trinity School, New York*; Larry Watson, *South Carolina State University*; ; Barbara Woods, formerly of *South Carolina State University*; Andrew Workman, *Mills College*; Deborah Wright, *Avery Research Center, College of Charleston*.

We are grateful to the reviewers through seven editions who devoted valuable time to reading and commenting on *The African-American Odyssey*. Their insightful suggestions greatly improved the quality of the text: Leslie Alexander, *The Ohio State University*; Carol Anderson, *University of Missouri, Columbia*; Abel A. Bartley, *Clemson University*; Jennifer L. Baszile, *Yale University*; James M. Beeby, *West Virginia Wesleyan College*; Richard A. Buckelew, *Bethune-Cookman College*; Claude A. Clegg, *Indiana University*; Gregory Conerly, *Cleveland State University*; Delia Cook, *University of Missouri at Kansas City*; Caroline Cox, *University of the Pacific*; Mary Ellen Curtin, *Southwest Texas State University*; Henry Vance Davis, *Ramapo College of NJ*; Roy F. Finkenbine, *Wayne State University*; Dr. Jessie Gaston, *California State University, Sacramento*; Abiodun Goke-Pariola, *Georgia Southern University*; Robert Gregg, *Richard Stockton College of NJ*; Keith Griffler, *University of Cincinnati*; John H. Haley, *University of North Carolina at Wilmington*; Robert V. Hanes, *Western Kentucky University*; Julia Robinson Harmon, *Western Michigan University*; Ebeneazer Hunter, *De Anza College*; Eric R. Jackson, *Northern Kentucky University*; Wali Rashash Kharif, *Tennessee Technological University*; John W. King, *Temple University*; Joseph Kinner, *Gallaudet University*; Lester C. Lamon, *Indiana University, South Bend*; Eric Love, *University of Colorado-Boulder*; John F. Marszalek, *Mississippi State University*; Kenneth Mason, *Santa Monica College*; Andrew T. Miller, *Union College*; Diane Batts Morrow, *University of Georgia*; Ruddy Pearson, *American College*; Walter Rucker, *University of Nebraska, Lincoln*; Josh Sides, *California State University, Northridge*; Manisha Sinha, *University of Massachusetts, Amherst*; John David Smith, *North Carolina State University at Raleigh*; Marshall Stevenson, *Ohio State University*; Betty Joe Wallace, *Austin Peay State University*; Matthew C. Whitaker, *Arizona State University*; Harry Williams, *Carleton College*; Vernon J. Williams, Jr., *Purdue University*; Leslie Wilson, *Montclair State University*; Andrew Workman, *Mills College*; Marilyn L. Yancy, *Virginia Union University*.

We wish to thank the following reviewers for their insightful comments in preparation for this seventh edition: Sele Adeyemi, *J Sargeant Reynolds Community College*; Daniel Anderson, *Cincinnati State Technical and Community College*; Latangela Crossfield, *Clark Atlanta University*; Linda Denkins, *Houston Community College District–Northeast*; Jennifer Harbour, *University of Nebraska–Omaha*; Misti Harper, *University of Arkansas*; Maurice Hobson, *University of Mississippi*; Lacey Hunter, *Rutgers University*; Ryan McMillen, *Santa Monica College*; Zacharia Nchinda, *University of Wisconsin–Milwaukee*; Charmayne Patterson, *Clark Atlanta University*; Matthew Schaffer, *Florence Darlington Technical College*; and Erica Woods-Warrior, *Hampton University*.

Leslie Alexander, *The Ohio State University*; Lila Ammons, *Howard University*; Beverly Bunch-Lyons, *Virginia Technical College*; Latangela Crossfield, *Clark Atlanta University*; Linda Denkins, *Houston Community College*; Lillie Edwards, *Drew University*; Jim Harper, *North Carolina Central University*; Dr. Maurice Hobson, *University of Mississippi*; Alyce Miller, *John Tyler Community College*; Zacharia Nchinda, *University of Wisconsin, Milwaukee*; Melinda Pash, *Fayetteville Technical Community College*; Charmayne Patterson, *Clark Atlanta University*; Matthew Schaffer, *Florence Darlington Technical College*; Denise Scifres, *City Colleges of Chicago, Center for Distance Learning*; Linda Tomlinson, *Fayetteville State University*; Angela Winand,

University of Illinois, Springfield; Erica Woods-Warrior, *Hampton University*.

Many librarians provided valuable help tracking down important material. They include Avery Daniels, Ruth Hodges, Doris Johnson, the late Barbara Keitt, Cathi Cooper Mack, Mary L. Smalls, Ashley Till, and Adrienne Webber, all of Miller F. Whittaker Library, South Carolina State University; James Brooks and Jo Cottingham of the interlibrary loan department, Cooper Library, University of South Carolina; and Allan Stokes of the South Carolina Library at the University of South Carolina. Dr. Marshanda Smith and Kathleen Thompson provided important documents and other source material.

Seleta Simpson Byrd of South Carolina State University; Marshanda Smith of Northwestern University provided valuable research assistance in the preparation of several content and statistical charts and timelines.

Each of us also enjoyed the support of family members, particularly Barbara A. Clark, Robbie D. Clark, Emily Harrold, Judy Harrold, Carol A. Hine, and Thomas D. Hine.

Finally, we gratefully acknowledge the essential help of the superb editorial and production team at Prentice Hall/Pearson Education: Charlyce Jones Owen, Publisher, whose vision got this project started and whose unwavering support saw it through to completion; Maureen Diana, Editorial Assistant; Rochelle Diogenes, Editor-in-Chief of Development; Maria Lange, Creative Design Director; Ann Marie McCarthy, Senior Managing Editor; and Emsal Hasan, Project Manager, who saw it efficiently through production; Marianne Gloriande, Manufacturing Buyer; Wendy Albert, Senior Marketing Manager; Beverly Fong, Program Manager; Tanisha Jackson, Program Editor at Ohlinger Publishing Services, for editorial and bibliographical suggestions and material contributions; and Ohlinger Publishing Services, who worked on this edition's development.

D.C.H.
W.C.H.
S.H.

About the Authors

Darlene Clark Hine

Darlene Clark Hine is Board of Trustees Professor of African American Studies and Professor of History at Northwestern University. She is a fellow of the American Academy of Arts and Sciences, as well as past president of the Organization of American Historians and of the Southern Historical Association. In 2014 President Barack Obama awarded Hine the National Humanities Medal (2013) for her work in African American and in Black Women's History. In 2015, the National Women's History Project honored Hine for her contributions to women's history. Hine received her BA at Roosevelt University in Chicago, and her MA and PhD from Kent State University, Kent, Ohio. Hine has taught at South Carolina State University and at Purdue University. She was a fellow at the Center for Advanced Study in the Behavioral Sciences at Stanford University and at the Radcliffe Institute for Advanced Studies at Harvard University. She is the author and/or coeditor of 20 books, most recently *The Black Chicago Renaissance* (Urbana: University of Illinois Press, 2012), *Black Europe and the African Diaspora* (Urbana: University of Illinois Press, 2010), coedited with Trica Danielle Keaton and Stephen Small; *Beyond Bondage: Free Women of Color in the Americas* (Urbana: University of Illinois Press, 2005), coedited with Barry Gaspar; and *The Harvard Guide to African-American History* (Cambridge, MA: Harvard University Press, 2000), coedited with Evelyn Brooks Higginbotham and Leon Litwack. She coedited a two-volume set with Earnestine Jenkins, *A Question of Manhood: A Reader in U.S. Black Men's History and Masculinity* (Bloomington: Indiana University Press, 1999, 2001); and with Jacqueline McLeod, *Crossing Boundaries: Comparative History of Black People in Diaspora* (Bloomington: Indiana University Press, 2000). With Kathleen Thompson she wrote *A Shining Thread of Hope: The History of Black Women in America* (New York: Broadway Books, 1998), and edited with Barry Gaspar *More Than Chattel: Black Women and Slavery in the Americas* (Bloomington: Indiana University Press, 1996). She won the Dartmouth Medal of the American Library Association for the reference volumes coedited with Elsa Barkley Brown and Rosalyn Terborg-Penn, *Black Women in America: An Historical Encyclopedia* (New York: Carlson Publishing, 1993). She is the author of *Black Women in White: Racial Conflict and Cooperation in the Nursing Profession, 1890–1950* (Bloomington: Indiana University Press, 1989). She continues to work on the forthcoming book project *The Black Professional Class: Physicians, Nurses, Lawyers, and the Origins of the Civil Rights Movement, 1890–1955*.

William C. Hine

Now retired, William C. Hine taught history for many years at South Carolina State University.

Stanley Harrold

Stanley Harrold is Professor of History at South Carolina State University and coeditor of *Southern Dissent*, a book series published by the University Press of Florida. Harrold has a BA from Allegheny College and an MA and PhD from Kent State University. He has received four National Endowment for the Humanities Fellowships, most recently in 2013–14. His books include *Gamaliel Bailey and Antislavery Union* (Kent State University Press, 1986), *The Abolitionists and the South* (University Press of Kentucky, 1995), *Antislavery Violence: Sectional, Racial, and Cultural Conflict in Antebellum America*, coedited with John R. McKivigan (University of Tennessee Press, 1999), *American Abolitionists* (Taylor & Francis, 2001), *Subversives: Antislavery Community in Washington, D.C., 1828–1865* (Louisiana State University Press, 2003), *The Rise of Aggressive Abolitionism: Addresses to the Slaves* (University Press of Kentucky, 2004), *Civil War and Reconstruction: A Documentary Reader* (Wiley, 2007), and *Border War: Fighting over Slavery before the Civil War* (University of North Carolina Press, 2010). In 2011, *Border War* won the Southern Historical Association's 2011 James A. Rawley Award and received an honorable mention for the Lincoln Prize. Harrold has recently published articles in *North & South*, *Organization of American Historian's Magazine of History*, and *Ohio Valley History*.

The African-American Odyssey

Part I
Becoming African American

Nzinga Mbemba

	to 1500	1500–1700

RELIGION

	to 1500
300s CE	Axum adopts Christianity
750s	Islam begins to take root in West Africa
1300s–1500s	Timbuktu flourishes as a center of Islamic learning
1324	Mansa Musa's pilgrimage to Mecca
c. 1500	Portuguese convert Kongo kings to Christianity

CULTURE

POEMS
ON
VARIOUS SUBJECTS,
RELIGIOUS AND MORAL.
BY
PHILLIS WHEATLEY,
NEGRO SERVANT to Mr. JOHN WHEATLEY,
of BOSTON, in NEW ENGLAND.

LONDON:
Printed for A. BELL, Bookseller, Aldgate; and Sold by
Messrs. COX and BERRY, King-Street, BOSTON.
MDCCLXXIII.

	1500–1700
1600s	African versions of English and French—Gullah, Geechee, and Creole—begin to develop
1600s–1700s	African-American folk culture appears among the slaves

POLITICS AND GOVERNMENT

	to 1500		1500–1700
c. 3150–30 BCE	Independence of Ancient Egypt	**1500s**	Rise of Akan states
1st century CE	Fall of Kush	**1607**	Jamestown founded
8th century CE	Decline of Axumite Empire in Ethiopia	**1696**	South Carolina Slave Code enacted
c. 750–1076	Empire of Ghana		
1230–1468	Empire of Mali		
1400s–1700s	Expansion of Benin		
1468–1571	Empire of Songhai		

SOCIETY AND ECONOMY

	to 1500		1500–1700
10th century	Islamic slave trade across the Sahara and Central Africa begins	**1502**	First mention of African slaves in the Americas
1472	First Portuguese slave traders in Benin	**1518**	Spanish *Asiento* begins
1481	First "slave factory" in Elmira on the Guinea coast	**c. 1520**	Sugar plantations begin in Brazil
		1619	First African slaves arrive in Jamestown
		1620s	Chesapeake tobacco plantations increase the demand for slaves
		1624	First black child reported born in British North America
		1660s	Chattel slavery emerges in the southern colonies

Phillis Wheatley

Richard Allen

James Forten

1700–1800	1800–1820	Noteworthy Individuals

1700–1800

c. 1738 First Great Awakening: George Whitefield preaches to African Americans

1780 Lemuel Haynes becomes first ordained black Congregationalist minister

1794 Mother Bethel Church founded in Philadelphia St. Thomas's Episcopal Church established under Absalom Jones

1740s Lucy Terry Prince publishes poetry

1760 Jupiter Hammon publishes a book of poetry

1773 Phillis Wheatley's Poems on Various Subjects

1775 Prince Hall founds first African-American Masonic Lodge

1780 First African-American mutual aid society founded in Newport, Rhode Island

1787 Free African Society founded in Philadelphia

1791–1795 Benjamin Banneker's Almanac published

1793 Philadelphia's Female Benevolent Society of St. Thomas founded

1773 Massachusetts African Americans petition the legislature for freedom

1775 Black militiamen fight at Lexington and Concord

1776 Declaration of Independence

1777 Vermont prohibits slavery

1782 Virginia allows manumission

1783 Massachusetts allows male black taxpayers to vote

1787 Congress bans slavery in the Northwest Territory

1789 U.S. Constitution includes the Three-Fifths clause

1793 Congress passes First Fugitive Slave Act

1712 New York City slave rebellion

1739 Stono slave revolt in South Carolina

1776–1783 100,000 slaves flee southern plantations

1781–1783 20,000 black Loyalists depart with British troops

1793 Eli Whitney invents the cotton gin

1800–1820

1808 Abyssinian Baptist Church organized in New York City

1811 African Presbyterian Church established in Philadelphia under Samuel E. Cornish

1816 African Methodist Episcopal Church established

1818 Mother Bethel Church establishes the Augustine School

1807 Britain abolishes the Atlantic slave trade

1808 U.S. abolishes the Atlantic slave trade

1820 Missouri Compromise First settlement of Liberia by African Americans

1800 Gabriel's rebellion in Charleston

1811 Deslondes's rebellion in Louisiana

Noteworthy Individuals

King Piankhy of Kush
(r. c. 750 BCE)

Sundiata of Mali
(c. 1235 CE)

Emperor Mansa Musa
of Mali (r. 1312–1337)

King Sunni Ali of Songhai
(r. 1464–1492)

King Askia Muhammed Toure
of Songhai (r. 1493–1528)

King Nzinga Mbemba (Afonso I)
of Kongo (r. 1506–1543)

Ayuba Suleiman Diallo
of Bondu (c. 1701–1773)

Jupiter Hammon
(1711–c. 1806)

Crispus Attucks
(1723–1770)

Benjamin Banneker
(1731–1806)

Prince Hall
(1735–1807)

Elizabeth Freeman
(1744–1811)

Absalom Jones
(1746–1818)

Olaudah Equiano
(c. 1745–1797)

James Forten
(1746–1818)

Peter Salem
(1750–1816)

Phillis Wheatley
(c. 1753–1784)

Richard Allen
(1760–1831)

Paul Cuffe
(1759–1817)

Daniel Coker
(1780–1846)

Gabriel
(d. 1800)

Charles Deslondes
(d. 1811)

Chapter 1

Africa

CA. 6000 BCE–CA. 1600 CE

West Africans were making iron tools long before Europeans arrived in Africa.

∨ Learning Objectives

After reading this chapter, you should be able to:

1.1 Recognize the geographical characteristics of Africa.

1.2 Be aware of current theories about where and how humans originated.

1.3 Understand why ancient African civilizations are important.

1.4 Appreciate West Africa's significance in regard to African-American history.

1.5 Analyze what Kongo and Angola had in common with West Africa.

1.6 Understand how legacies of West African society and culture influenced the way African Americans lived.

These [West African] nations think themselves the foremost men in the world, and nothing will persuade them to the contrary. They imagine that Africa is not only the greatest part of the world but also the happiest and most agreeable.

—Father Cavazzi, 1687

The ancestral homeland of most black Americans is West Africa. Other parts of Africa—Angola and East Africa—were caught up in the great Atlantic slave trade that carried Africans to the New World from the sixteenth to the nineteenth centuries. But West Africa was the center of the trade in human beings. Knowing the history of West Africa therefore is important for understanding the people who became the first African Americans.

That history, however, is best understood within the larger context of the history and geography of the African continent. This chapter begins, therefore, with a survey of the larger context. It emphasizes aspects of a broader African experience that shaped life in West Africa before the arrival of Europeans in that region. It then explores West Africa's unique heritage and the facets of its culture that have influenced the lives of African Americans from the Diaspora—the original forced dispersal of Africans from their homeland—to the present.

1.1 A Huge and Diverse Land

Recognize the geographical characteristics of Africa.

Africa, the second largest continent in the world (only Asia is larger), is bounded by the Mediterranean Sea to the north, the Atlantic Ocean to the west, and the Indian Ocean and the Red Sea to the east. A narrow strip of land in Africa's northeast corner connects it to the Arabian Peninsula and beyond that to Asia and Europe.

From north to south, Africa is divided into a succession of climatic zones (see Map 1-1). Except for a fertile strip along the Mediterranean coast and the agriculturally rich Nile River valley, most of the northern third of the continent consists of the Sahara Desert. For thousands of years, the Sahara limited contact between the rest of Africa—known as sub-Saharan Africa—and the Mediterranean coast, Europe, and Asia. South of the Sahara is a semidesert region known as the Sahel, and south of the Sahel is a huge grassland, or **savanna**, stretching from Ethiopia west to the Atlantic Ocean. Arab adventurers named this savanna *Bilad es Sudan*, meaning "land of the black people," and the term *Sudan* designates this entire region rather than simply the modern East African nations of Sudan and South Sudan. Much of the habitable part of West Africa falls within the savanna. The rest lies within the northern part of a **rain forest** that extends east from the Atlantic coast over most of the central part of the continent. Another region of savanna borders the rain forest to the south, followed by another desert—the Kalahari—and another coastal strip at the continent's southern extremity.

savanna

A flat, nearly treeless grassland typical of large portions of West Africa.

rain forest

A dense growth of tall trees characteristic of hot, wet regions.

Map 1-1 Africa: Climatic Regions and Early Sites

Africa is a large continent with several climatic zones. It is also the home of several early civilizations.

What impact did the variety of climatic zones have on the development of civilization in Africa?

1.2 The Birthplace of Humanity

Be aware of current theories about where and how humans originated.

Paleoanthropologists—scientists who study the evolution and prehistory of humans—have concluded that the origins of humanity lie in the savanna regions of Africa. All people today, in other words, are very likely descendants of beings who lived in Africa millions of years ago.

Fossil and genetic evidence suggests that both humans and the forest-dwelling great apes (gorillas and chimpanzees) descended from a common ancestor who lived in Africa about 5 to 10 million years ago. The African climate had grown, as forests gave way to savannas dotted with isolated patches of trees.

The earliest known *hominids* (the term designates the biological family to which humans belong) were the *Ardipithecines*, who emerged about 4.5 million years ago. These creatures walked upright but otherwise retained primitive characteristics and did not make stone tools. But by 3.4 million years ago, their descendants, known as *Australopithecus*, used primitive stone tools to butcher meat. By 2.4 million years ago, *Homo habilis*, the earliest creature designated as within the *homo* (human) lineage, had developed a larger brain than *Ardipithecus* or *Australopithecus*. *Homo habilis* (*habilis* means "tool using") used fire and built shelters with stone foundations. Like people in **hunting-and-gathering societies** today, members of the *Homo habilis* species probably lived in small bands in which women foraged for plant food and men hunted and scavenged for meat.

Recent discoveries suggest *Homo habilis* may have spread from Africa to the Caucasus region of southeastern Europe. A more advanced human, *Homo erectus*, spread even farther from Africa, reaching eastern Asia and Indonesia. *Homo erectus*, who emerged in Africa about 1.6 million years ago, may have been the first human to use rafts to cross large bodies of water and may have had a limited ability to speak.

Paleoanthropologists agree that modern humans, *Homo sapiens*, evolved from *Homo erectus*, but they disagree on how. According to a multiregional model, modern humans evolved throughout Africa, Asia, and Europe from ancestral regional populations of *Homo erectus* and archaic *Homo sapiens*. According to the currently stronger out-of-Africa model, modern humans emerged in Africa some 200,000 years ago and began migrating to the rest of the world about 100,000 years ago, eventually replacing all other existing hominid populations. Both of these models are consistent with recent genetic evidence, and both indicate that all living peoples are closely related. The "Mitochondrial Eve" hypothesis, which supports the out-of-Africa model, suggests that all modern humans are descended from a single African woman who lived in East Africa between 100,000 and 200,000 years ago. The multiregional model maintains that a continuous exchange of genetic material allowed archaic human populations in Africa, Asia, and Europe to evolve simultaneously into modern humans.

1.3 Ancient Civilizations and Old Arguments

Understand why ancient African civilizations are important.

The earliest civilization in Africa and one of the two earliest civilizations in world history is that of ancient Egypt (see Map 1-1), which emerged in the Nile River valley in the fourth millennium BCE. Mesopotamian civilization, the other of the two, emerged in the valleys of the Tigris and Euphrates rivers in southwest Asia. In both regions, civilization appeared at the end of a long process in which hunting and gathering gave way to agriculture. The settled village life that resulted from this transformation permitted society to become increasingly **hierarchical** and specialized. Similar processes gave rise to civilization in other parts of the world. Among them were the Indus valley in India around 2300 BCE, northeast China around 1500 BCE, and Mexico and Andean South America during the first millennium BCE.

The race of the ancient Egyptians and the nature and extent of their influence on later Western civilizations have long been a source of controversy. That controversy reflects more about the racial politics of recent history than it reveals about the Egyptians themselves, who did not regard themselves in ways related to modern racial terminology. It is not clear whether the Egyptians were an offshoot of their Mesopotamian contemporaries, whether they were part of a group of peoples whose origins were in both Africa and southwest Asia, or whether black Africans were ancestors of both the Egyptians and

hominids

The biological family to which humans belong.

hunting-and-gathering societies

Small societies dependent on hunting animals and collecting wild plants rather than on agriculture.

hierarchical

Refers to a social system based on class rank.

This drawing is based on a partial, fossilized skeleton discovered at Afar, Ethiopia, in 1994. The anthropologists who found the remains concluded in 2009 that the bones are those of a female *Ardipithecus ramidus* (nicknamed "Ardi") who lived 4.5 million years ago. Ardi fortifies existing evidence that human origins lay in Africa.

© '09 J.H. Matternes

Map 1-2 Ancient Egypt and Nubia

What does this map indicate about the relationship between ancient Egypt and Nubia/Kush?

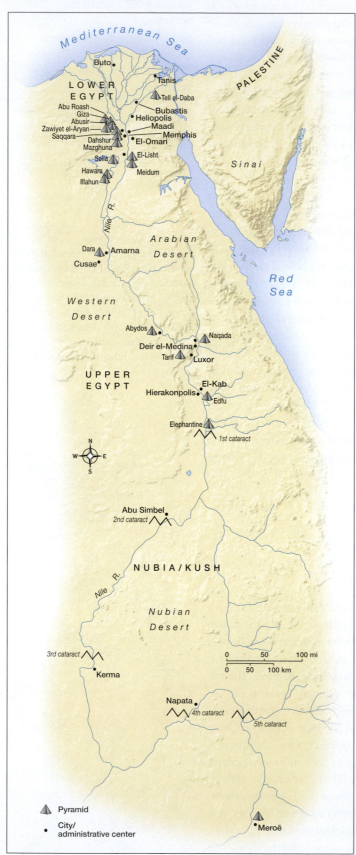

Mesopotamians. What is clear is that the ancient Egyptians exhibited a mixture of racial features and spoke a language related to the languages spoken by others in the fertile regions of North Africa and southwest Asia.

The argument over the Egyptians' race began in the nineteenth century when African Americans and white reformers sought to refute claims by racist pseudoscientists that people of African descent were inherently inferior to people of European descent. Unaware of the achievements of West African civilization, those who believed in human equality used evidence that the Egyptians were black to counter assertions that African Americans were incapable of civilization.

During the last two decades of the twentieth century, a more scholarly debate occurred between Afrocentricists and traditionalists. Afrocentricists regarded ancient Egypt as an essentially black civilization closely linked to other indigenous African civilizations to its south. They maintained not only that the Egyptians influenced later African civilizations but also that they had a decisive impact on the Mediterranean Sea region, including ancient Greece and Rome. Therefore, in regard to philosophy and science, black Egyptians originated Western civilization. In response, traditionalists claimed that modern racial categories have no relevance to the world of the ancient Egyptians. The ancient Greeks, they argued, developed the empirical method of inquiry and notions of individual freedom that characterize Western civilization. Not under debate, however, was Egypt's contribution to the spread of civilization throughout the Mediterranean region. No one doubts that in religion, commerce, and art, Egypt strongly influenced Greece and subsequent Western civilizations.

1.3.1 Egyptian Civilization

Egypt was, as the Greek historian Herodotus observed 2,500 years ago, the "gift of the Nile." This great river's gentle annual flooding regularly irrigated its banks, leaving behind deposits of fertile soil. This allowed Egyptians to cultivate wheat and barley and herd goats, sheep, pigs, and cattle in an otherwise desolate region. The Nile also provided the Egyptians with a transportation and communications artery, while their desert surroundings protected them from foreign invasion.

Egypt became a unified kingdom around 3150 BCE. Between 1550 and 1100 BCE, it expanded beyond the Nile valley, creating an empire over the coastal regions of southwest Asia as well as over Libya and Nubia in Africa. It was during this period that Egypt's kings began using the title *pharaoh*, which means "great house." After 1100 BCE, Egypt fell prey to a series of outside invaders. With the invasion of Alexander the Great's Macedonian army in 331 BCE, Egypt's ancient culture began a long decline under the pressure of Greek ideas and institutions (see Map 1-2). Finally the Roman Empire conquered Egypt in 30 BCE.

Before decline began, Egypt had resisted change for thousands of years. Pharaohs presided over a hierarchical society. Beneath them were classes of warriors, priests, merchants, artisans, and peasants. Scribes, who mastered Egypt's complex **hieroglyphic** writing system, staffed a large bureaucracy. Egyptian society was also **patrilineal** and **patriarchal**. Royal incest was customary, as pharaohs often chose one of their sisters to be their queen. Pharaohs also had numerous concubines, and other men could take additional wives if their first wife failed to produce children. Egyptian women nonetheless held a high status compared with women in much of the rest of the ancient world. They owned property independently of their husband, oversaw household slaves, controlled the education of their children, held public office, served as priests, and operated businesses. Several women became pharaoh, one of whom, Hatshepsut, reigned for 20 years (1478–1458 BCE).

A complex polytheistic religion shaped Egyptian life. Although there were many gods, two of the more important were the sun god Re (or Ra), who represented the immortality of the Egyptian state, and Osiris, the god of the Nile, who embodied each person's immortality. Personal immortality and the immortality of the state merged in the person of the pharaoh, as expressed in Egypt's elaborate royal tombs. The most dramatic examples of those tombs, the Great Pyramids at Giza near the modern city of Cairo, were built more than 4,500 years ago to protect the bodies of three Egyptian pharaohs, so that their souls might enter the life to come. The pyramids also symbolized the power of the Egyptian state. They endure as embodiments of the grandeur of Egyptian civilization.

1.3.2 Nubia, Kush, Meroë, and Axum

To the south of Egypt in the upper Nile valley, in what is today the nation of Sudan, lay the ancient region known as Nubia. As early as the fourth millennium BCE, the black people who lived there interacted with the Egyptians. Archaeological evidence suggests that grain production and the concept of monarchy may have arisen in Nubia and then spread north to Egypt. But Egypt always had a much larger population than Nubia's, and during the second millennium BCE, Egypt used its military power to make Nubia an Egyptian colony and control Nubian copper and gold mines. Egyptians also imported ivory, ebony, leopard pelts, and slaves from Nubia and required the sons of Nubian nobles to live in Egypt as hostages.

Egyptian religion, art, hieroglyphics, and political structure influenced Nubia. Then, with Egypt's decline during the first millennium BCE, the Nubians established

hieroglyphics

A writing system based on pictures or symbols.

patrilineal

Descent through the male line.

patriarchal

A society ruled by a senior man.

The ruined pyramids of Meroë on the banks of the upper Nile River are not as old as those at Giza in Egypt, and they differ from them stylistically. But they nonetheless attest to the cultural connections between Meroë and Egypt.

This giant stele at Axum demonstrates the spread of Egyptian architecture into what is today Ethiopia. Probably erected during the first century CE, before Axum converted to Christianity, this is the last of its kind still standing.

an independent kingdom known as Kush, which had its capital at Kerma on the Nile River. During the eighth century BCE, the Kushites took control of upper (meaning southern because the Nile flows from south to north) Egypt, and in about 750 BCE, the Kushite king Piankhy added lower Egypt to his realm. Piankhy became pharaoh and founded Egypt's twenty-fifth dynasty. This dynasty ruled Egypt until the Assyrians invaded from southwest Asia in 663 BCE and drove the Kushites out.

Kush itself remained independent for another thousand years. Its kings continued for centuries to call themselves pharaohs and had themselves buried in pyramid tombs covered with Egyptian hieroglyphics. They and the Kushite nobility practiced the Egyptian religion and spoke the Egyptian language. In 540 BCE a resurgent Egyptian army destroyed Kerma, and the Kushites moved their capital southward to Meroë. The new capital became wealthy from trade with East Africa, with regions to the west across Sudan, and with the Mediterranean world by way of the Nile River. The development of a smelting technology capable of exploiting local deposits of iron transformed the city into Africa's first industrial center.

Kush's wealth attracted powerful enemies, and in 23 BCE a Roman army invaded. But it was the decline of Rome and its Mediterranean economy that hurt Kush the most. As the Roman Empire grew weaker and poorer, its trade with Kush declined, and Kush, too, weakened. During the early fourth century CE, it fell to the neighboring Noba people, who in turn fell to the kingdom of Axum, whose warriors destroyed Meroë.

Located in what is today Ethiopia, Axum emerged as a nation during the first century BCE as **Semitic** people from the Arabian Peninsula settled among a local black population. By the time it absorbed Kush during the fourth century CE, Axum had become the first Christian state in sub-Saharan Africa. By the eighth century, shifting trade patterns, environmental depletion, and Islamic invaders combined to reduce Axum's power. It nevertheless retained its unique culture and its independence.

1.4 West Africa

Appreciate West Africa's significance in regard to African-American history.

For centuries, legend has held that the last kings of Kush retreated across the savanna to West Africa, bringing with them artistic motifs, the knowledge of iron making, and the concepts of divine kingship and centralized government. It is true that by the fifth century BCE, in what is today Libya, Garamantian **Berbers** introduced pyramids, Egyptian gods, and ancestor worship to the western Sahara region.

But no archaeological evidence supports the Kush kings legend. Instead, West African civilization had independent roots. Ironworking, for example, arose earlier in West Africa than it did at Meroë. Therefore the major early roots of African-American culture lay in the civilizations that emerged in West Africa during the first millennium BCE. This, however, does not mean that the Nile valley civilizations of Egypt and Kush did not contribute to the heritage of all Africans.

Like Africa as a whole, West Africa is physically, ethnically, and culturally diverse. Much of West Africa south of the Sahara Desert falls within the savanna that spans the continent from east to west. West and south of the savanna are extensive forests. They

Semitic

Refers to languages, such as Arabic and Hebrew, native to southwest Asia.

Berbers

A people native to North Africa and the Sahara Desert.

cover Senegambia (modern Senegal and Gambia), the southwest coast of West Africa, and the lands located along the coast of the Gulf of Guinea. These two environments—savanna and forest—were home to a variety of cultures and languages. Patterns of settlement in the region ranged from isolated homesteads and hamlets to villages, towns, and cities.

West Africans began cultivating crops and tending domesticated animals between 1000 BCE and 200 CE. Those who lived on the savanna usually adopted settled village life well before those who lived in the forests. The early farmers produced grains—millet, rice, and sorghum—while tending cattle and goats. By 500 BCE, beginning with the Nok people of the forest region, some West Africans produced iron tools and weapons.

From early times, the peoples of West Africa traded among themselves and with the peoples who lived across the Sahara Desert in North Africa. This extensive trade became an essential part of the region's economy and had two other important results. First, it served as the basis for the three great western Sudanese empires that successively dominated the region, from before 800 CE to the beginnings of the modern era. Second, it drew Arab merchants, and the Islamic religion, into the region.

1.4.1 Ancient Ghana

The first known kingdom in western Sudan was Ghana (see Map 1-3). Founded by the Soninke people in the area north of the modern republic of Ghana, the kingdom's origins are unclear. It may have arisen as early as the fourth century CE or as late as the

---

Map 1-3 The Empires of Ghana and Mali

The western Sudanese empires of Ghana and Mali helped shape West African culture. Ghana existed from as early as the fourth century CE to 1076. Mali dominated western Sudan from 1230 to 1468.

What does this map suggest concerning the historical relationship between ancient Ghana and Mali?

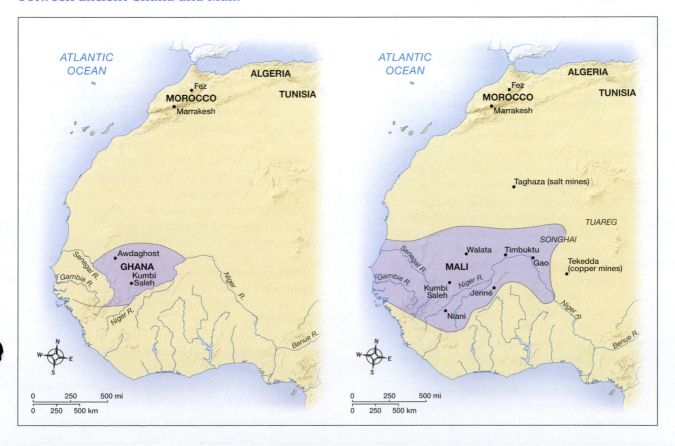

eighth century when Arab merchants began to praise its wealth. Its name comes from the Soninke word for "king," which Arab traders mistakenly applied to the entire kingdom.

Because they possessed superior iron weapons, the Soninke could dominate their neighbors and forge an empire through constant warfare. Ghana's boundaries reached into the Sahara Desert to its north and into modern Senegal to its south. But the empire's real power lay in commerce.

Ghana's kings had a reputation in Europe and southwest Asia as the richest of monarchs, and trade produced their wealth. Camels were key to this trade. Introduced into Africa from Asia during the first century CE, camels could carry heavy burdens over long distances while consuming small amounts of food and water. Reliance on them therefore allowed for a dramatic increase in trade across the Sahara between the western Sudan and coastal regions of North Africa.

Ghana traded in several commodities. From North Africa came silk, cotton, glass beads, horses, mirrors, dates, and especially salt—a scarce necessity in the torridly hot western Sudan. In return, Ghana exported pepper, slaves, and especially gold. The slaves were usually war captives, and the gold came from mines in the Wangara region to the southwest of Ghana. The Soninke did not mine the gold themselves. Instead, the kings of Ghana grew rich by taxing the gold as it passed through their lands.

Before the fifth century CE, Roman merchants and Berbers served as West Africa's chief partners in the trans-Sahara trade. As Roman power declined and Islam spread across North Africa during the seventh and eighth centuries, Arabs replaced the Romans. Arab merchants settled in Saleh, the Muslim part of Kumbi Saleh, Ghana's

Voices

Al Bakri Describes Kumbi Saleh and Ghana's Royal Court

Nothing remains of the documents compiled by Ghana's Islamic bureaucracy. As a result, accounts of the civilization are all based on the testimony of Arab or Berber visitors. In this passage, written in the eleventh century, Arab geographer Al Bakri describes the great wealth and power of the king of Ghana and suggests there were tensions between Islam and the indigenous religion of the Soninke.

The city of Ghana [Kumbi Saleh] consists of two towns lying in a plain. One of these towns is inhabited by Muslims. It is large and possesses twelve mosques. . . . There are imams and muezzins, and assistants as well as jurists and learned men. Around the town are wells of sweet water from which they drink and near which they grow vegetables. The town in which the king lives is six miles from the Muslim one, and bears the name Al Ghaba [the forest]. The land between the two towns is covered with houses. The houses of the inhabitants are of stone and acacia wood. The king has a palace and a number of dome-shaped dwellings, the whole surrounded by an enclosure like the defensive wall of a city. In the town where the king lives, and not far from the hall where he holds his court of justice, is a mosque where pray the Muslims who come on diplomatic missions. Around the king's town are domed buildings, woods, and copses where live the sorcerers of these people, the men in charge of the religious cult. . . .

Of the people who follow the king's religion, only he and his heir presumptive, who is the son of his sister, may wear sewn clothes. All the other people wear clothes of cotton, silk, or brocade, according to their means. All men shave their beards and women shave their heads. The king adorns himself like a woman, wearing necklaces and bracelets, and when he sits before the people he puts on a high cap decorated with gold and wrapped in a turban of fine cotton. The court of appeal [for grievances against officials] is held in a domed pavilion around which stand ten horses with gold embroidered trappings. Behind the king stand ten pages holding shields and swords decorated with gold, and on his right are the sons of the subordinate kings of his country, all wearing splendid garments and their hair mixed with gold. . . . When the people professing the same religion as the king approach him, they fall on their knees and sprinkle their heads with dust, for this is their way of showing him their respect. As for the Muslims, they greet him only by clapping their hands.

1. What does this passage indicate about life in ancient Ghana?

2. According to Al Bakri, in what ways do customs in Kumbi Saleh differ from customs in Arab lands?

SOURCE: Abu Abdullah al-Bakri (1068), *Book of Roads & Kingdoms.*

capital, which by the twelfth century had become an impressive city. There were stone houses and tombs and as many as 20,000 people. Visitors remarked on the splendor of Kumbi Saleh's royal court. Saleh had several mosques, and some Soninke converted to Islam, although it is unclear whether the royal family joined them. Muslims dominated the royal bureaucracy and introduced Arabic writing to the region.

Commercial and religious rivalries led to Ghana's decline during the twelfth century. The Almoravids, who were Islamic Berbers from what is today Morocco, had been Ghana's principal competitors for control of the trans-Sahara trade. In 992 Ghana's army captured Awdaghost, the Almoravid trade center northwest of Kumbi Saleh. Driven as much by religious fervor as by economic interest, the Almoravids retaliated in 1076 by conquering Ghana. The Soninke regained their independence in 1087, but a little over a century later the Sosso, a previously tributary people, destroyed Kumbi Saleh.

1.4.2 The Empire of Mali, 1230–1468

Following the defeat of Ghana by the Almoravids, western Sudanese peoples competed for political and economic power. This contest ended in 1235 when the Mandinka, under their legendary leader Sundiata (c. 1210–1260), defeated the Sosso at the Battle of Kirina. Sundiata then forged the Empire of Mali.

Mali, which means "where the emperor resides" in Mende, the language of the Mandinka, was socially, politically, and economically similar to Ghana. It was larger than Ghana, however—stretching 1,500 miles from the Atlantic coast to the region east of the Niger River. Its center lay farther south than Ghana's in a region of greater rainfall and more abundant crops. In addition, Sundiata gained control of the gold mines of Wangara, making his empire wealthier than Ghana had been. As a result, Mali's population grew to eight million.

Sundiata also had an important role in western Sudanese religion. According to legend, he wielded magical powers to defeat his enemies. This suggests he practiced an indigenous faith. But Sundiata was also a Muslim and helped make Mali—at least superficially—an Islamic state. As we have mentioned, West Africans had been converting to Islam since Arab traders arrived in the region centuries before. But many converts, like Sundiata, continued to practice indigenous religions. By his time, most merchants and bureaucrats were Muslims, and the empire's rulers gained stature among Arab states by converting to Islam.

To administer their vast empire at a time when communication was slow, Mali's rulers relied on personal and family ties with local chiefs. Commerce, bureaucracy, and scholarship also helped hold the empire together. Mali's most important city was Timbuktu, which had been established during the eleventh century beside the Niger River near the southern edge of the Sahara.

By the thirteenth century, Timbuktu had become a major hub for trade in gold, slaves, and salt. It attracted merchants from throughout the Mediterranean world and became a center of Islamic learning. The city had several mosques, 150 Islamic schools, a law school, and many book dealers. It supported a cosmopolitan community and impressed visitors with its religious and ethnic tolerance. Even though Mali enslaved war captives and traded slaves, an Arab traveler noted in 1352–1353, "the Negroes possess some admirable qualities. They are seldom unjust, and have a greater abhorrence of injustice than any other people."

Mali reached its peak during the reign of Mansa Musa (r. 1312–1337). One of the wealthiest rulers the world has known, Musa made himself and Mali famous when in 1324 he undertook a pilgrimage across Africa to the Islamic holy city of Mecca in Arabia. With an entourage of 60,000, a train of one hundred elephants, and a propensity for distributing huge amounts of gold to those who greeted him along the way, Musa amazed the Islamic world. After his death, however, Mali declined. In 1468, one of its formerly subject peoples, the Songhai, captured Timbuktu, and their leader, Sunni Ali, founded a new West African empire.

Mansa Musa, who ruled the West African Empire of Mali from 1312 to 1337, is portrayed at the bottom center of this portion of the fourteenth-century Catalan Atlas. Musa's crown, scepter, throne, and the huge gold nugget he displays symbolize his power and wealth.

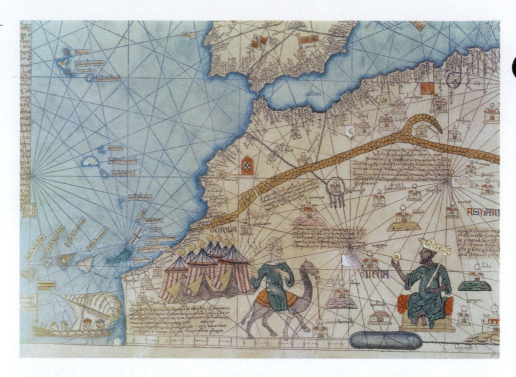

Map 1-4 West and Central Africa, c. 1500

This map shows the Empire of Songhai (1464–1591), the Kongo kingdom (c. 1400–1700), and the major kingdoms of the West African forest region.

How did the western Sudanese empires' geographical location make them susceptible to slave trading?

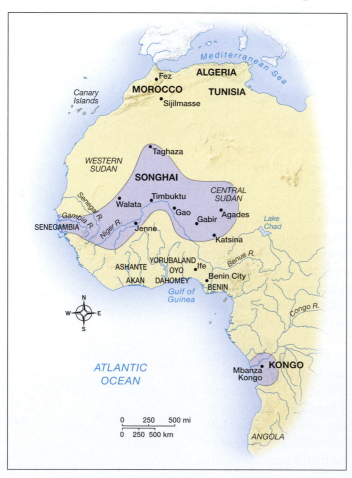

1.4.3 The Empire of Songhai, 1464–1591

Like the Mandinka and Soninke before them, the Songhai were great traders and warriors. The Songhai had seceded from Mali in 1375, and under Sunni Ali (r. 1464–1492), they built the last and largest of the western Sudanese empires (see Map 1-4). Sunni Ali required conquered peoples to pay tribute but otherwise let them control their own affairs. Nominally a Muslim, he—like Sundiata—was reputedly a great magician who derived power from the traditional spirits.

When Sunni Ali died by drowning, Askia Muhammad Toure led a successful revolt against Ali's son and made himself king of Songhai. The new king (r. 1492–1528) extended the empire north into the Sahara, west into Mali, and east to include the trading cities of Hausaland. He centralized the administration of the empire, replacing local chiefs with members of his family, substituting taxation for tribute, and establishing a bureaucracy to regulate trade.

A devout Muslim, Muhammad Toure used his power to spread the influence of Islam within the empire. During a pilgrimage to Mecca in 1497, he established diplomatic relations with Morocco and Egypt and recruited Muslim scholars to serve at the Sankore Mosque at Timbuktu. The mosque became a center for the study of theology, law, mathematics, and medicine. Despite these efforts, by the end of Muhammad Toure's reign—members of his family deposed the aging, senile, and blind ruler—Islamic culture remained weak in West Africa outside urban areas. Peasants, who made up 95 percent of the population, spoke a variety of languages, continued to practice indigenous religions, and remained loyal to their local chiefs.

Songhai reached its peak of influence under Askia Daud (r. 1549–1582). However, as the political balance of power in West Africa changed rapidly, Songhai failed to adapt, as it lacked new leaders as resourceful as Sunni Ali or Muhammad Toure. Since the 1430s, adventurers from the European country of Portugal had been establishing trading centers along the Guinea Coast, seeking gold and diverting it from the trans-Sahara trade. Their success threatened the Arab rulers of North Africa, Songhai's traditional partners in the trans-Sahara trade. In 1591 the king of Morocco, hoping to regain access to West African gold, sent an army of 4,000—mostly Spanish mercenaries armed with muskets and cannons—across the Sahara to attack Gao, Songhai's capital. Only 1,000 of the soldiers survived the grueling march to confront Songhai's elite cavalry at Tondibi on the approach to Gao. But the Songhai warriors' bows and lances were no match for firearms, and the mercenaries routed them. Its army destroyed, the Songhai empire fell apart. The center of Islamic scholarship in West Africa shifted east from Timbuktu to Hausaland. When the Moroccans soon departed, West Africa no longer had a government powerful enough to intervene when the Portuguese, other Europeans, and the African kingdoms of the Guinea Coast became more interested in trading for human beings than for gold.

1.4.4 The West African Forest Region

The area known as the forest region of West Africa extends 2,000 miles along the Atlantic coast from Senegambia in the northwest to the former kingdom of Benin (modern Cameroon) in the east. Among the early settlers of this region were the Nok, who, in what is today southern Nigeria, created around 500 BCE a culture noted for its ironworking technology and its terra-cotta sculptures. But significant migration into the forests began only after 1000 CE, as the western Sudanese climate became increasingly dry.

Some ancient customs survived in the forest region. They included dividing types of agricultural labor by gender and living in villages composed of extended families. But, because people migrated south from Sudan in small groups over an extended period, considerable cultural diversification occurred. A variety of languages, economies, political systems, and traditions came into existence. The region became a patchwork of diverse ethnic groups with related but various ways of life.

It took hard work to colonize a region covered with thick vegetation. In some portions of the forest, agriculture did not supplant hunting and gathering until the fifteenth and sixteenth centuries. In more open parts of the region, however, small kingdoms emerged centuries earlier. Benin City dates to the thirteenth century and Ife in Nigeria to the eleventh. Although none of these kingdoms ever grew as large as the empires of western Sudan, some became powerful. Their kings claimed semidivine status and sought to extend their power by conquering and assimilating neighboring peoples. Secrecy and elaborate ritual marked royal courts, which also became centers of patronage for art and religion. Meanwhile, nobility and urban elites worked to limit the kings' power.

The peoples of the forest region are of particular importance for African-American history because of the role they played in the Atlantic slave trade as both slave traders and victims. Space limitations permit only a survey of the most important of these peoples, beginning with those of Senegambia in the northwest.

The Nok people of what is today Nigeria produced terra-cotta sculptures like this one during the first millennium BCE. They also pioneered, between 500 and 450 BCE, iron smelting in West Africa.

The great mosque in the West African city of Jenne was first built during the fourteenth century CE. It demonstrates the importance of Islam in the region's trading centers.

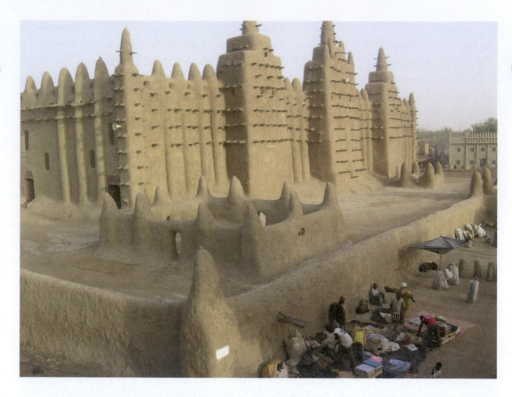

This carved wooden ceremonial offering bowl is typical of a Yoruba art form that has persisted for centuries. It reflects religious practices as well as traditional hairstyle and dress.

The inhabitants of Senegambia shared a common history and spoke closely related languages, but they were not politically united. Parts of the region had been incorporated within the empires of Ghana and Mali and had been exposed to Islamic influences. Senegambian society was strictly hierarchical, with royalty at the top and slaves at the bottom. Most people were farmers, growing rice, millet, sorghum, plantains, beans, and bananas. They supplemented their diet with fish, oysters, rabbits, and monkeys.

Southeast of Senegambia, the Akan states emerged during the sixteenth century as the gold trade provided local rulers with the wealth they needed to clear forests and initiate agricultural economies. The rulers used gold from mines they controlled to purchase slaves who did the difficult work of cutting trees and burning refuse. The rulers then distributed the cleared fields to settlers. In return the settlers gave the rulers a portion of their produce and provided services. When Europeans arrived, the rulers used gold to purchase guns. The guns in turn allowed the Akan states to expand. During the late seventeenth century, one of them, the Ashantee, created a well-organized and densely populated kingdom, comparable in size to the modern country of Ghana. By the eighteenth century, this kingdom dominated the central portion of the forest region and used its army to capture slaves for sale to European traders.

To the east of the Akan states (in modern Benin and western Nigeria) lived the people of the Yoruba culture. They gained ascendancy in the area as early as 1000 CE by trading kola nuts and cloth to the peoples of the western Sudan. The artisans of the Yoruba city of Ife gained renown for their fine bronze, brass, and terra-cotta sculptures. Ife was also notable for the prominent role women played in commerce. During the seventeenth century, the Oyo people, employing a well-trained cavalry, imposed political unity on part of the Yoruba region. They, like the Ashantee, became extensively involved in the Atlantic slave trade.

West of the Oyo were the Fon people, who formed the Kingdom of Dahomey, which rivaled Oyo as a center for the slave trade. The king of Dahomey was an absolute monarch who, to ensure the loyalty of potential rivals, took thousands of wives for himself from leading families.

At the eastern end of the forest region was the Kingdom of Benin, which controlled much of what is today southern Nigeria. The people of this kingdom shared a common heritage with the Yoruba, who played a role in the kingdom's formation during the thirteenth century. Throughout Benin's history, the Obas (kings), who claimed divine status, struggled for power with the kingdom's hereditary nobility.

After a reform of its army during the fifteenth century, Benin expanded to the Niger River in the east, to the Gulf of Guinea to the south, and into Yoruba country to the west. The kingdom peaked during the late sixteenth century. European visitors noted the size and sophistication of its capital, Benin City. There skilled artisans produced the fine bronze sculptures for which the region is still known. The city's wealthy class dined on beef, mutton, chicken, and yams. Its streets, unlike those of European cities of the time, had no beggars.

Benin remained little influenced by Islam or Christianity, but like other coastal kingdoms, it joined in the Atlantic slave trade. Beginning in the late fifteenth century, the Oba allowed Europeans to trade for gold, pepper, ivory, and slaves. Initially, the Oba forbade the sale of his subjects, but his large army—the first in the forest region to have European firearms—captured others for the trade as it conquered neighboring regions. By the seventeenth century, Benin's prosperity depended on the slave trade. As the kingdom declined during the eighteenth century, it began to sell its own people to European slave traders.

To Benin's east was Igboland, a densely populated but politically weak region along the Niger River. The Igbo people lived in one of the stateless societies common in West Africa. In these societies, families rather than central authorities ruled. Village elders provided local government, and life centered on family homesteads. Igboland had long exported fieldworkers and skilled artisans to Benin and other kingdoms. When Europeans arrived, they expanded this trade, which brought many Igbos to the Americas (see Map 1-5).

Map 1-5 Trans-Saharan Trade Routes

Ancient trade routes connected sub-Saharan West Africa to the Mediterranean coast. Among the commodities carried southward were silk, cotton, horses, and salt. Among those carried northward were gold, ivory, pepper, and slaves.

What was the significance of the trans-Sahara trade in West African history?

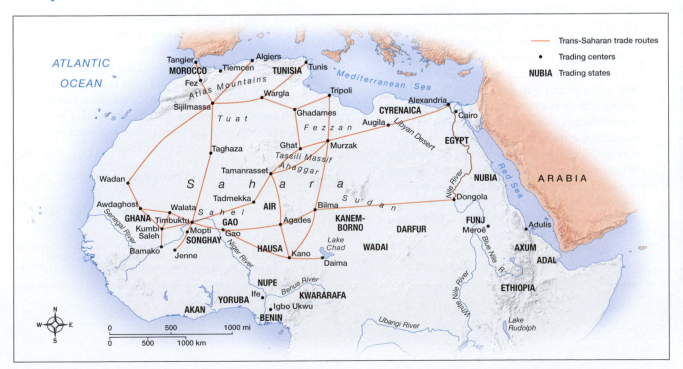

Voices

A Description of Benin City

Benin was a port city in southern Nigeria, where trade with European nations flourished during the 16th and 17th centuries. This description of Benin City, published in 1760, is based on two separate accounts by Dutch visitors during the 17th century. It indicates how impressive the city was.

Benin, the capital, is a city of great extent. *Artus of Dantzic* calls it eleven miles in circumference, containing 100,000 inhabitants. You enter it by a large street, which, according to the same writer, is eight times wider than any street in *Holland*. This we apprehend to be a sort of avenue or great road leading to the city, since other travellers, who have measured it, call it eight leagues in length. It passes through the city, dividing it into two equal parts, and is itself cut by innumerable other streets that traverse it.

For the whole eight leagues the houses stand so close on each side the road, that it may well be mistaken for a street. After advancing twelve miles, you come to a large gate, which divides the city from the suburbs. The gate is of wood; but it is defended by a strong bastion of mud and earth, surrounded by a deep ditch forty feet wide. Here a guard is constantly kept to receive the tolls, duties, and imposts, upon merchandize. All the streets of the city are strait, long, and broad, adorned with a variety of shops filled with *European* merchandize, as well as the commodities of the country.

Formerly the houses stood close, the whole street appearing like one complete building, every part of it in a manner surcharged with inhabitants; at present it is broke by numberless chasms and ruins, that seem to presage its short duration. As the country affords no stone, all the houses are built with mud and clay, covered with reeds, straw, or clay, with an elegance that is astonishing. Nor is the architecture of the principal buildings altogether contemptible; many of them being not unworthy of a more civilized people. Only natives are permitted to live here; several of whom are wealthy, and trade to a great extent. Here the women are employed in keeping the streets neat and clean; in which respect the inhabitants of Benin are not exceeded by the *Hollanders* themselves.

A principal part of the city is taken up by the royal palace, which is rather prodigious in its dimensions than commodious or elegant in the contrivance. The eye is first met by a long gallery, sustained by fifty-eight strong planks, rough and unpolished, above twelve feet in height, and three in circumference. Passing this gallery, you come to a high mud wall, which hath three gates. That in the center is decorated at the top with a wooden turret of a spiral form, 79 feet high. Upon the very extremity of this cone is fixed a large copper snake, well cast, carved, and bearing marks of a proficiency in the arts. Within the gate you are presented with an area of fine turf, a quarter of a mile in length, and near as broad; at the further end of which is another gallery in the same taste as the former, only that the pilasters, which sustain it, are ornamented with human figures, and many of them cut out in that form, but in a gross and awkward manner. Behind a canvas curtain are shewn four heads cast in brass, neither resembling the human or brute figure, each of them supported by a large elephant's tooth, the king's property.

Passing through this gallery and another gate, you have the king's dwelling-house in front; an appearance that by no means dazzles with its pomp and magnificence. Here is another snake over the porch, done probably by the same artist as that on the turret. In the first apartment is the king's audience-chamber, where, in presence of the chief nobility or officers of the court, he receives foreign ministers and ambassadors. His throne is of ivory, under a canopy of rich silk. This chamber of audience would likewise seem to be the repository of his majesty's merchandize (for here the king, as well as his subjects, is a trader), it being filled with loads of elephants teeth, and other commodities, lying in a confusion which plainly indicates they are not intended for ornament. The room is hung with fine tapestry, and the floor covered with mats and carpets of an indifferent manufacture. . . .

1. According to the Dutch visitors, how does Benin City compare to Holland?

2. What seems to impress the Dutch visitors most about Benin City?

SOURCE: [John Swinton, et al. eds.], *The Modern Part of an Universal History: From the Earliest Account of Time Compiled from Original Authors* . . . 43 vols. (London: S. Richardson and others, 1760), 16:360–61.

Profile

Nzinga Mbemba (Afonso I) of Kongo

DON ALVARE RIX CON

Nzinga Mbemba, baptized Dom Afonso, ruled as the Mani Kongo (r. c. 1506–1543 CE). His life illustrates the complex and tragic relationships between the African coastal kingdoms and Europeans in search of power, cultural hegemony, and wealth.

Mbemba was a son of Nzinga Knuwu, who, as Mani Kongo, established diplomatic ties with Portugal. Portuguese vessels had first reached Kongo in 1482, and in 1491 the Portuguese king sent a formal mission to Mbanza Kongo (the City of Kongo). Amid considerable ceremony, Knuwu converted to Christianity because conversion gave him access to Portuguese musketeers he needed to put down a rebellion. Mbemba served as his father's general in the ensuing successful campaign.

By 1495, internal politics and Knuwu's inability to accept Christian monogamy had led him to renounce his baptism and banish Christians—both Portuguese and Kongolese—from Mbanza Kongo. Mbemba, who was a sincere Christian, became their champion in opposition to a traditionalist faction headed by his half-brother Mpanza. Following Knuwu's death in 1506, the two princes fought over the succession. Mbemba's victory led to his coronation as Afonso and the execution of Mpanza.

By then Mbemba had learned to speak, read, and write Portuguese. He gained at least outward respect from the Portuguese monarchy as a ruler and Christian missionary. Soon hundreds of Portuguese advisers, priests, artisans, teachers, and settlers lived in Mbanza Kongo and its environs. In 1516 a Portuguese priest described Mbemba as "not . . . a man but an angel sent by the Lord to this kingdom to convert it. . . . Better than we, he knows the Prophets and the Gospel of Our Lord Jesus Christ." Mbemba destroyed images and shrines associated with Kongo's traditional religion, replaced them with crucifixes and images of saints, built Christian churches in Mbanza Kongo, and had some of his opponents burned.

While seeking the spiritual salvation of his nation, Mbemba hoped also to modernize it on a European model. He dressed in Portuguese clothing, had his sons and other young men educated in Portugal, and began schools for the children of Kongo's nobility. He corresponded with Portuguese kings, and his son Dom Henrique, who became a Christian bishop, represented Kongo at the Vatican, where he addressed the pope in Latin in 1513.

Mbemba put too much faith in his Portuguese patrons and too little in the traditions of his people. By 1508, Portuguese priests traded in slaves and lived with Kongolese mistresses. This disturbed Mbemba not because he opposed slavery but because the priests undermined his authority. He was supposed to have a monopoly over the slave trade, and he did not want his own people subjected to it.

Mbemba's complaints led to a formal agreement with Portugal in 1512 called the *Regimento*, which only made matters worse. It placed restrictions on the priests and pledged continued Portuguese military assistance. But it also recognized Portuguese merchants' right to trade for copper, ivory, and slaves, and it exempted the Portuguese from punishment under local law. Soon the slave trade and related corruption increased, as did unrest among Mbemba's increasingly unhappy subjects. In 1526, Mbemba created a commission to ensure that only war captives could be enslaved. When this strategy failed, he begged the Portuguese king, "In these kingdoms there should not be any trade in slaves or market for slaves."

In response, Portugal made alliances with Kongo's neighbors and withdrew much of its support from Mbemba, who died surrounded by scheming merchants, corruption, and dissension. In 1568—a quarter century after his death—Kongo became a client state of Portugal, and the slave trade expanded.

1.5 Kongo and Angola

Analyze what Kongo and Angola had in common with West Africa.

Although the forebears of most African Americans originated in West Africa, a large minority came from Central Africa. In particular, they came from the area around the Congo River and its tributaries and from the region to the south that the Portuguese called Angola. The people of these regions had much in common with those of the Guinea Coast. They divided labor by gender, lived in villages of extended families, and gave semidivine status to their kings. Also the Atlantic slave trade ensnared them, much as it did the peoples of West Africa.

During the fourteenth and fifteenth centuries, a number of states formed in the area to the north and south of what is today the border between the Democratic Republic of the Congo and Angola. Among them were Ndonga, Matamba, Ksanje, and Lunda. By far the most important was Kongo Kingdom, which controlled much of the Congo River system, with its fertile valleys and abundant fish. In addition to farming and fishing, this kingdom's wealth derived from access to salt, iron, and trade with the interior. Nzinga Knuwu was *Mani Kongo* (the Kongolese term for king) when Portuguese expeditions arrived in the late fifteenth century, seeking chiefly to trade for slaves. Knuwu surpassed other African rulers in welcoming the intruders. His son Nzinga Mbemba tried to convert the kingdom to Christianity and remodel it along European lines. The resulting unrest, combined with Portuguese greed and the effects of the slave trade, undermined royal authority. The ultimate result was the breakup of the kingdom and the disruption of the other Kongo-Angola states.

1.6 West African Society and Culture

Understand how legacies of West African society and culture influenced the way African Americans lived.

West Africa's great ethnic and cultural diversity makes it hazardous to generalize about the social and cultural background of the first African Americans. The dearth of written records from the region south of Sudan compounds the difficulties. But by working with a variety of sources, including oral histories, traditions, and archaeological studies, historians have pieced together a broad understanding of the way the people of West Africa lived at the beginning of the Atlantic slave trade.

1.6.1 Families and Villages

By the early sixteenth century, most West Africans were farmers. They usually lived in hamlets or villages of extended families and clans called **lineages**. Villages tended to be larger on the savanna than in the forest region, and usually one lineage occupied each village, although some large lineages peopled several villages. Each extended family descended from a common ancestor, and each lineage claimed descent from a mythical personage. Depending on the ethnic group involved, extended families and lineages were either patrilineal or **matrilineal**. In patrilineal societies, social rank and property passed in the male line from fathers to sons. In matrilineal societies, rank and property, although controlled by men, passed from generation to generation in the female line. A village chief in a matrilineal society was succeeded by his sister's son, not his own. According to the Arab chronicler Al Bakri, the succession to the throne of the empire of Ghana followed this pattern. But, like the people of Igboland, many West Africans lived in stateless societies with no government other than that provided by extended families and lineages.

Within extended families, **nuclear families** (husband, wife, and children) or in some cases **polygynous families** (husband, wives, and children) acted as economic units. In other words, nuclear and polygynous families existed in the context of broader family communities composed of grandparents, aunts, uncles, and cousins. Elders in

lineage

A type of clan, typical of West Africa, in which members claim descent from a single ancestor.

matrilineal

Descent traced through the female line.

nuclear family

A family unit consisting solely of one set of parents and their children.

polygynous family

A family unit consisting of a man, his wives, and their children.

these extended families had great power over the economic and social lives of their members. Each nuclear or polygynous family unit might have several houses. In nuclear households, the husband occupied the larger house and his wife the smaller. In polygynous households, the husband had the largest house, and his wives lived in smaller ones. In contrast with ancient Egypt, strict incest taboos prohibited people from marrying within their extended family.

Villagers' few possessions included cots, rugs, stools, and wooden storage chests. Their tools and weapons included bows, spears, iron axes, hoes, and scythes. Households used grinding stones, baskets, and ceramic vessels to prepare and store food. Villagers in both the savanna and forest regions produced cotton for clothing, but their food crops were distinct. West Africans in the savanna cultivated millet, rice, and sorghum as their dietary staples; kept goats and cattle for milk and cheese; and supplemented their diets with peas, okra, watermelons, and nuts. Yams, rather than grains, were the dietary staple in the forest region. Other important forest region crops included bananas and coco yams, both derived from Indonesia.

Farming in West Africa was not easy. Drought came often on the savanna. In the forest, diseases carried by the tsetse fly sickened draft animals, and agricultural plots (because they had to be cleared by hand) averaged just two or three acres per family. Although private landownership prevailed, West Africans generally worked land communally, dividing tasks by gender. Among the Akan of the Guinea Coast, for example, men cleared the land of trees and underbrush, and women tended the fields, planting, weeding, and harvesting. Women also cared for children, prepared meals, and manufactured household pottery.

1.6.2 Women

In general, men dominated women in West Africa. As previously noted, men often had two or more wives, and, to a degree, custom held women to be the property of men. But West African women also enjoyed an amount of freedom that impressed Arabs and Europeans. In ancient Ghana, women sometimes served as government officials. Later, in the forest region, they sometimes inherited property and owned land—or at least controlled its income. Women—including enslaved women—in the royal court of Dahomey held high government posts. Ashantee noblewomen could own property, although they themselves could be considered inheritable property. The Ashantee queen held her own court to administer women's affairs.

Women retained far more sexual freedom in West Africa than was the case in Europe or southwest Asia. Ibn Battuta, a Muslim Berber who visited Mali during the fourteenth century, was shocked to discover that in this Islamic country "women show no bashfulness before men and do not veil themselves, though they are assiduous in attending prayer." Battuta expressed even more surprise on learning that West African women could have male friends and companions other than their husbands or relatives.

Sexual freedom in West Africa was, however, more apparent than real. Throughout the region **secret societies** instilled in men and women ethical standards of behavior. The most important secret societies were the women's *Sande* and the men's *Poro*. They initiated boys and girls into adulthood and provided sex education. They established standards for personal conduct by emphasizing female virtue and male honor. Other secret societies influenced politics, trade, medical practice, recreation, and social gatherings.

secret societies

Social organizations that have secret ceremonies that only their members know about and can participate in.

1.6.3 Class and Slavery

Although many West Africans lived in stateless societies, most of them lived in hierarchically organized states headed by monarchs who claimed divine or semidivine status. Most of these monarchs' power was far from absolute, but they commanded armies, taxed commerce, and accumulated wealth. Beneath the royalty were classes of landed nobles, warriors, bureaucrats, and peasants. Lower classes included blacksmiths, butchers, weavers, woodcarvers, and tanners.

Slavery had been part of this hierarchical social structure since ancient times. Although common throughout West Africa, slavery was less so in the forest region than on the savanna. It took many forms and was not necessarily a permanent condition. Like people in other parts of the world, West Africans held war captives—including men, women, and children—to be without rights and suitable for enslavement. In Islamic regions, masters had obligations to their slaves similar to those of a guardian for a ward. They were, for example, responsible for their slaves' religious well-being. In non-Islamic regions, the children of slaves acquired legal protections, such as the right not to be sold away from the land they occupied.

Slaves who served either in the royal courts of a West African kingdom or in a kingdom's armies often exercised power over free people and could acquire property. Also, the slaves of peasant farmers often had standards of living similar to those of their masters. Slaves who worked under overseers in gangs on large estates were far less fortunate. However, the children and grandchildren of these enslaved agricultural workers gained employment and privileges similar to those of free people. Slaves retained a low social status, but in many respects slavery in West African societies functioned as a means of **assimilation**.

1.6.4 Religion

There were two religious traditions in fifteenth-century West Africa: Islamic and indigenous. Islam, which Arab traders introduced into West Africa, took root first in the Sudanese empires and remained more prevalent in the cosmopolitan savanna. Even there it was stronger in cities than in rural areas because it was the religion of merchants and bureaucrats. Islam fostered literacy in Arabic, the spread of Islamic learning, and the construction of mosques. Islam is resolutely monotheistic, asserting that Allah is the only God. It recognizes its founder, Muhammad, as well as Abraham, Moses, and Jesus, as prophets but regards none of them as divine.

West Africa's indigenous religions remained strongest in the forest region. They were **polytheistic** and **animistic**, recognizing many divinities and spirits. Beneath an all-powerful but remote creator god, lesser gods represented the forces of nature or were associated with particular mountains, rivers, trees, and rocks. Indigenous West African religion, in other words, saw the force of God in all things.

In part because practitioners of West African indigenous religions perceived the creator god to be unapproachable, they invoked the spirits of their ancestors and turned to magicians and oracles for assistance. Like the Chinese, they believed the spirits of their ancestors could influence their lives. Therefore, ceremonies to sustain ancestral spirits and their power over the earth became central to traditional West African religions. These rituals were part of everyday life, making organized churches and professional clergy rare. Instead, family members with an inclination to do so assumed religious duties. These individuals encouraged their relatives to participate in ceremonies that involved music, dancing, and animal sacrifice in honor of deceased ancestors. Funerals were especially important because they symbolized the linkage between the living and the dead.

1.6.5 Art and Music

As in other parts of the world, religious belief and practice influenced West African art. West Africans, seeking to preserve the images of their ancestors, excelled in woodcarving and sculpture in terra-cotta, bronze, and brass. Throughout the region, artists produced wooden masks representing in highly stylized manners ancestral spirits and gods. Wooden and terra-cotta figurines, sometimes referred to as "**fetishes**," were also common. West Africans used them in funerals, in rituals related to ancestral spirits, in medical practice, and in coming-of-age ceremonies. In contrast to masks and fetishes, the great bronze sculptures of Benin had political functions. They portrayed their subjects, which consisted of kings, warriors, and nobles rather than gods and spirits, realistically.

assimilation

The process by which people of different backgrounds become similar to each other in culture and language.

polytheistic

Many gods.

animistic

The belief that inanimate objects have spiritual attributes.

fetish

A natural object or an artifact believed to have magical power. A charm.

West African music also served religion. Folk musicians employed such instruments as drums, xylophones, bells, flutes, and mbanzas (predecessor to the banjo) to produce a highly rhythmic accompaniment to the dancing associated with religious rituals. A **call-and-response** style of singing also played a vital role in ritual. Vocal music, produced in a full-throated but often raspy style, had polyphonic textures and sophisticated rhythms.

1.6.6 Literature: Oral Histories, Poetry, and Tales

West African literature was part of an oral tradition that passed from generation to generation. At its most formal, trained poets and musicians who served kings and nobles created it. But it was also a folk art that expressed the views of the common people.

At a king's court there could be several poet-musicians who had high status and specialized in poems glorifying rulers and their ancestors by linking fact and fiction. Drums and horns often accompanied recitations of these poems. Court poets also used their trained memories to recall historical events and precise genealogies. The self-employed poets, called *griots*, who traveled from place to place were socially inferior to court poets but functioned in a similar manner. Both court poets and griots were men. Women were more involved in folk literature. They joined men in creating and performing work songs. They led in creating and singing dirges, lullabies, and satirical verses. Often these forms of literature used a call-and-response style.

This six-string wooden harp is a rare example of the type of instrument West African musicians and storytellers used to accompany themselves.

call-and-response

An African-American singing style rooted in Africa. A solo call tells a story to which a group responds, often with repeated lyrics.

griot

A West African self-employed poet and oral historian.

Just as significant for African-American history were the West African prose tales. Like similar stories in other parts of Africa, these tales took two forms: those with human characters and those with animal characters who represented humans. The tales centered on human characters dealt with such subjects as creation, the origins of death, worldly success, and romantic love. They frequently involved magical objects and potions.

The animal tales aimed to entertain and to teach lessons. They focused on small creatures, often referred to as "trickster characters," who struggled against larger beasts. Among the heroes were the hare, the spider, and the mouse. Plots centered on the ability of these weak animals to outsmart larger and meaner antagonists, such as the snake, leopard, and hyena. These animal characters had human emotions and goals. Storytellers presented them in human settings, although they retained animal characteristics.

In West Africa, these tales represented the ability of common people to counteract the power of kings and nobles. When the tales reached America, they became allegories for the struggle between enslaved African Americans and their powerful white masters.

1.6.7 Technology

West African technology was also distinctive and important. Although much knowledge about this technology has been lost, iron refining and forging, textile production, architecture, and rice cultivation helped shape life in the region.

As we previously mentioned, iron technology had existed in West Africa since ancient times. Smelting furnaces employing bellows turned ore into refined metal. Blacksmiths, who enjoyed an elevated almost supernatural status, produced tools for agriculture, weapons for hunting and war, ceremonial staffs, and religious amulets. These products encouraged the development of cities and kingdoms.

Architecture embodied Islamic and indigenous elements, with the former predominant on the savanna and the latter in the forest region. Building materials consisted of stone, mud, and wood. Builders in dry regions relied on stone and mud to build walls and relied on thatch supported by wooden beams for roofs. In some parts of the savanna, mud plaster covered stone walls. In other parts, walls consisted entirely of mud brick or packed earth. Public buildings reached large proportions, and some mosques served 3,000 worshippers. Massive stone or mud walls surrounded cities and towns.

Hand looms for household production existed throughout Africa for thousands of years, and cloth made from pounding bark persisted in the forest region into modern times. But trade and Islamic influences led to commercial textile production. By the ninth century CE, large looms, some equipped with pedals, produced narrow strips of wool or cotton. Men, rather than women, made cloth and tailored it into embroidered Islamic robes, shawls, hats, and blankets, which Muslim merchants traded over wide areas.

Of particular importance for African-American history, West Africans living along rivers in coastal regions had produced rice since approximately 1000 BCE. Portuguese who arrived during the fifteenth century CE reported large diked rice fields. Deliberate flooding of these fields, transplanting sprouts, and intensive cultivation were practices that reemerged in the colonial South Carolina low country.

Conclusion

In recent years, paleoanthropologists, archaeologists, and historians have revealed much about Africa's history and prehistory, but much remains to be learned concerning the past of this vast and diverse continent. The evolution of humans, the role of ancient Egypt in world history, and Egypt's relationship to Nubia and Kush are topics that continue to attract wide interest.

Although all of Africa contributed to their background, the history of African Americans begins in West Africa, the region from which the ancestors of most of them were unwillingly wrested. Historians have discovered, as subsequent chapters will show, that West Africans taken to America and their descendants in America preserved much more of their ancestral way of life than scholars once believed possible. West African family organization, work habits, language structures and some words, religious beliefs, legends and stories, pottery styles, art, and music all reached America. These African legacies, although often sharply modified, influenced the way African Americans and other Americans lived in their new land. They continue to shape American life.

Chapter Timeline

EVENTS IN AFRICA	WORLD EVENTS
10 million years ago	
5–10 million years ago	**1.6 million years ago**
Separation of hominids from apes	*Homo erectus* beginning to spread through Eurasia
4 million years ago	
Emergence of *australopithecines*	
2.4 million years ago	
Emergence of *Homo habilis*	
1.7 million years ago	
Emergence of *Homo erectus*	
1.5 million years ago	
100,000–200,000 years ago	**8000 BCE**
Appearance of modern humans	Appearance of the first agricultural settlements in southwest Asia
6000 BCE	
Beginning of Sahara Desert formation	

EVENTS IN AFRICA

WORLD EVENTS

5000 BCE

5000 BCE
First agricultural settlements in Egypt

3500 BCE
Sumerian civilization in Mesopotamia

3800 BCE
Predynastic period in Egypt

c. 3150 BCE
Unification of Egypt

2500 BCE

2700–2150 BCE
Egypt's Old Kingdom

2300 BCE
Beginning of Indus valley civilization

2100–1650 BCE
Egypt's Middle Kingdom

1500 BCE

1550–700 BCE
Egypt's New Kingdom

1600–1250 BCE
Mycenaean Greek civilization

c. 1500 BCE
Beginning of Shang dynasty in China

1000 BCE

750–670 BCE
Rule of Kushites over Egypt

600–336 BCE
Classical Greek civilization

540 BCE
Founding of Meroë

c. 500 BCE
Beginning of iron smelting in West Africa

50 CE
Destruction of Kush

500 CE

632–750 CE
Islamic conquest of North Africa

204 BCE–476 CE
Domination of Mediterranean by Roman Republic and Empire

c. 750–1076 CE
Empire of Ghana; Islam begins to take root in West Africa

500–1350 CE
European Middle Ages

c. 570 CE
Birth of Muhammad

1200 CE

1230–1468 CE
Empire of Mali

c. 1300 CE
Rise of Yoruba states

EVENTS IN AFRICA   WORLD EVENTS

1400 CE

1434 CE

Start of Portuguese exploration and
establishment of trading outposts on
West African coast

c. 1450 CE

Centralization of power in Benin

1464–1591 CE

Empire of Songhai

1492 CE

Christopher Columbus and European
encounter of America

1517 CE

Reformation begins in Europe

1600 CE

c. 1650 CE

Rise of Kingdom of Dahomey and the
Akan states

1610 CE

Scientific revolution begins in Europe

Review Questions

1. What was the role of Africa in the evolution of
modern humanity?

2. Discuss the controversy concerning the racial
identity of the ancient Egyptians. What is the
significance of this controversy for the history of
African Americans?

3. Compare and contrast the western Sudanese empires
with the forest civilizations of the Guinea Coast.

4. Discuss the role of religion in West Africa. What
was the African religious heritage of black
Americans?

5. Describe West African society on the eve of the
expansion of the Atlantic slave trade. What were
the society's strengths and weaknesses?

Retracing the Odyssey

National Museum of African Art, Smithsonian Institution,
Washington, D.C. The museum exhibits visual art from
African regions south of the Sahara Desert. It includes art
from ancient Benin and ancient Kerma in Nubia. There is
also an exhibit of African musical instruments.

**African Collection, National History Museum of Los
Angeles County,** Los Angeles, CA. This collection
includes about 5,000 objects representing African cultures.

**African Gallery, University of Pennsylvania Museum of
Archaeology and Anthropology,** Philadelphia, PA. The
gallery includes a collection of Benin bronzes.

Chattanooga African American Museum, Chattanooga,
TN. The museum includes an exhibit dealing with
African culture and history.

Recommended Reading

Emmanuel Kwaku Akyeampong, ed. *Themes in West Africa's History.* Athens: Ohio University Press, 2006. Provides an interdisciplinary approach to major themes in
West African history.

Robert W. July. *A History of the African People*, 5th ed. Prospect Heights, IL: Waveland, 1998. A comprehensive
social history with good coverage of West Africa and
West African women.

Roland Oliver. *The African Experience: From Olduvai Gorge
to the 21st Century.* Boulder, CO: Westview, 2000. Shorter
and less encyclopedic than July's book but innovative
in organization. It also provides insightful analysis of
cultural relationships.

John Reader. *Africa: A Biography of the Continent.*
New York: Knopf, 1998. The most up-to-date account
of early African history, emphasizing how the

continent's physical environment shaped human life there.

Christopher Stringer and Robin McKie. *African Exodus: The Origins of Modern Humanity.* New York: Henry Holt, 1997. A clearly written account favoring the out-of-Africa model.

John Thornton. *Africa and Africans in the Making of the Atlantic World, 1400–1689.* New York: Cambridge University Press, 1992. A thorough consideration of West African culture and its impact in the Americas.

Additional Bibliography

Prehistory, Egypt, and Kush

Martin Bernal. *Black Athena: The Afroasiatic Roots of Classical Civilization.* New Brunswick, NJ: Rutgers University Press, 1987.

Geoff Embering. *Nubia: Ancient Kingdoms of Africa.* New York: Institute for the Study of the Ancient World, 2011.

Nicholas C. Grimal. *A History of Ancient Egypt.* Oxford, UK: Blackwell, 1993.

Donald Johanson, Lenora Johanson, and Blake Edgar. *Ancestors: In Search of Human Origins.* New York: Villard Books, 1994.

Susan Kent. *Gender in African Prehistory.* Walnut Creek, CA: Altamira, 1998.

Mary R. Lefkowitz and Guy MacLean Rogers, eds. *Black Athena Revisited.* Chapel Hill: University of North Carolina Press, 1996.

Donald B. Redford. *From Slave to Pharaoh: The Black Experience of Ancient Egypt.* Baltimore: Johns Hopkins University Press, 2004.

Stuart Tyson Smith. *Wretched Kush: Ethnic Identities and Boundaries in Egypt's Nubian Empire.* New York: Routledge, 2003.

Derek A. Welsby. *The Kingdom of Kush: The Napatan and Merotic Empires.* Princeton, NJ: Markus Wiener, 1998.

Western Sudanese Empires

Nehemiah Levtzion. *Ancient Ghana and Mali.* London: Methuen, 1973.

Nehemiah Levtzion and J. F. Hopkins, eds. *Corpus of Early Arabic Sources for West African History.* New York: Cambridge University Press, 1981.

Roland Oliver and Brian M. Fagan. *Africa in the Iron Age.* New York: Cambridge University Press, 1975.

Roland Oliver and Caroline Oliver, eds. *Africa in the Days of Exploration.* Englewood Cliffs, NJ: Prentice Hall, 1965.

David Robinson. *Muslim Societies in African History.* New York: Cambridge University Press, 2004.

The Forest Region of the Guinea Coast

I. A. Akinjogbin. *Dahomey and Its Neighbors, 1708–1818.* New York: Cambridge University Press, 1967.

Edna G. Bay. *Wives of the Leopard: Gender, Politics, and Culture in the Kingdom of Dahomey.* Charlottesville: University of Virginia Press, 1998.

Daryll Forde, ed. *African Worlds.* New York: Oxford University Press, 1954.

Robert W. July. *Precolonial Africa.* New York: Scribner's, 1975.

Robin Law. *The Oyo Empire, c. 1600–c. 1836: West African Imperialism on the Eve of the Atlantic Slave Trade.* Oxford, UK: Clarendon, 1977.

T. C. McCaskie. *State and Society in Pre-Colonial Ashanti.* New York: Cambridge University Press, 1995.

Walter Rodney. *A History of the Upper Guinea Coast, 1545–1800.* Oxford, UK: Clarendon, 1970.

Robert Sydney Smith. *Kingdoms of the Yoruba.* 3rd ed. Madison: University of Wisconsin Press, 1988.

Culture

Harold Courlander, ed. *A Treasury of African Folklore.* New York: Marlowe, 1996.

Susan Denyer. *African Traditional Architecture: An Historical and Geographical Perspective.* London: Heinemann, 1978.

Paulin J. Hountondji. *African Philosophy: Myth and Reality.* Bloomington: Indiana University Press, 1984.

Elizabeth Allo Isichei. *The Religious Traditions of Africa: A History.* Westport, CT: Praeger, 2004.

J. H. Kwabena Nketia. *The Music of Africa.* New York: Norton, 1974.

Isidore Okpewho. *African Oral Literature: Backgrounds, Character, and Continuity.* Bloomington: Indiana University Press, 1992.

Oyekan Owomoyela. *Yoruba Trickster Tales.* Lincoln: University of Nebraska Press, 1977.

Frank Willett. *African Art.* 3rd ed. New York: Thames and Hudson, 2003.

Chapter 2

Middle Passage
CA. 1450–1809

After Great Britain banned the Atlantic slave trade in 1807, British warships enforced the ban. The people portrayed in this early nineteenth-century woodcut were rescued from a slave ship by the H.M.S. *Undine*.

 ## Learning Objectives

After reading this chapter, you should be able to:

2.1 Discuss how the arrival of the Europeans affected Africa.

2.2 Compare and contrast the slave trade in Africa with the Atlantic slave trade.

2.3 Evaluate the relationship between the Atlantic slave trade and the Industrial Revolution.

2.4 Trace the experiences of enslaved Africans from capture to arrival in the West Indies.

2.5 Analyze how Africans adapted to conditions in the Americas.

2.6 Describe "seasoning."

2.7 Describe the treatment of slaves in the Americas.

2.8 Discuss the factors involved in ending the Atlantic slave trade.

> . . . They felt the sea-wind tying them into one nation
> of eyes and shadows and groans, in the one pain
> that is inconsolable, the loss of one's shore.
>
> . . . They had wept, not for
> their wives only, their fading children, but for strange,
> ordinary things. This one, who was a hunter,
>
> wept for a sapling lance whose absent heft sang
> in his palm's hollow. One, a fisherman, for an ochre
> river encircling his calves; one a weaver, for the straw
>
> fishpot he had meant to repair, wilting in water.
> They cried for the little thing after the big thing.
> They cried for a broken gourd.
>
> —*Derek Walcott, Omeros*

The lines by Derek Walcott, a modern black West Indian poet, that open this chapter express the sorrow and loss the Atlantic slave trade inflicted on the Africans it tore from their homelands. This huge enterprise, which lasted for more than three centuries, brought millions of Africans 3,000 miles across the Atlantic Ocean to the Americas. It was the largest forced migration in history. By the eighteenth century, the voyage across the ocean in European ships called "slavers" had become known as the "**Middle Passage**." British sailors coined this innocuous phrase to describe the middle leg of a triangular journey first from England to Africa, then from Africa to the Americas, and finally from the Americas back to England. Yet today Middle Passage denotes an unbelievable descent into an earthly hell of cruelty and suffering. From the Middle Passage the first African Americans emerged.

Middle Passage
The voyage of slave ships (slavers) across the Atlantic Ocean from Africa to the Americas.

This chapter describes the Atlantic slave trade and the Middle Passage. It explores their origins both in European colonization of the Americas and in the slave trade that had existed in Africa itself for centuries. It focuses on the experience of the enslaved people whom the trade brought to America. For those who survived, the grueling journey led to servitude on huge agricultural factories called plantations. Many who became African Americans first experienced plantation life in the West Indies—the Caribbean islands—where a process called "seasoning" prepared them for lives as slaves in the Americas.

2.1 The European Age of Exploration and Colonization

Discuss how the arrival of the Europeans affected Africa.

The origins of the Atlantic slave trade and its long duration were products of Western Europe's expansion of power that began during the fifteenth century and continued into the twentieth century. For a variety of economic, technological, and demographic reasons, Portugal, Spain, the Netherlands, France, England, and other nations sought to explore, conquer, and colonize in Africa, Asia, and the Americas. Their efforts had important consequences for these areas.

Portugal took the lead during the early 1400s when its ships reached Africa's western coast. Portuguese captains hoped to find Christian allies there against the Muslims of North Africa and spread Christianity. But they were more interested in trade with African kingdoms, as were the Spanish, Dutch, English, and French who followed them.

Even more attractive than Africa to the Portuguese and their European successors as sources of trade and wealth were India, China, Japan, and the East Indies (modern

Indonesia and Malaysia). In 1487 Portuguese explorer Bartolomeu Dias discovered the Cape of Good Hope at the southern tip of Africa and thereby established that it was possible to sail around Africa to reach India and regions to its east. Ten years later Vasco da Gama initiated this route on behalf of Portuguese commerce. A similar desire to reach these eastern regions motivated the Spanish monarchy to finance Christopher Columbus's westward voyages that began in 1492.

Columbus, who believed the earth to be much smaller than it is, hoped to reach Japan or India by sailing west, thereby opening a direct trade route between Spain and these eastern countries. Columbus's mistake led to his accidental landfall in the Americas. In turn, that encounter led to the European conquest, settlement, and exploitation of North and South America and the Caribbean islands, where Columbus first landed. Columbus and those who followed him quickly enslaved indigenous Americans (American Indians) as laborers in fields and mines. Almost as quickly, many indigenous peoples either died of European diseases and overwork or escaped beyond the reach of European power. Consequently, European colonizers needed additional laborers. This demand for a workforce in the Americas caused the Atlantic slave trade.

2.2 The Slave Trade in Africa and the Origins of the Atlantic Slave Trade

Compare and contrast the slave trade in Africa with the Atlantic slave trade.

Slave labor was not peculiar to the European colonies in the Americas. Slavery and slave trading had existed in all cultures for thousands of years. As Chapter 1 indicates, slave labor was common in West Africa, although it was usually less oppressive than it became in the Americas.

When Portuguese voyagers first arrived at Senegambia, Benin, and Kongo, they found a thriving commerce in slaves. These kingdoms represented the southern extremity of an extensive trade conducted by Islamic nations that involved the capture and sale of Europeans and North African Berbers as well as people from south of the Sahara Desert. Although Arabs nurtured antiblack prejudice, race was not the major factor in this Islamic slave trade. Arab merchants and West African kings, for example, imported white slaves from Europe.

In West Africa, Sudanese horsemen conducted the Islamic slave trade. The horsemen invaded the forest region to capture people who could not effectively resist—often they belonged to stateless societies. The trade dealt mainly in women and children who as slaves were destined for lives as concubines and domestic servants in North Africa and southwest Asia. This pattern contrasted with that of the later Atlantic slave trade, which primarily sought young men for agricultural labor in the Americas. The West African men who constituted a minority of those subjected to the trans-Sahara slave trade were more likely to become soldiers than fieldworkers in such North African states as Morocco and Egypt.

The demand for slaves in Muslim countries remained high from the tenth through the fifteenth centuries because many slaves died from disease or gained freedom and assimilated into Arab society. The trans-Sahara slave trade therefore rivaled the trade in gold across the Sahara. It helped make such West African cities as Timbuktu, Walata, Jenne, and Gao wealthy. According to historian Roland Oliver, the Atlantic slave trade did not reach the proportions of the trans-Sahara slave trade until 1600 (see Figure 2-1).

When Portuguese ships first arrived off the **Guinea Coast**, their captains traded chiefly for gold, ivory, and pepper, but they also wanted slaves. As early as 1441, Antam Goncalvez of Portugal enslaved a Berber and his West African servant and took them home as gifts for a Portuguese prince. During the following decades,

Guinea Coast

The southward-facing coast of West Africa, from which many of the people caught up in the Atlantic slave trade departed for the Americas.

Figure 2-1 Estimated Annual Exports of Slaves from Western Africa to the Americas, 1500–1700

SOURCE: Based on John Thornton, *Africans in the Making of the Atlantic World, 1400–1680* (New York: Cambridge University Press, 1992), 118. © Darlene Clark Hine.

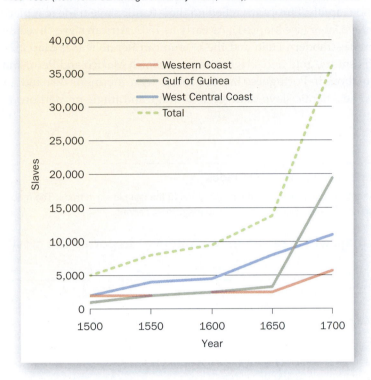

Portuguese raiders captured hundreds of Africans to work as domestic servants in Portugal and Spain.

But usually the Portuguese and the other European and white Americans who succeeded them did not capture and enslave people themselves. They instead purchased slaves from African traders. This arrangement began formally in 1472 when Portuguese merchant Ruy do Siqueira gained permission from the Oba (king) of Benin to trade for slaves, as well as for gold and ivory, within the borders of the Oba's kingdom. Siqueira and other Portuguese found that a commercial infrastructure already existed in West Africa that could distribute European trade goods and procure slaves. The rulers of Benin, Dahomey, and other African kingdoms restricted the Europeans to a few points on the coast, and the kingdoms raided the interior to supply the Europeans with slaves.

Interethnic rivalries in West Africa led to the warfare that produced these slaves during the sixteenth century. Although Africans initially resisted selling members of their own ethnic group to Europeans, they did not at first consider it wrong to sell members of their own race to foreigners. In fact, neither Africans nor Europeans had yet developed a concept of racial solidarity. However, by the eighteenth century, at least the victims of the trade believed that such solidarity *should* exist. Ottobah Cugoano, who had been captured and sold during that century, wrote, "I must own to the shame of my countrymen that I was first kidnapped and betrayed by [those of] my own complexion."

Until the early sixteenth century, Portuguese seafarers conducted the Atlantic slave trade on a tiny scale to satisfy a limited market for domestic servants in Portugal and Spain. Other European countries had no demand for slaves because their workforces

West African artists recorded the appearance of Europeans who came to trade in gold, ivory, and human beings. This Benin bronze relief sculpture, dating to the late sixteenth or early seventeenth century, portrays two Portuguese men.

were already too large. But the impact of Columbus's voyages drastically changed the slave trade. The Spanish and Portuguese—followed by the Dutch, English, and French—established colonies in the Caribbean, Mexico, Central America, and South America. Because disease and overwork caused the number of American Indians in these regions to decline rapidly, Europeans relied on the Atlantic slave trade to replace them as a source of slave labor (see Map 2-1). As early as 1502, African slaves lived on the island of Hispaniola—modern Haiti and the Dominican Republic (see Map 2-2). During the sixteenth century, gold and silver mines in Spanish Mexico and Peru, and especially sugar plantations in Portuguese Brazil, produced an enormous demand for labor. Consequently, the Atlantic slave trade grew to huge and tragic proportions to meet that demand.

Map 2-1 The Atlantic and Islamic Slave Trades

Not until 1600 did the Atlantic slave trade reach the proportions of the Islamic slave trade. The map shows the principal sources of slaves, primary routes, and major destinations.

According to this map, which region in the Americas imported the most slaves?

Map 2-2 Slave Colonies of the Seventeenth and Eighteenth Centuries

This map indicates regions in North America, the West Indies, and South America that had, during the seventeenth and eighteenth centuries, significant populations of enslaved people of African descent.

What European powers controlled the regions of North America and the Caribbean islands shown in this map?

Although the overwhelming majority of Africans who were caught up in the Atlantic slave trade went to the Americas, a few reached Europe. This sixteenth-century drawing by German artist Albrecht Durer depicts Katharina, a servant of a Portuguese official who lived in Antwerp.

2.3 Growth of the Atlantic Slave Trade

Evaluate the relationship between the Atlantic slave trade and the Industrial Revolution.

Because Europe provided an insatiable market for sugar, cultivation of this crop in the Americas became extremely profitable. Sugar plantations employing slave labor spread from Portuguese-ruled Brazil to the Caribbean islands. Later, the cultivation of coffee in Brazil and of tobacco, rice, and **indigo** in British North America added to the demand for African slaves. By 1510 Spain had joined Portugal in the enlarged Atlantic slave trade, and a new, harsher form of slavery had appeared in the Americas. Unlike slavery in Africa, Asia, and Europe, slavery in the Americas was based on race, as only Africans and American Indians were enslaved. Most of the slaves were men or boys who served as agricultural laborers rather than soldiers or domestic servants. They became **chattel**—meaning "personal property"—of their masters and lost their customary rights as human beings. Men and boys predominated in part because Europeans believed they were stronger laborers than women and girls. Another factor was that West Africans preferred to have women do agricultural work and therefore tended to withhold them from the Atlantic trade.

Portugal and Spain dominated the Atlantic slave trade during the sixteenth century. They shipped about 2,000 Africans per year to their American colonies, with most by far going to Brazil. From the beginning of the trade until its nineteenth-century

indigo

A bluish-violet dye produced from the indigo plant.

chattel

Enslaved people who were treated legally as property.

The Portuguese established the city of Luanda in 1575. This eighteenth-century print portrays the city when it was at its height as a center for shipment of enslaved Africans to Brazil.

Asiento

The monopoly over the slave trade from Africa to Spain's American colonies.

cash crop

A crop grown for sale rather than subsistence.

Industrial Revolution

An economic change that began in England during the early eighteenth century and spread to Continental Europe and the United States. Industry rather than agriculture became the dominant form of enterprise.

abolition, about 6,500,000 of the approximately 11,328,000 Africans taken to the Americas went to Brazil and Spain's colonies. Both the Portuguese and the Spanish monarchies granted monopolies over the trade to private companies. In Spain this monopoly became known in 1518 as the *Asiento* (meaning "contract"). The profits from the slave trade were so great that by 1550 the Dutch, French, and English were becoming involved. During the early seventeenth century, the Dutch drove the Portuguese from the West African coast and became the principal European slave-trading nation. For the rest of that century, most Africans came to the Americas in Dutch ships—including a group of 20 in 1619 who until recently were considered to have been the first of their race to reach British North America.

The Dutch also shifted the center of sugar production to the West Indies. England and France followed, with the former taking control of Barbados and Jamaica and the latter taking Saint Domingue (Haiti), Guadeloupe, and Martinique. With the development of tobacco as a **cash crop** in Virginia and Maryland during the 1620s and with the expansion of sugar production in the West Indies, the demand for African slaves continued to grow. The result was that England and France competed with the Dutch to control the Atlantic slave trade. After a series of wars, England emerged supreme. It had driven the Dutch out of the trade by 1674. Victories over France and Spain led in 1713 to English control of the *Asiento*, which allowed English traders the exclusive right to supply slaves to all of Spain's American colonies. After 1713, English ships dominated the slave trade, carrying about 20,000 slaves per year from Africa to the Americas. At the peak of the trade during the 1790s, they transported 50,000 per year.

The profits from the Atlantic slave trade, together with those from the sugar and tobacco produced in the Americas by slave labor, were invested in England and helped fund the **Industrial Revolution** during the eighteenth century. In turn, Africa became a market for cheap English manufactured goods (see Map 2-3). Eventually, two triangular trade systems developed. In one, traders carried English goods to West Africa and exchanged the goods for slaves. Then the traders carried the slaves to the West Indies and exchanged them for sugar, which they took back to England on the third leg of the triangle. In the other triangular trade, white Americans from Britain's New England colonies carried rum to West Africa to trade for slaves. From Africa they took the slaves to the West Indies to exchange for sugar or molasses—sugar syrup—which they then took home to distill into rum.

Map 2-3 Atlantic Trade Among the Americas, Great Britain, and West Africa During the Seventeenth and Eighteenth Centuries

Often referred to as a triangular trade, this map shows the complexity of early modern Atlantic commerce, of which the slave trade was a major part.

What does this map suggest about the economy of the Atlantic world between 1600 and 1800?

2.4 The African-American Ordeal from Capture to Destination

Trace the experiences of enslaved Africans from capture to arrival in the West Indies.

The availability of large numbers of slaves in West Africa resulted from the wars that accompanied the formation of states in that region. Captives suitable for enslavement were a by-product of these wars. Senegambia and nearby Sierra Leone, then Oyo, Dahomey, and Benin, became, in turn, centers of the trade. Meanwhile, on the west coast of Central Africa, slaves became available as a result of the conflict between the expanding Kingdom of Kongo and its neighbors. The European traders provided the aggressors with firearms but did not instigate the wars. Instead, they used the wars to enrich themselves.

Sometimes African armies enslaved the inhabitants of conquered towns and villages. At other times, raiding parties captured isolated families or kidnapped

In this nineteenth-century engraving, African slave traders conduct a group of bound captives from the interior of Africa toward European trading posts.

individuals. As warfare spread to the interior, captives had to march for hundreds of miles to the coast where European traders awaited them. The raiders tied the captives together with rope or secured them with wooden yokes about their necks. It was a shocking experience, and many captives died from hunger, exhaustion, and exposure during the journey. Others killed themselves rather than submit, and the captors killed those who resisted.

Once the captives reached the coast, those destined for the Atlantic trade went to fortified structures called **factories**. Portuguese traders constructed the first factory at Elmina on the Guinea Coast in 1481—the Dutch captured it in 1637. Such factories contained the headquarters of the traders, warehouses for their trade goods and supplies, and dungeons or outdoor holding pens for the captives. In these pens, slave traders divided families and—as much as possible—ethnic groups to prevent rebellion. The traders stripped captives naked and inspected them for disease and physical defects. Those considered fit for purchase were branded like cattle with a hot iron bearing the symbol of a trading company.

In a rare account of such proceedings from a captive's point of view, Olaudah Equiano described during the 1780s how horrifying such treatment could be. The white slave traders, with their "horrible looks, red faces, and long hair," appeared to be savages who acted with a "brutal cruelty" that went beyond anything their victims had previously experienced. Many of the captives feared the Europeans were cannibals who would take them to their country for food. According to historian Gary Nash, such fears resulted from deliberate European brutalization of the captives, part of an attempt to destroy the Africans' self-respect and self-identity.

factories

Headquarters for a European company that traded for slaves or engaged in other commercial enterprises on the West African coast.

2.4.1 The Crossing

After being held in a factory for weeks or months, captives faced the frightening prospect of leaving their native land for a voyage across an ocean that many of them had never before seen. Sailors rowed them out in large canoes to slave ships offshore. One English trader recalled that during the 1690s "the negroes were so wilful and loth to leave their own country, that they often leap'd out of the canoos, boat and ship, into the sea, and kept under water till they were drowned."

Once at sea, the slave ships followed the route Columbus had established during his voyages to the Americas: from the Canary Islands off West Africa to the Windward Islands in the Caribbean. Because ships taking this route enjoyed prevailing winds and westward currents, the passage normally lasted between two and three months. But the time required for the crossing varied widely. The larger ships were able to reach the Caribbean in 40 days, but some voyages could take up to six months.

Both human and natural causes accounted for such delays. During the three centuries that the Atlantic slave trade endured, Western European nations often fought each other, and slave ships became prized targets. As early as the 1580s, English "sea dogs," such as John Hawkins and Sir Francis Drake, attacked Spanish ships to steal their human cargoes. Outright piracy peaked between 1650 and 1725 when demand for slaves in the West Indies increased. There were also such potentially disastrous natural forces as doldrums—long windless spells at sea—and hurricanes, which could destroy ships, crews, and cargoes.

2.4.2 The Slavers and Their Technology

Slave ships (called **slavers**) varied in size but grew larger over the centuries. A ship's tonnage determined how many slaves it could carry, with the formula being two slaves per ton. A ship of 200 tons might therefore carry 400 slaves. But captains often ignored the formula. Some kept their human cargo light, calculating that smaller loads lowered mortality and made revolt less likely. But most captains were "tight packers" who squeezed human beings together hoping that large numbers would offset increased deaths. The 120-ton *Henrietta Marie*, a British ship that sailed from London on its final voyage in 1699, should have been fully loaded with 240 slaves. Yet it carried 350 from West Africa when it set out for Barbados and Jamaica. Another ship designed to carry 450 slaves usually carried 600.

The slavers' cargo space was generally only five feet high. Ships' carpenters halved this vertical space by building shelves, so slaves might be packed above and below on planks that measured only 5.5 feet long and 1.3 feet wide. Consequently, slaves had only about 20 to 25 inches of headroom. To add to the discomfort, the crews chained male slaves together in pairs to help prevent rebellion and lodged them away from women and children.

The most frequently reproduced illustration of a slaver's capacity for human cargo comes from the *Brookes*, which sailed from Liverpool, England, during the 1780s. At 300 tons, the *Brookes* was an exceptionally large ship for its time, and the diagrams show how tightly packed the slaves were that it transported. Although those who wished to abolish the Atlantic slave trade created the diagrams, their bias does not make the diagrams less accurate. In fact, as historian James Walvin points out, the precise, unemotional renderings of the *Brookes*'s geometrically conceived design scarcely indicate the physical suffering it caused. The renderings do not show the constant shifting, crushing, and chafing among the human cargo caused by the movement of the ship at sea. Also, during storms the crew often neglected to feed the slaves, empty the tubs used for excrement, take slaves on deck for exercise, tend to the sick, or remove the dead.

Mortality rates were high because the crowded, unsanitary conditions encouraged seaboard epidemics. Between 1715 and 1775, slave deaths on French ships averaged 15 percent. The highest recorded mortality rate was 34 percent. By the nineteenth century, the death rate had declined to 5 percent. Overall, one-third of the Africans subjected to the trade perished between their capture and embarkation on a slave ship. Another third died during the Middle Passage or during "seasoning" on a Caribbean island. It would have been slight consolation to the enslaved to learn that, because of the seaboard epidemics, the death rate among slaver crews was proportionally higher than their own.

slaver

A ship used to transport slaves from Africa to the Americas.

Plan of the British slave ship *Brookes*, 1788. This plan, which may undercount the human cargo the *Brookes* carried, shows how tightly Africans were packed aboard slave ships.

As historian Marcus Rediker notes, by the eighteenth century Europeans regarded slavers as "useful machines." The large three-masted, full-rigged vessels, with their "cast-iron cannon . . . harnessed unparalleled mobility, speed, and destructive power." They were not only well armed to protect against those who might attempt to steal their human cargo but also built to be durable and stable, although they rarely lasted more than 10 years. By 1750 shipbuilders in Liverpool built slavers to order. The ships combined varieties of wood to produce strength, flexibility, and resistance to tropical ship worms that could bore into hulls. By 1800 they used copper sheathing to provide better protection below water. They used lattice doors, portholes, and funnels to ventilate slave quarters, which became healthier as time passed. They also maintained a special "hardware of bondage," including iron manacles, shackles, collars, branding implements, and thumbscrews.

2.4.3 A Slave's Story

In his book *The Interesting Narrative of the Life of Olaudah Equiano or Gustavus Vassa, the African, Written by Himself*, published in 1789, former slave Olaudah Equiano provides a vivid account of a West African's capture, sale to traders, and voyage to America in 1755. Although recent evidence suggests Equiano *may* have been born in South Carolina rather than West Africa, scholars respect the accuracy of his account. He tells the story of a young Igbo, the dominant ethnic group in what is today southern Nigeria. African slave raiders capture him when he is 10 years old and force him to march along with other captives to the Niger River or one of its tributaries, where they trade him to other Africans. His new captors take him to the coast and sell him to European slave traders whose ships sail to the West Indies.

The boy's experience at the coastal slave factory convinces him he has entered a hell, peopled by evil spirits. The stench caused by forcing many people to live in close confinement makes him nauseated and emotionally agitated. His African and European captors try to calm him with liquor. But because he is not accustomed to alcohol, he becomes disoriented and more convinced of his impending doom. When the sailors lodge him with others below deck on the ship, he is so sick that he loses his appetite and hopes to die. Instead, because he refuses to eat, the sailors take him on deck and whip him. Later the boy witnesses the flogging of a white crewman. The man dies, and the sailors throw his body into the sea just as they disposed of dead Africans.

During the time the ship is in port awaiting a full cargo of slaves, the boy spends much time on deck. After putting to sea, however, he usually remains below deck with the other slaves where "each had scarcely room to turn himself." There, the smells of unwashed bodies and of the toilet tubs, "into which the children often fell and were almost suffocated," create a loathsome atmosphere. The darkness, the chafing of chains on flesh, and the shrieks and groans of the sick and disoriented provide "a scene of horror almost inconceivable."

When slaves are allowed to get fresh air and exercise on deck, the crew strings up nets to prevent them from jumping overboard. Even so, two Africans who are chained together evade the nets and jump into the ocean, preferring drowning to staying on board. The boy shares their desperation. As the ship goes beyond sight of land, he and the other captives believe they lose "even the least glimpse of hope of [re]gaining the shore" and returning to their country. Equiano, in his first-person narrative, insisted that "many more" would have jumped overboard "if they had not been prevented by the ship's crew."

Attempts to keep the slaves entertained and in good humor seldom succeeded. Crews sometimes forced the slaves to dance and sing, but their songs, as slave-ship surgeon Alexander Falconbridge testified, were "melancholy lamentations, of their exile from their native country." Depression among the Africans led to a catatonia that contemporary observers called melancholy or extreme nostalgia. Falconbridge noted

Profile

Olaudah Equiano

Portrait of a Negro Man, Olaudah Equiano, 1780s.

For many years historians have regarded Olaudah Equiano's autobiography, *The Interesting Narrative of the Life of Olaudah Equiano or Gustavus Vassa, the African, Written by Himself* (1789), as one of the few authentic descriptions of the trade from an African point of view. Recently, however, Equiano's African birth, if not his general accuracy, has been questioned. Vincent Carretta, author of *Equiano the African: Biography of a Self-Made Man* (2005), discovered two documents—a 1759 baptismal record and a 1777 ship muster roll—indicating that Equiano was born in South Carolina in about 1747 rather than—as Equiano claimed—in Nigeria in 1745. It appears that Equiano had not used an African name for himself before he published his autobiography. But, as several scholars have noted, an African in the Atlantic world during the eighteenth century had good reason to hide his true identity and claim to have been born in America. Even Carretta does not flatly assert that Equiano lied about his African birth. Carretta, in fact, validates Equiano's autobiography by treating Equiano's description of his capture, experience on the Middle Passage, and enslavement "as if it were true."

Although the controversy over Equiano's birthplace may never be resolved, it is certain that he was a young slave in Virginia when a visiting British sea captain named Michael Henry Pascal purchased him in 1754. Pascal commanded a merchant ship and employed Equiano as his personal servant. Pascal also gave him the name Gustavus Vassa (after the king of Sweden), which Equiano used for the rest of his life. Pascal and Equiano traveled extensively and served together in North America during the French and Indian War of 1754–1763. As a result, both of them were with General James Wolfe in 1759 at Quebec, Canada, where the British won the decisive battle of the war. Equiano also lived in England, where he received the schooling that allowed him to work as "a shipping clerk and amateur navigator on the ship of his . . . [third] master, the Quaker Robert King of Philadelphia, trading chiefly between [North] America and the West Indies."

In 1766 growing antislavery sentiment among Quakers led King to allow Equiano to purchase his freedom for 40 pounds sterling. This was more money than most eighteenth-century British laborers earned in a year. Thereafter, Equiano toured the Mediterranean, sailed to the Arctic and Central America, converted to Calvinism, and became a leader in the British movement against the slave trade. In 1787 he helped organize a colony for emancipated British slaves at Sierra Leone in West Africa. Just before embarking for that country, however, dissention and confusion in the enterprise cost him his position as Commissary for Stores for the Black Poor. His autobiography, which he wrote shortly thereafter, proved to be a greater contribution to the anti–slave trade cause. The book also became a major source of income for Equiano.

In April 1792 he married an Englishwoman, Susanna Cullen, with whom he had two daughters. Their marriage notice recognized him "as the champion and advocate for procuring the suppression of the slave trade." When Equiano died on March 31, 1797, he was, according to Carretta, "probably the wealthiest and most famous person of African descent in the Atlantic world."

Equiano is significant for his account of the Atlantic slave trade and his service in the British struggle against that trade. His extraordinary life reveals how baseless the assumption was among Europeans and persons of European descent that black people were naturally suited for slavery.

that the slaves had "a strong attachment to their native country" and a "just sense of the value of liberty."

Although the traders, seeking to lessen the possibility of shipboard conspiracy and rebellion, separated individuals who spoke the same language, the boy described by Equiano manages to find adults who speak Igbo. They explain to him the purpose of the voyage, which he learns is to go to the white people's country to labor for them rather than to be eaten by them. He does not realize that work on a West Indian island could be a death sentence.

2.4.4 A Captain's Story

indentured servant

An individual who sells or loses his or her freedom for a specified number of years.

John Newton, a white captain of a slave ship, who was born in London in 1725, provides another perspective on the Middle Passage. In 1745 Newton, as an **indentured servant**, joined the crew of a slaver bound for Sierra Leone. Indentured servants lost their freedom for a specified number of years either because they sold it or because they were being punished for debt or crime. In 1748, on the return voyage to England, Newton survived a fierce Atlantic storm and, thanking God, became an evangelical Christian. Like most people of his era, Newton saw no contradiction between his newfound faith and his participation in the enslavement and ill treatment of men, women, and children. When he became a slaver captain in 1750, he read Bible passages to his crew twice each Sunday and forbade swearing. But he treated his human cargoes as harshly as any other slaver captain.

Newton was just 25 years old when he became captain of the *Duke of Argyle*, an old 140-ton vessel that he converted into a slaver after it sailed from Liverpool on August 11, 1750. Near the Cape Verde Islands, off the coast of Senegambia, carpenters began making the alterations required for packing Africans below deck. Newton also added the ship's guns and ammunition in order to protect against pirates or African resistance. On October 23 the *Duke of Argyle* reached Frenchman's Bay, Sierra Leone, where Newton observed other ships from England, France, and New England anchored offshore. Two days later, Newton purchased two men and a woman from traders at the port, but he had to sail to several other ports to accumulate a full cargo. Leaving West Africa for the open sea on May 23, 1751, the ship delivered its slaves to Antigua in the West Indies on July 3.

Poor health forced Newton to retire from the slave trade in 1754. Ten years later he became an Anglican priest, and from 1779 until his death in 1807 Newton served as rector of St. Mary Woolnoth Church in London. By the late 1770s, he had repented his involvement in the slave trade and had become one of its leading opponents. Together with William Cowper—a renowned poet—Newton published the *Olney Hymns* in 1779. Among the selections included in this volume was "Amazing Grace," which Newton wrote as a reflection on divine forgiveness for his sins. For several reasons, Newton and other religious Britons had begun to perceive an evil in the slave trade that, despite their piety, they had failed to see earlier.

2.4.5 Provisions for the Middle Passage

Slave ships left Liverpool and other European ports provisioned with food supplies for their crews. These included beans, cheese, beef, flour, and grog—a mixture of rum and water. When the ships reached the Guinea Coast in West Africa, their captains purchased pepper, palm oil, lemons, limes, yams, plantains, and coconuts. Because slaves were not accustomed to European foods, the ships needed these staples of the African diet. Meat and fish were rare luxuries on board, and crews did not share them with slaves. In the voyage Equiano describes, crew members at one point caught far more fish than they could eat but threw what was left overboard instead of giving it to the Africans who were exercising on deck. The captives "begged and prayed for some . . . but in vain." The sailors whipped those Africans who filched a few fish for themselves.

This mezzotint, engraved by J.R. Smith in 1793, follows a 1788 painting by English artist George Morland. The title of the painting is "The Slave Trade." In what would have been an unusual event, Morland shows English sea captains abducting Africans. The picture reflects moral opposition to the trade.

The crew usually fed the slaves twice per day in shifts. Cooks prepared vegetable pulps, porridge, and stews for the crew to distribute in buckets as the slaves assembled on deck during good weather or below deck during storms. At the beginning of the voyage, each slave received a wooden spoon for dipping into the buckets, which about 10 individuals shared. But in the confined confusion below deck, slaves often lost their spoons. They then had to eat from the buckets with their unwashed hands, which spread disease.

Although slaver captains realized it was in their interest to feed their human cargoes well, they often skimped on supplies to save money and make room for more slaves. Therefore, the food on a slave ship was often insufficient to prevent malnutrition and weakened immune systems among people already traumatized by separation from their families and homelands. As a result, many Africans died during the Middle Passage from diseases amid the horrid conditions that were normal aboard the slave ships. Others died from depression: they refused to eat despite the crew's efforts to force food down their throats.

2.4.6 Sanitation, Disease, and Death

Diseases such as malaria, yellow fever, measles, smallpox, hookworm, scurvy, and dysentery constantly threatened African cargoes and European crews during the Middle Passage. Astronomical death rates prevailed on board the slave ships before 1750. Mortality dropped after that date because ships became faster and ships' surgeons knew more about hygiene and diet. There were also early forms of vaccinations against smallpox, which may have been the worst killer of slaves on ships. But, even after 1750, poor sanitation led to many deaths. It is important to remember that before the early twentieth century, no civilization had developed a germ theory of disease. Physicians blamed human illnesses on poisonous atmospheres and imbalances among bodily fluids.

Usually slavers provided only three or four toilet tubs below deck for enslaved Africans to use during the Middle Passage. They had to struggle among themselves to get to the tubs, and children had a particularly difficult time. Those too ill to reach the tubs excreted where they lay, and diseases such as dysentery, which are spread by human waste, thrived. Dysentery, known by contemporaries as "the bloody flux," vied with smallpox to kill the most slaves aboard ships. Alexander Falconbridge reported that during one dysentery epidemic, "the deck, that is, the floor of [the slaves'] rooms, was so covered with blood and mucus which had proceeded from them in consequence of the flux, that it resembled a slaughter house. It is not in the power of human imagination, to picture to itself a situation more dreadful or disgusting."

John Newton's stark, unimpassioned records of slave deaths aboard the *Duke of Argyle* indicate even more about how the Atlantic slave trade devalued human life. Newton recorded deaths at sea only by number. He wrote in his journal, "Bury'd a man slave No. 84 . . . bury'd a woman slave, No. 47." Yet Newton probably was more conscientious than other slaver captains in seeking to avoid disease. During his 1750 voyage, he noted only 11 deaths: 10 slaves—five men, one woman, three boys, and one girl—and one crewman. Compared with the usual high mortality rates, this was an achievement.

What role ships' surgeons—general practitioners in modern terminology—played in preventing or inadvertently encouraging deaths aboard slave ships is difficult to determine. Some of them were frauds. Even the best were limited by the era's primitive medical knowledge. Captains rewarded the surgeons with "head money" for the number of healthy slaves who arrived in the Americas, but the surgeons could also be blamed for deaths at sea that reduced the value of the human cargo.

Many surgeons recognized that African remedies worked better than European medications in alleviating the slaves' symptoms. Therefore, the surgeons collected herbs and foods along the Guinea Coast. They learned African nursing techniques, which they found more effective in treating onboard diseases than European procedures. What the surgeons did not understand and regarded as superstition was the holistic nature of African medicine. African healers maintained that body, mind, and spirit were interconnected elements of the totality of a person's well-being.

The enslaved Africans were often just as dumbfounded by the beliefs and actions of their captors. They thought they had entered a world of bad spirits when they boarded a slaver, and they attempted to counteract the spirits with rituals from their homeland. John Newton noted that during one voyage he feared slaves had tried to poison the ship's drinking water. He was relieved to discover that they were only putting what he called "charms" in the water supply. Such fetishes, representing the power of spirits, were important in West African religions. What the slaves hoped to accomplish is not clear. But Newton, as a Christian, held their beliefs in contempt. "If it please God [that] they make no worse attempts than to charm us to death, they will not harm us," he wrote.

2.4.7 Resistance and Revolt at Sea

Although Newton ridiculed African religion, he rejoiced that the slaves were not planning to poison the crew or mutiny. Because many enslaved Africans refused to accept their fate, slaver captains had to be vigilant. Uprisings occurred often, and Newton himself put down a potentially serious one aboard the *Duke of Argyle*. Twenty men had broken their chains below deck but were apprehended before they could assault the crew.

Most such rebellions took place while a ship prepared to set sail. The African coast was in sight, and the slaves could still hope to return home. But some revolts occurred on the open sea, where it was unlikely the Africans, even if their revolt succeeded, could return to their homes or regain their freedom. Both sorts of revolt indicate that not even capture, forced march to the coast, imprisonment, branding, and sale could break the spirit of many captives. These Africans preferred to face death rather than accept bondage.

Voices

The Journal of a Dutch Slaver

The following account of slave trading on the West African coast is from a journal kept on the Dutch slaver St. Jan *between March and November 1659. Although written from a European point of view, it describes the conditions Africans faced on such ships.*

We weighed anchor, by the order of the Hon'ble Director, Johan Valckenborch, and the Hon'ble Director, Jasper van Heussen to proceed on our voyage to Rio Reael [on the Guinea Coast] to trade for slaves for the hon'ble company.

March 8. Saturday. Arrived with our ship before Ardra, to take on board the surgeon's mate and a supply of tamarinds for refreshment for the slaves; sailed again next day on our voyage to Rio Reael.

17. Arrived at Rio Reael in front of a village called Bany, where we found the company's yacht, named the *Vrede*, which was sent out to assist us to trade for slaves.

In April. Nothing was done except to trade for slaves.

May 6. One of our seamen died. . . .

22. Again weighed anchor and ran out of Rio Reael accompanied by the yacht *Vrede*; purchased there two hundred and nineteen head of slaves, men, women, boys and girls, and set our course for the high land of Ambosius, for the purpose of procuring food there for the slaves, as nothing was to be had at Rio Reael.

June 29. Sunday. Again resolved to proceed on our voyage, as there also but little food was to be had for the slaves in consequence of the great rains which fell every day, and because many of the slaves were suffering from the bloody flux in consequence of the bad provisions we were supplied with at El Mina. . . .

July 27. Our surgeon, named Martyn de Lanoy, died of the bloody flux.

Aug. 11. Again resolved to pursue our voyage towards the island of Annebo, in order to purchase there some refreshments for the slaves. . . .

15. Arrived at the island Annebo, where we purchased for the slaves one hundred half tierces of beans, twelve hogs, five thousand coconuts, five thousand sweet oranges, besides some other stores.

Sept. 21. The skipper called the ships officers aft, and resolved to run for the island of Tobago and to procure water there; otherwise we should have perished for want of water, as many of our water casks had leaked dry.

24. Friday. Arrived at the island of Tobago and hauled water there, also purchased some bread, as our hands had had no ration for three weeks.

Nov. 1. Lost our ship on the Reef of Rocus [north of Caracas], and all hands immediately took to the boat, as there was no prospect of saving the slaves, for we must abandon the ship in consequence of the heavy surf.

4. Arrived with the boat at the island of Curaco; the Hon'ble Governor Beck ordered two sloops to take the slaves off the wreck, one of which sloops with eighty four slaves on board, was captured by a privateer [pirate vessel].

1. What dangers did the slaves and crew on board the *St. Jan* face?

2. What is the attitude of the author of the journal toward slaves?

SOURCE: *Voyages of the Slavers St. John and Arms of Amsterdam, 1659, 1663.* Translated from the Original Manuscripts with Introduction and Index by E.B. O'Callaghan.

John Atkins, an English slaver surgeon who made many voyages between Africa and the Americas during the 1720s, noted that although the threat of revolt diminished on the high seas, it never disappeared:

When we are slaved and out at sea, it is commonly imagined that the *Negroes*['] Ignorance of Navigation, will always be a Safeguard [against revolt]; yet, as many of them think themselves bought to eat, and more, that Death will send them into their own Country, there has not been wanting Examples of rising and killing a Ship's Company, distant from Land, though not so often as on the Coast: But once or twice is enough to shew, a Master's Care and Diligence should never be over till the Delivery of them.

Later in the eighteenth century, a historian used the prevalence of revolt to justify the harsh treatment of Africans on slave ships. Edward Long wrote that "the many acts of violence they [the slaves] have committed by murdering whole crews and destroying ships when they had it left in their power to do so, have made this rigour wholly chargeable on their own bloody and malicious disposition, which calls for the same confinement as if they were wolves or wild boars."

Failed slave mutineers could expect harsh punishment, although profit margins influenced sentences. Atkins chronicled how the captain of the *Robert*, which sailed from Bristol, England, punished the ringleaders, who were worth more, less harshly than their followers who were not as valuable. Atkins related that

> Captain Harding, weighing the Stoutness and Worth of the two [ringleaders], did, as in other Countries they do by Rogues of Dignity, whip and scarify them only; while three others, Abettors, but not Actors, nor of Strength for it, he sentenced to cruel Deaths; making them first eat the Heart and Liver of one of them killed. The Woman [who had helped in the revolt] he hoisted up by the Thumbs, whipp'd and slashed her with Knives, before the other Slaves, till she died.

Other slaves resisted their captors by drowning or starving themselves. Thomas Phillips, captain of the slaver *Hannibal* during the 1690s, commented, "We had about 12 negroes did wilfully drown themselves and others starved themselves to death; for 'tis their belief that when they die they return home to their own country and friends again." As we previously indicated, captains used nets to prevent suicide by drowning. To deal with self-imposed starvation, they used hot coals or a metal device called a *speculum oris* to force individuals to open their mouths for feeding.

2.4.8 Cruelty

The Atlantic slave trade required more capital than any other maritime commerce during the seventeenth and eighteenth centuries. The investments for the ships, the exceptionally large crews they employed, the navigational equipment, the armaments, the purchase of slaves in Africa, and the supplies of food and water needed to feed hundreds of passengers were phenomenal. The aim was to carry as many Africans in healthy condition to the Americas as possible in order to make the large profits that justified such expenditures. Yet, as we have indicated, conditions aboard the vessels were abysmal.

Scholars have debated how much deliberate cruelty the enslaved Africans suffered from ships' crews. West Indian historian Eric Williams asserts that the horrors of the Middle Passage have been exaggerated. Many writers, Williams contends, are led astray by the writings of those who, during the late eighteenth and early nineteenth centuries, sought to abolish the slave trade. In his view—and that of other historians—the difficulties of the Middle Passage were similar to those of European indentured servants who suffered high mortality rates on the voyage to America.

From this perspective the primary cause of death at sea on all ships carrying passengers across the Atlantic to the Americas was epidemic disease, against which medical practitioners had few tools before the twentieth century. Contributing factors included inadequate means of preserving food from spoilage and failure to prevent freshwater from becoming contaminated during the long ocean crossing. According to Williams, overcrowding by slavers was only a secondary cause for the high mortality rates.

Such observations help place conditions aboard the slave ships in a broader perspective. Cruelty and suffering are, to some degree, historically relative in that practices acceptable in the past are now considered inhumane. Yet cruelty aboard slavers must also be placed in a cultural context. Cultures distinguish between what constitutes acceptable behavior to their own people on the one hand and to strangers on the other. For Europeans, Africans were cultural strangers, and what became normal in the Atlantic slave trade was in fact exceptionally cruel compared to how Europeans treated each other. Slaves below deck received only one-half the space allocated on board to European soldiers, free emigrants, indentured servants, and convicts. Europeans regarded slavery itself as a condition suitable only for non-Christians. And as strangers, Africans were subject to brutalization by European crew members who often cared little about the physical and emotional damage they inflicted.

2.4.9 African Women on Slave Ships

For similar reasons, African women did not enjoy the same protection against unwanted sexual attention from European men that European women received. Consequently, sailors during long voyages attempted to sate their sexual appetites with enslaved women. African women caught in the Atlantic slave trade were worth half the price of African men in Caribbean markets, and as a result, captains took fewer of them on board their vessels. Perhaps because the women were less valuable commodities, crew members felt they had license to abuse them sexually. As historian Marcus Rediker points out, because women and children appeared less likely to revolt, they often had "more freedom of movement on slave ships." But that very ability to move about made them more vulnerable to sexual assault. The separate below-deck compartments for women on slave ships also made them easier targets than they otherwise might have been.

Profile

Ayuba Suleiman Diallo of Bondu

"The Fortunate Slave," an illustration of African slavery in the early eighteenth century by Douglas Grant (1968)

Ayuba Suleiman Diallo, known to Europeans as Job ben Solomon, was one of the many West Africans caught up in the Atlantic slave trade. But his experience was far from typical. Because he had family connections, was literate in Arabic, and used his aristocratic personality to gain favor among Europeans, Diallo was able to escape enslavement and return to his native land. His story reveals much about the bonds of wealth and class in the Atlantic world during the early eighteenth century.

Diallo was born in about 1701 at the village of Marsa located in the eastern Senegambian region of Bondu. His father, the imam of the local mosque and village head, taught

him Arabic and the Koran when he was a child and prepared him to become a merchant. That Samba Geladio Jegi, the future king of the nearby kingdom of Futa Toro, was a fellow student suggests the standing of Diallo's family. Diallo, following Muslim and West African custom, had two wives. He married the first of them when he was 15 and she was 11, the second when he was 28.

In February 1730, Diallo was on his way to the Gambia River to sell two slaves to an English trader when he was himself captured by Mandingo warriors and sold as well. Although the English slaver captain was willing to ransom Diallo, his ship sailed before Diallo's father could send the money. As a result, Diallo was shipped with other Africans to Annapolis, Maryland, and delivered to Vachell Denton, factor for William Hunt, a London merchant. Shortly thereafter, Diallo was sold to a Mr. Tolsey, who operated a tobacco plantation on Maryland's eastern shore.

Although Diallo was "about five feet ten inches high . . . and naturally of a good constitution," his "religious abstinence" and the difficulties he had experienced during the Middle Passage unsuited him for fieldwork. Therefore, Tolsey assigned him to tending cattle. In June 1731, however, after a young white boy repeatedly interrupted his prayers, Diallo escaped to Dover, Delaware, where he was apprehended and jailed. There, Thomas Bluett, who published in 1734 an account of Diallo's adventures, discovered that Diallo was literate in Arabic, pious in his religious devotions, and—according to Bluett's stereotypical notions—"no common slave." Bluett provided this information to Tolsey, who on Diallo's return allowed him a quiet place to pray and permitted him to write a letter in Arabic to his father.

The letter reached James Oglethorpe, the director of England's slave-trading Royal African Company, who arranged to purchase Diallo from Tolsey and in March 1733 transport him by ship to England. Accompanied by Bluett, Diallo learned during the long voyage to speak, read, and write English. In London, Bluett contacted several well-to-do gentlemen who raised 60 pounds to secure Diallo's freedom and, with the aid of

the Royal African Company, return him to Senegambia. Before he left England in July 1734, Diallo had an audience with King George II, met with the entire royal family, dined with members of the nobility, and received expensive gifts.

Diallo's wives and children greeted him on his return to his village, but much had changed during his absence. Futa Toro had conquered Bondu, and as a result Diallo's family had suffered economically. In addition, the slave trade in Senegambia had intensified and Morocco had begun to interfere militarily in the region. Grateful to his English friends, Diallo used his influence in these difficult circumstances to help the Royal African Company hold its share of the trade in slaves and gold until the company disbanded in 1752. Able to differentiate between his fortunes and those of others, he retained commercial ties to the British until his death in 1773.

Voices

Dysentery (or the Bloody Flux)

Alexander Falconbridge (d. 1792) served as ship's surgeon on four British slavers between 1780 and 1787. In 1788 he became an opponent of the trade and published An Account of the Slave Trade on the Coast of Africa. *Here he describes in gruesome detail conditions in slave quarters during a dysentery epidemic that he mistakenly attributes to stale air and heat.*

Some wet and blowing weather having occasioned the port-holes to be shut, and the grating to be covered, fluxes and fevers among the Negroes ensued. While they were in this situation, my profession requiring it, I frequently went down among them, till at length their apartments became so extremely hot, as to be only sufferable for a very short time. . . . It is not in the power of the human imagination, to picture to itself a situation more dreadful or disgusting. Numbers of the slaves having fainted, they were carried upon deck, where several of them died, and the rest were, with great difficulty, restored. It had nearly proved fatal to me also. The climate was too warm to admit the wearing of any clothing but a shirt, and that I had pulled off before I went down; notwithstanding which, by only continuing among them for about a quarter of an hour, I was so overcome with the heat, stench, and foul air, that I had nearly fainted; and it was not without assistance, that I could get upon deck. The consequence was, that I soon after fell sick of the same disorder, from which I did not recover for several months. . . .

The place allotted for the sick Negroes is under the half deck, where they lie on the bare planks. By this means, those who are emaciated, frequently have their skin, and even their flesh, entirely rubbed

off, by the motion of the ship, from the prominent parts of the shoulders, elbows, and hips, so as to render the bones in those parts quite bare. And some of them, by constantly lying in the blood and mucus, that had flowed from those afflicted with the flux, and which . . . is generally so violent as to prevent their being kept clean, have their flesh much sooner rubbed off, than those who have only to contend with the mere friction of the ship. The excruciating pain which the poor sufferers feel from being obliged to continue in such a dreadful situation, frequently for several weeks, in case they happen to live so long, is not to be conceived or described. Few, indeed, are ever able to withstand the fatal effects of it. The utmost skill of the surgeon is here ineffectual. . . .

The surgeon, upon going between decks, in the morning, to examine the situation of the slaves, frequently finds several dead; and among the men, sometimes a dead and living Negroe fastened by their irons together. When this is the case, they are brought upon the deck, and being laid on the grating, the living Negroe is disengaged, and the dead one thrown overboard. . . .

1. Could slave traders have avoided the suffering described in this passage?
2. What impact would such suffering have had on those who survived it?

SOURCE: Alexander Falconbridge, *An Account of the Slave Trade on the Coast of Africa* (London: privately printed, 1788), in John H. Bracey Jr. and Manisha Sinha, *African American Mosaic: A Documentary History from the Slave Trade to the Twenty-first Century* (Upper Saddle River, NJ: Prentice Hall, 2004), 1: 24.

Historian Barbara Bush speculates that the horrid experience of the Middle Passage may have influenced black women's attitudes toward sexuality and procreation. This, in turn, may help explain why slave populations in the Caribbean and Latin America failed to reproduce themselves: exhaustion, terror, and disgust can depress sex drives.

2.5 Landing and Sale in the West Indies

Analyze how Africans adapted to conditions in the Americas.

As a slaver neared the West Indies, the crew prepared its human cargo for landing and sale. Slaves shaved, washed with fresh water, and exercised. Those bound for the larger Caribbean islands or for the British colonies of southern North America often received some weeks of rest in the easternmost islands of the West Indies. French slave traders typically rested their slave passengers on **Martinique**. The English preferred **Barbados**. Sale to white plantation owners followed.

The process of landing and sale that ended the Middle Passage was often as protracted as the events that began it in Africa. After anchoring at one of the Lesser Antilles Islands—Barbados, St. Kitts, or Antigua—English slaver captains haggled with the agents of local planters over numbers and prices. They then determined whether to sell all their slaves at their first port of call, sell some of them, sail to another island, or sail to such North American ports as Charleston, Williamsport, or Baltimore. If the market looked good in the first port, the captain might still take a week or more to sell his cargo. The captain of the *James*, who landed at Barbados in 1676, just as the cultivation of cane sugar there was becoming extremely profitable, sold most of his slaves in three days. "May Thursday 25th . . . sold 163 slaves. May Friday 26th. We sold 70 slaves. May Saturday 27th. Sold 110 slaves," he recorded in his journal.

Often, captains and crew had to do more to prepare slaves for sale than allow them to clean themselves and exercise. The ravages of cruelty, confinement, and disease could not be easily remedied. According to legend, young African men and women arrived in the Americas with gray hair, and captains used dye to hide such indications of age before the slaves went to market. Slaves were also required to oil their bodies to conceal blemishes, rashes, and bruises. Ships' surgeons used hemp to plug the anuses of those suffering from dysentery to block the bloody discharge the disease caused.

Humiliation continued as the slaves went to market. Once again they suffered close physical inspection from potential buyers, which—according to Equiano—caused "much dread and trembling among us" and "bitter cries." Unless a single purchaser agreed to buy an entire cargo of slaves, auctions took place either on deck or in sale yards on shore. However, some captains employed "the scramble." In these barbaric spectacles, the captain established standard prices for men, women, and children; herded the Africans together in a corral; and then allowed buyers to rush pell-mell among them to grab and rope together the slaves they desired.

Martinique

An island in the eastern Caribbean Sea that was a French sugar-producing colony from the seventeenth into the nineteenth century.

Barbados

An island nation in the Lesser Antilles located to the southeast of Puerto Rico.

This nineteenth-century engraving suggests the humiliation Africans endured as they were subjected to physical inspections before being sold.

2.6 Seasoning

Describe "seasoning."

Seasoning followed sale. This term referred to a period of up to two years of **acculturating** slaves and breaking them in to plantation routines. On Barbados, Jamaica, and other Caribbean islands, planters divided slaves into three categories: **Creoles** (slaves born in the Americas), old Africans (those who had lived in the Americas for some time), and new Africans (those who had just survived the Middle Passage). Creole slaves were worth three times the value of unseasoned new Africans, whom planters and Creole slaves called "salt-water Negroes" or "Guinea-birds." Seasoning began the process of making new Africans more like Creoles.

In the West Indies, this process involved more than an apprenticeship in the work routines of the sugar plantations. It also prepared many new arrivals for resale to North American planters, who preferred "seasoned" slaves to "unbroken" ones who came directly from Africa. In fact, before 1720 most of the Africans who ended up in the British colonies of North America had gone first to the West Indies. After that date, the demand for slave labor in the islands had become so great that they could spare fewer slaves for resale to the North American market. As a result, henceforth most slave imports into the tobacco-, rice-, and later cotton-growing regions of the American South came directly from Africa and had to be seasoned by their American masters. But many slaves still came to North America from the Caribbean, to which they had been brought from Africa or where they had been born.

In either case, seasoning was a disciplinary process intended to modify the behavior and attitude of slaves and make them effective laborers. As part of this process, the slaves' new masters gave them new names: Christian names, generic African names, or names from classical Greece and Rome (such as Jupiter, Achilles, or Plato).

The seasoning process also involved learning European languages. Masters in the Spanish Caribbean were especially thorough teachers. Consequently, although Spanish-speaking African slaves and their descendants retained African words, they could be easily understood by any Spanish-speaking person. In the French and English Caribbean islands and in parts of North America, however, slave society produced Creole dialects that in grammar, vocabulary, and intonation had distinctive African linguistic features. These Africanized versions of French and English, including the Gullah dialect still prevalent on South Carolina's sea islands and the Creole most Haitians speak today, could not be easily understood by those who spoke more standard dialects.

During seasoning, masters or overseers broke slaves into plantation work by assigning them to one of several work gangs. The strongest men joined the first or "great gang," which did the heavy fieldwork of planting and harvesting. The second gang, including women and older men, did lighter fieldwork, such as weeding. The third gang, composed of children, worked shorter hours and performed such tasks as bringing food and water to the field gangs. Other slaves became domestic servants. New Africans served apprenticeships with old Africans from their same ethnic group or with Creoles.

Some planters looked for cargoes of young people, anticipating that they might be more easily acculturated than older Africans. One West Indian master in 1792 recorded his hopes for a group of children: "From the late Guinea sales, I have purchased altogether twenty boys and girls, from ten to thirteen years old." He emphasized that "it is the practice, on bringing them to the estate, to distribute them in the huts of Creole blacks, under their direction and care, who are to feed them, train them to work, and teach them their new language."

Planters had to rely on old Africans and Creoles to train new recruits because white people were a minority in the Caribbean. Later, a similar demographic pattern

seasoning

The process by which newly arrived Africans were broken in to slavery in the Americas.

acculturating

Change in individuals who are introduced to a new culture.

Creoles

Persons of African and/or European descent born in the Americas.

developed in parts of the cotton-producing American South. In both regions, therefore, African custom shaped the cooperative labor of slaves in gangs. But the use of old Africans and Creoles as instructors and the appropriation of African styles of labor should not suggest leniency. Although plantation overseers, who ran day-to-day operations, could be white, of mixed race, or black, they invariably imposed strict discipline. Drivers, who directed the work gangs, were almost always black. But they carried whips and punished those who worked too slowly or showed disrespect. Planters assigned recalcitrant new Africans to the strictest overseers and drivers.

Planters housed slaves undergoing seasoning with the old Africans and Creoles who instructed them. The instructors regarded such additions to their households as economic opportunities because the new Africans provided extra labor on the small plots of land that West Indian planters often allocated to slaves. Slaves could sell surplus root vegetables, peas, and fruit from their gardens and save to purchase freedom for themselves or others. Additional workers helped produce larger surpluses to sell at local markets, thereby reducing the time required to accumulate a purchase price.

New Africans also benefited from this arrangement. They learned how to build houses in their new land and how to cultivate vegetables to supplement the food the planter provided. Even though many Africans brought building skills and agricultural knowledge with them to the Americas, old Africans and Creoles helped teach them how to adapt their skills and knowledge to a new climate, topography, building materials, and social organization.

2.7 The End of the Journey: Masters and Slaves in the Americas

Describe the treatment of slaves in the Americas.

By what criteria did planters assess the successful seasoning of new Africans? The first criterion was survival. Already weakened and traumatized by the Middle Passage, many Africans did not survive seasoning. Historian James Walvin estimates that one-third died during their first three years in the West Indies. African men died at a greater rate than African women, perhaps because they did the more arduous fieldwork.

A second criterion was that the Africans had to adapt to new foods and a new climate. The foods included salted codfish traded to the West Indies by New England merchants, Indian corn (maize), and varieties of squash not available in West Africa. The Caribbean islands, like West Africa, were tropical, but North America was much cooler. Even within the West Indies, an African was unlikely to find a climate exactly like the one he or she had left behind.

A third criterion was learning a new language. Planters did not require slaves to speak the local language, which could be English, French, Spanish, Danish, or Dutch, fluently. But slaves had to speak a creole dialect well enough to obey commands. A final criterion was psychological. When new Africans ceased to be suicidal, planters assumed they had accepted their status and their separation from their homeland.

It would have suited the planters if their slaves had met all these criteria. Yet that would have required the Africans to have been thoroughly desocialized by the Middle Passage, and they were not. As traumatic as that voyage was—for all the shock of capture, separation from loved ones, and efforts to dehumanize them—most Africans who entered plantation society in the Americas had not been stripped of their memories or their culture. When their ties to their villages and families were broken, they created bonds with shipmates that simulated blood relationships. Such social bonds became the basis of new extended families. So similar were these new synthetic families to those that had existed in West Africa that slaves considered sexual relations among shipmates and former shipmates incestuous.

As this suggests, African slaves did not lose all their culture during the Middle Passage and seasoning in the Americas. Their value system never totally replicated that of the plantation. Despite their ordeal, the Africans who survived the Atlantic slave trade and slavery in the Americas were resilient. Seasoning did modify their behavior. Yet the claim that it obliterated African Americans' cultural roots is incorrect. In 1941 anthropologist Melville Herskovits raised questions about this issue that still shape debate about the African-American experience.

Herskovits asked, "What discussions of world view might not have taken place in the long hours when [Creole] teacher and [new African] pupil were together, reversing their roles when matters only dimly sensed by the American-born slave were explained [by his pupil] in terms of African conventions he had never analyzed?" How many African beliefs and methods of coping with life and the supernatural were retained and transmitted by such private discussions? How much did African cultural elements, such as dance, song, folklore, moral values, and etiquette, offset the impulse to accept European values?

2.8 The Ending of the Atlantic Slave Trade

Discuss the factors involved in ending the Atlantic slave trade.

The cruelties associated with the Atlantic slave trade contributed to its abolition in the early nineteenth century. A court decision in 1772 had ended slavery in Britain. By 1783 a religiously oriented antislavery crusade, dominated by members of the Society of Friends (Quakers), had organized. Known as *abolitionists*, those who joined the crusade hoped to end slavery in Britain's colonies, but centered most of their energies on the slave trade. Former slaves, such as Equiano, actively supported the effort. Its best known leaders, however, were Bristish natives Thomas Clarkson, Granville Sharp, and William Wilberforce.

Because the British had dominated the Atlantic trade since 1713, this nation's growing antipathy became crucial to the trade's destruction. But it is debatable whether moral outrage alone prompted the abolitionist effort. By the late 1700s, Britain's industrializing economy had become less dependent on the slave trade and the entire plantation system than previously. To maintain its prosperity, Britain needed raw materials and markets for its manufactured goods. Slowly but surely its ruling classes realized more profits lay in industry and other forms of trade, while leaving Africans in Africa.

So morals and economic self-interest combined when Britain abolished the Atlantic slave trade in 1807 and tried to enforce that abolition on other nations through a naval patrol off the African coast. The following year, the U.S. Congress joined in outlawing the Atlantic trade. Although American, Brazilian, and Spanish slavers defied these prohibitions for years, the forced migration from Africa to the Americas dropped to a tiny percentage of what it had been at its peak. Ironically, the coastal kingdoms of Guinea and western Central Africa fought most fiercely to keep the trade going because their economies had become dependent on it. This persistence gave the English, French, Belgians, and Portuguese an excuse to establish colonial empires in Africa during the nineteenth century in the name of suppressing the slave trade.

Conclusion

Over more than three centuries, the Atlantic slave trade brought about 11 million Africans to the Americas. About 2 million died in transit. Of those who survived, most came between 1701 and 1810, when more Africans than Europeans reached the New World. Most Africans went to the sugar plantations of the Caribbean and Brazil. According to David Eltis and David Richardson in *Atlas of the Transatlantic Save Trade*, only about 377,000 went to the British colonies of North America, either directly or after seasoning in the West Indies. From these Africans have come the nearly 40 million African Americans alive today.

This chapter has described the great forced migration across the Atlantic that brought Africans into slavery in the Americas. We still have much to learn about the origins of the trade, its relationship to the earlier trans-Sahara trade, and its involvement with state formation in West and western Central Africa. Historians continue to debate how cruel the trade was, the ability of transplanted Africans to preserve their cultural heritage, and why Britain abolished the trade in the early nineteenth century.

We are fortunate that a few Africans who experienced the Middle Passage recorded their testimony. Otherwise, we would not appreciate how horrible it was. Even more important, however, is that so many survived the terror of the Atlantic slave trade and carried on. Their struggle testifies to the human spirit that is at the center of the African-American experience.

Chapter Timeline

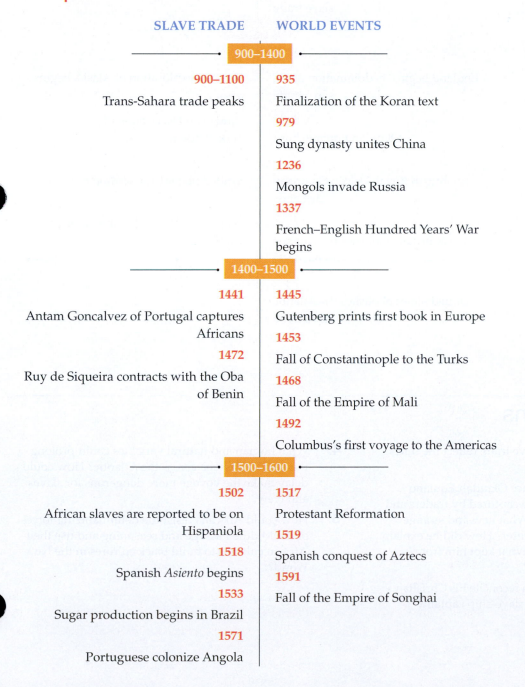

SLAVE TRADE	WORLD EVENTS
900–1400	
900–1100	**935**
Trans-Sahara trade peaks	Finalization of the Koran text
	979
	Sung dynasty unites China
	1236
	Mongols invade Russia
	1337
	French–English Hundred Years' War begins
1400–1500	
1441	**1445**
Antam Goncalvez of Portugal captures Africans	Gutenberg prints first book in Europe
1472	**1453**
Ruy de Siqueira contracts with the Oba of Benin	Fall of Constantinople to the Turks
	1468
	Fall of the Empire of Mali
	1492
	Columbus's first voyage to the Americas
1500–1600	
1502	**1517**
African slaves are reported to be on Hispaniola	Protestant Reformation
1518	**1519**
Spanish *Asiento* begins	Spanish conquest of Aztecs
1533	**1591**
Sugar production begins in Brazil	Fall of the Empire of Songhai
1571	
Portuguese colonize Angola	

SLAVE TRADE	WORLD EVENTS
1600–1700	
1610 Dutch drive Portuguese from Africa's west coast	**1607** Founding of Jamestown
1619 Africans reported to be in British North America	**1620** Pilgrims reach New England
1662 Portuguese destroy Kongo Kingdom	**1688** England's Glorious Revolution
1674 England drives the Dutch out of the slave trade	
1700–1800	
1713 England begins its domination of the slave trade	**1728** Russian exploration of Alaska begins
c. 1745 Olaudah Equiano born	**1776** American Declaration of Independence
1752 British Royal African Company disbands	**1789** United States Constitution ratified
1807 Great Britain abolishes the Atlantic slave trade	**1815** Napoleon defeated at the Battle of Waterloo
1808 United States abolishes the Atlantic slave trade	

Review Questions

1. How did the Atlantic slave trade reflect the times during which it existed?

2. Think about the experience Olaudah Equiano described of a young boy captured by traders and brought to a slave ship. What new and strange things did the boy encounter? How did he explain these things to himself? What kept him from descending into despair?

3. How could John Newton reconcile his Christian faith with his career as a slave-ship captain?

4. What human and natural variables could prolong the Middle Passage across the Atlantic? How could delay make the voyage more dangerous for slaves and crew?

5. How could Africans resist the dehumanizing forces of the Middle Passage and seasoning and use their African cultures to build black cultures in the New World?

Retracing the Odyssey

The *Henrietta Marie*. This is a slave ship placed on traveling display by the Museum of Southern Florida in Miami. The *Henrietta Marie* sank in 1701 after delivering slaves to Jamaica.

Chattanooga African American Museum, Chattanooga, TN. The museum includes an exhibit dealing with the Atlantic slave trade.

Recommended Reading

Barbara Bush. *Slave Women in Caribbean Society, 1650–1838.* 2nd ed. Bloomington: Indiana University Press, 2010. Contains an insightful discussion of African women, their introduction to slavery in the Americas, and their experience on sugar plantations.

Basil Davidson. *The African Slave Trade: Revised and Expanded Edition.* Boston: Little, Brown, 1980. Originally published in 1961, this book has been superseded in some respects by more recent studies, but it places the trade in both African and European contexts.

Herbert S. Klein. *The Atlantic Slave Trade.* 2nd ed. New York: Cambridge University Press, 2010. This is the most thorough and current study of the subject.

Marcus Rediker. *The Slave Ship: A Human History.* New York: Viking, 2007. Thoroughly and dramatically describes life on board slavers during the eighteenth century.

John Thornton. *Africa and Africans in the Making of the Atlantic World, 1400–1800,* 2nd ed. New York: Cambridge University Press, 1998. Emphasizes the contributions of Africans, slave and free, to the economic and cultural development of the Atlantic world during the slave trade centuries.

Additional Bibliography

The Slave Trade in Africa

Walter Hawthorne. *Planting Rice and Harvesting Slaves: Transformations along the Guinea-Bissau Coast, 1400–1900.* Portsmouth, NH: Heinemann, 2003.

Bernard Lewis. *Race and Slavery in the Middle East: An Historical Enquiry.* New York: Oxford University Press, 1990.

Patrick Manning. *Slavery and African Life: Occidental, Oriental, and African Slave Trades.* New York: Cambridge University Press, 1990.

Suzanne Miers and Richard Roberts. *The End of Slavery in Africa.* Madison: University of Wisconsin Press, 1988.

Claire C. Robertson and Martin A. Klein, eds. *Slavery in Africa.* Madison: University of Wisconsin Press, 1983.

Elizabeth Savage, ed. *The Human Commodity: Perspectives on the Trans-Saharan Slave Trade.* London: Frank Cass, 1992.

John K. Thornton. *The Kingdom of Kongo: Civil War and Transition, 1641–1718.* Madison: University of Wisconsin Press, 1983.

The Atlantic Slave Trade

Anne C. Bailey. *African Voices of the Atlantic Slave Trade: Beyond the Silence and the Shame.* Boston: Beacon, 2005.

Alexander X. Byrd. *Captives and Voyagers; Black Migrants Across the Eighteenth-Century British Atlantic World.* Baton Rouge: Louisiana State University Press, 2008.

Vincent Carretta. *Equiano the African: Biography of a Self-Made Man.* Athens: University of Georgia Press, 2005.

Emma Christopher. *Slave Ship Sailors and Their Captive Cargoes, 1730–1807.* New York: Cambridge University Press, 2006.

David Eltis and David Richardson. *Atlas of the Transatlantic Slave Trade.* New Haven: Yale University Press, 2010.

Rosemarie Robotham, ed. *Spirits of the Passage: The Transatlantic Slave Trade in the Seventeenth Century.* New York: Simon & Schuster, 1997.

Hugh Thomas. *The Slave Trade: The Story of the Atlantic Slave Trade, 1440–1870.* New York: Simon & Schuster, 1997.

Vincent Bakpetu Thompson. *The Making of the African Diaspora in the Americas, 1441–1900.* New York: Longman, 1987.

James Walvin. *Making the Black Atlantic: Britain and the African Diaspora.* New York: Cassell, 2000.

The West Indies

Edward Brathwaite. *The Development of Creole Society in Jamaica, 1770–1820.* New York: Oxford University Press, 1971.

William Claypole and John Robottom. *Caribbean Story: Foundations.* Kingston: Longman, 1980.

Melville J. Herskovits. *The Myth of the Negro Past.* Boston: Beacon, 1941.

Clarence J. Munford. *The Black Ordeal of Slavery and Slave Trading in the French West Indies, 1625–1715.* Lewiston, NY: Mellen, 1991.

Keith Albert Sandiford. *The Cultural Politics of Sugar: Caribbean Slavery and Narratives of Colonialism.* New York: Cambridge University Press, 2000.

Chapter 3

Black People in Colonial North America

1526–1763

This eighteenth-century woodcut shows enslaved black men, women, and children in the steps involved in the curing of tobacco.

∨ Learning Objectives

After reading this chapter, you should be able to:

3.1 Identify the various peoples of colonial North America.

3.2 Analyze the development of black servitude in the Chesapeake.

3.3 Describe the characteristics of plantation slavery as it existed between 1700 and 1750.

3.4 Discuss the factors that affected the way slaves lived in early America.

3.5 Discuss how miscegenation and creolization interacted in early African-American history.

3.6 Explain how African-American culture originated.

3.7 Compare and contrast slavery in the northern colonies with slavery in the southern colonies.

3.8 Compare and contrast the African-American experience under French and Spanish rule in North America with the African-American experience under British rule.

3.9 Describe African-American life in New Spain's northern borderlands.

3.10 Discuss how slavery affected black women in colonial America.

3.11 Describe the ways in which African Americans resisted slavery.

Whereas, the plantations and estates of this Province [of South Carolina] cannot be well and sufficiently managed and brought into use, without the labor and service of negroes and other slaves; and forasmuch as the said negroes and other slaves brought unto the People of the Province for that purpose, are of barbarous, wild, savage natures, and such as renders them wholly unqualified to be governed by the laws, customs, and practices of this Province; . . . it is absolutely necessary, that such other constitutions, laws and orders, should in this Province be made and enacted, for the good regulating and ordering of them, as may restrain the disorderly rapines and inhumanity, to which they are naturally prone and induced; and may also tend to the safety and security of the people of this Province and their estates.

—*From the introduction to the original South Carolina Slave Code of 1696*

African Americans lived in North America for nearly three centuries before the United States gained independence from Great Britain in 1783. During that long time period, most of them were slaves in British, French, and Spanish colonies. As a result, they left scant written testimony about their lives. Their history, therefore, must be learned through archaeology and the writings of the white settlers who enslaved and oppressed them.

The passage that begins this chapter is an example of what we can learn about African-American history by reading between the lines in the official publications of the colonial governments. As historian Winthrop D. Jordan points out, the founders of South Carolina in 1696 borrowed much of this section of the colony's law code from the British colony of Barbados in the Caribbean.

The code indicates that the British Carolinians believed they needed the labor of enslaved Africans for their colony to prosper. It also shows that the colonial British feared Africans and their African-American descendants. This ambivalence among white Americans concerning African Americans shaped life in colonial South Carolina and in other British colonies in North America. For nearly two centuries the dichotomy of white economic dependence on black labor and fear of black revolt remained a central fact of American history and provided a rationale for racial oppression.

The opening passage also reveals the willingness of British and other European settlers in North America to brand Africans and their American descendants as "barbarous, wild, [and] savage." Although real cultural differences underlay such negative perceptions, white people used them to justify oppressing black people. Unlike white people, black people by the 1640s could be enslaved for life. Black people did not enjoy the same legal protection as white people and received harsher punishment.

This chapter describes the history of African-American life in colonial North America from the early sixteenth century to the end of the **French and Indian War** in 1763. It concentrates on the British colonies that stretched along the eastern coast of the continent, but also briefly covers the black experience in Spanish Florida, in New Spain's southwestern borderlands, and in French Louisiana. During the seventeenth century, the plantation system that became a central part of black life in America for nearly two centuries took shape in the Chesapeake tobacco country and in the low country of South Carolina and Georgia. Unfree labor, which in the Chesapeake had originally involved both white and black people, solidified into a system of slavery based on race. Although the plantation system did not develop in Britain's northern colonies, race-based slavery existed in them as well. African Americans responded to these conditions by interacting with other groups, preserving parts of their African culture, seeking strength through religion, and resisting and rebelling against enslavement.

French and Indian War

A war between Great Britain and its American Indian allies and France and its American Indian allies, fought between 1754 and 1763 for control of the eastern portion of North America.

3.1 The Peoples of North America

Identify the various peoples of colonial North America.

In the North American colonies during the seventeenth and eighteenth centuries, African immigrants gave birth to a new African-American people. Born in North America and forever separated from their ancestral homeland, they preserved a surprisingly large core of their African cultural heritage. Meanwhile, a new natural environment and contacts with people of American Indian and European descent helped African Americans shape a way of life within the circumstances that slavery forced on them. To understand the early history of African Americans, we must first briefly discuss the other peoples of colonial North America.

3.1.1 American Indians

Historians and anthropologists group the original inhabitants of North America together as American Indians. (The terms *Amerinds* and *Native Americans* are also used, with the latter term including Inuits [Eskimos].) But when the British began to colonize the Atlantic coastal portion of this huge region during the early seventeenth century, the indigenous peoples who lived there had no such all-inclusive name. They spoke many different languages, lived in diverse environments, and considered themselves distinct from one another. Like other Indian peoples of the Western Hemisphere, they descended from Asians who, at least 15,000 years ago, had migrated eastward by coastal waterways and across a land bridge connecting Siberia and Alaska. Europeans called them Indians as a result of Christopher Columbus's mistaken assumption in 1492 that he had landed on islands near the "Indies," by which he meant near Southeast Asia.

In Mexico, Central America, and Peru, American Indian peoples developed complex, densely populated civilizations with hereditary monarchies, formal religions, armies, and social classes. Cultural developments in Mexico and the northward spread of the cultivation of maize (corn) influenced the indigenous peoples of what is today the United States. In the Southwest, the Anasazi and later Pueblo peoples developed farming communities. Beginning around 900 CE they produced pottery, studied astronomy, built large adobe towns, and struggled against a drying climate. Farther east in what is known as the Woodlands region, the Adena culture flourished in the Ohio River valley as early as 1000 BCE and attained the social organization required to construct large burial mounds. Between the tenth and fourteenth centuries CE, what is known as the Mississippian culture established a civilization, marked by extensive trade routes, division of labor, and urban centers. The largest such center was Cahokia—located near modern St. Louis, Missouri—which at its peak had a population of about 30,000.

Climate change and warfare destroyed the Mississippian culture during the fourteenth century, and only remnants of it existed when Europeans and Africans arrived in North America. By that time, a diverse variety of American Indian cultures existed in what is today the eastern portion of the United States. People resided in towns and villages, supplementing their agricultural economies with fishing and hunting. They held land communally, generally allowed women a voice in ruling councils, and—although warlike—usually regarded battle as an opportunity for young men to prove their bravery rather than as a means of conquest. Gravely weakened by diseases that settlers unwittingly brought from Europe, the woodlands Indians of North America's coastal regions could not effectively resist British settlers during the seventeenth century. Particularly in the Southeast, the British developed an extensive trade in Indian slaves.

Because American Indians were experts at living harmoniously with natural resources, they influenced the way people of African and European descent came to live in North America. Indian crops, such as corn, pumpkins, beans, and squash, became staples of the newcomers' diets. On the continent's southeastern coast, British cultivation of tobacco, another Indian crop, secured the economic survival of the Chesapeake colonies of Virginia and Maryland. Tobacco cultivation also led directly to the enslavement of Africans. The Indian canoe became a means of river transportation for black and white people, and everyone wore Indian moccasins.

The relationships between black people and American Indians during colonial times were complex. Although Indian nations often provided refuge to escaping black slaves, Indians sometimes became slaveholders and on occasion helped crush black revolts. Some black men assisted in the Indian slave trade and sometimes helped defend European colonists against Indian attacks. Meanwhile people of African and Indian descent frequently found themselves in similarly oppressive circumstances in Britain's American colonies. Although white officials attempted to keep them apart, social and sexual contacts between the two groups were frequent. Some interracial black–Indian settlements—and a few black–Indian–white settlements—have persisted to the present.

3.1.2 The Spanish, French, and Dutch

With one exception, European nations sent relatively few settlers to North America. Following Christopher Columbus's voyage in 1492, they recognized the great possibilities for gaining wealth and territory in the Americas. The Spanish, French, and Dutch thought in terms of trade with American Indians and expropriation of Indian labor.

Spain led the way. Beginning shortly after Columbus's first voyage Spanish adventurers, aided by a strong autocratic monarchy and internal peace at home, rapidly built a colonial empire in the Americas. Mining of gold and silver, as well as the production of sugar, tobacco, and leather goods, provided a firm economic foundation. But few Spaniards came to the Western Hemisphere. Consequently, Spain's colonial economy rested first on the forced labor of the Indian population and then increasingly on enslaved Africans when the Indian population declined from disease and overwork. African slaves arrived in the Spanish colonies as early as 1526 when Luis Vasquez de Ayllon employed 100 of them in an unsuccessful attempt to establish a settlement near what is now Georgetown, South Carolina. Later overseers in mines and fields often brutally worked Africans and Indians to death. But because the Spanish were few in number, some of the Africans and Indians who survived were able to gain freedom and become tradesmen, small landholders, and militiamen. Often they were of mixed race and identified with their former masters rather than with the oppressed people beneath them in society. African, Indian, and Spanish customs intermingled in what became a multicultural colonial society. Its center was in the West Indian islands of Cuba and Santo Domingo, Mexico, and northern South America. On its northern periphery were lands that are now part of the United States: Florida, Texas, Arizona, New Mexico, and California.

In part because of Spain's predominance and in part because of domestic religious strife, France did not establish a settlement in the Americas until 1604. That settlement centered on the St. Lawrence River and grew into what was known as either New France or Canada. It became a trading empire, based on acquiring beaver pelts and other furs from American Indians. The result was that throughout its existence New France's small French population depended on good commercial and military relations with Indian nations. There never were more than a few thousand slaves in New France, and most of them were Indian war captives. In the huge region of Louisiana, which France claimed from 1699 to 1763 and which stretched from the Gulf of Mexico to the Great Lakes, there were considerably larger numbers of Indian and African slaves. As in the Spanish colonies, although the death toll was extremely high for both groups of slaves, routes to freedom remained open.

Because the Netherlands—the Dutch homeland—spent much of the late sixteenth century in a struggle for independence from Spain, it, like France, did not succeed in establishing a colony in North America until the early seventeenth century. This colony, New Netherlands, centered on the Hudson River. Its chief settlement, New Amsterdam, located on Manhattan Island, later became New York City after the British conquered it in 1664. Like the French, the Dutch focused on the fur trade and attracted few European settlers beyond the area surrounding New Amsterdam. In that region the Dutch West Indian Company established African slavery in 1625. Under Dutch law, slaves retained basic human rights. Those rights and opportunities to work for wages led, as in the Spanish and French colonies, to the early appearance of a free black class.

3.1.3 The British and Jamestown

The Spanish had colonized warm, populous, and wealthy lands. The relatively less powerful French and Dutch acquired lands that were cooler, less populous, and deficient in easily acquired wealth. The British competed with the French and Dutch for these relatively less attractive lands. In addition, the British, like the Africans and the American Indians, were not a single nation. The British Isles—consisting principally of Britain and Ireland and located off the northwest coast of Europe—were the homeland of the English, Welsh, Scots, and Irish. By the seventeenth century, the English dominated the other ethnic groups. But at that time, the Kingdom of England was a poor country notable mainly for producing wool.

England's claim to the east coast of North America rested on the voyage of John Cabot, who sailed in 1497, just five years after Columbus's first westward voyage. But, unlike the Spanish who rapidly created an empire in the Americas, the English were slow to establish themselves in the region Cabot had reached. This was partly due to the harsher North American climate, with winters much colder than in England. In addition, the English monarchy was too poor to finance colonizing expeditions, and social turmoil associated with the Protestant Reformation absorbed its energies.

Attempts failed in the 1580s to colonize Newfoundland, a large island off the east coast of what is today Canada, and Roanoke Island, a small island off the coast of what is today North Carolina. It took the English naval victory over the **Spanish Armada** in 1588 and money raised by **joint-stock companies** to produce at Jamestown in 1607 the first successful British colony in North America. This settlement, established by the Virginia Company of London, was located in the Chesapeake region, which the British called Virginia—after Queen Elizabeth I (r. 1558–1603), the so-called Virgin Queen of England. The company hoped to make a profit at Jamestown by finding gold, trading with Indians, cutting lumber, or raising crops, such as rice, sugar, or silk, that could not be produced in Britain.

None of these schemes succeeded. There was no gold, and the climate was unsuitable for rice, sugar, and silk. Because of disease, hostility with the Indians, and especially economic failure, the settlement barely survived into the 1620s. By then, however,

Spanish Armada

A fleet that unsuccessfully attempted to carry out an invasion of England in 1588.

joint-stock companies

Primitive corporations that carried out British and Dutch colonization in the Americas during the seventeenth century.

English settler John Rolfe's experiments, begun in 1612 to cultivate a mild strain of tobacco that could be grown on the North American mainland, began to pay off. Smoking tobacco had become popular in Europe, and demand for it constantly increased. As a result, growing tobacco soon became the economic mainstay of Virginia and the neighboring colony of Maryland.

Sowing, cultivating, harvesting, and curing tobacco required considerable labor. Yet colonists in the Chesapeake could not follow the Spanish example of enslaving Indians to produce the crop. Disease had reduced the local Indian population, and those who survived eluded British conquest by retreating west.

Unlike the West Indian sugar planters, however, the North American tobacco planters did not immediately turn to Africa for laborers. British advocates of colonizing North America had always promoted it as a means to reduce unemployment, poverty, and crime in England. The idea was to send England's undesirables to America, where they could provide the cheap labor tobacco planters needed. Consequently, until 1700, white labor produced most of the tobacco in the Chesapeake colonies.

3.1.4 Africans Arrive in the Chesapeake

By early 1619, there were, nevertheless, 32 people of African descent—15 men and 17 women—living at Jamestown. Nothing is known about when they arrived or from where they came. They were all "in the service of sev[er]all planters." The following August a Dutch warship, carrying 17 African men and three African women, moored at Hampton Roads at the mouth of the James River. Historians long believed these were the first black people in British North America. They were part of a group of over 300 who had been taken from Angola by a Portuguese slaver that had set sail for the port of Vera Cruz in New Spain (Mexico). The Dutch warship, with the help of an English ship, had attacked the slaver, taken most of its human cargo, and brought these 20 Angolans to Jamestown. The Dutch captain traded them to local officials for provisions.

The Angolans became servants to Jamestown's officials and favored planters. For two reasons, the colony's inhabitants regarded both the new arrivals and those black people who had been in Jamestown earlier to be *unfree* but not slaves. First, unlike the Portuguese and the Spanish, the English had no law for slavery. Second, at least those Angolans who bore such names as Pedro, Isabella, Antoney, and Angelo were Christians, and—according to English custom and morality in 1619—Christians could not be enslaved. So, once these individuals worked off their purchase price, they regained their freedom. In 1623, Antoney and Isabella married. The next year they became parents of William, whom their master had baptized in the local **Church of England**. William may have been the first black person born in English America. He was almost certainly born free.

During the following years, people of African descent remained a small minority in the expanding Virginia colony. A 1625 census reported only 23 black people living in the colony, compared with a combined total of 1,275 white people and Indians. This suggests that many of the first black inhabitants had either died or moved away. By 1649 the total Virginia

Church of England

A Protestant church established in the sixteenth century as the English national or Anglican church with the English monarch as its head. After the American Revolution, its American branch became the Episcopal Church.

This painting by American illustrator Howard Pyle (1853–1911) is based on conjecture concerning the arrival of 20 African men and women at Jamestown in 1619.

population of about 18,500 included only 300 black people. The English, following the Spanish example, called them "negroes." (*Negro* means "black" in Spanish.) In neighboring Maryland, established in 1632 as a haven for persecuted English Catholics, the black population also remained small. In 1658 people of African descent accounted for only 3 percent of Maryland's population.

3.2 Black Servitude in the Chesapeake

Analyze the development of black servitude in the Chesapeake.

As these statistics suggest, during the early years of the Chesapeake colonies, black people represented a small part of a labor force composed mainly of white people. From the 1620s to the 1670s, black and white people worked in the tobacco fields together, lived together, and slept together (and also did these things with American Indians). They were all unfree indentured servants.

Indentured servitude had existed in Europe for centuries. In England, parents indentured—or, in other words, apprenticed—their children to "masters," who then controlled their lives and had the right to their labor for a set number of years. In return, the masters supported the children and taught them a trade or profession. Unrestrained by modern notions of human equality and democracy, masters could exercise brutal authority over those bound to them.

As the demand for labor to produce tobacco in the Chesapeake expanded, indentured servitude came to include adults who sold their freedom for two to seven years in return for the cost of their voyage to North America. Instead of training in a profession, the servants could improve their economic standing by remaining as free persons in America after completing their period of servitude.

When Africans first arrived in Virginia and Maryland, they entered into similar contracts, agreeing to work for their masters until the proceeds of their labor recouped the cost of their purchase. Indentured servitude could be harsh in the tobacco colonies because masters sought to get as much labor as they could from their servants before the indenture ended. Most indentured servants died from overwork or disease before regaining their freedom. But those who survived, black people as well as white people, could expect eventually to leave their masters and seek their fortunes as free persons.

The foremost example in early Virginia of a black man who emerged from servitude to become a tobacco planter himself is Anthony Johnson (see the Profile). But Johnson was not the only person of African descent who became a free property owner during the first half of the seventeenth century. Here and there, black men seemed to enjoy a status similar to their white counterparts. Free black men in the Chesapeake participated fully in the commercial and legal life of the colonies. They owned land, farmed, lent money, sued in the courts, served as jurors and minor officials, and at times voted.

This suggests that before the 1670s the English in the Chesapeake did not draw a strict line between white freedom and black slavery. Yet, beginning during the early 1600s, the ruling elite made decisions that limited the apparent social mobility Africans enjoyed. They treated black servants differently than they treated white servants. And, over the decades, the region's British population gradually came to believe that persons of African descent were inalterably alien. This sentiment did not become universal among the white poor during the colonial period. However, it provided a foundation for what historian Winthrop D. Jordan calls the "unthinking decision" among the British in the Chesapeake to establish **chattel slavery**. In this form of slavery, Africans and people of African descent became their master's private property on a level with livestock.

chattel slavery

A form of slavery in which the enslaved are treated legally as property.

Profile

Anthony Johnson

Little is known of the individual Africans and African Americans who lived in North America during the seventeenth and eighteenth centuries. A lack of contemporary accounts prevents us from truly understanding their personalities. In rare instances, however, black people emerge from bits and pieces of information preserved in court records. This is the case for Anthony Johnson and his family. Their accomplishments cast light on African-American life in the seventeenth-century Chesapeake.

Anthony Johnson arrived at Jamestown in 1621 from England, but his original home may have been Angola. He was fortunate the following year to escape death in an Indian attack on Jamestown. He was one of four out of 56 inhabitants on Edward Bennett's tobacco plantation, where he labored, to survive. He was also lucky to wed "Mary a Negro Woman," who in 1625 was the only woman residing at Bennett's. The couple had at least four children.

In 1635 Johnson's master, Nathaniel Littleton, released him from further service. Johnson, like other free men of this time and place, then scrambled to acquire wealth in the form of land, livestock, and human beings. He received his own 250-acre plantation in 1651 under the "headright system," by which the colonial government encouraged population growth by awarding 50 acres of land for every new servant a settler brought to Virginia.

This meant that Johnson had become the master of five servants; some of them were white. His property was on a neck of land between two creeks that flowed into the Pungoteague River in Northampton County. A few years later his relatives, John and Richard Johnson, also acquired land in this area. John brought 11 servants to the colony and received 550 acres, and Richard brought two and received one hundred acres.

The Johnson estates existed among white-owned properties in the same area. Like their white neighbors, the Johnsons did not belong to the planting elite. But they owned their own land, farmed, and had social, economic, and legal relations with other colonists. Anthony Johnson in particular engaged in litigation that tells us much about black life in early Virginia.

In 1654, his lawsuit against his black servant John Casor and a white neighbor set a precedent in favor of black slavery but also revealed Johnson's legal rights. Casor claimed that Johnson "had kept him his serv[an]t seven years longer than hee should or ought." Johnson, whom court records described as an "old Negro," responded that he was entitled to "ye Negro [Casor] for his life." Johnson momentarily relented when he realized that if he persisted in his suit, Casor could win damages against him. Shortly thereafter, however, Johnson brought suit against his white neighbor Robert Parker, whom Johnson charged had detained Casor "under pretense [that] the s[ai]d John Casor is a freeman." This time the court ruled in Johnson's favor. It returned Casor to him and required Parker to pay court costs.

During the 1660s, the extended Johnson family moved to Somerset, Maryland, where its members had acquired additional land. Anthony Johnson's estate became known as "Tonies Vinyard." He and Mary died there during the early 1670s. Their descendants continued to prosper as planters into the eighteenth century when records of the family in Maryland end. Some family members had moved on to New Jersey and others to Delaware, where some of them intermarried with the Nanticoke Indians. Historian John H. Russell exaggerated when he claimed in 1913 that black people in the seventeenth century had roughly the same opportunities as free white servants. But industrious and lucky black people at that time could achieve a social and economic standing that became nearly impossible for their descendants.

3.2.1 Race and the Origins of Black Slavery

Between 1640 and 1700, the British tobacco-producing colonies stretching from Delaware to northern Carolina underwent a social and demographic revolution. An economy once based primarily on the labor of white indentured servants became an economy based on the labor of black slaves. In Virginia, for example, the slave population in 1671 amounted to less than 5 percent of the colony's total non-Indian population. White indentured servants outnumbered black slaves by three to one. By 1700, however, slaves constituted at least 20 percent of Virginia's population. Most agricultural laborers were slaves.

Although historians debate how this change occurred, several interrelated factors brought it about. Some of these factors are easily understood. Others are more complicated and profound because they involve basic assumptions about the American nation.

Economic and demographic developments had major roles. During the second quarter of the seventeenth century, Britain's Caribbean sugar colonies set a precedent for enslaving Africans. Fewer poor white people came to the tobacco colonies as they found better opportunities for themselves in other regions of British North America. As Britain gained increased control over the Atlantic slave trade, African slaves became less costly.

These changing circumstances provide the context for the mass enslavement of people of African descent in the tobacco colonies. Race became crucial in shaping the *character* of unfree labor in the British mainland colonies. The English had historically distinguished between how they treated each other and how they treated those who differed physically and culturally from them. Such discrimination had been the basis of English colonial policies toward the Irish—whom England had been trying to conquer for centuries—and the American Indians. Because the English considered Africans even more different from themselves than either the Irish or the Indians, they had assumed from the beginning that Africans were especially inferior.

Therefore, although black and white servants residing in the Chesapeake during the early seventeenth century had much in common, their masters made distinctions between them based on race. The few women of African descent who arrived in the Chesapeake during those years worked in the tobacco fields with men, while most white women performed domestic duties. Also, unlike white servants, black servants usually did not have surnames, and early census reports listed them separately from white people. By the 1640s, black people could not bear arms, and local Anglican priests (unlike priests in England) maintained that persons of African descent could not become Christians. Although interracial sexual contacts among black, white, and Indian people were common, colonial authorities soon discouraged them. In 1662 Virginia's **House of Burgesses** (the colony's legislature) declared that "any christian [white person]" who committed "fornication with a negro man or woman, he or shee soe offending" would pay double the fine set for committing the same offense with a white person.

These distinctions suggest that the status of black servants had never been the same as that of white servants. But only starting in the 1640s do records indicate a predilection toward making black people slaves rather than servants. During that decade, courts in Virginia and Maryland began to assume that it was permissible for persons of African descent to serve their master for life rather than a set term. By then black men, women, and children often sold for higher prices than their white counterparts on the explicit provision that black people would serve "for their Life tyme," or "for ever."

3.2.2 The Legal Recognition of Chattel Slavery

Legal documents and statute books reveal that, during the 1660s, additional aspects of chattel slavery emerged in the Chesapeake colonies. Bills of sale began to stipulate that the children of black female servants would also be servants for life. In 1662 the House of Burgesses decreed that a child's condition—free or unfree—followed that of the mother. This ran counter to English common law, which assumed that a child's status derived from the father. The change permitted masters to exploit their black female servants sexually without having to acknowledge the children who might result from such contacts. Just as significant, by the mid-1660s statutes in the Chesapeake colonies assumed servitude to be the natural condition of black people.

With these laws, slavery in British North America emerged in the form that it retained until the American Civil War: a racially defined system of perpetual involuntary servitude that compelled almost all black people to work as agricultural labor-ers. **Slave codes** enacted between 1660 and 1710 further defined

House of Burgesses

A representative body established at Jamestown, Virginia, in 1619.

slave codes

Sometimes known as "black codes," a series of laws passed to define slaves as property and specify the legal powers of masters over slaves.

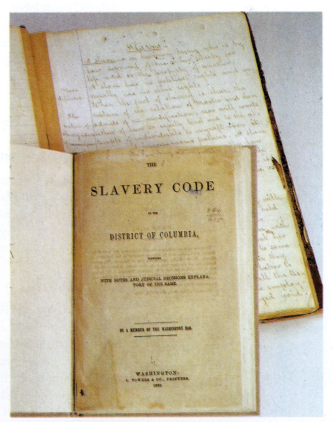

Slave codes regulated slaves and asserted the rights of slave owners.

American slavery as a system that sought as much to control persons of African descent as to exploit their labor. Slaves could not testify against white people in court, own property, leave their master's estate without a pass, congregate in groups larger than three or four, enter into contracts, or marry. They could not, of course, bear arms. Profession of Christianity no longer protected a black person from enslavement, nor was conversion a cause for **manumission**. In 1669 the House of Burgesses exempted from felony charges masters who killed a slave while administering punishment.

By 1700, just as the slave system began to expand in the southern colonies, enslaved Africans and African Americans had been reduced legally to the status of domestic animals. The only major exception was that, unlike animals (or masters who abused slaves), the law held slaves strictly accountable for crimes they committed.

manumission

The act of freeing a slave by the slave's master.

3.2.3 Bacon's Rebellion and American Slavery

The series of events that led to the enslavement of black people in the Chesapeake tobacco colonies preceded their emergence as the great majority of laborers in those colonies. The dwindling supply of white indentured servants, the growing availability of Africans, preexisting white racial biases, and legislation all affected this transformation. But the key event in bringing it about was the rebellion Nathaniel Bacon led in 1676.

Bacon was an English aristocrat who had recently migrated to Virginia. The immediate cause of his rebellion was disagreement over Indian policy between him and the colony's royal governor William Berkeley. Bacon, representing frontier interests, desired to attack and kill Indians. Berkeley, who profited from trade in furs with the Indians, refused to undertake such attacks. But white indentured servants, former indentured servants, and black slaves joined in the rebellion. This suggests that poor white and black people had a chance to unite against the **planter elite**.

Before such a class-based, biracial alliance could be realized, however, Bacon died of dysentery, and his rebellion collapsed. Even so, Bacon's uprising convinced the colony's elite that continued reliance on white agricultural laborers, who could become free and get guns, was dangerous. By moving rapidly toward full reliance on an enslaved black labor force that the planters assumed would never become free or have firearms, they hoped to avoid class conflict among white people. Increasingly thereafter, white Americans perceived that both their freedom from class conflict and their prosperity rested on denying freedom to black Americans.

planter elite

Those who owned the largest tobacco plantations.

3.3 Plantation Slavery, 1700–1750

Describe the characteristics of plantation slavery as it existed between 1700 and 1750.

The reliance of Chesapeake planters on slavery to meet their labor needs resulted from racial prejudice, the declining availability of white indentured servants, the increasing availability of Africans, and fear of white class conflict. When, following the shift from white indentured to enslaved black labor, the demand for tobacco in Europe increased sharply, the newly dominant slave labor system expanded rapidly.

3.3.1 Tobacco Colonies

Between 1700 and 1770, some 80,000 Africans arrived in the tobacco colonies, and even more African Americans were born into slavery there (see Figure 3-1). Tobacco planting spread from Virginia and Maryland to Delaware and North Carolina and from the coastal plain to the foothills of the Appalachian Mountains. In the process, American slavery assumed the form it kept for the next 165 years.

By 1750, 144,872 slaves lived in Virginia and Maryland, accounting for 61 percent of all the slaves in British North America. Another 40,000 slaves lived in the rice-producing

Figure 3-1 Africans Brought as Slaves to British North America, 1701–1775

The rise in the number of captive Africans shipped to British North America during the early eighteenth century reflects the increasing dependence of British planters on African slave labor. The declines in slave imports during the periods 1751–1760 and 1771–1775 resulted from disruptions to commerce associated with the French and Indian War (or Seven Years' War) and the struggle between the colonies and Great Britain that preceded the American War for Independence.

SOURCE: Based on the data from *The American Colonies: From Settlement to Independence,* by R. C. Simmons. © Darlene Clark Hine.

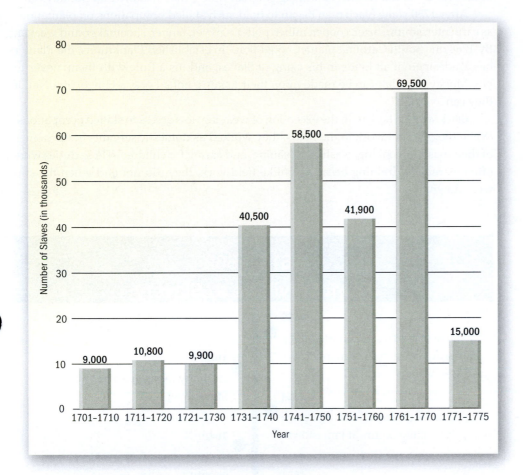

regions of South Carolina and Georgia, accounting for 17 percent. It is important to note that, unlike in the sugar colonies of the Caribbean where white people were a tiny minority, they constituted a majority in the tobacco colonies and a large minority in the rice colonies. Also, most white southerners did not own slaves. Nevertheless, the economic development of the region depended on black slaves.

The conditions under which slaves lived varied. Most slaveholders farmed small tracts of land and owned fewer than five slaves. These masters and their slaves worked together and developed close relationships. Other masters owned thousands of acres of land and rarely saw most of their slaves. During the early eighteenth century, the latter type of masters—great planters—divided their slaves among several small holdings. They did this to avoid concentrating potentially rebellious Africans in one area. As the proportion of newly arrived Africans in the slave population declined later in the century, larger concentrations of slaves became more common.

From the beginnings of slavery in North America, masters tried to make slaves work harder and faster while slaves sought to conserve their energy, take breaks, and socialize with each other. African men regarded field labor as women's work and tried to avoid it. But, especially if they had incentives, enslaved Africans could be efficient workers. One incentive to which both slaves and masters looked forward was the annual harvest festival. These festivals, derived from both Africa and Europe, became common throughout the British colonies early in the eighteenth century.

Before the mid-eighteenth century, nearly all slaves—both men and women—worked in the fields. On the smaller farms, they worked with their master. On larger estates, they worked for an overseer, who was usually white. Like other agricultural workers, enslaved African Americans normally worked from sunup to sundown with breaks for food and rest. Even during colonial times, they usually had Sunday off.

After 1750 some black men began to hold such skilled occupations on plantations as carpenter, smith, carter, cooper, miller, potter, sawyer, tanner, shoemaker, and weaver. By 1768 one South Carolina planter noted that "in established Plantations, the Planter has Tradesmen of all kinds in his Gang of Slaves, and 'tis a Rule with them, never to pay Money for what can be made upon their Estates, not a Lock, a Hinge, or a Nail if they can avoid it."

Black women had, with the exception of weaving, less access to skilled occupations. When they did not work in the fields, they worked as domestic servants in the homes of their masters, cooking, washing, cleaning, and caring for children. These duties were often extremely draining because, unlike fieldwork, they did not end when the sun went down.

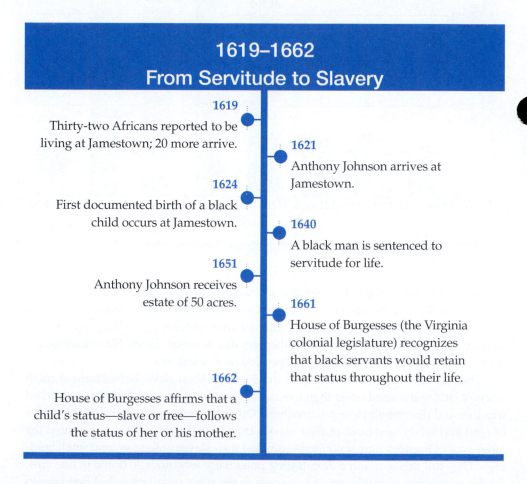

1619–1662
From Servitude to Slavery

1619
Thirty-two Africans reported to be living at Jamestown; 20 more arrive.

1621
Anthony Johnson arrives at Jamestown.

1624
First documented birth of a black child occurs at Jamestown.

1640
A black man is sentenced to servitude for life.

1651
Anthony Johnson receives estate of 50 acres.

1661
House of Burgesses (the Virginia colonial legislature) recognizes that black servants would retain that status throughout their life.

1662
House of Burgesses affirms that a child's status—slave or free—follows the status of her or his mother.

3.3.2 Low-Country Slavery

low country

The coastal regions of South Carolina and Georgia.

South of the tobacco colonies, on the coastal plain or **low country** of Carolina and Georgia, a distinctive slave society developed (see Map 3-1). The West Indian plantation system had much more influence here than in the Chesapeake, and rice, not tobacco, became the staple crop.

The first British settlers who arrived in 1670 at Charleston (in what would later become South Carolina) came mainly from Barbados, a sugar-producing island in the West Indies, rather than from England. Many of them had been slaveholders on that island and brought slaves with them. Therefore, in the low country, black people were never indentured servants. They were chattel from the start. The region's subtropical climate discouraged white settlement and encouraged dependence on black labor the way it did in the sugar islands. During the early years, nearly one-third of the settlers were African, most of them male. By the early eighteenth century, more Africans had arrived than white people. Carolina also became the center of an Indian slave trade. White Carolinians enslaved more American Indians than other British colonists did. During the early 1700s, Indians accounted for approximately one-quarter of the colony's slave population. Although official colonial policy sought to keep Africans and Indians apart, black slaves sometimes helped acquire and transport Indian slaves. Carolina exported Indian slaves to the West Indies and to other mainland British colonies.

By 1740 the Carolina low country had 40,000 slaves, who constituted 90 percent of the population in the region around Charleston. In all, 94,000 Africans arrived at Charleston between 1706 and 1776, which made it North America's leading port of entry for Africans during the eighteenth century. A Swiss immigrant commented in 1737 that the region "looks more like a negro country than like a country settled by white people."

During its first three decades, Carolina supplied Barbados with beef. Therefore, white settlers sought West Africans from the Gambia River region as slaves because they were skilled herders. Starting around 1700, when the low-country planters began concentrating on growing rice, they sought slaves skilled in growing that crop, which had been grown in West Africa for thousands of years. Economies of scale, in which an industry becomes more efficient as it grows larger, were more important in the production of rice than tobacco. Although tobacco could be profitably produced on small farms, rice required large acreages. Therefore, large plantations similar to those on the sugar islands of the West Indies became the rule in the low country.

In 1732 King George II of England chartered the colony of Georgia to serve as a buffer between South Carolina and Spanish Florida. James Oglethorpe, who received the royal charter, wanted to establish a refuge for England's poor, who were expected to become virtuous through their labor. Consequently, in 1734 Oglethorpe and the colony's other trustees banned slavery in Georgia. Economic difficulties, combined with land hunger among white South Carolinians, soon led to the ban's repeal. During the 1750s, rice cultivation and slavery spread into Georgia's coastal plain. By 1773 Georgia had as many black people—15,000—as white people.

Map 3-1 Regions of Colonial North America, 1683–1763

The British colonies on the North American mainland were divided into four regions. They were bordered on the south by Spanish Florida and to the west by regions claimed by France.

How did African Americans in the British colonies benefit from the close proximity of regions controlled by France and Spain?

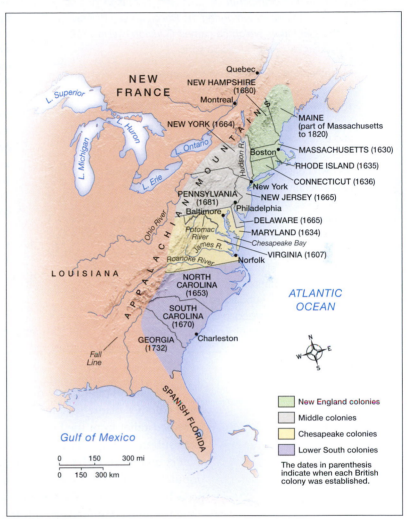

Voices

A Description of an Eighteenth-Century Virginia Plantation

The following eyewitness account of a large Virginia plantation in Fairfax County indicates the sorts of skilled labor slaves performed by the mid-eighteenth century. George Mason, one of Virginia's leading statesmen during the Revolutionary War era, owned this plantation, which he named Gunston Hall in 1758. The account is by one of Mason's sons.

My father had among his slaves carpenters, coopers, sawyers, blacksmiths, tanners, curriers, shoemakers, spinners, weavers and knitters, and even a distiller. His woods furnished timber and plank for the carpenters and coopers, and charcoal for the blacksmith, his cattle killed for his own consumption and for sale supplied skins for tanners, curriers, and shoemakers, and his sheep gave wool and his fields produced cotton and flax for the weavers and spinners, and his orchards fruit for the distiller. His carpenters and sawyers built and kept in repair all the dwelling-houses, barns, stables, ploughs, harrows, gates, &c., on the plantations and the outhouses at the home house. His coopers made the hogsheads the tobacco was prized in and the tight casks to hold the cider and other liquors. The tanners and curriers with the proper vats &c., tanned and dressed the skins as well for upper as for lower leather to the full amount of the consumption of the estate, and shoemakers made them into shoes for the negroes. . . . The blacksmith did all the iron work required by the establishment, as making and repairing ploughs, harrows, teeth chains, bolts, &c., &c. The spinners, weavers and knitters made all the coarse cloths and stockings used by the negroes, and nearly all worn by the children of it. The distiller made every fall a good deal of apple, peach and persimmon brandy. . . . Moreover, all the beeves and hogs for consumption or sale were driven up and slaughtered there at the proper seasons, and whatever was to be preserved was salted and packed away for after distribution.

1. What does this passage indicate about plantation life in mid-eighteenth-century Virginia?
2. How does the description of black people presented here compare to the passage from the South Carolina statute book that begins this chapter?

SOURCE: Speech Given in Gunston Hall by George Mason, 1830.

Absentee plantation owners became the rule in South Carolina and Georgia. In these colonies planters preferred to live in Charleston or Savannah where sea breezes provided relief from the heat. Meanwhile, enslaved Africans on low-country plantations suffered a high mortality rate from disease, overwork, and poor treatment, just as their counterparts did on Barbados and other sugar islands. Therefore, unlike the slave population in the Chesapeake colonies, the slave population in the low country did not grow by natural reproduction. Instead, until shortly before the American Revolution, it grew through continued arrivals from Africa.

Low-country slave society developed striking paradoxes in race relations. As the region's black population grew, white people became fearful of revolt, and by 1698 Carolina had the strictest slave code in North America. In 1721, Charleston organized a "Negro watch" to enforce a curfew on its black population, and watchmen could shoot recalcitrant Africans and African Americans on sight. Yet, as the passage that begins this chapter indicates, black people in Carolina faced the quandary of being both feared and needed by white people. Even as persons of European descent grew fearful of black revolt, the colony in 1704 authorized the arming of enslaved black men when needed for defense against Indian and Spanish raids.

Of equal significance was the appearance in Carolina, and to some extent in Georgia, of distinct classes among people of color. Like the low-country society itself, such classes were more similar to those in the Caribbean sugar islands than to the mainland colonies to the north. A Creole population that had absorbed European values lived alongside white people in Charleston and Savannah. Members of this Creole population were frequently mixed-race relatives of their masters and enjoyed social and economic privileges denied to slaves who labored on the nearby rice plantations. Yet this urban mixed-race class was under constant white supervision.

In contrast, slaves who lived in the country retained considerable autonomy in their daily routines. The intense cultivation required to produce rice encouraged the evolution of a "task system" of labor on the low-country plantations. Rather than working in gangs as in the tobacco colonies, slaves on rice plantations had daily tasks. When they completed these tasks, they could work on plots of land assigned to them or do what they pleased without white supervision. Because black people were the great majority in the low-country plantations, they also preserved more of their African heritage than did black people who lived in the region's cities or in the more northerly British mainland colonies.

3.3.3 Plantation Technology

During the American colonial era, most people of African descent living on southern plantations employed technologies associated with raising and processing crops for distant markets. A minority gained technical skills associated with a variety of trades.

In tobacco-growing regions, the harvest began a process of preparing leaves for market. Slaves hung plants in "tobacco houses," whose open construction kept out sunlight and rain while allowing breezes to circulate and dry the leaves. After six weeks, slaves removed the leaves and packaged them in wooden barrels for shipment. On low-country rice plantations, slaves built, operated, and maintained irrigation systems. They threshed, winnowed, and pounded rice to remove the husks. At first they performed these labor-intensive operations by hand. By the mid-eighteenth century, however, masters introduced "winnowing fans and pounding mills" powered by draft animals. Also, during the eighteenth century, low-country slave artisans built the vats, pumps, and structures required for turning indigo plants into a blue dye that was popular in Europe. As the indigo fermented in vats—releasing noxious fumes—slaves pumped in water, stirred and beat the plants into pulp, drained away blue liquid, solidified it with lime, dried it, and cut it into blocks.

Enslaved carpenters used a variety of hand tools to construct the buildings required for all these processes. They also built other plantation buildings. Slave sawyers operated water-powered mills to cut lumber. Other slaves made barrels. They cut and prepared oak staves—a process that took three years—trimmed the staves, soaked them, and bound them with iron hoops. Plantation blacksmiths used charcoal-burning hearths and billows to form the hoops from iron ingots and—using tongs and hammers—pounded the hoops into shape on anvils. They used a similar process to fashion nails, axe and hammer heads, hooks, horseshoes, hinges, and locks.

Like carpentry, tanning was essential. But, like indigo production, it was a laborious, smelly, and extended operation. Slaves cooked deer and cow hides in lime to remove fur and then washed off the lime with a mixture of animal dung, salt, and water. They used *tannin*, a chemical found in tree bark, to cure the hides. After drying, softening, stretching, and trimming, slave craftsmen used the leather to make shoes, boots, garments, and other articles.

3.4 Slave Life in Early America

Discuss the factors that affected the way slaves lived in early America.

Little evidence survives of the individual lives of enslaved black people in colonial North America. This is because they, along with American Indians and most white people of that era, were poor, illiterate, and kept no records. Yet recent studies provide a glimpse of their material culture.

Eighteenth-century housing for slaves was minimal and often temporary. In the Chesapeake, small log cabins predominated. They had dirt floors, brick fireplaces, wooden chimneys, and few, if any, windows. African styles of architecture were more

SLAVES' QUARTERS IN THE CELLAR OF THE OLD KNICKERBOCKER MANSION.

This 1876 drawing romanticizes the home life of slaves. The Knickerbocker Mansion is located in Schaghticoke, New York, and dates to 1770.

common in coastal South Carolina and Georgia. In these regions, slaves built the walls of their houses with tabby—a mixture of lime, oyster shells, and sand—or, occasionally, mud. In either case, the houses had thatched roofs. Early in the eighteenth century, when single African men made up the mass of the slave population, these structures served as dormitories. Later they housed generations of black families.

The amount of furniture and cooking utensils the cabins contained varied from place to place and according to how long the cabins were occupied. In some cabins, the only furniture consisted of wooden boxes for both storage and seating and planks for beds. But a 1697 inventory of items contained in a slave cabin in Virginia lists chairs, a bed, a large iron kettle, a brass kettle, an iron pot, a frying pan, and a "beer barrel." Enslaved black people, like contemporary Indians and white people, used hollowed-out gourds for cups and carted water in wooden buckets for drinking, cooking, and washing. As the eighteenth century progressed, slave housing on large plantations became more substantial, and slaves acquired tables, linens, chamber pots, and oil lamps. Yet primitive, poorly furnished log cabins persisted in many regions even after the abolition of slavery in 1865.

At first, slaves wore minimal clothing during summer. Men had breechcloths; women had skirts, leaving their upper bodies bare; and children went naked until puberty. Later men wore shirts, trousers, and hats while working in the fields. Women wore shifts (loose, simple dresses) and covered their heads with handkerchiefs. In winter, masters provided heavier cotton and woolen clothing and cheap leather shoes. In the early years, much of the clothing, or at least the cloth used to make it, came from England. Later, as the account of George Mason's Gunston Hall plantation indicated, homespun fabric made by slaves replaced English cloth. From the seventeenth century onward, slave women brightened clothing with dyes made from bark, decorated clothing with ornaments, and created African-style head wraps, hats, and hairstyles. In this manner, African Americans retained a sense of personal style compatible with West African culture.

Food consisted of corn, yams, salt pork, and occasionally salt beef and salt fish. Slaves caught fish and raised chickens and rabbits. When, during the eighteenth century, farmers in the Chesapeake began planting wheat, slaves baked biscuits. In the South Carolina low country, rice became an important part of African-American diets, but even there corn was the staple. During colonial times, slaves occasionally supplemented this limited diet with vegetables they raised in their gardens. They planted cabbage, cauliflower, black-eyed peas, turnips, collard greens, and rutabagas.

3.5 Miscegenation and Creolization

Discuss how miscegenation and creolization interacted in early African-American history.

When Africans first arrived in the Chesapeake during the early seventeenth century, they interacted culturally and physically with white indentured servants and with American Indians. This mixing of peoples changed all three groups. Interracial sexual contacts—miscegenation—produced people of mixed race. Meanwhile, cultural exchanges became an essential part of the process of creolization that led African parents to produce African-American children. When, as often happened, miscegenation and creolization occurred together, the result was both physical and cultural. However, the dominant British minority in North America during the colonial period defined persons of mixed race as black. Although enslaved mulattoes—those of mixed African and European ancestry—enjoyed some advantages over slaves who had a purely African ancestry, mulattoes as a group did not receive enhanced legal status.

Miscegenation between black people and white people, and black people and Indians, took place throughout British North America during the seventeenth and eighteenth centuries. But it was less extensive and accepted than in sugar colonies in the Caribbean, Latin America, or French Canada, where many French men married Indian women. British North America was exceptional because many more white women migrated there than to Canada, Latin America, or the Caribbean. Therefore, in British North America white men were far less likely to take black or Indian wives and concubines. Sexual relations between Africans and Indians were also more limited than they were elsewhere. This was because the coastal Indian population had drastically declined before large numbers of Africans arrived.

Yet miscegenation between black people and the remaining Indians certainly was extensive in British North America. There were also striking examples of black–white intermarriage. In 1656 in Northumberland County, Virginia, a mulatto woman named Elizabeth Kay successfully sued for her freedom and immediately thereafter married her white lawyer. In Norfolk County, Virginia, in 1671, Francis Skiper had to pay a tax on his wife Anne because she was black. In Westmoreland County, Virginia, in 1691, Hester Tate, a white indentured servant, and her husband James Tate, a black slave, had four children. One was apprenticed to her master and the other three to his.

Colonial assemblies banned such interracial marriages mainly to keep white women from bearing mulatto children. The assemblies feared that having free white mothers might allow persons of mixed race to sue and gain their freedom, thereby creating a legally recognized free mixed-race class. Such a class, wealthy white people feared, would blur the distinction between the dominant and subordinate races and weaken white supremacy. The assemblies did far less to prevent white male masters from sexually exploiting their black female slaves—although they considered such exploitation immoral—because the children of such liaisons would be slaves.

3.6 The Origins of African-American Culture

Explain how African-American culture originated.

Creolization and miscegenation transformed the descendants of the Africans who arrived in North America into African Americans. Historians long believed that in this process the Creoles lost their African heritage. But since Melville J. Herskovits published *The Myth of the Negro Past* in 1941 (see Chapter 2), scholars have found many African legacies not only in African-American culture but in American culture in general.

The second generation of people of African descent in North America did lose their parents' native languages and their ethnic identity as Igbos, Angolans, or Senegambians. But they retained a generalized West African heritage and passed it on to their descendants. Among the major elements of that heritage were family structure and notions of kinship, religious concepts and practices, African words and modes of expression, musical style and instruments, cooking methods and foods, folk literature, and folk arts.

This eighteenth-century painting of slaves on a South Carolina plantation provides graphic proof of the continuities between West African culture and the emerging culture of African Americans. The religious dance, the drum and banjo, and elements of the participants' clothing are all West African in origin.

The preservation of the West African extended family was the basis of African-American culture. Because most Africans imported into the British colonies during the late seventeenth and early eighteenth centuries were males, most black men of that era could not have wives and children. It was not until the Atlantic slave trade declined briefly during the 1750s that sex ratios became more balanced and African-American family life began to flourish. Without that family life, black people could not have maintained as much of Africa as they did.

During the Middle Passage, enslaved Africans created "fictive kin relationships" for mutual support. In dire circumstances, African Americans continued to improvise family structures. By the mid-eighteenth century, however, extended black families based on biological relationships dominated. Black people retained knowledge of these relationships to second and third cousins over several generations and wide stretches of territory. These extended families had roots in Africa but were also a result of—and a reaction to—slavery. West African **incest taboos** encouraged slaves to pick mates who lived on plantations other than their own. The sale of slaves away from their immediate families tended to extend families over wide areas. Once established, such far-flung kinship ties helped others, who had been forced to leave home, to adapt to new conditions under a new master. And kinfolk sheltered escapees.

incest taboos

Customary rules against sexual relations and marriage within family and kinship groups.

Extended families also influenced African-American naming practices, which in turn reinforced family ties. Africans named male children after close relatives. This custom survived in America because boys were more likely to be separated from their parents by being sold than girls were. Having the name of one's father or grandfather preserved one's family identity. Also, early in the eighteenth century, when more African Americans began to use surnames, they clung to the name of their original master. This reflected a West African predisposition to link a family name with a certain location. Like taking a parent's name, it helped maintain family relationships despite repeated scatterings.

The result was that African Americans preserved given and family names over many generations. Black men continued to bear such African names as Cudjo, Quash, Cuffee, and Sambo, and black women such names as Quasheba and Juba. Even when masters imposed demeaning classical names, such as Caesar, Pompey, Venus, and Juno, black Americans passed them on from generation to generation.

Bible names did not become common among African Americans until the mid-eighteenth century. This was because before that time masters often refused to allow slaves to be converted to Christianity. As a result, African religions—both indigenous and Islamic—persisted in parts of America well into the nineteenth century. The indigenous religions in particular maintained a premodern perception of the unity of the natural and the supernatural, the secular and the sacred, and the living and the dead. Black Americans continued to perform an African circle dance known as the "ring shout" at funerals, and they decorated graves with shells and pottery in the West African manner. They looked to recently arrived Africans for religious guidance, held bodies of water to be sacred, remained in daily contact with their ancestors through **spirit possession**, and practiced **divination** and magic. When they became ill, they turned to "herb doctors" and "root workers." Even when many African Americans began to convert to Christianity during the mid-eighteenth century, West African religious thought and practice shaped their lives.

spirit possession

A belief rooted in West African religions that spirits may possess human souls.

divination

A form of magic aimed at telling the future by interpreting a variety of signs.

3.6.1 The Great Awakening

The major turning point in African-American religion came in conjunction with the religious revival known as the Great Awakening. This extensive social movement of the mid- to late-eighteenth century grew out of growing dissatisfaction among white Americans with a deterministic and increasingly formalistic style of Protestantism that seemed to deny most people a chance for salvation. During the early 1730s in western Massachusetts, a Congregationalist minister named Jonathan Edwards began an emotional and participatory ministry aimed at bringing more people into the church. Later that decade, George Whitefield, an Englishman who along with John Wesley founded the Methodist Church, carried a similarly evangelical style of Christianity to the mainland colonies. In his sermons, Whitefield appealed to emotions, offered salvation to all who believed in Christ, and—although he did not advocate emancipation—preached to black people as well as white people.

Some people of African descent had converted to Christianity before Whitefield's arrival in North America. But two factors had prevented widespread black conversion. First, most masters feared that converted slaves would interpret their new religious status as a step toward freedom and equality. A South Carolina minister lamented in 1713, "The Masters of Slaves are generally of Opinion that a Slave grows worse by being a Christian; and therefore instead of instructing them in the principles of Christianity . . . malign and traduce those that attempt it." Second, many slaves remained so devoted to their ancestral religions that Christianity did not attract them.

With the Great Awakening, however, a process of general conversion began. African Americans did indeed link the spiritual equality preached by evangelical ministers with a hope for earthly equality. They tied salvation for the soul with liberation for the body. They recognized that the preaching style Whitefield and other evangelicals adopted had much in common with West African "spirit possession." As in West African religion, eighteenth-century revivalism in North America emphasized personal rebirth, singing, movement, and emotion. The practice of total body immersion during baptism in rivers, ponds, and lakes that gave the Baptist church its name paralleled West African water rites.

Because it drew African Americans into an evangelical movement that helped shape American society, the Great Awakening increased mutual black–white acculturation. Revivalists appealed to the poor of all races and emphasized spiritual equality. Evangelical Anglican, Baptist, Methodist, and Presbyterian churches welcomed black people. Members of these biracial churches addressed each other as *brother* and *sister*. Black members took communion with white members and served as church officers. The same church discipline applied to both races. By the late eighteenth century, a few black men gained ordination as priests and ministers and—often while still enslaved— preached to white congregations. They thereby influenced white people's perception of how services should be conducted.

Black worshipers also influenced white preachers and white religion. In 1756, a white minister in Virginia noted that African Americans spent nights in his kitchen. He recorded in his diary that "sometimes, when I have awakened about two-or three-a-clock in the morning, a torrent of sacred harmony poured into my chamber, and carried my mind away to Heaven."

Other factors, however, favored the development of a distinct African-American church. From the start, white churches seated black people apart from white people, belying claims to spiritual equality. Black members took communion *after* white members. Masters also tried to use religion to instill in their chattels such self-serving Christian virtues as meekness, humility, and obedience. Consequently, when they could, African Americans established their own churches. Dancing, shouting, clapping, and singing became especially characteristic of their religious meetings. Black spirituals probably date from the eighteenth century and, like African-American Christianity itself, they blended West African and European elements.

African Americans also retained the West African assumption that the souls of the dead returned to their homeland and rejoined their ancestors. Reflecting this family-oriented view of death, African-American funerals were often loud and joyous occasions with dancing, laughing, and drinking. Perhaps most important, the emerging black church reinforced black people's collective identity and helped them persevere in slavery.

3.6.2 Language, Music, and Folk Literature

Although African Americans did not retain their ancestral languages, those languages contributed to the **pidgins** and creolized languages that became **Black English** by the nineteenth century. It was in the low country, with its large and isolated black populations, that African-English creoles lasted the longest. The Gullah and Geechee dialects of the sea islands of South Carolina and Georgia, which combine African words and grammatical elements with a basically English structure, are still spoken today. In other regions, where black people were less numerous, creole languages did not last so long. Nevertheless, they contributed many words to American—particularly southern—English. Among them are *yam*, *banjo* (from mbanza), *tote*, *goober* (peanut), *buckra* (white man), *cooter* (tortoise), *gumbo* (okra), *nanse* (spider), *samba* (dance), *tabby* (a form of concrete), and *voodoo*.

Music was another essential part of West African life, and it remained so among African Americans, who preserved an antiphonal, call-and-response style of singing with an emphasis on improvisation, complex rhythms, and a strong beat. They sang while working and during religious ceremonies. Early on, masters banned drums and horns because of their potential for long-distance communication among slaves. But the African banjo survived in America, and African Americans quickly adopted the violin and guitar. At night, in their cabins or around communal fires, slaves accompanied these instruments with bones and spoons. Aside from family and religion, music may have been the most important aspect of African culture in the lives of American slaves. Eventually, African-American music influenced all forms of American popular music.

West African folk literature also survived in North America. African tales, proverbs, and riddles—with accretions from American Indian and European stories—entertained, instructed, and united African Americans. Just as the black people on the sea islands of South Carolina and Georgia were most able to retain elements of African language, so did their folk literature remain closest to its African counterpart. Africans used tales of how weak animals like rabbits outsmarted stronger animals like hyenas and lions to symbolize the power of the common people over unjust rulers (see Chapter 1). African Americans used similar tales to portray the ability of slaves to outsmart and ridicule their masters.

pidgin

A simplified mixture of two or more languages used to communicate between people who speak different languages.

Black English

A variety of American English that is influenced by West African grammar, vocabulary, and pronunciation.

Voices

Poem by Jupiter Hammon

Jupiter Hammon (1711–1806?) was a favored slave living in Long Island, New York, when on Christmas Day 1760 he composed "An Evening Thought: Salvation by Christ, with Penitential Cries," an excerpt of which appears here. A Calvinist preacher and America's first published black poet, Hammon was deeply influenced by the Great Awakening's emphasis on repentance and Christ's spiritual sovereignty.

Salvation comes by Jesus Christ alone,
The only Son of God;
Redemption now to every one,
That love his holy Word.
Dear Jesus we would fly to Thee,
And leave off every Sin,
Thy tender Mercy well agree;
Salvation from our King.
Salvation comes from God we know,
The true and only One;
It's well agreed and certain true,
He gave his only Son.

Lord hear our penitential Cry:
Salvation from above
It is the Lord that doth supply,
With his Redeeming Love.
Dear Jesus let the Nations cry,
And all the People say,
Salvation comes from Christ on high,
Haste on Tribunal Day.
We cry as Sinners to the Lord,
Salvation to obtain;
It is firmly fixt his holy Word,
Ye shall not cry in vain.

1. What elements in Hammond's poem might have appealed to African Americans of his time?

2. Does Hammond suggest a relationship between Christ and social justice?

SOURCE: Jupiter Hammon (1711–1806). *An Evening Thought: Salvation by Christ, with Penitential Cries.*

3.6.3 The African-American Impact on Colonial Culture

African Americans also influenced the development of white culture. As early as the seventeenth century, black musicians performed English ballads for white audiences in a distinctively African-American style. In the northern and Chesapeake colonies, people of African descent helped determine how all Americans celebrated. By the eighteenth century, slaves in these regions organized black election or coronation festivals that lasted for several days. Sometimes called *Pinkster* and ultimately derived from Dutch-American pre-Easter celebrations, these festivities included parades, athletics, food, music, dancing, and mock coronations of kings and governors. Although dominated by African Americans, they attracted white observers and a few white participants.

The African-American imprint on southern diction and phraseology is especially clear. Because black women often raised their master's children, generations of white children acquired African-American speech patterns and intonations. Black people also influenced white notions about portents, spirits, and folk remedies. Seventeenth- and eighteenth-century English lore about such things was not that different from West African lore, and white Americans consulted black conjurers and "herb doctors." Black cooks in early America influenced white southern eating habits. Preferences for barbecued pork, fried chicken, black-eyed peas, okra, and collard and mustard greens owed much to West African culinary traditions.

African Americans also used West African culture and skills to shape work habits in the American South during and after colonial times. Africans accustomed to collective agricultural labor imposed the **"gang system"** on most American plantations. Masters learned that their slaves worked harder and longer in groups. Their work songs were also an African legacy, as was the slow, deliberate pace of their labor. By the mid-eighteenth century, masters often employed slaves as builders. As a result, African styles and decorative techniques influenced southern colonial architecture. Black builders introduced African-style high-peaked roofs, front porches, wood carvings, and elaborate ironwork.

gang system

A mode of organizing labor that had West African antecedents. In this system American slaves worked in groups under the direction of a slave driver.

3.7 Slavery in the Northern Colonies

Compare and contrast slavery in the northern colonies with slavery in the southern colonies.

The British mainland colonies north of the Chesapeake had histories, cultures, demographics, and economies that differed considerably from those of the southern colonies. Organized religion played a much more important role in the foundation of most of the northern colonies than it did in those of the South (except for Maryland). In New England, where the Pilgrims settled in 1620 and the Puritans in 1630, religious utopianism shaped colonial life. The same was true in the West Jersey portion of New Jersey, where members of the English pietist Society of Friends (Quakers) settled during the 1670s, and in Pennsylvania, which William Penn founded in 1682 as a Quaker colony. Quakers, like other pietists, emphasized nonviolence and a divine spirit within all humans. These beliefs disposed some Quakers to become early opponents of slavery.

Even more important than religion in shaping life in northern British North America were a cooler climate, sufficient numbers of white laborers, lack of a staple crop, and a diversified economy. All these circumstances made black slavery in the colonial North less extensive than, and different from, its southern counterparts.

By the end of the colonial period during the 1770s, only 50,000 African Americans lived in the northern colonies in comparison to 400,000 in the southern colonies. In the North, black people amounted to 4.5 percent of the total population, compared with 40 percent in the South. But, as in the South, the northern black population varied in size from place to place. By 1770 enslaved African Americans constituted 10 percent of the population of Rhode Island, New Jersey, New York, and Pennsylvania (see Figure 3-2).

New York City had a particularly large black population. This dated to 1626 when the city bore the name New Amsterdam and served as the main port of New Netherlands. By 1638, free and enslaved Africans had become a large part of the city's

Figure 3-2 Africans as a Percentage of the Total Population of the British American Colonies, 1650–1770

SOURCE: *Time on the Cross: The Economics of Negro Slavery* by Robert W. Fogel and Stanley L. Engerman. Norton & Company, Inc. © Darlene Clark Hine.

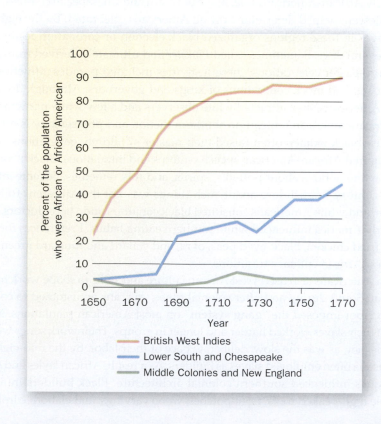

cosmopolitan population. They spoke a variety of European languages and converted to a variety of Christian churches. The English conquered New Netherlands in 1664, but as late as the 1810s many African Americans in and about New York City still spoke Dutch. By 1750, black residents constituted 20 percent of the city's population.

Like all Americans during the colonial era, most northern slaves performed agricultural labor. But, in contrast to those in the South, slaves in the North typically lived in their master's house. They worked with their master, his family, and one or two other slaves on a small farm. In northern cities, which were often home ports for slave traders, enslaved people of African descent worked as artisans, shopkeepers, messengers, domestic servants, and general laborers.

This eighteenth-century drawing of Philadelphia's London Coffee House suggests the routine nature of slave auctions in early America. The main focus is on architecture. The sale of human beings is merely incidental.

Consequently, most northern African Americans led lives that differed from their counterparts in the South. Mainly because New England had so few slaves, but also because of Puritan religious principles, slavery there was least oppressive. White people had no reason to suspect that the small and dispersed black population posed a threat of rebellion. The local slave codes were milder than in the South and, except for the ban on miscegenation, not rigidly enforced. New England slaves could legally own, transfer, and inherit property. From the early seventeenth century onward, Puritans converted Africans and African Americans who came among them to Christianity, recognizing their spiritual equality before God.

In the middle colonies of New York, New Jersey, and Pennsylvania, where black populations were larger and hence perceived by white people to be more threatening, slave codes were stricter and penalties harsher. But even in these colonies, the curfews imposed on Africans and African Americans, as well as the restrictions on their ability to gather together, were less well enforced than they were farther south.

These conditions encouraged rapid assimilation. Because of their small numbers, frequent isolation from others of African descent, and close association with their masters, northern slaves usually had fewer opportunities to preserve an African heritage. However, there was an increase in African customs among black northerners between 1740 and 1770. Before that time, most northern slaves had been born or "seasoned" in the South or the West Indies. Then, during the mid-eighteenth century, direct imports of African slaves into the North temporarily increased. With them came knowledge of African life. But overall, the less harsh and more peripheral nature of slavery in this region limited the retention of African perspectives, just as it allowed the slaves more freedom than most of their southern counterparts enjoyed.

3.8 Slavery in Spanish Florida and French Louisiana

Compare and contrast the African-American experience under French and Spanish rule in North America with the African-American experience under British rule.

Just as slavery in Britain's northern colonies differed from slavery in its southern colonies, slavery in Spanish Florida and French Louisiana—areas that later became parts of the United States—had distinctive characteristics. People of African descent, brought to Florida and Louisiana during the sixteenth, seventeenth, and eighteenth centuries, had different experiences from those who arrived in the British colonies. They and their descendants learned to speak Spanish or French rather than English. They became Roman Catholics rather than Protestants. The routes to freedom were also more plentiful in the Spanish and French colonies than they were in Britain's plantation colonies.

In 1565 Africans helped construct the Spanish settlement of St. Augustine in Florida, which is now the oldest city in the United States. But the Spanish monarchy regarded the settlement as primarily a military outpost, and plantation agriculture was not significant in Florida under Spanish rule. Therefore, the number of slaves in Florida remained small, and black men served more frequently as soldiers than as fieldworkers. As militiamen, they gained power that eluded slaves in most of the British colonies. As members of the Catholic Church, they acquired social status. By 1746 St. Augustine had a total population of 1,500, including about 400 black people. When the British took control of Florida in 1763, these local people of African descent retreated along with the city's white inhabitants to Cuba. Only with the British takeover did plantation slavery begin to grow in Florida.

When the French in 1699 established their Louisiana colony in the lower Mississippi River valley, their objective, like that of the Spanish in Florida, was primarily military. In 1720 few black people (either slave or free) lived in the colony. Then, during the following decade, Louisiana imported about 6,000 slaves, most of whom were men and boys from Senegambia. Although they faced harsh conditions and many died, by 1731 black people outnumbered white people in the colony. Some of the Africans worked on plantations growing tobacco and indigo. But most lived in the port city of New Orleans, where many became skilled artisans, lived away from their masters, became Roman Catholics, and gained freedom. Unfortunately, early in its history, New Orleans also became a place where white men exploited black women sexually with impunity. This custom eventually created a sizable mixed-race population with elaborate social gradations based on the amount of white ancestry a person had and the lightness of his or her skin. Unlike the case in Florida, Louisiana's distinctive black and mixed-race population did not leave when the colony became part of the United States in 1803.

3.9 African Americans in New Spain's Northern Borderlands

Describe African-American life in New Spain's northern borderlands.

What is today the southwestern United States was from the sixteenth century until 1821 the northernmost part of New Spain. Centered in Mexico, this Spanish colony reached into Texas, California, New Mexico, Colorado, and Arizona. The first people of African descent who entered this huge region were members of Spanish exploratory expeditions. The best known of them is Esteban, an enslaved Moor (the Spanish term for a dark-skinned Muslim) who survived a shipwreck on the Texas coast in 1529 and a brief captivity among Indians. He subsequently joined Spanish explorer Alvar Núñez Cabeza de Vaca in an arduous seven-year trek from Texas to Mexico City. Esteban, a skilled interpreter, later explored regions in what are today New Mexico and Arizona. Black men also accompanied Francisco Vásquez de Coronado's 1540–1542 search across the Southwest for the mythical Seven Cities of Cibola as well as Spanish expeditions along the upper regions of the Rio Grande in 1593 and 1598. During the seventeenth century, black soldiers participated in the Spanish conquest of Pueblo Indians. Some black and mulatto women also joined in Spanish military

This image shows the former slave Esteban, who, during the early 1500s, traveled through Texas to Mexico. Later he joined Spanish expeditions that explored what are now New Mexico and Arizona.

expeditions. The best known of them was Isabel de Olvena, who traveled with an expedition through New Mexico in 1600.

During the colonial era, however, New Spain's North American borderlands had far fewer black people than there were in the British colonies. In part this was because the total non-Indian population in the borderlands was extremely small. As late as 1792, only around 3,000 colonists lived in Texas, including about 450 described as black or mulatto. There were even fewer colonists in New Mexico and California, where people of mixed African, Indian, and Spanish descent were common. Black men in the borderlands gained employment as sailors, soldiers, tradesmen, cattle herders, and day laborers. Some of them were slaves, but others had limited freedom. In contrast to the British colonies, in New Spain's borderlands most slaves were Indians. They worked as domestics and as agricultural laborers or were marched south to Mexico, where they labored in gold and silver mines.

Also in contrast to the British mainland colonies, where no formal aristocracy existed but where white insistence on racial separation gradually grew in strength, both hereditary rank and racial fluidity existed in New Spain's borderlands. In theory, throughout the Spanish empire in the Americas, "racial purity" determined social status, with Spaniards of "pure blood" at the top and Africans and Indians at the bottom. In Texas free black people and Indians suffered legal disabilities. They paid special taxes and could not own guns or travel freely. But almost all of the Spaniards who moved north from Mexico were themselves of mixed race, and people of African and Indian descent could more easily acquire status than they could in the British colonies. In the borderlands black men held responsible positions at Roman Catholic missions. A few acquired large landholdings called *ranchos*.

3.10 Black Women in Colonial America

Describe how slavery affected black women in colonial America.

The lives of black women in early North America varied according to the colony in which they lived. The differences between Britain's New England colonies and its southern colonies are particularly clear. In New England religion and demographics

In this painting African Americans await sale to slave traders, who stand at the doorway on the left.

made the boundary between slavery and freedom permeable. There black women distinguished themselves in a variety of ways. The thoroughly acculturated Lucy Terry Prince of Deerfield, Massachusetts, published poetry in the 1740s and gained her freedom in 1756. Other black women succeeded as bakers and weavers. But in the South, where most black women of the time lived, they had few opportunities for work beyond tobacco and rice fields and the homes of their masters.

During the late seventeenth and the eighteenth centuries, approximately 90 percent of southern black women worked in the fields, as was customary for women in West Africa. White women also did fieldwork, but masters considered black women to be tougher than white women and therefore able to do more hard physical labor. Black women also mothered their children and cooked for their families, a chore that involved lugging firewood and water and tending fires as well as preparing meals. Like other women of their time, colonial black women suffered from inadequate medical attention while giving birth. But because black women worked until the moment they delivered, they were more likely than white women to experience complications in giving birth and to bear low-birth-weight babies.

As the eighteenth century passed, more black women became house servants. Yet most jobs as maids, cooks, and body servants went to the young, the old, or the infirm. Black women also wet-nursed their master's children. None of this was easy work. Those who did it were under constant white supervision and were particularly subject to the sexual exploitation that characterized chattel slavery.

European captains and crews molested and raped black women during the Middle Passage. Masters and overseers similarly used their power to force themselves on female slaves. The results were evident in the large mixed-race populations in the colonies and in the psychological damage it inflicted on African-American women and their mates. In particular, the sexual abuse of black women by white men disrupted the emerging black families in North America because black men usually could not protect their wives from it.

Although enslaved black women were more expensive than white indentured servants—because, unlike the children of white indentured servants, their children would become their master's property—slave traders and slaveholders never valued black women as highly as they did black men. Until 1660 the British mainland colonies imported twice as many African men as women. Thereafter, the ratio dropped to three African men for every two women. By the mid-eighteenth century, natural population growth among African Americans had corrected the sexual imbalance.

3.11 Black Resistance and Rebellion

Describe the ways in which African Americans resisted slavery.

That masters regularly used their authority to abuse black women sexually and thereby humiliate black men dramatizes the oppressiveness of a slave system based on race and physical force. Masters often rewarded black women who became their mistresses, just as masters and overseers used incentives to get more labor from field hands. But slaves who did not comply in either case faced a beating. Slavery in America was always a system that relied ultimately on physical force to deny freedom to African Americans. From its start, black men and women responded by resisting their masters as well as they could.

Such resistance ranged from sullen goldbricking (shirking assigned work) to sabotage, escape, and rebellion. Before the late eighteenth century, however, resistance and rebellion were not part of a coherent antislavery effort. Before the spread of ideas about natural human rights and universal liberty associated with the American and French revolutions, slave resistance and revolt did not aim to destroy slavery as a social system. Africans and African Americans resisted, escaped, and rebelled but not as part of an effort to free all slaves. Instead, they resisted to force masters to make concessions within the framework of slavery. They escaped and rebelled to relieve themselves, their friends, and their families from intolerable disgrace and suffering.

African men and women newly arrived in North America openly defied their masters. They frequently refused to work and often could not be persuaded by punishment to change their behavior. "You would really be surpris'd at their Perseverance," one frustrated master commented. "They often die before they can be conquered." Africans tended to escape in groups of individuals who shared a common homeland and language. When they succeeded, they usually became "outliers," living nearby and stealing from their master's estate. Less frequently, they headed west, where they found some safety among white frontiersmen, Indians, or interracial banditti. In 1672 Virginia's colonial government began paying bounties to anyone who killed outliers. Six decades later, the governor of South Carolina offered similar rewards. In some instances, escaped slaves, known as *maroons*—a term derived from the Spanish word *cimarron*, meaning "wild"—established their own settlements in inaccessible regions.

The most durable of such maroon communities in North America existed in the Spanish colony of Florida. In 1693 the Spanish king officially made this colony a refuge for slaves escaping from the British colonies, although he did not free slaves who were already there. Many such escapees joined the Seminole Indian nation and thereby gained protection between 1763 and 1783, when the British ruled Florida, and after 1821 when the United States took control. It was in part to destroy this refuge for former slaves that the United States fought the Seminole War from 1835 to 1842. Other maroon settlements existed in the South Carolina and Georgia backcountry and the **Great Dismal Swamp** of southern Virginia.

As slaves became acculturated, forms of slave resistance changed. To avoid punishment, African Americans replaced open defiance with more subtle day-to-day obstructionism. They malingered, broke tools, mistreated domestic animals, destroyed crops, poisoned their masters, and stole. Not every slave who acted this way, of

Great Dismal Swamp

A heavily forested area on the Virginia–North Carolina border that served as a refuge for fugitive slaves during the eighteenth and nineteenth centuries.

RUN away from the subscriber in *Albemarle*, a Mulatto slave called *Sandy*, about 35 years of age, his stature is rather low, inclining to corpulence, and his complexion light; he is a shoemaker by trade, in which he uses his left hand principally, can do coarse carpenters work, and is something of a horse jockey; he is greatly addicted to drink, and when drunk is insolent and disorderly, in his conversation he swears much, and in his behaviour is artful and knavish. He took with him a white horse, much scarred with traces, of which it is expected he will endeavour to dispose; he also carried his shoemakers tools, and will probably endeavour to get employment that way. Whoever conveys the said slave to me, in *Albemarle*, shall have 40 s. reward, if taken up within the county, 4 l. if elsewhere within the colony, and 10 l. if in any other colony, from
THOMAS JEFFERSON.

Announcement issued by Thomas Jefferson for a reward for a runaway slave, 14 September 1769.

course, was consciously resisting enslavement, but masters assumed they were. In 1770, Benjamin Franklin, who owned slaves, complained to a European friend, "Perhaps you may imagine the Negroes to be mild-tempered, tractable Kind of People. Some of them indeed are so. But the Majority are of plotting Disposition, dark, sullen, malicious, revengeful and cruel in the highest Degree." Acculturation also brought different escape patterns. Increasingly, the more assimilated slaves predominated among escapees. Most of them were young men who left on their own and relied on their knowledge of American society to pass as free. Although some continued to head for maroon settlements, most sought safety among relatives, in towns, or in the North Carolina piedmont, where there were few slaves.

In colonial North America, rebellions occurred far more rarely than resistance and escape. More and larger rebellions broke out during the early eighteenth century in Jamaica and Brazil. This discrepancy resulted mainly from demographics: in the sugar-producing colonies, black people outnumbered white people by six or eight to one, but in British North America black people were a majority only in the low country. The larger the proportion of slaves in a population, the more likely they were to rebel. Also, by the mid-eighteenth century, most male slaves in the British mainland colonies were Creoles with families. They had more to lose from a failed rebellion than did the single African men who made up the bulk of the slave population farther south.

Nevertheless there were waves of rebellion in British North America from 1710 to 1722 and 1730 to 1741. Men born in Africa took the lead in these revolts, and the two most notable of them occurred in New York City in 1712 and near Charleston, South Carolina, in 1739. In New York, 27 Africans, taking revenge for "hard usage," set fire to an outbuilding. When white men arrived to put out the blaze, the rebels attacked them with muskets, hatchets, and swords. They killed nine of the white men and wounded six. Shortly thereafter, local militia units captured the rebels. Six of the rebels killed themselves; the other 21 were executed—some brutally. In 1741 another revolt conspiracy in New York led to another mass execution. Authorities put to death 30 black people and four white people convicted of helping them.

Even more frightening for most white people was the rebellion that began at Stono Bridge within 20 miles of Charleston in September 1739. Under the leadership of a man named Jemmy or Tommy, 20 slaves who had recently arrived from Angola broke into a "weare-house, & then plundered it of guns & ammunition." They killed the warehousemen, left their severed heads on the building's steps, and fled toward Florida. Other slaves joined the Angolans until their numbers reached one hundred. They sacked plantations and killed approximately 30 more white people. But when they stopped to celebrate their victories and beat drums to attract other slaves, planters on horseback aided by Indians routed them, killing 44 and dispersing the rest. Many of the rebels, including their leader, remained at large for up to three years, as did the spirit of insurrection. In 1740 Charleston authorities arrested 150 slaves and hanged 10 daily to quell that spirit.

In South Carolina and other southern colonies, white people never entirely lost their fear of slave revolt. Whenever slaves rebelled or were rumored to rebel, the fear became intense. As the quotation that begins this chapter indicates, the unwillingness of many Africans and African Americans to submit to enslavement pushed white southerners into a siege mentality that became a determining factor in American history.

Profile

Francisco Menendez

Today Francisco Menendez is best known—if known at all—as a black pirate who used a Spanish ship to attack British vessels sailing on the Atlantic Ocean. But recent research into his life, and especially his battles on the border between Spanish Florida and British South Carolina, expand and clarify our understanding of African-American life on both sides of that border during the mid-eighteenth century.

Menendez was probably born in central Africa in the early 1700s. Kongolese soldiers captured him when he was a boy or young man. Shortly thereafter, he converted to Roman Catholicism, took a Portuguese name, and suffered enslavement. Along with thousands of others, he unwillingly crossed the Atlantic Ocean to work in South Carolina's low-country rice fields.

In 1724, Menendez, attracted by Spain's politically motivated offer of freedom to British slaves, escaped to Spanish Florida. He joined the St. Augustine militia, and in 1728 fought bravely in defense of that settlement against British invaders. Menendez's courage gained him promotion to the rank of captain.

Ten years later, Governor Manuel Montiano appointed Menendez to command at *Gracia Real de Mose*. Known as Fort Mose and located north of St. Augustine, the Spanish colonial government created this black settlement to defend Florida against British military threats from the north. Fort Mose's 100 inhabitants promised to "shed their last drop of blood in defense of the Great Crown of Spain and the Holy [Catholic] Faith."

Menendez led raids from Fort Mose into South Carolina. Such raids, of course, raised the specter of assisted slave revolt and frightened South Carolina's slaveholders and governors. The Stono Rebellion of September 1739 seemed to confirm such fears when—as the text of this chapter describes—100 armed low-country slaves attempted to march south to Florida and freedom. Although Menendez did not assist this effort, he likely gave aid and comfort to the rebels who reached Fort Mose. Months later, South Carolina militia invaded Florida in force. Under Menendez's command the Fort Mose militia drove the invaders back. But, during the fighting, the South Carolinians destroyed the fort.

Menendez then went to sea in what most likely was an effort to capture food and supplies from British ships. This led in 1741 to his capture under charges of piracy, perhaps to his torture, and—as punishment—his reenslavement. Subsequently, Menendez either escaped or Spanish authorities paid for his release. By 1752, he had resumed his militia duties at a rebuilt Fort Mose. He remained there until 1763, when Spain ceded Florida to Britain as part of the treaty ending the French and Indian War. Menendez and most black Floridians joined a Spanish removal to Cuba. Menendez may have organized a black community on that island and probably died in Havana.

Francisco Menendez's story, set in the eighteenth century, like that of Anthony Johnson's in the seventeenth century, is valuable largely because of its rarity. Sketchy as it is, it humanizes an exceptional individual who lived during a time from which few records of individuals have survived—or ever existed. Menendez's story also provides insight into black life in Spanish Florida and expands our understanding of the Stono Revolt, of the opportunities for freedom that international borders offered to slaves, and of slaveholders' determination to suppress those opportunities.

Conclusion

Studying the history of black people in early America is both painful and exhilarating. It is painful to learn of their enslavement, the emergence of racism in its modern form, and the loss of so much of the African heritage. But it is exhilarating to learn how much of that heritage Africans and African Americans preserved, how they resisted their oppressors and forged strong family bonds, and how an emerging African-American culture began to influence all aspects of American society.

The varieties of black life during the colonial period also help us understand the complexity of African-American society later in American history. Although they had much in common, black people in the Chesapeake, in the low country, in Britain's northern colonies, in Spanish Florida, in French Louisiana, and in New Spain's borderlands had different experiences, different relationships with white people and Indians, and different prospects. Those who lived in the fledgling colonial towns and cities differed from those who were agricultural laborers. The lives of those who worked on small farms differed from the lives of those who served on large plantations.

Finally, African-American history during the colonial era raises fundamental issues about contingency and determinism in human events. Did economic necessity, racism, and class interest make the development of chattel slavery in the Chesapeake inevitable? Or, had things gone otherwise (e.g., if Bacon's Rebellion had not occurred or had turned out differently), might African Americans in that region have retained more rights and access to freedom? What would have been the impact of that freedom on the colonies to the north and south of the Chesapeake?

Chapter Timeline

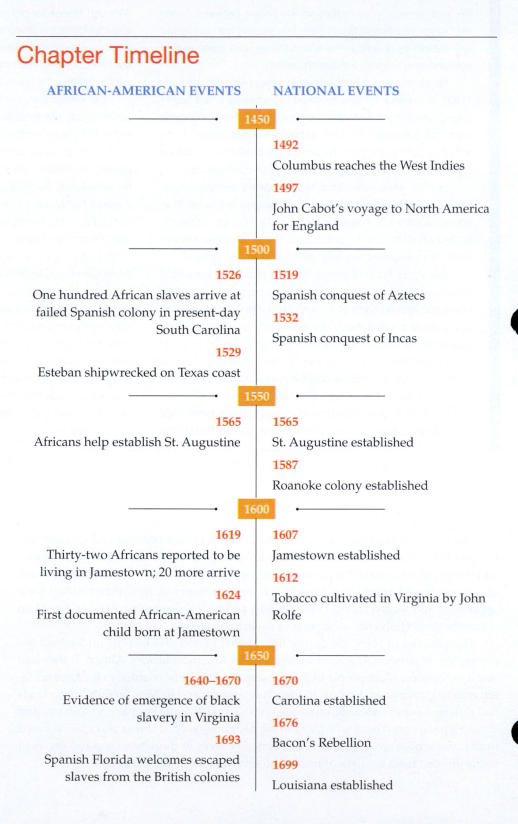

AFRICAN-AMERICAN EVENTS	NATIONAL EVENTS
	1450
	1492 Columbus reaches the West Indies
	1497 John Cabot's voyage to North America for England
	1500
1526 One hundred African slaves arrive at failed Spanish colony in present-day South Carolina	**1519** Spanish conquest of Aztecs
1529 Esteban shipwrecked on Texas coast	**1532** Spanish conquest of Incas
	1550
1565 Africans help establish St. Augustine	**1565** St. Augustine established
	1587 Roanoke colony established
	1600
1619 Thirty-two Africans reported to be living in Jamestown; 20 more arrive	**1607** Jamestown established
1624 First documented African-American child born at Jamestown	**1612** Tobacco cultivated in Virginia by John Rolfe
	1650
1640–1670 Evidence of emergence of black slavery in Virginia	**1670** Carolina established
1693 Spanish Florida welcomes escaped slaves from the British colonies	**1676** Bacon's Rebellion
	1699 Louisiana established

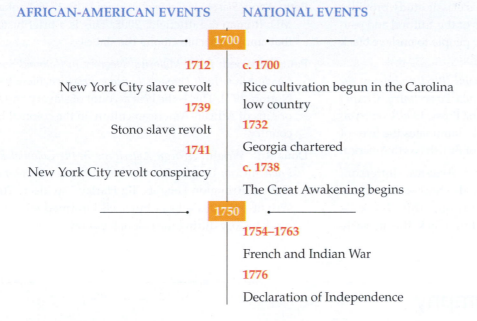

AFRICAN-AMERICAN EVENTS   NATIONAL EVENTS

1700

1712
New York City slave revolt

c. 1700
Rice cultivation begun in the Carolina low country

1739
Stono slave revolt

1732
Georgia chartered

1741
New York City revolt conspiracy

c. 1738
The Great Awakening begins

1750

1754–1763
French and Indian War

1776
Declaration of Independence

Review Questions

1. Based on your reading of this chapter, do you believe racial prejudice among British settlers in the Chesapeake led them to enslave Africans? Or did the unfree condition of the first Africans to arrive at Jamestown lead to racial prejudice among the settlers?

2. Why did vestiges of African culture survive in British North America? Did these vestiges help or hinder African Americans in dealing with enslavement?

3. Compare and contrast eighteenth-century slavery as it existed in the Chesapeake, in the low country of South Carolina and Georgia, and in the northern colonies.

4. What were the strengths and weaknesses of the black family in the eighteenth century?

5. How did enslaved Africans and African Americans preserve a sense of their own humanity?

Retracing the Odyssey

African Americans at Jamestown, Colonial National Historical Park, Jamestown and Yorktown, Virginia. This program covers the period from 1619, the date of the first reports concerning black inhabitants at Jamestown, to 1705, when Virginia formally adopted a slave code.

Colonial Williamsburg, Williamsburg, Virginia. The "Enslaving Virginia Tour" allows visitors to "explore [the] conditions that led to slavery's development in the Jamestown/Virginia colony."

Charles H. Wright Museum of African American History, Detroit, Michigan. The "Of the People: The African American Experience" exhibit includes material dealing with the memory of Africa and the "survival of the spirit."

Recommended Reading

Ira Berlin. *Many Thousands Gone: The First Two Centuries of Slavery in North America.* Cambridge, MA: Belknap Press, 1998. This impressive synthesis of black life in slavery during the seventeenth and eighteenth centuries emphasizes black people's ability to shape their lives in conflict with their masters' will.

Winthrop D. Jordan. *White over Black: American Attitudes Toward the Negro, 1550–1812.* Chapel Hill: University of

North Carolina Press, 1968. This classic study provides a probing and detailed analysis of the cultural and psychological forces that led white people to enslave black people in early America.

Philip D. Morgan. *Slave Counterpoint: Black Culture in the Eighteenth-Century Chesapeake and Lowcountry.* Chapel Hill: University of North Carolina Press, 1998. Comparative history at its best, this book illuminates the lives of black people in important parts of British North America.

Oscar Reiss. *Blacks in Colonial America.* Jefferson, NC: McFarland, 1997. Although short on synthesis and eccentric in interpretation, this book is packed with information about black life in early America.

Betty Wood. *Slavery in Colonial America 1619–1776.* Lanham, MD: Roman & Littlefield, 2005. This is a brief history that emphasizes life among the slaves.

Peter H. Wood. *Black Majority: Negroes in Colonial South Carolina from 1670 Through the Stono Rebellion.* New York: Norton, 1974. This is the best account of slavery and the origins of African-American culture in the colonial low country.

Donald R. Wright. *African Americans in the Colonial Era: From African Origins Through the American Revolution.* 2nd ed. Arlington Heights, IL: Harlan Davidson, 2000. Wright provides a brief but well-informed survey of black history during the colonial period.

Additional Bibliography

Colonial Society

Jack P. Greene. *Pursuits of Happiness: The Social Development of Early Modern British Colonies and the Formation of American Culture.* Chapel Hill: University of North Carolina Press, 1988.

Thomas S. Kidd. *The Great Awakening: The Roots of Evangelical Christianity in Colonial America.* New Haven, CT: Yale University Press, 2007.

John J. McCusker and Russell R. Menard. *The Economy of British America, 1607– 1789.* Chapel Hill: University of North Carolina Press, 1985.

Gary B. Nash. *Red, White, and Black: The Peoples of Early America.* 3rd ed. Englewood Cliffs, NJ: Prentice Hall, 1992.

Origins of Slavery and Racism in the Western Hemisphere

Robin Blackburn. *The Making of New World Slavery: From the Baroque to the Modern 1492–1800.* New York: Verso, 1997.

David Brion Davis. *Inhuman Bondage: The Rise and Fall of Slavery in the New World.* New York: Oxford University Press, 2006.

Seymour Drescher. *From Slavery to Freedom: Comparative Studies of the Rise and Fall of Atlantic Slavery.* New York: New York University Press, 1999.

David Eltis. *The Rise of African Slavery in the Americas.* New York: Cambridge University Press, 2000.

Frank Tannenbaum. *Slave and Citizen: The Negro in the Americas.* New York: Knopf, 1946.

Betty Wood. *The Origins of American Slavery: Freedom and Bondage in the English Colonies.* New York: Hill and Wang, 1997.

The Chesapeake

Barbara A. Faggins. *Africans and Indians: An Afrocentric Analysis of Contacts Between Africans and Indians in Colonial Virginia.* New York: Routledge, 2001.

Allan Kulikoff. *Tobacco and Slaves: The Development of Southern Cultures in the Chesapeake, 1680–1800.* Chapel Hill: University of North Carolina Press, 1986.

Gloria L. Main. *Tobacco Colony: Life in Early Maryland, 1650–1720.* Princeton, NJ: Princeton University Press, 1982.

Edmund S. Morgan. *American Slavery, American Freedom: The Ordeal of Colonial Virginia.* New York: Norton, 1975.

Isaac Rhys. *The Transformation of Virginia, 1740–1790.* New York: Norton, 1982.

Mechal Sobel. *The World They Made Together: Black and White Values in Eighteenth-Century Virginia.* Princeton, NJ: Princeton University Press, 1987.

The Carolina and Georgia Low Country

Judith Ann Carney. *Black Rice: The African Origins of Rice Cultivation in the Americas.* Cambridge, MA: Harvard University Press, 2001.

Alan Gallay. *The Indian Slave Trade: The Rise of the English Empire in the American South, 1670–1717.* New Haven, CT: Yale University Press, 2002.

Julia Floyd Smith. *Slavery and Rice Culture in Low Country Georgia, 1750–1860.* Knoxville: University of Tennessee Press, 1985.

Betty Wood. *Slavery in Colonial Georgia, 1730–1775.* Athens: University of Georgia Press, 1984.

Jeffrey R. Yount. *Domesticating Slavery: The Master Class in Georgia and South Carolina, 1670–1837*. Chapel Hill: University of North Carolina Press, 1999.

The Northern Colonies

Lorenzo J. Greene. *The Negro in Colonial New England, 1620–1776*. 1942. Reprint, New York: Atheneum, 1968.

Leslie M. Harris. *In the Shadow of Slavery: African Americans in New York City, 1626–1863*. Chicago: University of Chicago Press, 2003.

Graham R. Hodges. *Root and Branch: African Americans in New York and East Jersey, 1613–1863*. Chapel Hill: University of North Carolina Press, 1999.

William D. Piersen. *Black Yankees: The Development of an Afro-American Subculture in Eighteenth-Century New England*. Amherst: University of Massachusetts Press, 1988.

John Wood Sweet. *Bodies Politic: Negotiating Race in the American North 1730–1830*. Philadelphia: University of Pennsylvania Press, 2006.

Spanish Borderlands and Louisiana

Lynn Robinson Bailey. *Indian Slave Trade and the Southwest: A Study of Slave-Taking and the Traffic in Indian Captives*. Los Angeles: Westernlore, 1966.

Gwendolyn Midlo Hall. *Africans in Colonial Louisiana: The Development of Afro-Creole Culture in the Eighteenth Century*. Baton Rouge: Louisiana State University Press, 1992.

Thomas N. Ingersoll. *Mammon and Manon in Early New Orleans: The First Slave Society in the Deep South, 1718–1819*. Knoxville: University of Tennessee Press, 1999.

John L. Kessell. *Spain in the Southwest: A Narrative History of Colonial New Mexico, Arizona, Texas, and California*. Norman: University of Oklahoma Press, 2002.

Jane Landers. *Black Society in Spanish Florida*. Urbana: University of Illinois Press, 1999.

Michael M. Swann. *Migrants in the Mexican North: Mobility, Economy, and Society in a Colonial World*. Boulder, CO: Westview, 1989.

Quintard Taylor. *In Search of the Racial Frontier: African Americans in the American West, 1528–1990*. New York: Norton, 1998.

African-American Culture

John B. Boles. *Black Southerners, 1619–1869*. Lexington: University Press of Kentucky, 1983.

Joanne Brooks. *American Lazarus: Religion and the Rise of African American and Native American Literature*. New York: Oxford University Press, 2003.

Dickson D. Bruce. *The Origins of African American Literature, 1680–1865*. Charlottesville: University Press of Virginia, 2001.

Margaret W. Creel. *A Peculiar People: Slave Religion and Community Culture among the Gullahs*. New York: New York University Press, 1988.

Sylvaine A. Diouf. *Servants of Allah: African Muslims Enslaved in the Americas*. New York: New York University Press, 1998.

Michael Gomez. *Exchanging Our Country Marks: The Transformation of African Identities in the Colonial and Antebellum South*. Chapel Hill: University of North Carolina Press, 1998.

Melville J. Herskovits. *The Myth of the Negro Past*. 1941. Reprint, Boston: Beacon, 1990.

Linda Marinda Heywood. *Central Africans, Atlantic Creoles, and the Making of the Foundation of the Americas 1585–1660*. New York: Cambridge University Press, 2007.

Henry Mitchell. *Black Belief: Folk Beliefs of Blacks in America and West Africa*. New York: Harper & Row, 1975.

Sheila S. Walker, ed. *African Roots/American Culture: Africa and the Creation of the Americas*. Lanham: Rowman & Littlefield, 2001.

Joel Williamson. *New People: Miscegenation and Mulattoes in the United States*. New York: Free Press, 1980.

Black Women in Colonial America

Joan Rezner Gunderson. "The Double Bonds of Race and Sex: Black and White Women in a Colonial Virginia Parish." In Darlene Clark Hine, Wilma King, and Linda Reed, eds., *We Specialize in the Wholly Impossible: A Reader in Black Women's History*. Brooklyn, NY: Carlson, 1995.

Darlene Clark Hine and Kathleen Thompson. *A Shining Thread of Hope: The History of Black Women in America*. New York: Broadway, 1998.

Jane Kamensky. *The Colonial Mosaic: American Women, 1600–1760: Rising Expectations from the Colonial Period to the American Revolution*. New York: Oxford University Press, 1995.

Jenny Sharpe. *Ghosts of Slavery: A Literary Archaeology of Black Women's Lives*. Minneapolis: University of Minnesota Press, 2003.

Resistance and Revolt

Herbert Aptheker. *American Negro Slave Revolts*. 1943. Reprint, New York: International Publishers, 1974.

Merton L. Dillon. *Slavery Attacked: Southern Slaves and Their Allies, 1619–1865.* Baton Rouge: Louisiana State University Press, 1990.

Eugene D. Genovese. *From Rebellion to Revolution: Afro-American Slave Revolts in the Making of the Modern World.* Baton Rouge: Louisiana State University Press, 1979.

Michael Mullin. *Africa in America: Slave Acculturation and Resistance in the American South and the British Caribbean, 1736–1831.* Urbana: University of Illinois Press, 1992.

Walter C. Rucker. *The River Flows On: Black Resistance, Culture, and Identity Formation in Early America.* Baton Rouge: Louisiana State University Press, 2003.

Jack Shuler. *Calling Out Liberty: The Stono Slave Rebellion and the Universal Struggle for Human Rights.*Jackson: University Press of Mississippi, 2009.

John K. Thornton. *Africa and Africans in the Making of the Atlantic World, 1400–1800.* New York: Cambridge University Press, 1992.

Chapter 4

Rising Expectations: African Americans and the Struggle for Independence

1763–1783

African Americans fought on both sides in the American War for Independence. In this nineteenth-century painting, a black Patriot aims his pistol at a British officer during the Battle of Cowpens, fought in South Carolina in 1781.

Learning Objectives

After reading this chapter, you should be able to:

4.1 Analyze the factors involved in the crisis of the British Empire.

4.2 Describe what the Declaration of Independence meant to African Americans.

4.3 Discuss the African Americans who contributed to the Enlightenment.

4.4 Evaluate the African-American role in the War for Independence.

4.5 Explain how the American Revolution weakened slavery.

To the Honorable Legislature of the State of Massachusetts Bay, January 13, 1777: The petition of a great number of blacks detained in a state of slavery in the bowels of a free & Christian country humbly sheweth that your petitioners apprehend we have in common with all other men a natural and unalienable right to that freedom which the Great Parent of the Universe hath bestowed equally on all mankind, and which they have never forfeited by any compact or agreement whatever.

—Lancaster Hill, et al.

As the preceding quotation indicates, African Americans of the 1770s understood the revolutionary thought of their time. When a large minority of America's white population demanded independence from Britain on the basis of a natural human right to freedom, many black Americans asserted their right to be liberated from slavery. It took a momentous change in outlook from that of earlier ages for either group to perceive freedom as a right. Just as momentous was the dawning awareness among white people of the contradiction between claiming freedom for themselves and denying it to others.

The Great Awakening had nurtured humanitarian opposition to slavery. But secular thought, rooted in the European Enlightenment, shaped a revolutionary ethos in America. According to the precepts of the Enlightenment, all humans had natural, God-given rights that could not be taken from them without their consent. In 1777, the African-American petitioners in Massachusetts alluded to these precepts.

If the Enlightenment shaped the revolutionary discourse of the late eighteenth century, the French and Indian War, fought between 1754 and 1763, made the American struggle for independence possible. The outcome of that war, which pitted the British, Americans, and their American Indian allies against the French and their Indian allies, created a volatile situation in the Thirteen Colonies. That situation, in turn, produced the American War for Independence and efforts by many enslaved African Americans to gain their freedom.

In this chapter we explore the African-American quest for liberty during the 20 years between 1763, when the French and Indian War ended, and 1783, when Britain recognized the independence of the United States. During this period, African Americans exercised an intellectual and political leadership that had far-ranging implications. A few black writers and scientists emerged, black soldiers fought in battle, black artisans proliferated, and—particularly in the North—black activists publicly argued against enslavement. Most important, many African Americans used the War for Independence to gain their freedom. Some were Patriots fighting for American independence. Others were Loyalists fighting for the British. Still others used the dislocations of war to escape from their masters.

4.1 The Crisis of the British Empire

Analyze the factors involved in the crisis of the British Empire.

A great struggle for empire between Great Britain and France created the circumstances within which an independence movement and rising black hopes for freedom developed in America. Starting in 1689, the British and French fought a series of wars in Europe, India, North America, Africa, and the Caribbean. This conflict climaxed in the French and Indian War that began in North America in 1754, spread to Europe in 1756 (where it was called the Seven Years' War), and from there extended to other parts of the world.

The war sprang from competing British and French efforts to control the Ohio River valley and its lucrative **fur trade**. In 1754 and 1755, the French and their Indian allies defeated Virginian and British troops in this region and then attacked the western frontier of the British colonies. Not until 1758 did Britain undertake the vigorous and expensive military effort that by 1763 had forced France to withdraw from North America. Britain took Canada from France and Florida from France's ally Spain. In compensation, Spain received New Orleans and the huge French province of Louisiana in central North America (see Map 4-1).

fur trade

A North American colonial industry involving American Indians trapping fur-bearing animals (chiefly beavers) and exchanging their pelts for European products.

Map 4-1 European Claims in North America, 1750 (Left) and 1763 (Right)

These maps illustrate the dramatic change in the political geography of North America that resulted from the British victory in the French and Indian War (1754–1763). It eliminated France as a North American power. France surrendered Canada and the Ohio River valley to Britain. Spain ceded Florida to Britain and, as compensation, received Louisiana from France.

What was the significance for African Americans of these political changes and, in particular, of Great Britain's acquisition of Florida?

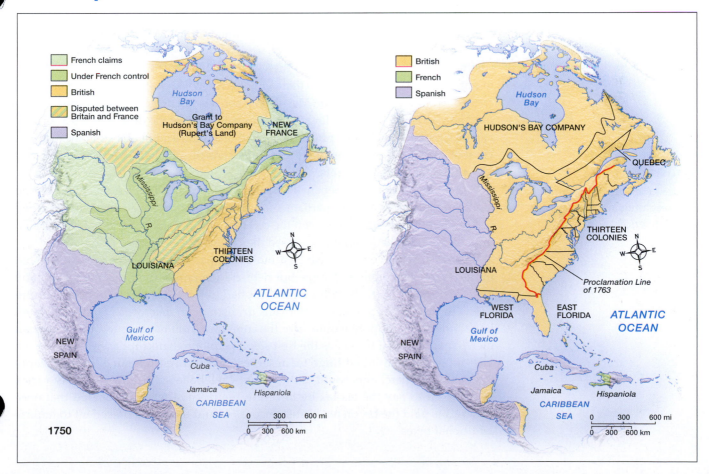

These changes had momentous consequences. Deprived of their ability to play off Britain against France and Spain, American Indian nations east of the Mississippi River had great difficulty resisting white encroachment. Meanwhile fugitive slaves escaping into Florida swamps lost their Spanish protection. Americans no longer had to face French and Spanish threats on their frontiers. The bonds between Britain and the Thirteen Colonies rapidly weakened.

The last two of these consequences were closely linked. The colonial assemblies had not always supported the war effort against the French. American merchants had traded with the enemy. Therefore, after the war ended, British officials decided that Americans should be taxed to pay their share of the costs of empire and that their commerce should be more closely regulated. In England it seemed entirely reasonable that the government should proceed in this manner. But white Americans had become accustomed to governing themselves, trading with whom they pleased, and paying only local taxes. They knew that with the French and Spanish gone, they no longer needed British protection. Therefore many resisted when the British Parliament asserted its power to tax and govern them.

During the 1760s Parliament passed laws that many Americans considered oppressive. The Proclamation Line of 1763 aimed to placate Britain's Indian allies by forbidding American settlement west of the crest of the **Appalachian Mountains**. The Sugar Act of 1764 levied **import duties** designed to raise revenue for Britain rather than simply regulate American trade. In 1765 the Stamp Act heavily taxed printed materials, such as deeds, newspapers, and playing cards.

In response, Americans at the Stamp Act Congress held in New York City in October 1765 moved toward united resistance. By agreeing not to import British goods, the congress forced Parliament in 1766 to repeal the Stamp Act. But the Sugar Act and Proclamation Line remained in force, and Parliament remained determined to exercise greater control in America.

In 1767 Parliament forced the New York assembly to provide quarters for British troops and enacted the Townshend Acts (named after the British finance minister Charles Townshend), which taxed glass, lead, paint, paper, and tea imported into the colonies from Britain. Resistance to these taxes in Boston led the British government to station two regiments of troops there in 1768. The volatile situation this deployment created led in 1770 to the Boston Massacre, when a small detachment of British troops fired into an angry crowd, killing five Bostonians. Among the dead was a black sailor named Crispus Attucks (see profile), who had taken the lead in accosting the soldiers. He soon became a martyr among those Americans dissatisfied with British rule, and who called themselves **Patriots**.

As it turned out, Parliament had repealed the Townshend duties, except the one on tea, before the massacre. This parliamentary retreat and reaction against the bloodshed in Boston reduced tension between the colonies and Britain. A period of calm lasted until May 1773, when Parliament passed the Tea Act.

The Tea Act gave the British East India Company a monopoly over all tea sold in the American colonies. A huge but debt-ridden entity, the East India Company governed India for the British Empire and had exclusive rights to import tea from China to Britain. At the time, Americans drank a great deal of tea, and Parliament hoped the tea monopoly would save the company from bankruptcy. But American merchants regarded the act as the first step in a plot to bankrupt them. Because the East India Company had huge tea reserves, it could sell tea much more cheaply than colonial merchants could. Other Americans believed the Tea Act was a trick to get them to pay the tea tax by lowering the price of tea. They feared that once Americans paid the tax on tea, British leaders would use it as a precedent to impose additional taxes.

Appalachian Mountains

A large mountain chain in eastern North America that stretches from Newfoundland in the north to central Alabama in the south.

import duties

Taxes on goods brought into a country or colony.

Patriots

Those Americans who, during the Revolutionary War, favored independence.

To prevent this, Boston's radical **Sons of Liberty** in December 1773 dumped a shipload of tea into the city's harbor. In response, Britain in early 1774 sent more troops to Boston and punished the city economically, sparking resistance throughout the colonies. Patriot leaders organized the **Continental Congress**, which met in Philadelphia in September 1774 and demanded the repeal of all "oppressive" legislation. By November, Massachusetts Minutemen—members of an irregular militia—had begun to stockpile arms in the villages surrounding Boston.

In April 1775 Minutemen clashed with British troops at Lexington and Concord near Boston. This was the first battle in what became a war for independence. Shortly thereafter, Congress appointed George Washington commander in chief of the Continental Army. Before he took command, however, the American and British forces at Boston fought the bloody Battle of Bunker Hill. After a year during which other armed clashes occurred and the British rejected a compromise, Congress in July 1776 declared the colonies to be independent states, and the war became a revolution.

Sons of Liberty

A secret American organization formed in the Northeast during the summer of 1765 and committed to forcible opposition to the Stamp Act.

Continental Congress

A representative assembly that first met in October 1775 and served as the de facto central government of the United States during the Revolutionary War.

4.2 The Declaration of Independence and African Americans

Describe what the Declaration of Independence meant to African Americans.

The Continental Congress adopted the Declaration of Independence on July 4, 1776. Thomas Jefferson, a Virginia slaveholder who regarded African Americans as an inferior people, served as the Declaration's principal author. Therefore, when Jefferson wrote "that all men are created equal; that they are endowed by their Creator with certain unalienable rights; that among these are life, liberty, and the pursuit of happiness," he did not mean to support black claims for freedom. Similarly John Adams, a Massachusetts nonslaveholder who helped Jefferson draft the Declaration, distinguished between the rights of white men of British descent and lack of rights for people of color. In 1765 Adams had written that God had "never intended the American colonists 'for Negroes . . . and therefore never intended us for slaves.'" So convinced were Jefferson, Adams, and other Patriot leaders that black people could not claim the same rights as white people; they felt no need to qualify their words proclaiming universal liberty.

The draft declaration that Jefferson, Adams, and Benjamin Franklin submitted to Congress for approval did denounce the Atlantic slave trade as a "cruel war against human nature itself, violating its most sacred rights of life and liberty in the persons of a distant [African] people." But Congress deleted this passage because delegates from South Carolina and Georgia objected to it. The final version of the Declaration referred to slavery only to accuse the British of arousing African Americans to revolt against their masters.

Yet, although Jefferson and the other delegates did not mean to encourage African Americans to hope the American War for Independence could become a war against slavery, that is what African Americans believed it could be. Black people heard Patriot speakers make unqualified claims for human equality and natural rights. They read accounts of such speeches or listened as white men discussed them. In response, African Americans began to assert that such principles applied as much to them as to the white population. They forced white people to confront the contradiction between the new nation's professed ideals and its reality. Most white Americans did not deny that black Americans were human beings. White Americans therefore had to choose between accepting the literal meaning of the Declaration, which meant changing American society, or rejecting the revolutionary **ideology** that supported their claims for independence.

ideology

A body of ideas that presents a coherent view of human society and politics.

Profile

Crispus Attucks

Crispus Attucks was a fugitive slave who escaped in 1750 from his Framingham, Massachusetts, master. He had a black father and an American Indian mother. His master described him as "a mulatto fellow, about 27 years old, named Crispus, 6 feet 2 inches height, short, curl'd hair, his knees nearer together than common." During his 20 years as a fugitive, Attucks worked as a sailor, with Boston as his home port.

Attucks shared the anti-British sentiment that developed after the French and Indian War. This is not surprising because the tightening restrictions Parliament placed on American trade affected his livelihood as a seaman. In Boston, British soldiers became the target of such resentment. Bostonians insulted and threw rocks at them for some time before Attucks joined a crowd that, armed with clubs and sticks, accosted a small detachment of troops on the chilly evening of March 5, 1770. Attucks was not the only African American in the crowd. One pro-British witness described those who gathered as "saucy boys, Negroes and mulattoes, Irish Teagues and outlandish Jack Tars [sailors]."

Although eyewitness accounts differ, Attucks probably took the lead in confronting Captain Thomas Preston and the nine soldiers under his command. A black witness maintained that Attucks, "a stout man with a long cordwood stick," hit a soldier, which led the troops to fire on the mob. John Adams, who defended the soldiers in court, credited this account, and Attucks almost certainly died first when the soldiers, with their backs to a wall, fired.

Samuel Adams, John's cousin, and other Patriots in Boston declared the 47-year-old Attucks the first martyr to British oppression. They carried his coffin, along with those of three of the other four men who were killed, to Faneuil Hall—called the "Cradle of Liberty" because of its association with revolutionary rhetoric. There Attucks lay in state for three days with the other victims of what Americans immediately called the Boston Massacre. From this hall 10,000 mourners accompanied four hearses to Boston's Middle Burying Ground. The inscription on the monument raised to commemorate the martyrs reads:

> Long as in freedom's cause the wise contend,
> Dear to your country shall your fame extend;
> While to the world the lettered stone shall tell
> Where Caldwell, Attucks, Gray, and Maverick fell.

Bostonians commemorated the anniversary of the massacre annually into the 1840s. They revived the practice in 1858 to protest the Supreme Court's decision in *Dred Scott v. Sanford* that African Americans were not citizens of the United States. At about the same time, African Americans in Cincinnati formed the "Attucks Guards" to resist enforcement of the Fugitive Slave Law. After the Civil War, black abolitionist William C. Nell linked the service of black men in defense of the Union to Attucks's sacrifice "in defense of this nation's freedom."

Attucks has remained a symbol of African-American patriotism. In 1967, at the height of the Vietnam War, the Newark, New Jersey, Board of Education, at the expressed desire of the city's large black community, made March 5 an annual holiday in honor of Attucks. This was the first holiday to recognize an African American.

The death of Crispus Attucks in the Boston Massacre.

4.2.1 The Impact of the Enlightenment

At the center of that ideology was the European Enlightenment. The roots of this intellectual movement, also known as the Age of Reason, lay in Renaissance secularism and humanism dating back to the fifteenth century. But it was Isaac Newton's *Principia Mathematica*, published in England in 1687, that shaped a new way of perceiving human beings and their universe.

Newton used mathematics to portray an orderly, balanced universe that ran according to natural laws that humans could discover through reason. Newton's insights supported the rationalized means of production and commerce associated with the Industrial Revolution that began in England during the early eighteenth century. An emerging market economy required the same sort of rational use of resources that Newton discovered in the universe. But what made the Enlightenment of particular relevance to the **Age of Revolution** was John Locke's application of Newton's ideas to politics.

Age of Revolution

A period in Atlantic history that began with the American Revolution in 1776 and ended with the defeat of Napoleonic France in 1815.

In his essay "Concerning Human Understanding," published in 1690, Locke maintained that human society—like the physical universe—ran according to natural laws. He contended that at the base of those laws were natural rights that all people shared. Human beings, according to Locke, created governments to protect their natural individual rights to life, liberty, and private property. If a government failed to perform this basic duty and became oppressive, he insisted, the people had the right to overthrow it. Although conceived nearly a century before the 1777 Massachusetts petition with which this chapter begins, Locke's ideas underlie its appeal on behalf of black liberty. Locke also maintained that the human mind at birth was a *tabula rasa* (i.e., knowledge and wisdom are not inherited but are acquired through experience). This suggested that with education *all* people could learn and advance. Locke saw no contradiction between these principles and human slavery. However, during the eighteenth century, such a contradiction became increasingly clear.

Most Americans became acquainted with Locke's ideas through **pamphlets** that a radical political minority in Britain produced during the early eighteenth century. This literature portrayed the British government of the day as a conspiracy aimed at depriving British subjects of their natural rights, reducing them to slaves, and establishing tyranny. After the French and Indian War, Americans, both black and white, interpreted British colonial policies and actions from the pamphlets' perspective.

pamphlet

A short published essay.

Such pamphlets clearly influenced white Patriot leaders who, between 1763 and 1776, charged that the British government sought to enslave Americans by depriving them of their rights as Englishmen. When such leaders made these charges, they had difficulty denying that they themselves deprived African Americans of natural rights. George Washington, for example, declared in 1774 that "the crisis is arrived when we must assert our rights, or submit to every imposition, that can be heaped upon us, till custom and use shall make us tame and abject, as the blacks we rule over with such arbitrary sway."

4.2.2 African Americans in the Revolutionary Debate

During the 1760s and 1770s, when powerful slaveholders such as George Washington talked of liberty, natural rights, and hatred of enslavement, African Americans listened. Most of them had been born in America and had absorbed English culture. They were united as a people and knew their way in colonial society. Those who lived in or near towns and cities had access to public meetings and newspapers. They knew about the disputes with Great Britain and the contradictions between demanding liberty for oneself and denying it to others. They understood that the ferment of the 1760s had shaken traditional assumptions about government. Many of them hoped for more changes.

The greatest source of optimism for African Americans was the expectation that white Patriot leaders would realize that their revolutionary principles were incompatible

This drawing depicts James Armistead (1760–1831) who, as an enslaved young man, served as a Patriot spy during the War for Independence. Under the command of the Marquis de Lafayette, whose name Armistead later added to his own, he infiltrated British camps in Virginia. He provided information that helped George Washington force the British surrender at Yorktown in 1781.

freedom suits

Legal cases in which slaves sued their master or master's heirs for freedom.

The drawing portrays a black youngster joining in a Boston demonstration against the Stamp Act of 1765.

with slavery. Those in England who believed white Americans must submit to British authority pointed out the contradiction. Samuel Johnson, London's most famous writer, asked, "How is it that we hear the loudest yelps for liberty among the drivers of negroes?" White Americans made similar comments. As early as 1763, James Otis of Massachusetts warned, "Those who every day barter away other mens['] liberty, will soon care little for their own." Thomas Paine, whose pamphlet *Common Sense* rallied Americans to endorse independence in 1776, asked them to contemplate "with what consistency, or decency they complain so loudly of attempts to enslave them, while they hold so many hundred thousands in slavery; and annually enslave many thousands more."

Such principled misgivings among white people about slavery helped improve the situation for black people in the North and upper South during the war. But African Americans acting on their own behalf had the key role. In January 1766 slaves marched through Charleston, South Carolina, shouting "Liberty!" In the South Carolina and Georgia low country and in the Chesapeake, slaves escaped in massive numbers throughout the revolutionary era.

Rumors of slave uprisings spread throughout the southern colonies. However, it was in New England—the heartland of anti-British radicalism—that African Americans formally made their case for freedom. As early as 1701, a Massachusetts slave won his liberty in court, and there were 11 similar suits before 1750. During the revolutionary era, such cases multiplied. In addition, although slaves during the seventeenth and early eighteenth centuries had based their **freedom suits** on contractual technicalities, during the revolutionary period they increasingly sued on the basis of principles of universal liberty. They did not always win their cases—John Adams, a future president, was the lawyer who defeated one such case in Boston in 1768—but they set precedents.

African Americans in Massachusetts, New Hampshire, and Connecticut, meanwhile, petitioned their colonial or state legislatures for gradual emancipation. These petitions, worded like the one at the start of this chapter, indicate that the black men who signed them adopted revolutionary rhetoric to their cause. They had learned the rhetoric as they joined white radicals to confront British authority.

In 1765 black men in Boston demonstrated against the Stamp Act. They rioted against British troops there in 1768 and joined Crispus Attucks in 1770. Black Minutemen stood with their white comrades at Lexington and Concord. In 1773 black petitioners from Boston told a delegate to the colonial assembly, "We expect great things from men who have made such a noble stand against the designs of their *fellow-men* to enslave them. . . . The divine spirit of *freedom*, seems to fire every human breast."

4.3 The Black Enlightenment

Discuss the African Americans who contributed to the Enlightenment.

Besides influencing radical political discourse during the revolutionary era, the Enlightenment also shaped the careers of America's first black intellectuals. Because it emphasized human reason, the Enlightenment led to the establishment of colleges, academies, and libraries in Europe and America. These institutions usually served a tiny elite, but newspapers and pamphlets made science and literature available to the masses. And the eighteenth century became an era in which amateurs could make serious contributions to human knowledge. Some of these amateurs, such as Thomas Jefferson and Benjamin Franklin,

Voices

Boston's Slaves Link Their Freedom to American Liberty

In April 1773 a committee of slaves from Boston submitted this petition to the delegate to the Massachusetts General Court from the town of Thompson. The petition, which overflows with sarcasm, demonstrates African-American familiarity with the principles of the Enlightenment and the irony of white Americans' contention that Britain aimed to enslave them. Its authors are of two minds about their society. They see both the potential for black freedom and the entrenched prejudice of white Americans. Note that the authors propose to go to Africa if they gain their freedom.

Boston, April 20th, 1773

Sir,

The efforts made by the legislative of this province in their last sessions to free themselves from slavery, gave us, who are in that deplorable state, a high degree of satisfaction. We expect great things from men who have made such a noble stand against the designs of their *fellow-men* to enslave them. We cannot but wish and hope Sir, that you will have the same grand object, we mean civil and religious liberty, in view in your next session. The divine spirit of *freedom*, seems to fire every humane breast on this continent, except such as are bribed to assist in executing the execrable plan.

We are very sensible that it would be highly detrimental to our present masters, if we were allowed to demand all that of *right* belongs to us for past services; this we disclaim. Even the *Spaniards*, who have not those sublime ideas of freedom that English men have, are conscious that they have no right to all the services of their fellow-men, we mean the *Africans*, whom they have purchased with their money; therefore they allow them one day in a week to work for themselves, to enable them to earn money to purchase the residue of their time. . . . We do not pretend to dictate to you Sir, or to the Honorable Assembly, of which you are a member. We acknowledge our obligations to you for what

you have already done, but as the people of this province seem to be actuated by the principles of equity and justice, we cannot but expect your house will again take our deplorable case into serious consideration, and give us that ample relief which, *as men*, we have a natural right to.

But since the wise and righteous governor of the universe, has permitted our fellow men to make us slaves, we bow in submission to him, and determine to behave in such a manner as that we can have reason to expect the divine approbation of, and assistance in, our peaceable and lawful attempts to gain our freedom.

We are willing to submit to such regulations and laws, as may be made relative to us, until we leave the province, which we determine to do as soon as we can, from our joyntlabours procure money to transport ourselves to some part of the Coast of *Africa*, where we propose settlement. We are very desirous that you should have instructions relative to us, from your town, therefore we pray you to communicate this letter to them, and ask this favor for us.

In behalf of our fellow slaves in this province, and by order of their Committee.

Peter Bestes,
Sambo Freeman,
Felix Holbrook,
Chester Joie.

For the Representative of the town of Thompson.

1. What is the object of this petition?
2. What Enlightenment principles does the petition invoke?
3. What is the significance of the slaves' vow to go to Africa if freed?

SOURCE: Gary B. Nash, *Race and Revolution* (Madison, WI: Madison House, 1990), 173–74.

were rich and well educated. They made discoveries in botany and electricity while pursuing political careers. What is striking is that some African Americans, with far more limited resources, also became scientists and authors.

Because they had easier access to evangelical Protestantism than to secular learning, most African Americans who gained intellectual distinction during the late eighteenth century owed more to the Great Awakening than to the Enlightenment. The best known of these is Jupiter Hammon, a Long Island slave who published religious poetry in the 1760s. There were also Josiah Bishop and Lemuel Haynes, black ministers to white church congregations in Virginia and New England. But the Enlightenment influenced Phillis Wheatley and Benjamin Banneker, who became the most famous black intellectuals of their time.

4.3.1 Phillis Wheatley and Poetry

Wheatley came to Boston from Africa—possibly near the Gambia River—in 1761 aboard a slaver. She was seven or eight years old, small, frail, and nearly naked. John Wheatley, a wealthy white merchant, purchased her as a servant for his wife. Although Phillis spoke no English when her ship docked, she soon began reading and writing in that language and studying Latin. She pored over the Bible and became a fervent Christian. She also read the fashionable poetry of British author Alexander Pope and became, by age 13, a poet herself. For the rest of her short life, Wheatley wrote poems to celebrate important events. Like Pope's, Wheatley's poetry reflected the values of the Enlightenment. She aimed to blend thought, image, sound, and rhythm to create perfectly balanced compositions. In 1773 the Wheatleys sent her to London where her first book of poems—the first book ever by an African-American woman and the second by any American woman—was published under the title *Poems on Various Subjects, Religious and Moral*. The Wheatleys freed Phillis after her return to Boston, although she continued to live in their house until they both had died. In 1778 she married John Peters, a black grocer, and soon became mired in illness and poverty. Two of her children died in infancy, and she died in December 1784 giving birth to her third child, who died with her.

In her writing Wheatley called on black people to adopt white culture. Before her marriage, she lived almost exclusively among white people and absorbed their values. Although she lamented the sorrow her capture had caused her parents, she was grateful to have been brought to America:

Twas mercy brought me from my Pagan land,
Taught my benighted soul to understand
That there's a God, that there's a Saviour too:
Once I redemption neither sought nor knew.

But Wheatley did not simply copy her masters' views. Although the Wheatleys remained loyal to Britain, she became a fervent Patriot. She attended Boston's Old North Church, a hotbed of anti-British sentiment, and wrote poems supporting the Patriot cause. In early 1776, she lavishly praised George Washington, "fam'd for thy valour, for thy virtues more," and received effusive thanks from the general.

Wheatley also became an advocate and symbol of John Locke's ideas concerning the influence of environment on human beings. White leaders of the Revolution and intellectuals debated whether black people were inherently inferior in intellect to white people or whether this perceived black inferiority resulted from enslavement. Some slaveholders, such as Thomas Jefferson—who held racist assumptions about innate black inferiority—dismissed Wheatley's work as "below the dignity of criticism." But those who favored an environmental perspective considered Wheatley an example of what people of African descent could achieve if freed from oppression. She made her own views clear:

Some view our sable race with scornful eye,
"Their colour is a diabolic dye."
Remember, Christians, Negroes, black as Cain,
May be refin'd, and join th' angelic train.

4.3.2 Benjamin Banneker and Science

In the breadth of his achievement, Benjamin Banneker is even more representative of the Enlightenment than Phillis Wheatley. Like hers, his life epitomizes a flexibility concerning race that the revolutionary era briefly promised to expand.

A frontispiece portrait of Phillis Wheatley precedes the title page of her first book of poetry, which was published in 1773. The portrait suggests Wheatley's small physique and studious manner.

Voices

Phillis Wheatley on Liberty and Natural Rights

Phillis Wheatley wrote the following letter to Samson Occom, an American-Indian minister, in 1774, after her return from England and as tensions between Britain and its American colonies intensified. In it, she links divine order, natural rights, and an inner desire for personal liberty. She expresses optimism that Christianity and the emergence of order in Africa will lead to the end of the Atlantic slave trade. And she hopes that God will ultimately overcome the avarice of American slaveholders ("our modern Egyptians") and let them see the contradiction between their words and deeds.

February 11, 1774

Rev'd and honor'd Sir,

I have this Day received your obliging kind Epistle, and am greatly satisfied with your Reasons respecting the Negroes, and think highly reasonable what you offer in Vindication of their natural Rights. Those that invade them cannot be insensible that the divine Light is chasing away the thick Darkness which broods over the Land of Africa; and the Chaos which has reign'd so long, is converting into beautiful Order, and reveals more and more clearly, the glorious Dispensation of civil and religious Liberty, which are so inseparably united, that there is little or no Enjoyment of one without the other. Otherwise, perhaps, the Israelites had been less solicitous for their Freedom from Egyptian Slavery; I don't say they would have been contented without it. By no Means, for in every human Breast, God has implanted a Principle, which we call Love of Freedom; it is impatient of Oppression, and pants for Deliverance. And by the leave of our modern Egyptians, I will assert that the same principle lives in us. God grant Deliverance in his own Way and Time, and get him honor upon all those whose Avarice impels them to countenance and help forward the Calamities of their fellow Creatures. This I desire not for their Hurt, but to convince them of the strange Absurdity of their Conduct whose Words and Actions are so diametrically opposite. How well the cry for Liberty, and the reverse Disposition for the exercise of oppressive Power over others agree, I humbly think it does not require the Penetration of a Philosopher to determine.

Phillis Wheatley

1. How does this letter reflect principles associated with the Enlightenment?
2. What insights does this letter provide into Wheatley's views on slavery and its abolition?

SOURCE: Phillis Wheatley in 1774 (*Connecticut Gazette,* March 11, 1774, written by Wheatley to Reverend Samson Occum, 11 February 1774).

Banneker was born free in Maryland in 1731 and died in 1806. The son of a mixed-race mother and an African father, he inherited a farm near Baltimore from his white grandmother. As a child, Banneker attended a racially integrated school. Later his farm gave him a steady income and the leisure to study literature and science.

With access to the library of his white neighbor George Ellicott, Banneker "mastered Latin and Greek and had a good working knowledge of German and French." By the 1770s he had a reputation as a man "of uncommonly soft and gentlemanly manners and of pleasing colloquial powers." Like Jefferson, Franklin, and others of his time, mechanics fascinated Banneker and in 1770 he constructed a clock. He also wrote a treatise on bees. However, he gained international fame as a mathematician and astronomer. Because of his knowledge in these disciplines, he became a member of the survey commission for Washington, D.C. This made him the first black civilian employee of the U.S. government. Between 1791 and 1796, he used his astronomical observations and mathematical calculations to publish an almanac predicting the positions in the earth's night sky of the sun, moon, and constellations.

Like Wheatley, Banneker thoroughly assimilated white culture and well understood the fundamental issues of human equality raised by the American Revolution. In 1791 he sent Thomas Jefferson, who was then U.S. secretary of state, a copy of his almanac to refute Jefferson's claim in *Notes on the State of Virginia* that black people were inherently inferior intellectually to white people. Noting Jefferson's commitment to the biblical statement that God had created "us all of one flesh" and Jefferson's words in the Declaration of Independence, Banneker called the great man to account concerning slavery.

Benjamin Banneker's
PENNSYLVANIA, DELAWARE, MARY-
LAND, AND VIRGINIA
ALMANAC,
FOR THE
YEAR of our LORD 1795;
Being the Third after Leap-Year.

BANNEKER.

PHILADELPHIA:
Printed for WILLIAM GIBBONS, Cherry Street.

The title page of the 1795 edition of Benjamin Banneker's *Pennsylvania, Delaware, Maryland, and Virginia Almanac*. Banneker was widely known during the late eighteenth century as a mathematician and astronomer.

Loyalists

Those Americans who, during the Revolutionary War, wished to remain within the British Empire.

Continental Army

The army created by the Continental Congress in June 1775 to fight British troops. George Washington was its commander in chief.

Referring to the Declaration, Banneker wrote, "You were then impressed with proper ideas of the great valuation of liberty, and the free possession of those blessings, to which you were entitled by nature; but, Sir, how pitiable is it to reflect, that altho you were so fully convinced of the benevolence of the Father of Mankind, and of his equal and impartial distribution of these rights and privileges . . . that you should at the Same time counteract his mercies, in detaining by fraud and violence so numerous a part of my brethren, under groaning captivity and cruel oppression."

4.4 African Americans in the War for Independence

Evaluate the African-American role in the War for Independence.

In the words of historian Benjamin Quarles, "The Negro's role in the Revolution can best be understood by realizing that his major loyalty was not to a place nor to a people, but to a principle." When it came to fighting between Patriots on one side and the British and their **Loyalist** American allies on the other, African Americans joined the side that offered freedom. In the South, where the British held out the promise of freedom in exchange for military service, black men eagerly fought on the British side as Loyalists. In the North, where white Patriots were more consistently committed to human liberty than in the South, black men just as eagerly fought on the Patriot side (see Map 4-2). In contrast, American Indians, hoping to counter white expansion westward, almost always fought on the British side.

The war began in earnest in August 1776 when the British landed a large army at Brooklyn, New York, and drove Washington's **Continental Army** across New Jersey into Pennsylvania. The military and diplomatic turning point in the war came the following year at Saratoga, New York, when a poorly executed British strategy to take control of the Hudson River resulted in British general John Burgoyne's surrender of his entire army to Patriot forces. This victory led France and other European powers to enter the war against Britain. Significant fighting ended in October 1781 when Washington and the French forced Lord Cornwallis to surrender another British army at Yorktown, Virginia.

When Washington had organized the Continental Army in July 1775, he forbade the enlistment of new black troops and the reenlistment of black men who had served at Lexington and Concord, Bunker Hill, and other early battles. Shortly after Washington announced his ban on black service, all 13 states followed his example. Several factors account for Washington's decision and its ratification by the Continental Congress. Although black men had served during the French and Indian War, the colonies had traditionally excluded African Americans from militia service. Like others before them, Patriot leaders feared that if they enlisted African-American soldiers, it would encourage slaves to leave their masters without permission. White people—especially in the South—feared that armed black men would endanger the social order. Paradoxically, white Americans simultaneously believed black men were too cowardly to be effective soldiers. Although apparently contradictory, these last two beliefs persisted into the twentieth century.

4.4.1 Black Loyalists

Because so many Patriot leaders resisted employing black troops, by mid-1775 the British had taken the lead in recruiting African Americans. During the spring of that year, from Maryland southward, rumors had circulated that the British planned to instigate slave revolt. In North Carolina, for example, the white populace believed that British agents promised to reward black individuals who murdered their masters. However, no such uprisings occurred.

Instead, many slaves escaped and sought British protection as Loyalists. Thomas Jefferson later claimed that 30,000 slaves escaped in Virginia alone. The British employed most black men who escaped to their lines as laborers and foragers. During the siege at Yorktown in 1781, the British used the bodies of black laborers who had died of smallpox in a primitive form of biological warfare to try to infect the Patriot army. Even so, many black refugees fought for British or Loyalist units.

Black Loyalists were most numerous in the low country of South Carolina and Georgia. At the end of the war in 1783, approximately 20,000 African Americans left with the British forces as they evacuated Savannah and Charleston. A few who remained became known as "the plunderers of Georgia." They carried out guerrilla warfare there until 1786.

The most famous British appeal to African Americans to fight for the empire in return for freedom came in Virginia. On November 7, 1775, Lord Dunmore, the last royal governor of the Old Dominion, issued a proclamation offering to liberate slaves who joined "His Majesty's Troops . . . for the more speedily reducing this Colony to a proper sense of their duty to His Majesty's crown and dignity."

Ralph Henry, a 26-year-old slave of Patrick Henry, joined those who responded to Dunmore's offer. Perhaps Ralph Henry recalled his famous master's "Give me liberty or give me death" speech. Another who joined Dunmore's troops was James Reid, who later became a leader of Britain's colony for former slaves in Sierra Leone in West Africa. Reid's 16-year-old wife came with him, and they both served with the Royal Artillery. In 1780 at least 20 of Thomas Jefferson's slaves joined Cornwallis's army when it invaded Virginia.

Map 4-2 Major Battles of the American War for Independence, Indicating Those in Which Black Troops Participated

Black troops fought on both sides during the American War for Independence and participated in most of the major battles.

SOURCE: Adapted from *The Atlas of African-American History and Politics, 1/e*, by A. Smallwood and J. Elliot. The McGraw-Hill Companies. Used by permission.

Why is it significant that most of these battles were in the North?

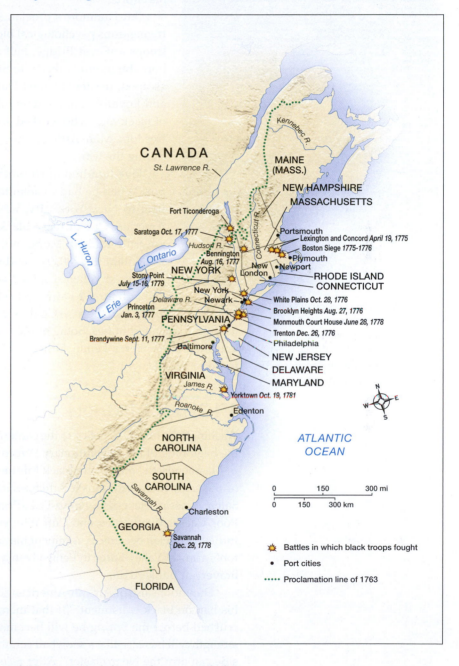

By his Excellency the Right Honourable JOHN Earl of DUNMORE, his Majesty's Lieutenant and Governour-General of the Colony and Dominion of Virginia, and Vice-Admiral of the same:

A PROCLAMATION.

AS I have ever entertained Hopes that an Accommodation might have taken Place between *Great Britain* and this Colony, without being compelled, by my Duty, to this most disagreeable, but now absolutely necessary Step, rendered so by a Body of armed Men, unlawfully assembled, firing on his Majesty's Tenders, and the Formation of an Army, and that Army now on their March to attack his Majesty's Troops, and destroy the well-disposed Subjects of this Colony: To defeat such treasonable Purposes, and that all such Traitors, and their Abetters, may be brought to Justice, and that the Peace and good Order of this Colony may be again restored, which the ordinary Course of the civil Law is unable to effect, I have thought fit to issue this my Proclamation, hereby declaring, that until the aforesaid good Purposes can be obtained, I do, in Virtue of the Power and Authority to me given, by his Majesty, determine to execute martial Law, and cause the same to be executed throughout this Colony; and to the End that Peace and good Order may the sooner be restored, I do require every Person capable of bearing Arms to resort to his Majesty's S T A N-DARD, or be looked upon as Traitors to his Majesty's Crown and Government, and thereby become liable to the Penalty the Law inflicts upon such Offences, such as Forfeiture of Life, Confiscation of Lands, &c. &c. And I do hereby farther declare all indented Servants, Negroes, or others (appertaining to Rebels) free, that are able and willing to bear Arms, they joining his Majesty's Troops, as soon as may be, for the more speedily reducing this Colony to a proper Sense of their Duty, to his Majesty's Crown and Dignity. I do farther order, and require, all his Majesty's liege Subjects to retain their Quitrents, or any other Taxes due, or that may become due, in their own Custody, till such Time as Peace may be again restored to this at present most unhappy Country, or demanded of them for their former salutary Purposes, by Officers properly authorised to receive the same.

GIVEN under my Hand, on Board the Ship William, off Norfolk, the 7th Day of November, in the 16th Year of his Majesty's Reign.

DUNMORE.

GOD SAVE THE KING.

This is a broadside version of Lord Dunmore's November 7, 1775, proclamation calling on black men in Virginia to fight on the British side in the American War for Independence in return for their freedom.

Dunmore initially recruited black soldiers out of desperation. Then he became the strongest advocate—on either the British or the Patriot side—of their fighting ability. When he issued his appeal, Dunmore had only 300 British troops and had been driven from Williamsburg, Virginia's colonial capital. Mainly because Dunmore had to seek refuge on British warships, only about 800 African Americans managed to reach his forces. Defeat by the Patriots at the Battle of Great Bridge in December 1775 curtailed his efforts.

But Dunmore's proclamation and the black response to it struck a tremendous psychological blow against his enemies. Of Dunmore's 600 troops at Great Bridge, half were African Americans whose uniforms bore the motto "Liberty to Slaves." As more and more Virginia slaves escaped, masters blamed Dunmore. Throughout the war, other British and Loyalist commanders followed his example, recruiting thousands of black men who worked and sometimes fought in exchange for their freedom. More African Americans became active Loyalists than Patriots during the war.

Five hundred of Dunmore's black troops died of typhus or smallpox. When he had to abandon Virginia, the remainder sailed with his fleet to New York City, which had become British headquarters in America. One of these black soldiers, the notorious Colonel Tye, led guerrilla raids in Monmouth County, New Jersey, for years. Until he was killed in 1780, Tye and his interracial band of about 25 Loyalists plundered villages, spiked cannons to make them incapable of firing, and kidnapped Patriot officers. When the war ended, many black Loyalists, like those in Charleston and Savannah, joined white Loyalists in leaving the United States. Some of them went first to Acadia—now Nova Scotia—and then on to Sierra Leone. Others went to the British West Indies, where some faced reenslavement.

4.4.2 Black Patriots

Washington's July 1775 policy to the contrary, black men fought on the Patriot side from the beginning of the Revolutionary War to its conclusion. Before Washington's arrival in Massachusetts, there were black Minutemen at Lexington and Concord, and some of the same men distinguished themselves at Bunker Hill. Among them were Peter Salem, Caesar Dickerson, Pomp Fisk, Prince Hall, Cuff Hayes, Barzillai Lew, Salem Poor, Caesar Weatherbee, and Cuff Whittemore. Lew was a veteran of the French and Indian War. Hall became a prominent black leader. Poor, who wintered with Washington's army at Valley Forge in Pennsylvania in 1777–1778, received a commendation for bravery at Bunker Hill.

Dunmore's use of African-American soldiers prompted Washington to reconsider his ban on black enlistment. "If that man, Dunmore," he wrote in late 1775, "is not crushed before the Spring he will become the most dangerous man in America. His strength will increase like a snowball running down hill. Success will depend on which side can arm the Negro faster." After receiving encouragement from black veterans, Washington, on December 30, 1775, allowed African-American reenlistment in the Continental Army. Troop shortages forced Congress and most state governments to go beyond this and allow recruitment of black soldiers for the Continental Army and state militias. Even then, South Carolina and Georgia continued to refuse to permit black men to serve in regiments raised within their boundaries, although black men from the two states joined other Patriot units.

The Patriot recruitment policy changed most quickly in New England. In early 1777 Massachusetts opened its militia to black men, and Rhode Island formed a black

1775
African Americans and the War
for Independence

April 18, 1775

Black Minutemen participate in the Battle of Lexington and Concord.

May 10, 1775

The Second Continental Congress convenes in Philadelphia.

June 15, 1775

Congress appoints George Washington commander in chief of the new Continental Army.

June 17, 1775

Black men fight with the Patriots at Bunker Hill.

July 9, 1775

George Washington bans African-American enlistment in the Continental Army.

November 7, 1775

Lord Dunmore, the royal governor of Virginia, offers freedom to slaves who will fight for the British.

December 30, 1775

Washington allows black reenlistments in the Continental Army.

regiment. Connecticut enabled masters to free their slaves to serve as substitutes for the masters or their sons in the militia or Continental Army. New York and New Jersey adopted similar statutes.

Also in 1777, when Congress set state enlistment quotas for the Continental Army, state recruitment officers began to fill those quotas with black men so that white men might serve closer to home in the militia. Meanwhile, the southern states of Delaware, Maryland, Virginia, and North Carolina reluctantly began enlisting free black men. Of these states, only Maryland allowed slaves to serve in return for freedom. But the other three states sometimes allowed slaves to enlist as substitutes for their masters, and this usually led to freedom. Black men asserted that if they were to fight in a war for liberty, their own liberty had to be ensured. When one master informed his slave that both of them would be fighting for liberty, the slave replied "that it would be a great satisfaction to know that he was indeed going to fight for his liberty."

Except for Rhode Island's black regiment and some companies in Massachusetts, black Patriots served in integrated military units. Enrollment officers often did not specify a man's race when he enlisted, so it is difficult to know precisely how many black men were involved. The figure usually given is 5,000 black soldiers out of a total Patriot force of 300,000. A few black men, such as Salem Poor, became junior officers. Others served as drummers and fifers, sailors on **privateers** commissioned by the Continental Congress, and informants and spies. Like others who gathered intelligence behind enemy lines, African Americans who informed and spied risked being hanged if captured.

Black men fought on the Patriot side in nearly every major battle of the war (see Map 4-2). Prince Whipple and Oliver Cromwell crossed the Delaware River with

privateers

Merchant vessels armed and authorized by a government to raid enemy shipping.

For many years, historians presumed that Peter Salem was the black soldier portrayed in this detail from John Trumbull's contemporary oil painting *The Battle of Bunker Hill*. Instead, the soldier was Asaba Grosvenor, a slave who accompanied his master in the fighting.

mercenaries

German troops hired to fight on the British side.

Washington on Christmas night 1776 to surprise Hessian **mercenaries** at Trenton, New Jersey. Others fought at Monmouth, Saratoga, Savannah, Princeton, and Yorktown. In 1777 a Hessian officer reported, "No [Patriot] regiment is to be seen in which there are not Negroes in abundance, and among them are able bodied, strong and brave fellows."

Black women also supported the Patriot cause. Like white women, black women, such as James Reid's wife, sometimes accompanied their soldier husbands into army camps, if not into battle. A few black women also demonstrated their sympathy for the Patriots in defiance of British authority. When the British occupied Philadelphia in 1777, they put Patriot prisoners of war in the city jail. The following year, a local Patriot correspondent reported that a free black woman, "having received two hard dollars for washing, and hearing of the distress of our prisoners in the goal, went to market and bought some neck beef and two heads, with some green[s], and made a pot of as good broth as she could; but having no more money to buy bread, she got credit of a baker for six loaves of bread, all of which she carried to our unfortunate prisoners."

4.5 The Revolution and Emancipation

Explain how the American Revolution weakened slavery.

The willingness of African Americans to risk their lives in the Patriot cause encouraged northern legislatures to emancipate slaves within their borders. By the late 1770s, most of these legislatures had begun debating abolition. Petitions and lawsuits initiated by black people in Massachusetts, Connecticut, New Hampshire, and elsewhere encouraged such consideration. But an emerging market economy, the Great Awakening, and the Enlightenment established the context in which people who believed deeply in the sanctity of private property could consider such a momentous change. Economic, religious, and intellectual change convinced many white Americans that slavery should be abolished.

Enlightenment rationalism was a powerful antislavery force. In the light of reason, slavery appeared to be inefficient, barbaric, and oppressive. But rationalism alone could not convince white Americans that black people should be released from slavery. White people also had to believe general emancipation was in their self-interest and their Christian duty.

In the North, where all these forces operated and the economic stake in slave labor was relatively small, emancipation made steady progress. In the Chesapeake, where some of these forces operated, emancipationist sentiment grew, and many masters manumitted their slaves; however, there was no serious threat to the slave system. In the low country of South Carolina and Georgia, where economic interests and white solidarity against large black populations outweighed intellectual and religious considerations, white commitment to black bondage remained absolute.

The movement among white Americans to abolish slavery began within the Society of Friends. This religious group, whose members were known as Quakers, had always emphasized conscience, human brotherhood, and nonviolence. Also, many leading Quaker families engaged in international business ventures that required educated, efficient, and moral workers. This predisposed such Quakers against a system that forced workers to be uneducated, recalcitrant, and often ignorant of Christian religion. Although Quakers had owned and traded slaves for generations, growing numbers of them concluded that slaveholding was sinful.

During the 1730s Benjamin Lay, a former slaveholder who had moved from Barbados to the Quaker-dominated colony of Pennsylvania, began to exhort his fellow Friends to disassociate themselves from owning and buying slaves. A decade later

John Woolman, who lived in southern New Jersey, urged northeastern and Chesapeake Quakers to emancipate their slaves. With assistance from British Quakers, Woolman and Anthony Benezet, a Philadelphia teacher, convinced the Society's 1758 annual meeting to condemn slavery and the slave trade.

When the conflict with Britain made human rights a political as well as a religious issue, Woolman and Benezet carried their abolitionist message beyond the Society of Friends. They thereby merged their sectarian crusade with the rationalist efforts of such northern white revolutionary leaders as former slaveholder Benjamin Franklin of Philadelphia and John Jay and Alexander Hamilton—who continued to own slaves—of New York. Under Quaker leadership, antislavery societies organized in the North and the Chesapeake. The societies joined African Americans in petitioning northern legislatures and, in one instance, the Continental Congress to act against slavery or the slave trade.

4.5.1 The Revolutionary Impact

In calling for emancipation, the antislavery societies emphasized black service in the war against British rule and the religious and economic progress of northern African Americans. They also contended that emancipation would prevent black rebellions. As a result, by 1784 all the northern states except New Jersey and New York had undertaken either immediate or gradual abolition of slavery. Delaware, Maryland, and Virginia made manumission easier. Even South Carolina and Georgia undertook to mitigate the most brutal excesses that slavery encouraged among masters. Many observers believed the Revolution had profoundly improved the prospects for African Americans.

In fact, the War for Independence dealt a heavy, although not mortal, blow to slavery (see Figure 4-1). While northern states prepared to abolish involuntary servitude, an estimated 100,000 slaves escaped from their masters in the South. In South Carolina alone, approximately 25,000 escaped—about 30 percent of the state's black population. Twenty thousand black people left with the British at the end of the war (see Map 4-3). Meanwhile, numerous escapees found their way to southern cities or to the North, where they joined an expanding free black class.

In the Chesapeake, as well as in the North, individual slaves gained freedom either in return for service in the war or because their masters had embraced Enlightenment principles. Philip Graham of Maryland freed his slaves, commenting that holding one's "fellow men in bondage and slavery is repugnant to the gold law of God and the unalienable right of mankind as well as to every principle of the late glorious revolution

Figure 4-1 The Free Black Population of the British North American Colonies in 1750 and of the United States in 1790 and 1800

The impact of revolutionary ideology and a changing economy led to a great increase in the free black population during the 1780s and 1790s.

SOURCE: *A Century of Population Growth in the United States. 1790–1900* (1909), 80. Data for 1750 Estimated.

Map 4-3 The Resettlement of Black Loyalists After the American War for Independence

Like their white Loyalist counterparts, many black Loyalists left with the British following the Patriot victory. Most of those settled in Nova Scotia soon moved on to Great Britain or the British free black colony Sierra Leone. Some black migrants to the British Caribbean were reenslaved.

SOURCE: Adapted from *The Atlas of African-American History and Politics, 1/e,* by A. Smallwood and J. Elliot. The McGraw-Hill Companies. Used by permission.

What does the arrival of some black Loyalists in Sierra Leone indicate about Great Britain's changing attitudes toward slavery?

which has taken place in America." The Virginia legislature ordered masters to free slaves who had fought for American independence.

Those Chesapeake slaves who did not become free also made gains during the Revolution because the war hastened the decline of tobacco raising. As planters switched to wheat and corn, they required fewer year-round, full-time workers. This encouraged the planters to free their excess labor force or to negotiate contracts that let slaves serve for a term of years rather than for life. Another alternative was for masters to allow slaves—primarily males—to practice skilled trades instead of doing fieldwork. Such slaves often **"hired their own time"** in return for giving their masters a large percentage of their wages.

Even those slaves who remained agricultural workers had more time to garden, hunt, and fish to supply themselves and their families with food and income. They gained more freedom to visit relatives who lived on other plantations, attend religious meetings, and interact with white people. Masters tended to refrain from the barbaric punishments used in the past, to improve slave housing, and to allow slaves more access to religion.

In South Carolina and Georgia, greater autonomy for slaves during the revolutionary era took a different form. The war increased absenteeism among masters and reduced contacts between the black and white populations. The black majorities in rice-producing regions grew larger, more isolated, and more African in culture as the two states imported more slaves from Africa. The constant arrival of Africans helped the regions' African-American population retain a distinctive culture and the Gullah dialect. The increase in master absenteeism also permitted the task system of labor to expand. As historian Peter Kolchin notes, although African Americans in the North and the Chesapeake lived near white people and interacted with them, "in the coastal region of the lower South, most blacks lived in a world of their own, largely isolated from whites, and developed their own culture and way of life."

hired their own time
Refers to a practice in which a master allowed slaves to work for wages paid by someone other than the master himself.

4.5.2 The Revolutionary Promise

Even though the northern states moved toward general emancipation during the revolutionary era, most newly free African Americans lived in the Chesapeake. They gained their freedom by serving in the war or escaping or because of economic and ideological change. As a result, a substantial free black population emerged in the Chesapeake after the war. Free African Americans had, of course, always lived there—Anthony Johnson is a prominent example—but before the Revolution they were few in number. In 1782 Virginia had only 1,800 free people within a total black population of 220,582. By 1790 the state had 12,766 free people within a total black population of 306,193. By 1810 it was 30,570 within 423,088. Free black populations also grew in Delaware and Maryland, where—unlike Virginia—the number of slaves began a long decline.

But in South Carolina and Georgia, the free black class remained tiny. Most lowcountry free black people were the children of white slave owners. They tended to be less independent of their former masters than their Chesapeake counterparts and lighter complexioned because their freedom was often a result of a family relationship to their masters.

In the North and the Chesapeake, free African Americans frequently moved to cities. Boston, New York, Philadelphia, Baltimore, Richmond, and Norfolk gained substantial free black populations after the Revolution. Black women predominated in this migration because they could more easily find jobs as domestics in the cities than in rural areas. Cities also offered free black people opportunities for community development that did not exist in thinly settled farm country. Although African Americans often used their new mobility to reunite families disrupted by slavery, relocating to a city could disrupt families that had survived enslavement. It took about a generation for stable, urban, two-parent households to emerge.

Newly freed black people also faced economic difficulty, and their occupational status often declined. Frequently they emerged from slavery without the economic resources needed to become independent farmers, shopkeepers, or tradespeople. In the North such economic restraints sometimes forced them to remain with their former masters long after formal emancipation. To make matters worse, white artisans used legal and extralegal means to protect themselves from black competition. Therefore, African Americans who had learned trades as slaves had difficulty employing their skills in freedom.

Yet, in the North and Chesapeake, most African Americans refused to work for their old masters and left the site of their enslavement. Those who had escaped had to leave. For others, leaving indicated a desire to put the stigma of servitude behind and embrace, despite the risks, the opportunities freedom offered. Many former masters did not understand this desire and criticized their former chattels for not staying on as hired hands. One white Virginian complained, "I cannot help thinking it is too generally the case with all those of colour to be ungrateful."

Many African Americans took new names to signify their freedom. They adopted surnames such as *Freedom*, *Liberty*, or *Justice* and dropped classical given names such as *Pompey* and *Caesar*. Some paid homage to their African ancestry and complexion by taking surnames such as *Africa*, *Guinea*, *Brown*, and *Coal*. Others, however, expressed their aspirations in a racially stratified society by replacing African given names, such as *Cuffee* and *Quash*,with Anglicized biblical names and the surnames of famous white people.

Conclusion

In the Peace of Paris signed in September 1783, Britain recognized the independence of the United States, acquiesced in American control of the territory between the Appalachian Mountains and the Mississippi River, and returned Florida to Spain (see Map 4-4). Both sides promised to return confiscated property—including slaves—to their owners, but neither side complied. As the United States gained recognition of its independence, African Americans could claim they had helped secure it. As soldiers in the Continental Army or in Patriot state militias, many black men fought and died for the revolutionary cause. Others supported the British. African Americans, like white Americans, had been divided over the War for Independence. Yet those black men and women who chose the Patriot side, as well as those who became Loyalists, had freedom as their goal.

This chapter has sought to place the African-American experience during the struggle for independence in the broad context of revolutionary ideology derived from the Enlightenment. Black men and women, such as Benjamin Banneker and Phillis Wheatley, exemplified the intellectually liberating impact of eighteenth-century rationalism and recognized its application to black freedom.

During the war, and with the assistance of white opponents of slavery, African Americans combined arguments for natural rights with action to gain freedom. The American Revolution seemed about to fulfill its promise of freedom to a minority of African Americans, and they were ready to embrace the opportunities it offered. By the war's end in 1783, slavery was dying in the North and seemed to be on the wane in the Chesapeake. The first steps toward forming free black communities had been taken. Black leaders and intellectuals had emerged. Although most of their brothers and sisters remained in slavery, although the slave system began to expand again during the 1790s, and although free black people achieved *at best* second-class citizenship, they had made undeniable progress. Yet African Americans were also learning how difficult freedom could be despite the new republic's embrace of revolutionary ideals.

Map 4-4 North America, 1783

This map shows the political geography of North America following British recognition of the independence of the United States in 1783.

Why was this division of territory important for African Americans?

Chapter Timeline

AFRICAN-AMERICAN EVENTS	NATIONAL EVENTS
1750–1754	
1750	**1754**
Crispus Attucks escapes from slavery	French and Indian War begins
1760–1765	
1760	**1763**
Jupiter Hammon publishes a book of poetry	Expulsion of French power from North America
1761	**1764**
Phillis Wheatley arrives in Boston	Parliament passes Sugar Act

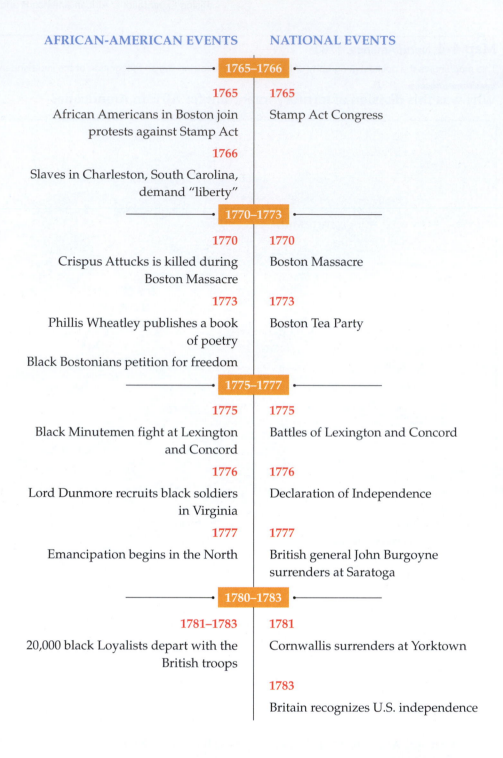

AFRICAN-AMERICAN EVENTS   NATIONAL EVENTS

1765–1766

1765

African Americans in Boston join protests against Stamp Act

1766

Slaves in Charleston, South Carolina, demand "liberty"

1765

Stamp Act Congress

1770–1773

1770

Crispus Attucks is killed during Boston Massacre

1773

Phillis Wheatley publishes a book of poetry

Black Bostonians petition for freedom

1770

Boston Massacre

1773

Boston Tea Party

1775–1777

1775

Black Minutemen fight at Lexington and Concord

1776

Lord Dunmore recruits black soldiers in Virginia

1777

Emancipation begins in the North

1775

Battles of Lexington and Concord

1776

Declaration of Independence

1777

British general John Burgoyne surrenders at Saratoga

1780–1783

1781–1783

20,000 black Loyalists depart with the British troops

1781

Cornwallis surrenders at Yorktown

1783

Britain recognizes U.S. independence

Review Questions

1. How did the Enlightenment affect African Americans during the revolutionary era?

2. What was the relationship between the American Revolution and black freedom?

3. What was the role of African Americans in the War for Independence? How did their choices in this conflict affect how the war was fought?

4. How did the American Revolution encourage assimilation among African Americans? How did it discourage assimilation?

5. Why did a substantial class of free African Americans emerge from the revolutionary era?

Retracing the Odyssey

Colonial Williamsburg, Williamsburg, Virginia. This is the largest historical restoration site in America. It emphasizes the period on the "eve of the American Revolution." Take the "Other Half Tour," which deals with "the lives and livelihoods of eighteenth-century African Americans."

Crispus Attucks' Grave, Granary Burial Ground, Boston, Massachusetts. Attucks is buried with the other victims of the Boston Massacre.

Recommended Reading

Ira Berlin and Ronald Hoffman, eds. *Slavery and Freedom in the Age of the American Revolution.* Charlottesville: University Press of Virginia, 1983. The essays in this collection center on black life in America during the revolutionary era.

David Brion Davis. *The Problem of Slavery in the Age of Revolution, 1770–1823.* Ithaca, NY: Cornell University Press, 1975. This magisterial study discusses the influence of the Enlightenment and the Industrial Revolution on slavery and opposition to slavery in the Atlantic world.

Douglas R. Egerton. *Death or Liberty: African Americans and Revolutionary America.* New York: Oxford University Press, 2009. Egerton focuses on individual initiative as central to the black experience during the late eighteenth century.

Sylvia R. Frey. *Water from the Rock: Black Resistance in a Revolutionary Age.* Princeton, NJ: Princeton University Press, 1991. This book portrays the War for Independence in the South as a three-way struggle among Patriots, British, and African Americans. It emphasizes the role of religion and community in black resistance to slavery.

Benjamin Quarles. *The Negro in the American Revolution.* 1961. Reprint, New York: Norton, 1973. This classic study remains the most comprehensive account of black participation in the War for Independence. It also demonstrates the impact of the war on black life.

Ellen Gibson Wilson. *The Loyal Blacks.* New York: G. P. Putnam's Sons, 1976. This book discusses why many African Americans chose the British side in the War for Independence. It also focuses on the fate of those loyal blacks who departed Nova Scotia in Canada for Sierra Leone.

Additional Bibliography

The Crisis of the British Empire

Stephen Conway. *The British Isles and the War of American Independence.* New York: Oxford University Press, 2000.

Edward Countryman. *The American Revolution.* Revised ed. New York: Hill and Wang, 2003.

Douglas E. Leach. *Roots of Conflict: British Armed Forces and Colonial Americans, 1677–1763.* Chapel Hill: University of North Carolina Press, 1986.

Pauline Maier. *From Resistance to Revolution: Colonial Radicals and the Development of American Opposition to Britain, 1765–1776.* New York: Knopf, 1972.

Peter David Garner Thomas. *Revolution in America: Britain and the Colonies, 1765–1776.* Cardiff, UK: University of Wales, 1992.

The Impact of the Enlightenment

Bernard Bailyn. *The Ideological Origins of the American Revolution.* Cambridge, MA: Harvard University Press, 1967.

Henry Steele Commager. *The Empire of Reason: How Europe Imagined and America Realized the Enlightenment.* Garden City, NY: Anchor, 1977.

Paul Finkelman. *Slavery and the Founders: Race and Liberty in the Age of Jefferson.* London: M. E. Sharpe, 1996.

Frank Shuffelton, ed. *The American Enlightenment.* Rochester, NY: University of Rochester Press, 1993.

Gordon S. Wood. *The Idea of America: Reflections on the Birth of the United States.* New York: Penguin, 2011.

African Americans and the American Revolution

Lerone Bennett Jr. *Before the Mayflower: A History of Black America*, 6th ed. Chicago: Johnson, 1987, Chapter 3.

Ira Berlin. "The Revolution in Black Life," in Alfred F. Young, ed., *The American Revolution: Explorations in the History of American Radicalism.* DeKalb: Northern Illinois University Press, 1976, 349–82.

Merton L. Dillon. *Slavery Attacked: Southern Slaves and Their Allies, 1619–1865.* Baton Rouge: Louisiana State University Press, 1990, Chapter 2.

Alan Gilbert. *Black Patriots and Loyalists: Fighting for Emancipation in the War for Independence.* Chicago: University of Chicago Press, 2012.

Woody Holton. *Forced Founders: Indians, Debtors, Slaves, and the Making of the American Revolution in Virginia.* Chapel Hill: University of North Carolina Press, 1999.

Sidney Kaplan and Emma Nogrady Kaplan. *The Black Presence in the Era of the American Revolution.* Amherst: University of Massachusetts Press, 1989.

Peter Kolchin. *American Slavery, 1619–1877.* New York: Hill and Wang, 1993, Chapter 3.

Duncan McLeod. *Slavery, Race, and the American Revolution.* New York: Cambridge University Press, 1974.

John W. Pulis. *Moving On: Black Loyalists in the Afro-Atlantic World.* New York: Garland, 1999.

Simon Schama. *Rough Crossings: Britain, the Slaves, and the American Revolution.* New York: Ecco, 2006.

David Waldstreicher. *Runaway America: Benjamin Franklin, Slavery, and the American Revolution.* New York: Hill and Wang, 2004.

Peter H. Wood. "'The Dream Deferred': Black Freedom Struggles on the Eve of White Independence," in Gary Y. Okihiro, ed., *In Resistance: Studies in African, Caribbean, and Afro-American History.* Amherst: University of Massachusetts Press, 1986, 166–87.

Antislavery and Emancipation in the North

Robin Blackburn. *The Overthrow of Colonial Slavery, 1776–1848.* New York: Verso, 1988, Chapter 3.

Merton L. Dillon. *The Abolitionists: The Growth of a Dissenting Minority.* New York: Norton, 1974, Chapter 1.

Joanne Pope Melish. *Disowning Slavery: Gradual Emancipation and "Race" in New England, 1780–1860.* Ithaca, NY: Cornell University Press, 1998.

Gary B. Nash. *The Forgotten Fifth: African Americans in the Age of Revolution.* Cambridge, MA: Harvard University Press, 2006.

Gary B. Nash and Jean R. Soderlund. *Freedom by Degrees: Emancipation in Pennsylvania and Its Aftermath.* New York: Oxford University Press, 1991.

James Brewer Stewart. *Holy Warriors: The Abolitionists and American Slavery.* Rev. ed. New York: Hill and Wang, 1997, Chapter 1.

Arthur Zilversmit. *The First Emancipation: The Abolition of Slavery in the North.* Chicago: University of Chicago Press, 1967.

Biography

Silvio A. Bedini. *The Life of Benjamin Banneker: The First African-American Man of Science.* Baltimore: Maryland Historical Society, 1999.

Vincent Carretta. *Phillis Wheatley: Biography of a Genius in Bondage.* Athens: University of Georgia Press, 2011.

Henry Louis Gates Jr. *The Trials of Phillis Wheatley.* New York: Basic Civitas Books, 2003.

Chapter 5

African Americans in the New Nation

1783–1820

This early twentieth-century photograph portrays pre-Civil War slave quarters on the Hermitage rice plantation located just north of Savannah, Georgia. Each small brick building housed two African-American families.

∨ Learning Objectives

After reading this chapter, you should be able to:

5.1 Describe the forces that, following the American Revolution, worked for black freedom.

5.2 Describe the forces that, following the American Revolution, worked to maintain slavery.

5.3 Discuss the characteristics of early free black communities.

5.4 Identify the early black leaders in the United States, and indicate their varying ideas, tactics, and solutions for the problems African Americans faced.

5.5 Evaluate the African-American role in the War of 1812.

5.6 Evaluate the Missouri Compromise's impact on African Americans.

> **Anytime, anytime while I was a slave, if one minute's freedom had been offered to me, and I had been told I must die at the end of that minute, I would have taken it—just to stand one minute on God's earth a free woman—I would.**
>
> *—Elizabeth Freeman*

> **This, my dear brethren, is by no means the greatest thing we have to be concerned about. Getting our liberty in this world is nothing to our having the liberty of the children of God . . . . What is forty, fifty, or sixty years, when compared to eternity?**
>
> *—Jupiter Hammon*

> **Death or Liberty.**
> **Proposed inscription for a flag to be used in Gabriel's planned rebellion of 1800.**
>
> *—Gabriel*

Except that they were all born slaves in eighteenth-century America, Elizabeth Freeman, Jupiter Hammon, and Gabriel had little in common. Freeman was an illiterate domestic servant when, in 1781, she sued for her freedom in Massachusetts. Hammon, who lived in Long Island, New York, was a poet and orthodox Calvinist preacher who enjoyed the support of his master and never sought his freedom. Gabriel was a literate, skilled slave who in 1800 masterminded a conspiracy to overthrow slavery in Virginia.

In this chapter, we explore how African Americans as diverse as Freeman, Hammon, and Gabriel helped shape the lives of black people during America's early years as an independent republic. We also examine how between 1783 and 1820 the forces for black liberty vied with the forces for slavery and inequality. The end of the War for Independence created great expectations among African Americans. But by 1820, when the Missouri Compromise confirmed the power of slaveholders in national affairs, black people in the North and the South had long known that the struggle for freedom was far from over.

That struggle took place at the state and local, as well as regional and national, levels. The forces involved in it were often impersonal. They included the emergence of a market economy in the North, based on wage labor, and an economy in the South, based on the production of cotton by slave labor. There was also a revolutionary ideology that encouraged African Americans to seek freedom, by force if necessary. In contrast, economic self-interest encouraged white northerners to limit black freedom, and fear of race war caused white southerners to strengthen the slave system.

Individual and group action also shaped African-American life in the new nation. As urban, church-centered black communities arose, men and women—both slave and free—influenced culture, politics, economics, and perceptions of race. This was particularly true in the North and the Chesapeake but also to a lesser degree in the Deep South. The years between 1783 and 1820 were years of considerable progress for African Americans, although they ended with free black people facing deteriorating conditions in the North and with slavery spreading westward across the South.

5.1 Forces for Freedom

Describe the forces that, following the American Revolution, worked for black freedom.

After the War for Independence ended in 1783, a strong trend in the North and the Chesapeake favored emancipation. It had roots in economic change, evangelical Christianity, and a revolutionary ethos based on the Enlightenment's natural rights doctrines. African Americans took advantage of these forces to escape from slavery, purchase the freedom of their families and themselves, sue for freedom in court, and petition state legislatures to grant them equal rights.

In the postrevolutionary North, slavery, although widespread, was not economically essential. Farmers could hire hands during the labor-intensive seasons of planting and harvesting more efficiently than they could maintain a year-round slave labor force. Northern slaveholders had wealth and influence, but they lacked the overwhelming authority of their southern counterparts. In addition, transatlantic immigration brought to the North plenty of white laborers, who worked cheaply and resented slave competition. As the Great Awakening initiated a new religious morality, as natural rights doctrines flourished, and as a market economy based on wage labor emerged, northern slaveholders had difficulty defending perpetual black slavery.

In Chapter 4, we saw that emancipation in the North was a direct result of the War for Independence. But the *process* of doing away with slavery unfolded in these states only after the war. Meanwhile, Congress set a precedent in discouraging the expansion of slavery, and antislavery societies proliferated in the North and Upper South.

5.1.1 Northern Emancipation

In comparison to other parts of the Atlantic world, emancipation in the northern portion of the United States began early. Its first stages preceded the revolt that had by 1804 ended slavery in Haiti, the first independent black republic. It preceded by a much greater margin the initiation in 1838 of peaceful, gradual abolition of slavery in the British Empire and the end of slavery in 1848 in the French colonies. Northern emancipation was exceptional in that it did not result from force or intervention by an imperial power. Although free black communities emerged throughout the Western Hemisphere during this period, those in the North stand out because they included the bulk of the region's black population.

Emancipation in the North did not follow a single pattern. Instead, the New England states of Massachusetts (which included Maine until it became a separate state in 1820), Connecticut, Rhode Island, New Hampshire, and Vermont moved more quickly than did the mid-Atlantic states of Pennsylvania, New York, and New Jersey (see Map 5-1). Slavery collapsed in the New England states because African Americans who lived there refused to remain in servitude and because most white New Englanders acquiesced. The struggle against slavery in the Mid-Atlantic states was longer and harder because more white people living there had a vested interest in maintaining it.

Vermont and Massachusetts—certainly—and New Hampshire—probably—abolished slavery immediately during the 1770s and 1780s. Vermont, where there had never been more than a few slaves, prohibited slavery in the constitution it adopted in 1777. Massachusetts, in its constitution of 1780, declared "that all men are born free and equal; and that every subject is entitled to liberty." Although this constitution did not specifically ban slavery, within a year Elizabeth Freeman and other slaves in Massachusetts sued under it for their freedom. Freeman, while serving as a waitress at her master's home in Sheffield, Massachusetts, overheard "gentlemen" discussing the "free and equal" clause of the new constitution. Shortly thereafter, she contacted a prominent local white lawyer, Theodore Sedgwick Sr., who agreed to represent her in court.

Map 5-1 Emancipation and Slavery in the Early Republic

This map indicates the abolition policies adopted by the states of the Northeast between 1777 and 1804, the antislavery impact of the Northwest Ordinance of 1787, and the extent of slavery in the South during the early republic.

Why did the states and territories shown in this map adopt different policies toward African Americans?

At about the same time, another Massachusetts slave, Quok Walker, left his master and began living as a free person. In response, Walker's master sought a court order to force Walker to return to slavery. This case led in 1783 to a Massachusetts Supreme Court ruling that "slavery is . . . as effectively abolished as it can be by the granting of rights and privileges wholly incompatible and repugnant to its existence." Another judge used similar logic to grant Freeman her liberty. These decisions encouraged other Massachusetts slaves to sue for their freedom or simply to leave their masters because the courts had ruled unconstitutional the master's claim to his human chattel.

As a result, the first U.S. census in 1790 found no slaves in Massachusetts. Even before then, black men in the state had gained the right to vote. In 1780 Paul and John Cuffe, free black brothers who lived in Dartmouth, had protested with five other free black men to the state legislature that they were being taxed without representation. By 1783 the courts had decided that African-American men who paid taxes in Massachusetts could vote there. This was a rare victory. Before the Civil War, only a few New England states permitted black men to vote on the same basis as white men.

This engraving originally appeared in Boston in 1793, with the caption, "Cuffe near him . . . grasps his hand." It suggests the progress African Americans had made in the North but also the contempt in which many white northerners held them. The object of the picture is to ridicule Massachusetts governor John Hancock for participating in a black celebration.

New Hampshire's record on emancipation is less clear than that of Vermont and Massachusetts. In 1779 black residents petitioned the New Hampshire legislature for freedom. A few years later, several New Hampshire court rulings based on that state's 1783 constitution, which was similar to Massachusetts's, refused to recognize human property. Nevertheless New Hampshire still had about 150 slaves in 1792. Slavery may have withered away there rather than having been abolished by the courts.

In Connecticut and Rhode Island, the state legislatures, rather than individual African Americans, took the initiative against slavery. In 1784 these states adopted gradual abolition plans that left adult slaves in bondage but proposed to free their children over a period of years. In Connecticut, all children born to enslaved mothers after March 1, 1784, became free at age 25. Rhode Island had a less gradual plan. Beginning that same March 1, it freed the children of enslaved women at birth. By 1790 only 3,763 slaves remained in New England out of a total black population there of 16,882. By 1800 only 1,339 slaves remained in the region, and by 1810 only 418—108 in Rhode Island and 310 in Connecticut.

In New Jersey, New York, and Pennsylvania, the investment in slaves was much greater than in New England. After considerable debate, the Pennsylvania legislature in 1780 voted that the children of enslaved mothers would be free at age 28. Under this scheme, Pennsylvania still had 403 slaves in 1830 (see Table 5-1). But many African Americans in the state gained their freedom much earlier by lawsuits or by leaving

Table 5-1 Slave Populations in the Mid-Atlantic States, 1790–1860

	1790	1800	1810	1820	1830	1840	1850	1860
New York	21,324	20,343	15,017	10,888	75	4		
New Jersey	11,432	12,343	19,851	7,557	2,243	674	236	18
Pennsylvania	3,737	1,706	795	211	403	64		

SOURCE: Based on Philip S. Foner, *History of Black Americans, from Africa to the Emergence of the Cotton Kingdom*, vol. 1 (Westport, CT: Greenwood, 1975), 374. © Darlene Clark Hine.

their masters. Emancipation came even more slowly in New York and New Jersey. In 1785 their legislatures *defeated* proposals for gradual abolition. White revolutionary leaders, such as Alexander Hamilton and John Jay, worked for abolition in New York, and Quakers had long advocated it in New Jersey. But these states had relatively large slave populations, powerful slaveholders, and white workforces fearful of free black competition.

In 1799 the New York legislature finally agreed that male slaves born after July 4 of that year were to be free at age 28 and females at age 25. In 1804 New Jersey adopted a similar law that freed male slaves born after July 4 of that year at age 25 and females at age 21. Under this plan, New Jersey still had 18 slaves in 1860.

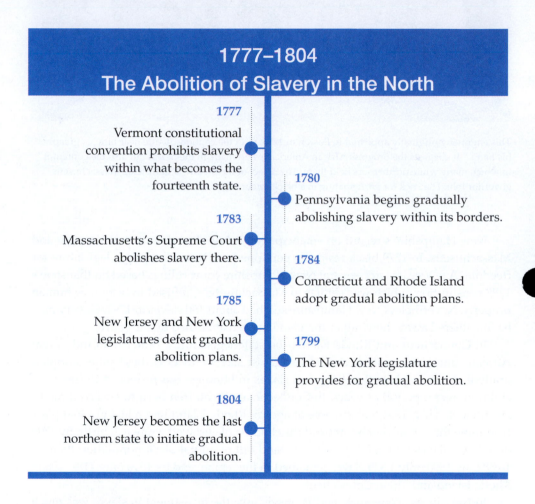

1777–1804
The Abolition of Slavery in the North

1777
Vermont constitutional convention prohibits slavery within what becomes the fourteenth state.

1780
Pennsylvania begins gradually abolishing slavery within its borders.

1783
Massachusetts's Supreme Court abolishes slavery there.

1784
Connecticut and Rhode Island adopt gradual abolition plans.

1785
New Jersey and New York legislatures defeat gradual abolition plans.

1799
The New York legislature provides for gradual abolition.

1804
New Jersey becomes the last northern state to initiate gradual abolition.

5.1.2 The Northwest Ordinance of 1787

Nearly as significant as the northern states' actions against slavery was Congress's decision to limit slavery's expansion. During the 1780s, Congress drew its authority from a constitution known as the Articles of Confederation. The Articles created a weak central government for the United States that lacked power to tax or to regulate commerce. This government did, however, acquire jurisdiction over the region west of the Appalachian Mountains and east of the Mississippi River, eclipsing several states' conflicting land claims.

During the War for Independence, increasing numbers of white Americans had migrated across the Appalachians into this huge region. The migrants—some of whom brought slaves with them—provoked hostilities with American Indian nations. Those who moved into the region's northern portion also faced British opposition, and those who moved into the region's southern portion contested for control against

Spanish forces. In response to these circumstances, Congress formulated policies to protect the migrants and provide for their government. The new nation's leaders also disparaged the westward expansion of slavery, and Thomas Jefferson sought to deal with both issues. First, he suggested that the western region be divided into separate territories and prepared for statehood. Second, he proposed that after 1800 slavery be banned from the entire region stretching from the Appalachians to the Mississippi River and from Spanish Florida—Spain had regained Florida in 1783—to British Canada.

In 1784 Jefferson's antislavery proposal failed by a single vote to pass Congress. Three years later, Congress adopted the **Northwest Ordinance**. This legislation applied the essence of Jefferson's plan to the region north of the Ohio River—what historians call the Old Northwest. The ordinance provided for the orderly sale of land, support for public education, territorial government, and the eventual formation of new states. Unlike Jefferson's plan, the ordinance banned slavery immediately. But, because it applied only to the Northwest Territory, the ordinance left the huge region south of the Ohio River open to slavery expansion.

Even in parts of the Old Northwest, some African Americans remained unfree after 1787. The first governor of the territory forced those who had been slaves before the adoption of the ordinance to remain slaves. Then in 1803, when Ohio became a state, the remainder of the Northwest Territory legalized indentured servitude. The result was that in southern parts of what became Illinois and Indiana, a few African Americans remained in bondage well into the nineteenth century.

Yet, by preventing slaveholders from taking slaves legally into areas north of the Ohio River, the ordinance set a precedent for excluding slavery from U.S. territories. Whether Congress had the power to do this became a contentious issue after President Jefferson annexed the huge Louisiana Territory in 1803 (see p. 114). The issue divided northern and southern politicians until the Civil War.

Northwest Ordinance

Based on earlier legislation drafted by Thomas Jefferson, it organized the Northwest Territory, providing for orderly land sales, public education, government, the creation of five to seven states out of the territory, and the prohibition of slavery within the territory.

5.1.3 Antislavery Societies in the North and the Upper South

While African Americans helped destroy slavery in the northeastern states and Congress blocked its advance into the Old Northwest, a few white people organized to spread antislavery sentiment. In 1775 Quaker abolitionist Anthony Benezet organized the first antislavery society in the world. In 1787 it became the Pennsylvania Society for Promoting the Abolition of Slavery, and Benjamin Franklin became its president. Similar societies emerged in Delaware in 1788 and Maryland in 1789. By 1800, abolition societies existed in New Jersey, Connecticut, and Virginia. Organized antislavery sentiment also arose in the new slave states of Kentucky and Tennessee. But such societies never appeared in the Deep South.

From 1794 to 1832, antislavery societies cooperated within the loose framework of the American Convention for Promoting the Abolition of Slavery and Improving the Condition of the African Race. Only white people participated in these Quaker-dominated organizations, although members often cooperated with black leaders. As the northern states adopted abolition plans, the societies focused their attention on Delaware, Maryland, and Virginia. They aimed at gradual, compensated emancipation. They encouraged masters to free their slaves, attempted to protect free black people from reenslavement, and often advocated sending freed black people out of the country.

Experience with emancipation in the northern states encouraged the emphasis on gradual abolition. So did the reluctance of white abolitionists to challenge the property rights of masters. Abolitionists also feared that immediate emancipation might lead masters to abandon elderly slaves and assumed that African Americans would require long training before they could be free. All of this played into the hands of slaveholders who, like Thomas Jefferson, opposed slavery in the abstract but had no intention of freeing their own slaves.

Profile

Elizabeth Freeman

This portrait of Elizabeth Freeman was painted in watercolor on ivory by Elizabeth Sedgwick in 1811, 30 years after Freeman initiated her famous lawsuit.

Known as Mum Bett, Elizabeth Freeman showed a strength of character that impressed everyone she met. She was probably born in 1744 in Claverack, New York. As her parents were African slaves, she was also a slave. After the death of her first master in 1758, Freeman and her sister became the property of Colonel John Ashley, a judge, in Sheffield, Massachusetts. She married young, gave birth to her only child—a daughter—and became a widow when her husband was killed fighting on the Patriot side in the War for Independence.

Freeman, who was illiterate, may have first learned of natural rights when in 1773 a group of men met at Ashley's home to draft a protest against British policies in the American colonies. "Mankind . . . have a right to the undisturbed Enjoyment of their lives, their Liberty and Property," the document declared. She took these words to heart, and when she learned while serving as a waitress in 1780 that Massachusetts had adopted a bill of rights asserting that all people were born free and equal, she was ready to apply the doctrine to herself.

In 1781 Freeman received "a severe wound" to her arm when she attempted to protect her sister from Ashley's wife, who "in a fit of passion" was threatening her with a hot kitchen shovel. Outraged at this attack, Freeman left the Ashley home and refused to return. Instead, she engaged the legal assistance of Theodore Sedgwick, Sr. in a suit for her freedom on the basis of Massachusetts's new bill of rights. The jury found in Freeman's favor and required Ashley to pay her 30 shillings in damages. It was at this point that Mum Bett changed her name legally to Elizabeth Freeman. Shortly thereafter, the Massachusetts Supreme Court declared slavery unconstitutional throughout the state.

For the remainder of her active life, Freeman worked as a paid domestic servant in the Sedgwick household and moved with the Sedgwicks to Stockbridge in 1785. Because Theodore Sedgwick, Sr.'s wife was emotionally unstable, Freeman became a surrogate mother to the Sedgwick children, who later testified to her "superior instincts," abilities as a nurse, efficiency, and bravery.

During the 1830s, Theodore Sedgwick, Jr. told British writer Harriet Martineau that in 1786 some participants in Shays's Rebellion entered the Sedgwick home while Theodore Sr. was away. Acting quickly to hide the family's silverware, Freeman confronted the men with a kitchen shovel similar to the one her former mistress had used against her. While advising the men "that they 'dare not strike a woman,' " she threatened to use the shovel against any one of them who disturbed the family possessions, and she managed to usher them out with only minor damage to the Sedgwicks' property.

Freeman earned enough while employed by the Sedgwicks to purchase her own home and retire. When she died, she left a small estate to her daughter, grandchildren, and great grandchildren. She left another legacy to the Sedgwick children. When Theodore Jr. became an abolitionist during the 1830s, he credited Freeman as the source of his conviction that black people were not inferior to white people. Earlier, his brother Charles had the following lines inscribed on Freeman's gravestone: "She never violated a trust, nor failed to perform a duty. In every situation of domestic trial, she was the most efficient helper, and the tenderest friend. Good mother fare well."

The antislavery societies of the Upper South tended to be small and short lived. A Wilmington, Delaware, society, established in 1788, peaked at 50 members and ceased to exist in 1800. The Maryland society organized in 1781 with six members, grew to 250 in 1797, and disbanded in 1798. African Americans and their white friends, nevertheless, hoped that antislavery sentiment was advancing southward.

5.1.4 Manumission and Self-Purchase

Another hopeful sign for African Americans was that after the Revolution most southern states liberalized their **manumission** laws. This meant that masters could free individual slaves by deed or will. Masters no longer had to go to court or petition a state legislature to prove that an individual they desired to free had performed a "meritorious service." Virginia led the way in 1782 by repealing its longstanding ban on private manumissions. Delaware followed in 1787, Maryland in 1790, Kentucky in 1792, and the slaveholding territory of Missouri in 1804.

As a result, hundreds of slaveholders in the Upper South freed slaves individually. Religious sentiment and natural rights principles motivated many of these masters. But there were limits to manumission as an antislavery measure. Most of the masters who manumitted slaves considered the slave system immoral but opposed general emancipation. And their motives were not always noble. Masters often profited from self-purchase agreements they negotiated with their slaves. Slaves raised money by marketing farm produce or hiring themselves out for wages and then paid their master in installments for their eventual freedom. Masters liked the installments because they provided income in addition to what they otherwise received from a slave's labor.

Masters also sometimes manumitted slaves who were no longer profitable investments. A master might be switching from tobacco to wheat or corn—crops that did not need a year-round workforce. Or a master might manumit older slaves whose best years as workers were behind them. Frequently, however, slaves—usually young men—presented their masters with the choice of either manumitting them after a term of years or having them escape immediately.

Self-purchase often left African Americans in precarious financial condition. Sometimes they used up their savings to buy their freedom. In other instances, they went into debt to their former masters, to white lawyers who acted as their agents, or to other white people who had loaned them money to cover their purchase price. After receiving money from a slave, some masters reneged on their agreement to manumit. Many of the freedom suits that became common in the Upper South during this period resulted from such unethical behavior by masters.

5.1.5 The Emergence of a Free Black Class in the South

As a result of manumission, self-purchase, and freedom suits, the free black population of the Upper South blossomed. Maryland and Virginia had the largest free black populations. Between 1790 and 1820, the number of free African Americans in Maryland climbed from 8,043 to 39,730 and in Virginia from 12,766 to 36,889. By 1820 the Upper South (Delaware, Maryland, Virginia, District of Columbia, Kentucky, Missouri, North Carolina, and Tennessee) had a free black population of 114,070, compared with a northern free black population of 99,281. However, most of the Upper South's black population remained in slavery while the North's was on the way to general emancipation. In the North, 83.9 percent of African Americans were free in 1820, compared with 10.6 percent of those in the Upper South.

In the Deep South (South Carolina, Georgia, Florida, Louisiana, Alabama, and Mississippi), both the percentage and the absolute numbers of free black people remained much smaller. During the eighteenth century, neither South Carolina nor Georgia restricted the right of masters to manumit their slaves. However, far fewer masters in these states exercised this right after the Revolution

manumission
The act of freeing a slave by the slave's master.

The title of this 1811 painting by German-American artist John Lewis Krimmel is *Pepper-Pot, A Scene in the Philadelphia Market*. Slavery still existed in Pennsylvania when Krimmel recorded this scene. It is likely, however, that the black woman who is selling pepper-pot (a type of stew) was free.

than was the case in the Chesapeake. Manumission declined in Louisiana following its annexation to the United States in 1804. Generally, masters in the Deep South freed only their illegitimate slave children, other favorites, or those unable to work. Only 20,153 free black people lived in the Deep South in 1820. In North Carolina, a transitional area between the Upper and Deep South, the state legislature made manumission more difficult after 1777. But many masters—especially those who were Quakers—nevertheless freed their slaves or let them live in quasi-freedom.

The emergence of a free black class in the South, especially in the Deep South, produced social strata more similar to those in Latin America than was the case in the North. As in the Caribbean, South America, and portions of Mexico, there were dominant white people, free people of color, and slaves. In southern cities, such as Charleston, Savannah, and New Orleans, some free African Americans not only identified economically and culturally with their former masters but also acquired slaves.

5.2 Forces for Slavery

Describe the forces that, following the American Revolution, worked to maintain slavery.

The forces for black freedom in the new republic rested on widespread African-American dissatisfaction with slavery, economic change, Christian morality, and revolutionary precepts. Most black northerners had achieved freedom by 1800, three-quarters were free by 1810, and by 1840 only 0.7 percent remained in slavery. Yet for the nation as a whole and for the mass of African Americans, the forces favoring slavery proved to be stronger. Abolition took place in the North, where slavery was weak. In the South, where it was strong, slavery thrived and expanded. Virginia, for example, had 293,427 slaves in 1790, and—despite manumissions and escapes—it had 425,153 in 1820. Even more significant, although Virginia continued to have the largest population of enslaved African Americans in the country, slave populations grew more quickly in North Carolina, South Carolina, and Georgia. Meanwhile, slavery expanded westward. Tennessee, as a territory in 1790, had 3,417 slaves. By 1820, as a state, it had 80,107 slaves.

5.2.1 The U.S. Constitution

The U.S. Constitution, which went into effect in 1789, became a major force in favor of the continued enslavement of African Americans. During the War for Independence, the Continental Congress had provided a weak central government for the United States, as each of the 13 states retained control over its own internal affairs. The Articles of Confederation, which served as the American constitution from 1781 to 1789, formalized this system of divided sovereignty.

However, by the mid-1780s, wealthy and powerful men perceived that the Confederation Congress was too weak to protect their interests. Democratic movements in the states threatened property rights. Congress's inability to regulate commerce led to trade disputes among the states. Congress's inability to tax prevented it from maintaining an army and navy. This meant it could not control the western territories and, most frightening to the wealthy, it could not help states suppress popular uprisings, such as that led by Daniel Shays in western Massachusetts in 1786.

The fears Shays's Rebellion caused led directly to the Constitutional Convention in Philadelphia that in 1787 produced the Constitution under which the United States is still governed. The new Constitution gave the central government power to regulate commerce, to tax, and to have its laws enforced in the states. But the convention could not create a more powerful central government without first making important concessions to southern slaveholders.

The delegates to the convention omitted the words *slave* and *slavery* from the Constitution. But they included clauses designed to maintain the enslavement of African Americans in the southern states. These clauses provided for continuing the Atlantic slave trade another 20 years, for national military aid in suppressing slave revolts, and for returning to their masters slaves who escaped to other states. The Constitution also enhanced representation for slaveholders in Congress and in the Electoral College that elected the president and vice president.

Humanitarian opposition to the Atlantic slave trade had mounted during the revolutionary era. Under pressure from black activists—such as Prince Hall of Boston—and Quakers, northern state legislatures during the 1780s forbade their citizens to engage in the slave trade. Rhode Island led the way in 1787. Massachusetts, Connecticut, and Pennsylvania followed in 1788. Economic change in the Upper South also prompted opposition to the trade. Virginia, for example, banned the importation of slaves from abroad nearly a decade before Rhode Island.

Yet convention delegates from South Carolina and Georgia maintained that their states had an acute labor shortage. They threatened that they would not tolerate a central government that could stop their citizens from importing slaves—at least not in the near future. Torn between these conflicting perspectives, the convention compromised by including a provision in the Constitution that prohibited Congress from abolishing the slave trade until 1808. During the 20 years before 1808, when Congress banned the trade, thousands of Africans came unwillingly into southern states. Between 1804 and 1808, 40,000 entered through Charleston alone. Overall, more slaves entered the United States between 1787 and 1808 than during any other 20-year period in American history. Such huge numbers helped fuel westward expansion of the slave system.

Other proslavery clauses of the Constitution aimed to counteract slave rebellion and escape. The Constitution gave Congress power to put down "insurrections" and "domestic violence." It provided that persons "held to service or labour in one State, escaping into another . . . shall be delivered up on claim of the party to whom such service or labour may be due." This clause was the basis for the **Fugitive Slave Act of 1793**, which allowed masters or their agents to pursue slaves across state lines, capture them, and take them before a magistrate. There, on presentation of satisfactory evidence, masters could regain legal custody of the person they claimed. This act did not stop slaves from escaping from Virginia and Maryland to Pennsylvania. It did extend the power of masters into the North, force the federal and northern state governments to uphold slavery, create personal tragedies for those who suffered recapture, and encourage the kidnapping of free black northerners falsely claimed as escapees.

Finally, the Constitution strengthened the political power of slaveholders through the **Three-Fifths Clause**. This clause resulted from another compromise between northern and southern delegates. Southern delegates had wanted slaves to be counted toward representation in the national government but not counted for purposes of taxation. Northern delegates had wanted just the opposite. The Three-Fifths Clause split the difference by providing that a slave be counted as three-fifths of a free person in determining a state's representation in the House of Representatives and in the Electoral College. Slaves would be counted similarly if and when Congress instituted a per capita tax.

This gave slaveholders increased representation on the basis of the number of slaves they owned—slaves who, of course, had no vote or representation. As a result, the South gained enormous political advantage. If not for the Three-Fifths Clause, northern nonslaveholder John Adams would have been reelected president in 1800 instead of losing the presidency to southern slaveholder Thomas Jefferson. Also, for many years, this clause contributed to the domination of the U.S. government by slaveholding southerners, even though the South's population steadily fell behind the North's. That Congress never instituted a per capita tax made this victory for slaveholders all the more remarkable.

Fugitive Slave Act of 1793

An act of Congress permitting masters to recapture escaped slaves who had reached the free states and, with the authorization of local courts, return with the slave or slaves to their home state.

Three-Fifths Clause

A clause in the U.S. Constitution providing that a slave be counted as three-fifths of a free person in determining a state's representation in Congress and the electoral college and three-fifths of a free person in regard to per capita taxes levied by Congress on the states.

THE FIRST COTTON-GIN.—DRAWN BY WILLIAM L. SHEPPARD.—[SEE PAGE 613.]

Harpers Weekly printed this "conjectural work" in 1869. Although the clothing worn by the men and women shown reflects styles of a later era, the machine suggests how slaves used the gin Eli Whitney invented in 1793.

cotton gin

A simple machine invented by Eli Whitney in 1793 to separate cotton seeds from cotton fiber. It greatly speeded this task and encouraged the westward expansion of cotton growing in the United States.

domestic slave trade

A trade dating from the first decade of the nineteenth century in American-born slaves purchased primarily in the border South and sent overland or by sea to the cotton growing regions of the Old Southwest.

Four other factors, however, were more important than constitutional provisions in fostering the continued enslavement of African Americans in the new republic. They included increased cultivation of cotton, the Louisiana Purchase, declining revolutionary fervor, and intensified white racism.

5.2.2 Cotton

The most obvious of the four developments was the increase in cotton production. By the late eighteenth century, Britain led the world in textile manufacturing. As mechanization made the spinning of cotton cloth more economical, Britain's demand for raw cotton increased dramatically. The United States led in filling that demand as a result of Eli Whitney's invention of the **cotton gin** in 1793. Seeds in cotton bolls had prevented commercial use of the type of cotton most easily grown in the South. Whitney's simple machine provided an easy and quick way to remove them.

Consequently, cotton production in the United States rose from 3,000 bales in 1790 to 178,000 bales in 1810—each bale of cotton weighed 480 pounds. Cotton became by far the most lucrative U.S. export. Southern cotton production also encouraged the development of textile mills in New England, thereby creating a proslavery alliance between the "lords of the lash and the lords of the loom."

Cotton reinvigorated the slave-labor system, which spread rapidly across Georgia and later into Alabama, Mississippi, Louisiana, and eastern Texas. Cotton cultivation also existed in South Carolina, North Carolina, Arkansas, and parts of Virginia and Tennessee. To make matters worse for African Americans, the westward expansion of cotton production encouraged a **domestic slave trade**. Masters in the old tobacco-growing regions of Maryland, Virginia, and other states began to support themselves by selling their slaves to the new cotton-growing regions (see Figure 5-1).

5.2.3 The Louisiana Purchase and African Americans in the Lower Mississippi Valley

The Jefferson administration's purchase of Louisiana from France in 1803 accelerated the westward expansion of slavery and the domestic slave trade, as the purchase nearly doubled the area of the United States. That slavery might extend over this vast region became an issue of great importance to African Americans. The purchase also brought under American sovereignty those black people, both free and slave, who lived in the portion of the territory that centered on the city of New Orleans. As Chapter 3 indicates, black life in the New Orleans area had developed a distinctive pattern under French rule from 1699 to 1763, under Spanish rule from 1763 to 1801, and again under French rule from 1801 to 1803. Although people of African descent were a majority of the area's population, they consisted of two distinct groups. First were the free people of color who called themselves Creoles. They were usually craftsmen and shopkeepers, spoke French, belonged to the Roman Catholic Church, and aspired to equal rights with other free inhabitants. Some of them bought and sold slaves. Their numbers had increased under Spanish rule as urban slaves purchased their freedom. This route to freedom became more difficult under American sovereignty, but, as a group, Louisiana's free people of color remained optimistically integrationist in outlook.

Nevertheless the second black group grew more rapidly. It consisted of slaves, most of whom had come directly from Africa and worked on Louisiana plantations. Spain had encouraged white Americans to settle in the lower Mississippi valley. The Americans, in turn, demanded more strictly enforced slave codes and the expansion of the external slave trade. At first the slaves produced tobacco and indigo, but by the 1790s sugar and cotton had emerged as the crops of the future. As demand for these crops grew, conditions for slaves in Louisiana became increasingly harsh, especially after the region became part of the United States. The slaves' rural location, their predominantly African culture, and, eventually, their Protestant religion cut them off from free people of color. In 1770 the region that later became the state of Louisiana had a slave population of 5,600. By 1810 it had 34,660, and by 1820 the slave population numbered 149,654. This tremendous growth, involving an extremely harsh form of slavery in a huge region, constituted a warning to all opponents of that institution. With the termination of the external slave trade, the notorious slave markets of New Orleans became the dreaded destination of thousands of African Americans "sold south" by their masters in the domestic slave trade.

5.2.4 Conservatism and Racism

The waning of revolutionary humanitarianism and the rise of a more intense racism among white people were less tangible forces than cotton production and the Louisiana Purchase, but they were just as important in strengthening slavery. They also made life more difficult for free African Americans.

By the 1790s white Americans had begun a long retreat from the egalitarianism of the revolutionary era. In the North and the Chesapeake, most white people became less willing to challenge the prerogatives of slaveholders and more willing to accept slavery as suitable for African Americans. Most Marylanders and Virginians came to think of emancipation as best left to the distant future. This outlook strengthened the slaveholders and their nonslaveholding white supporters in the Deep South who had never embraced the humanitarian precepts of the Enlightenment and Great Awakening.

Increasing proslavery sentiment among white Americans stemmed, in part, from revulsion against the radicalism of the French Revolution that had begun in 1789. Reports from France of bloody class and religious warfare, disruption of the social order, and redistribution of property led most Americans to value property rights—including rights to human property—and order above equal rights. In addition, as cotton production spread westward and the value of slaves soared, rationalist and evangelical criticism of human bondage withered. Antislavery sentiment in the Upper South that had flourished among slaveholders, nonslaveholders, Deists, Methodists, and Baptists became increasingly confined to African Americans and Quakers. During the early 1800s, manumissions began a long decline.

Using race to justify slavery became an important component of this conservative trend. Unlike white people, the argument went, black people were unsuited for freedom or citizenship. The doctrines embodied in the Declaration of Independence, therefore, did not apply to them. A new scientific racism supported this outlook. As early as the 1770s, some American intellectuals had challenged the Enlightenment theory that perceived racial differences were not essential or inherent but results of the different environments in which Africans and Europeans originated. Scientific racists began to propose that God had created a great chain of being from lesser creatures to higher creatures. In this chain, black people constituted a separate species as close to the great apes as to white people. During the 1780s Thomas Jefferson reflected this theory when

Figure 5-1 Distribution of the Southern Slave Population, 1800–1860

The demand for slaves in the cotton-growing Deep South produced a major shift in the distribution of the slave population.

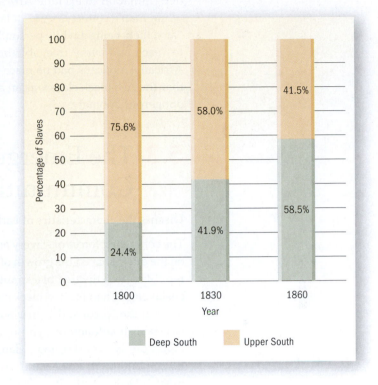

he argued that "scientific observation" supported the conclusion that black people were inherently "inferior to whites in the endowments of both body and mind."

Such views spread and became common among white northerners and southerners—and they had practical results. During the 1790s Congress expressed its determination to exclude African Americans from the benefits of citizenship in "a white man's country." A 1790 law limited the granting of naturalized citizenship to "any alien, being a white person." In 1792 Congress limited enrollment in state militias to "each and every free, able-bodied white male citizen." These laws implied that African Americans had no place in the United States except as slaves. They suggested that the free black class was an anomaly and, in the opinion of most white people, a dangerous anomaly.

5.3 The Emergence of Free Black Communities

Discuss the characteristics of early free black communities.

The competing forces of slavery and racism, on one hand, and freedom and opportunity, on the other, shaped the growth of African-American communities in the early American republic. A distinctive black culture had existed since the early colonial period. But enslavement had limited black community life. The advent of large free black populations in the North and Upper South after the Revolution allowed African Americans to establish autonomous and dynamic communities. They appeared in Philadelphia, Baltimore, Newport (Rhode Island), Richmond, Norfolk (Virginia), New York City, and Boston. Although smaller and less autonomous, there were also free black communities in such Deep South cities as Charleston, Savannah, and New Orleans. As free black people in these cities acquired a modicum of wealth and education, they established institutions that have shaped African-American life ever since.

A combination of factors encouraged African Americans to form these institutions. First, as they emerged from slavery, they realized they would have inferior status in white-dominated organizations or not be allowed to participate in them at all. Second, black people valued the African heritage they had preserved over generations in slavery. They wanted institutions that would perpetuate that heritage.

The earliest black community institutions were mutual aid societies. Patterned on similar white organizations, these societies were like modern insurance companies and benevolent organizations. They provided for their members' medical and burial expenses and helped support widows and children. African Americans in Newport, Rhode Island, organized the first black mutual aid society in 1780. Seven years later, Richard Allen and Absalom Jones established the more famous Free African Society in Philadelphia.

Most early free black societies admitted only men, but similar organizations for women appeared during the 1790s. In 1793 Philadelphia's Female Benevolent Society of St. Thomas took over the welfare functions of the city's Free African Society. Other black women's organizations in Philadelphia during the early republic included the Benevolent Daughters, established in 1796 by Sarah Allen (the wife of the Rev. Richard Allen); the Daughters of Africa, established in 1812; the American Female Bond Benevolent Society, formed in 1817; and the Female Benezet Society, formed in 1818.

These ostensibly secular societies maintained a decidedly Christian moral character. They insisted that their members meet standards of middle-class propriety and, in effect, became self-improvement as well as mutual aid societies. Members had to pledge to refrain from fornication, adultery, drunkenness, and other "disreputable behavior." By the early 1800s, such societies also organized resistance to kidnappers who sought to recapture fugitive slaves or enslave free African Americans.

Because the societies provided real benefits and reflected black middle-class aspirations, they spread to every black urban community. By 1830 more than 100 such organizations existed in Philadelphia alone. Although these societies were more common in the North than in the South, Baltimore had about 30 of them by that same year. Charleston, South Carolina, had at least two. One of them was the Brown Fellowship, founded in 1790, which admitted only black men with light complexions. The other was open to all free black men in Charleston.

Of particular importance were the black Freemasons because, unlike other free black organizations, the Masons united black men from several northern cities. Combining rationalism with secrecy and obscure ritual, Freemasonry constituted a major movement among European and American men during the late eighteenth and early nineteenth centuries. Opportunities for male bonding, wearing fancy regalia, and achieving prestige in a supposedly ancient hierarchy attracted both black and white men. As historians James Oliver Horton and Lois E. Horton suggest, black people drew special satisfaction from the European-based order's claims to have originated in ancient Egypt, which black people associated with their African heritage.

The most famous black Mason of his time was Prince Hall, the Revolutionary War veteran and abolitionist. During the 1770s he began in Boston what became known as the **Prince Hall Masons**. Hall's relationship to Masonry epitomizes the free black predicament in America.

In 1775 the local white Masonic lodge in Boston rejected Hall's application for membership because of his black ancestry. Therefore Hall, a Patriot, organized African Lodge No. 1 on the basis of a limited license he secured from a British Masonic lodge associated with the British army that then occupied Boston. The irony of this situation compounded when, after the War for Independence, American Masonry refused to grant the African Lodge a full charter. Hall again had to turn to the British Masons, who approved his application in 1787. Under this British charter, Hall in 1791 organized the African Grand Lodge of North America—later renamed the Prince Hall Grand Lodge—and became its first grand master. Even before this he had begun authorizing black lodges in other cities, including Philadelphia and Providence, Rhode Island.

This late eighteenth-century portrait of Prince Hall (1735?–1807) dressed as a gentleman places him among Masonic symbols. A former slave, a skilled craftsman and entrepreneur, an abolitionist, and an advocate of black education, Hall is best remembered as the founder of the African Lodge of North America, popularly known as the Prince Hall Masons.

5.3.1 The Origins of Independent Black Churches

Although black churches emerged at least a decade later than black benevolent associations, the churches quickly became the core of African-American communities. Not only did these churches attend to the spiritual needs of free black people and—in some southern cities—slaves, but their pastors also became the primary African-American leaders. Black church buildings housed schools, social organizations, and antislavery meetings.

During the late eighteenth century, as the egalitarian spirit of the Great Awakening waned among white Baptists, Methodists, and Episcopalians, separate but not independent black churches appeared in the South. The biracial churches the Awakening spawned had never embraced African Americans on an equal basis with white people, and as time passed, white people denied black people significant influence in church governance. White parishioners also subjected African Americans to segregated seating, communion services, Sunday schools, and cemeteries. In response, African Americans formed separate black congregations, usually headed by black ministers but subordinate to white church hierarchies. The first such congregations appeared during the 1770s in South Carolina and Georgia.

In contrast to these subordinate churches, a truly independent black church emerged gradually in Philadelphia between the 1780s and the early 1800s. The movement for such a church began within the city's white-controlled St. George's Methodist

Prince Hall Masons

A black Masonic order formed in 1791 in Boston under the leadership of Prince Hall. He became its first grand master and promoted its expansion to other cities.

Church. Richard Allen and Absalom Jones, who led the movement, could rely for help on the Free African Society they established in 1787.

Allen in 1780 and Jones in 1783 had purchased their freedom. In 1786 Allen, a fervent Methodist since the 1770s, received permission from St. George's white leadership to use the church in the evenings to preach to black people. Jones joined Allen's congregation. Soon they and other black members of St. George's chafed under policies they considered un-Christian and insulting. But, during the 1780s, Allen's and Jones's faith that Methodist egalitarianism would prevail over discrimination undermined their efforts to create a separate black Methodist church.

The break finally came in 1792 when St. George's white leaders grievously insulted the church's black members. An attempt by white trustees to prevent Jones from praying in what the trustees considered the white section of the church led black members to walk out. "We all went out of the church in a body," recalled Allen, "and they were no more plagued with us in the church."

St. George's white leaders fought hard and long to control the expanding and economically valuable black congregation. Yet other white Philadelphians, led by abolitionist Benjamin Rush, applauded the concept of an independent "African church." Rush and other sympathetic white people contributed to the new church's building fund. When construction began in 1793, Rush and at least 100 other white people joined with African Americans at a banquet to celebrate the occasion.

However, the black congregation soon split. When the majority determined that the new church would be Episcopalian rather than Methodist, Allen and a few others refused to join. The result was *two* black churches in Philadelphia. St. Thomas's Episcopal Church, with Jones as priest, opened in July 1794 as an African-American

Voices

Richard Allen on the Break with St. George's Church

It took an emotionally wrenching experience to convince Richard Allen, Absalom Jones, and other black Methodists that they must break their association with St. George's Church. Allen published posthumously the following account in 1833 as part of his autobiography, The Life Experiences and Gospel Labors of the Rt. Rev. Richard Allen. *Although many years had passed since the incident, Allen's account retains a strong emotional immediacy.*

A number of us usually attended St. George's church in Fourth street; and when the colored people began to get numerous in attending the church, they moved us from the seats we usually sat on, and placed us around the wall, and on Sabbath morning, we went to the church and the sexton stood at the door, and told us to go in the gallery. He told us to go, and we would see where to sit. We expected to take the seats over the ones we formerly occupied below, not knowing any better. We took those seats. Meeting had begun and they were nearly done singing, and just as we got to the seats, the elder said, "Let us pray." We had not been long upon our knees before I heard considerable scuffling and low talking. I raised my head up and saw one of the trustees, H M, having hold of the Rev. Absalom

Jones, pulling him up off his knees, and saying, "You must get up—you must not kneel here." Mr. Jones replied, "Wait until prayer is over." Mr. H M said, "No, you must get up now, or I will call for aid and force you away." Mr. Jones said, "Wait until prayer is over, and I will get up and trouble you no more." With that he [H M] beckoned to one of the other trustees, Mr. L S to come to his assistance. He came, and went to William White to pull him up. By this time prayer was over, and we all went out of the church in a body, and they were no more plagued with us in the church . . . . We then hired a storeroom, and held worship by ourselves. Here we were pursued with threats of being disowned, and read publicly out of meeting if we did continue worship in the place we had hired; but we believed the Lord would be our friend. We got subscription papers out to raise money to build the house of the Lord.

---

1. What sparked the confrontation Allen describes?
2. How did white leaders respond to the withdrawal of the church's black members?

SOURCE: *The Life Experiences and Gospel Labors of Rt. Rev. Richard Allen*, 1833.

congregation within the white-led national Episcopal Church. Then Allen's Mother Bethel congregation became the first truly independent black church. The white leaders of St. George's tried to control Mother Bethel until 1816. That year Mother Bethel became the birthplace of the **African Methodist Episcopal (AME) Church**. Allen became the first bishop of this organization, which spread to other cities in the North and the South.

The more significant among the other AME congregations were Daniel Coker's in Baltimore, the AME Zion in New York, and those in Wilmington, Delaware; Salem, New Jersey; and Attleboro, Pennsylvania. Other independent black churches formed at this time out of similar conflicts with white-led congregations. They included the African Baptist Church established in Boston in 1805 and led by Thomas Paul from 1806 to 1808, the Presbyterian Evangelical Society founded in 1811 by John Gloucester, the Abyssinian Baptist Church organized in New York City in 1808 by Paul, and the African Presbyterian Church established in Philadelphia in 1822 by Samuel E. Cornish.

5.3.2 The First Black Schools

Schools for African-American children, slave and free, date to the early 1700s. In both North and South, white clergy, including the Massachusetts Congregationalist Cotton Mather, ran the schools. So did Quakers, early abolition societies, and missionaries acting for the Anglican Society for the Propagation of the Gospel in Foreign Parts. But the first schools established by African Americans to instruct African-American children arose after the Revolution. The new black mutual aid societies and churches created and sustained them.

African Americans founded their own schools because local white authorities either refused to admit black children to public schools or provided only inadequate separate black schools. For example, in 1796, when Prince Hall failed to convince Boston's city council to provide a school for black students, he had the children taught in his home and that of his son Primus. By 1806 Hall's school met in the basement of the new African Meeting House, which housed Thomas Paul's African Baptist Church.

Hall was not the first to take such action. As early as 1790, Charleston's Brown Fellowship operated a school for its members' children. Free black people in Baltimore supported schools during the same decade, and during the early 1800s similar schools opened in Washington, D.C. Such schools frequently employed white teachers. Not until Philadelphia's Mother Bethel Church established the Augustine School in 1818 did a school for black children exist that was entirely administered and taught by African Americans.

These schools faced great difficulties. Because many black families could not afford the fees, the schools strained their meager resources by accepting charity cases. In addition, some black parents believed education was pointless when African Americans often could not get skilled jobs. And white Americans often reacted negatively to black schools. They feared competition from skilled black workers, believed black schools attracted undesirable populations, and—particularly in the South—feared that educated free African Americans would encourage slaves to revolt.

Therefore violent threats against black schools and efforts to suppress them became common. The case of Christopher McPherson serves as an example. In 1811 McPherson, a free African American, established a night school for black men at

Raphaelle Peale, the son of famous Philadelphia portraitist Charles Wilson Peale, completed this oil portrait of the Reverend Absalom Jones (1746–1818) in 1810. Reverend Jones is shown in his ecclesiastical robes holding a Bible in his hand.

African Methodist Episcopal (AME) Church

Founded in Philadelphia in 1816, this was the first black church and eventually became the largest independent black church.

This lithograph, c. 1887, portrays the New York African Free School, No. 2. The New York Manumission Society established the original school in 1787, at 137 Mulberry Street in New York City. Men who later became prominent black abolitionists, such as Henry Highland Garnet and James McCune Smith, attended the school during the 1820s.

Richmond, Virginia, and hired a white teacher. All went well until McPherson advertised the school in a local newspaper. In response, white residents forced the teacher to leave the city, and local authorities had McPherson committed to the state lunatic asylum. Nevertheless, similar schools continued to operate in the North and Upper South, producing a growing class of literate African Americans.

5.4 Black Leaders and Choices

Identify the early black leaders in the United States, and indicate their varying ideas, tactics, and solutions for the problems African Americans faced.

By the 1790s an educated black elite existed in the North and the Chesapeake. It provided leadership for African Americans in religion, economic advancement, and racial politics. Experience had driven members of this elite to a contradictory perception of themselves and of America. On the one hand, they were acculturated, patriotic Americans who had achieved some personal well-being and security. On the other hand, they knew that American society had not lived up to its revolutionary principles. They lamented the continued enslavement of the mass of African Americans, and they had misgivings about the future.

Prominent among these leaders were members of the clergy. Two of the most important of them were Richard Allen and Absalom Jones. Besides organizing his church, Allen opened a school in Philadelphia for black children, wrote against slavery and racial prejudice, and made his home a refuge for fugitive slaves. A year before his death in 1831, Allen presided over the first national black convention.

Jones, too, became an early abolitionist. In 1797 his concern for fugitives facing reenslavement led him to become the first African American to petition Congress. His petition anticipated later abolitionists' contention that because slavery violated the spirit of the U.S. Constitution Congress could abolish it.

Other influential black ministers of the late eighteenth and early nineteenth centuries included Jupiter Hammon of Long Island, Daniel Coker of Baltimore, John Chavis of Virginia, and Lemuel Haynes of New England. Hammon, who is quoted at

Voices

Absalom Jones Petitions Congress on Behalf of Fugitives Facing Reenslavement

Absalom Jones wrote his petition to Congress on behalf of four black men who had been manumitted in North Carolina. Because they were in danger of being reenslaved, they had taken refuge in Philadelphia. The men, under whose names the petition appears in the Annals of Congress, *were Jupiter Nicholson, Jacob Nicholson, Joe Albert, and Thomas Pritchet. Jones provided brief accounts of their troubles. Here we include only the important general principles that Jones invoked. Southern representatives argued that accepting a petition from alleged slaves would set a dangerous precedent, and Congress refused to accept the petition.*

To the President, Senate, and House of Representatives,

The Petition and Representation of the under-named Freemen, respectfully showeth:

That, being of African descent, the late inhabitants and natives of North Carolina, to you only, under God, can we apply with any hope of effect, for redress of our grievances, having been compelled to leave the State wherein we had a right of residence, as freemen liberated under the hand and seal of humane and conscientious masters, the validity of which act of justice in restoring us to our native right of freedom, was confirmed by judgment of the Superior Court of North Carolina . . . yet, not long after this decision, a law of that State was enacted, under which men of cruel disposition, and void of just principle, received countenance and authority in violently seizing, imprisoning, and selling into slavery, such as had been so emancipated; whereby we were reduced to the necessity of separating from some of our nearest and most tender connections, and seeking refuge in such parts of the Union where more regard is paid to the public declaration in favor of liberty and the common right of man, several hundreds, under our circumstances, having, in consequence of the said law, been hunted day and night, like beasts of the forest, by armed men with dogs, and made a prey of as free and lawful plunder . . .

We beseech your impartial attention to our hard condition, not only with respect to our personal sufferings, as freemen, but as a class of that people who, distinguished by color, are therefore with a degrading partiality, considered by many, even of those in eminent stations, as unentitled to that public justice and protection which is the great object of Government . . . .

If, notwithstanding all that has been publicly avowed as essential principles respecting the extent of human right to freedom; notwithstanding we have had that right restored to us, so far as was in the power of those by whom we were held as slaves, we cannot claim the privilege of representation in your councils, yet we trust we may address you as fellow-men, who, under God, the sovereign Ruler of the Universe, are entrusted with the distribution of justice, for the terror of evil-doers, the encouragement of protection of the innocent, not doubting that you are men of liberal minds, susceptible of benevolent

feelings and clear conception of rectitude to a catholic extent, who can admit that black people . . . have natural affections, social and domestic attachments and sensibilities; and that, therefore, we may hope for a share in your sympathetic attention while we represent that the unconstitutional bondage in which multitudes of our fellows in complexion are held, is to us a subject sorrowfully affecting; for we cannot conceive their condition (more especially those who have been emancipated and tasted the sweets of liberty, and again reduced to slavery by kidnappers and man-stealers) to be less afflicting or deplorable than the situation of citizens of the United States, captured and enslaved through the unrighteous policy prevalent in Algiers . . . may we not be allowed to consider this stretch of power, morally and politically, a Governmental defect, if not a direct violation of the declared fundamental principles of the Constitution; and finally, is not some remedy for an evil of such magnitude highly worthy of the deep inquiry and unfeigned zeal of the supreme Legislative body of a free and enlightened people?

---

1. On what principles does Jones believe the U.S. government is bound to act?
2. What does Jones's petition indicate concerning the legal status of African Americans?

SOURCE: *Annals of Congress*, 4 Cong., 2 sess. (January 23, 1797), 2015–18.

---

the beginning of this chapter, became a well-known poet. Coker, who was of mixed race, conducted a school, cofounded the AME Church, and advocated black migration to Africa. Chavis also combined preaching and teaching. Born free, he served on the Patriot side in the War for Independence and entered the College of New Jersey (Princeton) in 1792. Thereafter he became a Presbyterian missionary among African Americans in Virginia, Maryland, and North Carolina and gained a wide reputation as a biblical scholar. Haynes was perhaps even better known for his intellectual accomplishments. The son of a white mother and black father, Haynes served with the Minutemen and Continental Army, spoke against slavery, and in 1780 became the first ordained black Congregationalist minister serving as pastor to white congregations.

Vying with clergy for influence were African-American entrepreneurs. Prince Hall owned leather dressing and catering businesses in Boston. Peter Williams, principal founder of New York's AME Zion Church, was a prosperous tobacco merchant. Another prominent black businessman was James Forten of Philadelphia, described as "probably the most noteworthy free African-American entrepreneur in the early nineteenth century." Born to free parents in 1766, Forten was a Patriot during the War for Independence, learned the craft of sail making, and became the owner of his own business in 1798. For the rest of his life, he advocated equal rights and abolition.

American patriotism, religious conviction, organizational skill, intellectual inquisitiveness, and antislavery activism delineate the lives of most free black leaders in this era. Yet these leaders often disagreed among themselves regarding what was best for African Americans. Hammon and Chavis accommodated slavery and racial oppression. They condemned slavery and lauded human liberty, but they were not activists. They maintained that God would eventually end injustice. As late as 1836, Chavis, who lived in the South, wrote, "Slavery is a national evil no one doubts, but what is to be done? . . . All that can be done, is to make the best of a bad bargain . . . . I am clearly of the opinion that immediate emancipation would be to entail the greatest earthly curse upon my brethren according to the flesh."

Allen, Jones, Hall, and Forten expressed more optimism than Hammon and Chavis concerning the ability of African Americans to mold their destiny in the United States.

Profile

James Forten

James Forten was one of the few black leaders of the early American republic to live well beyond that era. His long career as a determined opponent of slavery linked the time of Prince Hall and Richard Allen to that of the militant abolitionists William Lloyd Garrison and Frederick Douglass(see Chapters 8 and 9). From the 1790s until his death in 1842, Forten used his wealth and organizational talents to build a cohesive black community in Philadelphia. But he also struggled to create a broader American community based on merit rather than on racial privilege.

Forten was born in Philadelphia in 1766. Family tradition held that one of his great grandfathers was an African who had been brought to Delaware in the late 1600s. His paternal grandfather was one of the first Pennsylvania slaves to purchase his freedom.

As a child, Forten learned to read and write at a school run by Quaker abolitionist Anthony Benezet and acquired Benezet's broad humanistic philosophy. In 1781 Forten volunteered to serve as a powder boy with a cannon crew on board the American privateer *Royal Louis*. He proved himself a brave sailor in battle. He was also deeply patriotic. When taken prisoner and offered special treatment by the son of a British officer, Forten declared, "No, NO! I am here a prisoner for the liberties of my country; *I never, NEVER, shall prove a traitor to her interests*." As a result of his defiance, Forten spent seven months on a rotting prison ship in New York Harbor.

After his release Forten walked back to Philadelphia and became an apprentice sail maker. He became foreman in 1786 and bought the business in 1798. By 1807 he employed an interracial workforce of 30 members and by 1832 had acquired a fortune of about $100,000—a large sum at the time.

Throughout the 1780s and most of the 1790s, Forten stood aloof from Philadelphia's developing black community. He did not join the Free African Society or help establish separate black churches. He only emerged as an active black leader in 1797 when he joined Richard Allen and Absalom Jones in establishing the African Masonic Lodge of Pennsylvania, which Prince Hall came to Philadelphia to install. Forten then joined 80 other Philadelphia African Americans to petition Congress to repeal the Fugitive Slave Law of 1793.

By 1817 Forten had become a major opponent of black migration to Africa. Although he had previously endorsed some colonization schemes, he had come to believe such efforts were racist because they assumed that black people were not suited for American citizenship. Rather than commit resources to sending African Americans to other parts of the world, he was determined to improve their standing in the United States. In 1809 he joined Allen and Jones in creating a self-improvement organization, the Society for the Suppression of Vice and Immorality. By 1830 he hoped to use the newly organized Black National Convention movement to train young black men for skilled trades.

Forten also became an important influence on white abolitionist leader William Lloyd Garrison. Forten welcomed Garrison to his home, introduced him to other black leaders, and helped finance his antislavery newspaper, the *Liberator*. In 1833 Forten joined Garrison, Arthur Tappan, Lewis Tappan, and other white and black abolitionists in organizing the American Anti-Slavery Society, pledged to the peaceful immediate abolition of slavery without colonization of the former slaves and without compensation to slaveholders. Increasingly radical during his remaining years, Forten advocated an end to war, favored equal rights for women, and resisted the enforcement of the Fugitive Slave Law. He also helped establish the American Moral Reform Society. He demonstrated his commitment to women's rights in the way he raised his daughters—Sarah, Margaretta, and Harriet—who carried on his activism.

Although Allen, Jones, Hall, and Forten each expressed misgivings, they believed that, despite setbacks, the egalitarian principles of the American Revolution would prevail if black people insisted on liberty. Forten never despaired that African Americans would be integrated into the larger American society on the basis of their individual talent and enterprise. Although he was often frustrated, Hall pursued for four decades a strategy based on the assumption that white authority would reward black protest and patriotism. In 1786, when Daniel Shays led his revolt of white farmers in western Massachusetts, Hall offered to raise 700 black volunteers to help defeat the insurgency. Allen and Jones put more emphasis on separate black institutions than did Forten or Hall. Yet they were just as willing to organize, protest, and petition to establish the rights of black people as American citizens.

5.4.1 Migration

African Americans, however, had another alternative: migration from the United States to establish their own society free from white prejudices. In 1787 British philanthropists, including Olaudah Equiano, had established Freetown in Sierra Leone on the West African coast as a refuge for former slaves. As we mentioned in Chapter 4, some African Americans who had been Loyalists during the American Revolution settled there. Other black and white Americans proposed that free black people should settle in western North America or the Caribbean islands. Great practical obstacles stood in the way of mass black migration to all of these regions. Migration was expensive, difficult to organize, and involved long, often fruitless negotiations with foreign governments. But no black leader during the early national period was immune to the appeal of migration proposals.

Aware of Freetown, Hall in 1787 petitioned the Massachusetts legislature to support efforts by black Bostonians to establish a colony in Africa. Although he recognized black progress in Massachusetts, Hall maintained that he and others found themselves "in many respects, in very disagreeable and disadvantageous circumstances; most of which must attend us so long as we and our children live in America." By the mid-1810s, a few influential white Americans had also decided that there was no place in the United States for free African Americans. In 1816 they organized the **American Colonization Society**. Under its auspices, Coker in 1820 led the first party of 86 African Americans to the new colony of Liberia on the West African coast.

The major black advocate of migration to Africa during this period was Paul Cuffe, the son of an Ashantee father and Wampanoag Indian mother. He became a prosperous New England sea captain and, by the early 1800s, cooperated with British humanitarians and entrepreneurs to promote migration. He saw African-American colonization in West Africa as a way to end the Atlantic slave trade, spread Christianity, create a refuge for free black people, and make profits. Before his death in 1817, Cuffe had influenced not only Coker but also—at least temporarily—Forten, Allen, and Jones to consider colonization as a viable alternative for African Americans.

American Colonization Society
An organization founded in Washington, DC, by prominent slaveholders. It claimed to encourage the ultimate abolition of slavery by sending free African Americans to its West African colony of Liberia.

5.4.2 Slave Uprisings

While, after the Revolution, black northerners grew increasingly aware of limits to their freedom, black southerners faced perpetual slavery. As cotton production expanded westward, as new slave states entered the Union, and as masters in such border slave states as Maryland and Virginia turned away from the revolutionary commitment to gradual emancipation, slaves pursued several strategies.

Some lowered their expectations and loyally served their masters. Most continued patterns of day-to-day resistance. Many escaped. A few risked their lives to join forceful revolutionary movements to destroy slavery. Just several hundred out of hundreds of thousands of slaves rallied behind Gabriel in 1800 near Richmond and behind Charles Deslondes in 1811 near New Orleans. But they frightened white southerners and raised hopes for freedom among countless African Americans.

Toussaint Louverture (1744–1803) led the black rebellion in the French colony of St. Domingue on the Caribbean island of Hispaniola that led to the creation of the independent black republic of Haiti in 1804. Louverture became an inspiration for black rebels in the United States.

The egalitarian principles of the American and French revolutions influenced Gabriel and Deslondes. Unlike earlier slave rebels, they acted not to revenge personal grievances or to establish maroon communities but to destroy slavery because it denied natural human rights to its victims. The American Declaration of Independence and the legend of Haiti's Toussaint Louverture provided the intellectual foundations for their efforts. Louverture, against great odds, had led the enslaved black people of the French sugar colony of Saint Domingue—modern Haiti—to freedom and independence. This bitter and bloody struggle lasted from 1791 to 1804. Many white planters fled the island with their slaves to take refuge in Cuba, Jamaica, South Carolina, Virginia, and, somewhat later, Louisiana. The Haitian slaves carried the spirit of revolution with them to their new homes.

During the early 1790s, black unrest and rumors of revolt mounted in Virginia. The state militia arrested suspected plotters and had them whipped. It was in this context that Gabriel, the human property of Thomas Prosser, Sr., prepared to lead a massive slave insurrection. An acculturated and literate blacksmith, Gabriel understood the rationalist and revolutionary currents of his time. He was also a large and powerful man with a violent temper. In 1799 a local court convicted him of "'biting off a considerable part of [the] left Ear' of a white neighbor."

While the ideology of the American Revolution shaped Gabriel's actions, he also perceived that white people were politically divided and distracted by an undeclared naval war between the United States and France. He enjoyed secret support from a few white people and hoped poor white people would rally to his cause as he and his associates planned to kill those who supported slavery and take control of central Virginia.

But on August 30, 1800—the day set for the uprising—two slaves revealed the plan to white authorities while a tremendous thunderstorm prevented Gabriel's followers from assaulting Richmond. Then Virginia governor—and future U.S. president—James Monroe had suspects arrested. Gabriel, who relied on white allies to get to Norfolk, was among the last captured. In October he and 26 others, convicted of "conspiracy and insurrection," were hanged. Yet by demonstrating that slaves could organize for large-scale rebellion, they left a legacy of fear among slaveholders and hope for liberation among southern African Americans.

The far less famous Louisiana Rebellion took place under similar circumstances. By the early 1800s, refugees from Haiti had settled with their slaves in what was then known as Orleans Territory. As they arrived, rumors of slave insurrection spread across the territory. The rumors became reality on January 8, 1811, when Deslondes, a Haitian native and slave driver on a plantation north of New Orleans, initiated a massive revolt in cooperation with maroons.

Although no record of Deslondes's rhetoric survives and his goals may have been less ideologically coherent than Gabriel's, he organized a force of at least 180 men and women. They marched south along the Mississippi River toward New Orleans, with leaders on horseback and with flags and drums but few guns. The revolutionaries plundered and burned plantations but killed only two white people and one recalcitrant slave. On January 10 a force of about 700 territorial militia, slaveholding vigilantes, and U.S. troops overwhelmed the rebels. The "battle" was a massacre. Well-armed white men slaughtered 66 rebels and captured 30. They tried the captives without benefit of counsel, found 22—including Deslondes—guilty of rebellion, and shot them. Then they cut off the executed men's heads and displayed them on pikes to warn other African Americans of the consequences of revolt.

5.4.3 The White Southern Reaction

Deslondes's uprising is one of the few major slave revolts in American history. But Gabriel's conspiracy and events in Haiti left a more significant legacy. For generations, enslaved African Americans regarded Louverture as a black George Washington and recalled Gabriel's revolutionary message. The networks among slaves that Gabriel established survived his death, and, as the domestic slave trade carried black Virginians southwestward, they carried his promise of liberation with them. White southerners responded to these black revolutionary currents by rejecting the egalitarian values of the Enlightenment. Because white southerners feared race war and believed emancipation would encourage African Americans to begin such a war, most of them determined to make black bondage stronger, not weaker.

Beginning with South Carolina in December 1800, southern states outlawed assemblies of slaves, placed curfews on slaves and free black people, and made manumissions more difficult. The old colonial practice of white men on horseback patrolling slave quarters revived. Assuming that revolutionaries like Gabriel received encouragement from northern white abolitionists, white southerners became suspicious of such outsiders as Yankee peddlers, evangelicals, and foreigners. Based on an assumption that local free African Americans were even more involved in slave uprisings than white outsiders, some white southerners advocated forcing them to leave. This brought about an odd alliance between white advocates of expulsion and black advocates of emigration to Africa.

5.5 The War of 1812

Evaluate the African-American role in the War of 1812.

Many of the themes developed in this chapter—African-American patriotism, opportunities for freedom, migration sentiment, and influences pushing slaves toward revolutionary action—are reflected in the black experience during the American war with Britain that began in 1812 and lasted until early 1815. This conflict, known as the War of 1812, was a late development in a massive military and economic struggle between Britain and France for mastery over the Atlantic world. It began in 1793, during the French Revolution, and ended with the defeat of Napoleon Bonaparte by a British-led coalition in 1815.

British military support for American Indian resistance in the Old Northwest, an American desire to annex Canada, and especially Britain's interference with American ships trading with Europe drew the United States into the Franco-British war. Many Americans regarded the War of 1812 as a second war for independence, and American forces won important victories. But the United States failed to conquer Canada; suffered the burning of Washington, D.C.; and allowed the war to end in a draw. It was also a war in which black military service, and white fear of slave revolt, had important roles (see Map 5-2).

By 1812 prejudice and fear of revolt had nearly obliterated positive white memories of black Patriot soldiers during the Revolution. The Militia Act of 1792 eliminated armed black participation in all state militias except that of North Carolina. In 1798 the

Map 5-2 The War of 1812

As during the War for Independence, African Americans fought on both sides during the War of 1812. Some joined the British army that burned Washington, D.C. Others helped the United States win control of Lake Erie in 1813 and stop British invasion of Louisiana at the Battle of New Orleans in 1815.

What was at stake for African Americans in the War of 1812?

secretary of the navy ended black service on American warships. Because of the news from Haiti and because of Gabriel's conspiracy, most white southerners joined John Randolph of Virginia in regarding African Americans as "an internal foe." Therefore, when the War of 1812 began, southern states refused to enlist black men for fear they would use their guns to aid slave revolts. Meanwhile, a lack of enthusiasm for the war, combined with the absence of a British threat to their part of the country, kept northern states from mobilizing black troops in 1812 and 1813.

Southern fears of slave revolt mounted during the spring of 1813 when the British invaded the Chesapeake. As they had during the Revolution, British generals offered slaves freedom in Canada or the British West Indies in return for help. In response, African Americans joined the British army that burned Washington, D.C., in 1814 and attacked Baltimore.

The threat this British army posed to Philadelphia and New York led to the first active black involvement in the war on the American side. The New York state legislature authorized two black regiments, offered freedom to slaves who enlisted, and promised compensation to their masters. African Americans in Philadelphia and New York City volunteered to help build fortifications. In Philadelphia, James Forten,

Richard Allen, and Absalom Jones patriotically raised a "Black Brigade." The brigade never saw action because the British halted when they failed to capture Baltimore.

African-American men did fight, however, at two of the war's most important battles. During the naval engagement at Put-in-Bay on Lake Erie in September 1813, which secured control of the Great Lakes for the United States, one-quarter of Commandant Oliver Hazard Perry's 400 sailors were black. Although Perry had been prejudiced against using black men, after the battle he praised their valor. At the Battle of New Orleans—fought in January 1815, about a month after a peace treaty had been negotiated but not ratified—African Americans also fought bravely. Yet white memories of Deslondes's uprising almost prevented them from being allowed to fight on the American side. Many white people feared that the local free black militia, which dated back to the Spanish occupation of Louisiana from 1763 to 1801, would make common cause with slaves and the British rather than take the American side. In defiance of such fears, General Andrew Jackson included the black militia in his force defending New Orleans and offered its members equal pay and benefits. At least 600 free black men fought on the American side in the battle, and Jackson lived up to his promise of equal treatment. It was a choice, he later informed President James Madison, between having the free African Americans "in our ranks or . . . in the ranks of the enemy."

5.6 The Missouri Compromise

Evaluate the Missouri Compromise's impact on African Americans.

After 1815, as the United States emerged from a difficult war, sectional issues between the North and South, which constitutional compromises and the political climate had pushed into the background, revived. The nation's first political parties—the Federalist and the Republican—had failed to confront slavery as a national issue. The northern wing of the modernizing Federalist Party had abolitionist tendencies. But during the 1790s when they controlled the national government, the Federalists did not raise the slavery issue. Then the victory of the agrarian and state rights–oriented Republican Party in the 1800 elections fatally weakened the Federalists as a national organization. A series of proslavery presidential administrations in Washington resulted.

It took innovations in transportation and production that began during the 1810s, as well as the rapid disappearance of slavery in the northern states, to transform the North into a region consciously at odds with the South's traditional culture and slave-labor economy. The first major expression of intensifying sectional differences over slavery and its expansion came in 1819 when the slaveholding Missouri Territory, which had been carved out of the Louisiana Territory, applied for admission to the Union as a slave-labor state. Northerners expressed deep reservations about such an application. Many in the North feared that admitting a new slaveholding state would destroy the political balance between the sections and encourage the expansion of slavery elsewhere. The aged Thomas Jefferson called this negative northern reaction a "fire bell in the night." He meant that henceforth slaveholders had to be on guard in national politics to protect their interests.

African Americans recognized the significance of the Missouri crisis. Black residents of Washington, D.C., crowded into the U.S. Senate gallery as that body debated the issue. Finally, Henry Clay of Kentucky, the slaveholding Speaker of the House of Representatives, directed an effort that in 1820 produced a compromise that temporarily quieted North–South discord. Clay's Missouri Compromise (see Map 5-3) permitted Missouri to become a slave-labor state; maintained a sectional political balance by admitting Maine, which had been part of Massachusetts, as a free-labor state; and banned slavery north of the 36° 30' line of latitude in the old Louisiana Territory. Yet sectional relations would never be the same, and a new black and white antislavery militancy soon confronted the white South.

Map 5-3 The Missouri Compromise of 1820

Under the Missouri Compromise, Missouri entered the Union as a slave state, Maine entered as a free state, and Congress banned slavery in the huge unorganized portion of the old Louisiana Territory north of the 36° 30' line of latitude.

Which section of the United States did the Missouri Compromise favor?

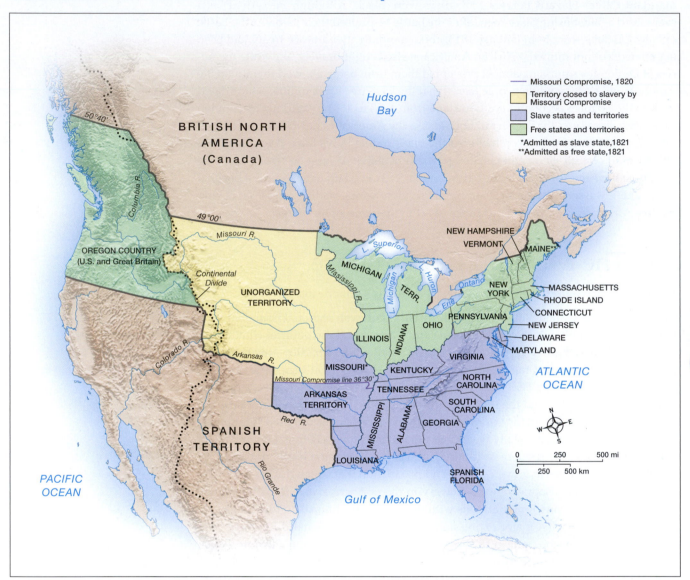

Conclusion

The period between the War for Independence and the Missouri Compromise was a time of transition for African Americans. On one hand, the legacy of the American Revolution brought emancipation in the North and a promise of equal opportunity with white Americans. On the other hand, during the 1790s slavery and racism had grown stronger. Through a combination of antiblack prejudice among white Americans and African Americans' desire to preserve their cultural traditions, black urban communities arose in the North, Upper South, and, occasionally—in Charleston and Savannah, for example—in the Deep South.

Spreading freedom in the North and Upper South, and the emergence of black communities in the North and South, were heartening developments. New opportunities opened for black education, spiritual expression, and economic growth. But the mass of

African Americans remained in slavery. The forces for human bondage became stronger. And freedom for those who had gained it in the Upper South and North remained marginal and precarious.

Gabriel's conspiracy in Virginia and Deslondes's rebellion in Louisiana indicated that revolutionary principles persisted among black southerners. But these rebellions and British recruitment of slaves during the War of 1812 convinced most white southerners that black bondage had to be permanent. In these circumstances, African Americans looked to the future with mixed emotions. A few determined that the only hope for real freedom lay in migration from the United States.

Chapter Timeline

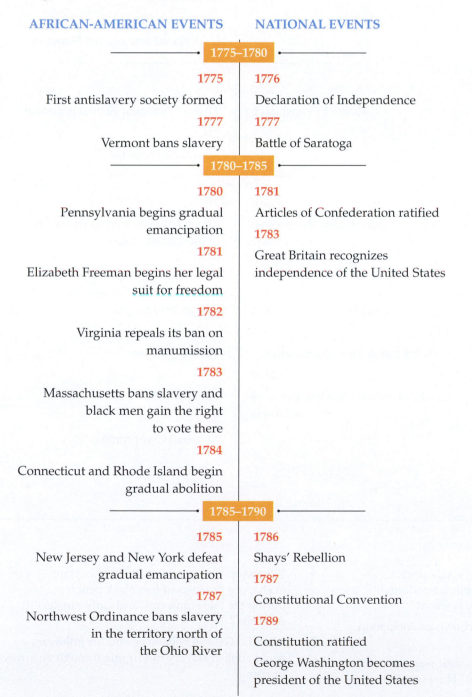

AFRICAN-AMERICAN EVENTS   **NATIONAL EVENTS**

1775–1780

1775
First antislavery society formed

1776
Declaration of Independence

1777
Vermont bans slavery

1777
Battle of Saratoga

1780–1785

1780
Pennsylvania begins gradual emancipation

1781
Articles of Confederation ratified

1781
Elizabeth Freeman begins her legal suit for freedom

1783
Great Britain recognizes independence of the United States

1782
Virginia repeals its ban on manumission

1783
Massachusetts bans slavery and black men gain the right to vote there

1784
Connecticut and Rhode Island begin gradual abolition

1785–1790

1785
New Jersey and New York defeat gradual emancipation

1786
Shays' Rebellion

1787
Northwest Ordinance bans slavery in the territory north of the Ohio River

1787
Constitutional Convention

1789
Constitution ratified

George Washington becomes president of the United States

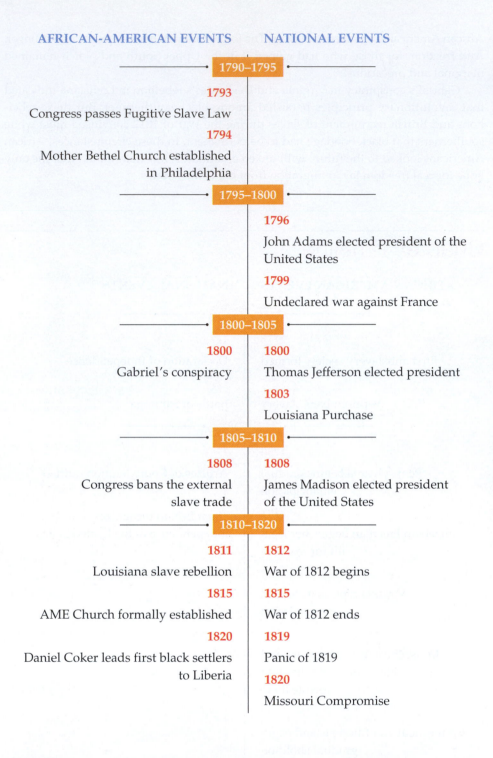

AFRICAN-AMERICAN EVENTS   NATIONAL EVENTS

1790–1795

1793

Congress passes Fugitive Slave Law

1794

Mother Bethel Church established
in Philadelphia

1795–1800

1796

John Adams elected president of the
United States

1799

Undeclared war against France

1800–1805

1800   **1800**

Gabriel's conspiracy   Thomas Jefferson elected president

1803

Louisiana Purchase

1805–1810

1808   **1808**

Congress bans the external   James Madison elected president
slave trade   of the United States

1810–1820

1811   **1812**

Louisiana slave rebellion   War of 1812 begins

1815   **1815**

AME Church formally established War of 1812 ends

1820   **1819**

Daniel Coker leads first black settlers Panic of 1819
to Liberia

1820

Missouri Compromise

Review Questions

1. Which were stronger in the early American republic, the forces in favor of black freedom or those in favor of continued enslavement?

2. How did African Americans achieve emancipation in the North?

3. How was the U.S. Constitution, as it was drafted in 1787, a proslavery document? How was it an antislavery document?

4. Why were separate institutions important in shaping the lives of free black people during the late eighteenth and early nineteenth centuries?

5. Why did Gabriel believe he and his followers could abolish slavery in Virginia through an armed uprising?

Retracing the Odyssey

Monticello, Charlottesville, Virginia. One hundred and thirty African Americans worked on this plantation during the late eighteenth and early nineteenth centuries.

Amherst History Museum, Amherst, Massachusetts. An exhibit on free black people who lived in eighteenth-century Amherst.

Afro-American Historical and Cultural Museum, Philadelphia, Pennsylvania. The collection includes an exhibit on black churches, 1740–1977.

Recommended Reading

Ira Berlin. *Slaves without Masters: The Free Negro in the Antebellum South.* New York: New Press, 1974. The early chapters of this classic study indicate the special difficulties the first large generation of free black southerners faced.

Douglas R. Egerton. *Gabriel's Rebellion: The Virginia Slave Conspiracies of 1800 and 1802.* Chapel Hill: University of North Carolina Press, 1993. This account of Gabriel's conspiracy emphasizes both the revolutionary context within which he acted and his legacy.

Philip S. Foner. *History of Black Americans, from Africa to the Emergence of the Cotton Kingdom.* Westport, CT: Greenwood, 1975. This is the first volume of a comprehensive three-volume history of African Americans. It is detailed and informative about black life between 1783 and 1820.

James Oliver Horton and Lois E. Horton. *In Hope of Liberty: Culture, Community, and Protest among Northern Free Blacks, 1700–1860.* New York: Oxford University Press, 1997. This is a well-written interpretation of the northern free black community and its origins.

Sidney Kaplan and Emma Nogrady Kaplan. *The Black Presence in the Era of the American Revolution*, Rev. ed. Amherst: University of Massachusetts Press, 1989. This delightfully written book provides informative accounts of black leaders who lived during the early American republic.

Gary B. Nash. *Forging Freedom: The Formation of Philadelphia's Black Community, 1720–1840.* Cambridge, MA: Harvard University Press, 1988. This path-breaking study of a black community analyzes the origins of separate black institutions.

Donald R. Wright. *African Americans in the Early Republic, 1789–1831.* Arlington Heights, IL: Harlan Davidson, 1993. This is a brief but comprehensive account.

Additional Bibliography

Emancipation in the North

James D. Essig. *The Bonds of Wickedness: American Evangelicals Against Slavery, 1770–1808.* Philadelphia: Temple University Press, 1982.

David N. Gellman. *Emancipating New York: The Politics of Slavery and Freedom, 1777–1827.* Baton Rouge: Louisiana State University Press, 2006.

Joanne Pope Melish. *Disowning Slavery: Gradual Emancipation and "Race" in New England, 1780–1860.* Ithaca, NY: Cornell University Press, 1998.

Gary B. Nash and Jean R. Soderlund. *Freedom by Degrees: Emancipation in Pennsylvania and Its Aftermath.* New York: Oxford University Press, 1991.

Arthur Zilversmit. *The First Emancipation: The Abolition of Slavery in the North.* Chicago: University of Chicago Press, 1967.

Proslavery Forces

Paul Finkelman. *Slavery and the Founders: Race and Liberty in the Age of Jefferson.* Armonk, NY: M. E. Sharpe, 1996.

Charles F. Irons. *The Origins of Proslavery Christianity: White and Black Evangelicals in Colonial and Antebellum Virginia.* Chapel Hill: University of North Carolina Press, 2008.

Donald G. Nieman. *Promises to Keep: African Americans and the Constitutional Order, 1776 to the Present.* New York: Oxford University Press, 1991.

Donald L. Robinson. *Slavery in the Structure of American Politics, 1765–1820.* New York: Harcourt Brace Jovanovich, 1971.

Larry E. Tise. *Proslavery: A History of the Defense of Slavery in America, 1701–1840.* Athens: University of Georgia Press, 1987.

Free Black Institutions, Migration Movements, and the War of 1812

Eddie S. Glaude. *Exodus!: Religion, Race, and Nation in Early Nineteenth-Century Black America.* Chicago: University of Chicago Press, 2000.

Leon Litwack. *North of Slavery: The Negro in the Free States.* Chicago: University of Chicago Press, 1961.

William A. Muraskin. *Middle-Class Blacks in a White Society: Prince Hall Freemasonry in America.* Berkeley: University of California Press, 1975.

Richard S. Newman. *Freedom's Prophet: Bishop Richard Allen, the AME Church, and the Black Founding Fathers.* New York: New York University Press, 2008.

Gene A. Smith. *The Slave's Gamble: Choosing Sides in the War of 1812.* New York: Palgrave Macmillan, 2013.

Lamont D. Thomas. *Paul Cuffe: Black Entrepreneur and Pan-Africanist.* Urbana: University of Illinois Press, 1988.

Heather Andrea Williams. *Self-Taught: African American Education in Slavery and Freedom.* Chapel Hill: University of North Carolina Press, 2005.

Julie Winch. *Between Slavery and Freedom: Free People of Color in America from Settlement to the Civil War.* Lanham, MD: Rowman and Littlefield, 2014.

———. *A Gentleman of Color: The Life of James Forten.* New York: Oxford University Press, 2002.

The South

John Hope Franklin. *The Free Negro in North Carolina, 1790–1860.* 1943. Reprint, New York: Russell and Russell, 1969.

Peter Kolchin. *American Slavery, 1619–1877.* New York: Hill and Wang, 1993.

John Chester Miller. *The Wolf by the Ears: Thomas Jefferson and Slavery.* 1977. Reprint, Charlottesville: University Press of Virginia, 1991.

T. Stephen Whitman. *The Price of Freedom: Slavery and Manumission in Baltimore and Early National Maryland.* Lexington: University of Kentucky Press, 1997.

Slave Revolts, Resistance, and Escapes

Merton L. Dillon. *Slavery Attacked: Southern Slaves and Their Allies, 1619–1865.* Baton Rouge: Louisiana State University Press, 1990.

Eugene D. Genovese. *From Rebellion to Revolution: Afro-American Slave Revolts in the Making of the Modern World.* Baton Rouge: Louisiana State University Press, 1979.

John R. McKivigan and Stanley Harrold, eds. *Antislavery Violence: Sectional, Racial, and Cultural Conflict in Antebellum America.* Knoxville: University of Tennessee Press, 1999.

Gerald W. Mullin. *Flight and Rebellion: Slave Resistance in Eighteenth-Century Virginia.* New York: Oxford University Press, 1972.

Daniel Rasmussen. *American Uprising: The Untold Story of America's Largest Slave Revolt.* New York: Harper, 2012.

James Sidbury. *Ploughshares into Swords: Race, Rebellion, and Identity in Gabriel's Virginia, 1730–1810.* New York: Cambridge University Press, 1998.

Connecting the Past

The Great Awakening and the Black Church

Preacher meeting in the African Church, Cincinnati, Ohio.

The Great Awakening and African-American life and culture are closely connected. Black Christianity, often called "the black church," both shaped the huge evangelical revival that flourished in British North America during the mid-eighteenth century—*and* sprang from it. Black Christians, and *especially* black preachers, combined African and Christian religious beliefs and practices. Their churches became community centers that guided and supported families, nurtured resistance to oppression, pointed the way to freedom, and encouraged cultural expression.

No single event or movement, no matter how pervasive, can shape all aspects of something as large and dependent on personal interpretation as religious belief, practice, and organization. In the Virginia colony, people of African descent converted to Christianity as early as the 1620s. After that and

Richard Allen (1760–1831), an American Methodist bishop and founder of the African Methodist Episcopal Church.

before the Great Awakening, some colonial masters allowed their slaves to become Christians. During the nearly three centuries since the Awakening, slavery, segregation, poverty, urbanization, the civil rights movement, and activist theology have expanded and modified black Christianity. New ideas and circumstances continue to change it.

Nevertheless, the Great Awakening fundamentally shaped African-American religious institutions and culture. Under its influence, nearly all African Americans affiliated with Christian churches. Just as important, most of them became evangelical Protestants (Baptists and Methodists) rather than Episcopalians, Presbyterians, or Roman Catholics. They believed God's spirit dwelt in each human, that they could participate in a holy community, achieve brotherhood, gain salvation, and bring on the millennium. Black theology became liberation theology, with early spirituals expressing a yearning for freedom. Plantation slaves held services in secret to avoid the master's suppression.

The Great Awakening also initiated the chain of events that produced separate black congregations and independent black churches. Separate black congregations within larger white church organizations date to the 1770s. Independent churches, such as the African Methodist Episcopal (AME) Church and African Methodist Episcopal Zion (AME Zion) Church, arose between 1790 and 1822. Racial discrimination and segregation among white Methodists (and later Baptists)

helped shape these developments. Yet the creation of separate congregations and independent churches freed black Christians to preserve African beliefs and rituals that contributed so much to their religious sensibilities. Separation also allowed black church buildings to become centers of antislavery activism, powerbases for abolitionist ministers, and venues for abolitionist meetings that white churches often barred.

During the Civil War, black churches supported the Union cause, encouraged black men to enlist in Union armies, and urged emancipation as a war aim. During Reconstruction, black northern churches (along with many of their white counterparts) sent missionaries and teachers south to serve the freed people. As a result, the black churches expanded southward during the late nineteenth century. In the South, as earlier in the North, the churches housed schools, community organizations, mutual aid societies, benevolent groups, women's clubs, and fraternal societies. Black ministers provided political leadership. After Reconstruction, black churches helped their communities endure decades of oppression. By the mid-twentieth century, they had become centers for and leaders of the civil rights movement. Throughout these years, the black experience during the Great Awakening exerted its influence.

Not all black leaders praised the black church. In 1848, Frederick Douglass, who opposed all racial segregation, criticized the church as too emotional, too focused on heaven, too expensive, and too conservative. Black ministers, Douglass charged, were often unqualified. He preferred a black struggle for equality within white churches.

Other black leaders have also called for a better-educated clergy. But most have been more supportive than Douglass of the black church. In 1903, W. E. B. Du Bois declared, "The Negro church of today is the social center of Negro life in the United States, and the most characteristic expression of African character." Du Bois also thought the black church influenced "poor whites." Their religion, he claimed, "is a plain copy of Negro thought and methods." He added caustically, "The mass of 'gospel' hymns which has swept through American churches and well-nigh ruined our sense of song consists largely of debased imitations of Negro melodies." More broadly, he asserted, "The study of Negro religion is not only a vital part of the history of the Negro in America, but no uninteresting part of American history."

Du Bois also valued black ministers: "The Preacher is the most unique personality developed by the Negro on American soil . . . . The combination of a certain adroitness with a deep-set earnestness, of tact with consummate ability, gave him his preeminence, and helps him maintain it." By the time Du Bois died in 1963, the leadership such ministers provided to the civil rights movement had borne out this view. That leadership is also a legacy of the Great Awakening.

---

1. How has the black church changed since the Great Awakening?

2. How has the black church remained the same since the Great Awakening?

Part II

Slavery, Abolition, and the Quest for Freedom: The Coming of the Civil War, 1793–1861

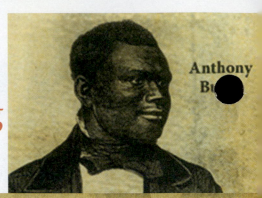

Anthony Burns

	1770–1800		1800–1830	
RELIGION	1775	Philadelphia Quakers organize first antislavery society in America	1819	Episcopal Diocese of New York excludes black delegates from annual conventions
	Late 1700s–1830s	Second Great Awakening	1820s	Semisecret churches spread among slaves
			1829	Oblate Sisters of Providence founded in Baltimore, first African-American order of Roman Catholic nuns
CULTURE 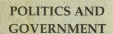	Early 1800s	Growth of folk tales among slaves	1820s–1830s	Numerous black literary societies established in northern cities
POLITICS AND GOVERNMENT			1804–1849	Black laws in midwestern states restrict rights of African Americans
			1807	New Jersey disfranchises black voters
			1818	Connecticut bans new black voters
			1820	Missouri Compromise
			1821	New York retains property qualification for black voters
			1822	Rhode Island disfranchises black voters
SOCIETY AND ECONOMY	1784	Society for the Promotion of the Abolition of Slavery founded	1800	Gabriel's conspiracy
			1812	African schools become part of Boston's public schools
			1816	American Colonization Society founded
			1822	Denmark Vesey's conspiracy
			1827	*Freedom's Journal* begins publication

Harriet Tubman   **Frederick Douglass**   **Sojourner Truth**

| 1830–1850 | 1850–1870 | Noteworthy Individuals |

| 1840s | Mother Bethel Church in Philadelphia has largest black congregation in the United States |
| 1853 | Episcopal Diocese of New York readmits black delegates |

1840s–1850s	Paintings of Robert Duncanson
1845	*Narrative of the Life of Frederick Douglass* published
1848	Okah Tubee's fictionalized autobiography published

1852	*Uncle Tom's Cabin* published
1853	William W. Brown, first African-American novelist, publishes *Clotel*
	Elizabeth Taylor Greenfield makes her singing debut in New York before a white audience
	Solomon Northup publishes *Twelve Years as a Slave*
1854	Frances Ellen Watkins Harper publishes *Poems*
1855	William C. Nell publishes *The Colored Patriots of the American Revolution*
1859	Harriet Wilson publishes first novel by an African-American woman

1832	Virginia rejects gradual emancipation
1836–1841	"Gag rule" prohibits Congress from considering petitions regarding slavery
1838	Pennsylvania disfranchises black voters
1846	Wilmot Proviso
1846–1848	Mexican War
1847	Liberia becomes an independent republic
1848	Free Soil party founded

1850	Compromise of 1850 includes stronger Fugitive Slave Act
1851	Indiana bans African Americans from residing in the state
1855–1856	"Bleeding Kansas"
1857	*Dred Scott* decision
1858	Arkansas reenslaves free blacks who refuse to leave the state
1859	John Brown raids Harpers Ferry
1860	Lincoln elected president
1860–1861	Eleven southern states secede and form the Confederacy
1861	Civil War begins

1831	Nat Turner's revolt William Lloyd Garrison begins publication of *The Liberator*
1832	First black women's abolitionist organization founded
1833	American Anti-Slavery Society founded
1834	African Free Schools become part of New York's public schools
1835	Abolitionist postal campaign begins
1836	Elijah P. Lovejoy killed by antiabolitionist mob
1839	Amistad mutiny
1843	Henry H. Garnet's *Address to the Slaves*
1847	Frederick Douglass begins publication of the *North Star*
	Missouri bans education of free blacks

1851	"Battle" of Christiana
1853	Rochester Convention
1854	Ashmun Institute, first black institution of higher education in the United States, founded
1860	U.S. slave population put at 3,953,760

Chapter 6

Life in the Cotton Kingdom
1793–1861

PICKING COTTON ON A GEORGIA PLANTATION.

In this engraving, which dates to about 1858, slaves harvest cotton on a southern plantation. Note the division of labor with women picking and men packing and carrying.

 ## Learning Objectives

After reading this chapter, you should be able to:

6.1 Discuss the growth and expansion of slavery in the South.

6.2 Compare and contrast how slaves produced the South's various crops.

6.3 Describe how the work of house slaves and skilled slaves differed from the work of agricultural slaves.

6.4 Evaluate the role of punishment in slavery.

6.5 Describe the character and impact of the domestic slave trade as it existed between 1820 and 1860.

6.6 Discuss the various factors that shaped black life in the Cotton Kingdom.

6.7 Analyze how African Americans adapted to life in slavery, and the role religion played in this adaption.

6.8 Evaluate the different ways in which historians have portrayed the black experience in slavery.

> **There may be humane masters, as there certainly are inhumane ones; there may be slaves well-clothed, well-fed, and happy, as there surely are those half-clad, half-starved, and miserable; nevertheless, the institution that tolerates such wrong and inhumanity . . . is a cruel, unjust, and barbarous one.**
>
> —*Solomon Northup, Twelve Years a Slave: Narrative of Solomon Northup*

Solomon Northup, a free black man, had been kidnapped into slavery during the 1840s. After 12 years in bondage, he finally escaped. In the passage above, he identifies the central cruelty of slavery. It was not that some masters failed to provide slaves with adequate food, clothing, and shelter while others did. Nor was it that some masters treated their slaves brutally while others did not. The central cruelty of slavery was that it gave masters nearly absolute power over their slaves. In other words, the root cause of black suffering in slavery lay not in abuses, but in the institution of slavery itself.

In this chapter we describe the life of black people in the slave South from the rise of the Cotton Kingdom during the 1790s to the eve of the Civil War in 1860. As we indicate in previous chapters, African Americans suffered brutal oppression on southern plantations. But they also developed means of coping with that oppression, resisting it, and escaping from it. During the period this chapter covers, slavery in the South peaked as a productive system and means of white control over black southerners. We describe the extent of that slave system, how it varied across the South, and how it operated. The chapter also investigates the slave communities that African-American men, women, and children built.

6.1 The Expansion of Slavery

Discuss the growth and expansion of slavery in the South.

Eli Whitney's invention of the cotton gin in 1793 made the cultivation of cotton profitable on the North American mainland (see Chapter 5). It led to the rapid and extensive expansion of slavery from the Atlantic coast to Texas. By 1811 cotton growing had spread across South Carolina, Georgia, and parts of North Carolina and Virginia. By 1821 it had crossed Alabama and reached Mississippi, Louisiana, and parts of Tennessee. It then expanded again into Arkansas, Florida, and eastern Texas (see Map 6-1). Enslaved black labor cleared forests and drained swamps to make these lands fit for cultivation.

The expansion of the cotton culture led to the removal of the American Indians— some of them slaveholders—who inhabited this vast region. During the 1830s and 1840s, the U.S. Army forced the Cherokee, Chickasaw, Choctaw, Creek, and most Seminole to leave their ancestral lands for Indian Territory in what is now Oklahoma. Many Indians died during this forced migration, and the Cherokee remember it as "The Trail of Tears." Yet the Cherokees created in Oklahoma an economy dependent on black slave labor. By 1860 there were 7,000 slaves there, which accounted for 14 percent of the population.

Map 6-1 Cotton Production in the South, 1820–1860

Cotton production expanded westward between 1820 and 1860 into Alabama, Mississippi, Louisiana, Texas, Arkansas, and western Tennessee.

SOURCE: Sam Bowers Hilliard, *Atlas of Antebellum Southern Agriculture* (Louisiana State University Press, 1984), 67–71.

Why did cotton production spread westward?

Far fewer slaves lived in the other western territories. Kansas never had more than a few dozen slaves during the 1850s and had none after 1858. In New Mexico in 1850, there were about 40 black slaves and 3,000 American Indian slaves. When Utah Territory legalized slavery in 1852, only about 26 enslaved black people were living there, and by 1860 Utah had just 29 black people. Although California entered the Union as a state in 1850 under a constitution that banned slavery, two years later more than 300 illegally held slaves worked there as prospectors or servants.

6.1.1 Slave Population Growth

In contrast to the Far West, during the period of territorial expansion a tremendous increase in the number of African Americans in bondage occurred in the region stretching from the Atlantic coast to Texas. There the slave population grew almost six-fold between 1790 and 1860, from 697,897 to 3,953,760 (see Table 6-1). But slaves were not equally distributed across the region. Western North Carolina, eastern Tennessee, western Virginia, and most of Missouri never had many slaves. Their numbers grew fastest in the newer cotton-producing states, such as Alabama and Mississippi (see Map 6-2).

Virginia had the largest slave population throughout the period. But between 1820 and 1860, that population increased by only 15 percent, from 425,153 to 490,865. During the same 40 years, the slave population of Georgia increased by 209 percent, from 149,654 to 462,198, and that of Mississippi by 1,231 percent, from 32,814 to 436,631. By 1860 Mississippi and South Carolina were the only states with more slaves than free inhabitants. But it is important to note that this great increase took place even as the predominantly male slave populations in Latin America failed to reproduce themselves, and declined drastically before general emancipation.

6.1.2 Ownership of Slaves in the Old South

Slaveholders were as unevenly distributed across the South as slaves and, unlike slaves, declined in number. In 1830, 1,314,272 white southerners (36 percent of a total white southern population of 3,650,758) owned slaves. In 1860 only 383,673 white southerners (4.7 percent of a total white southern population of 8,097,463) owned slaves. Even counting the immediate families of slaveholders, only 1,900,000 (or less than 25 percent of the South's white population) had a direct interest in slavery in 1860.

Almost half of the South's slaveholders owned fewer than five slaves, only 12 percent owned more than 20 slaves, and just 1 percent owned more than 50 slaves. Yet more than half the slaves belonged to masters who had 20 or more slaves. So, although the typical slaveholder owned few slaves, the typical slave lived on a sizable plantation.

Since the time of Anthony Johnson in the mid-1600s, a few black people had been slaveholders, and this class continued to exist. In 1830, only 2 percent of free African Americans owned slaves. This amounted to 3,775 individuals. Many of them became slaveholders to protect their families from sale and disruption. This was because, as the nineteenth century progressed, southern states made it more difficult for masters to manumit slaves and for slaves to purchase their freedom. The states also threatened to expel former slaves from their territory. In response, black men and women sometimes purchased relatives who were in danger of sale to traders and who—if legally free—might be forced by white authorities to leave a state.

Some African Americans, however, purchased slaves for financial reasons and passed those slaves on to their heirs. Most black people who became masters for financial reasons owned five or fewer slaves. But William Johnson, a wealthy free black barber who lived in Natchez, Louisiana, owned many slaves whom he employed on a plantation he purchased. Some black women, such as Margaret Mitchell Harris of South Carolina and Betsy Somayrac of Natchitoches, Louisiana, also became slaveholders for economic reasons. Harris was a successful rice planter who inherited 21 slaves from her white father. She prospered by carefully managing her resources in land and slaves. By the time she sold out in 1849, she had more than 40 slaves and nearly 1,000 acres that produced 240,000 pounds of rice per year.

Table 6-1 U.S. Slave Population, 1820 and 1860

	1820	1860
United States	1,538,125	3,953,760
North	19,108	64
South	1,519,017	3,953,696
Upper South	965,514	1,530,229
Delaware	4,509	1,798
Kentucky	127,732	225,483
Maryland	107,397	87,189
Missouri	10,222	114,931
North Carolina	205,017	331,059
Tennessee	80,107	275,719
Virginia	425,153	490,865
Washington, D.C.	6,377	3,185
Lower South	553,503	2,423,467
Alabama	41,879	435,080
Arkansas	1,617	111,115
Florida	*	61,745
Georgia	149,654	462,198
Louisiana	69,064	331,726
Mississippi	32,814	436,631
South Carolina	258,475	402,406
Texas	*	182,566

*Florida and Texas were not states in 1820.

SOURCE: The U.S. Bureau of the Census, *Historical Statistics of the United States, Colonial Times to 1970*, vol. 2.

Map 6-2 Slave Population, 1820–1860

Slavery spread southwestward from the Upper South and the eastern seaboard following the spread of cotton cultivation.

SOURCE: Sam Bowers Hilliard, *Atlas of Antebellum Southern Agriculture* (Louisiana State University Press, 1984). Used with permission from Louisiana State University Press.

What does this map suggest about black life in the South?

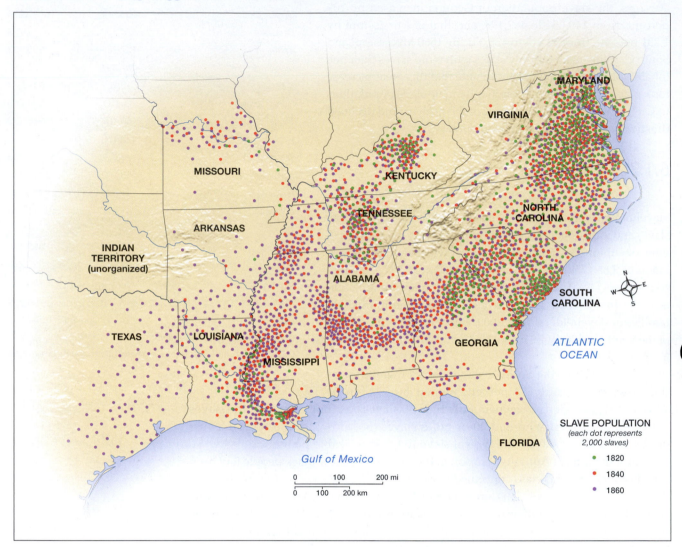

6.2 Slave Labor in Agriculture

Compare and contrast how slaves produced the South's various crops.

Agricultural laborers constituted 75 percent of the South's slave population. About 55 percent of the slaves cultivated cotton, 10 percent grew tobacco, and 10 percent produced sugar, rice, or hemp. About 15 percent were domestic servants, and the remaining 10 percent worked in trades and industries.

6.2.1 Tobacco

During the 1800s, tobacco remained important in Virginia, Maryland, Kentucky, and parts of North Carolina and Missouri (see Map 6-3). A difficult crop to produce, tobacco required a long growing season and careful cultivation. In the spring slaves had to transfer seedlings from sterilized seedbeds to well-worked and manured soil. Then they had to hoe weeds, pick off insects, and prune lower leaves so the topmost leaves grew to their full extent. Slaves also built scaffolds to cure the tobacco leaves and made the barrels used in shipping tobacco to market.

Profile

Solomon Northup

Solomon Nor Theep

IN HIS PLANTATION SUIT.

Solomon Northup's aspirations as a musician led in 1841 to his kidnapping and sale into slavery. For 12 years, he labored in the cotton and sugar regions of Louisiana, interacted with slaves and masters, and experienced firsthand what it was like to be caught up in a brutal labor system.

Northup was born free at Minerva, New York, in about 1808. His parents were prosperous farmers, and he became a farmer too, although he also worked occasionally as a violinist. He lived in Saratoga Springs, New York, with his wife and three children until March 1841, when two white men suggested that he become a musician in their circus, which was performing in Washington, D.C.

Enticed by the prospect of good wages and a chance to perform, Northup left with the two men without informing his wife or anyone else. Within two days of arriving in Washington, he was drugged, robbed of his money and free papers, chained, and sold to slave traders. After experiencing a terrible beating with a wooden paddle and a rope, Northup was shipped to New Orleans and sold to William Ford, who owned a cotton plantation and sawmill in Louisiana's Red River region.

As Ford's slave, Northup worked at the mill "piling lumber and chopping logs." Northup liked Ford and regarded him to be a "model master" who treated his slaves well and read scripture to them each Sunday. But when Ford became insolvent and sold his slaves, Northup had to deal with a series of brutal masters. They employed him as a carpenter, as a field hand on cotton and sugar plantations, and finally as a slave driver.

At one point when he was cutting lumber and building cabins, Northup was surprised to have several "large and stout" black women join in the forestry work. Later he observed women performing other demanding physical labor. "There are lumberwomen as well as lumbermen in the forests of the South," he reported. "In fact . . . they perform their share of all the labor required by the planters. They plough, dray, drive team, clear wild lands, work on the highway and so forth."

Subsequently, Northup spent 10 years as a slave of Edwin Epps, a cotton planter, who when drunk enjoyed forcing his slaves to dance. Northup noted that Epps's slaves received a meager diet of corn and bacon. They slept in crude, crowded cabins on planks of wood. During harvest season, "it was rarely that a day passed by without one or more whippings" as slaves failed to pick their quota. During a three-year period, Epps hired Northup out to "sugar plantations during the season of cane-cutting and sugar making" for $1.00 per day.

Northup had become Epps's slave driver by 1852, when he set in motion the events that led to his rescue. Deeply disturbed by being forced to whip other slaves, Northup conspired with a Canadian carpenter to smuggle a letter to two white businessmen in Saratoga Springs. The letter led the governor of New York to send Henry B. Northup—a member of the family that had owned Solomon Northup's father—to Louisiana to present evidence that Solomon Northup was a free man. By January 1853, he had been reunited with his family in New York. In July of that year he published *Twelve Years a Slave*, which sold over 30,000 copies and earned him enough money to purchase a home for his family in Glens Falls, New York, where he died in 1863.

Map 6-3 Agriculture, Industry, and Slavery in the Old South, 1850

The experience of the African American in slavery varied according to their occupation and the region of the South in which they lived.

To what degree did climate affect the type of crop slaves produced?

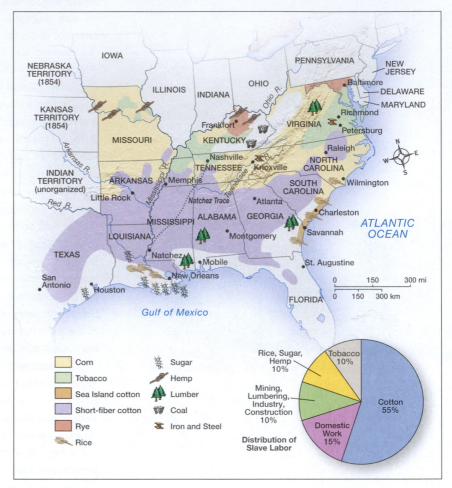

Robert Ellett, a former slave, recalled that when he was just eight years old he worked in Virginia "a-worming tobacco." He "examined tobacco leaves, pull[ed] off the worms, if there were any, and killed them." He claimed that if an overseer discovered that slaves had overlooked worms on the tobacco plants, the overseer had the slaves whipped or forced them to eat the worms. Nancy Williams, another Virginia slave, recalled that sometimes as a punishment slaves had to inhale burning tobacco until they became nauseated.

6.2.2 Rice

Unlike the cultivation of tobacco, which spread west and south from Maryland and Virginia, rice production remained confined to the South Carolina and Georgia low country. As they had since colonial times (see Chapter 3), slaves in these coastal regions worked according to task systems that allowed them considerable autonomy. But that did not make their work easy. Because rice fields needed to be flooded for the seeds to germinate, slaves maintained elaborate systems of dikes and ditches. Influenced by West African methods, they sowed, weeded, and harvested the rice crop.

Rice cultivation required intensive labor, and rice plantations needed large labor forces to grow and harvest the crop and maintain the fields. By 1860, 20 rice plantations had 300 to 500 slaves each, and eight others had between 500 and 1,000 slaves each. The only

American plantation employing more than 1,000 slaves was in the rice-producing region. Such vast plantations represented sizable capital investments, and masters or overseers carefully monitored slave productivity. Although slaves had considerable leeway in how they performed their assigned duties, those who missed a day's work risked forfeiting their weekly allowance "of either bacon, sugar, molasses, or tobacco."

6.2.3 Sugar

Another important crop that grew in a restricted region was sugar, which slaves cultivated on plantations along the Mississippi River in southern Louisiana. Commercial production of sugarcane did not begin in Louisiana until the 1790s. It required a consistently warm climate, a long growing season, and at least 60 inches of rain per year.

Raising sugarcane and refining sugar also required constant labor. Together with the great profitability of the sugar crop, these demands encouraged masters to work their slaves hard. Slave life on sugar plantations was harsh, and African Americans across the South feared being sent to labor on them. Historian Paul W. Gates details the work of slaves on sugar plantations:

> Fresh land was constantly being cleared, and the wood was used for fuel in the sugarhouses or was sold to steamboats. Levees had to be raised; ditching and draining was never completed. Planting, numerous hoeings, cutting, loading and unloading the cane, putting it through the mill, feeding the boilers, moving the huge hogsheads of sugar and molasses and drawing them to the boat landing, setting aside the seed cane, hauling the bagasse to the fields—all this took much labor.

Slaves did this work in hot and humid conditions, adding to the toll it took on their strength and health. Because cane could not be allowed to stand too long in the fields, harvest time was hectic. As one former slave recalled, "On cane plantations in sugar time, there is no distinction as to the days of the week. They [the slaves] worked on the Sabbath as if it were Monday or Thursday."

6.2.4 Cotton

Although tobacco, rice, and sugar were economically significant, cotton was by far the South's and the country's most important staple crop. By 1860 cotton exports amounted to more than 50 percent of the annual dollar value of all U.S. exports (see Figure 6-1). This was almost 10 times the value of cotton's nearest export competitors, wheat and wheat flour.

Cotton as a crop did not require cultivation as intensive as that needed for tobacco, rice, or sugar. However, the cotton culture was so extensive that cotton planters as a group employed the most slave labor. By 1860, out of the 2,500,000 slaves employed in agriculture in the United States, 1,815,000 of them produced cotton. Cotton drove the South's economy and its westward expansion. Even in rice-producing South Carolina and sugar-producing Louisiana, cotton dominated, and cotton plantations employed the bulk of the slave populations.

Demand for cotton fiber in the textile mills of Britain and New England stimulated the westward spread of cotton cultivation. Between 1830 and 1860, this demand increased by at least 5 percent per year. In response—and with the essential aid of Whitney's cotton gin—American production of cotton rose

Figure 6-1 Cotton Exports as a Percentage of all U.S. Exports, 1800–1860

Cotton rapidly emerged as the country's most important export crop after 1800 and was key to its prosperity. Because slave labor produced the cotton, increasing exports strengthened the slave system itself.

from 3,000 bales in 1790 to 731,000 in 1830 to 3,837,000 in 1860. The new states of Alabama, Louisiana, and Mississippi led in this mounting production.

Picturesque scenes of ripening cotton fields are part of the romantic image of the Old South that novels, songs, and movies perpetuated. Even a former slave could recall that "few sights are more pleasant to the eye than a wide cotton field when it is in full bloom. It presents an appearance of purity, like an immaculate expanse of light, new-fallen snow." Yet such scenes mask the backbreaking labor enslaved African Americans performed and the anxiety and fear they experienced.

During the early nineteenth century, potential profits drew white farmers to the rich Black Belt lands of Mississippi and Alabama. Rapid population growth allowed Mississippi to gain statehood in 1817 and Alabama in 1819. By 1860 these states had become the leading cotton producers. They also had the greatest concentration of plantations with one hundred or more slaves. Twenty-four of Mississippi's slaveholders each owned between 308 and 899 slaves.

As huge agricultural units drew in labor, the price of slaves increased. During the 1830s, a prime male field hand sold in the New Orleans slave market for $1,250 (about $32,000 today). Prices dipped during the hard times of the early 1840s. But, by the 1850s, such slaves cost $1,800 (more than $52,000 today). Young women usually sold for up to $500 less than young men. Elderly slaves, unless they were highly skilled, sold for far less.

The enslaved men and women who worked in the cotton fields rose before dawn when the master or overseer sounded the plantation bell or horn. They ate breakfast and then assembled in work gangs of 20 or 25 under the control of black slave drivers. They plowed and planted in the spring. They weeded with heavy hoes in the summer and harvested in the late fall. During harvest season, adult slaves picked about 200 pounds of cotton per day. Regardless of the season, the work was hard, and white overseers whipped those who seemed to be lagging. Slaves usually had a two-hour break at midday in the summer and an hour to an hour and a half in the winter. Then they returned to the fields until sunset, when they went back to their cabins for dinner and an early bedtime enforced by the master or overseer.

Frederick Law Olmsted, a northern traveler, described a large gang of Mississippi slaves he saw in 1854 marching home early because of rain:

> First came, led by an old driver carrying a whip, forty of the largest and strongest women I ever saw together; they were all in a single uniform dress of a bluish check stuff, the skirts reaching little below the knee; their legs and feet were bare; they carried themselves loftily, each having a hoe over the shoulder, and walking with a free, powerful swing. Behind them came the [plow hands and their mules], thirty strong, mostly men, but a few of them women. . . . A lean and vigilant white overseer, on a brisk pony, brought up the rear. The men wore small blue Scotch bonnets; many of the women handkerchiefs, turban fashion. . . . They were evidently a picked lot. I thought every one could pass for a "prime" cotton hand.

6.2.5 Cotton and Technology

Agricultural technology in the Cotton Kingdom was primitive compared to that in the Old Northwest. Free northwestern farmers by the 1840s used a variety of machines, drawn by teams of horses and constructed of wood and iron, to plant, cultivate, and harvest crops. In contrast, southern slave workers relied on simple plows and harrows, drawn by a single mule—as well as handheld shovels, rakes, and heavy hoes—to perform similar work. Masters did not trust slaves with expensive machinery. They also preferred to invest in slaves and land rather than labor-saving devices. And the nature of the South's major crop had an essential impact. Because cotton ripened unevenly, nineteenth-century mechanical harvesters could not discern which plants were ready

By the early nineteenth century many slaves in Delaware, Maryland, and Virginia were cultivating wheat rather than tobacco. This 1831 lithograph portrays a demonstration of Cyrus McCormick's automatic reaper. It indicates the adaptability of slave labor to new technology.

for harvest. Therefore, three times each harvest season, enslaved men, women, and children picked cotton bolls by hand. They had long sacks tied to their waists or hung from their shoulders to hold the bolls.

Nineteenth-century technology nevertheless impacted slaves' lives. Although the South lagged behind the North and Britain in applying steam power to transportation, it surpassed continental Europe and other regions of the world. After 1811 the Mississippi River teamed with steamboats. Railroads helped open the Old Southwest to cotton production, which encouraged the growth of the domestic slave trade and the disruption of black families.

In some instances technology improved plantation conditions. Early in the nineteenth century, cotton gins became much larger and more efficient than the ones Eli Whitney designed during the 1790s. Enslaved men operated gins powered by mules attached to long "sweeps" walking in circles. Once bolls had been cleaned of their seeds, slaves used presses, driven by huge screws turned by either man or mule power, to form bales. Slaves packaged the bales in cloth bagging and took them by wagon to river steamboat landings for shipment to market.

The technology available to enslaved women on cotton plantations was less sophisticated. They used heavy cast-iron kettles for cooking food and washing clothes. Washing involved boiling garments in soapy water, beating them with "battling sticks" on "battling blocks," and returning them for another boiling before hanging them out to dry.

6.2.6 Other Crops

Besides cotton, sugar, tobacco, and rice, slaves in the Old South produced hemp, corn, wheat, oats, rye, white potatoes, and sweet potatoes. They also raised cattle, hogs, sheep, and horses. The hogs and corn were mainly for consumption on the plantations. But all the hemp and much of the other livestock and wheat went to market. In fact, wheat replaced tobacco as the main cash crop in much of Maryland and Virginia. The transition to wheat encouraged many planters to substitute free labor for slave labor, but slaves continued to grow wheat in the South until the Civil War.

The hemp industry centered in Kentucky. Before the Civil War, planters used hemp, which is closely related to marijuana, to make rope and bagging for cotton bales. This tied Kentucky economically to the Deep South. But, because hemp required much less labor than rice, sugar, or cotton, Kentucky developed a distinctive slave system. Three slaves could tend 50 acres of hemp, so slave labor forces were much smaller there than elsewhere. Robert Wickliffe, the largest Kentucky slaveholder during the 1840s, owned 200 slaves—a large number but far fewer than his counterparts in the Cotton Belt.

6.3 House Servants and Skilled Slaves

Describe how the work of house slaves and skilled slaves differed from the work of agricultural slaves.

About 75 percent of the slave workforce in the nineteenth century consisted of field hands. But because masters wanted to make their plantations as self-sufficient as possible, they also employed slaves as house servants and skilled craftsmen. Slaves who did not have to do field labor were an elite group. Those who performed domestic duties, drove carriages, or learned a craft considered themselves privileged. However, they were also suspended between two different worlds.

House slaves worked as cooks, maids, butlers, nurses, and gardeners. Their work was less physically demanding than fieldwork, and they often received better food and clothing. Nevertheless nineteenth-century kitchen work was grueling, and maids and butlers were on call at all hours. House servants' jobs were also more stressful than field hands' jobs because the servants were under closer white supervision.

In addition, house servants were by necessity cut off from the slave community centered in the slave quarters. Yet, as Olmsted pointed out during the 1850s, house servants rarely sought to become field hands. Conversely, field hands had little desire to be exposed to the constant surveillance house servants had to tolerate. As Olmsted put it,

> Slaves brought up to housework dread to be employed at field-labor; and those accustomed to the comparatively unconstrained life of the Negro-settlement detest the close control and careful movements required of the house-servants. It is a punishment of a lazy field hand to employ him in menial duties at the house . . . and it is equally a punishment to a neglectful house-servant, to banish him to the field-gangs.

Skilled slaves tended to be even more a slave elite than house servants were. As had been true earlier, black men had a decided advantage over black women—apart from those who were seamstresses—in becoming skilled. Slave carpenters, blacksmiths, and millwrights built and maintained plantation houses, slave quarters, and machinery. Because they might need to travel to get tools or spare parts, such skilled slaves gained a more cosmopolitan outlook than field hands or house servants. They got a taste of freedom, which from the masters' point of view was dangerous.

As plantation slavery declined in the Chesapeake, skilled slaves could leave their master's estate to "hire their time." Either they or their masters negotiated labor contracts with employers who needed their expertise. In effect, these slaves worked for money. Although masters often kept all or most of what they earned, some of these skilled slaves merely paid their master a set rate and lived as independent contractors.

6.3.1 Urban and Industrial Slavery

Most skilled slaves who hired their time lived in the South's towns and cities, where they interacted with free black communities. Many of them resided in Baltimore and New Orleans, which were major ports and the Old South's largest cities. But there were others in such smaller southern urban centers as Richmond and Norfolk, Virginia;

Atlanta and Augusta, Georgia; Washington, D.C.; Charleston, South Carolina; Louisville, Kentucky; and Memphis, Tennessee.

Slave populations in southern cities were often large, although they tended to decline between 1800 and 1860. In 1840 slaves were a majority of Charleston's population of 29,000. They nearly equaled white residents in Memphis and Augusta, which had total populations of 14,700 and 6,000, respectively. Slaves constituted almost one-quarter of New Orleans's population of 145,000 (see Map 6-4).

As the young Frederick Douglass found when his master sent him from rural Maryland to Baltimore during the late 1830s, life in a city could be much more complicated for a slave than life on a plantation. When urban slaves were not working for their masters, they could earn money for themselves. As a result, masters had a harder time controlling their lives. Those who contracted to provide their masters with a certain amount of money per year could live on their own, buying their food and clothing. "You couldn't pay me," observed one enslaved woman, "to live at home if I could help myself."

Urban slaves served as domestics, washwomen, waiters, artisans, stevedores, drayers, hack drivers, and general laborers. In general, they did the urban work that foreign immigrants undertook in northern cities. If urban slaves purchased their freedom, they usually continued in the same work they had done as slaves. Particularly in border cities like Baltimore, Louisville, and Washington, urban slaves increasingly relied on their free black neighbors—and sympathetic white people—to escape north. Urban masters often let slaves purchase their freedom over a term of years to keep them from leaving. In Baltimore, during the early nineteenth century, this "**term slavery**" was gradually replacing slavery for life.

term slavery

A type of slavery prevalent in the Chesapeake from the late 1700s to the Civil War in which slaves were able to purchase their freedom from their masters by earning money over a number of years.

Map 6-4 Population Percentages in the Southern States, 1850

The percentage of slaves, free African Americans, and white people varied from state to state. In the Upper South, white populations were substantially larger than black populations. In the Deep South, however, the races were more in balance.

SOURCE: Faragher, John Mack; Buhle, Mari Jo; Czitrom, Daniel H.; Armitage, Susan H., *Out of Many: A History of the American People,* 4th ed., p. 333. Reprinted and Electronically Reproduced by Permission of Pearson Education, Inc.

In which two states were there black majorities in 1850, and why?

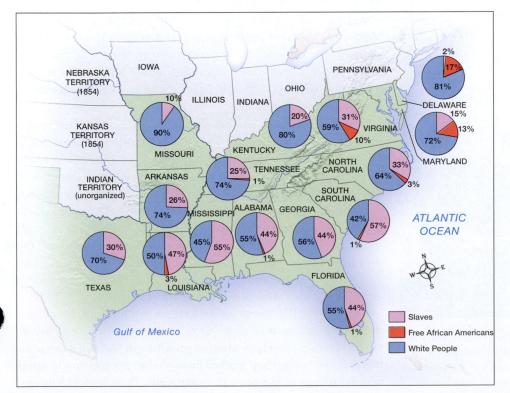

Industrial slavery overlapped with urban slavery, but southern industries that employed slaves were often in rural areas. By 1860 about 5 percent of southern slaves—approximately 200,000 people—worked in industry. Enslaved men, women, and children worked in textile mills in South Carolina and Georgia, sometimes beside white people. In Richmond and Petersburg, Virginia, during the 1850s, about 6,000 slaves, most of whom were men, worked in factories producing chewing tobacco. Richmond's famous Tredegar Iron Works also employed a large slave workforce. So did earlier southern ironworks in Virginia, Maryland, northern Tennessee, and southern Kentucky.

The bulk of the 16,000 people who worked in the South's lumber industry in 1860 were slaves. Under the supervision of black drivers, they felled trees, operated sawmills, and delivered lumber. Slaves also did most of the work in the naval stores industry of North Carolina and Georgia, manufacturing tar, turpentine, and related products. In western Virginia, they labored in the salt works of the Great Kanawha River Valley, producing the salt used to preserve meat—especially the southern mainstay salt pork. During the 1820s many workers in the Maryland Chemical Works in Baltimore, which manufactured industrial chemicals, pigments, and medicines, were slaves.

Most southern industrialists did not purchase slaves. Instead, they hired slaves from their masters. The industrial work slaves performed was often dangerous and tiring. But, as historian John B. Boles points out, slaves came to prefer industrial jobs to plantation labor. Like urban slaves, industrial slaves had more opportunities to advance themselves, enjoyed more autonomy, and often received cash incentives. Industrial labor, like urban labor, was a path to freedom for some.

Enslaved black women often had the responsibility of raising their masters' young children. The women's duties sometimes forced them to neglect the needs of their own children.

6.4 Punishment

Evaluate the role of punishment in slavery.

Those who used slave labor, whether on plantations, on small farms, in urban areas, or in industry, frequently offered incentives to induce slaves to perform well. Yet slave labor by definition is forced labor based on the threat of physical punishment. Masters denied that this brutal aspect detracted from what they claimed was the essentially benign and paternalistic character of the South's "peculiar institution." After all, Christian masters found support in the Bible for using corporal punishment to chastise servants.

White southerners also believed that African Americans would not work unless threatened with beatings. Olmsted reported that in Mississippi he had observed a young girl subjected to "the severest corporal punishment" he had ever seen. The white overseer, who had administered the flogging with a rawhide whip "across her naked loins and thighs," told Olmsted that the girl had been shirking her duties. He claimed that "if I hadn't [punished her so hard] she would have done the same thing again to-morrow, and half the people on the plantation would have followed her example. Oh, you've no idea how lazy these niggers are. . . . They'd never do any work at all if they were not afraid of being whipped."

Fear of the lash drove slaves to work *and* to cooperate among themselves for mutual protection. Parents and older relatives taught slave children how to avoid punishment and still resist masters and overseers. They worked slowly—but not too slowly—and feigned illness to maintain their strength. They broke tools and

In this 1863 photograph, a former Louisiana slave displays the scars that resulted from repeated whippings. Although this degree of scarring is exceptional, few slaves were able to avoid being whipped at least once in their lives.

Voices

Frederick Douglass on the Readiness of Masters to Use the Whip

This passage from the Narrative of the Life of Frederick Douglass, An American Slave, *published in 1845, suggests the volatile relationship between slaves and masters that could quickly result in violence. As Douglass makes clear, masters and overseers used the whip not just to force slaves to work but also to enforce a distinction between what was proper and even laudable for white men and what was forbidden behavior for slaves.*

It would astonish one, unaccustomed to a slaveholding life, to see with what wonderful ease a slaveholder can find things of which to make occasion to whip a slave. A mere look, word, or motion—a mistake, accident, or want of power—are all matters for which a slave may be whipped at any time. Does a slave look dissatisfied? It is said, he has the devil in him, and it must be whipped out. Does he speak loudly when spoken to by his masters? Then he is getting high-minded, and should be taken down a button-hole lower. Does he forget to pull off his hat at the approach of a white person? Then he is wanting in reverence, and should be whipped for it. Does he ever venture to vindicate his conduct, when censured for it? Then he is guilty of impudence—one of the greatest crimes of which a slave can be guilty. Does he ever venture to suggest a different mode of doing things from that pointed out by his master? He is indeed presumptuous, and getting above himself; and nothing less than a flogging will do for him. Does he, while plowing, break a plough—or, while hoeing, break a hoe? It is owing to his carelessness, and for it a slave must always be whipped.

1. Why did masters and overseers whip slaves?
2. Given the behavior by masters that Douglass describes, how were slaves likely to act around white people?

SOURCE: *The Narrative of the Life of Frederick Douglass, An American Slave,* Published in 1845.

injured mules, oxen, and horses to tacitly protest their condition. This interplay of covert resistance and physical punishment caused anxiety for both masters and slaves. Resistance (described in more detail in Chapter 3) often forced masters to reduce work hours and improve conditions. Yet few slaves escaped being whipped at least once during their lives in bondage.

6.5 The Domestic Slave Trade

Describe the characteristics and impact of the domestic slave trade as it existed between 1820 and 1860.

The expansion of the Cotton Kingdom south and west, combined with the decline of slavery in the Chesapeake, stimulated the domestic slave trade. As masters in Delaware, Maryland, Virginia, North Carolina, and Kentucky trimmed excess slaves from their workforces—or switched entirely from slave to wage labor—they sold men, women, and children to slave traders. The traders in turn shipped these unfortunate people to the slave markets of New Orleans and other cities for resale. Masters also sold slaves as punishment, and fear of being "sold down river" led many slaves in the Chesapeake to escape. A vicious circle resulted: Masters sold slaves south to prevent their escape, and slaves escaped to avoid being sold south.

Some slave songs record the anxiety of those facing separation from loved ones as a result of the domestic trade. One song laments the sale of a man sold away from his wife and family:

William Rino sold Henry Silvers;
Hilo! Hilo!
Sold him to de Gorgy [Georgia] trader;
Hilo! Hilo!
His wife she cried, and children bawled

A slave-coffle passing the Capitol.

coffle

A file of slaves chained together that was typical of the domestic slave trade.

Hilo! Hilo!
Sold him to de Gorgy trader;
Hilo! Hilo!
. . .
See wives and husbands sold apart,
Their children's screams will break my heart;—
There's a better day coming,
Will you go along with me?
There's a better day a coming,
Go sound the jubilee!

The number of people traded was huge and, considering that many of them were ripped away from their families, tragic. Starting in the 1820s, about 150,000 slaves per decade moved toward the southwest either with their masters or traders. Between 1820 and 1860, an estimated 50 percent of the slaves of the Upper South moved involuntarily into the Southwest.

Traders operated compounds called slave prisons or slave pens in Baltimore; Washington, D.C.; Alexandria and Richmond, Virginia; Lexington, Kentucky; Charleston, South Carolina; and in smaller cities. Most of the victims of the trade moved on foot in groups called **coffles**, chained or roped together. From the 1810s onward, northern and European visitors to Washington noted the coffles passing by the U.S. Capitol. There was also a considerable coastal trade in slaves from Chesapeake ports to New Orleans, and by the 1840s some traders transported their human cargoes in railroad cars.

The domestic slave trade demonstrated the falseness of slaveholders' portrayal of slavery as a benign institution. Driven by economic necessity, profit, or a desire to frustrate escape plans, masters in the upper South irrevocably separated husbands and wives, mothers and children, and brothers and sisters. Traders sometimes tore babies from their mothers' arms. The journey from the Chesapeake to Mississippi, Alabama, or Louisiana could be long and hard, and some slaves died along the way. A few managed to keep in touch with those they had left behind through letters and travelers, but most could not. After the abolition of slavery in 1865, many African Americans used their new freedom to travel across the South looking for relatives from whom they had been separated long before.

6.6 Slave Families

Discuss the various factors that shaped black life in the Cotton Kingdom.

The families that enslaved African Americans sought to preserve had been developing in America since the seventeenth century. However, such families had no legal standing. Most enslaved men and women could choose their mates, although masters sometimes arranged such things. Masters encouraged pairings among female and male slaves because they assumed correctly that husbands and fathers would be less rebellious than single men. Masters also knew that they would benefit if their human chattel reproduced. As Thomas Jefferson put it, "I consider a [slave] woman who brings [gives birth to] a child every two years as more profitable than the best man on the farm. What she produces is an addition to the capital, while his labors disappear in mere consumption."

For African Americans, however, a family's importance transcended economics. Families were the core of the black community. Even though no legal sanctions supported slave marriages and the domestic slave trade could sunder them, many such marriages endured. Before they wed, some couples engaged in courting rituals, while others rejected

Profile

William Ellison

The life of William Ellison, who was born a slave in the Fairfield district of South Carolina in 1790 and named *April* by his master, exemplifies several of the themes of this chapter. He was a skilled slave, used what he knew to save enough to purchase his freedom, and subsequently became a slaveholder himself. His story came to light in 1935 when three white children, playing in the crawlspace under his former home, discovered his personal papers.

The son of a slave mother and an unknown white father, Ellison received special treatment from his owner, who apprenticed him at age 12 to a skilled white craftsman named William McCreight. Together with several white apprentices, Ellison learned carpentry, blacksmithing, and how to repair cotton gins. He also learned how to conduct a business. He did so well that in 1816, when he was 26, he purchased his freedom.

Once free, Ellison petitioned a court to change his name from his slave name *April* to *William*, in honor of his mentor—or perhaps his father. With freedom, skills, and a new name, Ellison opened a gin-making and gin-repair shop in Statesburg, South Carolina. Like the Natchez, Mississippi, barber William Johnson, Ellison achieved a respectable reputation among his white clients and neighbors as a churchgoing businessman. On the surface at least, his ties to his slave past diminished as he prospered. Because his income depended on white slaveholders, he did nothing to antagonize them.

As a result, Ellison became one of the wealthiest owners of real and personal property in the South. He owned hundreds of acres of farmland and woodland worth at least $8,250 (about $231,000 today). As early as 1820, he owned two slaves. In 1830 he owned four, and in 1840 he owned 26. By 1860 he owned 63 and was worth in personal property alone $53,000 (about $1,500,000 today).

Ellison assigned tasks to his slaves according to their gender and age. The field hands—mostly women and children—produced 80 bales of cotton each in 1850. They also raised thousands of bushels of corn, sweet potatoes, and other vegetables each year. The gin shop workers—men and adolescent boys—worked as blacksmiths, carpenters, and mechanics.

When South Carolina seceded from the Union in December 1860 and the Civil War began a few months later, Ellison and his family were caught between two contradictory forces. During the war, South Carolina's state government considered free African Americans potential traitors and curtailed their liberty. Meanwhile, the Union moved relentlessly toward immediate, uncompensated emancipation. Ellison, who died on December 5, 1861, did not live to see the emancipation of his slaves in 1865. But his children did. They also saw the destruction of his business when its newly emancipated workers refused to continue to work for the Ellisons as free men and women.

"such foolishness." Similarly, slave pairings ranged from simply "taking up" and living together to religious wedding ceremonies replete with food and frolics.

These ceremonies often included "jumping the broom," although this custom was not African but European. During the 1930s former slave Tempie Herndon recalled her wedding ceremony conducted by "de nigger preacher dat preached at de plantation church." In particular, she remembered that after the religious ceremony, "Marse George got to have his little fun" by having the newlyweds jump backward over a broomstick. "You got to do dat to see which one gwine be boss of your household," she commented. "If both of dem jump over without touchin' it, dey won't gwine be no bossin', dey just gwine be congenial." In fact, more equality existed between husbands and wives in slave marriages than in those of the masters. Southern white concepts of patriarchy required male dominance. But because black men lacked power, their wives were more like partners than servants.

Enslaved couples usually lived together in cabins on their master's property. They had little privacy because

This woodcut of a black father being sold away from his family appeared in *The Child's Anti-Slavery Book* in 1860. Family ruptures, like the one shown, were among the more common and tragic aspects to slavery, especially in the Upper South, where masters claimed slavery was "mild."

nineteenth-century slave cabins were crude, small, one-room dwellings that two families might have to share. But couples who shared cabins were generally better off than husbands and wives who lived on different plantations as the property of different masters. In these cases, children lived with their mother, and their father visited when he could in the evenings. Work patterns that changed with the seasons or with the mood of a master could interfere with such visits. So could the requirement that slaves have passes to leave home.

6.6.1 Children

Despite these difficulties, enslaved parents instructed their children in family history, religion, and the skills required to survive in slavery. They sang to their children and told them stories full of folk wisdom. In particular, they impressed on them the importance of extended family relationships. The ability to rely on grandparents, aunts and uncles, cousins, and honorary relatives served as a hedge against the family disruption that the domestic slave trade might inflict. In this manner, too, the extended black family provided slaves with the resources they needed to avoid complete physical, intellectual, cultural, and moral subjugation to their masters.

During an age when infant mortality rates were much higher than they are today, those rates for black southerners were even higher than they were for white people. There were several reasons for this. Enslaved black women usually performed field labor up to the time they delivered a child, and their diets lacked necessary nutrients. Consequently, they tended to have babies whose weights at birth were less than normal. Enslaved infants were also more likely than other children to be subject to such postpartum maladies as rickets, tetany, tetanus, high fevers, intestinal worms, and influenza. More than 50 percent of slave children died before the age of five.

Slaveholders contributed to high infant mortality rates probably more from ignorance than malevolence. It was, after all, in the master's economic self-interest to have slave mothers produce healthy children. Masters often allowed mothers a month

Voices

A Slaveholder Describes a New Purchase

In this letter to her mother, a white Louisiana woman, Tryphena Blanche Holder Fox, describes her husband's purchase of a slave woman and her children. Several things are apparent in the letter—that investing in slaves was expensive, that the white woman's only concern for the slave woman and her children was their economic value, that it was up to the white woman to supervise the new slaves, and that the slave woman showed her displeasure with her situation.

Hygiene [Jesuit Bend, Louisiana]

Sunday, Dec 27, 1857

Dear Mother,

We are obliged to save every dollar he can "rake & scrape" to pay for a negro woman. . . . She has two likely children . . . and is soon to have another, and he only pays fourteen hundred for the three. She is considered an excellent bargain . . . he would not sell her and the children for less than $2,000. She came & worked two days, so we could see what she was capable of. . . . She was sold by a Frenchman. . . . He has a family of ten & she had all the work to do besides getting her own wood & water from the river. She was not used to do this, and gave them a great deal of trouble. . . . How much trouble she will give me, I don't know, but I think I can get along with her, passable well any how. Of course it increased my cares, for having invested so much in one purchase, it will be to my interest to see that the children are well taken care of clothed and fed. All of them give more or less trouble. . . .

1. What does Tryphena reveal about the management of slaves?

2. What does she indicate about the ability of slaves to force concessions from their masters?

SOURCE: Tryphena Blanche Holder Fox to Anna Rose Holder, December 27, 1857, Mississippi Department of Archives and History, Jackson, Mississippi.

to recuperate after giving birth and several months thereafter off from fieldwork to nurse their babies. Although this reduced the mother's productivity, the children's labor might make up the loss when they entered the plantation workforce. Unfortunately, many infants needed more than a few months of breast-feeding to survive.

The care of enslaved children varied with the size of a slave-holder's estate, the region it was in, and the mother's work. House servants could carry their babies with them while they worked. On small farms, enslaved women strapped their babies to their backs or left them at the edge of fields, so they could nurse them periodically, although the latter practice risked exposing an infant to ants, flies, or mosquitoes. On larger plantations, mothers could leave a child with an elderly or infirm adult. This encouraged the sense of black community, as it rested on shared responsibility among the slaves for all black children on a plantation.

As children grew older, they spent much time in unsupervised play, often with white children. Boys played marbles and ball games; girls skipped rope and tended to their dolls. A game of hiding and whipping, similar to the more recent cops and robbers game, amounted to a childish commentary on a violent system.

Black children began doing "light chores" in cotton fields at an early age. These girls are collecting cotton bolls that older workers missed.

Slave childhood was short. Early on, parents and others taught youngsters about the realities of plantation life. As early as age six, children undertook so-called light chores. Work became more taxing as they grew older, until, between the ages of 8 and 12, they performed adult fieldwork. Sale away from families, particularly in the Upper South, accelerated transition to adulthood.

6.6.2 Sexual Exploitation

As with forced separations, masters' sexual exploitation of black women disrupted enslaved families. Abuse of black women began during the Middle Passage and continued after the abolition of slavery in the United States in 1865.

Long-term relationships between masters and enslaved women were common in the nineteenth-century South. Such continuing relationships rested not on overt coercion but on masters' implicit power and authority. The relationship between Thomas Jefferson and his slave Sally Hemings is the most infamous of these. DNA and circumstantial evidence indicate that Jefferson and Hemings had a long sexual relationship that produced four children who survived to adulthood. It began in 1787 when Hemings served as caretaker to one of Jefferson's daughters at his household in Paris, where he was U.S. ambassador to France. At that time Jefferson was 44 and Hemings about 14. She was pregnant when she returned to Virginia in 1789, although the child probably died in infancy.

There is evidence that Hemings and her children enjoyed special privileges on Jefferson's Monticello plantation. But, by modern standards, her relationship to Jefferson began with statutory rape, and Hemings's unfree status and that of her children limited her ability to resist his sexual advances. Two of Hemings's children, a man named Beverly and a woman named Harriet, were "allowed" to escape in 1821 or 1822. Thereafter, they lived as white people in Washington, D.C. Two others, Madison and Eston, gained freedom as young men under Jefferson's will. Jefferson never freed Sally Hemings. Instead, his daughter permitted her to leave Monticello shortly after his death in 1826. She lived with Madison and Eston in Charlotte, Virginia, until her death in 1835.

Even more common than relationships like that of Jefferson and Hemings were instances in which masters, overseers, and their sons forced slave women to have

Throughout its existence, slavery in America encouraged white men to exploit black women for sexual purposes and to abuse black men and women physically. *Virginian Luxuries*, painted c. 1810, aimed to expose and ridicule these practices.

sex against their will. This routine rape caused great distress. Former slave Harriet Jacobs wrote in her autobiography, "I cannot tell how much I suffered in the presence of these wrongs, nor how I am still pained by the retrospect." One of the more notorious antebellum—pre–Civil War—cases of forced sexual exploitation occurred in Missouri during the 1850s. It involved 60-year-old Robert Newsom and Celia, a 14-year-old girl he had purchased in 1850. Newsom repeatedly raped Celia until she killed him in 1855. Celia's attorneys put up a spirited defense at her trial. They argued that an 1845 Missouri law that made it a crime to "take any woman unlawfully against her will and by force, menace or duress, compel her to be defiled" gave Celia a right to defend her virtue. But the white male jury convicted her of murder, and she was executed.

White southerners justified sexual abuse of black women in several ways. They maintained that black women were naturally promiscuous and seduced white men. Some proslavery apologists argued that the sexual exploitation of black women by white men reduced prostitution and promoted purity among white women. These apologists ignored the devastating emotional impact of sexual exploitation on black women. They failed to note that the rape of black women by white men emphasized in the most degrading manner the inability of black men to protect their wives and daughters.

6.6.3 Diet

The slaves' diet hardly raised the moral issues associated with the sexual exploitation of black women by white men. The typical plantation's weekly ration of one peck of cornmeal (about 14 pounds) and three to four pounds of salt pork or bacon was enough to maintain an adult's body weight and, therefore, appeared to be adequate. But even when black men and women added vegetables, eggs, and poultry that they raised or fish and small game that they caught, this diet was (according to modern medical science) deficient in calcium, vitamin C, riboflavin, protein, and iron and other minerals. Because these nutrients are essential to the health of people who perform hard labor in a hot climate, slaves frequently suffered from chronic illnesses.

They often complained about being hungry and the poor quality of their food. As one song went,

> We raise de wheat,
> Dey gib us de corn;
> We bake de bread,
> Dey gib us de crust;
> We sif' de meal,
> Dey gib us de huss;
> We peel de meat,
> Dey gib us de skin

Yet masters and white southerners generally consumed the same sort of food that slaves ate, and, in comparison to people in other parts of the Atlantic world, enslaved African Americans were not undernourished. Although adult slaves were on average an inch shorter than white northerners, they were three inches taller than new arrivals from Africa, two inches taller than slaves who lived in the West Indies, and one inch taller than British Royal Marines.

African-American cooks, primarily women, developed a distinctive cuisine based on African culinary traditions. They seasoned foods with salt, onions, pepper, and other spices and herbs. They fried meat and fish, served sauce over rice, and flavored vegetables with bits of smoked meat. The availability in the South of such African foods as okra, yams, collard greens, benne seeds, and peanuts strengthened their culinary ties to that continent. Cooking also gave black women the ability to control part of their lives and demonstrate their creativity.

6.6.4 Clothing

Enslaved men and women had less control over what they and their children wore than how they cooked. Although skilled slaves often produced the shoes and clothing plantation workers wore, slaves in general rarely had the time or skill to make their clothes. They went barefoot during the warm months and wore cheap shoes, usually made by local cobblers, in the winter. Slaveholding women, with the help of trained female house servants, sewed the clothes slaves wore. They usually used homespun cotton or wool to make the clothing. Some slaves also received hand-me-downs from masters and overseers.

Although distribution of clothing varied widely over time and space and according to the generosity of masters, slaves usually received clothing allotments twice a year. In the fall, enslaved men received two outfits for the approaching cold weather along with a jacket and a wool cap. In the spring, they received two cotton outfits. Slave drivers wore garments of finer cloth and greatcoats during the winter. Butlers and carriage drivers wore liveries appropriate to their public duties. Enslaved women received at each distribution two simple dresses of calico or homespun. In the winter they wore capes or cloaks and covered their heads with kerchiefs or bonnets.

Because masters gave priority to clothing adult workers, small children often went naked during the warm months. Depending on their ages and the season, children received garments called *shirts* if worn by boys and *shifts* if worn by girls. "I ain' neber had no pants 'till de year befo' de [Civil] war. All de li'l boys wo' shu't-tail shu'ts, jes' a slip to de knees," recalled former Louisiana slave Jacob Branch. This androgynous garb lasted until children reached "about twelve or fourteen," when they began doing adult work.

Although enslaved women received standard-issue clothing, they sought to individualize what they wore. They changed the colors of clothes with dyes they extracted from roots, berries, walnut shells, oak leaves, and indigo. They wove threads of different colors into their clothes to make "checkedy" and other patterns. Former slave Morris Sheppard remembered that with his mother "everything was stripedy."

6.6.5 Health

Low birth weight, diet, and clothing all affected the health of slaves. Before the 1830s diseases were endemic among them, and death could come quickly. Much of this ill health resulted from overwork in the South's hot, humid summers; exposure to cold during the winter; and poor hygiene. Slave quarters rarely had privies; human waste could contaminate drinking water; and food was prepared under unsanitary conditions. Dysentery, typhus, food poisoning, diarrhea, hepatitis, tuberculosis, typhoid fever, salmonella, and intestinal worms were common and often fatal maladies.

The South's warm climate encouraged mosquito-borne diseases such as yellow fever and malaria, the growth of bacteria, and the spread of viruses. Interaction between people of African and European descent increased the types of illnesses. Smallpox, measles, and gonorrhea came from Europe. Malaria, hookworm, and yellow fever came from Africa. The sickle-cell blood trait protected people of African descent from malaria but could cause sickle-cell anemia, a painful, debilitating, and fatal disease.

African Americans also had greater susceptibility to certain other afflictions than did persons of European descent. Black people suffered from lactose intolerance, which greatly limited the amount of calcium they could absorb from dairy products, and from a limited ability to acquire vitamin D from sunlight in temperate regions. Because many slaves lost calcium through perspiration while working, these tendencies led to a high incidence of debilitating diseases. They included, according to historian Donald R. Wright, "blindness or inflamed and watery eyes; lameness or crooked limbs; loose, missing or rotten teeth; and skin sores. Also, they made African Americans much more apt than whites to suffer from a number of often fatal diseases—tetanus, intestinal worms, diphtheria, whooping cough, pica (or dirt eating), pneumonia, tuberculosis, and dysentery."

However, black southerners constituted the only New World slave population that grew by natural reproduction. Although slaves had a higher mortality rate than white southerners, they had a similar one to that of Europeans. Slave health also improved after 1830, when their rising economic value persuaded masters to improve slave quarters, provide warmer winter clothing, reduce overwork, and hire physicians. During the 1840s and 1850s, slaves were more likely than white southerners to be cared for by a physician, although often nineteenth-century doctors could do little to combat disease.

Enslaved African Americans also used traditional remedies—derived from Africa and passed down by generations of women—to treat the sick. Wild cherry bark and herbs such as pennyroyal or horehound went into teas to treat colds. Slaves used jimsonweed tea to counter rheumatism and chestnut leaf tea to relieve asthma. One former slave recalled that her grandmother dispensed syrup to treat colic and teas to cure fevers and stomachaches. Some of these folk remedies were more effective than those prescribed by white physicians. This was especially true of kaolin, a white clay that black women used to treat dysentery.

6.7 The Socialization of Slaves

Analyze how African Americans adapted to life in slavery, and the role religion played in this adaption.

African Americans had to acquire the skills needed to protect themselves and their loved ones from a brutal slave system. Folktales, often derived from Africa but on occasion from American Indians, helped pass such skills from generation to generation. Parents, other relatives, and elderly slaves generally told such tales to teach survival, mental agility, and self-confidence.

The heroes of the tales are animal tricksters with human personalities. Most famous is Brer Rabbit, who in his weakness and cleverness represents African Americans in slavery. Although the tales portray Brer Rabbit as far from perfect, he uses his wits to overcome threats from strong and vicious antagonists, principally Brer Fox, who represents slaveholders. By hearing these stories and rooting for Brer Rabbit, slave children learned how to conduct themselves in a difficult environment.

They learned to watch what they said to white people, not to talk back, to withhold information about other African Americans, and to dissemble. In particular, they refrained from making antislavery statements and camouflaged their awareness of how masters exploited them. As Henry Bibb, who escaped from slavery, put it, "The only weapon of self defense that I could use successfully was that of deception." Another former slave, Charshee Charlotte Lawrence-McIntyre, summed up the slave strategy in rhyme: "Got one mind for the boss to see; got another for what I know is me."

Masters tended to miss the subtlety in their bond peoples' divided consciousness. When slaves refused to do simple tasks correctly, masters saw it as black stupidity rather than resistance. Sometimes outsiders, such as white northern missionary Charles C. Jones, understood more clearly what was going on. In 1842 Jones observed,

> Persons live and die in the midst of Negroes and know comparatively little of their real character. The Negroes form a distinct class in the community, and keep themselves very much to themselves. They are one thing before the whites and another before their own color. Deception towards the former is characteristic of them, whether bond or free. . . . It is habit—long established custom, which descends from generation to generation.

6.7.1 Religion

Along with family and socialization, religion helped African Americans cope with slavery. Some masters denied their slaves access to Christianity, and some slaves ignored the religion. But most slaves did not. In New Orleans, Baltimore, and a few other locations, there were Roman Catholic slaves, who were usually the human property of Roman Catholic masters. In Maryland during the 1830s, the Jesuits, an order of Roman Catholic priests and brothers, collectively owned approximately 300 slaves. By the mid-nineteenth century, however, most American slaves practiced a Protestantism similar but not identical to that of most white southerners.

British artist John Antrobus completed this painting in about 1860. It is named *Plantation Burial* and suggests the importance of religion among enslaved African Americans.

Biracial Baptist and Methodist congregations persisted in the South longer than they did in northern cities. The southern congregations usually had racially segregated seating, but black and white people joined in communion and church discipline. They shared cemeteries. Many masters during the nineteenth century sponsored plantation churches for slaves, and white missionary organizations also supported such churches.

In the plantation churches, white ministers told their black congregations that Christian slaves must obey their earthly masters as they did God. This was not what slaves wanted to hear. Cornelius Garner, a former slave, recalled that "dat ole white preacher jest was telling us slaves to be good to our marsters. We ain't keer'd a bit 'bout dat stuff he was telling us 'cause we wanted to sing, pray, and serve God in our own way." At times slaves walked out on ministers who preached obedience.

Instead of services sponsored by masters, slaves preferred a semisecret black church they conducted themselves. They did so under the leadership of self-called, often illiterate black preachers who were little concerned with consistent theology or Christian meekness. Services involved singing, dancing, shouting, moaning, and clapping. According to historian Peter Kolchin, slaves mixed aspects of African culture into Christianity. Among those aspects were "potions, concoctions, charms, and rituals [used] to ward off evil, cure sickness, harm enemies, and produce amorous behavior." European settlers in America during the previous century had also melded Christian and non-Christian beliefs and practices. So it is not surprising that white as well as black people sought the help of African-American conjurers.

6.8 The Character of Slavery and Slaves

Evaluate the different ways in which historians have portrayed the black experience in slavery.

For over a century, historians have debated the character of the Old South's slave system and the people it held in bondage. During the 1910s southern historian Ulrich B. Phillips portrayed slavery as a benign, paternalistic institution in which Christian slaveholders cared for largely content slaves. Slavery, Phillips argued—as had the slaveholders themselves—rescued members of an inferior race from African barbarism and permitted them to rise as far as they possibly could toward civilization. With different emphasis, historian Eugene D. Genovese, between the 1960s and his death in 2012, also placed paternalism at the heart of southern plantation slavery.

Other historians, however, deny paternalism had much to do with a system that rested on force and raw capitalism. Since the 1950s they have contended that slaveholders exploited their bond people in a selfish quest for profits. Although some slaveholders cared about the welfare of their slaves, this brutal portrait of slavery is persuasive in the twenty-first century. Many masters never met their slaves face to face. Most slaves suffered whippings at some point in their lives, and over half the slaves caught up in the domestic slave trade were separated from their families.

Scholars have also compared slavery in the American South with its counterpart in Latin America. Historians note that slaves in Latin American countries influenced by Roman law and the Roman Catholic Church enjoyed more protection from abusive masters than did slaves in the United States, where English law and Protestant Christianity dominated. Routes to freedom, through self-purchase and manumission, were more available in Latin America than in the Old South. More interracial marriage also existed in Latin America. Therefore, some historians maintain, less racism existed in Latin America than in the United States. Other historians, however, have established that protections offered by law and religion to slaves in Latin America were more theoretical than practical. They argue that racism there merely took a different form than it did in the United States. Certainly Latin American slaves had a far greater mortality rate than their counterparts in the American South. This implies that the conditions under which slaves labored in Latin America were even harsher than the grim conditions slaves often faced in the United States.

Another debate has centered on the character of enslaved African Americans. Historians such as Phillips argued that African Americans were genetically predisposed to being slaves and were therefore usually content. In 1959 Stanley M. Elkins changed the debate by arguing that black people were not inherently inferior or submissive but that concentration-camp-like conditions on plantations made them into childlike "Sambos." Elkins portrayed slaves in the Cotton Kingdom as dependent on their masters as were inmates in Nazi extermination camps on their guards.

A scholarly reaction to Elkins's study led to current understandings of the character of African Americans in slavery. Since the 1960s historians have argued that rather than defeating black people, slavery led them to create institutions that allowed them some control over their lives. Slaves built families, churches, and communities. According to these historians, African-American resistance forced masters to accept African work patterns and black autonomy in the slave quarters. Although these historians may idealize the strength of slave communities within a brutal plantation context, they have enriched our understanding of slave life.

Conclusion

African-American life in slavery during the time of the Cotton Kingdom is a vast subject. As slavery expanded westward before 1860, it varied from region to region and according to the crops that slaves cultivated. Although cotton became the South's most important product, many African-American slaves continued to produce tobacco, rice, sugar, and hemp. In the Chesapeake, slaves grew wheat. Others tended livestock or worked in cities and industry. Meanwhile, enslaved African Americans continued to build the community institutions that allowed them to maintain their cultural autonomy and persevere within a brutal system.

The story of African Americans in southern slavery is one of labor, perseverance, and resistance. Black labor was responsible for the growth of a southern economy that helped produce prosperity throughout the United States. Black men and women preserved and expanded an African-American cultural heritage that included African, European, and American Indian roots. They resisted determined efforts to dehumanize them. They developed family relationships, communities, churches, and traditions that helped them preserve their character as a people.

Chapter Timeline

AFRICAN-AMERICAN EVENTS	NATIONAL EVENTS
	1810–1820
1816	**1812**
William Ellison purchases his freedom	Louisiana becomes a state
1818	**1817**
Suppression of Charleston's AME Church	Mississippi becomes a state
	1819
Frederick Douglass born in Maryland	Alabama becomes a state

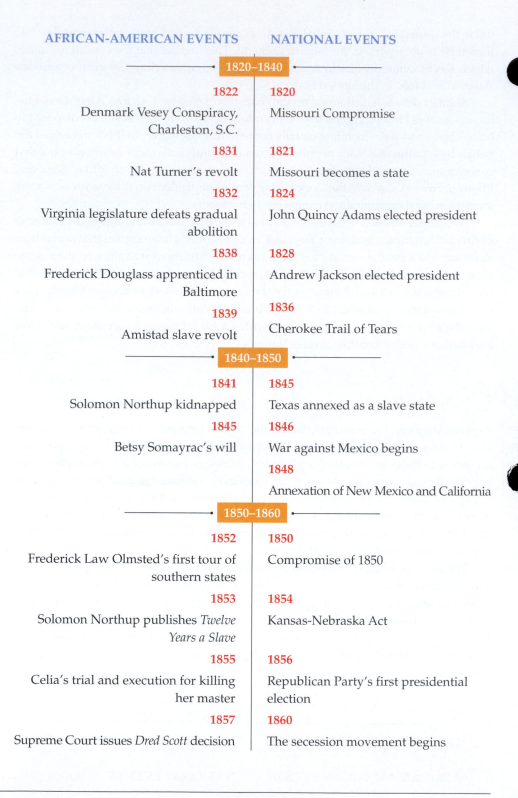

AFRICAN-AMERICAN EVENTS	NATIONAL EVENTS
1820–1840	
1822	**1820**
Denmark Vesey Conspiracy, Charleston, S.C.	Missouri Compromise
1831	**1821**
Nat Turner's revolt	Missouri becomes a state
1832	**1824**
Virginia legislature defeats gradual abolition	John Quincy Adams elected president
1838	**1828**
Frederick Douglass apprenticed in Baltimore	Andrew Jackson elected president
1839	**1836**
Amistad slave revolt	Cherokee Trail of Tears
1840–1850	
1841	**1845**
Solomon Northup kidnapped	Texas annexed as a slave state
1845	**1846**
Betsy Somayrac's will	War against Mexico begins
	1848
	Annexation of New Mexico and California
1850–1860	
1852	**1850**
Frederick Law Olmsted's first tour of southern states	Compromise of 1850
1853	**1854**
Solomon Northup publishes *Twelve Years a Slave*	Kansas-Nebraska Act
1855	**1856**
Celia's trial and execution for killing her master	Republican Party's first presidential election
1857	**1860**
Supreme Court issues *Dred Scott* decision	The secession movement begins

Review Questions

1. How did the domestic slave trade and the exploitation of black women by white males affect slave families?

2. How significant were black slaveholders in the history of slavery?

3. How did urban and industrial slavery differ from plantation slavery in the Old South?

4. What impact did housing, nutrition, and disease have on the lives of slaves between 1820 and 1860?

5. How did black Christianity differ from white Christianity in the Old South? How did black Christianity in the South differ from black Christianity in the North?

Retracing the Odyssey

William Johnson House (not currently open to the public) **and Melrose Plantation,** Natchez, Mississippi. Johnson was one of the rare black slaveholders, and John T. McMurrin, the owner of Melrose Plantation, was a northern white man who became a slaveholder.

Hampton Plantation State Park, McClellanville, South Carolina. The plantation house dates to about 1750, and the outbuildings include slave cabins.

Magnolia Mound Plantation, Baton Rouge, Louisiana. This historic site includes a plantation house, outbuildings, an overseer's house, and a separate kitchen building.

Zephaniah Kingsley Plantation, Fort George Island, Florida. Kingsley's was an interracial family. Buildings on the plantation include the oldest standing plantation house in Florida and 32 slave quarters.

Recommended Reading

Ira Berlin. *Generations in Captivity: A History of African-American Slaves.* Cambridge, MA: Harvard University Press, 2003. Portrays slavery in the Cotton Kingdom as the product of a series of negotiations between masters and slaves over the terms of captivity.

Charles B. Dew. *Bonds of Iron: Masters and Slaves at Buffalo Forge.* New York: Norton, 1994. Dew offers an excellent account of one type of industrial slavery in the Old South.

Michael P. Johnson and James L. Roark. *Black Masters: A Free Family of Color in the Old South.* New York: Norton, 1984. This book provides a full account of William Ellison and his slaveholding black family.

Norrece T. Jones Jr. *Born a Child of Freedom, Yet a Slave: Mechanisms of Control and Strategies of Resistance in Antebellum South Carolina.* Middleton, CT: Wesleyan University Press, 1990. This book explores how masters controlled slaves and how slaves resisted.

Wilma King. *Stolen Childhood: Slave Youth in Nineteenth-Century America.* Bloomington: Indiana University Press, 1995. This is the most up-to-date account of enslaved black children. It is especially useful concerning the children's work.

Melton A. McLaurin. *Celia, a Slave.* Athens: University of Georgia Press, 1991. This is the most complete study of an enslaved woman's response to sexual exploitation. MacLaurin establishes the social and political contexts for this famous case.

Additional Bibliography

Slavery and Its Expansion

Edward Baptist. *The Half Has Never Been Told: Slavery and the Making of American Capitalism.* New York: Basic Books, 2014.

Diane Mutti Burke. *On Slavery's Border: Missouri's Small-Slaveholding Households 1815–1865.* Athens: University of Georgia Press, 2010.

Stanley M. Elkins. *Slavery: A Problem in American Institutional and Intellectual Life.* 3rd ed. Chicago: University of Chicago Press, 1976.

Eugene D. Genovese. *The Political Economy of Slavery: Studies in the Economy and Society of the Slave South.* 1961. Reprint, New York: Random House, 1967.

Roger G. Kennedy. *Mr. Jefferson's Lost Cause: Land, Farmers, Slavery, and the Louisiana Purchase.* New York: Oxford University Press, 2003.

Larry Koger. *Black Slaveowners: Free Black Slave Masters in South Carolina, 1790–1860.* 1985. Reprint, Columbia: University of South Carolina Press, 1994.

Peter Kolchin. *American Slavery 1619–1877.* New York: Hill and Wang, 1993.

John H. Moore. *The Emergence of the Cotton Kingdom in the Old Southwest.* Baton Rouge: Louisiana State University Press, 1988.

Larry Eugene Rivers. *Slavery in Florida: Territorial Days to Emancipation.* Gainesville: University Press of Florida, 2000.

Kenneth M. Stampp. *The Peculiar Institution: Slavery in the Antebellum South.* 1956. Reprint, New York: Vintage Books, 1989.

Urban and Industrial Slavery

Ronald L. Lewis. *Coal, Iron, and Slaves: Industrial Slavery in Maryland and Virginia, 1715–1865*. Westport, CT: Greenwood, 1979.

Robert S. Starobin. *Industrial Slavery in the Old South*. New York: Oxford University Press, 1970.

Midori Takagi. *Rearing Wolves to Our Own Destruction: Slavery in Richmond, Virginia, 1782–1865*. Charlottesville: University Press of Virginia, 1999.

Richard C. Wade. *Slavery in the Cities: The South 1820–1860*. 1964. Reprint, New York: Oxford University Press, 1967.

The Domestic Slave Trade

Steven Deyle. *Carry Me Back: The Domestic Slave Trade in American Life*. New York: Oxford University Press, 2005.

Walter Johnson. *Soul by Soul: Life Inside the Antebellum Slave Market*. Cambridge, MA: Harvard University Press, 1999.

Damian Alan Pargas. *Slavery and Forced Migration in the Antebellum South*. New York: Cambridge University Press, 2015.

Michael Tadman. *Speculators and Slaves: Masters, Traders, and Slaves in the Old South*. 1989. Reprint, Madison: University of Wisconsin Press, 1996.

The Slave Community

John W. Blassingame. *The Slave Community: Plantation Life in the Antebellum South*. 2nd ed. New York: Oxford University Press, 1979.

Wilma A. Dunaway. *The African-American Family in Slavery and Emancipation*. New York: Cambridge University Press, 2003.

Eugene D. Genovese. *Roll, Jordan, Roll: The World the Slave Made*. 1974. Reprint, Vintage Books, 1976.

Herbert Gutman. *The Black Family in Slavery and Freedom*. 1976. Reprint, Vintage Books, 1977.

Ann Patton Malone. *Sweet Chariot: Slave Family and Household Structure in Nineteenth-Century Louisiana*. Chapel Hill: University of North Carolina Press, 1992.

Todd L. Savitt. *Medicine and Slavery: The Diseases and Health Care of Blacks in Antebellum Virginia*. Urbana: University of Illinois Press, 1978.

Maria Jenkins Schwartz. *Born in Bondage: Growing Up Enslaved in the Antebellum South*. Cambridge, MA: Harvard University Press, 2000.

Enslaved Women

Stephanie M. H. Camp. *Closer to Freedom: Enslaved Women and Everyday Resistance in the Plantation South*. Chapel Hill: University of North Carolina Press, 2004.

David Barry Gaspar and Darlene Clark Hine, eds. *More Than Chattel: Black Women and Slavery in the Americas*. Bloomington: Indiana University Press, 1996.

Thavolia Glymph. *Out of the House of Bondage: The Transformation of the Plantation Household*. New York: Cambridge University Press, 2008.

Renee K. Harrison. *Enslaved Women and the Art of Resistance in Antebellum America*. Basingstroke, NY: Palgrave Macmillan, 2009.

Darlene Clark Hine, Wilma King, and Linda Reed, eds. *"We Specialize in the Wholly Impossible": A Reader in Black Women's History*. Brooklyn, NY: Carlson, 1996.

Joshua D. Rothman. *Notorious in the Neighborhood: Sex and Families Across the Color Line in Virginia 1787–1861*. Chapel Hill: University of North Carolina Press, 2003.

Jean Fagan Yellin. *Harriet Jacobs: A Life*. New York: Basic Civitas, 2003.

Slave Culture and Religion

John B. Boles, ed. *Masters and Slaves in the House of the Lord: Race and Religion in the American South, 1740–1870*. Lexington: University Press of Kentucky, 1988.

Ras Michael Brown. *African-Atlantic Cultures and the South Carolina Lowcountry*. New York: Cambridge University Press, 2012.

———. *Slave Missions and the Black Church in the Antebellum South*. Columbia: University of South Carolina Press, 1999.

Sharla M. Fett. *Working Cures: Healing, Health, and Power on Southern Slave Plantations*. Chapel Hill: University of North Carolina Press, 2002.

Daniel L. Fountain. *Slavery, Civil War, and Salvation: African American Slaves and Christianity 1830–1870*. Baton Rouge: Louisiana State University Press, 2010.

Albert J. Raboteau. *Slave Religion: The "Invisible Institution" in the Antebellum South*. New York: Oxford University Press, 1978 (updated ed. 2004).

Chapter 7

Free Black People in Antebellum America
1820–1861

Barbering was one of the skilled trades open to black men during the antebellum years. Several wealthy African Americans began their careers as barbers.

Learning Objectives

After reading this chapter, you should be able to:

7.1 Describe the demographics of black freedom.

7.2 Discuss how the policies of the Jacksonian Democrats impacted African Americans.

7.3 Describe the limits northern states placed on black freedom between 1820 and 1861.

7.4 Discuss the characteristics of northern black communities as they existed between 1820 and 1861.

7.5 Compare and contrast the roles of free black institutions between 1820 and 1861.

7.6 Compare and contrast the ways in which free African Americans lived in the North, South, and West during the decades prior to the Civil War.

Our vices and our degradation are ever arrayed against us, but our virtues are passed by unnoticed. And what is still more lamentable, our [white] friends, to whom we concede all the principles of humanity and religion, from these very causes seem to have fallen into the current of popular feeling and are imperceptibly floating on the stream—actually living in the practice of prejudice, while they abjure it in theory, and feel it not in their hearts.

—*Freedom's Journal, March 16, 1827*

Journalist Samuel Cornish wrote the passage above in 1827 when he introduced himself to his readers as the coeditor of the first African-American newspaper. He knew that pervasive white prejudice limited the lives of black people. During the 40 years before the Civil War, such prejudice was less rigid but nearly as common in the North as in the South. The northern states had abolished slavery, and free black people living in those states enjoyed more rights than their counterparts in the South. Yet these very rights made many white northerners hostile toward African Americans.

While southern legislatures considered expelling free black people from their states, northern legislatures—particularly in the Old Northwest—restricted black people's ability to move into their states. White workers, North and South, fearing competition for jobs, sponsored legislation that limited most free African Americans to menial employment. White people also required most black people to live in segregated areas of cities. African Americans responded to these conditions by forming and maintaining communities that cultivated a dynamic cultural legacy and built enduring institutions.

This chapter picks up the story of free black communities that began in Chapter 5. It provides a portrait of free African Americans between 1820 and the start of the Civil War. Like the revolutionary era, the antebellum period was a time of hope and fear. The numbers of free African Americans steadily increased. But the number of slaves increased much faster.

7.1 Demographics of Freedom

Describe the demographics of black freedom.

In 1820 there were 233,504 free African Americans in the United States. In comparison, there were 1,538,125 slaves and 7,861,931 white people. Of the free African Americans, 99,281 lived in the North, 114,070 in the Upper South, and only 20,153 in the Deep South (see Map 7-1). Free people of color accounted for 2.4 percent of the American population and 3 percent of the southern population. More black women than black men were free in 1820, and—particularly in urban areas—this remained true throughout the period.

As southern states made freedom suits and manumission more difficult, the northern free black population increased more rapidly than the free black populations in either the Upper or the Deep South.

By 1860 the free African-American population had reached 488,070. Of these, 226,152 lived in the North, 224,963 in the Upper South, and 36,955 in the Deep South

Map 7-1 The Slave, Free Black, and White People of the United States in 1830

This map does not distinguish the slave from the free black population of the free states, although the process of gradual emancipation in several northeastern states was still under way and some black northerners remained enslaved.

SOURCE: For slave states, Ira Berlin, *Slaves without Masters: The Free Negro in the Antebellum South* (New York: New Press, 1971); for free states, *Historical Statistics of the United States* (Washington: GPO, 1960). © Darlene Clark Hine.

Which states had the largest and smallest free black populations in 1830?

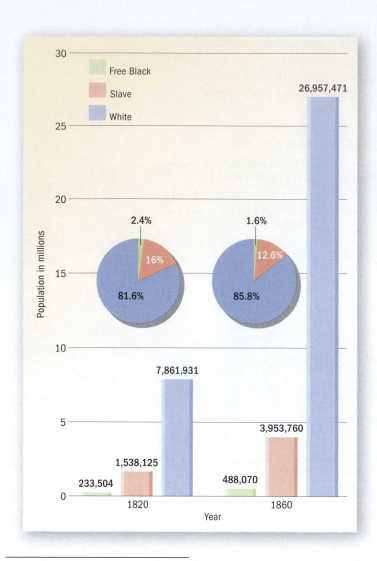

Figure 7-1 The Free Black, Slave, and White Populations of the United States in 1820 and 1860

The bar graph shows the relationship among the free black, slave, and white populations in the United States in the years 1820 and 1860. The superimposed pie charts illustrate the percentages of these groups in the population in the same year.

market revolution

The process between 1800 and 1860 by which an American economy based on subsistence farming, production by skilled artisans, and local markets changed into an economy marked by commercial farming, factory production, and national markets.

(see Figures 7-1 and 7-2). A few thousand free black people lived in the west beyond Missouri, Arkansas, and Texas. Meanwhile, the number of slaves had increased to just under four million, and massive immigration had tripled the white population to 26,957,471. Because the white population grew so quickly, the proportion of free African Americans dropped to just 1.6 percent of the total American population and to 2.1 percent of the southern population. A year later the Civil War began the process of making all black people free.

A larger portion of the free black population than of the white population lived in cities. By 1860, 47.3 percent of free African Americans lived in urban areas compared to 32.9 percent of the white population. And of the total number of African Americans who lived in cities, 62.5 percent lived in cities with populations over 100,000. Therefore free African Americans accounted for a significantly larger percentage of the population of large cities than they did of the total American population. In Baltimore, free black people represented 12 percent of the 212,418 residents. There, as well as in Richmond, Norfolk, and other smaller cities of the Upper South, free African Americans interacted with enslaved populations to create communities embracing both groups. The largest black urban population in the North existed in Philadelphia, where 22,185 African Americans made up 4.2 percent of its approximately 533,000 residents. Other important northern cities—such as New York; Boston; Providence; Cincinnati; New Haven, Connecticut; and New Bedford, Massachusetts—had smaller black populations, but they were still large enough to develop dynamic communities.

7.2 The Jacksonian Era

Discuss how the policies of the Jacksonian Democrats impacted African Americans.

After the War of 1812, free African Americans—like other Americans of the time—witnessed rapid economic, social, and political change. Between 1800 and 1860, a **market revolution** transformed the North into an industrial society. An economy based on subsistence farming, goods produced by skilled artisans, and local markets changed into one based on commercial farming, factory production, and national markets. The Industrial Revolution that began in Britain a century earlier encouraged these changes. But it took improved transportation to bring the changes to America. In 1807, Robert Fulton demonstrated the practicality of steam-powered river vessels. Thereafter steamboats speeded travel on the country's inland waterways. During the 1820s a system of turnpikes and canals began to unite the North and parts of the South. Of particular importance were the National Road (extending west from Baltimore) and the Erie Canal, which in 1825 opened a water route from New York City to the Great

Figure 7-2   The Free Black, Slave, and White Populations by Region, 1860

These pie charts compare the free black, slave, and white populations of the North, Upper South, and Lower South in 1860. Note the near balance of the races in the Lower South.

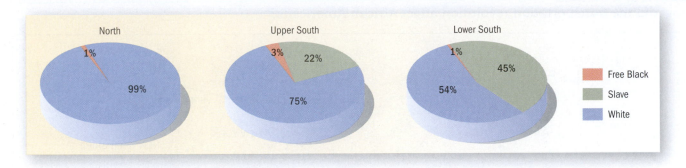

Lakes. By the 1830s, railroads linked urban and agricultural regions in much of the country (see Map 7-2).

As faster transportation expanded trade, as a factory system began to replace small shops run by artisans, and as cities grew, northern society profoundly changed. A large urban working class arose. Artisans and small farmers feared for their future. Entrepreneurs began to replace the traditional social elite. Foreign immigrants, mostly from Ireland and Germany, poured in as entrepreneurs sought cheap labor. By the 1820s northern states bristled with religiously inspired reform movements designed to deal with the social dislocations the market revolution caused. Together these developments made the North increasingly different from the agrarian South.

The market revolution had a major political impact as communications improved, populations became more concentrated, and wage workers became more assertive. By 1810 states had begun dropping the property qualifications that had limited citizens' right to vote. One by one, states moved toward universal white manhood suffrage. This trend doomed the openly elitist Federalist Party and disrupted its foe, the Republican Party. As the market revolution picked up during the 1820s, unleashing hopes and fears among Americans, politicians recognized the need for more broadly based mass political parties.

In the 1824 presidential election all four candidates ran as Republicans, and none received a majority of the popular or electoral vote. War hero Andrew Jackson of Tennessee led the field, but in early 1825 Congress—exercising its power to decide such elections—chose Secretary of State John Quincy Adams of Massachusetts to be president. Adams paradoxically represented both the old elitist style of politics and the entrepreneurial spirit of emerging northern capitalism. Along with Henry Clay— his secretary of state—Adams, as president, promoted industrialization through a national program of federal aid. Meanwhile, Jackson's supporters claimed that Clay and Adams, by combining their forces in Congress, had cheated the general out of the presidency. Led by Martin Van Buren of New York, the Jacksonians organized a new Democratic Party to counter the Adams–Clay program. By appealing to slaveholders, who believed economic nationalism favored the North over the South, and to "the common [white] man" throughout the country, the Democrats defeated Adams and elected Jackson in 1828.

Jackson was a strong but controversial president. In what became known as "Jacksonian Democracy," he claimed to stand for the people against an antidemocratic wealthy elite. During the **Nullification Crisis** of 1832–1833, he acted as a nationalist in facing down South Carolina's attempt to nullify—block—the collection of the U.S. tariff

Nullification Crisis

Occurred between 1832 and 1833; arose when the South Carolina legislature declared the United States tariff "null and void" within the state's borders.

Map 7-2 Transportation Revolution

This map shows the principal American canals and roads built by 1830 and the principal railroad lines built by 1850. A growing transportation network cut travel time and shipping costs, which encouraged commerce.

How did the transportation revolution affect African Americans?

on imports within the state. Otherwise Jackson, who owned as many as 150 slaves, followed a pro-southern agenda. He promoted state rights, economic localism, and the territorial expansion of slavery. In opposition to Jackson, Clay (a Kentucky slaveholder), Adams, and others formed the Whig Party.

A national organization that fought the Democrats for power from 1834 to 1852, the Whig Party mixed traditional and modern politics. It was a mass political party, but many of its leaders questioned the legitimacy of mass parties. It favored a nationalist approach to economic policy, which made it more successful in the North than in the South. It opposed territorial expansion, worried about the growing number of immigrants, and endorsed the moral values of evangelical Protestantism. In contrast to Democratic politicians who increasingly made racist appeals to antiblack prejudices among white voters, Whigs often adopted a more conciliatory tone on race. By the late 1830s, a few northern Whigs claimed their party opposed slavery and racial oppression. They, however, exaggerated. The Whig Party usually nominated slaveholders for the presidency, and few Whig politicians defended black rights.

7.3 Limited Freedom in the North

Describe the limits northern states placed on black freedom between 1820 and 1861.

Addressing an interracial audience in Boston in 1846, white abolitionist Joseph C. Lovejoy described the North as a land "partially free." Lovejoy emphasized that the Fugitive Slave Law of 1793 extended into the northern states the power of southern masters to enslave African Americans. This law endangered the freedom of northern black men, women, and children. Those who had escaped from slavery lived in fear that as long as they stayed in the United States they might be seized and returned to their erstwhile masters. And, under the aegis of this law, any black northerner could be kidnapped, taken to a southern state, and enslaved. Throughout the antebellum period, northern black people had to be vigilant against kidnapping. In this vigilance, they sometimes had the support of their white neighbors and employers. But white northerners also limited black freedom. They enacted **black laws**. They rarely allowed black men to vote. They often demanded segregated housing, schools, and transportation. And they limited African Americans' employment opportunities.

black laws

Laws passed in states of the Old Northwest during the early nineteenth century banning or restricting black settlement and limiting the rights of black residents.

7.3.1 Black Laws

As indicated in previous chapters, the racially egalitarian impulse of the revolutionary era had by the 1790s begun to wane among white Americans. Meanwhile, the dawning Romantic Age—characterized by a sentimental fascination with uniqueness—encouraged a general belief that each ethnic and racial group had an inherent spirit that set it apart from others. As white Americans began to perceive self-reliance, intellectual curiosity, the capacity for self-government, military valor, and an energetic work ethic as inherently "Anglo-Saxon" characteristics, they began to believe other racial groups lacked these virtues. As Samuel Cornish suggested, even those white people who befriended black people considered them outsiders in a "white man's country."

Most white northerners wanted nothing to do with African Americans. They paradoxically dismissed black people as incapable of honest work and feared black competition for jobs. Contact with African Americans, they believed, had degraded white southerners and would corrupt white northerners if permitted. Therefore, as historian Leon Litwack puts it, "Nearly every northern state considered, and many adopted, measures to prohibit or restrict the further immigration of Negroes."

Such measures were more prevalent in the Old Northwest than in the Northeast. Ohio, Illinois, Indiana, Michigan, Iowa, and Wisconsin all limited or banned black immigration and discriminated against black residents. But in 1821 a bill to keep black people from entering Massachusetts failed to reach a vote in the state legislature on the grounds that it was inconsistent with "love of humanity." In Pennsylvania, which had a much larger influx of southern African Americans than Massachusetts, the legislature defeated attempts to limit their entry.

W. M. Prior painted this portrait of Eliza, Nellie, and Margaret Copeland in 1854. The Copeland family was one of the few African-American families affluent enough to commission such a portrait. Note the girls' fine clothing.

Free Soil Party

An almost entirely northern political coalition from 1848 to 1853 opposed to the expansion of slavery into western territories. It included former supporters of the Whig, Democratic, and Liberty parties.

But in the Old Northwest, state legislatures passed such laws, which became known as "black laws." Between 1804 and 1849, Ohio's black laws required African Americans entering the state to produce legal evidence of their free status. They also had to register with a county clerk and post a $500 bond "to pay for their support in case of want." State and local authorities rarely enforced these provisions, and by the time the Ohio **Free Soil Party** brought about their repeal in 1849, about 25,000 African Americans lived in the state. But Ohio authorities rigorously enforced other black law provisions. Among them were those prohibiting black testimony against white people in court, black service on juries, and black enlistment in the state militia. In 1829 Cincinnati used the laws to force between 1,100 and 2,200 of the city's black residents to depart.

Other governments in the Old Northwest placed even more extreme limits on black freedom than Ohio did. In 1813, Illinois Territory threatened African Americans who tried to settle within its borders with repeated whipping until they left. In 1847, the state of Illinois mandated that African Americans who sought to become permanent residents could be fined. Those who could not pay the fine could be sold at public auction into indentured servitude. In neighboring Indiana, citizens ratified a state constitution in 1851 that explicitly banned all African Americans from the state, and Michigan, Iowa, and Wisconsin followed Indiana's example. Yet, like Ohio, these states rarely enforced such restrictive laws. As long as white northerners did not feel threatened, they usually tolerated a few black people in their midst (see Table 7-1).

Table 7-1 Black Population in the States of the Old Northwest, 1800–1840

	1800	1810	1820	1830	1840
Ohio	337	1,899	4,723	9,574	17,345
Michigan	144	174	293	707	
Illinois		781	1,374	2,384	3,929
Indiana	298	630	1,420	3,632	7,168
Iowa					188

SOURCE: Based on the data from James Oliver Horton and Lois E. Horton, *In Hope of Liberty: Culture, Community, and Protest among Northern Free Blacks, 1700–1860* (New York: Oxford University Press, 1997), 104.

7.3.2 Disfranchisement

Disfranchisement of black voters occurred throughout the North—except in most of New England—during the antebellum decades. The same white antipathy to African Americans that led to exclusionary legislation supported a movement to deny black men the right to vote. (No women could vote anywhere in the United States during most of the nineteenth century.) At no time before the Civil War could black men vote in the Old Northwest states of Ohio, Indiana, Illinois, Michigan, and Wisconsin, nor could they ever vote in Iowa. However, the northeastern states initially allowed black male suffrage, and efforts to curtail it in that region came as by-products of the Jacksonian Democrats' championing of the common white man.

From the eighteenth century into the early nineteenth, the northeastern elite used property qualifications to prevent the poorest black *and* white men from voting. Because black people were generally less wealthy than white people, these property qualifications gave most white men the right to vote and denied it to most black men. Under such circumstances, white people saw no danger in letting a few relatively well-to-do black men exercise the franchise. It was ironically the Jacksonian movement to end property qualifications that led to the outright disfranchisement of most black voters in the Northeast.

In the political struggle over ending the qualifications, advocates and opponents of universal white male suffrage opposed allowing all black men to vote. They claimed allowing all black men to vote would lead in certain districts to black men being elected to office. That in turn, they maintained, would encourage morally suspect African Americans to corrupt the political process and try to mix socially with white people. Then, they predicted, justifiably angry white people would react violently. In this manner, what had been an argument regarding class became an argument over race, and the outcomes varied.

Those northeastern states with the larger black populations tended to be most determined to deny black men the right to vote. At one extreme were New Jersey and Connecticut. New Jersey stopped allowing black men to vote in 1807 and in 1844 adopted a white-only suffrage provision in its state constitution. In 1818 Connecticut determined that, although black men who had voted before that date could continue to vote, no new black voters would be allowed. At the other extreme were Maine, New Hampshire, Vermont, and Massachusetts. None of these states had a significant African-American population, and they made no effort to deprive black men of the right to vote. In the middle were Rhode Island, New York, and Pennsylvania, which had protracted struggles over the issue.

In 1822 Rhode Island denied that black men were eligible to vote in its elections. Then, in 1842, a popular uprising against the state's conservative government extended the franchise to all men, black and white. In New York, an 1821 state constitutional convention defeated an attempt to disfranchise all black men. Instead, it raised the property qualification for black voters while eliminating it for white voters. To vote in New York, black men had to have property worth $250 (approximately $159,000 today) and pay taxes, whereas white men simply had to pay taxes or serve in the state militia. This provision denied the right to vote to nearly all of the 10,000 black men who had previously voted in the state. African Americans nevertheless remained active in New York politics. As supporters of the Liberty Party in 1844, the Whig Party in 1846, and the Free-Soil Party in 1848, they fought unsuccessfully to regain equal access to the polls.

A similar protracted struggle in Pennsylvania resulted in a more absolute elimination of black suffrage. From 1780 to 1837, black men who met property qualifications could vote in some of this state's counties but not in others. Then, in 1838, delegates to a convention to draft a new state constitution voted 77 to 45 to enfranchise all white men and disfranchise all black men. Such African-American leaders as Robert Purvis, Peter Gardner, and Frederick Hinton organized to defeat the new constitution.

But Pennsylvanians ratified it by a vote of 113,971 to 112,759. Black Pennsylvanians continued to argue that without the right to vote they faced mounting repression. In 1855 they unsuccessfully petitioned Congress to help them gain equal access to the polls. And, just before the Civil War, 93 percent of black northerners lived in states that either denied or limited black men's right to vote.

7.3.3 Segregation

Only the Old Northwest states passed laws designed to exclude African Americans. Not all northern states disfranchised black men. But no black northerner could effectively counter a determination among most white northerners to segregate society.

Northern hotels, taverns, and resorts turned black people away unless they were servants of white guests. Public lecture halls, art exhibits, and religious revivals either banned African Americans or allowed them to attend only at certain times. Those white churches and theaters that allowed black people to enter required them to sit in segregated sections. Ohio excluded African Americans from state-supported poorhouses and insane asylums. In relatively enlightened Massachusetts, prominent black abolitionist and orator Frederick Douglass was "within the space of a few days . . . turned away from a menagerie on Boston Common, a **lyceum** and revival meeting in New Bedford, [and] an eating house."

African Americans faced especial difficulty in trying to use public transportation. They could ride in a stagecoach only if it had no white passengers. As rail travel became more common during the late 1830s, companies set aside special cars for African Americans. In Massachusetts in 1841, a railroad first used the term **Jim Crow**, which derived from a blackface minstrel act, to describe these cars. Later the term came to define other forms of racial segregation as well. In cities, many omnibus and streetcar companies barred African Americans entirely, even though urban black people had little choice but to try to use these means of transportation. Steamboats refused to rent cabins to African Americans. They had to remain on deck at night and during storms. All African Americans, regardless of their wealth or social standing, endured such treatment.

In this atmosphere, black people learned to distrust white people. A correspondent of Frederick Douglass's newspaper, the *North Star*, wrote in 1849 that there seemed "to be a fixed determination on the part of our oppressors in this country to destroy every vestige of self-respect, self-possession, and manly independence left in the colored people." Even when African Americans interacted with white people on an ostensibly equal basis, there were underlying tensions. James Forten's wealthy granddaughter Charlotte Forten, who attended an integrated school in Boston, wrote in her diary, "It is hard to go through life meeting contempt with contempt, hatred with hatred, fearing with too good reason, to love and trust hardly any one whose skin is white—however lovable, attractive, and congenial."

African Americans in northern cities also faced residential segregation. A few wealthy black people lived in white urban neighborhoods, and a few northern cities, such as Cleveland and Detroit, had no patterns of residential segregation. But in most cases, a white belief that black neighbors led to lowered property values produced such patterns. Neighborhoods existed such as "Nigger Hill" in Boston, "Little Africa" in Cincinnati, "Hayti" in Pittsburgh, and Philadelphia's "Southside." Conditions in these ghettoes were often dreadful. On the other hand, they provided a refuge from constant insult and a place where black institutions could develop.

Because African Americans representing all social and economic classes lived in segregated neighborhoods, the quality of housing in them varied. At its worst, it was bleak and dangerous. One visitor called the black section of New York City's Five Points "the worst hell of America." Other black urban neighborhoods were as bad. People lived in unheated shacks and shanties, in dirt-floored basements, or in houses without doors and windows. These conditions nurtured disease, infant mortality, alcoholism, and crime.

lyceum

A public lecture hall.

Jim Crow

Term used to describe railroad cars set aside for black people.

FIVE POINTS, 1827.

This engraving, created by American artist George Catlin, depicts New York City's notorious Five Points neighborhood. Catlin portrays black people caught up in poverty and crime.

Southern visitors to northern cities blamed the victims, insisting that the plight of many urban black northerners proved that African Americans were better off in slavery.

7.4 Black Communities in the Urban North

Discuss the characteristics of northern black communities as they existed between 1820 and 1861.

Northern African Americans lived in both rural and urban areas during the antebellum decades, but it was urban black neighborhoods, poor as they might be, that had the concentrated populations required to nurture community life (see Table 7-2). African-American urban communities of the antebellum period developed from the free black communities that had emerged from slavery in the North during the late eighteenth century (see Chapter 5). The communities varied from city to city and from region to region, yet they had much in common and interacted with each other. Resilient families, poverty, class divisions, active church congregations, the continued development of voluntary organizations, and concern for education characterized them. Particularly in the Northeast, urban black communities attracted people of American Indian descent, who often married African Americans.

Table 7-2 Free Black Population of Selected Cities, 1800–1850

City	1800	1850
Baltimore	2,771	25,442
Boston	1,174	1,999
Charleston	951	3,441
New Orleans	800 (estimated)	9,905
New York	3,499	13,815
Philadelphia	4,210	10,736
Washington	123	8,158

SOURCE: Adapted from "The Free Black in Urban America, 1800–1850: The Shadow of a Dream," by Dr. Leonard P. Curry, p. 250. 1981 University of Chicago Press, Chicago, IL. © Darlene Clark Hine.

7.4.1 The Black Family

As they became free, northern African Americans left their masters and established their own households. Some left more quickly than others, and in states such as New York and New Jersey, where gradual emancipation extended into the nineteenth century, the process continued into the 1820s. By then the average black family in northern cities had two parents and between two and four children. However, in the Northeast and Old Northwest, single-parent black families, usually headed by women, became increasingly common during the antebellum period. In Cincinnati black families headed by women increased from 11 percent in 1830 to more than 22 percent in 1850. The difficulty black men had gaining employment may have influenced this trend. A high mortality rate among black men certainly contributed, and many black women became widows during their 40s.

Meanwhile financial need and African-American culture encouraged black northerners to take in boarders and create extended families. By 1850 approximately one-third of black adults in such cities as Boston, Buffalo, Chicago, Detroit, and Cincinnati boarded. Economic considerations determined such arrangements, but friendship and family relationships also played a part. Sometimes entire nuclear families boarded, but most boarders were young, single, and male. As historians James Oliver Horton and Lois E. Horton put it, "The opportunity to rely on friends and family for shelter enhanced the mobility of poor people who were often forced to move to find employment. It provided financial assistance when people were unemployed; it provided social supports for people who faced discrimination; and it saved those who had left home or run away from slavery from social isolation."

7.4.2 Poverty

The rising tide of immigration from Europe hurt northern African Americans economically. Before 1820 black craftsmen had been in demand, but, given the choice, white people preferred to employ other white people, and black people suffered. To make matters worse for African Americans, white workers excluded young black men from apprenticeships, refused to work with black people, and used violence to prevent employers from hiring black workers when white workers were unemployed. By the 1830s these practices had driven African Americans from the skilled trades. For the rest of the antebellum period, most northern black men performed menial day labor, although a few worked as coachmen, teamsters, waiters, barbers, carpenters, masons, and plasterers. During the 1850s black men lost (to Irish immigrants) unskilled work as longshoremen, drayers, railroad workers, hod carriers, porters, and shoe shiners, as well as positions in such skilled trades as barbering.

By 1847, 80 percent of employed black men in Philadelphia did unskilled labor. Barbers and shoemakers predominated among those black workers with skills. Only 0.5 percent held factory jobs. Among employed black women, 80 percent either washed clothes or worked as domestic servants. Three-quarters of the remaining 20 percent worked as seamstresses. During the 1850s black women, too, lost work to Irish immigrants. A few became prostitutes. About 5 percent of black men and women were self-employed, selling food or secondhand clothing.

Unskilled black men often could not find work. When they did work, they received low wages. To escape such conditions in Philadelphia and other ports, they became sailors. By 1850 black men constituted about 50 percent of the crewmen on American merchant and whaling vessels. Not only did these sailors leave their families for months at a time and endure brutal conditions at sea, they also risked imprisonment if their ship anchored at southern ports.

7.4.3 The Northern Black Elite

Despite the poor prospects of most northern African Americans, a northern black elite emerged during the first six decades of the nineteenth century. Membership in this elite could be achieved through talent, wealth, occupation, family connections, complexion, and education. The elite led in the development of black institutions and culture, in the antislavery movement, and in the struggle for racial justice. It also served as the bridge between the black community and sympathetic white people.

Although few African Americans achieved financial security during the antebellum decades, black individuals could become rich. Segregated neighborhoods gave rise to a black professional class of physicians, lawyers, ministers, and undertakers who served an exclusively black clientele. Black merchants gained wealth by selling to black communities. Other relatively well-off African Americans included skilled tradesmen, such as carpenters, barbers, waiters, and coachmen, who generally found employment among white people.

Although less so than in the South, complexion also influenced social standing among African Americans in the North, especially in cities like Cincinnati located close to the South. White people often preferred to hire people of mixed race, successful black men often chose light-complexioned brides, and African Americans generally accepted white notions of human beauty.

By the 1820s the black elite had become better educated and more socially polished than its less wealthy black neighbors, yet it could never disassociate itself from them. Segregation and discriminatory legislation in the North applied to all African Americans regardless of class and complexion, and all African Americans shared a common culture and history.

Conspicuous among the black elite were entrepreneurs who, against considerable odds, gained wealth and influence. As we noted in Chapter 5, James Forten was one of the first of them, and several other examples indicate the character of such people. John Remond—who as a child migrated from Curacao, a Dutch-ruled island in the Caribbean, to Salem, Massachusetts—and his wife, Nancy Lenox Remond, became prosperous restaurateurs, caterers, and retailers. Their fortune subsidized the abolitionist careers of their son Charles Lenox Remond and daughter Sarah Parker Remond. Louis Hayden, who escaped from slavery in Kentucky in 1845, had by 1849 become a successful Boston haberdasher and abolitionist. Perhaps most successful were Stephen Smith and his partner William Whipper, who had extensive business interests in southeast Pennsylvania (see the Profile on page 187).

7.4.4 Inventors

In some cases, members of the black elite owed their success to technological innovations. Some black inventors had been born in slavery; others had not. Some participated in black community life; others did not.

In 1834 Henry Blair of Maryland became the first African American to patent an invention—a horse-drawn mechanized corn seed planter. In 1836 he patented a similar cotton seed planter. Henry Boyd, born in Kentucky in 1802, apprenticed as a cabinetmaker, purchased his freedom in 1826, and moved to Cincinnati. In 1835, as that city's leading bed manufacturer, he patented the "Boyd Bedstead." Versions of this "corded four poster" sold from between $8.00 and $125.00 (about $208 and $3,250 today). In 1844 Boyd produced more than 1,000 of them.

Lewis Temple was another prominent black inventor of the period. Born free in Richmond, Virginia, Temple moved to New Bedford, Massachusetts. In 1845, at this whaling port, Temple, a blacksmith, devised the toggle harpoon. Set with a wooden pin,

Voices

Maria W. Stewart on the Condition of Black Workers

Maria W. Stewart (1803–1879) was the first black female public speaker in the United States. She was strong willed and spoke without qualification what she believed to be the truth. At times she angered both black and white people. In the following speech, which she delivered in Boston in September 1831, Stewart criticized the treatment accorded to black workers—especially black female workers—in the North.

Tell us no more of southern slavery; for with few exceptions, although I may be very erroneous in my opinion, yet I consider our condition but little better than that. . . . After all, methinks there are no chains so galling as those that bind the soul, and exclude it from the vast field of useful and scientific knowledge. . . .

I have asked several [white] individuals of my sex, who transact business for themselves, if providing our girls were to give them the most satisfactory references, they would not be willing to grant them an equal opportunity with others? Their reply has been—for their own part, they had no objection; but as it was not the custom, were they to take them into their employ, they would be in danger of losing the public patronage.

And such is the powerful force of prejudice. Let our girls possess whatever amiable qualities of soul they may; let their characters be fair and spotless as innocence itself; let their natural taste and ingenuity be what they may; it is impossible for scarce an individual of them to rise above the condition of servants. . . .

I observed a piece . . . respecting us, asserting that we were lazy and idle. I confute them on that point. Take us generally as a people, we are neither lazy nor idle: and considering how little we have to excite or stimulate us, I am almost astonished that there are so many industrious and ambitious ones to be found. . . .

Again it was asserted that we were "a ragged set, crying for liberty." I reply to it, the whites have so long and so loudly proclaimed the theme of equal rights and privileges, that our souls have caught the flame also, ragged as we are. As far as our merit deserves, we feel a common desire to rise above the condition of servants and drudges. I have learnt, by bitter experience, that the continual hard labor deadens the energies of the soul, and benumbs the faculties of the mind; the ideas become confined, the mind barren, and, like the scorching sands of Arabia, produces nothing: or like the uncultivated soil, brings forth thorns and thistles. . . .

Most of our color have dragged out a miserable existence of servitude from the cradle to the grave. . . . Do you [women] ask, why are you wretched and miserable? I reply, look at many of the most worthy and most interesting of us doomed to spend our lives in gentlemen's kitchens. Look at our young men, smart, active, and energetic, with souls filled with ambitious fire; if they look forward, alas! What are their prospects? They can be nothing but the humblest laborers, on account of their dark complexions; hence many of them lose their ambition, and become worthless. . . .

1. Is Stewart correct in assuming that conditions for black northerners were little better than those for slaves?

2. According to Stewart, what was the impact of northern white prejudice on black workers?

SOURCE: Maria W. Stewart, "Lecture Delivered at the Franklin Hall, Boston, September 21, 1831," as quoted in Roy Finkenbine, *Sources of the African-American Past: Primary Sources in American History* (New York: Longman, 1997), 30–32.

the barbed toggle secured a whale to a harpooner's line on impact. Although Temple did not patent this invention, he made a good living manufacturing it before his death in 1854. At the same time Temple devised his harpoon, Joseph Hawkins of West Windsor, New Jersey, patented "a gridiron used to broil meat," which preserved juices as the meat cooked.

One of the best-known stories of early nineteenth-century black inventions, however, has been called into question. James Forten's biographer finds no evidence to substantiate a contemporary claim that Forten "invented an improvement in the management of sails" that "came into general use."

7.4.5 Professionals

The northern black elite also included physicians and lawyers. Among the physicians, some, such as James McCune Smith and John S. Rock, received medical degrees. Smith,

Profile

Stephen Smith and William Whipper, Partners in Business and Reform

William Whipper, c. 1835

Black people in antebellum America had great difficulty succeeding in business. In most states, northern and southern, African-American entrepreneurs faced limited educational opportunities, inequality before the law, disfranchisement, and pervasive prejudice. To make their fortunes, they had to compete in a marketplace white people dominated. Yet a few African Americans, aided by skill, determination, and luck, acquired great wealth. Some who did, such as William Ellison of South Carolina (see Profile on page 159 in Chapter 6), had little sympathy for the less fortunate. But others used their affluence to improve conditions for other African Americans. Black Pennsylvanians Stephen Smith and William Whipper, who linked their commercial success to reform efforts, illustrate this point.

Both Smith and Whipper were children of black mothers and white fathers. Both of their mothers were domestic servants in white households. Smith was born unfree in Dauphin County, south-central Pennsylvania, in about 1795. Whipper was born free in nearby Lancaster, Pennsylvania, in about 1804. Nothing suggests that either of them had a formal education.

When Smith was five years old, his master apprenticed him to Thomas Boule, who owned a lumber business. During his late teens, Smith became manager of Boule's business. In 1816 he purchased his freedom, married, and began his own lumber company. Shortly thereafter, he began purchasing real estate. Not far away, Whipper grew up and struck out on his own. During the 1820s, he worked as a steam scourer in Philadelphia. In 1834 he opened a grocery store in the same city.

The two men became partners in 1835. They had phenomenal success despite a mob attack that same year on their office. They operated one of the largest lumbering businesses in southeast Pennsylvania and expanded into selling coal. By 1842, when Smith moved to Philadelphia and left Whipper in charge of their Columbia operations, the two men had invested $9,000 (approximately 252,000 current dollars) in a bridge company and had bank deposits totaling $18,000 (about $504,000 today). By 1850, they owned—in addition to their lumber and coal business—22 railroad cars and $27,000 (about $756,000 today) worth of bank stock. They grossed $100,000 (nearly $2,800,000 today) per year. Smith continued to excel in real-estate acquisition, owning at one point 52 brick houses in Philadelphia. He was, perhaps, the richest African American in antebellum America.

The two men were partners in reform as well as business. Both of them began during the 1830s as integrationists who, based on their experience, believed that white society would accept African Americans who worked to uplift themselves. Early on, Whipper made his grocery a center for temperance and antislavery activities. He became a leader at the Black National Conventions, while Smith became an African Methodist Episcopal minister and builder of churches. They were both active in the underground railroad and opened their homes to escaped slaves. Despite their business success, however, during the 1850s they grew more pessimistic about peaceful reform as a way to gain black rights in the United States. Whipper began to promote black migration to Canada. In 1858 Smith hosted a meeting at which white antislavery activist John Brown discussed his plan to incite slave revolt in the South. Clearly, Smith and Whipper as African Americans experienced the double consciousness that W. E. B. Du Bois later so eloquently identified.

the first African American to earn this degree, graduated from the University of Glasgow in Scotland in 1837. He practiced in New York City until his death in 1874. Rock, who had been a dentist in Philadelphia, graduated from the American Medical College in 1852 and practiced medicine in Boston until 1860 when he undertook the study of law. In 1865 he became the first African American to argue a case before the U.S. Supreme Court.

Either because they had been forced out of medical school or they chose not to go, other prominent black physicians practiced medicine without having earned a degree.

John S. Rock, portrayed in an 1860 *Harper's Weekly* illustration, was born free in Salem, New Jersey, in 1825. He earned a medical degree in 1852 and practiced law beginning in 1861.

(This was legal in the nineteenth century.) James Still of Medford, New Jersey, had meager formal education but used natural remedies to develop a successful practice among black and white people. The multitalented Martin R. Delany, who had been born free in Charles Town, Virginia, in 1812, practiced medicine in Pittsburgh after having been expelled from Harvard Medical School at the insistence of two white classmates.

Prominent black attorneys included Macon B. Allen, who gained admission to the Maine bar in 1844, and Robert Morris, who qualified to practice law in Massachusetts in 1847. Both Allen and Morris apprenticed with white attorneys, and Morris had a particularly successful and lucrative practice. Yet white residents thwarted his attempt to purchase a mansion in a Boston suburb.

7.4.6 Artists and Musicians

Although they rarely achieved great wealth and have not become famous, black artists and musicians were also part of the northern African-American elite. Among the best-known artists are Robert S. Duncanson, Robert Douglass, Patrick Reason, and Edmonia Lewis. Several of them supported the antislavery movement through their artistic work.

Douglass, a painter who studied in England before establishing himself in Philadelphia, and Reason, an engraver, created portraits of abolitionists during the 1830s. Reason also etched illustrations of the sufferings of slaves. Duncanson, who was born in Cincinnati and worked in Europe between 1843 and 1854, painted landscapes and portraits. Lewis, the daughter of a black man and an Ojibwe woman, enrolled with abolitionist help at Oberlin College in Ohio and studied sculpture in Rome. Her works, which emphasized African-American themes, came into wide demand after the Civil War.

The reputations of black professional musicians of the antebellum period have suffered in comparison with the great tradition of black folk music epitomized by spirituals. But in Philadelphia a circle of black musicians wrote and performed a wide variety of music for orchestra, voice, and solo instruments. Similar circles existed in New Orleans, Boston, Cleveland, New York, Baltimore, and St. Louis. The best-known professional black singer of the period was Elizabeth Taylor Greenfield, born into slavery in Mississippi and raised by Quakers in Philadelphia. Known as the "Black Swan," Taylor gained renown for her vocal range.

Educated at Oberlin College, Edmonia Lewis (1843–1911?) studied sculpture in Rome and emerged as one of the more prolific American artists of the late nineteenth century.

7.4.7 Authors

The antebellum era was a golden age of African-American literature. Driven by suffering in slavery and limited freedom in the North, black authors portrayed an America that had not lived up to its revolutionary ideals. Black autobiography recounted life in bondage and dramatic escapes. Although the antislavery movement promoted the publication of scores of such narratives, the best known is Frederick Douglass's classic *Narrative of the Life of Frederick Douglass, an American Slave*, published in 1845.

African Americans also wrote history, novels, and poetry. In 1855 William C. Nell published *The Colored Patriots of the American Revolution*, which reminded its readers that black men had fought for American freedom. William Wells Brown, who had escaped from slavery in Kentucky, became the first African-American novelist. His *Clotel, or the President's Daughter*, published in 1853, used the affair between Thomas Jefferson and Sally Hemings to explore in fiction the moral ramifications of slaveholders who fathered children with their bondwomen. Another black novelist of the antebellum years was Martin R. Delany. His *Blake, or the Huts of America*, a story of emerging revolutionary consciousness among southern slaves, ran as a serial in the *Weekly Anglo-African* during 1859.

Black poets included George M. Horton, a slave living in North Carolina, who in 1829 published *The Hope of Liberty*. There was also James W. Whitfield of Buffalo, New York, who in 1853 lampooned the song "My Country 'tis of Thee." Whitfield's poem includes the lines:

America, it is to thee
Thou boasted land of liberty,—
Thou land of blood, and crime, and wrong.

African-American women who published fiction during the period include Frances Ellen Watkins Harper and Harriet E. Wilson. Harper was born free in Baltimore in 1825. Associated with the antislavery cause in Pennsylvania and Maine, she published poems depicting the sufferings of slaves. Her first collection, *Poems on Various Subjects*, appeared in 1854. Wilson published *Our Nig: Or, Sketches from the Life of a Free Black, in a Two-Story White House, North* in 1859. This is the first novel published by a black woman in the United States. In the genre of autobiographical fiction, it compared the lives of black domestic workers in the North with those of southern slaves. Wilson's book, however, received little attention during her lifetime, and until the 1980s critics believed a white author had written it.

At about the same time that Wilson wrote *Our Nig*, Hanna Crafts, who had recently escaped from slavery in North Carolina, wrote *The Bondwoman's Narrative*. Unpublished until 2002, this melodramatic autobiographical novel tells the story of a house slave and her escape to freedom.

Frances Ellen Watkins Harper (1825–1911) was born free in Baltimore. During the 1850s, she published antislavery poetry and traveled across the North as an antislavery speaker.

7.5 African-American Institutions

Compare and contrast the roles of free black institutions between 1820 and 1861.

During the antebellum decades, the black institutions that had appeared during the revolutionary era in urban areas of the North, Upper South, and—to a lesser extent—the Deep South grew in strength, numbers, and variety. Growing black populations, exertions of the African-American elite, and persistence of racial exclusion and segregation contributed to this phenomenon. Black institutions included schools, mutual aid organizations, benevolent and fraternal societies, self-improvement and temperance associations, literary groups, newspapers and journals, and theaters. But, aside from families, the most important black institutions remained the churches.

7.5.1 Churches

Black church buildings served as community centers. They housed schools and meeting places for other organizations. Antislavery societies often met in churches, and the churches harbored fugitive slaves. All of this went hand in hand with the community leadership black ministers provided. The ministers began schools and voluntary associations. They spoke against slavery, racial oppression, and what they considered weaknesses among African Americans. However, black ministers never spoke with one voice. Throughout the antebellum decades, many followed Jupiter Hammon (see Chapter 5) in admonishing their congregations that preparing one's soul for heaven had more importance than gaining equal rights on Earth.

This lithograph depicts the bishops of the African Methodist Episcopal Church and suggests both the church's humble origins and its remarkable growth during the antebellum years. Founder Richard Allen is portrayed at the center.

By 1846 the independent African Methodist Episcopal (AME) Church had 296 congregations in the United States and Canada totaling 17,375 members. In 1848 Frederick Douglass maintained that the AME Mother Bethel Church in Philadelphia was "the largest church in this Union," with 2,000–3,000 worshipers each Sunday. The AME Zion Church of New York City was probably the second largest black congregation, with about 2,000 members.

Most black Baptist, Presbyterian, Congregationalist, Episcopal, and Roman Catholic congregations remained affiliated with white denominations, although they rarely sent delegates to regional and national church councils. For example, the Episcopal Diocese of New York in 1819 excluded black ministers from its annual conventions, maintaining that African Americans "*are* socially degraded, and are not regarded as proper associates for the class of persons who attend our convention." Not until 1853 was white abolitionist William Jay able to convince New York Episcopalians to admit black representatives.

Many northern African Americans continued to attend white churches. To do so, they had to submit to the same second-class status that had driven Richard Allen and Absalom Jones to establish separate black churches in Philadelphia during the 1790s (see Chapter 5). Throughout the antebellum years, northern white churches required their black members to sit in separate sections during services, provided separate Sunday schools for black children, and insisted that black people take communion after white people. Even Quakers, who spearheaded white opposition to slavery in the North and South, often provided separate seating for black people at their meetings.

During the 1830s and 1840s, some black leaders criticized the existence of separate black congregations and denominations. Frederick Douglass called them "negro pews, on a higher and larger scale." Such churches, Douglass and others maintained, were part and parcel of a segregationist spirit that divided America according to complexion. Douglass also denounced what he considered the illiteracy and anti-intellectual bias of most black ministers. Growing numbers of African Americans, nevertheless, regarded such churches as sources of spiritual integrity and legitimate alternatives to second-class status among white Christians. (See Connecting the Past: The Great Awakening and the Black Church in Chapter 5.)

7.5.2 Schools

As we noted earlier in this chapter, education, like religion, was racially segregated in the North between 1820 and 1860. Tax-supported compulsory public education for children in the United States began in Massachusetts in 1827 and spread throughout the Northeast and Old Northwest during the 1830s. Some public schools, such as those in Cleveland, Ohio, during the 1850s, admitted black students. But usually, as soon as 20 or more African-American children appeared in a school district, white parents demanded that they attend separate schools. White people claimed that black children lacked mental capacity and lowered the quality of education. White people also feared that opening schools to black children would encourage more black people to live in a school district.

How to educate African-American children who were not allowed to attend school with white children became a persistent issue in the North. Until 1848 Ohio and the other states of the Old Northwest simply excluded black children from public schools and refused to allocate tax revenues to support separate facilities. The northeastern states were more willing to undertake such expenditures. But, even in these states, white residents resisted using tax dollars to fund education for African Americans. As a result, appropriations for black public schools lagged far behind those for public schools white children attended.

This tendency extended to cities where African-American leaders and white abolitionists had created private schools for black children. In 1812 the African School, established by Prince Hall in 1798, became part of Boston's public school system. As a result, like newly created black public schools in the city, it began to suffer from inadequate funding and a limited curriculum. The African Free Schools, opened in New York City in 1787 by the New York Society for Promoting the Manumission of Slaves, had a similar fate. In 1834, when these schools became part of New York's public school system, funding and attendance declined. By the 1850s public support for the city's black schools had become negligible.

Voices

The Constitution of the Pittsburgh African Education Society

Compared with black southerners, black northerners were fortunate to have access to education, and education societies were prominent among black self-improvement organizations. In January 1832 a group headed by John B. Vashon, a local black barber and philanthropist, met at Pittsburgh's African Church to establish such a society and a school. The following extracts from its constitution indicate the group's motives and plans.

> Whereas, ignorance in all ages has been found to debase the human mind, and to subject its votaries to the lowest vices, and most abject depravity— and it must be admitted, that ignorance is the sole cause of the present degradation and bondage of the people of color in these United States—that the intellectual capacity of the black man is equal to that of the white, and that he is equally susceptible of improvement, all ancient history makes manifest; and even modern examples put beyond a single doubt.
>
> We, therefore, the people of color, of the city and vicinity of Pittsburgh, and State of

Pennsylvania, for the purpose of dispersing the moral gloom that has so long hung around us, have, under Almighty God, associated ourselves together, which association shall be known by the name of the *Pittsburgh African Education Society*. . . .

> It shall be the duty of the Board of Managers . . . to purchase such books and periodicals as the Society may deem it expedient, they shall have power to raise money by subscription or otherwise, to purchase ground, and erect thereon a suitable building or buildings for the accommodation and education of youth, and a hall for the use of the Society. . . .

1. Why would this group claim that black ignorance was the "sole cause" of black degradation and enslavement?

2. Why was the Pittsburgh African Education Society necessary?

SOURCE: Dorothy Porten, ed., *Early Negro Writing, 1760–1837* (1971; reprint, Baltimore: Black Classics, 1995), 120–22.

Woefully inadequate public funding resulted in poor education or none at all for most black children across the North. The few black schools were dilapidated and overcrowded. White teachers who taught in them received lower pay than those who taught in white schools, and black teachers received even less, so teaching was generally poor. Black parents, however, often did not know their children received an inadequate education. Even black and white abolitionists tended to expect less from black students than from white students.

Some black leaders defended segregated schools as better for black children than integrated ones. They probably feared that the real choice was between separate black schools or none at all. But, by the 1830s, most northern African Americans favored racially integrated public education, and during the 1840s Frederick Douglass became a leading advocate for such a policy. Douglass, other black leaders, and their white abolitionist allies made the most progress in Massachusetts, where by 1845 all public schools, except those in Boston, had been integrated. After a 10-year struggle, the Massachusetts legislature finally ended segregated schools in that city. This victory encouraged the opponents of segregated public schools across the North. By 1860 integration had advanced among the region's smaller school districts. But, except for those in Boston, urban schools remained segregated on the eve of the Civil War.

In fact, the black elite had more success gaining admission to northern colleges during the antebellum period than most African-American children had in gaining an adequate primary education. Some colleges served African Americans exclusively. In 1854, white Presbyterian minister John Miller Dickey and his Quaker wife Sarah Emlen Cresson established Ashmun Institute in Oxford, Pennsylvania, to educate black missionaries who would go to Africa. Ashmun, later renamed Lincoln University, became the first black institution of higher learning in the United States. In 1855 the AME Church founded Wilberforce University, located near Columbus, Ohio, as another exclusively black college. Earlier some northern previously all-white colleges had begun to admit a few black students. They included Bowdoin in Maine, Dartmouth in New Hampshire, Harvard and Mount Pleasant in Massachusetts, Oneida Institute in New York, and Western Reserve University in Ohio. Because of its association with the anti-slavery movement, Oberlin College in Ohio became the most famous biracial institution of higher learning during the era. By 1860 many northern colleges, law schools, medical schools, and seminaries admitted black applicants, although not on an equal basis with white applicants.

7.5.3 Voluntary Associations

The African-American mutual aid, benevolent, self-improvement, and fraternal organizations that originated during the late eighteenth century proliferated during the antebellum decades. So did black literary and temperance associations.

Mutual aid societies became especially attractive to black women. In 1830 black women in Philadelphia had 27 such organizations, compared with 16 for black men. By 1855 Philadelphia had 108 black mutual aid societies. They enrolled 9,762 members, and had a combined annual income of $29,600 (approximately $9,770,000 today). Among black benevolent societies, African Dorcas Associations became especially prevalent. Started in 1828 in New York City by black women, these societies distributed used clothing to the poor, especially poor schoolchildren. During the early 1830s, black women also began New York City's Association for the Benefit of Colored Orphans. The association operated an orphanage that by 1851 had helped 524 children. Other black benevolent organizations in New York maintained the Colored Seaman's Home and a home for the elderly.

During the same period, the Prince Hall Masons created new lodges in the cities of the Northeast and the Chesapeake. Beginning during the 1840s, Black Odd Fellows lodges also became common. Even more prevalent were self-improvement, library, literary, and temperance organizations. These manifested the reform spirit that swept the North and the Upper South during the antebellum decades. Closely linked to evangelical Protestantism, reformers maintained that the moral regeneration of individuals was essential to perfecting society. African Americans shared this belief and formed organizations to put it into practice.

Among the more prestigious of the societies for black men were the Phoenix Literary Society, established in New York City in 1833, and the Philadelphia Library Company of Colored Persons, founded in 1833. There were also Pittsburgh's Theban Literary Society, founded in 1831, and Boston's Adelphi Union for the Promotion of Literature and Science, established in 1836. Black women formed the Female Literary Society of Philadelphia in 1831, and New York City's Ladies Literary Society in 1834. The Ladies Literary Society of Buffalo emerged in the mid-1830s, and Boston's Afric-American Female Intelligence Society began in 1832.

Black temperance societies spread even more widely than literary and benevolent organizations, although they also tended to be more short-lived. Like their white counterparts, black temperance advocates were middle-class activists who sought to stop those lower on the social ladder from abusing alcoholic beverages. The temperance societies organized lecture series and handed out literature that portrayed the negative physical, economic, and moral consequences of liquor. The societies' effectiveness is debatable, but they helped unite black communities.

7.6 Free African Americans in the Upper South

Compare and contrast the ways in which free African Americans lived in the North, South, and West during the decades prior to the Civil War.

Life for free black people in the South during the antebellum period differed from that in the North. The free black experience in the Upper South also differed from what it was in the Deep South. In general, free African Americans in the North, despite the limits on their liberty, had opportunities their southern counterparts did not enjoy. Each of the southern regions, nevertheless, offered some advantages to free black residents.

The free black people of the Upper South had much in common with their northern counterparts. In particular, African Americans in the Chesapeake cities of Baltimore, Washington, Richmond, and Norfolk had ties to black northerners, ranging from family and church affiliations to business connections and membership in fraternal organizations. Nevertheless the South's agricultural economy and slavery set free black workers in the Upper South apart from their northern counterparts. Although nearly half the free black population in the North lived in cities, only one-third did so in the Upper South, hampering the development there of black communities.

The impact of slavery on the lives of free African Americans in the Upper South also caused more basic differences. Unlike black northerners, free black people in the Upper South lived alongside slaves. Many had family ties to slaves and were more directly involved than black northerners in the slaves' suffering. They did so in several capacities, including efforts to prevent the sale south of relatives and friends, reimbursing masters for manumissions, and funding freedom suits. They earned a reputation among white southerners as harborers of escaped slaves. Southern white politicians and journalists used the close connection between free black southerners and slaves to justify limiting the freedom of the former group.

Free black people of the Upper South also faced more risk of being enslaved than black northerners did. Except for Louisiana, with its French and Spanish heritage, all southern states' legal systems assumed African Americans to be slaves unless they could prove otherwise. Free black people had to carry **free papers** and renew them

free papers

Proof of freedom that free black people had to carry at all times in the southern states prior to emancipation. The papers, issued by state governments, identified an individual by name, age, sex, color, height, and so forth.

periodically. They could be enslaved if they lost their papers or had them stolen. Sheriffs routinely arrested free African Americans on the assumption that they might be fugitive slaves. Even when those arrested proved they were free, their jailors sometimes sold them into slavery to pay the cost of imprisoning them. Free African Americans who got into debt in the South similarly risked being sold into slavery to pay off their creditors.

As the antebellum period progressed, the distinction between free and enslaved African Americans narrowed in the Upper South. Although a few northern states allowed black men to vote, no southern state did after 1835 when North Carolina followed Tennessee—the only other southern state to allow black suffrage—in revoking the right to vote among property-owning black men. Free black people of the Upper South also had more difficulty traveling, owning firearms, congregating in groups, and being out after dark than did black northerners. Although residential segregation was less pronounced in southern cities than in the North, African Americans of the Upper South faced a more thorough exclusion from hotels, taverns, trains and coaches, parks, theaters, and hospitals.

Free black people in the Upper South experienced various degrees of hardship in earning a living, although, during the nineteenth century, their employment expanded as slavery declined in Maryland and northern Virginia. Free persons of color in rural areas generally worked as tenant farmers. Some had to sign labor contracts that reduced them to semislavery. But others owned land, and a few owned slaves. Rural free African Americans also worked as miners, lumberjacks, and teamsters. In Upper South urban areas, most free black men worked as unskilled day laborers, waiters, whitewashers, and stevedores. Free black women worked as laundresses and domestic servants. As in the North, the most successful African Americans were barbers, butchers, tailors, caterers, merchants, and those teamsters and hack drivers who owned their own horses and vehicles. Before 1850 free black people in the Upper South had less competition from European immigrants for jobs than was the case in northern cities. Therefore, although the Upper South had fewer factories than the North, more free black men worked in them. This changed during the 1850s when Irish and German immigrants competed against free black people in the Upper South just as they did in the North for all types of employment. As in the North, immigrants often used violence to drive African Americans out of skilled trades.

These circumstances made it difficult for free black people in the Upper South to maintain community institutions. In addition, the measures white authorities adopted to prevent slave revolt limited free black autonomy, and such measures became pervasive after the revolt Nat Turner led in southern Virginia in 1831. Many black churches and schools had to close or curtail their activities. The Baltimore Conference of the AME Church, which had been expanding during the 1820s, declined during the early 1830s. Some states required that black churches have white ministers, and some black ministers left for the North. Yet free African Americans persevered. During the late 1830s, new black churches organized in Louisville and Lexington, Kentucky, and in St. Louis, Missouri. Between 1836 and 1856, the Baltimore AME Conference rebounded and more than doubled its membership. By 1860 Baltimore had 15 black churches. Louisville had nine, and Nashville, St. Louis, and Norfolk had four each. Most of these churches ministered to both enslaved and free members.

Black schools and voluntary associations in the Upper South also survived white efforts to suppress them, although the schools faced great challenges. Racially integrated schools and public funding for segregated black schools were out of the question in the South. Most black children received no formal education. Black churches, a few white churches, and a scattering of black and white individuals maintained what educational facilities the Upper South had for black children. The schools met—often sporadically—in churches or private homes. They generally lacked books, chalkboards, and desks. Particularly noteworthy are the educational efforts of the Oblate Sisters

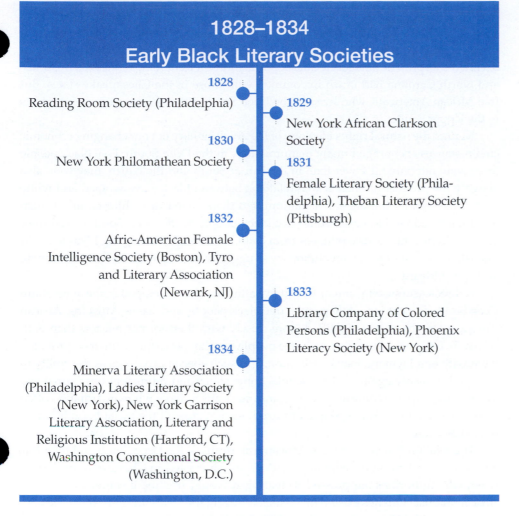

1828–1834
Early Black Literary Societies

1828
Reading Room Society (Philadelphia)

1829
New York African Clarkson Society

1830
New York Philomathean Society

1831
Female Literary Society (Philadelphia), Theban Literary Society (Pittsburgh)

1832
Afric-American Female Intelligence Society (Boston), Tyro and Literary Association (Newark, NJ)

1833
Library Company of Colored Persons (Philadelphia), Phoenix Literacy Society (New York)

1834
Minerva Literary Association (Philadelphia), Ladies Literary Society (New York), New York Garrison Literary Association, Literary and Religious Institution (Hartford, CT), Washington Conventional Society (Washington, D.C.)

of Providence and John F. Cook. The Oblate Sisters established the first black Roman Catholic religious order in the United States. Cook was an AME and Presbyterian minister who lived in Washington, D.C.

Elizabeth Clovis Lange, who was of Haitian descent, established the Oblate Sisters in Baltimore in 1829 to provide a free education to the children of French-speaking black refugees from the Haitian Revolution. The sisters taught English, math, composition, and religion. In 1836 the Sisters also built a chapel that became the first black Catholic church in the United States. At his Union Seminary, Cook, from 1834 until his death in 1854, taught subjects similar to those that the Sisters taught. Both the Sisters and Cook confronted persecution and inadequate funding. Cook had to flee Washington temporarily in 1835 to avoid being killed by a mob. Nevertheless, he passed his school on to his son, who kept it going through the Civil War. Meanwhile, the Oblate Sisters had increased their influence in the black community.

Black voluntary associations, particularly in urban areas of the Upper South, fared better than black schools. By 1838 Baltimore had at least 40 such organizations, including chapters of the Prince Hall Masons, Black Odd Fellows, literary societies, and temperance groups. In Norfolk, the Masons enrolled slaves as well as freemen. As in the North, black women organized their own voluntary associations. Washington's Colored Female Roman Catholic Beneficial Society, for example, provided death benefits for its members. Black benevolent organizations in the Upper South also sought to apprentice orphans to black tradesmen; sponsored fairs, picnics, and parades; and provided protection against kidnappers.

7.6.1 Free African Americans in the Deep South

More than half the South's free black population lived in Maryland, Delaware, and Virginia. To the west and south of these states, the number of free people of color declined sharply. The smaller free black populations in Kentucky, Tennessee, Missouri, and North Carolina had much in common with those in the Chesapeake states. But free African Americans who lived in the Deep South differed from their counterparts in the Upper South.

Neither the natural rights ideology of the revolutionary era nor changing economic circumstances encouraged many manumissions in the Deep South. Free black people there were not only far fewer than in the Upper South and the North, they were also "largely the product of illicit sexual relations between black slave women and white men." Slaveholder fathers either manumitted their mixed-race children or let them buy their freedom. However, some free black people of the Deep South traced their ancestry to free mixed-race refugees from Haiti, who sought during the 1790s to avoid that island nation's bloody revolutionary struggle by fleeing to Charleston, Savannah, and New Orleans.

A three-caste system similar to that in Latin America developed in the antebellum Deep South. It included white people, free black people, and slaves. Most free African Americans in the region identified more closely with their former masters than with slaves. To ensure the loyalty of such free people of color, powerful white men provided them with employment, loans, protection, and such special privileges as the ability to vote and to testify against white people. Some states and municipalities formalized this relationship by requiring free African Americans to have white guardians—often their blood relatives. Some people of mixed descent crossed the racial boundary and passed as white.

The relationship between free African Americans of the Deep South and their former masters extended to religion. An AME church existed in Charleston until 1818, when city authorities suppressed it, fearing it would become a center of sedition. African Baptist churches existed in Savannah during the 1850s. In 1842 New Orleans's Sisters of the Holy Family became the second Roman Catholic religious order for black women in the United States. But free black people in the region were more likely than those farther north to remain in white churches largely because they identified with the white elite.

In the Deep South, free African Americans—over half of whom lived in cities—concentrated more in urban areas than did their counterparts in the North and Upper South. Although Deep South cities restricted their employment opportunities, free black people in Charleston, Savannah, Mobile, and New Orleans maintained stronger positions in the skilled trades than free black people in the Upper South or the North. By 1860 in Charleston, three-quarters of the free black men worked in skilled trades. Free African Americans made up only 15 percent of Charleston's male population, yet they constituted 25 percent of its carpenters, 40 percent of its tailors, and 75 percent of its millwrights. In New Orleans, free black men predominated as carpenters, masons, bricklayers, barbers, tailors, cigar makers, and shoemakers. In both cities, free African Americans compared favorably to white people in their ratio of skilled to unskilled workers. The close ties between free black people and the white upper-class explain much of this success.

Despite this relationship, free black communities comparable to those in the Upper South and North arose in the cities of the Deep South. Although they usually lacked separate black churches as community centers, free African Americans in the region created other institutions. In Charleston the Brown Fellowship Society survived throughout the antebellum period. Charleston also had a chapter of the Prince Hall Masons, and free black men and women in the city maintained other fraternal and benevolent associations. In addition to similar sorts of organizations, the free black elite in

New Orleans published literary journals and supported an opera house. During the 1850s, Savannah—where black churches existed—had at least three black volunteer fire companies, a porters' association, and several benevolent societies.

Because black churches were rare, wealthy African Americans and black fraternal organizations led in organizing private schools for black children in the cities of the Deep South. In Charleston, the Brown Fellowship Society organized an academy. New Orleans had several black schools, most of which were conducted in French—the first or second language for many free black people in the city. Some of the wealthier free black families in these cities sent their children to Europe for education, and the literacy rate among free black people in both Charleston and New Orleans reached markedly high levels for the antebellum period.

In all, free people of color in the Deep South differed substantially from those in the Upper South and the North. Their ties to the white slaveholding class gave them tangible advantages. Yet they were not without sympathy for those who remained in slavery, and white authorities never fully trusted them to be loyal to the slave system. In particular, white people feared contact between free African Americans who lived in the ports of the Deep South and black northerners—especially black sailors. As a new round of slave unrest began in the South and a more militant northern antislavery movement got under way during the 1820s, free black people in the Deep South faced difficult circumstances.

7.6.2   Free African Americans in the Far West

Free black communities in the North, Upper South, and Deep South each had unique features, and all of them had existed for decades by the antebellum period. In the huge region stretching from the Great Plains to the Pacific coast, which had become part of the United States during the 1840s, free black people were rare. Black communities there were just emerging in a few isolated localities. As historian Quintard Taylor notes, the 4,000 "nominally free" African Americans who lived in California in 1860 constituted "75 percent of the free black population of the West." In the major slaveholding state of Texas, census figures indicate that a tiny free black population decreased from 397 in 1850 to 355 in 1860. The prevalence of discriminatory "black laws" in the region's states and territories partially explains the small number of free black westerners. Like similar laws in the Old Northwest, these laws either banned free African Americans or restricted the activities of those allowed to settle. Nevertheless a few black families sought economic opportunities in the West. During the 1840s they joined white Americans in settling Oregon. The California gold rush of 1849 had by 1852 attracted about 2,000 African Americans, most of whom were men, among hundreds of thousands of white Americans.

Usually black Californians lived and worked in multicultural communities that also included people of Chinese, Jamaican, Latin American, and white American descent. But in a few localities, African Americans predominated. Some black Californians prospered as gold prospectors. Others worked as steamship stewards, cooks, barbers, laundresses, mechanics, saloonkeepers, whitewashers, porters, and domestics. By the early 1850s, there were black communities centered on churches in San Francisco, Sacramento, and Los Angeles. In 1851 Bernard Fletcher established an AME church in Sacramento. The following year, John Jamison Moore established an AME Zion church in San Francisco. As in the East, these black communities organized benevolent and self-help societies. Although most African Americans who went west were men, black women sometimes accompanied their husbands and families. Those black women who were better off raised funds for AME churches and voluntary associations. Others worked as cooks, laundresses, and prostitutes. (For more on free African Americans in California, see Chapter 10.)

Painted in 1858 by Thomas Waterman Wood, *Market Woman* portrays a young woman carrying produce she has purchased. There is no indication of her status as either free or enslaved. The portrait provides an example of how black women dressed in antebellum America.

Conclusion

During the antebellum period, free African-American communities that had emerged during the revolutionary era grew and fostered black institutions. Particularly in the urban North, life in these segregated communities foreshadowed the pattern of black life from the end of the Civil War into the twentieth century. Although the black elite could gain education, professional expertise, and wealth despite white prejudices, most northern people of color remained poor. Extended families, churches, segregation, political marginality, and limited educational opportunities shaped their lives.

Free black people in the Upper South and Deep South faced even greater difficulties. Presumed to be slaves if they could not prove otherwise, they confronted more danger of enslavement and harsher restrictive legislation than their counterparts in the North. Even so, energetic black communities existed in the Upper South throughout the antebellum period. In the Deep South, the small free black population was better off economically than were free black people in other regions. But it depended on white slaveholders, who proved to be unreliable allies as sectional controversy mounted. The antislavery movement, secession, and the Civil War would have a more profound impact on the free black communities in the South than in the North. Although it is not wise to generalize about free black people in the trans-Mississippi West, their presence on the Pacific coast in particular demonstrates their involvement in the westward expansion that characterized the United States during the antebellum years. Their West Coast communities indicate the adaptability of black institutions to new circumstances.

Chapter Timeline

AFRICAN-AMERICAN EVENTS	NATIONAL EVENTS
1800–1810	
1807 New Jersey disfranchises black men	**1803** Louisiana Purchase **1807** Robert Fulton's steamboat is launched in New York Harbor
1810–1820	
1812 African School becomes part of the Boston public school system **1818** Connecticut bars new black voters	**1812** War of 1812 begins **1815** War of 1812 ends **1819** Panic of 1819 begins
1820–1830	
1821 New York retains property qualification for black voters	**1825** John Quincy Adams becomes president Erie Canal opens

AFRICAN-AMERICAN EVENTS	NATIONAL EVENTS
1822	**1827**
Rhode Island disfranchises black voters	Massachusetts pioneers compulsory public education
1824	**1828**
Massachusetts defeats attempt to ban black migration to that state	Andrew Jackson is elected president
1827	
Freedom's Journal begins publication	
1828	
African Dorcas Association is established	
1829	
Cincinnati expels black residents	

1830–1840

1831	**1832**
Maria W. Stewart criticizes treatment of black workers	Surge in European immigration begins
1834	**1832–1833**
African Free Schools become part of New York City public school system	Nullification Crisis
1838	**1837**
Pennsylvania disfranchises black voters	Panic of 1837
1842	
Rhode Island revives black male voting	
1843	
Edmonia Lewis born	

1840–1850

1845	**1846–1848**
Narrative of the Life of Frederick Douglass is published	War against Mexico
1849	**1850**
Ohio black laws repealed	Compromise of 1850

Review Questions

1. How was black freedom in the North limited in the antebellum decades?

2. How did northern African Americans deal with these limits?

3. What was the relationship of the African-American elite to urban black communities?

4. How did African-American institutions fare between 1820 and 1861?

5. Compare black life in the North to free black life in the Upper South, Deep South, and California.

Retracing the Odyssey

Boston African-American National Historic Site: Black Heritage Trail and Museum of Afro-American History, Boston, Massachusetts. Visitors may follow the Black Heritage Trail to historic locations located in Boston's antebellum black community on Beacon Hill. Of particular interest are the African Meeting House and the Abiel Smith School.

New Bedford Whaling Museum, New Bedford, Massachusetts. Exhibits include "Heroes in the Ships: African Americans in the Whaling Industry, 1840–1900."

Chattanooga African American Museum, Chattanooga, Tennessee. A major exhibit focuses on free black businessmen in antebellum Chattanooga.

Recommended Reading

Ira Berlin. *Slaves without Masters: The Free Negro in the Antebellum South.* New York: New Press, 1971. This classic study is still the most comprehensive treatment of free African Americans in the antebellum South.

W. Jeffrey Bolster. *Black Jacks: African American Seamen in the Age of Sail.* Cambridge, MA: Harvard University Press, 1997. *Black Jacks* explores the lives of black seamen between 1740 and 1865.

Leonard Curry. *The Free Black in Urban America, 1800–1850: The Shadow of the Dream.* Chicago: University of Chicago Press, 1981. Curry provides a comprehensive account of urban African-American life in the antebellum period.

Philip S. Foner. *History of Black America: From the Emergence of the Cotton Kingdom to the Eve of the Compromise of 1850.* Westport, CT: Greenwood, 1983. This second volume of Foner's three-volume series presents a wealth of information about African-American life between 1820 and 1861, especially about the northern black community.

James Oliver Horton and Lois E. Horton. *In Hope of Liberty: Culture, Community, and Protest among Northern Free Blacks, 1700–1860.* New York: Oxford University Press, 1997. The authors focus on how the northern black community responded to difficult circumstances, especially during the antebellum decades.

Leon F. Litwack. *North of Slavery: The Negro in the Free States, 1790–1860.* Chicago: University of Chicago Press, 1961. This book emphasizes how northern white people treated African Americans. It is a useful guide to the status of African Americans in the antebellum North.

Quintard Taylor. *In Search of the Racial Frontier: African Americans in the American West, 1528–1990.* New York: Norton, 1998. This is the first book-length study of black westerners.

Additional Bibliography

Community Studies

Tommy L. Bogger. *Free Blacks in Norfolk, Virginia, 1790–1860: The Darker Side of Freedom.* Charlottesville: University Press of Virginia, 1997.

Letitia Woods Brown. *Free Negroes in the District of Columbia, 1790–1846.* New York: Oxford University Press, 1972.

Melvin Patrick Ely. *Israel on the Appomattox: A Southern Experiment in Black Freedom from the 1790s Through the Civil War.* New York: Knopf, 2004.

Leslie M. Harris. *In the Shadow of Slavery: African Americans in New York City, 1626–1863.* Chicago: University of Chicago Press, 2003.

James Oliver Horton and Lois E. Horton. *Black Bostonians: Family Life and Community Struggle in the Antebellum North.* New York: Holmes and Meier, 1979.

Bobby L. Lovett. *The African-American History of Nashville,Tennessee, 1780–1930: Elites and Dilemmas.* Fayetteville: University of Arkansas Press, 1999.

Gary B. Nash. *Forging Freedom: The Formation of Philadelphia's Black Community, 1720–1840.* Cambridge, MA: Harvard University Press, 1988.

Christopher Phillips. *Freedom's Port: The African-American Community of Baltimore, 1790–1860.* Urbana: University of Illinois Press, 1997.

Bernard E. Powers Jr. *Black Charlestonians: A Social History, 1822–1885*. Fayetteville: University of Arkansas Press, 1994.

Harry Reed. *Platform for Change: The Foundations of the Northern Free Black Community, 1775–1865*. East Lansing: Michigan State University Press, 1994.

Judith Kelleher Schafer. *Becoming Free, Remaining Free: Manumission and Enslavement in New Orleans, 1846–1862*. Baton Rouge: Louisiana State University Press, 2003.

Julie Winch. *Philadelphia's Black Elite: Activism, Accommodation, and the Struggle for Autonomy, 1787–1848*. Philadelphia: Temple University Press, 1988.

State-Level Studies

Barbara Jeanne Fields. *Slavery and Freedom on the Middle Ground: Maryland During the Nineteenth Century*. New Haven, CT: Yale University Press, 1985.

John Hope Franklin. *The Free Negro in North Carolina, 1790–1860*. Chapel Hill: University of North Carolina Press, 1943.

Graham Russell Hodges. *Root and Branch: African Americans in New York and East Jersey, 1613–1863*. Chapel Hill: University of North Carolina Press, 1999.

John H. Russell. *The Free Negro in Virginia, 1619–1865*. 1913. Reprint, New York: Negro Universities Press, 1969.

H. E. Sterkx. *The Free Negro in Antebellum Louisiana*. Rutherford, NJ: Fairleigh Dickinson University Press, 1972.

Marina Wilkramangrake. *A World in Shadow—The Free Black in Antebellum South Carolina*. Columbia: University of South Carolina Press, 1973.

Race Relations

Francis D. Adams. *Alienable Rights: The Exclusion of African Americans in a White Man's Land, 1619–2000*. New York: HarperCollins, 2003.

Noel Ignatiev. *How the Irish Became White*. New York: Routledge, 1995.

Stephen Middleton. *The Black Laws: Race and the Legal Process in Ohio 1787–1860*. Athens: Ohio University Press, 2005.

Rita Roberts. *Evangelicalism and the Politics of Reform in Northern Black Thought 1776–1863*. Baton Rouge: Louisiana State University Press, 2010.

David Roediger. *The Wages of Whiteness: Race and the Making of the American Working Class*. New York: Verso, 1991.

Joel Williamson. *New People: Miscegenation and Mulattoes in the United States*. New York: Free Press, 1980.

Carol Wilson. *Freedom at Risk: The Kidnapping of Free Blacks in America, 1780–1865*. Lexington: University Press of Kentucky, 1994.

Women and Family

Erica Armstrong Dunbar. *A Fragile Freedom: African American Women and Emancipation in the Antebellum City*. New Haven, CT: Yale University Press, 2008.

Virginia Meacham Gould, ed. *Chained to the Rock of Adversity: To Be Free, Black, and Female in the Old South*. Athens: University of Georgia Press, 1998.

Herbert G. Gutman. *The Black Family in Slavery and Freedom, 1750–1925*. New York: Pantheon Books, 1977.

Lynn M. Hudson. *The Making of "Mammy Pleasant": A Black Entrepreneur in Nineteenth-Century San Francisco*. Urbana: University of Illinois Press, 2003.

Wilma King. *Free Black Women during the Slave Era*. Columbia: University of Missouri Press, 2006.

Suzanne Lebsock. *The Free Women of Petersburg: Status and Culture in a Southern Town, 1784–1860*. New York: Norton, 1984.

T. O. Madden Jr., with Ann L. Miller. *We Were Always Free: The Maddens of Culpeper County, Virginia, a 200 Year Family History*. New York: Norton, 1992.

Institutions and the Black Elite

Douglas Walter Bristol. *Knights of the Razor: Black Barbers in Slavery and Freedom*. Baltimore: Johns Hopkins University Press, 2009.

Carlton Mabee. *Black Education in New York State*. Syracuse, NY: Syracuse University Press, 1979.

Eileen Southern. *The Music of Black America*. 2nd ed. New York: Norton, 1983.

Loretta J. Williams. *Black Freemasonry and Middle-Class Realities*. Columbia: University of Missouri Press, 1980.

Chapter 8

Opposition to Slavery
1730–1833

This drawing, known as "Nat Turner Preaches Religion," portrays Turner telling "friends and brothers" in August 1831 that God has chosen them to lead a violent "struggle for freedom."

 Learning Objectives

After reading this chapter, you should be able to:

8.1 Explain how abolitionism began in America.

8.2 Analyze the forces and events that fueled a more radical antislavery movement.

8.3 Evaluate the goals of the American Colonization Society.

8.4   Discuss the role of black women in the abolition movement.

8.5   Compare and contrast David Walker and Nat Turner.

> **Beloved brethren—here let me tell you, and believe it, that the Lord our God, as true as he sits on his throne in heaven, and as true as our Savior died to redeem the world, will give you a Hannibal [an ancient Carthaginian general], and when the Lord shall have raised him up, and given him to you for your possession, O my suffering brethren! . . . Read the history particularly of Hayti, and see how they were butchered by the whites, and do you take warning. The person whom God Shall give you, give him your support and let him go his length, and behold in him the salvation of your God. God will indeed, deliver you through him from your deplorable and wretched condition under the Christians of America.**

—David Walker's Appeal

In Boston in 1829, black abolitionist David Walker wrote the words that begin this chapter. They suggest the sense early nineteenth-century Americans had of the nearness of God and the anguish a free black man felt about his brothers and sisters in bondage.

In his harsh language and demands for action, Walker anticipated the militant black and white abolitionists of the 1830s, 1840s, and 1850s. He bluntly portrayed the oppression African Americans suffered. He urged black men to redeem themselves by defending their loved ones from abuse. If that led to violence and death, he asked, "Had you not rather be killed than be a slave to a tyrant, who takes the life of your mother, wife and dear little children?" Through his provocative language and efforts to have his *Appeal . . . to the Colored Citizens of the World* distributed in the South, Walker became a prophet of violent revolution against slaveholders.

Walker's *Appeal* was not just a reaction to slavery; it was also a response to a conservative brand of antislavery reform. This chapter explores the emergence, during the eighteenth century, of abolitionism in America; its transformation during the early nineteenth century; and the beginning of a more radical antislavery movement by the late 1820s. Slave revolt conspiracies; political, social, and religious turmoil; and wide-ranging reform shaped this process. Black leaders, including Walker, Denmark Vesey, and Nat Turner, were major contributors. So was white abolitionist William Lloyd Garrison.

8.1 Antislavery Begins in America

Explain how abolitionism began in America.

The antislavery movement in its broadest context reflected economic, intellectual, and moral changes that affected the Atlantic world during the Age of Revolution that began during the 1760s. In the United States, that age forged *two* antislavery movements that survived until the end of the Civil War. Although separate, the two movements influenced each other. The first movement arose in the South among slaves with the help of free African Americans and a few sympathetic white people. As we mentioned in earlier chapters, from the seventeenth century onward enslaved African Americans, individually and in groups, sought their freedom through violent and nonviolent means. Before the revolutionary era, however, they only wanted to free themselves. They did not seek to destroy slavery as a social system.

The second antislavery movement consisted of black and white abolitionists in the North, with outposts in the Upper South. Although abolitionists were always a small minority, far more white people engaged in this movement than in the one southern slaves conducted. In the North, white people controlled the larger antislavery organizations, although African Americans led in direct action against slavery. In the Upper South, African Americans could not openly establish or participate in antislavery organizations, but they cooperated covertly and informally with white abolitionists.

This second antislavery movement began during the 1730s when white Quakers in New Jersey and Pennsylvania realized slaveholding contradicted their belief in spiritual equality. Therefore, they advocated the abolition of slavery—at least among their fellow Quakers—in their home states and in the Chesapeake. As members of a denomination that emphasized nonviolence, Quakers generally expected slavery to be abolished peacefully and gradually.

Quakers remained prominent in the northern antislavery movement for the next 130 years. But the American Revolution, together with the French Revolution that began in 1789 and the Haitian struggle for independence between 1791 and 1804 (see Chapter 5), revitalized the northern and southern antislavery movements and changed their nature. The revolutionary doctrine, endorsed by all three revolutions, that all men had a natural right to life, liberty, and property led other northerners besides Quakers and African Americans to support the antislavery cause.

In 1775 Philadelphia Quakers organized the first antislavery society in the world. But their organization lapsed during the War for Independence. When they regrouped in 1784 as the Society for the Promotion of the Abolition of Slavery, they attracted non-Quakers. Among the first of these were Benjamin Rush and Benjamin Franklin, both of whom embraced natural rights doctrines. Revolutionary principles also influenced Alexander Hamilton and John Jay, who helped organize New York's first antislavery society. Similarly Prince Hall, the most prominent black abolitionist of his time, based his effort to abolish slavery in Massachusetts on universal rights. He contended that African Americans "have in common with all other men a natural right to our freedom."

Black and white abolitionists led in abolishing slavery in the North. However, the early northern antislavery movement had several limiting features. First, black and white abolitionists had similar goals but worked in separate organizations. Even white Quaker abolitionists rarely mixed socially with African Americans or welcomed them to their meetings. Second, except in parts of New England, northern abolitionists supported *gradual* emancipation because they believed they had to protect slaveholders' economic interests. Third, despite natural rights rhetoric, white abolitionists did not advocate equal rights for black people. As we discussed in Chapter 7, in most northern states, laws kept free black people from enjoying such rights. Fourth, early northern abolitionists did little on behalf of abolition in the South, where most slaves lived.

All this indicates that neither Quaker piety nor natural rights principles created a truly egalitarian or sectionally aggressive northern abolitionism. Instead, it took major antislavery efforts carried out by black southerners, widespread religious revivalism, demands for reform, and the growth of northern black institutions to establish a framework for a more biracial and wide-ranging antislavery movement.

8.1.1 From Gabriel to Denmark Vesey

Gabriel's abortive slave revolt conspiracy of 1800 in Virginia (discussed in Chapter 5) owed as much to revolutionary ideology as did the northern antislavery movement. The arrival of Haitian refugees in that state led to slave unrest throughout the 1790s, and Gabriel hoped to attract French revolutionary support. Although he was betrayed, and he and 26 of his followers executed, the revolutionary spirit and insurrectionary network he established lived on (see Map 8-1). Virginia authorities had to suppress another slave conspiracy in 1802, and for years sporadic minor revolts erupted.

Gabriel's conspiracy had two other consequences. The first involved the Quaker-led antislavery societies of the Chesapeake. These organizations had always been small and weak compared with antislavery societies in the North. Unlike their northern counterparts, the Chesapeake societies concentrated more on helping free people illegally held as slaves than on promoting emancipation. The revelation of Gabriel's plot worsened conditions for these organizations. State and local governments suppressed them, or they withered under negative public opinion. The chance that Maryland, Virginia, and North Carolina would follow the northeastern states' example in abolishing slavery gradually and peacefully all but vanished.

The second consequence involved most white southerners and many white northerners. Gabriel's conspiracy convinced them that, so long as African Americans lived among them, a race war like the one in Haiti could erupt in the United States. Slaveholders and their defenders argued that this threat did not result from the oppressiveness of slavery. Instead, they claimed, people of African descent were naturally suited for bondage. Slaves, they asserted, would be content if a growing free black class did not instigate resistance and revolt.

Slavery's defenders contended that free African Americans were dangerous, criminal, and potentially revolutionary. They had to be regulated, subdued, and ultimately expelled from the country to prevent catastrophe. No system of emancipation that would increase the number of free black people in the United States could be tolerated. Slaveholders who had never shown a willingness to free their slaves began to claim they would favor emancipation if it

Map 8-1 Major Slave Conspiracies and Uprisings, 1800–1831

Major slave conspiracies and revolts were rare between 1800 and 1860. This was in part because those that took place frightened masters and led them to adopt policies aimed at preventing recurrences.

Does the geographical distribution of slave revolts suggest anything about their nature?

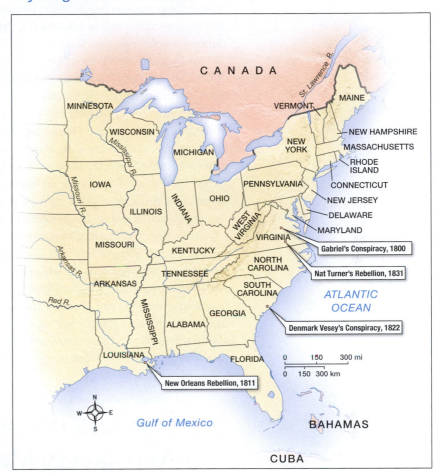

were not for fear of enlarging such a dangerous group. As an elderly Thomas Jefferson put it, white southerners had "the wolf by the ear": once they had enslaved black people, it was impossible to free them safely. Without the restrictions slavery placed on African Americans, southern politicians and journalists argued, they would become economic competitors to white workers, a perpetual criminal class, and a revolutionary threat to white rule.

Events in and about Charleston, South Carolina, in 1822 appeared to confirm the threat. In that year black informants revealed to local authorities that Denmark Vesey, a free black carpenter, had organized a massive slave revolt conspiracy. Like Gabriel before him, Vesey could read and was well aware of the revolutions that had shaken the Atlantic world. Born most likely on the Danish-ruled Caribbean island of St. Thomas, Vesey—a former sailor—had been to Haiti and hoped for Haitian aid for an antislavery revolution in the South Carolina low country. He understood the significance of the July 14, 1789, storming of the Bastille—a fortress-prison in Paris— that marked the start of the French Revolution and planned to start his revolution on July 14, 1822. He had read the antislavery speeches of northern members of Congress during the 1820 debates over the admission of Missouri to the Union, and he may have hoped for northern aid.

However, religion had a more prominent role in Vesey's plot than in Gabriel's. Vesey, a Bible-quoting Methodist who conducted religious classes, resented white authorities' attempts in 1818 to suppress Charleston's African Methodist Episcopal (AME) Church. He believed passages in the Bible about the enslavement of Hebrews in Egypt and their deliverance promised freedom for African Americans. Vesey also relied on aspects of African religion that had survived among low-country slaves to promote his revolutionary efforts. To reach slaves whose Christian convictions blended in with West African spiritualism, he relied on Jack Pritchard—known as Gullah Jack. A "conjure-man" born in East Africa, Pritchard distributed charms and cast spells he claimed would make black revolutionaries invincible.

Vesey and his associates planned to capture arms and ammunition and seize control of Charleston. But Gullah Jack's charms failed to protect against white vigilance and black informers. About a month before the revolt was to begin, the arrest of one of Vesey's lieutenants put authorities on guard. Vesey moved the date of the uprising up to June 16. Then on June 14 a house servant told his master about the plot, the local government called in the state militia, and arrests followed. Over several weeks, law officers rounded up 131 suspects. The accused received public trials, and juries convicted 76 of them. Thirty-five, including Vesey and Gullah Jack, were hanged. Thirty-seven were banished. Courts convicted four white men—three of them foreigners—of inciting slaves to revolt. These four received prison sentences and fines.

After the executions, Charleston's city government destroyed what remained of the local AME church, and white churches assumed responsibility for supervising other black congregations. In addition, white South Carolinians sought to make slave patrols more efficient. The state legislature outlawed assemblages of slaves and banned teaching slaves to read. Local authorities jailed black seamen whose ships docked in Charleston until the ships prepared to leave. Assuming that free black and white abolitionists inspired slave unrest, white South Carolinians became more suspicious of local free African Americans and of white Yankees who visited their state.

8.2 The Path toward a More Radical Antislavery Movement

Analyze the forces and events that fueled a more radical antislavery movement.

Gabriel's conspiracy, Vesey's conspiracy, and the publication of Walker's *Appeal* all took place during a long period of economic, political, and social turmoil. As we describe in earlier chapters, the invention of the cotton gin in 1793 led to a vast westward expansion of cotton cultivation. Where cotton went, so did slavery. By the late 1820s, southern slaveholders and their slaves had pushed into what was then the Mexican province of Texas. Meanwhile, the states of the Old Northwest passed from frontier conditions to commercial farming. By 1825 the Erie Canal linked this region economically to the Northeast. Later railroads carried the Old Northwest's agricultural products to East Coast cities. An enormous amount of grain and meat also flowed down the Ohio and Mississippi Rivers. This commerce encouraged the growth of such cities as Pittsburgh, Cincinnati, Louisville, St. Louis, Memphis, and New Orleans. As steamboats became common and networks of macadam turnpikes (paved with crushed stone and tar), canals, and railroads spread, travel time diminished. Americans became more mobile, families scattered, and ties to local communities weakened. For African Americans, subject to the domestic slave trade, mobility came with a high price.

The factory system, which arose in urban areas of the Northeast and spread to parts of the Old Northwest and Upper South, also caused disruption. As cities grew and immigration from Europe increased, native black and white Americans had to compete for employment with foreign-born workers. Farmers became more dependent on urban markets to sell their crops. The money economy expanded, banks became essential, and private fortunes influenced public policy. Many Americans came to believe that forces beyond their control threatened their way of life and the nation's republican values. They distrusted change and wanted someone to blame for the uncertainties they faced. This outlook encouraged American politics to become paranoid—dominated by fear of hostile conspiracies.

8.2.1 Slavery and Politics

The charge (see Chapter 7) that John Quincy Adams and Henry Clay had cheated Andrew Jackson out of the presidency in early 1825 reflected this fear of conspiracies. What Jackson's supporters called "the corrupt bargain," alongside claims that Adams favored a wealthy and intellectual elite at the expense of the common white man, led to the organization of the Democratic Party and the election of Jackson to the presidency in 1828. The Democrats claimed to stand for the natural rights and economic well-being of American workers and farmers against what they called the "money power," a conspiratorial alliance of bankers and businessmen.

Yet, from its start, the Democratic Party also represented the interests of the South's slaveholding elite. Democratic politicians, North and South, favored a state rights doctrine that protected slavery from national government interference. They sought (through legislation, judicial decisions, and diplomacy) to make the right to hold human property inviolate. They became the most ardent supporters of expanding slavery into new regions, leading their opponents to claim they were part of a "**slave power**" conspiracy. Most Democratic politicians openly advocated white supremacy. Although their rhetoric demanded equal rights for all and special privileges for none, they really cared only about the rights of white men.

slave power

A key concept in abolitionist and northern antislavery propaganda that depicted southern slaveholders as the driving force in a political conspiracy to promote slavery at the expense of white liberties.

The Democratic Party's outlook toward American Indians, women, and African Americans demonstrated this. Democratic politicians led in demanding the removal of Indians to the area west of the Mississippi River. This led to the Cherokee "Trail of Tears" in 1838 (see Chapter 6). Democrats also supported patriarchy, a subservient role for women in family life and the church, and the exclusion of women from the public sphere. (Reformers did not begin to propose equal rights for women until the late 1830s.) Similarly almost all Democratic leaders believed God and nature had designed African Americans to be slaves. During the 1820s and early 1830s, only a few radicals like Walker saw the hypocrisy of this outlook and contended that real democracy would embrace all men, regardless of race.

By the mid-1830s, those Americans who favored a more enlightened political program turned—often reluctantly—to the Whig Party, which opposed Jackson and the Democrats. The Whigs also attracted those who had supported the Anti-Masonic Party during the early 1830s. This third party epitomized political paranoia by contending that Freemasons conspired to subvert republican government. Whig politicians, such as Henry Clay, Daniel Webster, William H. Seward, and John Quincy Adams, emphasized Christian morality and an active national government. They regarded themselves as conservatives, did not seek to end slavery in the South, and included many wealthy slaveholders within their ranks. But in the North, the party's moral orientation and its opposition to territorial expansion by the United States made it attractive to slavery's opponents.

A major reason why Whig politicians, especially in the North, emphasized Christian morality is that they wished to appeal to evangelical Christian voters. They thereby served as a channel through which evangelicalism influenced politics. Often evangelicals themselves, some northern Whig politicians and journalists defended the human rights of African Americans and American Indians. They criticized the inhumanity of slaveholders and tried to limit federal support for the "peculiar institution." When and where black men could, they voted for Whig candidates.

The Trail of Tears, painted in 1942 by Robert Lindneux, dramatizes the westward journey of Cherokees from their homeland in Georgia to what is now Oklahoma. The Democratic Party, which championed the rights of white men, was chiefly responsible for the forced westward relocation of the Cherokees and other southeastern Indian peoples.

8.2.2 The Second Great Awakening

As the evangelicals' influence on the Whig Party suggests, Christian morality had an impact during the 1830s. Religion, of course, had always been important in America. During the 1730s and 1740s, the revival known as the Great Awakening used emotional preaching and hymn singing to encourage men and women to embrace Jesus and reform their lives. American churches converted black people, and African Americans in turn helped shape the revival. At the end of the eighteenth century, a new, emotional revivalism began. Known as the **Second Great Awakening**, it lasted through the 1830s. It led laymen to replace clergy as leaders, and it sought to impose moral order on America's turbulent society.

The Second Great Awakening also influenced Richard Allen and Absalom Jones's efforts to establish separate black churches in Philadelphia during the 1790s (see Chapter 5). It helped shape the character of other black churches that emerged during the 1800s and 1810s. These churches became an essential part of the antislavery movement. However, the Second Great Awakening did not peak until the 1820s. During that decade, Charles G. Finney, a white Presbyterian, and other revivalists helped

Second Great Awakening

A series of religious revivals in the first half of the nineteenth century characterized by great emotionalism in large public meetings.

This print, published in *Harper's Weekly* in August 1972, depicts what *Harper's* calls "A Negro Camp Meeting in the South." Although the print comes from a much later time, it suggests the spirit of revival meetings during the Second Great Awakening.

democratize religion in America. At days-long camp meetings, revivalists preached that all men and women—not just a few—could become faithful Christians and save their souls. Just as Jacksonian democracy revolutionized politics in America, the Second Great Awakening revolutionized the nation's spiritual life and—especially in the Northeast and Old Northwest—led many Americans, black and white, to join reform movements.

8.2.3 The Benevolent Empire

Evangelicals emphasized "practical Christianity." Those who were truly among the saved, they maintained, must through their deeds oppose sin and save others. Black evangelicals, in particular, called for "a *liberating* faith" applied in ways that advanced material and spiritual well-being. This emphasis on action led during the 1810s and 1820s to what became known as the **Benevolent Empire**, a network of church-related organizations designed to fight sin and rescue souls. The Benevolent Empire launched what is now known as antebellum or Jacksonian reform.

Centered in the Northeast, this broad social movement flourished through the 1850s. Voluntary associations organized on behalf of a host of causes. Among them were public education, self-improvement, limiting or abolishing alcohol consumption and sales (the temperance movement), prison reform, and aid to the intellectually and physically challenged. Other associations distributed Bibles and religious tracts, funded missionary activities, and discouraged prostitution. Still others sought to improve health through diet and medical fads, alleviate shipboard conditions for sailors, and—by the 1840s—gain equal rights for women. The self-improvement, temperance, and missionary associations that free black people—and sometimes slaves—formed in urban areas in conjunction with their churches were part of this movement (see Chapter 7).

The most important of these reform associations addressed the problem of African-American bondage. During the eighteenth and early nineteenth centuries, people referred to the associations as societies for promoting the abolition of slavery. By the 1830s they had become known as antislavery societies. Whatever they called themselves, their members were abolitionists, people who favored abolishing slavery in their respective states and throughout the country.

This 1844 lithograph by Peter S. Duval, derived from a painting by Alfred Hoffy, portrays Julianne Jane Tillman. Tillman was an AME preacher and one of the few women of her time to be employed in such a capacity.

Benevolent Empire

Network of reform associations affiliated with Protestant churches in the early nineteenth century dedicated to the restoration of moral order.

8.3 Colonization

Evaluate the goals of the American Colonization Society.

The **American Colonization Society (ACS)** was the most prominent organization of the 1810s and 1820s that *claimed* to be opposed to slavery. Whether it honestly aimed at emancipation is debatable. In late 1816, white leaders met in Washington, D.C., to form this organization, formally named the American Society for Colonizing Free People of Colour of the United States. Among these white leaders were prominent slaveholders, including Henry Clay and Bushrod Washington—a nephew of George Washington.

The ACS had a twofold program. First, it proposed to abolish slavery gradually in the United States, perhaps giving slaveholders financial compensation for giving up their human property. Second, it proposed to send former slaves *and* previously free African Americans to Africa. To achieve this second goal, the ACS—with the support of the U.S. government—in 1822 established the colony of Liberia on West Africa's coast. The founders of the ACS claimed that free African Americans had to go to Liberia because masters would never emancipate their slaves if they thought doing so would

American Colonization Society (ACS)

An organization founded in Washington, D.C. (1816–1912), by prominent slaveholders. It claimed to encourage the ultimate abolition of slavery by sending free African Americans to its West African colony of Liberia.

increase the size of what they regarded as a shiftless and dangerous free black class. Despite this questionable agenda, the ACS became an integral part of the Benevolent Empire. It commanded widespread support among many who regarded themselves as friends of humanity. At first black and white abolitionists did not perceive the moral and practical objections to the ACS program.

The ACS always had its greatest strength in the Upper South and enjoyed the support of slaveholders, including—besides Washington and Clay—Francis Scott Key (who wrote the lyrics for "The Star-Spangled Banner"), James Monroe, Andrew Jackson, John Tyler, and John Randolph. But, by the 1820s, the society had branches in every northern state. During that decade, such northern white abolitionists as Arthur and Lewis Tappan, Gerrit Smith, and William Lloyd Garrison supported colonization. They emphasized the ACS's abolitionist aspects and hoped free and soon-to-be-emancipated African Americans would be able to choose whether to stay in the United States or go to Liberia. In either case, they assumed black people would become free.

8.3.1 African-American Advocates of Colonization

Prominent black abolitionists initially shared this positive assessment of the ACS. They perpetuated a black nationalist tradition dating back to Prince Hall that, disappointed with repeated rebuffs from white people, endorsed black migration to Africa. During the early 1800s, Paul Cuffe of Massachusetts was the most prominent advocate of this point of view. In 1811, six years before the ACS organized, Cuffe, a Quaker of African and American Indian ancestry, addressed Congress on the subject of African-American Christian colonies in Africa.

The colonization argument that appealed to Cuffe and many other African Americans was that white prejudice would never allow black people to enjoy full citizenship, equal protection under the law, and economic success in the United States. Black people born in America, this argument held, could enjoy equal rights only in the land of their ancestors. American evangelicalism also led many African Americans to embrace the prospect of relocated black people bringing Christianity to African nations. Like white Americans, they considered Africa a pagan, barbaric land that could benefit from Christianity and republican government. Other black leaders who favored colonization objected to this view of Africa. They considered African cultures superior to those of America and Europe. They were often Africans themselves, the children of African parents, or individuals who had been influenced by Africans.

In 1815 Cuffe, who owned and commanded a ship, took 34 African-American settlers to the British free black colony of Sierra Leone, located just north of what became Liberia. Cuffe's American-Indian wife's reluctance to leave her native land and his death in 1817 prevented him from transporting more settlers to West Africa. Instead, former AME bishop Daniel Coker in 1820 led the first 86 African-American colonists to Liberia. Coker led in part because pro-ACS sentiment was especially strong among African Americans in his home city of Baltimore and other nearby urban areas. By 1838 approximately 2,500 colonists had made the journey. They lived less than harmoniously with Liberia's 28,000 indigenous inhabitants (see Map 8-2).

In 1847 Liberia became an independent republic. But, despite the efforts of such **black nationalist** advocates as

black nationalist

African Americans who hold the belief that they must seek their racial destiny by establishing separate institutions and, perhaps, migrating as a group to a location (often Africa) outside the United States.

Map 8-2 The Founding of Liberia

This map shows the location of Sierra Leone and Liberia in West Africa. British abolitionists established Sierra Leone as a colony for former slaves in 1800. The American Colonization Society established Liberia for the same purpose in 1821.

Why were Sierra Leone and Liberia established in West Africa?

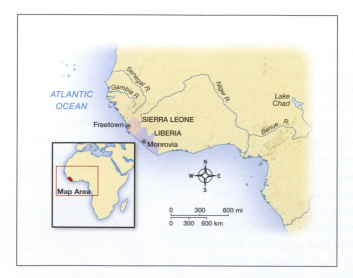

Henry Highland Garnet and Alexander Crummell, only about 10,000 African-American immigrants had gone there by 1860. This number amounted to just 3 percent of the *increase* of America's black population since 1816. Well before 1860, facts demonstrated that African colonization would never fulfill the dreams of its black or white advocates.

Other African American and white leaders regarded Haiti as a potential refuge from the oppression black people suffered in the United States. African Americans whose ancestors had lived in the Caribbean and those who admired Haiti's revolutionary history found moving there especially attractive. In 1824 about 200 men, women, and children from Philadelphia, New York City, and Baltimore went to Haiti. By the end of the 1820s, between 8,000 and 13,000 African Americans had arrived there. But many of the emigrants found Haitian culture alien. They had difficulty learning French and Creole and distrusted the Roman Catholic Church, to which most Haitians at least nominally belonged. About one-third of the emigrants returned to the United States.

8.3.2 Black Opposition to Colonization

Some African Americans had always opposed overseas colonization, and, as early as 1817, such influential black leaders as James Forten wavered in their support of the ACS. Although in private Forten continued to endorse colonization, he led a meeting that year of 3,000 black Philadelphians who denounced it. By the mid-1820s, many black abolitionists in cities from Richmond to Boston had criticized colonization in general and the ACS in particular.

Such critics included Samuel Cornish, who in New York City in 1827 began publishing *Freedom's Journal,* the first African-American newspaper. Cornish, a young Presbyterian minister, called for independent black action against slavery. The *Journal*—reflecting the values of antebellum reform (see Chapter 7)—also encouraged northern black self-improvement, education, civil rights, and sympathy for slaves. However, John Russwurm—the *Journal*'s cofounder—was less opposed than Cornish to the ACS. This disagreement contributed to the suspension of the newspaper in 1829. That same year Russwurm, one of the first African Americans to earn a college degree, moved to Liberia.

In contrast to Russwurm, people like Cornish wanted to improve black life in the United States. They considered Liberia to be foreign and unhealthy. They had no desire to go to Africa or send other African Americans there. They also distrusted ACS proposals for *voluntary* colonization because nearly every southern state *required* the expulsion of slaves individually freed by their masters. The Maryland and Virginia legislatures had been considering legislation designed to require *all* free black people to leave those states or be enslaved. These efforts failed, but they added to African-American fears that colonization would be forced on them, much the way state and federal governments forced American Indians from their land.

By the mid-1820s, most black abolitionists had concluded that the ACS represented a proslavery effort to drive free African Americans from the United States. The ACS, they maintained, was not an antislavery organization at all but a proslavery scheme to force free black people to choose between reenslavement or banishment. America, they argued, was their native land. They knew nothing of Africa. Efforts to have them go there rested on a racist assumption that they had no right to live in freedom in the land of their birth. David Walker asked, "Do they think to drive us from our country and homes, after having enriched it with our blood and tears?"

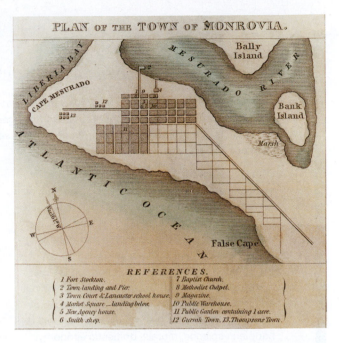

Monrovia, Liberia, c. 1830. This map shows the American Colonization Society's main Liberian settlement as it existed about 10 years after its founding.

Voices

William Watkins Opposes Colonization

In response to a white clergyman who argued that migration to Africa would help alleviate the plight of African Americans, William Watkins stressed black unity, education, and self-improvement in this country.

[The Reverend Mr. Hewitt says] "Let us unite into select societies for the purpose of digesting a plan for raising funds to be appropriated to this grand object" [African colonization]. This we cannot do; we intend to let the burden of this work rest upon the shoulders of those who wish us out of the country. We will, however, compromise the matter with our friend. We are willing and anxious to "unite into select societies for the purpose of digesting a plan": for the improvement of our people in science, morals, domestic economy, &c. We are willing and anxious to form union societies . . . that shall discountenance and

destroy, as far as possible, those unhappy schisms which have too long divided us, though we are brethren. We are willing to unite . . . in the formation of temperance societies . . . that will enable us to exhibit to the world an amount of moral power that would give new impetus to our friends and "strike alarm" into the breasts of our enemies, if not wholly disarm them of the weapons they are hurling against us.

1. According to Watkins, how will black self-improvement societies help counter colonization?
2. What difficulties does Watkins believe African Americans must overcome to make themselves stronger in the United States?

SOURCE: "A Colored American [Watkins] to Editors," n.d., in *Genius of Universal Emancipation*, December 18, 1829.

8.4 Black Abolitionist Women

Discuss the role of black women in the abolition movement.

Black women joined black men in opposing slavery. In considering their role, it is important to understand that the United States in the early nineteenth century had a rigid gender division. Law and custom proscribed women from engaging in politics, the professions, and most businesses. In this view, women deemed respectable by black and white Americans—the women of wealthy families—were expected to devote themselves exclusively to domestic concerns and remain socially aloof. Church and benevolent activities constituted their only opportunities for public action. Even in these arenas, custom relegated women to work in auxiliaries to men's organizations.

This was true of the first *formal* abolitionist groups of black women. Among the leaders were Charlotte Forten, the wife of James Forten, and Maria W. Stewart, the widow of a well-to-do Boston ship outfitter. In 1833 Charlotte and her daughters Sarah, Margaretta, and Harriet joined other black and white women to found the **Philadelphia Female Anti-Slavery Society**. A year earlier, other black women had established in Salem, Massachusetts, the first women's antislavery society. Women of the black elite also supported the education of black children. They hoped that, as African Americans gained knowledge, white prejudice that supported slavery would diminish.

Stewart's brief career as an antislavery orator provoked far more controversy than those of the Fortens or other early black abolitionist women. Influenced by Walker's *Appeal* and encouraged by William Lloyd Garrison, Stewart in 1831 and 1832 became the first American woman publicly to address male audiences. Although she directed some of her remarks to "Afric's daughters" and to "ye fairer sisters," she—as had Walker before her—pointedly called on black men to act against slavery. "It is true," she told a group assembled at the African Masonic Hall

Philadelphia Female Anti-Slavery Society

A biracial abolitionist organization (1833–1870) aligned with the American Anti-Slavery Society. White Quaker women dominated the society, but it included a significant number of black women.

Profile

Maria W. Stewart

Maria W. Stewart had a brief but striking career as an abolitionist, feminist, and advocate of racial justice. She was born Maria Miller in Hartford, Connecticut, in 1803 to free parents, and she was orphaned at age five. Raised in the home of a minister, she had little formal education until she began attending "sabbath schools" when she was 15. In 1826 she married James W. Stewart, a successful Boston businessman nearly twice her age, in a ceremony conducted by Thomas Paul at his Boston church. When Stewart died in 1829, he left her with limited means.

In 1830, caught up in the Second Great Awakening, Maria W. Stewart determined to dedicate herself to Christian benevolence. When William Lloyd Garrison began publishing *The Liberator* in 1831, she visited him at his office. Later that year, Garrison published her pamphlet *Religion and Pure Principles of Morality, the Sure Foundation on Which We Must Build*, in which she advocated abolition and black autonomy. The following year, Garrison published her second and last pamphlet, which dealt more narrowly with religion.

Meanwhile, Stewart began speaking to black organizations. In early 1832 she addressed Boston's Afric-American Female Intelligence Society. Using prophetic rhetoric, she noted that the world had entered a revolutionary age and called on African-American women to influence their husbands and children on behalf of the cause of black freedom, equality, education, and economic advancement in America. In regard to African colonization, she said, "Before I go, the bayonet shall press me through."

But in February 1833, when she addressed Boston's African Masonic Lodge, Stewart overplayed her role as a prophet. She invoked the glories of ancient Africa and black service in the American Revolution to chastise black men of her time for not being more active on behalf of the liberty of their people. By claiming that black men lacked "ambition and requisite courage," she provoked her audience to respond with hoots, jeers, and a barrage of rotten tomatoes.

Daunted by this stunning rejection, Stewart determined to leave Boston for New York City. In her farewell address of September 1833, which she delivered at a schoolroom in Paul's church, she asserted that her advice had been rejected because she was a woman. Nevertheless, while acknowledging that black men must lead, she called on black women to promote themselves, their families, and their race.

During the rest of her life, Stewart sought to fulfill that role in a less flamboyant manner. In New York she joined the Female Literary Society and became a schoolteacher. She moved to Baltimore in 1852 to start a school for black children. During the Civil War, with the assistance of black seamstress Elizabeth Keckley, she organized a black school in Washington, D.C. Later she worked as a matron at that city's Freedmen's Hospital and organized a Sunday school for poor black children. She died at Freedmen's Hospital in December 1879.

in Boston in 1833, "our fathers bled and died in the revolutionary war, and others fought bravely under the command of [General Andrew] Jackson [at New Orleans in 1815], in defense of liberty. But where is the man that has distinguished himself in these modern days by acting wholly in the defense of African rights and liberty?" Such remarks from a woman cut deeply. Thereafter Stewart met such hostility from the black community that in September 1833 she retired as a public speaker. Henceforth, she labored in more conventional and respectable female ways for the antislavery cause.

Many black women—and white women—did not fit the early nineteenth-century criteria for respectability that applied to the Fortens, Stewart, and others among the African-American elite. Most free black women lacked wealth and education. They worked outside their homes. Particularly in the Upper South, these women became *practical* abolitionists.

From the revolutionary era onward, countless anonymous black women, both slave and free, living in such southern border cities as Baltimore, Louisville, and Washington, risked everything to harbor fugitive slaves. Others saved their meager earnings to purchase freedom for themselves and their loved ones. Among them was Alethia Tanner of Washington, who purchased her freedom in 1810 for $1,400 (about $25,600 today). During the 1820s she purchased the freedom of her sister, her sister's

William Lloyd Garrison (1805–1879) was the most prominent American abolitionist during the 1830s. He called for immediate emancipation of American slaves, without compensation to their masters, and led the American Anti-Slavery Society.

10 children, and her sister's five grandchildren. During the 1830s Tanner purchased the freedom of seven more slaves. Meanwhile, according to an account written in the 1860s, "Mrs. Tanner was alive to every wise scheme for the education and elevation of her race."

8.4.1 The Baltimore Alliance

Among the stronger black abolitionist opponents of the ACS were William Watkins, Jacob Greener, and Hezekiah Grice. All three worked in Baltimore with Benjamin Lundy, a white Quaker abolitionist who published an antislavery newspaper named the *Genius of Universal Emancipation*. By the mid-1820s, Watkins, a schoolteacher, had emerged, in letters he published in *Freedom's Journal* and in Lundy's paper, as one of the more articulate critics of colonization. Greener, a whitewasher and schoolteacher, helped Lundy publish the *Genius* and promoted its circulation. Grice, who later changed his mind about colonization, became the principal founder of the National Black Convention Movement, which during the 1830s, 1840s, and 1850s served as a forum for black abolitionists.

In 1829 Watkins, Greener, and Grice profoundly influenced William Lloyd Garrison, who a few years later became the most influential American antislavery leader. Lundy had convinced Garrison—a young reform journalist—to leave his native Massachusetts to come to Baltimore as the associate editor of the *Genius*. Garrison, a deeply religious product of the Second Great Awakening, had decided before he came to Baltimore that *gradual* abolition was neither practical nor moral. Gradualism was impractical, he said, because it continually put off the

---

Voices

A Black Woman Speaks Out on the Right to Education

Historians generally believe the antebellum women's rights movement emerged from the antislavery movement during the late 1830s. But as the following letter, published in Freedom's Journal *on August 10, 1827, indicates, some black women advocated equal rights for women much earlier:*

Messrs. Editors,

Will you allow a female to offer a few remarks upon a subject that you must allow to be all-important? I don't know that in any of your papers, you have said sufficient upon the education of females. I hope you are not to be classed with those, who think that our mathematical knowledge should be limited to "fathoming the dish-kettle," and that we have acquired enough of history, if we know that our grandfather's father lived and died. . . . The diffusion of knowledge has destroyed those degraded opinions, and men of the present age, allow, that we have minds that are capable and deserving of culture. There are difficulties . . . in the way of our advancement;

but that should only stir us to greater efforts. We possess not the advantages with those of our sex, whose skins are not coloured like our own, but we can improve what little we have, and make our one talent produce two-fold. . . . Ignorant ourselves, how can we be expected to form the minds of our youth, and conduct them in the paths of knowledge? I would address myself to all mothers. . . . It is their bounden duty to store their daughters' minds with useful learning. They should be made to devote their leisure time to reading books, whence they would derive valuable information, which could never be taken from them . . . Matilda

---

1. How does Matilda use sarcasm to make her point?
2. What special difficulties did black women like Matilda face in asserting their rights?

SOURCE: Messrs. Editors, *Freedom's Journal*, August 10, 1827.

date of general emancipation. It was immoral because it encouraged slaveholders to continue sinfully and criminally oppressing African Americans.

Garrison, however, tolerated the ACS until he came under the influence of Watkins, Greener, and Grice. They set him on a course that transformed the abolitionist movement in the United States during the early 1830s. They also initiated a bond between African Americans and Garrison that—although strained at times—shaped the rest of his antislavery career. That bond intensified in 1830 when Garrison served 49 days in Baltimore Jail on charges he had libeled a slave trader. While in jail, Garrison met imprisoned fugitive slaves. When the slaves' masters came to the jail to retrieve them, Garrison denounced the masters *to their faces*.

In 1831, when he began publishing his abolitionist newspaper, *The Liberator*, in Boston, Garrison led the antislavery movement in a radical direction. It was radical not so much because Garrison rejected gradual abolition and called for immediate emancipation. He had earlier rejected gradualism, and he was not the first to endorse **immediatism**. Instead, the insight he gained from his association with African Americans in Baltimore made his brand of abolitionism revolutionary. He learned from Watkins, Greener, and others that immediate emancipation must be combined with a commitment to racial justice in the United States. Watkins and Greener convinced Garrison that African Americans must have equal rights in America and not be sent to Africa after their emancipation. Immediate emancipation without compensating slaveholders and without expatriating African Americans became the core of Garrison's program for the rest of his long antislavery career.

immediatism

Refers to an antislavery movement that began in the United States during the late 1820s, which demanded that slavery be abolished immediately rather than gradually.

8.5 David Walker and Nat Turner

Compare and contrast David Walker and Nat Turner.

Two other black abolitionists, David Walker and Nat Turner, helped shape Garrison's brand of abolitionism. Walker and Turner had several things in common. They were from the South—Walker from North Carolina and Turner from Virginia—and they were deeply religious. They also advocated employing violent means against slavery and had an impact on both the white South and northern abolitionists. Otherwise their circumstances differed, as did the form of their antislavery efforts.

This chapter began with a quote from Walker's *Appeal . . . to the Colored Citizens of the World*, which he published in Boston in 1829. As historian Clement Eaton commented in 1936, this *Appeal* became "a dangerous pamphlet in the Old South." In it Walker, who in his youth may have been influenced by Denmark Vesey, furiously attacked slavery and white racism. He suggested that slaves use violence to secure their liberty. "I do declare," he wrote, "that one good black can put to death six white men."

The *Appeal* shaped the struggle over slavery in three ways. First, although Garrison advocated only peaceful means, Walker's harsh writing style influenced the tone of Garrison and other advocates of immediate abolition. Second, Walker's effort to instill hope and pride in an oppressed people inspired an increasingly militant black abolitionism. Third, his pamphlet and his ability to have it circulated among free African Americans in the South contributed to white southern fear of encirclement from without and subversion from within. This fear encouraged the section's leaders to make demands on the North that helped bring on the Civil War.

In this last respect, Nat Turner's contribution exceeded Walker's in its impact. Slave conspiracies had not ended with Denmark Vesey's execution in 1822. But in 1831 Turner, a privileged slave from eastern Virginia, became the first to initiate a large-scale slave uprising since Charles Deslondes's revolt in Louisiana in 1811. As a result, Turner inspired far greater fear among white southerners than Walker had.

Profile

David Walker

Title page and facing page illustration of David Walker's *Appeal in Four Articles*, 1848.

David Walker was born free in Wilmington, North Carolina, in 1796 or 1797. Although he learned to read and write, we know nothing of his early life. He may have attended a biracial Methodist church in Wilmington. As a young man, he traveled widely and, according to his *Appeal*, spent time in Charleston, South Carolina, where he attended a religious camp meeting in 1821. This has led historians to conjecture that Walker knew something about Denmark Vesey's conspiracy or, if he was still in Charleston in 1822, that he may even have participated in it.

By 1825 Walker was in Boston dealing in second-hand clothes. He had his own shop, lived in the city's black neighborhood, was married, and had a daughter and a son. At a time when many occupations were closed to African Americans, Walker was doing relatively well. He associated with well-established local black people, including Thomas Paul, an abolitionist minister, and William C. Nell, a foe of Boston's segregated public schools. During the late 1820s, Walker worked as a circulation agent in Boston for John Russwurm and Samuel Cornish's *Freedom's Journal*.

Walker also wrote for the *Journal* and recognized the legal disabilities African Americans faced in Boston as well as the oppressiveness of slavery. In December 1828 he addressed the Massachusetts General Colored Association on the topic of black cooperation with white abolitionists to improve the conditions of free black people and to liberate the slaves.

Not long after this, Walker became more radical. He wrote his *Appeal* and in September 1829 implemented a clandestine method to circulate it among slaves. He had black and white sailors, to whom he sold used clothes in Boston, take copies of the pamphlet to southern ports and distribute them to African Americans.

When white southerners discovered that slaves had copies of the pamphlet, southern officials demanded that the mayor of Boston stop Walker from publishing. When the mayor refused, rumors circulated that a group of white southerners had offered a reward for Walker, dead or alive. It is not surprising, therefore, that when Walker's daughter and then Walker himself died during the summer of 1830, many assumed they had been poisoned. The most recent biography of Walker, however, indicates that they died of tuberculosis.

During the years before Turner's uprising, unrest among slaves in Virginia had increased, and Walker's *Appeal* may have contributed to this. So may have class and regional divisions among white Virginians. In anticipation of a state constitutional convention in 1829, white people in western Virginia, where there were few slaveholders, had called for emancipation. Poorer white men demanded an end to the property qualifications that denied them the vote. As the convention approached, a "spirit of dissatisfaction and insubordination" became manifest among slaves. Some armed themselves and escaped north. As proslavery Virginians grew fearful, they demanded additional restrictions on the ability of local free black people and northern abolitionists to influence slaves.

Yet no evidence indicates that Turner or any of his associates had read Walker's *Appeal*, had contact with northern abolitionists, or knew about divisions among white Virginians. Also, although Turner *did* know about the successful slave revolt in Haiti, he was more a religious visionary than a political revolutionary. Born in 1800, he learned to read as a child. As a young man, he spent much of his time studying and memorizing the Bible. He became a lay preacher and a leader among local slaves. By the late 1820s, he had begun to have visions that convinced him God intended him to lead his people to freedom through violence.

This recently colorized drawing of the capture of Nat Turner dates to the 1830s. Turner avoided apprehension for nearly two months following the suppression of his revolt. The artist conveys how Turner maintained his dignity in surrender.

1829–1831
The Radical Turn in the Abolition Movement

July 1829

William Lloyd Garrison joins Benjamin Lundy in Baltimore as associate editor of the *Genius of Universal Emancipation*

September 1829

David Walker's *Appeal* is published in Boston and then circulated in the South

November 1829

William Watkins's anticolonization letters first appear in the *Genius*

June 1830

Garrison is sentenced to jail in Baltimore for libeling a slave trader

August 1830

Walker dies of tuberculosis in Boston

January 1831

Garrison begins publication of *The Liberator* in Boston

August 1831

Nat Turner's revolt occurs

After considerable planning, Turner began his uprising on the evening of August 21, 1831. His band, which numbered between 60 and 70, killed 57 white men, women, and children—the largest number of white Americans that slave rebels ever killed—before militia put down the revolt the following morning. That November, Turner and 17 others, convicted on charges of insurrection and treason, died on the gallows. In addition, panicked white people in nearby parts of Virginia and North Carolina killed more than 100 African Americans whom they—almost always incorrectly—suspected of being in league with the rebels.

The bloodshed in Virginia inspired general revulsion. White southerners—and some northerners—accused Garrison and other abolitionists of inspiring the revolt. In response, northern abolitionists of both races asserted their commitment to a *peaceful* struggle against slavery. Yet black and white abolitionists respected Turner. Black abolitionists accorded him the same heroic stature they gave Toussaint Louverture and Gabriel. White abolitionists compared Turner to George Washington and other leaders of national liberation movements. This tension between lip service to peaceful means and admiration for violence against slavery characterized the antislavery movement for the next 30 years.

Conclusion

This chapter has focused on the two principal antislavery movements in the United States before 1833. One movement existed in the South among slaves. The other centered in the North and the Chesapeake among free African American and white abolitionists. The two movements shared roots in the age of revolution, and each gained vitality from evangelical Christianity. The black church, the Bible, and elements of African religion helped inspire slave revolutionaries. The Second Great Awakening and the reforming spirit of the Benevolent Empire shaped the northern antislavery effort.

The antislavery movement that existed in the North and portions of the Upper South was always biracial and emphasized peaceful means to end slavery. During the 1810s and for much of the 1820s, many black abolitionists embraced a form of nationalism that encouraged them to cooperate with the conservative white people who led the ACS. As the racist and proslavery nature of that organization became clear, most northern black and white abolitionists, led by Garrison, called for immediate, uncompensated general emancipation that would not force former slaves to leave the United States.

Unlike northern abolitionists, Gabriel, Vesey, and Turner had to rely on violence to fight slavery. However, the two movements had similarities and influenced each other. Walker's life in Charleston at the time of Vesey's conspiracy very likely shaped his beliefs. In turn, Walker's *Appeal* may have influenced slaves. Turner's revolt helped determine the course of northern abolitionism after 1831. During the subsequent decades, the efforts of slaves to resist their masters, to rebel, and to escape influenced radical black and white abolitionists in the North.

Slavery, the legal disabilities imposed on free African Americans, and the widespread religious revivalism of the early nineteenth century created conditions different from those that exist today. But some similarities between then and now are striking. As it was in the 1810s and 1820s, the United States today is in turmoil. Technological innovation and corporate restructuring have contributed to economic fluctuation and a volatile job market that disproportionately affects members of minority groups. As they did in the early nineteenth century, African-American leaders today advocate various strategies to deal with such developments.

Cornish, Watkins, and others who opposed the ACS sought through peaceful means to abolish slavery and gain recognition of African Americans as American citizens. Walker advocated a more forceful strategy to achieve the same ends. Cornish, Watkins, and Walker all cooperated with white abolitionists. Others took a position closer to black nationalism by linking the abolition of slavery to an independent black destiny in Africa. Each of these strategies had virtues, weaknesses, and dangers.

Chapter Timeline

AFRICAN-AMERICAN EVENTS	NATIONAL AND WORLD EVENTS

1790–1800

1796 or 1797 David Walker born	**1791** Haitian Revolution begins
	1796 John Adams elected president
	1798 Undeclared Franco-American naval war

1800–1810

1800 Gabriel's conspiracy is exposed	**1800** Thomas Jefferson elected president
1803 Maria W. Stewart born	**1803–1806** Lewis and Clark Expedition
1805 William Lloyd Garrison born	**1807** Britain bans Atlantic slave trade
	1808 United States bans Atlantic slave trade

1810–1820

1811 Louisiana slave revolt	**1812** War of 1812 begins
1815 Paul Cuffe leads African Americans to Sierra Leone	**1815** War of 1812 ends
1816 American Colonization Society is formed	**1816** James Madison elected president

1820–1830

1822 Denmark Vesey's conspiracy exposed	**1820** Missouri Compromise passed
1824 Benjamin Lundy comes to Baltimore	**1824** John Quincy Adams elected president
1827 *Freedom's Journal* begins publication	**1828** Andrew Jackson elected president
1829 William Lloyd Garrison comes to Baltimore; David Walkers's *Appeal*	

1830–1850

1831 Nat Turner's Revolt is suppressed	**1832** Great increase in migration to United States begins
	1846–1848 Indian Removal Act passed by Congress

Review Questions

1. What did the program of the ACS mean for African Americans? How did they respond to this program?

2. Analyze the role played in abolitionism (1) by Christianity and (2) by the revolutionary tradition in the Atlantic world. Which was more important in shaping the views of black and white abolitionists?

3. Evaluate the interaction of black and white abolitionists during the early nineteenth century. How did their motives for becoming abolitionists differ?

4. How did Gabriel, Denmark Vesey, and Nat Turner influence the northern abolitionist movement?

5. What risks did Maria W. Stewart take when she called publicly for antislavery action?

Retracing the Odyssey

National Afro-American Museum and Cultural Center, Wilberforce, Ohio. Exhibits on African-American history include the antislavery struggle.

Oberlin College, Oberlin, Ohio. Oberlin, one of the first racially integrated and coeducational institutions of higher learning in the United States, was an antislavery and underground railroad center. The college maintains a collection of antislavery publications.

The Amistad Research Center, Tulane University, New Orleans, Louisiana. This institution maintains the archives of the American Missionary Association, the largest American antislavery organization of the 1840s and 1850s.

Recommended Reading

Eric Burin. *Slavery and the Peculiar Solution: A History of the American Colonizaton Society.* Gainesville: University Press of Florida, 2005. This is the most recent account of the ACS.

Merton L. Dillon. *Slavery Attacked: Southern Slaves and Their Allies, 1619–1865.* Baton Rouge: Louisiana State University Press, 1990. Integrates slave resistance and revolt with the northern abolitionist movement.

Eugene D. Genovese. *From Rebellion to Revolution: Afro-American Slave Revolts in the Making of the Modern World.* Baton Rouge: Louisiana State University Press, 1979. Places the major American slave revolts and conspiracies in an Atlantic context.

Peter P. Hinks. *To Awaken My Afflicted Brethren: David Walker and the Problem of Antebellum Slave Resistance.* University Park: Pennsylvania State University Press, 1997.

The most recent biography of Walker, which places him within the black abolitionist movement and attempts to clarify what little we know about his life.

Benjamin Quarles. *Black Abolitionists.* New York: Oxford University Press, 1969. A classic study that emphasizes cooperation between black and white abolitionists.

Harry Reed. *Platform for Change: The Foundations of the Northern Free Black Community, 1775–1865.* East Lansing: Michigan State University Press, 1994. An excellent study of the relationship between free black culture in the North and antislavery action.

Shirley J. Yee. *Black Women Abolitionists: A Study in Activism, 1828–1860.* Knoxville: University of Tennessee Press, 1992. Concentrates on the period after 1833, but it is the best place to start reading about black abolitionist women.

Additional Bibliography

The Relationship Among Evangelicalism, Reform, and Abolitionism

Robert H. Abzug. *Cosmos Crumbling: American Reform and the Religious Imagination.* New York: Oxford University Press, 1994.

Gilbert H. Barnes. *The Antislavery Impulse, 1830–1844.* 1933. Reprint, Gloucester, MA: Peter Smith, 1973.

Rita Roberts. *Evangelicalism and the Politics of Reform in Northern Black Thought 1776–1863.* Baton Rouge: Louisiana State University Press, 2010.

Douglas M. Strong. *Perfectionist Politics: Abolitionism and the Religious Tensions of American Democracy.* Syracuse, NY: Syracuse University Press, 1999.

American Abolitionism before 1831

David Brion Davis. *The Problem of Slavery in Western Culture.* Ithaca, NY: Cornell University Press, 1966.

———. *Slavery and Human Progress.* Ithaca, NY: Cornell University Press, 1987.

———. *The Problem of Slavery in the Ages of Emancipation.* New York: Knopf, 2014.

Merton L. Dillon. *The Abolitionists: The Growth of a Dissenting Minority.* New York: Norton, 1974.

Richard S. Newman. *The Transformation of American Abolitionism: Fighting Slavery in the Early Republic.* Chapel Hill: University of North Carolina Press, 2002.

Beverly C. Tomek. *Colonization and Its Discontents: Emancipation, Emigration, and Antislavery in Antebellum Pennsylvania.* New York: New York University Press, 2010.

Slave Revolts and Conspiracies

Herbert Aptheker. *American Negro Slave Revolts.* 1943. New ed., New York: International Publishers, 1974.

Douglas R. Egerton. *He Shall Go Out Free: The Lives of Denmark Vesey.* Madison, WI: Madison House, 1999.

David P. Feggus, ed. *The Impact of the Haitian Revolution on the Atlantic World.* Columbia: University of South Carolina Press, 2001.

Kenneth S. Greenberg, ed. *Nat Turner: A Slave Rebellion in History and Memory.* New York: Oxford University Press, 2003.

John Lofton. *Denmark Vesey's Revolt: The Slave Plot That Lit a Fuse to Fort Sumter.* Kent, OH: Kent State University Press, 1983.

Stephen B. Oates. *The Fires of the Jubilee: Nat Turner's Fierce Rebellion.* New York: Harper & Row, 1975.

T. Stephen Whitman. *Challenging Slavery in the Chesapeake: Black and White Resistance to Human Bondage.* Baltimore: Maryland Historical Society, 2007.

Black Abolitionism and Black Nationalism

Rodney Carlisle. *The Roots of Black Nationalism.* Port Washington, NY: Kennikat, 1975.

Eddie S. Glaude. *Exodus!: Religion, Race, and Nation in Early Nineteenth-Century Black America.* Chicago: University of Chicago Press, 2000.

Leroy Graham. *Baltimore: Nineteenth-Century Black Capital.* Washington, DC: University Press of America, 1982.

Vincent Harding. *There Is a River: The Black Struggle for Freedom in America.* New York: Harcourt, Brace, Jovanovich, 1981.

Floyd J. Miller. *The Search for Black Nationality: Black Colonization and Emigration, 1787–1863.* Urbana: University of Illinois Press, 1975.

Marilyn Richardson. *Maria W. Stewart: America's First Black Woman Political Writer.* Bloomington: Indiana University Press, 1987.

Sterling Stuckey. *Slave Culture: Nationalist Theory and the Foundations of Black America.* New York: Oxford University Press, 1987.

Lamont D. Thomas. *Rise to Be a People: A Biography of Paul Cuffe.* Urbana: University of Illinois Press, 1986.

Julie Winch. *Philadelphia's Black Elite: Activism, Accommodation, and Struggle for Autonomy, 1787–1840.* Philadelphia: Temple University Press, 1988.

Chapter 9

Let Your Motto Be Resistance

1833–1850

A group of women and children prepare to ford a river as they escape from slavery. Most escapees were young men, but people of both sexes and all age groups tried to reach freedom in the North or Canada.

 ## Learning Objectives

After reading this chapter, you should be able to:

9.1 Describe how racism and violence during the 1830s and 1840s affected the antislavery movement.

9.2 Discuss the roles of black institutions and moral suasion in the antislavery movement.

9.3 Evaluate the impact of black churches and black newspapers on the abolitionist movement.

9.4 Discuss the breakup of the American Anti-Slavery Society and the organizations that emerged from it.

9.5 Explain why abolitionism became more aggressive during the 1840s and 1850s.

9.6 Compare and contrast the views of Frederick Douglass and those of Henry Highland Garnet.

It is in your power to torment the God-cursed slaveholders, that they would be glad to let you go free. . . . But you are a patient people. You act as though you were made for the special use of these devils. You act as though your daughters were born to pamper the lusts of your masters and overseers. And worse than all, you tamely submit, while your lords tear your wives from your embraces, and defile them before your eyes. In the name of God we ask, are you men? . . . Heaven, as with a voice of thunder, calls on you to arise from the dust. Let your motto be Resistance! Resistance! Resistance! no oppressed people have ever secured their Liberty without resistance.

—*Henry Highland Garnet, "Address to the Slaves of the United States of America"*

When black abolitionist Henry Highland Garnet spoke the words printed above at the National Convention of Colored Citizens, held in Buffalo, New York, on August 16, 1843, he caused a tremendous stir among those assembled. In 1824, when he was a boy, Garnet had escaped with his family from slavery in Maryland. Thereafter he received an excellent education while growing up in New York. By the 1840s, he had become a powerful speaker. But some of the delegates in his audience pointed out that he was far away from the slaves he claimed to address. Others believed he risked encouraging a potentially disastrous slave revolt. Therefore, by a narrow margin, the convention refused to endorse his speech.

In fact, Garnet had not called for slave revolt. He had rhetorically told slaves, "We do not advise you to attempt a revolution with the sword, because it would be INEXPEDIENT. Your numbers are too small, and moreover the rising spirit of the age, and the spirit of the gospel, are opposed to war and bloodshed." Instead, he advocated a general strike. This, he contended, would put the onus of initiating violence on masters. Nevertheless, Garnet's speech reflected a new militancy among black and white abolitionists that shaped the antislavery movement during the two decades before the Civil War.

This chapter investigates the causes of that militancy and explores the role of African Americans in the antislavery movement from the establishment of the American Anti-Slavery Society in 1833 to the **Compromise of 1850**. Largely in response to changes in American culture, unrest among slaves, and sectional conflict between North and South, the biracial northern antislavery movement during this period became splintered and diverse. Yet it also became more powerful.

Compromise of 1850

An attempt by the U.S. Congress to settle divisive issues between the North and South, including slavery expansion, apprehension in the North of fugitive slaves, and slavery in the District of Columbia.

9.1 A Rising Tide of Racism and Violence

Describe how racism and violence during the 1830s and 1840s affected the antislavery movement.

Garnet spoke correctly about the peaceful spirit of the gospel. But he erred concerning the spirit of his time. Militancy among abolitionists reflected increasing American racism and violence during a period stretching from the 1830s through the

Manifest Destiny

Doctrine, first expressed in 1845, that the expansion of white Americans across the continent was inevitable and ordained by God.

Civil War. White Americans' embrace of an exuberant nationalism called **Manifest Destiny** contributed to this trend. This doctrine, which defined political and economic progress in racial terms, held that God intended the United States to expand its territory, by war if necessary. Meanwhile, the American School of Ethnology continued the development of the "scientific" racism that had begun during the late eighteenth century (see Chapter 5). According to the School of Ethnology, white people—particularly white Americans—were a superior race culturally, physically, economically, politically, and intellectually. Therefore they had a right to rule over other races.

As Manifest Destiny gave divine sanction to imperialism, the School of Ethnology justified white Americans in their continued enslavement of African Americans and extermination of American Indians. Prejudice against European immigrants to the United States also increased during this period. By the late 1840s, a movement known as *nativism* pitted native-born Protestants against foreign-born Roman Catholics, whom the natives saw as competitors for jobs and as cultural subversives.

A wave of racially motivated violence, committed by the federal and state governments as well as by white vigilantes, accompanied these intellectual and demographic developments. Starting in the 1790s, the United States Army waged a systematic campaign to remove American Indians from the states and relocate them west of the Mississippi River (see Chapter 6). This campaign is epitomized by the Trail of Tears, when in 1838 the army forced 16,000 Cherokees from Georgia to move to what is now Oklahoma. During the same decade, antiblack riots became common in northern cities. White mobs wreaked havoc in African-American neighborhoods and attacked abolitionist newspaper presses. Wealthy "gentlemen of property and standing," who believed they defended the social order, led the rioters.

Figure 9-1 Mob Violence in the United States, 1812–1849

This graph illustrates the rise of mob violence in the North in reaction to abolitionist activity. Attacks on abolitionists peaked during the 1830s and then declined as antislavery sentiment spread in the North.

9.1.1 Antiblack and Antiabolitionist Riots

Antiblack riots coincided with the start of immediate abolitionism during the late 1820s. The riots became more common as abolitionism gained strength during the 1830s and 1840s (see Figure 9-1 and Map 9-1). Although few northern cities escaped attacks on African Americans and their property, riots in Cincinnati, Providence, New York City, and Philadelphia were the worst.

In 1829 a three-day riot instigated by local politicians led many black Cincinnatians to flee to Canada. In 1836 and 1841, mob attacks on the *Philanthropist*, Cincinnati's white-run abolitionist newspaper, expanded into attacks on African-American homes and businesses. During each riot, black residents defended their property with guns. In 1831 white sailors led a mob in Providence that literally tore that city's black neighborhood to pieces. With spectators cheering them on, rioters pulled down the chimneys of black residences and then "with a fire hook and plenty of axes and iron bars" wrecked the buildings and dragged the occupants into the streets. The Rhode Island militia finally stopped the mayhem. In New York City in 1834, a mob destroyed 12 houses owned by black residents, a black church, a black school, and the home of white abolitionist Lewis Tappan.

No city had more or worse race riots than Philadelphia—the City of Brotherly Love. In 1820, 1829, 1834, 1835, 1838, 1842, and 1849, antiblack rampages broke out. In 1838 a white mob burned Pennsylvania Hall, which abolitionists had just built and dedicated to free discussion. The ugliest riot came in 1842 when Irish immigrants led a mob that assaulted members of a black temperance society, who were commemorating the abolition of slavery in the British colony of Jamaica. When African Americans defended themselves with muskets, the mob responded by looting and burning Philadelphia's principal black neighborhood. Among those who successfully defended their homes was Robert Purvis, the abolitionist son-in-law of James Forten.

9.1.2 Texas and the War against Mexico

Not only northern cities experienced violence. Under President James K. Polk, the United States adopted a belligerent foreign policy, especially toward the Republic of Mexico, located on its southwestern border. Mexico had gained its independence from Spain in 1822 and in 1829 had abol-

Map 9-1 Antiabolitionist and Antiblack Riots During the Antebellum Period

African Americans faced violent conditions in both the North and South during the antebellum years. Fear among whites of growing free black communities and white antipathy toward spreading abolitionism sparked numerous antiblack and antiabolitionist riots.

Why did most of these riots occur in the Northeast?

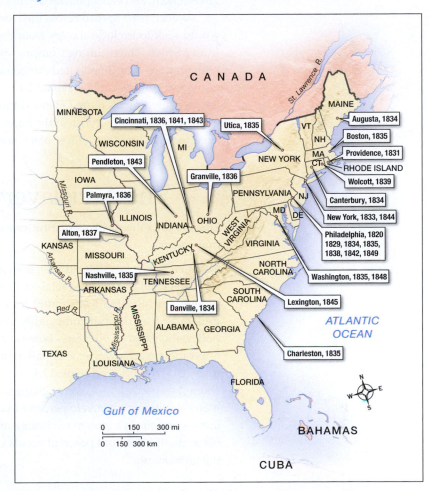

ished slavery within its bounds. Meanwhile, American slaveholders settled in the Mexican province of Texas. At the time, the gigantic regions then known as California and New Mexico (now comprising the states of California, Arizona, New Mexico, Utah, and part of Colorado) also belonged to Mexico. In 1836 Texas won independence and, as a slaveholding republic, applied for annexation to the United States as a large slave-labor state. At first Democratic and Whig politicians, who realized that adding a large state to the Union would divide the country along North–South lines, rebuffed the application. But the desire for new territory, encouraged by Manifest Destiny and an expanding slave-labor economy, could not be denied. In 1844 Polk, then the Democratic presidential candidate, called for the annexation of Texas and Oregon, a huge territory in the Pacific Northwest that the United States and Britain had been jointly administering. After Polk defeated Whig candidate Henry Clay, who favored delaying annexation, Congress in early 1845 annexed Texas by joint resolution as a slaveholding state.

In early 1846 Polk backed away from confronting Britain over Oregon, agreeing to split its territory along the 49th degree of latitude. Then, a few months later, Polk provoked a war against Mexico that by 1848 forced Mexico to recognize American sovereignty over Texas and to cede New Mexico and California to the United States (see Map 10-1 in Chapter 10). Immediately, the major American political question became: Would slavery expand into these territories? If it did, many northerners expected slaveholders to push for new slave-labor states in the Southwest, use such states' votes to dominate the federal government, and enact policies detrimental to northern workers and farmers.

As such fears spread across the North, slaveholders in turn feared that northerners would seek to exclude slavery from the western lands southerners had helped wrest from Mexico. The resulting Compromise of 1850 (see Chapter 10) attempted to satisfy both sections. But it subjected African Americans to additional violence because part of the Compromise met slaveholders' demands for a stronger fugitive slave law. This law provided much more federal aid to masters in recapturing bond people who had escaped to the North than had the Fugitive Slave Law of 1793. The new law also encouraged more kidnapping of free black northerners into slavery.

9.2 The Antislavery Movement

Discuss the roles of black institutions and moral suasion in the antislavery movement.

The increase in race-related violence caused difficulties for an antislavery movement that was itself not free of racial strife and officially limited to peaceful means. Even though African Americans found loyal white allies within the movement, interracial understanding did not come easily. As white abolitionists assumed they should set policy, their black colleagues became resentful. During the same period, abolitionist opposition to achieving emancipation through the use of force weakened. Opposition to force had arisen as a principled rejection of the violence that pervaded America and as a shrewd response to proslavery charges that abolitionists encouraged slave revolt. Now many abolitionists began to perceive that rejection of forceful means limited their movement's options in a violent environment. By the end of the 1830s, greater autonomy for black abolitionists and peaceful versus violent means became contentious issues within the movement.

9.2.1 The American Anti-Slavery Society

American Anti-Slavery Society (AASS; 1833–1870)

The umbrella organization for immediate abolitionists during the 1830s and the main Garrisonian organization after 1840.

Before the era of Manifest Destiny, the **American Anti-Slavery Society (AASS)**—the most significant abolitionist organization of the 1830s—emerged from a turning point in the abolitionist cause. This was William Lloyd Garrison's decision in 1831 to create a movement dedicated to immediate, uncompensated emancipation and to equal rights for African Americans in the United States (see Chapter 8). To reach these goals, abolitionists organized the AASS in December 1833 at Philadelphia's Adelphi Hall. Well aware of the fears Nat Turner's revolt had raised, those assembled declared, "The society will never, in any way, countenance the oppressed in vindicating their rights by resorting to physical force."

No white American worked harder than Garrison to bridge racial differences. He spoke to black groups, stayed in the homes of African Americans when he traveled, and welcomed them to his home. Black abolitionists responded with affection and loyalty. They provided financial support for his newspaper, *The Liberator*; worked as subscription agents; paid for his speaking tour in England in 1833; and served as his bodyguards. But Garrison, like most other white abolitionists, remained stiff and condescending in conversation with black colleagues, and the black experience in the AASS reflected this.

On one hand, it is remarkable that the AASS allowed black men to participate in its meetings without formal restrictions. At the time, no other American organization did so. On the other hand, that black participation in the AASS was paltry. Three African Americans—James McCrummell, Robert Purvis, and James G. Barbadoes—helped found the AASS, and McCrummell presided at its first meeting. But, among 60 white people attending that meeting, these three were the only African Americans. Although three white women also participated in the meeting, no black women did. Throughout the AASS's existence, it rarely allowed black people to hold positions of authority.

Wealthy black abolitionist Robert Purvis is at the very center of this undated photograph of the Philadelphia Anti-Slavery Society. The famous Quaker abolitionist Lucretia Mott and her husband James Mott are seated to Purvis's left. Equally significant as Purvis's central location in the photograph is that he is the *only* African American pictured.

As state and local auxiliaries of the AASS organized across the North during the early 1830s, these patterns repeated themselves. Black men participated but did not lead, although a few held prominent offices. Among them were Barbadoes and Joshua Easton, who in 1834 joined the board of directors of the Massachusetts Anti-Slavery Society. Also, in 1837 seven black men, including James Forten, helped organize the Pennsylvania Anti-Slavery Society. Black and white women—with some exceptions—could observe the proceedings of these organizations but not participate in them. It took a three-year struggle between 1837 and 1840 over "the woman question" before an AASS annual meeting elected a woman to a leadership position, and that victory helped split the organization.

9.2.2 Black and Women's Antislavery Societies

In these circumstances, black men, black women, and white women formed auxiliaries to the AASS. Often African Americans belonged to all-black *and* to integrated, predominantly white organizations. Black men's auxiliaries to the AASS formed across the North during the mid-1830s. As mentioned in Chapter 8, the earliest black women's abolitionist organization appeared in Salem, Massachusetts, in 1832, a year before the AASS formed.

The black organizations arose in part because of racial discord in the predominantly white organizations and because of a black desire for racial solidarity. But, as historian Benjamin Quarles notes, during the 1830s "the founders of Negro societies did not envision their efforts as distinctive or self-contained; rather they viewed their role as that of a true auxiliary—supportive, supplemental, and subsidiary." Despite their differences, black and white abolitionists belonged to a single movement.

The women's racially integrated organizations exemplified Quarles's point. Although these organizations did not overcome antiblack prejudice, they surpassed men's societies in elevating African Americans to prominent positions. Black abolitionist Susan Paul became a member of the board of the Boston Female Anti-Slavery Society when it organized in 1833. Later that year, Margaretta Forten became recording secretary of the Female Anti-Slavery Society of Philadelphia, founded by white Quaker abolitionist Lucretia Mott. In May 1837 black Quaker Sarah M. Douglass of Philadelphia and Sarah Forten—Margaretta's sister—served as delegates to the First Anti-Slavery Convention of American Women in New York City. At the second convention, Susan Paul became a vice president, and Douglass became treasurer.

Profile

Sojourner Truth

I SELL THE SHADOW TO SUPPORT THE SUBSTANCE.
SOJOURNER TRUTH.

Sojourner Truth does not fit easily into the history of the antislavery movement. She did not identify with a particular group of abolitionists. Instead, as her biographer Nell Irvin Painter points out, Truth served the cause by making herself a symbol of the strength of all black women.

Originally named Isabella, Truth was born a slave—probably in 1797—in a Dutch-speaking area north of New York City. She had several masters, one of whom beat her brutally. Always a hard worker, she grew into a tall, muscular woman. She had a deep voice, and throughout her career enemies charged she was a man—despite her five children.

In 1827 Truth escaped to an antislavery family that purchased her freedom. Two years later, she became a revivalist preacher in New York City. Later she joined a communal religious cult, became an ardent millenarian—predicting that Judgment Day was rapidly approaching—and in 1843 took the name Sojourner Truth. A few years later, while working at a commune in Northampton, Massachusetts, she met abolitionists Frederick Douglass and David Ruggles. This meeting led to her career as a champion of abolition and women's rights.

During the late 1840s and the 1850s, she lectured across the North and as far west as Kansas. Blunt but eloquent, Truth appealed to common sense in arguing that African Americans and women deserved the same rights as white men because they could work as hard as white men. Truth almost always addressed white audiences and had a strong impression on them. During the Civil War, she volunteered to work among black Union troops, and President Abraham Lincoln invited her to the White House in 1864. She continued to advocate black and women's rights until her death in 1883.

As Painter and others note, Truth probably never used the phrase "Ar'n't I a Woman?" for which she is most widely remembered. A white female journalist attributed the phrase to Truth years after the 1851 women's rights meeting in Akron, Ohio, where Truth was supposed to have used it. Contemporary accounts indicate that she did not. Truth did, however, tell those assembled in Akron, "I have as much muscle as any man, and I can do as much work as any man. I have plowed and reaped and husked and chopped and mowed, and can any man do more than that?"

All of the women's antislavery societies concentrated on fundraising. They held bake sales, organized antislavery fairs and bazaars, and sold antislavery memorabilia. The proceeds went to the AASS or to antislavery newspapers. The women's societies also inspired feminism by creating awareness that women had rights and interests that a male-dominated society had to recognize. By writing essays and poems on political subjects and making public speeches, abolitionist women challenged a culture that relegated *respectable* women to domestic duties. During the 1850s famous African-American speaker Sojourner Truth emphasized that all black women, through their physical labor and the pain they suffered in slavery, had earned equal standing with men and their more favored white sisters.

Black men and women also formed auxiliaries during the early 1830s to the Quaker-initiated Free Produce Association, which tried to put economic pressure on slaveholders by boycotting agricultural products produced by slaves. James Cornish led the Colored Free Produce Society of Pennsylvania, which marketed meat, vegetables, cotton, and sugar produced by free labor. With a similar aim, Judith James and Laetitia Rowley organized the Colored Female Free Produce Society of Pennsylvania. Other black affiliates to the Free Produce Association existed in New York and Ohio, and black abolitionist William Whipper operated a free produce store in Philadelphia in 1834. During the 1850s Frances Ellen Watkins Harper, one of the few prominent black female speakers of the time, always included the free produce movement in her abolitionist lectures and wrote newspaper articles on its behalf.

9.2.3 Moral Suasion

During the 1830s the AASS adopted a reform strategy based on **moral suasion**—what we would today call moral *persuasion*. This was an appeal to Americans North and South to support abolition and racial justice on the basis of their Christian consciences. Slaveholding, the AASS argued, was a sin and a crime that deprived African Americans of the freedom of conscience they needed to save their souls. Slaveholding led masters to damnation through their indolence, sexual exploitation of black women, and brutality. Abolitionists also argued that slavery was an inefficient labor system that enriched a few masters while impoverishing black and white southerners and hurting the American economy.

moral suasion

A tactic endorsed by the American Anti-Slavery Society during the 1830s. It appealed to slaveholders and others to support immediate emancipation on the basis of Christian principles.

Abolitionists did not just criticize white southerners. They noted as well that northern industrialists thrived by manufacturing cloth from cotton produced by slave labor. They pointed out that the U.S. government protected the interests of slaveholders in the District of Columbia, in the territories, in the interstate slave trade, and through the Fugitive Slave Act of 1793. Northerners who profited from slave-produced cotton and supported the national government with their votes and taxes bore their share of guilt for slavery and faced divine punishment.

The AASS hoped to convince masters to begin freeing their slaves immediately. The organization also hoped to persuade northerners and nonslaveholding white southerners to put pressure on slaveholders to do so. To reach a white southern audience, the AASS in 1835 launched the Great Postal Campaign to send antislavery literature to southern post offices and individual slaveholders. At about the same time, the AASS organized a petitioning campaign aimed to agitate the slavery issue in Congress. Antislavery women led in circulating and signing the petitions. In 1836 over 30,000 petitions reached Washington.

In the North, AASS agents lectured against slavery and distributed antislavery literature. Often a pair of agents—one black and one white—traveled together. Ideally, the black agent would be a former slave, so he could testify from personal experience to the brutality and immorality of slavery. During the early 1840s, the AASS paired fugitive slave Frederick Douglass with William A. White, a young white Harvard graduate, in a tour through Ohio and Indiana. In 1843 the Eastern New York Anti-Slavery Society paired white Baptist preacher Abel Brown with "the noble colored man," Lewis Washington. At first, only men served as agents. Later, abolitionist organizations also employed women.

In an effort to stir antiabolitionist feelings, this broadside announces an upcoming abolitionist lecture at a local New York church.

The reaction to these efforts in the North and the South was not what the leaders of the AASS anticipated. As the story in the Voices box on Frederick Douglass relates, by speaking of racial justice and exemplifying interracial cooperation, abolitionists trod new ground. This created awkward situations that are—in retrospect—humorous. But audiences often reacted very negatively. Southern postmasters burned antislavery literature, and southern state governments censored the mail. Vigilantes drove off white southerners who openly advocated abolition. Black abolitionists, of course, did not dare denounce slavery when and if they visited the South.

In 1836 southern representatives and their northern allies in Congress passed the Gag Rule forbidding petitions related to slavery from being

An increase in slaves helped inspire the more aggressive abolitionist tactics of the 1840s and 1850s. In this 1845 cover illustration for sheet music composed by white antislavery minstrel Jesse Hutchinson, Jr., Frederick Douglass is shown in an idealized rendition of his escape from slavery in Maryland.

introduced in the House of Representatives. In response, the AASS sent 415,000 petitions in 1838, and Congressman (and former president) John Quincy Adams began his struggle against the Gag. Technically not an abolitionist but a defender of the First Amendment right to petition Congress, Adams succeeded in having the Gag repealed in 1844.

Meanwhile northern mobs continued to assault abolitionist agents, disrupt their meetings, destroy their newspaper presses, and attack black neighborhoods. In 1837 a proslavery mob killed white abolitionist journalist Elijah P. Lovejoy as he defended his printing press in Alton, Illinois. On another occasion, as Douglass, White, and older white abolitionist George Bradburn held an antislavery meeting in the small town of Pendleton, Indiana, an enraged mob attempted to kill Douglass. Some of the rioters shouted, "Kill the nigger, kill the damn nigger." Douglass suffered a broken hand. A rock hit White's head. Finally, the two men fled. Years later, Douglass told White, "I shall never forget how like very brothers we were ready to dare, do, and even die for each other. . . . How I looked running you can best describe but how you looked bleeding I shall always remember."

9.3 Black Community Support

Evaluate the impact of black churches and black newspapers on the abolitionist movement.

A maturing African-American community undergirded the antislavery movement and helped it survive violent opposition. The free black population of the United States grew from 59,000 in 1790 to 319,000 in 1830 and 434,449 in 1850. Gradual emancipation in the northern states, acts of individual manumission in the Upper South, escapes, and a high birthrate accounted for this sevenfold increase. The concentration of a growing black population in such cities as New York, Philadelphia, Baltimore, Boston, and Cincinnati strengthened the black communities. These cities had enough African Americans to support the independent churches, schools, benevolent organizations, and printing presses that such communities required. They became bedrocks of abolitionism.

9.3.1 The Black Convention Movement

The dozens of local, state, and national black conventions held in the North between 1830 and 1864 helped inspire a black community that transcended localities. These conventions manifested the antebellum American reform impulse, and their agenda transcended the antislavery cause. Nevertheless, the conventions provided forums for prominent black abolitionist men, such as Garnet, Frederick Douglass, and Martin R. Delany. They provided a setting in which abolitionism could grow and adapt to meet the demands of a sectionally polarized and violent time.

Hezekiah Grice, a young black man who had worked with Benjamin Lundy and William Lloyd Garrison in Baltimore during the 1820s (see Chapter 8), organized the first Black National Convention. It met on September 24, 1830, at the Bethel Church in Philadelphia with the venerable churchman Richard Allen presiding. The national convention became an annual event for the next five years, with all but one held in Philadelphia. During the same period, many state and local black conventions met across the North. All the conventions were small and informal—particularly those at the local level—and had no guidelines for choosing delegates. Still, they provided attractive venues for discussing and publicizing black concerns. They called for the abolition of slavery and improved conditions for northern African Americans. Among other reforms, they advocated integrated public schools and the rights of black men to vote, serve on juries, and testify against white people in court.

The conventions also stressed black self-help through temperance, sexual morality, education, and thrift. These causes remained important parts of the black agenda throughout the antebellum years. But by the mid-1830s, the national convention movement faltered as black abolitionists placed their hopes in the AASS.

9.3.2 Black Churches in the Antislavery Cause

Black churches were more important than black conventions in the antislavery movement. With few exceptions, leading black abolitionists were ministers. Among them were Garnet, Jehiel C. Beman, Samuel E. Cornish, Theodore S. Wright, Charles B. Ray, James W. C. Pennington, Nathaniel Paul, Alexander Crummell, Daniel A. Payne, and Samuel Ringgold Ward. Some of these men led congregations affiliated with African-American churches, such as the African Baptist Church or the African Methodist Episcopal (AME) Church. Others preached to black congregations affiliated with predominantly white churches. A few black ministers, such as Amos N. Freeman of Brooklyn, New York, served white antislavery congregations. In all cases, they used their pulpits to attack slavery, racial discrimination, proslavery white churches, and the American Colonization Society (ACS). Having covered most of these topics in a sermon to a white congregation in 1839, Daniel Payne, who had grown up free in South Carolina, declared, "Awake! AWAKE! to the battle, and hurl the hottest thunders of divine truth at the head of this cruel monster [slavery], until he shall fall to rise no more; and the groans of the enslaved are converted into the songs of the free!" Black churches also provided forums for abolitionist speakers, such as Douglass and Garrison, and meeting places for predominantly white antislavery organizations, which frequently could not meet in white churches.

9.3.3 Black Newspapers

Although less influential than black churches, black antislavery newspapers had an important role in the antislavery movement, particularly by the 1840s. Like their white counterparts, they almost always faced financial difficulties, and few survived for long. This was because *reform*—as opposed to *commercial*—newspapers were a luxury that not many subscribers, black or white, could afford. Black newspapers faced added difficulties finding readers because most African Americans were poor, and many were illiterate. Moreover, white abolitionist newspapers, such as *The Liberator*, served a black clientele. They published speeches by black abolitionists and reported black convention proceedings. Some black abolitionists argued, therefore, that a separate black press was unnecessary. An additional, self-imposed burden was that publishers eager to get their message out almost never required subscribers to pay in advance.

Yet several influential black abolitionist newspapers existed between the late 1820s and the Civil War. The first black newspaper, *Freedom's Journal*, owned and edited by Samuel Cornish and John B. Russwurm, lasted from 1827 to 1829. It proved African Americans could produce interesting, competent journalism that attracted black and white subscribers. The *Journal* also established a framework for black journalism during the antebellum period by emphasizing opposition to slavery, support for racial justice, and devotion to Christian and democratic values.

Philip A. Bell became the most ubiquitous black journalist of the period. Bell published or co-published the *New York Weekly Advocate* in 1837, the **Colored American** from 1837 to 1842, and the San Francisco *Pacific Appeal* and the San Francisco *Elevator* during the 1860s. But black clergyman Charles B. Ray of New York City provided the real spirit behind the *Colored American*. Aware of the need for financial success, Ray declared in

Colored American

Published in New York from 1837 to 1842, the leading African-American newspaper of its time.

Voices

Frederick Douglass Describes an Awkward Situation

Frederick Douglass wrote this passage during the mid-1850s. It is from My Bondage and My Freedom, *the second of his three autobiographies. It relates with humor not only the racial barriers that black and white abolitionists had to break but also primitive conditions they took for granted.*

In the summer of 1843, I was traveling and lecturing in company with William A. White, Esq., through the state of Indiana. Anti-slavery friends were not very abundant in Indiana . . . and beds were not more plentiful than friends. . . . At the close of one of our meetings, we were invited home with a kindly-disposed old farmer, who, in the generous enthusiasm of the moment, seemed to have forgotten that he had but one spare bed, and that his guests were an ill-matched pair. . . . White is remarkably fine looking, and very evidently a born gentleman; the idea of putting us in the same bed was hardly to be tolerated; and yet there we were, and but the one bed for us, and that, by the way, was in the same room occupied by the other members of the family. . . . After witnessing the confusion as long as I liked, I relieved the kindly-disposed family by playfully saying, "Friend White, having got entirely rid of my prejudice against color, I think, as proof of it, I must allow you to sleep with me to-night." White kept up the joke, by seeming to esteem himself the favored party, and thus the difficulty was removed.

1. What does this passage reveal about American life during the 1840s?
2. What does Douglass tell us about his personality?

SOURCE: Douglass, F. (1855). *My Bondage and My Freedom.* London, England: Partridge and Oakey.

1838, "If among the few hundred thousand free colored people in the country—to say nothing of the white population from whom it ought to receive a strong support—a living patronage for the paper cannot be obtained, it will be greatly to their reproach."

Other prominent, if short-lived, black newspapers of the 1840s and 1850s included Garnet's *United States Clarion*, published in his home city of Troy, New York; Stephen Myers's *Northern Star and Freeman's Advocate*, published in Albany, New York; Samuel Ringgold Ward's *True American*, of Cortland, New York, which in 1850 became the *Impartial Citizen*; Martin Delany's *Mystery*, published in Pittsburgh during the 1840s; and Thomas Van Rensselaer's *Ram's Horn*, which appeared in New York City during the 1850s.

Frederick Douglass's **North Star** and its successor *Frederick Douglass' Paper* were the most influential black antislavery newspapers of the late 1840s and the 1850s. Heavily subsidized by wealthy white abolitionist Gerrit Smith and attracting more white than black subscribers, Douglass's weeklies gained the support of many black abolitionist organizations. His papers were well edited and attractively printed. They also employed able assistant editors, including Martin R. Delany during the late 1840s, and insightful correspondents, such as William J. Wilson of Brooklyn and James McCune Smith of New York City.

North Star

A weekly newspaper published and edited by Frederick Douglass from 1847 to 1851. *Frederick Douglass' Paper* (1851–1860) succeeded it.

American and Foreign Anti-Slavery Society (AFASS; 1840–1855)

An organization of church-oriented abolitionists.

Liberty Party (1840–1848)

The first antislavery political party. Most of its supporters joined the Free Soil Party in 1848, although its radical New York wing maintained a Liberty organization into the 1850s.

9.4 The American and Foreign Anti-Slavery Society and the Liberty Party

Discuss the breakup of the American Anti-Slavery Society and the organizations that emerged from it.

In 1840 the AASS splintered. Most of its members left to establish the **American and Foreign Anti-Slavery Society (AFASS)** and the **Liberty Party**, the first antislavery political party. In part, the split resulted from long-standing disagreements about the role of women in abolitionism and William Lloyd Garrison's broadening radicalism. By

Profile

Henry Highland Garnet

Henry Highland Garnet (1815–1882)

Henry Highland Garnet rivaled Frederick Douglass as a black leader during the antebellum decades. While Douglass emphasized assimilation, Garnet advocated black nationalism. The two men had much in common, however, and by the Civil War their views were almost indistinguishable.

In 1824, when Garnet was nine, his family fled a Maryland plantation for freedom in the North. His father led the family to New York City, where Garnet enrolled in the Free African School. Influenced by his father's pride in their African heritage, by his vigilance against slave catchers, and by a lameness that led to the amputation of one of his legs in 1840, Garnet brought a profound determination to all he undertook. In 1835 he was among 12 black students admitted to Noyes Academy at Canaan, New Hampshire. When shortly thereafter local farmers reacted by tearing down the school buildings, Garnet defended his black classmates with a shotgun. The following year he enrolled at Oneida Theological Institute near Utica, New York. There, guided by white abolitionist Beriah Green, Garnet

prepared for the ministry. In 1842 he became pastor of the black Presbyterian church in Troy, New York.

By that time, he had become an active abolitionist. He worked closely with Gerrit Smith's radical New York wing of the Liberty Party. He also advocated independent antislavery action among African Americans. Referring to white abolitionists, he said, "They are our allies—*Ours* is the battle." But it was within the interracial context of the New York Liberty Party's determination to challenge slavery on its home ground that Garnet delivered his famous "Address to the Slaves" at the 1843 National Convention of Colored Citizens. By demanding that slaves claim their freedom and acknowledging that violence could result, Garnet highlighted his differences with Frederick Douglass and other African Americans who endorsed nonviolence.

Garnet's conviction that African Americans ultimately must free themselves led him to promote migration to Africa. He always regarded the American Colonization Society (ACS) as proslavery and racist. But by 1848 he had come to believe African colonization could be a powerful part of the struggle for emancipation in the United States. Garnet's years abroad during the early 1850s strengthened this outlook. He served as a delegate to the World Peace Conference in Frankfurt, Germany, in 1850; spent 1851 in Great Britain; and was a Presbyterian missionary in Jamaica from 1853 to 1856. Garnet returned to the United States in 1856 and in 1858 organized the African Civilization Society, designed to build an independent Africa through black emigration from America and the cultivation of cotton in Africa.

Few African-American leaders shared Garnet's views, and the Civil War effectively ended his nationalist efforts. Early in the war, he advocated enlisting black troops in the Union armies. In 1863 he became pastor of the 15th Street Presbyterian Church in Washington, D.C., and in 1865 became the first African American to deliver a sermon in Congress. Like Douglass, Garnet was a staunch Republican after the Civil War. In January 1882, he became U.S. ambassador to Liberia and died there a month later.

declaring that slavery had irrevocably corrupted the existing American society, by denouncing organized white churches as irrevocably proslavery, by becoming a feminist, and by embracing a form of Christian anarchy that precluded formal involvement in politics, Garrison seemed to have lost sight of abolitionism's main concern. However, the failure of moral suasion to make progress against slavery—particularly in the South—and the question of how abolitionists should respond to slave unrest also helped fracture the AASS.

Garrison and a minority of New England–centered abolitionists who agreed with his radical critique of America retained control of the AASS, which became known as the "Old Organization." By 1842 they had deemphasized moral suasion and begun calling for disunion—the separation of the North from the South—as the only means of ending northern support for slavery. The U.S. Constitution, Garrison declared, was a proslavery document that had to be replaced before African Americans could gain freedom.

Those who withdrew from the AASS took a more traditional stand on the role of women, believed white churches could be converted to abolitionism, and asserted that the Constitution could be used on behalf of emancipation. Under the leadership of Lewis Tappan, a wealthy white New York City businessman, some of these non-garrisonians formed the church-oriented AFASS. Others created the Liberty Party and nominated James G. Birney, a slaveholder-turned-abolitionist, as their candidate in the 1840 presidential election. Birney received only 7,069 votes out of a total cast of 2,411,187, and William Henry Harrison, the Whig candidate, became president. But the Liberty Party began what became an increasingly powerful political crusade against slavery.

Black abolitionists joined in the disruption of the Old Organization. As might be expected, most black clerical abolitionists joined the AFASS. Eight, including Jehiel C. Beman and his son Amos G. Beman, Christopher Rush, Samuel E. Cornish, Theodore S. Wright, Stephen H. Gloucester, Andrew Harris, and Garnet helped create the new organization. After 1840 African Americans were always more prominent as leaders in the AFASS than the AASS. Only in New England did most black abolitionists remain loyal to the AASS. Among the loyalists were Frederick Douglass, William Wells Brown, Robert Purvis, Charles L. Remond, Susan Paul, and Sarah Douglass.

The Liberty Party also attracted black support, although few black men could vote. The platform of the radical New York wing of the party, led by Gerrit Smith, especially appealed to black abolitionists. Philip A. Bell, Charles B. Ray, Samuel E. Cornish, Jermain Wesley Loguen, and Garnet endorsed the New York Liberty Party and influenced its program. Of all the antislavery organizations, the New York party advocated the most aggressive action against slavery in the South and became most involved in helping slaves escape.

9.5 A More Aggressive Abolitionism

Explain why abolitionism became more aggressive during the 1840s and 1850s.

The New York Liberty Party maintained that the U.S. Constitution, interpreted in the light of the Bible and natural law, outlawed slavery throughout the country. While other Liberty abolitionists recognized Congress's power over slavery only in the District of Columbia, the territories, and interstate commerce, the New Yorkers held Congress could also act against slavery in the states. They contended that neither northern state militias nor the U.S. Army should help suppress slave revolts. Most important, they argued that, since masters had no legal right to own human beings, slaves who escaped and those who aided them acted within the law.

This body of thought, which dated to the late 1830s, reflected northern abolitionist empathy with slaves as they struggled for freedom. At that time, the domestic slave trade in the Border South states of Maryland, Virginia, Kentucky, and Missouri tore black families apart to fill the demand for labor in new cotton-producing areas farther south. That some slaves responded by escaping or staging minor rebellions encouraged Garnet to deliver his "Address to the Slaves." Slave actions also inspired the New York Liberty Party's constitutional interpretation, and the party's encouragement of black and white northerners to go south to help escapees. Two major seaborne revolts had a similar impact.

9.5.1 The *Amistad* and the *Creole*

In particular, two maritime slave revolts encouraged northern abolitionist militancy. The first of these revolts, however, did not involve enslaved Americans. In June 1839, 54 African captives, under the leadership of Joseph Cinque, seized control of the Spanish schooner *Amistad* (meaning "friendship"), which had been carrying them to slavery in Honduras. After the Africans lost their way in an attempt to return to their homeland, a U.S. warship captured them off the coast of Long Island, New York. Imprisoned in New Haven, Connecticut, the Africans soon gained the assistance of Lewis Tappan and other abolitionists. As a result of that aid and arguments presented by Congressman John Quincy Adams, the Supreme Court in November 1841 freed Cinque and the others.

Later that November, Madison Washington led a revolt aboard the brig *Creole* as it transported 135 American slaves from Richmond to New Orleans. Washington had earlier escaped from Virginia to Canada. When he returned to Virginia to rescue his wife, white Virginians captured him, reenslaved him, and put him on the *Creole*. At sea, Washington and about a dozen other black men seized control and sailed the vessel to the Bahamas, a British colony where slavery had been abolished. There local black fishermen protected the *Creole* by surrounding it with their boats, and most of those on board immediately gained their freedom under British law. Four months later, so did Washington and the other rebels. Although Washington soon vanished from the public eye, the *Creole* revolt made him a hero among abolitionists and a symbol of black bravery.

Cinque and Washington inspired others to risk their lives and freedom to help African Americans escape bondage. The New York Liberty Party reinforced this commitment by declaring their revolts divinely ordained and strictly legal.

Amistad

A Spanish schooner on which West African Joseph Cinque led a successful slave revolt in 1839.

9.5.2 The Underground Railroad

The famous **underground railroad** must be placed within the context of increasing southern white violence against black families, slave resistance, and aggressive northern abolitionism. Because the underground railroad had to be secret, details about how it operated are difficult to uncover. Slaves, since colonial times, had escaped from their masters, and free black people and some white people had assisted them. But organized slave escape from the Chesapeake, Kentucky, and Missouri along predetermined routes to Canada became common only after the mid-1830s. A united national underground railroad with a president or unified

underground railroad

Refers to several loosely organized, semi-secret biracial networks that helped slaves escape from the Border South to the North and Canada. The earliest networks appeared during the first decade of the nineteenth century; others operated into the Civil War years.

Death of Capt. Ferrer, the Captain of the Amistad, July, 1839.

Don Jose Ruiz and Don Pedro Montez, of the Island of Cuba, having purchased fifty-three slaves at Havana, recently imported from Africa, put them on board the Amistad, Capt. Ferrer, in order to transport them to Principe, another port on the Island of Cuba. After being out from Havana about four days, the African captives on board, in order to obtain their freedom, and return to Africa, armed themselves with cane knives, and rose upon the Captain and crew of the vessel. Capt. Ferrer and the cook of the vessel were killed; two of the crew escaped; Ruiz and Montez were made prisoners.

This 1840 engraving provides a dramatic portrayal of the successful uprising of African slaves on board the Spanish schooner *Amistad* in 1839.

Map 9-2 The Underground Railroad

This map illustrates approximate routes traveled by escaping slaves through the North to Canada. Although some slaves escaped from the Deep South, most of those who utilized the underground railroad network came from the border slave states.

What difficulties did escaping slaves face as they attempted to reach Canada?

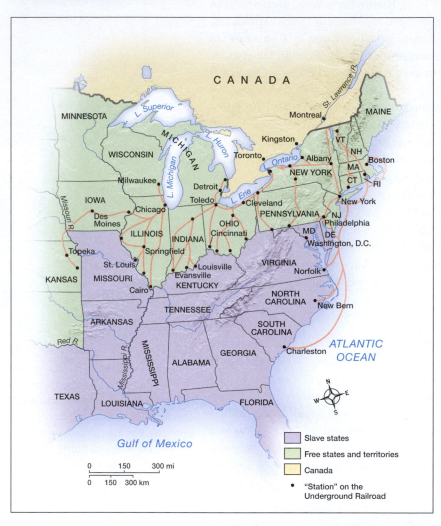

Slave states

Free states and territories

Canada

● "Station" on the Underground Railroad

command never existed. Instead, different organizations separated in time and space from one another operated the network (see Map 9-2). Even during the 1840s and 1850s, most of the slaves who escaped did so on their own. Sometimes they fought pursuing masters.

The best-documented underground railroad organizations centered in Ripley, Ohio, and Washington, D.C. In southern Ohio and Indiana, some residents, black and white, had helped fugitive slaves since the 1810s as the escapees headed north from Kentucky. By the late 1820s John Rankin, a white Presbyterian minister, lit a lantern each night at his Ripley, Ohio, home—located on a hill above the north shore of the Ohio River—to serve as a beacon for escaping slaves. During the late 1840s, former slave John P. Parker became the most aggressive agent of the Ripley-based underground railroad. With Rankin's support, Parker, who had purchased his freedom in 1845, repeatedly went into Kentucky to lead others north. In Washington, Charles T. Torrey, a white Liberty Party abolitionist from Albany, New York, and Thomas Smallwood, a free black resident of Washington, began in 1842 to help slaves escape along a northward route. Between March and November of that year, they sent at least 150 enslaved men, women, and children to Philadelphia. From there, a local black vigilance committee provided the fugitives with transportation to Albany, where a local, predominantly white, vigilance group helped them get to Canada.

The escapees were by no means passive "passengers" in the underground railroad networks. They raised money to pay for their transportation, recruited and aided other escapees, and helped plan escapes. During the mid-1850s, Arrah Weems of Rockville, Maryland, whose freedom had been recently purchased by black and white abolitionists and whose daughter Ann Maria had been rescued by underground railroad agents, became an agent herself. She brought an enslaved infant from Washington through Philadelphia to Rochester, New York, where she met Frederick Douglass.

Weems's trek north was not an easy journey. She and others who helped slaves escape took great risks. In 1843 Smallwood had to flee to Canada as Washington police closed in on his home. In 1846 Torrey died of tuberculosis in a Maryland prison while serving a six-year sentence for helping slaves escape. Parker recalled "real warfare" in southern Ohio between underground railroad operators and slaveholders from Kentucky. "I never thought of going uptown without a pistol in my pocket, a knife in my belt, and a blackjack handy," he recalled.

During the early 1850s, Harriet Tubman, a fugitive slave, became the most active worker on the eastern branch of the underground railroad. Born in 1820 on a Maryland plantation, she suffered years of abuse at the hands of her master. When in 1849 he threatened to sell her and her family south, she escaped to the North. Then she returned about 13 times to Maryland to help others flee. She had the help of Thomas Garrett, a white Quaker abolitionist who lived in Wilmington, Delaware, and William Still, the black leader of the Philadelphia Vigilance Association. During the 1850s, Still, who as a child had been a fugitive slave, coordinated the work of many black and white underground agents between Washington and Canada.

Harriet Tubman, standing at the left, is shown in this undated photograph with a group of people she helped escape from slavery. Because she worked in secret during the 1850s, she was known only to others engaged in the underground railroad, the people she helped, and few other abolitionists.

9.5.3 Technology and the Underground Railroad

Historian Fergus M. Bordewich notes that before the late 1830s those who helped slaves escape referred to their networks as "lines of posts" or "chains of friends." Only as railroad mileage expanded in the eastern United States did railroad power, speed, and organization serve as a metaphor for escape networks.

But the link between slave escapes and technology was more than a metaphor. Steam engines, whether used to power locomotives or vessels, promoted northward escapes. By the early 1840s, police in Border South cities patrolled steamboat wharves to prevent fugitive slaves from boarding. In 1842 in Washington, D.C., Torrey and Smallwood often helped escapees get on steamboats. When the two men led parties north on foot or by carriage, they headed for Philadelphia, where fugitives boarded northbound trains. As rail lines spread, masters in Maryland and Virginia despaired of recapturing slaves who crossed the Mason-Dixon Line.

Railroads and steamboats had essential roles in two famous escapes of the late 1840s. In December 1848, Ellen and William Craft (see Chapter 10) used both means of transportation to reach Philadelphia from Macon, Georgia. A few months later, Henry Brown—encased in a shipping box—traveled by train from Richmond to the Potomac River "where the tracks ended." He went by steamer to Washington, and once again by train to freedom in Philadelphia. Improving transportation technology posed a threat to slavery.

9.5.4 Canada West

The ultimate destination for many African Americans on the underground railroad was Canada West (present-day Ontario) located between Buffalo and Detroit on the northern shore of Lake Erie. Black Americans began to settle in Canada West as early as the 1820s. When the British Empire prohibited slavery after 1833, fugitive slaves became safer in Canada. When Congress passed a stonger fugitive slave law as part of the Compromise of 1850 (see Chapter 10), Canada became an even more important refuge for African Americans. Between 1850 and 1860, the number of black people in Canada West rose from approximately 8,000 to at least 20,000.

Several communal black settlements existed in Canada West. They included the Refugee Home Society in Sandwich and Maidstone Townships, the Buxton Community at Elgin, and the Dawn Settlement in Dresden. However, most black immigrants lived

This is the only surviving photograph of Mary Ann Shadd Cary (1823–1893). An advocate, during the 1850s, of black migration to Canada, Cary also promoted racial integration.

and worked in Toronto and Chatham. They usually worked as craftsmen and laborers. A few were entrepreneurs or professionals.

Mary Ann Shadd Cary became the chief advocate of black migration to Canada West, and she was the only advocate of black migration who supported racial integration. Between 1854 and 1858, she edited the *Provincial Freeman*, an abolitionist paper published in Toronto, and lectured in northern cities promoting emigration to Canada. Cary knew, however, that by the 1850s black people faced the same sort of segregation and discrimination in Canada that existed in the northern United States.

9.6 Black Militancy

Compare and contrast the views of Frederick Douglass and those of Henry Highland Garnet.

As we mentioned earlier in this chapter, during the 1840s growing numbers of northern black abolitionists advocated forceful action against slavery. This resolve accompanied a trend toward separate black antislavery action. The black convention movement revived during the 1840s, and well-attended meetings took place in Buffalo in 1843 (where Garnet presented his "Address to the Slaves"); in Troy, New York, in 1844; and in Cleveland in 1848. In addition, more black-owned and -edited abolitionist newspapers appeared.

The rise in militancy had several causes. First, the breakup of the AASS weakened abolitionist loyalty to the national antislavery organizations. Second, all abolitionists, black and white, explored new antislavery tactics. Third, many black abolitionists came to believe that most white abolitionists enjoyed antislavery debate and theory more than action.

Influenced by the examples of Cinque, Madison Washington, and other rebellious slaves, many black abolitionists during the 1840s and 1850s wanted to do more to encourage slaves to resist and escape. This outlook inspired Garnet, who, as we have described, supported the radical New York wing of the Liberty Party. That organization's willingness to act rather than just talk attracted other black leaders. However, black abolitionists, like white abolitionists, approached the subjects of violence and slave rebellion cautiously. As late as 1857, Garnet and Frederick Douglass described slave revolt as "inexpedient."

The black abolitionist desire to go beyond rhetoric found its best outlet in local vigilance organizations. Such associations appeared during the mid-1830s and often had white as well as black members. As the 1840s progressed, African Americans formed more of them and led those that already existed. In this they reacted against a facet of the growing violence in the United States: the use of force by "slave catchers" to recapture fugitive slaves in northern cities. In Philadelphia, during the late 1840s and 1850s, William Still led the most famous of the vigilance associations.

Charges that white abolitionists did not live up to their words in favor of racial justice also contributed to black militancy. Economic slights rankled the most. At the annual meeting of the AFASS in 1852, a black delegate demanded to know why Lewis Tappan did not employ a black clerk in his business. In 1855 Samuel Ringgold Ward denounced Garrison and his associates for failing to have an African American "as clerk in an anti-slavery office, or editor, or lecturer to the same extent . . . as white men of the same calibre." These charges reflected factional struggles between the AASS and the AFASS. But they also represented real grievances among black abolitionists and inconsistencies among white abolitionists.

9.6.1 Frederick Douglass

Frederick Douglass's career illustrates the impact of the failure of some white abolitionists to live up to their egalitarian ideals. Douglass was born a slave in Maryland in 1818. Brilliant, ambitious, and charming, he resisted brutalization, learned to read, and acquired a trade before escaping to New England in 1838. By 1841 he had, with

Garrison's encouragement, become an antislavery lecturer, which led to the travels with William White discussed earlier.

Douglass had remained loyal to Garrison during the 1840s when most other black abolitionists left the AASS. But, as time passed, Douglass suspected that his white colleagues wanted him to continue in the role of a fugitive slave even as he became a premier American orator. A white colleague advised him, "People won't believe you ever was a slave, Frederick, if you keep on this way."

Finally Douglass decided he had to free himself from the AASS. In 1847 he asserted his independence by leaving Massachusetts for Rochester, New York, where he began publishing the *North Star*. This decision angered Garrison and his associates but enabled Douglass to chart his course as a black leader. Although Douglass continued to work closely with white abolitionists, especially Gerrit Smith, he could now do it on his own terms and be more active in the black convention movement, which he considered essential to gaining general emancipation and racial justice. In 1851 he completed his break with the AASS by endorsing the constitutional arguments and tactics of the New York Liberty Party as better designed than Garrison's "disunionism" to achieve emancipation.

By the mid-1840s, Frederick Douglass had emerged as one of the more powerful speakers of his time. He began publishing his influential newspaper, the *North Star*, in 1847.

9.6.2 Revival of Black Nationalism

Douglass always believed black people constituted part of a larger American nation and that their best prospects for political and economic success lay in the United States. He was, despite his differences with some white abolitionists, an ardent integrationist.

1839–1846
The Antislavery Struggle Intensifies

June 1839
Joseph Cinque leads a successful revolt of enslaved Africans aboard the Spanish schooner *Amistad*

April 1840
The Liberty Party nominates James G. Birney for U.S. president

November 1841
Madison Washington leads a successful revolt of American slaves aboard the *Creole*

March 1842
Charles T. Torrey and Thomas Smallwood organize an underground railroad network to help slaves escape from Washington, D.C., and its vicinity

August 1843
Henry Highland Garnet in Buffalo, New York, delivers his "Address to the Slaves"

December 1843
Smallwood flees to Canada to avoid arrest

June 1844
Torrey is arrested in Baltimore on multiple charges of having helped slaves escape

May 1846
Torrey dies in a Maryland penitentiary

Voices

Martin R. Delany Describes His Vision of a Black Nation

This excerpt comes from the appendix of Martin R. Delany's The Condition, Elevation, Emigration and Destiny of the Colored People of the United States, Politically Considered, *which he published in 1852. It embodies Delany's black nationalist vision.*

Every people should be the originators of their own designs, the projectors of their own schemes, and creators of the events that lead to their destiny—the consummation of their desires.

Situated as we are in the United States, many, and almost insurmountable obstacles present themselves. We are four-and-a-half millions in numbers, free and bond; six hundred thousand free, and three-and-a-half millions bond.

We have native hearts and virtues, just as other nations; which in their pristine purity are noble, potent, and worthy of example. We are a nation within a nation. . . .

But we have been, by our oppressors, despoiled of our purity, and corrupted in our native characteristics, so that we have inherited their vices, and but few of their virtues, leaving us in character, really a broken people.

Being distinguished by complexion, we are still singled out—although having merged in the habits and customs of our oppressors—as a distinct nation of people. . . . The claims of no people, according to established policy and usage, are respected by any nation, until they are presented in a national capacity.

To accomplish so great and desirable an end, there should be held, a great representative gathering of the colored people of the United States; not what is termed a National Convention, representing en masse, such as have been, for the last few years, held at various times and places; but a true representation of the intelligence and wisdom of the colored freemen. . . . A Confidential Council. . . .

By this Council to be appointed, a Board of Commissioners . . . to go on an expedition to the EASTERN COAST OF AFRICA, to make researches for a suitable location on that section of the coast, for the settlement of colored adventurers from the United States, and elsewhere.

The whole continent is rich in minerals, and the most precious metals, as but a superficial notice of the topographical and geological reports from that country, plainly show. . . . The land is ours—there it lies with inexhaustible resources; let us go and possess it. In Eastern Africa must rise up a nation, to whom all the world must pay commercial tribute.

1. How does this document express black nationalism?
2. What is Delany's view of Africa?

SOURCE: *The Condition, Elevation, Emigration, and Destiny of the Colored People of the United States* (1852), Martin Robison Delany.

He opposed separate black churches and predicted that African Americans would eventually merge into a greater American identity. Most black abolitionists did not go that far, but they believed racial oppression in all its forms could be defeated in the United States.

During the 1840s and 1850s, however, an influential minority of black leaders disagreed with this point of view. Prominent among them were Garnet and Douglass's sometime colleague on the *North Star*, Martin R. Delany. Although they disagreed over important details, Delany and Garnet both favored African-American migration and nationalism as the best means to realize black aspirations.

Since the postrevolutionary days of Prince Hall and Paul Cuffe, some black leaders had believed African Americans could thrive only as a separate nation. They suggested sites in Africa, Latin America, and the American West as possible places to pursue this goal. But it took the rising tide of racism and violence emphasized in this chapter to induce a respectable minority of black abolitionists to reconsider migration. Almost all of them opposed the ACS's African migration scheme, which they regarded as proslavery and racist. Nevertheless, Garnet conceded in 1849 that he would "rather see a man free in Liberia [the ACS colony], than a slave in the United States."

Douglass and most black abolitionists rejected this outlook, insisting the aim must be freedom in the United States. Yet emigration plans Garnet and Delany developed during the 1850s became a significant part of African American reform culture. Delany, a physician and novelist, was born free in western Virginia in 1812. He grew up in Pennsylvania and by the late 1840s championed black self-reliance. To further this cause, he promoted mass black migration to Latin America or Africa. "We must MAKE an ISSUE, CREATE an EVENT, and ESTABLISH a NATIONAL POSITION for OURSELVES," he declared in 1852.

In contrast, Garnet welcomed white assistance for his plan to foster Christianity and economic development in Africa by encouraging *some*—not all—African Americans to migrate there under the patronage of his African Civilization Society. In 1858 he wrote, "Let those who wished to stay, stay here—and those who had enterprise and wished to go, go and found a nation, if possible, of which the colored Americans could be proud."

Little came of these nationalist visions, largely because of the successes of the antislavery movement. Black and white abolitionists, although not perfect allies, awoke many in the North to the brutalities of slavery. They helped convince most white northerners that the slave-labor system and slaveholder control of the national government threatened their economic and political interests. At the same time, abolitionist aid to escaping slaves and their defense of fugitive slaves from recapture pushed southern leaders to adopt policies that led to secession and the Civil War. The northern victory in the war, general emancipation, and constitutional protection for black rights made most African Americans—for a time—optimistic about their future in the United States.

Conclusion

This chapter has focused on the radical movement for the immediate abolition of slavery. The movement flourished in the United States from 1831, when William Lloyd Garrison began publishing *The Liberator*, through the Civil War. Garrison hoped slavery could be abolished peacefully. But during the 1840s abolitionists adjusted their antislavery tactics to deal with increasing racism and antiblack violence, both of which grew out of the existence of slavery. Slave resistance also inspired a more confrontational brand of abolitionism. Many black abolitionists and their white colleagues concluded that the tactic of moral suasion, typical of abolitionism during the 1830s, could not by itself achieve their goals. Most black abolitionists came to believe they needed a combination of moral suasion, political involvement, and direct action to end slavery and improve the lives of African Americans in the United States. By the late 1840s, a minority of black abolitionists contended they had to establish an independent nation beyond the borders of the United States to promote African-American rights, interests, and identity.

Although much has changed since the abolitionist era, these two perspectives remain characteristic of the African-American community. Most African Americans prefer integration within a larger American nation. But black nationalism still has an appeal. Black people often endorse parts of both views, just as Frederick Douglass embraced some facets of black nationalism and Henry Highland Garnet some integrationism. Reformers still debate whether persuasion is more effective than confrontation.

Chapter Timeline

AFRICAN-AMERICAN EVENTS	NATIONAL EVENTS
1830–1833	
1831	**1832**
Publication of *The Liberator* begun by William Lloyd Garrison	Andrew Jackson reelected president
	1833
1833	End of Nullification Controversy
Formation of AASS	
1835–1839	
1835	**1836**
Abolitionist postal campaign	Martin Van Buren elected president; Texas independence from Mexico
1839	
Amistad mutiny	
1840–1844	
1840	**1840**
Breakup of AASS	William H. Harrison elected president
1841	
Creole revolt	**1844**
1843	James K. Polk elected president
Henry Highland Garnet's "Address to the Slaves"	
1845–1849	
1847	**1845**
Publication of the *North Star* begun by Frederick Douglass	Annexation of Texas
	1846
1849	War against Mexico begins
Harriet Tubman's career begins	**1848**
	Annexation of Mexico's California and New Mexico provinces
1850–1851	
1851	**1850**
Start of resistance to the Fugitive Slave Act of 1850	Compromise of 1850
Black migration advocated by Martin Delany	

Review Questions

1. What was the historical significance of Henry Highland Garnet's "Address to the Slaves"? How did Garnet's attitude toward slavery differ from that of William Lloyd Garrison?

2. Evaluate Frederick Douglass's career as an abolitionist. How was he consistent? How was he inconsistent?

3. How did black women contribute to the antislavery movement? How did participation in this movement alter their lives?

4. How did the integrationist views of Frederick Douglass compare with the nationalist views of Martin Delany and Henry Highland Garnet?

5. Why did so many black abolitionists leave the AASS in 1840?

Retracing the Odyssey

Frederick Douglass National Historic Site, Washington, D.C. This is Douglass's Cedar Hill home, which he purchased in 1878. It contains materials related to his career as an abolitionist and advocate of black rights.

"Free at Last: A History of the Abolition of Slavery in America." A "National Touring Exhibition" sponsored by the Lincoln Home National Historic Site, Springfield, Illinois, that shows how "abolition became a national issue, how the slavery issue drew politicians and moral reformers together, [and] how the efforts of escaped slaves contributed a human face to the horrors of slavery."

National Underground Railroad Freedom Center, Cincinnati. Ohio. Exhibits, programs, and events dealing with "slavery and freedom," with emphasis on the underground railroad.

National Underground Railroad Museum, Maysville, Kentucky. Houses artifacts associated with, and provides information on, the underground railroad.

Recommended Reading

Stanley Harrold. *The Abolitionists and the South, 1831–1861.* Lexington: University Press of Kentucky, 1995. Emphasizes the formative impact of slave resistance on northern abolitionism and the aggressiveness of that movement toward the South.

Jane H. Pease and William H. Pease. *They Who Would Be Free: Blacks' Search for Freedom, 1830–1861.* New York: Athenaeum, 1974. Deals with cooperation and conflict between black and white abolitionists. The book emphasizes conflict.

Benjamin Quarles. *Black Abolitionists.* New York: Oxford University Press, 1969. A classic study that emphasizes cooperation between black and white abolitionists.

Harry Reed. *Platforms for Change: The Foundations of the Northern Free Black Community, 1776–1865.* East Lansing: Michigan State University Press, 1994. Places black abolitionism and black nationalism within the context of community development.

Shirley J. Yee. *Black Women Abolitionists: A Study of Activism.* Knoxville: University of Tennessee Press, 1992. Discusses the activities of black women abolitionists in both white and black organizations.

R. J. Young. *Antebellum Black Activists: Race, Gender, Self.* New York: Garland, 1996. A sophisticated study of black abolitionists' motivation.

Additional Bibliography

General Studies of the Antislavery Movement

Herbert Aptheker. *Abolitionism: A Revolutionary Movement.* Boston: Twayne, 1989.

Lawrence J. Friedman. *Gregarious Saints: Self and Community in American Abolitionism, 1830–1870.* New York: Cambridge University Press, 1982.

Stanley Harrold. *American Abolitionists.* Harlow, UK: Longman, 2001.

———. *The Rise of Aggressive Abolitionism: Addresses to the Slaves.* Lexington: University Press of Kentucky, 2004.

James Brewer Stewart. *Holy Warriors: The Abolitionists and American Slavery.* 2nd ed. New York: Hill and Wang, 1997.

The Black Community

John Brown Childs. *The Political Black Minister: A Study in Afro-American Politics and Religion.* Boston: G. K. Hall, 1980.

Leonard P. Curry. *The Free Black in Urban America, 1800–1850: The Shadow of a Dream.* Chicago: University of Chicago Press, 1981.

Martin E. Dann. *The Black Press, 1827–1890.* New York: Capricorn, 1971.

James Oliver Horton and Lois E. Horton. *In Hope of Liberty: Culture, Community, and Protest among Northern Free Blacks, 1700–1860.* New York: Oxford University Press, 1997.

Patrick Rael. *Black Identity and Black Protest in the Antebellum North.* Chapel Hill: University of North Carolina Press, 2002.

David E. Swift. *Black Prophets of Justice: Activist Clergy before the Civil War.* Baton Rouge: Louisiana State University Press, 1989.

Black Abolitionists

Howard Holman Bell. *A Survey of the Negro Convention Movement, 1830–1861.* New York: Arno, 1969.

R. J. M. Blackett. *Building an Antislavery Wall: Blacks in the Atlantic Abolitionist Movement, 1830–1860.* Baton Rouge: Louisiana State University Press, 1983.

Christopher Webber. *American to the Backbone: The Life of W. C. Pennington, the Fugitive Slave Who Became One of the First Black Abolitionists.* New York: Pegasus Books, 2011.

Women

Blanch Glassman-Hersh. *Slavery of Sex: Feminist-Abolitionists in Nineteenth-Century America.* Urbana: University of Illinois Press, 1978.

Darlene Clark Hine, ed. *Black Women in American History: From Colonial Times through the Nineteenth Century.* 4 vols. New York: Carlson, 1990.

Julie Roy Jeffrey. *The Great Silent Army of Abolitionism: Ordinary Women in the Antislavery Movement.* Chapel Hill: University of North Carolina Press, 1998.

Gayle Tate. *Unknown Tongues: Black Women's Political Activism in the Antebellum Era 1830–1860.* East Lansing: Michigan State University Press, 2003.

Jean Fagan Yellin. *Women and Sisters: Antislavery Feminists in American Culture.* New Haven, CT: Yale University Press, 1990.

Biography

Catherine Clinton. *Harriet Tubman: The Road to Freedom.* New York: Little, Brown, 2003.

Henry Mayer. *All on Fire: William Lloyd Garrison and the Abolition of Slavery.* New York: St. Martin's Press, 1998.

William S. McFeely. *Frederick Douglass.* New York: Simon and Schuster, 1991.

Nell Irvin Painter. *Sojourner Truth: A Life, a Symbol.* New York: Norton, 1996.

Joel Schor. *Henry Highland Garnet: A Voice of Black Radicalism in the Nineteenth Century.* Westport, CT: Greenwood, 1977.

Victor Ullman. *Martin R. Delany: The Beginnings of Black Nationalism.* Boston: Beacon, 1971.

Underground Railroad

Fergus M. Bordewich. *Bound for Canaan: The Underground Railroad and the War for the Soul of America.* New York: Amistad, 2005.

Stanley Harrold. *Border War: Fighting Over Slavery Before the Civil War.* Chapel Hill: University of North Carolina Press, 2010.

———. *Subversives: Antislavery Community in Washington, D.C., 1828–1865.* Baton Rouge: Louisiana State University Press, 2003.

William Still. *The Underground Railroad.* 1871. Reprint, Chicago: Johnson Publishing, 1970.

Black Nationalism

Rodney Carlisle. *The Roots of Black Nationalism.* Port Washington, NY: Kennikat, 1975.

Floyd J. Miller. *The Search for Black Nationality: Black Emigration and Colonization, 1787–1863.* Urbana: University of Illinois Press, 1975.

Chapter 10

"And Black People Were at the Heart of It": The United States Disunites Over Slavery

1846–1861

In January 1856, Margaret Garner, her husband Robert, and their four children escaped from Kentucky to Ohio across the frozen Ohio River. They were pursued to the home of a black man by slave owners as well as deputy marshals. The Garners fiercely resisted. Robert Garner shot and wounded one of the deputies. But when it became clear that they were about to be captured, Margaret killed her daughter rather than have the child return to slavery.

Learning Objectives

After reading this chapter, you should be able to:

10.1 State the major differences between northern and southern political leaders on the issue of the expansion of slavery.

10.2 Describe the reaction of African Americans to the passage and enforcement of the Fugitive Slave Law of 1850.

10.3 Compare the responses of slave owners and opponents of slavery to the U.S. Supreme Court decision in the *Dred Scott* case.

10.4 Explain the importance of John Brown in the controversy over slavery.

10.5 Distinguish the ways in which white northerners, white southerners, and African Americans reacted to the election of Abraham Lincoln in 1860.

The Fugitive Slave Bill, (exhibited in its hideous deformity at our previous meeting,) has already in hot haste commenced its bloody crusade o'er the land, and the liability of ourselves and our families becoming its victims at the caprice of Southern menstealers, imperatively demands an expression, whether we will tamely submit to chains and slavery, or whether we will, at all and every hazard, Live and Die freemen.

—*Robert C. Nell, "Declaration of Sentiments of the Colored Citizens of Boston on the Fugitive Slave Bill!!!," 1850*

By the end of the 1840s in the United States, no issue was as controversial as slavery. Slavery or, more accurately, its expansion deeply divided the American people and led to the bloodiest war in American history. Try as they might from 1845 to 1860, political leaders could not solve, evade, or escape slavery, nor could they agree on whether to allow it to expand into the nation's western territories.

Caught in this monumental dispute were the South's nearly four million enslaved men, women, and children. Their future, as well as the fate of the country, was at stake. As many as 750,000 Americans—northern and southern, black and white—would die before a divided nation would be reunified and slavery would be abolished.

Whether slavery should be permitted in the western territories was not a new issue. As early as 1787, Congress had prohibited slavery in the Northwest Territory, the area north of the Ohio River that became the states of Ohio, Indiana, Illinois, Michigan, and Wisconsin. Then in 1819 a major political controversy erupted when Missouri applied for admission to the Union as a slave state. The Missouri Compromise—which admitted Maine as a free state, Missouri as a slave state, and outlawed slavery north of the 36° 30' line of latitude (see Chapter 5)—settled that controversy, but only postponed for 25 years further conflict over the expansion of slavery.

The country's desire to acquire western lands intensified in the 1830s and 1840s. Most white Americans and many free black Americans assumed that the American people should occupy the entire North American continent from the Atlantic to the Pacific. It was their future, their Manifest Destiny (see Chapter 9). In 1846–1847, U.S. troops fought an 18-month conflict that resulted in the acquisition of more than half of Mexico and was a major step toward the fulfillment of Manifest Destiny.

10.1 The Lure of the West

State the major differences between northern and southern political leaders on the issue of the expansion of slavery.

Even before the war with Mexico, hundreds of Americans made the long journey west, drawn by the opportunity to settle the fertile valleys of California and the Oregon Territory, which included what is today the states of Oregon and Washington. African Americans shared these hopes and dreams. In 1844 a black Missouri farmer with the improbable name of George Washington Bush caught "Oregon fever" and set out with his wife, six children, and four other families on the 1,800-mile trek by wagon train to Oregon. Bush settled north of the Columbia River in what later became the Washington Territory because Oregon's territorial constitution forbade black settlement. Although the law was rarely enforced, black residents were legally subject to whipping every six months until they departed. The statute remained Oregon state law until the 1920s.

10.1.1 Free Labor versus Slave Labor

Westward expansion revived the issue of slavery's future in the territories. Should slavery be legal or prohibited in western lands? Most white Americans held thoroughly ingrained racist beliefs that people of African descent were not and could never be their intellectual, political, or social equals. Yet those same white Americans disagreed vehemently on where those unfree African Americans should be permitted to work and reside.

Most northern white people adamantly opposed allowing southern slaveholders to take their slaves into the former Mexican territories, and they detested the prospect of slavery spreading westward and limiting their opportunities to settle and farm those lands. Except for the increasing number of militant abolitionists, white northerners detested both slavery as a labor system and the black people who were enslaved.

By the mid-nineteenth century, northern black and white people embraced the system of **free labor**—that is, free men and women who worked for compensation to earn a living and improve their lives. If southern slave owners managed to gain a foothold for their unfree labor on the western plains, in the Rocky Mountains, or on the Pacific coast, then the future for free white laborers would be severely restricted, if not destroyed.

free labor

Mid-nineteenth-century Americans who were free and worked for income or compensation to advance themselves, as opposed to slave labor, which was work done with no financial compensation by people who were not free.

10.1.2 The Wilmot Proviso

In 1846, during the Mexican War, a Democratic congressman from Pennsylvania, David Wilmot, introduced a measure in Congress, the so-called Wilmot Proviso, to prohibit slavery in any lands acquired from Mexico. Wilmot later explained that he wanted neither slavery nor black people to taint territory that should be reserved exclusively for whites: "The negro race already occupy enough of this fair continent. . . . I would preserve for free white labor a fair country . . . where the sons of toil, of my own race and own color, can live without the disgrace which association with negro slavery brings upon free labor."

The **Wilmot Proviso** failed to become law. Nonetheless, white southerners were enraged, and they saw the proviso as a blatant attempt to prevent them from moving west and enjoying the prosperity and way of life that an expanding slave-labor system would create. They considered any attempt to limit the growth of slavery to be the first step toward eliminating it. And the possibility that slavery might be abolished, as remote as that may have seemed in the 1840s, was too awful for them to contemplate.

White southerners had convinced themselves that black people were a childlike and irresponsible race wholly incapable of surviving as a free people if they were emancipated and compelled to compete with white Americans. Most white people believed the black

Wilmot Proviso

A measure initially introduced in Congress in 1845 to prohibit slavery in any lands acquired from Mexico. It did not pass.

race would decline and disappear if slaves were freed. Virginia lawyer George Fitzhugh wrote in 1854, "The negro race is inferior to the white race, and living in their midst, they would be far outstripped or outwitted in the chase of free competition. Gradual, but certain, extermination would be their fate." Thus, southern white people considered slavery "a positive good"—in the words of Senator John C. Calhoun of South Carolina—that benefited both races and resulted in a society vastly superior to that of the North.

To prevent slavery's expansion, the Free-Soil Party was formed in 1848. It was composed mainly of white people who vigorously opposed slavery's expansion and the supposed harm that the presence of black men and women might bring to the new western lands. But some black and white abolitionists also supported the Free-Soilers as a way to oppose slavery. They reasoned that even though many Free-Soil supporters were hostile to black people, the party still represented a serious challenge to slavery and its expansion. Frederick Douglass felt comfortable enough with the Free-Soil Party to attend its convention in 1848. The Free-Soil candidate for president that year was former Democratic president Martin Van Buren. He came in a distant third behind Whig candidate and hero of the Mexican War, Zachary Taylor, who won, and Democrat Lewis Cass. Nevertheless, 10 Free-Soil congressmen were elected, and the party provided a growing forum to oppose slavery's advance.

Forty-Niners

The men and women who rushed to California in 1849 after gold had been discovered there.

Although white miners often resented the presence of black men during the gold rush, these two black men and two white men are operating a sluice together as they mine for gold in Spanish Flat in northern California in 1852.

10.1.3 African Americans and the Gold Rush

The discovery of gold in California in 1848 sent thousands of Americans hurrying west in 1849. The **Forty-Niners**, as these migrants were called, were almost exclusively male, and most were white Americans. But the desire to get rich had universal appeal, and the gold rush attracted Europeans, Asians (mostly Chinese), and African Americans. By 1850 nearly 900 black men (and fewer than 100 black women) were living in California, including people of African descent from Mexico, Peru, Chile, and Jamaica.

A black sailor known only as Hector deserted a naval vessel, the USS *Southampton*, in 1848 in Monterey, California, and headed for the gold fields. He returned with

$4,000, a large sum at the time. Another African American, Dick, brought $100,000 in gold, a veritable fortune, out of Tuolumne County, only to lose it all gambling in San Francisco.

Most of the Forty-Niners—whatever their race or nationality—were placer miners. Using the most basic technology—little more than a pan, a pick, and a shovel—they sought the chips and flakes of gold deposited in the icy streams that flowed down the western slopes of the Sierra Nevada Mountains. By swishing the water with their pan, they separated the tiny specks and pieces of gold from the sand and gravel. The more enterprising miners built a sluice to wash the rock and gravel more efficiently. Few of these placer miners struck it rich, but many of them made a modest living from the gold they recovered.

The richer veins of the precious metal were deeper underground and required more sophisticated technology and expensive equipment to mine it. Hydraulic mining used high-pressure hoses that sent powerful streams of water into the sides of hills and mountains, scarring the landscape as the sand and soil were ripped away and revealing the rock, stone, and sometimes gold embedded below. A black man known only as Smith worked his mining claim in Amador County with hydraulic equipment. He earned a respectable five to six dollars a day.

Quartz mining involved heavy and costly machinery that crushed huge quantities of rock and boulders. Only larger corporations—not individual miners—had the financial resources to buy and install the machinery and to hire the workers to operate it. Moses L. Rodgers was an ex-slave from Missouri who became knowledgeable and successful in quartz mining operations in the late 1860s. He was both an investor and superintendent of several California gold mines, including the Washington Mine, which was producing $500,000 in gold annually by the early 1870s. Most of the laborers under Rodgers's supervision were Chinese immigrants.

10.1.4 California and the Compromise of 1850

With the gold rush, California's population soared to more than 100,000, and its new residents quickly applied for admission to the Union as a free state. White southerners were horrified at the prospect of California prohibiting slavery, and they refused to consider its admission unless slavery was lawful there. Most northerners would not accept this.

Into this dispute stepped Whig Senator Henry Clay, who 30 years earlier had forged the Missouri Compromise. In 1850 the aging Clay put together an elaborate piece of legislation, the **Compromise of 1850**, designed not only to settle the controversy over California but also to resolve the issue of slavery's expansion once and for all. Clay attempted to satisfy both sides. To placate northerners, he proposed admitting California as a free state and eliminating the slave trade (but not slavery) in the District of Columbia. To satisfy white southerners, he offered a stronger fugitive slave law to make it easier for slave owners to apprehend runaway slaves and return them to slavery. New Mexico and Utah would be organized as territories with no mention of slavery (see Map 10-1).

Compromise of 1850

An attempt by the U.S. Congress to settle divisive issues between the North and South, including slavery expansion, apprehension in the North of fugitive slaves, and slavery in the District of Columbia.

Clay's measures were hammered into a single bill that produced one of the most remarkable debates in the history of the Senate, but it did not pass. Southern opponents like Senator John C. Calhoun of South Carolina could not tolerate the admission of California without slavery. Northern opponents like Senator William Seward of New York could not tolerate a tougher fugitive slave law. President Zachary Taylor shocked his fellow southerners and insisted that California should be admitted as a free state and that Clay's compromise was unnecessary. Taylor promised to veto the compromise if Congress passed it.

Clay's effort had failed—or so it seemed. But in the summer of 1850, Taylor died unexpectedly and was succeeded by Millard Fillmore, who was willing to accept the compromise. Senator Stephen Douglas, an ambitious Democrat from Illinois, guided Clay's compromise through Congress by breaking it into separate bills. California entered the Union as a free state, and a stronger fugitive slave law entered the federal legal code.

10.1.5 Fugitive Slave Laws

Those who may have hoped the compromise would forever resolve the dispute over slavery were mistaken. The **Fugitive Slave Law of 1850** created bitter resentment among black and white abolitionists and made slavery a more emotional and personal issue for many white people who had previously considered slavery a remote southern institution.

Fugitive Slave Law of 1850

Part of the Compromise of 1850. It required law enforcement officials as well as civilians to assist in capturing runaway slaves.

Had runaway slaves not been an increasingly frustrating problem for slave owners—particularly those in the Upper South states of Maryland, Virginia, and Kentucky—the federal fugitive slave law would not have needed to be strengthened in 1850. The U.S. Constitution and the fugitive slave law passed in 1793 would seem to have provided ample authority for slave owners to recover runaway slaves.

The Constitution in Article IV, Section 2, stipulates that "any person held to service or labor in one State" who ran away to another state "shall be delivered up on claim

Map 10-1 The Compromise of 1850

As a result of the war against Mexico, the United States acquired the regions shown on this map in California, Utah Territory, New Mexico Territory, and the portions of Texas not included in the Province of Texas.

With the Compromise of 1850 California entered the Union as a free state. In which remaining western lands would slavery be accepted or rejected?

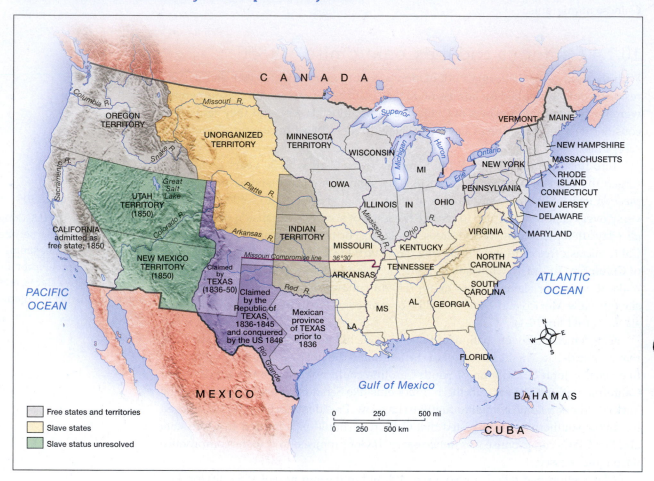

Free states and territories
Slave states
Slave status unresolved

---

of the party to whom such service or labor may be due." The Fugitive Slave Law of 1793 permitted slave owners to recover slaves who had escaped to other states. The escaped slave had no rights—no right to a trial, no right to testify, and no guarantee of *habeas corpus* (the legal requirement that a person be brought before a court and not imprisoned illegally).

But by the 1830s and 1840s, hundreds if not thousands of slaves had escaped to freedom by way of the underground railroad, and white southerners increasingly found the 1793 law too weak to overcome the resistance of northern communities to the return of escapees. For example, in January 1847 four Kentuckians and a local law officer attempted to capture Adam Crosswhite, his wife, and their four children after the family had escaped from slavery in Kentucky and settled on a farm near Marshall, Michigan. When the would-be abductors arrived, an old black man mounted a horse and galloped through town ringing a bell warning that the Crosswhites were in danger. Having been aroused by this "black Paul Revere," about one hundred people helped rescue the family and put them on a railroad train to Canada. The local citizens who had aided the Crosswhites were later successfully sued by the slave owner and fined an amount equal to the estimated value of the Crosswhites had the family been sold as slaves.

Northern states had enacted personal liberty laws that made it illegal for state law enforcement officials to help capture runaways. (Michigan passed such a law in 1855

habeas corpus
A court order that a person arrested or detained by law enforcement officers must be brought to court and charged with a crime and not held indefinitely.

Voices

African Americans Respond to the Fugitive Slave Law

These two passages reflect the outrage the Fugitive Slave Law of 1850 provoked among black Americans. In the first, John Jacobs, a fugitive slave from South Carolina, urges black people to take up arms to oppose the law. In the second, from a speech he delivered a few days after the passage of the law, Martin Delany defies authorities to search his home for runaway slaves.

> My colored brethren, if you have not swords, I say to you, sell your garments and buy one. . . . They said that they cannot take us back to the South; but I say, under the present law they can; and now they say unto you; let them take only dead bodies. . . . I would, my friends, advise you to show a front to our tyrants and arm yourselves . . . and I would advise the women to have their knives too.

SOURCE: William F. Cheek, *Black Resistance Before the Civil War* (Beverly Hills, CA: Glencoe Press, 1970), 148–49.

> Sir, my house is my castle; in that castle are none but my wife and my children, as free as the angels of heaven, and whose liberty is as sacred as the pillars of God. If any man approaches that house in search of a slave—I care not who he may be, whether the constable, or sheriff, magistrate or even judge of the Supreme Court—nay, let it be he who sanctioned this act to become law [President Millard Fillmore] surrounded by his cabinet as his bodyguard, with the Declaration of Independence waving above his head as his banner, and the constitution of this country upon his breast as his shield—if he crosses the threshold of my door, and I do not lay him a lifeless corpse at my feet, I hope the grave may refuse my body a resting place, and righteous Heaven my spirit a home. O, no! He cannot enter that house and we both live.

1. How and why did these two black men justify the use of violence against those who were enforcing a law passed by Congress?

2. Under what circumstances is it permissible to violate the law or threaten to kill another human being?

SOURCE: Victor Ullman, *Martin R. Delany: The Beginnings of Black Nationalism* (Boston: Beacon, 1971), 112.

---

after the Crosswhites escaped to Canada.) Not only did many northerners refuse to cooperate in returning fugitives to slavery under the 1793 law, but they also encouraged and assisted the fleeing slaves. The local black vigilance committees that were created in many northern communities and discussed in Chapter 9—among them the League of Freedom in Boston and the Liberty Association in Chicago—were especially effective in these efforts. These actions infuriated white southerners and prompted their demand for a stricter fugitive slave law.

The Fugitive Slave Law of 1850 was one of the toughest and harshest measures the U.S. Congress ever passed. Anyone apprehended under the law was almost certain to be sent back to slavery. The law required U.S. marshals, their deputies, and even ordinary citizens to help seize suspected runaways. Those who refused to help apprehend fugitives or who helped the runaways could be fined or imprisoned. The law made it nearly impossible for black people to prove they were free. Slave owners and their agents only had to provide legal documentation from their home state or the testimony of white witnesses before a federal commissioner that the captive was a runaway slave. The federal commissioners were paid $10 for captives returned to bondage but only $5 for those declared free. Supporters of the law claimed the additional paperwork involved in returning a fugitive to slavery necessitated the higher fee. Opponents saw it as a bribe to encourage federal authorities to return men and women to bondage. While the law was in effect, 332 captives were returned to the South and slavery, and only 11 were released as free people.

The new fugitive slave law outraged many black and white northerners. An angry Frederick Douglass insisted in October 1850 that "the only way to make the Fugitive Slave Law a dead letter is to make a half dozen or more dead kidnappers." White abolitionist Wendell Phillips exhorted his listeners to disobey the law, declaring that "we must trample this law under our feet."

10.2 Fugitive Slaves

Describe the reaction of African Americans to the passage and enforcement of the Fugitive Slave Law of 1850.

The fugitive slave law did more than anger black and white northerners. It exposed them to cruel and heart-wrenching scenes as southern slave owners and slave catchers took advantage of the new law and—with the vigorous assistance of federal authorities—relentlessly pursued runaway slaves. Many white people and most black people were disappointed and disgusted over this crackdown on those who had fled from slavery to freedom.

In September 1850 and only eight days after the law went into effect, U.S. marshals in Brooklyn, New York, captured James Hamlet, a black porter, and immediately returned him to slavery in Baltimore, even though he insisted that because his mother was a free woman he had not been a slave. (In each of the slave states, the law stipulated the status of the mother determined a child's legal status—free or slave.) Soon thereafter 2,000 black people and a handful of white people assembled in New York City's African Methodist Episcopal Zion church, and they contributed $800 to purchase Hamlet's freedom. Days later he was back in Brooklyn, reunited with his wife and children.

In Poughkeepsie, New York, slave catchers captured a well-to-do black tailor and returned him to slavery in South Carolina. In Indiana, a black man was apprehended while his wife and children looked on, and he was sent to Kentucky, where his owner claimed he had escaped 19 years earlier.

Not all fugitives were forced back into bondage, however. A Maryland slave owner attempted to recover a black woman in Philadelphia who, he asserted, had escaped 22 years earlier. Since then, she had given birth to six children, and the slave owner insisted they were also his property. In this instance, the federal commissioner ruled that the woman and her children were free.

Even California was not immune to the furor over fugitive slaves. Although the new state prohibited slavery, several hundred black people were illegally held there as slaves in the 1850s. Nevertheless, some slaves ran away to the far West rather than to the North. Black abolitionist Mary Ellen Pleasant hid fugitive Archy Lee in San Francisco

Leaflets like this reflected the outrage many northerners felt in response to the capture and reenslavement of African Americans that resulted from the passage of a tougher fugitive slave law as part of the Compromise of 1850.

Effects of the Fugitive-Slave-Law.

in 1858. Other black Californians provided security for runaways from as far east as Maryland.

10.2.1 William and Ellen Craft

Black and white abolitionists had organized vigilance committees to resist the fugitive slave law and to prevent—by force if necessary—the return of fugitives to slavery. In October 1850 slave catchers arrived in Boston prepared to capture and return William and Ellen Craft to slavery in Georgia. In 1848 the Crafts had devised an ingenious escape. Ellen's fair complexion enabled her to disguise herself as a sickly young white man who, accompanied by "his" slave, was traveling north for medical treatment. They journeyed to Boston by railroad and ship and thus escaped from slavery—or so they thought.

Slave catchers vowed to return the Crafts to servitude no matter how long it took: "If [we] have to stay here to all eternity, and if there are not enough men in Massachusetts to take them, [we] will bring some from the South." While white abolitionists protected Ellen and black abolitionists hid William, the vigilance committee plastered posters around Boston describing the slave catchers, calling them "man-stealers," and threatening their safety. Within days (which must have seemed slightly less than eternity), the slave catchers left without the Crafts. Soon thereafter, the Crafts sailed to security in England.

Profile

Mary Ellen Pleasant

Mary Ellen Pleasant was an influential woman of many accomplishments. But her life is shrouded in mystery and uncertainty. She may have been born in Georgia or Louisiana. She claimed she was born in Philadelphia in 1814 to a free woman of color. Her father may have been Asian, Native American, or even a white planter.

She did live for a time on Nantucket Island off the Massachusetts coast and then in Boston. She was an educated woman. In New England she became acquainted with black and white abolitionists. She married John W. Smith, who was said to have been a Cuban planter. They had a daughter, Elizabeth. Her husband died in 1844. During the gold rush in 1849, she moved to California where she married John Pleasant and became prominent in San Francisco's African-American community. San Francisco had about 500 black residents in the mid-1850s.

The entrepreneurial spirit struck Pleasant who was soon operating three laundries and a boarding house. She also invested in mining stock. She remained committed to abolition and assisted fugitive slaves who fled to the far West. She may have attended the 1855 Colored Convention in San Francisco, and she almost certainly met Mifflin Gibbs, who ran the first black newspaper on the Pacific coast, *The Mirror of the Times*. (See Chapter 13 for a profile on the Gibbs brothers.)

By the late 1850s, Pleasant was in Chatham, Canada West (Ontario), where she collaborated with Martin Delany, Mary Ann Shadd Cary, and other black abolitionists. They had formed the

Chatham Vigilance Committee that aided fugitive slaves escaping from the United States. She met John Brown in Chatham and reportedly donated $30,000 to his efforts to organize a slave rebellion.

Pleasant returned to California by the mid-1860s and presided over her daughter's elegant wedding at San Francisco's AME Zion Church. Ever the entrepreneur, Pleasant operated a fashionable restaurant and a well-appointed boarding house that some people insisted was a brothel patronized by prominent white men.

Through her contacts with powerful politicians and businessmen, she accumulated information—some might call it gossip—about influential white families and the men who governed them. She used her connections to help black Californians find employment. She also worked as a housekeeper for two well-to-do white families, the Woodworths and then the Bells. Believed by some to be a voodoo queen, she was said to have developed peculiar powers over people, especially men.

Pleasant fought racial discrimination and supported legislation to permit black people to testify in California courts. She was loved and respected as well as hated and resented. She twice sued a San Francisco streetcar company that did not allow her to ride in its vehicles. She won $500 in her second suit, but the verdict was overturned on appeal.

She became renowned as "Mammy Pleasant," but she detested the nickname and did not hesitate to tell people so. At age 87 she curtly informed a journalist, "Listen: I don't like to be called Mammy by everybody. Put that down. I'm not Mammy to everybody in California. I got a letter from a minister in Sacramento. It was addressed to Mammy Pleasant. I wrote back to him on his own paper that my name was Mrs. Mary E. Pleasant. . . . If he didn't have better sense he should have had better manners."

Mrs. Mary E. Pleasant died in 1904. Her estate included diamond jewelry, 114 acres in Sonoma County, and a lot on Octavia Street in San Francisco. Even in death she remained a puzzling and curious figure to many people. There was no mystery, however, to her request that her gravestone simply be inscribed: "She was a friend of John Brown."

10.2.2 Shadrach Minkins

Some black and white abolitionists urged caution and patience. They counseled others to respect the new law even if they were absolutely opposed to it. But many abolitionists and vigilance committee members were fully prepared to take up arms and use force against the U.S. government and slave owners and their agents. Sometimes the abolitionists succeeded, sometimes they did not. In early 1851, a few months after the Crafts left Boston, federal marshals apprehended there a black waiter who had escaped from slavery and given himself the name Shadrach Minkins. However, a well-organized band of black and white men led by Lewis Hayden invaded the courthouse and rescued Minkins.

Federal authorities brought charges against Hayden, as well as three other black men and four white men who were indicted by a grand jury for helping Minkins escape, but local juries refused to convict them. Hayden himself had fled from slavery in Kentucky six years earlier and became an influential leader of the vigilance committee in Boston. Minkins, in the meantime, made it to Canada and settled in Montreal where he operated a restaurant.

10.2.3 The Battle at Christiana

In September 1851 a battle erupted in the little town of Christiana, in southern Pennsylvania, when a Maryland slave owner, Edward Gorsuch, arrived to recover two runaway slaves. Accompanied by family members and three deputy U.S. marshals, he confronted a well-armed crowd of at least 25 black men and several white men. Black leader William Parker told Gorsuch to give up any plans to take the runaway slaves. Gorsuch refused, and a battle ensued. Gorsuch was killed, and several black and white men were hurt. The runaway slaves escaped to Canada.

President Fillmore sent U.S. Marines to Pennsylvania, and they helped round up the alleged perpetrators of the violence. Thirty-six black men and five white men were arrested and indicted for treason by a federal grand jury. But after the first trial ended in acquittal, the remaining cases were dropped.

10.2.4 Anthony Burns

Of all the fugitive slave cases, none elicited more support or sorrow than that of Anthony Burns. In 1854 Burns escaped from slavery in Virginia by stowing away on a ship to Boston. After gaining work in a clothing store, he unwisely sent a letter to his brother, who was still a slave. The letter was confiscated, and Burns's former owner set out to capture him. Burns was arrested by a deputy marshal who, recalling Shadrach Minkins's escape, placed him under guard in chains in the federal courthouse. Efforts by black and white abolitionists to break into the courthouse with axes, guns, and a battering ram failed, although a deputy U.S. marshal was killed during the assault.

President Franklin Pierce, a northern Democrat who in 1852 had been elected with southern support, sent U.S. troops to Boston—including marines, cavalry, and artillery—to uphold the law and return Burns to Virginia. Black minister Leonard A. Grimes and the vigilance committee tried to purchase Burns's freedom, but the U.S. attorney refused. In June 1854, with church bells tolling and buildings draped in black, thousands of Bostonians watched silently—many in tears—as Anthony Burns was marched through the streets to a ship that would take him to Virginia.

The spectacle of a lone black man, escorted by hundreds of armed troops, as he trudged from freedom to slavery moved even those people who had shown no special interest in or sympathy for fugitives or slaves. One staunchly conservative white man remarked, "When it was all over, and I was left alone in my office, I put my face in my hands and I wept. I could do nothing less." William Lloyd Garrison burned a copy of the Constitution on the Fourth of July as thousands looked on with approval.

Yet the government was unrelenting. A federal grand jury indicted seven black men and white men for riot and inciting a riot in their attempt to free Burns. One indictment was set aside on a technicality, and the other charges were then dropped because no Boston jury would convict the accused. Several months later, black Bostonians led by the Rev. Grimes purchased Burns for $1,300. He settled in St. Catherines, Ontario, in Canada, where he died in 1862.

The "trial" and subsequent return of Anthony Burns to slavery in 1854 resulted in the publication of a popular pamphlet in Boston. Documents like this generated increased support—and funds—for the abolitionist cause.

10.2.5 Margaret Garner

If the Burns case was the most moving, then Margaret Garner's was one of the most tragic examples of the lengths to which slaves might go to gain freedom for themselves and their children. In the winter of 1856, Margaret Garner and seven other slaves escaped from Kentucky across the Ohio River to freedom in Cincinnati. But their owner, Archibald Grimes, pursued them. Grimes, accompanied by a U.S. deputy marshal and several other people, attempted to arrest the fugitives at a small house where they had hidden. Refusing to surrender, the slaves were overpowered and subdued.

Before the fugitives were captured, Garner slit the throat of her daughter with a butcher knife rather than see the child returned to slavery. She was disarmed before she could kill her two sons. Ohio authorities charged her with murder, but by that time she had been returned to Kentucky and then sent to Arkansas with her surviving children to be sold. On the trip down the river, her youngest child and 24 other people drowned

Profile

Thomas Sims, a Fugitive Slave

U.S. military forces were sometimes employed to enforce a law that an increasing number of northerners had come to regard as unjust.

By stowing away on a ship in Savannah, Georgia, in 1851, Thomas Sims, a 23-year-old slave who was a bricklayer, escaped to Boston, where he worked briefly as a waiter. Sims unwisely sent a telegram to his wife who was free and still in Georgia, asking her to send money. The telegram was intercepted, and his owner, James Potter, quickly had agents locate and apprehend the young man. Sims was confined in chains on the third floor of the federal courthouse in Boston. Black leader Lewis Hayden tried to free Sims, but failed. Hayden had difficulty attracting support because many of the men whom he would ordinarily have depended on had fled when authorities began to search for those who had freed fugitive slave Shadrach Minkins a few weeks earlier.

One plan involved piling mattresses under Sims's window and having him jump about 30 feet to freedom. It was abandoned when bars were installed in the window. Neither Sims's lawyers' attempts to win a writ of *habeas corpus* nor public protests succeeded in gaining his freedom.

On April 11, 1851, a federal commissioner ordered Sims returned to his owner and slavery. At 5:00 A.M. on April 12 he was marched in the predawn darkness from the courthouse, "protected" by 200 Boston police and other armed law enforcement personnel, and taken to a ship in the harbor. A desperate plan to free him by 20 armed men aboard another vessel failed because Sims's ship sailed for Savannah before the other ship could get underway.

Opponents of the fugitive slave law and defenders of Sims were stunned and enraged that they, the people of Boston, had been unable to help a man whose sole desire was for freedom. Boston was their cherished home of liberty. It was where a black man, Crispus Attucks, was among those slain in the Boston Massacre in 1770. It was also where the Tea Party took place in 1773, and where Paul Revere set out on his midnight ride in 1775.

Henry David Thoreau, the transcendental writer and author of *Walden*, who preferred calm reflection to angry denunciation, reacted in fury to the forcible return of Thomas Sims. He wrote, "A government which deliberately enacts injustice—& persists in it!—it will become the laughing stock of the world." Later that summer, Sims was sent to Charleston, and then to New Orleans, where he was auctioned off to a brick mason from Vicksburg, Mississippi. Sims spent the next 12 years enslaved as a mason in Mississippi. In 1863, during the Civil War, when Union forces under Gen. Ulysses S. Grant laid siege to Vicksburg, Sims again fled to freedom. This time his wife, child, and four black men joined him in the escape. Sims and his family returned to Boston, where they witnessed the return in 1865 of the all-black 54th Massachusetts Regiment from combat in South Carolina, Georgia, and Florida.

By 1877 Sims was in Washington, D.C. He obtained a job as a messenger in the Department of Justice through the intervention of U.S. Attorney General Charles Devens—the federal marshal who had arrested him in Boston in 1851.

in a shipwreck, thereby cruelly fulfilling her wish that the child not grow up to be a slave. Margaret Garner was later sold at a slave market in New Orleans. (Her story was the basis of Toni Morrison's novel *Beloved*, which won the 1988 Pulitzer Prize for fiction and was made into a film by Oprah Winfrey in 1998.)

10.2.6 Freedom in Canada

For many of those people fleeing from slavery, the underground railroad ended in Canada. Slavery had been abolished in Canada in the late eighteenth century. By escaping to Canada West—now the Province of Ontario—former slaves were far less likely to be captured by slave catchers and returned to slavery. Following the passage of the Fugitive Slave Law, the black population of Chatham, Ontario, for example, increased from 353 in 1851 to 1,259 in 1861.

Although many white Canadians detested the arrival of black people who sought freedom, black residents of Canada did possess some legal rights. They could own property, sue in a court of law, serve on juries, and vote. Black men served in the provincial militia. The public schools were, however, usually segregated.

The freed people took up farming, cultivating corn, wheat, oats, and hemp, and raising livestock in rural communities such as Buxton and Dawn. Others took up residence in black neighborhoods in towns including Chatham and St. Catherines where those who possessed skills worked as carpenters, shoemakers, seamstresses, and barbers while many were unskilled laborers. They joined black churches that were mostly Baptist and Methodist congregations. Two black newspapers circulated in the 1850s. Mary Ann Shadd Cary edited the *Provincial Freeman* and Henry Bibb ran the *Voice of the Fugitive* until fire destroyed the enterprise.

Many black men returned to the United States during the Civil War and joined the all-black Union Army regiments that were formed in 1863 and 1864. Triumph in the war and the end of slavery in the United States prompted many of those who had fled from bondage to return to the nation of their birth. Approximately 60 to 70 percent of black residents of Ontario left after the Civil War to take advantage of economic opportunities and equal rights that they thought awaited them in the United States.

10.2.7 The Rochester Convention, 1853

In 1853, while northern communities grappled with the consequences of the fugitive slave law, African-American leaders gathered for a national convention in Rochester, New York. The **Rochester Convention** warned that black Americans were not prepared to submit quietly to a government more concerned about the interests of slave owners than people seeking to free themselves from bondage. The delegates looked past the grim conditions of the times to call for greater unity among black people and to find ways to improve their economic prospects. They asserted their claims to the rights of citizenship and equal protection before the law, and they worried that the wave of European immigrants entering the country would deprive poor black northerners of the menial and unskilled jobs on which they depended. Frederick Douglass spoke of the need for a school to provide training in the skilled trades and manual arts. There was even talk of establishing a Negro museum and library.

Rochester Convention

African-American leaders assembled in Rochester, New York, in 1853 to discuss slavery, abolition, the recently passed fugitive slave law, and their prospects for life in America.

10.2.8 Nativism and the Know-Nothings

Not only did many white Americans look with disfavor and often outright disgust at African Americans, but they were also distressed by and opposed to the increasing numbers of white immigrants coming to the United States. Hundreds of thousands of Europeans—mostly Germans and Irish—arrived in the 1840s and 1850s. In one year—1854—430,000 people arrived on American shores.

Beginning in 1830 and continuing until the end of the nineteenth century, black leaders held a series of national conventions like the one pictured above, which took place in New Orleans on May 4, 1872. Those that were held prior to the Civil War focused on the abolition of slavery and met in northern cities such as Philadelphia, Cleveland, and Rochester. Following the war, the gatherings occurred in Washington, D.C., and Nashville, among other places, with the emphasis on the rights and opportunities of African Americans.

"Know-Nothing Party"

This nickname applied to members of the American Party, which opposed immigration in the 1850s.

The mass starvation that accompanied the potato famine of the 1840s in Ireland drove thousands of Irish people to the United States, where they often encountered intense hostility. Native-born, Protestant, white Americans considered the Catholic Irish crude, ignorant drunks. Irish immigrants also competed with Americans for low-paying unskilled jobs. Anti-Catholic propaganda warned that the influence of the Vatican would weaken American institutions. Some even charged there was a Roman Catholic conspiracy to take over the United States. Mobs attacked Catholic churches and convents.

These anti-immigrant, anti-Catholic, antialcohol sentiments helped foster in 1854 the rise of a nativist third political party, the American Party—better known as the **"Know-Nothing Party."** (Its members were supposed to reply "I know nothing" if someone asked if they belonged to the party.) The Know-Nothings attracted considerable support. Feeding on resentment and prejudice, the party grew to one million strong. Most Know-Nothings were in New England, and they even for a short time took political control of Massachusetts, where many of the Irish had settled. The party was also strong in Kentucky, Texas, and elsewhere.

Although Know-Nothings opposed immigrants and Catholics, they disagreed among themselves over slavery and its expansion. As a result, the party soon split into northern and southern factions and collapsed.

10.2.9 *Uncle Tom's Cabin*

No one contributed more to the growing opposition to slavery among white northerners than Harriet Beecher Stowe. Raised in a religious environment—her father, brothers, and husband were ministers—Stowe developed a hatred of slavery that she converted into a melodramatic but moving novel about slaves and their lives.

Uncle Tom's Cabin

This antislavery novel by Harriet Beecher Stowe was a best-seller in the 1850s and it helped inflame the controversy over slavery.

Uncle Tom's Cabin, or Life among the Lowly, was first published in installments in the antislavery newspaper *The National Era*. When it appeared as a book in 1852, it sold an astonishing 300,000 copies in a year. In the novel, Stowe depicted slavery's cruelty, inhumanity, and destructive impact on families through characters and a plot that appealed to the sentimentality of nineteenth-century readers. There was Little Eliza, with a babe in her arms, barely escaping across the icy Ohio River from a slave owner in hot pursuit. There was Uncle Tom, the noble and devout Christian. Financial necessity forces Tom's decent master to sell the kindly slave to Simon Legree, a vicious brute and a northerner who had embraced slavery. Legree takes perverse delight in beating Tom until the gentle old man dies.

Uncle Tom's Cabin moved northerners to tears and made slavery more emotional to readers who had previously considered it only a distant system of labor that exploited black people. In stage versions of the book that were later produced across the North, Uncle Tom was transformed from a dignified man into a pitiful and fawning figure eager to please white people—hence the emergence of the derogatory term "Uncle Tom."

Uncle Tom's Cabin infuriated white southerners. They condemned it as a grossly false depiction of slavery and their way of life. They pointed out correctly that Stowe had little firsthand knowledge of slavery and had never even visited the Deep South. But she had lived in Cincinnati for 18 years and witnessed with anguish the desperate attempts of slaves to escape across the Ohio River. In response to her southern critics, Stowe wrote *A Key to Uncle Tom's Cabin*, citing the sources for her novel. Many of those sources were southern newspapers.

Harriet Beecher Stowe was a prolific writer. She wrote travel accounts, children's books, and 10 adult novels. Easily, her best-known work was *Uncle Tom's Cabin*. It was first published in serial form in the antislavery weekly newspaper *The National Era* when Stowe was 40 years old.

10.2.10 The Kansas-Nebraska Act

After the Compromise of 1850, the disagreement over slavery's expansion intensified and became violent. In 1854 Senator Stephen Douglas introduced a bill in Congress to organize the Kansas and Nebraska Territories that soon provoked white settlers in Kansas to kill each other over slavery. Douglas's primary concern was to secure the Kansas and Nebraska region for the construction of a transcontinental railroad. Until 1853 it had been part of the Indian Territory that the federal government had promised would not be open to white settlement. To win the support of southern Democrats, who wanted slavery in at least one of the two new territories, Douglas's bill would permit Kansas residents to decide for themselves whether to allow slavery (see Map 10-2).

This proposal—known as "**popular sovereignty**"—angered many northerners because it created the possibility that slavery might expand to areas where it had been prohibited. The Missouri Compromise of 1820 banned slavery north of the 36° 30' line of latitude. Douglas's **Kansas-Nebraska Act** would repeal that limitation and allow settlers in Kansas, which was north of that line, to vote on slavery there. Thus, if enough proslavery people moved to Kansas and voted for slavery, slaves and their owners would be legally permitted to dwell on land that had been closed to them for more than 30 years.

Douglas managed to muster enough votes in Congress to pass the bill, but its enactment destroyed an already divided Whig Party and drove a wedge between the North and the South. The Whig Party disintegrated. Northern Whigs joined supporters of the Free-Soil Party to form the Republican Party, which was organized expressly to oppose the expansion of slavery. Southern Whigs drifted, often without enthusiasm, to the Democrats or Know-Nothings.

Violence soon erupted in Kansas between proslavery and antislavery forces. "**Border ruffians**" from Missouri invaded Kansas to attack antislavery settlers and to vote illegally in Kansas elections. The New England Emigrant Aid Society dispatched people to the territory, and the Rev. Henry Ward Beecher encouraged them to pack "Beecher's Bibles," which were firearms and not the Word of the Lord. By 1856 Kansas had 8,500 settlers, including 245 slaves, and two rival territorial governments. Civil war had erupted—prompting the press to label the territory "Bleeding Kansas."

More than 200 people died in the escalating violence. Some 500 border ruffians attacked the antislavery town of Lawrence, damaging businesses and killing one person. Abolitionist John Brown and four of his sons sought revenge by hacking five proslavery men (none of whom actually owned slaves) to death in Pottawattamie. A proslavery firing squad executed nine Free-Soilers. John Brown reappeared in Missouri, killed a slave owner, and freed 11 slaves. Then he fled to plan an even larger and more dramatic attack on slavery.

popular sovereignty

A proposal in which the residents of a territory (such as Kansas) would vote to legalize or prohibit slavery in that territory.

Kansas-Nebraska Act

Legislation introduced by Democratic Senator Stephen Douglas in 1854 to organize the Kansas and Nebraska territories. It provided for "popular sovereignty," whereby settlers would decide whether slavery would be legal or illegal.

border ruffians

Proslavery advocates and vigilantes from Missouri who crossed the border into Kansas in 1855–1857 to support slavery in Kansas by threatening and attacking antislavery settlers.

Map 10-2 The Kansas-Nebraska Act

This measure, guided through Congress by Democratic Senator Steven A. Douglas, opened up the Great Plains to settlement and to railroad development. It also deeply divided the nation by repealing the 1820 Missouri Compromise line of 36° 30' and permitting—through popular sovereignty—the people of Kansas to determine slavery's fate in that territory. Eastern Kansas became a bloody battleground between proslavery and antislavery forces.

Where exactly could slavery conceivably exist where it had previously been prohibited?

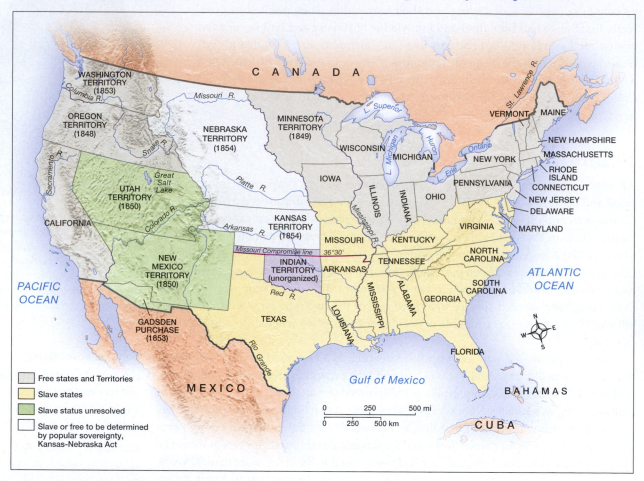

Free states and Territories
Slave states
Slave status unresolved
Slave or free to be determined by popular sovereignty, Kansas-Nebraska Act

"Border ruffians" were armed men from Missouri who crossed the border to support proslavery forces in the Kansas territory. These men sought the legalization of slavery in Kansas. They—as well as the opponents of slavery—were willing to resort to violence to achieve their aims.

10.2.11 Preston Brooks Attacks Charles Sumner

The violence in Kansas spread to Congress. In May 1856, Massachusetts Senator Charles Sumner delivered a tirade in the Senate denouncing the proslavery settlers in Kansas and the southerners who supported them. Speaking of "The Crime against Kansas," Sumner accused South Carolina Senator Andrew P. Butler of keeping slavery as his lover. Butler "has chosen a mistress to whom he has made his vows, and who . . . though polluted in the sight of the world, is chaste in his sight—I mean the harlot slavery." Butler was not present for the speech, but his distant cousin, South Carolina Congressman Preston Brooks, was in the chamber, and Brooks did not appreciate Sumner's verbal assault on a member of his family.

Two days later, Brooks exacted his revenge. Waiting until the Senate adjourned, Brooks strode to the desk where Sumner was seated and attacked him with a rattan cane. The blows rained down until the cane shattered and Sumner tumbled to the floor, bloody and semiconscious. Brooks proudly recalled, "I gave him about thirty first-rate stripes." Sumner suffered lingering physical and emotional effects from the beating and did not return to the Senate for almost four years. Brooks resigned from the House of Representatives, paid a $300 fine, and went home to South Carolina a hero. He was easily reelected to his seat.

In the 1856 presidential election, the Democrats—although divided over the debacle in Kansas—nominated James Buchanan of Pennsylvania, another northern Democrat who was acceptable to the South. The Republicans supported a handsome army officer, John C. Fremont. Their slogan was "Free Soil, Free Speech, Free Men, and Fremont." But the Republicans were exclusively a northern party, and, with the demise of the Whigs, the South had become largely a one-party region. Almost no white southerners would support the Republicans, a party whose very existence was based on its opposition to slavery's expansion. Buchanan won the presidency with nearly solid southern support and enough northern votes to carry him to victory, but the Republicans gained enough support and confidence to give them hope for the 1860 election. Before then, however, the U.S. Supreme Court intervened in the controversy over slavery.

10.3 The *Dred Scott* Decision

Compare the responses of slave owners and opponents of slavery to the U.S. Supreme Court decision in the *Dred Scott* case.

Like most slaves, Dred Scott did not know his exact age. But when the Supreme Court accepted his case in 1856, Scott was in his 50s and had been entangled in the judicial system for more than a decade. Scott was born in Virginia, but by the 1830s he belonged to John Emerson, an army doctor in Missouri. Emerson took Scott to military posts in Illinois and to Fort Snelling in what is now Minnesota. While at Fort Snelling, Scott married Harriet, a slave woman, and they had a daughter, Eliza, before Emerson returned with the three of them to St. Louis. In 1846, after Emerson's death and with the support of white friends, Scott and his wife filed separate suits for their freedom. By agreement, her suit was set aside pending the outcome of her husband's litigation. Scott and his lawyers contended that because Scott had been taken to territory where slavery was illegal, he had become a free man.

Scott lost his first suit, won his second, but lost again on appeal to the Missouri Supreme Court. His lawyers then appealed to the federal courts where they lost again. The final appeal in **Dred Scott v. Sandford** was to the U.S. Supreme Court. Although 79-year-old Chief Justice Roger Taney of Maryland had freed his own slaves, he was an unabashed advocate of the southern way of life. Moreover, Taney, a majority of the other justices, and President Buchanan were convinced that the prestige of the Court would enable it to render a decision about slavery that might be controversial but would still be accepted as the law of the land.

Dred Scott v. Sandford
The 1857 U.S. Supreme Court case that ruled against Missouri slave Dred Scott by declaring that black people were not citizens, possessed no constitutional rights, and were considered to be property.

10.3.1 Questions for the Court

Taney framed two questions for the Court to decide in the Scott case: Could Scott, a black man, sue in a federal court? And was Scott free because he had been taken to a state and a territory where slavery was prohibited? In response to the first question, the Court, led by Taney, ruled that Scott—and every other black American—could not sue in a federal court because black people were not citizens. Speaking for the majority (two of the nine justices dissented), Taney emphatically stated that black people had no rights: "They had for more than a century before been regarded as beings of an inferior order; and altogether unfit to associate with the white race, either in social or political relations; and so far inferior that they had no rights which the white man was bound to respect; and that the negro might justly and lawfully be reduced to slavery for his benefit."

Taney was wrong. Although not treated as equals, free black people in many states had enjoyed rights associated with citizenship since the ratification of the Constitution

The *Dred Scott* decision was front-page news on *Frank Leslie's Illustrated Newspaper* in 1857. Harriet and Dred with their two daughters are depicted sympathetically as members of the middle class rather than as abused and mistreated slaves.

in 1788. Black men had entered into contracts, held title to property, sued in the courts, and voted at one time in five of the original 13 states.

A majority of the Court also answered no to the second question. Scott was not a free man, although he had lived in places where slavery was illegal. Scott, Taney maintained, again speaking for the Court, was slave property—and the slave owner's property rights took precedence. To the astonishment of those who opposed slavery's expansion, the Court also ruled that Congress could not pass measures—including the Missouri Compromise or the Kansas-Nebraska Act—that might prevent slave owners from taking their property into any territory. To do so, Taney implied, would violate the Fifth Amendment of the Constitution, which protected people from the loss of their life, liberty, or property without due process of law.

Following the decision, a new owner freed Dred and Harriet Scott. They settled in St. Louis, where he worked as a porter at Barnum's Hotel until he died of tuberculosis in 1858.

10.3.2 Reaction to the *Dred Scott* Decision

The Court had spoken. Would the nation listen? White southerners were delighted with Taney's decision. Republicans were horrified. But instead of earning the acceptance—let alone the approval—of most Americans, the case further inflamed the controversy over slavery. But if white Americans were divided in their reaction to the *Dred Scott* decision, black Americans were discouraged, disgusted, and defiant. Taney's decision delivered another setback to a people—already held in forced labor—who believed that their toil, sweat, and contributions over the previous 250 years to what had become the United States gave them a legitimate role in American society. Now the Supreme Court said they had no rights. They knew better.

At rallies across the North, black people condemned the decision. Black writer, abolitionist, and women's rights advocate Frances Ellen Watkins Harper heaped scorn on the U.S. government as "the arch traitor to liberty, as shown by the Fugitive Slave Law and the Dred Scott decision."

Black leader H. Ford Douglas vented his rage at an American government and a constitution that could produce such a decision:

> To persist in supporting a government which holds and exercises the power . . . to trample a class under foot as an inferior and degraded race is on the part of the colored man at once the height of folly and the depth of pusillanimity. . . . The only duty the colored man owes to a constitution under which he is declared to be an inferior and degraded being . . . is to denounce and repudiate it, and to do what he can by all proper means to bring it into contempt.

Only Frederick Douglass found a glimmer of hope. He believed—and events proved him right—that the decision was so wrong that it would help destroy slavery:

> The Supreme Court . . . [was] not the only power in the world. We, the abolitionists and the colored people, should meet this decision, unlooked for and monstrous as it appears, in a cheerful spirit. The very attempts to blot out forever the hopes of an enslaved people may be one necessary link in the chain of events preparatory to the complete overthrow of the whole slave system.

10.3.3 White Northerners and Black Americans

Many white northerners were genuinely concerned by the struggles of fugitive slaves, moved by *Uncle Tom's Cabin*, and disturbed by the *Dred Scott* decision. Yet as sensitive and sympathetic as some of them were to the plight of black people, most white Americans—including northerners—remained indifferent to, fearful of, or hostile to people of color. By the 1850s, 200,000 black people lived in the northern states, and many white people there were not pleased with their presence. Many white northerners, especially those living in southern Ohio, Indiana, and Illinois, supported the fugitive slave law and were eager to help return runaway slaves to bondage.

The same white northerners who opposed the expansion of slavery to California or Kansas also opposed the migration of free black people to northern states and communities. In 1851 Indiana and Iowa outlawed the emigration of black people, slave or free, to their territory. Illinois did likewise in 1853. White male voters in Michigan in 1850 voted overwhelmingly—32,000 to 12,000—against permitting black men to vote. Only Ohio was an exception. In 1849 it repealed legislation excluding black people from the state.

These restrictive measures were not new. Most northern states had begun to restrict or deny the rights of black Americans in the early 1800s (see Chapter 7). Although only loosely enforced, the laws reflected the prevailing racial sentiments among many white northerners, as did the widespread antiblack rioting of the 1830s and 1840s. During the debate over excluding black people from Indiana, a state senator explained that the Bible revealed God had condemned black people to inferiority. "The same power that has given him a black skin, with less weight or volume of brain, has given us a white skin, with greater volume of brain and intellect; and that we can never live together upon an equality is as certain as that no two antagonistic principles can exist together at the same time."

Foreign observers were struck by northern racism. Alexis de Tocqueville, a French aristocrat, toured America in 1831 and wrote a perceptive analysis of American society. He considered northerners more antagonistic toward black people than southerners. "The prejudice of race appears to be stronger in the states that have abolished slavery than in those where it still exists; and nowhere is it so intolerant as in those states where servitude has never been known."

10.3.4 The Lincoln–Douglas Debates

In 1858 Senator Stephen Douglas of Illinois, a Democrat, ran for reelection to the Senate against Republican Abraham Lincoln. The main issues in the campaign were slavery and race, which the two candidates addressed in debates around the state. In carefully reasoned speeches and responses, these experienced and articulate lawyers focused almost exclusively on slavery's expansion and its future in the Union. At Freeport, Illinois, Lincoln, a former Whig congressman, attempted to trap Douglas by asking him if slavery could expand now that the *Dred Scott* decision had ruled slaves were property whom their owners could take into any federal territory. In reply, Douglas, who wanted to be president and had no desire to offend northern or southern voters, cleverly defended "popular sovereignty" and the *Dred Scott* decision. He insisted that slave owners could indeed take their slaves where they pleased. But, he contended, if the people of a territory failed to enact slave codes to protect and control slave property, slave owners were not likely to settle there with their slaves.

10.3.5 Abraham Lincoln and Black People

The **Lincoln–Douglas debates** did not always turn on the fine points of constitutional law or the fate of slavery in the territories. Thanks mainly to Douglas, who accused Lincoln and the Republicans of promoting the interests of black people over those of white people, the debates sometimes degenerated into crude exchanges about which

Lincoln–Douglas debates
Abraham Lincoln and Stephen Douglas debated seven times in the 1858 U.S. Senate race in Illinois. They spent most of their time arguing over slavery, its expansion, the *Dred Scott* decision, and the character of African Americans. Douglas won the election.

Profile

Martin Delany

Martin R. Delany played a key role in the emergence of black nationalism in the nineteenth century. He was an abolitionist, a medical doctor, and a journalist. As a major, he was the highest-ranking black military officer commissioned during the Civil War.

I thank God for making me a man, but Delany thanks Him for making him a black man.

—Frederick Douglass on Martin Delany

Martin Delany (1812–1885) was one of the first individuals to insist that African Americans should control their own destiny. In speeches, articles, and books, he evoked pride in his African heritage and stressed black people's need to rely on themselves and not on the white majority.

Delany was a medical doctor, a journalist, an explorer, an anthropologist, an army officer, and a political leader. He was born free in Charlestown, Virginia (now West Virginia), but the family moved to Chambersburg, Pennsylvania, in 1822. In 1831 Martin went to Pittsburgh, where he spent most of the next 25 years. His education was strongly influenced by Lewis Woodson, a young African Methodist Episcopal minister. He also studied medicine as an apprentice under two white physicians.

Delany was active in the Pittsburgh Anti-Slavery Society and helped slaves escape on the underground railroad. In 1843 he married Catherine Richards, the daughter of a well-to-do black butcher, and by 1860 they had six children, each named for a well-known black figure: Toussaint Louverture, Alexander Dumas, Saint Cyprian, Faustin Soulouque, Charles L. Redmond, and their only daughter, Ethiopia Halle.

In 1843, Delany began publishing *The Mystery*, a four-page weekly newspaper devoted to abolition. It did not thrive, and in 1847 he joined Frederick Douglass briefly as the coeditor of the *North Star* (see Chapter 9). In 1850 Delany was admitted to Harvard Medical School with two other black students for formal training, but they were forced to leave after one term because of the protests of white students.

In 1852, he wrote and published *The Condition, Elevation, Emigration and Destiny of the Colored People of the United States*—the first major statement of black nationalism. Delany observed, "We are a nation within a nation." He recommended that people of African descent abandon the United States and migrate to Central America, South America, or Hawaii. Delany was the key figure in organizing the National Emigration Convention in Cleveland in 1854.

He and his family left the United States for Canada and lived in Canada West (Ontario), where he organized a meeting of black people and John Brown in 1858. He also wrote a novel, *Blake*, about a West Indian slave who promotes revolution in the United States and Cuba. In 1859–1860, Delany visited Liberia and explored what is today Nigeria.

Once the United States began to enlist black troops in the Civil War, Delany helped recruit black men. His son Toussaint joined the famed 54th Massachusetts Regiment. Delany himself became one of the few black officers. In Charleston, South Carolina, he helped recruit two regiments of former slaves. After the war, he remained in South Carolina, where he entered politics. But he grew disillusioned with the Republicans—both black and white—who dominated southern governments during Reconstruction. He ran for lieutenant governor on a reform party ticket but lost. In 1876 he astounded many black people when he supported white Democrats who favored the restoration of white political control over South Carolina. When Democrats won the election, Governor Wade Hampton rewarded Delany by naming him to a minor political office. In 1878, a group of black South Carolinians and Georgians proposed migrating to Liberia. Delany became their treasurer, but he did not join them. The venture largely failed.

After he unsuccessfully sought an appointment to a federal position in Washington, D.C., Delany went to Xenia, Ohio, and Wilberforce University, where his family had lived since the late 1860s. He died there in 1885.

candidate favored white people more and black people less. Douglas proudly advocated white supremacy: "The signers of the Declaration [of Independence] had no reference to the Negro . . . or any other inferior or degraded race when they spoke of the equality of men." He later charged that Lincoln and the Republicans wanted black and white equality: "If you, Black Republicans, think the negro ought to be on social equality with your wives and daughters, . . . you have a perfect right to do so. . . . Those of you who believe the negro is your equal . . . of course will vote for Mr. Lincoln."

Lincoln did not believe in racial equality, and he made that plain. In exasperation, he explained that merely because he opposed slavery did not mean he believed in equality. "I do not understand that because I do not want a negro woman for a slave I must necessarily have her for a wife." He bluntly added,

> I am not, nor ever have been in favor of bringing about in any way the social and political equality of the white and black races—that I am not nor ever have been in favor of making voters or jurors of negroes, nor of qualifying them to hold office, nor to intermarry with white people; and I will say in addition to this that there is a physical difference between the races which I believe will forever forbid the two races living together on terms of social and political equality.

But without repudiating these views, Lincoln later tried to transcend this blatant racism. "Let us discard all this quibbling about this man and the other man—this race and that race and the other race being inferior." Instead, he added, let us "unite as one people throughout this land, until we shall once more stand up declaring that all men are created equal." Lincoln stated unequivocally that race had nothing to do with whether a man had the right to be paid for his labor. He pointed out that the black man, "in the right to eat the bread, without leave of anybody else, which his own hand earns, he is my equal and the equal of Judge Douglas, and the equal of every living man."

Lincoln may have won the debate in the minds of many, but Douglas won the election. (State legislators—not voters—elected U.S. senators until the ratification of the Seventeenth Amendment in 1917.) Lincoln, however, made a name for himself that would work to his political advantage in the near future, and Douglas, despite his best efforts, had thoroughly offended many southerners by suggesting that slave owners would not risk taking their human property to a territory that lacked a slave code. Douglas also antagonized white southerners when he opposed the proslavery Kansas Lecompton constitution that he and many others believed had been fraudulently adopted. In two years, these disagreements over slavery would contribute to a decisive split in the Democratic Party.

10.4 John Brown and the Raid on Harpers Ferry

Explain the importance of John Brown in the controversy over slavery.

While Lincoln and Douglas were debating, John Brown was plotting. Following his attack on Pottawattamie in Kansas, Brown began to plan the overthrow of slavery in the South itself. In Canada in May 1858, accompanied by 11 white followers, he met 34 black people led by Martin Delany and appealed for their support. Brown was determined to invade the South and end slavery. He hoped to attract legions of slaves as his "army" moved down the Appalachian Mountains into the heart of the plantation system.

10.4.1 Planning the Raid

Only one man at the Canadian gathering—Osborne P. Anderson—agreed to join the raid. Brown returned to the United States and garnered financial support from prosperous white abolitionists. Contributing money rather than risking their lives seemed more realistic to these men, who preferred to keep their identities confidential and thus came to be known as the Secret Six: Gerrit Smith, Thomas Wentworth Higginson, Samuel Gridley Howe, George L. Stearns, Theodore Parker, and Franklin Sanborn.

Brown also asked Frederick Douglass and Harriet Tubman to join him. They declined. By the summer of 1859, at a farm in rural Maryland, Brown had assembled an "army" consisting of 17 white men (including three of his adult sons) and five black men. The black men who enlisted were Osborne Anderson; Sheridan Leary, an escaped slave who had become a saddle and harness maker in Oberlin, Ohio; Leary's nephew John A. Copeland, an Oberlin College student; and two escaped slaves, Shields Green and Dangerfield Newby.

Newby was determined to rescue his pregnant wife Harriet and their six children, who were about to be sold from nearby Warrenton, Virginia, down the river to Louisiana. Harriet sent her husband a letter begging for him, "Oh Dear Dangerfield, com this fall . . . without fail . . . I want to see you so much that is one bright hope I have before me."

10.4.2 The Raid

Brown's invasion began on Sunday night, October 16, 1859, with a raid on Harpers Ferry, Virginia, and the federal arsenal there. Brown hoped to secure weapons and then advance south, but the operation went awry from the start. The dedication and devotion of Brown and his men were not matched by their strategy or his leadership. The first person Brown's band killed was ironically a free black man, Heyward Shepard, who was a baggage handler at the train station. The alarm went out, and opposition gathered.

Although they had lost the initiative, Brown and his men neither advanced nor retreated. Instead, they remained in Harpers Ferry while Virginia and Maryland militia converged on them. Fighting began, and two townspeople, the mayor, and eight of Brown's men, including Sheridan Leary, Dangerfield Newby, and two of Brown's sons, were killed. Newby died carrying his wife's letter. But Brown managed to seize hostages, including Lewis W. Washington, the great grandnephew of George Washington.

By Tuesday morning, Brown, with his hostages and what remained of his "army," were holed up in an engine house. U.S. Marines under the command of Robert E. Lee arrived, surrounded the building, and demanded Brown's surrender. He refused. The marines broke in. Brown was wounded and captured.

About 150 adult slaves lived near Harpers Ferry. Most of them were aware of the raid, and many of them joined the insurrection. Osborne Anderson provided pikes to slaves. Some of them acquired firearms. Several slaves managed to flee to freedom in the North. Perhaps a dozen black men—in addition to those who accompanied Brown—died during and after the raid.

There was no massive slave uprising. Shields Green and John A. Copeland fled but were caught. Osborne Anderson eluded capture and later fought in the Civil War. Virginia tried Brown, Green, and Copeland for treason. They were found guilty and sentenced to hang. But the violence did not end. In the weeks that followed, the barn of every juror who convicted Brown was burned. Many horses and cattle died. They were apparently poisoned.

10.4.3 The Reaction

John Brown's raid had not proceeded as planned. Still, Brown and his men succeeded in intensifying the deep emotions of those who supported and those who opposed slavery. At first regarded as crazed zealots and insane

John Brown's raid

Brown's raid on Harpers Ferry, Virginia, in October 1859 failed to lead to a major slave insurrection, but it inflamed the controversy over slavery in the North and South.

John Brown was captured in the Engine House at Harpers Ferry on October 18, 1859. He was quickly tried for treason and convicted. On December 2, 1859, he was hanged. His raid helped catapult the nation toward civil war.

fanatics, they showed they were willing—even eager—to die for the antislavery cause. The dignity and assurance that Brown, Green, and Copeland displayed as they awaited the gallows impressed many black and white northerners.

Black teacher and abolitionist Frances Ellen Watkins Harper wrote to John Brown's wife two weeks before Brown was executed to express compassion and admiration for both husband and wife:

> Belonging to the race your dear husband reached forth his hand to assist, I need not tell you that my sympathies are with you. I thank you for the brave words you have spoken. A republic that produces such a wife and mother may hope for better days. Our heart may grow more hopeful for humanity when it sees the sublime sacrifice it is about to receive from his hands. Not in vain had your dear husband periled all, if the martyrdom of one hero is worth more than the life of a million cowards.

John A. Copeland wrote his family that he was proud to die:

> I am not terrified by the gallows, which I see staring me in the face, and upon which I am soon to stand and suffer death for doing what George Washington was made a hero for doing. . . . Could I die in a manner and for a cause which would induce true and honest men more to honor me, and the angels more ready to receive me to their happy home of everlasting joy above? . . . I imagine that I hear you, and all of you, mother, father, sisters and brothers, say—"No, there is not a cause for which we, with less sorrow, could see you die."

Brown also eloquently and calmly announced his willingness to die as so many had died before him. "Now, if it is deemed necessary that I should forfeit my life for the furtherance of the ends of justice, and mingle my blood further with the blood of my children and with the blood of millions in this slave country whose rights are disregarded by wicked, cruel, and unjust enactments, I say, let it be done."

For many northerners, the day Brown was executed, December 2, 1859, was a day of mourning. Church bells tolled, and people bowed their heads in prayer. One unnamed black man later solemnly declared, "The memory of John Brown shall be indelibly written upon the tablets of our hearts, and when tyrants cease to oppress the enslaved, we will teach our children to revive his name, and transmit it to the latest posterity, as being the greatest man in the 19th century."

White southerners were traumatized by the raid and outraged that northerners made Brown a hero and a martyr. A wave of hysteria and paranoia swept the South as incredulous white people wondered how northerners could admire a man who sought to kill slave owners and free their slaves.

Brown's raid and the reaction to it further divided a nation already badly split over slavery. Although neither he nor anyone else realized it at the time, Brown and his "army" had propelled the South toward secession from the Union—and thereby moved the nation closer to his goal of destroying slavery.

10.5 The Election of Abraham Lincoln

Distinguish the ways in which white northerners, white southerners, and African Americans reacted to the election of Abraham Lincoln in 1860.

With the country fracturing over slavery, four candidates ran for president in the election of 1860. The Democrats split into a northern faction, which nominated Stephen Douglas, and a southern faction, which nominated John C. Breckenridge of Kentucky. The Constitutional Union Party, a new party formed by former Whigs, nominated John Bell of Tennessee. The breakup of the Democratic Party assured victory for the Republican candidate, Abraham Lincoln (see Map 10-3).

Map 10-3 The Election of 1860

The results reflect the sectional schism over slavery. Lincoln carried the election, although he won only in northern states. His name did not even appear on the ballot in most southern states.

How was Lincoln able to win without getting any electoral votes from the South?

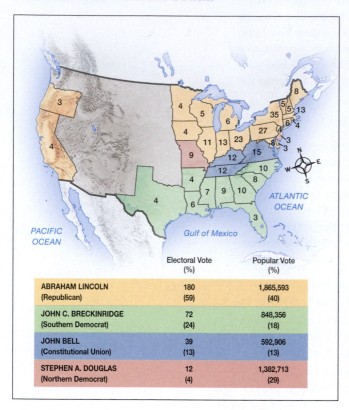

	Electoral Vote (%)	Popular Vote (%)
ABRAHAM LINCOLN (Republican)	180 (59)	1,865,593 (40)
JOHN C. BRECKINRIDGE (Southern Democrat)	72 (24)	848,356 (18)
JOHN BELL (Constitutional Union)	39 (13)	592,906 (13)
STEPHEN A. DOUGLAS (Northern Democrat)	12 (4)	1,382,713 (29)

Lincoln's name was not even on the ballot in most southern states because his candidacy was based on the Republican Party's adamant opposition to the expansion of slavery into any western territory. Although Lincoln took pains to reassure white southerners that slavery would continue in states where it already existed, they were not persuaded. A South Carolina newspaper was convinced Lincoln would abolish slavery: "[Lincoln] has openly proclaimed a war of extermination against the leading institutions of the Southern States. He says that there can be no peace so long as slavery has a foot hold in America."

A Georgia newspaper preferred a bloody civil war to a Lincoln presidency: "Let the consequences be what they may—whether the Potomac is crimsoned in human gore, and Pennsylvania Avenue is paved ten fathoms deep with mangled bodies . . . the South will never submit to such humiliation and degradation as the inauguration of Abraham Lincoln."

10.5.1 Black People Respond to Lincoln's Election

Although they were less opposed to Lincoln than white southerners, black northerners and white abolitionists were not eager to see Abraham Lincoln become president. Dismayed by his contradictions and racism—he opposed slavery, but he tolerated it; he was against slavery's expansion, but he condemned black Americans as inferiors—many black people refused to support him or did so reluctantly. The New York *Anglo-African* opposed both Republicans and Democrats in the 1860 election, telling its readers to depend on each other. "We have no hope from either [of the] political parties. We must rely on ourselves, the righteousness of our cause, and the advance of just sentiments among the great masses of the . . . people."

Abolitionists such as William Lloyd Garrison and Wendell Phillips believed Lincoln was too willing to tolerate slaveholding interests. But Frederick Douglass wrote, "Lincoln's election will indicate growth in the right direction," and his presidency "must and will be hailed as an anti-slavery triumph."

After Lincoln's election, black leaders almost welcomed the secession of southern states. H. Ford Douglas urged the southern states to leave the Union. "Stand not upon the order of your going, but go at once. . . . There is no union of ideas and interests in this country, and there can be no union between freedom and slavery." Frederick Douglass was convinced that there were men prepared to follow in the footsteps of John Brown's "army" to destroy slavery. "I am for dissolution of the Union—decidedly for a dissolution of the Union! . . . In case of such a dissolution, I believe that men could be found . . . who would venture into those states and raise the standard of liberty there."

10.5.2 Disunion

When South Carolina seceded on December 20, 1860, it began a procession of southern states out of the Union. By February 1861 seven states—South Carolina, Mississippi, Alabama, Florida, Louisiana, Georgia, and Texas—had seceded and formed the

Confederate States of America in Montgomery, Alabama. Before there could be the kind of undertaking against slavery that Douglass had proposed, Abraham Lincoln tried to persuade the seceding states to reconsider. In his inaugural address of March 4, 1861, Lincoln attempted to calm the fears of white southerners but informed them he would not tolerate their withdrawal from the Union. Lincoln repeated his assurance that he would not tamper with slavery in the states where it was already legal: "I have no purpose, directly or indirectly, to interfere with the institution of slavery in the States where it exists. I believe I have no lawful right to do so, and I have no inclination to do so."

Lincoln added that the "only" dispute between the North and South was over the expansion of slavery. He emphatically warned, however, that he would enforce the Constitution and not permit secession. "Plainly, the central idea of secession is the essence of anarchy." He pleaded with white southerners to contemplate their actions patiently and thoughtfully, actions that might provoke a civil conflict. "In your hands, my dissatisfied fellow-countrymen, and not in mine, is the monumental issue of civil war."

Southern whites did not heed him. Slavery was too essential to give up merely to preserve the Union. Arthur P. Hayne of South Carolina had succinctly summed up its importance in an 1860 letter to President James Buchanan: "Slavery with us is no abstraction—but a great and vital fact. Without it our every comfort would be taken from us. Our wives, our children, made unhappy—education, the light of knowledge—all lost and our people ruined forever. Nothing short of separation from the Union can save us."

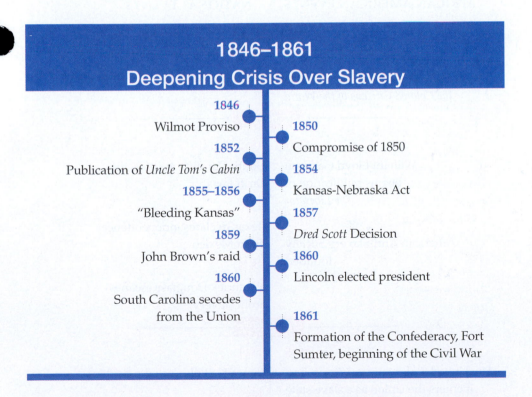

1846–1861
Deepening Crisis Over Slavery

1846	
Wilmot Proviso	**1850**
1852	Compromise of 1850
Publication of *Uncle Tom's Cabin*	**1854**
1855–1856	Kansas-Nebraska Act
"Bleeding Kansas"	**1857**
1859	*Dred Scott* Decision
John Brown's raid	**1860**
1860	Lincoln elected president
South Carolina secedes from the Union	**1861**
	Formation of the Confederacy, Fort Sumter, beginning of the Civil War

Barely a month after Lincoln's inauguration, Confederate leaders demanded that U.S. Army Major Robert Anderson surrender Fort Sumter in the harbor of Charleston, South Carolina. Anderson refused, and on April 12, 1861, Confederate artillery fired on the fort. In the aftermath, Virginia, North Carolina, Tennessee, and Arkansas joined the Confederacy. The Civil War had begun.

Conclusion

Virtually every event and episode of major or minor consequence in the United States between 1846 and 1861 involved black people and the expansion of slavery. From the Wilmot Proviso and the Compromise of 1850 to the *Dred Scott* decision and John Brown's raid, white Americans were increasingly perplexed about how the nation could remain half slave and half free. They were unable to resolve the problem of slavery's expansion.

Without the presence of black people in America, neither secession nor civil war would have occurred. Yet the Civil War began because white Americans had developed contradictory visions of the future. White southerners contemplated a future that inextricably linked their security and prosperity to slavery. The South, they believed, could neither advance nor endure without slavery.

Northern white people believed their future rested on the opportunities for white men and their families to flourish as independent, self-sufficient farmers, shopkeepers, and skilled artisans. For their future to prevail, they insisted the new lands in the American West should exclude the slave system that white southerners considered so vital. Neither northern nor southern white people—except for some abolitionists—ever believed people of color should fully participate as free people in American society or in the future of the American nation.

Chapter Timeline

AFRICAN-AMERICAN EVENTS	NATIONAL EVENTS
1820–1830	
1829	**1820**
David Walker publishes his *Appeal to the Colored Citizens of the World*	Missouri Compromise
1830–1840	
1831	**1832**
William Lloyd Garrison begins publication of *The Liberator*	South Carolina nullifies the tariff laws
1833	**1836**
American Anti-Slavery Society founded	Texas declares independence from Mexico
	1838
	Frederick Douglass escapes from slavery
1840–1850	
1845	**1844**
The United States annexes Texas, and it enters the Union as a slave state	James K. Polk elected president
	1846–1847
1847	Mexican War
Crosswhite family eludes capture in Michigan	**1846**
	Wilmot Proviso
1848	**1847**
William and Ellen Craft escape from slavery in Georgia	Mormons begin settlement of Utah

AFRICAN-AMERICAN EVENTS   **NATIONAL EVENTS**

1848

Formation of the Free-Soil Party

Zachary Taylor elected president

Women's rights convention at Seneca
Falls, New York

1850–1860

1850   **1850**

Fugitive Slave Act   Compromise of 1850

1850–1860   **1852**

Fugitive slaves captured   Publication of *Uncle Tom's Cabin*

1850   Franklin Pierce elected president

James Hamlet returned to   **1854**
slavery and then purchased
and freed   Kansas-Nebraska Act

1851   **1855–1856**

Shadrach Minkins eludes capture   "Bleeding Kansas"
in Boston
                                         1856
Thomas Sims returned to slavery
                                         James Buchanan elected president
"Battle" at Christiana
                                         Congressman Preston Brooks assaults
1853   Senator Charles Sumner

Black convention at Rochester,   **1858**
New York
                                         Lincoln–Douglas debates
1854

Anthony Burns returned
to slavery from Boston

1856

Margaret Garner kills her daughter in
unsuccessful escape

1857

Dred Scott decision

1859

John Brown's raid on Harpers Ferry

1860–1865

1861   **1860**

Free black men in Charleston offer   Abraham Lincoln elected president
their support to South Carolina
                                         South Carolina secedes from
                                         the Union

                                         1861

                                         Six more southern states secede and
                                         form the Confederacy

                                         Civil War begins after firing on
                                         Fort Sumter

                                         Four more southern states join
                                         the Confederacy

Review Questions

1. How and why did southern and northern white people differ over slavery? On what did white people of both regions agree and disagree about race and slavery?

2. If you were a northern African American in the 1850s, how would you have responded to the policies of the U.S. government?

3. If you were a white southerner in the 1850s, would you have been encouraged or discouraged by U.S. government policies?

4. Why did seven southern states secede from the Union within three months after Abraham Lincoln was elected president in 1860?

5. If you were a black person—either a slave or free—would you have welcomed the secession of the southern states? How might secession affect the future of your people?

Retracing the Odyssey

Black Heritage Trail, Boston, Massachusetts. This is a 1.6-mile walking tour of 14 sites. It begins at the Africa Meeting House (built in 1806) and includes the four-story home of black leader Lewis Hayden and his wife Harriet as well as Augustus Saint-Gaudens's powerful 1897 *Memorial to Robert Gould Shaw and the 54th Massachusetts Regiment*.

The Old St. Louis Court House, St. Louis, Missouri. This restored structure was the scene of two of Dred Scott's trials. It contains some of the legal papers and newspaper articles involving the case.

The First Baptist Church, Chatham, Ontario, Canada. On May 8, 1858, John Brown met with members of Chatham's black community—many of whom had fled to Canada to escape the fugitive slave law. Brown appealed for support to begin an armed uprising of slaves in the South. Fire destroyed the original structure in 1907, and the current church was built in 1908.

Harpers Ferry National Park, West Virginia. Picturesquely situated in the Blue Ridge Mountains at the confluence of the Shenandoah and Potomac Rivers, this is where John Brown and his "army" in October 1859 attempted to secure weapons to begin a slave rebellion.

Recommended Reading

Eric Foner. *Free Soil, Free Labor and Free Men: The Ideology of the Republican Party Before the Civil War.* New York: Oxford University Press, 1970. An excellent overview of attitudes on free soil, slavery, and race.

Vincent Harding. *There Is a River: The Black Struggle for Freedom in America.* New York: Harcourt, Brace, Jovanovich, 1981. A tribute to and a masterful narrative about the black people who challenged the white majority in nineteenth-century America.

Stanley Harrold, *Border War: Fighting Over Slavery Before the Civil War.* Chapel Hill: University of North Carolina Press, 2010. This is a deft and riveting analysis of the violence and bloodshed that erupted along the border between slave and free states in the 30 years prior to the Civil War.

Leon Litwack. *North of Slavery: The Negro in the Free States, 1790–1860.* Chicago: University of Chicago Press, 1961. A story of black northerners and the discrimination they encountered.

James McPherson. *Battle Cry of Freedom: The Civil War Era.* New York: Oxford University Press, 1988. A superb account of the crisis leading up to the Civil War and of the war itself.

David Potter. *The Impending Crisis, 1848–1861.* New York: Harper & Row, 1976. Another fine account of the events leading up to the Civil War.

Additional Bibliography

California and the Compromise of 1850

Eugene H. Berwanger. *The Frontier Against Slavery: Western Anti-Negro Prejudice and the Slave Extension Controversy.* Urbana: University of Illinois Press, 1967.

Fergus Bordewich. *America's Great Debate: Henry Clay, Stephen A. Douglas, and the Compromise That Preserved the Union.* New York: Simon and Schuster, 2012.

Holman Hamilton. *Prologue to Conflict: The Crisis and Compromise of 1850.* Lexington: University Press of Kentucky, 1964.

Lynn M. Hudson. *The Making of "Mammy Pleasant," a Black Entrepreneur in Nineteenth-Century San Francisco.* Urbana: University of Illinois Press, 2003.

Rudolph M. Lapp. *Blacks in Gold Rush California.* New Haven, CT: Yale University Press, 1977.

The Fugitive Slave Law and Resistance to It

Stanley W. Campbell. *The Slave Catchers: Enforcement of the Fugitive Slave Law, 1850–1860.* Chapel Hill: University of North Carolina Press, 1968.

Gary Collison. *Shadrach Minkins.* Cambridge, MA: Harvard University Press, 1998.

Eric Foner. *Gateway to Freedom: The Hidden History of the Underground Railroad.* New York: W. W. Norton, 2015.

Albert J. von Frank. *The Trials of Anthony Burns: Freedom and Slavery in Emerson's Boston.* Cambridge, MA: Harvard University Press, 1998.

Jonathan Katz. *Resistance at Christiana: The Fugitive Slave Rebellion at Christiana, Pennsylvania, September 11, 1851: A Documentary Account.* New York: Crowell, 1974.

Thomas P. Slaughter. *Bloody Dawn: The Christiana Riot and Violence in the Antebellum North.* New York: Oxford University Press, 1991.

Jacqueline Tobin with Hettie Jones. *From Midnight to Dawn: The Last Tracks of the Underground Railroad.* New York: Doubleday, 2007.

The 1850s

Walter Ehrlich. *They Have No Rights: Dred Scott's Struggle for Freedom.* Westport, CT: Greenwood, 1979.

Don E. Fehrenbacher. *The Dred Scott Case: Its Significance in American Law and Politics.* New York: Oxford University Press, 1978.

William W. Freehling. *The Road to Disunion: Secessionists Triumphant, 1854–1861.* New York: Oxford University Press, 2008.

Henry Lewis Gates Jr. and Donald Yacovone, eds. *Lincoln on Race and Slavery.* Princeton, NJ: Princeton University Press, 2009.

Michael F. Holt. *The Fate of Their Country: Politicians, Slavery Extension, and the Coming of the Civil War.* New York: Hill and Wang, 2005.

Robert W. Johannsen. *Stephen A. Douglas.* New York: Oxford University Press, 1973.

Kenneth M. Stampp. *America in 1857: A Nation on the Brink.* New York: Oxford University Press, 1990.

Eric Walther. *The Shattering of the Union: America in the 1850s.* Wilmington, DE: Scholarly Resources, 2004.

John Brown and the Raid on Harpers Ferry

Louis A. DeCaro Jr. *"Fire from the Midst of You": A Religious Life of John Brown.* New York: New York University Press, 2002.

Paul Finkelman. *And His Soul Goes Marching On: Responses to John Brown and the Harpers Ferry Raid.* Charlottesville: University of Virginia Press, 1995.

Tony Horwitz. *Midnight Rising: John Brown and the Raid That Sparked the Civil War.* New York: Henry Holt, 2011.

Truman Nelson. *The Old Man John Brown at Harpers Ferry.* New York: Holt, Rinehart and Winston, 1973.

Stephen Oates. *To Purge This Land with Blood: A Biography of John Brown.* New York: Harper and Row, 1970.

Benjamin Quarles. *Blacks on John Brown.* Urbana: University of Illinois Press, 1972.

Secession

William L. Barney. *The Road to Secession.* New York: Praeger, 1972.

Steven A. Channing. *Crisis of Fear: Secession in South Carolina.* New York: Simon and Schuster, 1970.

Kenneth M. Stampp. *And the War Came: The North and the Secession Crisis, 1860–1861.* Baton Rouge: Louisiana State University Press, 1950.

Abraham Lincoln

Gabor Boritt, ed. *The Lincoln Enigma.* New York: Oxford University Press, 2001.

Orville Vernon Burton. *The Age of Lincoln.* New York: Hill and Wang, 2007.

David Herbert Donald. *Lincoln*. New York: Simon and Schuster, 1995.

Eric Foner. *The Fiery Trial: Abraham Lincoln and Slavery*. New York: W. W. Norton, 2010.

Stephen B. Oates. *With Malice Toward None: A Life of Abraham Lincoln*. New York: Harper and Row, 1977.

Benjamin Thomas. *Abraham Lincoln: A Biography*. New York: Alfred A. Knopf, 1952.

Ronald C. White Jr. *A. Lincoln: A Life*. New York: Random House, 2009.

Novels

Martin R. Delany. *Blake or the Huts of America*. Boston: Beacon Press, 1970.

Harriet Beecher Stowe. *Uncle Tom's Cabin, or Life among the Lowly*. New York: Modern Library, 1985.

Connecting the Past

Narrative of the Life of Frederick Douglass and Black Autobiography

NARRATIVE

OF THE

LIFE

OF

FREDERICK DOUGLASS,

AN

AMERICAN SLAVE.

WRITTEN BY HIMSELF.

BOSTON:
PUBLISHED AT THE ANTI-SLAVERY OFFICE,
No. 25 CORNHILL.
1845.

Shortly after the *Narrative of the Life of Frederick Douglass, An American Slave, Written by Himself* appeared in 1845, white author and feminist Margaret Fuller reviewed this autobiography in the *New York Tribune*. Comparing Douglass to the famous French novelist Alexandre Dumas, whom

Fuller also considered to be black because his grandmother was Haitian, she declared of the *Narrative*, "We have never read one more simple, true, coherent, and warm with genuine feeling. It is an excellent piece of writing, and on that score to be prized as a specimen of the powers of the Black Race, which Prejudice persists in disparaging." Today Douglass's *Narrative* is part of the American literary canon.

Black Americans wrote autobiographies long before 1845. In 1760, Briton Hammon, a Boston slave captured in 1747 by American Indians, published *A Narrative of the Uncommon Suffering, and Surprising Delivery of Briton Hammon, a Negro Man*. In 1798, Venture Smith, a former slave who had purchased his freedom, published *A Narrative of the Life and Adventures of Venture, a Native of Africa, but Resident Above Sixty Years in the United States, Related by Himself*. In 1825, William Grimes published *Life of William Grimes, the Runaway Slave, Written by Himself*. By the 1830s, former slaves' autobiographies were common. Through accounts of suffering in bondage and escape from it, they aimed to reach a white northern audience and gain support for the antislavery movement.

Douglass followed the pattern of these earlier life stories, and like them his *Narrative* sought to increase opposition to slavery. Yet Douglass's is by far the best of the slave narratives. Rather than simple antislavery propaganda, it is a psychological and intellectual portrayal of a slave's struggle for human identity. Douglass's *Narrative* was also immensely successful, selling 30,000 copies within five years of its publication. That number, while not impressive by today's standards, surpassed the *combined* sales of Herman Melville's *Moby-Dick*, Henry David Thoreau's *On Walden Pond*, and Walt Whitman's *Leaves of Grass* during a similar period after their publication. Most important, the *Narrative* remains compelling. As Douglass's biographer William S. McFeely observed in 1991, "The person we come to know in these brief pages is unforgettable."

Black leaders have followed Douglass in using autobiography to define themselves and their goals. Douglass himself wrote two more autobiographies: *My Bondage and My Freedom* (1855) and *Life and Times of Frederick Douglass,*

Written by Himself (1892). These cover his later career and provide additional information about his life in slavery, but do not match the literary stature of the *Narrative*. In 1868, Elizabeth Keckley, who led the Washington, D.C., Contraband Relief Association during the Civil War and worked for Mary Todd Lincoln, published *Behind the Scenes, Or, Thirty Years a Slave and Four Years in the White House*.

Booker T. Washington's *Up from Slavery: An Autobiography* (1901) is organized more like Douglass's *Narrative* than is Keckley's book. Like Douglass, Washington emphasizes education and influencing white opinion. In addition, during the last years of his life, Douglass directly influenced Mary Church Terrell, Washington's young contemporary. Increasingly aware of racism's negative impact, Terrell, like Douglass, became a renowned speaker for civil rights. In 1940, she published her autobiography, *A Colored Woman in a White World*.

Like Douglass, W. E. B. Du Bois, the most influential black activist and intellectual from the 1910s through the 1940s, wrote three autobiographies. He published the first of them, *Darkwater: Voices from within the Veil*, in 1920. Du Bois's themes of the color-line and divided black consciousness are more psychologically sophisticated than Douglass's. Yet Douglass's revelation that in 1841, when he first addressed a white audience, "I felt myself a slave, and the idea of speaking to white people weighed me down," anticipates Du Bois's portrayal of interracial unease.

Martin Luther King, Jr. and Malcolm X were less in Douglass's autobiographical tradition. King shared Douglass's commitment to racial integration. Yet *The Autobiography of Martin Luther King* (1998) is not really an autobiography. Instead, it is a selection of King's writings compiled by black historian Clayborne Carson that appeared long after King died. Malcolm was the author of *The Autobiography of Malcolm X* (1965), but black author Alex Haley had a major role in shaping the book. Malcolm's life also differed greatly from Douglass's, although both of their autobiographies stress resistance to conditions white people forced on black people.

In 1966, poet Langston Hughes reflected on Douglass's impact: "Douglass was someone who, had he walked with wary foot and frightened tread, from very indecision, might be dead. . . . He is not dead." Neither is his autobiographical legacy among black leaders. In *Dreams of My Father: A Story of Race and Inheritance* (1995), Barack Obama wrote

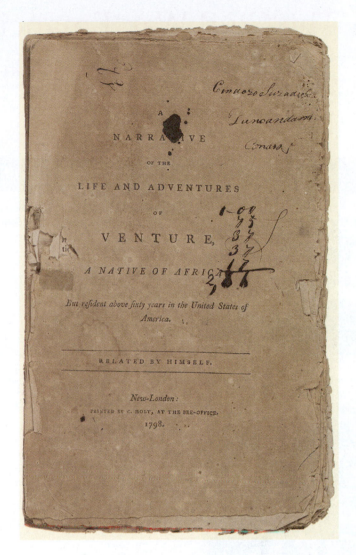

an autobiography in the Douglass manner, as Obama defined himself, despite his biracial and international roots, as a black American.

---

1. Does black autobiography have a central historical theme?

2. How is the *Narrative of the Life of Frederick Douglass* relevant today?

Part III

The Civil War, Emancipation, and Black Reconstruction

The Second American Revolution

Robert Brown Elliot

| 1860–1865 | 1865–1870 |

RELIGION

| 1865–1870s | Former slaves organize their own religious congregations across the South | 1866–1870s | Numerous black ministers elected to political office and leadership positions in the South |

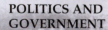

CULTURE

		1865–1870s	More than 40 black colleges founded in the South
		1867	Howard University established
		1868	Elizabeth Keckley publishes *Behind the Scenes, or, Thirty Years a Slave and Four Years in the White House*
		1869	More than 100,000 students attend Freedmen's Bureau schools in the ●

POLITICS AND GOVERNMENT

1861	Union Army rejects black volunteers. First Confiscation Act frees slaves who had been used by the Confederate Army	1865–1866	Black conventions held across the South
1862	Militia Act authorizes recruitment of black troops for the Union Army. First black troops fight for Union at Island Mountain, MO	1867	Reconstruction Acts passed by Congress
1863	Emancipation Proclamation issued. Black troops assault Battery Wagner in Charleston Harbor	1867–1868	Black people participate in southern states' constitutional conventions
1864	Fort Pillow Massacre	1868	Fourteenth Amendment gives black people the rights of citizenship
1865	Confederate Congress votes to enlist 300,000 black troops. U.S. Congress creates the Freedmen's Bureau. Thirteenth Amendment abolishes slavery. Congress passes a Civil Rights Act. Southern states rejoin the Union and enact black codes		

SOCIETY AND ECONOMY

1862	Port Royal Experiment begins in South Carolina	1866	Ku Klux Klan organized. New Orleans Massacre. White mob lynches 24 black men near Pine Bluff, AR
1863	New York City draft riots attack African Americans		
1864	Black National Convention meets in Syracuse, NY		
1865	Freedmen's Savings Bank and Trust Company established	1869	Isaac Myers organizes the Colored National Labor Union

Susie King Taylor

Blanche K. Bruce

P. B. S. Pinchback

1870–1880

1880–1900

Noteworthy Individuals

1870 Colored Methodist Episcopal Church established

1870s Black people organize St. Mark's, the first African-American Episcopal congregation in Charleston, SC

1872 Charlotte Ray becomes the first African-American woman lawyer
Alcorn A&M College, the first black state university, founded in Mississippi

1902 Susie K. Taylor publishes her memoir of nursing black troops in the Union Army

1870 Fifteenth Amendment prohibits disfranchisement because of race
Hiram R. Revels, first African-American U.S. senator, elected
Joseph Rainey, first African-American congressman, elected

1870–1871 Enforcement Acts against Klan terrorism passed by Congress

1877 Reconstruction ends

1883 U.S. Supreme Court strikes down the Civil Rights Act of 1875

1872 Colfax Massacre in Louisiana

1874 Freedmen's Savings Bank closes

1876 Hamburg Massacre and Ellenton Riot in South Carolina

Aaron A. Bradley
(1815–1881)
Elizabeth Keckley
(1818–1907)
Hiram R. Revels
(1822–1901)
Mifflin W. Gibbs
(1823–1915)
Richard H. Cain
(1825–1887)
Jonathan C. Gibbs
(c. 1827–1874)
Isaac Myers
(1835–1901)
William Whipper
(1835–1907)
James T. Rapier
(1837–1883)
Francis L. Cardozo
(1837–1903)
Charlotte Forten
(1837–1914)
P. B. S. Pinchback
(1837–1921)
Robert Smalls
(1839–1915)
Jonathan J. Wright
(1840–1885)
William H. Carney
(1840–c. 1901)
Blanche K. Bruce
(1841–1898)
Robert Brown Elliott
(1842–1884)
Frances Rollin
(1844–1901)
Susie King Taylor
(1848–1912)
Charlotte Ray
(1850–1911)
Katherine Rollin
(1851–1876)

Chapter 11

Liberation: African Americans and the Civil War

1861–1865

The band of 107th U.S. Colored Infantry at Fort Corcoran in Arlington, Virginia.

Learning Objectives

After reading this chapter, you should be able to:

11.1 Explain the primary objective of President Abraham Lincoln when the Civil War began in 1861.

11.2 Describe the responses of African Americans to the outbreak of the Civil War.

11.3 Compare Abraham Lincoln's policy on slavery when the Civil War began in 1861 to his policy contained in the Emancipation Proclamation.

11.4   Summarize the contributions of African-American men and women to the Union war effort.

11.5   Analyze the positions that Confederate leaders as well as African Americans themselves took on the employment of black men to fight for the Confederacy.

If the muse were mine to tempt it
And my feeble voice were strong,
If my tongue were trained to measures,
I would sing a stirring song.
I would sing a song heroic
Of those noble sons of Ham,
Of the gallant colored soldiers
Who fought for Uncle Sam! . . .
Ah, they rallied to the standard
To uphold it by their might;
None were stronger in the labors,
None were braver in the fight.
From the blazing breach of Wagner
To the plains of Olustee,
They were foremost in the fight
Of the battles of the free. . . .
And their deeds shall find a record
In the registry of Fame;
For their blood has cleansed completely
Every blot of Slavery's shame.
So all honor and all glory
To those noble sons of Ham—
The gallant colored soldiers
Who fought for Uncle Sam!

*—From "The Colored Soldiers," 1895, by Paul Laurence Dunbar, whose father,
Joshua, served with the all-black 55th Massachusetts Regiment*

Slavery caused the Civil War. Yet when the war began in 1861, neither the Union nor the Confederacy entered the conflict with any intention or desire to change the status of black Americans. It was supposed to be a white man's war. White southerners would wage war to make the **Confederacy** a separate and independent nation free to promote slavery. White northerners took up arms to maintain the Union but not to free a single slave. African Americans who wanted to enlist in 1861 were rejected. The Union might be disrupted, but slavery was not going to be disturbed.

Both North and South expected a quick victory. No one anticipated that 48 months of brutal war would rip the nation apart. When the Civil War ended in April 1865, approximately 750,000 Americans were dead—including nearly 50,000 black men. The Union was preserved. Four million people had been freed. Nothing in American history compares with it.

Confederacy
Association of slave states that left the Union in 1861.

11.1 Lincoln's Aims

Explain the primary objective of President Abraham Lincoln when the Civil War began in 1861.

Throughout the war, President Lincoln's unwavering objective was to preserve the Union. Any policies that helped or hindered black people were subordinate to that goal. Following the attack on Fort Sumter in April 1861 and Lincoln's call for state militias to help suppress the rebellion, four more slave states—North Carolina, Virginia, Tennessee, and Arkansas—seceded from the Union and joined the Confederacy. For most of 1861, Lincoln was determined to do nothing that would drive the four remaining slave states—Delaware, Maryland, Kentucky, and Missouri—into the Confederacy. Lincoln feared that if he did or said anything that could be interpreted as interfering with slavery, those four states would leave the Union too.

Meanwhile, Lincoln called for 75,000 men to enlist in the military for 90 days of service to the national government. Many thousands of black and white men, far more than 75,000, responded. White men were accepted. Black men were rejected. Despite being spurned by federal and state authorities, black men remained determined to aid the cause.

11.2 Black Men Volunteer and Are Rejected

Describe the responses of African Americans to the outbreak of the Civil War.

Black people recognized long before most white northerners that the fate of the Union was inextricably tied to the issue of slavery and the future of slavery was tied to the outcome of the war. "Talk as we may," insisted the *Anglo-African*, a black New York newspaper,

> we are concerned in this fight and our fate hangs upon its issues. The South must be subjugated, or we shall be enslaved. In aiding the Federal government in whatever way we can, we are aiding to secure our own liberty; for this war can end only in the subjugation of the North or the South.

Black men in New York formed their own military companies and began to drill. In Boston, they drew up a resolution modeled on the Declaration of Independence and appealed for permission to go to war:

> Our feelings urge us to say to our countrymen that we are ready to stand by and defend our Government as equals of its white defenders; to do so with "our lives, our fortunes, and our sacred honor," for the sake of freedom, and as good citizens; and we ask you to modify your laws, that we may enlist—that full scope may be given to patriotic feelings burning in the colored man's breast.

Black men in Philadelphia volunteered to infiltrate the South to incite slave revolts but were turned down. In Washington, D.C., Jacob Dodson, a black employee of the Senate, wrote to Secretary of War Simon Cameron shortly after the fall of Fort Sumter volunteering the services of local black men. "I desire to inform you that I know of some 300 reliable colored free citizens of this city who desire to enter the service for the defense of the city." Cameron curtly rejected Dodson, "This Department has no intention at the present to call into the service of the government any colored soldiers."

11.2.1 Union Policies toward Confederate Slaves

Slaves started to liberate themselves as soon as the war began, but Union leaders had no coherent policy for dealing with them. To the disappointment of black northerners and white abolitionists, Union military commanders showed more concern for the interests of Confederate slave owners than for the people in bondage. In May 1861 General George B. McClellan reassured Virginia slave owners, "Not only will we abstain from all interferences with your slaves, but we will, with an iron hand, crush any attempt at insurrection on their part."

General Henry Halleck ordered slaves who escaped in the Ohio valley to be returned to their owners, and General Winfield Scott, the army's chief of staff, asked that Confederate slave owners be permitted to recover slaves who crossed the Potomac River to what they believed was the freedom of Union lines. In Tennessee in early 1862, General Ulysses S. Grant returned runaway slaves to their owners if the owners supported the Union cause but put them to work on fortifications if their owners favored secession.

11.2.2 "Contraband"

Not all Union commanders were so callous. A month after the war began, three bond-men working on Confederate fortifications in Virginia escaped to the Union's Fortress Monroe on the coast. Their owner, a Confederate colonel, appeared at the fortress the next day under a flag of truce and demanded the return of his slaves under the 1850 Fugitive Slave Act. The incredulous Union commander, General Benjamin Butler, informed him that because Virginia had seceded from the Union, that law was no longer in force. Butler did not free the three slaves, but he did not reenslave them either. He declared them "**contraband**"—enemy property—and put them to work for the Union. Soon, over a thousand slaves fled to Fortress Monroe. The white authorities may have thought of them as contraband, but it is doubtful that while crossing Union lines any slaves declared, "We are contraband." Rather, they were apt to insist, "We are free!"

On August 6, 1861, Congress clarified the status of runaway slaves when it passed the **First Confiscation Act**. Through this act, federal forces could seize any property that belonged to Confederates used in the war effort. Any slaves their masters used to benefit the Confederacy—and only those slaves—would be freed. Almost immediately, Union General John C. Fremont (the 1856 Republican presidential candidate) exceeded the strict limits of the act by freeing all the slaves belonging to Confederates in Missouri. President Lincoln countermanded the order and told Fremont that only slaves actively used to aid the Confederate war effort were to be freed. Lincoln worried that Fremont's decision would drive Missouri or Kentucky into the Confederacy.

Black leaders were—to put it mildly—displeased with Lincoln and with federal policies that both prohibited the enlistment of black troops and ignored the plight of the enslaved. To fight a war against the South without fighting against slavery, the institution on which the South was so dependent, seemed absurd. As Frederick Douglass stated, "To fight against slaveholders, without fighting against slavery, is but a half-hearted business, and paralyzes the hands engaged in it. . . . Fire must be met with water. . . . War for the destruction of liberty must be met with war for the destruction of slavery."

Others were less charitable. Joseph R. Hawley, a white Connecticut Republican, thought Lincoln was foolish to worry about whether the border states might leave the Union: "Permit me to say damn the border states. . . . A thousand Lincolns cannot stop the people from fighting slavery." In the New York *Anglo-African*, a letter writer who identified himself as "Ivanhoe" urged northern black men to decline any request to serve in

contraband

Slaves who escaped to the Union or were captured by Union troops early in the Civil War; these slaves were considered enemy property.

First Confiscation Act

This 1861 Act stated that any slaves used by their masters to benefit the Confederacy would be freed.

These African-American troops served as teamsters for the Union Army in Virginia. Most northern white people—including political leaders—believed that black men lacked the courage and fortitude for combat. They expected black men would do little more as soldiers than haul freight, erect fortifications, serve guard duty, and prepare food.

Union military forces until the slaves were freed and black northerners received treatment equal to that of white people: "And suppose we were invited [to enlist], what duty would we then owe to ourselves and our posterity? . . . Our enslaved brethren must be made freedmen. . . . We of the North must have all of the rights which white men enjoy; until then we are in no condition to fight under the flag [which] gives us no protection."

Lincoln was unmoved. Union military forces occupied an enclave on South Carolina's southern coast and the sea islands in late 1861, and on May 9, 1862, General David Hunter ordered slavery abolished in South Carolina, Georgia, and Florida. Lincoln revoked Hunter's order and reprimanded him. Nevertheless, thousands of slaves along the South Carolina and Georgia coast threw off their shackles and welcomed Union troops as plantation owners fled to the interior.

11.2.3 Lincoln's Initial Position

For more than a year, Lincoln remained reluctant to strike decisively against slavery. He believed the long-term solution to slavery and the race problem in the United States was the **compensated emancipation** of slaves followed by their colonization outside the country. That is, slave owners would be paid for their slaves. The slaves would be freed but forced to settle in the Caribbean, Latin America, or West Africa.

compensated emancipation

Emancipation accompanied by the monetary compensation of former slave owners.

As a Whig congressman in 1849, Lincoln voted for a bill that would have emancipated slaves and compensated their owners in the District of Columbia if it had passed. In 1861 he tried—but failed—to persuade the Delaware legislature to support compensated emancipation. Then in April 1862, at Lincoln's urging, Republicans in Congress (against almost unanimous Democratic opposition) voted to provide funds to "any state which may adopt gradual abolishment of slavery." Lincoln wanted to eliminate slavery from the border states with the approval of slave owners there and thus diminish the likelihood that those states would join the Confederacy.

But leaders in the border states rejected the proposal. Lincoln brought it up again in July. This time he warned congressmen and senators from the border states that if their states opposed compensated emancipation, they might have to accept emancipation without compensation. They ignored his advice and denounced compensated emancipation as a "radical change in our social system" and an intrusion by the federal government into a state issue.

To many white Americans, Lincoln's support for compensated emancipation and colonization was a misguided attempt to link the war to the issue of slavery. But to black Americans, abolitionists, and an increasing number of Republicans, Lincoln's refusal to abolish slavery immediately was tragic. Antislavery advocates regarded Lincoln's willingness to purchase the freedom of slaves as an admission that he considered those human beings to be property. They deplored his seeming inability to realize the Union would not win the war unless slaves were liberated.

11.2.4 Lincoln Moves toward Emancipation

However, by the summer of 1862, after the border states rejected compensated emancipation, Lincoln concluded that victory and the future of the Union were tied directly to the issue of slavery. Therefore, slavery became the instrument Lincoln would use to hasten the end of the war and restore the Union. He told Secretary of the Navy Gideon Welles, "We must free the slaves or be ourselves subdued. The slaves were undeniably an element of strength to those who had their service, and we must decide whether that element should be with us or against us." Emancipation, Lincoln stressed, would "strike at the heart of the rebellion."

In cabinet meetings in July 1862, Lincoln discussed abolishing slavery. Except for Postmaster General Montgomery Blair, cabinet members supported emancipation.

Blair feared that eliminating slavery would cost the Republicans control of Congress in the fall elections. Secretary of State William H. Seward supported abolition but advised Lincoln not to issue a proclamation until the Union Army won a major victory. Otherwise, emancipation might look like the desperate gesture of the leader of a losing cause. Therefore, Lincoln accepted Seward's advice and postponed emancipation.

11.2.5 Lincoln Delays Emancipation

Nevertheless, word circulated that Lincoln intended to abolish slavery. However, weeks passed and slavery did not end. Frustrated abolitionists and Republicans attacked Lincoln. Frederick Douglass was exasperated with a president who had shown inexcusable deference to white southerners who had rebelled against the Union:

> Abraham Lincoln is no more fit for the place he holds than was [previous president] James Buchanan. . . . The country is destined to become sick of both [General George B.] McClellan and Lincoln, and the sooner the better. The one plays lawyer for the benefit of the rebels, and the other handles the army for the benefit of traitors. We should not be surprised if both should be hurled from their places before the rebellion is ended.

In his *Prayer of Twenty Millions*, Horace Greeley, editor of the *New York Tribune*, expressed his disappointment that the president had not moved promptly against slavery, the issue that had led the southern states to leave the Union and go to war: "We ask you to consider that Slavery [is the] inciting cause and sustaining base of treason. . . . We think timid counsels in such a crisis [are] calculated to prove perilous, probably disastrous." Greeley insisted that Lincoln should have long ago warned white southerners that secession would endanger slavery.

On August 22, 1862, Lincoln replied to Greeley and explained his priorities. Placing the preservation of the Union before freedom for the enslaved, Lincoln declared, "My paramount object in this struggle is to save the Union, and is not either to save or destroy slavery. If I could save the Union without freeing any slave I would do it; and if I could save it by freeing all the slaves, I would do it; and if I could do it by freeing some and leaving others alone, I would also do that." He concluded, "I have here stated my purpose according to my view of *official* duty, and I intend no modification of my oft-expressed *personal* wish that all men, everywhere, could be free."

11.2.6 Black People Reject Colonization

Lincoln's policy on emancipation had shifted dramatically, but he remained committed to colonization. On August 14, 1862, Lincoln invited black leaders to the White House and appealed for their support for colonization. After condemning slavery as "the greatest wrong inflicted on any people," he explained that white racism made it unwise for black people to remain in the United States. "Your race suffers very greatly, many of them, by living among us, while ours suffer from your presence. There is an unwillingness on the part of our people, harsh as it may be, for you free colored people to remain among us. . . . I do not mean to discuss this, but to propose it as a fact with which we have to deal. I cannot alter it if I would." Lincoln asked the black leaders to begin enlisting volunteers for a colonization project in Central America.

Most black people were unimpressed by Lincoln's words and unmoved by his advice. A black leader from Philadelphia condemned the president. "This is our country as much as it is yours, and we will not leave it." Frederick Douglass accused Lincoln of hypocrisy and claimed that support for colonization would lead white men "to commit all kinds of violence and outrage upon the colored people."

Lincoln would not retreat from his support for colonization. Attempts were already under way to put compensated emancipation and colonization into effect. In April 1862 Congress enacted a bill to pay District of Columbia slave owners up to $300 for each slave they freed and to provide $100,000 to support the voluntary colonization of the freed people in Haiti or Liberia. In 1863 the government tried to settle 453 black American colonists at Ile à Vache, an island near Haiti. The settlers suffered terribly from disease and starvation. This sorry attempt at government-sponsored colonization ended in 1864 when the navy returned 368 survivors to the United States.

11.2.7 The Preliminary Emancipation Proclamation

Preliminary Emancipation Proclamation

Proclamation issued on September 22, 1862, declaring that slaves residing in states still in rebellion on January 1, 1863, would be freed.

Finally, on September 22, 1862—more than two months after Lincoln first seriously considered freedom for the enslaved—the president issued the **Preliminary Emancipation Proclamation**. It came five days after General George B. McClellan's Army of the Potomac turned back an invasion of Maryland at Antietam by General Robert E. Lee's Army of Northern Virginia. This bloody but indecisive victory allowed Lincoln to justify emancipation. But his first proclamation freed no people that September—or during the rest of 1862; rather, it stipulated that anyone in bondage in states or parts of states still in rebellion on January 1, 1863, would be "thenceforward, and forever free." Lincoln's announcement gave the Confederate states 100 days to return to the Union. If any or all of those states rejoined the Union, the slaves there would remain in bondage. The Union would be preserved, and slavery would be maintained.

What were Lincoln's intentions? It might seem that he expected the Confederate leaders to give his offer serious consideration and perhaps return to the Union and thus was willing to free the slaves only as a last resort. But Lincoln knew there was virtually no chance that white southerners would return to the Union just because he had threatened to free their slaves. Most Confederates expected to win the war, thereby maintaining secession and safeguarding slavery. White southerners ridiculed the preliminary proclamation. Lincoln hoped, however, that the preliminary emancipation proclamation would prepare white northerners to accept freedom for slaves.

11.2.8 Northern Reaction to Emancipation

In the Union, the Preliminary Emancipation Proclamation was greeted with little enthusiasm. Most black people and abolitionists were, of course, gratified that Lincoln had finally issued the proclamation. Frederick Douglass was ecstatic. "We shout for joy that we live to record this righteous decree." In *The Liberator*, William Lloyd Garrison

During the Civil War, Abraham Lincoln met with a free black family on the lawn of the Executive Mansion. A white woman and Union soldier are observers.

wrote that it was "an act of immense historical consequence." But they also worried that—however remote the possibility—some slave states would return to the Union by January 1, denying freedom to those enslaved.

Many white northerners resented emancipation. One New York soldier, more concerned with defeating the South than freeing the slaves, reflected these views: "We must first conquer & then it's time enough to talk about the *dam'd niggers*." A northern newspaper editor vilified Lincoln as a "half-witted usurper" and the Proclamation as "monstrous, impudent, and heinous . . . insulting to God as to man, for it declares those 'equal' whom God created unequal."

Even before the announcement of emancipation, antiblack riots flared in the North. In Cincinnati in the summer of 1862, Irish dockworkers invaded black neighborhoods after black men had replaced the striking wharf hands along the city's riverfront. In Brooklyn, New York, Irish Americans burned a tobacco factory that employed black women and children.

11.2.9 Political Opposition to Emancipation

Northern Democrats almost unanimously opposed emancipation. They accused Lincoln and the Republicans of "fanaticism" and regretted that emancipation would liberate "two or three million semi savages" who would "overrun the North" and compete with white working people. The Democratic-controlled lower houses of the legislatures in Indiana and Illinois condemned the Proclamation as "wicked, inhuman, and unholy." Republicans recognized the hostility among many white northerners to black people. Senator Lyman Trumbull of Illinois conceded that "there is a very great aversion in the West—I know it to be so in my state—against having free negroes come among us. Our people want nothing to do with the negro."

And as some Republicans had predicted and feared, the Democrats capitalized on dissatisfaction with the war's progress and with Republican support for emancipation to make gains in the fall elections. New York and New Jersey elected Democratic governors, and Democrats won 34 more seats in the U.S. House of Representatives, although the Republicans retained a majority. Overjoyed Democrats proclaimed, "Abolition Slaughtered!" Republicans took solace that their losses were not greater.

11.3 The Emancipation Proclamation

Compare Abraham Lincoln's policy on slavery when the Civil War began in 1861 to his policy contained in the Emancipation Proclamation.

On January 1, 1863, Abraham Lincoln issued the **Emancipation Proclamation**. It was not the first step toward freedom; since 1861, several thousand slaves had already freed themselves. However, it was the first significant effort by Union authorities to assure freedom to nearly four million people of African descent who, with their ancestors, had been enslaved for 250 years in North America. The Civil War was now a war to make people free.

Black communities and many white people across the North celebrated. Church bells rang. Poems were written, and prayers of thanksgiving offered. Many considered it the most momentous day in American history since July 4, 1776. Frederick Douglass had difficulty describing the emotions of people in Boston when word reached the city late on the night of December 31 that Lincoln would

Emancipation Proclamation

Issued by President Abraham Lincoln on January 1, 1863, the Emancipation Proclamation freed slaves in areas of the Confederate states not under Union control.

The Emancipation Proclamation was essentially a military directive and not a ringing declaration of liberation. Nevertheless, its uninspiring words would free more than three million people from bondage by 1865. Decorative copies such as this circulated for many decades after the Civil War.

issue the Proclamation the next day. "The effect of this announcement was startling beyond description, and the scene was wild and grand. Joy and gladness exhausted all forms of expression, from shouts of praise to sobs and tears. . . . A Negro preacher, a man of wonderful vocal power, expressed the heartfelt emotion of the hour, when he led all voices in the anthem, 'Sound the loud timbrel o'er Egypt's dark sea, Jehovah hath triumphed, his people were free.'" Well into the twentieth century, New Year's Day was commemorated as Emancipation Day, a holiday black Americans zealously observed.

11.3.1 Limits of the Proclamation

Despite this excitement, the language of the Emancipation Proclamation was uninspired and unmoving. It lacked the eloquence of the Declaration of Independence or the address Lincoln would deliver after the Union victory at Gettysburg in July 1863. Lincoln dryly wrote that "as a fit and necessary measure for suppressing said rebellion . . . I do order and declare that all persons held as slaves within said designated States, and parts of States, are, and henceforth shall be free."

Moreover, by limiting emancipation to those states and areas still in rebellion, Lincoln did not include enslaved people in the four border states still in the Union or in areas of Confederate states that Union forces had already occupied. This included 48 counties in western Virginia that would soon become the state of West Virginia, parts of Tennessee, and 13 parishes (counties) in Louisiana, including New Orleans (see Map 11-1). Thus, thousands of people would remain in bondage despite the Proclamation. Slave owners in the Confederacy did not recognize Lincoln's authority, and

Map 11-1 Effects of the Emancipation Proclamation

When Abraham Lincoln issued the Emancipation Proclamation on January 1, 1863, it applied only to slaves in those portions of the Confederacy not under Union authority. No southern slave owners freed their slaves at Lincoln's command. But many black people already had freed themselves as well as family and friends in the aftermath of Lincoln's order. The Emancipation Proclamation was of extreme importance. It helped the Union win the war. It meant that at long last the U.S. government had joined the abolitionist movement.

Where, according to the map, did slaves reside who were to be freed under the terms of the Proclamation?

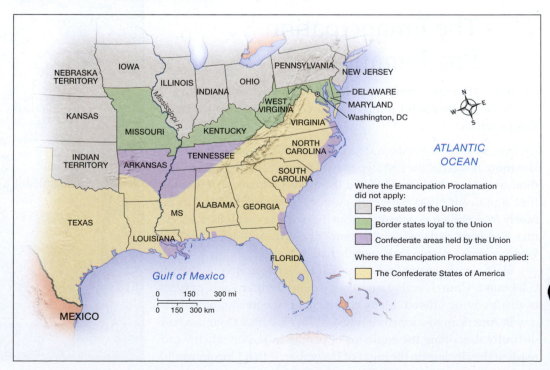

they certainly did not free their slaves on January 1 or anytime soon thereafter. Nevertheless, as many as 50,000 slaves liberated themselves in the days and weeks following Lincoln's proclamation. The Emancipation Proclamation remains one of the most important documents in American history. It made the Civil War a war to free people as well as to preserve the Union, and it gave the Union cause moral authority. And as many black people had freed themselves before the Proclamation, many more would liberate themselves after.

11.3.2 Effects of the Proclamation on the South

The Emancipation Proclamation destroyed any chance that Britain or France would offer diplomatic recognition to the Confederate government. Diplomatic recognition would have meant accepting the Confederacy as a legitimate state equal in international law to the Union, and it would almost surely have led to financial and military assistance for the South. British leaders, who had considered recognizing the Confederacy, now declined to support a "nation" that relied on slavery while its opponent moved to abolish it. In this sense, the Proclamation weakened the Confederacy's ability to prosecute the war.

Even more important, it undermined slavery in the South and contributed directly to the Confederacy's defeat. While the Proclamation may not have freed any of those in bondage on January 1, 1863, word of freedom spread rapidly across the South. Black people—aware a Union victory in the war meant freedom—were far less likely to labor for their owners or for the Confederacy. More slaves ran away, especially as Union troops

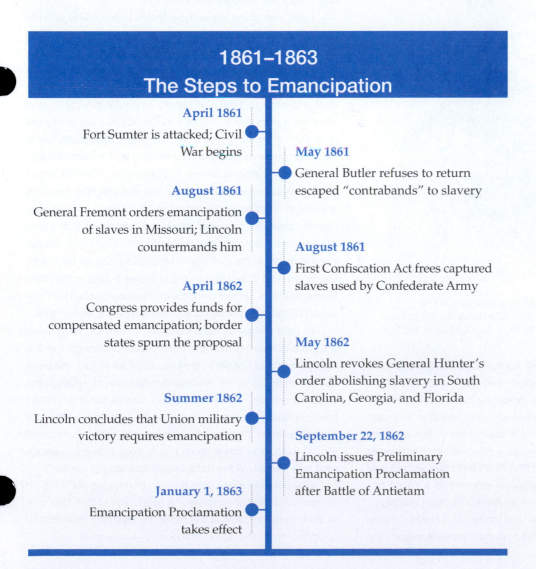

1861–1863
The Steps to Emancipation

April 1861
Fort Sumter is attacked; Civil War begins

May 1861
General Butler refuses to return escaped "contrabands" to slavery

August 1861
General Fremont orders emancipation of slaves in Missouri; Lincoln countermands him

August 1861
First Confiscation Act frees captured slaves used by Confederate Army

April 1862
Congress provides funds for compensated emancipation; border states spurn the proposal

May 1862
Lincoln revokes General Hunter's order abolishing slavery in South Carolina, Georgia, and Florida

Summer 1862
Lincoln concludes that Union military victory requires emancipation

September 22, 1862
Lincoln issues Preliminary Emancipation Proclamation after Battle of Antietam

January 1, 1863
Emancipation Proclamation takes effect

approached. Slave resistance became more likely, although Lincoln cautioned against insurrection in the Proclamation: "And I hereby enjoin upon the people so declared to be free to abstain from all violence, unless in necessary self-defence." The institution of slavery cracked, crumbled, and collapsed after January 1, 1863.

Without emancipation, the United States would not have survived as a unified nation. Abraham Lincoln, after first failing to make the connection between eliminating slavery and preserving the Union, came to understand it fully and grasped what freedom meant to both black and white people. In his annual message to Congress in December 1862, one month before the Proclamation, Lincoln described the importance of emancipation with

Profile

Elizabeth Keckley

Elizabeth Keckley employed 20 seamstresses in her Washington, D.C., shop by 1860. She designed the gown that Mary Todd Lincoln wore to the inaugural ball in 1861.

Born a slave in 1818, Elizabeth Keckley became a dressmaker for First Lady Mary Todd Lincoln and later wrote one of the first personal accounts of life inside the Lincoln White House. Elizabeth Keckley had experienced the exploitation and degradation common to thousands of slave women. She was born in Dinwiddie Court House, Virginia, and spent her childhood as a slave of the Burwell family. She saw slaves beaten and sold away from their families. She even watched as a young boy was sold away from his mother so his owner could buy pigs.

During adolescence, she was loaned to a North Carolina slave owner, where she was beaten and eventually raped. She described what happened: "I was regarded as fair-looking for one of my race, and for four years a white man—I spare the world his name—had base designs upon me. I do not care to dwell upon this subject for it is one that is fraught with pain. Suffice it to say that he persecuted me for four years, and I—I became a mother. The child of which he was the father was the only child I ever brought into the world."

Later, one of the Burwell daughters took Keckley and her son George to St. Louis. She already knew how to sew, and she became a proficient seamstress. She also married a slave, James Keckley, but they soon separated. Keckley was able to purchase herself and her son for $1,200. She also learned to read and write. In 1860 she moved to Washington, D.C., and attracted a prosperous clientele that included such prominent politicians' wives as Varma Davis, the wife of Mississippi Senator Jefferson Davis, soon to be president of the Confederacy.

After the Lincolns arrived in Washington, Keckley began making dresses for the First Lady and became Mrs. Lincoln's confidante and traveling companion. She helped convert Mrs. Lincoln, whose family owned slaves in Kentucky, to strong antislavery views. Both women lost sons. Keckley's son George was killed early in the Civil War in Missouri fighting for the Union. Eleven-year-old Willie Lincoln died of a fever in 1862 in the White House. With Mrs. Lincoln's assistance, Keckley founded the Contraband Relief Association to help former slaves in Washington.

In 1868 she published *Behind the Scenes: Or, Thirty Years a Slave and Four Years in the White House*. Although it was a favorable account of life in the Lincoln White House, the book upset the Lincoln family. Keckley denied she had violated Mrs. Lincoln's privacy. "If I have betrayed confidence in anything I have published it has been to place Mrs. Lincoln in better light before the world. My own character as well as the character of Mrs. Lincoln, is at stake, since I have been intimately associated with the lady in the most eventful periods of her life."

Elizabeth Keckley spent the rest of her own life living off the pension from her son's service as a Union soldier. She died in Washington in 1907 at the Home for Destitute Women and Children, which she had helped found years earlier.

a passion and with feelings that were absent in the Proclamation itself. "We know how to save the Union. The world knows we do know how to save it. We—even we here—hold the power, and bear the responsibility. In giving freedom to the slave, we assure freedom to the free—honorable alike in what we give, and what we preserve."

11.4 Black Men Fight for the Union

Summarize the contributions of African-American men and women to the Union war effort.

The Emancipation Proclamation not only marked the beginning of the end of slavery but also authorized the enlistment of black troops in the Union Army. Just as white leaders in the North came to realize the preservation of the Union necessitated the abolition of slavery, they also began to understand that black men were needed for the military effort if the Union was to triumph in the Civil War.

By early 1863 the war had not gone well for the all-white Union Army. Although Union forces had won victories in Kentucky and Tennessee and had captured New Orleans, the war in the east was a different matter (see Map 11-2). The Union's Army of the Potomac faced a smaller but highly effective Confederate Army—the Army of Northern Virginia—led by General Robert E. Lee. Confederate troops forced a Union retreat from Richmond during the 1862 Peninsular Campaign. Union forces lost at the first and second battles of Bull Run. Their only victory over Lee at Antietam was followed by a crushing Union loss at Fredericksburg.

Like the decision to free the slaves, the decision to employ black troops proceeded neither smoothly nor logically. The commitment to the Civil War as a white man's war was entrenched, and many white northerners opposed the initial attempts to enlist black troops. As with emancipation, Lincoln moved slowly from outright opposition to cautious acceptance to enthusiastic support for enlisting black men in the Union Army.

Although black men had fought well in the War for Independence and the War of 1812, they were legally prohibited from joining the regular U.S. Army. The Militia Act of 1792 also barred them from the state militias. In 1861 a few black men were able to join Union units and go off to war. H. Ford Douglas, who had a fair complexion, enlisted in the all-white 95th Illinois Infantry, a volunteer regiment.

11.4.1 The First South Carolina Volunteers

Some Union officers recruited black men long before emancipation was proclaimed and before most white northerners were prepared to accept, much less welcome, black troops. In May 1862 General David Hunter began recruiting former slaves along the South Carolina coast and the sea islands, an area Union forces had captured in late 1861. But some black men did not want to enlist, and Hunter used white troops to force black men to "volunteer" for military service. He managed to organize a 500-man regiment—the **First South Carolina Volunteers**.

The former slaves were outfitted in bright red pants, with blue coats and broad-brimmed hats. Through the summer of 1862, Hunter trained and drilled the regiment while awaiting official authorization and funds to pay them. When Congress balked, Hunter disbanded all but one company of the regiment that August. The troops were dispersed, unpaid and disappointed. The surviving company was sent to St. Simon's Island off the Georgia coast to protect former slaves.

Although Congress failed to support Hunter, it did pass the **Second Confiscation Act** and the **Militia Act of 1862**, which authorized President Lincoln to enlist black men. General Rufus Saxton gained the approval of Secretary of War Edwin Stanton to revive Hunter's dispersed regiment and to recall the company that had been sent to St. Simon's Island.

First South Carolina Volunteers

This black military unit consisted of former slaves recruited in the South Carolina and Georgia low country in 1862 and 1863 for service with Union military forces in the Civil War.

Second Confiscation Act

The 1862 Act freeing all slaves of rebel owners.

Militia Act of 1862

The 1862 Act authorizing Lincoln to enlist black soldiers.

Map 11-2 The Course of the Civil War

Although the outcome of the Civil War remained in doubt until the autumn of 1864, Union armies, as well as Union naval blockade, applied increasing pressure on the 11 Confederate states beginning in 1862. Black people freed themselves as Union forces carved out an enclave on the South Carolina coast, captured New Orleans, and pushed through Kentucky and Tennessee into Mississippi and Arkansas. Following the successful Union siege of Vicksburg in 1863, the Confederacy was divided along the Mississippi River. In 1864 General Ulysses S. Grant's Army of the Potomac drove General Robert E. Lee's Army of Northern Virginia into entrenchment around Richmond and Petersburg. General William Tecumseh Sherman marched from Atlanta to Savannah and then into the Carolinas. Several thousand more black people liberated themselves. The war ended in April 1865 with Lee's surrender to Grant at Appomattox Court House and Joseph E. Johnston's capitulation to Sherman near Durham, North Carolina.

Based on an examination of these maps, what appears to have been the strategy of Union military forces to defeat the Confederacy?

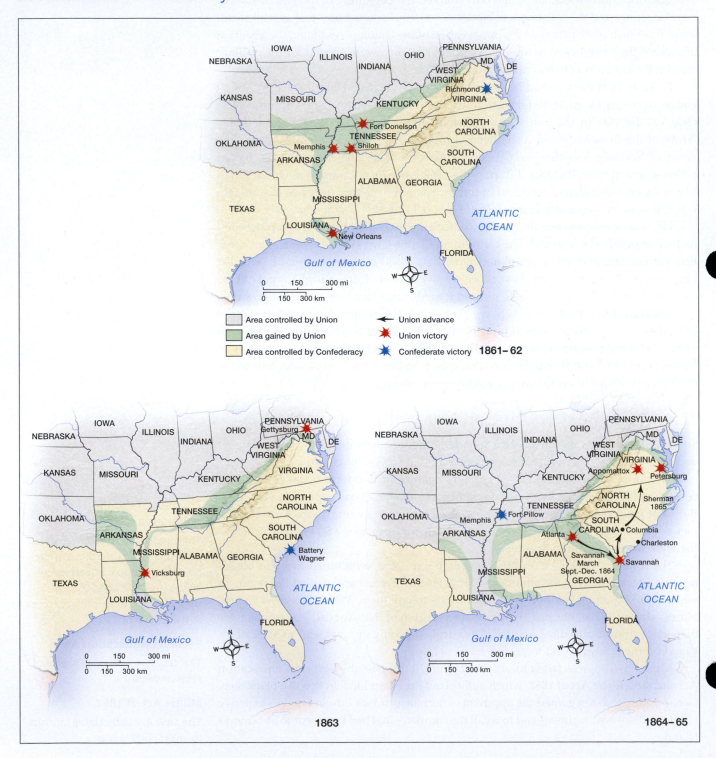

As commander, Saxton appointed Thomas Wentworth Higginson. Higginson was an ardent white abolitionist, one of the Secret Six who had provided financial support for John Brown's raid on Harpers Ferry. He was determined not merely to end slavery but to prove that black people were equal to white people, a proposition most white people regarded as preposterous. Disposing of the unit's gaudy red trousers, Higginson set out to mold this regiment of mostly former slaves into an effective fighting force. On Emancipation Day, January 1, 1863, near Beaufort, South Carolina, the First South Carolina Volunteer Regiment was inducted into the U.S. Army and later became the 33rd U.S. Colored Infantry.

11.4.2 The Louisiana Native Guards

After Louisiana seceded from the Union and joined the Confederacy, the governor called for men to volunteer for service in the state militia. More than 1,500 free men of color declared their willingness to serve Louisiana and the Confederacy in April 1861, and they joined the Louisiana Native Guards. Some of them were slave own-ers. Louisiana's legislature later that year enacted a measure that limited service in the militia to white males. The Native Guards were forced to disband—temporarily as it turned out.

In September 1862 the Louisiana Native Guards reorganized in support of the Union cause. It now consisted of black men who had been free before the war as well as others who had been slaves. They were led by black officers. In time the 1st, 2nd, and 3rd Louisiana Native Guards became the 73rd, 74th, and 75th U.S. Colored Infantry. But they lost most of their black officers. Union military commander General Nathaniel Banks had little confidence in the leadership abilities of the black officers, and most of them were replaced by white men.

The Louisiana troops joined white Union military forces in May 1863 in a frontal assault on Port Hudson, a key Confederate fortification overlooking the Mississippi River north of New Orleans. The attack failed, but the black soldiers distinguished themselves. One observer reported: "They fought with great desperation, and carried all before them. They had to be restrained for fear they would get too far unsupported. They have shown they can and will fight."

One of the men killed at Port Hudson was Captain Andre Cailloux, one of the few black officers who did not lose his position to a white man. Cailloux had been prominent among free people of color in New Orleans prior to the Civil War. Edu-cated in Paris, he was fluent in English and French. Proud of his African heritage, Cailloux declared that he was the blackest man in New Orleans. His right arm was shattered at Port Hudson, but he continued to lead his troops until he was killed by a second shell.

The bodies of the black men who fell at Port Hudson remained on the bat-tlefield for weeks after the remains of Confederate and white Union soldiers had been recovered under a flag of truce that did not apply to black troops. Thousands of black people turned out to honor Cailloux when his funeral was finally held in New Orleans.

11.4.3 The Second South Carolina Volunteers

In early 1863 the Second South Carolina Volunteers began enrolling ex-slaves, many from Georgia and Florida. James Montgomery, another former financial supporter of John Brown, commanded them. Montgomery was determined that the regiment would wipe out all vestiges of slavery, especially the homes, plantations, and per-sonal possessions of families who owned slaves. Montgomery found that many for-mer slaves were reluctant to volunteer for military service, so he also used force to recruit them. He concluded that black men responded to the call to arms much the way white men did, except black men were less likely to desert once they joined the army:

> Finding it somewhat difficult to induce Negroes to enlist, we resolved to the draft. The negroes reindicate their claim to humanity by shirking the draft in every possible way; acting exactly like white men under similar circumstances. . . . The only difference that I notice is, the negro, after being drafted does not desert; but once dressed in the uniform with arms in his hands he feels himself a man; and acts like one.

11.4.4 The 54th Massachusetts Regiment

54th Massachusetts Regiment

This all-black volunteer infantry regiment was recruited in the northern states for service with Union military forces in the Civil War. It was made up almost entirely of black men who had been free. It was commanded by white officers.

Black Committee

An organization of prominent black men in the North who assisted in recruiting African Americans to fight for the Union in the Civil War.

While ex-slaves joined the Union ranks in Louisiana and South Carolina, free black men in the North enlisted in what would become the most famous black unit, the **54th Massachusetts Regiment**. In January 1863 Governor John A. Andrew received permission from Secretary of War Stanton to raise a black regiment; however, because few black men lived in Massachusetts, Andrew asked prominent black men across the North for help. The **Black Committee**—as it became known—included Frederick Douglass, Martin Delany, Charles Remond, and Henry Highland Garnet.

These black leaders were convinced that by serving in the military, black men would prove they deserved to be treated as equals and had earned the right to be citizens. Frederick Douglass put it succinctly: "Once let the black man get upon his person the brass letters, U.S.; let him get an eagle on his button, and a musket on his shoulder and bullets in his pocket, and there is no power on earth which can deny that he has earned the right to citizenship." Douglass's sons, Charles and Lewis, joined the 54th.

Lincoln, who had opposed emancipation and resisted enlisting black troops, became an enthusiastic supporter of black men in the Union Army. Writing to Andrew Johnson, the Union military governor of Tennessee, Lincoln perhaps overoptimistically predicted that, "the bare sight of fifty thousand armed, and drilled black soldiers on the banks of the Mississippi, would end the rebellion at once. And who doubts that we can present that sight, if we but take hold in earnest."

Governor John A. Andrew selected 25-year-old Robert Gould Shaw to command the 54th Massachusetts Regiment. Shaw was a Harvard graduate from a prominent Massachusetts family, and he had already been wounded at the Battle at Antietam. Although not an active abolitionist, he opposed slavery and was determined to prove that black men would fight well. The men the Black Committee recruited came from most of the northern states. Their average age was around 25, and virtually all of them were literate. They were farmers, seamen, butchers, blacksmiths, and teamsters. Only one of them had grown up in a slave state. As the ranks of the 54th filled, the 55th Massachusetts Regiment and the all-black 5th Massachusetts Cavalry Regiment were also formed.

On May 28, 1863, the 54th paraded through Boston to board a ship for the trip to South Carolina and the war. Thousands turned out to see the black men in blue uniforms. As they passed the home of fiery abolitionist William Lloyd Garrison, he stood erect with a bust of John Brown. As they passed the Old Statehouse where Crispus Attucks and four others had been killed in the Boston Massacre in 1770, the regiment sang "John Brown's Body." The departure of the 54th from the city was perhaps the most emotional event Boston had witnessed since Anthony Burns had been forcibly returned to slavery in 1854.

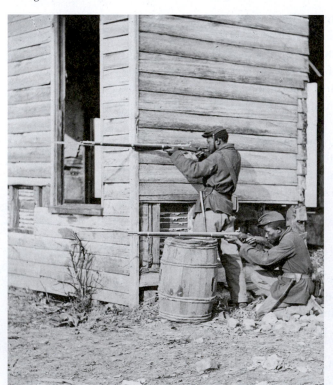

Poised with their rifles, these African-American soldiers were members of the Twenty-first U.S. Colored Infantry at the battle of Dutch Gap in Virginia in August 1864.

11.4.5 Black Soldiers Confront Discrimination

However, the enthusiastic departure could not disguise the discrimination and hostility that black troops faced during the war. Many white northerners would accept neither the presence of black troops nor the idea that black men could endure combat. Many white people tolerated black troops only because they preferred that a black man die rather than a white man. A crude bit of verse in an Irish dialect that reflected this racism circulated during the war:

Sambo's Right to Be Kilt

Some tell us 'tis a burnin' shame
To Make the naygers fight;
And that the thrade of bein' kilt
Belongs but to the white;
But as for me, upon my sowl!
So liberal are we here,
I'll let Sambo be murthered instead of myself,
On every day of the Year.

In the same vein, a white Union soldier wrote that a "Negro can fall from a rebel shot as well as me or my friends, and better them than us."

That black troops would serve in separate, all-black units was a matter of course. No one seriously proposed that black men integrate all-white regiments. In 1863 the War Department created the Bureau of Colored Troops, and the Union Army remained segregated throughout the war. The only exceptions were the officers of the black regiments.

Almost all black troops had white officers. Yet many white officers, convinced such service would taint their military record, refused to command black troops. Others believed black men could not be trained for combat. Even those white officers who were willing to command black troops sometimes regarded their men as "niggers" suited only for work or fatigue duty. When the 110th U.S. Colored Infantry joined General William Tecumseh Sherman's army on its march through Georgia and South Carolina in 1864 and 1865, Sherman kept them out of combat. Some were armed with picks and axes. Others served as hospital guards and teamsters.

Black soldiers were paid less than white soldiers. Based on the assumption that black troops would be used almost exclusively for construction, transportation, cooking, and burial details, and not for fighting, the War Department authorized a lower pay scale for them. A white private earned $13 per month, a black private $10 per month. This demoralized black soldiers, particularly after they had shown they were more than capable of fighting.

The 54th Massachusetts Regiment refused to accept their pay until they received equal pay. To take no compensation was an enormous sacrifice for men who had wives, children, and families to support. For some, however, it was more than a monetary loss. Sergeant William Walker insisted—despite orders—that the men in his company take no pay until they received equal pay. He was charged with mutiny, convicted, and executed by firing squad. In Texas, a soldier in a black artillery unit from Rhode Island threatened a white officer in the dispute over pay. The white lieutenant shot and killed him, and the regiment's commander declined to press charges.

The pay issue festered for nearly two years. Finally, near the end of the war, Congress enacted a compromise, but many black soldiers remained dissatisfied. The law equalized pay between black and white troops but made it retroactive only to January 1, 1864—except for black men who had never been slaves. Therefore, the thousands of black men who had been slaves and had joined the military before January 1, 1864, would not be entitled to equal pay for the entire period of their service. The War Department compounded the problem with bureaucratic delays.

11.4.6 Black Men in Combat

Once black men put on the Union uniform, they took part in almost every battle that was fought during the rest of the Civil War. Black troops not only faced an enemy dedicated to the belief that black people belonged in slavery but also confronted white northerners' doubts about their willingness to fight. Yet by war's end, black units had suffered disproportionately more casualties than white units.

In October 1862, the first black unit went into combat in Missouri. James H. Lane, a white Free-Soiler, recruited 500 black men in Kansas. Most were runaway slaves from Missouri and Arkansas. After hasty training, they advanced against a Confederate position at Island Mountain. The black troop held off an attack until reinforcements repulsed the Confederates. Soon thereafter the black unit became the First Kansas Colored Infantry.

On July 17, 1863, at Honey Springs in Indian Territory (now Oklahoma), the Kansas soldiers attacked a Confederate force of white Texans and Cherokee Indians. After a 20-minute battle, the black troops broke through the southern line, won a victory, and captured the flags of a Texas regiment. In January 1863, Thomas Wentworth Higginson led the First South Carolina Volunteers on raids on the Georgia and Florida coasts. At one point, they were surrounded at night by Confederate cavalry but fought their way out and escaped. And in May 1863, the Louisiana Native Guards had joined with white Union troops in the failed attempt to capture Port Hudson on the Mississippi River. On June 3, 1863, the 54th Massachusetts Regiment arrived in South Carolina and joined the raids in Georgia. Other raids in the Carolina low country devastated rice plantations and liberated hundreds of slaves.

11.4.7 The Assault on Battery Wagner

Since 1861 and the Confederate capture of Fort Sumter in Charleston Harbor, Union leaders had been determined to retake the fort and occupy nearby Charleston—the heart of secession. In 1863 Union commanders began a land and sea offensive to seize

This young man is Jackson. In the first photo he is shown as a slave who worked as a servant in the Confederate Army. In the second photo he has been freed and has joined the U.S. Colored Troops as a drummer.

the fort. But **Battery Wagner**, a fortified installation on the northern tip of Morris Island, guarded the entrance to the harbor.

Frustrated in their efforts to enter the harbor, Major General Quincy A. Gilmore and Rear Admiral John Dahlgren decided on a full-scale assault on Wagner. After an unsuccessful attack by white troops, Colonel Shaw volunteered to lead the 54th in a second attack on the battery.

To improve the Union's chances, artillery fired more than 9,000 shells on Wagner on July 18, 1863. Everyone but the fort's Confederate defenders was convinced that no one could survive the bombardment. In fact, it had killed only eight of the 1,620 defenders.

At sunset, 650 men of the first brigade of the 54th prepared to lead more than 5,000 Union troops in storming the battery. The regiment was tired and hungry but eager for the assault. Colonel Shaw told his troops, "Now I want you to prove yourselves men."

At 7:45 P.M., the 54th charged and was met by heavy rifle and artillery fire. Within minutes, the sand was littered with injured and dying men. Sergeant Major Lewis Douglass (the son of Frederick Douglass) was among those who took part. The 54th reached the walls, only to be thrown back in hand-to-hand combat. Shaw was killed.

Sergeant Major William H. Carney, although wounded four times, saved the regiment's flags. In May 1900, he was awarded the Medal of Honor for his gallantry that night.

Although white troops supported the 54th, the attack could not be sustained, and the battle was over by 1:00 A.M. But within days, the courage of the 54th was known across the North, putting to rest—for a time—the myth that black men lacked the nerve to fight.

The day after the attack, Shaw and 20 of his men were buried in a trench outside Wagner. Several wounded men had drowned when the tide came in. Altogether 246 black and white men were killed, 890 were wounded, and 391 were taken prisoner. Forty-two percent of the men of the 54th were killed or injured, and 80 men were taken prisoner.

Union forces never took Wagner. The Confederates abandoned Charleston as the war was ending in February 1865. Black Union troops—the 21st U.S. Colored Infantry and the 55th Massachusetts Regiment—occupied the city. Years later Charles Crowley recalled the scene: "Never, while memory holds power to retain anything, shall I forget the thrilling strain of music of the Union, as sung by our sable soldiers when marching up Meeting Street with the battle stained banners flapping in the breeze."

Battery Wagner

This defensive fortification guarded Fort Sumter near the entrance to Charleston Harbor in South Carolina. It was the scene in July 1863 of a major Union assault by the 54th Massachusetts Regiment, a black unit. The assault failed, but the bravery and valor of the black troops earned them fame and glory.

On the evening of July 18, 1863, more than 600 black men led by their white commander, Colonel Robert Gould Shaw, attacked the heavily fortified Battery Wagner on Morris Island near the southern approach to Charleston harbor. They made a frontal assault through withering fire and managed to breach the battery before Confederate forces threw them back. Shaw was killed, and the 54th suffered heavy losses. It was a defining moment of the Civil War, demonstrating to skeptical white people the valor and determination of black troops.

Voices

Lewis Douglass Describes the Fighting at Battery Wagner

After the failed assault on Battery Wagner, Lewis Douglass wrote this letter home to his wife Amelia.

July 20 [1863]

Lewis Douglass

My Dear Amelia:

I have been in two fights, and am unhurt. I am about to go in another I believe tonight. Our men fought well on both occasions. The last one was desperate. We charged that terrible battery on . . . Fort Wagner and were repulsed. . . . I escaped unhurt from amidst that perfect hail of shot and shell. It was terrible. . . . This regiment has established its reputation as a fighting regiment. Not a man flinched, though it was a trying time. Men fell all around me. . . . Our men would close

up again, but it was no use. . . . How I got out of that fight alive I cannot tell, but I am here. My dear girl, I hope again to see you. I must bid you farewell should I be killed. Remember if I die, I die in a good cause. I wish we had a hundred thousand colored troops. We would put an end to this war.

Your own loving

Lewis

1. How does Douglass describe combat?
2. What motivated him and his fellow troops?
3. Does this account of combat differ in any way from the way a white soldier might describe it?

SOURCE: Lewis Douglass's letter to his wife Amelia, July 20, 1863.

11.4.8 Olustee

On February 20, 1864, the 54th fought again and was joined by two black regiments—the First North Carolina and the Eighth U.S. of Pennsylvania—and six white regiments at the Battle at Olustee in northern Florida. After almost five hours of combat, Confederate troops forced a Union retreat. The 54th had marched 110 miles in 100 hours before entering the engagement.

11.4.9 The Crater

As impressive as black troops often were in battle, northern commanders sometimes hesitated to commit them to combat. In 1864, after Union troops laid siege to Petersburg, Virginia, white soldiers of the 48th Pennsylvania, who had been coal miners before the war, offered to dig a tunnel and set off an explosion under Confederate lines. General Ambrose Burnside assigned black troops to prepare to lead the attack after the blast.

Four tons of powder were placed in the tunnel; however, only hours before the blast was set to go off, Burnside's superior, General George Meade, replaced the black troops with inadequately trained white soldiers commanded by an alcoholic. Meade either lacked confidence in the black unit or was worried he would be blamed for using black men as shields for white soldiers if the attack failed.

On July 30, 1864, at 4:45 A.M., what was perhaps the largest man-made explosion in history up to that time buried a Confederate regiment and an artillery battery and created a crater 170 feet long, 60 feet wide, and 30 feet deep. But the white Union troops rushed down into the crater instead of fanning out around it in pursuit of the stunned enemy. While the Union soldiers marveled at the destruction, the Confederates counterattacked and threw back the Union troops, including the black troops, who were finally brought forward. Some black men were murdered after they surrendered. More than 4,000 Union troops, many of them black, were killed or wounded.

11.4.10 The Confederate Reaction to Black Soldiers

On June 7, 1863, Confederate forces attempting to relieve the Union siege of Vicksburg attacked black Union troops at Milliken's Bend on the Mississippi River. Although armed with outdated muskets and not fully trained, the defenders fought off the Confederate attack. Assistant Secretary of War Charles A. Dana claimed that their valor would change the attitudes of white people toward the use of black troops: "The bravery of the blacks completely revolutionized the sentiment of the army with regard to the employment of negro troops. I heard prominent officers who formerly in private sneered at the idea of negroes fighting express themselves after that as heartily in favor of it."

The southern soldiers who lost at Milliken's Bend, however, felt differently. Enraged by having to fight black troops, they executed several black prisoners and sold others into slavery.

11.4.11 The Abuse and Murder of Black Troops

Confederate leaders and troops refused to recognize black men as legitimate soldiers. Captured black soldiers were abused and even murdered rather than treated as prisoners of war. Confederate Secretary of War James A. Seddon ordered that captured black soldiers be executed: "We ought never to be inconvenienced with such prisoners . . . summary execution must therefore be inflicted on those taken."

Protests erupted across the North after Confederate authorities decided to treat 80 men of the 54th Massachusetts Regiment who had been captured in the attack on Battery Wagner not as prisoners of war but as rebellious slaves. Frederick Douglass refused to recruit any more black men and held Abraham Lincoln personally responsible for tolerating the mistreatment of black prisoners: "How many 54ths must be cut to pieces, its mutilated prisoners killed, and its living sold into slavery, to be tortured to death by inches, before Mr. Lincoln shall say, 'Hold, enough!' "

Lincoln issued **General Order 11**, threatening to execute southern troops or confine them to hard labor: "For every soldier of the United States killed in violation of the laws of war a rebel soldier shall be executed, and for every one enslaved by the enemy or sold into slavery a rebel soldier shall be placed at hard labor on the public works, and continued at such labor until the other shall be released and receive the treatment due to a prisoner of war."

General Order 11

Order threatening retaliation for the mistreatment of black soldiers by Confederate forces.

Lincoln's order did not prevent the Confederates from sending the men of the 54th to trial by the state of South Carolina. The state regarded the black soldiers as either rebellious slaves or free black men inciting rebellion. Four black soldiers went on trial in Charleston police court, but the court declared it lacked jurisdiction. The black prisoners were eventually sent to prisoner-of-war camps.

11.4.12 The Fort Pillow Massacre

The war's worst atrocity against black troops occurred at **Fort Pillow** in Tennessee on April 12, 1864. Confederates under the command of Nathan Bedford Forrest slaughtered 300 black troops and their white commander, William F. Bradford, after many of them had surrendered. (After the Civil War, Forrest gained notoriety as a founder of the Ku Klux Klan. Before the war he had been a slave trader.) The Fort Pillow Massacre became the subject of an intense debate in Lincoln's cabinet. But rather than retaliate indiscriminately—as General Order 11 required—the cabinet decided to punish only those responsible for the killings, if and when they were apprehended. But no one was punished during or after the war. Instead, black troops exacted revenge themselves. In fighting around Petersburg later that year, black soldiers shouting "Remember Fort Pillow!" reportedly murdered several Confederate prisoners. Captain Charles Francis Adams, Jr. reported, "The darkies fought ferociously. . . . If they murdered prisoners, as I hear they did . . . they can hardly be blamed." Confederate troops committed many other racial atrocities during the remainder of the war.

Fort Pillow

This fort on the east bank of the Mississippi River north of Memphis, Tennessee, was the scene of a massacre of black Union troops as well as some white soldiers and officers by Confederate cavalry in April 1864.

On their own, Union commanders in the field also retaliated for the Confederate treatment of captured black troops. When captured black men were virtually enslaved and forced to work at Richmond and Charleston on Confederate fortifications that were

In April 1864 1,500 Confederate forces under General Nathan Bedford Forrest attacked and captured Fort Pillow, a Union installation on the Mississippi River 40 miles north of Memphis, Tennessee, that was defended by 550 black and white troops. After the Union forces surrendered, Confederate troops executed some of the black soldiers. Forrest and his men denied the atrocity, but there is little doubt it occurred.

under Union attack, Union officers put Confederate prisoners to work on Union installations that were under fire. Aware they were not likely to be treated as well as white soldiers if they were captured, black men often fought desperately.

11.4.13 Black Men in the Union Navy

Black men had a tradition of serving at sea and had been in the U.S. Navy almost continuously since its creation in the 1790s. In the early nineteenth century, there were so many black sailors that some white people tried to ban black men from the navy. However, black sailors did not serve in segregated units. Naval crews were integrated.

Voices

A Black Nurse on the Horrors of War and the Sacrifice of Black Soldiers

Susie King Taylor was born a slave in Georgia and learned to read and write in Savannah. She escaped to Union forces in 1862 and served as a nurse and laundress with the First South Carolina Volunteers. In these passages, written years later, she recalls her service with the black men who went into combat and pays tribute to them.

It seems strange how our aversion to seeing suffering is overcome in war,—how we are able to see the most sickening sights, such as men with their limbs blown off and mangled by the deadly shells, without a shudder; and instead of turning away, how we hurry to assist in alleviating their pain, bind up their wounds, and press the cool water to their parched lips, with feelings only of sympathy and pity. . . .

I look around now and see the comforts that our younger generation enjoy, and think of

the blood that was shed to make these comforts possible for them, and see how little some of them appreciate the old soldiers. My heart burns within me at this want of appreciation. There are only a few of them left now, so let us all, as the ranks close, take a deeper interest in them. Let the younger generation take an interest also, and remember that it was through the efforts of these veterans that we older ones enjoy our liberty today.

1. How does Taylor describe what men in combat endure?
2. Who is the object of Taylor's criticism, and why does she offer it?

SOURCE: Susie King Taylor, *Reminiscences of My Life in Camp* (Boston: Taylor, 1902), 31–32, 51–52.

Nonetheless, black sailors encountered rampant discrimination and exploitation during the Civil War. They were paid less than white sailors. They were assigned the hardest and filthiest tasks, such as loading coal and tending the boilers, on the navy's new steam-powered vessels. Many were stewards who waited on white officers. White officers and sailors often treated black sailors with contempt. On the USS *Constellation* in 1863, white crew members regularly referred to the 33 black sailors as "God-damned nigger," "black dog," and "black bitches" and kicked and swore at them.

Some white men, however, admired the black sailors. One observed, "We never were betrayed when we trusted one of them, they were always our friends and were ready, if necessary, to lay down their lives for us." (He did not say whether white men were willing to lay down their lives for black men.) About 17,000, or over 20 percent, of the men who served in the Union Navy during the war were black sailors.

11.4.14 Liberators, Spies, and Guides

Besides serving as soldiers and sailors, black men and women aided themselves and the Union cause as liberators, spies, guides, and messengers. At about 3:00 A.M. on May 13, 1862, Robert Smalls, a 23-year-old slave, fired the boiler on the *Planter*, a Confederate supply ship moored in Charleston Harbor. With the aid of seven black crewmen, Smalls sailed the *Planter* past Confederate fortifications, including Fort Sumter, to the Union fleet outside the harbor and to freedom. Smalls liberated himself and 15 other slaves, including the families of several crewmen and his own wife, daughter, and son.

Smalls managed the daring escape because he knew the South Carolina coast and was familiar with Confederate navigation signals and regulations. He became an overnight hero in the North, a slave who wanted freedom and had possessed the leadership, knowledge, and tenacity to liberate 16 people.

In 1863 Harriet Tubman organized a spy ring in the South Carolina low country, and in cooperation with the all-black Second South Carolina Volunteer Regiment, she helped organize an expedition that destroyed plantations and freed nearly 800 slaves, many of whom joined the Union Army.

In Richmond in 1864, slaves helped more than 100 escaped Union prisoners of war. Other slaves drew sketches and maps of Confederate fortifications and warned Union forces about troop movements. A black couple near Fredericksburg, Virginia, cleverly transmitted military intelligence to Union general Joseph Hooker. The woman washed laundry for a Confederate officer and hung shirts and blankets in patterns that conveyed information to her husband, a cook and groom for Union troops, and he relayed the information to Union officers.

Mary Elizabeth Bowser was a former slave who worked as a servant at the Confederate White House in Richmond. She overheard conversations by President Jefferson Davis and his subordinates, and—because she was literate—she covertly examined Confederate correspondence. She relayed the information to Union agents until the Confederates became suspicious. Bowser and slave Jim Pemberton fled after trying to burn down the mansion to distract their pursuers.

Robert Smalls was born a slave in Beaufort, South Carolina in 1839. In May 1862 while still a slave and working as a pilot in Charleston on a 150-foot Confederate vessel, the *Planter*, Smalls devised an audacious plan to seize the ship. With the ship's white officers enjoying a night on the town, Smalls sailed the *Planter* with family and friends aboard to the Union Navy outside the harbor. Smalls's exploits created a sensation in the North. He went on to become a successful Republican politician in South Carolina in the decades following the Civil War.

Profile

Harriet Tubman

Harriet Tubman ca. 1819–1913, African-American abolitionist and activist in the Underground Railroad.

Long before her death in 1913, Harriet Tubman had achieved legendary status. Although she never led a slave revolt like Nat Turner or Joseph Cinque, she freed more slaves than any other individual in American history.

Thomas Wentworth Higginson, commander of the First South Carolina Volunteers, called her "the greatest heroine of the age. Her tales of adventure are beyond anything in fiction and her ingenuity and generalship are extraordinary. I have known her for some time—the slaves call her Moses."

Tubman was born in 1821 or 1822 on Maryland's eastern shore, one of 11 slave children of Harriet Greene and Benjamin Ross. While a teenager, she was struck in the head by a rock or chunk of metal hurled by an overseer at a fleeing slave. The incident left her plagued by seizures and with an ugly scar that she sometimes covered with a turban.

In 1849 she married John Tubman, a free black man. Fearing that she would be sold after the death of her owner, she escaped to Pennsylvania, but her husband refused to go with her. He married another woman and died after the Civil War.

Tubman—like Sojourner Truth—never learned to read or write. However, her religious faith sustained her and helped inspire her return to slave states again and again to free people held in bondage. She made at least 15 trips south in 10 years as a conductor on the Underground Railroad.

With the support of William Still and the General Vigilance Committee in Philadelphia and Quaker abolitionist Thomas Garrett in Wilmington, Delaware, she led between 70 and 80 people to freedom on 14 trips to Maryland's Eastern Shore between 1849 and 1860. Among them were her sister, her sister's two children, and her parents. Tubman also helped as many as 200 other people escape slavery. She never lost a passenger.

Aware that she had a reward on her head, Tubman devised detailed plans and elaborate disguises to elude capture. She feigned insanity, pretended to be feeble, forged passes, and acquired real railroad tickets. She also packed a gun, as much to goad any of her charges whose courage might waver as to protect herself.

In 1862, during the Civil War, Tubman journeyed to the South Carolina low country, where Union military forces had established a base. She worked as a nurse, cook, scout, and liberator. She made her way up the Combahee River and helped more than 700 slaves to freedom. She was on Morris Island in 1863 when the 54th Massachusetts Regiment attacked Battery Wagner.

After the war, she married Nelson Davis, a Union veteran who died in 1888. She and her supporters spent years in an effort to gain her federal pension. She finally secured an award of $20 a month that was based on her husband's military service rather than her own contributions to the Union cause.

Tubman was active in the women's rights movement of the late nineteenth century. She attended several women's rights conventions and befriended Susan B. Anthony. She also helped elderly ex-slaves who faced insecurity and uncertainty after emancipation. She bought a home in Auburn, New York, and eventually died there.

Many Americans talk about freedom, but not many have done as much to make it a reality for as many people as did Harriet Tubman.

In Virginia's Shenandoah Valley, slave John Henry Woodson was a guide for Union General Philip H. Sheridan's cavalry in 1864 and 1865. Woodson was the father of Carter G. Woodson, who would become the "father" of black history in the twentieth century.

11.4.15 Violent Opposition to Black People

No matter how well black men fought, no matter how much individual black women contributed, and no matter how many people—black and white—died "to make men free," many white northerners, both civilian and military, remained bitter and often violently hostile to black people. They used intimidation, threats, and terror to injure and kill people of color.

THE NEW YORK CITY DRAFT RIOT   Irish Catholic Americans, themselves held in contempt by prosperous white Protestants, indulged in an orgy of violence in New York City in July 1863. The New York draft riot arose from racial, religious, and class antagonisms. Democrats, including New York Governor Horatio Seymour, convinced poor, unskilled Irish workers and other white northerners that the war had become a crusade to benefit black people.

The violence began when federal officials prepared to select the first men to be drafted by the Union for military service. An enraged mob of mostly Irish men attacked the draft offices and any black people who were around. Many of the Irish men were angry because black men had replaced striking Irish stevedores on the city's wharves the month before and because rich white northerners could purchase an exemption from the draft.

The riot went on for four days. The police could not control it. Black people were beaten and lynched. The Colored Orphan Asylum was burned to the ground, although the children had already fled. The mob attacked businesses that employed black people. Protestant churches were burned. Rioters set fire to Horace Greeley's *New York Tribune*. The houses of Republicans and abolitionists were destroyed. The violence did not end until the army arrived. Soldiers who had been fighting Confederates at Gettysburg two weeks earlier found themselves firing on New York rioters.

THE RIOTS IN NEW YORK: THE MOB LYNCHING A NEGRO IN CLARKSON-STREET.—SEE PAGE 142.

During the draft riot in New York City in July 1863, black people were attacked, beaten, and killed. A mob lynched this black man near Clarkson Street.

11.4.16 Union Troops and Slaves

White Union troops who brutalized southern freedmen sometimes exceeded the savagery of northern civilians. In November 1861 men from the 47th New York Regiment raped an eight-year-old black girl. Later, in Virginia, a Connecticut soldier revealed what men in his regiment did to a pair of black women. They took "two niger wenches . . . turned them on their heads, & put tobacco, chips, sticks, lighted cigars & sand into their behinds." On Sherman's march through Georgia in 1864, a drunken Irish soldier from an Ohio regiment shot into a crowd of black children, wounding one youngster. He was tried and convicted but released on a technicality and returned to the army.

However, some Union soldiers wanted to fight for the liberation of black people. One Wisconsin private wrote, "I have no heart in this war if the slaves cannot be free." The desire of slaves for freedom moved many. A Union officer noted that those who believed slaves were satisfied with slavery were wrong. "It is claimed the negroes are so well contented with their slavery; if it ever was so, that day has ceased." Several Union soldiers wept when they witnessed a daughter reunited with her mother 10 years after a slave sale had separated them.

11.4.17 Refugees

Throughout the war, black people freed themselves. It was not easy. Confederate authorities did not hesitate to reenslave or even execute black people who sought freedom. In 1862, six black people were hanged near Georgetown, South Carolina, when they were captured trying to reach Union forces.

As Union armies plunged deep into the Confederacy in 1863 and 1864, thousands of black people liberated themselves and became refugees. When General William Tecumseh Sherman's army of 60,000 troops laid waste to Georgia in 1864, an estimated 10,000 former slaves followed his troops to Savannah, although they lacked adequate food, clothing, and housing. Sherman did not like black people, and his troops tried to discourage the refugees. As one elderly black couple prepared to leave a plantation, Union soldiers as well as their master urged them to remain. They declined: "We must go, freedom is as sweet to us as it is to you."

11.5 Black People and the Confederacy

Analyze the positions that Confederate leaders as well as African Americans themselves took on the employment of black men to fight for the Confederacy.

The Confederacy was based on the defense of slavery, and it benefited from the usually coerced but sometimes willing labor of black people. Slaves toiled in southern fields and factories during the Civil War. The greater the burden of work the slaves took on, the more white men there were who could become soldiers. When the war began, southern whites believed their disadvantage in manpower—the 22 northern states had 22,339,989 people, and the 11 Confederate states had 9,103,332 (5,449,462 white people, 3,521,110 slaves, and 132,760 free black people)—would be partly offset by the slaves whose presence would free a disproportionately large number of white southerners to go to war. While slaves would tend cotton, corn, and cattle, white southern men would fight.

11.5.1 Skilled and Unskilled Slaves in Southern Industry

Slave labor helped sustain the Confederate war effort. More than 800 slaves and several hundred free black people, for example, worked at the South's largest industrial complex in Richmond, Virginia. The sprawling Tredegar Iron Works along the James River produced half of the 2,200 cannons that Confederate military forces used. It also furnished locomotives, iron plates, boilers, and nails.

As white men departed for military service, the Tredegar operators relied increasingly on slaves for skilled and unskilled labor. The company typically hired slaves from their owners for one-year terms. By 1864, slaves represented half of the workforce at Tredegar. They toiled in the machine shop, rolling mill, foundry, and as blacksmiths. After a white man quit in a pay dispute, a black engineer operated the Tredegar steam engine. Ed Taylor, who was one of the blacksmiths, performed the highly specialized task of hammering out iron bands that were fixed on artillery pieces to strengthen them. The company paid Taylor's owner the extraordinary sum of $1,000 a year for his technical expertise. Most slaves at Tredegar were hired from their owners at $200 per year. Unfortunately for Tredegar and the Confederacy but fortunately for its slave laborers, many of them escaped as Union military forces closed in on Richmond in 1864. Other black men across the South loaded and unloaded ships, worked on the railroads, and labored in salt mines.

11.5.2 The Impressment of Black People

As the war went on, the Confederacy needed more troops and laborers. Slave owners were first asked—and then compelled—to contribute their slave laborers to the war effort. In July 1861, the Confederate Congress required free black people to register and enroll for military labor. In the summer of 1862 the Virginia legislature authorized the **impressment** of 10,000 slaves between the ages of 18 and 45 for up to 60 days. The owners would receive $16 per month per slave. Despite protests by Tredegar's management, slave laborers were taken from the factory and forced to build fortifications for 60-day terms.

But many slave owners who enjoyed the benefits of forced labor did not want to be forced to turn their slaves over to state authorities. In October 1862, President Davis asked Virginia to draft 4,500 black people to build fortifications around Richmond so that "whites could fight more and dig less."

In South Carolina in 1863, Confederate officials appealed to slave owners for 2,500 slaves to help fortify Charleston. The owners offered fewer than 1,000. During the Union bombardment of Fort Sumter, 500 slaves did the difficult, dirty, and dangerous work of building and rebuilding the fort. Slaves were even forced into combat. Two Virginia slaves who were compelled to load and fire Confederate cannons near Yorktown were shot and killed.

Although many slave owners resisted the impressment of their bondmen, other white southerners who did not own slaves were infuriated when the Confederate **conscription law** in 1862 exempted men who owned 20 or more slaves from military service. This "20 nigger law" (later reduced to 15) meant that poor white men were drafted while wealthier planters remained home, presumably to supervise and discipline their slaves. One Mississippi soldier deserted the Confederate Army, claiming he "did not propose to fight for the rich men while they were home having a good time." Although the law was widely criticized, planters—always a small percentage of the white southern population—dominated the Confederate government and would not permit the repeal of the exemption.

impressment

During the Civil War, Southern states and the Confederate government required slave owners to provide slaves to work on such public projects as fortifications, roads, and wharves. The owners (not the slaves) were usually compensated for the work.

conscription law

The 1862 Confederate law defining who was required to provide military service.

11.5.3 Confederates Enslave Free Black People

After Lincoln's Emancipation Proclamation, Confederate President Jefferson Davis issued a counter proclamation in February 1863 declaring that free black people would be enslaved, "all free negroes within the limits of the Southern Confederacy shall be placed on the slave status, and be deemed to be chattels . . . forever." This directive was not widely enforced. Davis, however, also ordered Confederate armies that invaded Union states to capture free black people in the North and enslave them: "All negroes who shall be taken in any of the States in which slavery does not now exist, in the progress of our arms, shall be adjudged, immediately after their capture, to occupy slave status."

This was done. Several hundred northern black people were taken south after Confederate forces invaded Pennsylvania in 1863 and fought at Gettysburg. Robert E. Lee's Army of Northern Virginia at Greensburg, Pennsylvania, captured at least 50 black people. A southern victory in the Civil War could have led to the enslavement of more than 132,000 free black residents of the Confederate States.

11.5.4 Black Confederates

Most of the labor black people did for the Confederacy was involuntary; however, a few free black men and women offered their services to the southern cause. In Lynchburg, Virginia, in the spring of 1861, 70 free black people volunteered "to act in whatever capacity may be assigned them." In Memphis in the fall, several hundred black residents cheered for Jefferson Davis and sang patriotic songs. These demonstrations of black support were made early in the conflict when the outcome was in doubt and long before the war became a crusade against slavery.

The status of many free black southerners remained precarious. In Virginia in 1861, impressment laws, like those applying to slaves, compelled free black men to work on Confederate defenses around Richmond and Petersburg. Months before the war, South Carolina considered forcing its free black population to choose between enslavement and exile. The legislature rejected the proposal, but it terrified the state's free black people. Many people of color there had been free for generations. Fair in complexion, they had education, skills, homes, and businesses. Some even owned slaves. When the war came, many were willing to demonstrate their devotion to the South in a desperate attempt to gain white acceptance before they lost their freedom and property.

In early 1861, before the formation of the Confederacy but after the secession of South Carolina, 82 free black men in Charleston petitioned Governor Francis W. Pickens "to be assigned any service where we can be useful." To distinguish themselves from slaves and show their solidarity with white southerners, they proclaimed, "We are by birth citizens of South Carolina, in our veins is the blood of the white race in some half, in others much more, our attachments are with you, our hopes of safety and protection is in South Carolina, our allegiance is due alone to her, in her defence we are willing to offer up our lives and all that is dear to us." Pickens rejected the petition, but white South Carolinians were pleased at this show of loyalty.

White southern leaders generally ignored offers of free black support unless it was for menial labor. But when Charleston was under siege between 1863 and 1865, black and white residents were grateful that volunteer fire brigades composed of free black men turned out to fight fires caused by Union artillery.

11.5.5 Personal Servants

Other black men contributed in different ways to the Confederate military effort. Black musicians in Virginia played for Confederate regiments and received the same pay as white musicians. Wealthy white men often took their slaves—personal servants—with them when they went off to war. The servants cooked, cleaned uniforms, cared for weapons, maintained horses, and even provided entertainment. Some were loyal and devoted. They cared for owners who were wounded or fell sick. They accompanied the bodies of dead masters home.

Being the personal servant for a soldier was hard and sometimes dangerous work. Those close to combat could be killed or injured. One white father warned his son not to take Sam, a valuable slave, into battle. "I hear you are likely to have a big battle soon, and I write to tell you not to let Sam go into the fight with you. Keep him in the rear, for that nigger is worth a thousand dollars." The father evidently placed a higher value on the slave than on his son.

11.5.6 Black Men Fighting for the South

Approximately 144,000 black men from the southern states fought with the Union Army. Most had been slaves. Although it was technically not legal until almost the end of the war, a much smaller number of black men also fought for the Confederacy. White New York troops claimed to have encountered about 700 armed black men in late 1861 near Newport News, Virginia. In 1862 a black Confederate sharpshooter positioned himself in a chimney and shot several Union soldiers before he was killed. Fifty black men served as pickets for the Confederates along the Rappahannock River in Virginia in 1863.

John Wilson Buckner, a free black man with a light complexion, enlisted in the First South Carolina Artillery. As a member of the well-regarded free black Ellison family of Stateburg, South Carolina, Buckner was considered an "honorary white man." He fought for the Confederacy in the defense of Charleston at Battery Wagner in July 1863 and was wounded just before the 54th Massachusetts Regiment assaulted the fort.

Some black civilians supported the war effort and stood to profit if the South won. Buckner's uncles grew corn, sweet potatoes, peas, sorghum, and beans on the Ellison family plantation to feed Confederate troops. By hiring out horses, mules, and slaves they owned, the Ellisons had earned nearly $1,000 by 1863. By 1865 they had paid almost $5,000 in taxes to the Confederacy, nearly one-fifth of their total income. They

Black troops were among the first Union military forces to "liberate" the devastated city of Charleston, South Carolina, in the waning weeks of the Civil War. On February 21, 1865, the 55th Massachusetts Regiment occupied Charleston. Black residents—many of them former slaves—eagerly welcomed the soldiers. Defeated and discouraged white residents remained secluded indoors.

also patriotically invested almost $7,000 in Confederate bonds and notes. Like prosperous white families, the Ellisons lost most of this investment with the defeat of the Confederacy. At war's end, the bonds were as worthless as Confederate cash, and the 80 slaves the Ellisons owned—worth approximately $100,000—were free people (see Chapter 6).

Other black southerners also suffered economically from the Confederate defeat. Richard Mack, a South Carolina slave, went off to war as a personal servant. After his master died, he became an orderly for another Confederate officer. He worked hard and accumulated a large sum in Confederate currency. He later joked, "If we had won, I would be rich."

In Virginia, free black people and slaves also contributed to the Confederate cause. Pompey Scott of Amelia County gave $20 to the war effort. William, a slave who had amassed $150, invested in Confederate State Loan Bonds. Lewis, a Mecklenburg County slave, was not permitted to join a cavalry unit as a bugler, so he donated his bugle and $20 to the Confederacy.

White southerners praised the few black people who actively supported the South. Several states awarded pensions to black men who served in the war and survived. Henry Clay Lightfoot, a slave in Culpeper, Virginia, went to war as a body servant of Captain William Holcomb. After the war, he bought a house, raised a family, and was elected to the Culpeper town council. He collected a pension from Virginia, and when he died in 1931, the United Daughters of the Confederacy draped his coffin in a Confederate flag.

11.5.7 Black Opposition to the Confederacy

Although many white southerners and some northerners believed most slaves would support their masters, in fact most slaves did not. When a slave named Tom was asked if slaves would fight for their masters, he replied, "I know they say dese tings, but dey lies. Our masters may talk now all dey choose; but one ting's sartin,—dey don't dare to try us. Jess put de guns in our hans, and you'll soon see dat we not only knows how to shoot, but who, to shoot. My master wouldn't be wuff much ef I was a soldier."

11.5.8 The Confederate Debate on Black Troops

By late 1863 and 1864, prospects for the Confederacy had become grim. The Union naval blockade had become increasingly effective, and the likelihood of British aid had all but vanished. Confederate armies suffered crushing defeats at Vicksburg and Gettysburg in 1863 and absorbed terrible losses in Tennessee, Georgia, and Virginia in 1864.

As defeat loomed, white southerners began to discuss the possibility of arming black men. Several newspapers advocated it. In September 1863, the Montgomery (Alabama) *Weekly Mail* admitted it would have been preposterous to contemplate the need for black troops earlier in the war, but it had now become necessary to save the white South:

> We are forced by the necessity of our condition—by the insolence and barbarity of the enemy, by his revengeful and demoniacal spirit—to take a step which is revolting to every sentiment of pride, and to every principle that governed our institutions before the war. But the war has made great changes, and we must meet those changes, for the sake of preserving our very existence. It is a matter of necessity, therefore, that we should use every means within our reach to defeat the enemy. One of these, and the only one which will checkmate him, is the employment of negroes in the military service of the Confederacy.

In early 1864 General Patrick Cleburne recommended enlisting slaves and promising them their freedom if they remained loyal to the Confederacy. Cleburne argued that this policy would gain recognition and aid from Britain and would disrupt Union military efforts to recruit black southerners. Yet the prospect of arming slaves and free black men appalled most white southerners. Jefferson Davis ordered military officers, including Cleburne, to cease discussing it.

Most white southerners were convinced that to arm slaves and put black men in gray uniforms defied the assumptions on which southern society was based. Black people were inferior, and their proper status was to be slaves. The *Richmond Whig* declared in 1864 that "servitude is a divinely appointed condition for the highest good of the slave." It was absurd to contemplate black people as soldiers and as free people. Georgia politician Howell Cobb explained that slaves could not be armed. "If slaves will make good soldiers our whole theory of slavery is wrong."

The Civil War for white southerners was a war to prevent the abolition of slavery. Now white southern voices were proposing abolition to preserve the southern nation. North Carolina Senator Robert M. T. Hunter opposed any attempt to enlist slaves and free them. "If we are right in passing this measure we were wrong in denying to the old government the right to interfere with the institution of slavery and to emancipate slaves. Besides, if we offer slaves their freedom . . . we confess that we were insincere, were hypocritical, in asserting that slavery was the best state for the negroes themselves."

Nevertheless, as the military situation deteriorated, the South moved toward employing black troops. In November 1864, Virginia Governor William Smith enthusiastically supported the idea. "There is not a man that would not cheerfully put the negro in the Army rather than become a slave himself. . . . Standing before God and my country, I do not hesitate to say that I would arm such portion of our able-bodied slaves population as may be necessary." In February 1865, Jefferson Davis and the Confederate cabinet conceded, "We are reduced to choosing whether the negroes shall fight for us or against us."

The opinion of General Robert E. Lee was critical to determining whether the Confederacy would decide to arm black men. No southerner was more revered and respected. Lee had freed nearly 200 slaves in keeping with the instructions of his father-in-law George Washington Parke Custis's will in 1862, which provided that the slaves be emancipated within five years of Custis's death in 1857.

With his army struggling to survive a desperate winter around Petersburg and Richmond, Lee announced in February 1865 that he favored both enrolling and emancipating black troops. "My own opinion is that we should employ them without delay." Their service as slaves would make them capable soldiers. "They possess the physical qualities in an eminent degree. Long habits of obedience and subordination, coupled with moral influence which in our country the white man possesses over the black, furnish an excellent foundation for that discipline which is the best guarantee of military efficiency."

Less than a month later in March 1865, although many white southerners still opposed it, the Confederate Congress voted to enlist 300,000 black men between the ages of 18 and 45. They would receive the same pay, equipment, and supplies as white soldiers. But those who were slaves would not be freed unless their owner consented and the state where they served agreed to their emancipation.

It was a desperate measure by a nearly defeated government and did not affect the outcome of the conflict. Before the war ended in April, authorities in Virginia managed to recruit some black men and send a few into combat. By the end of March, one company of 35 black men—12 free black men and 23 slaves—was organized. On April 4, 1865, Union troops attacked Confederate supply wagons that the black troops were guarding in Amelia County. Less than a week later, Lee surrendered to Grant at Appomattox Court House, and the Civil War ended.

Conclusion

The Civil War ended with the decisive defeat of the Confederacy. The Union was preserved. The ordeal of slavery for millions of people of African descent was over. Slavery—having thrived in America for nearly 250 years—was finally abolished by an amendment to the Constitution. Congress passed the Thirteenth Amendment on January 31, 1865. It was ratified by 27 states and declared in effect on December 18, 1865.

Were it not for the presence and labors of more than four million black people, there would have been no Civil War. Had it not been for the presence and contributions of nearly 200,000 black soldiers and sailors, the Union would not have won. Almost 50,000 of those black men died in combat and of disease during the war. Twenty-one black men were awarded the Medal of Honor for heroism.

Abraham Lincoln represented the dramatic shift in attitudes and policies toward African Americans during the Civil War. When the war began, Lincoln insisted it was a white man's conflict to suppress rebellious white southerners. Black people, Lincoln remained convinced, would be better off outside the United States. But the war went on, and thousands of white men died. Lincoln issued the Emancipation Proclamation and welcomed the enlistment of black troops. The president came to appreciate the achievements and devotion of black troops and condemned the mean-spiritedness of white northerners who opposed the war. Lincoln wrote in 1863, "And then there will be some black men who can remember that, with silent tongue, and clenched teeth, and steady eye, and well-poised bayonet, they have helped mankind on to this great consummation; while, I fear, there will be some white ones, unable to forget that, with malignant heart, and deceitful speech, they have strove to hinder it."

Chapter Timeline

AFRICAN-AMERICAN EVENTS	NATIONAL EVENTS
1860–1861	
April–May 1861	**November 1860**
Black men volunteer for military service and are rejected	Abraham Lincoln elected president
Black men in Louisiana join the Native Guards in support of the Confederacy	**December 1860**
	South Carolina secedes from the Union
The Louisiana legislature limits military service to white men	**February 1861**
	The Confederate States of America is formed
August 1861	**March 1861**
First Confiscation Act	Lincoln inaugurated
	April 1861
	The firing on Fort Sumter begins the Civil War
	November 1861
	Union forces capture the sea islands and coastal areas of South Carolina and Georgia

AFRICAN-AMERICAN EVENTS	NATIONAL EVENTS

1862–1863

May 1862

Robert Smalls escapes with the *Planter* and 16 slaves

May–August 1862

The First South Carolina Volunteers, an all-black regiment, forms

September 1862

The Louisiana Native Guards reorganize in support of the Union

Lincoln announces the Preliminary Emancipation Proclamation

October 1862

Black troops see combat for the first time in Missouri

January 1, 1863

Lincoln issues the Emancipation Proclamation

January–March 1863

Troops recruited for the 54th and the 55th Massachusetts Regiments

May 1863

Black Louisiana troops join white Union forces in the attack on Port Hudson

June 1863

Battle of Milliken's Bend

July 1863

Assault on Battery Wagner; New York City draft riots

September 1862

Battle of Antietam

March 1863

The U. S. government enacts a Conscription Act

July 1863

Battles of Vicksburg and Gettysburg

1864–1965

February 1864

Battle at Olustee

April 1864

Fort Pillow Massacre

February 1865

Black troops lead the occupation of Charleston

March 1865

Confederate Congress approves the enlistment of black men

December 1865

Thirteenth Amendment ratified

November 1864

Lincoln is reelected

November–December 1864

Sherman's march to the sea

February 1865

Charleston falls

March 1865

Richmond falls

April 1865

Lee surrenders at Appomattox

Lincoln is assassinated

Review Questions

1. How did the Union's goals in the Civil War change between 1861 and 1865? What accounts for those changes?

2. How did the Confederate government's policies toward slaves change during the Civil War? When and why did those changes occur?

3. When the Civil War began, why did northern black men volunteer to serve in the Union army if the war had not yet become a war to end slavery?

4. How did Abraham Lincoln's policies and attitudes toward black people change during the Civil War? Does Lincoln deserve credit as "the Great Emancipator"? Why or why not?

5. What did the Emancipation Proclamation seek to achieve? Why was it issued? What did it actually accomplish?

6. What did black men and women contribute to the Union war effort? Was it in their interests to participate in the Civil War? Why or why not?

7. Why did some black people support the Confederacy?

8. Was the result of the Civil War worth the loss of 750,000 lives?

Retracing the Odyssey

The Penn Center, St. Helena Island, South Carolina. Beginning in 1862, black and white teachers from the North began offering instruction to former slaves on the Carolina coast. Laura Towne and Ellen Murray helped establish Penn school amid the oak trees draped in Spanish moss. The school closed in 1948. During the 1950s and 1960s, civil rights leaders, including Dr. Martin Luther King, Jr., gathered at Penn to discuss strategy. Today Penn Center provides programs on health, literacy, landownership, and agriculture. It serves as a cultural and community center, and there is a museum among the historic buildings.

Olustee Battlefield State Historic Site, Olustee, Florida. In February 1864 the largest Civil War battle in Florida was fought at Olustee, which is almost 50 miles west of Jacksonville. About one-third of the Union troops were black men. There is a museum with exhibits and artifacts.

Fort Pillow State Park, Tennessee. This was the scene of the April 1864 battle in which Confederate forces attacked the black and white Union defenders of the fort. About 238 black men were killed, some during the battle and others after they surrendered. There is a visitor center, museum, and trail to the fortifications.

The Crater, Petersburg National Battlefield, Virginia. The longest siege in American military history occurred in and around the town of Petersburg in 1864 and 1865. Union forces attempted to break Confederate lines by setting off an enormous explosion in July 1864. Poor leadership and inept execution turned the Union advantage to disaster for the white and black troops who took part. Portions of the trenches and the crater are still visible.

Harriet Tubman Museum, Auburn, New York. In 1896 the famed liberator of slaves bought this property and made it her home. She died here in 1913. The African Methodist Episcopal Zion Church operates the house as a museum. Harriet Tubman is buried nearby at Fort Hill Cemetery.

Recommended Reading

Lerone Bennett. *Forced into Glory: Abraham Lincoln's White Dream.* Chicago: Johnson, 2000. Bennett is highly critical of Lincoln in this thought-provoking account.

Dudley Taylor Cornish. *The Sable Arm: Negro Troops in the Union Army, 1861–1865.* New York: W. W. Norton, 1956. The best single study of black men in the military during the war.

John Hope Franklin. *The Emancipation Proclamation.* Garden City, NY: Doubleday, 1963. A work written to commemorate the centennial of the Proclamation.

Thavolia Glymph. *Out of the House of Bondage: The Transformation of the Plantation Household.* Cambridge, UK: Cambridge University Press, 2008. Destroys the myth that white mistresses and slave women maintained a feminine bond during slavery and following emancipation.

Michael P. Johnson and James L. Roark. *Black Masters: A Free Family of Color in the Old South.* New York: W. W. Norton, 1984. A splendid depiction of life among prosperous free black people before and during the Civil War.

Ervin Jordon. *Black Confederates and Afro-Yankees in Civil War Virginia*. Charlottesville: University of Virginia Press, 1995. A rich and informative study of life and society among African Americans in Virginia during the war.

James McPherson. *Battle Cry of Freedom: The Civil War Era*. New York: Oxford University Press, 1988. A superb one-volume account of the Civil War.

George W. Williams. *History of the Negro Troops in the War of the Rebellion*. New York: Harper and Row, 1888. An account of black soldiers in the war by America's first African-American historian.

Additional Bibliography

Military

Joseph T. Glatthaar. *Forged in Battle: The Civil War Alliance of Black Soldiers and White Officers*. New York: Free Press, 1990.

_____. *The March to the Sea and Beyond: Sherman's Troops in the Savannah and Carolina Campaign*. New York: New York University Press, 1985.

Herman Hattaway and Archer Jones. *How the North Won: A Military History of the Civil War*. Urbana: University of Illinois Press, 1983.

John Keegan. *The American Civil War: A Military History*. New York: Alfred A. Knopf, 2009.

Geoffrey Ward and Ken Burns. *The Civil War*. New York: Alfred A. Knopf, 1990.

Stephen R. Wise. *Gate of Hell: Campaign for Charleston Harbor, 1863*. Columbia: University of South Carolina Press, 1994.

African Americans and the War

Iver Bernstein. *The New York City Draft Riots: Their Significance for American Society and Politics in the Age of the Civil War*. New York: Oxford University Press, 1991.

Peter Burchard. *One Gallant Rush: Robert Gould Shaw and His Brave Black Regiment*. New York: St. Martin's Press, 1965.

George S. Burkhardt. *Confederate Wrath: No Quarter in the Civil War*. Carbondale: Southern Illinois University Press, 2007.

John Cimpach. *Fort Pillow: A Civil War Massacre and Public Memory*. Baton Rouge: Louisiana State University Press, 2005.

Catherine Clinton. *Harriet Tubman: The Road to Freedom*. Boston: Little, Brown, 2004.

Charles B. Dew. *Ironmaker to the Confederacy: Joseph R. Anderson and the Tredegar Iron Works*. New Haven, CT: Yale University Press, 1966.

Jennifer Fleischner. *Mrs. Lincoln and Mrs. Keckley: The Remarkable Story of the Friendship Between a First Lady and a Former Slave*. New York: Broadway Books, 2004.

Eric Foner. *Forever Free: The Story of Emancipation and Reconstruction*. New York: Vintage Books, 2006.

Ella Forbes. *African American Women During the Civil War*. New York: Garland, 1998.

James G. Hollandsworth. *The Louisiana Native Guards*. Baton Rouge: Louisiana State University Press, 1996.

Kate Clifford Larson. *Bound for the Promised Land: Harriet Tubman, Portrait of an American Hero*. New York: Ballantine, 2004.

Leon Litwack. *Been in the Storm So Long: The Aftermath of Slavery*. New York: Alfred A. Knopf, 1979.

Edward A. Miller. *Gullah Statesman: Robert Smalls from Slavery to Congress, 1839–1915*. Columbia: University of South Carolina Press, 1995.

Benjamin Quarles. *The Negro in the Civil War*. Boston: Little, Brown, 1953.

Willie Lee Rose. *Rehearsal for Reconstruction: The Port Royal Experiment*. Indianapolis, IN: Bobbs Merrill, 1964.

Milton C. Sernett. *Harriet Tubman: Myth, Memory, and History*. Durham, NC: Duke University Press, 2007.

Richard Slotkin. *No Quarter: The Battle of the Crater, 1864*. New York: Random House, 2009.

John David Smith. *Lincoln and the U.S. Colored Troops*. Carbondale: Southern Illinois University Press, 2013.

Noah A. Trudeau. *Like Men of War: Black Troops in the Civil War, 1862–1865*. Boston: Little, Brown, 1998.

Gregory J. W. Urwin, ed. *Black Flag over Dixie: Racial Atrocities and Reprisals in the Civil War*. Carbondale: Southern Illinois University Press, 2004.

Bell I. Wiley. *Southern Negroes, 1861–1865*. New Haven, CT: Yale University Press, 1938.

Documents, Letters, and Other Sources

Virginia M. Adams, ed. *On the Altar of Freedom: A Black Soldier's Civil War Letters from the Front.* [Corporal James Henry Gooding]. Amherst: University of Massachusetts Press, 1991.

Ira Berlin et al., eds. *Freedom: A Documentary History of Emancipation, 1861–1867.* Series 1, Volume I, *The Destruction of Slavery.* New York: Cambridge University Press, 1985.

_____. *Freedom: A Documentary History of Emancipation, 1861–1867.* Series 1, Volume III, *The Wartime Genesis of Free Labor: The Lower South.* New York: Cambridge University Press, 1990.

Robert F. Durden. *The Gray and the Black: The Confederate Debate on Emancipation.* Baton Rouge: Louisiana State University Press, 1972.

Michael P. Johnson and James L. Roark, eds. *No Chariot Letdown: Charleston's Free People of Color on the Eve of the Civil War.* Chapel Hill: University of North Carolina Press, 1984.

James McPherson. *The Negro's Civil War: How American Negroes Felt and Acted During the War for the Union.* New York: Pantheon, 1965.

Edwin S. Redkey, ed. *A Grand Army of Black Men: Letters from African American Soldiers in the Union Army, 1861–1865.* New York: Cambridge University Press, 1992.

Reminiscences

Thomas Wentworth Higginson. *Army Life in a Black Regiment.* Boston: Beacon, 1962.

Elizabeth Keckley. *Behind the Scenes: Or, Thirty Years a Slave and Four Years in the White House.* New York: Oxford University Press, 1968.

Susie King Taylor. *Reminiscences of My Life in Camp.* Boston: Taylor, 1902.

Chapter 12

The Meaning of Freedom: The Promise of Reconstruction

1865–1868

African-American children crowded into primary schools such as this one that the Freedmen's Bureau opened in Richmond, Virginia, following the Civil War.

⌄ Learning Objectives

After reading this chapter you should be able to:

12.1 Explain exactly what freedom meant to former slaves.

12.2 Discuss the importance that acquiring land had to people who had been slaves.

12.3 Explain how African Americans gained an education.

12.4 Characterize the extent of violence confronted by African Americans after the Civil War.

12.5 Analyze the impact that President Andrew Johnson's policies had on African Americans.

Many Thousand Gone

No more auction block for me,

No more, no more,

No more auction block for me,

Many thousand gone.

No more driver's lash for me,

No more, no more,

No more driver's lash for me,

Many thousand gone.

No more peck of salt for me,

No more, no more,

No more peck of salt for me,

Many thousand gone.

No more iron chain for me,

No more, no more.

No more iron chain for me,

Many thousand gone.

—An African-American emancipation song

What did freedom mean to a people who had endured and survived 250 years of enslavement in America? What did the future hold for nearly four million African Americans in 1865? Freedom meant many things to many people. But to most former slaves, it meant that families would stay together. Freedom meant that women would no longer be sexually exploited. Freedom meant learning to read and write. Freedom meant organizing churches. Freedom meant moving around without having to obtain permission. Freedom meant that labor would produce income for the laborer and not the master. Freedom meant working without the whip. Freedom meant land to own, cultivate, and live on. Freedom meant a trial before a jury if charged with a crime. Freedom meant voting. Freedom meant citizenship and having the same rights as white people.

Years after slavery ended, a former Texas slave, Margrett Nillin, was asked if she preferred slavery or freedom. She answered unequivocally, "Well, it's dis way, in slavery I owns nothin' and never owns nothin'. In freedom I's own de home and raise de family. All dat causes me worryment and in slavery I has no worryment, but I takes freedom."

12.1 The End of Slavery

Explain exactly what freedom meant to former slaves.

With the collapse of slavery, many black people were quick to inform white people that whatever loyalty, devotion, and cooperation they might have shown as slaves had never reflected their inner feelings and attitudes. Near Opelousas, Louisiana, a Union officer asked a young black man why he did not love his master, and the youth responded sharply, "When my master begins to lub me, den it'll be time enough for me to lub him. What I wants is to get away. I want to take me off from dis plantation, where I can be free."

In North Carolina, planter Robert P. Howell was disappointed that a loyal slave named Lovet fled at the first opportunity. "He was about my age and I had always treated him more as a companion than a slave. When I left I put everything in his charge, told him that he was free, but to remain on the place and take care of things. He promised me faithfully that he would, but he was the first one to leave . . . and I did not see him for several years."

Emancipation was traumatic for many former masters. A Virginia freedman remembered that "Miss Polly died right after the surrender, she was so hurt that all the negroes was going to be free." Another former slave, Robert Falls, recalled that his master assembled the slaves to inform them they were free. "I hates to do it, but I must. You all ain't my niggers no more. You is free. Just as free as I am. Here I have raised you all to work for me, and now you are going to leave me. I am an old man, and I can't get along without you. I don't know what I am going to do." In less than a year, he was dead. Falls attributed his master's death to the end of slavery: "It killed him."

12.1.1 Differing Reactions of Former Slaves

Other slaves bluntly displayed their reaction to years of bondage. Aunt Delia, a cook with a North Carolina family, revealed that she secretly had been gaining retribution for the indignity of servitude. "How many times I spit in the biscuits and peed in the coffee just to get back at them mean white folks." In Goodman, Mississippi, a slave named Caddy learned she was free and rushed from the field to find her owner. "Caddy threw down that hoe, she marched herself up to the big house, then, she looked around and found the mistress. She went over to the mistress, she flipped up her dress and told the white woman to do something. She said it mean and ugly. This is what she said: 'Kiss my ass!' "

In contrast, some slaves, especially elderly ones, were apprehensive about freedom. On a South Carolina plantation, an older black woman refused to accept emancipation. "I ain' no free nigger! I is got a marster and mistiss! Dee right dar in de great house. Ef you don' b'lieve me, you go dar an' see."

12.1.2 Reuniting Black Families

As slavery ended, the most urgent need for many freed people was finding family members who had been sold away from them. Slavery had not destroyed the black family. Husbands, wives, and children went to great lengths to reassemble their families after the Civil War. For years and even decades after the end of slavery, advertisements in black newspapers appealed for information about missing kinfolk. For example, the *Colored Tennessean* published the following notice on August 5, 1865:

> Saml. Dove wishes to know of the whereabouts of his mother, Areno, his sisters Maria, Neziah and Peggy, and his brother Edmond, who were owned by Geo. Dove of Rockingham County, Shenandoah Valley, Va. Sold in Richmond, after which Saml. and Edmond were taken to Nashville, Tenn., by Joe Mick; Areno was left at the Eagle Tavern, Richmond. Respectfully yours, Saml. Dove, Utica, New York.

In North Carolina a northern journalist met a middle-aged black man "plodding along, staff in hand, and apparently very footsore and tired." The nearly exhausted freedman explained that he had walked almost 600 miles looking for his wife and children, who had been sold four years earlier.

There were emotional reunions as family members found each other after years of separation. Ben and Betty Dodson had been apart for 20 years when Ben found her in a refugee camp after the war. "Glory! glory! hallelujah," he shouted as he hugged his wife. "Dis is my Betty, shuah. I foun' you at las'. I's hunted and hunted till I track you up here. I's boun' to hunt till I fin' you if you's alive."

Other searches had more heart-wrenching results. Husbands and wives sometimes learned that their spouses had remarried during the separation. Believing his wife had died, the husband of Laura Spicer remarried—only to learn after the war that Laura was still alive. Sadly, he wrote to her but refused to meet: "I would come and see you but I know I could not bear it. I want to see you and I don't want to see you. I love you just as well as I did the last day I saw you, and it will not do for you and I to meet."

Tormented, he wrote again pledging his love: "Laura I do not think that I have change any at all since I saw you last—I thinks of you and my children every day of my life. Laura I do love you the same. My love to you never have failed. Laura, truly, I have got another wife, and I am very sorry that I am. You feels and seems to me as much like my dear loving wife, as you ever did Laura."

One freedman testified to the close ties that bound many slave families when he replied bitterly to the claim that he had had a kind master who had fed him and never used the whip: "Kind! yes, he gib men corn enough, and he gib me pork enough, and he neber gib me one lick wid de whip, but whar's my wife?—whar's my chill'en? Take away de pork, I say; take away de corn, I can work and raise dese for myself, but gib me back de wife of my bosom, and gib me back my poor chill'en as was sold away."

12.2 Land

Discuss the importance that acquiring land had to people who had been slaves.

As people embraced freedom and left their masters, they wanted land. Nineteenth-century Americans of virtually every background associated economic security with owning land. Families wanted to work land and prosper as self-sufficient yeomen. Former slaves believed their future as a free people was tied to the possession of land. But just as it had been impossible to abolish slavery without federal intervention, it would not be possible to acquire land without the assistance of the U.S. government. At first, federal authorities seemed determined to make land available to freedmen.

12.2.1 Special Field Order #15

Special Field Order #15

General William Tecumseh Sherman issued this military directive in January 1865. It set aside lands along the coast from Charleston, South Carolina, to Jacksonville, Florida, for former slaves. President Andrew Johnson revoked the order six months later.

Shortly after his army arrived in Savannah—after having devastated Georgia—Union General William T. Sherman announced that freedmen would receive land. On January 16, 1865, he issued **Special Field Order #15**. This military directive set aside a 30-mile-wide tract of land along the Atlantic coast from Charleston, South Carolina, 245 miles south to Jacksonville, Florida. White owners had abandoned the land, and Sherman reserved it for black families. The head of each family would receive "possessory title" to 40 acres of land. Sherman also gave the freedmen the use of army mules—hence the

FREEDMAN'S VILLAGE, ARLINGTON, VIRGINIA.—[SEE PAGE 294.]

Former slaves in a village near Washington, D.C. Black people welcomed emancipation, but without land, education, or employment, they faced an uncertain future.

slogan, "Forty acres and a mule." (Mules, horses, and other draft animals were essential for plowing fields and harvesting many crops before agriculture became mechanized.)

Within six months, 40,000 freed people were working 400,000 acres in the South Carolina and Georgia low country and on the sea islands. Former slaves generally shunned the slave crops of cotton and rice and instead planted sweet potatoes and corn. They also worked together as families and kinfolk. They avoided the gang labor associated with slavery. Most husbands and fathers preferred that their wives and daughters not work in the fields as slave women had been forced to do. Black women who worked in the homes of white families were increasingly willing to resist what they considered the unreasonable demands of white women.

12.2.2 The Port Royal Experiment

Meanwhile, hundreds of former slaves had been cultivating land for three years. In late 1861 Union military forces carved out an enclave around Beaufort and Port Royal, South Carolina, that remained under federal authority for the rest of the war. White planters fled to the interior, leaving their slaves behind. Under the supervision of U.S. Treasury officials and northern reformers and missionaries who hurried south in 1862, ex-slaves began to work the land in what came to be known as the "**Port Royal Experiment**." When Treasury agents auctioned off portions of the land for nonpayment of taxes, freedmen purchased some of it. But northern businessmen bought most of the real estate and then hired black people to raise cotton.

White owners sometimes returned to their former lands only to find that black families had taken charge. Black farmers told one former owner, "We own this land now, put it out of your head that it will ever be yours again." And on one South Carolina sea island, white men were turned back by armed black men.

Port Royal Experiment

An effort by northern white missionaries, educators, and businessmen in the Sea Islands near Beaufort, South Carolina, to transform former slaves into educated, reliable, and industrious wage earners. Most of the freedmen did not acquire the land they worked.

12.2.3 The Freedmen's Bureau

As the war ended in early 1865, Congress created the Bureau of Refugees, Freedmen, and Abandoned Lands—commonly called the **Freedmen's Bureau**. Created as a temporary agency to assist freedmen to make the transition to freedom, the bureau was placed under the control of the U.S. Army, and General Oliver O. Howard was put in command. Howard, a devout Christian who had lost an arm in the war, was eager to aid the freedmen.

The bureau was given enormous responsibilities. It was designed to help freedmen obtain land, gain an education, negotiate labor contracts with white planters, settle legal and criminal disputes involving black and white people, and provide food, medical care, and transportation for black and white people left destitute by the war. However, Congress never provided sufficient funds or personnel to carry out these tasks.

The Freedmen's Bureau never had more than 900 agents spread across the South from Virginia to Texas. Mississippi, for example, had 12 agents in 1866. One agent often served a county with a population of 10,000 to 20,000 freedmen. Few of the agents were black because few military officers were black. John Mercer Langston of Virginia was an inspector of schools assigned to the bureau's main office in Washington, D.C.; Major Martin R. Delany worked with freedmen on the South Carolina sea islands. Large portions of the South had been devastated by the war. Richmond, Atlanta, Columbia (South Carolina), and Charleston were in ruins. Railroads had been torn up. Factories were destroyed. Sherman's army laid waste to farms, plantations, and towns in Georgia and the Carolinas. Southern planters lost nearly four million human beings they had owned as property and had controlled as labor.

The need for assistance was desperate as thousands of black and white southerners endured disease and extreme privation as the Civil War ended. A terrible smallpox epidemic swept through the South and killed thousands of newly freed people.

Freedmen's Bureau

Congress established the Bureau of Refugees, Freedmen, and Abandoned Lands in February 1865 to assist black and white Southerners left destitute by the Civil War.

The Bureau was overwhelmed as it tried to provide medical care to freedmen and thousands of white people who were suffering and dying from malnutrition, cholera, yellow fever, and pneumonia, as well as smallpox. The bureau established camps for the homeless, fed the hungry, and cared for orphans and the sick as best it could. By 1866 it had distributed more than 13 million rations, consisting of flour, cornmeal, and sugar.

In July 1865 the bureau took a first step toward distributing land when General Howard issued Circular 13 ordering agents to "set aside" 40-acre plots for freedmen. But the allocation had hardly begun when the order was revoked, and authorities announced that land already distributed under Sherman's Special Field Order #15 was to be returned to its white owners.

The reason for this reversal was that Andrew Johnson, who had become president after Lincoln's assassination in April 1865, began to pardon hundreds and then thousands of former Confederates and restore their lands to them. General Howard had to tell black people that they had to relinquish the land they thought they had acquired. Speaking to some 2,000 freedmen on South Carolina's Edisto Island in October 1865, Howard pleaded with them to "lay aside their bitter feelings, and to become reconciled to their old masters." A black man shouted a response, "Why, General Howard, why do you take away our lands? You take them from us who are true, always true to the Government! You give them to our all-time enemies. This is not right!"

A committee rejected Howard's appeal for reconciliation and forgiveness and an unhappy black man insisted the government provide land:

> You ask us to forgive the landowners of our island. You only lost your right arm in war and might forgive them. The man who tied me to a tree and gave me 39 lashes and who stripped and flogged my mother and my sister and who will not let me stay in his empty hut except I will do his planting and be satisfied with his price and who combines with others to keep away land from me well knowing I would not have anything to do with him if I had land of my own—that man I cannot well forgive.

These appeals moved Howard. He returned to Washington and attempted to persuade Congress to provide land. Congress refused, and President Johnson was determined that white people would get their lands back. It seemed so sensible to most white people. Property that had belonged to white families for generations simply

Freedmen's Bureau agents often found themselves in the middle of angry disputes over land and labor that erupted between black and white southerners. Too often the bureau officers sided with the white landowners in these disagreements with former slaves.

THE FREEDMEN'S BUREAU.—Drawn by A. R. Waud.—[See Page 417.]

could not be given to freedmen. Freedmen saw it differently. They deserved land that they and their families had worked without compensation for generations. Freedmen believed it was the only way to make freedom meaningful and to gain independence from white people. As it turned out, most freedmen were forced off land they thought should belong to them.

12.2.4 Southern Homestead Act

In early 1866 Congress attempted to provide land for freedmen with the passage of the **Southern Homestead Act**. More than three million acres of public land were set aside for black people and white southerners who had remained loyal to the Union. Much of this land, however, consisted of swampy wetlands or unfertile pinewoods unsuitable for farming. More than 4,000 black families—three-quarters of them in Florida—did claim some of this land, but many lacked the financial resources to cultivate it. Eventually timber companies acquired much of it, and the Southern Homestead Act largely failed.

Southern Homestead Act

Congress passed this measure in 1866 that set aside over three million acres of land for former slaves and loyal white Southerners to farm following the Civil War. Most of the land was not fertile or suitable for agriculture, and the act largely failed.

Voices

Jourdon Anderson's Letter to His Former Master

Not long after the Civil War ended, Tennessee planter Patrick H. Anderson wrote a letter to his former slave, Jourdon Anderson, and asked that the freed man and his family return to Tennessee and become laborers once again. Now they would be paid for their work. Here is Jourdon Anderson's response.

Dayton, Ohio, August 7, 1865

To My Old Master, Colonel P. H. Anderson

Big Spring, Tennessee

Sir: I got your letter and was glad to find you had not forgotten Jourdon, and that you wanted me to come back and live with you again, promising to do better for me than anybody else can. I have often felt uneasy about you. I thought the Yankees would have hung you long before this for harboring Rebs they found at your house. I suppose they never heard about you going to Col. Martin's to kill the Union soldier that was left by his company in their stable. Although you shot at me twice before I left you, I did not want to hear of your being hurt, and am glad you are still living. It would do me good to go back to the dear old home again and see Miss Mary and Miss Martha, and Allen, Esther, Green, and Lee. Give my love to them all, and tell them I hope we meet in the better world, if not in this. I would have come back to see you all when I was working in Nashville, but one of the neighbors told me Henry intended to shoot me if he ever got a chance.

I want to know particularly what the good chance is you propose to give me. I am doing tolerably well here; I get $25 a month, with victuals

and clothing; have a comfortable home for Mandy (the folks here call her Mrs. Anderson), and the children, Milly, Jane and Grundy, go to school and are learning well; the teacher says Grundy has a head for a preacher. They go to Sunday-School, and Mandy and me attend church regularly. We are kindly treated; sometimes we hear others saying, "Them colored people were slaves" down in Tennessee. The children feel hurt when they hear such remarks, but I tell them it was no disgrace in Tennessee to belong to Col. Anderson. Many darkies would have been proud, as I used to was, to call you master. Now, if you will write and say what wages you will give me, I will be better able to decide whether it would be to my advantage to move back again.

As for my freedom, which you say I can have, there is nothing to be gained on that score, as I got my free-papers in 1864 from the Provost-Marshall-General of the Department of Nashville. Mandy says she would be afraid to go back without some kind of proof that you are sincerely disposed to treat us justly and kindly—and we have concluded to test your sincerity by asking you to send our wages for the time we served you. This will make us forget and forgive old scores; and rely on your justice and friendship in the future. I served you faithfully for thirty-two years and Mandy twenty years. At $25 a month for me, and $2 a week for Mandy, our earnings would amount to $11,680. Add to this interest for the time our wages has been kept back and deduct what you would paid for our clothing and three doctor's visits to me, and pulling a tooth for Mandy, and the balance will show what we are in justice entitled to. Please send the money by Adams Express, in care of V. Winters, esq, Dayton, Ohio. If you fail to pay us for faithful labors in the past we can have little faith in your promises in the future. We trust the good Maker has opened your eyes to the wrongs which you and your fathers have done to me and my fathers, in making us toil for you for generations without recompense. Here I draw my wages every Saturday night, but in Tennessee there was never any pay day for the negroes any more than for the horses and cows. Surely there will be a day of reckoning for those who defraud the laborers of his hire.

In answering this letter please state if there would be any safety for my Milly and Jane, who are now grown up and both good-looking girls. You know how it was with poor Matilda and Catherine. I would rather stay here and starve and die if it comes to that than have my girls brought to shame by the violence and wickedness of their young masters. You will also please state if there has been any schools opened for the colored children in your neighborhood, the great desire of my life now is to give my children an education, and have them form virtuous habits.

P.S.—Say howdy to George Carter, and thank him for taking the pistol from you when you were shooting at me.

From our old servant,
Jourdon Anderson

The $11,680 that Anderson mentioned would be approximately $165,000 in 2015 dollars. Patrick Anderson died in 1867. Jourdon Anderson lived with his family in Dayton until his death in 1907.

1. Under what specific terms would Jourdon Anderson agree to return to work for his former master?

2. What fears did Jourdon Anderson have for his daughters if the family agreed to return to Tennessee?

3. In your judgment, why was it highly unlikely that Jourdon Anderson seriously considered going back to Col. Patrick Anderson?

SOURCE: Jourdan Anderson's Letter to His Former Master. (Dayton, Ohio, August 7, 1865. To My Old Master, Colonel P. H. Anderson, Big Spring, Tennessee.)

12.2.5 Sharecropping

To make matters worse, by 1866 bureau officials tried to force freedmen to sign labor contracts with white landowners—returning black people to white authority. Black men who refused to sign contracts could be arrested. Theoretically, these contracts were legal agreements between two equals: landowner and laborer. But they were seldom freely concluded. Bureau agents usually sided with the landowner and pressured freedmen to accept unequal terms.

Occasionally, the landowner would pay wages to the laborer. But because most landowners lacked cash to pay wages, they typically agreed to provide the laborer with part of the crop. The laborer, often grudgingly, agreed to work under the supervision of the landowner. The contracts required labor for a full year, and the laborer could neither quit nor strike. Landowners demanded that the laborers work the fields in gangs. Freedmen, however, resisted this system. They sometimes insisted on making decisions involving planting, fertilizing, and harvesting as they sought to exercise independence (see Map 12-1).

Thus, it took time for a new form of agricultural labor to develop. But by the 1870s, the system of **sharecropping** dominated most of the South. There were no wages. Freedmen worked land as families—not in gangs—and not under direct white supervision. The landowner provided seed, tools, fertilizer, and work animals (mules, horses, oxen), and the black family received one-third of the crop. There were many variations on these arrangements, and black families were often cheated out of their fair share of the crop. Without land of their own, they remained under white authority well into the twentieth century.

sharecropping

The system following the Civil War in which former slaves worked land owned by white people and "paid" for the use of the land and for tools, seeds, fertilizer, and mules by sharing the crop—usually cotton—with the owner.

12.2.6 The Black Church

In the years after slavery, the church became the most important institution among African Americans other than the family. It filled deep spiritual needs, offered enriching music, provided charity and compassion to those in need, developed community and political

Map 12-1 The Effect of Sharecropping on the Southern Plantation: The Barrow Plantation, Oglethorpe County, Georgia

With the end of slavery, and advent of sharecropping, black people would no longer agree to work in fields as gangs. They preferred to have each family cultivate separate plots of land, thereby distancing themselves as much as possible from slavery and white supervision.

Although many freed people worked the same land that they had as slaves, how does this map suggest the changes experienced by black people in family life, religion, education, and their relationships with white people?

1860

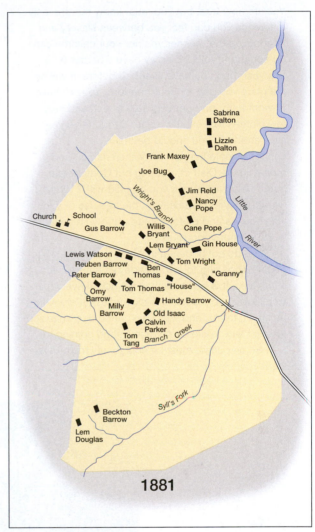

1881

leaders, and was free of white supervision. Before slavery's demise, free black people and slaves often attended white churches where they participated in religious services conducted by white clergymen and where they were treated as second-class Christians.

Once liberated, black men and women organized their own churches with their own ministers. Most black people considered white ministers incapable of delivering a meaningful message. Nancy Williams recalled, "Ole white preachers used to talk wid dey tongues widdout sayin' nothin', but Jesus told us slaves to talk wid our hearts."

Northern white missionaries were sometimes appalled by the unlettered and ungrammatical black preachers who nevertheless communicated effectively and emotionally with their parishioners. A visiting white clergyman was impressed and humbled on hearing a black preacher who lacked education but more than made up for it with his devout faith. "He talked about Christ and his salvation as one who understood what he said . . . . Here was an unlearned man, one who could not read, telling of the love of Christ, of Christian faith and duty in a way which I have not learned."

Voices

A Freedmen's Bureau Commissioner Tells Freed People What Freedom Means

In June 1865 Charles Soule, the commissioner of contracts for the Freedmen's Bureau, told freedmen in Orangeburg, South Carolina, what to expect and how to behave in the coming year:

You are now free, but you must know that the only difference you can feel yet, between slavery and freedom, is that neither you nor your children can be bought or sold. You may have a harder time this year than you have ever had before; it will be the price you pay for your freedom. You will have to work hard, and get very little to eat, and very few clothes to wear. If you get through this year alive and well, you should be thankful . . . . You cannot be paid in money, for there is no good money in the District, nothing but Confederate paper. Then, what can you be paid with? Why, with food, with clothes, with the free use of your little houses and plots. You do not own a cent's worth except yourselves.

You do not understand why some of the white people who used to own you do not have to work in the field. It is because they are rich. If every man were poor, and worked in his own field, there would be no big farms, and very little cotton or corn raised to sell; there would be no money, and nothing to buy. Some people must be rich, to pay the others, and they have the right to do no work except to look out after their property.

Remember that all of your working time belongs to the man who hires you: therefore you must not leave work without his leave not even to nurse a child, or to go and visit a wife or husband. When you wish to go off the place, get a pass as you used to, and then you will run no danger of being taken up by our soldiers.

In short, do just about as the good men among you have always done. Remember that even if you are badly off, no one can buy and sell you: remember that if you help yourselves, GOD will help you, and trust hopefully that next year and the year after will bring some new blessing to you.

---

1. According to Soule, what is the difference between slavery and freedom?

2. Does freedom mean that freed people will have economic opportunities equal to those of white people?

3. How should freed people have responded to Soule's advice?

SOURCE: Ira Berlin et al., "The Terrain of Freedom: The Struggle over the Meaning of Free Labor in the U.S. South," *History Workshop* 22 (Autumn 1986): 108–30.

Freedwomen washing laundry.

Hundreds of black churches were founded across the South following the Civil War, and they grew spectacularly in the decades that followed. This illustration shows a congregation crowded into Richmond's First African Baptist Church in 1874.

Other black and white religious leaders anguished over what they considered moral laxity and displaced values among the freed people. They preached about honesty, thrift, temperance, and elimination of sexual promiscuity. They demanded an end to "rum-suckers, bar-room loafers, whiskey dealers and card players among the men, and to those women who dressed finely on ill gotten gain."

Church members struggled, scrimped, and saved to buy land and build churches. Most former slaves founded Baptist and Methodist churches. These denominations tended to be more autonomous and less subject to outside control. Their doctrine was usually simple and direct without complex theology. Of the Methodist churches, the African Methodist Episcopal (AME) Church made giant strides in the South after the Civil War.

In Charleston the Emanuel AME Church was resurrected 40 years after it had been forced to disband during the turmoil over the Denmark Vesey plot in 1822 (see Chapter 8). (Nine members of the Emanuel congregation including the Reverend Clementa Pinckney were killed in a hate crime on June 17, 2015.) By the 1870s, three AME congregations were thriving in Charleston. In Wilmington, North Carolina, the 1,600 members of the Front Street Methodist Church decided to join the AME Church soon after the Civil War ended. They replaced the longtime white minister with a black man.

White Methodists initially encouraged cooperation with black Methodists and helped establish the Colored (now Christian) Methodist Episcopal (CME) Church. However, the white Methodists lost some of their fervor after they failed to persuade the black Methodists to keep political issues out of the CME Church and to dwell instead solely on spiritual concerns.

12.2.7 Class and Status

Issues of class and status often prevailed among African Americans after the Civil War. Wealth and prewar status were critical markers among black people. Often African Americans who were of fair complexion and had been free—and sometimes slave owners—before the war separated themselves from darker people who had been slaves and lacked education and financial resources.

The Presbyterian, Congregational, and Episcopal churches appealed to the more prosperous members of the black community. Their services tended to be more formal and solemn. Black people who had been free before the Civil War were usually affiliated with these congregations and remained so after the conflict. Well-to-do free black people in Charleston organized St. Mark's Protestant Episcopal Church when they separated from the white Episcopal Church, but they retained their white minister Joseph Seabrook as rector. Poorer black people found churches like St. Mark's unappealing. Ed Barber visited, but only one time:

> "When I was trampin' 'round Charleston, dere was a church dere called St. Mark, dat all de society folks of my color went to. No black nigger welcome dere, they told me. Thinkin' as how I was bright 'nough to git in, I up and goes dere one Sunday, Ah, how they did carry on, bow and scrape and ape de white folks . . . . I was uncomfortable all de time though, 'cause they were too "hifalootin" in de ways, in de singin', and all sorts of carryin' ons."

The Roman Catholic Church made modest in-roads among black southerners. There were all-black parishes in St. Augustine, Savannah, Charleston, and Louisville after the Civil War. For generations before the conflict, many well-to-do free people of color in New Orleans had been Catholics, and their descendants remained faithful to the church. On Georgia's Skidaway Island, Benedictine monks established a school for black youngsters in 1878 that survived for nearly a decade.

Religious differences notwithstanding, the black churches, their parishioners, and their clergymen would play a vital role in Reconstruction politics. More than 100 black ministers were elected to political office after the Civil War.

12.3 Education

Explain how former slaves gained an education.

Freedom and education were inseparable. To remain illiterate after emancipation was to remain enslaved. One ex-slave master bluntly told his former slave, Charles Whiteside, "Charles, you is a free man they say, but Ah tells you now, you is still a slave and if you lives to be a hundred, you'll STILL be a slave, cause you got no education, and education is what makes a man free!" Almost every freed black person—young or old—desperately wanted to learn. Elderly people were especially eager to read the Bible. During the war and before slavery ended, black people began to establish schools. In 1861 Mary Peake, a free black woman, opened a school in Hampton, Virginia. On South Carolina's sea islands, a black cabinetmaker began teaching openly after having covertly operated a school for years. In 1862 northern missionaries arrived on the sea islands to begin teaching. Laura Towne and Ellen Murray, two white women, and Charlotte Forten, a black woman, opened Penn School on St. Helena's Island as part of the Port Royal Experiment. They enrolled 138 children and 58 adults. By 1863 there were 1,700 students and 45 teachers at 30 schools in the South Carolina low country.

With the end of the Civil War, northern religious organizations, in cooperation with the Freedmen's Bureau, organized hundreds of schools. Classes were held in stables, homes, former slave cabins, taverns, churches, and even—in Savannah and New Orleans—the old slave markets. Former slaves spent hours in the fields and then trudged to a makeshift school to learn the alphabet and arithmetic. In 1865 black ministers created the Savannah Educational Association, raised $1,000, employed 15 black teachers, and enrolled 600 students.

In 1866 the Freedmen's Bureau set aside $500,000 for education. The Bureau furnished the buildings, while former slaves hired, housed, and fed the teachers. By 1869 the Freedmen's Bureau was involved with 3,000 schools and 150,000 students. Even more impressive, by 1870 black people had contributed $1 million to educate their people.

12.3.1 Black Teachers

Although freedmen appreciated the dedication of the white teachers affiliated with the missionary societies, they usually preferred black teachers. The Rev. Richard H. Cain, an AME minister who came south from Brooklyn, New York, said that black people needed to learn to control their own futures: "We must take into our own hands the education of our race . . . . Honest, dignified whites may teach ever so well, but it has not the effect to exalt the black man's opinion of his own race, because they have always been in the habit of seeing white men in honored positions, and respected."

Black men and women responded to the call to teach. Virginia C. Green, a northern black woman, felt compelled to go to Mississippi: "Though I have never known servitude they are . . . my people. Born as far north as the lakes I have felt no freer because so many were less fortunate . . . . I look forward with impatience to the time when my people shall be strong, blest with education, purified and made prosperous by virtue and industry." Hezekiah Hunter, a black teacher from New York, commented in 1865 on the need for black teachers: "I believe we best can instruct our own people, knowing our own peculiarities—needs—necessities. Further—I believe we that are competent owe it to our people to teach them our speciality." And in Malden, West Virginia, when black residents found that a recently arrived 18-year-old black man could read and write, they hired him to teach.

In some areas of the South, the sole person available to teach was a poorly educated former slave equipped primarily with a willingness to teach fellow freedmen. One such teacher explained, "I never had the chance of goen to school for I was a slave until freedom . . . . I am the only teacher because we can not doe better now." Many northern teachers, black and white, provided more than the basics of elementary education. Black life and history were occasionally read about and discussed. Abolitionist Lydia Maria Child wrote *The Freedmen's Book*, which offered brief biographies of Benjamin Banneker, Frederick Douglass, and Toussaint Louverture. More often northern teachers, dismayed at the backwardness of the freedmen, struggled to modify behavior and to impart cultural values by teaching piety, thrift, cleanliness, temperance, and timeliness.

Many former slaves came to resent some of these teachers as condescending, self-righteous, and paternalistic. Sometimes the teachers, especially those who were white, became frustrated with recalcitrant students who did not readily absorb middle-class values. Others, however, derived enormous satisfaction from teaching freedmen. A Virginia teacher commented, "I think I shall stay here as long as I live and teach this people. I have no love or taste for any other work, and I am happy only here with them."

Charlotte Forten came from a prominent Philadelphia family of color. She joined hundreds of black and white teachers who migrated South during and after the Civil War to instruct the freed people. Some teachers remained for a few months. Others stayed for a lifetime. Charlotte Forten—shown here in an 1866 photograph—taught on the South Carolina sea islands from 1862 to 1864.

Black and white land-grant colleges stressed training in agriculture and industry. In this late nineteenth-century photograph, Hampton Institute students learn milk production. The men are in military uniforms, which was typical for males at these colleges. Military training was a required part of the curriculum.

American Missionary Association

This religious organization sent teachers and clergymen throughout the South following the Civil War to tend to the spiritual and educational needs of former slaves. It was instrumental in establishing dozens of schools, including Fisk, Hampton, and Avery.

12.3.2 Black Colleges

Northern churches and religious societies established dozens of colleges, universities, academies, and institutes across the South in the late 1860s and the 1870s. Most of these institutions provided elementary and secondary education. Few black students were prepared for actual college or university work. The **American Missionary Association**—an abolitionist and Congregationalist organization—worked with the Freedmen's Bureau to establish Fisk in Tennessee, Hampton in Virginia, Tougaloo in Alabama, and Avery in South Carolina. The primary purpose of these schools was to educate black students to become teachers.

In Missouri, the black enlisted men and white officers of the 62nd and 65th Colored Volunteers raised $6,000 to establish Lincoln Institute in 1866, which would become Lincoln University. The American Baptist Home Mission Society founded Virginia Union, Shaw in North Carolina, Benedict in South Carolina, and Morehouse in Georgia. Northern Methodists helped establish Claflin in South Carolina, Rust in Mississippi, and Bennett in North Carolina. The Episcopalians were responsible for St. Augustine's in North Carolina and St. Paul's in Virginia. These and similar institutions formed the foundation for the historically black colleges and universities.

12.3.3 Response of White Southerners

White southerners considered black people's efforts to learn absurd. For generations, white Americans had considered people of African descent abjectly inferior. When efforts were made to educate former slaves, white southerners reacted with suspicion, contempt, and hostility. One white woman told a teacher, "I do assure you, you might as well try to teach your horse or mule to read, as to teach these niggers. They can't learn."

Most white people were well aware that black people could learn. Otherwise, the slave codes that prohibited educating slaves would have been unnecessary. After slavery's end, some white people went out of their way to prevent black people from learning. Countless schools were burned, mostly in rural areas. In Canton, Mississippi, black people collected money to open a school—only to have white residents inform them that the school would be burned and the prospective teacher lynched if it opened. The female teacher at a freedmen's school in Donaldsonville, Louisiana, was shot and killed.

Other white southerners grudgingly tolerated black people's desire to acquire an education. One planter conceded in 1870, "Every little negro in the county is now going to school and the public pays for it. This is one hell of [a] fix but we can't help it, and the best policy is to conform as far as possible to circumstances."

Most white people refused to attend school with black people. No integrated schools were established in the immediate aftermath of emancipation. Most black people were more interested in gaining an education than in whether white students attended school with them. When black youngsters tried to attend a white school in Raleigh, North Carolina, the white students stopped going to it. For a brief time in Charleston, black and white children attended the same school, but they were taught in separate classrooms.

Profile

Charlotte E. Ray

Charlotte E. Ray became the first African-American woman to earn a law degree and the first woman admitted to practice law in Washington, D.C. She was born on January 13, 1850, in New York City, one of seven children. Her parents were the Rev. Charles B. Ray and his second wife, Charlotte Augusta Burroughs Ray. They were firm believers in the rights of African Americans and in their potential for success.

Charlotte attended Myrtilla Miner's Institution for the Education of Colored Youth in Washington, D.C., where Myrtilla Miner, a white educator from New York, was determined to demonstrate that black women were as capable of high moral and mental development as white women.

Charlotte completed high school at Miner's in 1869 and taught at the Normal and Preparatory Department of the recently established Howard University. She also enrolled in law classes at Howard and wrote a thesis analyzing corporations.

She graduated from the law school in 1872 and a month later was admitted to the bar in Washington. She opened an office and planned to practice real estate law. As a real estate lawyer, she could avoid court appearances and the discrimination that women attorneys encountered. She often used her initials, C. E. Ray, so that her clients would not suffer because their legal counsel could be identified as a woman.

Because of the Panic of 1873 and the ensuing economic depression, as well as the difficulties of being a black woman in a white male profession, Ray gave up the practice of law. She supported women's rights and, in 1876, attended the annual meeting of the National American Woman Suffrage Association in New York City. By 1879, she had returned to New York and taught school in Brooklyn. Sometime before 1886, she had married, but little is known of her husband. Charlotte Ray died of acute bronchitis on January 11, 1911.

Voices

A Northern Black Woman on Teaching Freedmen

Blanche Virginia Harris was born in 1842 in Monroe, Michigan, and graduated from Oberlin College in 1860. She became the principal of a black school in Norfolk, Virginia, attended by 230 students. She organized night classes for adults and a sewing society to provide clothing for impoverished students. Later, she taught in Mississippi, North Carolina, and Tennessee. In the following letter she describes her experiences in Mississippi:

23 January 1866

Natchez, Miss.

I have been in this city now nearly five months . . . . The colored teachers three in number, sent out by the [American Missionary] Association to this city, have been brought down here it is true. And then left to the mercy of the colored people or themselves. The distinction between the two classes of teachers (white and colored) is so marked that it is the topic of conversation among the better class of colored people.

My school is very large, some of them pay and some do not. And from the proceeds I pay the board of my sister and myself, and also for the rent of two rooms; rent as well as board is very high so I have to work quite hard to meet my expenses. I also furnish lights, wood and coal. I do not write this as fault-finding, far from it. I shall be thankful if I can in any way help. I sometimes get discouraged . . . .

I have become very much attached to my school; the interest they manifest in their studies pleases me. I will now tell you how I employ my time. From 8 A.M. until 2 P.M. I teach the children. At 3 P.M. I have a class of adults and at night I have night school.

One afternoon we have prayer meeting, another sewing school. And another singing school. I hope my next letter may be more interesting to you.

Very Respectfully,
Blanche Harris

1. Why was the race of the teacher of such concern?
2. What did Harris find difficult about teaching, and what did she find rewarding?

SOURCE: Blanche Virginia Harris, 23 January 1866.

12.4 Violence

Characterize the extent of violence confronted by African Americans after the Civil War.

In the days, weeks, and months after the end of the Civil War, an orgy of brutality and violence swept across the South. White southerners—embittered by their defeat and unable to adjust to the end of slave labor and the loss of millions of dollars' worth of slave property—lashed out at black people. There were beatings, murders, rapes, and riots, often with little or no provocation.

Black people who demanded respect, wore better clothing, refused to step aside for white people, or asked to be addressed as "mister" or "missus" were attacked. In South Carolina, a white clergyman shot and killed a black man who protested when another black man was removed from a church service. In Texas, one black man was killed for not removing his hat in the presence of a white man and another for refusing to relinquish a bottle of whiskey. A black woman was beaten for "using insolent language," and a black worker in Alabama was killed for speaking sharply to a white overseer. In Virginia, a black veteran was beaten after announcing he had been proud to serve in the Union Army.

In South Carolina, a white man asked a passing black man whom he belonged to. The black man replied that he no longer belonged to anybody, "I am free now." With that, the white man roared, "Sas me? You black devil!" He then slashed the freedman with a knife. The sheriff of DeWitt County, Texas, shot a black man who was whistling "Yankee Doodle." A Freedmen's Bureau agent in North Carolina explained the intense white hostility: "The fact is, it's the first notion with a great many of these people, if a Negro says anything or does anything that they don't like, to take a gun and put a bullet into him, or a charge of shot." In Texas another Freedmen's Bureau officer claimed that white people simply killed black people "for the love of killing."

There was also large-scale violence. In 1865 University of North Carolina students twice attacked peaceful meetings of black people. Near Pine Bluff, Arkansas, in 1866, a white mob burned a black settlement and lynched 24 men, women, and children. An estimated 2,000 black people were murdered around Shreveport, Louisiana. In Texas, white people killed 1,000 black people between 1865 and 1868.

In May 1866 white residents of Memphis went on a rampage after black veterans forced police to release a black prisoner. The city was already beset with economic difficulties and racial tensions caused in part by an influx of rural refugees. White people, led by Irish policemen, destroyed hundreds of homes, cabins, shacks, churches, and schools in the black section of Memphis. Altogether, 46 black people and two white men died.

On July 30, 1866, in New Orleans, white people—angered that black men were demanding political rights—assaulted black people on the street and in a convention hall. City policemen, who were mostly Confederate veterans, shot down the black delegates as they fled in panic waving white flags in a futile attempt to surrender. In the assault, 34 black people and three of their white allies died. Federal troops eventually stopped the bloodshed. General Philip H. Sheridan called the riot "an absolute massacre."

Little was done to stem the violence. Most Union troops had been withdrawn from the South and demobilized after the war. The Freedmen's Bureau was usually unwilling and unable to protect the black population. Black people left to defend themselves were usually in no position to retaliate. Instead, they sometimes attempted to bring the perpetrators to justice. In Orangeburg, South Carolina, armed black men brought three white men who had been wreaking violence in the community to the local jail. In Holly Springs, Mississippi, a posse of armed black men apprehended a white man who had murdered a freedwoman.

For black people, the system of justice was thoroughly unjust. Although black people could now testify against white people in court, southern juries remained all white and refused to convict white people charged with harming black people. In Texas during 1865 and 1866, 500 white men were indicted for murdering black people. None were convicted.

12.4.1 The Crusade for Political and Civil Rights

In October 1864 in Syracuse, New York, 145 black leaders gathered in a national convention. Some of the century's most prominent black men and women attended, including Henry Highland Garnet, Frances E. W. Harper, William Wells Brown, Francis L. Cardozo, Richard H. Cain, Jonathan J. Wright, and Jonathan C. Gibbs. They embraced the basic tenets of the American political tradition and proclaimed that they expected to participate fully in it.

Anticipating a future free of slavery, Frederick Douglass optimistically declared "that we hereby assert our full confidence in the fundamental principles of this government . . . the great heart of this nation will ultimately concede us our just claims, accord us our rights, and grant us our full measure of citizenship under the broad shield of the Constitution."

Even before the **Syracuse Convention**, northern Republicans met in Union-controlled territory around Beaufort, South Carolina, and nominated the state's delegates to the 1864 Republican national convention. Among those selected were Robert Smalls and Prince Rivers, former slaves who had exemplary records with the Union Army. The probability of black participation in postwar politics seemed promising.

But northern and southern white leaders who already held power would largely determine whether black Americans would gain political power or acquire the same rights as white people. As the Civil War ended, President Lincoln was more concerned with restoring the seceded states to the Union than in opening political doors for black people. Yet Lincoln suggested that at least some black men deserved the right to vote. On April 11, 1865, he wrote, "I would myself prefer that [the vote] were now conferred on the very intelligent, and on those who serve our cause as soldiers." Three days later he was assassinated.

Syracuse Convention

A meeting of black leaders in Syracuse, New York, to discuss the future of African Americans following the abolition of slavery. They insisted that black people had earned and deserved the same political and legal rights as white Americans.

12.5 Presidential Reconstruction under Andrew Johnson

Analyze the impact that President Andrew Johnson's policies had on African Americans.

Vice President Andrew Johnson became president following Lincoln's assassination and initially seemed inclined to impose stern policies on the white South while befriending the freedmen. He announced that "treason must be made odious, and traitors must be punished and impoverished." In 1864 he had told black people, "I will be your Moses, and lead you through the Red Sea of War and Bondage to a fairer future of Liberty and Peace." Nothing proved to be further from the truth. Andrew Johnson was no friend of black Americans.

Born poor in eastern Tennessee and never part of the southern aristocracy, Johnson opposed secession and was the only senator from the seceded states to remain loyal to the Union. He had nonetheless acquired five slaves and the conviction that black people were so inferior that white men must forever govern them. In 1867 Johnson argued that black people could not exercise political power and that they had "less capacity for government than any other race of people. No independent government of any form has ever been successful in their hands. On the contrary, wherever they have been left to their own devices they have shown a constant tendency to relapse into barbarism."

Johnson quickly lost his enthusiasm for punishing traitors. Indeed, he began to placate white southerners. In May 1865 Johnson granted blanket amnesty and pardons to former Confederates willing to swear allegiance to the United States. The main exceptions were high former Confederate officials and those who owned property valued in excess of $20,000, a large sum at the time. Yet even these leaders could appeal for individual pardons. And appeal they did. By 1866 Johnson had pardoned more than 7,000 high-ranking former Confederates and wealthier southerners. Moreover, he had restored land to those white people who had lost it to freedmen.

Johnson's actions encouraged those who had supported secession, owned slaves, and opposed the Union. He permitted longtime southern leaders to regain political influence and authority only months after the end of America's bloodiest conflict. As black people and Radical Republicans watched in disbelief, Johnson appointed provisional governors in the former Confederate states. Leaders in those states then called constitutional conventions, held elections, and prepared to regain their place in the Union. Johnson merely insisted that each former Confederate state formally accept the **Thirteenth Amendment** (ratified in December 1865, it outlawed slavery) and repudiate Confederate war debts.

The southern constitutional conventions excluded black people from the political system and denied them equal rights. As one Mississippi delegate explained, "'Tis nature's law that the superior race must rule and rule they will."

12.5.1 Black Codes

After the election of state and local officials, white legislators gathered in state capitals across the South to determine the status and future of the freedmen. With little debate, the legislatures drafted the so-called **black codes**. Southern politicians gave no thought to providing black people with the political and legal rights associated with citizenship.

The black codes sought to retain the availability of a subservient agricultural labor supply controlled by white people. They imposed severe restrictions on freedmen, who had to sign annual labor contracts with white landowners. To discourage black people from becoming self-employed tradesmen or entrepreneurs, South Carolina's black code required black people who wanted to establish a business to purchase licenses costing from $10 to $100. Black youngsters could be apprenticed even against their will to the age of 21 for males and to 18 for females. Apprentices could be punished "moderately" by whipping as white people sought to maintain discipline and control over "their" laborers. Employers were designated "masters" and employees "servants." The black codes also restricted black people from loitering or vagrancy, using alcohol or firearms, and set limits on hunting, fishing, and grazing livestock.

However, the codes did guarantee rights that slaves had not possessed. Freedmen could marry legally, engage in contracts, purchase property, sue or be sued, and testify in court. But black people could not vote or serve on juries. South Carolina's code established a separate court system for black people—with white judges and white jurors. The black codes conceded—barely—freedom to black people.

12.5.2 Black Conventions

Alarmed by these threats to their freedom, black people met in conventions across the South in 1865 and 1866 to protest, appeal for justice, and chart their future. Men who had been free before the war dominated the conventions. Many were ministers, teachers, and artisans. Few had been slaves. Women and children also attended—as spectators, not delegates—but women were often influential as they offered comments, suggestions, and criticism. These meetings were hardly militant or radical affairs. Delegates respectfully insisted that white people live up to the principles and rights embodied in the Declaration of Independence and the Constitution.

At the AME church in Raleigh, North Carolina, delegates asked for equal rights and the right to vote. At Georgia's convention, they protested against white violence and appealed for leaders who would enforce the law without regard to color: "We ask not

Thirteenth Amendment

This amendment to the U.S. Constitution outlawed slavery and involuntary servitude.

black codes

Laws that were passed in each of the former Confederate states following the Civil War that applied only to black people. While conceding such rights as the right to marry, to contract a debt, or to own property, the codes severely restricted the rights and opportunities of former slaves in terms of labor and mobility.

Bearing a remarkable resemblance to a slave auction, this scene in Monticello, Florida, shows a black man auctioned off to the highest bidder shortly after the Civil War. Under the terms of most southern black codes, black people arrested and fined for vagrancy or loitering could be "sold" if they could not pay the fine. Such spectacles infuriated many northerners and led to demands for more rigid Reconstruction policies.

for a Black Man's Governor, nor a White Man's Governor, but for a People's Governor, who shall impartially protect the rights of all, and faithfully sustain the Union."

Delegates at the Norfolk meeting reminded white Virginians that black people were patriotic: "We are Americans. We know no other country. We love the land of our birth." But they protested that Virginia's black code caused "invidious political or legal distinctions, on account of color merely." They requested the right to vote and added that they might boycott the businesses of "those who deny to us our equal rights."

Two conventions were held in Charleston, South Carolina—one before and one after the black code was enacted. At the first, delegates stressed the "respect and affection" they felt toward white Charlestonians. They even proposed that only literate men be granted the right to vote if it were applied to both races. The second convention denounced the black code and insisted on its repeal. Delegates again asked for the rights to vote and testify in court: "These two things we deem necessary to our welfare and elevation." They also appealed for public schools and for "homesteads for ourselves and our children." White authorities ignored the black conventions and their petitions. Instead, they were confident they had relegated the freedmen to a subordinate and manageable role.

By late 1865 President Johnson's Reconstruction policies had aroused black people. One black Union veteran summed up the situation: "If you call this Freedom, what do you call Slavery?" Republicans in Congress also opposed Johnson's policies toward the freedmen and the former Confederate states.

12.5.3 The Radical Republicans

Radical Republicans, as the more militant Republicans were called, were especially disturbed that Johnson seemed to have abandoned the ex-slaves to their former masters. They considered white southerners disloyal and unrepentant, despite their military defeat. Moreover, Radical Republicans—unlike moderate Republicans and Democrats— were determined to transform the racial fabric of American society by including black people in the political and economic system.

Radical Republicans

Members of the Republican Party during Reconstruction who vigorously supported the rights of African Americans to vote, hold political office, and have the same legal and economic opportunities as white people.

Among the most influential Radical Republicans were Senators Charles Sumner, Benjamin Wade, and Henry Wilson, as well as Congressmen Thaddeus Stevens, George W. Julian, and James M. Ashley. Few white Americans were as dedicated to the rights of black people as these men. They had fought to abolish slavery and were reluctant to compromise. They were honest, tough, and articulate but also abrasive, difficult, self-righteous, and vain. Black people appreciated them, whereas many white people hated them. One black veteran wrote to Charles Sumner in 1869, stating, "Your name shall live in our hearts forever." A white Philadelphia businessman said that Thaddeus Stevens "seems to oppose any measure that will not benefit the nigger."

12.5.4 Radical Proposals

To provide freedmen with land, Stevens introduced a bill in Congress in late 1865 to confiscate 400 million acres from the wealthiest 10 percent of southerners and distribute it free to freedmen. The remaining land would be auctioned off in plots no larger than 500 acres. Few legislators supported the proposal. Even those who wanted fundamental change considered confiscation a violation of property rights.

Instead, Radical Republicans supported voting rights for black men. They were convinced that black men—to protect themselves and to secure the South for the Republican Party—had to have the right to vote.

Moderate Republicans, however, found the prospect of black voting almost as objectionable as the confiscation of land. They preferred to build the Republican Party in the South by cooperating with President Johnson and attracting loyal white southerners.

The thought of black suffrage appalled northern and southern Democrats. Most white northerners—Republicans and Democrats—favored denying black men the right to vote in their states. After the war, proposals to guarantee the right to vote to black men were defeated in New York, Ohio, Kansas, and the Nebraska Territory. In the District of Columbia, a vote to permit black suffrage lost 6,951 to 35. However, five of the six New England states as well as Iowa, Minnesota, and Wisconsin allowed black men to vote.

As much as they objected to black suffrage, most white northerners objected even more strongly to defiant white southerners. Journalist Charles A. Dana described the attitude of many northerners: "As for negro suffrage, the mass of Union men in the Northwest do not care a great deal. What scares them is the idea that the rebels are all to be let back . . . and made a power in government again, just as though there had been no rebellion."

In December 1865 Congress created the Joint Committee on Reconstruction to determine whether to readmit the southern states to the Union. The committee confirmed reports of widespread mistreatment of black people and white arrogance.

12.5.5 The Freedmen's Bureau Bill and the Civil Rights Bill

In early 1866 Senator Lyman Trumbull, a moderate Republican from Illinois, introduced two major bills. The first was to provide more financial support for the Freedmen's Bureau and extend its authority to defend the rights of black people.

The second proposal became the first **Civil Rights Act** in American history. It made any person born in the United States a citizen (except Indians) and entitled them to rights protected by the U.S. government. Black people would possess the same legal rights as white people. The bill was clearly intended to invalidate the black codes.

12.5.6 Johnson's Vetoes

Both measures passed in Congress with nearly unanimous Republican support. President Johnson, however, vetoed them. He claimed that the bill to continue the Freedmen's Bureau would greatly expand the federal bureaucracy and permit too "vast a number of agents" to exercise arbitrary power over the white population. He insisted that the Civil Rights Bill

Civil Rights Act

This act nullified the black codes and made African Americans citizens with the basic rights of life, liberty, and due process. It was passed over President Andrew Johnson's veto. Its main features were subsequently embedded in the Fourteenth Amendment to the Constitution.

Profile

Aaron A. Bradley

At a time when many white people considered it a disgrace that even the most reserved, refined, and well-educated black man might serve in political office, Aaron Bradley's presence in politics was outrageous. White southerners regarded him as a dangerous revolutionary. White Republicans, who normally would have been his allies, considered him belligerent and uncooperative. But most freedmen admired and supported him. Like him or not, he was a major figure in Georgia politics during Reconstruction.

Bradley was born a slave in about 1815 in South Carolina. His father was probably white. He belonged to Francis W. Pickens, who was South Carolina's governor when the state seceded (see Chapter 10). For a time, Bradley worked as a shoemaker in nearby Augusta, Georgia. At about age 20, he escaped and went to Boston, where he studied law and met black and white abolitionists.

In 1865 Bradley moved to Savannah, where he took up the cause of the freedmen and opened a school. He worked closely with the city's black longshoremen and low country and sea island rice field workers.

Bradley demanded that black families keep the land they had occupied under Sherman's Special Field Order #15. He believed that they had to have land to prosper. He criticized the Freedmen's Bureau for attempting to force black people off the land and argued that President Johnson should be impeached for supporting Confederate landowners rather than black and white people who were loyal to the Union.

Bradley also insisted that black people deserved the rights to vote, testify in court, and have jury trials. After he urged black farmers to defend their land by force, federal authorities charged him with advocating insurrection. He was sentenced to a year's confinement but was soon paroled. Almost immediately, another fiery speech got him in trouble again, and he had to leave Georgia.

He returned to Boston and renewed his pleas for land for the freedmen. He wrote the head of the Freedmen's Bureau, "My great object is, to give you Back-bone, and as the Chief Justice of 4 millions of Colored people, and Refugees; You can not, and must not, be a Military Tool, in the hands of Andrew Johnson."

In 1867 Bradley returned to Savannah and attacked the system of sharecropping. He complained that freedmen were compelled to work involuntarily and asked that black men be permitted to arm themselves. He also argued that justice would be fairer if the courts included black men. Although the Freedmen's Bureau considered Bradley a troublemaker, he never backed down.

In 1867, black voters elected Bradley to the state constitutional convention, but he was soon expelled. Then he was elected to the state senate—only to be expelled again along with all the black members of the Georgia legislature.

Meanwhile, Bradley carried on a running battle with Savannah's mayor, a former Confederate colonel affiliated with the Ku Klux Klan. He threatened the "KKK and all Bad Men, . . . if you strike a blow the man or men will be followed, and the house in which he or they shall take shelter, will be burned to the ground."

In 1868 Bradley organized black workers to arm themselves to retain the lands that they believed belonged to them. For a month, black men controlled parts of Chatham County outside Savannah. Eventually, federal authorities jailed 100 of them. Bradley again fled north.

He returned to Georgia in 1870 and reclaimed his senate seat after Congress forced the legislature to seat its black members. He supported measures to remove Savannah's mayor, reduce taxes on workers, and institute an eight-hour workday.

Democrats regained control of Georgia politics in 1872, and Bradley and the Republicans were swept from power. He ran for Congress in South Carolina in 1874 but lost. He supported black migration to Liberia and Florida, but he moved to St. Louis and died there in 1881.

Aaron Bradley was certainly not a typical Reconstruction leader. He maintained few close ties to black or white politicians. He was constantly embroiled in disputes, he did not cooperate with middle-class black leaders, and had no ties with local churches and their clergymen—a rarity among black politicians.

He dressed in expensive and flashy clothes, and he could be pompous, abrasive, and intemperate. White people universally detested him. Yet Bradley remained popular among freedmen.

---

benefited black people at the expense of white people: "In fact, the distinction of race and color is by the bill made to operate in favor of the colored and against the white race."

The Johnson vetoes stunned Republicans. Although he had not meant to, Johnson drove moderate Republicans into the radical camp and strengthened the Republican Party. The president did not believe Republicans would oppose him to support the freedmen. He was wrong. Congress overrode both vetoes. The Republicans broke with Johnson in 1866, defied him in 1867, and impeached him in 1868 (failing to remove him from office by only one vote in the Senate).

12.5.7 The Fourteenth Amendment

Fourteenth Amendment

This amendment ratified during Reconstruction made any person born in the United States a citizen of the United States and of the state in which he or she lived.

To secure the legal rights of freedmen, Republicans passed the **Fourteenth Amendment**. This amendment fundamentally changed the Constitution by compelling states to accept their residents as citizens and to guarantee that their rights as citizens would be safeguarded.

Its first section guaranteed citizenship to every person born in the United States. This included virtually every black person. In addition, it made each person a citizen of the state in which he or she resided, defined the specific rights of citizens, and protected those rights against the authority of state governments. Citizens had the right to due process (usually a trial) before they could lose their life, liberty, or property:

> All persons born or naturalized in the United States, and subject to the jurisdiction thereof, are citizens of the United States and of the State wherein they reside. No State shall make or enforce any law which shall abridge the privileges or immunities of citizens of the United States; nor shall any State deprive any person of life, liberty, or property, without due process of law; nor deny to any person within its jurisdiction the equal protection of the laws.

Eleven years after Chief Justice Roger Taney declared in the *Dred Scott* decision that black people were "a subordinate and inferior class of beings" who had "no rights that white people were bound to respect," the Fourteenth Amendment vested African Americans with the same rights of citizenship other Americans possessed.

The amendment also threatened to deprive states of representation in Congress if they denied black men the vote. The end of slavery had also made obsolete the Three-Fifths Clause in the Constitution, which had counted slaves as only three-fifths (or 60 percent) of a white person in calculating a state's population and in determining the number of representatives each state was entitled to in the House of Representatives. Republicans feared that southern states would count black people in their populations without permitting them to vote, thereby gaining more representatives than those states had before the Civil War. The amendment mandated that if any state—northern or southern—did not allow adult male citizens to vote, then the number of representatives it was entitled to in Congress would be reduced in proportion to the number of men denied the right to vote.

1865–1867
Federal Reconstruction Legislation

1865
Freedmen's Bureau established

1865
Thirteenth Amendment passed and ratified

1866
Freedmen's Bureau Bill and the Civil Rights Act of 1866 passed over Johnson's veto

1866
Fourteenth Amendment passed (ratified 1868)

1867
Reconstruction Acts passed over Johnson's veto

Democrats almost unanimously opposed the Fourteenth Amendment. Andrew Johnson denounced it, although he could not prevent its adoption. Except for Tennessee, southern states refused to ratify it. Women's suffragists felt betrayed because the amendment limited suffrage to males. Despite this opposition, the amendment was ratified in 1868.

12.5.8 Radical Reconstruction

By 1867 Radical Republicans in Congress had wrested control over **Reconstruction** from Johnson, and they then imposed policies that brought black men into the political system as voters and officeholders. It was a dramatic development, second in importance only to emancipation and the end of slavery.

Republicans swept the 1866 congressional elections despite the belligerent opposition of Johnson and the Democrats. With two-thirds majorities in the House and Senate, Republicans easily overrode presidential vetoes. Two years after the Civil War, Republicans dismantled the state governments established in the South under Johnson's authority and instituted a new Reconstruction policy.

Republicans passed the first of three **Reconstruction Acts** over Johnson's veto in March 1867. It divided the South into five military districts, each under the command of a general (see Map 12-2). Troops would protect lives and property while new civilian governments were formed. Elected delegates in each state would draft a new constitution and submit it to the voters.

12.5.9 Universal Manhood Suffrage

The Reconstruction Act stipulated that all adult males in the states of the former Confederacy were eligible to vote, except for those who had actively supported the Confederacy or were convicted felons. Once each state had formed a new government and approved the Fourteenth Amendment, it would be readmitted to the Union with representation in Congress.

The advent of Radical Reconstruction was the culmination of the struggle of black people to gain legal and political rights. Since the 1864 black national convention in Syracuse and the meetings and conventions in the South in 1865 and 1866, black leaders had argued that one of the consequences of the Civil War should be the inclusion of black men in the body politic. The achievement of that goal was due to their persistent and persuasive efforts, the determination of Radical Republicans, and, ironically, the obstructionism of Andrew Johnson, who had played into their hands.

12.5.10 Black Politics

Full of energy and enthusiasm, black men and women rushed into the political arena in the spring and summer of 1867. Although women could not vote, they joined men at the meetings, rallies, parades, and picnics that accompanied political organizing in the South. For many freed men and women, politics became as important as religious activities. Black people flocked to the Republican Party and the new Union Leagues.

Map 12-2 Congressional Reconstruction

Under the terms of the First Reconstruction Act of 1867, the former Confederate states (except Tennessee) were divided into five military districts and placed under the authority of military officers. Commanders in each of the five districts were responsible for supervising the reestablishment of civilian governments in each state.

SOURCE: Robert C. Nell, "Declaration of Sentiments of the Colored Citizens of Boston on the Fugitive Slave Bill, 1850." © Darlene Clark Hine.

In which states were African Americans a majority of delegates to that state's constitutional convention?

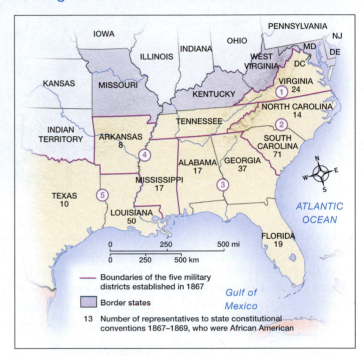

Reconstruction

The 12 years (1865–1877) following the Civil War, during which the former Confederate states were restored to the Union and former slaves became citizens and gained the right to vote and hold political office. It was also a time of violence and terrorism as many southern white people resisted the change in the status of African Americans.

Reconstruction Acts

Led by Radical Republicans, Congress divided the South into five military districts. Each former Confederate state (except Tennessee) was to frame a new state constitution and establish a new state government. The first Reconstruction Act provided for universal manhood suffrage, which granted the right to vote to all adult males, including black men.

With the adoption of Radical Republican policies, most black men eagerly took part in political activities. Political meetings, conventions, speeches, barbecues, and other gatherings also attracted women and children.

Union League

A social and fraternal organization that stirred political interest and support among black and white Republicans in the South during Reconstruction.

The **Union Leagues** had been established in the North during the Civil War, but they expanded across the South as quasi-political organizations in the late 1860s. The Leagues were social, fraternal, and patriotic groups in which black people often but not always outnumbered white people. League meetings featured ceremonies, rituals, initiation rites, and oaths. They gave people an opportunity to sharpen leadership skills and gain a political education by discussing issues from taxes to schools.

12.5.11 Sit-Ins and Strikes

Political progress did not induce apathy, satisfaction, or contentment among black people. Instead, gaining citizenship, legal rights, and the vote generated more expectations and demands for advancement. For example, black people insisted on equal access to public transportation. In Charleston, South Carolina, black people were permitted to ride only on the outside running boards of the horse- and mule-drawn streetcars. After a Republican rally there in April 1867, black men staged a "sit-in" on one of the vehicles before they were arrested. They wanted to sit on the seats inside. Within a month, after military authorities intervened, the streetcar company gave in. Similar protests occurred in Richmond and New Orleans.

Black workers also struck across the South in 1867. Black longshoremen in New Orleans, Mobile, Savannah, Charleston, and Richmond walked off the job. Black laborers were usually paid less than white men for the same work, which led to labor unrest during the 1860s and 1870s. Sometimes the strikers won, sometimes they lost. In 1869 a black Baltimore longshoreman, Isaac Myers, organized the National Colored Labor Union.

12.5.12 The Reaction of White Southerners

White southerners grimly opposed Radical Reconstruction. They were outraged that black people could claim the same legal and political rights they themselves possessed. Such a possibility seemed preposterous to people convinced of the absolute inferiority of black people. Benjamin F. Perry, whom Johnson had appointed provisional governor of South Carolina in 1865, captures the depth of this racist conviction. "The African,"

Perry declared, "has been in all ages, a savage or a slave. God created him inferior to the white man in form, color and intellect, and no legislation or culture can make him his equal . . . . His hair, his form and features will not compete with the caucasian race, and it is in vain to think of elevating him to the dignity of the white man. God created differences between the two races, and nothing can make him equal."

Some white people, taking solace in their belief in the innate inferiority of black people, concluded they could turn black suffrage to their advantage. White people, they assumed, should easily be able to control and manipulate black voters just as they had controlled black people during slavery. White southerners who believed this, however, would be disappointed, and their disappointment would turn to fury.

Conclusion

Why were black southerners able to gain citizenship and access to the political system by 1868? Most white Americans did not suddenly abandon 250 years of deeply ingrained beliefs that people of African descent were their inferiors. The advances that African Americans achieved fit into a series of complex political developments after the Civil War. Black people themselves had fought and died to preserve the Union, and they had earned the grudging respect of many white people and the open admiration of others. Black leaders in meetings and petitions insisted that their rights be recognized.

White northerners—led by the Radical Republicans—were convinced that President Johnson was wrong to support policies that permitted white southerners to retain pre–Civil War leaders while the black codes virtually made freedmen slaves again. Republicans were determined that white southerners realize that their defeat had doomed the prewar status quo. Republicans established a Reconstruction program to disfranchise key southern leaders while providing legal rights to freedmen. The right to vote, they reasoned, would enable black people to deal more effectively with white southerners and strengthen the Republican Party in the South.

The result was to make the mid to late 1860s one of the few high points in African-American history. During this period, not only was slavery abolished, but black southerners were able to organize schools and churches, and black people throughout the South acquired legal and political rights that would have been incomprehensible before the war. Yet black people did not stand on the brink of utopia. Most freedmen still lacked land and had no realistic hope of obtaining much, if any, of it. In addition, white violence and cruelty continued almost unabated across much of the South. Still, for millions of African Americans, the future looked more promising than ever before in American history.

Chapter Timeline

AFRICAN-AMERICAN EVENTS	NATIONAL EVENTS
	1862–1864
March 1862	**February 1862**
The Port Royal Experiment in South Carolina begins	Julia Ward Howe publishes the first version of "Battle Hymn of the Republic" in the *Atlantic Monthly*
October 1864	
Black national convention in Syracuse, New York	**July 1862**
	Morrill Land-Grant College Act signed into law
	November 1864
	President Lincoln reelected

AFRICAN-AMERICAN EVENTS	NATIONAL EVENTS
1865–1866	
January 1865	**April 1865**
General Sherman's Special Field Order #15	Lincoln is assassinated; Andrew Johnson succeeds to presidency
March 1865	**May 1865**
Freedmen's Bureau established	Johnson begins presidential Reconstruction
September–November 1865	**June–August 1865**
Black codes enacted	Southern state governments reorganized
February 1866	**December 1865**
Southern Homestead Act	Thirteenth Amendment to the Constitution ratified
March 1866	**November 1866**
President Johnson vetoes bill to extend the Freedman's Bureau and the Civil Rights Bill	Republicans gain greater than two-thirds majorities in House and Senate
April 1866	
Congress overrides Johnson's veto of the Civil Rights Bill	
May 1866	
Memphis riot	
July 1866	
Congress enacts new Freedmen's Bureau bill over Johnson's veto; New Orleans riot	
1867–1869	
Spring–Summer 1867	**March 1867**
Union Leagues and the Republican Party organized in southern states	Congress passes the first Reconstruction Act over President Johnson's veto
1869	The United States purchases Alaska from Russia
The National Colored Labor Union established under the leadership of Isaac Myers	**February 1868**
	House impeaches President Johnson
	May 1868
	Senate acquits Johnson by one vote
	July 1868
	Fourteenth Amendment to the Constitution ratified
	November 1868
	Ulysses S. Grant elected president
	May 1869
	Transcontinental railroad completed

Review Questions

1. What did freedom mean to ex-slaves? How did their priorities differ from those of African Americans who had been free before the Civil War?

2. What did the former slaves and the former slaveholders want after emancipation? Were these desires realistic? How did former slaves and former slaveholders disagree after the end of slavery?

3. Why did African Americans form separate churches, schools, and social organizations after the Civil War? What role did the black church play in the black community?

4. How effective was the Freedmen's Bureau? How successful was it in assisting ex-slaves to live in freedom?

5. Why did southern states enact black codes?

6. Why did Radical Republicans object to President Andrew Johnson's Reconstruction policies? Why did Congress impose its own Reconstruction policies?

7. Why were laws passed to enable black men to vote?

8. Why did black men gain the right to vote but not possession of land?

9. Did congressional Reconstruction secure full equality for African Americans as American citizens?

Retracing the Odyssey

The Avery Research Center for African-American History and Culture, Charleston, South Carolina. In 1865 the American Missionary Association opened a private school for black youngsters that served the Charleston community until 1954. The renovated structure currently contains an archive, a restored classroom, and exhibits devoted to African-American life in the Carolina low country.

Shaw University and St. Augustine's College, Raleigh, North Carolina. These are two of the many black colleges established during Reconstruction. The Baptists founded Shaw in 1865, and its impressive Estey Hall has survived almost 130 years. The Episcopal Church and the Freedmen's Bureau collaborated to found St. Augustine's in 1867.

Fisk University, Nashville, Tennessee. The American Missionary Association established Fisk in 1866. Magnificent Jubilee Hall is the nation's oldest building dedicated to the higher education of black students. It was completed in 1876. There is an impressive collection of European and American art on the campus at the Carl Van Vechten Art Gallery.

St. Stephen African Methodist Episcopal Church, Wilmington, North Carolina. Following the Civil War, black members of the Front Street Methodist Church withdrew and founded their own church on Red Cross Street. In 1880 they began construction of the current building. For a time parishioners met in the basement while work continued on the imposing and ornate sanctuary above them.

Gullah/Geechee Cultural Heritage Corridor. In 2006 Congress established this 12,000-square-mile corridor that extends along the South Atlantic coast from Wilmington, North Carolina, through South Carolina and Georgia, to Jacksonville, Florida. It was created to recognize the cultural contributions, language, and way of life that has prevailed among people of African descent on the sea islands and the low country since the seventeenth century.

Recommended Reading

Ira Berlin and Leslie Rowland, eds. *Families and Freedom: A Documentary History of African-American Kinship in the Civil War Era.* New York: Cambridge University Press, 1997. A collection of documents that conveys the aspirations and frustrations of freedmen.

David W. Blight. *Race and Reunion: The Civil War in American Memory.* Cambridge, MA: Harvard University Press, 2001. This outstanding study shows how white Americans "remembered" the Civil War and reconciled their sectional differences by essentially forgetting the role and contributions of African Americans.

Jim Downs. *Sick From Freedom: African American Illness and Suffering During the Civil War and Reconstruction.* New York: Oxford University Press, 2012. This thought-provoking account traces the devastating impact that smallpox and other diseases had on African Americans as they gained their freedom.

W. E. B. Du Bois. *Black Reconstruction in America: An Essay Toward a History of the Part Which Black Folk Played in the Attempt to Reconstruct Democracy in America, 1860–1880.* New York: Russell and Russell, 1935. A classic account of Reconstruction challenging the traditional interpretation that it was a tragic era marked by corrupt and inept black rule of the South.

Douglas R. Egerton. *The Wars of Reconstruction: The Brief, Violent History of America's Most Progressive Era.* New York: Bloomsbury, 2014. This is an evocative account of the lives and experiences of African Americans as they sought freedom and inclusion in American society.

Eric Foner. *Reconstruction: America's Unfinished Revolution, 1863–1877.* New York: Harper and Row, 1988. The best and most comprehensive account of Reconstruction.

Herbert G. Gutman. *The Black Family in Slavery and Freedom, 1750–1925.* New York: Oxford University Press, 1976. An illustration of how African-American family values and kinship ties forged in slavery endured after emancipation.

Steven Hahn. *A Nation Under Our Feet: Black Political Struggles in the Rural South from Slavery to the Great Migration.* Cambridge, MA: Harvard University Press, 2003. In a sophisticated analysis, Hahn explores how African Americans conceived of themselves as political people and organized from slavery through Reconstruction and disfranchisement to the 1920s.

Tera W. Hunter. *To 'Joy My Freedom: Southern Black Women's Lives and Labors after the Civil War.* Cambridge, MA: Harvard University Press, 1997. An examination of the interior lives of black women, their work, social welfare, and leisure.

Gerald D. Jaynes. *Branches Without Roots: Genesis of the Black Working Class in the American South, 1862–1882.* New York: Pantheon, 1986. Examines the changes in work patterns and the labor of African Americans after slavery.

Leon F. Litwack. *Been in the Storm So Long: The Aftermath of Slavery.* New York: Alfred A. Knopf, 1979. A rich and detailed account of the transition to freedom largely based on recollections of former slaves.

Additional Bibliography

Education

James D. Anderson. *The Education of Blacks in the South, 1860–1935.* Chapel Hill: University of North Carolina Press, 1988.

Ronald E. Butchart. *Northern Schools, Southern Blacks, and Reconstruction: Freedmen's Education, 1862–1875.* Westport, CT: Greenwood, 1981.

Edmund L. Drago. *Initiative, Paternalism, and Race Relations: Charleston's Avery Normal Institute.* Athens: University of Georgia Press, 1990.

Robert C. Morris. *Reading, 'Riting, and Reconstruction: The Education of the Freedmen in the South, 1861–1890.* Chicago: University of Chicago Press, 1981.

Joe M. Richardson. *Christian Reconstruction: The American Missionary Association and Southern Blacks, 1861–1890.* Athens: University of Georgia Press, 1986.

Brenda Stevenson, ed. *The Journals of Charlotte Forten Grimke.* New York: Oxford University Press, 1988.

Heather Andrea Williams. *Self Taught: African-American Education in Slavery and Freedom.* Chapel Hill: University of North Carolina Press, 2005.

Land and Labor

Paul A. Cimbala and Randall M. Miller, eds. *The Freedmen's Bureau and Reconstruction.* Bronx, NY: Fordham University Press, 1999.

Barbara J. Fields. *Slavery and Freedom on the Middle Ground: Maryland During the Nineteenth Century.* New Haven, CT: Yale University Press, 1985.

Jacqueline Jones. *Labor of Love, Labor of Sorrow: Black Women, Work and Family, from Slavery to the Present.* New York: Basic Books, 1985.

Edward Magdol. *A Right to the Land: Essays on the Freedmen's Community.* Westport, CT: Greenwood Press, 1977.

Claude F. Oubre. *Forty Acres and a Mule: The Freedmen's Bureau and Black Landownership.* Baton Rouge: Louisiana State University Press, 1978.

Dylan C. Penningroth. *The Claims of Kinfolk: African American Property and Community in the Nineteenth-Century South.* Chapel Hill: University of North Carolina Press, 2003.

Roger L. Ransom and Richard Sutch. *One Kind of Freedom: The Economic Consequences of Emancipation.* New York: Cambridge University Press, 1977.

Elizabeth Regosin. *Freedom's Promise: Slave Families and Citizenship in the Age of Emancipation.* Charlottesville: University of Virginia Press, 2002.

Willie Lee Rose. *Rehearsal for Reconstruction: The Port Royal Experiment.* Indianapolis, IN: Bobbs-Merrill, 1964.

Julie Saville. *The Work of Reconstruction: From Slave to Wage Labor in South Carolina, 1860–1870.* New York: Cambridge University Press, 1994.

James D. Schmidt. *Free to Work: Labor, Law, Emancipation, and Reconstruction, 1815–1880.* Athens: University of Georgia Press, 1998.

Leslie A. Schwalm. *A Hard Fight for We: Women's Transition From Slavery to Freedom in South Carolina.* Urbana: University of Illinois Press, 1997.

Black Communities

John W. Blassingame. *Black New Orleans, 1860–1880.* Chicago: University of Chicago Press, 1973.

Orville Vernon Burton, Jerald Podair, and Jennifer L. Weber, eds. *The Struggle for Equality: Essays on the Sectional Conflict, the Civil War, and the Long Reconstruction.* Charlottesville: University of Virginia Press, 2011.

Cyprian Davis. *The History of Black Catholics in the United States.* New York: Crossroad, 1990.

Robert F. Engs. *Freedom's First Generation: Black Hampton, Virginia, 1861–1890.* Philadelphia: University of Pennsylvania Press, 1979.

William E. Montgomery. *Under Their Own Vine and Fig Tree: The African American Church in the South 1865–1900.* Baton Rouge: Louisiana State University Press, 1993.

Bernard E. Powers Jr. *Black Charlestonians: A Social History, 1822–1885.* Fayetteville: University of Arkansas Press, 1994.

Clarence E. Walker. *A Rock in a Weary Land: The African Methodist Episcopal Church During the Civil War and Reconstruction.* Baton Rouge: Louisiana State University Press, 1982.

James M. Washington. *Frustrated Fellowship: The Black Baptist Quest for Social Power.* Macon, GA: Mercer University Press, 1986.

Chapter 13

The Meaning of Freedom: The Failure of Reconstruction

1868–1877

These are the first African Americans to serve in the U.S. Congress. Standing, left to right: Robert C. DeLarge, representative, South Carolina; Jefferson Long, representative, Georgia; Seated, left to right: U.S. Senator Hiram R. Revels, Mississippi; Benjamin S. Turner, representative, Alabama; Josiah T. Walls, representative, Florida; Joseph H. Rainey, representative, South Carolina; Robert B. Elliott, representative, South Carolina.

 Learning Objectives

After reading this chapter, you should be able to:

13.1 Identify the political offices that African Americans held during Reconstruction.

13.2 Describe the major issues that were of most concern to black political leaders.

13.3 Explain the purpose of the Ku Klux Klan and the actions it took to achieve that purpose.

13.4 State the purpose of the Fifteenth Amendment.

13.5 Analyze the impact that Redemption had on African Americans.

> **Let us with a fixed, firm, hearty, earnest, and unswerving determination move steadily on and on, fanning the flame of true liberty until the last vestige of oppression shall be destroyed, and when that eventful period shall arrive, when, in the selection of rulers, both State and Federal, we shall know no North, no East, no South, no West, no white nor colored, no Democrat nor Republican, but shall choose men because of their moral and intrinsic value, their honesty and integrity, their love of unmixed liberty, and their ability to perform well the duties to be committed to their charge.**
>
> *From a speech delivered in 1872, by Jonathan J. Wright, Associate Justice of the South Carolina Supreme Court*

In 1868, for the first time in American history, thousands of black men would elect hundreds of black and white leaders to state and local offices across the South. Would this newly acquired political influence enable freedmen to complete the transition from slavery to freedom? Would political power propel black people into the mainstream of American society? Equally important, would white southerners and northerners accept black people as fellow citizens?

Events from 1867 to 1877 generated hope that black and white Americans might learn to live together on a compatible and equitable basis. But these developments also raised the possibility that black people's new access to political power would fail to resolve the racial animosity and intolerance that persisted in American life after the Civil War.

13.1 Constitutional Conventions

Identify the political offices that African Americans held during Reconstruction.

Black men as a group first entered politics as delegates to constitutional conventions in the southern states in 1867 and 1868. Each of the former Confederate states—except Tennessee, which had already been restored to the Union—elected delegates to these conventions. Most southern white men were Democrats. They boycotted these elections to protest Congress's assumption of authority over Reconstruction and the extension of voting privileges to black men. Thus, the delegates to the conventions that met to frame new state constitutions to replace those drawn up in 1865 under President Johnson's authority were mostly Republicans joined by a few conservative southern Democrats. The Republicans represented three constituencies. One consisted of white northern migrants who moved to the South after the war. They were disparagingly called **carpetbaggers** because they were said to have arrived in the South with all their possessions in a single carpetbag. A second group consisted of native white southerners, mostly small farmers in devastated upland regions of the South who hoped for economic relief from Republican governments. Other southern white people denigrated them as **scalawags**, or scoundrels. African Americans made up the third and most influential Republican constituency.

Of the 1,000 men elected as delegates to the 10 state conventions, 265 were black. Black delegates were a majority only in the South Carolina and Louisiana conventions. In most states, including Alabama, Georgia, Mississippi, Virginia, North Carolina, Arkansas, and Texas, black men made up 10 to 20 percent of the delegates. At least 107 of the 265 black delegates had been born slaves. About 40 had served

carpetbagger

The derogatory term used during Reconstruction to describe northerners who came South following the Civil War to take advantage of political and economic opportunities. They were labeled "carpetbaggers" because they ostensibly carried all of their possessions in a solitary carpetbag.

scalawag

The derogatory term used during Reconstruction to identify a native white southerner who supported black and white Republicans. They were considered traitors to their people and the Democratic Party.

Southern black men cast ballots for the first time in 1867 in the election of delegates to state constitutional conventions. The ballots were provided by the candidates or political parties, not by state or municipal officials. Most nineteenth-century elections were not by secret ballot.

in the Union Army. Several were well-educated teachers and ministers. Others were tailors, blacksmiths, barbers, and farmers. Most went on to hold other political offices.

These delegates produced impressive constitutions. Unlike previous state constitutions in the South, the new constitutions ensured that all adult males could vote, and except in Mississippi and Virginia, they did not disfranchise many former Confederates. They conferred broad guarantees of civil rights. In several states they provided the first statewide systems of public education. These constitutions were progressive, not radical. Black and white Republicans hoped to attract support from white southerners for the new state governments these documents created by encouraging state support for private businesses, especially railroad construction.

13.1.1 Elections

Elections were held in 1868 to ratify the new constitutions and elect men to political office. The white Democratic response varied. In some states, Democrats boycotted the elections. In others, they participated but voted against ratification, and in still other states they supported ratification and attempted to elect as many Democrats as possible. Congress required only a majority of those voting—not a majority of all registered voters—to ratify the constitutions. In each state, a majority of those voting eventually voted to ratify, and in each state, black men were elected to office.

13.1.2 Black Political Leaders

Over the next decade, 1,465 black men held political office in the South. Although black leaders individually and collectively enjoyed significant political leverage, white Republicans dominated politics during Reconstruction. In general, the number of black officials in a state reflected the size of that state's African-American population. Black people were a substantial majority of the population in just Mississippi and South Carolina, and most of the black officeholders came from those two states and

Table 13-1 African-American Population and Officeholding During Reconstruction in the States Subject to Congressional Reconstruction

	African-American Population in 1870	African-Americans as Percentage of Total Population	Number of African-American Officeholders During Reconstruction
South Carolina	415,814	58.9	314
Mississippi	444,201	53.6	226
Louisiana	364,210	50.1	210
North Carolina	391,650	36.5	180
Alabama	475,510	47.6	167
Georgia	545,142	46.0	108
Virginia	512,841	41.8	85
Florida	91,689	48.7	58
Arkansas	122,169	25.2	46
Texas	253,475	30.9	46
Tennessee	322,331	25.6	20

SOURCE: Based on Eric Foner, *Freedom's Lawmakers: A Directory of Black Officeholders During Reconstruction* (New York: Oxford University Press, 1993), xiv; *The Statistics of the Population of the United States,* Ninth Census (1873), xvii. © Darlene Clark Hine.

Louisiana, where black people were a slight majority. In most states, such as Arkansas, North Carolina, Tennessee, and Texas, where black people made up between 25 and 40 percent of the population, far fewer black men were elected to office (see Table 13-1).

Initially, black men chose not to run for the most important political offices because they feared their election would further alienate angry white southerners. But as white Republicans swept into office in 1868, black leaders reversed their strategy, and by 1870 black men had been elected to many key positions. No black man was elected governor, but Lieutenant Governor P. B. S. Pinchback served one month (December 1872 to January 1873) as governor in Louisiana after the white governor was removed from office. Blanche K. Bruce and Hiram Revels represented Mississippi in the U.S. Senate. Beginning with Joseph Rainey in 1870 in South Carolina, 14 black men served

Profile

The Gibbs Brothers

Mifflin Gibbs was probably the only African American in the nineteenth century elected to political office in two nations. He served as a city councilman in Victoria, British Columbia, in Canada in the late 1860s, and he was elected a judge in Little Rock, Arkansas, in 1873.

Among the many black leaders who emerged during Reconstruction were the Gibbs brothers, who had political careers in Arkansas and Florida. Mifflin W. Gibbs and Jonathan C. Gibbs grew up in a well-to-do, free black family in Philadelphia, where their father was a Methodist minister. But their paths diverged, and they spent little time together as adults.

Mifflin was born in 1823 and became a building contractor. By the 1840s, he was an active abolitionist. With the discovery of gold in California in 1849, he went west and eventually established California's first black newspaper, the *Mirror of the Times*. He led a protest in 1851 against a California constitution

provision that denied black men the right to vote. In 1858 he left California for Canada, again because gold had been discovered. He spent more than 10 years in Canada as a businessman involved in real estate and a coal company. In 1866 he was elected to the Victoria City Council in British Columbia. He returned to the United States in 1869, and graduated from the law program at Oberlin College in 1870.

Mifflin moved to Arkansas in 1871 and was elected municipal judge in Little Rock in 1873. Although defeated for reelection, he remained involved in the Republican Party and was a delegate to every Republican national convention from 1876 to 1904. In 1897, Republican President William McKinley appointed him U.S. consul to Madagascar, a French island colony off the east coast of Africa, where he served until 1901. He died in 1915, and a black high school in Little Rock was named in his honor.

Jonathan, born in 1827 or 1828, also joined the abolitionist movement. Rejected by 18 colleges because of his color, he finally graduated from Dartmouth in 1852. He then went to Princeton Theological Seminary and became a Presbyterian minister in Troy, New York.

Jonathan attended the 1864 National Black Convention in Syracuse, New York; taught at a freedmen's school in North Carolina; and then spent two years in Charleston, South Carolina. There he joined those black leaders who favored limiting the right to vote to literate men if that restriction were applied both to black and white people.

In 1867, Jonathan moved to Florida, where he became a key Republican leader and the state's highest-ranking black official. He was elected to the 1868 Florida constitutional convention, and the Republican governor appointed him secretary of state. Although defeated for a seat in Congress in 1868, he remained one of Florida's most visible black leaders and was repeatedly threatened by the Ku Klux Klan. In 1873, another Republican governor appointed him state superintendent of education. Jonathan Gibbs died in 1874, but his son Thomas served in the Florida House of Representatives, where he was instrumental in establishing Florida A&M University.

Hiram R. Revels represented Mississippi in the U.S. Senate from February 1870 until March 1871, completing an unexpired term. He went on to serve as Mississippi's secretary of state. He was born free in Fayetteville, North Carolina, in 1822. He attended Knox College in Illinois before the Civil War. In 1874 he abandoned the Republican Party and became a Democrat. By the 1890s he had acquired a sizable plantation near Natchez.

in the U.S. House of Representatives during Reconstruction. Six black men served as lieutenant governors. In Mississippi and South Carolina, a majority of the representatives in state houses were black men, and each of these states had two black speakers of the house in the 1870s. Jonathan J. Wright, quoted at the beginning of this chapter, served seven years as a supreme court justice in South Carolina. Four black men served as state superintendents of education, and Francis L. Cardozo served as South Carolina's secretary of state and then treasurer. During Reconstruction, 112 black state senators and 683 black representatives were elected. There were also 41 black sheriffs, five black mayors, and 31 black coroners. Tallahassee, Florida, and Little Rock, Arkansas, had black police chiefs.

Many of these men—by background, experience, and education—were well qualified. However, others were not. Of the 1,465 black officeholders, at least 378 had been free before the Civil War, 933 were literate, and 195 were illiterate (we lack information about the remaining 337). In addition, 64 had attended college or professional school. In fact, 14 of the leaders had been students at Oberlin College in Ohio, which began admitting both black and female students before the Civil War.

Black farmers and artisans—tailors, carpenters, and barbers—were well represented among those who held political office. There were also 237 ministers and 172 teachers. At least 129 had served in the Union Army, and 46 had worked for the Freedmen's Bureau.

Several black politicians were wealthy, and a few were former slave owners. Antoine Dubuclet, who became Louisiana's treasurer, had owned more than one hundred slaves and land valued at more than $100,000 before the Civil War. Former slave Ferdinand Havis became a member of the Arkansas House of Representatives. He owned a saloon, a whiskey business, and 2,000 acres near Pine Bluff, where he became known as "the Colored Millionaire."

Although black men did not take over any state politically, a few did dominate districts with sizable black populations. Before he was elected to the U.S. Senate, Blanche K. Bruce all but controlled Bolivar County, Mississippi, where he served as sheriff, tax collector, and superintendent of education. Former slave and Civil War hero Robert Smalls was the political "kingpin" in Beaufort, South Carolina. He served in the South Carolina house and senate and in the U.S. House of Representatives. He was also a member of the South Carolina constitutional conventions in 1868 and 1895.

13.2 The Issues

Describe the major issues that were of most concern to black political leaders.

Many but not all black and white Republican leaders favored increasing the authority of state governments to promote the welfare of all the state's citizens. Before the Civil War, most southern states did not provide schools, medical care, assistance for the mentally impaired, or prisons. Such concerns—if attended to at all—were left to local communities or families.

13.2.1 Education and Social Welfare

Black leaders were eager to increase literacy and promote education among black people. Republicans created statewide systems of public education throughout the South. It was a difficult and expensive task, and the results were only a limited success. Schools had to be built, teachers employed, and textbooks provided. To pay for it, taxes were increased in states still reeling from the war.

In many rural areas, schools were not built. In other places, teachers were not paid. Some people—black and white—opposed compulsory education laws, preferring to let parents determine whether their children should attend school or work to help the family. Some black leaders favored a poll tax on voting to fund the schools. Thus, although Reconstruction leaders established a strong commitment to public education, the results they achieved were uneven.

Furthermore, white parents refused to send their children to integrated schools. Although no laws required segregation, public schools during and after Reconstruction were invariably segregated. However, black parents were usually more concerned that their children attend school, and were less concerned that the schools were integrated. In any case, the schools in New Orleans were mixed.

Reconstruction leaders also supported higher education. In 1872 Mississippi legislators took advantage of the 1862 federal Morrill Land-Grant Act, which provided states with funds for agricultural and mechanical colleges, to found the first historically black state university: Alcorn A&M College. Although the university was named after white Republican Governor James L. Alcorn, former U.S. Senator Hiram Revels was its first president. The South Carolina legislature created a similar college and attached it to the Methodist-sponsored Claflin University.

Black leaders in the state legislature compelled the University of South Carolina, which had been all white, to admit black students and hire black faculty. As a result, many of the white students and faculty left. Several black politicians enrolled in the law and medical programs at the university. Richard Greener, a black Harvard graduate, served on the university's faculty and was its librarian.

Despite the costs, Reconstruction leaders also created the first state-supported institutions for the insane, the blind, and the deaf in much of the South. Some southern states during Reconstruction began to offer medical care and public health programs. Some states established orphanages and built prisons. Black leaders also supported revisions to state criminal codes, the elimination of corporal punishment for many crimes, and a reduction in the number of capital crimes.

13.2.2 Civil Rights

Black politicians were often the victims of racial discrimination when they tried to use public transportation and accommodations such as hotels and restaurants. Rather than provide separate arrangements for black customers, white-owned businesses simply excluded black patrons. This was true in the North as well as the South. The Civil War hero Robert Smalls, for example, was ejected from a Philadelphia streetcar in 1864. After protests, the company agreed to accept black riders. In Arkansas, Mifflin Gibbs (see Profile: The Gibbs Brothers) and W. Hines Furbish successfully sued a local saloon after they had been denied service. In South Carolina, Jonathan J. Wright won $1,200 in a lawsuit against a railroad after he had purchased a first-class ticket but had been forced to ride in the second-class coach.

Black leaders' determination to open public facilities to all people revealed deep divisions between themselves and white Republicans. In several southern states they introduced bills to prevent proprietors from excluding black people from restaurants, barrooms, hotels, concert halls, and auditoriums, as well as railroad coaches, streetcars, and steamboats. Many white Republicans and virtually every Democrat attacked such proposals as efforts to promote social equality and gain access for black people to places where they were not welcome. White politicians blocked these laws in most states. Only South Carolina—with a black majority in the house and many black senators—enacted such a law, but it was not effectively enforced. In Mississippi, the Republican Governor James L. Alcorn vetoed a bill to outlaw racial discrimination by railroads. In Alabama and North Carolina, civil rights bills were defeated, and Georgia and Arkansas enacted measures that encouraged segregation.

13.2.3 Economic Issues

Black politicians sought to promote economic development in general and for black people in particular. For example, white landowners sometimes fired black agricultural laborers near the end of the growing season and then did not pay them. Some of these landowners were dishonest, but others were in debt and could not pay their workers. To prevent such abuses, black politicians secured laws that required laborers to be paid before the crop was sold or when it was sold. Some black leaders who had been slaves also wanted to regulate wages, but these proposals failed because most Republicans did not believe states had the authority to regulate wages and prices.

Legislators also enacted measures that protected the land and property of small farmers against seizure for nonpayment of debts. Black and white farmers who lost land, tools, animals, and other property because they could not pay their debts were unlikely to recover financially. "Stay laws" prohibited, or "stayed," authorities from taking property. Besides protecting poor farmers, Republicans hoped these laws would weaken support among white yeomen for the Democratic Party and draw them into the Republican Party.

13.2.4 Land

Black leaders were unable to provide land to landless black and white farmers. Many black and white political leaders believed the state had no right to distribute land. Again, South Carolina was the exception. Its legislature created a state land commission in 1869.

The commission could purchase and distribute land to freedmen. It also gave the freedmen loans on generous terms to pay for the land. Unfortunately, the commission was corrupt and inefficiently managed and had little fertile land to distribute. Yet despite its many difficulties, the commission enabled more than 14,000 black families and a few white families to acquire land in South Carolina. Their descendants still possess some of this land today.

Although some black leaders were reluctant to use the states' power to distribute land, others had no qualms about raising property taxes so high that large landowners would be forced to sell some of their property to pay their taxes. Abraham Galloway of North Carolina explained, "I want to see the man who owns one or two thousand acres of land, taxed a dollar on the acre, and if they can't pay the taxes, sell their property to the highest bidder . . . and then we negroes shall become the land holders."

13.2.5 Business and Industry

Black and white leaders had an easier time enacting legislation to support business and industry. Like most Americans after the Civil War, Republicans believed that expanding the railroad network would stimulate employment, improve transportation, and generate prosperity. State governments approved the sale of state-supported bonds to finance railroad construction. In Georgia, Alabama, Texas, and Arkansas, the railroad network did expand; however, the bonded debt of these states soared, and taxes increased to pay for it. Moreover, railroad financing was often corrupt. Most of the illegal money wound up in the pockets of white businessmen and politicians. Black politicians rarely had access to large financial transactions.

So attractive were business profits that some black political leaders formed corporations. They invested modest sums and believed—like so many capitalists—that the rewards outweighed the risks. In Charleston, 28 black leaders (and two white politicians) formed a horse-drawn streetcar line they called the Enterprise Railroad to carry freight between the city wharves and the railroad terminal. Black leaders in South Carolina also created a company to extract the phosphate used for fertilizer from riverbeds and riverbanks in the low country. Neither business lasted long. Black men found it far more difficult than white entrepreneurs to finance their corporations.

13.2.6 Black Politicians: An Evaluation

Southern black political leaders on the state level did create the foundation for public education; for state assistance for the blind, deaf, and insane; and for reforming the criminal justice system. They tried (but mostly failed) to outlaw racial discrimination in public facilities and encouraged state support for economic expansion.

But black leaders could not significantly improve the lives of their constituents. Because white Republicans almost always outnumbered them, they could not enact an agenda of their own. Moreover, black leaders often disagreed among themselves about issues and programs. Class and prewar status frequently divided them. Those leaders who had not been slaves and had not been raised in rural isolation were less likely to be concerned with land and agricultural labor. More prosperous black leaders showed more interest in civil rights and encouraging business. Even when they agreed about the need for public education, black leaders often disagreed about how to finance it and whether it should be compulsory.

13.2.7 Republican Factionalism

Disagreements among black leaders paled compared to the conflicts that divided the Republican Party during Reconstruction. Black and white Republicans often disagreed on political issues and strategy, but the lack of party cohesion and discipline was even more harmful. The Republican Party in the South constantly split as factions within the party fought with each other. Most disagreements were over who should run for and hold political office.

Hundreds of would-be Republican leaders—black and white—sought public offices. If they lost the Republican nomination, they often formed a competing slate of candidates. Then Republicans ran against each other and against the Democrats in the general election. It was not a recipe for political success.

These bitter and angry contests were based less on race and issues than on the desperate desire to gain an office that would pay even a modest salary. Most black and white Republicans were not well off. Public office assured them a modicum of economic security.

Ironically, these factional disputes led to a high turnover in political leadership and the loss of that very economic security. It was difficult for black leaders (and white leaders too) to be renominated and reelected to more than one or two terms. Few officeholders served three or four consecutive terms in the same office during Reconstruction. This made for inexperienced leadership and added to Republican woes.

13.2.8 Opposition

Even if black and Republican leaders had been less prone to fighting among themselves and more effective in adopting a political platform, they might still have failed to sustain themselves for long. Most white southerners led by conservative Democrats remained absolutely opposed to letting black men vote or hold office. As a white Floridian put it, "The damned Republican Party has put niggers to rule us and we will not suffer it." Of course, just because black people voted did not mean they ruled

Profile

The Rollin Sisters

MISS FRANCES ANNE ROLLIN

Few women, black or white, were as influential in Reconstruction politics as the Rollin sisters of South Carolina. Although they could not vote or hold political office, the five sisters, and especially Frances and Katherine, were closely associated with the black and white Republican leadership in South Carolina. With their education, knowledge, and charm, these black women affected political decisions and policies.

The sisters were born and raised in the elite antebellum free black community in Charleston. Their father, William Rollin, a prosperous lumber dealer, was descended from French Catholic Haitians and insisted that his daughters obtain a first-rate education. Frances, who was born in 1844, was sent to Philadelphia to take the "ladies course" at the Quaker's Institute for Colored Youth. At least two of the other sisters attended school in Boston. After the war, Frances joined other members of Charleston's prominent people of color and taught at schools sponsored by the American Missionary Association. She also wrote the biography of the black abolitionist leader Martin Delany. This was the first major nonfiction work a black woman published in America, but she felt compelled to conceal her identity under a male name, Frank A. Rollin.

In 1867 and 1868, as black men were entering the political arena, the Rollin sisters also gravitated to politics. Against her father's wishes, Frances married one of South Carolina's most controversial figures, William Whipper, a black attorney from Philadelphia who settled in Beaufort, South Carolina, after the war. (Whipper was the nephew of the antebellum black Pennsylvania businessman, also named William Whipper, profiled in Chapter 7.) He was elected to the state constitutional convention and then to the South Carolina House of Representatives. Whipper was a tough, able, shrewd, and not altogether honest politician. He enjoyed an expensive lifestyle. Most white people detested him.

While the legislature was in session, the Whippers and the Rollin sisters lived in Columbia, the state capital. There, the sisters were extraordinarily popular. They were well educated, intelligent, refined, and sophisticated. One observer described them as "ravishingly beautiful." Katherine Rollin was frequently seen with white State Senator George W. McIntyre.

The Rollin sisters were enthusiastic proponents of women's rights and women's suffrage who enlisted the wives of prominent black and white Republicans in their cause. Charlotte and Katherine organized a women's rights convention in Columbia in 1870 and formed the South Carolina branch of the American Women's Suffrage Association.

Charlotte Rollin pleaded for the right to vote:

> We ask suffrage not as a favor, not as a privilege, but as a right based on the grounds that we are human beings and as such entitled to human rights. While we concede that woman's ennobling influence should be confined chiefly to the home and society, we claim that public opinion has had a tendency to limit a woman's sphere to too small a circle and until woman has the right of representation this will last, and other rights will be held by insecure tenure.

Their black and white male allies tried to amend South Carolina's constitution to enable women to vote, but the legislature rejected it after a bitter debate.

After the Democrats regained political power in 1877, the Rollin sisters left for the North. Charlotte and Louise settled with their mother in Brooklyn, New York. William and Frances Whipper and their five children moved to Washington, DC, in 1882, where he practiced law and she was a clerk in the General Land Office. Three of their children survived to adulthood. Their sole son, Leigh Whipper, was a prominent stage and screen actor in the 1940s and 1950s. Sometime in the 1890s, Frances joined her husband in Beaufort. She died there in 1901.

during Reconstruction; however, many white people failed to grasp that. Instead, for most white southerners, the only acceptable political system was one that excluded black men and the Republican Party.

As far as most white people were concerned, the end of slavery and the enfranchisement of black men did not make black people their equals. They did not accept the Fourteenth Amendment, and they attacked Republican governments and their leaders unrelentingly. White southerners blamed the Republicans for an epidemic of waste and corruption in state government. But most of all, they considered it preposterous and outrageous that former slaves could vote and hold office.

James S. Pike spoke for many white people when he ridiculed black leaders in the South Carolina House of Representatives in 1873:

> The body is almost literally a Black Parliament. . . . The Speaker is black, the Clerk is black, the door-keepers are black, the little pages are black, the chairman of the Ways and Means is black, and the chaplain is coal-black. At some of the desks sit colored men whose types it would be hard to find outside of Congo; whose costume, visages, attitudes, and expression only befit the forecastle of a buccaneer. It must be remembered, also, that these men, with not more than a half a dozen exceptions, have been themselves slaves, and that their ancestors were slaves for generations.

Pike's observations circulated widely in both the North and the South.

White southerners were determined to rid themselves of Republicans and the disgrace of having to live with black men who possessed political rights. White southerners would "redeem" their states by restoring white Democrats to power. This meant not just defeating black and white Republicans in elections but removing them from politics entirely. White southerners believed any means—fair or foul—were justified in exorcising this evil.

13.3 The Ku Klux Klan

Explain the purpose of the Ku Klux Klan and the actions it took to achieve that purpose.

If the presence of black men in politics was illegitimate—in the eyes of white southerners—then it was acceptable to use violence to remove them. This thinking gave rise to militant terrorist organizations, such as the **Ku Klux Klan**, the Knights of the White Camellia, the White Brotherhood, and the Whitecaps. They were terrorists who resorted to threats, intimidation, beatings, rapes, and murder to restore conservative white Democratic rule and to force black people back into subordination.

The Ku Klux Klan, founded in Pulaski, Tennessee, in 1866, was originally a social club for Confederate veterans who adopted secret oaths and rituals—similar to the Union Leagues but with far more deadly consequences. One of the key figures in the Klan's rapid growth was former Confederate General Nathan Bedford Forrest, who became its leader or grand wizard. The Klan drew its members from all classes of white society, not merely from among the poor. Businessmen, lawyers, physicians, and politicians, as well as farmers and planters, were active in the Klan. The Klan and other armed groups functioned mainly where black people were a large minority and where their votes could affect elections. Klansmen virtually took over areas of western Alabama, northern Georgia, and Florida's Panhandle. The Klan controlled the up-country of South Carolina and the area around Mecklenburg County, North Carolina. However, in the Carolina and Georgia low country where there were huge black majorities, the Klan rarely, if ever, appeared.

Although the Klan and similar societies were neither well organized nor unified, they did reduce support for the Republican Party and helped eliminate its leaders. Often wearing hoods and masks to hide their faces, white terrorists embarked on a campaign of violence rarely matched and never exceeded in American history.

Ku Klux Klan

A secret society founded by former Confederates in Pulaski, Tennessee, in 1866. It transformed itself into a terrorist organization during Reconstruction to drive black and white Republicans from political power in southern states.

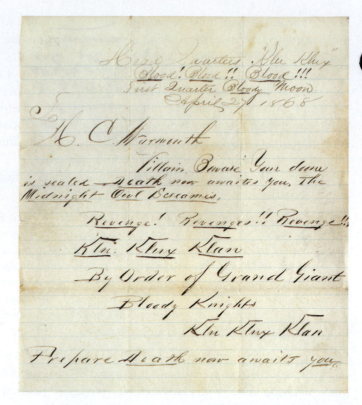

The flowing white robes and cone-shaped headgear associated with the Ku Klux Klan today are mostly a twentieth-century phenomenon. The Klansmen of the Reconstruction era, like these two men in Alabama in 1868, were well armed, disguised, and prepared to intimidate black and white Republicans. The note is a Klan death threat directed at Louisiana's first Republican governor, Henry C. Warmoth.

Mobs of marauding terrorists beat and killed hundreds of black people—and many white people. Black churches and schools were burned. Republican leaders were threatened or killed. In South Carolina in 1868, the black chairman of the Republican Party, Benjamin F. Randolph, was murdered as he stepped off a train. Black legislator Lee Nance and white legislator Solomon G. W. Dill were later slain. In 1870 black lawmaker Richard Burke was killed in Sumter County, Alabama, because he was considered too influential among "people of his color."

As his wife looked on, Jack Dupree—a local Republican leader—had his throat cut and was eviscerated in Monroe County, Mississippi. In 1870 North Carolina Senator John W. Stephens, a white Republican, was murdered. After Alabama freedman George Moore voted for the Republicans in 1869, Klansmen beat him, raped a girl who was visiting his wife, and attacked a neighbor. An Irish-American teacher and four black men were lynched in Cross Plains, Alabama, in 1870. The outlaw John Wesley Hardin openly acknowledged he had killed black Texas state policemen.

White men attacked a Republican campaign rally in Eutaw, Alabama, in 1870, killing four black men and wounding 54 other people. After three black leaders were arrested in 1871 in Meridian, Mississippi, for delivering what many white people considered inflammatory speeches, shooting broke out in the courtroom. The Republican judge and two of the defendants were killed, and in a wave of violence, 30 black people were murdered, including every black leader in the small community. In the same year, a mob of 500 men broke into the jail in Union County, South Carolina, and lynched eight black prisoners accused of killing a Confederate veteran.

Nowhere was the Klan more active and violent than in York County, South Carolina. Almost the entire adult white male population joined in threatening, attacking, and murdering the black population. Hundreds were beaten and at least 11 were killed.

Voices

An Appeal for Help against the Klan

H. K. Roberts, a black lieutenant in the South Carolina militia, described Klan terror in York County in late 1870 to Governor Robert K. Scott. Roberts desperately appealed for aid to protect Republicans and defend the black community.

Dec. the 6th 1870.

Antioch P.O. York County S.C.

To Your Excelency R. K. Scott

Sir I will tell you that on last friday night the 2nd day of this [month] 8 miles from here thier was one of the worst outrages Commited that is on record in the state from 50 to 75 armed men went to the house of Thomas Blacks a colored man fired shots into the house and cald for him he clibed up in the loft of the house they fired up their and he came down jumped out at a window ran about 30 steps was shot down then they shot him after he fell they then draged him about 10 steps and cut his throat from ear to ear their was about 30 bullet holes in his body some 50 to one hundred shots in the house. . . . [They] abused his wife and enquired for one or two more colored men some of the colored people are leaving and a great many lying out in the woods and they reports comes to me evry day that they Ku Kluxs intend to kill us all out and I heard yesterday that they had 30 stands of arms. . . . I wish you would give me 20 or 25 men or let me enroll that many and I will stop it or catch some of them or send some U S Soldiers on for I tell you their must be something don and that quick to for I do believe that they intend to beat and kill out the Radical party in the upper Counties of the state where the vote is close if we was to have the ellection now the Radicals would turn [out] to vote their ticket I leave the matter with you I hope you will wright back to me by return mail and let me heare what you think you can do for us up here I cant tell whether I can hold my own or not I know some men that stay with us at night for safety but if they come as strong as they were the other night they may kill me and all of my men I remain yours truly as ever.

H.K. Roberts, Lieut.
Commanding Post of State Guards Kings Mountain

1. Why did Roberts write this letter?
2. Would Roberts have had any reason to exaggerate the violence in York County?
3. According to Roberts, what motivated white men to attack?

SOURCE: H. K. Roberts to Governor Robert K. Scott, South Carolina Department of Archives and History.

Terrified families fled into the woods. Black leaders sent appeals for help to Governor Robert K. Scott (see Voices: An Appeal for Help against the Klan).

But Scott did not send aid. He had already sent the South Carolina militia into areas of Klan activity, and even more violence had resulted. The militia was made up mostly of black men, and white terrorists retaliated by killing militia officers. Scott could not send white men to York County because most of them sympathized with the Klan. Thus, Republican governors like Scott responded ineffectually. Republican-controlled legislatures passed anti-Klan measures that made it illegal to appear in public in disguises and masks, and they strengthened laws against assault, murder, and conspiracy. Nonetheless, enforcement was weak.

A few Republican leaders did deal harshly and effectively with terrorism. Governors in Tennessee, Texas, and Arkansas declared martial law and sent in hundreds of well-armed white and black men to quell the violence. Hundreds of Klansmen were arrested, many fled, and three were executed in Arkansas. But when Governor William W. Holden of North Carolina sent the state militia after the Klan, he provoked an angry reaction. Subsequent Klan violence in 10 counties helped Democrats carry the 1870 legislative elections, and the legislature then removed Holden from office.

Outnumbered and outgunned, black people in most areas did not retaliate against the Klan, and the Klan was rarely active where black people were in a majority and prepared to defend themselves. In the cause of white supremacy, the Klan usually attacked those who could not defend themselves.

1869–1875
Federal Reconstruction Legislation

1869
Fifteenth Amendment passed
(ratified 1870)

1870
Enforcement Act passed

1871
Ku Klux Klan Act passed

1875
Civil Rights Act of 1875 passed

13.3.1 The West

During the 1830s the U.S. government forced the Five Civilized Tribes—the Cherokee, Chickasaw, Choctaw, Creek, and Seminole—from their southern homelands to Indian Territory in what is now Oklahoma. By 1860 Native Americans there held 7,367 African Americans in slavery. Many of the Indians fought for the Confederacy during the Civil War. Following the war, the former slaves encountered nearly as much violence and hostility from Native Americans as they did from southern white people. Indians were reluctant to share their land with freedmen, and they vigorously opposed policies that favored black voting rights.

Gradually and despite considerable Indian prejudice, some African Americans managed to acquire tribal land. Also, the Creeks and the Seminoles permitted former slaves to take part in tribal government. Black men served in both houses of the Creek legislature—the House of Warriors and the House of Kings. An African American, Jesse Franklin, served as a justice on the Creek tribal court in 1876. In contrast, the Chickasaw and Choctaw were absolutely opposed to making concessions to freed people. Therefore, the U.S. government ordered federal troops onto Chickasaw and Choctaw lands to protect the former slaves.

Elsewhere on the western frontier, black people struggled for legal and political rights and periodically participated in territorial governments. In 1867, 200 black men voted—although white men protested—in the Montana territorial election. In the Colorado Territory, William Jefferson Hardin, a barber, campaigned with other black men for the right to vote, and in 1865 they persuaded 137 African Americans (91 percent of Colorado's black population) to petition the territorial governor to abolish a white-only voting provision. In 1867 black men in Colorado finally gained the right to vote. Hardin later moved to Cheyenne and was elected to the Wyoming territorial legislature in 1879.

Fifteenth Amendment

This constitutional amendment stipulated that the right to vote could not be denied on account of race, color, or because a person had been a slave.

This optimistic 1870 illustration exemplifies the hope and aspirations generated during Reconstruction as black people gained access to the political system, suggesting that African Americans would soon assume their rightful and equitable role in American society.

13.4 The Fifteenth Amendment

Discuss the purpose of the Fifteenth Amendment.

The federal government under Republican domination tried to protect black voting rights and defend Republican state governments in the South. In 1869 Congress passed the **Fifteenth Amendment**, which was ratified in 1870. It stipulated that a person could not be deprived of the right to vote because of race: "The right of citizens of the United States to vote shall not be denied or abridged by the United States or by any State on account of race, color, or previous condition of servitude." Black people, abolitionists, and reformers hailed the amendment as the culmination of the crusade to end slavery and give black people the same rights as white people.

Northern black men were the amendment's immediate beneficiaries because, before its adoption, black men could vote in only eight northern states. Yet to the disappointment of many, the amendment said nothing about women voting and did not outlaw poll taxes, literacy tests, and property qualifications that could disfranchise citizens.

13.4.1 The Enforcement Acts

In direct response to the terrorism in the South, Congress passed the **Enforcement Acts** in 1870 and 1871; the federal government thereby expanded its authority over the states. The 1870 act outlawed disguises and masks and protected the civil rights of citizens. The 1871 act—known as the Ku Klux Klan Act—made it a federal offense to interfere with a person's right to vote, hold office, serve on a jury, or enjoy equal protection of the law. Those accused of violating the act would be tried in federal court. For extreme violence, the act authorized the president to send in federal troops and suspend the writ of *habeas corpus*. (*Habeas corpus* is the right to be brought before a judge and not be arrested and jailed without cause.)

Black congressmen, who had long advocated federal action against the Klan, endorsed the Enforcement Acts. Representative Joseph Rainey of South Carolina wanted to suspend the Constitution to protect citizens: "I desire that so broad and liberal a construction be placed on its provisions, as will insure protection to the humblest citizen. Tell me nothing of a constitution which fails to shelter beneath its rightful power the people of a country."

Armed with this new legislation, the Justice Department and Attorney General Amos T. Ackerman moved vigorously against the Klan. Hundreds of Klansmen were arrested—700 in Mississippi alone. Faced with a full-scale rebellion in late 1871 in South Carolina's up-country, President Ulysses S. Grant declared martial law in nine counties, suspended the writ of *habeas corpus,* and sent in the army. Mass arrests and trials followed, but federal authorities permitted many Klansmen to confess and thereby escape prosecution. The government lacked the human and financial resources to bring hundreds of men to court for lengthy trials. Some white men were tried, mostly before black juries, and were imprisoned or fined. Comparatively few Klansmen, however, were punished severely, especially considering the enormity of their crimes.

13.4.2 The North and Reconstruction

Although the federal government did reduce Klan violence for a time, white southerners remained convinced that white supremacy must be restored and Republican governments overturned. Klan violence did not overthrow any state governments, but it undermined freedmen's confidence in the ability of these governments to protect them. Meanwhile, Radical Republicans in Congress grew frustrated that the South and especially black people continued to demand so much of their time and attention year after year. There was less and less sentiment in the North to continue support for the freedmen and involvement in southern affairs.

Many northern Republicans lost interest in civil rights issues and principles and became more concerned with winning elections and the economy. By the mid-1870s, there was more discussion in Congress of patronage, veterans' pensions, railroads, taxes, tariffs, the economy, and monetary policy than about rights for black people or the future of the South.

By the 1870s, the American political system was also awash in corruption, which further detracted from concerns over the South. Although President Grant was a man of integrity, many men in his administration were not. They were implicated in scandals

Enforcement Acts

Also known as the Force Acts, these measures were passed by Congress in the early 1870s to undermine the Ku Klux Klan and other terrorist organizations by authorizing the president to use military force and to suspend the writ of *habeas corpus.*

habeas corpus

A court order that a person arrested or detained by law enforcement officers must be brought to court and charged with a crime, not just held indefinitely.

involving the construction of the transcontinental railroad, federal taxes on whiskey, and fraud within the Bureau of Indian Affairs. Nor was the dishonesty limited to Republicans. William Marcy "Boss" Tweed and the Democratic machine that dominated New York City were notoriously corrupt.

Many Republicans began to question the necessity for more moral, military, and political support for African Americans. They were convinced that African Americans had demanded too much for too long from the national government. Former slaves had become citizens and had the right to vote and hold political office. Therefore, they did not need additional help or legislation from the federal government. Equality for black people would come from their labor as free men, which would produce wealth and acceptance by white people. Federal legislation, many northern white people believed, could not create equality.

The *Chicago Tribune*, a Republican newspaper, had wearied of black agitation by 1874: "Is it not time for the colored race to stop playing baby? The whites of America have done nobly in outgrowing old prejudices against them. They cannot hurry this process by law. Let them obtain social equality as every other man, woman, and child in the world obtain it,—by showing themselves in their lives the social equals of those with whom they wish to consort. If they do this, year by year the prejudices will die away."

Other northern white people, swayed by white southerners' views of black people, began to doubt the wisdom of universal manhood suffrage. Many white people who had nominally supported black suffrage began to believe the exaggerated complaints about corruption among black leaders and the unrelenting claims that freedmen were incapable of self-government. Some white northerners began to conclude that Reconstruction had been a mistake.

Economic conditions contributed to changing attitudes. A financial crisis—the Panic of 1873—sent the economy into a long slump. Businesses and financial institutions failed, unemployment soared, and prices fell. In 1874 the Democrats recaptured a majority in the House of Representatives for the first time since 1860 and also took control of several northern states.

13.4.3 The Freedmen's Bank

Freedmen's Savings Bank

A private financial institution chartered by Congress in 1865. Many black people and organizations deposited funds in the bank, which went bankrupt in 1874.

One of the casualties of the financial crisis was the **Freedmen's Savings Bank**, which failed in 1874. Founded in 1865 when hope flourished, the Freedmen's Savings and Trust Company had been chartered by Congress but was not connected to the Freedmen's Bureau. However, the bank's advertising featured pictures of Abraham Lincoln, and many black people assumed it was a federal agency. Freedmen and black veterans, churches, fraternal organizations, and benevolent societies opened thousands of accounts in the bank. Most of the deposits totaled under $50, and some amounted to only a few cents.

Although the bank had many black employees, its board of directors consisted of white men. They invested the bank's funds in risky ventures, including Washington, DC, real estate. With the Panic of 1873, the bank lost large sums in unsecured railroad loans. To restore confidence, its directors persuaded Frederick Douglass to serve as president and invest $10,000 of his own money to help shore up the bank. Douglass lost his money, and African Americans across the South lost more than $1 million when the bank closed in June 1874. Eventually about half the depositors received three-fifths of the value of their accounts, but many African Americans believed the U.S. government owed them a debt. Well into the twentieth century, they wrote to Congress and the president in unsuccessful efforts to retrieve their hard-earned money.

13.4.4 The Civil Rights Act of 1875

Civil Rights Act of 1875

This federal legislation outlawed racial discrimination in public accommodations such as hotels and restaurants, and in transportation, including railroad coaches and steamboats. The Supreme Court invalidated it in 1883.

Before Reconstruction expired, Congress made one final—some said futile—gesture to protect black people from racial discrimination when it passed the **Civil Rights Act of 1875**. Championed by Senator Charles Sumner of Massachusetts, it was originally intended to open public accommodations—including schools, churches, cemeteries, hotels, and transportation—to all people regardless of race. It passed in the

Voices

Black Leaders Support the Passage of a Civil Rights Act

Black Congressmen Robert Brown Elliott of South Carolina and James T. Rapier of Alabama spoke passionately in favor of the Sumner civil rights bill in 1874. Both men had been free before the war. Both were also lawyers, and although each accumulated considerable wealth, they died in poverty in the 1880s.

[James T. Rapier]

I must confess it is somewhat embarrassing for a colored man to urge the passage of this bill, because if he exhibit an earnestness in the matter and expresses a desire for its immediate passage, straightaway he is charged with a desire for social equality, as explained by the demagogue and understood by the ignorant white man. But then it is just as embarrassing for him not to do so, for, if he remains silent while the struggle is being carried on around, and for him, he is liable to be charged with a want of interest in a matter that concerns him more than anyone else, which is enough to make his friends desert his cause. So in steering away from Scylla I may run upon Charybdis. But the anomalous, and I may add the supremely ridiculous, position of the Negro at this time, in this country, compel me to say something. Here his condition is without comparison, parallel alone to itself. Just that the law recognizes my right upon this floor as a lawmaker, but that there is no law to secure to me any accommodations whatever while traveling here to discharge my duties as a Representative of a large and wealthy constituency. Here I am the peer of the proudest, but on a steamboat or car I am not equal to the most degraded. Is not this most anomalous and ridiculous?

[Robert Brown Elliott]

The results of the war, as seen in Reconstruction, have settled forever the political status of my race. The passage of this bill will determine the civil status, not only of the Negro but of any other class of citizens who may feel themselves discriminated against. It will form the capstone of that temple of liberty begun on this continent under discouraging circumstances, carried on in spite of the sneers of monarchists and the cavils of pretended friends of freedom, until at last it stands in all its beautiful symmetry and proportions, a building the grandest which the world has ever seen, realizing the most sanguine expectations and the highest hopes of those who in the name of equal, impartial and universal liberty, laid the foundation stone.

---

1. If black men had the right to vote and serve in Congress, why was a civil rights law needed?
2. Who would benefit most from the passage of this bill?
3. What distinction do the congressmen draw between social discrimination and political rights?

SOURCE: *Congressional Record*, 43rd Congress, 1st sess., 1874, vol. II, pt. 1, 565–67; Peggy Lamson, *The Glorious Failure* (New York: Norton, 1973), 181.

On January 6, 1874, Robert Brown Elliott delivered a ringing speech in the U.S. House of Representatives in support of the Sumner civil rights bill. Elliott was responding in part to words uttered the day before by Virginia Congressman John T. Harris, who claimed that "there is not a gentleman on this floor who can honestly say he really believes that the colored man is created his equal."

Republican-controlled Senate in 1874, but House Democrats held up passage. It was not enacted until 1875 and then largely as a memorial to Sumner, who had died in 1874. In its final form, the bans on discrimination in churches, cemeteries, and schools were deleted.

The act stipulated "That all persons . . . shall be entitled to the full and equal enjoyment of the accommodations, advantages, facilities, and privileges of inns, public conveyances on land or water, theaters, and other places of public amusement." After its passage, no attempt was made to enforce these provisions, and in 1883 the Supreme Court declared it unconstitutional. Justice Joseph Bradley wrote that the Fourteenth Amendment protected black people from discrimination by states but not by private businesses. Black newspapers likened the decision to the *Dred Scott* case a quarter century earlier.

redemption

The term used for the process, often violent, by which white conservative Democrats regained political control of a southern state from black and white Republicans during Reconstruction.

13.5 The End of Reconstruction

Analyze the impact that Redemption had on African Americans.

Reconstruction ended as it began—in violence and controversy. Democrats demanded "**redemption**"—a word with biblical and spiritual overtones. They wanted southern states restored to conservative, white political control. By 1875 they had regained authority in all the former Confederate states except Mississippi, Florida, Louisiana, and South Carolina (see Map 13-1). Democrats had redeemed Tennessee in 1870 and Georgia in 1871. Democrats had learned two lessons. First, few black men would vote for the Democratic Party—no matter how much white leaders wanted to believe former slaves were easy to manipulate. Second, intimidation and violence would win elections in areas where the number of black and white voters was nearly equal. The federal government had stymied Klan violence in 1871, but by the mid-1870s the government had become reluctant to send troops to the South to protect black citizens.

Map 13-1 Dates of Readmission of Southern States to the Union and Reestablishment of Democratic Party Control

Once conservative white Democrats regained political control of a state government from black and white Republicans, they considered that state "redeemed." The first states the Democrats "redeemed" were Georgia, Virginia, and North Carolina. Louisiana, Florida, and South Carolina were the last. (Tennessee was not included in the Reconstruction process under the terms of the 1867 Reconstruction Act.)

In which states did black and white Republicans hold political control for the shortest and longest periods of time?

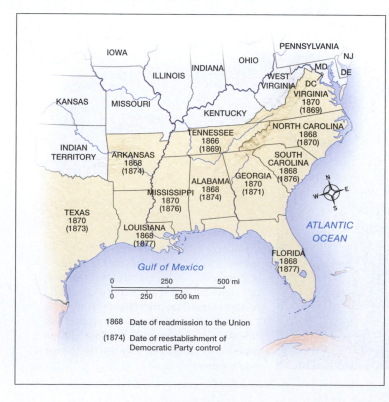

1868   Date of readmission to the Union

(1874) Date of reestablishment of Democratic Party control

13.5.1 Violent Redemption and the Colfax Massacre

In Alabama in 1874, black and white Republican leaders were murdered, and white mobs destroyed crops and homes. On election day in Eufaula, white men killed seven and injured nearly 70 unarmed black voters. Black voters were also driven from the polls in Mobile. Democrats won the election and "redeemed" Alabama.

White violence marred every election in Louisiana from 1868 to 1876. After Republicans and Democrats each claimed victory in the 1872 elections, black people seized the small town of Colfax along the Red River to protect themselves against a Democratic takeover. They held out for three weeks. Then on Easter Sunday in 1873, a well-armed white mob attacked the black defenders. At least 105 were killed in the **Colfax Massacre**, the worst single day of bloodshed during Reconstruction. In 1874 the White League almost redeemed Louisiana in a wave of violence. Black people were murdered, courts were attacked, and white people refused to pay taxes to the Republican state government. Six white and two black Republicans were murdered at Coushatta. In September, President Grant finally sent federal troops to New Orleans after 3,500 White Leaguers nearly wiped out the black militia and the Metropolitan Police. But the stage had been set for the 1876 campaign.

Colfax Massacre

At least 105 African Americans were murdered on Easter Sunday in 1873 in Colfax, Louisiana, in the single worst episode of racial violence during Reconstruction.

13.5.2 The Shotgun Policy

In 1875 white Mississippians, no longer afraid the national government would intervene in force, declared open warfare on the black majority. The masks and hoods of the Klan were discarded. One newspaper proclaimed that Democrats would carry the election, "peaceably if we can, forcibly if we must." Another paper carried a bold banner: "Mississippi is a white man's country, and by the eternal God we'll rule it."

White Mississippi unleashed a campaign of violence known as the "**shotgun policy**" that was extreme even for Reconstruction. Many Republicans fled, and others were murdered. In late 1874 an estimated 300 black people were hunted down outside Vicksburg after black men armed with inferior weapons had lost a "battle" with white men. In 1875, 30 teachers, church leaders, and Republican officials were killed in Clinton. The white sheriff of Yazoo County, who had married a black woman and supported the education of black children, fled the state.

Governor Adelbert Ames appealed for federal help, but President Grant refused: "The whole public are tired out with these annual autumnal outbreaks in the South . . . [and] are ready now to condemn any interference on the part of the Government." The terrorism intensified, and many black voters went into hiding on election day, afraid for their lives and those of their families. Democrats redeemed Mississippi and prided themselves that they—a superior race representing the most civilized of all people—were back in control.

In Florida in 1876, white Republicans noted that support for black people in the South was fading. They nominated an all-white Republican slate and even refused to renominate black Congressman Josiah Walls.

shotgun policy

In Mississippi in 1875, white men resorted to violence and intimidation against black and white Republicans to regain political control of the state for conservative Democrats.

13.5.3 The Hamburg Massacre and the Ellenton Riot

South Carolina Democrats were divided between moderate and extreme factions, but they united to nominate former Confederate General Wade Hampton for governor after the **Hamburg Massacre**. The prelude to this event occurred on July 4, 1876—the nation's centennial—when two white men in a buggy confronted the black militia that was drilling on a town street in Hamburg, a small, mostly black town. Hot words were exchanged, and days later, Democrats demanded the militia be disarmed. White rifle club members from around the state arrived in Hamburg and attacked the armory, where 40 black members of the militia defended themselves. The rifle companies brought up a cannon and reinforcements from Georgia. After the militia ran low on ammunition, white men captured the armory. One white man was killed, 29 black men were taken prisoner, and the other 11 fled. Five of the black men identified as leaders were shot down in cold blood. The rifle companies wrecked the town. Seven white men were indicted for murder. All were acquitted.

Two months after the Hamburg killings a false allegation that African Americans had assaulted an elderly white woman gave armed bands of white men the excuse to attack black people in the rural community of Ellenton about 30 miles south of Hamburg. Between 30 and 100 African Americans were slain in the **Ellenton Riot**, including state legislator Simon Coker. Two white men died. Had it not been for the timely arrival of U.S. troops, more lives would have been lost. No one was charged much less convicted in the Ellenton affair.

Hamburg Massacre

White Democrats attacked black Republicans in July 1876 in the village of Hamburg, South Carolina. Five black men were murdered as the Democrats began a violent effort to redeem the state.

Ellenton Riot

Between 30 and 100 African Americans were killed by marauding white men in September 1876 in Aiken County, South Carolina, after an alleged assault by a black man on an elderly white woman.

The Hamburg Massacre and Ellenton Riot represented the determined effort of South Carolina Democrats to imitate Mississippi's "shotgun policy." It also had forced a reluctant President Grant to send federal troops to South Carolina. In the 1876 election campaign, hundreds of white men in red flannel shirts turned out on mules and horses to support Wade Hampton against incumbent Republican Governor Daniel Chamberlain and his black and white allies. When Chamberlain and fellow Republicans tried to speak in Edgefield, 600 Red Shirts—many of them armed—ridiculed, threatened, and shouted them down.

Democrats beat and killed black people to prevent them from voting. Democratic leaders instructed their followers to treat black voters with contempt: "In speeches to negroes you must remember that argument has no effect on them. They can only be influenced by their fears, superstition, and cupidity. . . . Treat them so as to show them you are a superior race and that their natural position is that of subordination to the white man."

As the election approached, black people in the up-country of South Carolina knew it would be dangerous if they tried to vote. But in the low country, black people went on the offensive and attacked Democrats. In Charleston, a white man was killed in a racial melee. At a campaign rally at Cainhoy, a few miles outside Charleston, armed black men killed five white men.

A few black men supported Hampton and the Red Shirts. Hampton had a paternalistic view of black people, and, although he considered them inferior, he promised to respect their rights. Martin Delany believed Hampton and the Democrats were more trustworthy than unreliable Republicans; Delany campaigned for Hampton and was later rewarded with an appointment to a minor political post. A few conservative black men during Reconstruction also supported the Democrats and curried their favor and patronage. However, most black people despised them. When one black man gave his support to the Democrats, his wife threw him and his clothes out, declaring she would prefer to "beg her bread" than live with a "Democratic nigger."

13.5.4 The "Compromise" of 1877

Threats, violence, and bloodshed accompanied the elections of 1876 in the South, but the national results were confusing and contradictory. Samuel Tilden, the Democratic presidential candidate, won the popular vote by more than 250,000 and had a large lead—185 to 167—over Republican Rutherford B. Hayes in the electoral vote. The 20 remaining electoral votes were in dispute. Both Democrats and Republicans claimed to have won in Florida, Louisiana, and South Carolina, the last three southern states that had not been redeemed. (There was also one contested vote from Oregon.) Unless Hayes managed to capture all 20 electoral votes of the three contested states (and Oregon), Tilden would be the next president (see Map 13-2).

The constitutional crisis over the outcome of the 1876 election was not resolved until shortly before Inauguration Day in March 1877. An informal understanding known as the **Compromise of 1877** ended the dispute. Democrats accepted a Hayes victory, but Hayes let southern Democrats know he would not support Republican governments in Florida, Louisiana, and South Carolina. In 1877 Hayes withdrew the last federal troops from the South, and the Republican administration in those states collapsed. Democrats immediately took control.

Redemption was now complete. White Democrats controlled each of the former Confederate states. Henry Adams, a black leader from Louisiana, explained what had happened: "The whole South—every state in the South had got into the hands of the very men that held us as slaves."

Compromise of 1877

This informal arrangement between national Democrats and Republicans settled the disputed presidential election of 1876 by permitting Republican Rutherford B. Hayes to become president while allowing Democrats to complete redemption by taking political control of Louisiana, Florida, and South Carolina.

Map 13-2 The Election of 1876

Although Democrat Samuel Tilden appeared to have won the election of 1876, Rutherford B. Hayes and the Republicans were able to claim victory after a prolonged political and constitutional controversy involving the disputed Electoral College votes from Louisiana, Florida, and South Carolina (and one from Oregon). In an informal settlement in 1877, Democrats agreed to accept electoral votes for Hayes from those states, and Republicans agreed to permit those states to be "redeemed" by the Democrats. The result was to leave the entire South under the political control of conservative white Democrats. For the first time since 1867, black and white Republicans no longer effectively controlled any former Confederate state.

What factors explain the loss of political power by southern Republicans?

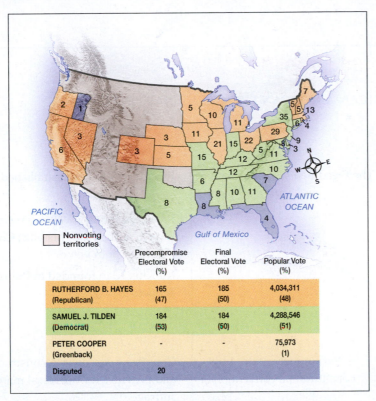

	Precompromise Electoral Vote (%)	Final Electoral Vote (%)	Popular Vote (%)
RUTHERFORD B. HAYES (Republican)	165 (47)	185 (50)	4,034,311 (48)
SAMUEL J. TILDEN (Democrat)	184 (53)	184 (50)	4,288,546 (51)
PETER COOPER (Greenback)	-	-	75,973 (1)
Disputed	20		

Conclusion

The glorious hopes that emancipation and the Union victory in the Civil War had aroused among African Americans in 1865 appeared forlorn by 1877. To be sure, black people were no longer slave laborers or property. They lived in close-knit families that white people no longer controlled. They had established hundreds of schools, churches, and benevolent societies. The Constitution now endowed them with freedom, citizenship, and the right to vote. Some black people had even acquired land.

But no one can characterize Reconstruction as a success. The epidemic of terror and violence made it one of the bloodiest eras in American history. Thousands of black people had been beaten, raped, and murdered since 1865 simply because they had acted as free people. Too many white people were determined that black people could not and would not have the same rights that white people enjoyed. White southerners would not tolerate either the presence of black men in politics or white Republicans who accepted black political involvement. Most white northerners and even Radical Republicans grew weary of intervening in southern affairs and became convinced again that black men and women were their inferiors and were not prepared to participate in government. Reconstruction, they concluded, had been a mistake.

Furthermore, black and white Republicans hurt themselves by indulging in fraud and corruption and by engaging in angry and divisive factionalism. But even if Republicans had been honest and united, white southern Democrats would never have accepted black people as worthy to participate in the political system.

Southern Democrats would accept black people in politics only if Democrats could control black voters. But black voters understood this, rejected control by former slave owners, and were loyal to the Republican Party—as flawed as it was.

As grim a turn as life may have taken for black people by 1877, it would get even worse in the decades that followed.

Chapter Timeline

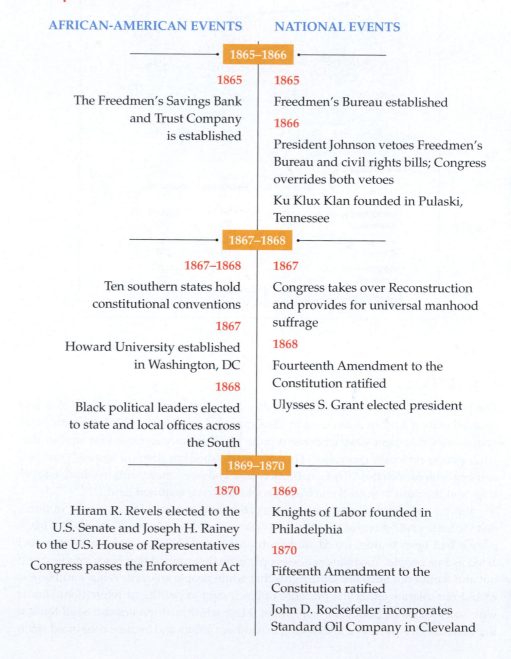

AFRICAN-AMERICAN EVENTS	NATIONAL EVENTS
1865–1866	
1865	**1865**
The Freedmen's Savings Bank and Trust Company is established	Freedmen's Bureau established
	1866
	President Johnson vetoes Freedmen's Bureau and civil rights bills; Congress overrides both vetoes
	Ku Klux Klan founded in Pulaski, Tennessee
1867–1868	
1867–1868	**1867**
Ten southern states hold constitutional conventions	Congress takes over Reconstruction and provides for universal manhood suffrage
1867	**1868**
Howard University established in Washington, DC	Fourteenth Amendment to the Constitution ratified
1868	Ulysses S. Grant elected president
Black political leaders elected to state and local offices across the South	
1869–1870	
1870	**1869**
Hiram R. Revels elected to the U.S. Senate and Joseph H. Rainey to the U.S. House of Representatives	Knights of Labor founded in Philadelphia
Congress passes the Enforcement Act	**1870**
	Fifteenth Amendment to the Constitution ratified
	John D. Rockefeller incorporates Standard Oil Company in Cleveland

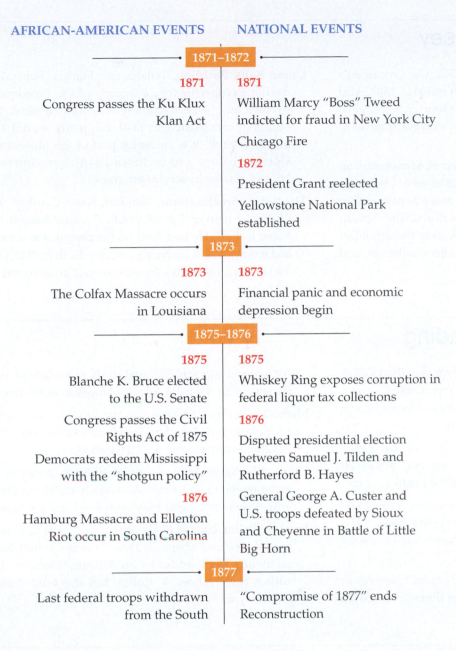

AFRICAN-AMERICAN EVENTS   **NATIONAL EVENTS**

1871–1872

1871
Congress passes the Ku Klux Klan Act

1871
William Marcy "Boss" Tweed indicted for fraud in New York City

Chicago Fire

1872
President Grant reelected

Yellowstone National Park established

1873

1873
The Colfax Massacre occurs in Louisiana

1873
Financial panic and economic depression begin

1875–1876

1875
Blanche K. Bruce elected to the U.S. Senate

Congress passes the Civil Rights Act of 1875

Democrats redeem Mississippi with the "shotgun policy"

1876
Hamburg Massacre and Ellenton Riot occur in South Carolina

1875
Whiskey Ring exposes corruption in federal liquor tax collections

1876
Disputed presidential election between Samuel J. Tilden and Rutherford B. Hayes

General George A. Custer and U.S. troops defeated by Sioux and Cheyenne in Battle of Little Big Horn

1877

Last federal troops withdrawn from the South

"Compromise of 1877" ends Reconstruction

Review Questions

1. What issues most concerned black political leaders during Reconstruction?

2. What did black political leaders accomplish and fail to accomplish during Reconstruction? What contributed to their successes and failures?

3. Were black political leaders unqualified to hold office so soon after the end of slavery?

4. To what extent did African Americans dominate southern politics during Reconstruction? Should this era be referred to as "Black Reconstruction"?

5. Why did the Republican Party fail to maintain control of southern state governments during Reconstruction?

6. What was "redemption"? What happened when redemption occurred? What factors contributed to redemption?

7. How and why did Reconstruction end?

8. How effective was Reconstruction in assisting black people to move from slavery to freedom? How effective was it in restoring the southern states to the Union?

Retracing the Odyssey

Howard University, Washington, DC. The Freedmen's Bureau founded this national university in 1867. Also located on the campus is the Moorland-Spingarn Research Center, one of the country's richest archives in African-American history.

Wilberforce University and the National Afro-American Museum and Cultural Center, Wilberforce, Ohio. Wilberforce University opened in 1856 and was named after English abolitionist William Wilberforce. The African Methodist Episcopal Church took over the school in 1863. It contains exhibits, an art gallery, a theater, and has a picnic area.

Union Bank Building, Tallahassee, Florida. For a time during Reconstruction, a branch of the Freedmen's Savings and Trust Company was located here. The building, constructed in 1840, originally served as a planters' bank. It is currently part of the Museum of Florida History and includes its African-American History teacher in-service program.

The Robert Smalls Home, Beaufort, South Carolina. The Civil War hero and black political leader bought this house in 1863. He had lived on the premises as a slave, and it remained in his hands until his death in 1915. (The former Smalls house is a privately owned dwelling today.)

Recommended Reading

Eric Foner. *Freedom's Lawmakers: A Directory of Black Office-holders During Reconstruction.* New York: Oxford University Press, 1993. Biographical sketches of every known southern black leader during the era.

John Hope Franklin. *Reconstruction after the Civil War.* Chicago: University of Chicago Press, 1961. An excellent summary and interpretation of the postwar years.

William Gillette. *Retreat from Reconstruction, 1869–1879.* Baton Rouge: Louisiana State University Press, 1979. An analysis of how and why the North lost interest in the South.

Thomas Holt. *Black over White: Negro Political Leadership in South Carolina.* Urbana: University of Illinois Press, 1979.

A masterful and sophisticated study of black leaders in the state with the most African-American politicians.

Michael L. Perman. *Emancipation and Reconstruction, 1862–1879.* Arlington Heights, IL: Harlan Davidson, 1987. Another excellent survey of the period.

Howard N. Rabinowitz, ed. *Southern Black Leaders of the Reconstruction Era.* Urbana: University of Illinois Press, 1982. A series of biographical essays on black politicians.

Frank A. Rollin. *Life and Public Services of Martin R. Delany.* Boston: Lee and Shepard, 1883. This is the first biography of a black leader by an African American. The author was Frances A. Rollin, but she used a male pseudonym.

Additional Bibliography

Reconstruction in Specific States and Territories

M. Thomas Bailey. *Reconstruction in Indian Territory: A Story of Avarice, Discrimination, and Opportunism.* Port Washington, NY: Kennikat Press, 1972.

Jane Dailey. *Before Jim Crow: The Politics of Race in Post Emancipation Virginia.* Chapel Hill: University of North Carolina Press, 2000.

Edmund L. Drago. *Black Politicians and Reconstruction in Georgia.* Athens: University of Georgia Press, 1982.

———. *Hurrah for Hampton!: Black Red Shirts in South Carolina During Reconstruction.* Fayetteville: University of Arkansas Press, 1998.

Luther P. Jackson. *Negro Officeholders in Virginia, 1865–1895.* Norfolk, VA: Guide Quality Press, 1945.

Peter Kolchin. *First Freedom: The Responses of Alabama's Blacks to Emancipation and Reconstruction.* Westport, CT: Greenwood Press, 1972.

Merline Pitre. *Through Many Dangers, Toils, and Snares: The Black Leadership of Texas, 1868–1900.* Austin, TX: Eakin Press, 1985.

Joe M. Richardson. *The Negro in the Reconstruction of Florida, 1865–1877.* Tallahassee: Florida State University Press, 1965.

Buford Stacher. *Blacks in Mississippi Politics, 1865–1900.* Washington, DC: University Press of America, 1978.

Ted Tunnell. *Crucible of Reconstruction: War, Radicalism and Race in Louisiana, 1862–1877*. Baton Rouge: Louisiana State University Press, 1984.

Charles Vincent. *Black Legislators in Louisiana During Reconstruction*. Baton Rouge: Louisiana State University Press, 1976.

Joel Williamson. *After Slavery: The Negro in South Carolina: 1861–1877*. Chapel Hill: University of North Carolina Press, 1965.

National Politics: Andrew Johnson and the Radical Republicans

Michael Les Benedict. *A Compromise of Principle: Congressional Republicans and Reconstruction*. New York: Norton, 1974.

Dan T. Carter. *When the War Was Over: The Failure of Self-Reconstruction in the South, 1865–1867*. Baton Rouge: Louisiana State University Press, 1983.

Hugh Davis. *We Will Be Satisfied with Nothing Less: The African American Struggle for Equal Rights in the North During Reconstruction*. Ithaca, NY: Cornell University Press, 2011.

Michael W. Fitzgerald. *The Union League Movement in the Deep South*. Baton Rouge: Louisiana State University Press, 1989.

———. *Splendid Failure: Postwar Reconstruction in the American South*. Chicago: Ivan R. Dee, 2007.

Eric L. McKitrick. *Andrew Johnson and Reconstruction, 1865–1867*. Chicago: University of Chicago Press, 1960.

James M. McPherson. *The Struggle for Equality: Abolitionists and the Negro in the Civil War and Reconstruction*. Princeton, NJ: Princeton University Press, 1964.

Hans L. Trefousse. *The Radical Republicans: Lincoln's Vanguard for Racial Justice*. Baton Rouge: Louisiana State University Press, 1969.

Education, Land, Labor, and the Freedmen's Bank

Elizabeth Bethel. *Promiseland: A Century of Life in a Negro Community*. Philadelphia: Temple University Press, 1981.

Carol R. Bleser. *The Promised Land: The History of the South Carolina Land Commission, 1869–1890*. Columbia: University of South Carolina Press, 1969.

Sharon Ann Holt. *Making Freedom Pay: North Carolina Freed People Working for Themselves, 1865–1900*. Athens: University of Georgia Press, 2000.

Ward McAfee. *Religion, Race and Reconstruction: The Public Schools in the 1870s*. Albany: State University of New York Press, 1998.

Lynda J. Morgan. *Emancipation in Virginia's Tobacco Belt*. Athens: University of Georgia Press, 1992.

Donald G. Nieman. *To Set the Law in Motion: The Freedmen's Bureau and Legal Rights for Blacks, 1865–1869*. Millwood, NY: KTO, 1979.

Carl R. Osthaus. *Freedmen, Philanthropy and Fraud: A History of the Freedman's Savings Bank*. Urbana: University of Illinois Press, 1976.

Heather Cox Richardson. *The Death of Reconstruction: Race, Labor, and Politics in the Post–Civil War North, 1865–1901*. Cambridge, MA: Harvard University Press, 2001.

Violence and the Ku Klux Klan

Charles Lane. *The Day Freedom Died: The Colfax Massacre, the Supreme Court and the Betrayal of Reconstruction*. New York: Henry Holt, 2008.

George C. Rable. *But There Was No Peace: The Role of Violence in the Politics of Reconstruction*. Athens: University of Georgia Press, 1984.

Allen W. Trelease. *White Terror: The Ku Klux Klan Conspiracy and Southern Reconstruction*. New York: Harper & Row, 1973.

Christopher Waldrep and Donald G. Nieman, eds. *Local Matters: Race, Crime, and Justice in the Nineteenth Century South*. Athens: University of Georgia Press, 2011.

Lou Falkner Williams. *The Great South Carolina Ku Klux Klan Trials, 1871–1872*. Athens: University of Georgia Press, 1996.

Autobiography and Biography

Mifflin Wistar Gibbs. *Shadow and Light: An Autobiography*. Lincoln: University of Nebraska Press, 1995.

David Joens. *From Slave to State Legislator: John W. E. Thomas: Illinois' First African American Lawmaker*. Carbondale: Southern Illinois University Press, 2012.

Peter D. Klingman. *Josiah Walls*. Gainesville: University Press of Florida, 1976.

Peggy Lamson. *The Glorious Failure: Black Congressman Robert Brown Elliott and Reconstruction in South Carolina*. New York: Norton, 1973.

Edward A. Miller. *Gullah Statesman: Robert Smalls: From Slavery to Congress, 1839–1915*. Columbia: University of South Carolina Press, 1995.

Loren Schweninger. *James T. Rapier and Reconstruction*. Chicago: University of Chicago Press, 1978.

Okon E. Uya. *From Slavery to Public Service: Robert Smalls, 1839–1915*. New York: Oxford University Press, 1971.

Connecting the Past

Voting and Politics

The Fifteenth Amendment to the Constitution, ratified in 1870, explicitly states that the right "to vote shall not be denied or abridged by the United States or any State on account of race, color, or previous condition of servitude." Why then was it necessary for Congress to pass the Voting Rights Act of 1965?

Race and the right to vote have been volatile issues since the creation of the American republic. The Founding Fathers betrayed a deep mistrust of permitting white men to vote who lacked education and had no stake in society through the possession of property or wealth. Slaves could not vote. Women were disfranchised. But in the late 1700s, a few free black men in the Northeastern states of Pennsylvania, New York, Connecticut, Rhode Island, Massachusetts, New Hampshire, and Vermont did vote. In the early nineteenth century, however, as the political system became more democratic for white men, black men in Pennsylvania and Connecticut—and most black men in New York—lost the right to vote.

Following the Civil War, white Southerners and northern Democrats were outraged when Republicans in Congress granted black men the right to vote through Reconstruction legislation and the Fifteenth Amendment. As southern Democrats "redeemed" the former Confederate states, they systematically disfranchised black voters and evaded the Fifteenth Amendment.

To do this, they devised a variety of schemes. Among them were the poll tax, the literacy test, and a requirement that illiterate men could vote only if they could "understand" the Constitution. Several southern states also adopted the grandfather clause, which stipulated that only men who were eligible to vote before 1867 or had fathers or grandfathers who were eligible to vote at that time would be eligible to vote in the late nineteenth century. Violence and intimidation were also used to "persuade" black men and their white allies that they did not want to vote. The U.S. Supreme Court acquiesced in disfranchisement by narrowly defining voting rights for African Americans in a series of cases in the late nineteenth and early twentieth centuries that nullified the Fifteenth Amendment. In tortured logic in one of these cases, Chief Justice Morrison Waite declared that, "The Fifteenth Amendment does not confer the right of suffrage upon anyone." Instead, he claimed, "It prevents the States, or United States, however, from giving preference . . . to one citizen of the United States over another, on account of race, color or previous condition of servitude."

By the early twentieth century, Democrats and Republicans began to hold primary elections to nominate party candidates to run in the general election. Southern Democrats took advantage of this innovation to limit membership in the Democratic Party to white men—and later white women. Only members of the Democratic Party were eligible to vote in the Democratic primary. Because the Republican Party had all but ceased to exist in the South after Reconstruction and rarely ran candidates for statewide offices, victory in the Democratic primary meant victory in the fall election. Black voters who could still vote in the general election found it a meaningless gesture because the "real" election had been the Democratic primary.

As black men and women migrated North and West in the early and mid-twentieth century, they were able to vote in their new communities. Their increasing political strength enabled them to elect black men and women to local and state offices. They also elected black men from northern cities, including Oscar DePriest, Robert Nix, Adam Clayton Powell, and Charles Diggs, to serve in the U.S. House of Representatives. With the New Deal in the 1930s, black voters began to support Democratic candidates as they abandoned their longstanding loyalty to the Republican Party. In turn, the Democratic Party increasingly relied on those black voters to support their presidential candidates, such as Franklin D. Roosevelt, Harry S Truman, and John F. Kennedy. In the meantime, the Supreme Court declared the grandfather clause unconstitutional in 1915 and outlawed the South's white Democratic primary elections in 1944.

During the civil rights movement and with unrelenting pressure from President Lyndon B. Johnson, northern Democrats and Republicans in Congress passed—over the bitter opposition of southern Democrats—the Civil Rights Act of

1964 and the Voting Rights Act of 1965. The Voting Rights Act authorized the U.S. Department of Justice to dispatch federal registrars to states and communities that had a history of suppressing voting rights. As a result, the number of black voters and then black officeholders expanded exponentially across the South.

Yet voting rights still is not a dead issue. In 2013 the U.S. Supreme Court in *Shelby County v. Holder* invalidated a key provision of the Voting Rights Act. Chief Justice John Roberts stated that "entrenched racial discrimination in voting" was no longer evident in the states where it had prevailed 50 years earlier. In the meantime, the Republican Party launched a campaign in 30 states to require voter photo identification at the polls.

President Barrack Obama weighed into the controversy over voting rights in 2015 by supporting 94-year-old Rosanell Eaton's lawsuit brought by the NAACP to overrule North Carolina's new legal restrictions limiting voting rights. "I am," Obama wrote, "where I am today because men and women like Rosanell Eaton refused to accept anything less than a full measure of equality. Their efforts made our country a better place. It is now up to us to continue those efforts. Congress must restore the Voting Rights Act. Our state leaders and legislatures must make it easier—not harder—for more Americans to have their voices heard. Above all, we must exercise our right as citizens to vote, for the truth is that too often we disenfranchise ourselves."

1. Who should be denied the right to vote? Why?
2. To prevent fraud in elections, should voters be required to present photo identification to cast a ballot?

Part IV
Searching for Safe Spaces

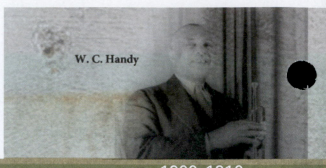

W. C. Handy

	1860–1900	1900–1910

RELIGION

1880s–1890s Holiness Movement and Pentecostal churches spread among African Americans
1854 James A. Healey ordained first African-American Roman Catholic priest in Paris
1890 Baptist churches count 1,300,000 southern black members, making them the largest African-American denomination

CULTURE

1887 Black players banned from major league baseball
1890s–1920s Emergence of jazz and the blues among southern blacks
1899 Scott Joplin writes the "Maple Leaf Rag"
1900 James W. Johnson writes "Lift Every Voice and Sing"

1901 Booker T. Washington publishes *Up from Slavery*
1903 W. E. B. Du Bois publishes *The Souls of Black Folk*
1905 The *Defender* begins publication in Chicago
1908 Jack Johnson wins heavyweight championship in boxing

POLITICS AND GOVERNMENT

1869–1889 Four black regiments stationed on the Western frontier
1881 First Jim Crow law segregates trains in Tennessee
1882 South Carolina begins to disfranchise black voters
1892 Populist Party attracts many black voters
1896 *Plessy v. Ferguson* upholds "separate but equal" doctrine of racial segregation
1898 First black officers command black troops in the Spanish-American War
1899–1901 George H. White serves as the South's last black congressman to be elected until 1972

SOCIETY AND ECONOMY

1867 Independent Order of St. Luke founded
1868 Hampton Institute founded
1870 Howard University Law School founded
1881 Tuskegee Institute founded
1886 Washington County, Texas, race riot
1887 National Colored Farmers' Alliance formed
1892 155 African Americans lynched in the United States
1895 Booker T. Washington addresses the Cotton States Exposition in Atlanta
1896 National Association of Colored Women founded

1903 St. Luke Penny Savings Bank established in Richmond
1904 Boule (Sigma Pi Phi) formed
1905 Niagara Movement begins
1906 Brownsville Affair Atlanta riot
1908 Springfield riot National Association of Colored Graduate Nurses founded
1909 NAACP established

Zora Neale Hurston

Countee Cullen

Anna Julia Cooper

George H. White
(1852–1918)
Booker T. Washington
(1856–1915)
Johnson C. Whittaker
(1858–1931)
Anna Julia Cooper
(1858–1964)
Ida Wells Barnett
(1862–1931)
Mary Church Terrell
(1863–1954)
C. J. Walker
(1867–1919)
Scott Joplin
(1868–1917)
W. E. B. Du Bois
(1868–1963)
William J. Seymour
(1870–1922)
James W. Johnson
(1871–1938)
W. C. Handy
(1873–1958)
Carter Woodson
(1875–1950)
Jack Johnson
(1878–1946)
Gertrude "Ma" Rainey
(1886–1939)
Marcus Garvey
(1887–1940)
A. Philip Randolph
(1889–1979)
Jelly Roll Morton
(1890–1941)
Claude McKay
(1890–1948)
Bessie Smith
(1894–1937)
Jean Toomer
(1894–1962)
Florence Mills
(1895–1927)
Paul Robeson
(1898–1976)
Duke Ellington
(1899–1974)
Zora Neale Hurston
(1901–1960)
Langston Hughes
(1902–1967)
Countee Cullen
(c. 1903–1946)
Fats Waller
(1904–1943)

1920 Baseball's Negro League organized
1922 Claude McKay publishes *Harlem Shadows*
1924 Jessica R. Faucet publishes *There Is Confusion*
1925 Countee Cullen publishes *Color*
     Alain Locke publishes *The New Negro*
1926 Carter Woodson organizes Negro History Week
     Langston Hughes publishes *The Weary Blues*
1927 James W. Johnson publishes *God's Trombones*
1928 Duke Ellington debuts at the Cotton Club
     Claude McKay publishes *Home to Harlem*
1929 Fats Waller's "Ain't Misbehavin" opens on Broadway
1930 James W. Johnson publishes *Black Manhattan*
1933 James W. Johnson publishes his autobiography
     Along the Way
1937 Zora Neale Hurston publishes *Their Eyes Were
     Watching God*

1914 President Woodrow Wilson defends
     racial segregation
1917–1918 Over 1,000 black men serve as
     officers in World War I

1920 Nineteenth Amendment grants female suffrage
     with support from black women
1927 *Nixon v. Herndon* strikes down the white primary
     laws

1910 Urban League founded
     Negro Fellowship League founded
1914 Universal Negro Improvement
     Association founded
1915 Reemergence of the Ku Klux Klan
1917 East St. Louis riot
     Houston riot
1919 Chicago riot
     Elaine, Arkansas, riot
     Pan-African Congress meets in Paris
     Marcus Garvey founds the Black
     Star Line

1925 National Bar Association founded
     A. Philip Randolph founds the Brotherhood
     of Sleeping Car Porters

Chapter 14

White Supremacy Triumphant: African Americans in the Late Nineteenth Century

1877–1895

The Moses Speese family acquired a homestead near Westerville in Custer County, Nebraska.
This 1888 photograph shows the extended family assembled in front of their sod house. They have
installed a windmill to provide power to pump water from a well. They also possess two teams
of horses.

 ## Learning Objectives

After reading this chapter, you should be able to:

14.1   Explain the role of African Americans in the political system
in the late nineteenth century.

14.2   Discuss the methods employed to disfranchise black voters.

14.3   Describe the emergence of laws and customs that required racial segregation.

14.4   Analyze the scope and extent of racial violence and brutality in maintaining white supremacy.

14.5   Explain how law enforcement and the court system affected African Americans.

The supremacy of the white race of the South must be maintained forever, and the domination of the negro race resisted at all points and at all hazards—because the white race is the superior race. This is the declaration of no new truth. It has abided forever in the marrow of our bones, and shall run forever with the blood that feeds Anglo-Saxon hearts.

—*Henry Grady, editor of the Atlanta Constitution, 1887*

I remember a crowd of white men who rode up on horseback with rifles on their shoulders. I was with my father when they rode up, and I remember starting to cry. They cursed my father, drew their guns and made him salute, made him take off his hat and bow down to them several times. Then they rode away. I was not yet five years old, but I have never forgotten them.

—*Benjamin E. Mays on his childhood in Epworth, South Carolina, in 1898*

Black people struggled against a rising tide of white supremacy in the late nineteenth century. White southerners—and most white northerners—had long been convinced that as a race they were superior to black people intellectually and culturally. They were certain that black people—because of their inferiority—could play only a subservient role in society. During slavery, white southerners had taken that subservience for granted. With slavery's end, black people had allied themselves with radical Republicans during Reconstruction and challenged white supremacy as they became citizens and participated in the political system. The federal government established and enforced—although unevenly—the rights of all citizens to enjoy equal protection of the law and due process of law. But the commitment of the Republicans and the federal government wavered, waned, and then collapsed by the mid-1870s.

With vivid recollections of the Civil War receding by the late 1800s, antagonism lessened between white southerners and white northerners. Many northern white people had previously expressed considerable sympathy for former slaves and bitter hostility toward southern rebels. But white Americans increasingly came to remember the Civil War less as a conflict directly involving the destiny of four million African Americans and more as a war that was marked by the terrible sacrifices and losses endured by white people. The same white Americans were increasingly preoccupied with the frontier West and with the Industrial Revolution that was transforming American society.

Congress, the president, and especially the Supreme Court abandoned the commitment to protect African Americans' civil and legal rights. Political and judicial leaders embraced a laissez-faire approach to social and economic issues. The government would keep its hands off the expanding railroad, steel, and petroleum industries. Neither would government intervene to safeguard the rights of black citizens. The Supreme Court interpreted the Fourteenth Amendment to protect corporations from government regulation, but it failed to protect the basic rights of black people.

As a result, the conservative white Democrats who had regained power in the South were no more than mildly fearful that the U.S. government or Republicans would intrude as white authority expanded over the lives of southern African Americans in the late nineteenth century. Between 1875 and 1900, black people in the South were gradually excluded from politics, segregated in public life, and denied equal—even basic—rights. They were forced to behave in a demeaning and deferential manner to white people. Most of them were limited to menial agricultural and domestic jobs that left them poor and dependent on white landowners and merchants. They were often raped, lynched, and beaten. Southern justice was systematically unjust.

Unwilling and unable to tolerate such conditions, some African Americans left the South for Africa or the American West. However, most black people remained in the South, where many acquired a semblance of education, some managed to purchase land, and a few even prospered.

14.1 Politics

Explain the role of African Americans in the political system in the late nineteenth century.

In the late nineteenth century, black people remained important in southern politics. Black men served in Congress, state legislatures, and local governments. They received federal patronage appointments to post offices and custom houses. But as southern Democrats steadily disfranchised black voters in the 1880s and 1890s, the number of black politicians declined until the political system was virtually all white by 1900 (see Figure 14-1).

When Reconstruction ended in 1877 and the last Republican state governments collapsed, black men who held major state offices were forced out. In South Carolina, Lieutenant Governor Richard H. Gleaves resigned under protest in 1877: "I desire to place on record, in the most public and unqualified manner, my sense of the great wrong which thus forces me practically to abandon rights conferred on me, as I fully believe by a majority of my fellow citizens of this State."

For a time, some conservative white Democrats accepted limited black participation in politics as long as no black leader had power over white people and black participation did not challenge white domination. South Carolina's Governor Wade Hampton even assured black people that he respected their rights and would appoint qualified black men to minor offices. Hampton condescendingly told black people in 1878, "We propose to protect you and give you all your rights; but while we do this you cannot expect that we should discriminate in your favor, and say because you are a colored man, you have the right to rule the State. We say to you that we intend to take the best men we can find to represent the State, and you must qualify yourselves to do so before you can expect to be chosen."

Paternalistic Democrats like Hampton did appoint black men to lower-level positions. Hampton, for example, appointed Richard Gleaves and Martin Delany as trial justices. In turn, some black men supported the Democrats. A few black Democrats were elected to state legislatures in the 1880s. Some had been Democrats throughout Reconstruction. Others had abandoned the Republicans.

Most black voters, however, remained loyal Republicans even though the party had become a hollow shell of what it had been during Reconstruction. Its few white supporters usually shunned black Republicans. The party rarely fielded candidates for statewide elections, limiting itself to local races in regions where Republicans remained strong.

14.1.1 Black Congressmen

Democrats created oddly shaped congressional districts to confine much of the black population of a state to one district, such as Mississippi's third, South Carolina's seventh, Virginia's fourth, and North Carolina's second. A black Republican usually represented these districts, while the rest of the state elected white Democrats to Congress. This diluted black voting strength and reduced the number of white people represented by a black congressman. Thus Henry Cheatham and George H. White of North Carolina, John Mercer Langston of Virginia, and Thomas E. Miller of South Carolina were elected to the House of Representatives long after Reconstruction ended (see Table 14-1).

Figure 14-1 African-American Representation in Congress, 1867–1900

Black men served in the U.S. Congress from Joseph Rainey's election in 1870 until George H. White's term concluded in 1901. All were Republicans.

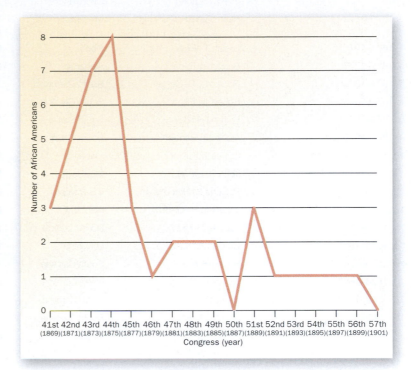

But these black men wielded only limited power in Washington. They could not persuade their white colleagues to enact significant legislation to benefit their black constituents. They did, however, get Republican presidents to appoint black people to federal positions in their districts—including post offices and custom houses—and they denounced the plight of African Americans. George H. White, for example, rebuked white leaders for their readiness to label black people as inferior while denying them the means to prove otherwise: "It is rather hard to be accused of shiftlessness and idleness when the accuser . . . closes the avenues for labor and industrial pursuits to us. It is hardly fair to accuse us of ignorance when it was made a crime under the former order of things to learn enough about letters to even read the Word of God."

14.1.2 Democrats and Farmer Discontent

Black involvement in southern politics survived Reconstruction, but it did not survive the nineteenth century. Divisions within the Democratic Party and the rise of a new political party—the Populists—accompanied successful efforts to remove black people entirely from southern politics.

Militant Democrats opposed the more paternalistic conservatives who took charge after Reconstruction. For the militants, these redeemers seemed too willing to tolerate limited black participation in politics while showing little interest in the needs of white yeoman farmers. Dissatisfied independents, "readjusters," and other disaffected white people resented the domination of the Democratic Party by former planters, wealthy businessmen, and lawyers who often favored limited government and reduced state support for schools, asylums, orphanages, and prisons while encouraging industry and railroads. Nor did the redeemer and paternalistic

Table 14-1 Black Members of the U.S. Congress, 1860–1901

Dates	Name	State	Occupation	Prewar Status
1. 1870–1879	Joseph H. Rainey	South Carolina	Barber	Slave, then free
2. 1870–1873	Jefferson Long	Georgia	Tailor, storekeeper	Slave
3. 1870–1873	Hiram Revels*	Mississippi	Barber, minister, teacher, college president	Free
4. 1871–1877	Josiah T. Walls	Florida	Editor, planter, teacher, lawyer	Slave
5. 1871–1873	Benjamin Turner	Alabama	Businessman, farmer, merchant	Slave
6. 1871–1873	Robert C. DeLarge	South Carolina	Tailor	Free
7. 1871–1875	Robert B. Elliott	South Carolina	Lawyer	Free
8. 1873–1879	Richard H. Cain	South Carolina	African Methodist Episcopal minister	Free
9. 1873–1875	Alonzo J. Ransier	South Carolina	Shipping clerk, editor	Free
10. 1873–1875	James T. Rapier	Alabama	Planter, editor, lawyer, teacher	Free
11. 1873–1877, 1882–1883	John R. Lynch	Mississippi	Planter, lawyer, photographer	Slave
12. 1875–1881	Blanche K. Bruce*	Mississippi	Planter, teacher, editor	Slave
13. 1875–1877	Jeremiah Haralson	Alabama	Minister	Slave
14. 1875–1877	John A. Hyman	North Carolina	Storekeeper, farmer	Slave
15. 1875–1877	Charles E. Nash	Louisiana	Mason, cigar maker	Free
16. 1875–1887	Robert Smalls	South Carolina	Ship pilot, editor	Slave
17. 1883–1887	James E. O'Hara	North Carolina	Lawyer	Free
18. 1889–1893	Henry P. Cheatham	North Carolina	Lawyer, teacher	Slave
19. 1889–1891	Thomas E. Miller	South Carolina	Lawyer, college president	Free
20. 1889–1891	John M. Langston	Virginia	Lawyer	Free
21. 1893–1897	George W. Murray	South Carolina	Teacher, farmer	Slave
22. 1897–1901	George H. White	North Carolina	Lawyer	Slave

*Revels and Bruce served in the Senate. The 20 remaining black legislators served in the House.

Democrats always agree among themselves. Some favored agricultural education, boards of health, and even separate colleges for black students. This disunity permitted insurgent Democrats and even Republicans to exploit economic and racial issues to undermine Democratic solidarity.

Many farmers felt betrayed as the Industrial Revolution transformed society. They fed and clothed America, but large corporations, banks, and railroads dominated economic life. Wealth was concentrated in the hands of big industrialists and financiers. Farmers were no longer self-sufficient, admired for hard work and self-reliance. They now depended on banks for loans, were exploited when they bought and sold goods, and were at the mercy of railroads when they shipped their commodities. As businessmen got richer, farmers got poorer.

A sharp decline in the price of cotton between 1865 and 1890 hurt small independent (yeomen) farmers in the South. Many lost their land and were forced into tenant farming and sharecropping. By 1890 most farmers in the Deep South, black and white, worked land they did not own.

In response to their woes, farmers organized. In the 1870s they formed the Patrons of Husbandry, or Grange. Initially a fraternal organization, the Grange promoted economic cooperatives and political involvement. Grangers especially favored government regulation of the rates railroads charged to transport crops. By the 1880s, many hard-pressed farmers turned to Farmers' Alliances, which soon spread from the South into the Midwest and Great Plains. These organizations favored railroad regulation, currency inflation (to increase crop prices and reduce debt), and support for agricultural education. By 1888 many of them joined in the National Farmers' Alliance.

14.1.3 The Colored Farmers' Alliance

The alliances, however, were conservative on racial issues and did not challenge the racial status quo. Excluded from the Southern Alliance, black farmers formed their own **Colored Farmers' Alliance**, which expanded across the South and became one of the largest black organizations in American history. When the white alliances met in St. Louis in 1889, so did the black alliance—in a separate convention. The alliances maintained strict racial distinctions but promised to cooperate to resolve their economic woes.

However, black and white alliance members did not always see their economic difficulties from the same perspective. Some white farmers owned the land that the black farmers lived on and worked. Black men saw their alliance as a way of getting a political education. In 1891, 16 black men organized a branch of the Colored Farmers' Alliance in St. Landry Parish in Louisiana. Their purpose was to help their race and their families and acquire enough information to vote effectively: "This organization is for the purpose of trying to elevate our race, to make us better citizens, better husbands, better fathers and sons, to educate ourselves so that we may be able to vote more intelligently on questions that are of vital importance to our people."

But white people were not certain they wanted black men to vote at all—intelligently or otherwise—and they opposed electing black men to office. Paradoxically, they also encouraged black men to vote as long as the black voters supported candidates the alliances backed. By the late 1880s, alliance-backed candidates in the South were elected to state legislatures, to Congress, and to four governorships.

Colored Farmers' Alliance

A large organization of black southern farmers in the 1880s and 1890s that had as many as one million members who agitated for improved conditions and income for black landowners, renters, and sharecroppers.

14.1.4 The Populist Party

By 1892 many alliance members threw their political support to a new political party—the People's Party—generally known as the **Populist Party**. Convinced that neither the Democrats nor the Republicans cared about American farmers and industrial workers, the Populists hoped to wrestle control of the economy from bankers, industrialists, and their allies in the traditional parties and let the "people" shape the country's destiny. The Populists wanted the federal government to take over railroad, telegraph, and telephone companies and to operate a loan and marketing program, known as the subtreasury system, to benefit farmers. They urged southern white men to abandon the Democrats and southern black men to reject the Republicans and unite politically to support the Populists.

The foremost proponent of black and white political unity was Thomas Watson of Georgia. He and other Populist leaders believed economic and political cooperation could transcend racial differences. During the 1892 presidential campaign, Watson explained that black and white farmers faced the same economic exploitation, but that they failed to cooperate with each other because of race:

Populist Party

Also known as the People's Party, the Populists supported inflation; the free and unlimited coinage of silver and gold; government ownership of railroads, telephone, and telegraph companies; and an eight-hour workday. They won state and congressional elections but lost the presidential contests in 1892 and 1896.

> The white tenant lives adjoining the colored tenant. Their homes are almost equally destitute of comforts. Their living is confined to bare necessities. They are equally burdened with heavy taxes. They pay the same high rent for gullied and impoverished land. . . .
>
> Now the Peoples' Party says to these two men, You are kept apart that you may be separately fleeced of your earnings. You are made to hate each other because upon that hatred is rested the keystone of the arch of financial despotism which enslaves you both. You are deceived and blinded that you may not see how this race antagonism perpetuates a monetary system which beggars both.

Watson, however, was not calling for improved race relations. He opposed economic exploitation that was disguised by race; however, when Democrats accused him of promoting racial reconciliation, he bluntly supported segregation to a black audience:

> They say I am an advocate of social equality between the whites and the blacks. THAT IS AN ABSOLUTE FALSEHOOD, and the man who utter[s] it knows it, I have done no such thing, and you colored men know it as well as the men

who formulated the slander. It is best for your race and my race that we dwell apart in our private affairs. It is best for you to go to your churches, and I will go to mine; it is best that you send your children to the colored school, and I'll send my children to mine; you invite your colored friends to your home, and I'll invite my friends to mine.

Watson eventually became a racial demagogue who thoroughly supported white supremacy. But in 1892 he desperately wanted black and white voters to support Populist candidates. The Populists lost the national election that year and again in 1896, although they did win several congressional and governor's races. Southern Democrats, outraged at the Populist appeal for black votes, resorted again to fraud and terror to prevail. When a biracial coalition of black and white Populists took control of Grimes County in east Texas in 1900, Democrats massacred first the black and then the white leaders.

Nor is it a coincidence that in the election of 1892, when the Democrats carried every southern state, there was an explosion of violence. Democrats were determined to destroy the Populist challenge. That year a record 235 people were lynched in the United States.

The Populist challenge heightened southern Democrats' fears that black voters could decide elections if the white vote split. But many black people were suspicious of the Populists and remained loyal to the Republicans. The Republican Party in the South, however, was much weaker than it had been during Reconstruction because many of its supporters could no longer vote. Years before the alliances and the Populists emerged, southern Democrats had begun to eliminate the black vote.

14.2 Disfranchisement

Discuss the methods employed to disfranchise black voters.

As early as the late 1870s, southern Democrats worked to undermine black political power. Violence and intimidation, so effective during Reconstruction, continued in the 1880s and 1890s. Frightened, discouraged, or apathetic, many black men stopped voting. White landlords could sometimes intimidate or bribe black sharecroppers and renters not to vote or to vote for the landlord's candidates.

There was also simple injustice. In 1890 black Congressman Thomas E. Miller ran for reelection and won—or so he thought. But he was charged with using illegal ballots and declared the loser. He appealed to the South Carolina Supreme Court, which ruled that although his ballots were printed on the required white paper, it was "of a distinctly yellow tinge." He did not return to Congress.

14.2.1 Evading the Fifteenth Amendment

More militant and determined southern Democrats were unwavering in their efforts to find some "legal" means to prevent black men from voting. However, the Fifteenth Amendment stated that the right to vote could not be denied on "account of race, color, or previous condition of servitude."

White leaders worried that if they imposed what were then legally acceptable barriers to voting—literacy tests, poll taxes, and property qualifications—they would also disfranchise many white voters. But resourceful Democrats found

A rural black man "freely" exercises his right to vote. Notice the bottle of whisky next to the ballot box.

ways around this problem. In 1882, for example, South Carolina passed the Eight Box Law, a primitive literacy test that required voters to deposit separate ballots for separate election races in the proper ballot box. Illiterate voters could not identify the boxes unless white officials assisted them.

14.2.2 Mississippi

Mississippi made the most successful effort to eliminate black voters without openly violating the Fifteenth Amendment. Black men had continued to vote in Mississippi despite intimidation. In 1889 black leaders from 40 Mississippi counties protested the "violent and criminal suppression of the black vote." In response, white men called a constitutional convention to do away with the black vote.

With a single black delegate and 134 white delegates, the convention adopted complex voting requirements that—without mentioning race—disfranchised black voters. Voting required proof of residency and payment of all taxes, including a $2 poll tax. A person convicted of arson, bigamy, or petty theft—crimes the delegates associated with black people—could not vote. People convicted of so-called white crimes—murder, rape, and grand larceny—could vote.

The new Mississippi constitution also required voters to be literate, but illiterate men could still qualify to vote by demonstrating that they understood the constitution if it was read to them. It was taken for granted that white voting registrars would accept almost all white applicants and fail black applicants seeking to register under this provision.

14.2.3 South Carolina

Black voting had been declining in South Carolina since the end of Reconstruction. In 1876, 91,870 black men voted. In 1888, only 13,740 did. Unhappy that even so few voters might decide an election, U.S. Senator Benjamin R. Tillman won approval for a constitutional convention in 1895. The convention followed Mississippi's lead and created an "understanding clause," but not without a protest from black leaders.

Six black men and 154 white men were elected to the South Carolina convention. Two of the black men—Robert Smalls and William Whipper (see Chapter 13)—had been delegates to the 1868 constitutional convention. The six black men protested black disfranchisement. Thomas E. Miller explained that the basic rights of citizens were at stake: "The Negroes do not want to dominate. They do not and would not have social equality, but they do want to cast a ballot for the men who make their laws and administer the laws. I stand here pleading for justice to a people whose rights are about to be taken away with one fell swoop."

It was for naught. Black voters were disfranchised in South Carolina. White delegates did not even pretend that elections should be fair. William Henderson of Berkeley County admitted,

> We don't propose to have fair elections. We will get left at that every time. . . . I tell you, gentlemen, if we have fair elections in Berkeley we can't carry it. There's no use to talk about it. The black man is learning to read faster than the white man. And if he comes up and can read you have got to let him vote. Now are you going to throw it out. . . . We are perfectly disgusted with hearing so much about fair elections. Talk all around, but make it fair and you'll see what'll happen.

14.2.4 The Grandfather Clause

In 1898 Louisiana added a new twist to **disfranchisement**. Its **grandfather clause** stipulated that only men who had been eligible to vote before 1867—or whose father or

disfranchisement

White southern Democrats devised a variety of techniques in the late nineteenth and early twentieth centuries to prevent black people from voting. Those techniques included literacy tests, poll taxes, and the grandfather clause as well as intimidation and violence.

grandfather clause

A method southern states used to disfranchise black men. It stipulated that only men whose grandfathers were eligible to vote were themselves eligible to vote. The U.S. Supreme Court invalidated the grandfather clause in 1915.

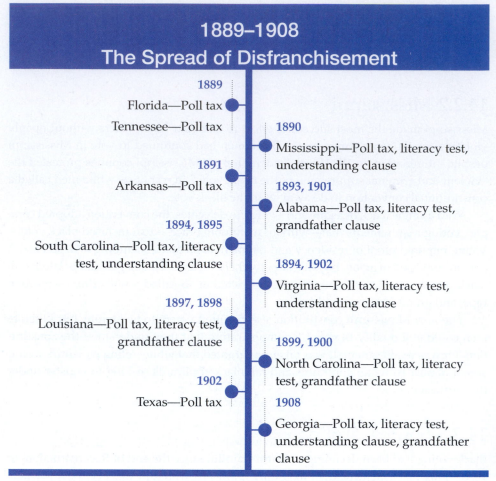

1889–1908
The Spread of Disfranchisement

1889
Florida—Poll tax
Tennessee—Poll tax

1890
Mississippi—Poll tax, literacy test, understanding clause

1891
Arkansas—Poll tax

1893, 1901
Alabama—Poll tax, literacy test, grandfather clause

1894, 1895
South Carolina—Poll tax, literacy test, understanding clause

1894, 1902
Virginia—Poll tax, literacy test, understanding clause

1897, 1898
Louisiana—Poll tax, literacy test, grandfather clause

1899, 1900
North Carolina—Poll tax, literacy test, grandfather clause

1902
Texas—Poll tax

1908
Georgia—Poll tax, literacy test, understanding clause, grandfather clause

SOURCE: Goldfield et al., *The American Journey* (Upper Saddle River, NJ: Prentice Hall, 2004), 550.

grandfather had been eligible before that year—would be qualified to vote. Because virtually no black men had been eligible to vote before 1867—most had just emerged from slavery—the law immediately disfranchised almost all black voters. In Louisiana in 1896, 130,000 black men voted. In 1904, 1,342 voted.

Except for Kentucky and West Virginia, each southern state had enacted elaborate restrictions on voting by the 1890s. As a result, few black men continued to vote, and none were elected to office.

14.2.5 The "Force Bill"

Republicans in Congress in the meantime had made a final, futile attempt to protect black voting rights. In 1890 Massachusetts Congressman Henry Cabot Lodge introduced a bill to require federal supervision of elections in congressional districts where fraud and intimidation were alleged. White southerners were enraged and labeled it the "Force bill" because they believed—incorrectly—that it would force black rule over white people.

This **Federal Elections Bill** easily passed the House, but it failed in the Senate after a 33-day Democratic filibuster. That ended the last significant congressional attempt to protect black voting rights in the South until the passage of the Voting Rights Act in 1965.

Federal Elections Bill

A measure, also known as the Force bill, to protect the voting rights of black men in the South by providing federal supervision of elections. It passed in the House of Representatives but failed in the Senate.

14.3 Segregation

Describe the emergence of laws and customs that required racial segregation.

When black attorney T. McCants Stewart visited Columbia, South Carolina, in 1885, he told readers of the *New York Age* that he had been pleasantly received and had encountered little discrimination: "I can ride in first class cars on the railroads and in the streets. I can go into saloons and get refreshments even as in New York. I can stop in and drink a glass of soda and be more politely waited upon than in some parts of New England." Stewart's visit occurred before most segregation laws had been enacted. In fact, the word *segregation* was almost never used before the twentieth century.

Not that black and white people typically mingled freely in the 1880s and 1890s. They did not. Since Reconstruction, schools, hospitals, asylums, and cemeteries had been segregated. Many restaurants and hotels did not admit black people, and many black people did not venture where they felt unwelcome or were likely to meet hostility. But "Jim Crow" had not yet become legally embedded in southern life.

14.3.1 Jim Crow

The term **Jim Crow** originated with a minstrel show routine called "Jump Jim Crow" that a white performer, Thomas "Daddy" Rice, created in the 1830s and 1840s. Rice blackened his face with charcoal and ridiculed black people. How Rice's character became synonymous with segregation, discrimination, and white supremacy is unclear, but by the end of the nineteenth century Jim Crow and segregation were rapidly expanding in the South, greatly restricting the lives of African Americans.

In the decades following slavery's demise, segregation evolved gradually as a way to enforce white domination. Many white southerners resented the presence of black people in public facilities, places of entertainment, and businesses. If black people were—as white southerners believed—a subordinate race, then their proximity in shops, in parks, and on trains suggested an unacceptable equality in public life.

Moreover, many black people acquiesced in some facets of racial separation. During Reconstruction, people of color formed their own churches and social organizations. Black people were more comfortable around people of their own race than they were among white people. Furthermore, black southerners often accepted separate seating in theaters, concert halls, and other facilities that had been previously closed to them. Segregation, they felt, was better than exclusion.

14.3.2 Segregation on the Railroads

Many white people particularly objected to the presence of black people in the first-class coaches of trains. Before segregation laws, white passengers and railroad conductors sometimes forced black people who had purchased first-class tickets into second-class coaches. In 1889 black Baptists from Savannah bought first-class tickets to travel to a convention in Indianapolis. News was telegraphed ahead, and a white mob threatened and beat them at a railroad stop in Georgia. A white man shoved a pistol into the breast of a black woman who had screamed in fear. He demanded, "You G-d d-n heffer, if you don't hush your mouth and get out of here, I will blow your G-d d-n brains out."

In another instance, a young black woman, Mary Church (later Mary Church Terrell), was traveling alone in a first-class coach when the conductor attempted to move her to the second-class car. She stayed but only after warning the conductor that she would send a telegram to her father telling him "you are forcing me to ride all night in a Jim

segregation
The separation of people based on their race in the use of such public facilities as hotels, restaurants, restrooms, drinking fountains, parks, and auditoriums. In many instances segregation meant the exclusion of black people.

Jim Crow
"Jump Jim Crow" was a nineteenth-century dance ridiculing black people that was transformed by the twentieth century into a term meaning racial discrimination and segregation.

To enforce segregation on a railroad coach, a rather shabbily attired conductor evicts a well-dressed black man from a first-class coach so that he will not pose a danger to a white woman and her child.

Plessy v. Ferguson

In 1896, in an 8-to-1 decision, the U.S. Supreme Court ruled that segregation did not violate the equal protection clause of the Fourteenth Amendment. The "separate but equal" doctrine remained the supreme law of the land until the 1954 *Brown v. Board of Education* decision overturned *Plessy.*

Crow car. He will sue the railroad for compelling his daughter who has a first-class ticket to ride in a second-class car."

The first segregation laws involved passenger trains. Despite the opposition of black politicians, the Tennessee legislature mandated segregation on railroad coaches in 1881. Florida passed a similar law in 1887. The railroads opposed these laws but not because they wanted to protect the rights of black people. Rather, they were concerned about the expense of maintaining separate cars or sections within cars for black and white people. Whether they could pay for a first-class ticket or not, most black passengers were confined to grimy second-class cars crowded with smoking and tobacco-chewing black and white men. Hitched just behind the smoke-belching locomotive, these cars were filthy with soot and cinders.

14.3.3 *Plessy v. Ferguson*

In 1891 the Louisiana legislature required segregated trains within the state, despite opposition from a black organization, the American Citizens' Equal Rights Association of Louisiana, the state's 18 black legislators, and the railroads.

In a test case, black people challenged the law and hoped to demonstrate its absurdity by enlisting the support of a black man who was almost indistinguishable from a white person. In 1892 Homer A. Plessy bought a first-class ticket and attempted to ride on the coach designated for white people. Plessy, who was only one-eighth black, was arrested for violating the new law.

In the case—***Plessy v. Ferguson***—Plessy's lawyers argued that segregation deprived their client of equal protection of the law guaranteed by the Fourteenth Amendment. But in 1896 the Supreme Court, in an 8-to-1 decision, upheld Louisiana's segregation statute. Speaking for the majority, Justice Henry Brown ruled that the law, merely because it required separation of the races, did not deny Plessy his rights, nor did it imply he was inferior. The lone dissenter from this "separate but equal" doctrine, Justice John Marshall Harlan—whose father had owned slaves—likened the majority opinion to the *Dred Scott* decision 39 years earlier. Thus, with the complicity of the Supreme Court, the Fourteenth Amendment no longer afforded black Americans equal treatment under the law. After the *Plessy* decision, southern states and cities created an American apartheid—an elaborate system of racial separation.

14.3.4 Streetcar Segregation

Before the automobile, the electric streetcar was the primary form of public transportation in American cities and towns. Beginning with Georgia in 1891, states and cities across the South segregated these vehicles. In some communities, the streetcar companies had to operate separate cars for black and white passengers. In others, they designated separate sections within cars. The companies often resisted segregation, citing the expense of duplicating equipment and hiring more employees.

But black people were bitterly opposed to Jim Crow streetcars. During Reconstruction, they had fended off streetcar discrimination with boycotts and sit-ins. Thirty years later, they tried the same techniques. There were boycotts in at least 25 southern cities between 1891 and 1910. Black people refused to ride segregated cars in Atlanta, Augusta, Jacksonville, Montgomery, Mobile, Little Rock, and Columbia. The boycotts seriously hurt the streetcar companies, and segregation was briefly abandoned in Atlanta and Augusta.

Black people also attempted to form alternative transportation companies in Portsmouth and Norfolk, Virginia, and in Chattanooga and Nashville, Tennessee. In 1905 the black community in Nashville organized a black-owned bus company and committed $25,000 to it. They purchased five buses, but the company failed after a few months.

14.3.5 Segregation Proliferates

Jim Crow proceeded inexorably. "White" and "colored" signs appeared in railroad stations, theaters, auditoriums, and restrooms, and over drinking fountains. Southern white people went to any length to keep black and white people apart. Courtrooms maintained separate Bibles for black and white witnesses "to swear to tell the truth." By 1915 Oklahoma mandated white and colored public telephone booths. New Orleans

Voices

Majority and Dissenting Opinions on *Plessy v. Ferguson*

The Supreme Court's 8-to-1 decision in Plessy v. Ferguson *sanctioned legal segregation and opened the way for segregation laws throughout the South. The majority opinion ruled that segregation was constitutional so long as both races were provided equal facilities. In practice, of course, the facilities for African Americans were invariably inferior to those for white people. From Justice Henry Brown of Michigan's majority opinion:*

> The object of the [Fourteenth] amendment was undoubtedly to enforce the absolute equality of the two races before the law, but in the nature of things it could not have been intended to abolish distinctions based upon color, or to enforce social, as distinguished from political, equality, or a commingling of the two races upon terms unsatisfactory to either.
>
> We consider the underlying fallacy of the plaintiff's argument to consist in the assumption that the enforced separation of the two races stamps the colored race with a badge of inferiority. If this be so, it is not by the reason of anything found in the act, but solely because the colored race chooses to put that construction upon it. . . . If the two races are to meet on terms of social equality, it must be the result of natural affinities, a mutual appreciation of each other's merits and a voluntary consent of individuals. . . . Legislation is powerless to eradicate racial instincts or to abolish distinctions based upon physical differences. . . . If one race be inferior to the other socially, the Constitution of the United States cannot put them upon the same plane.

From Justice John Marshall Harlan of Kentucky, the lone dissent:

> In my opinion, the judgment this day rendered will, in time, prove to be quite as pernicious as the decision made by this tribunal in the Dred Scott Case. . . . But it seems that we have yet, in some of the states, a dominant race, a superior class of citizens, which assumes to regulate the enjoyment of civil rights, common to all citizens, upon the basis of race. The present decision, it may well be apprehended, will not only stimulate aggressions, more or less brutal and irritating, upon the admitted rights of colored citizens, but it will encourage the belief that it is possible, by means of state enactments, to defeat the beneficent purposes which the people of the United States had in view when they adopted the recent amendments of the Constitution, by one which the blacks of this country were made citizens of the United States and of the states in which they respectively reside and whose privileges and immunities, as citizens, the states are forbidden to abridge. . . . What can more certainly arouse race hate, what more certainly create and perpetuate a feeling of distrust between these races, than state enactments which in fact proceed on the ground that the colored citizens are so inferior and degraded that they cannot be allowed to sit in public coaches occupied by white citizens? . . . But in view of the Constitution, in the eyes of the law, there is in this country no superior, dominant, ruling class of citizens. There is no caste here. Our Constitution is color-blind, and neither knows nor tolerates classes among citizens. In respect of civil rights, all citizens are equal before the law.

1. What does Justice Brown mean when he distinguishes between political and social equality? How does his position compare to that of Congressmen Rapier and Elliott when they argued for civil rights in 1874? (see p. 358)

2. How does Justice Harlan counter the majority opinion?

SOURCE: 163 U.S. 537 United States Reports: *Cases Adjudged in the Supreme Court* (New York: Banks and Brothers, 1896).

attempted to segregate customers of black and white prostitutes, but with mixed results.

Although *Plessy v. Ferguson* required "separate but equal" facilities for black and white people, when facilities were made available to black people, they were inferior to those afforded white people. Often, people of color were offered no facilities at all. They were simply excluded. Few hotels, restaurants, libraries, bowling alleys, public parks, amusement parks, swimming pools, golf courses, or tennis courts would admit black people. The only exceptions were black people who accompanied or assisted white people. For example, a black woman caring for a white child could visit a "white-only" public park with the child, but she dare not visit it with her own child.

14.3.6 Racial Etiquette

During slavery, white people had insisted that black people act in a subservient manner. Such behavior made white dominance clear. After emancipation, white southerners sought to maintain that dominance through a pattern of racial etiquette that determined how black and white people dealt with each other in their day-to-day affairs.

Black and white people did not shake hands. Black people did not look white people in the eyes. They were supposed to stare at the ground when addressing white men and women. Black men removed their hats in the presence of white people. White men did not remove their hats in a black home or in the presence of a black woman. Black people went to the back door, not the front door, of a white house. A black man or boy was never to look at a white woman. A black man in Mississippi observed, "You couldn't smile at a white woman. If you did you'd be hung from a limb." Touching a white woman, even inadvertently, was a serious offense for a black man.

White customers were always served first, even if a black customer had been the first to arrive. Black women could not try on clothing in white businesses. White people did not use titles of respect—Mr., Mrs., Miss—when addressing black adults. They used first names, "boy" or "girl," or sometimes even "nigger." Older black people were sometimes called "auntie" or "uncle." But black people were expected to use Mr., Mrs., or Miss when addressing white people, including adolescents. "Boss" or "cap'n" might do for a white man.

14.4 Violence

Analyze the scope and extent of racial violence and brutality in maintaining white supremacy.

The late nineteenth-century South was a violent place. Political and mob violence, so prevalent during Reconstruction, continued unabated into the 1880s and 1890s as Democrats often used force to drive the dwindling number of black and white Republicans out of politics.

14.4.1 Washington County, Texas

In 1886 in Washington County in Texas, Democrats were determined to keep the control they had won in 1884 through fraud. Masked Democrats tried to seize ballot boxes in a Republican precinct. But armed black men resisted and killed one of the white men. Eight black men were arrested. A mob of white men in disguise broke into the jail and lynched three of the black men. Three white Republicans fled but convinced federal authorities to investigate. The U.S.

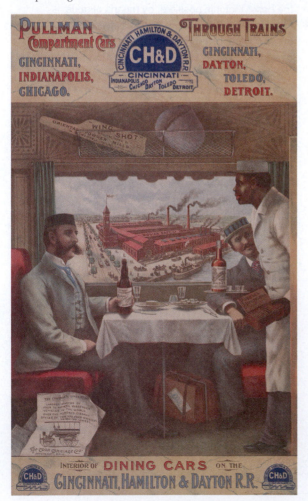

The Pullman Company manufactured and operated passenger, sleeping, and dining cars for the nation's railroads. The company employed black men to serve and wait on passengers, who were usually white people. Black porters and attendants were expected to be properly deferential as they dealt with passengers.

attorney twice tried to secure convictions for election fraud. The first trial ended in a hung jury, the second in acquittal. The white Democratic sheriff did not investigate the lynching. But the black man charged with the killing of a white man was sentenced to 25 years in prison.

14.4.2 The Phoenix Riot

In the tiny South Carolina community of Phoenix in 1898, a white Republican candidate for Congress urged black men to fill out an affidavit if they were not permitted to vote. This produced a confrontation with Democrats. Words were exchanged, shots were fired, and the Republican candidate was wounded. White men then went on a rampage through rural Greenwood County. Black men were killed—how many is unknown. Others, including Benjamin Mays's father, as related in one of the quotes that opens this chapter—had to humiliate themselves by bowing down and saluting white men.

14.4.3 The Wilmington Riot

While white men roamed Greenwood County for black victims, an even bloodier riot erupted in Wilmington, North Carolina. Black and white men shared power as Republicans and Populists in Wilmington's government, and white Democrats resented it. With the encouragement of the *Wilmington News and Observer*, the Democrats were determined to drive the legitimately elected political leaders from power. Alfred Moore Waddell, a former Confederate and U.S. congressman, vowed in a speech to "choke the Cape Fear [River] with carcasses."

In the midst of this tense situation, Alex Manly, the young editor of a local black newspaper, the *Daily Record*, wrote an editorial condemning white men for the sexual exploitation of black women. Manly also suggested that black men had sexual liaisons with rural white women, which infuriated the white community: "Poor white men are careless in the matter of protecting their women, especially on the farms. . . . Tell your men that it is no worse for a black man to be intimate with a white woman than for a white man to be intimate with a colored woman. . . . Don't think ever that your women will remain pure while you are debauching ours."

A white mob destroyed the newspaper office. Black and white officials resigned in a vain attempt to prevent further violence, but at least a dozen black men—and perhaps more—were murdered. Some 1,500 black residents of Wilmington fled. White people then bought up black homes and property at bargain rates. Waddell was installed as Wilmington's new mayor. Black Congressman George H. White, who represented Wilmington and North Carolina's second district, served the remainder of his term and then moved north. He remarked, "I can no longer live in North Carolina and be a man." White was the last black man to serve in Congress from the South until the election of Andrew Young in Atlanta in 1972.

14.4.4 The New Orleans Riot

Robert Charles was a 34-year-old literate laborer who had migrated to New Orleans from rural Mississippi. Infuriated by lynching, he was tantalized by the prospect of emigration to Liberia promoted by African Methodist Episcopal (AME) Bishop Henry M. Turner. On July 23, 1900, white New Orleans police officers harassed Charles and a friend. One of the officers attempted to beat Charles with a nightstick. Failing to subdue the large black man, the officer then drew a gun. Charles pulled out his own gun, and each man wounded the other. Charles fled but was tracked down to a rooming house where he had secluded himself with a rifle, with which he proceeded to shoot his tormentors. Eventually, a white mob that numbered as many as 20,000 gathered. In the meantime, Charles—an expert marksmen—methodically shot 27 white people, killing seven, including four policemen. Finally, burned out of the dwelling, Charles

Figure 14-2 Lynching in the United States, 1889–1932

Depending on the source, statistics on lynching vary. It was difficult to assemble information on lynching, particularly in the nineteenth century. Not every lynching was recorded.

SOURCE: Based on the data from *Negro Year Book, 1931–32*, by Monroe Nathan Work and Jessie Parkhurst Guzman, p. 293. © Darlene Clark Hine.

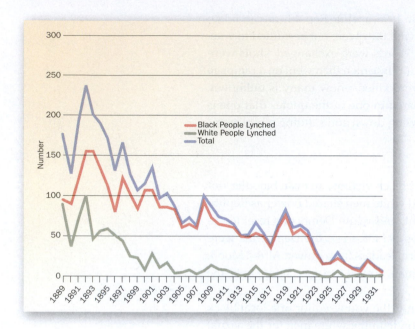

Lynchings were common and public events in the South. Jesse Washington, a 17-year-old, was accused and found guilty of the rape and murder of a white woman in Waco, Texas, in 1916. Before the sentence could be carried out, he was lynched in front of a crowd of several thousand people.

was shot, and enraged white people stomped his corpse beyond recognition. Four days of rioting ensued. At least a dozen black people were killed and many more injured.

14.4.5 Lynching

Between 1889 and 1932, 3,745 people were lynched in the United States (see Figure 14-2). Two or three people were lynched, on average, every week for 30 years. Most lynchings happened in the South, and black men were usually the victims. Sometimes white people were lynched. In 1891 in New Orleans, 11 Italians were lynched for alleged involvement with the Mafia and for the murder of the city's police chief. For black southerners, violence was an ever-present possibility. Rarely did a sheriff or police officer protect a potential victim; even if one did, that protection was often not enough.

Lynchers were never apprehended, tried, or convicted. Prominent community members frequently encouraged and even participated in lynch mobs. White politicians, journalists, and clergymen rarely denounced lynching in public. The *Atlanta Constitution* dismissed lynching as relatively inconsequential: "There are places and occasions when the natural fury of men cannot be restrained by all the laws in Christendom."

Lynchings were barbaric, savage, and hideous. Such mob brutality was another manifestation of white supremacy. Black people were murdered, beaten, burned, and mutilated for trivial reasons—or for no reason. Most white southerners justified lynching as a response to the raping of white women by black men. But many lynchings involved no alleged rape. Even in cases when a rape occurred, the person or persons lynched rarely were involved in the crime.

After a white family was murdered in Statesboro, Georgia, in 1904, Paul Reed and Will Cato were convicted of murder and then seized by a mob that invaded the courtroom. They were burned alive in front of a large crowd. Then the violence spread. Albert Roger and his son were lynched "for being Negroes." A black man named McBride attempted to protect his wife who had had a baby three days earlier. He "was beaten, killed, and shot to death."

Mobs often attacked black people who had achieved economic success. In Memphis, Thomas Moss with two friends opened the People's Grocery Company in a black neighborhood. The store flourished, but it competed with a white-owned grocery. "They were succeeding too well," one of Moss's friends observed. After the white grocer had the three black men indicted for conspiracy, black people organized a protest, and violence followed. The three black men were jailed. A white mob attacked the jail, lynched them, and looted their store. Ida B. Wells, a newspaper editor and a friend of Moss, was heartbroken: "A finer, cleaner man than he never walked the streets of Memphis." She considered his lynching an "excuse to get rid of Negroes who were acquiring wealth and property and thus keep the race terrorized and keep the nigger down." Wells began a lifelong crusade against lynching. (See *Profile: Ida Wells Barnett*.)

Although less often than men, black women were also lynched. In 1914 in Wagoner County, Oklahoma, 17-year-old Marie Scott was lynched because her brother had killed a white man who had raped her. In Valdosta, Georgia, in 1918, after Mary Turner's husband was lynched, she publicly vowed to bring those responsible to justice. Although she was eight months pregnant, a mob seized her, tied her ankles together, and hanged her upside down from a tree. Someone slit her abdomen, and her nearly full-term child fell to the ground. The mob stomped the infant to death. They then set Turner's clothes on fire and shot her.

14.4.6 Rape

Although white people often justified lynching as a response to the presumed threat black men posed to the virtue of white women, white men routinely harassed and abused black women. There are no statistics on such abuse, but it surely was more common than lynching. Like lynching, rape demonstrated the power of white men over black men and women.

Black men tried to keep their wives and daughters away from white men. For example, they often refused to permit black women to work as servants in homes where white men were present. One black man commented in 1912, "I believe nearly all white men take, and expect to take, undue liberties with their colored female servants, not only the fathers, but in many cases the sons also." A black man could not easily protect a black woman. He might be killed trying to do so, as an Alabama clergyman pointed out: "White men on the highways and in their stores and on the trains will insult our women and we are powerless to resent it as it would only be an invitation for our lives to be taken."

Many white people believed black women "invited" white males to take advantage of them. Black women were considered inferior, immoral, and lascivious. Therefore, white people reasoned it was impossible to defend the virtue of black women because they had none. Governor Coleman Blease of South Carolina pardoned black and white men found guilty of raping black women. "I am of the opinion," he said in 1913, "as I have always been, and have very serious doubts as to whether the crime of rape can be committed upon a negro."

14.4.7 Migration

In 1900 AME Minister Henry McNeal Turner despaired for black people in America: "Every man that has the sense of an animal must see that there is no future in this

Profile

Ida Wells Barnett

Ida Wells Barnett began life as a slave in 1862 and grew up during Reconstruction. As a young woman, she saw the worst indignities and cruelties that the Jim Crow South could inflict, but she fought back as a journalist, agitator, and reformer.

Wells was one of eight children born to Jim and Lizzie Wells in Holly Springs, Mississippi. After the Civil War, she and her mother learned to read and write at a school for freed people. Her parents and one of her brothers died in the yellow fever epidemic of 1878. Sixteen-year-old Ida became mother and father to her five surviving siblings. She attended Shaw University in Holly Springs (now Rust College) and taught school in Mississippi and Tennessee.

In 1884, a railroad conductor removed Wells from a first-class car. She sued the railroad and won a $500 settlement. "Dusky Damsel Gets Damages," a Memphis newspaper reported. But a higher court reversed the decision.

Ida Wells Barnett (1862–1931)

Wells then took up journalism and wrote a weekly column for the *Living Way*. In 1889, she bought a one-third interest in the *Memphis Free Speech and Headlight*. She wrote about racial issues and criticized black educators for the quality of black schools. In 1892 her friend Thomas Moss was lynched with two other men for the crime of running a successful grocery store. Wells expressed her rage and horror in a fiery editorial, thus beginning a lifelong crusade against lynching.

Wells blamed the white people of Memphis for her friend's murder and pointed out that more black men were lynched for challenging the myth of white superiority than for allegedly raping a white woman. She angered white people even more by writing that white women could be attracted to black men.

She blamed white clergymen and their parishioners for tolerating lynching: "Our American Christians are too busy saving the souls of white Christians from burning in hell-fire to save the lives of black ones from present burning in fires kindled by white Christians."

Wells moved to Chicago and helped draft a pamphlet that criticized the exclusion of black people from the local groups that organized the 1893 World's Fair. In 1895 she married Ferdinand Barnett, the owner of the *Chicago Conservator*.

After a white journalist from Missouri wrote that black women were immoral, "having no sense of virtue and altogether without character," black women including Wells Barnett founded the National Association of Colored Women in 1896.

In 1909, Wells Barnett was one of two black women who supported the founding of the National Association for the Advancement of Colored People (NAACP), although she later broke with the group because of its mostly white board of directors and what she considered its cautious stands. She also helped organize the Negro Fellowship League in 1910.

Wells Barnett became an ardent supporter of black voting rights. She believed that if enough black men and women could vote, their political power would end lynching. In 1913 she helped found the Alpha Suffrage Club, the first black women's suffrage organization in Illinois, and was a delegate to the National American Woman's Suffrage Association meeting in Washington, DC.

Ever an agitator, she found Booker T. Washington's philosophy too timid. She was influenced by the Universal Negro Improvement Association in the 1920s and praised Marcus Garvey as a black leader who "made an impression on this country as no Negro before him had ever done."

She continued to write, campaign, speak out, and organize. She protested the execution of black soldiers after the 1917 Houston riot. She exposed the injustice 12 poor black farmers experienced after the Elaine riot and massacre in 1919 (see p. 466). She supported A. Phillip Randolph and the formation of the Brotherhood of Sleeping Car Porters (see p. 488). In 1928 she ran as a Republican for the state senate. Only death from kidney failure in 1931 ended her efforts to secure justice for black Americans.

country for the Negro. [W]e are taken out and burned, shot, hanged, unjointed and murdered in every way. Our civil rights are taken from us by force, our political rights are a farce."

It is therefore surprising that more African Americans did not flee poverty, powerlessness, and brutality in the South. As late as 1910, 90 percent of black Americans still lived in the southern states. And of those who left the South, most did not head north along the old underground railroad route. The Great Migration to the northern industrial states did not begin until about 1915. Emigrants of the 1870s or 1880s were more likely to strike out for Africa; move west to Kansas, Oklahoma, and Arkansas; or move from farms to southern towns or cities.

14.4.8 The Liberian Exodus

When in 1875 white Democrats redeemed Mississippi with the "shotgun policy," a group of black people from Winona, Mississippi, wrote to Governor Adelbert Ames "to inquire about the possibility of moving to Africa. [W]e the colored people of Montgomery County are in a bad fix for we have no rights in the county and we want to know of you if there is any way for us to get out of the county and go to some place where we can get homes . . . so will you please let us know if we can go to Africa?"

They did not go to Africa, but some black Georgians and South Carolinians did. In 1877 black leaders in South Carolina, including Congressman Richard H. Cain, probate judge Harrison N. Bouey, and Martin Delany, urged black people to migrate to Liberia. Black communities and churches caught "Liberia Fever" while black people in upper South Carolina still felt the trauma of the terror that had ended Reconstruction.

A white journalist described the situation in Chester County: "At some places in this county the desire to shake off the dust of their feet against this Democratic State is so great, that they are talking of selling out their crops and their personal effects, save what they would need in their new home." They were given promising although sometimes inaccurate information about Liberia. One potato in Liberia, they were told, could feed an entire family.

Several black men organized the Liberian Exodus Joint Stock Steamship Company. They raised $6,000 and hired a ship, the *Azor*. The ship left Charleston in April 1878 with 206 migrants aboard, leaving 175 behind because there was not enough room for them. With inadequate food and fresh water and no competent medical care, 23 migrants died at sea. The ship arrived in Liberia on June 3.

In Liberia, several of the migrants prospered. Sam Hill established a 700-acre coffee plantation, and C. L. Parsons became the chief justice of the Liberian Supreme Court. But others did less well, and some returned to the United States. The Liberian Exodus Company experienced financial difficulties and could not pay for further voyages.

In a paradoxical twist in 1890, South Carolina Democrat Matthew C. Butler introduced an emigration bill in the U.S. Senate to appropriate $5 million per year to transport African Americans who volunteered to migrate to Africa. Butler was a former Confederate general who had helped redeem South Carolina. Most African Americans—including Frederick Douglass and Robert Smalls—opposed the legislation, but some, including Henry McNeal Turner, supported it. Butler's bill never passed. (See the Profile on Turner in Chapter 15.)

14.4.9 The Exodusters

In May 1879 black delegates from 14 states met in a convention in Nashville presided over by Congressman John R. Lynch of Mississippi. The delegates declared that "the colored people should emigrate to those States and Territories where they can enjoy all the rights which are guaranteed by the laws and Constitution of the United States." They also asked Congress—in vain—for $500,000 for this venture.

Nevertheless, black people headed west. Between 1865 and 1880, 40,000 black people known as "**Exodusters**" moved to Kansas. Benjamin "Pap" Singleton, a charismatic ex-slave from Tennessee, persuaded several hundred to migrate. Six black men were instrumental in founding the Kansas town of Nicodemus in 1877. Named after an African prince who bought his freedom, Nicodemus thrived in the 1880s with a hotel, two newspapers, a general store, a drugstore, a school, and three churches. Several of the businesses were white owned. Edwin P. McCabe, a black native of Troy, New York, settled for a time in Nicodemus, and in 1882 Kansas voters elected him state auditor.

By 1890, however, Nicodemus went into a decline from which it never recovered. Three railroads were built across Kansas, but each avoided Nicodemus, spelling economic ruin for the community. Edwin McCabe moved to Oklahoma and helped found the black town of Langston. Eventually more black people settled in Oklahoma than in

Exodusters

Black migrants who left the South during and after Reconstruction and settled in Kansas, often in all-black towns.

Kansas. By 1900 African Americans possessed 1.5 million acres in Oklahoma worth $11 million. In 1889 Congress enacted legislation eliminating Indian Territory in Oklahoma, dispossessing the Five Civilized Tribes of their land, and dismantling tribal government. More than two dozen black towns, including Boley and Liberty, were founded in Oklahoma. There were nearly 50 black towns in the West by the early twentieth century, including Allensworth, California; Blackdom, New Mexico; and Dearfield, Colorado. Other black migrants settled in rural and isolated portions of Nebraska, the Dakotas, and Colorado (see Map 14-1).

Many people who moved west after the Civil War took advantage of the 1862 Homestead Act, which provided 160 acres of federal land free to those who would settle on it and farm it for at least five years. (Alternatively, a settler could buy the land for $1.25 per acre and possess it after six months' residency.) Life on the frontier was often bleak, dreary, and lonely. People lived in sod houses and relied on cow (or buffalo) chips for heat and cooking fuel as they struggled to endure.

Map 14-1 African-American Population of Western Territories and States, 1880–1900

Although most African Americans remained in the South following the Civil War, thousands of black people moved west and settled on farms and ranches. Others migrated to small towns that were populated mostly by former slaves.

What motivated several thousand African Americans to move to the Great Plains, Rocky Mountains, and West Coast in the late nineteenth century?

With their meager belongings, these African Americans await the arrival of a steamboat in about 1878 to transport them to Kansas or perhaps another western location.

Railroads encouraged migration by offering reduced fares. Some western farmers and agents were eager to sell land, but some of it was of little value. Some white residents of Mississippi and South Carolina, which had large black majorities, were glad to see the black people go. However, the loss of cheap black labor alarmed others.

Some black leaders urged black people to stay put. In 1879 Frederick Douglass insisted that more opportunities existed for black people in the South than elsewhere: "Not only is the South the best locality for the Negro on the ground of his political powers and possibilities, but it is best for him as a field of labor. He is there, as he is nowhere else, an absolute necessity." Robert Smalls urged black people to come to his home county of Beaufort, South Carolina, "where I hardly think it probable that any prisoner will ever be taken from jail by a mob and lynched."

14.4.10 Migration within the South

Many black people left the poverty and isolation of farms and moved to villages and towns in the South. Others went to growing black neighborhoods in larger southern cities like Atlanta, Richmond, and Nashville. Urban areas offered more economic opportunities than rural areas. Although black people were usually confined to menial labor—from painting and shining shoes to domestic service—city work paid cash on a fairly regular basis, whereas rural residents received no money until their crops were sold. Towns and cities also had more entertainment and religious and educational activities. Black youngsters in towns spent more time in school than rural children, who had to work the farms.

Black women had a better chance than black men of finding regular work in a town, although it was usually as a domestic or cleaning woman. This economic situation damaged the black family. Before the increase in migration, a husband and wife headed 90 percent of black families. But with migration, many black men remained in rural areas where they could get farm work, while women went to urban communities. Often these women became single heads of households.

14.4.11 Black Farm Families

Most black people remained poverty-stricken sharecroppers and renters on impoverished, white-owned land. They were poorly educated. They lacked political power.

They were invariably in debt. Many rural black families remained close to involuntary servitude in the decades after Reconstruction.

Many black and white southerners were hardly better off than medieval serfs. They lived in drafty, leaky cabins without electricity or running water. Outdoor toilets created health problems. Medical care was often unavailable. Diets were dreary and unbalanced—mostly pork and cornbread—and deficient in vitamins and protein.

14.4.12 Cultivating Cotton

By the late 1800s, farmers in the Midwest and on the Great Plains had access to expensive labor-saving machinery such as reapers, threshers, and combines that enabled them to cultivate hundreds if not thousands of acres of grain. In the South cotton was unaffected by mechanization until the 1930s and 1940s. From the end of slavery into the twentieth century, black farm families annually grew millions of pounds of cotton by spending hundreds of millions of hours in the fields.

Each spring an older youth or adult walked behind a mule and broke the ground with a plow. At the end of a row, the farmer might shout "haw!" to the mule, and the animal then made a left turn to plow another row. Men, women, and children then planted cotton seeds and supplied fertilizer—guano—to the soil. When the green cotton plants emerged, the weaker plants were removed. From May until July, the field was hoed or chopped repeatedly to remove weeds that competed with the cotton for nutrients.

"Lay-by" time came in July and August as the cotton plants matured and the "fruit" or the cotton bolls grew. There was less work during lay-by time, and children sometimes went to school in July and August. The cotton was then picked by hand beginning in the oppressive heat and humidity of August and continuing into September and October. Family members carried large baskets or enormous sacks through the fields as they removed the cotton from the spiny bolls. Because the bolls did not open simultaneously, the fields had to be picked more than once. The larger the family, the larger the labor force, and the more cotton they could harvest.

Benjamin Mays described his experience in the fields as a 12-year-old in early twentieth-century South Carolina: "When it came to picking cotton, my brother Hezekiah and I were the best in the family, and among the best cotton pickers in the county. We often competed with each other to see which could pick the most cotton. . . . 'H. H.' as we called him and I competed all day, from sunup to sundown, . . . when father weighed the cotton that evening, H. H. had picked 424 pounds and I had picked 425."

For generations after the Civil War, African-American men, women, and children planted, tended, and picked cotton.

Picked cotton was stored before it was transported by wagon to the local ginnery. A few cotton gins were still operated with animal or water power; however, by the late nineteenth century steam engines ran the equipment at most ginneries. The modern facility was typically a two-story frame building that featured a large hose-like device that suctioned the cotton from the wagon. A separator then removed debris before a conveyor belt sent the clean cotton to gins that removed the cotton seeds. Then a large hydraulic press compressed the cotton into bales that weighed approximately 500 pounds each. Wagons took the bales to a nearby railroad depot where they were shipped to a textile mill.

14.4.13 Sharecroppers

Most of these black farm families (and many white families) were sharecroppers. Sharecropping had emerged during Reconstruction as landowners allowed the use of their land for a share of the crop. The landlord also usually provided housing, horses or mules, tools, seed, and fertilizer, as well as food and clothing. In return, the landowner received from one-half to three-quarters of the crop.

Sharecropping lent itself to exploitation. By law, verbal agreements were considered contracts. In any case, many sharecroppers were illiterate and could not have read written contracts. The landowner informed the sharecropper of the value of the product raised—typically cotton—and the value of the goods provided to the sharecropping family. Black farmers who disputed white landowners put themselves in peril. Although many sharecroppers knew the proprietor's calculations were wrong, they could do nothing about it. Also, cotton brokers and gin owners routinely paid black farmers less than white farmers per pound for cotton. A forlorn ditty in the late nineteenth century captured this inequity:

A naught's a naught, and a figger's a figger—

All fer de white man—none fer de nigger!

Black men were forced to accept the white man's word. One Mississippi sharecropper explained, "I have been living in this Delta thirty years, and I know that I have been robbed every year; but there is no use jumping out of the frying pan into the fire. If we ask any questions we are cussed, and if we raise up we are shot, and that ends it."

RENTERS   Black farmers preferred renting to sharecropping. As tenants, they paid a flat charge to rent a given number of acres. Payment would be made in either cash—perhaps $5 per acre—or, more typically, in a specified amount of the crop—two bales of cotton per 20 acres. Tenants usually owned their own animals and tools. As Bessie Jones explained, "You see, a sharecropper don't ever have nothing. Before you know it, the man done took it all. But the renter always have something, and then he go to work when he want to go to work. He ain't got to go to work on the man's time. If he didn't make it, he didn't get it."

CROP LIENS   Many sharecroppers and renters were also indebted to a merchant for food, clothing, and farm supplies. The merchant advanced the merchandise on credit but took out a **lien** on the crop. If the sharecropper or renter failed to repay the merchant, the merchant was entitled to all or part of the crop once the landowner had received his payment. Merchants tended to charge high prices and interest rates. They usually insisted that farmers plant cotton before they would agree to a lien. Cotton could be sold quickly for cash.

PEONAGE   Many farmers fell deeply into debt, which led to their virtual reenslavement. They were cheated. Bad weather destroyed crops. Crop prices declined. Landless farmers could not leave the land until their debts were paid. If they tried to depart without the land owner's permission, the owner swore out a warrant for their arrest

lien

Black and white farmers purchased goods on credit from local merchants. The merchant demanded collateral in the form of a lien on the crop, typically cotton. If the farmer failed to repay the loan, the merchant had a legal right to seize the crop.

Voices

Cash and Debt for the Black Cotton Farmer

Benjamin E. Mays was born in 1895 in Epworth, South Carolina. He was the youngest and eighth child of parents who had been slaves and whose lives revolved around agriculture. Mays went on to South Carolina State College, to Bates College in Maine, and to the University of Chicago. He became the president of Morehouse College in Atlanta, where he served as a mentor to Martin Luther King, Jr. Mays delivered the eulogy at King's funeral in 1968. Here he explains his family's economic situation as renters.

As I recall, Father usually rented forty acres of land for a two-mule farm, or sixty acres if we had three mules. The rent was two bales of cotton weighing 500 pounds each, for every twenty acres rented. So the owner of the land got his two, four, or six bales of cotton out of the first cotton picked and ginned.

To make sixteen bales of cotton on a two-mule farm was considered excellent farming. After four bales were used to pay rent, we would have twelve bales left. The price of cotton fluctuated. If we received ten cents a pound, we would have somewhere between five and six hundred dollars, depending on whether the bales of cotton weighed an average of 450, 475, or 500 pounds. When all of us children were at home we, with our father and mother, were ten. We lived in a four-room house, with no indoor plumbing—no toilet facilities, no running water.

We were never able to clear enough from the crop to carry us from one September to the next. We could usually go on our own from September through February; but every March a lien had to be placed on the crop so that we could get money to buy food and other necessities from March through August, when we would get some relief by selling cotton. Strange as it may seem, neither we nor our neighbors ever raised enough hogs to have meat year round, enough corn and wheat to insure having our daily bread, or cows in sufficient numbers to have enough milk. The curse was cotton. It was difficult to make farmers see that more corn, grain, hogs, and cows meant less cash but more profit in the end. Cotton sold instantly, and that was cash money. Negro farmers wanted to feel the cash—at least for that brief moment as it passed through their hands into the white man's hands!

1. What might have led to greater independence for people like the Mays family?

2. Why were southern black and white families so large?

SOURCE: Mays, B. E. (2003) *Born to Rebel: An Autobiography* by Benjamin Elijah Mays. The University of Georgia Press.

peonage

The system that forbade southern farmers, usually sharecroppers and renters, who accumulated debts to leave the land until the debt was repaid—often an impossible task.

and the county sheriff pursued them. If they were apprehended—and they often were—they were returned to the land. This was **peonage**, and it amounted to enslavement, holding thousands of black people across the South in perpetual bondage. Peonage violated federal law, but the law was rarely enforced. White juries acquitted landowners and merchants who were prosecuted for keeping black people in peonage.

14.4.14 Black Landowners

Considering the incredible obstacles against them, black farm families acquired land at an astonishing rate after the Civil War. Many white people refused to sell land to black buyers, preferring to keep them dependent. Black people also found it difficult to save enough money to purchase land even when they could find a willing seller. Still, they managed to accumulate land.

A white Georgia farmer sourly commented that African Americans were desperate to get their own land: "They will almost starve and go naked before they will work for a white man, if they can get a patch of ground to live on and get from under his control."

Some black families had kept land that had been distributed in the Carolina and Georgia low country under the Port Royal Experiment and Sherman's Special Field Order #15 (see Chapter 12). In 1880 black people on South Carolina's sea islands held 10,000 acres of land worth $300,000.

By 1900 more than 100,000 black families owned their own land in the eight states of the Deep South. Black landownership increased more than 500 percent between

1870 and 1900. Most black people possessed small farms of about 20 acres. These small plots were often subsequently subdivided among sons and grandsons, making it harder for their families to prosper. But some black farmers owned impressive estates. Prince Johnson had 360 acres of excellent Mississippi delta land. Freedman Leon Winter was the richest black man in Tennessee, with real estate worth $70,000 in 1889. In Florida, J. D. McDuffy raised melons, cabbages, and tomatoes on an 800-acre farm near Ocala. Texas freedman Daniel Webster Wallace had a 10,000-acre cattle ranch. Few black people inherited large estates. Most of these landowners had been born into slavery. After emancipation, they managed to accumulate land—usually just a few acres at a time.

14.4.15 White Resentment of Black Success

Most white Southerners considered African Americans to be a woefully inferior race unable to compete with the superior race. Nevertheless, white Southerners incessantly urged black people to acquire manual skills, work hard, and be thrifty. Prosperity would be their reward. Therefore, it was a cruel irony that many white southerners could not tolerate black economic success and lashed out at those who achieved it. For example, when one rural black resident of Arkansas built an attractive new house, white people told him not to paint it—lest it look better than theirs. He accepted the advice and left the dwelling bare.

In the early twentieth century, Henry Watson, a well-to-do black farmer in Georgia, drove a new car to town. Enraged white people forced Watson and his daughter out at gunpoint and burned the vehicle. Watson was told, "From now on, you niggers walk into town, or use that ole mule if you want to stay in this city."

In 1916 Anthony Crawford, the owner of 427 acres of prime cotton land in Abbeville, South Carolina, secretary of the Chapel AME Church, a married man with 16 children, was arrested and then released after he quarreled with a local white merchant over the price of cotton seed. But a mob, infuriated that Crawford spoke so bluntly to a white man, went after him. "When a nigger gets impudent we stretch him out and paddle him a bit," exclaimed one white man. But Crawford resisted and crushed the skull of a white attacker. The mob then stabbed and beat Crawford before the sheriff rescued him and put him in jail. But a second mob broke into the jail and beat him to death. His body was left hanging at the fairgrounds. After his first beating, Crawford had told a friend, "I thought I was a good citizen." The coroner's jury ruled that his death had occurred at the hands of persons unknown.

While pursuing a master's degree at the University of Chicago, Benjamin E. Mays briefly taught English at South Carolina State College in Orangeburg. This is a photo taken from the 1926 college yearbook. He met his second wife, Sadie Grey, while teaching in Orangeburg. She was teaching sociology and also working on a graduate degree at the University of Chicago. Mays's first wife, Ellen Harvin, had died from complications due to child birth in 1923.

14.5 African Americans and the Legal System

Explain how law enforcement and the court system affected African Americans.

The southern criminal justice systems yielded nothing but injustice to black people. Southern lawmakers worried incessantly about what they considered the black crime problem and enacted laws to control the black population. Vagrancy laws made it easy to arrest idle black men or one who was passing through a community. Contract evasion laws ensnared black people who attempted to escape peonage and perpetual servitude.

14.5.1 Segregated Justice

The legal system also became increasingly white after Reconstruction. Black police officers were eliminated, and white policemen acquired a deserved reputation for brutality. Juries were all white by 1900. (No women served on southern juries.) In Alabama, a black man called for a local grand jury insisted on serving until he was beaten and forced to step down. Judges were white men. Most attorneys were white. The few black lawyers faced daunting hurdles. Some black defendants believed—correctly—that they would be convicted and sentenced to a longer term if they retained a black attorney rather than a white one. Court personnel treated black plaintiffs, defendants, and witnesses with contempt, calling them "niggers," "boy," and "gal." Black people were rarely "Mr." or "Mrs." in court proceedings.

A black defendant could not get justice. Black people were more often charged with crimes than white people. They were almost always convicted, regardless of the strength of the evidence or the credibility of witnesses. In one of the few instances when a black man was found not guilty of killing a white man, his attorney advised him to leave town because white people were unlikely to accept the verdict. He fled but returned 20 years later and was castrated by two white men.

Race took precedence in the legal system. Black victims of crime found the law turned against them. In 1897 in Hinds County, Mississippi, a white man beat a black woman with an axe handle. She took him to court, only to have the justice of the peace rule that he knew of "no law to punish a white man for beating a negro woman."

Juries rarely found white people guilty of crimes against black people. In a Georgia case in 1911, the evidence against several white people for holding black families in peonage was so overwhelming that the judge virtually ordered the jury to return a guilty verdict. Nonetheless, after five minutes of deliberation, the jury found the defendants not guilty. Many black and white people were astonished in 1898 in Shreveport, Louisiana, when a jury found a white man guilty of murdering a black man. He was sentenced to five years in prison.

Black people could receive leniency from the judicial system, but it was not justice. They were much less likely to be charged with a crime against another black person, such as raping a black woman, than against a white person. Black people often were not charged with crimes such as adultery and bigamy because white people considered such offenses typical black behavior.

Black defendants who had some personal or economic connection to a prominent white person were less likely to be treated or punished the same way as black people who had no such relationship. In Vicksburg, Mississippi, a black woman watched as the black man who had murdered her husband was acquitted because a white man intervened. Those black people known as "a white man's nigger" had an advantage in court.

Black people received longer sentences and larger fines than white people. In Georgia, black convicts served much longer sentences than white convicts for the

Black and white men serve on a jury together during Reconstruction but they segregate themselves.

Profile

Johnson C. Whittaker

Shortly after 6:00 A.M. on April 6, 1880, West Point's lone black cadet, Johnson C. Whittaker, was found lying unconscious on the floor of his room in the barracks. He was splattered with blood. His hands were tied together, and his feet were tied to the bed. In the months that followed, Whittaker's case attracted nationwide attention.

Whittaker was born a slave in 1858 near Camden, South Carolina, the son of a house slave and a free man. In 1876 white Republican Congressman Solomon L. Hoge nominated Whittaker to West Point.

During his first year at the military academy, Whittaker roomed with the only other black cadet, Henry O. Flipper. But Flipper graduated in 1877—the first black man to graduate from the academy—and Whittaker spent the next four years completely ostracized as the only remaining black cadet. White cadets refused to associate or room with him. Quiet and studious, he had a creditable academic record, but when he failed an exam in 1878, he had to repeat a year.

When he was found bloody and bound, Whittaker claimed he had been assaulted by three masked men after receiving a warning note the day before. A court of inquiry, however, declared that he had mutilated himself. Whittaker then insisted on a court-martial to prove his innocence. In February 1881, that court-martial convened in New York City.

Whittaker was charged with conduct unbecoming an officer and with lying. After four months of testimony, the court found him guilty. It determined that Whittaker was "shamming"—making it up to avoid failing an exam. Major Asa Bird Gardiner told the court, "Negroes are noted for their ability to sham and feign." Gardiner maintained that Whittaker was unfit: "By his own story the accused has shown himself a coward without one redeeming quality . . . his mental attitude [was] inferior to the average Anglo-Saxon."

The court ordered Whittaker dishonorably discharged, fined $1, and sentenced to a year's hard labor. But in March 1882, President Chester Arthur overturned the verdict. On the same day, Secretary of War Robert Lincoln (Abraham's son) ordered Whittaker discharged from West Point.

Whittaker spent most of the rest of his life working with young black people at South Carolina State College and at Douglass High School in Oklahoma City. He died in South Carolina in 1931. Whittaker had two sons. Both were commissioned officers and served in all-black units in World War I.

Whittaker summed up the meaning of his experience at West Point in a speech after the court-martial found him guilty:

> West Point has tried to take from me honor and good name, but West Point has failed. I have honor and manhood still left in me. I have an education which none can take from me. That education has come to me at fearful cost. The government may not wish me to use it in her service, but I shall use it for the good of my fellow men and for the good of those around me. . . . Poverty and sneers can never crush manhood. With God as my guide, duty will be my watchword, I can, I must, I will win a place in life!

In July 1995, President Bill Clinton posthumously awarded Johnson C. Whittaker his commission in the U.S. Army.

---

same offense—five times as long for larceny, for example. An 80-year-old black preacher went to prison "for what a white man was fined five dollars." In New Orleans, a black man was sentenced to 90 days in jail for petty theft. A black newspaper said it was "three days for stealing and eighty-seven days for being colored."

14.5.2 The Convict Lease System: Slavery by Another Name

At least 100,000 African Americans were re-enslaved in the last decades of the nineteenth century and the early years of the twentieth century. The **convict lease system** emerged as a key source of cheap labor in every former Confederate state except Virginia. Southern states and counties found that it was lucrative to lease prisoners— the vast majority were black men—to timber companies, coal mines, railroads, and plantation owners. The state or the county was freed of the responsibility of feeding, housing, and guarding inmates. Businessmen, industrialists, and planters paid the states and counties for the convict labor. South Carolina, for example, collected $3 per month for each leased prisoner. There was no incentive to maintain the health and strength of the laborers. Leased convicts endured appalling conditions. They were

convict lease system

Southern states and communities leased prisoners to privately operated mines, railroads, and timber companies. These businesses forced the prisoners, who were usually black men, to work in brutal, unhealthy, and dangerous conditions. Many convicts died of abuse and disease.

shackled and beaten, overworked, and underfed. They slept on vermin-infested straw mattresses and received little or no medical care. They sustained terrible injuries on the job and at the hands of guards. Diseases proliferated in the camps. Hundreds died. They had, in effect, been sentenced to death for petty crimes. As one employer explained in 1883, "But these convicts; we don't own em. One dies, get another."

Leasing prisoners became such an attractive source of revenue for sheriffs, counties, and states that they simply rounded up black men and sent them into involuntary servitude. They were arrested for a variety of felonies and misdemeanors, ranging from murder and larceny to drunkenness, loitering, and vagrancy. Sometimes no charges were levied against them. Petty crimes or no crime meant virtual enslavement.

As horrific as the convict lease system was for black men, it was worse for black women. In much smaller numbers than men, African American women were leased to businesses and agricultural enterprises. In states like Georgia they were forced into the same jobs and working conditions in mines, lumber operations, and fields as men. But unlike men, they were sexually abused, raped, and became pregnant while under the harsh domination of white guards and supervisors. Convict leasing became such a notorious scandal that most states outlawed it by the 1930s.

Conclusion

With the end of the Civil War and slavery in 1865, more than four million African Americans had looked with hope and anticipation to the future. Four decades later, there were more than nine million African Americans, and more than eight million of them lived in the South. The crushing burden of white supremacy limited their hopes and aspirations. The U.S. government abandoned black people to white southerners and their state and local governments. The federal government that had affirmed their rights as citizens during Reconstruction ignored the legal, political, and economic situation that entrapped most black southerners.

Although the Thirteenth Amendment abolished slavery, thousands of black people were trapped in peonage or labored as sharecroppers and renters, indebted to white landowners and merchants. Yet more than 100,000 black families managed to acquire their own farms by 1900. Many black farmers had also organized and participated in the Colored Farmers' Alliance and the Populist Party, although it brought few tangible benefits.

Still well over 100,000 African American men and women were held in bondage through the convict lease system while thousands of other landless black families were kept in involuntary servitude through peonage.

The Fourteenth Amendment had guaranteed the rights of citizenship that included due process of law. No state could deprive a person of life, liberty, or property without a court proceeding. The amendment also ensured each citizen equal protection of the law. But the Supreme Court had ruled that racial segregation in public places did not infringe on the right to equal protection of the law. And as for the right to life, by the early 1900s, mobs had lynched hundreds of black people.

The Fifteenth Amendment stipulated that race could not be used to deprive a man of the right to vote. But southern states circumvented the amendment with poll taxes, literacy tests, and the grandfather clause. Thus, by 1900, after black men had held political offices across the South for 30 years, no black person served in an elected political position in any southern state.

White people regarded black Americans as an inferior race not entitled to those rights that the Constitution supposedly guaranteed. What could black people do about the discrimination, violence, and powerlessness they had to endure? What strategies, ideas, and leadership could overcome the burdens they were forced to bear? What chances did they have of overcoming white supremacy? How could black people organize to gain fundamental rights that were guaranteed to them?

Chapter Timeline

AFRICAN-AMERICAN EVENTS	NATIONAL EVENTS

1875–1880

1880

Cadet Johnson C. Whittaker assaulted at West Point

1877

Reconstruction ends

1880

James Garfield elected president

1880–1890

1881

Tennessee segregates passenger trains

Tuskegee Institute founded

1886

Riot in Washington County, Texas

1887

National Colored Farmers' Alliance formed

Florida segregates passenger trains

1889–1908

Southern states disfranchise black voters

1880s

Southern Farmers' Alliance forms

1881

President Garfield assassinated

Clara Barton establishes the Red Cross

1884

Grover Cleveland elected president

1886

Haymarket affair in Chicago

1887

Congress creates the Interstate Commerce Commission

Dawes Act permits individual Indian families to own reservation land

1888

Benjamin Harrison elected president

1889

Wall Street Journal established

1890–1895

1891

Georgia segregates streetcars

1892

235 people lynched in the United States, 155 of them African American

1890

Eleven Italians lynched in New Orleans

James A. Naismith invents basketball

1892

Populist Party challenges the Democrats and Republicans in national elections

Homestead strike at the Carnegie steel plant near Pittsburgh

Grover Cleveland elected to a second term as president

1893

Panic of 1893 begins economic depression

AFRICAN-AMERICAN EVENTS	NATIONAL EVENTS
	1895–1900	
1896	**1896**
In *Plessy v. Ferguson*, Supreme Court upholds legal segregation	William McKinley elected president
	Populist Party's last national campaign
1898	**1898**
Phoenix riot in South Carolina	Eugene V. Debs helps found
Wilmington riot in North Carolina	Socialist Party
1899–1901	United States annexes Hawaii
George H. White of North Carolina—the South's last black congressman until 1972	Spanish-American War
	1900
1900	William McKinley reelected president
New Orleans riot	

Review Questions

1. How were black people prevented from voting despite the Fifteenth Amendment?

2. How did white Americans justify segregation?

3. Why did the South experience an epidemic of violence and lynching in the late nineteenth century?

4. Why didn't more black people leave the South in this period?

Retracing the Odyssey

Nicodemus National Historic Site, Nicodemus, Kansas. W. R. Hill was a black real estate agent who founded Nicodemus in 1877. By 1887 over 250 people lived in the town. The absence of a railroad led to a prolonged decline of what had been a small thriving community. Most of the town's original structures have not survived.

Langston, Oklahoma, and Langston University. Langston was one of the many all-black towns established after the Civil War. In 1897 the town set aside 40 acres to create a black land-grant university. The town and university are named for John Mercer Langston, a prominent nineteenth-century black leader and congressman from Virginia.

Historic District, Boley, Oklahoma. Boley was an all-black town incorporated in 1905. Many of the town's residents left when the economy collapsed during the Great Depression. Some of the historic black businesses and buildings still stand.

Black American West Museum and Heritage Center, Denver, Colorado. Founded by Paul Stewart, this museum is dedicated to the black pioneers of the frontier West, including cowboys, soldiers, barbers, and homesteaders. It has artifacts, photographs, recordings, and other memorabilia of nineteenth- and early twentieth-century African Americans. It is located in the former home of Dr. Justina Ford, a pioneer and black woman physician who delivered 7,000 babies of virtually every ethnic background.

Recommended Reading

Edward L. Ayers. *The Promise of the New South: Life After Reconstruction.* New York: Oxford University Press, 1992. An excellent overview of life in the late nineteenth-century South.

Douglas A. Blackmon. *Slavery by Another Name: The Re-Enslavement of Black Americans from the Civil War to World War II.* New York: Random House, 2009. In harrowing

detail, this account describes the lives of thousands of black people who were taken into custody and forced into labor through the convict lease system in the decades following the Civil War.

Talitha L. LeFlouria. *Chained in Silence: Black Women and Convict Labor in the New South.* Chapel Hill: University of North Carolina Press, 2015. A grim but revealing examination of lives of African American women who were caught up in the convict lease system.

Leon Litwack. *Trouble in Mind: Black Southerners in the Age of Jim Crow.* New York: Alfred A. Knopf, 1998. In moving words, black people describe life in a white supremacist society.

Rayford Logan. *The Negro in American Life and Thought: The Nadir, 1877–1901.* New York: Dial Press, 1954. Explorations of the contours and oppressiveness of racism.

Benjamin E. Mays. *Born to Rebel: An Autobiography.* New York: Charles Scribner, 1971. Graphic recollection of growing up black in the rural South at the turn of the century.

C. Vann Woodward. *The Strange Career of Jim Crow.* New York: Oxford University Press, 1955. The evolution of legal segregation in the South.

Additional Bibliography

Regional, State, and Local Studies

Charles S. Aiken. *The Cotton Plantation South Since the Civil War.* Baltimore: Johns Hopkins University Press, 1998.

Eric Anderson. *Race and Politics in North Carolina, 1872–1901: The Black Second.* Baton Rouge: Louisiana State University Press, 1981.

David Cecelski and Timothy B. Tyson, eds. *Democracy Betrayed: The Wilmington Race Riot and Its Legacy.* Chapel Hill: University of North Carolina Press, 1998.

Helen G. Edmonds. *The Negro and Fusion Politics in North Carolina, 1894–1901.* Chapel Hill: University of North Carolina Press, 1951.

William Ivy Hair. *Carnival of Fury: Robert Charles and the New Orleans Riot of 1900.* Baton Rouge: Louisiana State University Press, 1976.

Neil R. McMillen. *Dark Journey: Black Mississippians in the Age of Jim Crow.* Urbana: University of Illinois Press, 1989.

David M. Oshinsky. *"Worse Than Slavery": Parchman Farm and the Ordeal of Jim Crow Justice.* New York: Free Press, 1999.

H. Leon Prather. *We Have Taken a City: Wilmington Racial Massacre and Coup of 1898.* Rutherford, NJ: Fairleigh Dickinson University Press, 1984.

George B. Tindall. *South Carolina Negroes, 1877–1900.* Columbia: University of South Carolina Press, 1952.

Vernon Wharton. *The Negro in Mississippi, 1865–1890.* Chapel Hill: University of North Carolina Press, 1947.

Biographies and Autobiographies

Mia Bay. *To Tell the Truth Freely: The Life of Ida B. Wells.* New York: Hill and Wang, 2009.

Albert S. Broussard. *African-American Odyssey: The Stewarts, 1853–1963.* Lawrence: University Press of Kansas, 1998.

Alfreda Duster, ed. *Crusade for Justice: The Autobiography of Ida B. Wells.* Chicago: University of Chicago Press, 1972.

Henry O. Flipper. *The Colored Cadet at West Point.* New York: Arno Press, 1969.

Paula Giddings. *Ida: A Sword Among Lions: Ida B. Wells and the Campaign Against Lynching.* New York: HarperCollins, 2008.

John F. Marszalek, Jr. *Court Martial: The Army vs. Johnson Whittaker.* New York: Scribner, 1972.

_____. *A Black Congressman in the Age of Jim Crow: South Carolina's George Washington Murray.* Gainesville: University Press of Florida, 2006.

Linda McMurry. *To Keep the Waters Troubled: The Life of Ida B. Wells.* New York: Oxford University Press, 1998.

Patricia A. Schechter. *Ida B. Wells-Barnett and American Reform, 1882–1930.* Chapel Hill: University of North Carolina Press, 2001.

Politics and Segregation

Grace Hale. *Making Whiteness: The Culture of Segregation in the South, 1890–1940.* New York: Pantheon Books, 1998.

Williamjames Hull Hoffer. *Plessy v. Ferguson: Race and Inequality in Jim Crow America.* Lawrence: University of Kansas Press, 2012.

J. Morgan Kousser. *The Shaping of Southern Politics: Suffrage Restriction and the Establishment of the One-Party South, 1880–1910.* New Haven, CT: Yale University Press, 1974.

Michael Perman. *Struggle for Mastery: Disfranchisement in the South, 1888–1908.* Chapel Hill: University of North Carolina Press, 2001.

Thomas Adams Upchurch. *Legislating Racism: The Billion Dollar Congress and the Birth of Jim Crow.* Lexington: University Press of Kentucky, 2004.

Lynching

James Allen, Hinton Als, John Lewis, and Leon F. Litwack. *Without Sanctuary: Lynching Photography in America.* Santa Fe, NM: Twin Palms Books, 2000.

W. Fitzhugh Brundage. *Lynching in the New South: Georgia and Virginia, 1880–1930.* Urbana: University of Illinois Press, 1993.

_____, ed. *Under Sentence of Death: Lynching in the South.* Chapel Hill: University of North Carolina Press, 1997.

Sandra Gunning. *Race, Rape, and Lynching: The Red Record of American Literature, 1890–1912.* New York: Oxford University Press, 1996.

National Association for the Advancement of Colored People. *Thirty Years of Lynching in the United States, 1889–1918.* New York: NAACP, 1919.

Diane Sommerville. *Rape and Race in the Nineteenth Century South.* Chapel Hill: University of North Carolina Press, 2004.

Stewart E. Tolnay and E. M. Beck. *A Festival of Violence: An Analysis of Southern Lynchings, 1882–1930.* Urbana: University of Illinois Press, 1995.

The West

Robert G. Athearn. *In Search of Canaan: Black Migration to Kansas, 1879–80.* Lawrence: Regents Press of Kansas, 1978.

Jacob U. Gordon. *Narratives of African Americans in Kansas, 1870–1992.* Lewiston, NY: Edward Mellon Press, 1993.

Nell Irvin Painter. *Exodusters: Black Migration to Kansas After Reconstruction.* New York: Alfred A. Knopf, 1977.

Quintard Taylor. *In Search of the Racial Frontier: African Americans in the American West, 1528–1990.* New York: W. W. Norton, 1998.

Migration, Mobility, and Land Ownership

William Cohen. *At Freedom's Edge: Black Mobility and the Southern White Quest for Racial Control, 1861–1915.* Baton Rouge: Louisiana State University Press, 1991.

Pete Daniel. *The Shadow of Slavery: Peonage in the South, 1901–1969.* Urbana: University of Illinois Press, 1972.

Edward Royce. *The Origins of Southern Sharecropping.* Philadelphia: Temple University Press, 1993.

Loren Schweninger. *Black Property Owners in the South, 1790–1915.* Urbana: University of Illinois Press, 1990.

Chapter 15

African Americans Challenge White Supremacy
1877–1918

Several hundred African-American cowboys participated in the development of the western cattle empire in the decades after the Civil War. This photo depicts a group of those cowboys near Bonham, Texas, in 1909.

 ## Learning Objectives

After reading this chapter, you should be able to:

15.1 Explain how scientific and scholarly ideas were used to support and promote racism.

15.2 Compare and contrast the main purposes of education according to Booker T. Washington to those of his critics.

15.3   Analyze the ways in which African Americans used religious faith and church services to benefit themselves and their communities.

15.4   Explain what motivated African-American men to serve in U.S. military forces that fought against Native Americans, the Spanish, and the Filipinos.

15.5   Describe opportunities that both existed and were denied to African Americans in business, professions, entertainment, and athletics.

> The Anglo-Saxon said to the negro, in most haughty tones: "in this great 'battle for bread,' you must supply the brute force while I will supply the brain." . . . He will contribute the public funds to educate the negro and then exert every possible influence to keep the negro from earning a livelihood by means of that education.
>
> They pay our teachers poorer salaries than they do their own; they give us fewer and inferior school buildings and they make us crawl in the dust before the very eyes of our children in order to secure the slightest concessions. . . .
>
> In school, they are taught to bow down and worship at the shrine of men who died for the sake of liberty, and day by day they grow to disrespect us, their parents[,] who have made no blow for freedom. But it will not always be thus!
>
> —*Black novelist Sutton E. Griggs in Imperio in Imperio, 1899*

Industrialization and the rise of large, powerful corporations transformed the American economy in the late nineteenth century. As millions of European immigrants crowded into the cities of the North and Midwest to find jobs in the new factories, agricultural production increased and prices declined, impoverishing many rural southerners. Most black people—nearly eight million—remained in the South, where they struggled to confront white supremacy. Living in a society that sought to disregard their rights and exclude them from its institutions and culture, black Americans increasingly relied on their own resources to forge a path into the future.

Some African Americans turned to education to elevate themselves and their people, but they disagreed about exactly what knowledge and training would be most effective. Some African-American men sought to advance themselves and prove their worth to American society through military service. By the late nineteenth century, however, black Americans mostly relied on each other and their own communities to sustain themselves. As they had during Reconstruction, they continued to support churches, schools, and colleges. They established businesses and sometimes formed labor unions and went on strike. They founded their own hospitals. They expressed themselves in music by creating ragtime, jazz, and blues. At times they were allowed to participate with white people in organized sports such as professional boxing, baseball, horse racing, and college football. More often, they formed their own athletic teams and leagues. African Americans refused to allow white supremacy to prevent them from creating a meaningful place for themselves in American society.

15.1 Social Darwinism

Explain how scientific and scholarly ideas were used to support and promote racism.

Pseudoscientific evidence and academic scholarship bolstered the conviction of many Americans that white people, especially those of English and Germanic descent—Anglo-Saxons—were culturally and racially superior to nonwhites and even other Europeans. Sociologists Herbert Spencer and William Graham Sumner drew on Charles Darwin's theory of evolution and concluded that life in modern industrial societies mirrored life in the animal kingdom. This theory, called **social Darwinism**, held that through natural selection, the strong would thrive, prosper, and reproduce, while the weak would falter, fail, and die. Life was a struggle. Only the fittest survived.

Social Darwinism applied to both individuals and "races." It justified great disparities in wealth, suggesting that such men as John D. Rockefeller and Andrew Carnegie were rich because they were "fit," whereas many European immigrants and most African Americans were poor and unlikely to succeed because they were "unfit." The same logic explained why the United States, Britain, and Germany were stronger and more prosperous than countries such as Spain and Italy and why African, Asian, and Latin American societies seemed backward and primitive. In absorbing this ideology of class and race, many Americans and Europeans came to believe they had a responsibility—a duty—to introduce the political, economic, and religious benefits and values of Western cultures to the "less advanced" and usually darker peoples of the globe. The English poet Rudyard Kipling called this supposed responsibility "the white man's burden."

Social Darwinism led most Protestant white Americans to believe that other Americans could be ranked from superior to inferior based on their race, nationality, and ethnicity. Black people invariably occupied the bottom of this hierarchy, and the eastern and southern European immigrants who were flooding the country ranked slightly above them. Black people were capable, so the reasoning went, of only a subordinate role in a complex and advanced society as it rushed into the twentieth century. And if their position was biologically ordained, why should society devote substantial resources to educating them?

social Darwinism

Derived from Charles Darwin's theory of evolution, Herbert Spencer and William Graham Sumner asserted that life in modern society was competitive and only those individuals who were mentally, emotionally, and physically strong would prevail.

15.2 Education and Schools: The Issues

Compare and contrast the main purposes of education according to Booker T. Washington to those of his critics.

A black youngster who wanted an education in the late nineteenth century faced formidable obstacles. Most black people were poor farmers who had few opportunities for an education and even fewer prospects for a career in business or in a profession. It is a testimony to black perseverance that so many black people did manage to acquire an education and free themselves from illiteracy (see Figure 15-1).

Gaining even a rudimentary education was not easy. Rural schools for black children rarely operated for more than 30 weeks a year. Because of the demands of fieldwork, most black youngsters could not attend school on a regular basis. Brothers and sisters sometimes alternated work and school with each other on a daily basis. Benjamin Mays was 19 years old before he went to school for more than four months a year—and even then he had to defy his father's demand that he leave school in February to work on the farm.

Figure 15-1 Black and White Illiteracy in the United States and the Southern States, 1880–1900

Although more than half of adult black southerners were still illiterate in 1900, black people had made substantial progress in education during the last two decades of the nineteenth century. This progress is especially remarkable considering the difficulties black youngsters and adults faced in acquiring even an elementary education.

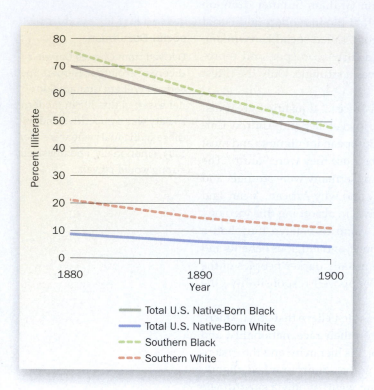

Schools were often dilapidated shacks. They lacked plumbing, electricity, books, and teaching materials. Some schools were in churches and homes. Teachers were poorly paid and often poorly prepared. Septima Clark remembered her first teaching experience on Johns Island on the South Carolina coast in the early twentieth century:

> Here I was, a high-school graduate, eighteen years old, principal in a two-teacher school with 132 pupils ranging from beginners to eighth graders, with no teaching experience, a schoolhouse constructed of boards running up and down, with no slats on the cracks, and a fireplace at one end of the room that cooked the pupils immediately in front of it but allowed those in the rear to shiver and freeze on their uncomfortable, hard, back-breaking benches.

15.2.1 Segregated Schools

Although southern states could not afford to support even one first-rate public school system, each of them operated separate schools for black and white children (see Table 15-1). The South had almost no public black high schools. In 1915, not one public black high school existed in 23 southern cities with populations of more than 20,000, including Tampa, New Orleans, Charleston, and Charlotte. But these 23 cities had 36 high schools for white youngsters. In 1897—over the vehement protests of the black community—white officials in Augusta, Georgia, transformed Ware High School, the black secondary school, into a black primary school. The U.S. Supreme Court in 1899 in *Cumming v. Richmond County [Georgia] Board of Education* unanimously refused to accept black parents' contention that this violated the "separate but equal" doctrine announced in the *Plessy v. Ferguson* case three years earlier. Augusta was left with two white high schools—one for males and one for females—and none for black people.

Table 15-1 South Carolina's Black and White Public Schools, 1908–1909

Black Schools		White Schools
2,354	Public schools	2,712
894	Men teachers	933
1,802	Women teachers	3,247
181,095	Total pupils	153,807
123,481	Average attendance	107,368
77	Pupils per school	55
63	Pupils per teacher	35
14.7	Average number of weeks of school	25.2
$118.17	Average yearly salary for male teachers	$479.79
$91.45	Average yearly salary for female teachers	$249.13
$308,153.16	Total expenditures	$1,590,732.51

SOURCE: Department of Education Annual Report, South Carolina, 1908–09, 935, 961.

Young black people who sought a secondary education often had to travel to a black college or university that offered a high school program. For example, in 1911, at the age of 16, Benjamin Mays traveled 100 miles to South Carolina State College and enrolled in the seventh grade. He graduated from high school there in 1916 at the age of 22 and then graduated from Maine's Bates College four years later.

In many communities, black people, with the assistance of churches and northern philanthropists, operated private academies and high schools, such as the Fort Valley High and Industrial School in Georgia and Mather Academy in Camden, South Carolina, to fill the void the lack of public schools created. Typically students were charged a modest tuition and came from more prosperous families. In 1890, 3,106 black youngsters between the ages of 15 and 19 attended black public or private high schools in the South. By 1910, 26,553 did.

School for most southern black students and teachers was a part-time activity. Because of the demands of agriculture, few rural students, black or white, attended school more than six months a year. Few teachers were graduates of four-year college programs. In urban communities and the Upper South, the school year lasted longer and education was better financed. But all public southern schools were segregated.

15.2.2 The Hampton Model

Some black and many white people regarded education for black youngsters as pointless. Benjamin Mays's father put little value in education: "My greatest opposition to going away to school was my father. When I knew that I had learned everything that I could in the one-room Brickhouse School and realized how little that was, my father felt . . . that it was all I needed. . . . He was convinced that education went to one's head and made him a fool and dishonest." In 1911 South Carolina's Governor Coleman Blease was even more blunt: "Instead of making an educated negro, you are ruining a good plow hand and making a half-trained fool."

Others were convinced the most appropriate education for a black child was industrial or domestic training. Black youngsters, these people maintained, should learn skills they could teach others and use to become productive members of the community.

Hampton Normal and Agricultural Institute was founded in 1868 in Virginia and was dominated for decades by Samuel Chapman Armstrong, a white missionary with paternalistic inclinations. Hampton trained legions of African Americans and Native Americans to teach skills and embrace hard work, diligence, and Christian morality. Armstrong stressed learning trades, such as shoemaking, carpentry, tailoring, and sewing. Hampton placed little emphasis on critical or independent thinking. Instead, students were taught to conform to middle-class values. Armstrong cautioned against black involvement in politics and acquiesced to Jim Crow racial practices. The chapel walls at Hampton featured pictures of Robert E. Lee and Andrew Johnson.

Young African-American children being taught washing and ironing at a primary school in Hampton, Virginia, in the 1890s.

15.2.3 Booker T. Washington and the Tuskegee Model

Hampton's foremost graduate was Booker T. Washington, who became the nation's leading apostle of industrial training and one of the most remarkable men—black or white—in American history. Washington was born a slave in western Virginia in 1856. His father was an unknown white man. His mother, Jane, raised him in an unimpressive but tidy cabin built of split logs on a small farm. As a child, he worked at a salt works, in coal mines, and as a houseboy for a prominent white family. He learned to read and write at a local school.

Intensely ambitious, Washington set off for Hampton Institute in 1872. While there, he was much affected by Armstrong, his curriculum, and his method of instruction. Washington worked his way through school and taught for two years at Hampton after graduating. In 1881 he accepted an invitation to found a black college in Alabama—Tuskegee Institute. The result was an institution that he forged almost single-handedly and that reflected his experience at Hampton and the influence of Armstrong.

From his arrival at Tuskegee until his death in 1915, Washington worked tirelessly to persuade black and white people that the surest way for black people to advance was by learning skills and demonstrating a willingness to do manual labor. In a famous speech at the Cotton States Exposition in Atlanta in 1895 (see Chapter 16), Washington told his segregated audience, "No race can prosper till it learns that there is as much dignity in tilling a field as in writing a poem. It is at the bottom of life we must begin, and not at the top." He believed that if black people acquired skills and became prosperous small farmers, artisans, and shopkeepers, they would earn the respect and acceptance of white Americans and eradicate the race problem—all without unseemly protest and agitation.

White political leaders and philanthropists, who were more inclined to support the promotion of trades and skills among black people than an academic and liberal education, praised Washington's message. Steel magnate Andrew Carnegie, impressed by Washington, financed the construction of 29 buildings on the campuses of black schools and colleges. White railroad executive William H. Baldwin provided millions of dollars for black industrial education, and the John F. Slater Fund poured money into vocational education. Julius Rosenwald, the longtime head of Sears and Roebuck, consulted with Washington and contributed liberally to black education across the South. Disciples of Washington and graduates of Tuskegee fanned out across the South as industrial and agricultural training for black youngsters proliferated.

The Morrill Act, which Congress passed in 1862, entitled each state to the proceeds from the sale of federal land (most of it in the West) for establishing land-grant colleges to provide agricultural and mechanical training. However, southern states did not admit black students to their A&M (Agricultural and Mechanical) schools. In 1890, however, a second Morrill Act permitted states to establish and fund separate black land-grant colleges. The 1890 act accelerated the development of practical education through the appropriation of federal money to such institutions as Alcorn A&M in Mississippi, Florida A&M, Southern University in Louisiana, Langston in Oklahoma, and Tuskegee Institute. By 1915 there were 16 black land-grant colleges.

Most of the institutions were not actually colleges. Few of their students graduated with bachelor's degrees, and many of them were enrolled in primary and secondary programs. Most students at the black land-grant schools had to take courses in trades, agriculture, and domestic sciences. Most of the schools required students to do manual labor for which they were paid small sums. Students built and maintained the campuses and raised the food served in the school cafeteria. Many students were in the "normal"

Booker T. Washington was by 1900 the most influential black leader in America. White business and political leaders were reassured by his message that black people themselves were responsible for their economic progress and that people of color should avoid a direct challenge to white supremacy. Although W. E. B. Du Bois appreciated Washington's commitment to the advancement of black people, he believed more emphasis should be placed on developing an educated elite who would take the lead in solving the race problem. Washington was a southerner who looked for practical solutions to the problems of everyday life; Du Bois was a northerner who stressed the need for intellectual advancement.

curriculum, which prepared them to teach at a time when most states did not require a college degree for a teaching certificate. Students in "normal" schools or programs earned a licentiate of instruction that certified them to teach.

15.2.4 Critics of the Tuskegee Model

Not everyone shared Washington's stress on industrial and agricultural training to the near exclusion of the liberal arts, including literature, history, philosophy, and languages. Washington's program, critics charged, seemed designed to train black people for a subordinate role. Black people, they worried, would continue to labor much as they had in slavery and not far removed from it.

W. E. B. Du Bois, a Fisk- and Harvard-trained scholar, and African Methodist Episcopal (AME) Bishop Henry M. Turner believed education went beyond mere training and the acquisition of skills. It involved intellectual growth. It would confront racial problems, and it would create wise men. According to Du Bois, "The function of the Negro college, then, is clear, it must maintain standards of popular education, it must seek the social regeneration of the Negro, and it must help in the solution of problems of race contact and cooperation. And finally, beyond all this, it must develop men."

Many of the private black colleges resisted the emphasis on agricultural and mechanical training. American Missionary Association schools such as Fisk, Talladega, and Tougaloo; AME schools such as Allen, Paul Quinn, and Morris Brown; and Methodist institutions such as Claflin, Bennett, and Rust still promoted the liberal arts and taught Latin, Greek, mathematics, and natural sciences. Henry L. Morehouse of the American Baptist Home Missionary Society explained that the purpose of education was to develop strong minds. He believed gifted intellectuals—a "talented tenth" as he characterized them in 1896—could lead people forward. Du Bois likewise stressed the need for the best-educated 10 percent of the black population to promote progress and advance the race.

Washington did not deny the importance of a liberal arts education, but he believed industry was the foundation to progress:

> On such a foundation as this will grow habits of thrift, a love of work, economy, ownership of property, bank accounts. Out of it in the future will grow practical education, professional education, and positions of public responsibility. Out of it will grow moral and religious strength. Out of it will grow wealth from which alone can come leisure and the opportunity for the enjoyment of literature and the fine arts.

Ultimately, however, Washington was wrong to believe education for black people that focused on economic progress would earn the respect of most white Americans. As Du Bois explained, most white people preferred ignorant and unsuccessful black people to educated and prosperous ones:

> If my own city of Atlanta had offered it to-day the choice between 500 Negro college graduates—forceful, busy, ambitious men of property and self-respect— and 500 black cringing vagrants and criminals, the popular vote in favor of the criminals would be simply overwhelming. Why? Because they want Negro crime? No, not that they fear Negro crime less, but that they fear Negro ambition and success more. They can deal with crime by chain gang and lynch law, or at least they think they can, but the South can conceive neither machinery nor place for the educated, self-reliant, self-assertive black man.

As Chapter 16 discusses, the disagreement among black leaders over education would expand by the early twentieth century into a larger controversy. What began as a conversation over the value of practical education became a passionate debate among Washington, Du Bois, and others over the most effective strategy—accommodation or confrontation—for overcoming Jim Crow and white supremacy.

Voices

Thomas E. Miller and the Mission of the Black Land-Grant College

In 1896 the South Carolina General Assembly established the Colored Normal, Industrial, Agricultural and Mechanical College of South Carolina. It derived funds from the Morrill Acts of 1862 and 1890 and from the state itself. Its first president was former black congressman and lawyer Thomas E. Miller. In an address to the Bamberg County Colored Fair in 1897, Miller embraced the Hampton and Tuskegee models as he described the mission of his institution:

> The work of our college is along the industrial line. We are making educated and worthy school teachers, educated and reliable mechanics, educated, reliable and frugal farmers. We teach your sons and daughters how to care for and milk the cows, how to make gilt-edged butter, how to make cheese, what kind of fertilizer each crop needs, the natural strength and productive qualities of the various soils, and last to make a compost heap and how to take care of it. We teach them how to make a wagon, plow and hoe, how to shoe a horse and nurse him when sick. We teach your children how to keep books and typewrite, we teach your girls how to make a dress or undergarment, how to cook, wash and iron. We teach your boys how to make and run an engine, how to make and control electricity, we teach them mechanical and artistic drawing, house and sign painting.

1. Given the racism of the 1890s, why was or wasn't agricultural and mechanical training the most suitable education for most black youngsters?

2. If a young black person did learn the skills Miller mentioned, was he or she educated for an inferior place in society?

SOURCE: Thomas E. Miller, the Bamberg County Colored Fair in 1897.

15.3 Church and Religion

Analyze the ways in which African Americans used religious faith and church services to benefit themselves and their communities.

In a world in which white people so thoroughly dominated the lives and limited the possibilities of black people, the church had long been the most important institution—after the family—that African Americans controlled for themselves. After the Civil War, black people organized their own churches and religious denominations, which thrived as sources of spiritual comfort and centers of social activity. Black clergymen were often the most influential members of the black community.

In 1890 the South had more black Baptists than all other denominations combined. Baptist congregations were more independent and under less supervision by church hierarchy than other denominations. Bishops, for example, in the African Methodist Episcopal Zion Church and the AME Church, exercised considerable authority over congregations, as did Methodist and Presbyterian leaders. Many black people (and many southern white people) preferred the autonomy of the Baptist churches (Figure 15-2).

But whatever the denomination, the church was integral to the lives of most black people. It fulfilled spiritual needs through sermons and music. It enabled black people, free from white interference, to plan, organize, and lead. It was a sanctuary for black women, who immersed themselves in church activities. Although church members usually had little money to spare, they helped the sick, the bereaved, and those in need. Congregations also helped thousands of youngsters attend school and college.

The church service itself was the most important aspect of religious life for most black congregations. Parishioners were expected to participate and not merely listen quietly to the minister's sermon. Black people had long considered white church services too sedate. One black school principal believed black people gave added meaning to Christianity; whereas "the white man gives it system, logic and abstraction, the Negro is necessary to impart feeling, sanctioned emotions, heart throes and ecstasy."

Figure 15-2   Church Affiliation Among Southern Black People, 1890

The vast majority of black southerners belonged to Baptist, Methodist, and Presbyterian congregations in the late nineteenth century, although there were about 15,000 black Episcopalians and nationwide perhaps 200,000 black Roman Catholics.

SOURCE: Based on Edward L. Ayers, *The Promise of the New South,* 160–61. © Darlene Clark Hine.

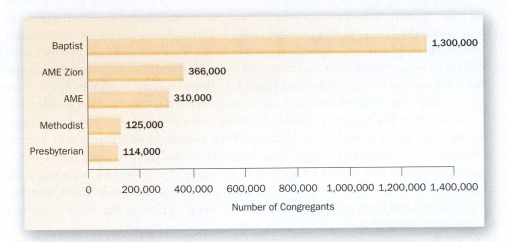

In most black churches, members punctuated the minister's call with many an "Amen." They testified, shouted, laughed, cried, and sometimes fainted. Choirs provided joyful music and solemn songs.

Most congregations did not want scholarly sermons or theologically sound addresses. When Frederick Jones, a well-dressed new black minister in North Carolina, offered a deliberate message brimming with rationality, he was met with silence and rebuked by a senior member of the congregation: "Dese fellers comes out heah wid dere starched shirts, and dey' beaver hats, and dere kid gloves, but dey don't know nuffin b[o]ut 'ligion." The next time Jones preached, he had changed his clothes and delivered a passionate sermon.

Many black ministers had little or no education. Benjamin E. Mays's father told him the clergy did not need an education: "God called men to preach; and when He called them, He would tell them what to say!" Unqualified clergymen who relied on ungrammatical and rhetorical appeals disturbed some black leaders. In 1890 Booker T. Washington claimed that "three-fourths of the Baptist ministers and two-thirds of the Methodists are unfit, either mentally or morally, or both, to preach the Gospel to any one or to attempt to lead any one." W. E. B. Du Bois wanted black churches free of "the noisy and unclean leaders of the thoughtless mob" and the clergy replaced by thoughtful "apostles of service and sacrifice." But a black Alabama farmer observed that solemn and erudite preachers would not survive: "You let a man preach de true Gospel and he won't git many nickels in his pocket; but if he hollers and jumps he gits all the nickels he can hold and chickens besides."

A few black women led congregations. Nannie Helen Burroughs established

Nannie Helen Burroughs and other black women came together at the Banner State Woman's National Baptist Convention in the early twentieth century. In addition to her involvement with the Baptist women's movement, Burroughs was devoted to industrial education as well as voting rights for black men and women. She was also active with the National Association of Colored Women, serving as the chair of its anti-lynching committee.

Women's Day in Baptist churches. Women delivered sermons and guided the parishioners. But she complained that Women's Day quickly became more an occasion to raise money than to raise women.

15.3.1 The Church as Solace and Escape

For many black people, the emotional involvement in church services was an escape from their dreary and oppressive daily lives. Growing up in rural South Carolina, Benjamin E. Mays admitted that his Baptist preacher, James F. Marshall, who barely had a fifth-grade education, "emphasized the joys of heaven and the damnation of hell" and that the "trials and tribulations of the world would all be over when one got to heaven." But such messages helped to assuage the impact of white supremacy: "Beaten down at every turn by the white man, as they were, Negroes could perhaps not have survived without this kind of religion."

Clergymen like Marshall refused to challenge white supremacy. Even veiled comments might invite retaliation or lynching. When a visiting minister began to criticize white people to Marshall's congregation, Marshall immediately stopped him. Despite the reluctance of many black clergymen to advocate improvement in race relations, many white people still viewed black religious gatherings as a threat. Black churches were burned and black ministers assaulted and killed with tragic regularity in the late nineteenth-century South.

Black clergymen, like their white counterparts, often stressed middle-class values to their congregations while suggesting that many black people found themselves in shameful situations because of their sinful ways. They urged them to improve their behavior. The black clergyman at Mount Ever Rest Colored Church in rural Mississippi warned his congregation to stop "cussin; lyin; stealin; crap shootin; whisky drinkin; and backbiting one another to de white folks." Black people who had acquired sinful reputations sometimes received funeral sermons that consigned them to eternal damnation. As Benjamin Mays recalled, "The church was usually full at funerals, especially if the deceased had been well known; and when a man of bad reputation died the church was jammed."

Some black clergy publicly opposed white supremacy and insisted that black people stand up for their rights. Bishop Henry M. Turner persistently spoke out on racial matters. In 1883, after the Supreme Court declared the 1875 Civil Rights Act unconstitutional, Turner called the Constitution "a dirty rag, a cheat, a libel and ought to be spit upon by every Negro in the land."

15.3.2 The Holiness Movement and the Pentecostal Church

Not all black people belonged to mainline denominations. For example, the Holiness movement and the emergence of Pentecostal churches affected Methodist and Baptist congregations. Partly in reaction to the elite domination and stiff authority of white Methodism, the Holiness movement gained a foothold among white people and spilled over among black southerners. Holiness churches ordained women such as Neely Terry to lead them. Holiness clergy preached that sanctification allowed a Christian to receive a "second blessing" and feel the "perfect love of Christ." Believers thus achieved an emotional reaffirmation and a new state of grace.

The Church of God in Christ (COGIC) became the leading black Holiness church. After successful revivals in Mississippi and Memphis, two black former Baptists—Charles Harrison Mason and C. P. Jones—founded COGIC in 1907. However, Mason was expelled after reporting that "a flame touched [his] tongue," and his "language changed." He had spoken in tongues. Mason then organized the Pentecostal General Assembly of the Church of God in Christ, and he assigned black men as bishops in Mississippi, Arkansas, Texas, Missouri, and California. In 1911 Mason appointed Lizzie Woods Roberson to lead the Woman's Department, a post she held until 1945. She transformed it into a financial powerhouse for COGIC.

In the meantime, Charles Fox Parham, a white minister, had founded the Pentecostal church in the early twentieth century in Texas. William J. Seymour, who was born a slave in Louisiana, played a key role in the development of the church. After hearing black people speak in tongues in Houston, he went to Los Angeles, where he and others also began to speak in tongues. There he founded what became the Pentecostal church, which grew rapidly.

Charles Harrison Mason joined the Pentecostal movement, and under his leadership the Reorganized COGIC became the leading Pentecostal denomination. It soon spread across the South among black and white people. Although there were tensions between black and white believers, the Pentecostal church was the only significant movement that crossed the racial divide in early twentieth-century America.

15.3.3 Roman Catholics and Episcopalians

Most African Americans belonged to one of the Baptist or Methodist churches. Booker T. Washington reportedly observed that "if a black man is anything but a Baptist or Methodist, someone has been tampering with his religion." Nevertheless, black people also belonged to other churches and denominations—or to no organized religious group.

About 200,000 African Americans were Roman Catholics in 1890. However, they were rarely fully accepted by the church or white Catholics. In the South, they were segregated in separate churches with separate parish schools.

The most prominent black Catholics came from the Healy family. Eliza Clark was a slave who had nine children by Michael Healy, an Irish-Catholic plantation owner in Georgia. Unlike many white men, Healy genuinely cared for Eliza and their children, although by law he could not marry her. The children were educated in northern schools. James A. Healy graduated from the Jesuit-run Holy Cross College in Massachusetts and was ordained a priest in Paris in 1854. He later became a bishop in Portland, Maine.

Patrick Healy also attended Holy Cross and became the first black Jesuit priest in the United States. He served eight years as president of Georgetown University in Washington. Eliza Healy took vows as a nun and was the headmistress of a Catholic school in Vermont. Most white people were unaware of the racial ancestry of the Healys, and members of the family did not openly acknowledge being African American even when other black Catholics asked for their support. Bishop James Healy, for example, refused on three occasions to speak to the Congress of Colored Catholics, an association of black Catholics that met at least four times in northern cities between 1889 and 1893. Its members were mainly concerned with the discrimination they faced in the church and with the educational opportunities that were available—or more often not available—to black Catholic children in church schools.

Augustus Tolton was another African-American priest, and there was no question about his color. Because no American seminary would accept him, he was educated and ordained in 1886 in Rome. For a time, he presided over a parish in Quincy, Illinois, made up mainly of Irish and German Catholics. Unlike Bishop Healy, Tolton did speak to the Congress of Colored Catholics in Philadelphia in 1892.

Mother Mathilda Beasley came from a prominent free black family in Savannah. Her efforts to establish a community of Franciscan nuns in rural Georgia ultimately failed.

Although he rarely mentioned it, James A. Healy's mother was black and a slave. He graduated from Holy Cross College, was ordained a Roman Catholic priest in Paris in 1854, and became the Bishop of Portland, Maine, in 1875.

Profile

Henry McNeal Turner

Henry McNeal Turner began as a supporter of racial harmony and a patriot. As he aged, however, he became disenchanted with the way white Americans contradicted their professed dedication to the principles of fairness and justice by their treatment of black Americans.

Turner was born to free black parents in Newberry, South Carolina, in 1834. After his father's death, he worked in cotton fields and learned to be a blacksmith and carriage maker. He also learned to read and write. Drawn to religion, he was licensed to preach by the Methodist Episcopal Church, a white denomination. In 1859 he moved to Baltimore and was ordained in the AME Church. He then became pastor of Union Bethel Church, the largest black congregation in Washington, D.C. During the Civil War, he was a chaplain with the First Regiment of U.S. Colored Troops.

After the war, he briefly worked for the Freedmen's Bureau in Georgia. In an Emancipation Day address in Savannah in 1866 he praised the American flag and predicted that white people would soon accept black people.

Turner became active in Republican politics and was elected to the 1867–1868 Georgia constitutional convention, where he was the only black delegate to favor a literacy requirement for voting. He also supported a measure to help white planters who had not paid their taxes to keep their land. He conceded that "no man in Georgia has been more conservative than I. Anything to please white folks has been my motto."

In 1868 Turner was elected to the Georgia House of Representatives. When white legislators voted to remove the 32 black representatives, he objected: "I shall neither fawn nor cringe before any party, nor stoop to beg for my rights. . . . I am here to demand my rights, and to hurl thunderbolts at the men who dare to cross the threshold of my manhood." The black lawmakers were reinstated.

In 1880 he was elected one of the 12 bishops in the AME Church and became president of Morris Brown College in Atlanta, where he served until 1900. He also became an advocate of emigration to Africa and the Liberian Exodus of 1877. Turner supported women's suffrage and ordained a woman as a deacon in the AME Church in 1888, but the AME Council of Bishops withdrew the appointment.

Turner had little tolerance for those who considered Christianity a white man's religion. He asserted that "God is a Negro" and attacked those who "believe God is a white-skinned, blue-eyed, projecting-nosed, compressed-lipped, and finely-robed white gentleman."

He helped establish and edited a monthly AME newspaper, the *Voice of Missions*. In its pages he took a black nationalist stance and criticized white supremacy and lynching. Growing older and angrier, he told black readers to attack white predators: "Let every Negro in this country who has a spark of manhood in him supply his house with one, two, or three guns . . . and when your domicile is invaded . . . turn loose your missiles of death and blow the fiendish wretches into a thousand giblets."

He denounced black soldiers who fought to suppress the Philippine Insurrection: "I boil over with disgust when I remember that colored men from this country . . . are there fighting to subjugate a people of their own color. . . . I can scarcely keep from saying that I hope the Filipinos will wipe such soldiers from the face of the earth. . . . To go down there and shoot innocent men and take the country away from them, is too much for me to think about."

Embittered and tired, Turner lost faith in the intentions of white people and no longer praised the flag: "I used to love what I thought was the grand old flag, and sing with ecstasy about the Stars and Stripes, but to the Negro in this country the American flag is a dirty and contemptible rag. . . . Without multiplying words, I wish to say that hell is an improvement on the United States where the Negro is concerned."

Turner died of a heart attack in 1915. He was married four times, outliving three wives and all but two of his children.

In New Orleans, where there were many black Catholics of French and Spanish descent, the Sisters of the Blessed Sacrament established a black high school in 1915 that became Xavier University in 1925.

Fairly or not, most African Americans identified black Episcopalians with wealth and privilege. Many black Episcopalians traced their heritage to free black families before the Civil War. By 1903 approximately 15,000 members of black Episcopal parishes worshipped in Richmond, Raleigh, Charleston, and other cities in the North and South.

15.4 Red versus Black: The Buffalo Soldiers

Explain what motivated African-American men to serve in U.S. military forces that fought against Native Americans, the Spanish, and the Filipinos.

After the Civil War, the U.S. Army was reduced to fewer than 30,000 troops. Congressional Democrats tried to eliminate black soldiers from this small force, but Radical Republicans, led by Massachusetts Senator Henry Wilson, kept the military open to black men. The Army Reorganization Act of 1869 maintained 21 white regiments and four all-black regiments: the 9th and 10th Cavalry Regiments and the 24th and 25th Infantry Regiments. These four regiments spent most of the next three decades on the western frontier. Nearly 12,500 black men served during the late nineteenth century in these segregated units commanded—as black troops had been during the Civil War—by white officers. Unlike in the Civil War, however, many of these white officers were southerners who frequently held black men in low regard.

Military service in the West was wretched for white troops and worse for black soldiers. Too often officers considered black troops lazy, undisciplined, and cowardly. Black regiments were assigned mainly to the New Mexico and Arizona territories and to west Texas because the army thought black people tolerated heat better than white people did. The ancestors of the slaves were "from the tropics," claimed Quartermaster General Montgomery C. Meigs, and "not from the Northern or Southern extremities of Africa but from the Torrid Zone almost entirely." Most black soldiers were thus compelled to endure the hot, dry, and dusty Southwest desert. Others were sent to Kansas, Colorado, and the Dakotas, where they confronted howling blizzards, subzero temperatures, and frostbite (see Map 15-1).

15.4.1 Discrimination in the Army

Black troops faced more hardships than adverse weather. The army provided them inferior food and inadequate housing. Whereas white soldiers received dried apples and peaches, canned tomatoes, onions, and potatoes, black troops were given foul beef, bad bread, and canned peas unfit for human consumption. In 1867 white troops at Fort Leavenworth in Kansas lived in barracks while black troops slept in tents on wet ground. Black regiments were allotted used weapons and equipment. The army sent its worst horses—often old and lame—to the black cavalry.

Long stretches of boredom, tedious duty, and loneliness marked army life for black and white men in the West. Months might pass without combat. Desertion and alcoholism were endemic, although black soldiers were less likely to desert or turn to drink than were white troops. In 1877, for example, 18 men deserted from the all-black 10th Regiment, and 184 white soldiers deserted from the all-white 4th Regiment. Black troops realized that although army life could be harsh and dangerous, it compared favorably to the civilian world, which held few opportunities for them. Army food was poor, but the private's pay of $13 per month was regular. Moreover, black troops developed immense pride as professional soldiers.

Map 15-1   Military Posts Where Black Troops Served, 1866–1917

Black troops in the 9th and 10th Cavalaries and the 24th and 25th Infantries were assigned almost exclusively to western military posts from the end of the Civil War until the early twentieth century.

Why were African-American troops assigned largely to isolated posts on the western frontier?

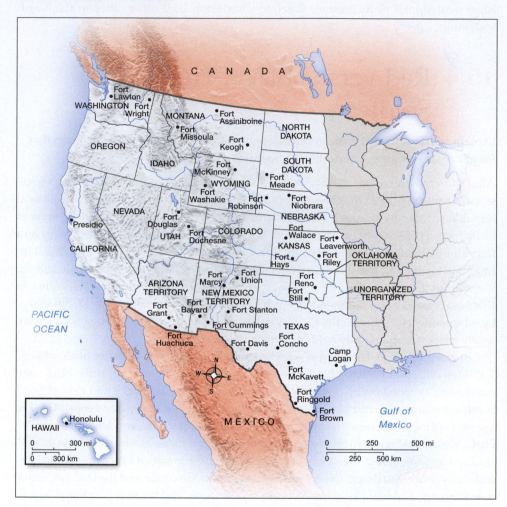

---

buffalo soldiers

Named by the Plains Indians for the four regiments of black soldiers that served with the U.S. Army on the western frontier from the 1870s to the 1890s.

How African-American troops came to be identified as buffalo soldiers is uncertain. Comanche and Cheyenne Indians began to refer to black troops as "**buffalo soldiers**" in the 1870s, perhaps because the Plains Indians associated the hair of black men with the shaggy coat of the buffalo, a sacred animal. The wife of a white officer on the western frontier referred to buffalo soldiers in her personal correspondence. Famed artist and sculptor Frederic Remington described black troops as buffalo soldiers in an article in *Century Magazine* in 1889. The 10th Cavalry later displayed a buffalo in their unit emblem.

15.4.2 The Buffalo Soldiers in Combat

It was ironic that white military authorities would employ black men to subdue red people. Most black soldiers, however, had no qualms about fighting Indians, protecting white settlers and railroad construction gangs, or apprehending bandits and cattle rustlers. From the late 1860s to the early 1890s, the four black regiments repeatedly engaged hostile Indians. In September 1867, 700 Cheyenne attacked 50 Army scouts along a dry riverbed in eastern Colorado. The scouts held out for over a week until the 10th Cavalry rescued them. For more than 12 months in 1879 and 1880, the 9th and 10th Cavalries fought the Apaches under Chief Victorio in New Mexico and Texas in a campaign of raid and counterraid. The Apaches slipped across the Mexican border and then returned to southwest Texas. In clashes at Rattlesnake Springs and near Fresno Spring, the 10th killed more than 30 Apaches before Victorio fled again to Mexico, where the Mexican Army killed him. But the 9th and 10th Cavalries deserve most of the credit for his defeat, with their dogged pursuit for months over hundreds of miles of rugged terrain.

In 1879, however, 10th Cavalry troops protected Kiowa women and children from Texas Rangers. Black troops also protected Chickasaw and Cherokee farmers from Kiowa and Comanche bands.

In 1890 the 9th Cavalry was sent to the Pine Ridge Reservation in South Dakota, where Sioux Indians were holding a religious ceremony known as the Ghost Dance. Confined to reservations, some Indians—out of desperation and yearning for the past— believed their participation in the Ghost Dance would bring their ancestors and huge herds of buffalo back to the Great Plains. White people would vanish, and Indian life would return to what it had been decades earlier. White authorities considered the Ghost Dance an act of defiance.

On December 29, the 7th Cavalry attempted to disarm the Sioux at Wounded Knee on the Pine Ridge Reservation. Shooting erupted, and 146 Indian men, women, and children—along with 26 soldiers—were killed. The 9th Cavalry, 108 miles away, rode the next day through a blizzard and arrived tired and freezing to come to the aid of the 7th Cavalry. The 9th spent the remainder of the winter guarding the Sioux. A black private, W. H. Prather, observed, "The Ninth, the Ninth were the first to come, will be the last to leave, we poor devils, and the Sioux are left to freeze."

15.4.3 Civilian Hostility to Black Soldiers

Despite the gallant performance of the buffalo soldiers, civilians frequently treated them with hostility. In Texas in 1875, Mexicans ambushed five black soldiers, killed two of them, and mutilated their bodies. The next day the infuriated white commander of the 9th Cavalry, Colonel Edward Hatch, rode out with 60 soldiers and apprehended the Mexicans. A local grand jury indicted nine of them for murder, but one was acquitted, and the other eight were released without a trial. Hatch, another white officer, and three buffalo soldiers were then indicted for breaking into and burglarizing the shack where the Mexicans had sought refuge. The charges were dropped, but the five men had to hire their own lawyers.

In 1877, 54 black troops from the 9th Cavalry intervened successfully in a political and ethnic dispute between white and Mexican residents of El Paso, Texas. The 9th was also dispatched to police the so-called Johnson County War in Wyoming between big and small ranchers in 1890. One of the state's U.S. senators, who favored the big ranchers, arranged the deployment of black troops; their presence angered the small ranchers, as it was intended to do. Racial violence and bloodshed soon erupted between residents of the town of Suggs, who had run two black soldiers out of town, and several of the soldiers who had disobeyed orders. The troops were withdrawn after the town was shot up and one soldier killed.

A west Texas newspaper, the *Bellville Countryman*, summarized the attitudes of many white westerners when it complained that "the

Several black men who were in the 10th Cavalry enjoy some time to themselves near St. Mary's, Montana, in 1894. Within four years they would be in combat against Spanish troops in Cuba during the Spanish-American War.

idea of a gallant and high-minded people being ordered and pushed around by an inferior, ignorant race is shocking to the senses."

15.4.4 Brownsville

Brownsville affair

In 1906, a shooting in Brownsville, Texas, was blamed on black soldiers from the 25th Infantry Regiment. President Theodore Roosevelt summarily dismissed 167 black men from the U.S. Army. Later investigations exonerated the men.

One of the worst examples of hostility to black troops, the so-called **Brownsville affair**, also occurred in Texas. In 1906 the 1st Battalion of the 25th Infantry was transferred from Nebraska to Fort Brown in Brownsville, Texas, along the Rio Grande. The black soldiers immediately encountered discrimination from both white people and Mexicans in this border community. More than four out of five of Brownsville's residents were Hispanic. Black people were not permitted in public parks, and white businesses refused to serve them. Civilians provoked and attacked black soldiers.

Shortly after midnight on August 14, about 150 shots were fired in Brownsville. One man died, and a Hispanic policeman and the editor of a Spanish-language newspaper were injured. Black troops were blamed for the violence when clips and cartridges from the army's Springfield rifles were found in the street. Two military investigations concluded that black soldiers did the shooting. The army could not identify the specific soldiers responsible because no one would confess or name the alleged perpetrators.

With no hearing or trial, President Theodore Roosevelt dismissed three companies of black men—167 soldiers—from the army. They were barred from rejoining the military and from government employment and were denied veterans' pensions or benefits. The black community, which had supported Roosevelt, reacted angrily. Booker T. Washington, a Roosevelt supporter, wrote, "There is no law, human or divine, which justifies the punishment of an innocent man." Washington added, "I have the strongest faith in the President's honesty of intention, high mindedness of purpose, sincere unselfishness and courage, but I regret for all these reasons all the more that this thing has occurred."

Republican Senator James B. Foraker of Ohio led a Senate investigation that upheld Roosevelt's dismissals. But Foraker, an opponent of Roosevelt, questioned the guilt of the black men. The clips and cartridges that served as evidence were apparently planted. After Roosevelt left office in 1909, the War Department reinstated 14 of the soldiers. In 1972 the Justice Department determined that an injustice had occurred. The black soldiers were posthumously awarded honorable discharges. Congress awarded the only survivor of the Brownsville affair—Dorsie Willis—$25,000 and the right to treatment at veterans' facilities.

15.4.5 African Americans in the Navy

Naval service was even more unappealing than life in the army. In the late nineteenth century, as the navy made the transition from timber and sail to steam and steel, approximately one sailor in 10 was a black man. Although warships were technically integrated, in that black and white sailors served on them together, white sailors were often hostile to black sailors. They would not eat or bunk with them or take orders from them. Increasingly, and to enforce a de facto shipboard segregation, black sailors were restricted to stoking boilers and to cooking and serving food to white sailors.

James Conyers was the first black man to enroll as a midshipman at the U.S. Naval Academy in 1872. He faced intense ostracism, and resigned in 1873. Seventy-six years later, in 1949, Wesley A. Brown became the first African American to graduate from the Naval Academy.

15.4.6 The Black Cowboys

Black men before, during, and after the Civil War were familiar with horses and mules. As slaves, some black men had tended and cared for the animals. Black cavalrymen gained experience with horses. By the 1870s and 1880s, black men joined Mexicans, Native Americans, and white men on the long cattle drives from Texas to Kansas,

Nebraska, and Missouri. There were probably no more than a few hundred black cowboys in the late nineteenth and early twentieth centuries.

Tending cattle was monotonous, difficult, and dirty work. Yet it required skill as a rider to manage hundreds of ornery and stinking animals. Cowboys had to tolerate weather that ranged from incredibly hot to bitter cold. They had to eat unappetizing food. There was no bed to sleep in each night, and their closest companion was often the horse they rode.

Black cowhands sometimes endured discrimination and abuse. They had to tame the toughest horses, work the longest hours, and face hostility in saloons, hotels, brothels, and shops in towns like Dodge City, Abilene, or Cheyenne. Still, black cowboys earned the respect of white ranchers and cattle barons. Bose Ikard had been born a slave in Mississippi and went to work for Texas cattleman Charles Goodnight after the Civil War. Goodnight praised Ikard: "He was my detective, banker, and everything else in Colorado, New Mexico, and the other wild country I was in. . . . We went through some terrible trials during those four years on the trail. . . . [Ikard] was the most skilled and trustworthy man I had."

15.4.7 The Black Cowgirls

Several African-American women were "cowgirls." Johanna "Aunt Chona" was of black and Seminole Indian descent, and she rode side saddle and broke untamed horses in Texas. She called it "gentling" them. Henrietta Williams Foster—"Aunt Rittie"—was born a slave in Mississippi and sold to Texas slave owners. As an ex-slave she became an expert rider who could take control of a herd of cattle. Although lacking formal education, she served as a midwife and also treated injured animals. Small in stature, she could be tough, mean, and would out-cuss most men.

Mary Fields—otherwise known as "Stagecoach Mary"—operated a stagecoach in Montana for eight years. An imposing woman at six feet tall and 200 pounds, she carried a 38 Smith and Wesson and took part in at least one shooting with an angry cowboy. She lived in Cascade, Montana, into the twentieth century.

15.4.8 The Spanish-American War

With the West subdued by 1890, many Americans concluded that the United States should expand overseas. European nations had already carved out colonies in Africa and Asia. Many, but by no means all, Americans favored the extension of U.S. authority to Latin America and the Pacific. In 1893 the navy and American businessmen toppled the monarchy in Hawaii, and the United States annexed those islands in 1898.

The same year, the United States went to war to liberate Cuba from Spain. As in the Civil War, black men enlisted, fought, and died. Twenty-two black sailors were among the 266 men who died when the battleship USS *Maine* blew up in Havana harbor; this event helped trigger the war. Many black Americans were convinced, as they had been during previous wars, that their support for the war against Spain would reduce or even eliminate white hostility. E. E. Cooper, editor of the *Washington Colored American*, declared that the war would "cement the races into a more compact brotherhood through perfect unity of purpose and patriotic affinity." The war, he asserted, would help white Americans "unloose themselves from the bondage of race prejudice."

Bill Pickett was an authentic cowboy who became one of the first black movie stars. "The Bull-Dogger" was a 1922 black-and-white silent film aimed at attracting black audiences. (No copies of the film are known to have survived.) Pickett's skill as a bull-dogger was legendary. He would ride alongside a steer, jump off the horse, and grab the animal by the horns. He then wrestled it to the ground by sharply biting the animal's upper lip or nose. Pickett was the hit of the 1904 Cheyenne Frontier Days rodeo in Wyoming.

"Stagecoach" Mary Fields was born a slave in Tennessee before she moved to Montana and drove a stagecoach carrying U.S. mail. She later opened a restaurant in Cascade, Montana, that failed—not because of the poor quality of the food, but because she fed so many people who could not afford to pay for their meals.

Many black and white Americans, however, questioned the American cause. Some black people saw the war as an effort to extend American racial practices, including Jim Crow, beyond U.S. borders. The Rev. George W. Prioleau, chaplain of the 9th Cavalry, wondered why black Americans supported what he considered a hypocritical war:

> Talk about fighting and freeing poor Cuba and of Spain's brutality. . . . Is America any better than Spain? Has she not subjects in her very midst who are murdered daily without a trial of judge or jury? Has she not subjects in her own borders whose children are half-fed and half-clothed, because their father's skin is black. . . . Yet the Negro is loyal to his country's flag.

Whether or not they harbored doubts, black men by the thousands served in the Spanish-American War and in the Philippine Insurrection that followed it. Shortly before war was declared, the army transferred its four black regiments from the West to Florida to prepare for combat in Cuba. President William McKinley also appealed for volunteers. The War Department designated four of the black volunteer units "immune regiments" because it believed that black men would tolerate the heat and humidity of Cuba better than white troops and that black people were immune or at least less susceptible to yellow fever, which was endemic to Cuba. (Mosquitoes carry yellow fever, but in 1898 most people believed the tropical Caribbean climate caused the disease.)

State militia (national guard) units were also called into federal service, and several states—including Alabama, Ohio, Massachusetts, Illinois, Kansas, Virginia, Indiana, and North Carolina—sent all-black militias, as well as white units. But Georgia's governor refused to permit that state's black militia to serve, and New York would not permit black men to enlist in its militia. The states typically followed the federal example and confined black men to all-black units commanded by white officers, but there were exceptions.

15.4.9 Black Officers

The buffalo soldiers of the 9th and 10th Cavalries and the 24th and 25th Infantries remained under white officers. But the men of several volunteer units insisted they be led by black officers: "No officers, no fight." So for the first time in American history, black men commanded all-black units: the 8th Illinois, the 23rd Kansas, and the 3rd North Carolina. Mindful that many people doubted black men's ability to lead, the colonel of the 8th Illinois cautioned his men, "If we fail, the whole race will have to shoulder the burden." The War Department also permitted black men to serve as lieutenants with other black volunteer units; however, all higher-ranking officers were white men. Charles Young, a black graduate of West Point, was given command of Ohio's 9th Battalion. He served with distinction and was promoted to colonel.

As black and white troops assembled in Georgia and Florida, black men soon realized a U.S. uniform did not lessen white prejudice. White civilians in Georgia killed four black men of the 3rd North Carolina. All-white juries acquitted those who were charged with the murders. After the white proprietor of a drug store in Lakeland, Florida, refused to serve a black soldier at the soda fountain, a mob of black troops gathered. The proprietor was pistol whipped, and a stray bullet killed another white man before the troops were disarmed. In Tampa, where the troops were embarking for Cuba, an all-night riot broke out after drunken white soldiers from Ohio used a black child for target practice. Twenty-seven black soldiers and three white soldiers were seriously wounded. When black troops of the 3rd Alabama regiment adopted an injured crow as the unit mascot, they named it Jim.

Most of the black units never saw combat. White military authorities considered black men unreliable and inadequately trained. Black volunteer units stayed behind in Florida when white units embarked for Cuba. However, the buffalo soldiers did go to Cuba, where they performed well despite the doubts and criticism of some white men. The Spanish troops were impressed enough to give the black men the nickname "smoked yankees."

15.4.10 "A Splendid Little War"

In the summer of 1898, U.S. troops arrived in Cuba. Black men of the 10th Cavalry fought alongside Cuban rebels, many of whom were black. Four black American privates earned the Congressional Medal of Honor. Black and white troops were best remembered for their role in the assault on San Juan and Kettle Hills overlooking Santiago in eastern Cuba. Santiago was the main Spanish naval base in Cuba, and its capture would break Spain's hold over the island.

In this assault, black soldiers from the 24th Infantry and the 9th and 10th Cavalries fought alongside white troops including Theodore Roosevelt's volunteer unit, the Rough Riders. In the fiercest fighting of the war, black and white men were thrown together under withering Spanish fire. Although the outcome was in doubt, they took the high ground overlooking Santiago harbor. White soldiers praised the black troops. One commented, "I am not a negro lover. My father fought with Mosby's Rangers [in the Confederate Army] and I was born in the South, but the negroes saved that fight." In his campaign for vice president in 1900, Theodore Roosevelt stated that black men saved his life during the battle. Later, however, he accused black men of cowardice.

AFTER THE WAR As hostilities concluded, men of the 24th Infantry agreed to work in yellow fever hospitals after white regiments refused the duty. Some 471 black soldiers contracted yellow fever. Other black troops arrived in Cuba after the war to serve garrison duty. The 8th Illinois and the 23rd Kansas built roads, bridges, schools, and hospitals. The black men were especially pleased at the absence of Jim Crow in Cuba. Some black soldiers considered organizing emigration to Cuba, but nothing came of it. Still other black troops from the 6th Massachusetts joined in the invasion of Puerto Rico as the United States took that island from Spain.

Voices

Black Men in Battle in Cuba

On October 1, 1898, a letter appeared in the Illinois Record, *a black newspaper, from one of the men in the 10th Cavalry. The author was probably John E. Lewis, and he wrote the letter from Montauk Point on Long Island in New York, where black and white troops were sent after the war. Lewis described the enthusiastic reaction of the Rough Riders to the 9th and 10th Cavalries, but he complained that the black soldiers' contributions were too often ignored.*

The Rough Riders were mustered out on the 12th and 13th [of September], and when Colonel Roosevelt bade the regiment good-bye he paid a glowing tribute to the 9th and 10th Cavalry, especially in saving them from ambush.

Mr. Editor, if your readers could have heard the Rough Riders yell when the 10th Cav. was mentioned as the 'Smoked Yankees' and that they were of a good breed, they would have been doubly proud of the members of their race who rendered such signal service on the battle field. . . .

When a troop of the 10th made their famous charge of 3,000 yards under the command of Capt. [William J.] Beck, the non-commissioned officers, all colored, distinguished themselves in a manner that will redound to the glory of the race. Among those who distinguished themselves are Carter Smith, acting 1st Sergeant, Sgts. Geo. Taylor, James F. Cole, James H. Williams, Smith Johnson and Corpl. Joseph G. Mitchell who was wounded at San Juan.

All are soldiers whose names should go down in history. They never faltered in the thickest of the battle; they encouraged on in a rain of shot and shell and showed by their actions that they were the leaders. They did not hesitate to take the lead, and when that charge was made it was "save your cartridges, don't waste a shot."

The half will never be told of their deeds upon the battlefield. All deserve praise from the private up, but the praise has been given those who should have been in the lead instead of laying in the rear under cover. And yet they say that the black is not fit to lead.

If our war reports would only give credit where credit is due there would be no need writing these poorly composed lines that your readers might know of the deeds and hardships their dear ones have passed through.

You will read that colored troops, or companies did so and so, but the white papers never mention a name and the world only knows one who has done an act of bravery as a Negro soldier, nameless and friendless. It was never mentioned how, at that famous charge of the 10th Cav. and the rescue of the Rough Riders at San Juan Hill, the yell was started by a single trooper of C Troop, 10th Cav. and was carried down the line.

Brave 1st Sgt. Adam Huston at the head of his troop commanded "forward" which seemed into almost certain death. In him the troop found an able leader; Lieut. [E. D.] Anderson who was in command and fell to the rear and when the command "Forward March" was given, the brave Major [Theodore J.] Wint only smiled, for he admired bravery and did not change the command although he knew that the troops was in a desperate position. The troops were carried safely through. . . .

Will it ever be known how Sgt. Thomas Griffith of Troop C cut the wire fence along the line so that the 10th Cav. and Rough Riders could go through?

Never once did these brave men give thought to danger. . . .

The Spaniard would have sent our army home in disgrace had it not been for the daring and almost reckless charge of the Negro regiments. God was with them in that charge and no man who has ever seen the place will say that it was possible to make the charge without being slaughtered. . . .

[Unsigned]

1. Why is the author of this letter bitter?
2. Why did black men fight in the Spanish-American War?
3. Does any of this account seem exaggerated or unreliable? Why or why not?

SOURCE: Courtesy of John E. Lewis, 1898.

THE PHILIPPINE INSURRECTION   With the resounding victory in the war, many Americans decided their nation had an obligation to uplift those less fortunate peoples who had been part of the Spanish empire. Thus, President William McKinley insisted the United States acquire Guam, Puerto Rico, and the Philippines from Spain in the Treaty of Paris that ended the war in December 1898. The Filipinos, like the Cubans, had opposed Spanish rule and expected the American government to support their independence. When they learned that the United States intended to annex the Philippines, the Filipinos, under Emilio Aguinaldo, switched from fighting the Spanish to fighting the occupying U.S. forces.

WOULD BLACK MEN FIGHT BROWN MEN?   Many black and white Americans denounced the effort to take the Philippines. They were unconvinced the Filipinos would benefit from American benevolence. Some wondered how African-American soldiers were helping to lessen racial oppression in the United States by oppressing the Filipinos. AME Bishop Henry Turner termed U.S. intervention in the Philippines an "unholy war of conquest," and Booker T. Washington believed the Filipinos "should be given an opportunity to govern themselves." In a grim attempt to taunt those who proclaimed the superiority of white civilization, a group of black men formed the "Black Man's Burden Association."

Nonetheless, black soldiers served throughout the campaign in the Pacific islands. The black troops included the regular 25th and 24th Infantries, the 9th Cavalry, and the 48th and 49th Volunteer Regiments. The Filipino rebels attempted to convince black troops to abandon the cause. Posters reminded "The Colored American Soldier" of injustice and lynching in the United States. White troops did not help by calling Filipinos "niggers." Although many black soldiers had reservations about the fighting, they remained loyal. By the time the conflict subsided and the Americans declared victory in 1902, only five black men had deserted. David Fagen of the 24th Infantry joined Filipino forces and became an officer, fighting American troops for two years before he was killed. Two black men from the 9th Cavalry were executed for desertion. Fifteen white deserters had their death sentences commuted.

Although black men had served with distinction as professional soldiers for 40 years after the Civil War—on the frontier, in Cuba, and in the Philippines—the army little valued their achievements and sacrifice, as the Brownsville affair showed. White military and political leaders relied on passions and prejudices over evidence of achievement. These circumstances dashed the hopes of those black civilians and soldiers who believed the performance of black troops would demonstrate that black citizens had earned the same rights as other Americans.

15.5 African Americans and Their Role in the American Economy

Describe the opportunities that both existed and were denied to African Americans in business, professions, entertainment, and athletics.

As the nineteenth century ended, the American people had become enthralled by their country's scientific, industrial, and agricultural progress. Their enthusiasm for these achievements was exemplified by the fairs and expositions held around the country between 1876 and 1916. Municipal leaders in Philadelphia, New Orleans, Atlanta, Nashville, Buffalo, and St. Louis, among others, were eager to capitalize on the curiosity of thousands of people who would visit these fairs and leave millions of dollars behind to enrich local businesses.

15.5.1 African Americans and the World's Columbian Exposition

There is no better example of this mania for fairs than the World's Columbian Exposition held in Chicago in 1893 to commemorate the 400th anniversary of Christopher Columbus's first voyage to America. The Chicago fair was spectacular. Located on 600 acres on the city's south side, it featured 200 buildings and exhibits from 46 nations. At the center was the White City, a group of white buildings that were illuminated at night by electric lights. The fair's featured attraction was a huge 264-foot-high steel wheel designed by George Ferris that could carry 2,160 riders in its 36 passenger cars. The fair drew 27 million visitors between May and October 1893.

In promoting the technological progress of the American people, visitors enjoyed comparing their society to the other nations that had exhibits. The Dahomey village and its 69 Fon people was perhaps the most sensational and controversial among the fair's black and white visitors. One journalist captured the reaction of many white people to these Africans from a French colony when he wrote, "Sixty-nine of them are here in all their barbaric ugliness." Some African Americans were plainly embarrassed by what they considered a display of primitive culture. However, African Americans who visited the exposition found little overt discrimination or segregation as they took in the exhibits and attractions and dined in the restaurants.

Three black colleges created exhibits that were intended to depict the advances African Americans had achieved since the end of slavery. Wilberforce College won a Columbian Medal and Diploma for its display of academic work by its students that included examples of math, logic, and rhetoric as well as needlecraft and woodwork. The Atlanta University exhibit had photos of the campus with students engaged in nursing, home economics, and crafts. Hampton Institute's display featured dressmaking, tailoring, and woodwork. The Atlanta University representative at the fair proudly proclaimed that his institution's 300 feet of exhibition floor space showed "better than any others, what is being done for the race and what the race is doing for itself."

Colored American Day at the fair was held on August 25, 1893. Some African Americans, including Ida B. Wells, resented having a separate day for black people, and she criticized Frederick Douglass for agreeing to speak at that day's festivities. But the 75-year-old Douglass delivered a blunt address about race in America. He denounced Americans' commitment to white supremacy and their unjust treatment of people of color: "Men talk of the Negro problem. There is no Negro problem. The problem is whether the American people have honesty enough, loyalty enough, honor enough, patriotism enough to live up to their own Constitution."

15.5.2 Obstacles and Opportunities for Employment among African Americans

During planning for the Chicago fair, African Americans, including Ida B. Wells, complained that black people had been excluded on the committees that organized the exposition. But white people rarely elevated African Americans to positions of authority. Well-educated black men and women stood no chance of gaining employment with any major business or industrial corporation in the 1890s. White males not only monopolized management and supervisory positions, but also took nearly every job that did not involve manual labor. In 1899 black novelist Sutton E. Griggs described the frustrations that an educated black man encountered:

> He possessed a first class college education, but that was all. He knew no trade nor was he equipped to enter any of the professions. . . . He would have made an excellent drummer, [salesman] clerk, cashier, government official (county, city, state, or national), telegraph operator, conductor, or anything of such a nature. But the color of his skin shut the doors so tight that he could not even peep in. . . . It is true that such positions as street laborer, hod carrier, cart driver, factory hand, railroad hand were open to him; but such menial tasks were uncongenial to a man of his education and polish.

Although white supremacy and Jim Crow restricted opportunities for educated black people, those same limitations enabled enterprising black men and women to open and operate businesses that served black clientele. By the early twentieth century, black Americans had established banks, newspapers, insurance companies, retail businesses, barbershops, beauty salons, and funeral parlors. Virtually every black community had its own small businesses, markets, street vendors, and other entrepreneurs.

Some black men and women established substantial businesses. In Atlanta, Union Army veteran Alexander Hamilton was a successful building contractor. He supervised construction of the Good Samaritan Building, oversaw the erection of buildings on the Morris Brown College campus, and built many impressive houses on Peachtree Street. Hamilton employed both black and white workmen.

Alonzo Herndon was a former slave who also thrived in Atlanta. His fashionable barbershop on Peachtree Street served well-to-do white men. The shop had crystal chandeliers and polished brass spittoons. Herndon opened two other shops, eventually employing 75 men. He also founded the Atlanta Life Insurance Company, the largest black stock company in the world.

In Montgomery, Alabama, H. A. Loveless, a former slave, became a butcher and then diversified by opening an undertaking establishment and a hack and dray company. By 1900, he also ran a coal and wood yard and sold real estate.

In Richmond, Maggie Lena Walker—the secretary-treasurer of the Independent Order of St. Luke, a mutual benefit society, and a founder of the St. Luke's Penny Savings Bank—became the wealthiest black woman in America. Also in Richmond, former slave John Dabney owned a catering business that served wealthy white Virginians. He catered two state dinners for President Grover Cleveland. He purchased houses and invested in real estate.

Madam C. J. Walker may have been the most successful black entrepreneur of them all. Born Sarah Breedlove in 1867 on a Louisiana cotton plantation, she married at age 14 and was a widowed single parent by age 20. She spent the next two decades struggling to make ends meet. In 1905 with $1.50, she developed a formula to nourish and enrich the hair of black women.

The business rapidly became a thriving enterprise that employed hundreds of black women. She established the company's headquarters in Indianapolis. In the meantime, she married Charles Joseph Walker and took his name and the title Madam. As she accumulated wealth, she shared it generously with Bethune Cookman College and Tuskegee Institute. She was a major contributor to the NAACP's antilynching campaign. When she died at age 51 in 1919, she was reportedly a millionaire.

Despite such successes, most black people who went into business had difficulty surviving. Too often they depended on black customers who were themselves poor. White-owned banks were unlikely to provide credit to black business people. And even the wealthiest black entrepreneurs did not come close to possessing the wealth the richest white Americans accumulated.

15.5.3 African Americans and Labor

Thousands of black southerners worked in factories, mills, and mines. Although most textile mills refused to hire black people except as janitors, many black laborers toiled in tobacco and cigar-making facilities, flour mills, coal mines, sawmills, and turpentine camps, and on railroads. Black women worked for white families as servants. Black workers usually were paid less than white men employed in the same capacity. Conversely, white working people frequently complained they were not hired because employers retained black workers who worked for less pay. In 1904 in Georgia, white railroad firemen struck in an attempt to compel management to dismiss black firemen. Antagonism between black and white laborers was chronic.

In less than two decades in the early twentieth century, Sarah Breedlove rose from abject poverty to become extraordinarily wealthy as Madam C. J. Walker.

UNIONS   When white workers formed labor unions, they usually excluded black workers. The Knights of Labor, however, founded in 1869, was open to all workers (except whiskey salesmen, lawyers, and bankers), and by the mid-1880s counted 50,000 women and 70,000 black workers among its nearly 750,000 members. But by the 1890s, after unsuccessful strikes and a deadly riot in Chicago, the Knights had lost influence to a new organization, the American Federation of Labor (AFL). Founded in 1886, the AFL was ostensibly open to all skilled workers, but most of its local craft unions barred women and black tradesmen. In contrast, the United Mine Workers (UMW), formed in 1890, encouraged black coal miners to join the union rather than serve as strikebreakers. By 1900 approximately 20,000 of the 91,000 members of the UMW were black men. The Industrial Workers of the World, a revolutionary labor organization founded in 1905, brought black and white laborers together in, among other places, the Brotherhood of Timber Workers in the Piney Woods of east Texas.

In 1869 a Baltimore ship caulker, Isaac Myers, organized the National Colored Labor Union, which lasted for seven years. It discouraged strikes and encouraged its members to work hard and be thrifty. However, it lost whatever effectiveness it had when Republican leaders took it over during Reconstruction.

STRIKES   During the late nineteenth and early twentieth centuries, most strikes failed because business owners could rely on strikebreakers and the police or national guard to bring the strikes to an often violent end. For a time, black shipyard workers in southern ports achieved success. Black stevedores who loaded and unloaded ships endured oppressive conditions and long hours for low pay. They periodically went on strike in Charleston, Savannah, and New Orleans. The Longshoremen's Protective Union in Charleston won several strikes in the 1870s. In Nashville in 1871 black dockyard workers went on strike, demanding 20 cents an hour. Steamboat owners broke the strike by hiring state convicts for 15 cents an hour.

Black and white laborers who toiled in the Louisiana sugarcane fields earned an average of $13 a week in the 1880s. They were paid in scrip—not cash—that was redeemable only in stores the planters owned, where prices were exorbitant. Workers lived in 12-by-15-foot cabins that they rented from the planters. In some ways, it was worse than slave labor.

Although the state militia had broken previous strikes, 9,000 black and 1,000 white workers responded in 1887 to a call by the Knights of Labor for a new strike. They quit the sugar fields in four parishes (as Louisiana counties are called) to demand more pay. The strike was peaceful, but the governor sent in the militia. The troops fired into a crowd at Pattersonville and killed four people. Local officials killed several strikers who had been taken prisoner. In Thibodaux, "prominent citizens" organized and armed themselves and had martial law declared. More than 35 unarmed black people, including women and children, were killed in their homes and churches. Two black strike leaders were lynched. The strike was broken.

Black washerwomen went on strike in Atlanta in 1881. The women, who washed laundry by hand for white families, refused to do any more until they were guaranteed $1 per 12 pounds of laundry. The strike was well organized through black churches, and it spread to cooks and domestics. A strike committee used persuasion and intimidation to ensure support. Some 3,000 black people joined the strike, and white families went two weeks without clean clothes. However, Atlanta's white community broke the strike. Police arrested strike leaders for disorderly conduct. Black women were fined from $5 to $20. The city council threatened to require each washerwoman to purchase a $25 business license. Although the strike ended without achieving its goal, it demonstrated that poor black women could organize effectively.

15.5.4 Black Professionals

Like business and labor, the medical and legal professions were strictly segregated. Most black physicians, nurses, and lawyers attended all-black professional schools in the late nineteenth century. Black people in need of medical care were either excluded from white hospitals or confined to all-black wards. Since black physicians were denied staff privileges at white hospitals, black people often formed their own hospitals. Most were small with 50 or fewer beds.

MEDICINE In 1891 Dr. Daniel Hale Williams established Provident Hospital and Training Institute in Chicago, the first black hospital operated solely by African Americans. In 1894 the Freedmen's Hospital was organized in Washington, D.C., and later affiliated with Howard University. Frederick Douglass Memorial Hospital and Training School was founded in Philadelphia in 1895. Dr. Alonzo McClennan and other black physicians established the Hospital and Training School for Nurses in Charleston, South Carolina, in 1897.

In 1900 Williams explained why black medical institutions were necessary:

> In view of this cruel ostracism, affecting so vitally the race, our duty seems plain. Institute Hospitals and Training Schools. Let us no longer sit idly and inanely deploring existing conditions. Let us not waste time trying to effect changes or modifications in the institutions unfriendly to us, but rather let us seek to promote the doctrine of helping and stimulating our race.

By 1890, 909 black (most of whom were male) physicians were practicing in the United States. They served a black population of 7.5 million people. Barred from

Profile

Maggie Lena Walker

Maggie Mitchell graduated from a normal school in 1883 and taught primary school. She was a lifelong member of the First African Baptist Church. In 1886 she married Armstead Walker. Her views on marriage were progressive: "Since marriage is an equal partnership, I believe that the woman and the man are equal in power and should by consultation and agreement, mutually decide as to the conduct of the home and the government of the children."

The Independent Order of St. Luke was one of many black mutual aid societies that flourished in the nineteenth century. Black people contributed small sums, and the Order paid benefits either to members who became sick or to their survivors. But the Order was also a fraternal and social organization that stressed racial pride as well as compassion, generosity, and charity.

Maggie Lena Walker became active in the Order at age 14 in 1881. She was elected Grand Matron and became the Right Worthy Grand Secretary in 1899. When she assumed her duties, the Order had $31.61 and 1,080 members. She was a dynamic leader and an inspirational speaker. She traveled extensively and spoke to members. She stressed racial concerns and attacked discrimination and lynching. She appealed to audiences to patronize black enterprises. By the early twentieth century, under Walker's guidance, the Order operated in 22 states. Its membership had increased, and its financial standing had improved. In 1924 its funds totaled $3,480,540.

The Order ran a newspaper, the *St. Luke Herald*, and a bank with Walker as president. She was the first black woman to serve as the chief executive of a bank in the United States. The bank subsequently merged with two other banks and became the Consolidated Bank and Trust Company, with Walker as president. She was especially pleased that the bank enabled black customers to purchase homes. By 1920, 645 black families had acquired their houses with the bank's assistance.

Walker was concerned with the plight of black women and made certain that the Order employed black women in significant positions. In 1909 she paid homage to women of color:

> And the great all absorbing interest, this thing which has driven sleep from my eyes and fatigue from my body, is the love I bear women, our Negro women, hemmed, circumscribed, with every imaginable obstacle in our way, blocked and held down by the fears and prejudices of the whites, ridiculed and sneered at by the intelligent blacks.

Walker became wealthy and lived in a 22-room house. She was involved in community affairs and organizations. She supported Virginia Union University and the Industrial School for Colored Girls. She worked with the Piedmont Tuberculosis

By the early twentieth century, Maggie Lena Walker was a successful businesswoman, community leader, and one of the wealthiest black women in America. She was also an ardent advocate for her race and her gender. She was born Maggie Mitchell in Richmond on July 15, 1867, to Elizabeth Draper, a laundress. Her mother married William Mitchell in 1870. Young Maggie was greatly influenced by the determination, fortitude, and hard work of her mother. Throughout her childhood, she helped her mother wash, iron, and carry laundry.

Sanitarium for Negroes, served on Richmond's Council for Colored Women and with the Virginia Federation of Colored Women's Clubs, and was among the prominent women who helped organize the Council of Women of the Darker Races. She joined the National Association of Colored Women in 1912 and was active in the NAACP. She was also a committed Republican and ran unsuccessfully for state superintendent of public instruction. She died on December 15, 1934.

membership in the American Medical Association, black doctors organized the National Medical Association in Atlanta in 1895. Most black doctors had been educated at seven black medical schools that included Leonard Medical School at Shaw University in Raleigh, Flint-Goodridge Medical College in New Orleans, Meharry Medical School in Nashville, and the Howard University School of Medicine in Washington, D.C.

In 1910, in a report issued by the Carnegie Foundation for the Advancement of Teaching, Abraham Flexner recommended improving medical education in the United States by eliminating weaker medical schools. He suggested raising admission standards and expanding laboratory and clinical training in the stronger schools. As a result of these recommendations, 60 of 155 white medical schools closed; among black medical schools, only Howard and Meharry survived. By 1920 there were 3,885 black physicians. Many had completed medical school before the Flexner report was compiled.

The number of black women physicians was declining. In 1890, 90 black women were practicing medicine. By 1920 only 65 were. There were fewer medical schools, and most black and white men considered medicine an inappropriate profession for women. But black women also had to contend with the opposition of white women. Isabella Vandervall was a graduate of New York Medical College and Hospital who was accepted for an internship at the Hospital for Women and Children in Syracuse. When she appeared in person, however, the hospital's female administrator rejected Vandervall, declaring, "We can't have you here! You are colored!"

Nursing was different. By 1920 there were 36 black nurse training schools and 2,150 white nursing schools. White nurses resented the competition from black nurses for positions as private duty nurses. In addition, the black physicians who ran nurse training schools exploited their students by hiring them out, as part of their training, for private duty work but requiring them to relinquish their pay to the schools. Moreover, many people—black and white—regarded black nurses more as domestics than as trained professionals. To confront such obstacles, 52 black nurses met in New York City in 1908 and formed the National Association of Colored Graduate Nurses (NACGN). By 1920 the NACGN had 500 members.

Black physicians and nurses struggled to provide medical care to people who were often desperately ill and sought treatment only as a last resort. Disease and sickness flourished among people who were ill nourished, poorly clad, and inadequately housed. Tuberculosis, pneumonia, pellagra, hookworm, and syphilis afflicted many poor black people—as they also did poor white people. Bessie Hawes, a 1918 graduate of Tuskegee Institute's Nurse Training program, described the situation she faced in rural Alabama:

> A colored family of ten were in bed and dying for the want of attention. No one would come near. I was glad of the opportunity. As I entered the little country cabin, I found the mother in bed. Three children were buried the week before. The father and the remainder of the family were running a temperature of 102–104. Some had influenza, others had pneumonia. No relatives or friends would come near. I saw at a glance I had work to do. I rolled up my sleeves and killed chickens and began to cook. . . . I milked the cow, gave medicine, and did everything I could to help conditions. I worked day and night trying to save them for seven days. I had no place to sleep. In the meantime the oldest daughter had a miscarriage and I delivered her without the aid of any physicians. . . . I only wished that I could have reached them earlier and been able to have done something for the poor mother.

THE LAW Unlike black physicians and nurses, who were excluded from white hospitals, black lawyers were permitted to practice in what was essentially a white male court system. But white judges and attorneys did not welcome them. Black defendants and plaintiffs often retained white lawyers in the hope that white legal counsel might improve their chances of receiving justice. As a result, many black attorneys had a hard time making a living from the practice of law.

The American Bar Association (ABA) would not admit black attorneys to membership. William H. Lewis, a graduate of Amherst College and the Harvard Law School who was appointed an assistant U.S. attorney general by President William Howard Taft in 1911, was expelled by the ABA in 1912 when its leaders discovered he was black. They defended his expulsion by claiming the association was mainly a social organization. In 1925 black lawyers—led by Howard Law School graduate George H. Woodson—organized the National Bar Association.

Few black women were lawyers. Charlotte Ray was the first (see Chapter 12). In 1900 there were 10 black women practicing law compared to over 700 black men and 112,000 white men. Lutie A. Lytle, who graduated from Central Tennessee Law School in 1897, returned to her alma mater and became the first black woman law professor in the United States.

15.5.5 Music

In the half century after the Civil War, music created and performed by black people evolved into the uniquely American art forms of ragtime, jazz, blues, and gospel. The roots of these extraordinary musical innovations are difficult to pin down precisely. Some late nineteenth-century music can be traced to African styles and rhythms. Other sources are slave work songs and spirituals. There were also European musical influences.

Traveling groups of black men, some of them ex-slaves, put on minstrel shows that featured "coon songs" after the Civil War. Many black Americans resented these popular shows as caricatures and exaggerations of black behavior. At least 600 "coon songs" that attracted a predominantly white audience were published by 1900, including "All Coons Look Alike to Me," "Mammy's Little Pickaninny," and "My Coal Black Lady."

Lutie A. Lytle graduated from the Central Tennessee College of Law and passed the bar examination. She became a member of the faculty at the same institution, and thus was the first African-American woman to become a professor of law in an American law school.

Profile

A Man and His Horse: Dr. William Key and Beautiful Jim Key

More than five million people visited the 1904 St. Louis World's Fair. Perhaps the most popular attraction was a horse, Beautiful Jim Key, and his African-American owner, Dr. William Key.

On the fair's opening day, President Theodore Roosevelt's feisty 20-year-old daughter Alice, accompanied by Congressman Nicholas Longworth, went to see the horse that had captured the hearts and minds of hundreds of thousands of Americans over the previous seven years. Using his mouth, Beautiful Jim Key plucked the correct letters from a metal frame that contained the alphabet and arranged them to spell "Alice Roosevelt." Then, prompted by a member of the audience, the horse added "Longworth" to Roosevelt's name. It was prophetic. Two years later the Republican congressman married the president's daughter, and she became Alice Roosevelt Longworth.

William Key was born a slave in Winchester, Tennessee, in 1833, the son of a slave woman who had Cherokee ancestry and a white man. From childhood, Key demonstrated an ability to work with and care for animals. He became a self-taught veterinarian whom local black and white people called "Dr. Key."

He also learned the art of diplomacy. During the Civil War he simultaneously helped slaves escape while protecting his owner's two sons who went off to fight for the Confederacy. For these latter efforts, he was arrested by Union officials and threatened with hanging.

Following the war and emancipation, Key acquired enough wealth as a veterinarian to purchase land near Shelbyville, Tennessee. A shrewd businessman and gambler, he sold patent medicine—Keystone Liniment—and regularly won at poker. Dr. Key also purchased an Arabian horse that had been relegated to circus acts in Mississippi. He bred the neglected and weary mare, and she produced a sickly, scrawny colt in 1889 that he named Beautiful Jim Key. Through years of kind training, Key transformed this unimpressive horse into a splendid, talented animal.

The veterinarian had an uncanny capacity to communicate with Beautiful Jim Key, sometimes through indecipherable Cherokee and African words. The horse could add, subtract, multiply, and divide numbers that totaled less than 30. In one show he was asked to multiply four times five, then add five, and subtract three. He promptly plucked the card with 22 from the rack, causing one journalist to wonder, "What will he learn next, square roots?" The brainy horse learned the alphabet and how to read basic names and words. Asked by audience members, he spelled such words as "physics," "constitution," and "Pennsylvania." He could make change by selecting the correct coins out of a specially built National Cash Register.

In 1897 a white entrepreneur and showman from Cincinnati, Albert Rogers, persuaded Dr. Key to collaborate with him, and Rogers managed and promoted the black veterinarian and his horse for the next decade. Key and Rogers stressed the kind and gentle treatment of animals before virtually every audience. (Key never used a whip.) Beautiful Jim Key was eventually inducted into honorary membership in the American Humane Association, its only nonhuman member.

But Beautiful Jim Key's intelligence and knowledge attracted the crowds. In 1897 President William McKinley visited the Nashville World's Fair and sat amazed in the Negro Building as Beautiful Jim Key selected the names of cabinet members from a rack as they were read to him.

With the emergence of Jim Crow, Dr. Key and his horse performed before segregated audiences across the South. When William Key would hold special shows "open to all," the audience was invariably all black.

There were those who doubted the intelligence of Beautiful Jim Key. Some thought the doctor had devised secret means of communicating answers to the horse. In 1901 a group of Harvard professors scrutinized Beautiful Jim Key. After witnessing two performances, the scholars declared that no trickery was involved. Dr. Key had simply educated an intelligent animal.

The man and his horse finally retired to the Key estate near Shelbyville. William Key died at age 76 in 1909. His magnificent horse died at age 23 in 1912.

Most black people had other forms of musical entertainment. "The Civil Rights Juba," published in 1874, was a precursor to ragtime. In 1871 the Fisk University Jubilee Singers began the first of many fundraising concert tours that entertained black and white audiences in the United States and Europe for years thereafter with slave songs and spirituals. Other black colleges and universities sent choirs and singers on similar trips.

RAGTIME   Ragtime, which emerged in the 1890s, was composed music, written down for performance on the piano. Ragtime pieces were not accompanied by lyrics and not meant to be sung. The creative genius of ragtime, Scott Joplin, was born in Texarkana, Texas, in 1868. He learned to play on a piano his mother bought from her earnings as a maid, and he may have had training in classical music. Joplin learned to transfer complex banjo syncopations to the piano as he fused European harmonies and African rhythms. He played at the World's Columbian Exposition in Chicago in 1893 and soon wrote ragtime sheet music that sold well. In 1899 he composed his best-known tune, the "Maple Leaf Rag," named after a social club (brothel) in Sedalia, Missouri. It sold an astonishing one million copies.

JAZZ   Jazz gradually replaced ragtime in popularity in the early twentieth century. Unlike ragtime, jazz was mostly improvised, not composed, and it was not confined to the piano. Jazz incorporated African and European musical elements drawn from such diverse sources as plantation bands, minstrel shows, riverboat ensembles, and Irish and Scottish folk tunes. The first jazz bands emerged around New Orleans where they played at parades, funerals, clubs, and outdoor concerts. Instead of the banjos, pipes, fifes, and violins of earlier black musical groups, these bands relied more on brass, reeds, and drums.

Ferdinand J. La Menthe, regarded as the first prominent jazz musician, was born in 1890 and grew up in a French-speaking family in New Orleans. Young La Menthe played several musical instruments before settling on the piano. He was also a superb composer and arranger. Later he changed his name to Morton and came to be known as Jelly Roll Morton. He played in the "red light" district of New Orleans known as Storyville, where he was also a pool shark and gambler. He moved to Los Angeles in 1917 and to Chicago in 1922, where he led and recorded with "Morton's Red Hot Peppers." He died in 1941.

THE BLUES   In rural, isolated areas of the South, poor black people composed and sang songs about their lives and experiences. W. C. Handy, the father of the blues, later recalled, "Southern Negroes sang about everything. Trains, steamboats, steam whistles, sledge hammers, fast women, mean bosses, stubborn mules." They accompanied themselves on anything from a guitar to a harmonica to a washboard. They played in juke joints (rural nightclubs), at picnics, in lumber camps, and in urban nightclubs.

Handy, who was born in Florence, Alabama, in 1873, took up music despite the opposition of his devoutly Christian parents. He learned to play the guitar, although his mother and father regarded it as the "devil's plaything." He later led his own nine-man band. In the Mississippi delta in 1903, Handy encountered "primitive," or "boogie," music unlike anything he had heard before. Handy was not initially impressed by the mostly unskilled and itinerant musicians whose lives swirled around cheap whiskey, gambling, prostitution, and violence: "Then I saw the beauty of primitive music. They had the stuff people wanted. It touched the spot. Their music wanted polishing, but it contained the essence. People would pay money for it." Handy composed many tunes, including "Memphis Blues" and "St. Louis Blues."

Handy was not the only musician to "discover" the blues. Gertrude Pridget sang in southern minstrel shows. In 1902 she heard a young black woman in Missouri sing about a lover who had left her. Pridget included the song in her shows. In 1904 she married William "Pa" Rainey and became "Ma" Rainey. She created other "blues" songs based on ballads, hymns, and the experiences of black people. As "Mother of the Blues," Rainey recorded extensively in the 1920s and 1930s.

GOSPEL   What came to be known as gospel music emerged at about the same time as ragtime and the blues in the late nineteenth century. The roots of gospel were embedded in spirituals and slave work songs. But gospel singers usually infused their music and songs with greater rhythm, harmony, and repetition than the spirituals. First performed in Pentecostal, Holiness, and Sanctified churches, gospel singers moved, danced, clapped their hands, and stomped their feet. Often they were accompanied by musical instruments such as the guitar and tambourine.

Mainline congregations, especially Baptists and Methodists, were offended by the "carrying-on" and un-Christian-like behavior of gospel performances, regarding it—like the blues—as "devil's music." But it was a black Methodist Episcopal minister

Scott Joplin (1868–1917) was one of America's most prolific composers, and his name is indelibly linked with ragtime. Although ragtime's popularity faded by the 1920s, Joplin's reputation and compositions were resurrected in 1974 when the Hollywood film *The Sting* relied on Joplin's 1902 rag "The Entertainer" for its soundtrack. In 1976 Scott Joplin was posthumously awarded the Pulitzer Prize for music.

in Philadelphia, Charles Albert Tindley, who wrote and popularized early gospel songs including "Stand By Me," "(Take Your Burden to the Lord) Leave it There," and "I'll Overcome Someday" that was later transformed into the anthem of the civil rights movement, "We Shall Overcome."

With the migration of thousands of rural black Southerners to Northern cities, gospel came to be identified with the urban experience. Vinyl recordings and establishment of black radio stations in the 1920s and 1930s expanded the audience for gospel music and groups. In 1930 the National Baptist Convention finally agreed to recognize gospel music as it continued to grow and expand.

By the 1920s three distinctive yet similar forms of American music were developing—jazz, blues, and gospel. They drew on African and American musical elements and European musical traditions. But most of all, jazz, blues, and gospel represented the experiences of African Americans and the creativity of the musicians who developed and performed the music.

15.5.6 Sports

While talented black musicians were making dramatic innovations, black athletes found that white athletes and sports entrepreneurs increasingly opposed the presence of black men in the boxing ring and on the playing field.

BOXING AND JACK JOHNSON   Black boxers regularly fought white boxers through the end of the nineteenth century, but this offended many white people—especially southerners. In 1892 George Dixon, a black boxer, won the world featherweight title, and some white men cheered his victory, distressing a Chicago journalist: "It was not pleasant to see white men applaud a negro for knocking another white man out. It was not pleasant to see them crowding around 'Mr.' Dixon to congratulate him on his victory, to seek an introduction with 'the distinguished colored gentleman' while he puffed his cigar and lay back like a prince receiving his subjects." Despite such opinions, there was never any official prohibition of interracial bouts.

The success of another black boxer, heavyweight Jack Johnson, angered many white Americans. Johnson was born in Galveston, Texas, in 1878. Between 1902 and 1907 he won 57 bouts against black and white fighters. In 1908 he beat the white heavyweight champion, Tommy Burns, in Australia. Many white fans were unwilling to accept Johnson as the champion and looked desperately for "a great white hope" who could defeat him. Jim Jeffries, a former champion, came out of retirement to take on Johnson. In a brutal fight in Reno, Nevada, in 1910, Johnson knocked out Jeffries in the 15th round.

Johnson's personal life, as well as his prowess in the ring, provoked white animosity. Having divorced his black wife, he married a white woman in 1911. Several months later, overwhelmed by social ostracism, she committed suicide. After Johnson married a second white woman, he was convicted of violating the Mann Act, which made it illegal to transport a woman across state lines for immoral purposes. The "immorality" was Johnson's marriage to a white woman. Sentenced to a year in prison and fined $1,000, Johnson fled to Canada and then to France to avoid punishment. He lost his title to Jesse Willard in 1915 in Havana in the 26th round in a fight many people believe that Johnson threw. He returned to the United States in 1920 and served 10 months in Leavenworth Prison.

Jack Johnson spars with Marty Cutler in the early twentieth century. Johnson was a superb fighter whose ability to defeat white boxers rankled many white men. But Johnson's involvement with white women infuriated them even more and led to his imprisonment.

BASEBALL   Baseball became popular after the Civil War. As professional baseball developed in the 1870s and 1880s, both black and white men competed to earn money playing the game. It was not easy. They were the nation's first professional athletes, but professional baseball was unstable. Teams were formed and dissolved with depressing regularity. Players moved from team to team. Some 30 black men played professional baseball in the quarter century after the Civil War.

Led by A. C. "Cap" Anson of the Chicago White Stockings, white players tried to get club owners to stop signing black men to contracts. Anson, who was from Iowa, resented having to play against black men. In 1887 International League officials rescinded a rule that had permitted them to sign black players. One black player, Weldy Wilberforce Walker, protested the exclusion in a letter to *Sporting Life*: "There should be some broader cause—such as lack of ability, behavior, and intelligence—for barring a player, rather than his color. It is for these reasons and because I think ability and intelligence should be recognized first and last—at all times and by everyone—I ask the question again, 'Why was the law permitting colored men to sign repealed, etc.?' " There was no intelligent answer to Walker's question. But Jim Crow was now on the baseball diamond. Moses Fleetwood Walker—Weldy's brother—was the last black man to play major league baseball with white men until Jackie Robinson joined the Brooklyn Dodgers in 1947.

In reaction to their exclusion, black men formed their own teams. By 1900 there were five black professional teams including the Norfolk Red Stockings, the Chicago Unions, and the Cuban X Giants of New York. The Negro Leagues would be an integral (but not integrated) part of sports for the next half century.

BASKETBALL AND BICYCLING   James Naismith invented basketball in 1891 in Springfield, Massachusetts. Black youngsters were playing organized basketball by 1906 in the YMCA in New York City and later in YMCAs in Philadelphia and Washington, D.C. By 1910–1911 Howard University and Hampton Institute had basketball teams. Bicycling and bicycle racing were enormously popular by the 1890s, and in 1899 a black rider, Marshall W. "Major" Taylor, won the world championship.

HORSE RACING   From its beginnings in colonial America into the early decades of the twentieth century, African American men were an integral part of horse racing. Long before boxing, baseball, and basketball attracted attention, horse racing—and the gambling associated with it—was the sport of choice of many Americans. Thoroughbred race horses were a topic of conversation, a source of entertainment, and a sign of status among well-to-do white men.

Yet before the Civil War it was an elite group of black men—most of them slaves—who groomed, trained, and rode the valuable animals. Black men developed a keen and close understanding of the often temperamental race horses. It was ironic that the white men who owned both the horses and the slaves came to depend on the advice and knowledge of the experienced and skilled black horse men when it came to evaluating and preparing the horses for competition.

Following the Civil War horse racing expanded as a profitable and popular enterprise that attracted wealthy businessmen and bankers. Black men—now free—remained a constant presence at race tracks from Saratoga to Churchill Downs. The first Kentucky Derby in 1875 was won by *Aristides* ridden by a black jockey, Oliver Lewis, and trained by a black man, Ansel Williamson. No fewer than 12 jockeys in that first Derby were African Americans.

Perhaps the greatest jockey of that era was Isaac Murphy, who won the Kentucky Derby three times. But as Jim Crow pervaded American society by the early twentieth century, it also infected horse racing. Black jockey Jimmy Winkfield won the Kentucky Derby in 1901 and 1902. But black men were steadily eased out of thoroughbred racing. Winkfield moved to Europe and rode horses at tracks in Russia and France. Between 1921 and 2000 no black jockey rode in the Kentucky Derby. As of 2015, 5 percent of the jockeys in the United States are African Americans.

Isaac Murphy became one of the finest jockeys in the history of horse racing. Born a slave in Lexington, Kentucky in 1861, he rode in at least 1538 races and won a phenomenal 530 of them. That winning percentage of nearly 35% has never been surpassed. Murphy died in Lexington in 1896. He was inducted into the Horse Racing Hall of Fame in 1955.

COLLEGE ATHLETICS Generally, white colleges and universities in the North that admitted black students would not let them participate in intercollegiate sports. (Southern colleges and universities did not admit black students.) There were, however, exceptions. In 1889, W. T. S. Jackson and William Henry Lewis played football for Amherst College. Lewis was the captain of the team in 1890. As a law school student, Lewis played for Harvard and was named to the Walter Camp All-American team in 1892. (Lewis was later forced out of the American Bar Association because of his color. See the section "The Law" in this chapter.) White institutions with black players often encountered rampant racism. In 1907 the University of Alabama baseball team canceled a game with the University of Vermont because the Vermont squad had two black infielders. Moreover, opposing teams and their fans frequently abused black players.

White colleges and universities occasionally played black institutions. The Yale Law School baseball team, for example, played Howard in 1898. But black college teams were far more likely to play each other. The first football game between two black colleges took place on December 27, 1892, when Biddle University (today Johnson C. Smith University) defeated Livingston College in Salisbury, North Carolina.

Eventually black athletic conferences were formed. The Central Intercollegiate Athletic Association was organized in 1912 with Hampton, Howard, Virginia Union, and Shaw College in Raleigh among its early members. The Southeastern Conference was established in 1913 and consisted of Morehouse, Fisk, Florida A&M, and Tuskegee, among others. It would become the Southern Intercollegiate Athletic Conference (SIAC). In Texas in 1920, five black colleges founded the Southwestern Athletic Conference: Prairie View A&M, Bishop College, Paul Quinn College, Wiley College, and Sam Houston College.

Conclusion

White supremacy was debilitating, discouraging, and dangerous, but black Americans could sometimes turn Jim Crow to their advantage. To combat white racism and improve the economic status of black people, educators like Samuel Chapman Armstrong and Booker T. Washington recommended agricultural and mechanical training for black Americans. But critics such as W. E. B. Du Bois stressed the need to cultivate the minds as well as the hands of black people to develop leaders.

Black men served with distinction in all-black military units in the Indian wars, the Spanish-American War, and the Philippine Insurrection. But no matter how loyal or committed black soldiers were, the white majority never fully trusted or displayed confidence in them. African Americans could only react with outrage when President Theodore Roosevelt dismissed 167 black soldiers in 1906 in the Brownsville affair.

As they tried to shape their own destinies in the late nineteenth century, black Americans organized a variety of institutions. Mostly barred from white schools, churches, hospitals, labor unions, and places of entertainment, they developed businesses and facilities to serve their communities in an environment mostly free from white interference. Black people relied on their own experiences and imaginations to create new music. They occasionally participated in sports with white athletes but more often played separately from them as segregation and white hostility spread.

Although black people recognized their churches, hospitals, schools, and businesses were often inadequately financed and usually less imposing than those of white people, they also knew that at a black school or church, in a black store, or in the care of a black physician or nurse, they would not be abused, mistreated, or ridiculed because of their color.

Chapter Timeline

AFRICAN-AMERICAN EVENTS

NATIONAL EVENTS

1860–1870

1867

Independent Order of St. Luke founded in Baltimore

1868

Hampton Institute founded

1869–1898

Four regiments of black soldiers serve on the western frontier

1862

Morrill Land-Grant Act is passed to support agricultural and mechanical education

1867

United States purchases Alaska from Russia

1869

Cincinnati "Red Stockings" organized as the first professional baseball team

Rutgers and Princeton play the first college football game

1870–1880

1870

Howard University Law School established

1875

Black jockey Oliver Lewis wins the first Kentucky Derby

1873

Panic of 1873 is followed by major depression

1880–1890

1881

Tuskegee Institute founded

1887

Black players barred from major league baseball

1881

Clara Barton establishes the Red Cross

1890–1900

1891

Dr. Daniel Hale Williams founds Provident Hospital in Chicago

1892

First black college football game: Biddle vs. Livingstone

1895

Booker T. Washington addresses the Cotton States Exposition in Atlanta

1899

Scott Joplin composes the "Maple Leaf Rag"

1890

Second Morrill Act passed

1891

John D. Rockefeller funds the establishment of the University of Chicago

1892

Grover Cleveland elected to a second term as president

1893

World's Columbian Exposition in Chicago

1895

Sears, Roebuck and Company form a retail mail-order business

AFRICAN-AMERICAN EVENTS | **NATIONAL EVENTS**

1896

William McKinley elected president

1898

Spanish-American War

1899

Cumming v. Richmond County [Georgia] Board of Education eliminates Augusta's black high school

1900–1910

1903

St. Luke Penny Savings Bank established in Richmond with Maggie Lena Walker as president

1906

Brownsville affair

1908

National Association of Colored Graduate Nurses is founded in New York City; Jack Johnson wins the heavyweight championship in boxing

1900

William McKinley reelected president

1901

President McKinley assassinated; Vice President Theodore Roosevelt becomes president

1903

Henry Ford organizes the Ford Motor Company

Wilbur and Orville Wright launch the first powered aircraft at Kitty Hawk, North Carolina

1904

Theodore Roosevelt reelected president

1908

William Howard Taft elected president

Review Questions

1. How and why did the agricultural and mechanical training that Hampton Institute and Tuskegee Institute offered gain so much support among both black and white people? Why did black colleges and universities emphasize learning trades and acquiring skills?

2. How compatible was the educational philosophy of the late nineteenth century with the era's racial ideology?

3. Of what value was an education for a black person in the 1890s or early 1900s? To what use could a black person put an education?

4. What purpose did the black church serve? What were the strengths and weaknesses of the black church? What roles did black clergymen play in late nineteenth-century America?

5. How could a black soldier justify participating in wars against Native Americans, the Spanish, and the Filipinos? Why did black soldiers serve? How well did they serve?

6. Did black people derive any benefits from the expansion of segregation and Jim Crow?

7. Why did ragtime, jazz, the blues, and gospel emerge and become popular?

8. How did segregation affect amateur and professional athletics in the United States?

Retracing the Odyssey

Hampton University, Hampton, Virginia. Founded by Samuel Chapman Armstrong with the assistance of the American Missionary Association, Hampton Normal and Agricultural Institute opened in 1868 to train former slaves (and later Native Americans) in agricultural and mechanical skills. Virginia Hall (1874), Memorial Church (1886), the Hampton Museum, and the giant Emancipation Oak are all located on this picturesque campus overlooking Chesapeake Bay and Hampton Roads.

Tuskegee Institute National Historic Site, Tuskegee, Alabama. What is now Tuskegee University opened in 1881 and remained under the leadership of Booker T. Washington until his death in 1915. His home—The Oaks—was built by students and is now a museum. His grave and memorial are also on the campus, as is the George Washington Carver Museum.

Alonzo F. Herndon Home, Atlanta, Georgia. Herndon was the founder of the Atlanta Life Insurance Company and one of the wealthiest black men in America by the early 1900s. His 15-room mansion with immense white pillars was finished in 1910 and is open to the public. It is furnished with antiques, Roman and Venetian glass, and ornate artwork.

Maggie L. Walker National Historic Site, Richmond, Virginia. Built in 1883, this 22-room Victorian mansion was home to the Walker family from 1904 to 1934 and is now open for tours. There is a visitor center that contains exhibits on the life of Maggie Lena Walker and the Jackson Ward community.

Madame C. J. Walker Center, Indianapolis, Indiana. In 1910 C. J. Walker (Sarah Breedlove) moved her thriving hair care and beauty products business from Denver to Indianapolis. The four-story triangular building was completed in 1919 shortly after Walker's death. It housed manufacturing facilities and was home to a beauty college that trained Walker's agents to care for the hair of African-American women and to sell Walker's products. It is currently a community center and theater.

Dunbar Hospital, Detroit, Michigan. This red brick structure was built in 1892 and served as a hospital for Detroit's black community from 1918 to 1928. It is currently operated by the Detroit Medical Society, and it has exhibits, medical devices, photographs, and papers documenting the medical care available to black Detroit.

Recommended Reading

James D. Anderson. *The Education of Blacks in the South, 1860–1931.* Chapel Hill: University of North Carolina Press, 1988. Anderson is highly critical of the education and philosophy promoted and provided by Hampton Institute and Tuskegee Institute.

Edward L. Ayers. *The Promise of the New South: Life After Reconstruction.* New York: Oxford University Press, 1992. This wide-ranging study encompasses almost every aspect of life in the late nineteenth-century South, including religion, education, sports, and music.

Sutton E. Griggs. *Imperium in Imperio.* New York: Arno Press, 1899. This novel describes the formation of a separate black nation in Texas at the end of the nineteenth century.

Leon Litwack. *Trouble in Mind: Black Southerners in the Age of Jim Crow.* New York: Alfred A. Knopf, 1998. The author lets the words of black people of the time, including lawyers, physicians, and musicians, explain what life was like in an age of intense white supremacy.

Leon Litwack and August Meier, eds. *Black Leaders in the Nineteenth Century.* Urbana: University of Illinois Press,

1988. This volume contains 18 brief but valuable biographical essays.

Benjamin E. Mays. *Born to Rebel.* New York: Scribner, 1971. Mays's autobiography includes penetrating insights into religion and education among rural black southerners.

Katherine C. Mooney. *Race Horse Men: How Slavery and Freedom were made at the Racetrack.* Cambridge, MA: Harvard University Press, 2014. A superb analysis of horse racing and the essential role that African-American men played in its development and popularity.

Howard N. Rabinowitz. *Race Relations in the Urban South, 1865–1890.* New York: Oxford University Press, 1978. The author examines black life in Atlanta, Montgomery, Nashville, Raleigh, and Richmond.

Christopher Robert Reed. *"All the World Is Here!": The Black Presence at White City.* Bloomington: Indiana University Press, 2000. Although African Americans were not involved in the planning or management of the World's Columbian Exposition, they did take part in the fair's exhibits and activities.

Mim Eichler Rivas. *Beautiful Jim Key: The Lost History of a Horse and a Man Who Changed the World.* New York: William Morrow, 2005. A fascinating and warm account of how a former slave and an exceptional horse became hugely successful entertainers.

Quintard Taylor. *In Search of the Racial Frontier: African Americans in the American West, 1528–1990.* New York: W. W. Norton, 1998. A fine survey and analysis of African Americans in the West from the sixteenth century to 1990.

Additional Bibliography

Education

Eric Anderson and Alfred A. Moss, Jr. *Dangerous Donations: Northern Philanthropy and Southern Black Education, 1902–1930.* Columbia: University of Missouri Press, 1999.

James D. Anderson and V. P. Franklin, eds. *New Perspectives on Black Educational History.* Boston: G. K. Hall, 1978.

Peter M. Ascoli. *Julius Rosenwald: The Man Who Built Sears, Roebuck and Advanced the Cause of Black Education in the American South.* Bloomington: Indiana University Press, 2006.

Henry A. Bullock. *A History of Negro Education in the South from 1619 to the Present.* Cambridge, MA: Harvard University Press, 1967.

Stephanie Deutsch. *"You Need a School House": Booker T. Washington, Julius Rosenwald, and Building Schools for the Segregated South.* Evanston, IL: Northwestern University Press, 2011.

Mary S. Hoffschwelle. *The Rosenwald Schools in the American South.* Gainesville: University Press of Florida, 2006.

Religion

Stephen W. Angell. *Bishop Henry McNeal Turner and African American Religion in the South.* Knoxville: University of Tennessee Press, 1992.

Cyprian Davis. *The History of Black Catholics in the United States.* New York: Crossroad, 1990.

Harold T. Lewis. *Yet with a Steady Beat: The African American Struggle for Recognition in the Episcopal Church.* Valley Forge, PA: Trinity Press International, 1996.

Iain MacRobert. *The Black Roots and White Racism of Early Pentecostalism in the USA.* Basingstoke, UK: Macmillan, 1988.

James M. O'Toole. *Passing for White: Race, Religion, and the Healy Family, 1820–1920.* Amherst: University of Massachusetts Press, 2002.

Edwin S. Redkey, ed. *The Writings and Speeches of Henry McNeal Turner.* New York: Arno Press, 1971.

Clarence E. Walker. *A Rock in a Weary Land: The African Methodist Episcopal Church During the Civil War and Reconstruction.* Baton Rouge: Louisiana State University Press, 1982.

The Military and the West

John M. Carroll, ed. *The Black Military Experience in the American West.* New York: Liveright, 1973.

Willard B. Gatewood, ed. *Smoked Yankees and the Struggle for Empire: Letters from Negro Soldiers, 1898–1902.* Urbana: University of Illinois Press, 1971.

William Loren Katz. *The Black West.* New York: Touchstone Books, 1996.

William H. Leckie. *The Buffalo Soldiers: A Narrative of the Negro Cavalry in the West.* Norman: University of Oklahoma Press, 1967.

Sara R. Massey, ed. *Black Cowboys of Texas.* College Station: Texas A&M University Press, 2000.

Frank N. Schubert. *Voices of the Buffalo Soldier: Records, Reports, and Recollections of Military Life and Service in the West.* Albuquerque: University of New Mexico Press, 2003.

Paul W. Stewart and Wallace Yvonne Ponce. *Black Cowboys.* Broomfield, CO: Phillips, 1986.

John D. Weaver. *The Brownsville Raid.* New York: W. W. Norton, 1971.

Labor

Tera W. Hunter. *To 'Joy My Freedom: Southern Black Women's Lives and Labors After the Civil War.* Cambridge, MA: Harvard University Press, 1997.

Gerald D. Jaynes. *Branches Without Roots: Genesis of the Black Working Class in the American South, 1862–1882.* New York: Oxford University Press, 1986.

The Professions

V. N. Gamble. *The Black Community Hospital: Contemporary Dilemmas in Historical Perspective.* New York: Garland, 1989.

Darlene Clark Hine. *Speak Truth to Power: Black Professional Class in United States History.* Brooklyn, NY: Carlson, 1996.

Gertrude Woodruff Marlowe. *A Right Worthy Grand Mission: Maggie Lena Walker and the Quest for Black Economic Empowerment.* Washington, DC: Howard University Press, 2003.

J. Clay Smith, Jr. *Emancipation: The Making of the Black Lawyer, 1844–1944.* Philadelphia: University of Pennsylvania Press, 1993.

_____, ed. *Rebels in Law: Voices in History of Black Women Lawyers.* Ann Arbor: University of Michigan Press, 1998.

Susan L. Smith. *Sick and Tired of Being Sick and Tired: Black Women's Health Activism in America, 1890–1950.* Philadelphia: University of Pennsylvania Press, 1995.

Thomas J. Ward, Jr. *Black Physicians in the Jim Crow South.* Fayetteville: University of Arkansas Press, 2003.

Music

W. C. Handy. *Father of the Blues: An Autobiography.* New York: Macmillan, 1941.

John Edward Hasse, ed. *Ragtime, Its History, Composers, and Music.* London: Macmillan, 1985.

William Howland Kenney. *Jazz on the River.* Chicago: University of Chicago Press, 2005.

Alan Lomax. *Mr. Jelly Roll: The Fortunes of Jelly Roll Morton, New Orleans Creole and "Inventor of Jazz."* New York: Grove Press, 1950.

Gunther Schuller. *Early Jazz: Its Roots and Musical Development.* New York: Oxford University Press, 1968.

Sports

Ocania Chalk. *Black College Sport.* New York: Dodd, Mead, 1976.

Neil Lanctot. *Negro League Baseball: The Rise and Ruin of a Black Institution.* Philadelphia: University of Pennsylvania Press, 2004.

Robert W. Peterson. *Only the Ball Was White: Negro Baseball: A History of Legendary Black Players and All-Black Professional Teams Before Black Men Played in the Major Leagues.* New York: Prentice Hall, 1970.

Andrew Ritchie. *Major Taylor: The Extraordinary Career of a Championship Bicycle Racer.* San Francisco: Bicycle Books, 1988.

Randy Roberts. *Papa Jack: Jack Johnson and the Era of White Hopes.* New York: Free Press, 1983.

Chapter 16

Conciliation, Agitation, and Migration: African Americans in the Early Twentieth Century

1895–1925

Although Tuskegee Institute stressed agricultural and vocational subjects, students did enroll in math, science, and English courses. Here students in a U.S. history class are involved in a discussion of Virginia's founding in the early seventeenth century. Notice that the male and female students are segregated and that the classroom features portraits of three U.S. presidents and several American flags.

Learning Objectives

After reading this chapter, you should be able to:

16.1   Describe Booker T. Washington's program for the advancement of African Americans.

16.2   Describe W. E. B. Du Bois's program for the advancement of African Americans.

16.3   Explain the role of middle-class black women in the advancement of African Americans.

16.4   Explore the defining characteristics of the black elite.

16.5   Evaluate the contributions of African Americans to U.S. military forces in the early twentieth century.

16.6   Analyze the reasons for the widespread outbreak of race riots during the first quarter of the twentieth century.

16.7   Explain why African Americans began to leave the rural South in the early twentieth century, and describe the types of lives they made for themselves in urban communities.

The wisest among my race understand that the agitation of questions of social equality is the extremest folly, and that progress in the enjoyment of all privileges that will come to us must be the result of severe and constant struggle rather than of artificial forcing. No race that has anything to contribute to the markets of the world is long in any degree ostracized. It is important and right all privileges of the law be ours, but it is vastly more important that we be prepared for the exercises of these privileges.

—*Booker T. Washington, Atlanta Cotton States and International Exposition, September 18, 1895*

Mr. Washington distinctly asks that black people give up, at least for the present three things,—First, political power, Second, insistence on civil rights, Third, higher education of Negro youth,—and concentrate all their energies on industrial education, the accumulation of wealth, and the conciliation of the South.

—*W. E. B. Du Bois, The Souls of Black Folk (1903)*

As the twentieth century dawned, black and white Americans had profoundly different views on the future of black people in America. Most white people believed African Americans were an inferior race capable of little more than manual labor and entitled to only the most basic legal rights. Black Americans rejected those assertions and worked for a more equitable place in society. Black scholar W. E. B. Du Bois announced in 1903 that race would be the century's critical issue: "The problem of the twentieth century is the problem of the color line—the relation of the darker to the lighter races of men in Asia and Africa, in America and the islands of the sea."

Black people refused to accept the inferiority to which they had been consigned. They devised strategies and organized institutions to enable them to prosper in a hostile society. However, African Americans and their leaders disagreed about how to secure the constitutional rights and the material comforts that so many white Americans took for granted. Some, following Du Bois, a founder of the Niagara Movement and the National Association for the Advancement of Colored People (NAACP), favored a frontal assault on discrimination, disfranchisement, and Jim Crow. Others, following Booker T. Washington of the Tuskegee Institute, cautioned against the vigorous pursuit of civil rights and political power and insisted that agricultural and industrial training would generate prosperity and self-sufficiency among people of color.

The emergence of the club movement among black women and other self-help organizations enabled more prosperous black people to aid those suffering from poverty and prejudice. The black elite, often reviled for ostentatious social displays, came to be designated the **Talented Tenth**, and many of them took seriously their responsibilities to aid their brethren.

When the United States entered World War I in 1917, black men responded patriotically, as they had in previous conflicts. They joined a Jim Crow military that was fighting to make the world safe for democracy. But black people in America were not safe, and democracy did not include them. Racial violence erupted before, during, and after the war.

In the meantime, one of the most important episodes in American history—a vast and prolonged migration of hundreds of thousands of rural black southerners to northern cities—began in earnest after 1910. Drawn mainly by economic opportunities, black people moved to New York, Philadelphia, Cleveland, Chicago, and other urban centers where they became the core of the black working class.

By the 1910s, many Americans were anxious about the rapid economic and social changes that confronted the United States, including industrialization, the rise of powerful corporations, the explosive growth of cities, and the influx of millions of immigrants. Their apprehensions spawned a disparate collection of reform efforts known as the progressive movement. In general, progressives believed America needed a new social awareness to deal with the new social and economic problems. But most of the middle- and upper-class white people who formed the core of the movement showed little interest in white racism and its impact. Indeed, many were racists themselves. They were primarily concerned with the concentration of wealth in monopolies such as Standard Oil, with the pervasive political corruption in state and local governments, and with the plight of working-class immigrants in American cities. They cared deeply about the debilitating effects of alcohol, tainted food, and prostitution, but little about the grim impact of white supremacy. When Upton Sinclair wrote his muckraking novel *The Jungle* in 1906 to expose the exploitation of European immigrants in Chicago meatpacking houses, he depicted black people as brute laborers and strikebreakers.

The reforms of the progressive movement nonetheless offered a glimmer of hope that racial advancement was possible. If efforts were made to improve America, was it not possible also to improve the policies and conditions affecting black Americans? But how much militancy or forbearance was necessary to achieve racial progress? Did it even make sense for black people to demand a meaningful role in a nation that despised them? Perhaps it was wiser to rely on each other rather than plead for white recognition and respect.

Talented Tenth

Term coined by W. E. B. Du Bois for the educated black elite of the late nineteenth and early twentieth centuries. The upper 10 percent was supposed to assume responsibility for the leadership and advancement of the remaining 90 percent of African Americans.

16.1 Booker T. Washington's Approach

Describe Booker T. Washington's program for the advancement of African Americans.

Booker T. Washington's commitment to agricultural and industrial education was the basis for his approach to "the problem of the color line." By 1900, Washington was convinced that black men and women who had mastered skills acquired at institutions like Tuskegee and Hampton would be recognized, if not welcomed, as productive contributors to the southern economy. He believed economic acceptance would lead to political and social acceptance.

The Tuskegee leader eloquently outlined his philosophy in the speech he delivered at the opening ceremonies of the Cotton States Exposition in Atlanta in 1895 (see Chapter 15). Black people, he told his segregated audience, would find genuine opportunities in the South: "When it comes to business, pure and simple, it is in the South that the Negro is given a man's chance in the commercial world." Washington added that black people should not expect too much but should welcome menial labor as a first step in the struggle for progress. Ever optimistic, he looked hopefully at what was possible while deprecating those who complained: "Nor should we permit our grievances to overshadow our opportunities." He told white listeners that the lives of black and white southerners were historically linked and that black people were far more loyal and steadfast than newly arrived immigrants: "In our humble way, we shall stand by you with a devotion that no foreigner can approach, ready to lay down our lives, if need be, in defence of yours, interlacing our industrial, commercial, civil, and religious life with yours in a way that shall make the interests of both races one."

Washington reassured white people that cooperation between the races in the interest of prosperity did not endanger segregation: "In all things that are purely social we can be as separate as the fingers, yet one as the hand in all things essential to mutual progress." Finally, Washington implied that black people need not protest because they were denied rights that white men possessed. Instead, he urged his black listeners to struggle steadily rather than make defiant demands: "The wisest among my race understand that the agitation of questions of social equality is the extremest folly, and that progress in the enjoyment of all the privileges that will come to us must be the result of severe and constant struggle rather than of artificial forcing." Washington was convinced that as African Americans became productive and made economic progress, white people would concede them their rights.

The speech was warmly received by both white and black listeners and by those who read it when it was widely reprinted. T. Thomas Fortune, the black editor of the *New York Age*, told Washington that he had replaced Frederick Douglass (who died in 1895) as a leader: "It looks as if you are our Douglass, the best equipped of the lot of us to be the single figure ahead of the procession."

But not everyone was complimentary. The black editor of the *Washington Bee*, W. Calvin Chase, complained, "He said something that was death to the Afro-American and elevating to white people." Bishop Henry M. Turner added that Washington "will have to live a long time to undo the harm he has done our race."

White people regarded Washington's speech as moderate, sensible, and praiseworthy. Almost overnight he was designated the spokesman for African Americans. Washington took full advantage of the recognition.

16.1.1 Washington's Influence

Booker T. Washington was a complex man. Many people found him unassertive, dignified, and patient. Yet he was ambitious, aggressive, and opportunistic as well as shrewd, calculating, and devious. He had an uncanny ability to elicit a positive response from other people. He became extraordinarily powerful, "the wizard of Tuskegee," in the words of his assistant, Emmett J. Scott.

After the Atlanta speech, Washington's influence soared. He received extensive and mostly positive coverage in black newspapers. Some of that popularity stemmed from admiration for his leadership and agreement with his ideas. But Washington also flattered editors, paid for advertisements for Tuskegee, and financially assisted struggling African-American journalists.

He was especially effective in dealing with prominent white businessmen and philanthropists. Washington's management of Tuskegee so impressed William H. Baldwin, vice president of the Southern Railroad, that Baldwin agreed to serve as the chairman of Tuskegee's board. Washington developed support among the nation's industrial elite including steel magnate Andrew Carnegie and Julius Rosenwald, the head of Sears, Roebuck and Company. They trusted Washington's judgment and consulted him before contributing to black colleges and universities. Washington assured them of the wisdom of training black men and women in agricultural and mechanical skills. These students, he reminded donors, would be self-sufficient and productive members of southern society.

For example, Rosenwald traveled to Tuskegee, consulted with Washington, and agreed to contribute several million dollars to construct public schools for black youngsters across the southern states. Between 1913 and 1932, over 5,300 schools ranging in size from one to six classrooms were built. Rosenwald insisted that local communities provide a substantial portion of the funds. Of the $28 million spent on constructing these Rosenwald schools, black communities contributed 19 percent, Rosenwald donated 16.5 percent, white people provided 4.5 percent, and state and local governments provided 60 percent. Some white communities, however, refused to have these schools built even after black people and Rosenwald agreed to share the financial responsibility for the schools. Black children in those communities received little, if any, education.

16.1.2 The Tuskegee Machine

Washington advised black people to avoid politics, but he ignored his own advice. Although he never ran for office or was appointed to a political position, Washington was a political figure to be reckoned with. His connections to white businesspeople and politicians gave him enormous influence. With his influence, connections, and organizational skills, Washington operated what came to be known as the "**Tuskegee Machine**." In 1896 he supported winning Republican presidential candidate William McKinley over the Democratic and Populist William Jennings Bryan. Washington got along superbly with McKinley's successor, Theodore Roosevelt. Although Roosevelt subscribed to social Darwinism (see Chapter 15) and regarded black Americans as inferiors, he respected Washington.

In 1901 Roosevelt invited Washington to dinner at the White House, where Roosevelt's family and a Colorado businessman joined them. Black people applauded, but the white South recoiled in disgust from such a flagrant breach of racial etiquette. Under no circumstances did white people and black people dine together at the same table. South Carolina Senator Benjamin R. Tillman declared, "The action of President Roosevelt in entertaining that nigger will necessitate our killing a thousand niggers in the South before they will learn their place again." Roosevelt was unmoved, and he continued to correspond and meet with Washington. Still, Roosevelt never invited Washington for another meal at the Executive Mansion.

Washington and Roosevelt consulted each other on political appointments. In the most notable case, Washington urged Roosevelt to appoint William D. Crum, a black medical doctor, as the collector of customs for the port of Charleston. White southerners, led by Senator Benjamin R. Tillman, delayed confirmation by the Senate for nearly three years. With Washington's assent, Roosevelt appointed black attorney William Lewis as U.S. attorney in Boston. President William Howard Taft later appointed Lewis assistant attorney general. (For more on Lewis, see Chapter 15.)

Most of Washington's political activities were not public. He secretly helped finance an unsuccessful court case against the Louisiana grandfather clause. (The statute disfranchised those voters—black men—whose grandfathers had not possessed the right to vote. See Chapter 14.) Washington funded two cases that were appealed to the U.S. Supreme Court that challenged Alabama's grandfather clause. But the Supreme Court justices rejected both cases on a

Tuskegee Machine

As the president of Tuskegee Institute, Booker T. Washington developed an extensive network of contacts that gave him extraordinary influence with white political leaders and philanthropists as well as with black businesspeople, journalists, and college presidents.

Booker T. Washington had access to and influence among the most powerful political and business leaders in the United States. Here he shares the podium with President Theodore Roosevelt. Washington persuaded Republican leaders like Roosevelt to appoint black men to an assortment of federal offices and convinced businessmen to contribute sizable sums to black colleges and universities. Nevertheless, some African Americans criticized the Tuskegee leader for not speaking out more candidly in opposition to white supremacy and Jim Crow.

technicality. He tried to persuade railroad executives to improve the conditions on segregated coaches and in station waiting rooms. He worked covertly with white attorneys to free a black farm laborer imprisoned under Alabama's peonage law. In many of these secret activities, Washington used code names in correspondence to hide his involvement. In the Louisiana case he was identified only as X.Y.Z.

Washington was a conservative leader who did not directly or publicly challenge white supremacy. He was willing to accept literacy and property qualifications for voting if they were equitably enforced regardless of race. He also opposed women's suffrage. He attacked lynching only occasionally. But he did write an annual letter to white newspapers filled with data on lynchings that had been compiled at Tuskegee. Washington let the grim statistics speak for themselves rather than denounce the injustice himself.

Washington founded the National Negro Business League in 1900 and served as its president until he died in 1915. The league brought together merchants, retailers, bankers, funeral directors, and other owners and operators of small enterprises. It promoted black businesses in the black community and brought businessmen together to exchange information. Moreover, the league's annual meetings allowed Washington to develop support for the Tuskegee Machine from black community leaders from across the nation. Similarly, he worked closely with leaders in black fraternal orders such as the Odd Fellows and Pythians.

16.1.3 Opposition to Washington

Years before Washington became prominent, there were black leaders who favored a direct challenge to racial oppression. In 1889 delegates from 23 states met to form the Afro-American League in Chicago. Its main purpose was to press for civil and political rights guaranteed by the Constitution: "The objects of the League are to encourage State and local leagues in their efforts to break down color bars, and in obtaining for the Afro-American an equal chance with others in the avocations of life . . . in securing the full privileges of citizenship." But the league did not flourish, and the Niagara Movement eventually displaced it.

Opposition to Washington's conciliatory stance on racial matters intensified. William Monroe Trotter, the Harvard-educated editor of the *Boston Guardian*, attacked Washington as "the Great Traitor," "the Benedict Arnold of the Negro Race," and "Pope Washington." At a 1903 meeting of the National Negro Business League in Boston, Trotter stood on a chair and interrupted a speech by Washington, defiantly asking, "Are the rope and the torch all the race is to get under your leadership?" Washington ignored him, and the police arrested the editor for disorderly conduct. He spent 30 days in jail for what newspapers labeled "the Boston Riot."

16.2 W. E. B. Du Bois

Describe W. E. B. Du Bois's program for the advancement of African Americans.

William Edward Burghardt Du Bois, who was 12 years younger than Booker T. Washington, would eventually eclipse the influence and authority of the Wizard of Tuskegee. Du Bois became the most significant black leader in America during the first half of the twentieth century. Whereas slavery, poverty, and the industrial work ethic fostered at Hampton Institute had shaped Washington's life, Du Bois was born and raised in the largely white town of Great Barrington, Massachusetts. It was a small community where he encountered little overt racism and developed a passion for knowledge.

Du Bois possessed, as he put it, "a flood of Negro blood, a strain of French, a bit of Dutch, but, thank God! no Anglo-Saxon." He graduated from Great Barrington High School at a time when few white and still fewer black youngsters attended more than

Voices

W. E. B. Du Bois on Being Black in America

W. E. B. Du Bois's The Souls of Black Folk (1903) contained perhaps the most eloquent statement ever written on being black in white America. The difficulties of their circumstances, Du Bois believed, create a double consciousness among Americans of African descent.

After the Egyptian and Indian, the Greek and Roman, the Teuton and Mongolian, the Negro is a sort of seventh son, born with a veil, and gifted with second-sight in this American world,—a world which yields him no true self-consciousness, but only lets him see himself through the revelation of the other world. It is a peculiar sensation, this double-consciousness, this sense of always looking at one's self through the eyes of others, of measuring one's soul by the tape of a world that looks on in an amused contempt and pity. One ever feels his two-ness,—an American, a Negro; two souls, two thoughts, two unreconciled strivings; two warring ideals in one dark body, whose dogged strength alone keeps it from being torn asunder.

The history of the American Negro is the history of this strife,—this longing to attain self-conscious manhood, to merge his double self into a better and truer self. In this merging he wishes neither of the older selves to be lost. He would not Africanize America, for America has too much to teach the world and Africa. He would not bleach his Negro soul in a flood of white Americanism, for he knows that Negro blood has a message for the world. He simply wishes to make it possible for a man to be both a Negro and an American, without being cursed and spit upon by his fellows, without having the doors of Opportunity closed roughly in his face.

---

1. Why does Du Bois maintain that a black person cannot be simply an American?
2. Would Du Bois agree, based on his concept of double consciousness, that African Americans have a separate identity and culture from other Americans?

SOURCE: W. E. B. Du Bois, *The Souls of Black Folk* (New York: Library of America, 1903), 8–9.

---

primary school. He went to Fisk University in Nashville and graduated at age 20. He was the first black man to earn a Ph.D. (in history) at Harvard in 1895, and he pursued additional graduate study in Germany.

Du Bois was perhaps the greatest scholar-activist in American history. He was an intellectual, at ease with words and ideas. He wrote 16 nonfiction books, five novels, and two autobiographies. He was a fearless activist determined to confront disfranchisement, Jim Crow, and lynching. Whereas Washington solicited the goodwill of powerful white leaders and was comfortable with a gradual approach to eradicating white supremacy, Du Bois was impatient with white people who accepted or ignored white domination and had little tolerance for black people who were unwilling to demand their civil and political rights.

Du Bois was well aware that he and Washington came from dissimilar backgrounds:

> I was born free. Washington was born a slave. He felt the lash of an overseer across his back. I was born in Massachusetts, he on a slave plantation in the South. My great-grandfather fought with the Colonial Army in New England in the American Revolution. I had a happy childhood and acceptance in the community. Washington's childhood was hard. I had many more advantages: Fisk University, Harvard, graduate years in Europe. Washington had little formal schooling.

16.2.1 The Du Bois Critique of Washington

Du Bois was not always critical of Washington. Following Washington's speech at the Cotton States Exposition in 1895, Du Bois, then a young Harvard Ph.D. teaching at Ohio's Wilberforce University, wrote to praise him: "Let me heartily congratulate you upon your phenomenal success at Atlanta—it was a word fitly spoken." But in 1903,

Du Bois, by then an Atlanta University professor, published *The Souls of Black Folk*. One of the major literary works of the twentieth century, it contained the first formal attack on Washington and his leadership.

In a provocative essay, "Of Booker T. Washington and Others," Du Bois conceded it was painful to challenge Washington, a man so highly praised and admired: "One hesitates, therefore, to criticise a life which, beginning with so little, has done so much. And yet the time is come when one may speak in all sincerity and utter courtesy of the mistakes and shortcomings of Mr. Washington's career, as well as the triumphs." Du Bois proceeded to attack Washington for failing to stand up for political and civil rights and higher education for black Americans. Du Bois found even more infuriating Washington's willingness to compromise with the white South and Washington's apparent agreement with white southerners that black people were not their equals: "Mr. Washington represents in Negro thought the old attitude of adjustment and submission . . . and Mr. Washington's programme practically accepts the alleged inferiority of the Negro races."

In concluding, Du Bois stressed that he agreed with Washington on some issues, but he so disagreed on other significant issues that it was vital to oppose Washington's positions:

> So far as Mr. Washington preaches Thrift, Patience, and Industrial Training for the masses, we must hold up his hands and strive with him. . . . But so far as Mr. Washington apologizes for injustice, North or South, does not rightly value the privilege and duty of voting, belittles the emasculating effects of caste distinctions, and opposes higher training and ambition of our brighter minds,— so far as he, the South, or the Nation, does this,—we must unceasingly and firmly oppose them.

Washington worried that the opposition of Trotter, Du Bois, and others would jeopardize the flow of funds from white philanthropists to black colleges and universities. To reconcile with his opponents, he organized a meeting with them, funded by white philanthropists, at Carnegie Hall in New York City in 1904. But Du Bois and other opponents of Washington came to the gathering determined to adopt a radical agenda. When Washington loyalists monopolized the proceedings, Du Bois quit in disgust.

16.2.2 *The Souls of Black Folk*

W. E. B. Du Bois's *The Souls of Black Folk* contained much more than a scathing analysis of Booker T. Washington's ideology. It was a perceptive and sensitive account that combined history, personal reminiscences, and sociology. "Herein lie buried many things," Du Bois wrote in the book's preface, "which if read with patience may show the strange meaning of being black here at the dawning of the Twentieth Century."

In 14 essays and in less than 200 pages, the 35-year-old Du Bois provided a largely positive evaluation of the work of the Freedmen's Bureau during Reconstruction. He went on to discuss his experiences as a summer school teacher in a rural Tennessee primary school where he encountered a shy and innocent young girl named Josie. He reflected in another essay on the music of Negro religion—"The one true expression of a people's sorrow, despair, and hope." Du Bois sadly tried to fathom the death of his first-born child in the book's eleventh essay.

This early twentieth-century photograph depicts a dapper young W. E. B. Du Bois (1868–1963). He was a key figure in opposing Booker T. Washington's Tuskegee Machine. Du Bois helped found the NAACP and edited its publication, *The Crisis*, for two decades.

The Souls of Black Folk is an American classic. No work in more than 100 years since its publication matches its language, its insights, and its capacity to explain what it meant to be a man of learning and a man of color in a Jim Crow nation.

16.2.3 The Talented Tenth

Du Bois, joined by a small cadre of black intellectuals, set out to organize an aggressive effort to secure the rights of black citizens. He was convinced that the advancement of black people was the responsibility of the black elite, those he called the Talented Tenth, meaning the upper 10 percent of black Americans. Education, he believed, was the key:

> Work alone will not do it unless inspired by the right ideals and guided by intelligence. Education must not simply teach work—it must teach Life. The Talented Tenth of the Negro race must be made leaders of thought and missionaries of culture among people. No others can do this work, and Negro colleges must train men for it. The Negro race, like all other races, is going to be saved by its exceptional men.

16.2.4 The Niagara Movement

In 1905 Du Bois carried the anti-Washington crusade a step further and invited a select group to meet at Niagara Falls in Canada. The 29 delegates to this meeting insisted that black people no longer quietly accept the loss of the right to vote: "We believe that [Negro] American citizens should protest emphatically and continually against the curtailment of their political rights." They also demanded an end to segregation: "All American citizens have the right to equal treatment in places of public entertainment." They appealed for better schools, health care, and housing; protested the discrimination black soldiers endured; and criticized the racial prejudice of most churches as "wrong, unchristian and disgraceful to the twentieth century civilization." Perhaps most important, the Niagara gathering insisted that white people did not know what was best for black people: "We repudiate the monstrous doctrine that the oppressor should be the sole authority as to the rights of the oppressed."

The founders of the Niagara Movement posed in front of a photograph of the falls when they met in Niagara Falls, Ontario, Canada, in 1905. W. E. B. Du Bois is second from the right in the middle row.

The Niagara Movement that emerged from this meeting attracted 400 members and remained active for years. Du Bois composed annual addresses to the nation designed to arouse black and white support. But the Niagara Movement was no match for the powerful, well-financed Tuskegee Machine. Washington used every means at his disposal to undermine the movement. Black newspaper editors like the *Washington Bee*'s W. Calvin Chase, who had earlier attacked Washington's Atlanta address, were paid to attack Du Bois and praise Washington. Washington dispatched spies to Niagara meetings to report on the organization's activities.

Washington sent a telegram requesting that black lawyer Clifford Plummer infiltrate the first Niagara meeting: "See Plummer at once. Give him fifty dollars. Tell him to go to Buffalo tonight or tomorrow morning ostensibly to attend Elks convention but to report fully what goes on at meeting. . . . Get into meeting, if possible but be sure [to get] name of all who attend and what they do." Washington let it be known that black federal employees might be dismissed if they joined the Niagara Movement.

Niagara members also quarreled among themselves. Du Bois was an inexperienced leader, and difficulties developed between him and Trotter. In 1908 the Niagara Movement virtually collapsed. Most black and white Americans would not support an organization that seemed so uncompromising in its demands.

16.2.5 The NAACP

As the Niagara Movement expired, the National Association for the Advancement of Colored People (NAACP) came to life. There was no direct link between the demise of the Niagara Movement and the rise of the NAACP. However, the relatively few people—black and white—who felt comfortable with the Niagara Movement's assertive stance on race were inclined to support the NAACP. In its early years the NAACP was a militant organization dedicated to racial justice. White leaders dominated it, and white contributors largely financed it.

A few white progressives were concerned about the rampant racial prejudice manifested so graphically in lynchings, Jim Crow, black disfranchisement, and a vicious riot in 1908 in Springfield, Illinois—Abraham Lincoln's hometown. After a gathering of leaders in January 1909 in New York City, on February 12—Lincoln's birthday—Oswald Garrison Villard called on "all believers in democracy to join a national conference to discuss present evils, the voicing of protests, and the renewal of the struggle for civil and political liberty."

Villard was the president and editor of the *New York Evening Post* and the grandson of abolitionist William Lloyd Garrison. Prominent progressives endorsed the call, including social workers Lillian Wald and Jane Addams, literary scholar Joel E. Spingarn, and respected attorneys Clarence Darrow and Moorfield Storey. Du Bois, Ida Wells Barnett, and Mary Church Terrell were the black leaders most involved in forming the NAACP.

The first issue of *The Crisis* monthly magazine was published in November 1910.

16.2.6 Using the System

The NAACP was determined that black citizens should fully enjoy the civil and political rights the Constitution guaranteed to all citizens. It relied on the judicial and legislative systems in what would be a persistent and decades-long effort to secure those rights. The NAACP won its first major legal victory in 1915 when the Supreme Court overturned Oklahoma's grandfather clause in *Guinn v. United States*. But poll taxes and literacy tests continued to disfranchise black citizens.

In 1917, in a case brought by the Louisville NAACP, the Supreme Court struck down a local law that enforced residential segregation by prohibiting black people and white people from selling real estate to people of the other race. The NAACP also tried in 1918 to secure a federal law prohibiting lynching. With the assistance of Congressman Leonidas Dyer, a white St. Louis Republican, the antilynching measure—the Dyer bill—passed in the House of Representatives in 1922 over vigorous Democratic opposition. But the Senate blocked it, and it never became law.

16.2.7 Du Bois and *The Crisis*

Du Bois was easily the most prominent black figure associated with the NAACP during its first quarter century. He became director of publicity and research and edited the NAACP publication called *The Crisis*, while largely leaving leadership and administrative tasks to others.

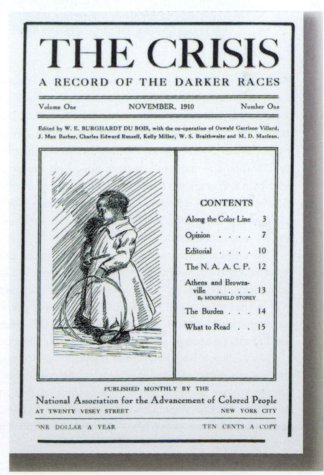

THE CRISIS
A RECORD OF THE DARKER RACES

Volume One   NOVEMBER, 1910   Number One

Edited by W. E. BURGHARDT DU BOIS, with the co-operation of Oswald Garrison Villard, J. Max Barber, Charles Edward Russell, Kelly Miller, W. S. Braithwaite and M. D. Maclean.

CONTENTS

Along the Color Line   3
Opinion   7
Editorial   10
The N. A. A. C. P.   12
Athens and Brownsville   13
    By MOORFIELD STOREY
The Burden . . .   14
What to Read . .   15

PUBLISHED MONTHLY BY THE
National Association for the Advancement of Colored People
AT TWENTY VESEY STREET   NEW YORK CITY

ONE DOLLAR A YEAR   TEN CENTS A COPY

Profile

Mary Church Terrell

Mary Church Terrell lived from the year of the Emancipation Proclamation (1863) to the year that the Supreme Court declared segregated schools unconstitutional (1954). During those nine decades, she exemplified the African-American leaders whom Du Bois called the Talented Tenth. The daughter of slaves, she acquired a superb education and became prominent in Washington's black elite. She was ever conscious of her social status, education, and fair complexion. She was dedicated to eliminating Jim Crow and also to the cause of African-American women.

Mary Church was born in Memphis and raised during Reconstruction. She went to Oberlin College where she studied classics, became proficient in languages, and earned an M.A. In 1891 she married Robert H. Terrell, who had earned a law degree at Howard. He was an auditor in the U.S. Treasury Department and became a District of Columbia municipal judge.

Mary Church Terrell immersed herself in literary, social, and political activities. She spearheaded the creation of the Colored Women's League and in 1896 became the first president of the National Association of Colored Women (NACW). She believed that well-to-do black women had a responsibility to assist struggling and poorer women of color.

Terrell was an inspirational speaker. She spoke in 1904 at the International Congress of Women in Berlin—in German, French, and English. Mamie Garvin Fields recalled a speech Terrell delivered in Charleston in 1916:

> Oh, my, when I saw her walk onto that podium in her pink evening dress and long white gloves, with her beautifully done hair, she was the Modern Woman. . . . Regal, intelligent, powerful, reaching out from time to time with that long glove, she looked and sounded like the Modern Woman that she talked about.

Terrell was active in the NAACP, which was not easy given her close relationship with Booker T. Washington and his wife, Margaret Murray Washington. She could not afford to alienate Washington because he could prevent her husband's reappointment as judge. Terrell managed to convince Washington that she supported him; in fact, she was devoted to the NAACP and its program. She served on its board and spoke forcefully on civil rights. She risked the wrath of President Theodore Roosevelt after she criticized his dismissal of three companies of black soldiers following the Brownsville incident (see Chapter 15). She presented President William Howard Taft with NAACP petitions against lynching. She wrote articles attacking chain gangs, peonage, disfranchisement, and lynching. She worked with progressive organizations, such as the Women's International League for Peace and Freedom, and supported women's suffrage and the Nineteenth Amendment.

The Terrells were active in Washington's black elite—the Four Hundred. They attended balls, concerts, and parties, traveled extensively, and belonged to Washington's most exclusive black congregation, the Lincoln Temple Congregational Church. She was also active in the Delta Sigma Theta sorority.

Mary Church Terrell consistently opposed racial discrimination. She protested to Oberlin College when her daughters encountered more prejudice as students than she had. A lifelong Republican, she opposed Democratic President Franklin Roosevelt's inaction on civil rights in the 1930s. At age 87 she demonstrated against an all-white restaurant in Washington, D.C.

Mary Church Terrell summed up her legacy in her 1940 autobiography, *A Colored Woman in a White World*: "This is the story of a colored woman living in a white world. It cannot possibly be like a story written by a white woman. A white woman has only one handicap to overcome—that of sex. I have two—both sex and race. I belong to the only group in this country which has two such huge obstacles to surmount. Colored men have only one—that of race."

With *The Crisis*, Du Bois the scholar became Du Bois the propagandist. He denounced white racism and atrocities and demanded that black people stand up for their rights: "Agitate, then, brother; protest, reveal the truth and refuse to be silenced. . . . A moment's let up, a moment's acquiescence, means a chance for the wolves of prejudice to get at our necks." He would not provoke violence, but he would not tolerate mistreatment either: "I am resolved to be quiet and law abiding, but to refuse to cringe in body or in soul, to resent deliberate insult, and to assert my just rights in the face of wanton aggression." These were not the even-tempered, cautious words of Booker T. Washington to which so many Americans had grown accustomed. *The Crisis* became required reading in many black homes. By 1913 it had 30,000 subscribers, whereas the NAACP had only 3,000 members.

16.2.8 Washington versus the NAACP

Villard tried to reassure Washington that the NAACP posed no threat and to gain his support for the new association: "It is not to be a Washington movement, or a Du Bois movement. The idea is that there shall grow out of it, first, an annual conference . . . for the discussion by men of both races of the conditions of the colored people, politically, socially, industrially and educationally."

Many black leaders and members of the NAACP, however, despised Washington and his ideology, and Washington returned the sentiment and worked to subvert the new organization. Washington considered Du Bois little more than the puppet of white people, who dominated the leadership of the NAACP, and the Tuskegee leader declined to debate Du Bois. One of Washington's aides commented that "it would be entirely out of place for Dr. Washington to enter into any discussion with a man occupying the place that Dr. Du Bois does, for the reason that Dr. Washington is at the head of a large institution. . . . Dr. Du Bois, on the other hand, is a mere hired man, as it were, in an institution completely controlled by white people."

Charles Anderson, a Tuskegee loyalist in New York City, wrote to Washington in 1909 that the NAACP was meeting secretly, and he would attempt to disrupt its efforts: "I will find out as much about them as possible and let you know the facts. I am doing all I can to discredit this affair." Washington relied again on allies who were editors of black newspapers to criticize the NAACP.

He also wrote Clark Howell, the white editor of the *Atlanta Constitution*, to attack Du Bois: "I think that it is too bad that an institution like Atlanta University has permitted Dr. Du Bois to go on from year to year stirring up racial strife in the South." Washington told an alumnus of Tuskegee that the main aim of the NAACP was to destroy Washington and Tuskegee: "As a matter of straight fact, this organization is for the purpose of tearing down our work wherever possible and I think none of our friends should give it comfort."

Washington became so obsessed with the NAACP that he was not above manipulating white supremacists to damage those connected with it. When he learned that black and white progressives associated with the NAACP were going to gather at the Café Boulevard in New York City in 1911, he allowed Charles Anderson to alert the hostile white press, which described the multiracial dinner in the most inflammatory terms: "Fashionable White Women Sit at Board with Negroes, Japs and Chinamen to Promote 'Cause' of Miscegenation," proclaimed one headline. The *New York Press* added, "White women, evidently of the cultured and wealthier classes, fashionably attired in low-cut gowns, leaned over the tables to chat confidentially with negro men of the true African type."

Ultimately, Washington's efforts to ruin the NAACP and reduce its supporters' influence failed. By the time of his death in 1915, the NAACP had 6,000 members and 50 local branches. Its aggressive campaign for civil and political rights replaced Washington's strategy of progress through conciliation and accommodation.

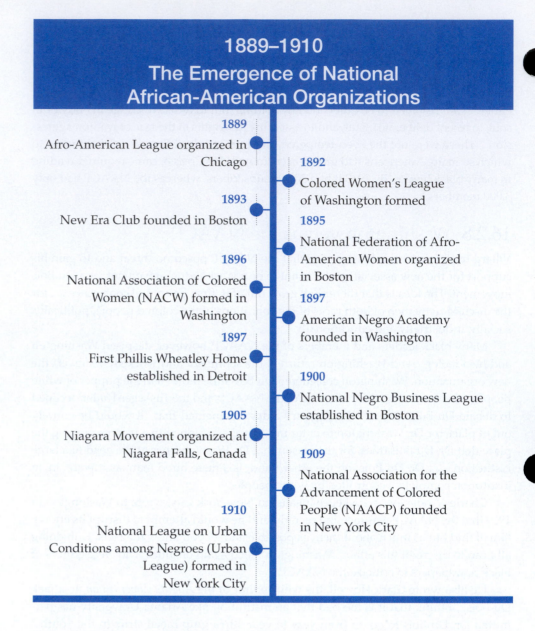

1889–1910
The Emergence of National African-American Organizations

1889
Afro-American League organized in Chicago

1892
Colored Women's League of Washington formed

1893
New Era Club founded in Boston

1895
National Federation of Afro-American Women organized in Boston

1896
National Association of Colored Women (NACW) formed in Washington

1897
American Negro Academy founded in Washington

1897
First Phillis Wheatley Home established in Detroit

1900
National Negro Business League established in Boston

1905
Niagara Movement organized at Niagara Falls, Canada

1909
National Association for the Advancement of Colored People (NAACP) founded in New York City

1910
National League on Urban Conditions among Negroes (Urban League) formed in New York City

16.2.9 The Urban League

In 1910, black and white progressives founded the National League on Urban Conditions among Negroes in New York City. Soon known simply as the Urban League, its goal was to alleviate conditions black people encountered as they moved into large cities in ever-increasing numbers during the early twentieth century. The Urban League worked to improve housing, medical care, and recreational facilities among black residents who lived in segregated neighborhoods in New York, Philadelphia, Atlanta, Nashville, Norfolk, and other cities. The league also assisted youngsters who ran afoul of the law, and it helped establish the Big Brother and Big Sister movements.

16.3 Black Women and the Club Movement

Explain the role of middle-class black women in the advancement of African Americans.

Years before the Urban League and the NAACP were founded, black women began creating clubs and organizations. The local groups that began forming in the 1870s and 1880s, such as the Bethel Literary and Historical Association in Washington, D.C., were mainly concerned with cultural, religious, and social matters. But many of the mostly middle-class women active in these clubs eventually became less interested in tea and gossip and more involved with community problems. In 1893 black women in Boston founded the New Era Club. Their monthly magazine, *Woman's Era*, featured articles on fashion, health, and family life.

In 1895 a New Era Club member, Josephine St. Pierre Ruffin, enraged by white journalist James W. Jack's vilification of black women as "prostitutes, thieves, and liars," issued a call to "Let Us Confer Together" that drew 104 black women to a meeting in Boston. The result was the formation of the National Federation of Afro-American Women, which soon included 36 clubs in 12 states. In the meantime, the Colored Women's League of Washington, D.C., which had been founded in 1892, appealed in *Woman's Era* for black women to organize a national association at the 1895 meeting of the National Council of Women. At that gathering, representatives from black women's clubs organized the National Colored Woman's League.

16.3.1 The NACW: "Lifting as We Climb"

The two groups—the National Federation of Afro-American Women and the National Colored Woman's League—merged in 1896 to form the National Association of Colored Women (NACW), with Mary Church Terrell elected the first president. The NACW adopted the self-help motto "Lifting as We Climb," and in the reforming spirit of the progressive age they stressed moral, mental, and material advancement. By 1914 the NACW had 50,000 members in 1,000 clubs nationwide.

Middle- and upper-class black club women were sometimes more concerned with the morality and behavior of black men and women than with civil rights and white supremacy. They opposed premarital sex and warned against the evils of alcohol.

There were occasionally unpleasant disagreements and conflicts among the club women. Margaret Murray Washington—Booker T. Washington's wife—served as NACW president from 1912 to 1916, and the organization's *National Notes* was published at Tuskegee until 1922. Not everyone was fond of this arrangement. Ida Wells Barnett claimed that the Tuskegee Machine censored the publication. Meanwhile, Mary Church Terrell found Barnett abrasive and contentious and managed to exclude her from the initial NACW meeting in 1896. There were also regional rivalries, ideological disputes, and sensitivity over the light complexion of leaders like Terrell.

More important than these internal struggles were the efforts of black women to confront the problems black people encountered in urban areas as rural southerners migrated to the cities by the thousands in the second and third decades of the twentieth century. The NACW clubs worked to eradicate poverty, end racial discrimination, and promote education. Members cared for older people, especially former slaves. They aided orphans; provided nurseries, health care, and information on childrearing for working mothers; and established homes for delinquent and abandoned girls.

16.3.2 Phillis Wheatley Clubs

Black women also formed Phillis Wheatley clubs and homes across the nation, named in honor of the eighteenth-century African-American poet (see Chapter 4). The residences offered living accommodations for single, black working women in many cities where YWCAs refused to admit them. Some Phillis Wheatley clubs also provided nurseries and classes in domestic skills. In Cleveland, a nurse named Jane Edna Hunter organized a residence for single, black working women who could not find comfortable and affordable housing. In 1911, she formed the Working Girls' Home Association for cleaning women, laundresses, and private duty nurses. With association members contributing five cents a week, Hunter opened a 23-room residence in 1913 that expanded to a 72-room building in 1917.

Profile

Jane Edna Hunter and the Phillis Wheatley Association

In the early twentieth century, no one was more committed to improving the lives of young black women than Jane Edna Hunter. Trained as a nurse, she migrated to Cleveland, where she founded the Phillis Wheatley Association.

Born Jane Harris in 1882 in Pendleton, South Carolina, she had a fair complexion because her father was the son of a slave woman and a white overseer. For a time she believed that her light color made her superior to darker friends and family members, especially her mother.

Her beloved father died when she was 10. She had little schooling as a child, but she was able to enroll at Ferguson Williams College in Abbeville, South Carolina, at age 14. Later her mother prodded her to marry Edward Hunter, a man 40 years her senior. The marriage lasted all of 15 months. Jane Edna Hunter never remarried.

She came to reject her color consciousness and embraced her heritage as a black woman: "—I was to be overwhelmed by the realization that I was, above and beyond all, my Mother's child—a Negro; that I was proud of the blood of my ancestors; that my life henceforth was to be a solemn dedication to the people of my Mother's race!"

She received training as a nurse in Charleston at the Canon Street Hospital and Training School for Nurses and then at the Dixie Hospital and Training School at Hampton Institute. In 1905 she moved to Cleveland, Ohio. She immediately encountered difficulties as a young black woman in a big city.

In search of a place to stay, she unintentionally knocked on the door of a brothel.

No white hospital would hire her as a nurse, and she worked as a cleaning woman while living in an unsavory boarding house: "In the average rooming house of that period . . . the Negro girl had to pay a dollar and a quarter a week for a small, low-roofed, poorly furnished room. She was charged extra for the use of the laundry and gas. If she wished to invite a caller, she was frequently required to clean the whole house in payment for the privilege. The use of the bath tub, when there was one, was discouraged."

The YWCA in Cleveland did not extend its benevolence to black women, and they were not permitted to live at YWCA residential facilities. Jane Edna Hunter took it upon herself to persuade the white women who ran the YWCA to support the establishment of a separate housing facility for black women. But some black people—"a small group of club women, who blessed with prosperity, had risen from the servant class and now regarded themselves as the arbiters and guardians of colored society"—opposed her efforts.

Nevertheless, the Phillis Wheatley Home opened in 1911. It was named in honor of the former slave who had become a prominent poet in colonial America. The first facility had 23 rooms. Hunter worked with white leaders to expand the size and services of what became the Phillis Wheatley Association. In doing so, black leaders attacked her for being too conciliatory and subservient to white people simply to gain access to their funds.

Ambitious and determined, she earned a law degree and passed the bar in 1926. She presided over the construction of an 11-story residence for black women that was completed in 1927. It featured a beauty school, dining facilities, a nursery school, and the Booker T. Washington Playground. The Phillis Wheatley Association also operated a summer camp for children and served as an employment agency for black women. Critics complained because many of the jobs were as domestics for well-to-do white families and accused Hunter of providing dead-end positions that kept black people in a subordinate status.

Hunter also shrewdly invested in Cleveland real estate and was active for decades in the NACW, even though it included many of the same women who had opposed her efforts. She served as a trustee of Ohio's Central State University. In 1937 she was awarded the NAACP's Spingarn Medal. She retired in 1946. When she died in 1971 she left most of her estate of nearly $500,000 to the Phillis Wheatley Foundation.

16.3.3 Anna Julia Cooper and Black Feminism

"Only the BLACK WOMAN can say 'when and where I enter, in the quiet, undisputed dignity of my womanhood, without violence and without suing or patronage, then and there the whole Negro race enters with me.'" So wrote Anna Julia Cooper in the late nineteenth century. Not only was Cooper convinced that black women would play a decisive role in shaping the destiny of their people, she labored against the stereotype that black women lacked refinement, grace, and morality.

Cooper was born a slave in Raleigh, North Carolina, in 1858 and graduated from St. Augustine's School. She then earned a bachelor's degree from Oberlin College in 1884. Speaking and writing with increasing confidence and authority, she published *A Voice From the South, by a Black Woman of the South* in 1892. In these essays she stressed the pivotal role that black women would play in the future and chastised white women for their lack of support. In 1900 she addressed the Pan African Conference in London.

Cooper was principal of Washington's famed M Street Colored High School (later Paul Laurence Dunbar High School) from 1901 to 1906. She was forced out in 1906 amid allegations that supporters of the Tuskegee Machine resented her emphasis on academic preparation over vocational training. She went on to teach for four years at Missouri's Lincoln University before returning to M Street High as a teacher. Fluent in French, she earned a Ph.D. at the Sorbonne in Paris.

She was active with the NACW, the NAACP, and the YWCA. Married in 1877, her husband died only two years later. Cooper found time following his death to take in and raise five children. She died in 1964 at age 105.

16.3.4 Women's Suffrage

Historically, many black women had supported women's suffrage. Before the Civil War, many abolitionists, including Mary Ann Shadd Cary, Sojourner Truth, and Frederick Douglass, had also backed women's suffrage. Cary and Truth tried unsuccessfully to vote after the war. Black women, such as Caroline Remond Putnam of Massachusetts, Lottie Rollin of South Carolina, and Frances Ellen Watkins Harper of Pennsylvania, attended conventions of the mostly white American Woman's Suffrage Association in the 1870s.

Black women were also involved in the long struggle for women's suffrage on the state level. Ida Wells Barnett was a leader in the Illinois suffrage effort. By 1900 Wyoming, Utah, Colorado, and Idaho permitted women to vote, and by 1918 women in 17 northern and western states had gained the vote. Black Chicago leader Fannie Barrier Williams predicted in 1914 that "when Colored women as well as white women begin to realize the real significance and power of the ballot, respect for the race will wonderfully increase."

But as more women won voting rights, women's suffrage became more controversial. The proposed Nineteenth Amendment to the Constitution instead drove a wedge between black and white advocates of women's political rights. Many opponents of women's suffrage, especially white southerners, warned that granting women the right to vote would increase the number of black voters. Some white women advocated strict literacy and educational requirements for voting to limit the number of black voters, both women and men.

Only two southern states—Kentucky and Tennessee—ratified the Nineteenth Amendment before its adoption in 1920. Black suffragists understood that the right to vote meant political power, and political power could be exercised to acquire civil rights, improve education, and gain respect. White southerners also grasped the importance of voting rights. Thus, despite the Nineteenth Amendment, most black people in the South—both men and women—remained unable to vote.

16.4 The Black Elite

Explore the defining characteristics of the black elite.

Many of the black leaders described by Du Bois as the Talented Tenth formed protest organizations, joined reform efforts, and organized self-help groups. The leaders were middle- and upper-class black people who were better educated than most Americans—black or white.

16.4.1 The American Negro Academy

In 1897, Episcopal priest Alexander Crummell met with 16 other black men in Washington, D.C., to form the American Negro Academy. This scholarly organization was made up of "men of African descent" who assembled periodically to discuss and publish works on history, literature, religion, and science. Among those who attended the initial gathering were Du Bois, Paul Laurence Dunbar, Kelly Miller, and Francis Grimke.

Crummell was an elderly but dynamic and distinguished leader who did not hesitate to express his convictions on race, religion, and Africa. He had been born in 1818 in New York and lived in Liberia in the 1850s and 1860s as an Episcopal missionary. Crummell died in 1898, but the Academy survived as a vibrant intellectual and elitist society.

Carter G. Woodson, Alain Locke, Arthur Schomburg, and James Weldon Johnson joined its ranks before the Academy disbanded in 1928. It afforded black intellectuals an opportunity to ponder what it meant to be black in America and develop their racial consciousness, thus nurturing ideas and concepts that would mature during the Harlem Renaissance.

Most members of the Academy supported women's rights and women's suffrage. Consequently, it was ironic that black women were not invited to become members of the Academy, although several black women, including Anna Julia Cooper, Ida Wells Barnett, and Mary Church Terrell, were easily the intellectual equals of the male participants.

16.4.2 The Upper Class

By the early twentieth century, there were several hundred wealthy African Americans. These black aristocrats were as sophisticated, refined, and status conscious as any group in American society. They distanced themselves from less affluent black and white people and lived in expensive houses. Many of them had fair complexions. They were medical doctors, lawyers, and businessmen. Although they possessed vastly more wealth than most Americans, their wealth paled compared to the huge fortunes of the richest American families, such as the Rockefellers, Carnegies, and Vanderbilts.

The black elite formed exclusive organizations that jealously limited membership to the small black upper class. In the 1860s the Ugly Fishing Club was made up of New York City's wealthiest black men. It soon came to be known simply as the Ugly Club, and its membership spread to Newport, Rhode Island; Baltimore; and Philadelphia. In 1904 two wealthy Philadelphia physicians, a dentist, and a pharmacist formed Sigma Pi Phi, better known as Boulé, to provide "inspiration, relaxation, intellectual stimulation, and brotherhood: for male college graduates." Boulé expanded to seven chapters in cities that included Chicago and Memphis, but its membership totaled a mere 177.

Organizations like the Diamondback Club and the Cosmos Club in Washington, the Loendi Club in Pittsburgh, and the Bachelor-Benedict Club in New York sponsored luxurious banquets, dances, and debutante balls. Several of these groups owned ornate clubhouses. These elite societies and cliques competed to demonstrate social exclusivity and preeminence.

16.4.3 Fraternities and Sororities

Among the black elite were also the African Americans who established the Greek-letter black fraternities and sororities. In 1906 seven students at Cornell University formed Alpha Phi Alpha, the first college fraternity for black men. Within a few years, it had chapters at the University of Michigan, Yale, Columbia, and Ohio State. The first black sorority, Alpha Kappa Alpha, was founded in 1908 at Howard University.

Other Greek-letter organizations were launched at Howard: Omega Psi Phi fraternity in 1911, Delta Sigma Theta sorority in 1913, Phi Beta Sigma fraternity in 1914, and Zeta Phi Beta sorority in 1920. In 1911 Kappa Alpha Psi fraternity was founded at Indiana University, and Sigma Gamma Rho sorority was formed in Indianapolis in 1922.

Besides providing college students with an opportunity to enjoy each other's company, the black fraternities and sororities stressed scholarship, social graces, and community involvement. Alpha Phi Alpha created the "Go to High School, Go to College" campaign in 1919. Kappa Alpha Psi adopted the "Guide Right" program to assist black youngsters in 1922. In 1923 Alpha Kappa Alpha opened a mobile health clinic in Mississippi. From 1935 to 1941, during the Great Depression, Alpha Kappa Alpha sponsored free health clinics in Mississippi under the guidance of Dr. Dorothy Ferebee of the Howard University Medical School. It was the first time many black people in that state had received professional medical attention.

16.4.4 African-American Inventors

Among the black elite were inventors and innovators who contributed to the technical and industrial transformation of America during the late nineteenth and early twentieth centuries. Like Thomas Edison, Henry Ford, and Harvey Firestone, these African Americans were mostly self-taught and not college educated. But there was an exception. Shelby J. Davidson had graduated from Howard University and was a lawyer.

As a longtime employee of the auditing department of the Post Office Division of the U.S. Treasury, Davidson became an expert on the new and complex adding machines used to maintain post office accounts. In 1908 he received a patent for an electric device that fed paper into the machines. He worked diligently for years to create a mechanism that would enable large Burroughs adding machines to calculate the ascending rates that post offices charged for money orders. But the attempt to secure a joint patent with Edwin Dowling for their invention failed when it was challenged. Davidson had not maintained the paperwork and drawings to sustain their claim.

As prejudice and discrimination against black federal employees intensified, Davidson resigned his auditing position in 1912. He believed that a less qualified white man was promoted while he was not. He complained to Assistant U.S. Attorney William H. Lewis, who was black, "Had I been white instead of colored I do not doubt at all that I would have been chief of one of the divisions instead of now being on trial, hounded, persecuted and expected to make another record in order to maintain my present rating and this under the most painful and adverse conditions."

Granville Woods was born in Australia in 1856 and grew up in Columbus, Ohio. He developed mechanical skills and became a locomotive engineer. His extensive knowledge of electricity enabled him to win 45 patents. His Synchronous Multiplex Railway Telegraph improved communication among trains and with stations, thereby increasing railroad safety. His invention of an electric railway brake also enhanced safe operations. Thomas Edison challenged Woods's claim to have invented the Multiplex Telegraph, but Woods prevailed. It was one of the rare patent cases that Edison lost.

Lewis Latimer's parents were slaves who had escaped from Virginia to Boston in 1842. Lewis was born in 1848, and as a youngster he sold copies of William Lloyd Garrison's abolitionist newspaper, the *Liberator*. During the Civil War at age 15, Latimer joined the Union Navy. After the war he became a skilled draftsman for a patent law

Lewis H. Latimer's *Incandescent Lighting: A Practical Description of the Edison System*, published in 1896, was one of the first books on electric lighting.

firm. In 1874 Latimer received a patent for a flushing mechanism that improved toilets on railway coaches.

He went on to draft diagrams for Alexander Graham Bell's patent application for the telephone. While working for the U.S. Electric Lighting Company, Latimer invented an improved process for manufacturing carbon filaments for light bulbs that he patented in 1882. He went to work for the Edison Electric Light Company in 1883, and in 1890 he published *Incandescent Lighting: A Practical Description of the Edison System*. He served as the chief draftsman for the General Electric/Westinghouse Board of Patent Control after it was formed in 1896.

The men who worked for Thomas Edison before 1885 joined together in 1918 as Edison Pioneers to reminisce about their early experiences and experiments. Latimer was the only African American among them.

Madam C. J. Walker was more an entrepreneur than an inventor (see Chapter 15). However, she did develop a secret chemical formula to nourish and promote the growth of hair among black women. She also created an improved hot comb and the Anti-Kink Walker System to straighten black hair.

16.4.5 Presidential Politics

Since Reconstruction, black voters had supported the Republican Party and its presidential candidates. "The Party of Lincoln" welcomed that support and rewarded black men with federal jobs. Republican presidents Theodore Roosevelt (1901–1909) and William Howard Taft (1909–1913) continued that policy.

FRUSTRATED BY THE REPUBLICANS However, other presidential actions offset whatever goodwill these appointments generated. Roosevelt discharged three companies of black soldiers after the Brownsville incident in 1906, and Taft tolerated restrictions on black voters in the South and encouraged the development of a "lily white" Republican Party, removing black people from federal jobs in the region.

In 1912 the Republican Party split in a bitter feud between President Taft and Theodore Roosevelt, and Roosevelt's supporters formed the Progressive Party, which nominated him to run against Taft and the Democratic candidate, Woodrow Wilson. But as the delegates at the Progressive convention in Chicago sang the "Battle Hymn of the Republic," southern black men who had come to the gathering stood outside the hall, denied admission by white Progressives.

WOODROW WILSON It was not a complete shock that militant black leaders like William Monroe Trotter and W. E. B. Du Bois urged black voters to break with the Republican Party and support Woodrow Wilson. Wilson was the reform governor of New Jersey and had been president of Princeton University. Wilson's academic background and his promise to pursue a progressive policy toward black Americans impressed Trotter and Du Bois. Du Bois wrote,

> Wilson is a cultivated scholar and he has brains. We have, therefore, a conviction that Mr. Wilson will treat black men and their interests with foresighted fairness. He will not advance the cause of an oligarchy in the South, he will not seek further means of "jim crow" insult, he will not dismiss black men wholesale from office, and he will remember that the Negro has a right to be heard and considered.

But President Wilson was no friend of black people. Born in Virginia and raised in South Carolina, Wilson had absorbed white southern racial views. Federal agencies

Profile

George Washington Carver and Ernest Everett Just

George Washington Carver, 1864 or 1865–1943

George Washington Carver and Ernest Everett Just rose from humble beginnings to become eminent biologists. Carver was born in 1864 or 1865 to slave parents in Diamond Grove, Missouri. Eager to learn, he spent much of his youth engaged in menial labor around Missouri, Iowa, and Kansas as he acquired an uneven education. He attended Simpson College and then enrolled at Iowa State University in 1891 at age 25 as its sole black student. He had a superb academic record and took charge of the campus greenhouse. He became fascinated with botany and focused on mycology (the study of fungi) and cross-fertilization.

Just was born in Charleston in 1883 and grew up on nearby James Island, where his mother toiled in phosphate mines after the death of his father. He attended local schools and earned a teacher training certificate in 1899 from what is now South Carolina State University. Just went on to Kimball Union Academy in New Hampshire and graduated with honors from Dartmouth College in 1907 with a major in biology and minors in Greek and history.

Just was hired by Howard University and spent the rest of his teaching career there. In 1911 he helped establish Omega Psi Phi, which became a major black fraternity. Although hired

to teach English and rhetoric, he soon changed to zoology and biology, the subjects in which he had an abiding interest. He spent several summers at the Marine Biology Laboratory at Woods Hole, Massachusetts, and earned a Ph.D. in zoology from the University of Chicago in 1916.

While Just felt more at home doing research in a laboratory, Carver felt more comfortable experimenting with crops in a field. At the invitation of Booker T. Washington, Carver left a promising career at Iowa State in 1896 to take charge of the agriculture program at Tuskegee Institute. Having studied with two men at Iowa State—James Wilson and Henry C. Wallace—who later became U.S. secretaries of agriculture, Carver established political ties that benefitted Tuskegee. He became the director of the nation's only black agricultural experiment station.

Carver was a superb teacher in and out of the classroom, but he was a less-than-efficient administrator who clashed with Booker T. Washington. Carver sought to make impoverished black farmers more productive and less dependent on cotton. He sponsored outreach programs and farmers' institutes. He discovered hundreds of uses for the protein-rich peanut. And he experimented extensively with sweet potatoes.

Carver became a folk hero by the 1930s with his gregarious personality and self-effacing demeanor. He never married and lived in a student dormitory at Tuskegee. He wore a tattered coat with a fresh flower in the lapel. Though he never earned more than $1,200 a year, he gave more than $60,000 to Tuskegee before he died in 1943.

Just, confronted with the lack of opportunities available to a dedicated black scientist at white universities, pursued his research in the fertilization of marine animals at Woods Hole. But even there he was shunned and patronized. Nevertheless, by 1928 he had published 35 articles, mostly on fertilization. Awarded a grant from the Julius Rosenwald Foundation, he spent much of the 1930s engaged in research in Italy, Germany, and France. In 1939 he published *Biology of the Cell Surface*.

Just married Ethel Highwarden, a Howard faculty member, in 1912. They had three children but later divorced. In 1939 he married Maid Hedwig Schnetzler, a German scientist. Just died of cancer in 1941.

Both George Washington Carver and Ernest Everett Just were awarded the NAACP's Spingarn Medal—Just in 1915 and Carver in 1923.

and buildings were fully segregated early during Wilson's tenure. In 1914 Trotter and a black delegation met with Wilson to protest segregation in the Treasury Department and the Post Office. Wilson defended separation of the races as a means to avoid friction. Trotter strongly disagreed. Wilson became visibly irritated with Trotter and abruptly ended the meeting.

16.5 Black Men and the Military in World War I

Evaluate the contributions of African Americans to U.S. military forces in the early twentieth century.

In 1915–1916 Wilson faced more than problems with dissatisfied black people. Relations with Mexico had steadily deteriorated after a revolution and civil war there. War in Europe threatened to draw the United States into conflict with Germany.

16.5.1 The Punitive Expedition to Mexico

In 1914 war almost broke out between the United States and Mexico when U.S. Marines landed at Vera Cruz after an attack on American sailors. Then in March 1916, Francisco "Pancho" Villa, one of the participants in Mexico's civil war, led a force of Mexican rebels across the border into New Mexico in an effort to provoke war with the United States. Fifteen Americans were killed, including seven U.S. soldiers. In response, Wilson dispatched a "punitive expedition" that eventually numbered 15,000 troops under General John J. Pershing. Pershing had acquired the nickname "Black Jack" after commanding black troops in Cuba during the Spanish-American War.

U.S. forces, including the black 10th Cavalry, spent 10 months in Mexico in 1916–1917 in a futile effort to capture Villa. White officers commanded the 10th Cavalry, as had been the case with black troops since the Civil War. But Lieutenant Colonel Charles Young, an 1889 black graduate of West Point, helped lead the regiment.

Young led the black troops against a contingent of Villa's rebels who had ambushed an element of the 13th Cavalry, a white unit, at Santa Cruz de Villegas. Major Frank Tompkins of the 13th was so relieved to be rescued that he reportedly exclaimed to Young, "By God, Young, I could kiss every black face out there." Young supposedly replied, "If you want to, you may start with me." As the probability increased that the United States would enter World War I against Germany, U.S. troops were withdrawn from Mexico in 1917.

Lieutenant Colonel Charles D. Young, an 1889 graduate of the U.S. Military Academy at West Point who served in Cuba, the Philippines, Haiti, and Mexico, was not permitted to command troops during World War I. He returned to military service at the end of the war and was sent to Liberia to help train that country's army. He died on furlough in Nigeria in 1922.

16.5.2 World War I

When World War I erupted in Europe in August 1914, most Americans had no intention or desire to participate. Wilson issued a proclamation of neutrality. Running for reelection in 1916 on the slogan "He Kept Us Out of War," Wilson narrowly defeated Republican Charles Evans Hughes. But German submarine attacks on civilian vessels and the loss of American lives infuriated Wilson and many Americans as a gross violation of U.S. neutrality rights. On April 6, 1917, Congress declared war on Germany. Most African Americans supported the war effort. As in previous conflicts, black people sought to demonstrate their loyalty and devotion to the country through military service. "If this is our country," declared W. E. B. Du Bois, "then this is our war. We must fight it with every ounce of blood and treasure."

Some white leaders were less enthusiastic about the participation of black men. One southern governor wondered about the wisdom of having the military train and arm thousands of black men at southern camps and posts. General Pershing insisted on white leadership: "Under capable white officers and with sufficient training, Negro soldiers have always acquitted themselves creditably."

16.5.3 Black Troops and Officers

There were about 10,000 black regulars in the U.S. Army in 1917: the 9th and 10th Cavalry Regiments and the 24th and 25th Infantry Regiments. There were more than 5,000 black men in the navy, but virtually all of them were waiters, kitchen attendants, and stokers for the ships' boilers. The Marine Corps did not admit black men. During World War I, the new Selective Service system drafted more than 370,000 black men—13 percent of all draftees—although none of the local draft boards had black members. Several all-black state National Guard units were also incorporated into federal service.

Although the military remained rigidly segregated, black newspapers and the NAACP campaigned to commission black officers to lead black troops. The War Department created an officer training school at Fort Des Moines, Iowa. Nearly 1,250 black men enrolled—1,000 were civilians, and 250 were enlisted men from the regular regiments—and over 1,000 received commissions. Black officers, however, were confined to the lower ranks. None of the new black officers were promoted above captain, and the overall command of black units remained in white hands.

Lieutenant Colonel Charles Young was eligible to lead black and white troops in World War I. He had already served in Cuba, the Philippines, Haiti, and Mexico. White soldiers complained, however, that they did not want to take orders from a black man, and, over Young's protests, military authorities forced him to retire by claiming he had high blood pressure. Young rode a horse from his home in Xenia, Ohio, to Washington, D.C., to prove he was in good health. But he remained on the retired list until he was given command of a training unit in Illinois five days before the war ended.

16.5.4 Discrimination and Its Effects

Most white military leaders, politicians, and journalists embraced racial stereotypes and expected little from black soldiers. As in earlier wars, black troops were discriminated against, abused, and neglected. Some had to drill with picks and shovels rather than rifles. At Camp Hill, Virginia, black troops lived through a cold winter in tents with no floors, no blankets, and no bathing facilities. White men failed to salute black officers, and black officers were denied admission to officers' clubs. Morale among black troops was low, and their performance sometimes reflected it.

Military authorities did not expect to use black troops in combat. The army preferred to employ black troops in labor battalions, as stevedores, in road construction, and as cooks and bakers. Of more than 380,000 black men who served in World War I, only 42,000 went into combat. Black troops represented 3 percent of U.S. combat strength. The army did not prepare black soldiers adequately for combat, but military leaders complained when black soldiers who did face combat performed poorly.

The 368th Infantry Regiment of the 92nd Division came in for especially harsh criticism. Fighting alongside the French in September 1918, the regiment's second and third battalions fell back in disorder. Some men ran. The white regimental commander blamed black officers, and 30 of them were relieved of command. Five officers were court-martialed for cowardice; four were sentenced to death and one to life in prison. All were later freed. But black Lieutenant Howard H. Long argued that the perceptions of white officers caused the poor performance: "Many of the [white] field officers seemed far more concerned with reminding their Negro subordinates that they were Negroes than they were in having an effective unit that would perform well in combat."

Even the white commander of the 92nd Division, General Charles C. Ballou, identified white officers as the main problem: "It was my misfortune to be handicapped by many white officers who were rabidly hostile to the idea of a colored officer, and who continually conveyed misinformation to the staff of the superior units, and generally created much trouble and discontent. Such men will never give the Negro the square deal that is his just due."

White officials stressed the weaknesses of the 368th Infantry Regiment and mostly ignored the commendable records of the 369th, 370th, 371st, and 372nd Regiments. The 369th compiled an exemplary combat record. Sent to the front for 91 consecutive days, these "Men of Bronze"—as they came to be known—consisted mainly of soldiers from the 15th Regiment of the New York National Guard. They fought alongside the French and were given French weapons, uniforms, helmets, and food (but not the wine that French soldiers received). They had an outstanding military band led by Jim Europe, one of the finest musical leaders of the early twentieth century. The 369th lived up to their motto, "Let's Go," as they took part in heavy fighting. They never lost a trench or gave up a prisoner. By June 1918 French commanders were asking for all the black troops the Americans could send.

Most French civilians and troops, unfazed by racist warnings from white American officials about the presumed danger black men posed to white women, praised the conduct of black soldiers and accepted them as equals. Following the triumph of the Allies in World War I, French authorities awarded the Croix de Guerre, France's highest military medal, to the men of the 369th, the 371st, and the 372nd Regiments.

Black troops returned to America on segregated ships. The 15th New York National Guard Unit from the 369th Regiment and its famed band were not permitted to join the farewell parade in New York City. Even praise from white Americans was riddled with racist stereotypes. The *Milwaukee Sentinel* was typical: "Those two colored regiments fought well, and it calls for special recognition. Is there no way of getting a cargo of watermelons over there?"

African-American troops on the march near Verdun in France in 1918.

16.5.5 Du Bois's Disappointment

The treatment of black soldiers embittered black leaders who had supported American entry in the war. During the war in 1918, Du Bois appealed to black people in *The Crisis* to "close ranks" and support the war:

> We of the colored race have no ordinary interest in the outcome. That which the German power represents today spells death to the aspirations of Negroes and all darker races for equality, freedom and democracy. Let us not hesitate. Let us, while this war lasts, forget our special grievances and close ranks with our own white fellow citizens and the allied nations that are fighting for democracy.

Du Bois's unequivocal support may have been connected to his effort to secure an officer's commission in military intelligence through the intervention of Joel E. Spingarn, chairman of the NAACP board of directors. Du Bois did not get his commission; instead, what he got was criticism for his "close ranks" editorial. William Monroe Trotter said that Du Bois had "finally weakened, compromised, deserted the fight, [and] betrayed the cause of his race." To Trotter, Du Bois was "a rank quitter in the cause for equal rights."

In 1930, Du Bois confessed that he should not have supported U.S. intervention in the war. He admitted that he had allowed his emotions to get the best of him as he was swept up in the patriotic fervor for war in 1917. He later decided that the conflict had not been fought as a war to end all wars or a war to preserve democracy, but instead it was a war pursued for selfish and greedy nationalistic reasons.

By the end of World War I, Du Bois—who had visited black troops in France—could see that black loyalty and sacrifice had not eroded white racism. He wrote defiantly in *The Crisis* that black people were determined to make America yield to its democratic ideals:

> But by the God of heaven, we are cowards and jackasses if now that the war is over, we do not marshal every ounce of our brain and brawn to fight a sterner, longer, more unbending battle against the forces of hell in our own land.
>
> We return.
>
> We return from fighting.
>
> We return fighting.
>
> Make way for Democracy! We saved it in France, and by the Great Jehovah, we will save it in the United States of America, or know the reason why.

16.6 Race Riots

Analyze the reasons for the widespread outbreak of race riots during the first quarter of the twentieth century.

Despite the reformist impulse of the progressive era and the democratic ideals trumpeted as the United States went to war against Germany, most white Americans clung to social Darwinism and white supremacy. White people reacted with contempt and violence to demands by black people for fairer treatment and equal opportunities in American society. The campaigns of the NAACP, the efforts of the black club women, and the services and sacrifices of black men in the war not only failed to alter white racial perceptions but were sometimes accompanied by a backlash against African Americans. Ten black men still in uniform were lynched in 1919.

Many white Americans concurred with Mississippi Senator James K. Vardaman when he declared in 1914 that white people would not accept black claims for a meaningful political and legal role in America:

> God Almighty never intended that the negro should share with the white man in the government of this country. . . . Do not forget that. It matters not what I may say or others may think; it matters not what constitutions may contain or statutes provide, wherever the negro is in sufficient numbers to imperil the white man's civilization or question the white man's supremacy the white man is going to find some way around the difficulty. And that is just as true in the North as it is in the South. You need not deceive yourselves about that. The feeling against the negro in Illinois when he gets in the white man's way is quite as strong, more bitter, less regardful of the negro's feelings and conditions than it is in Mississippi.

The racial violence that permeated southern life expanded into northern communities as many white Americans responded with hostility to the arrival of black migrants from the South. Black people defended themselves, and casualties among both races escalated (see Map 16-1).

Map 16-1 Major Race Riots, 1900–1923

In the years between 1900 and 1923, race conflicts and riots occurred in dozens of American communities as black people migrated in increasing numbers to urban areas. The violence reached a peak in the immediate aftermath of World War I during the Red Summer of 1919. White Americans—in the North and South—were determined to keep black people confined to a subordinate role as menial laborers and restricted to well-defined all-black neighborhoods. Afrian Americans who had made significant economic and military contributions to the war effort and who had congregated in large numbers in American cities insisted on participating on a more equitable basis in American society.

Were the causes of each of these riots similar, or were the reasons for the upsurge in racial violence unique to each situation?

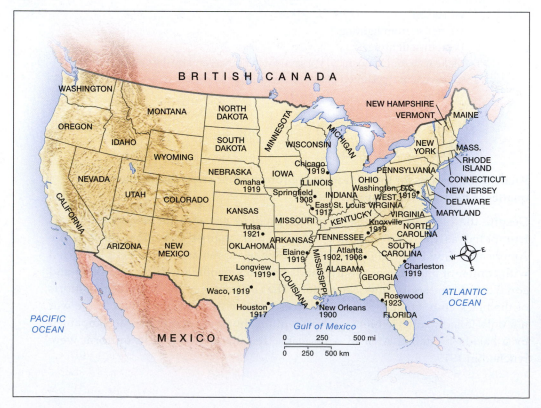

16.6.1 Atlanta, 1906

In 1906—11 years after Booker T. Washington delivered his Cotton States Exposition address there—white mobs attacked black residents in Atlanta. Several factors aggravated white racial apprehensions in the city. In 1902 four black and four white people had been killed in a riot there. Many rural black people, attracted by economic opportunities, had moved to Atlanta. But white residents considered the newcomers more lawless and immoral than the longtime black residents. The Atlanta newspapers—the *Constitution*, the *Journal*, and the *Georgian*—ran inflammatory accounts about black crime and black men who brutalized white women. However, many of these stories were false or exaggerated. Two white Democrats—Hoke Smith and Clark Howell—were engaged in a divisive campaign for a U.S. Senate seat in 1906, and both candidates stirred up racial animosity. There were also determined and ultimately successful efforts under way to disfranchise black voters in Georgia.

On a warm Saturday night, September 22, 1906, a white man jumped on a box on Decatur Street, one of Atlanta's main thoroughfares, and waved an Atlanta newspaper emblazoned with the headline THIRD ASSAULT. He hollered, "Are white men going to stand for this?" The crowd roared, "No! Save our women!" "Kill the niggers." A five-day orgy of violence followed.

The mayor, police, and fire departments vainly tried to stop the mob. Thousands of white people roamed the streets in search of black victims. Black people were tortured, beaten, and killed. White men pulled black passengers off streetcars. They destroyed black businesses. As white men armed themselves, the police disarmed black men. Black men and women who surrendered to marauding white mobs in hopes of mercy were not spared. Black men who fought back only infuriated the crazed white crowd. Twenty-five black people and one white person died, and hundreds were injured, in the riot.

Du Bois hurried home to Atlanta from Alabama to defend his family. He waited on his porch with a shotgun for a mob that never came: "I would without hesitation have sprayed their guts over the grass." In New York, black editor T. Thomas Fortune called for a violent black response: "It makes my blood boil. I would like to be there with a good force of armed men to make Rome howl. I cannot believe that the policy of non-resistance in a situation like that of Atlanta can result in anything but contempt and massacre of the race."

Booker T. Washington looked for a silver lining in the awful affair by noting that "while there is disorder in one community there is peace and harmony in thousands of others." He said that black resistance would merely result in more black fatalities. Washington went to Atlanta and appealed for racial reconciliation.

A Committee of Safety of 10 black and 10 white leaders was formed. Charles T. Hopkins, an influential white Atlantan, warned in strong paternalist terms: "If we let this dependent race be butchered before our eyes, we cannot face God in the judgment day." But little real racial cooperation resulted. Black minister Henry Hugh Proctor worked with white leaders and often seemed to agree with them that Atlanta's main problem was black crime, not white racism.

No members of the white mob were brought to justice. Black Georgia voters were disfranchised. Atlanta's streetcars were segregated. The city had no public high school for black youngsters. The Carnegie Library did not admit black people, and the Atlanta police force had no black officers.

16.6.2 Springfield, 1908

Two years later in August 1908, white citizens of Springfield, Illinois, attacked black residents in an episode that led to the creation of the NAACP in 1909. George Richardson, a black man, was falsely accused of raping a white woman. Although the sheriff got

Richardson out of town, a mob tore into Springfield's small black population. Six black people were shot and killed, two were lynched, dozens were injured, and black homes and businesses were wrecked. About 2,000 black people were driven out of Springfield.

Major racial conflicts occurred between 1917 and 1921 in East St. Louis, Illinois; Houston; Chicago; Elaine, Arkansas; and Tulsa. Smaller violent confrontations occurred in Washington, D.C.; Charleston; Knoxville, Tennessee; Omaha; and Waco and Longview, Texas. Although different incidents sparked each riot, the underlying causes were similar. White residents feared that black migrants would compete for jobs and housing.

16.6.3 East St. Louis, 1917

East St. Louis, Illinois, was a gritty industrial town of nearly 60,000 across the Mississippi River from St. Louis, Missouri. About 10 percent of the inhabitants were black. The town's schools, public facilities, and neighborhoods were segregated. Racial tensions increased in February 1917 after 470 black workers were hired to replace white members of the American Federation of Labor who had gone on strike against the Aluminum Ore Company. On July 1, white people drove through a black neighborhood firing guns. Shortly after, two white plainclothes police officers drove into the same neighborhood and were shot and killed by residents who may have believed the drive-by shooters had returned.

Angry white mobs sought revenge. Black people were mutilated and killed and their bodies thrown into the river. Black homes, many of them little more than cabins and shacks, were burned. Hundreds of black people were left homeless. The police joined the rioters. Thirty-five black people and eight white people died in the violence.

The NAACP sent W. E. B. Du Bois and Martha Gruening to East St. Louis. They compiled a report, "Massacre at East St. Louis," that documented instance after instance of brutality: "Negroes were 'flushed' from the burning houses, and ran for their lives, screaming and begging for mercy. A Negro crawled into a shed and fired on the white men. Guardsmen started after him, but when they saw he was armed, one of them turned to the mob and said: 'He's armed boys. You can have him. A white man's life is worth the lives of a thousand Negroes.' "

To protest the riot, the NAACP organized a silent demonstration in New York City, and thousands of well-dressed black people marched to muffled drums down Fifth Avenue.

16.6.4 Houston, 1917

A month after the East St. Louis riot, black soldiers in Houston attacked police officers and civilians. The Third Battalion of the 24th Infantry recently had been transferred from Wyoming and California to Camp Logan near Houston, where the black troops came face-to-face with Jim Crow. Streetcars and public facilities were segregated. White and Hispanic people regularly called the black troops "niggers."

On August 23 a black soldier tried to prevent a police officer, Lee Sparks, from beating a black woman. Sparks clubbed the soldier and hauled him off to jail. Corporal Charles W. Baltimore attempted to determine what had happened, and he was also beaten and incarcerated. Although both soldiers were later released, a rumor circulated that Baltimore had been slain. Led by Sergeant Vida Henry, black men sought revenge.

About 100 armed black soldiers mounted a two-hour assault on the police station. Fifteen white residents—including five policemen—and one Mexican American, four black soldiers, and two black civilians were killed. The army arrested 118 black soldiers and charged 63 of them with mutiny. Three separate court-martials were held. The NAACP retained the son of Texas legend Sam Houston to help defend them. Eight black men, however, agreed to testify against the defendants. Thirteen black troops were hanged (including Corporal Baltimore) after the first court-martial. Later

On July 28, 1917, the NAACP organized a silent march in New York City to protest the East St. Louis, Illinois, race riot, in which 35 black people died, as well as to denounce the ongoing epidemic of lynchings. The marchers were accompanied by the beat of muffled drums.

seven more were executed, seven others were acquitted, and the rest were sentenced to prison terms.

While the Houston violence prompted some political and military leaders to call for the abolition of the black regiments, Du Bois eulogized the first 13 black soldiers to be executed: "Thirteen young men, strong men, soldiers who have fought for a country which never was wholly theirs; men born to suffer ridicule, injustice and, at last, death itself." In the meantime, Lee Sparks remained on the Houston police force and killed two black people later that year.

16.6.5 Chicago, 1919

Between 1916 and 1919, the black population of Chicago doubled as migrants from the South moved north in search of jobs, political rights, and humane treatment. Many encountered a violent reception. A housing shortage strained the boundaries between crowded, segregated black neighborhoods and white residential areas. After World War I ended in November 1918, racial tensions increased as black men were hired to replace striking white workers in Chicago.

With summer temperatures rising and racial tensions escalating, Ida B. Wells anticipated a major conflict in the pages of the *Chicago Tribune* in early July. "With one Negro dead as a result of the race riot last week, another one very badly injured in the county hospital; with a half-dozen attacks upon Negro children, and one on the Thirty-fifth street car Tuesday, in which four white men beat one colored man, it looks very much like Chicago is trying to rival the south in its race hatred against the Negro."

The Chicago riot began on Sunday, July 27, 1919—one day after black troops were welcomed home with a parade down the city's Michigan Avenue. Eugene Williams, a young black man, was swimming in Lake Michigan and inadvertently crossed the invisible boundary that separated the black and white beaches and bathing areas. He was stoned by white people and drowned. Instead of arresting the alleged perpetrators, the police arrested a black man who complained about police inaction.

Williams's death set off a week of violence that left 23 black people and 15 white people dead. More than 500 were injured, and nearly 1,000 were left homeless after fire raged through a Lithuanian neighborhood. Police often joined white mobs as they attacked black pedestrians and streetcar passengers. Black men formed a barrier along State Street to stop white gangs from the stockyard district. Three regiments of the Illinois National Guard were sent into the streets, but the violence did not end until August 1, when heavy rains kept people indoors.

During the riot, the *Chicago Defender*, the city's black newspaper, reported many violent incidents: "In the early [Tuesday] morning a thirteen-year-old lad standing on his porch at 51st and Wabash Avenue was shot to death by a white man who, in an attempt to get away, encountered a mob and his existence became history. A mounted policeman, unknown, fatally wounded a small boy in the block of Dearborn Street and was shot to death by some unknown rioter."

16.6.6 Elaine, 1919

In 1919, black sharecroppers in and around Elaine, Arkansas, attempted to organize a union and withhold their cotton from the market until they received a higher price. Deputy sheriffs tried to break up a union meeting in a black church, and one of the deputies was killed. In retaliation, white people killed dozens of black people. No white people were prosecuted, but 12 black men were convicted of the deputy's murder. They were sentenced to death, and 67 other black men received prison terms of up to 20 years. Many were tortured and beaten in jail. Ida Wells Barnett and the Equal Rights League generated enormous publicity about the case. The NAACP appealed the convictions, and in 1923 the Supreme Court overturned them.

16.6.7 Tulsa, 1921

Violence erupted in Tulsa on May 31, 1921, after still another black man was accused of rape. Dick Rowland allegedly assaulted a white woman elevator operator, and rumors circulated that white men intended to lynch him. To protect Rowland, who was later found innocent, black men assembled at the jail as white men also gathered there. Angry words were exchanged, and shooting erupted. Several black and white men died in the chaos that ensued.

Black men retreated to their neighborhood, known as Greenwood, to protect their families and homes. The governor dispatched the National Guard, and the sheriff sent Rowland to an unknown location. By the morning of June 1, 500 white men confronted about 1,000 black men across a set of railroad tracks. White men in automobiles were cruising around the black residential area. Approximately 50 armed black people defended themselves in a black church near the edge of Greenwood as white men advanced on them. The attackers set fire to the church. As black people fled the burning building, they were shot. More fires were set. About 2,000 black residents managed to escape to a convention hall. Forty square blocks and more than 1,000 of Greenwood's homes, churches, schools, and businesses went up in flames. White men even used aircraft for reconnaissance and to drop incendiary devices on Greenwood. As many as 300 black people and 20 white people may have perished in what was one of the worst episodes of civilian violence in American history until September 11, 2001.

In 2001, a biracial commission recommended that the Oklahoma legislature offer restitution. The legislators declined to set aside funds for

The Greenwood neighborhood of Tulsa, Oklahoma, in flames during the riot in June 1921.

survivors, but they did appropriate $750,000 to formulate plans for a museum and memorial. They also created a Greenwood Redevelopment Authority and a scholarship program.

16.6.8 Rosewood, 1923

In January 1923, the small town of Rosewood, Florida, was destroyed, and its black residents were driven out or killed. Rosewood was a mostly black community—it had a few white inhabitants—in the pinewoods of west-central Florida not far from the Gulf of Mexico. On New Year's Day, Fannie Taylor, a married white woman from a nearby town, claimed a black man had raped and beaten her. White people assumed Jessie Hunter was responsible. Other white people believed Mrs. Taylor wanted to divert attention away from herself because she had a white lover who was not her husband.

White men sought Hunter and vengeance. Unable to find him, they beat Aaron Carrier, who may have helped Taylor's white lover escape. The mob killed Samuel Carter after mutilating him. Tensions escalated.

On January 4 an angry mob invaded Rosewood, but the black people there were prepared to defend themselves. Led by Sylvester Carrier and his mother Sarah, many townspeople had congregated in the Carrier home. The mob fired on the residence, killing Sarah Carrier. Two white men who attempted to enter the home were killed. Shooting continued until the mob ran out of ammunition on January 5.

The next day a mob of 250, including Ku Klux Klan members from Gainesville, invaded, burned, and destroyed Rosewood. The community's black residents fled to the woods and swamps with little more than the clothes on their backs, never to return. Rosewood was no more.

The precise number of black people who died will never be known. It may have exceeded 100. In 1994 the Florida legislature appropriated $2.1 million to survivors of Rosewood and to families who lost property in the assault. Ten survivors were still alive and collected $150,000 each. But many black people could not verify that they had been in Rosewood in 1923 or that they were kin to people who had owned property there. As a result, much of the money was not disbursed.

16.7 The Great Migration

Explain why African Americans began to leave the rural South in the early twentieth century, and describe the types of lives they made for themselves in urban communities.

The Great Migration of African Americans from the rural South to the urban North began as a trickle after the Civil War and became a flood by the second decade of the twentieth century (see Table 16-1). Between 1910 and 1940, 1.75 million black people left the South. As a result, the black population outside the South doubled by 1940. Most of the initial wave of migrants were younger people born in the 1880s and 1890s who had no recollection of slavery but anticipated a better future for themselves and their families in the North.

16.7.1 Why Migrate?

People moved for many reasons. Often they were both pushed from their rural homes and pulled toward urban areas. The push resulted from disasters in southern agriculture in the 1910s. The boll weevil destroyed cotton crops across the South, and floods devastated Mississippi and Alabama in 1915. The pull resulted from labor shortages created by World War I in northern industry and manufacturing. The war interrupted European immigration to the United States, eliminating a main source of cheap labor. At the same time, European governments and the United States placed huge orders for

Table 16-1 Black Population Growth in Selected Northern Cities, 1910–1920

	1910		1920		
	Number	Percentage*	Number	Percentage*	Percentage Increase
New York	91,709	1.9%	152,467	2.7%	66.3%
Chicago	44,103	2.0	109,458	4.1	148.2
Philadelphia	84,459	5.5	134,229	7.4	58.9
Detroit	5,741	1.2	40,838	4.1	611.3
St. Louis	43,960	6.4	69,854	9.0	58.9
Cleveland	8,448	1.5	34,451	4.3	307.8
Pittsburgh	25,623	4.8	37,725	6.4	47.2
Cincinnati	19,739	5.4	30,079	7.5	53.2
Indianapolis	21,816	9.3	34,678	11.0	59.0
Newark	9,475	2.7	16,977	4.1	79.2
Kansas City	23,566	9.5	30,719	9.5	30.4
Columbus	12,739	7.0	22,181	9.4	74.1
Gary	383	2.3	5,299	9.6	1,283.6
Youngstown	1,936	2.4	6,662	5.0	244.1
Buffalo	1,773	.4	4,511	.9	154.4
Toledo	1,877	1.1	5,691	2.3	203.2
Akron	657	1.0	5,580	2.7	749.3

*"Percentage" refers to percentage of city's population; "Percentage Increase" refers to growth of the black population.

SOURCE: U.S. Department of Commerce.

war material with northern factories. Thousands of jobs became available in steel mills, railroads, meatpacking plants, and the automobile industry. Northern businessmen sent labor agents to recruit southern workers.

Many southern white people reacted ambivalently to the loss of black residents. They welcomed the departure of people for whom they had contempt, but they also worried about the loss of tenants and sharecroppers. Southern states and municipalities required labor agents to obtain licenses to recruit workers. Angry white landowners and businessmen forced some of these agents to leave southern towns.

Black newspapers, such as the *Pittsburgh Courier* and especially the *Chicago Defender*, encouraged black southerners to move north. Black railroad porters and dining car employees distributed thousands of copies of the *Defender* throughout the South. One unnamed black man wrote in the *Defender* that sensible men would leave the poverty, injustice, and violence of the South for the cold weather of the North: "To die from the bite of frost is far more glorious than that of the mob. I beg of you, my brothers, to leave that benighted land. You are free men."

A black resident of South Carolina's sea islands explained in 1917 that he left to earn more money: "I could work and dig all year on the Island and best I could do would be to make $100 and take a chance of making nothin'. Well, I figured I could make 'roun' thirty or thirty-five dollars every week and at that rate save possibly $100 every two months." Like many migrants, he moved more than once. He first went to Savannah and then to Philadelphia before finally settling in New York.

Black people who departed the South (see Table 16-2) escaped the most blatant forms of Jim Crow and the injustice in the judicial system. Black women fled the sexual exploitation of white and black men. Black people in the North could vote. The North also offered better public schools. In the early twentieth century the South had almost no public high schools for black youngsters, and the longer school year in the urban North was not tied to the demands of planting and harvesting crops.

Some black people migrated to escape the dull, bleak, impoverished life and culture of the rural South. One young woman left South Carolina's St. Helena Island in 1919: "[I] got tired of the Island. Too lonesome. Go to bed at six o'clock. Everything dead.

Table 16-2 African-American Migration from the South

1910s	550,000
1920s	903,000
1930s	480,000
1940s	1,600,000
1950s	1,400,000
1960s	1,000,000
Total	5,933,000

SOURCE: Based on Isabel Wilkerson, *The Warmth of Other Suns: The Epic Story of America's Great Migration*. New York: Random House, Vintage Books, 2010, pp. 161, 217, 218. © Darlene Clark Hine.

No dances, no moving picture show, no nothing. 'Coz every once in a while they would have a dance, but here you could go to 'em every Saturday night. That's why people move more than anything else."

The decision to migrate could take years of pondering and planning. To depart was to leave family, friends, and familiar surroundings behind for the uncertainty, confusion, and rapid pace of urban communities. Migrants often first moved to southern towns or cities and then headed for a larger city. Writer Langston Hughes was born in Joplin, Missouri, in 1902 and moved to Lincoln, Illinois: "I had no sooner graduated from grammar school in Lincoln than we moved from Illinois to Cleveland. My stepfather sent for us. He was working in a steel mill during the war, and making lots of money. But it was hard work, and he never looked the same afterwards."

Some people made the decision to move impulsively. After she was fired from her nursing position at Hampton Institute in Virginia in 1905, Jane Edna Hunter decided to go to Florida but changed her mind:

> En route, I stopped at Richmond, Virginia, to visit with Mr. and Mrs. William Coleman, friends of Uncle Parris.
>
> They were at church when I arrived; so I sat on the doorstep to await their return. After these good friends had greeted me, Mrs. Coleman said, 'Our bags are packed to go to Cleveland, Jane. We are going to take you with us.' I was swept off my feet by the cheerful determination of the Colemans. My trunk, not yet removed from the station, was rechecked to Cleveland.

Most migrants maintained a fondness for their southern homes and kinfolk. They returned for holidays, weddings, and funerals. Kelly Miller, who had grown up in South Carolina, spent years as a scholar and teacher at Howard University, but he still had "an attachment for the old state that time and distance cannot destroy. After all, we love to be known as a South Carolinian." Thousands of black migrants routinely sent money home. Over the years, millions of dollars earned in the North flowed into southern communities.

16.7.2 Destinations

Although many black southerners went to Florida, most migrants from the Carolinas and Virginia settled in Washington, D.C., Philadelphia, and New York (see Map 16-2). Black people who left Georgia, Alabama, and Mississippi tended to move to Pittsburgh, Cleveland, and Detroit. Migrants from Louisiana, Mississippi, and Arkansas often rode the Illinois Central Railroad to Chicago. Once they experienced a metropolis, many black people then resettled in smaller communities. Migrants to Philadelphia, for example, moved on to Harrisburg or Altoona, Pennsylvania, or to Wilmington, Delaware.

Few black southerners moved west to California, Oregon, or Washington. California had only 22,000 black residents in 1910. Substantial black migration west did not occur until the 1930s and 1940s. But in 1920 Mallie Robinson made the long trek west. Deserted by her husband, she set out with her five children (including one-year-old Jackie, who would become a baseball legend) and eight other relatives. They boarded a train in Cairo, Georgia; traveled to Los Angeles; and settled in nearby Pasadena. Mallie's half brother, who had already moved west, assured her she would be closer to heaven in California.

However, most black migrants found their destination was near neither heaven nor the Promised Land. As early as 1899 Black Chicago leader Fannie Barrier Williams observed "the negroes in the south have learned from the experiences of those who have already come north that there is a distressing scarcity of the milk and honey which they dreamed of. They have begun to learn that the prejudice from which they would flee has been here all the time, and is ready to confront them in this rose colored haven of liberty and equality."

Map 16-2 The Great Migration and the Distribution of the African-American Population in 1920
Although several hundred thousand black southerners migrated north during the second and third decades of the twentieth century in the largest internal migration in American history, most African Americans remained in the southern states.

Why did most African Americans stay in the South if so many opportunities beckoned in the North?

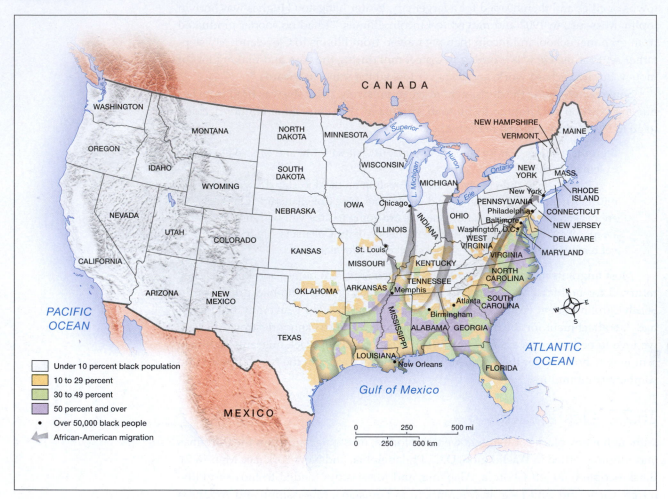

Black people congregated in all-black neighborhoods—Harlem in New York City, Chicago's South Side, Paradise Valley in Detroit, Cleveland's East Side, and the Hill District of Pittsburgh—that later would be called ghettoes. White owners resisted selling or renting property to black people outside of these neighborhoods. And many southern black migrants themselves, wary of white hostility, preferred to live among black people, often friends and family who had preceded them north.

16.7.3 Migration from the Caribbean

Many descendants of Africans who had been slaves in the sugarcane fields of the West Indies joined the migration of black southerners to the North. Between 1900 and 1924, 102,000 West Indians came to the United States. Most came from British colonies including Jamaica, Barbados, Montserrat, and Trinidad and Tobago. But black immigrants also arrived from French-held Guadeloupe and Martinique, the Dutch colonies of Aruba and Curacao, and the Danish Virgin Islands (which the United States acquired in 1917). Some of these migrants were middle-class professionals and skilled workers, but many had been employed as laborers building the Panama Canal from 1904 to 1914.

Although white Americans tended to lump all people of color together, regardless of their complexion or origin, the West Indians often did not mix comfortably with African Americans. Some spoke Dutch and French. Those who came from British islands were usually Anglicans (Episcopalians) and not Baptists or Methodists. Almost all of the newcomers sent money home to families in the West Indies. Moreover, many of the Caribbean arrivals were temporary residents; as many as one-third of them would return to the West Indies. In 1924 Congress restricted immigration to the United States, and migration from the Caribbean dropped drastically.

16.7.4 Northern Communities

Even before the Civil War, most northern cities had small free black populations. By the late nineteenth century, southern migrants began to gravitate to these urban areas and make their presence felt. Black residents established churches, social organizations, businesses, and medical facilities. They gained representation in community and political affairs.

There was less overt segregation in the North. Most northern states and California prohibited racial discrimination in public transportation, hotels, restaurants, theaters, and barbershops. Most of these states also forbade segregated schools. However, enacting such laws and enforcing them were two different matters. Many white businesses and communities ignored the statutes and embraced Jim Crow, especially along the Ohio River in southern Ohio, Indiana, and Illinois.

CHICAGO   As early as 1872, Chicago had a black policeman, and in 1876 John W. E. Thomas became the first black man elected to the Illinois Senate. Black physician Daniel

Voices

A Migrant to the North Writes Home

People who migrated to northern communities often wrote home to describe their new surroundings and experiences and to confess they missed their old homes. One unidentified black man who had moved to Philadelphia made his feelings known to a medical doctor.

> Oct. 7, 1919
>
> Philadelphia, Pa.,
>
> Dear Sir:
>
> I take this method of thanking you for yours early responding and the glorious effect of the treatment. Oh. I do feel so fine. Dr. the treatment reach me almost ready to move I am now housekeeping again I like it so much better than rooming. Well Dr. with the aid of God I am making very good I make $75 per month. I am carrying enough insurance to pay me $20 per week if I am not able to be on duty. I don't have to work hard. dont have to mister every little white boy comes along I havent heard a white man call a colored nigger you no now—since I been in the state of Pa. I can ride in the electric street and steam cars any where I get a seat. I dont care to mix with white what I mean I am not crazy about being with white folks, but if I have to pay the same fare I have learn to want the same accomodation. and if you are the first in a place here shoping you dont have to wait until the white folks get thro tradeing yet amid all this I shall ever love the good old South and I am praying that God may give every well wisher a chance to be a man regardless of his color, and if my going to the front [World War I] would bring about such conditions I am ready any day—well Dr. I dont want to worry you but read between the lines; and maybe you can see a little sense in my weak statement the kids are in school every day I have only two and I guess that all. Dr. when you find time I would be delighted to have word from the good old home state. Wife join me in sending love you and yours.

1. What is the writer's main reason for having migrated?
2. What was more important to this man, better living standards or the sense of liberation he enjoyed in Philadelphia?

SOURCE: Emmett J. Scott, ed., "Letters of Negro Migrants of 1916–1918," *Journal of Negro History* 4 (July 1, 1919), in Fishel and Quarles, *The Negro American: A Documentary History*, 398–99.

Hale Williams established African-American-staffed Provident Hospital on Chicago's South Side in 1891. By 1900 black Chicagoans were the twelfth largest ethnic group in the city, behind such European immigrant groups as the Irish, Poles, and Germans.

Chicago's black population surged from 1900 to 1930 as migrants poured into the city. Black institutions flourished. In 1912 an NAACP branch was established. By 1920 black Chicago had 80 Baptist and 36 Methodist churches. The Olivet Baptist Church grew from 3,500 members in 1916 to 9,000 by 1922. Because the downtown YMCA barred black men, black people raised $50,000 and Julius Rosenwald of Sears, Roebuck and Company contributed $25,000 to build the Wabash YMCA for the black community in 1913. However, many black Chicagoans considered this a surrender to segregation and insisted that they should be admitted to the white YMCA.

The *Chicago Defender* was the city's leading black newspaper. Its founder, Robert S. Abbott, the son of slaves, began publishing the *Defender* in 1905, and by 1920 it had a nationwide circulation of 230,000. Chicago's first black bank, Jesse Binga's State Bank, was established in 1908, and in 1919 Frank L. Gillespie organized the Liberty Insurance Company.

In 1915 black Chicago's political influence expanded when Oscar DePriest was elected second-ward alderman. Two other black men were elected to the city council by 1918. DePriest was then elected to the U.S. House of Representatives as a Republican in 1928, becoming the first black congressman since North Carolina's George White left the House in 1901.

As the number of black Chicagoans swelled, racial tensions exploded in the 1919 race riot. Competition for jobs was a critical issue. White employers, such as the meatpacking companies, regularly replaced white strikers with black workers. Black men took such jobs because most labor unions would not admit them. But a few weeks before the riot in 1919, the Amalgamated Meatcutters Union tried to sponsor a unity parade of black and white stockyard workers. The police prohibited it because, some observers believed, the meatpacking companies feared that black and white working men might unite.

Housing was an even more divisive issue than employment. Chicago's black population was almost entirely confined to an eight-square-mile area on the South Side east of State Street. Prosperous black people who could afford more expensive housing outside the area could not purchase it because of their race. As the black population grew, housing became more congested, and crime and vice increased.

Langston Hughes described the similar situation his family experienced in Cleveland:

> Rents were very high for colored people in Cleveland, and the Negro district was extremely crowded, because of the great migration. It was difficult to find a place to live. We always lived, during my high school years, either in an attic or a basement, and paid quite a lot for such inconvenient quarters. White people on the east side of the city were moving out of their frame houses and renting them to Negroes at double and triple the rents they could receive from others. An eight room house with one bath would be cut up into apartments and five or six families crowded into it, each two-room kitchenette apartment renting for what the whole house had rented for before.

HARLEM   Harlem was a white community in upper Manhattan that had declined by the latter 1800s. It then enjoyed a building boom that occurred in anticipation of the construction of the subway that would link upper Manhattan to downtown New York City by the early twentieth century. But real estate speculators overbuilt and were left with empty houses and apartments. Facing foreclosure, many white property owners sold or rented to black people in Harlem. In 1904 Philip A. Payton formed the Afro American Realty Company, which sold homes and rented apartments to black clients before it failed in 1908.

Harlem's white residents opposed the influx of black people. Some of them formed the Harlem Property Owners' Improvement Corporation in 1910 to block black settlement. Its founder, John G. Taylor, warned in 1913, "We are approaching a crisis, it is a question of whether the white man will rule Harlem or the Negro." However, many white property owners—eager for a profit—preferred to sell to black people rather than maintain white unity.

As thousands of black people moved to Harlem, many left the "Tenderloin" and "San Juan Hill" areas of Manhattan's West Side, where New York's black residents had lived in the nineteenth century. The construction of Pennsylvania Station forced many to vacate the "Tenderloin." Black churches took the lead in the "On to Harlem" movement as they occupied churches white denominations had formerly used. Some black churches were among the largest property owners in Harlem.

St. Philip's Protestant Episcopal Church, the wealthiest black church in the United States—and noted for its solemn services and elite parishioners—moved in 1910 from West 25th Street in the "Tenderloin" to Harlem. In 1911 St. Philip's purchased 10 apartment houses on West 135th Street between Lennox and Seventh Avenues for $640,000. The Rev. Adam Clayton Powell, Sr. and the Abyssinian Baptist Church, St. Mark's Episcopal Church, and the African Methodist Episcopal Zion Church ("Mother Zion") also moved to Harlem and acquired extensive real estate holdings there. The black churches helped make Harlem a black community.

As Harlem's black population increased, large houses and apartments were often subdivided among working families that could not rent or buy in other areas of New York. They paid higher prices for real estate than white people did. The average Harlem family paid $9.50 a room per month. White working families paid $6.50 for similar accommodations elsewhere in New York.

By 1920, 75,000 black people lived in Harlem (see Map 16-3). Harlem became the "Negro Capital of the World." Black businesses and institutions, including the Odd Fellows, Masons, Elks, Pythians, the NAACP, the Urban League, and the YMCA and YWCA, moved to Harlem. Black newspapers—the *New York News* and *Amsterdam News*—opened in Harlem to compete with the older *New York Age*. One resident exclaimed, "If my race can make Harlem, good lord, what can't it do?"

FAMILIES Migration placed black families under enormous strains. Relatives frequently moved north separately. Fathers or mothers would leave a spouse and children behind as they sought employment and housing. Children might be left with grandparents. Extended family members—cousins, in-laws, brothers, and sisters—crowded into limited living space.

Men generally found more opportunities for work in northern industries than women did. Unskilled labor during and after World War I was in huge demand. In 1915 Henry Ford astounded industrial America when he began to pay employees of the Ford Motor Company in Detroit the unprecedented sum of $5 per day, and that included black men and occasionally black women. Rarely, however, was a black man promoted beyond menial labor. Except for some opportunities in manufacturing during the war, black women were confined to domestic and janitorial work. Mary Ellen Washington recalled the experience in her family: "In the 1920s my mother and five aunts migrated to Cleveland, Ohio, from Indianapolis and, in spite of their many talents, they found every door except the kitchen door closed to them."

Black women employed as domestics lived with white families, worked long hours, and saw more of their white employer's children than they did their own. One maid explained her dreary and unhappy situation:

> I am now past forty years of age and am the mother of three children. My husband died nearly fifteen years ago. . . . For more than thirty years—or since I was ten years old—I have been a servant in one capacity or another in white families.

Map 16-3   The Expansion of Black Harlem, 1911–1930

Before the American Revolution, Harlem was a small Dutch village located at the northern end of Manhattan island. In the early twentieth century, African Americans transformed it into a thriving black metropolis. Migrants who arrived either after a short trip of just a few miles from the "Tenderloin" or "San Juan Hill" sections of midtown Manhattan or after much longer journeys from the Carolinas or Georgia took over block after block of Harlem homes and apartments.

Why did most African Americans settle in Harlem and not elsewhere in New York City?

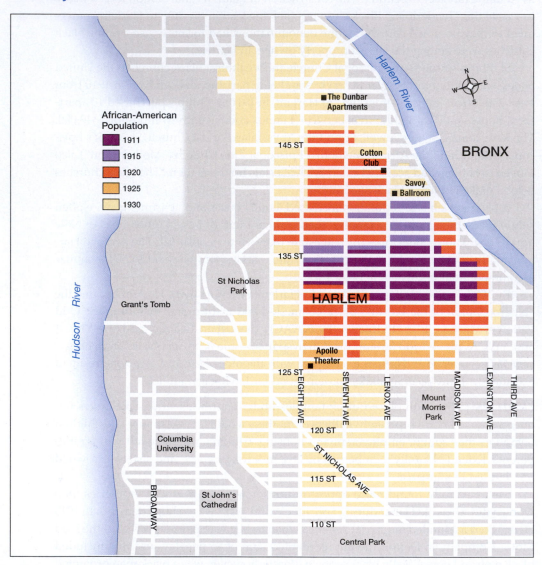

I frequently work from fourteen to sixteen hours a day. I am compelled . . . to sleep in the house. I am allowed to go home to my own children, the oldest of whom is a girl of 18 years, only once in two weeks, every other Sunday afternoon—even then I'm not permitted to stay all night. . . . I don't know what it is to go to church; I don't know what it is to go to a lecture or entertainment of any kind; I live a treadmill life. . . . You might as well say that I'm on duty all the time—from sunrise to sunrise, every day in the week. I am the slave, body and soul, of this family.

Some vulnerable younger women were lured into prostitution in the intimidating urban environment. Black women's organizations worked to prevent newly arrived migrants from being sexually exploited. They did not always succeed. Some women made a calculated decision to turn sex to their economic advantage. Sara Brooks caustically commented, "Some women woulda had a man to come and live in the house and had an outside boyfriend too, in order to get the house paid for and the bills. They meet a man and if he promises 'em four or five dollars to go to bed, they's grab it. That's called sellin' your own body, and I wasn't raised like that."

Despite the stresses and pressures, most black families survived intact. Most northern black families, although hardly well to do, were two-parent households. Women headed comparatively few families. Fathers were present in 7 of 10 black families in New York City in 1925. But the Great Migration transformed southern peasants into an urban proletariat.

Conclusion

In 1900 Booker T. Washington was the nation's most influential black leader. He soothed white people and reassured black Americans as he counseled conciliation, patience, and agricultural and mechanical training as the most effective means to bridge the racial divide. His 1895 speech at the Cotton States Exposition in Atlanta elicited praise from both white and black listeners.

The Wizard of Tuskegee, as Washington was known, had little appreciation for criticism and did not hesitate to attack his opponents, including William Monroe Trotter and W. E. B. Du Bois. He worked to subvert the Niagara Movement and the NAACP. But support for Washington and his conservative strategy diminished as the NAACP openly confronted racial discrimination. Washington died in 1915. By 1920 the NAACP took the lead in the struggle for civil rights as it fought in the courts and legislatures.

The Talented Tenth of black Americans, distinguished by their educational and economic resources, promoted "self-help" through a variety of organizations—from women's groups to fraternities and sororities—to enhance their own status and help less affluent black people.

As black men served in World War I and as thousands of black southerners migrated north, many white Americans became alarmed that African Americans were not as content with their subordinate and isolated status as Booker T. Washington had suggested they were. Some white Americans responded with violence in race riots as they attempted to prevent black Americans from assuming a more equitable role in American society. By 1920, despite white opposition, black Americans had demonstrated they would not accept economic subservience and the denial of their rights.

Chapter Timeline

AFRICAN-AMERICAN EVENTS	NATIONAL EVENTS

1895–1900

AFRICAN-AMERICAN EVENTS	NATIONAL EVENTS
1895	**1896**
Frederick Douglass dies; Booker T. Washington delivers Cotton States Exposition address	William McKinley is elected president
1896	**1898**
Plessy v. Ferguson	Spanish-American War
	1899
1898	Philippine insurrection begins
Riot erupts in Wilmington, North Carolina	**1900**
	President McKinley reelected
1900	
New Orleans riot	

AFRICAN-AMERICAN EVENTS	NATIONAL EVENTS
1900–1905	
1903	**1901**
W. E. B. Du Bois publishes *The Souls of Black Folk*	McKinley is assassinated; Theodore Roosevelt becomes president
	1904
	Theodore Roosevelt elected president
1905–1910	
1905	**1905**
Niagara Movement founded at Niagara Falls, Canada; the *Defender* founded in Chicago	Thomas Dixon publishes *The Clansman*; the film *Birth of a Nation* is based on the novel
1906	**1908**
Brownsville affair; Atlanta riot	William Howard Taft elected president
1908	
Springfield riot	
1909	
NAACP is founded	
1910–1915	
1910	**1912**
Urban League founded in New York City	Woodrow Wilson elected president
1912	**1914**
Du Bois endorses Woodrow Wilson for president	World War I breaks out in Europe
1915–1920	
1915	**1916**
Guinn v. United States overturns the Oklahoma grandfather clause; Booker T. Washington dies	President Wilson reelected
1917	**1917**
East St. Louis riot; Houston riot	United States enters World War I
1919	**1918**
Chicago riot; Elaine, Arkansas, riot	World War I ends
1920	**1919**
Harlem becomes "The Negro Capital of the World"	Treaty of Versailles
1921	**1920**
Tulsa riot occurs	Nineteenth Amendment (women's suffrage) ratified; Warren Harding elected president
1923	
Rosewood destroyed	

Review Questions

1. How did the strategies promoted by Booker T. Washington differ from those of W. E. B. Du Bois and the NAACP? Which were more effective?

2. Assess Washington's contributions to the advancement of black people.

3. How did middle-class and prosperous black people try to contribute to progress for their race? Were their efforts effective?

4. Why did most African Americans support U.S. participation in World War I? Was that support justified?

5. What factors contributed to race riots and violence in the World War I era?

6. Why did many black people leave the South in the 1920s? Why didn't this migration begin earlier or later?

7. Why did migrants decide to leave or to stay?

Retracing the Odyssey

The Booker T. Washington National Monument, Hardy, Virginia. Booker T. Washington lived his first nine years on this farm. A museum and restored schoolhouse depict rural life in nineteenth-century America, especially for slaves.

The George Washington Carver National Monument, Diamond, Missouri. George Washington Carver was born a slave here in 1864 or 1865 in a cabin that no longer exists. The 210-acre park has a visitor center that has exhibits on Carver's life as well as a short film about his boyhood. There are also nature trails and the Carver Science Discovery Center.

The 369th Historical Society, New York, New York. The 369th Regiment distinguished itself during World War I in combat alongside French units. Previously it had been the 15th Infantry Regiment of the New York National Guard. The 369th Armory contains a museum that features weapons, equipment, and photos of black troops from World War I to Operation Desert Storm of 1991.

The Greenwood Cultural Center, Tulsa, Oklahoma. The Greenwood Cultural Center has a permanent exhibit of 45 photos taken during the 1921 riot that devastated the Greenwood community. There is also a replica of one of the houses that was destroyed. The center maintains exhibits on other aspects of local black history as well, and it is home to a Jazz Hall of Fame.

Recommended Reading

W. E. B. Du Bois. *The Souls of Black Folk*. New York: Library of America, 1903. An essential collection of superb essays.

John Hope Franklin and August Meier. *Black Leaders of the Twentieth Century*. Urbana: University of Illinois Press, 1982. Fifteen "minibiographies," including those of Washington, Du Bois, T. Thomas Fortune, and Ida Wells Barnett.

Willard Gatewood. *Aristocrats of Color: The Black Elite, 1880–1920*. Bloomington: Indiana University Press, 1990. An examination of the lives and activities of well-to-do black people.

Lawrence Otis Graham. *One Kind of People: Inside America's Black Upper Class*. New York: HarperCollins, 1999. An informative history and analysis of black America's wealthiest families and organizations.

Louis R. Harlan. *Booker T. Washington: The Making of a Black Leader, 1856–1901*. New York: Oxford University Press, 1972; and *Booker T. Washington: The Wizard of Tuskegee, 1901–1915*. New York: Oxford University Press, 1983. The definitive two-volume biography.

David Levering Lewis. *W. E. B. Du Bois: Biography of a Race, 1868–1919*. New York: Henry Holt, 1993; and *W. E. B. Du Bois: The Fight for Equality and the American Century,*

1919–1963. New York: Henry Holt, 2001. A magisterial and exhaustive account of Du Bois's life and times.

Robert J. Norrell. *Up From History: The Life of Booker T. Washington.* Cambridge, MA: Harvard University Press, 2009. A positive assessment of the Wizard of Tuskegee.

Deborah Gray White. *Too Heavy a Load: Black Women in Defense of Themselves.* New York: W. W. Norton, 1999.

An exploration of black women's history in the twentieth century.

Isabel Wilkerson. *The Warmth of Other Suns: The Epic Story of America's Great Migration.* New York: Random House, 2010. This is an outstanding discussion and analysis of the people who migrated based on extensive research and marvelous oral histories.

Additional Bibliography

Leadership Conflicts and the Emergence of African-American Organizations

Tamara L. Brown, Gregory Parks, and Clarenda M. Phillips, eds. *African American Fraternities and Sororities: The Legacy and the Vision.* Lexington: University Press of Kentucky, 2005.

Deborah Davis. *Guest of Honor: Booker T. Washington, Theodore Roosevelt, and the White House Dinner That Shocked a Nation.* New York: Atria Books, 2012.

Kevin K. Gaines. *Uplifting the Race: Black Leadership, Politics, and Culture in the Twentieth Century.* Chapel Hill: University of North Carolina Press, 1996.

Charles F. Kellogg. *NAACP: A History of the National Association for the Advancement of Colored People.* Baltimore: Johns Hopkins University Press, 1967.

August Meier. *Negro Thought in America, 1880–1915.* Ann Arbor: University of Michigan Press, 1967.

Michele Mitchell. *Righteous Propagation: African Americans and the Politics of Racial Destiny After Reconstruction.* Chapel Hill: University of North Carolina Press, 2004.

Jacqueline Moore. *Booker T. Washington and W. E. B. Du Bois and the Struggle for Racial Uplift.* Wilmington, DE: Scholarly Resources, 2003.

Alfred A. Moss, Jr. *American Negro Academy: Voice of the Talented Tenth.* Baton Rouge: Louisiana State University Press, 1981.

B. Joyce Ross. *J. E. Spingarn and the Rise of the N.A.A.C.P.* New York: Atheneum, 1972.

Lawrence C. Ross, Jr. *The Divine Nine: The History of African-American Fraternities and Sororities.* New York: Kensington Books, 2000.

Elliott Rudwick. *W. E. B. Du Bois.* New York: Atheneum, 1968.

Nancy Weiss. *The National Urban League, 1910–1940.* New York: Oxford University Press, 1974.

Shamoon Zamir. *Dark Voices: W. E. B. Du Bois and American Thought, 1888–1903.* Chicago: University of Chicago Press, 1995.

African-American Women in the Early Twentieth Century

Elizabeth Clark-Lewis. *Living In, Living Out: African American Domestics in Washington, D.C., 1910–1940.* Washington, DC: Smithsonian Institution Press, 1994.

Bettye Collier-Thomas. *Jesus, Jobs, and Justice; African American Women and Religion.* New York: Alfred A. Knopf, 2010.

Anna Julia Cooper. *A Voice from the South.* New York: Oxford University Press, 1988.

Wanda A. Hendricks. *Fannie Barrier Williams: Crossing the Borders of Region and Race.* Urbana: University of Illinois Press, 2014.

Cynthia Neverdon-Morton. *Afro-American Women of the South and the Advancement of the Race, 1895–1925.* Knoxville: University of Tennessee Press, 1998.

Jacqueline A. Rouse. *Lugina Burns Hope: A Black Southern Reformer.* Athens: University of Georgia Press, 1989.

Stephanie J. Shaw. *What a Woman Ought to Be and to Do: Black Professional Women Workers During the Jim Crow Era.* Chicago: University of Chicago Press, 1996.

Rosalyn Terborg-Penn. *African American Women in the Struggle for the Vote, 1850–1920.* Bloomington: Indiana University Press, 1998.

African Americans in the Military in the World War I Era

Arthur E. Barbeau and Florette Henri. *Black American Troops in World War I.* Philadelphia: Temple University Press, 1974.

Edward M. Coffman. *The War to End All Wars: The American Military Experience in World War I.* Madison: University of Wisconsin Press, 1986.

Arthur W. Little. *From Harlem to the Rhine: The Story of New York's Colored Volunteers.* New York: Covici, Friede, 1936.

Bernard C. Nalty. *Strength for the Fight: A History of Black Americans in the Military.* New York: Free Press, 1986.

Cities and Racial Conflict

Michael D'Orso. *Like Judgment Day: The Ruin and Redemption of a Town Called Rosewood.* New York: Boulevard Press, 1996.

St. Clair Drake and Horace R. Clayton. *Black Metropolis: A Study of Negro Life in a Northern City.* 2 vols. Chicago: Harcourt, Brace, 1945.

Sherry Sherrod Dupree. *The Rosewood Massacre at a Glance.* Gainesville, FL: Rosewood Forum, 1998.

Scott Ellsworth. *Death in a Promised Land: The Tulsa Race Riot of 1921.* Baton Rouge: Louisiana State University Press, 1982.

David Fort Godshalk. *Veiled Visions: The 1906 Atlanta Race Riot and the Reshaping of American Race Relations.* Chapel Hill: University of North Carolina Press, 2005.

Robert V. Haynes. *A Night of Violence: The Houston Riot of 1917.* Baton Rouge: Louisiana State University Press, 1976.

Hannibal Johnson. *Black Wall Street, from Riot to Renaissance in Tulsa's Historic Greenwood District.* Austin, TX: Eakin Press, 1998.

David M. Katzman. *Before the Ghetto: Black Detroit in the Nineteenth Century.* Urbana: University of Illinois Press, 1973.

David F. Krugler. *1919, The Year of Racial Violence: How African Americans Fought Back.* New York: Cambridge University Press, 2015.

Kenneth L. Kusmer. *A Ghetto Takes Shape: Black Cleveland, 1870–1930.* Urbana: University of Illinois Press, 1976.

Gregory Mixon. *The Atlanta Riot: Race, Class, and Violence in a New South City.* Gainesville: University Press of Florida, 2005.

Kevin J. Mumford. *Interzones: Black/White Sex Districts in Chicago and New York in the Early Twentieth Century.* New York: Columbia University Press, 1997.

Gilbert Osofsky. *Harlem: The Making of a Ghetto, 1890–1930.* New York: Harper and Row, 1966.

Christopher Reed. *The Chicago NAACP and the Rise of Black Professional Leadership, 1910–1966.* Bloomington: Indiana University Press, 1997.

Elliott M. Rudwick. *Race Riot at East St. Louis, July 2, 1917.* Cleveland, OH: World, 1966.

Roberta Senechal. *The Sociogenesis of a Race Riot: Springfield, Illinois, in 1908.* Urbana: University of Illinois Press, 1990.

Allan H. Spear. *Black Chicago: The Making of a Negro Ghetto, 1890–1920.* Chicago: University of Chicago Press, 1967.

Joe William Trotter, Jr. *Black Milwaukee: The Making of an Industrial Proletariat, 1915–1945.* Urbana: University of Illinois Press, 1985.

William Tuttle. *Chicago in the Red Summer of 1919.* New York: Atheneum, 1970.

Lee E. Williams. *Anatomy of Four Race Riots: Racial Conflict in Knoxville, Elaine (Arkansas), Tulsa, and Chicago, 1919–1921.* Hattiesburg: University and College Press of Mississippi, 1972.

The Great Migration

Peter Gottlieb. *Making Their Own Way: Southern Blacks' Migration to Pittsburgh, 1916–1930.* Urbana: University of Illinois Press, 1987.

James Gregory. *The Southern Diaspora: How the Great Migrations of Black and White Southerners Transformed America.* Chapel Hill: University of North Carolina Press, 2005.

James R. Grossman. *Land of Hope: Chicago, Black Southerners, and the Great Migration.* Chicago: University of Chicago Press, 1989.

Florette Henri. *Black Migration, 1900–1920.* Garden City, NY: Anchor Press, 1975.

Carole Marks. *Farewell—We're Good and Gone: The Great Black Migration.* Bloomington: Indiana University Press, 1989.

Milton C. Sernett. *Bound for the Promised Land: African American Religion and the Great Migration.* Durham, NC: Duke University Press, 1997.

Joe William Trotter, Jr., ed. *The Great Migration in Historical Perspective.* Bloomington: Indiana University Press, 1991.

Autobiography and Biography

W. E. B. Du Bois. *Dusk of Dawn.* New York: Harcourt, Brace & Co., 1940.

———. *The Autobiography: A Soliloquy on Viewing My Life from the Last Decade of Its First Century.* New York: International Publishers, 1968.

Rayvon Fouché. *Black Inventors in the Age of Segregation: Granville T. Woods, Lewis H. Latimer & Shelby J. Davidson.* Baltimore: Johns Hopkins University Press, 2003.

Stephen R. Fox. *The Guardian of Boston: William Monroe Trotter.* New York: Atheneum, 1970.

Jane Edna Hunter. *A Nickel and a Prayer.* Cleveland, OH: Elli Kani Publishing, 1940.

Adrienne Lash Jones. *Jane Edna Hunter: A Case Study of Black Leadership, 1910–1950.* Brooklyn, NY: Carlson Publishing, 1990.

Kenneth R. Manning. *Black Apollo of Science: The Life of Ernest Everett Just.* New York: Oxford University Press, 1983.

Linda O. McMurry. *George Washington Carver: Scientist and Symbol.* New York: Oxford University Press, 1981.

Arnold Rampersad. *The Art and Imagination of W. E. B. Du Bois.* Cambridge, MA: Harvard University Press, 1976.

Mary Church Terrell. *A Colored Woman in a White World.* New York: Arno Press reprint, 1940.

Emma Lou Thornbrough. *T. Thomas Fortune.* Chicago: University of Chicago Press, 1970.

Booker T. Washington. *Up from Slavery.* New York: Doubleday, 1901.

Chapter 17

African Americans and the 1920s

1918–1929

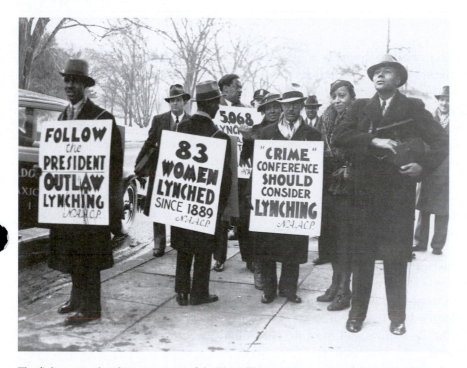

The fight to stop lynchings was one of the NAACP's most important campaigns in the early twentieth century. In the 1920s the NAACP fought unsuccessfully to secure antilynching legislation in Congress. To keep the issue in the public arena, the NAACP persisted with demonstrations and protests like this one at the Crime Conference in Washington, D.C.

⌄ Learning Objectives

After reading this chapter, you should be able to:

17.1 Describe the various forms of intolerance that dominated in the 1920s.

17.2 Analyze the competing strategies and effectiveness of black organizations in the 1920s.

17.3 Explain the origins and development of the Brotherhood of Sleeping Car Porters.

17.4 Identify the most significant people involved in the Harlem Renaissance and explain their lasting contributions.

17.5 Describe both the opportunities and discrimination experienced by black athletes in the 1920s.

> But jazz to me is one of the inherent expressions of Negro life in America; the eternal tom-tom beating in the Negro soul—the tom-tom of revolt against weariness in a white world, a world of subway trains, and work, work, work; the tom-tom of joy and laughter, and pain swallowed with a smile.
>
> —*Langston Hughes*

Many Americans had difficulty adjusting to life after World War I. The Allied victory brought little long-term satisfaction or security, and the Senate's rejection in 1919 of the Treaty of Versailles—and therefore membership in the League of Nations—left many Americans disillusioned. The Bolshevik Revolution in Russia in 1917 and labor agitation at home increased anxiety and heightened fears of radicals. Racial and ethnic intolerance escalated as thousands of rural black southerners continued to stream into northern cities, and more than 800,000 immigrants, mostly from Europe, arrived in America in 1920 and 1921.

Americans shunned Europe and its problems and closed their eyes to the imperfections of American society. Enthusiasm for progressive reforms faded as many Americans concluded that government efforts to mitigate poverty, control vice, improve working conditions, and regulate big business had been excessive. Middle-class Americans became preoccupied with making money and acquiring material possessions—usually on credit and for the first time. They were drawn to newly available technological devices—automobiles, radios, and home appliances—that would revolutionize daily living in the twentieth century. Middle-class black consumers also bought these products, but most African Americans in the 1920s were too poor to afford them.

Many native white Americans, convinced that black people and immigrants—especially Jewish and Catholic immigrants—threatened their Anglo-Saxon ethnic purity, ever more fervently embraced social Darwinism. Many sought reassurance in organizations that stressed religious, racial, and national pride. Millions of white Americans joined the revived Ku Klux Klan in the 1920s as it promoted white supremacy, American patriotism, and Protestant values.

Led by the NAACP, African Americans denounced injustice and pressed for inclusion in society, the enforcement of civil rights, and economic opportunities. Black workers—notably the members of the **Brotherhood of Sleeping Car Porters**—organized and demanded recognition and improved working conditions, hours, and wages. But the 1920s also saw hundreds of thousands of African Americans enthusiastically support Marcus Garvey and the **Universal Negro Improvement Association (UNIA)**. Garvey celebrated black nationalism and urged his followers to forsake white America, take pride in themselves, and look to Africa. In addition, the 1920s saw black culture blossom and flourish as the artists, writers, musicians, and entertainers of the Harlem Renaissance celebrated black life and society.

In 1919 and 1920, Americans were bewildered and angered by labor unrest and afraid the communists (or "Reds") in the new Soviet Union would try to incite a revolution in America. There were 3,600 strikes in 1919 as workers who, during the war, had deferred demands for pay raises and improved working conditions walked off their

Brotherhood of Sleeping Car Porters (BSCP)

Black men and women who worked on Pullman passenger coaches on the nation's railroads organized this labor union in 1925 with A. Philip Randolph as its leader.

Universal Negro Improvement Association (UNIA)

Established in 1914 in Jamaica by Marcus Garvey, it fostered racial pride, African heritage, Christian faith, and economic uplift.

jobs. More than 300,000 steelworkers in Pittsburgh and Gary, Indiana, struck, including 7,000 unskilled black steelworkers in Pittsburgh. In a demonstration of solidarity with striking shipyard workers, most of Seattle's working people shut the city down in a general strike. Americans were even more alarmed when police officers in Boston went on strike. Many worried that labor agitation was a prelude to revolution.

Political leaders exacerbated these feelings by warning that communists and foreign agents were plotting to overthrow the government. Woodrow Wilson's attorney general, A. Mitchell Palmer, grimly warned Americans of the Red menace and the threat that aliens posed. He ordered 249 aliens deported and some 6,000 arrested and imprisoned, in gross violation of their rights, but it was an action that many Americans approved. Palmer went too far, however, when he predicted the Red revolution would begin in the United States on May 1, 1920. There was no revolution, and confidence in Palmer waned. There were, however, several terrorist bombings, including one on Wall Street in September 1920 that killed 33 people. Moreover, evidence indicates that some business leaders supported the Palmer raids to discourage workers from forming and joining labor unions and participating in strikes.

Prompted in part by the **Red Scare**, xenophobia (fear of foreigners) swept the nation in the 1920s. Two Sicilian immigrants who were anarchists, Nicola Sacco and Bartolomeo Vanzetti, were charged in 1920 with a murder that had occurred during a payroll robbery near Boston. They were found guilty and, after a prolonged controversy, were executed in 1927. But their supporters believed the guilty verdict was due more to their foreign origins and radical beliefs than to conclusive proof they had committed the murder.

Red Scare

The widespread fear among many Americans in the years immediately after World War I from about 1918 to about 1924 that Russia's 1917 Bolshevik Revolution might result in communists attempting to take over the U.S. government.

17.1 Varieties of Racism

Describe the various forms of intolerance that dominated in the 1920s.

The entrenched racism of American society found expression in more than one form in the 1920s. There was the sophisticated racism associated with supposedly scholarly studies that reflected the ideology of social Darwinism. There was also the raw bigotry that manifested itself in popular culture and the ideology of the increasingly popular Ku Klux Klan.

17.1.1 Scientific Racism

Many white Americans believed the United States was under siege as European immigrants and black migrants flooded American cities. Pseudoscholars warned about the peril these "inferior" peoples posed. In 1916 Madison Grant published *The Passing of the Great Race*. Grant warned that America was committing "race suicide" because northern Europeans and their descendants—the "Great Race"—were being diluted by inferior people from eastern and southern Europe. Lothrop Stoddard's *The Rising Tide of Color* in 1920 argued that people of color would never be equal to white Americans. Stoddard stated his case unequivocally in 1927:

> Even a general knowledge of historical and scientific facts suffices to show the need for a racial basis to our national life,—as it has been, and as we intend that it shall be. We know that our America is a White America. "America," in the traditional sense of the word, was founded by White men, who evolved institutions, ideals, and cultural manifestations which were spontaneous expressions of their racial temperament and tendencies. And the overwhelming weight of both historical and scientific evidence shows that only so long as the American people remains White will its institutions, ideals, and culture continue to fit the temperament of its inhabitants,—and hence continue to endure.

White sociologists who taught at elite academic institutions including the University of Chicago and Columbia University reinforced these ideas in their classrooms and in books they wrote. They maintained that biological differences separated the races. People of color including Asians but especially African peoples were innately inferior to Caucasians. Black sociologist and scholar W. E. B. Du Bois rejected this as nonsense. Du Bois contended that there were no genetic differences between the races, but that cultural differences explained the disparity among the races. That is, economic and educational factors—not science—created the perception of black inferiority.

But the racist claims of the white scholars were accepted and passed for legitimate scholarship. This served to strengthen the cause of white supremacy in the 1920s and thereby helped to "protect" America from the "threat" of immigration. In 1921 and in 1924, Congress severely restricted immigration from southern and eastern Europe, Latin America, and the Caribbean and prohibited it entirely from Asia.

The glorification of the Ku Klux Klan in D.W. Griffith's *The Birth of a Nation*, reflected in this publicity poster, outraged African Americans. The NAACP protested when the silent film was first distributed in 1915 and again when a sound version was released in 1930. The demonstrations attracted publicity to both the film and the NAACP.

17.1.2 *The Birth of a Nation*

In 1915 D. W. Griffith released *The Birth of a Nation*, a cinematic masterpiece and historical travesty based on Thomas Dixon's 1905 novel *The Clansman*. Both the book and the film purported to depict Reconstruction in South Carolina. This was a three-hour black-and-white film without sound. In this epic, immoral and ignorant Negroes joined by shady mulattoes and greedy white Republicans ruthlessly seize control of state government until the heroic and honorable Ku Klux Klan saves the state and rescues its white womanhood. The film was enormously popular. President Wilson had it screened in the White House. It grossed $18 million ($310 million in 2016 dollars) and helped assure a future for Metro Goldwyn Mayer, the studio that produced it. It also distorted perceptions about Reconstruction and black Americans.

The NAACP was enraged by *The Birth of a Nation* and fought to halt its presentation. W. E. B. Du Bois complained in the *Crisis* that in the film "the Negro [was] represented either as an ignorant fool, a vicious rapist, a venal or unscrupulous politician or a faithful but doddering idiot." The film unleashed racist violence. After seeing it in Lafayette, Indiana, an infuriated white man killed a young black man. In Houston, white theatergoers shouted, "Lynch him!" during a scene in which a white actor in blackface pursued the film's star, Lillian Gish. In front of a St. Louis theater, white real estate agents passed out circulars calling for residential segregation.

Thanks largely to NAACP opposition, the film was banned in Pasadena, California; Wilmington, Delaware; and Boston. With an election looming in Chicago, Republican Mayor "Big Bill" Thompson appointed American Methodist Episcopal Bishop Archibald Carey to the board of censors, which temporarily banned the film there. When the sound version of *The Birth of a Nation* was released in 1930, the NAACP renewed its opposition. Ironically, the NAACP campaign may have provided publicity that attracted more viewers to the film. However, the campaign also helped increase NAACP membership.

17.1.3 The Ku Klux Klan

The Ku Klux Klan, which had disappeared after Reconstruction, was resurrected a few months after *The Birth of a Nation* was released. On Thanksgiving night in 1915, William J. Simmons and 34 other men gathered at Stone Mountain near Atlanta; in the flickering shadows of a fiery cross, they brought the Klan back to life.

The Ku Klux Klan in the 1920s stood for white supremacy—and more. Klansmen styled themselves as "100 percent Americans" who opposed perceived threats from immigrants as well as black Americans. The Klan claimed to represent white, Anglo-Saxon, Protestant America. With European immigrants flocking to America, William Simmons announced that the United States was no melting pot; rather, "It is a garbage can! . . . When the hordes of aliens walk to the ballot box and their votes outnumber yours, then that alien horde has got you by the throat."

The Klan found enormous support among apprehensive white middle-class Americans in the North and West. Many of them believed the liberal, immoral, and loose lifestyles they associated with urban life, immigrants, and African Americans threatened their religious beliefs and conservative values. The Klan attacked the theory of evolution, fought for the prohibition of alcoholic beverages, and claimed to uphold the "sanctity" of white womanhood. The Ku Klux Klan opposed Jews, Roman Catholics, and black people. Klansmen often used violence. They burned synagogues and Catholic churches. They beat, branded, and lynched opponents.

By 1925 the Klan had an estimated five million members, and 40,000 of them marched in Washington, D.C., that year. The Klan attracted small businessmen, shop-keepers, clerks, Protestant clergymen, farmers, and professional people. It was open only to native-born white men, but it also had a Women's Order, a Junior Order for boys, and a Tri K Klub for girls. The Klan was active in Oregon, Colorado, Illinois, and Maine, and it became a potent political force in Indiana, Oklahoma, and Texas, where candidates for office who refused to support or join the Klan stood little chance of election.

The Klan was also a moneymaking machine. Its leaders collected millions of dollars in initiation fees, membership dues, and sales of Klan paraphernalia. But the Klan declined rapidly in the late 1920s when its leaders fought among themselves. Its claim to uphold the purity of white womanhood was damaged when one of its leaders, D. C. Stephenson, was charged in Indiana with raping a young woman who subsequently committed suicide. Stephenson was sentenced to life in prison, and the Klan never fully recovered.

17.2 Protest, Pride, and Pan-Africanism: Black Organizations in the 1920s

Analyze the competing strategies and effectiveness of black organizations in the 1920s.

African Americans responded to racism and to cultural and economic developments in the 1920s in several ways. The NAACP continued its efforts to secure constitutional rights and guarantees by advocacy in the political and judicial systems. Many working-class black people who had migrated to northern cities were attracted to the racial pride that Marcus Garvey and the UNIA promoted. There were also attempts to foster racial cooperation among peoples of African descent and to exert diplomatic influence through the work of Pan-African Congresses that were held during the first three decades of the twentieth century.

17.2.1 The NAACP

During its second decade, the NAACP expanded its influence and increased its membership. In 1916 James Weldon Johnson (who wrote "Lift Every Voice and Sing") joined the NAACP as field secretary. He played a pivotal role in the organization's development and in its growth from 9,000 members in 1916 to 90,000 in 1920. Johnson traveled tirelessly, recruiting members and establishing branches.

Johnson impressed both black and white people. He got along well with Du Bois—not always an easy task, considering Du Bois's sometimes haughty and acerbic demeanor. Johnson was an excellent diplomat who could negotiate and compromise, but he could also be blunt when necessary. He methodically reported the gruesome details of lynchings, and when some NAACP directors complained in 1921 that these graphic descriptions offended people, Johnson stood his ground: "What we need to do is to root out the thing which makes possible these horrible details. I am of the opinion that this can be done only through the fullest publicity."

In 1918 Johnson hired Walter White to assist him. White was from Atlanta and, like Johnson, a graduate of Atlanta University. White's fair complexion permitted him to move easily among white people to investigate racial discrimination and violence. Although his domineering personality offended some NAACP officials and supporters, White devoted his life to the organization and to racial justice.

Johnson and the NAACP fought hard in Congress to secure passage of the Dyer antilynching bill in 1921 and 1922 (see Chapter 16). The legislation ultimately failed, but the NAACP publicized the persistence of barbaric mob behavior in a nation supposedly devoted to fairness and the rule of law. It was the first campaign by a civil rights organization to lobby Congress, and—like the attempt to block *The Birth of a Nation*—it won goodwill for the NAACP.

Voices

The Negro National Anthem: "Lift Every Voice and Sing"

In 1900, to celebrate Abraham Lincoln's birthday, James Weldon Johnson wrote "Lift Every Voice and Sing." His younger brother John Rosamond Johnson composed music to accompany the words. It was published in 1921 and soon thereafter—with the encouragement of the NAACP—the song was embraced as the Negro national anthem.

Lift every voice and sing, 'til earth and heaven ring,
Ring with the harmonies of liberty
Let our rejoicing rise, high as the list'ning skies,
Let it resound loud as the rolling sea.
Sing a song full of the faith that the dark past has taught us,
Sing a song full of the hope that the present has brought us;
Facing the rising sun of our new day begun
Let us march on till victory is won.

Stony the road we trod, bitter the chast'ning rod
Felt in the days when hope unborn had died
Yet with a steady beat, have not our weary feet
Come to the place for which our fathers sighed?
We have come over a way that with tears has been watered,
We have come, treading our path thro' the blood of
the slaughtered

Out from the gloomy past, 'til now we stand at last
Where the white gleam of our bright star is cast.

God of our weary years, God of our silent tears
Thou who has brought us thus far on the way
Thou who hast by Thy might, led us into the light
Keep us forever in the path, we pray.
Lest our feet stray from the places, our God, where we
met Thee
Lest our hearts, drunk with the wine of the world, we
forget Thee
Shadowed beneath Thy hand, may we forever stand
True to our God, true to our native land.

1. To what native land does Johnson refer in the last line: "True to our God, true to our native land"?

2. Do the lyrics apply to all Americans or only to African Americans? Would the song be appropriate as the American national anthem? Why or why not?

SOURCE: James Weldon Johnson wrote "Lift Every Voice and Sing." His younger brother John Rosamond Johnson composed music to accompany the words.

Johnson blamed the Dyer bill's failure on Republican senators. He charged that the Republican Party took black support for granted because southern Democrats remained committed to white supremacy, and therefore black people had little choice but to vote Republican: "The Republican Party will hold the Negro and do as little for him as possible, and the Democratic Party will have none of him at all." He warned, however, that black voters in the North would abandon the Republicans:

> The Negro can serve notice that he is no longer a part of the agreement by voting in the coming elections in each State against Republicans who have betrayed him, who are in league with the Ku Klux Klan, who are found to be hypocrites and liars on the question of the Negro's essential rights, and by letting them know he has done it. I am in favor of doing the job at once.

Johnson pointed out that black voters in Harlem had elected a black Democrat to the state legislature.

The NAACP continued to rely on the judicial system to protect black Americans and enforce their civil rights. By the 1920s the Democratic Party in virtually every southern state barred black people from membership, which excluded them from voting in Democratic primaries. The result was what was known as "white primaries." Because the Republican Party had almost disappeared in most of the South, victory in the Democratic primary led invariably to victory in the general election. In 1924 the NAACP, in cooperation with its El Paso branch, filed suit over the exclusion of black voters from the Democratic primary in Texas. In 1927 the Supreme Court ruled in *Nixon v. Herndon* that the Democratic primary was unconstitutional—the first victory in what would become a 20-year legal struggle to permit black men and women to vote in primary elections across the South.

In Detroit in 1925, black physician Ossian Sweet and his family moved into an all-white neighborhood. For several nights a mob threatened the Sweet family and other people who defended them. One evening, shots fired from the Sweet home killed a white man. As a result, 12 occupants of the house were charged with murder. The NAACP retained Clarence Darrow and Arthur Garfield Hayes, two of the nation's finest criminal attorneys, to defend the Sweets. The Sweets pleaded self-defense and after two trials were acquitted.

Profile

James Weldon Johnson

James Weldon Johnson was a man of immense talents: lawyer, diplomat, journalist, teacher, and gifted writer. Most important, he was an effective and dynamic civil rights leader.

Johnson was born in 1871 in Jacksonville, Florida, to parents who had not been slaves. His father was a waiter in a fashionable hotel, and his mother was a schoolteacher. He received his secondary and collegiate education at Atlanta University, where he also earned a master's degree. He read law in the office of a white Jacksonville attorney and was admitted to the Florida bar. In 1902 he moved to New York City.

With his brother John Rosamond and black entertainer Robert Cole, he became part of a successful songwriting team. They contributed two musical numbers to Theodore Roosevelt's 1904 presidential campaign: "You're All Right Teddy" and "The Old Flag Never Touched the Ground." Johnson's connection to the Republican Party and his support for Booker T. Washington helped secure diplomatic appointments for him. Johnson spent seven years as a U.S. consul in Venezuela and Nicaragua. In 1910 he married Grace Neal, the sister of a prominent New York real estate broker.

With the 1912 election of Woodrow Wilson, a Democrat, Johnson's diplomatic career ended. He became an editorial writer for the *New York Age*. He also published anonymously *The Autobiography of an Ex-Colored Man*. In 1916 Joel Spingarn, the president of the NAACP, asked Johnson to take a leadership role with that organization, and Johnson—who had not openly supported the NAACP before Booker T. Washington's death in 1915—became its field secretary.

Johnson spent the next 14 years with the NAACP. In 1920 he became chief executive, responsible for the association's day-to-day operations. He had organized the silent march on Fifth Avenue on July 28, 1917, to protest the East St. Louis riot (see Chapter 16). He publicized lynchings. He recruited members and established new branches. In 1920 in *The Nation*, he documented the mistreatment of Haitians by U.S. troops who had occupied that Caribbean nation. He supported black

workers and A. Philip Randolph and the Brotherhood of Sleeping Car Porters. He arranged legal counsel for Ossian Sweet in Detroit in 1925 after Sweet and several of his supporters were charged with murder.

Johnson also managed to write prolifically and imaginatively. In 1920, he wrote "The Creation: A Negro Sermon." He wrote "God's Trombones: Seven Negro Sermons in Verse" in 1927 and many other works of prose and poetry. In 1930 he finished *Black Manhattan*, which traced the cultural contributions of black people to New York City in music, poetry, and theater from the seventeenth to the twentieth century.

Like so many civil rights leaders, Johnson could be inconsistent about racial issues. Though dedicated to the proposition that black and white people should enjoy equal access to public facilities, he supported an all-black YMCA in Harlem and the separate training of black military officers during World War I. He opposed moving the NAACP headquarters from Fifth Avenue to Harlem. He supported building an all-black veteran's hospital at Tuskegee, Alabama, as long as it would be staffed by black physicians and nurses. He appreciated Marcus Garvey's emphasis on black pride, but he considered the back-to-Africa movement to be an attempt to escape from America's racial problems rather than a solution to them.

In 1930 Johnson became a professor of creative writing at Fisk University in Nashville. He left the NAACP as a far more visible and strong organization than he had found it in 1916. At Fisk, he worked with some of the twentieth century's leading black scholars, including Horace Mann Bond, Alrutheus A. Taylor, and E. Franklin Frazier. Historian John Hope Franklin was one of his students. Johnson published his autobiography, *Along the Way*, in 1933. Johnson died in an automobile accident in 1938.

17.2.2 "Up You Mighty Race": Marcus Garvey and the UNIA

With several million enthusiastic followers, Marcus Garvey's UNIA became the largest mass movement of black people in American history. The UNIA enabled black people—often dismissed by the white majority for having no genuine history or culture—to celebrate one another and their heritage and to anticipate a glorious future. Garvey was an energetic, charismatic, and flamboyant leader who wove racial pride, Christian faith, and economic cooperation into a black nationalist organization that by the early 1920s had spread throughout the United States.

Garvey was born in 1887 in the British colony of Jamaica, the eleventh child in a rural family. He quit school at age 14 and became a printer in Kingston, the island's capital. He was promoted to foreman before he was fired during a strike in 1907. He traveled to Costa Rica, Panama, Ecuador, and Nicaragua and became disturbed over the conditions black workers endured in fields, factories, and mines. He returned to Jamaica and set out to educate himself. He spent two years in London, where he sharpened his oratorical and debating skills discussing the plight of black people with Africans and people from the Caribbean.

He returned to Jamaica and founded the UNIA in 1914. With the slogan "One God! One Aim! One Destiny!" he stressed the need for black people to organize for their own advancement. Garvey had read Booker T. Washington's *Up From Slavery* and was much impressed with Washington's emphasis on self-help and progress through education and the acquisition of skills. Garvey also—like Washington—could criticize black people for their lack of progress: "The bulk of our people are in darkness and are really unfit for good society." They had "done nothing to establish the right to equality."

Garvey came to the United States in 1916 just as thousands of African Americans were migrating to cities. A dynamic speaker whose message resonated among the disaffected urban working class, Garvey built the UNIA into a major movement. He urged his listeners to take pride in themselves as they restored their race to its previous greatness: "We must canonize our own saints, create our own martyrs, and elevate to positions of fame and honor black men and women who have made their distinct contributions to our racial history." He reminded people that Africa had a remarkable past: "Africa was peopled with a race of cultured black men, who were masters in art, science and literature; men who were cultured and refined; men, who, it was said, were like the gods. . . . Black men, you were once great; you shall be great again." He insisted that his followers change their thinking: "We have outgrown slavery, but our minds are still enslaved to the thinking of the Master Race. Now take these kinks out of your mind, instead of out of your hair."

With the formation of the New York division of the UNIA in Harlem in 1917, Garvey exhorted, "Up you mighty race!" as he commanded black people to take control of their destiny. Still, he blamed them for their predicament: "That the Negro race became a race of slaves was not the fault of God Almighty . . . it was the fault of the race." Their salvation would result from their own exertion and not from concessions by white people.

Garvey's message and the UNIA spread to black communities large and small. He regularly couched his rhetoric in religious terms, and he came to be known as the Black Moses, a messiah. Garvey dwelled on Christ's betrayal as he identified himself with Jesus: "If Garvey dies, Garvey lives." "Christ died to make men free, I shall die to give courage and inspiration to my race."

Garvey's followers enjoyed the pageantry, ceremonies, and titles that were a part of the UNIA. The African Legionnaires and the Black Cross Nurses, resplendent in their uniforms, assembled in New York's Liberty Hall and paraded through Harlem. They prayed from *The Universal Negro Catechism* and reflected on their connection to Africa: "O Blessed Lord Jesus, redeem Africa from the hands of those who exploit and ravish her."

Garvey and the UNIA also established businesses that employed nearly 1,000 black people. The weekly newspaper *Negro World* promoted Garvey's ideology. In New York City, the Negro Factories Corporation operated three grocery stores, two restaurants, a printing plant, a steam laundry, and a factory that turned out clothes for UNIA members. The association also owned property in other cities. Garvey proudly declared to white Americans that the UNIA "employs thousands of black girls and black boys. Girls who could only be washer women in your homes, we made clerks, stenographers. . . . You will see from the start we tried to dignify our race."

Although Garvey and the UNIA are most frequently associated with urban communities in the North, the UNIA also

Jamaican-born Marcus Garvey arrived in the United States in 1916 and quickly rose to prominence as the head of the UNIA. Garvey appears here in the 1924 parade in Harlem attired in a uniform similar to those worn by British colonial governors in Jamaica, Trinidad, and elsewhere.

spread rapidly through the rural South in the 1920s. Black farmers and sharecroppers established UNIA chapters from Virginia to Louisiana, and the Garvey movement and the *Negro World* could be found in such remote communities as Kinston, North Carolina; Ty Ty, Georgia; and Cotton Plant, Arkansas.

Garvey may be best remembered for his proposal to return black people to Africa on the Black Star Line, a steamship company he founded in 1919. Garvey sold stock in the company for $5 a share, and he hoped to establish a fleet with black officers and crews. In 1920 the company purchased the *Yarmouth*, a dilapidated vessel that became the first ship in the fleet. Garvey bought two more ships, the *Kanawha* and the *Booker T. Washington*, but he lacked the money to maintain them or transport anyone to Africa.

Moreover, Garvey knew it was unrealistic to expect several million black residents of the Western Hemisphere to join the back-to-Africa enterprise, but he did believe that the UNIA could liberate Africa from European colonial rule: "Wake up Ethiopia! Wake up Africa! Let us work towards the one glorious end of a free, redeemed and mighty nation." The UNIA adopted a red, green, and black flag for the proposed African republic that represented the blood, land, and race of the African people.

The UNIA attempted to establish a settlement on the Cavalla River in southern Liberia. Garvey also petitioned the League of Nations to permit the UNIA to take over the former German colony of Tanganyika (today's Tanzania) in East Africa. But the major colonial powers in Africa—Britain and France—and the United States thwarted Garvey's plans, and the UNIA never gained a foothold on the continent.

The U.S. government and several black American leaders also worked diligently to undermine Garvey and the UNIA. J. Edgar Hoover and the Bureau of Investigation (the predecessor of the FBI) considered Garvey a threat to the racial status quo. Hoover employed black agents to infiltrate the UNIA and compile information that could be used to deport Garvey, who had never become an American citizen.

Garvey had few friends or admirers among African-American leaders because he and they differed fundamentally on strategy and goals. Garvey deplored efforts to gain legal and political rights within the American system. By appealing to the black masses, he rejected Du Bois's notion that the Talented Tenth would lead the race to liberation. He mocked the NAACP as the "National Association for the Advancement of Certain People." Not long after he arrived in the United States, Garvey visited the NAACP office in New York and disliked what he saw: "There was no representation of the race there that any one could recognize. . . . [Y]ou had to be as near white as possible, otherwise there was no place for you as stenographer, clerk or attendant in the office of the National Association for the Advancement of 'Colored' People."

Garvey called Du Bois a "lazy, dependent mulatto." In return, Du Bois described Garvey as "a little, fat black man, ugly but with intelligent eyes and big head," who was "the most dangerous enemy of the Negro race in America and the world . . . either a lunatic or a traitor." A. Philip Randolph, the black labor leader, called Garvey "the supreme Negro Jamaican Jackass," an "unquestioned fool and ignoramus."

Unlike African-American leaders, Garvey believed black and white people had separate destinies, and he regarded interracial cooperation as absurd. Thus, Garvey considered a meeting he had with Ku Klux Klan leaders in Atlanta in 1922 consistent with his racial views: "They are better friends to my race, for telling us what they are, and what they mean, thereby giving us a chance to stir for ourselves . . . every whiteman is a Klansman . . . and there is no use lying about it."

In 1922 Garvey and three other UNIA leaders were indicted on 12 counts of mail fraud in connection with the sale of stock in the Black Star Line. Eight African-American leaders wrote to the U.S. attorney general to insist on his prosecution. Although Garvey was guilty of no more than mismanagement and incompetence, he was found guilty and sent to prison in 1925. President Calvin Coolidge commuted his sentence in 1927, and he was then deported.

Voices

Marcus Garvey Appeals for a New African Nation

Marcus Garvey and the UNIA offered hope to African Americans in the 1920s. In the following words, Garvey passionately calls for African Americans and West Indians to support the creation of a new African nation:

For five years the Universal Negro Improvement Association has been advocating the cause of Africa for the Africans—that is, that the Negro peoples of the world should concentrate upon the object of building up for themselves a great nation in Africa. . . .

It is only a question of a few more years when Africa will be completely colonized by Negroes, as Europe is by the white race. What we want is an independent African nationality, and if America is to help the Negro peoples of the world establish such a nationality, then we welcome the assistance.

It is hoped that when the time comes for American and West Indian Negroes to settle in Africa, they will realize their responsibilities and duty. It will not be to go to Africa for the purpose of exercising an over-lordship over the natives, . . .

It will be useless, as stated before, for bombastic Negroes to leave America and the West Indies to go to Africa, thinking that they will have privileged positions to inflict upon the race that bastard aristocracy that they have tried to maintain in this Western world at the expense of the masses. Africa shall develop an aristocracy of its own, but it shall be based upon service and loyalty to race. Let all Negroes work toward that end. . . .

The time has really come for the Asiatics to govern themselves in Asia, as the Europeans are in Europe and the Western world, so also is it wise for the Africans to govern themselves at home, and thereby bring peace and satisfaction to the entire human family.

So Negroes, I say, through the Universal Negro Improvement Association, that there is much to live for. I have a vision of the future, and I see before me a picture of a redeemed Africa, with her dotted cities, with her beautiful civilization, with her millions of happy children going to and fro. Why should I lose hope, why should I give up and take a back place in this age of progress? . . .

Africa shall reflect a splendid demonstration of the worth of the Negro, of the determination of the Negro, to set himself free and to establish a government of his own.

---

1. Why does Garvey call for a black homeland in Africa? How realistic was this call in the 1920s for nationhood in Africa?
2. Who does Garvey believe should lead (or should not lead) the new African nation? What are the qualifications for such leadership?
3. What does Garvey think the globe will look like in the future? How will peoples of various colors coexist?

SOURCE: Amy Jacques Garvey (1923). *The Philosophy and Opinions of Marcus Garvey. Or, Africa for the Africans.* The Majority Press.

With the loss of its inspirational leader, the UNIA declined steadily in the late 1920s and the 1930s. UNIA businesses closed, and its property—including the *Yarmouth*—was sold. Garvey was never permitted to return to the United States, and he died in London in 1940. However, his legacy persisted. The Rev. Earl Little, a Baptist minister and the father of Malcolm X, belonged to the UNIA and admired Garvey. Malcolm X recalled his father's association with Garvey: "I remember hearing that he had black followers not only in the United States but all around the world, and I remember how the meetings always closed with my father saying, several times, and the people chanting after him, 'Up, you mighty race, you can accomplish what you will!'"

17.2.3 Amy Jacques Garvey

Although she never held an official position with the UNIA, Amy Jacques Garvey was second only in importance to Marcus Garvey in the organization. Like Marcus, she was born in Jamaica, but unlike Marcus, she was brought up in a middle-class family and attended a private high school.

Amy Jacques moved to the United States in 1918, settled in Harlem, and quickly immersed herself in the activities of the UNIA. After Marcus Garvey divorced his first wife, he and Amy married in 1922. She had a major impact on his thinking, assisting him in writing speeches and helping with administrative tasks in the UNIA.

After Marcus Garvey was sent to prison in 1925, Amy helped to manage the UNIA in his absence. She wrote a weekly column, "Our Women and What They Think," for the UNIA newspaper, the *Negro World*. She promoted the bond not only among women of African descent, but with women of color including those from Turkey, Egypt, China, Japan, and elsewhere.

Despite the commitment of the UNIA to equality between the sexes, she found that Marcus Garvey and other men in the organization could be haughty and demeaning in their conduct toward women. In one of her columns in the *Negro World*, she sharply criticized black men: "The doom of the race lies in the lethargy of its men. Black men you are failing on your jobs! Be honest enough to admit your laziness. Now shake yourselves, lift your head high, expand your chests, put right foot forward, then left, don't be afraid, now step right off and tackle your jobs. The world expects you to play a man's part, and is fed up on your whinings and 'can't be done' moans."

After Marcus Garvey was released from prison in 1927, he and Amy returned to Jamaica and then settled in London. They had two sons, but the relationship between the couple became more distant. She left him and with her sons returned to Jamaica. After the death of Marcus Garvey in 1940, she continued to promote his work and his legacy until her death in Kingston in 1973.

17.2.4 The African Blood Brotherhood

In 1919 black men who had migrated to New York City from the Caribbean formed the African Blood Brotherhood as a radical alternative to Marcus Garvey and the UNIA. Cyril Briggs, who had been born in St. Kitts-Nevis in 1888, was the founder. The brotherhood rejected Garvey's reliance on capitalism and his devotion to Christianity. The brotherhood supported Marxism and had ties to the Communist Party.

Edited by Briggs, the African Blood Brotherhood briefly published the *Crusader* in the early 1920s. Unlike the UNIA, the Brotherhood's rejection of private enterprise and mainstream religion prevented it from becoming a mass movement. It never had more than 3,000 supporters.

17.2.5 Hubert Harrison

Described by A. Philip Randolph as the "Father of Harlem Radicalism," Hubert Harrison was perhaps the most outspoken figure to emerge in the cultural and political ferment of Harlem in the 1920s.

Harrison was born in 1883 in St. Croix in the Danish West Indies (today the U.S. Virgin Islands). He migrated to New York City in 1900 where he attended high school. But he was largely self-educated. After he criticized Booker T. Washington's cautious approach to racial matters in the early twentieth century, Washington's extensive political network, the Tuskegee Machine, got Harrison fired from his position with the U.S. Post Office.

Harrison despised white supremacy and capitalism. There was an inseparable link, he believed, between racism and the rigid class system that made a sham of claims that the United States was a democracy based on equality. However, unlike Marcus Garvey, Harrison became a U.S. citizen. He married Irene Louise Horton in 1909, and they had four daughters and one son.

Speaking on Harlem street corners and writing for black and white newspapers, Harrison agitated for greater class consciousness and racial awareness among urban residents. He became an atheist and vigorously denounced organized religion. "Show me a population that is deeply religious, and I will show you a servile population, content with whips and chains, contumely and giblet, content to eat the bread of sorrow and drink from the waters of affliction."

For a time Harrison supported Marcus Garvey and the UNIA. He edited the *Negro World* for two years. But he grew disenchanted with Garvey's support for capitalism. Harrison called for a Negro state in America, and not in Africa as Garvey favored. Not only a superb orator, Harrison was a vociferous reader and a writer who contributed numerous essays and book reviews to a variety of publications. He read and spoke six languages. He supported the Lafayette Theater, a black theatrical company, convinced that it would stimulate critical thinking and cultural awareness among black people.

In the prime of his life, Hubert Harrison died of appendicitis at age 44 in 1927.

17.2.6 Pan-Africanism

While Garvey, Du Bois, Biggs, and Harrison differed on the most appropriate strategy for advancing African Americans, they shared an abiding interest in Africa. Garvey, Du Bois, Briggs, Harrison, and other black leaders believed people of African descent from around the world should come together to share their heritage, discuss their ties to the continent, and explore ways to moderate—if not eliminate—colonial rule in Africa, a concept termed **Pan-Africanism**.

By 1914 Britain, France, Germany, Portugal, Belgium, Spain, and Italy had established colonies across almost all of Africa. Only Liberia and Ethiopia (then called Abyssinia) remained independent. The Europeans assumed the "white man's burden" in their imperialist "scramble" for Africa. Christian missionaries sought to convert Africans, and European companies exploited Africa's human and natural resources. As they gained control over the continent, the European powers confirmed their conviction that they represented a superior race and culture.

The first Pan-African Congress convened in London in 1900 and was organized principally by Henry Sylvester Williams, a lawyer from Trinidad who had lived in Canada and then London. Du Bois chaired the Committee on the Address to the Nations of the World. He called for the creation of "a great central Negro state of the world." But Du Bois did not insist on the immediate withdrawal of the European powers from Africa. Instead, he offered a modest recommendation that would provide "as soon as practicable the rights of responsible self-government to the black colonies of Africa and the West Indies."

The second Pan-African Congress met in Paris for three days in February 1919 near Versailles, where the peace conference ending World War I was assembled. There were 58 delegates from 16 nations. Du Bois was among the 16 African Americans in attendance. (None of them had been to Africa.) Marcus Garvey did not attend. The delegates took seriously the Fourteen Points that President Wilson had proposed to create a new postwar world. They were especially interested in Wilson's fifth point, which called for the interests of colonial peoples to be given "equal weight" in the adjustment of colonial claims after the war. The congress recommended that the League of Nations assume authority over the former German colonies in Africa. The League later established mandates over those colonies but delegated authority to administer those mandates to Britain, France, and Belgium. Two more Pan-African Congresses met in Brussels and London in the 1920s but also failed to influence the policies of the colonial powers.

Pan-Africanism

A movement of people of African descent from sub-Saharan Africa in the early twentieth century that emphasized their identity, shared experiences, and the need to liberate Africa from its European colonizers.

17.3 Labor

Explain the origins and development of the Brotherhood of Sleeping Car Porters.

The arrival of thousands of black migrants in American cities during and after World War I changed the composition of the industrial workforce and intensified pressure on labor unions to admit black members. By 1916, 12,000 of the nearly 50,000 workers in the Chicago stockyards were black people. In Detroit, black laborers made up nearly 14 percent of the workforce in the automobile industry. The Ford Motor Company employed 50 black people in 1916 and 2,500 by 1920.

Yet even with the Industrial Revolution and the Great Migration, more than two-thirds of black workers in 1920 were employed in agriculture and domestic service (see Figure 17-1). Less than 20 percent were engaged in manufacturing. Many black men and women remained confined to the rural South. Those who were part of industrial America disproportionately worked in the dreary, dirty, and sometimes dangerous unskilled jobs that paid the least. Still, work in the factories, mills, and mines paid more than agriculture (Figure 17-2). But even those with skills were usually not admitted to the local craft unions that made up the American Federation of Labor (AFL). More than 50 trade unions within the AFL had no black members. Unions that did admit black workers included those representing cigar makers, coal miners, garment workers, and longshoremen.

By the World War I years, the NAACP and the Urban League regularly appealed to employers and unions to accept black laborers. The Urban League attempted to convince business owners that black employees would be efficient and reliable. But many employers preferred to divide black and white workers by hiring black men and women

---

Figure 17-1 Black Workers by Major Industrial Group, 1920

By 1920 thousands of African Americans had moved to northern cities and were employed in a variety of mostly unskilled and low-paying industrial jobs that nonetheless paid more than farm labor. Still, agriculture remained the largest single source of employment among black people, and agriculture and domestic service together employed more than two-thirds of African-American men and women. About 5 percent were employed in "white-collar" jobs.

SOURCE: Based on *The Black Worker: The Negro and the Labor Movement* by Sterling Denhard Spero, Abram Lincoln Harris. Columbia University Press, 1931. © Darlene Clark Hine.

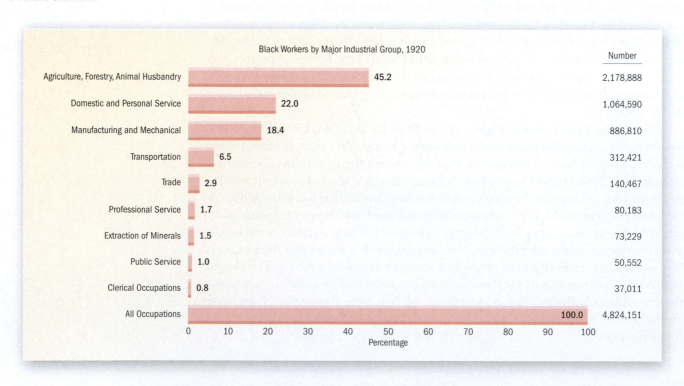

Black Workers by Major Industrial Group, 1920

Industrial Group	Percentage	Number
Agriculture, Forestry, Animal Husbandry	45.2	2,178,888
Domestic and Personal Service	22.0	1,064,590
Manufacturing and Mechanical	18.4	886,810
Transportation	6.5	312,421
Trade	2.9	140,467
Professional Service	1.7	80,183
Extraction of Minerals	1.5	73,229
Public Service	1.0	50,552
Clerical Occupations	0.8	37,011
All Occupations	100.0	4,824,151

Figure 17-2 Black and White Workers by Skill Level, 1920

Only one-third of black workers, compared to slightly more than one-half of white workers, found employment in skilled or semiskilled jobs in 1920.

SOURCE: Based on Sterling D. Spero and Abram L. Harris, *The Black Worker: The Negro and the Labor Movement* (1928), 85. © Darlene Clark Hine.

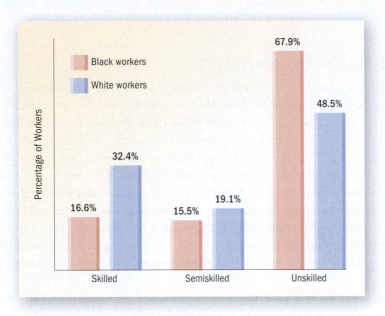

as strikebreakers, thereby enraging striking white workers. In 1918 Urban League officials met with Samuel Gompers, the longtime president of the AFL, and he agreed to bring more black people into the federation, but there were few tangible results. The Urban League did persuade the Department of Labor to establish a Division of Negro Economics to advise the secretary of labor on issues involving black workers.

17.3.1 The Brotherhood of Sleeping Car Porters

By the 1920s the Pullman Company, which owned and operated passenger railroad coaches, was the single largest employer of black people in the United States. More than 12,000 black men were porters on Pullman railroad cars. After founding the Pullman Palace Car Company in 1867, George Pullman decided to employ only black men as porters—on the assumption that prosperous white people were accustomed to being waited on by black servants. Furthermore, black employees could be and were paid less than white workers.

Pullman porters toiled for upward of 400 hours each month to maintain the coaches and serve the passengers. Porters had to prepare the cars before the train's departure and service them after the train arrived at its destination, although they were paid only for the duration of the trip. They assisted passengers, shined shoes (they had to purchase the polish themselves), and arranged sleeping compartments. Considered mere servants by most passengers, porters had little time for rest. To add to the indignity, white travelers invariably referred to these black men as "George," no matter what their actual name was. Porters were paid an average of $67.50 per month—about $810 per year. But with tips that might average $600 annually, a porter could earn $1,400 in a year ($19,141 in 2016 dollars), a decent wage at the time. They had to buy their own uniforms during their first 10 years of employment.

Although strenuous and time-consuming, Pullman employment was the most satisfactory work many black men could hope to achieve. Barred from business and industry, black men with college degrees often worked as sleeping car porters. As poorly paid as they were compared with many white workers, they still earned more than most black schoolteachers. Most of these Pullman employees regarded themselves as solid, respectable members of the middle class.

It seemed unlikely that men as subservient and unobtrusive as the Pullman porters would form a labor union to challenge one of America's most powerful corporations. But they did. The key figure in this effort was A. Philip Randolph. In 1925 Pullman porters in Harlem invited Randolph to become their "general organizer" as they formed the Brotherhood of Sleeping Car Porters (BSCP). Randolph accepted.

17.3.2 A. Philip Randolph

Randolph was a socialist with superb oratorical skills who had earned a reputation as a radical on the streets of Harlem. He was born in 1889 in Crescent City, Florida. He attended high school at Cookman Institute (later Bethune-Cookman College) and migrated in 1911 to New York City, where he attended City College and joined the Socialist Party. In 1913 he married Lucille Campbell Greene. She was a prosperous beauty shop owner who contributed financially to many of her husband's causes. With Chandler Owen, he founded the *Messenger*, a monthly socialist journal that drew the attention of federal agents because they regarded it as the only radical Negro magazine in the country. Randolph opposed American involvement in World War I. In 1919 Department of Justice officials arrested Randolph and Owen for violating the Espionage Act and held them briefly. They labeled Randolph the most dangerous Negro in America.

Randolph was an improbable radical. He was handsome, dignified, impeccably dressed, and aloof. Save for his color, he could have been mistaken for the sort of Wall Street broker or powerful corporate attorney he detested. But blessed with a rich baritone voice, he "damned the classes and exalted the masses" and maintained an unwavering commitment to economic and racial change. He was one of the nation's foremost protest leaders for more than five decades.

Randolph faced the daunting task of recruiting support for the brotherhood, winning recognition from the Pullman Company, and gaining the union's acceptance by the American Federation of Labor (AFL). There was considerable opposition, much of it from within the black community. Many porters were too frightened to join the brotherhood. Black clergymen counseled against union activities. Black newspapers, including the *Chicago Defender*, opposed the BSCP.

But Randolph persevered with the assistance of Milton Webster, who became vice president of the brotherhood after Randolph assumed the presidency. With the slogan "Service not servitude," the two men recruited members, organized the brotherhood, and attempted to negotiate with the Pullman Company. Pullman executives ignored Randolph's overtures. They instead fired porters who joined the union, infiltrated union meetings with company agents, and organized the Employees' Representation Plan—an alternative company union that they claimed actually represented the black employees.

Although the NAACP and the Urban League supported the BSCP, progress was slow. In 1928 Randolph threatened to call a strike against the Pullman Company, but he called it off after AFL president William Green promised modest assistance to the as-yet-unrecognized union. Green's offer simply saved face for Randolph. It is unlikely that a strike would have succeeded or that most porters would have followed

In this painting by Betsy G. Reyneau, A. Philip Randolph hardly resembles the militant agitator, activist, and labor leader that he was. He became the head of the BSCP, and he eventually rose to power in the AFL. He planned the first March on Washington in 1941 and was responsible for organizing the 1963 March on Washington.

Randolph's leadership and left the trains. The Great Depression of the 1930s brought layoffs and mass resignations from the brotherhood. The AFL barely responded to repeated charges of discrimination by Randolph, the NAACP, and the Urban League. The BSCP nearly collapsed. Not until the passage of legislation during President Franklin D. Roosevelt's New Deal in the mid-1930s did the BSCP make substantial gains.

17.4 The Harlem Renaissance

Identify the most significant people involved in the Harlem Renaissance and explain their lasting contributions.

For most of American history, most Americans have shown little interest in serious literature or intellectual developments. The 1920s were no exception. People were far more fascinated by sports, automobiles, the radio, and popular music than they were by poetry, plays, museums, or novels. Still, the 1920s witnessed a proliferation of creative works by a remarkable group of gifted writers and artists. Among white writers, T. S. Eliot, Ezra Pound, Edith Wharton, Ernest Hemingway, Sinclair Lewis, Eugene O'Neill, Willa Cather, and F. Scott Fitzgerald produced literary works that explored a range of themes but were mostly critical of American life and society. Eliot, Pound, Wharton, Fitzgerald, and Hemingway found American culture so unappealing that they exiled themselves to Europe.

Black intellectuals congregated in Manhattan and gave rise to the creative movement known as the **Harlem Renaissance**. Alain Locke promoted *The New Negro*. Poets, novelists, and painters probed racial themes and grappled with what it meant to be black in America. This renaissance had no precise beginning. As early as 1920, Du Bois wrote in the *Crisis* that the nation was on the verge of a "renaissance of American Negro literature." In 1925 the *New York Herald Tribune* declared that America was "on the edge, if not already in the midst of, what might not improperly be called a Negro renaissance." No matter when it began, the Harlem Renaissance produced stunning artistic works, especially in creative writing, that continued into the 1930s.

Harlem Renaissance

As New York City became a destination for black migrants before, during, and after World War I, most of them settled in Harlem—a large neighborhood in the northern portion of Manhattan Island—which by the 1920s became a center of African-American cultural activities including literature, art, and music.

17.4.1 Before Harlem

There had certainly been serious cultural developments among African Americans before the 1920s. From 1897 to 1928, the American Negro Academy was a forum for the Talented Tenth as men such as Alain Locke, Kelly Miller, and Du Bois reflected on race and color.

At the turn of the century, novelist Charles W. Chesnutt depicted a young black woman's attempt to pass for white in *The House Behind the Cedars*, and he wrote about racist violence in the post-Reconstruction South in *The Marrow of Tradition*. Ohio poet Paul Laurence Dunbar wrote evocatively of black life, frequently relying on black dialect, before he died at age 34 in 1906. Henry Ossawa Tanner had an illustrious career as a painter. Shortly after he produced "The Banjo Lesson" in 1893, Tanner left for Paris and spent most of the rest of his life in Europe. He died there in 1937.

Carter G. Woodson, the son of Virginia slaves, earned a Ph.D. in history at Harvard and founded in 1915 the Association for the Study of Negro Life and History. He stressed the need for the scholarly examination of Negro history and established the *Journal of Negro History* (now the *Journal of African American History*) and the *Negro History Bulletin*. He also founded Associated Publishers to publish books on black history. Woodson wrote several major works, including *The Negro in Our History*. In 1926 he established Negro History Week during February. Not surprisingly, Woodson became known as the "father of Negro history."

Carter G. Woodson was born in 1875, the son of slaves. As a young man he toiled in West Virginia coal mines. He worked his way through Berea College and then earned a doctorate in history from Harvard in 1912. In 1915 he founded the Association for the Study of Negro Life and History. In 1926 Woodson founded Negro History Week, which would become Negro History Month. He died in 1950.

During the bloody Red Summer of 1919 when racial violence erupted in Chicago and elsewhere, Claude McKay, a Jamaican who settled—like Marcus Garvey—in New York City, wrote a powerful poem, "If We Must Die," in response to the attacks by white people in Chicago on black residents:

> If we must die, let it not be like hogs
> Hunted and penned in an inglorious spot,
> While round us bark the mad and hungry dogs,
> Making their mock at our accursèd lot.
> If we must die, O let us nobly die,
> So that our precious blood may not be shed
> In vain; then even the monsters we defy
> Shall be constrained to honor us though dead!
> O kinsmen! We must meet the common foe!
> Though far outnumbered let us show us brave,
> And for their thousand blows deal one deathblow!
> What though before us lies the open grave?
> Like men we'll face the murderous, cowardly pack,
> Pressed to the wall, dying, but fighting back!

McKay left the United States for the Soviet Union in 1922 and spent the next 12 years in Europe. In 1928, while in France, he wrote *Home to Harlem*, a novel that depicted life among pimps, prostitutes, loan sharks, and petty criminals. McKay was not on cordial terms with the African-American intellectuals who formed the core of the Harlem Renaissance, and he did not consider himself part of the Talented Tenth: "I was an older man and not regarded as a member of the renaissance, but more as a forerunner."

17.4.2 Writers and Artists

Few white Americans and still fewer black Americans had access to a college education in the early twentieth century. Only about 2,000 African Americans were pursuing college degrees by 1920. Yet the writers and artists associated with the Harlem Renaissance were the products of some of the nation's finest schools, and, with the exception of Zora Neale Hurston, they did not come from isolated, rural southern communities. Hurston was born in Notasulga, Alabama, and raised near Orlando in the all-black town of Eatonville, Florida. She attended Morgan State University and Howard University, and graduated from Barnard College. Alain Locke was a native of Philadelphia and a Phi Beta Kappa graduate of Harvard. He was the first African American to win a Rhodes scholarship to Oxford University, and he also earned a Ph.D. in philosophy from Harvard. Aaron Douglas was born in Kansas and was an art major at the University of Nebraska.

Langston Hughes was born in Joplin, Missouri; graduated from high school in Cleveland; and attended Columbia University before he graduated from Pennsylvania's Lincoln University. Jessie Fauset came from a prominent Philadelphia family of color. She was a graduate of Cornell University and a member of Phi Beta Kappa. She earned an M.A. from the University of Pennsylvania in romance languages. Jean Toomer was born in Washington, D.C., and was raised largely by his grandparents in a fashionable white neighborhood. Toomer went to the University of Wisconsin and then the Massachusetts College of Agriculture. Wallace Thurman was born in Salt Lake City and attended both the University of Utah and the University of Southern California. Countee Cullen was a native of Lexington, Kentucky, and a Phi Beta Kappa graduate of New York University. Nella Larsen was the only major writer connected to the Harlem

Artist Aaron Douglas (1899–1979) was born in Topeka, Kansas, and was the sole black student at the University of Nebraska when he graduated in 1922. He moved to Harlem in 1925 and shortly after that visited Paris, where he met celebrated black artist Henry Ossawa Tanner. Douglas returned to Harlem and then taught art at Fisk University in Nashville from 1937 to 1966. His paintings reflected his deep interest in the African-American experience. Notice the Ku Klux Klan as well as black soldiers in this work.

Renaissance who did not have a college degree. A native of Chicago, she graduated from the nurse training program at New York City's Lincoln Hospital.

The Harlem Renaissance gradually emerged in the early 1920s and then expanded as more creative figures were drawn to Harlem. In 1923 Jean Toomer published *Cane*, a collection of stories and poetry about southern black life. It sold a mere 500 copies, but it had a major impact on Jessie Fauset and Walter White. Fauset was the literary editor of the *Crisis*, and in 1924 she finished *There Is Confusion*, the first novel published during the renaissance. Her novels explored the manners and color consciousness among well-to-do Negroes. Walter White, who was James Weldon Johnson's assistant at the NAACP, published in 1924 *The Fire in the Flint*, a novel about a black physician who confronted white brutality in Georgia.

In the meantime, the *Crisis*, as well as *Opportunity*, a new publication of the Urban League, published the poetry and short stories of black authors, including Langston Hughes, Countee Cullen, and Zora Neale Hurston. White publishers were also attracted to black literary efforts. In 1925 *Survey Graphic* published a special edition on black life and culture called "Harlem: Mecca of the New Negro." Howard University professor Alain Locke then edited *The New Negro*, which drew much of its material from *Survey Graphic* as well as *Opportunity* and included silhouette drawings with Egyptian motifs by Aaron Douglas. In his opening essay, Locke explained Harlem's literary significance: "Harlem has the same role to play for the new Negro as Dublin has had for the New Ireland or Prague for the New Czechoslovakia."

Disagreements erupted during the Harlem Renaissance over the definition and purpose of black literature. Some, such as Alain Locke, Du Bois, Jessie Fauset, and Benjamin Brawley, wanted black writers to promote positive images of black people in their works. They hoped inspirational literature could help resolve racial conflict in America, and they believed black writers should be included in the larger (and mostly white) American literary tradition. Claude McKay, Langston Hughes, and Zora Neale Hurston disagreed. Their work portrayed the streets and shadows of Harlem and the lives of poor black people. In *The Ways of White Folks*, Hughes ridiculed the notion that writers could promote racial reconciliation. One of his characters derisively declares, "Art would break down color lines, art would save the race and prevent lynchings! Bunk!"

1919–1937
The Harlem Renaissance

1919

Claude McKay publishes "If We Must Die"

1920

Eugene O'Neill's *The Emperor Jones* opens, featuring Charles Gilpin; Langston Hughes publishes *The Negro Speaks of Rivers*

1922

Shuffle Along, by Noble Sissle and Eubie Blake, opens on Broadway with Florence Mills and Josephine Baker; Claude McKay publishes *Harlem Shadows*

1923

Jean Toomer publishes *Cane*; the Cotton Club opens; *Opportunity: A Journal of Negro Life,* edited by Charles S. Johnson and supported by the Urban League, begins publication

1924

Jessie R. Fauset publishes *There Is Confusion*; Walter White publishes *The Fire in the Flint*; Paul Robeson stars in Eugene O'Neill's *All God's Chillun Got Wings*

1925

Countee Cullen publishes *Color*; James Weldon Johnson publishes *The Book of American Negro Spirituals*; *The New Negro,* edited by Alain Locke, is published

1926

Langston Hughes publishes *The Weary Blues*; George Schuyler's "The Negro-Art Hokum" appears in *The Nation*; The Savoy Ballroom opens; Wallace Thurman publishes one issue of *Fire*; Florence Mills dies

1927

Langston Hughes publishes *Fine Clothes to the Jew*; James Weldon Johnson publishes *God's Trombones: Seven Negro Sermons in Verse*

1928

Claude McKay publishes *Home to Harlem*; Duke Ellington's band appears at the Cotton Club; Nella Larsen publishes *Quicksand*

1929

Jessie R. Fauset publishes *Plum Bun*; Wallace Thurman publishes *The Blacker the Berry . . .* ; Claude McKay publishes *Banjo*; Countee Cullen publishes *The Black Christ*; Nella Larsen publishes *Passing*; Fats Waller's *Ain't Misbehavin'* opens on Broadway

1930

James Weldon Johnson publishes *Black Manhattan*

1931

Jessie R. Fauset publishes *The Chinaberry Tree*

1933

Jessie R. Fauset publishes her last novel, *Comedy American Style*; James Weldon Johnson publishes his autobiography, *Along the Way*

1934

Wallace Thurman dies

1935

Zora Neale Hurston publishes *Mules and Men*

1937

Zora Neale Hurston publishes *Their Eyes Were Watching God*

Du Bois commented caustically after he read McKay's bawdy *Home to Harlem*, "I feel distinctly like taking a bath." Du Bois was less than impressed with Jake, the novel's protagonist, who is intimately involved with the reality of life in Harlem that included opium, alcohol, and sex. Alain Locke dismissed McKay as a mere propagandist, and McKay in turn called Locke "a dyed-in-the-wool pussy-footing professor." Black critic George Schuyler's "The Negro-Art Hokum" in *The Nation* ridiculed black writers who contended that black people even had their own expressive culture that was separate from that of white people: "As for the literature, painting, and sculpture of Afroamericans—such as there is—it is identical in kind with the literature, painting, and sculpture of white Americans."

Langston Hughes, meanwhile, defended the authenticity of black art and literature but insisted the approval or disapproval of white people and black people was of little consequence:

> We younger Negro artists who create now intend to express our individual dark-skinned selves without fear or shame. If white people are pleased, we are glad. If they are not, it doesn't matter. We know we are beautiful. And ugly too. The tom-tom cries and the tom-tom laughs. If colored people are pleased we are glad. If they are not, their displeasure doesn't matter either. We build our temples for tomorrow, strong as we know how, and we stand on top of the mountain, free within ourselves.

Even more upsetting to those who wanted to safeguard the reputation of black people was Wallace Thurman, who arrived in New York in 1925. Thurman worked briefly at the *Messenger*, the socialist publication that A. Philip Randolph's BSCP had absorbed. He was a voracious reader with a brilliant mind and an eccentric personality who attracted many admirers. He wrote, "I cannot bear to associate with the ordinary run of people. I have to surround myself with individuals who for the most part are more than a trifle insane."

In 1926 Thurman published *Fire*, a journal that lasted only one issue but managed to incite enormous controversy and leave Thurman deeply in debt. *Fire* included Thurman's short story "Cordelia the Crude," about a prostitute, and a one-act play by Zora Neale Hurston, *Color Struck*. Hurston replicated the speech of rural black southerners while depicting the jealousy a darker woman feels when a light-skinned rival tries to take her man. Black critic Benjamin Brawley complained that with *Fire* "vulgarity had been mistaken for art."

Thurman, who was a dark black man, antagonized still more people when *The Blacker the Berry . . .* was published in 1929. In it he described the tribulations and sorrows of Emma Lou, a young woman who did not mind being black, "but she did mind being too black." The book made it plain that many black people had absorbed a color prejudice that they did not hesitate to inflict on darker members of their own race.

Unlike Thurman, Nella Larsen wrote about black people who were indistinguishable from white people. Her novel *Quicksand* depicted the life of Helga Crane, who, like Larsen herself, had a Danish mother and a black father. In *Passing*, Larsen dealt with a young black woman who passed for white and, indeed, married a white racist.

17.4.3 White People and the Harlem Renaissance

Like many of the writers associated with the Harlem Renaissance, Zora Neale Hurston's pen sliced like a scalpel. She called the white people who took an interest in Harlem "Negrotarians" and her black literary colleagues the "Niggerati." But no matter how they were described, black and white people developed pleasant but often uneasy relationships during the renaissance.

No white man was more attracted to the cultural developments in Harlem than photographer and writer Carl Van Vechten. In 1926 he caused a furor with his novel *Nigger Heaven*. The title, which referred to the balcony where black patrons had to sit in segregated theaters and auditoriums, offended many people. The novel dealt with the coarser aspects of life in Harlem, which irritated Du Bois, Fauset, and Countee Cullen. But Van Vechten wanted a more honest depiction of the black experience, and James Weldon Johnson, Walter White, and Langston Hughes approved of the novel.

Most black writers and artists welcomed the encouragement and financial backing they received from white authors, critics, and publishers. White writers, including Eugene O'Neill, Sherwood Anderson, Sinclair Lewis, and Van Wyck Brooks, were fascinated by black people and interested in the works of black authors. Major publishers, such as Alfred A. Knopf, published the works of Harlem writers. Black and white literary figures gathered for cocktails, small talk, and music at Carl Van Vechten's apartment on West 55th Street.

White attention and support were sometimes accompanied by condescension and disdain. Too many "Negrotarians" considered Harlem and its inhabitants exotic, curious, and uncivilized. They found life in Harlem—its clubs, music, and entertainers, as well as its poetry, prose, and painting—more energetic, lively, and sensual than white life and culture. Black culture was also—many white people believed—unsophisticated and primitive, which is what made it so appealing. Black writers like Langston Hughes, Claude McKay, and Countee Cullen wanted to depict black life realistically—from its gangsters to its gamblers. But they resented the notion that black culture was inherently crude and unrefined.

Claude McKay was a major figure of the Harlem Renaissance, a writer whose work provides frank portrayals of black life. His first and most famous work, *Home to Harlem*, was published in 1928 and depicted the gritty, intense nightlife of Harlem.

White patrons like Amy Spingarn, whose husband Joel was president of the NAACP board of directors, and Charlotte Osgood "Godmother" Mason supported black writers and artists. Spingarn helped finance Langston Hughes's education at Lincoln University. "Godmother" Mason was a wealthy widow who financially supported black artists. She worked closely with Alain Locke, who helped identify Langston Hughes, Zora Neale Hurston, and Aaron Douglas, among others, who became her "godchildren." Mason wanted no publicity for herself, but her patronage had its costs. Mason gave Hurston $200 a month and an automobile. She gave Hughes $150 a month plus expensive clothing and writing supplies. In return, Mason demanded that the black writers keep her informed about their activities, and she did not hesitate to tell them when they were not productive enough. She also tried to influence what they wrote. She preferred that black writers confine themselves to exotic themes. As helpful as Mason's financial assistance and personal encouragement were, she created a system of dependency, and Hughes and Hurston finally severed the arrangement. Hughes later fondly recalled, "I can only say that those months when I lived by and through her were the most fascinating and fantastic I have ever known."

Harlem's cultural icons sometimes congregated away from the curiosity and paternalism of white admirers. The plush twin townhouses of A'Lelia Walker at 108–110 West 136th Street also attracted Harlem's literary figures as well as entertainers. Walker was the daughter of black cosmetics millionaire Madam C. J. Walker. Although she read little herself, A'Lelia Walker enjoyed hosting musicians, writers, and artists at "The

Dark Tower," named for Countee Cullen's column, "The Dark Tower," that appeared regularly in *Opportunity*. But Harlem artists also gathered in the much less luxurious surroundings of "Niggerati Manor," a rooming house on 267 West 136th Street where Thurman, Hurston, and Hughes resided in the late 1920s.

The profusion of literary works associated with the Harlem Renaissance did not so much end as fade away. Black writers remained active into the 1930s. Hurston wrote her two most important works in the 1930s—*Mules and Men* in 1935 and *Their Eyes Were Watching God* in 1937. Although McKay and Hughes continued to have their work published, the Great Depression that began in 1929 devastated book and magazine sales. Subscriptions to the *Crisis* and *Opportunity* declined, and both journals published fewer works by creative writers. Many black intellectuals left Harlem. James Weldon Johnson and Aaron Douglas went to Fisk University in Nashville.

Du Bois quarreled with the NAACP and returned to Atlanta University. Alain Locke remained on the faculty at Howard University. Jessie Fauset married an insurance executive and took up housekeeping after her last novel was published in 1931. Nella Larsen was charged unjustly with plagiarism. She quit writing and resumed her career as a nurse. Wallace Thurman died an alcoholic in 1934. Countee Cullen taught French at DeWitt Clinton High School in New York City, where James Baldwin was one of his students in the late 1930s.

17.4.4 Harlem and the Jazz Age

As powerful and important as these black literary voices were, they were less popular than the entertainers, musicians, singers, and dancers who were also part of the Harlem Renaissance. Without Harlem, the 1920s would not have been the Jazz Age. From wailing trumpets, beating drums, dancing feet, and plaintive and mournful songs, Harlem's clubs, cabarets, theaters, and ballrooms echoed with the vibrant and soulful sounds of African Americans. By comparison, white music seemed sedate and bland.

Black and white people flocked to Harlem to enjoy themselves—and to break the law. In 1919–1920, the Eighteenth Amendment and the Volstead Act prohibited the manufacture, distribution, and sale of alcoholic beverages. But liquor flowed freely in Harlem's fancy establishments and smoky dives. Musicians and entertainers, like Harlem's working-class residents, had migrated there. The blues and their sorrowful tales of troubled and broken relationships arrived from the Mississippi delta and rural South. Jazz had its origins in New Orleans, but it drew on ragtime and spirituals as it moved up the Mississippi River to Kansas City and Chicago on its way to Harlem.

The Cotton Club was Harlem's most exclusive and fashionable nightspot. Opened in 1923 by white gangster Owney Madden to peddle illegal beer, it catered to well-to-do white people who regarded a trip to Harlem as a foreign excursion. The club's entertainers and waiters were black, but the customers were white. Black patrons were not admitted. The club featured well-choreographed and fast-paced two-hour revues that included a chorus line of attractive young women—all brown skinned, all under age 21, and all over five feet six inches tall. No dark women appeared. Assorted ensembles provided the music. Cab Calloway might sing "She's Tall, She's Tan and She's Terrific" or "Cotton Colored Gal of Mine."

In 1928 Edward K. "Duke" Ellington and his orchestra began a 12-year association with the Cotton Club. Although Ellington had not yet begun to compose his own music in earnest, his band already had an elegant, sophisticated, and recognizable African-American sound. Another club, Connie's Inn, also served a mostly white clientele. Thomas "Fats" Waller played a rambunctious piano at Connie's. Waller's father was the deacon at the Abyssinian Baptist Church in Harlem, and his mother was the organist. The songs and music their son wrote, including "Honeysuckle Rose" and "Ain't Misbehavin," were hardly sacred, but they were popular. Connie's also put on stunning musical revues, perhaps the best known of which was *Hot Chocolates*. Dancers who performed at Connie's included the legendary Bill "Bojangles" Robinson and Earl "Snakehips" Tucker. A young trumpeter from New Orleans, Louis Armstrong, played briefly at Connie's. Armstrong amazed listeners with his virtuoso trumpet and gravelly voice.

Harlem's black residents were more likely to step into one of Harlem's less pretentious and inexpensive establishments, such as the Sugar Cane. In these places, the beer and liquor were cheap, the food was plentiful, the music was good, and there were no elaborate production numbers. Even less impressive clubs and bars remained open after the legal closing hour of 3:00 A.M. "Arrangements" were made with the police, who looked the other way as the music and alcohol continued through the night. Musicians from "legal" clubs drifted into the after-hours joints and played until dawn.

Another popular—and sometimes necessary—form of entertainment among Harlemites was the rent party. Housing costs in Harlem were extravagant, and white people and real estate agents refused to rent or sell to black people in most other areas of New York City. To make the steep monthly rent payments, apartment dwellers would push the furniture aside and begin cooking chicken, chitterlings, rice, okra, and sweet potatoes. They would distribute a few flyers and hire a musician or two. The party was usually on a Saturday or a Thursday night. (Most domestic servants had Thursdays off.) Partygoers paid 10 to 50 cents for admission. Food and liquor were sold. With a decent crowd, the month's rent was paid.

17.4.5 Song, Dance, and Stage

Black women became popular as singers and dancers in Harlem and then often appeared in Broadway shows and revues. Florence Mills entranced audiences with her diminutive singing voice in several Broadway productions including *Plantation Review*, *Dixie to Broadway*, and *Blackbirds* before she died of appendicitis in 1927. Adelaide Hall also appeared in *Blackbirds* and later opened her own nightclubs in London and Paris. Ethel Waters worked her way up from smoky gin joints in Harlem basements, where she sang risqué and comic songs, to Broadway shows, and then to films. Years later she toured with Billy Graham's religious revivals.

White men wrote many of the popular Broadway productions that starred black entertainers. In 1921, however, Eubie Blake and Noble Sissle put on *Shuffle Along*, which became a major hit. Its most memorable tune was "I'm Just Wild About Harry." Sissle and Blake's *Chocolate Dandies* in 1924 was created especially for a thin, lanky, dark, and funny young lady named Josephine Baker. But in 1925 Baker moved to Paris, where she starred in the *Revue Nègre*, which created a sensation in the French capital. She remained in France for the rest of her life.

White playwright Eugene O'Neill wrote serious drama involving black people. Charles Gilpin and then Paul Robeson appeared in O'Neill's *Emperor Jones*. Robeson—who had an

Noble Sissle and Eubie Blake were the first two black entertainers who dressed elegantly in tuxedos and not as minstrel players. They collaborated on writing the lyrics and composing the music for *Shuffle Along*, which opened on Broadway in 1921 and played for 504 performances. The show's hit tune was "I'm Just Wild About Harry." In 1948 Harry Truman resurrected it as his campaign song. Truman went on to defeat Republican Thomas Dewey and win the presidency.

Profile

Bessie Smith

Bessie Smith knew the blues. She sang the blues. She lived the blues. She was the "Empress of the Blues." During the 1920s no singer in America was more popular than she was.

Bessie was born in poverty in 1894 in Chattanooga, Tennessee. She was one of seven children of a Baptist preacher, William Smith, and his wife, Laura. Bessie's parents and two brothers died while she was a child, and an older sister, Viola, raised the surviving children.

With her brother Andrew accompanying her on the guitar, Bessie began to sing on Chattanooga street corners to earn money for the family, an apprenticeship that shaped her career. In 1912 she toured with a musical group that featured Gertrude "Ma" Rainey. In 1913 she worked in Atlanta for $10 a week plus tips. Her fame spread, and soon she was touring the South. By the 1920s she was singing in Philadelphia and Atlantic City.

Initially her voice was considered too rough for the infant recording industry. But in 1923 Frank Walker signed her to a contract with Columbia Records. She recorded what were known in the 1920s as "race" records, produced for black audiences by white recording companies. Her first recordings included "Downhearted Blues" and "Gulf Coast Blues." Her second session brought "Tain't Nobody's Business If I Do." She sold 780,000 records within months.

In 1925 she recorded "St. Louis Blues" and "Careless Love" with Louis Armstrong—their only recordings together. She toured major cities, including Pittsburgh, Cleveland, and Chicago, in a private railroad coach, and huge crowds lined up at clubs and theaters to hear her. Though it could sound coarse, her striking and appealing voice conveyed her emotions and experiences.

She also knew of what she sang. When she sang "Money Blues," "Pickpocket Blues," or "Empty Bed Blues," she revealed the pathos, but also the humor, that so many black people had experienced. Smith's blues tore at the raw feelings that sociologists and academics missed when they discussed poverty, unemployment, alcoholism, or sexual relationships. Her blues were firmly grounded in African-American oral and musical traditions.

Bessie Smith was not a delicate woman. She was married twice. Her first husband, Earl Love, died shortly after they married. Her second marriage, to Jack Gee, was marked by jealousy, drinking, and physical conflict. They separated in 1930. She had a profusion of lovers—male and female. Her warmest and most enduring relationship was with Richard Morgan, a Chicago bootlegger.

People did not trifle with Bessie Smith. A large lady, over 200 pounds, she ate, drank, and fought to excess. She could be mean, contentious, and violent. She physically attacked others and was herself attacked. But she also had a sweet and loyal side and could be generous and compassionate. However, she seemed fond of some of the sleaziest, most dangerous nightclubs in America. She could not resist Detroit's Koppin Theater, a den of debauchery. She admitted wanting to go where "the funk was flying."

She continued to record even after record sales declined during the Depression. Her last recording session included "Nobody Knows You When You're Down and Out." Bessie Smith died at age 43 in 1937 in an automobile accident near Clarksdale, Mississippi. Perhaps Louis Armstrong summed up her musical legacy best: "She used to thrill me at all times, the way she could phrase a note with a certain something in her voice no other blues singer could get. She had music in her soul and felt everything she did."

illustrious career—was a graduate of Rutgers University, where he was an all-American football player. He earned a law degree at Columbia University but abandoned the law for the stage. He appeared in numerous productions, including O'Neill's *All God's Chillun Got Wings*, Shakespeare's *Othello*, Gershwin's *Porgy and Bess*, and Kern and Hammerstein's *Showboat*. He often sang spirituals in his rich voice and later recorded many of them.

17.5 Sports

Describe the opportunities and discrimination experienced by black athletes in the 1920s.

Sports flourished in the 1920s. Americans worshiped their athletic heroes. Babe Ruth and Jack Dempsey were as well known as President Coolidge. Professional athletics, especially baseball and boxing, expanded dramatically. Professional football and basketball emerged later. Black men had been banned from major league baseball in 1887 (see Chapter 15). Nevertheless, in 1901 Baltimore Orioles manager John J. McGraw signed a black man, Charlie Grant, to play second base. McGraw claimed that Grant was "Chief Tokohoma," a full-blooded Cherokee Indian. Chicago White Sox owner Charles Comiskey knew otherwise, and Grant did not play in the major leagues.

Playing among themselves, black baseball players barely made a living as they moved from team to team in an ever-fluctuating and disorganized system that saw teams come and go with monotonous regularity. No leagues functioned effectively for the black teams and players. Owners of the black teams were sometimes involved in organized crime. William A. Greenlee, for example, the proprietor of the Pittsburgh Crawfords, made most of his money from the numbers racket.

Black players crisscrossed the country on trains and in automobiles as they played each other in small towns and large cities for meager money shared from gate receipts. It was an insecure and nomadic life. The black clubs kept few individual or team statistics, and their financial records were frequently in disarray.

Negro National League

A professional baseball league for black players and teams organized in 1912.

Andrew "Rube" Foster was the father of black baseball. An outstanding pitcher, he reportedly taught major-league-great Christy Mathewson how to throw the screwball. He became the owner and manager of the Chicago American Giants and he was the founder of the Negro National League. His teams won the pennant in 1920, 1921, and 1922. He was elected to the Baseball Hall of Fame in Cooperstown in 1981.

17.5.1 Rube Foster

Andrew "Rube" Foster was the father of black baseball in twentieth-century America. He was a crafty pitcher from Texas who combined athletic skills with mental dexterity. In 1911 he founded the Chicago American Giants, and he pitched with them regularly until 1915; after that, he mainly managed the team. A fine athlete, Foster was an even more talented organizer and administrator.

In 1919 in the *Chicago Defender*, he argued for a Negro baseball league. In 1920 he was the catalyst in the formation of the eight-team **Negro National League** and became its president and secretary. It was the first stable black league, with franchises in Kansas City, St. Louis, Indianapolis, Detroit, Dayton, and two teams in Chicago. The eighth team was the Cuban Stars.

Foster and the new league took advantage of the migration of black people to northern cities. The black ball clubs usually played late in the afternoon or in the early evening so fans could attend after a day's work. (This was before night baseball.) Sunday doubleheaders in Chicago or Kansas City might draw 8,000 to 10,000 people. Players were paid regularly, and athletes on

Foster's Giants earned at least $175 a month. The biggest obstacle that black teams faced was the lack of their own fields or stadiums. They were forced to rent, often at exorbitant rates, from major league clubs, which frequently kept the profits from concessions.

Black baseball thrived—more or less—in the 1920s, thanks mostly to Foster's dedication. He was a tireless worker and strict disciplinarian, but the pressure may have been too much. He suffered a mental breakdown in 1926 and died in 1930. The loss of Foster—combined with the Depression—disrupted the league system.

17.5.2 College Sports

Football, baseball, basketball, and track and field were popular at the collegiate level. Amateur sports were less rigidly segregated than professional baseball. Black men played for white northern universities, although few teams had more than one black player. For example, Paul Robeson was on the Rutgers football team in 1916 that played against Frederick Douglass "Fritz" Pollard and Brown University. Pollard was the first black man to play in the Rose Bowl, where Brown lost to Washington State in 1916.

Pollard played professional football in the 1920s. He played for four early National Football League (NFL) teams, including Milwaukee and Providence. In 1921 he became the first African-American head coach in the league when he took charge of the Akron team. Later he coached an independent all-black team, the Chicago Black Hawks. Pollard, who died in 1986, was inducted into the NFL Hall of Fame in 2005.

Black college players on white teams encountered discrimination when the teams traveled. Spectators taunted and threatened them. The Big Ten had an unwritten agreement that basketball coaches would not accept black players. All-white college teams sometimes refused to play schools with black players. In 1920, for example, Virginia's Washington and Lee University canceled a football game against Washington and Jefferson College of Pennsylvania because Charles West, a black man, played in the Washington and Jefferson backfield.

Sports in black colleges and universities thrived in the 1920s. Baseball and football were the most popular spectator events. Traditional rivalries attracted large crowds. Several schools played baseball religiously each Easter Monday. In 1926 Livingstone College defeated Biddle University (now Johnson C. Smith University) before a crowd of 6,000 in Charlotte, North Carolina. With the migration of black people to the North, black colleges began to play football in northern cities. Howard and Lincoln played to a scoreless tie before 18,000 people in Philadelphia on Thanksgiving in 1925. Hampton and Lincoln played at New York's Polo Grounds on the edge of Harlem in 1929 in a game Lincoln won 13–7 before 10,000 spectators.

Conclusion

For African Americans, the 1920s must have seemed little more than a depressing continuation of earlier decades. Little appeared to have changed. Racial violence and lynching persisted. *The Birth of a Nation* mocked black people and inflamed racial animosity. "Experts" offered "proof" that people of color were inferior and threatened America's ethnic purity. The Ku Klux Klan became a formidable organization again. Millions of white men joined the Klan, and millions more supported it.

Nevertheless, positive developments in the 1920s gave hope for a more promising future. The NAACP became an organization to be reckoned with as it fought for antilynching legislation in Congress and for civil and political rights in the courts.

Its membership exceeded 100,000 during the 1920s. Although many black and white Americans ridiculed Marcus Garvey for his flamboyant style and excessive rhetoric, he offered racial pride and self-respect as he enrolled hundreds of thousands of black people in the UNIA.

Black workers made little progress as they sought concessions from big business and representation within the ranks of organized labor. A. Philip Randolph founded the BSCP and began a struggle with both the Pullman Company and the AFL that would begin to pay off in the 1930s.

The Harlem Renaissance was a cultural awakening in literature and the arts that was unprecedented in African-American history. A torrent of words poured forth from novelists, essayists, and poets. Although they disagreed—sometimes vehemently—on the purposes of black art, the writers and artists who were a part of the renaissance had an enduring impact. The renaissance allowed thoughtful and creative men and women to grapple with what it meant to be black in a society in which the white majority had defined the black minority as inferior, incapable, and backward. Hereafter, African Americans were less likely to let other people characterize them in demeaning ways.

Black musicians, dancers, singers, entertainers, and athletes made names for themselves and contributed to popular culture in a mostly urban environment. As the 1930s began, it remained to be seen whether the modest but real progress of the 1920s would be sustained.

Chapter Timeline

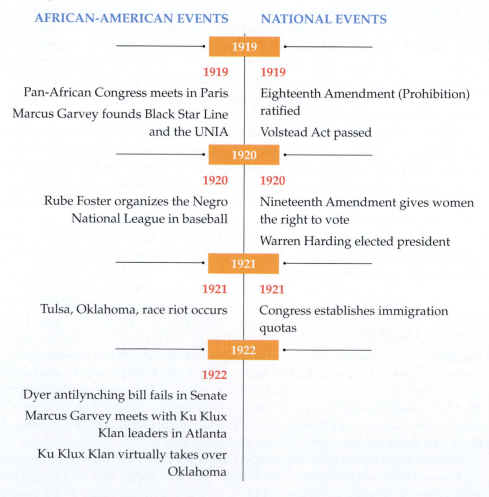

AFRICAN-AMERICAN EVENTS	NATIONAL EVENTS
1919	
1919	**1919**
Pan-African Congress meets in Paris	Eighteenth Amendment (Prohibition) ratified
Marcus Garvey founds Black Star Line and the UNIA	Volstead Act passed
1920	
1920	**1920**
Rube Foster organizes the Negro National League in baseball	Nineteenth Amendment gives women the right to vote
	Warren Harding elected president
1921	
1921	**1921**
Tulsa, Oklahoma, race riot occurs	Congress establishes immigration quotas
1922	
1922	
Dyer antilynching bill fails in Senate	
Marcus Garvey meets with Ku Klux Klan leaders in Atlanta	
Ku Klux Klan virtually takes over Oklahoma	

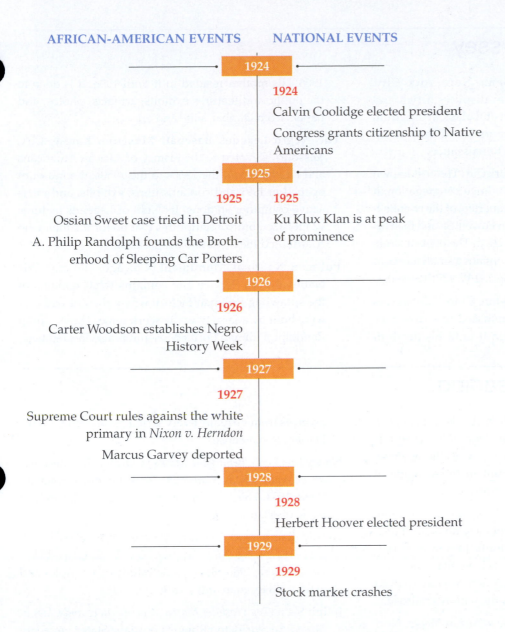

AFRICAN-AMERICAN EVENTS   **NATIONAL EVENTS**

1924

1924

Calvin Coolidge elected president

Congress grants citizenship to Native
Americans

1925

1925   **1925**

Ossian Sweet case tried in Detroit   Ku Klux Klan is at peak
                                     of prominence
A. Philip Randolph founds the Brotherhood of Sleeping Car Porters

1926

1926

Carter Woodson establishes Negro
History Week

1927

1927

Supreme Court rules against the white
primary in *Nixon v. Herndon*

Marcus Garvey deported

1928

1928

Herbert Hoover elected president

1929

1929

Stock market crashes

Review Questions

1. To what extent, if any, had the intensity of white supremacy changed by the 1920s from what it had been two to three decades earlier?

2. What examples of progress could leaders like W. E. B. Du Bois, James Weldon Johnson, A. Philip Randolph, and Marcus Garvey point to in the 1920s?

3. Why did so many African-American leaders reject Marcus Garvey?

4. How did the black nationalism of the Universal Negro Improvement Association differ from the white nationalism of the Ku Klux Klan?

5. What economic opportunities existed for African Americans who had migrated to northern cities?

6. Why did the literary and artistic movement known as the Harlem Renaissance emerge?

7. What was distinctive about black writers, artists, and musicians? Were their creative works essentially a part of American culture or separate from it?

8. Did African Americans have any reason to be optimistic by the late 1920s?

Retracing the Odyssey

The Studio Museum of Harlem, New York City. Founded in 1967, this museum displays a rich and diverse array of art and artifacts by black artists from Africa, the Caribbean, and America and thus maintains the legacy of the Harlem Renaissance.

Abyssinian Baptist Church, New York City. The best-known church in Harlem and home to a huge congregation, it was led for most of the first three-quarters of the twentieth century by the Rev. Adam Clayton Powell, Sr. and then his son, the Rev. Adam Clayton Powell, Jr. The present structure was completed in 1923 and contains a small museum at 132 Odell Clark Place (formerly 132 W. 138th Street).

Paul Laurence Dunbar Home, Dayton, Ohio. Dunbar was born in 1872 in Dayton. He purchased this two-story brick house in 1903 and lived in it until his death in 1906. His mother resided in it until 1936. It is open to the public and features exhibits, artifacts, photos, and papers from Dunbar's life and era.

The Negro Leagues Baseball Museum, Kansas City, Missouri. Devoted to the history of African Americans and baseball from the 1860s to the 1950s, the museum opened in 1991 and contains films, exhibits, and interactive computer stations. Its Field of Legends features 12 life-sized bronze sculptures that honor the men who contributed the most to black baseball.

Pullman National Monument, Chicago, Illinois. This National Park Service site contains what remains of the sprawling Pullman factory where the railroad cars were built by a largely white work force. The A. Philip Randolph Pullman Porter Museum is also located here.

Recommended Reading

William H. Harris. *Keeping the Faith: A. Philip Randolph, Milton P. Webster and the Brotherhood of Sleeping Car Porters, 1925–1937.* Urbana: University of Illinois Press, 1977. This is an excellent account of the struggle of Randolph and the BSCP for recognition.

Theodore Kornweibel, Jr. *Railroads in the African American Experience.* Baltimore: Johns Hopkins University Press, 2010. From slaves who largely built the southern railroad network to contemporary black women who operate Amtrak locomotives, African Americans have played a key role in the development of the nation's railroads.

David Levering Lewis. *When Harlem Was in Vogue.* New York: Alfred A. Knopf, 1981. Lewis captures the life and vitality of Harlem in the 1920s.

———, ed. *The Portable Harlem Renaissance Reader.* New York: Penguin Books, 1994. Contains essays, poems, and excerpts from virtually every writer associated with the Harlem Renaissance.

Nancy MacLean. *Behind the Mask of Chivalry: The Making of the Second Ku Klux Klan.* New York: Oxford University Press, 1994. This is the most recent study of the revived Ku Klux Klan.

Arnold Rampersad. *The Life of Langston Hughes, Vol. 1, 1902–1941: I, Too, Sing America.* New York: Oxford University Press, 1986. Here is a rich study of a complex and extraordinary man and writer.

Judith Stein. *The World of Marcus Garvey: Race and Class in Modern Society.* Baton Rouge: Louisiana State University Press, 1991. This is an effective examination of Garvey and the UNIA.

Additional Bibliography

The Ku Klux Klan

David M. Chalmers. *Hooded Americanism: A History of the Ku Klux Klan.* New York: Franklin Watts, 1965.

Kenneth T. Jackson. *The Ku Klux Klan in the City.* New York: Oxford University Press, 1967.

The NAACP

Kevin Boyle. *Arc of Justice: A Saga of Race, Civil Rights, and Murder in the Jazz Age* [the Ossian Sweet case]. New York: Henry Holt, 2004.

Charles F. Kellogg. *NAACP: A History of the National Association for the Advancement of Colored People.* Baltimore: Johns Hopkins University Press, 1967.

Robert L. Zangrando. *The NAACP Campaign Against Lynching, 1909–1950.* Philadelphia: Temple University Press, 1980.

Black Workers

Eric Arnesen. *The Black Worker: Race, Labor, and Civil Rights Since Emancipation.* Urbana: University of Illinois Press, 2007.

———. *Brotherhoods of Color: Black Railroad Workers and the Struggle for Equality.* Cambridge, MA: Harvard University Press, 2001.

David E. Bernstein. *Only One Place of Redress: African Americans, Labor Regulations and the Courts from Reconstruction to the New Deal,* Durham, NC: Duke University Press, 2001.

William Powell Jones. *The Tribe of Black Ulysses: African American Lumber Workers in the Jim Crow South.* Urbana: University of Illinois Press, 2005.

Philip F. Rubio. *There's Always Work at the Post Office: African American Postal Workers and the Fight for Jobs, Justice, and Equality.* Chapel Hill: University of North Carolina Press, 2010.

A. Philip Randolph and the Brotherhood of Sleeping Car Porters

Jervis B. Anderson. *A. Philip Randolph: A Biographical Portrait.* New York: Harcourt, Brace, Jovanovich, 1973.

Beth Tompkins Bates. *Pullman Porters and the Rise of Protest Politics in Black America, 1925–1945.* Chapel Hill: University of North Carolina Press, 2001.

Melinda Chateauvert. *Marching Together: Women of the Brotherhood of Sleeping Car Porters.* Urbana: University of Illinois Press, 1998.

Paula F. Pfeffer. *A. Philip Randolph: Pioneer of the Civil Rights Movement.* Baton Rouge: Louisiana State University Press, 1990.

Jack Santino. *Miles of Smiles, Years of Struggle: Stories of Black Pullman Porters.* Urbana: University of Illinois Press, 1989.

Larry Tye. *Rising From the Rails: Pullman Porters and the Making of the Black Middle Class.* New York: Henry Holt, 2004.

Marcus Garvey and the Universal Negro Improvement Association

Randall K. Burkett. *Garveyism as a Religious Movement: The Institutionalization of a Black Civil Religion.* Metuchen, NJ: Scarecrow Press, 1978.

E. David Cronon. *Black Moses: The Story of Marcus Garvey and the Universal Negro Improvement Association.* Madison: University of Wisconsin Press, 1955.

Marcus Garvey. *Philosophy and Opinions of Marcus Garvey.* New York: Atheneum, 1969.

Theodore Kornweibel, Jr. *Seeing Red: Federal Campaigns Against Black Militancy, 1919–1925.* Bloomington: Indiana University Press, 1998.

The Harlem Renaissance

Arna W. Bontemps, ed. *The Harlem Renaissance Remembered.* New York: Dodd, Mead, 1972.

Nathan Huggins. *Harlem Renaissance.* New York: Oxford University Press, 1971.

Bruce Kellner, ed. *The Harlem Renaissance: A Historical Dictionary of the Era.* Westport, CT: Greenwood Press, 1984.

Joyce Moore Turner. *Caribbean Crusaders and the Harlem Renaissance.* Urbana: University of Illinois Press, 2004.

Steven Watson. *The Harlem Renaissance: Hub of African American Culture, 1920–1930.* New York: Pantheon, 1995.

Biographies and Autobiographies

Pamela Bordelon, ed. *Go Gator and Muddy the Water: Writings by Zora Neale Hurston from the Federal Writers' Project.* New York: Norton, 1999.

Wayne F. Cooper. *Claude McKay, Rebel Sojourner in the Harlem Renaissance: A Biography.* Baton Rouge: Louisiana State University Press, 1987.

Robert C. Cottrell. *The Best Pitcher in Baseball: The Life of Rube Foster, Negro League Giant.* New York: New York University Press, 2001.

Thadious M. Davis. *Nella Larsen, Novelist of the Harlem Renaissance: A Woman's Life Unveiled.* Baton Rouge: Louisiana State University Press, 1994.

Robert Hemenway. *Zora Neale Hurston: A Literary Biography.* Urbana: University of Illinois Press, 1977.

Gloria T. Hull. *Color, Sex, and Poetry: Three Women Writers of the Harlem Renaissance.* Bloomington: Indiana University Press, 1987.

George Hutchinson. *In Search of Nella Larsen: A Biography of the Color Line.* Cambridge, MA: Harvard University Press, 2006.

James Weldon Johnson. *Along the Way.* New York: Viking Press, 1933.

Cynthia E. Kerman. *The Lives of Jean Toomer: A Hunger for Wholeness.* Baton Rouge: Louisiana State University Press, 1987.

Eugene Levy. *James Weldon Johnson: Black Leader, Black Voice.* Chicago: University of Chicago Press, 1973.

Aldon D. Morris. *The Scholar Denied: W. E. B. Du Bois and the Birth of Modern Sociology.* Berkley: University of California Press, 2015.

Jeffrey B. Perry. *Hubert Harrison: The Voice of Harlem Radicalism, 1883–1918.* New York: Columbia University Press, 2009.

Michelle R. Scott. *Black Empress in Black Chattanooga: Bessie Smith and the Emerging Urban South.* Urbana: University of Illinois Press, 2008.

Ula Y. Taylor. *The Veiled Garvey: The Life and Times of Amy Jacques Garvey.* Chapel Hill: University of North Carolina Press, 2002.

Connecting the Past

Migration

African-American men, women, and children who participated in the Great Migration to the north, with suitcases and luggage placed in front, Chicago, 1918.

Chicago had slightly more than 40,000 black residents in 1910. By 2010, more than one million African Americans lived in Chicago and its suburbs. This huge growth in the city's black population was part of the Great Migration, the largest internal movement of people in American history. Yet this massive shift in population was only one of many instances over the long course of history that Africans and their descendants have willingly or unwillingly changed locations.

Early humans roamed from Africa into Asia and Europe as hunters and gatherers about 100,000 years ago. Between the sixteenth and nineteenth centuries, 12 million Africans were forced to endure the horrors of the Middle Passage and the Atlantic slave trade. In the decades before the Civil War, thousands of southern slaves escaped to freedom in the northern states and Canada by way of the underground railroad. In the late 1870s, economic and political oppression led as many as 40,000 former slaves known as Exodusters to leave the South and move west to Kansas and Oklahoma. About the same time a small number of freedmen left the United States and went to Liberia in West Africa.

But it was the twentieth century's Great Migration that prompted recent and profound political and economic changes in American society. Most of these migrants boarded segregated passenger trains in southern towns to travel on the overground railroad to northern and western communities. Unlike the nineteenth-century abolitionist movement and the civil rights movement of the 1950s and 1960s, no dynamic organizations or inspirational leaders were involved in this remarkable resettlement. Instead, individuals, husbands, wives, and friends made what was often a heart-wrenching decision to leave the southern communities where they had been born and raised for a strange and distant destination like Chicago, Pittsburgh, or New York City. They did so because, like the slaves who had fled to freedom a century earlier, the migrants wanted a better life. They hoped to liberate themselves from economic dependence, and to escape the segregation and violence that exemplified life in the Jim Crow South.

While life in the North and the West may have been an improvement, black migrants did not suddenly find themselves residing in the Promised Land. White workers resented black competition for unskilled jobs in manufacturing. Labor unions prohibited black membership. White employers' use of black workers as strikebreakers or scabs further alienated white workingmen. Black women were confined to domestic work and denied employment as retail clerks, bank tellers, waitresses, or secretaries. But the "white" and "colored" signs that saturated the South rarely were seen in the North. Buses, streetcars, and passenger trains had open seating. Black people did not have to step aside when white people passed on city sidewalks.

By the middle of the twentieth century, several million African Americans lived in densely populated urban communities throughout the nation. Here are residents of Harlem on Seventh Avenue on a cold February day in 1956.

Many myths accompanied the migrants. Black people who already lived in northern cities looked down on the "countrified" ways of the new arrivals and ridiculed the way they talked, dressed, and carried themselves. They disparaged the newcomers' supposed lack of education, low incomes, and inability to maintain stable families. But these perceptions proved to be inaccurate. Migrants had a sense of purpose and commitment. They were better educated than the people they left behind. They had higher incomes and were less likely to be on welfare than African Americans who already resided in the North. They were more likely to be married and remain married. Their children lived in two-parent households.

The development of black political power was one of the unexpected consequences of the Great Migration. Black men and women voted freely in the North and West. Living together in black neighborhoods afforded them the opportunity to elect black city councilmen, aldermen, and congressmen. By the 1950s, black men from Chicago, Detroit, Philadelphia, and Harlem served in the U.S. House of Representatives. In the 1960s and 1970s, black mayors were elected in Cleveland, Newark, Detroit, and Los Angeles. Democratic presidential candidates Harry Truman in 1948 and John F. Kennedy in 1960 relied on black voters in northern cities to provide them with margins of victory.

The Civil Rights Act of 1964 and the Voting Rights Act of 1965 eradicated Jim Crow in the South. The Great Migration began to reverse itself. Black people who had migrated to northern communities in the 1940s and 1950s began to retire in the 1980s and 1990s to towns and communities they had left as young people. Now, with a shifting racial dynamic in the United States that included the election of an African-American president, there is a new migration. Black people from Africa and the Caribbean increasingly come to America. Between 2000 and 2010, 216,900 Africans moved to the United States. Not all of them will remain, but more will come, attracted to a place where their predecessors were sold and toiled as slaves. Those predecessors and their descendants helped create a vibrant nation that now draws immigrants from nearly every corner of the globe.

1. What specific factors account for the Great Migration?
2. Under what circumstances would you move hundreds of miles from your friends and family?

Part V
The Great Depression and World War II

Dizzy Gillespie

	1900–1930	1930–1935

RELIGION

1900–1930
1919 Father Divine begins what comes to be known as the Peace Mission Movement
1929 Nation of Islam emerges

1930–1935
1933 Father Divine establishes his Peace Mission in Harlem
1934 Elijah Muhammad becomes leader of the Detroit Temple of Islam

CULTURE

1930–1935
1930s–1940s Heyday of Chicago's Black Renaissance
1930 Duke Ellington's "Mood Indigo"; Langston Hughes publishes *Not Without Laughter*
1931 Katherine Dunham forms the Negro Dance Group
1933 Paul Robeson stars in *The Emperor Jones*
1935 Marvel Cooke and Ella Baker publish "The Bronx Slave Market" in the *Crisis*

POLITICS AND GOVERNMENT

1900–1930
1925 U.S. War College concludes that African Americans are not fit for combat
Clifton R. Wharton, Sr. (1899–1990) becomes the nation's first black Foreign Service officers for the U.S. Department of State. In 1960 President John F. Kennedy would appoint him U.S. Ambassador to Norway.
1928 Oscar DePriest elected, first African-American congressman from the North

1930–1935
1930 NAACP helps block John J. Parker's appointment to the Supreme Court
1932 "Scottsboro Boys" arrested
1933 Franklin D. Roosevelt's "black cabinet" formed

SOCIETY AND ECONOMY

1900–1930
1899 North Carolina Mutual Life Insurance Company becomes the largest black-owned business in the United States
1908 Binga Bank opens in Chicago

1930–1935
1930 Fannie Peck founds Detroit Housewives League
1932 Tuskegee Experiment begins
1935 Mary M. Bethune founds the National Council of Negro Women
National Negro Congress founded
NAACP sues to integrate University of Maryland School of Law

Mahalia Jackson   James Baldwin   Ralph Bunche

1935–1940   **1940–1950**   **Noteworthy Individuals**

1936 Jesse Owens wins four gold medals at the Berlin Olympics
1937 Joe Louis wins heavyweight championship
1939 Billie Holiday premiers "Strange Fruit"
Marian Anderson sings at the Lincoln Memorial
"Bojangles" Robinson organizes Black Actors Guild
1940s Black musicians introduce bebop
1940–1948 Oscar Micheaux's films

1940 Richard Wright publishes *Native Son*
1941 Mary Dawson founds the National Negro Opera Company
1942 Margaret Walker publishes *For My People*
1945 Nat King Cole becomes the first black star to have his own radio variety show
1947 Jackie Robinson becomes the first black National League baseball player
Larry Doby becomes the first black American League baseball player
1948 Alice Coachman becomes the first African-American woman to win an Olympic gold medal
1952 Ralph Ellison publishes *Invisible Man*

1936 African-American voters switch to the Democratic Party
1937 William Hastie named first black federal judge

1941 U.S. Army forms Tuskegee Air Squadron
1942 Marine Corps accepts first African Americans
1943 Navy officer schools accept African Americans
1944 Adam Clayton Powell elected to Congress
Port of Chicago "mutiny"
U.S. Supreme Court declares "white primaries" unconstitutional
1945 U.S. Army desegregates its Nurse Corps
1946 President Truman creates the Committee on Civil Rights
1948 Executive Order 9981 desegregates the U.S. military
1950 State Department revokes Paul Robeson's passport
1951 House Un-American Activities Committee indicts W. E. B. Du Bois
1954 *Brown v. Board of Education* declares "separate but equal" unconstitutional

1936 First National Negro Congress held
1937 Mary M. Bethune organizes conference on the Negro and Negro youth
1940s Many African Americans move from agriculture to jobs in industry

1941 A. Philip Randolph organizes the March on Washington Movement
1942 CORE founded
1943 Detroit race riots
1944 *An American Dilemma* published
Southern Regional Council established
1946 Journey of Reconciliation begins
1950 Ralph Bunche becomes the first African-American recipient of the Nobel Peace Prize

Chapter 18

Black Protest, Great Depression, and the New Deals

1929–1940

WORLD'S HIGHEST STANDARD OF LIVING

There's no way like the American Way

Photographer Margaret Bourke White may not have intended to contrast the American dream of prosperity—for white families—and the harsh realities of life for black Americans in this Depression photograph, but it has become representative of existing racial disparity. The collapse of the economy spurred the search for radical critiques and solutions to deal with the desperate conditions millions of African Americans endured. Separate economic development and the creation of parallel institutions and organizations was one option. But was it practicable?

Learning Objectives

After reading this chapter students will be able to:

18.1   Discuss the reasons why the American economic system collapsed into the Great Depression during the 1930s. Account for the disastrous impact it had on African Americans in the South and in the North.

18.2   Compare and contrast the different individual and group forms of resistance to derogatory images of African Americans in mainstream American culture and society in the 1930s.

18.3   Describe the different ways in which the New Deal created new opportunities for African Americans both in terms of economic development and in the cultural arena.

18.4   Discuss the relationship between Mary McLeod Bethune and President Roosevelt and First Lady Eleanor Roosevelt.

18.5   Explain the purpose of the Tuskegee Study and evaluate its lasting impact on race relations and black health care status.

18.6   Delineate the significant role that organized labor played in the radicalization of black Americans during the 1930s.

18.7   Discuss the issues that were at the core of the *Scottsboro* case and the consequences of the U.S. Supreme Court decisions delivered in the case.

The Depression brought everyone down a peg or two. And the Negro had but a few pegs to fall.

—*Langston Hughes*

The only thing that we not only can, but must do, is voluntarily and insistently to organize our economic and social power, no matter how much segregation it involves. Learn to associate with ourselves and to train ourselves in methods of democratic control within our own group. Run and support our own institutions.

—*W. E. B. Du Bois*

For African Americans, the Great Depression was an era of suffering made worse by the horrors and burdens of American racism as well as a time of profound political change, demographic shifts, and social activism that would lay the foundation for the progress of ensuing decades. At the beginning of the economic collapse in late 1929, most African Americans were either trapped in the failing southern agricultural system or eking out a bare existence at the margins of the booming urban economy. The economy's fall pushed many black Americans to the edge of starvation, throwing them off the land and out of the small niches they had carved out in other occupations. Coming out of the southern-dominated Democratic Party, President Franklin Roosevelt's New Deal programs for fighting the Depression might have simply reinforced existing racism, as in fact it did to some extent. But from another perspective, the emerging political power of African-American voters in the North, the development of civil rights organizations, and the growth of an antiracist agenda among radicals and labor unions created the preconditions for a profound change in American politics. Amid economic despair, peonage, lynchings, and labor conflicts, black men, women, and their children saw glimmers of hope in protests against racial segregation and radical critiques of capitalist exploitation. Their protests helped shape the policies and programs of the New Deal. The 1930s were thus the dark dawn of a new era that witnessed, among other significant changes, the rise to prominence of a remarkable cadre of black social scientists.

18.1 The Cataclysm, 1929–1933

Discuss the reasons why the American economic system collapsed into the Great Depression during the 1930s. Account for the disastrous impact it had on African Americans in the South and in the North.

The Great Depression was a cataclysm. National income fell from $81 billion in 1929 to $40 billion in 1932. Americans lost faith in banks, and the resulting panic deepened the despair. Overnight millions of Americans lost their life savings in bank closings and home foreclosures. Americans responded by buying fewer consumer goods; in turn, businesses cut back production, investment, and payrolls. The result was a downward spiral of economic activity made worse by increasing numbers of unemployed. According to the American Federation of Labor (AFL), the number of unemployed people increased from 3,216,000 in January 1930 to 13,689,000 in March 1933 (see Figure 18-1). The standard of living of nearly everyone, from farmers to small businessmen and entrepreneurs to wage laborers, dropped to a fraction of what it had been before 1929.

Most people blamed the stock market crash and Republican President Herbert Hoover for the hard times, but the true explanation is more complicated. Although its causes are hotly debated, the Great Depression was probably the result of several factors, including rampant speculation, corporate capitalism's drive for markets and profits unchecked by federal regulation, the failure of those in the government or private sector to understand how the economy worked, a weak international trading system, overproduction of—and low prices for—many agricultural goods and raw materials, and—most important—the great inequality of wealth and income that limited the purchasing power of millions of Americans.

Figure 18-1 Unemployment, 1925–1945

With the collapse of the American economy, unemployment soared in the 1930s. New Deal programs alleviated some of the suffering, but full recovery did not come until the defense industries swung into action with the U.S. entry into World War II.

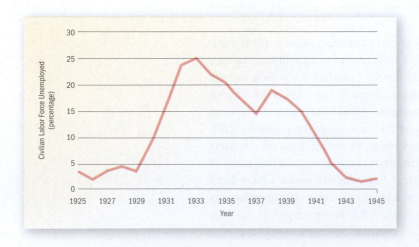

18.1.1 Harder Times for Black America

The economic collapse hit African Americans particularly hard. Most black people remained in the rural South mired in an exploitive agricultural system. Indeed, the Depression worsened the key problems besetting cash-crop production in the 1920s. Consumer demand for cotton and sugar fell with the depressed economy; however, as farmers grew more of these crops to make ends meet, the supply of these staples increased. The result was a catastrophe, with prices for cotton—still the mainstay of the southern economy—plunging from 18 cents a pound in 1929 to six cents in 1933. Black sharecroppers and tenant farmers, nearly powerless in the rural South, were reduced to starvation or thrown off the land.

The hard times also struck those 1.5 million African Americans who had escaped the South for northern urban communities (see Table 18-1). Even during the prosperous 1920s, black Americans had suffered layoffs, and their living standards had steadily fallen. After 1929 the same forces that impoverished rural Americans swept those in urban areas further toward the economic margins as waves of refugees from the farms crowded into the cities and competed for scarce jobs (see Table 18-2). By 1934, when the federal government noted that 17 percent of white citizens could not support themselves, the figure for black Americans had increased to 38 percent overall. In Chicago, 40 percent of African-American men were unemployed; in Pittsburgh, 48 percent; in Harlem, 50 percent; in Philadelphia, 56 percent; and in Detroit, 60 percent. The figures were even more dire for black workers in southern cities. In Atlanta, Georgia, 65 percent of black workers needed public assistance, and in Norfolk, Virginia, a stunning 80 percent had to apply for welfare.

African Americans lost jobs in those parts of the economy where they had gained a tenuous foothold. Before 1929, jobs in low-status or poorly paid occupations, such as garbage collection, foundries, or domestic service, had been regarded as "Negro work" and hence were generally immune from white competition. As desperation set in, however, white southerners not only competed for these jobs but also used the old tactics of terror and intimidation to compel employers to fire black people. Unions, north and south, continued to exclude African Americans from membership and pressured manufacturers to hire white people.

Black women workers, overwhelmingly concentrated in domestic service and laundry work, were affected even more than black men. There were fewer jobs because many families could no longer afford domestic help. With many impoverished women coming into the cities, those white people who could hire help found they could employ these desperate women for almost nothing. In 1935 two black women, Marvel Cooke and Ella Baker, published an exposé of the exploitation of these women laborers in the *Crisis*. They titled the article "The Bronx Slave Market" because the buying and selling of labor in New York City reminded them of the old slave marts in the antebellum South. Cooke and Baker described how the street corner market worked: "The Simpson avenue block exudes the stench of the slave market at its worst. Not only is human labor bartered and sold for a slave wage, but human love also is a marketable commodity." The black women gathered on particular street corners and waited as well-to-do white women selected them for a day's labor. They received "wages as low as 15 to 25 cents an

Table 18-1 Demographic Shifts: The Second Great Migration, 1930–1950

Year	Region	Black Population	Total Population	% Black
1930	Northeast	1,146,985	34,427,091	3.33
	Midwest	1,262,234	38,594,100	3.27
	Southeast	7,079,626	25,680,803	27.57
	South Central	2,281,951	12,176,830	18.74
	Mountain	30,225	3,701,789	0.82
	Pacific	90,122	8,622,047	1.05
1950	Northeast	2,018,182	39,477,986	5.11
	Midwest	2,227,876	44,460,762	5.01
	Southeast	7,793,379	32,659,516	23.86
	South Central	2,432,028	14,517,572	16.73
	Mountain	66,429	5,074,998	1.31
	Pacific	507,043	15,114,964	3.35

SOURCE: *Historical Statistics of the United States, 1789-1945: A Supplement to the Statistical Abstract of the United States, Part 1.* Retrieved from http://www2.census.gov/library/publications/1949/compendia/hist_stats_1789-1945/hist_stats_1789-1945-chB.pdf

Table 18-2 Median Income of Black Families Compared to the Median Income of White Families for Selected Cities, 1935–1936

City and Type of Family	Black	White	Black Income as a Percentage of White Income
Husband–Wife Families			
New York	$980	$1,930	51%
Chicago	$726	$1,687	43%
Columbus	$831	$1,622	51%
Atlanta	$632	$1,876	34%
Columbia	$576	$1,876	31%
Mobile	$481	$1,419	34%
Other Families			
Atlanta	$332	$940	35%
Columbia	$254	$1,403	18%
Mobile	$301	$784	38%

SOURCE: Based on the data from Median Income of Black Families . . . White Families for Selected Cities, 1935–1936 from *An American Dilemma: The Negro Problem and Modern Democracy* by Gunnar Myrdal. © Darlene Clark Hine.

hour, some working only two or three hours a day." Some black people were hired but never paid.

African Americans were no strangers to adversity, and many used the survival strategies developed through centuries of hardship to eke out an existence during the first years of the Great Depression. Survival demanded that black women pool their resources and adhere to a collective spirit that found fertile ground in segregated northern neighborhoods. In Chicago, for example, women and their families lived in crowded tenements in which they shared bathrooms and other facilities including hot plates, stoves, and sinks. They bartered and exchanged goods and services because money was so scarce. One woman might dress the hair of a neighbor in return for permission to borrow her dress or use her pots and pans. Another woman might trade bread and sugar or another household staple for milk, beans, or soap. Grandmothers watched over children as their mothers went to look with rising futility for a domestic job. They helped each other as best they could.

Rural black women, like their urban sisters, had to rely on their individual and collective ingenuity to survive. As one observer of black women household heads in rural Georgia noted, "In their effort to maintain existence, these people are catching and selling fish, reselling vegetables, sewing in exchange for old clothes, letting out sleeping space, and doing odd jobs. They understand how to help each other. Stoves are used in common, wash boilers go their rounds, and garden crops are exchanged and shared." Nonetheless, the depth and duration of this downturn strained these mutual aid strategies to the breaking point. By 1933 the clock seemed to have been turned back to 1865, when many African Americans could claim to own little more than their bodies.

18.1.2 Black Businesses in the Depression: Collapse and Survival

Black businessmen and professionals also suffered. African Americans who had built successful businesses and professional practices in medicine and law, for example, faced the same Depression-borne problems as other businesses, but they suffered even more because the communities on which they depended were poorer. Two types of black-owned businesses, banks and insurance companies, illustrate how black enterprises stood or fell during the economic crisis.

The Binga Bank, Chicago's first black-owned-and-operated financial institution, had been founded in 1908 by its president, Jesse Binga (1865–1950), a Detroit-born real estate broker who had worked as a barber and a Pullman porter. Binga had managed the bank so effectively that by 1930 its deposits had grown to more than $1.5 million. Binga once boasted he could lay claim to more footage on State Street, Chicago's principal thoroughfare, than any other man in the city. The Binga Bank was, during its early years, an important symbol of successful black capitalism and as such represented the hopes and aspirations of black Chicagoans. But the bank's assets were too heavily invested in mortgages to black churches and fraternal societies, many of which could not meet their payments after their members lost their jobs. Binga refused to seize the properties of these community institutions, but his restraint, coupled with financial improprieties, led to the bank's failure. On July 31, 1930, Illinois state bank auditors padlocked the institution and filed a federal misuse-of-funds charge against the once proud financier. Sentenced to prison in 1933, Binga was pardoned by the Governor of Illinois Dwight H. Green on April 12, 1941. He never regained his fortune.

Some black businesses survived the economic cataclysm, although often in a much weakened state. Among the businesses still standing when prosperity finally returned in the 1940s were the leading black insurance companies, such as Atlanta Life, Supreme Life, Golden State, and North Carolina Mutual Life. Atlanta Life Insurance Company, for example—founded in 1905 by a former Georgia slave, Alonzo Franklin Herndon—not only survived the Depression but recorded substantial profit. Between 1931 and 1936, its assets increased by more than $1 million. This was in part because insurance companies such as Atlanta Life provided an essential service for African Americans, particularly in an era before government-provided social security, and could thus depend on a continued flow of premiums. And unlike the Binga Bank, Atlanta Life's officers drastically reduced their investments in mortgages in the black community.

The North Carolina Mutual Life Insurance Company, founded in Durham, weathered the Great Depression under the astute leadership of Charles Clinton Spaulding (1874–1952), a former manager of a black cooperative grocery store. In 1899 Spaulding joined with two other African Americans to transform the insurance company into the nation's largest black business. His partners were his uncle, Dr. Aaron McDuffie Moore, Durham's only black physician, and John Merrick, a former slave and leading real estate agent and barber (he owned six barbershops, three for whites and three for blacks). Following on the heels of the great migration to the North, Spaulding expanded the company's territory into Virginia, Maryland, and the District of Columbia. The company adhered to the thrift, hard work, and self-help philosophy so ardently expressed by Booker T. Washington. It is still one of the three largest black-owned insurance companies in the United States.

Many of the 250 black hospitals, clinics, and nursing training schools that black physicians, such as Dr. Daniel Hale Williams, had launched since the 1890s could not survive the ravages of the Depression. Confronting a diminishing clientele and worsening health among black people, some black physicians began encouraging their patients to demand admission to the segregated, government-operated hospitals and clinics. At the outset of the Depression, Dr. Matilda A. Evans (1872–1935) of Columbia, South Carolina, an 1897 graduate of the Woman's Medical College in Philadelphia, mobilized a diverse constituency of black parents, professionals, and religious and business leaders to persuade the state board of health to provide free inoculations and immunization shots to black schoolchildren. Other healthcare professionals volunteered to conduct free medical and dental examinations. When Evans's Columbia Clinic opened in July 1930, over 700 patients showed up. This short-lived clinic reflected Evans's belief that health care was a state responsibility just as important as the provision of free public education. The black South Carolina newspaper, the *Palmetto Leader*, declared in October 1930 that "evidence keeps on piling on top of evidence to the effect that the Columbia Clinic is just proving to be, and will yet stand as the most important effort sponsored for our group in Columbia within the last half century." The deteriorating economic conditions of both the state of South Carolina and its people made it impossible to sustain this effort. But the Columbia Clinic movement taught black people a powerful lesson about how to mobilize to achieve change and thus raised, as Evans anticipated it would, black consciousness about the need to apply pressure on the state for more access to public resources.

A remarkable black woman physician, Dr. Matilda A. Evans (1872–1935) of Columbia, South Carolina, believed in the importance of establishing institutions and organizations that would enable black people to survive and from which they could fight to end racial segregation and discrimination. In the opening decades of the twentieth century, Dr. Evans established two hospitals and founded a nursing training school. She organized the Good Health Association of South Carolina, edited the *Negro Health Journal*, and served a term as president of the Palmetto Medical Association.

18.1.3 The Failure of Relief

Before Franklin Roosevelt's New Deal, private charities or, as a last resort, state and local governments were responsible for providing relief from economic hardships. Even in good times these institutions provided too little for all those in need. Moreover, African Americans had a much harder time getting aid than white people and were given less when they did get it. The Depression made it impossible for the nation's charitable organizations to meet the needs of more than a small portion of the hungry, homeless, and unemployed millions. In turn, state and local governments could not or would not provide unemployment insurance or increased welfare benefits to ease the suffering of those most vulnerable to the economic disaster. Even when these governments wanted to help, the economic collapse so lowered tax receipts that it became nearly impossible for relief agencies to act.

Despite the need to alleviate the economic disaster, President Hoover hesitated to respond. Steeped in the free-market orthodoxy of his time, he believed government should do little to interfere with the workings of the economy. Nevertheless, Hoover did more to counteract a depression than any previous president had done. He tried to convince businesses that if they retained employees and did not cut wages, they would contribute to the health of the general economy and promote their own best interests. The president also approved loans to banks, railroads, and insurance companies by the Reconstruction Finance Corporation, a federal agency created to rescue large corporations. He hoped these businesses would reinvigorate production, create new jobs, and restore consumer spending. His faith was misplaced. Businesses took the government loans and still laid off workers, much the same way many banks behaved in 2009 after receiving government funds to prevent them from failing.

Hoover's reluctance to use the federal government to intervene in the economy extended to the provision of relief. He suggested that local governments and charities should address the needs of the unemployed, the homeless, and the starving masses. Hoover was not a callous person, but he was trapped in a rigid ideology. He watched with dismay the wandering groups of men, women, and children who began settling into what they called, with grim humor, "Hoovervilles"—sordid clusters of shacks made of tin, cardboard, and burlap next to railroad tracks and dumps. Still, he refused to allow the federal government to provide direct relief.

Hoover's inactivity was bad enough, but his politics were as racist as those of the Democratic Party. Wanting to create a white Republican Party in the South, he cultivated white southerners by attempting to appoint to the U.S. Supreme Court Judge John Parker of North Carolina, who believed in "separate but equal," and by displacing black Republican leaders. Hoover's policy was not new. For decades the national Republican Party had treated black voters with contempt and often declined to reward them with patronage appointments. This policy looked even worse during the early 1930s against the backdrop of black suffering. As NAACP director Walter White put it, Hoover

> sat stolidly in the White House, refusing bluntly to receive Negro citizens who wished to lay before him the facts of their steadily worsening plight or to consider any remedial legislation or governmental action. His attitude toward Negroes caused me to coin a phrase, which gained considerable currency, particularly in the Negro world, in which I described Hoover as "the man in the lily-White House."

18.2 Black Protest during the Great Depression

Compare and contrast the different individual and group forms of resistance to derogatory images of African Americans in mainstream American culture and society in the 1930s.

During the 1930s African-American men and women initiated their own agenda and determined to use every resource at their disposal to destroy the obstacles to racial justice and barriers to equal opportunity. The NAACP sponsored a legal campaign, led by

Charles Houston and Thurgood Marshall, against educational discrimination and political disfranchisement; mobilized black communities; and sustained hope in the struggle. Black people benefited from the New Deal but less than white people did. The disparity between black and white lives was a spur to action. The juxtaposition of black subordination and misery alongside the new forms of federal aid so willingly distributed to white citizens convinced black Americans to intensify their own struggle for their rights as Americans. Many embraced radical critiques of American capitalism, but few ever considered communism a viable alternative to American democracy. Black people would emerge from the Depression more determined than ever to make democracy work for them.

18.2.1 The NAACP and Civil Rights Struggles

During the 1930s the NAACP became a more effective advocate for African-American civil rights. The biracial organization took the lead in pressing the government to protect African-American rights and eliminate the blatant racism in government programs. Part of the reason for this new dynamism was the astute leadership of Walter White, a man whose physical characteristics—he had blond hair and blue eyes—could have easily permitted him to pass for white and turn away from the problems of black people. Instead, he became an insistent voice of protest, personally investigating 42 lynchings and eight race riots, and he was an ardent lobbyist for civil rights legislation and racial justice. Throughout the 1930s African Americans of all hues moved into leadership positions in the NAACP and joined its many branches.

The NAACP's new dynamism became apparent in 1930 when Walter White took a prominent role in the successful campaign to defeat Hoover's nomination of John J. Parker to the Supreme Court. Parker had openly embraced white supremacy, stating, for example, that the "participation of the Negro in politics is a source of evil and danger to both races." The NAACP formed a coalition with the AFL to persuade the Senate to reject Parker's nomination by a vote of 41 to 39. It was the first time since 1854 that the Senate had refused to confirm a nominee to the Court. Although the NAACP could take only part of the credit for Parker's defeat, White trumpeted the victory and let it be known that African Americans would not be silent while "the Hoover administration proposed to conciliate southern white sentiment by sacrificing the Negro and his rights."

18.2.2 Du Bois and the "Voluntary Segregation" Controversy

The NAACP had critics, even within its own ranks. Many younger black people criticized its focus on civil liberties and deplored it for ignoring the economic misery of most African Americans. In 1934 W. E. B. Du Bois, editor of the NAACP's journal the *Crisis*, joined the chorus. Criticizing what he considered the group's overemphasis on integration, Du Bois advocated a program of self-determination he hoped would permit black people to develop "an economic nation within a nation." Du Bois acknowledged that this internal economy could meet only part of the needs of the African-American community. But he insisted it could be developed and expanded in many ways: "This smaller part could be so important and wield so much power that its influence upon the total economy of Negroes and the total industrial organization of the United States would be decisive for the great ends towards which the Negro moves."

Black intellectuals attacked Du Bois for advocating "voluntary segregation." Sociologist E. Franklin Frazier, for example, called the idea of black businesses succeeding within a segregated economy a black upper-class fantasy and social myth. Nevertheless, Du Bois held fast to his position that, as long as discrimination persisted, the NAACP should combine its opposition to legal segregation with vigorous support to improve segregated institutions. He was eventually forced from the editorship of the *Crisis*, but his resignation did not end the controversy. By the late 1930s the NAACP had developed a greater emphasis on economic policy and stronger ties to the growing labor movement.

18.2.3 Legal Battles against Discrimination in Education and Voting

A dramatic expansion of its legal campaign against racial discrimination enhanced the NAACP's effectiveness. Central to this project was the hiring of Charles Hamilton Houston, a Harvard-trained African-American lawyer and scholar, to lead it. As vice dean of Howard University Law School, Houston had transformed it into a powerful institution for training black attorneys in civil rights law. At the NAACP, he laid out a plan for a legal program to challenge inequality in education and the exclusion of black people from voting in the South. Houston used lawsuits to force state and local governments to live up to the Constitution and to inspire community organization. "This is no star performance," he said of his strategy. "My ideal of administration is to make the movement self-perpetuating. . . . Our idea should be to press upon the opposition and public that what we have is a real program, sweeping up . . . [from] popular demand."

Houston did not focus directly on eliminating segregation but rather sought to force southern states to equalize their facilities. Studies by the NAACP had revealed great disparities in per capita expenditures for white and black students and huge differences in salaries for white and black teachers. In Georgia, for example, the average annual per pupil expenditure for white students was $36.29, compared with $4.59 for black students. White teachers' salaries averaged $97.88 per month, whereas black teachers received only $49.41. Houston was no supporter of segregation. He hoped to use litigation to secure judgments that would so increase the cost of separate institutions that states would be forced to abandon them.

To execute his agenda, in 1936 Houston convinced Walter White to hire his former student at Howard, Thurgood Marshall. Born in 1908, in Baltimore, Marshall's father was a dining-car waiter and club steward. His mother had been a teacher before her marriage. During the 1930s Marshall and Houston focused on bringing greater parity between the pay of black and white teachers, a project they hoped would increase NAACP membership among teachers, their students, and parents. The two men, working with a network of African-American attorneys, also fought

Thurgood Marshall (1908–1993), Charles Hamilton Houston (1895–1950), and Donald Gaines Murray. In 1935, attorneys Marshall and Houston handled Donald Murray's suit against the University of Maryland Law School. In 1938 Murray became the first African American to graduate from a southern state school. Thus began the relentless black attack against segregated education in America.

to end discrimination against black students in professional and graduate schools. Inequalities were obvious here because many southern states offered no graduate facilities of any kind to black students. Like other campaigns, this focus on graduate education was intended to establish precedents that might be used to gain equality in other areas and as an organizing tool to strengthen local NAACP branches. The first significant accomplishment in this campaign was the Supreme Court's 1938 decision in *Gaines v. Canada*. The Court ordered the state of Missouri to provide black citizens an opportunity to study law in a state-supported institution. Failure to do so, the Court held, would violate the equal protection of the law clause of the Fourteenth Amendment to the Constitution. Although Lloyd Gaines, the prospective student for whom the case was brought, disappeared before this challenge was resolved, Missouri hastily established a law school for African Americans at the historically black Lincoln University in Jefferson City, the state capital. In the 1940s several southern states, including North Carolina, Texas, Oklahoma, and South Carolina, also established law schools for their black citizens.

The *Gaines* decision encouraged Marshall and the NAACP to persist in challenging the constitutionality of the "separate but equal" doctrine in universities and professional schools. The case of *Sipuel v. Board of Regents of the University of Oklahoma* (1947) was another such effort. In this case Ada Lois Sipuel sought admission to the law school of the University of Oklahoma at Norman. In accordance with state statutes, she was refused admission but granted an out-of-state tuition award. Marshall argued that this arrangement failed to meet the needs of the state's black citizens. The Supreme Court declared that Oklahoma was obliged under the equal protection clause of the Fourteenth Amendment to provide a legal education for Sipuel. The case established the principle that the states had to provide a separate law school for African-American students in their home states.

18.2.4 Black Texans Fight for Educational and Voting Rights

Heman Sweatt, a black mail carrier, tested this principle in a suit against the University of Texas Law School. In *Sweatt v. Painter* (1950), the Supreme Court again sided with the NAACP lawyers. In response to Sweatt's initial challenge, Texas had created a separate law school that had inadequate library facilities, faculty, and support staff. It was separate but hardly equal. Marshall and black lawyers in Texas argued that the legal education offered Sweatt at the black law school was so inferior it violated the equal protection clause of the Fourteenth Amendment. Marshall declared, "Whether the University of Texas Law School is compared with the original or new law school for Negroes, we cannot find substantial equality in the educational opportunities offered white and Negro law students by the state. In terms of number of faculty, variety of courses and opportunity for specialization, size of the student body, scope of the library, availability of law review, and similar activities, the University of Texas Law School is superior." These early legal victories laid the legal foundation for the 1954 *Brown v. Topeka Board of Education* decision.

The fight against political disfranchisement also helped mobilize local and state communities and NAACP branches. Nowhere was this more apparent than in Texas. In 1923 the Texas legislature enacted the **white primary law**, which declared, "In no event shall a Negro be eligible to participate in a Democratic primary election . . . in . . . Texas." In the one-party South, the Democratic primaries were more important than the general elections, which usually merely rubber-stamped the choice made in the primary. Thus, to be denied the right to vote in Democratic Party primaries was to be disfranchised. The NAACP developed a case to test the constitutionality of the Terrell law and began a 20-year battle through the courts. The Texas branches of the NAACP raised money and coordinated local involvement in the campaign to overthrow the Democratic white primary that disfranchised black Texans.

white primary law

The white primary law was a Texas law banning African-American participation in the Democratic primary.

The Texas white primary fight was the most sustained and intense effort that any NAACP chapter undertook during the interwar period. It began in the 1920s and won its first victory when the Supreme Court ruled in 1927 in *Nixon v. Herndon* that the Texas Democratic primary was unconstitutional (see Chapter 17). At the national headquarters, Houston and Marshall orchestrated the assault, and subsequent decisions chipped away at the legal basis for the white primary. Finally, in 1944 the Supreme Court issued a ruling in *Smith v. Allwright* that ended the white primary altogether. It was the NAACP's greatest legal victory to that time. Many more would soon follow.

18.2.5 Black Women Community Organizers

Black women made exceptional contributions to the NAACP during the 1930s through their fundraising and membership drives. Three agitators for racial justice were Daisy Adams Lampkin (c. 1884–1965), Juanita Mitchell (1913–1992), and Ella Baker (1903–1986). These women worked closely with White and the NAACP throughout the Depression and World War II. Lampkin, a native of Washington, D.C., in 1915, became the president of the Negro Women's Franchise League, a group dedicated to fighting for the vote. During World War I, she sold some $2 million worth of government Liberty Bonds in black communities in Pennsylvania to help finance the war. In 1930 Walter White enlisted her as regional field secretary of the NAACP, a post she held until she was made national field secretary in 1935. She continued raising funds for the NAACP and played leading roles within organized black womanhood.

Juanita E. Jackson was born in Hot Springs, Arkansas, and raised in Baltimore. She earned a degree in education from the University of Pennsylvania in 1931 and then returned to Baltimore, where she helped found the City-Wide Young People's Forum. This organization encouraged young people to combat such scourges as unemployment, segregation, and lynching. The success of the group prompted Walter White to offer her the leadership of the NAACP's new youth program, which she directed from 1935 to 1938. In 1938 Jackson married fellow civil rights activist Clarence Mitchell, had four sons, and directed the NAACP's voter registration campaigns. In 1950 she received a law degree from the University of Maryland. As the first black woman admitted to practice law in Maryland, she embarked on a series of cases that helped destroy racial segregation on the state's public beaches and in its public schools.

Ella Baker, who became one of the most important women in the civil rights movement of the 1950s and 1960s, began her life's work during the Depression. Born in Norfolk, Virginia, Baker moved to New York City in 1927 and worked as a waitress and as an organizer in radical politics. She was also on the staff of two local newspapers, the *American West Indian News* and the *Negro National News*. Within two years after her arrival, she had cofounded with George Schuyler the Young Negroes' Cooperative League in Harlem. The group practiced collective decision making and attempted to involve all segments of the community in the cooperatives. As she worked with the young men and women, Baker developed a strong belief in grassroots mobilization. She also worked with women's and labor groups, such as the Harlem Housewives Cooperative, the Women's Day Workers and Industrial League, and the YWCA. In 1935 she served as publicity director of the Sponsoring Committee of the National Negro Congress. In 1936 she worked as a teacher with the Works Progress Administration (WPA)—a New Deal organization created to provide jobs for the unemployed—and eventually became one of its assistant supervisors. Walter White was impressed with her relentless organizing and management skills. In 1941, after much persuasion, Baker accepted White's offer to become an assistant field secretary of the NAACP. She traveled across the country and

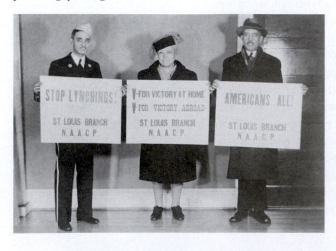

The NAACP in the 1930s and 1940s depended upon the fundraising and organizing efforts of black women. Daisy Lampkin stands here with Sidney R. Redmond and Elmer V. Mosee protesting lynching.

throughout the South, making friendships that would serve her well in the coming decades. From 1943 to 1946, Baker worked as director of NAACP branches and built up the organization's membership. After resigning from the NAACP, she joined the staff of the New York Urban League.

Other black women organized outside the NAACP. Black women in Detroit provide a potent illustration of this kind of activity. On June 10, 1930, 50 black women responded to a call issued by Fannie B. Peck, wife of Rev. William H. Peck, pastor of the 2,000-member Bethel African Methodist Episcopal Church and the president of the Booker T. Washington Trade Association. Out of this initial meeting emerged the Detroit Housewives' League, an organization that combined economic nationalism and black women's self-determination to help black families and businesses survive the Depression. Peck had been inspired by M. A. L. Holsey, secretary of the National Negro Business League. Holsey described the directed spending campaigns that enabled housewives in Harlem to consolidate their economic power to persuade businesses to hire black women and children. Fannie Peck became convinced that such an organization would also succeed in Detroit. An admirer recalled that Peck effectively "focused the attention of women on the most essential, yet most unfamiliar factor in the building of homes, communities, and nations, namely, 'The Spending Power of Women.' "

The Detroit organization grew rapidly. By 1934, 10,000 black women belonged to it. According to Peck, the black woman had finally realized "that she has been traveling through a blind alley, making sacrifices to educate her children with no thought as to their obtaining employment after leaving school." The only requirement for membership was a pledge to support black businesses, buy black products, and patronize black professionals, thereby keeping money in the community. The league quickly spread to other cities. Housewives' leagues in Chicago, Baltimore, Washington, Durham (North Carolina), Harlem, and Cleveland used boycotts of merchants who refused to sell black products and employ black children as clerks or stock persons to secure an estimated 75,000 new jobs for black people.

18.3 African Americans and the New Deal Era

Describe the different ways in which the New Deal created new opportunities for African Americans both in terms of economic development and in the cultural arena.

In 1932, the third year of the Great Depression, voters elected New York governor Franklin Delano Roosevelt to the presidency with a total of nearly 23 million votes. Roosevelt's lopsided victory over Hoover, who received fewer than 16 million votes, demonstrated the country's loss of faith in the Republican Party and its economic philosophy and heralded the emergence of a new electoral coalition. The new president appealed to the Democratic Party's base of support in the white South, but to this group he added a coalition of western farmers, industrial workers, white ethnic groups in northern cities, and reform-minded intellectuals. For the time being, however, black Americans still clung to the Republican banner. In Chicago, for example, less than 25 percent of black voters voted for Roosevelt. But this was the last election in which the party of Lincoln could take them for granted. To counter the Depression, in his first term Roosevelt inaugurated a multitude of programs—collectively known as the New Deal—that would shift the allegiance of African Americans. Initially his programs continued past patterns of discrimination against African Americans, but by 1935 the New Deal was providing more equal benefits and prompting profound social changes. The result was a new political order that ultimately undermined the edifice of American racism.

18.3.1 Roosevelt and the First New Deal, 1933–1935

During his first 100 days in office, Roosevelt pressed through Congress a profusion of bold new economic initiatives that came to be known as the first New Deal. To combat the Depression, Roosevelt, unlike Hoover, followed no predetermined plan. Instead, he favored experimentation—tempered by political expediency—over ideology as the guide to federal action. With little resistance Congress passed the president's sprawling and complex laws aimed at overhauling the nation's financial, agricultural, and industrial systems. Most hoped, vainly as it turned out, that these changes would eventually bring a return to prosperity. Meanwhile, Roosevelt moved to counter the immediate suffering of the unemployed with a massive emergency federal relief effort. Many of the first New Deal's programs benefited both white and black people, but the strength of white southerners in the Democratic Party and the nearly complete lack of African-American political power in the South caused much of this early program to be unfairly administered.

Agricultural Adjustment Act (AAA)

A federal program that provided subsidies to farmers to grow less to help stabilize prices.

The **Agricultural Adjustment Act (AAA)**, designed to protect farmers by giving them subsidies to limit production and thereby stabilize prices, illustrates the key benefits and problems African Americans experienced during the first New Deal. The theory underlying the AAA was that lessening production would increase agricultural prices. Essentially, farmers would be paid to grow less. The program provided for sharecroppers and tenant farmers to get part of the subsidies and allowed new rural relief agencies to dispense supplementary income to off-season wageworkers.

This program helped many African Americans, mainly because it pumped billions of dollars into an economic sector on which over 4.5 million black people relied for their livelihood. Also, the AAA was designed to remedy the problems of those farmers—disproportionately African American—who were overreliant on such cash crops as cotton. By 1929 three out of four black farmers, compared with two out of five white farmers, received at least 40 percent of their gross income from cotton. The flow of money from the AAA did, for a time, slow the exodus of black people from farming. Fewer left the farms in the first two years of the program than in the two years before it began. Indeed, from a broader perspective, the New Deal appeared to have slowed the rate at which black people left the land. During the 1930s only 4.5 percent of African Americans abandoned farming, compared with the 8.6 percent who did so during the 1920s.

But if the AAA brought real benefits to black farmers, it was often contrary to protections written into the law, administered unfairly and corruptly. Local control of the AAA resided in the hands of the Extension Service and County Agricultural Conservation Committees, which were supposed to represent all farmers. The county agents, however, were often the planters themselves, and the committees mirrored southern politics as a whole by excluding black people. African Americans were further disadvantaged by the system of unilateral bookkeeping and oppressive credit relations between landlords and tenants. During the first two years of the AAA, black farmers complained bitterly that white landlords simply grabbed and pocketed the millions of dollars of benefit checks they were supposed to forward to tenants. To compound the injury, some planters then evicted the sharecroppers and tenants from the land.

National Industrial Recovery Act (NIRA)

Federal law intended to promote the revival of manufacturing by allowing for cooperation among industries.

The experience of African Americans with the **National Industrial Recovery Act (NIRA)** mimicked the problems with the AAA. The NIRA was intended to revive manufacturing by allowing industries to cooperate in establishing codes of conduct to govern prices, wage levels, and employment practices, all of which were to be overseen by a National Recovery Administration (NRA). The NRA oversaw the drafting of the codes but faced tremendous resistance from employers and unions in eliminating racial disparities in wage rates and working conditions. Even when African-American advocates did win wage increases for occupations in which black people predominated, the result was often a shift to white labor. These policies prompted some African-American

Voices

A Black Sharecropper Details Abuse in the Administration of Agricultural Relief

This is one of many letters black sharecroppers sent to the NAACP for assistance to halt the mass evictions and abuse of New Deal relief efforts.

ALABAMA

June 21, 1934

Dear Sir:—

I am writing you these few lines ask you if it is any possible chance of you fining out just why F.E.R.A. office here in . . . refuse to gave me work when I have six in family to care for and also my wife's mother who is over 65 years old and been under the Doctor care for the past seven years of course my wife has a little job but its not with the relief work which some weeks she makes five dollars and some weeks less with four children to take care off which range in age 8–6–4–3 years old and we have $5 per month rent and also $1.74 per week Insurance which that don't enclude Food and Clothing and Fuel to burn. Now Mr. White in the past two and half months I am being going to the relief office trying to get on the relief work and it seem like it is empossible and also just before the first of April I went up to the relief office and explain my case to Mr . . . , the man that gave out the work cards and he gave me a food order for the amount of $2—two dollars and also I got some work to do. But as soon as I got paid for the 24 hours work he came to me to collect $2 for the food order that he gave me and I refuse to gave him $2 and I havent been able to get any more work to do and I have been going up to the office each day sence. But they tell me at the office that they can't gave me work because my wife is working. Of course if that maybe the case I can gave you the name and the address of at least a hundred families where there is two and three in one family who are working on the relief project and I know of at least twenty single men with no one but theirself to take care of and are working twenty-four hours every week and they got to gave their foreman one dollar each every week if they want to stay on the job.

Now Mr. White the white man who my wife work for and my wife told him that they refuse to gave me work because she was working for me and he went up to relief office to see about it But they told him that they didnt cut me out of work because my wife were working but they cut me off because I were unable to do the work. And of course I know that to be very much untrue. The trouble is I refuse to be a fool like so many of my race here and else where around here to pay for a food order that is supose to be giving to the needy free of charge but lots are paying for them and also paying for their job. Of course Mr. White I am colored and when you go up to the relief office The Colored people is treated just as if they were dogs and not human beings. I have been up in the office and I have seen with my own eyes my color kicked and beaten down a whole flight of stairs. I have seen everything done except been murder. Understand Mr. White the little job that my wife has isn't on the relief is a private and everybody that is head of any thing here in the re-lief office is kin to one another. Now Mr. White the lady that is head of the relief is Mrs. . . . which I saw here once since I was cut off from work and I explained my case to her and she told that she would send a investigator around to my home the next morning whose name is Miss. el; and she told me that when I gave Mr. . . . the $2 for the food order she would O.K. my work card. Mr. White if possible will you please fine out for me just what is the reason they refuse to gave me work when I have six in family and rent to pay. Insurance, Doctor bill, milk bill, buy food and clothing and with only my wife at work it is impossible Mr. White.

---

1. Discuss the conditions that motivated the writer to seek help from Walter White and the NAACP.

2. Explain why more blacks did not protest economic inequality.

SOURCE: Aptheker, Bettina (1974). *A Documentary History of the Negro People in the United States, 1933–1945*, Vol. 4, Carol Publishing Group, pp. 58–60.

newspapers and protest organizations to claim that "NRA" really stood for the "Negro Removal Agency" or "Negroes Robbed Again." To the relief of many African-American advocates and workers, the Supreme Court declared the NIRA unconstitutional in 1935.

The New Deal's national welfare programs included the Federal Emergency Relief Administration (FERA), the Civilian Conservation Corps (CCC), the Public Works Administration, and the Civil Works Administration (CWA). Although inadequate and unfairly administered on local levels, these programs were often the only thing standing between black people and starvation. FERA provided funds for local and state relief operations to restart and expand their programs. The program pulled millions of people back from the brink of starvation. Because African Americans suffered greater economic devastation, they received benefits at a higher rate than white people. In most cities north and south, 25–40 percent of African Americans were on relief rolls that FERA funded wholly or in part. However, many in the Roosevelt administration deemed direct welfare to be morally debilitating, so the government emphasized hiring the unemployed for public works projects. The CWA was a temporary agency created to help people through the winter of 1933–1934. The CCC built segregated camps to employ young men and remove them from the poverty and hopelessness of urban areas.

Dayton Jones of the FERA in California devised an ingenious plan that negated the CCC's regulations prohibiting segregation. In a June 26, 1935, letter, Jones shared his proposal for effective internal segregation within the camps with W. Frank Persons, the CCC's director of selections:

> It is a known fact that colored boys make efficient kitchen and dining-room aides, and in addition the vast majority of colored youths enjoy this type of work. By being assigned to work as cooks' helpers, kitchen police and in the preparation of raw vegetables for the men such as peeling and slicing potatoes, a good proportion of the colored members in most camps could be absorbed in this manner. Segregation of the colored boys in the mess halls is prevalent in a number of camps by virtue of actual necessity to prevent racial difficulties. Under my plan this segregation would automatically be accomplished because of the fact that kitchen help must necessarily eat at a time other than when the rest of the enrollees take their meals. By assigning these colored boys to this particular type of work the segregation could be accomplished with no one realizing that segregation was being effected.

Despite protests from the NAACP, the California camps did institute segregation. Effective August 9, 1935, all CCC districts in California transferred their African-American enrollees into "five colored companies." Yet despite the segregation, former enrollees conceded that their experience in the CCC helped them secure better jobs and a middle-class life after World War II. By the time the CCC was abolished in 1945, more than 200,000 African-American youth had taken part in it.

These relief programs helped many African Americans through the worst parts of the Depression. However, the programs also tended to be less helpful to black people than they were to white people. For example, in its early days the CCC was a tightly segregated institution, with only about 5 percent of its slots going to black youths during its first year. Likewise, although FERA tended to be administered fairly in northern cities, in the South it reached few of those in need.

18.3.2 Black Officials and the First New Deal

The first New Deal was not completely bleak for African Americans. In addition to the benefits—however grudgingly disbursed—that New Deal relief programs provided, African Americans also gained new influence and allies within the Roosevelt administration. Their experience reflected the growing availability of highly trained African Americans for government service and the emerging consciousness among white liberals about the problems—and potential electoral power—of black people.

Black people found a staunch ally in First Lady Eleanor Roosevelt. She was revered for her relentless commitment to racial justice. She arranged meetings at the White House for black leaders. She cajoled her husband to consider legislation for black rights. She defied Jim Crow laws by refusing to sit in a "white only" section while attending a meeting in the South. Moreover, she wrote newspaper columns calling for "fair play and equal opportunity for Negro citizens." Roosevelt further endeared herself to black Americans when she resigned her membership in the Daughters of the American Revolution after that organization refused to allow a young black opera singer, Marian Anderson, to perform at its Constitution Hall in Washington in 1939. (Administration officials subsequently arranged for Anderson to perform in front of the Lincoln Memorial on Easter Sunday before a crowd of 75,000. The first song she sang was "My Country, 'Tis of Thee.")

Other liberals joined Eleanor Roosevelt to press for racial justice and seek the appointment of African Americans throughout the government. Early in 1933 President Roosevelt acceded to their request that he appoint someone in his administration to assume responsibility for ensuring that African Americans received fair treatment. He asked Secretary of the Interior Harold Ickes, a former president of the Chicago chapter of the NAACP and a white man whom most black Americans trusted as a friend, to make this happen. Ickes invited Clark Foreman, a young white Georgian who had rejected his region's racism, to handle the assignment. Foreman recognized the irony of a white man representing black people in the government and immediately began to recruit highly trained African Americans. Similar efforts to bring African Americans into government positions were made by Eleanor Roosevelt, Ickes, and other administration officials, such as Secretary of Commerce Daniel Roper and Harry Hopkins, President Roosevelt's relief administrator and confidant. The result was that doors to the government began opening in an unprecedented way.

Black Cabinet

Informal group of highly placed African-American advisers to President Franklin D. Roosevelt.

Mary McLeod Bethune and Eleanor Roosevelt, wife of the President of the United States, speaking before an NYA meeting. Bethune was a key figure in Franklin Roosevelt's black cabinet, which included Robert Weaver, Eugene Kinckle Jones, and William H. Hastie.

18.4 The Rise of Black Social Scientists

Discuss the relationship between Mary McLeod Bethune and President Roosevelt and First Lady Eleanor Roosevelt.

The Roosevelt administration employed professional black architects, lawyers, engineers, economists, statisticians, interviewers, office managers, and social workers. The Department of Commerce hired Eugene K. Jones, on leave from the National Urban League. The National Youth Administration brought in Mary McLeod Bethune, and the Department of Interior employed William H. Hastie and Robert Weaver. Ira De A. Reid joined the Social Security Administration, and Lawrence W. Oxley worked for the Department of Labor. Ambrose Caliver served in the WPA and the Office of Education.

A core of highly placed African-American social scientists thus became linked in a network called the Federal Council on Negro Affairs, more loosely known as Roosevelt's "**Black Cabinet.**" Mary McLeod Bethune was a leader of this body, which consisted primarily of "New Deal race specialists." It numbered 27 men and three women working mostly in temporary emergency agencies, and it included such stalwarts as housing administrator Robert Weaver. This group met every Friday in Bethune's Washington home. A smaller and younger

Profile

Mary McLeod Bethune

Mary Mcleod Bethune played a powerful role in Roosevelt's black cabinet, but this was only one of the many forums in which she exercised consummate leadership and diplomatic skill. Bethune's life and work link the social reform efforts of post-Reconstruction black women to the civil rights protest activities of the generation emerging after World War II. All the strands of black women's struggle for education, political rights, racial pride, and sexual autonomy are united in her writings, speeches, and organizational work.

Bethune, born on July 10, 1875, near Mayesville, South Carolina, graduated from Scotia Seminary in 1894 and entered Dwight Moody's Institute for Home and Foreign Missions in Chicago. After teaching in mission schools, she settled in Daytona, Florida, where she founded the Daytona Educational and Industrial Institute for Training Negro Girls. Reflecting on her work years later, Bethune recalled, "The school expanded fast. In less than two years I had two hundred fifty pupils. . . . I concentrated more and more on girls, as I felt that they especially were hampered by lack of educational opportunities." Eventually, however, she agreed to merge with Cookman Institute, an educational facility for black boys under the auspices of the Methodist Church. In 1923 the now coeducational institution was renamed Bethune-Cookman College.

During the 1920s Bethune became the leader of the National Association of Colored Women (NACW), a federation of women's clubs. As its president she attempted to turn the organization away from its focus on self-help and moral uplift and toward broader goals. Although she made progress, by 1935 she had become frustrated by the NACW's caution and founded the National Council of Negro Women (NCNW), an "organization of organizations." The women present at the creation of the NCNW were the who's who of black women's activism. They included educators Charlotte Hawkins Brown and Mary Church Terrell, executive director of the National Association of Colored Graduate Nurses Mabel K. Staupers, NAACP national field director Daisy Lampkin, and former president of the Empire State Federation of Women's Clubs Addie W. Hunton, who also led the International Council of Women of the Darker Race. Eventually, the NCNW had 20 national affiliates and 90 local councils in cities, towns, and rural communities across the country. Club engagement strengthened women's resolve to struggle for black rights and provided safe space for them to develop the skills and networks that proved critical in the post–World War II civil rights movement.

With the New Deal, Bethune became a Democratic Party activist and a government official. She had a close relationship with First Lady Eleanor Roosevelt that gave her access to the president that few others enjoyed. She and Eleanor Roosevelt had persuaded the president that the National Youth Administration (NYA) needed a Negro division to ensure that benefits would be distributed fairly, and Bethune was named the NYA's director of Negro affairs. She was the first African-American woman to hold a high position in the government. During the 1936 campaign, Bethune helped convince African Americans that their best interests lay with the Democratic rather than the Republican Party.

One of Bethune's many noteworthy accomplishments was the 1937 conference the Department of Labor held on the "Problems of the Negro and Negro Youth," at which Eleanor Roosevelt delivered a key speech. During the session titled "Security of Life and Equal Protection under the Law," the conference called for a federal antilynching law, equal access to the ballot in federal elections, and elimination of segregation and discrimination on interstate trains and buses. This was a virtual blueprint of the agenda of the civil rights movement. No other general meeting on civil rights during the Roosevelt administration generated so much interest, support, and publicity. With this conference, Bethune assumed the middle ground of black politics.

group met occasionally in Robert Weaver's apartment. This cadre of advisers pressured the president and the heads of federal agencies to adopt and support color-blind policies and lobbied to advance the economic, educational, and social status of black Americans.

18.4.1 Social Scientists and the New Deal

Many black intellectuals, scholars, and writers believed the social sciences could be used to adjudicate race relations, and during the New Deal they found greater receptiveness to their work than ever before. Nearly 200 African Americans received Ph.D.s during the 1930s, more than four times the combined total from the previous three decades. Several of these young scholars reached the top ranks of the social sciences, studying the economic, political, and sociological problems of black people with a depth of experience and theoretical sophistication earlier generations of scholars had lacked. In sociology E. Franklin Frazier and Charles S. Johnson took the lead. Frazier's pioneering studies of black families, although now dated, placed him at the forefront of debates on social policy. Throughout the 1930s, as the editor of *Opportunity*, the journal of the Urban League, Johnson published insightful critiques of American racial practices and policies, as well as the work of emerging black novelists, poets, and playwrights. Meanwhile, Ralph Bunche became well known within political science, and Abram Harris and Robert Weaver gained renown in economics.

The first generation of professional black historians included Carter G. Woodson, Lorenzo Greene, Benjamin Quarles, and John Hope Franklin. They argued that black people had been active agents in the past and not simply the passive objects of white people's actions. Through the Association for the Study of Negro Life and History and Negro History Week, Woodson and his coworkers Lorenzo Greene, Alrutheus Taylor, and Monroe Work deployed their scholarship to dismiss claims of black inferiority. Their scholarly emphasis on racial pride, achievement, and autonomy raised black morale.

The increasing importance of black scholars became apparent late in the 1930s when the Carnegie Corporation, a philanthropic foundation, sponsored a major study of black life. Although Swedish social scientist Gunnar Myrdal led the study, nearly half of the large staff of scholars were African Americans, and several, particularly Bunche, had a major impact on the work. Published in 1944 as *An American Dilemma*, this massive study profoundly affected public understanding of how racism undermined the progress of African Americans, and it helped set the agenda for the civil rights movement.

18.4.2 The Second New Deal

By late 1935, after two years marked by a slow recovery, much of the first New Deal lay in shambles. The Supreme Court had invalidated major parts of it, and a conservative backlash was emerging against the Roosevelt administration. In response, Roosevelt pressed for a second burst of legislation marked by the passage of the Social Security Act (SSA), the National Labor Relations Act (NLRA), the creation of the WPA, and other measures considerably more radical than those he had established in 1933. The NLRA, for example, helped unions get established and grow. The SSA provided the rudiments of a social welfare system as well as unemployment and retirement insurance. This new set of laws, known as the second New Deal, survived legal challenges and fundamentally changed the United States, particularly by strengthening the role of the federal government.

Roosevelt's leftward political shift helped him win the 1936 presidential election in a landslide. This election cemented a new electoral coalition that yoked the southern wing of the Democratic Party with more liberal farmers and working-class voters who were labor union members in the North and West. The Democratic Party began to win the votes of the large African-American populations in the great cities of the North.

Profile

Robert C. Weaver

Robert C. Weaver (1907–1997) was born in Washington, D.C. His parents and his teachers at the elite Dunbar High School (which boasted a host of distinguished black alumni, including Charles Houston and William Hastie) instilled in him pride in being a black American. After Dunbar, Weaver went to Harvard, where he earned his undergraduate degree in 1925 and a Ph.D. in economics in 1933, despite the hostility of professors who doubted that black people could do serious intellectual work. Such racist thinking only hardened Weaver's resolve to succeed.

Armed with impressive credentials but bleak job prospects, Weaver returned to Washington, where—together with his Harvard classmate John P. Davis—he founded the Negro Industrial League (NIL) and the Joint Committee on Economic Recovery (JCER) to advocate for black workers. They attracted sponsorships from 24 black and white organizations, including the National Baptist Convention, the African Methodist Episcopal Church, the NAACP, the United Mine Workers, the Elks, the Catholic Interracial Council, and the YWCA. Weaver could soon claim that the NIL and the JCER represented over one million black people.

This broad coalition demanded that the Roosevelt administration appoint black advisers or "experts" to key New Deal agencies. In 1935, Weaver succeeded a white southerner as the adviser on Negro affairs in the Department of the Interior and together with Mary McLeod Bethune became coleader of Roosevelt's "black cabinet."

Weaver remained in government service until 1944. As director of the Office of Race Relations at the United States Housing Authority, he established guidelines that ensured that black workers would be employed on all government-funded housing projects.

Under President John F. Kennedy, Weaver rejoined the government in 1961 and persuaded Kennedy to issue an executive order banning racial discrimination in federal housing programs. In 1966, under Kennedy's successor, Lyndon B. Johnson, Weaver became secretary of housing and urban development, the nation's first African-American cabinet secretary. He spearheaded the passage of the Housing Act of 1968, which expanded opportunities for black home ownership. Weaver died in New York City in 1997.

18.4.3 The Rise of Black Politicians

The Great Migration had relocated tens of thousands of prospective black voters to northern urban centers, the traditional strongholds of Democratic Party machines, such as in Chicago. Institutionalized housing segregation, combined with the often conscious choice to live in their own neighborhoods, concentrated the black electorate and increased its political power. This power had already appeared in the 1928 election of Republican Oscar De Priest to the U.S. House of Representatives, the first African-American congressman from the North. In 1934, reflecting a shift in partisan allegiance, Chicago's black voters replaced De Priest with Democrat Arthur W. Mitchell. Mitchell, a registered Republican when the Great Depression began, switched to the Democratic Party and thus became the first black Democrat to win a seat in Congress.

Mitchell's election was only the beginning of the change in black people's political identification. The black press fanned the shifting winds, and many more black urban dwellers developed an intense interest in politics. They began to connect political power with the prospect of improving their economic conditions. By the end of the 1930s, black urban voters garnered noteworthy influence in key states such as Illinois, Ohio, Pennsylvania, and New York. This political consciousness led to the election of black state legislators in California, Illinois, Indiana, Kansas, Kentucky, New Jersey, New York, Ohio, Pennsylvania, and West Virginia.

In another indication of change, some Democrats began supporting antilynching legislation. Congressman Mitchell gave a strong speech printed in the *Congressional Record* in 1935 supporting President Roosevelt as an antilynching advocate. "No President," he declared, "has been more outspoken against the horrible crime of lynching than has Mr. Roosevelt. In speaking of lynching some time ago he character-ized it as 'collective murder' and spoke of it as a crime which blackens the record of America." Mitchell told black audiences, "Let me say again, the attitude of the adminis-tration at the White House is absolutely fair and without prejudice, insofar as the Negro citizenry is concerned." The 1936 election results revealed that Roosevelt had captured the allegiance of most African Americans. Robert Vann, editor of the *Pittsburgh Courier*, urged black people, after casting their ballots, to go home and "turn Lincoln's picture to the wall." There are many complex reasons for this revolution in black political allegiance. The shift to the Democratic Party did not occur without anxiety. Some black people feared that by joining the party they would open the door for even more white southern Democrats to assume national power and thwart black advancement. But by 1936 most African-American voters were willing to take the risk.

18.4.4 Black Americans and the Democratic Party

The increased participation of African Americans in the Democratic Party sent chills down the spines of the white southern elite. The tension between black Democrats and white con-servative Democrats erupted at the party's 1936 convention in Philadelphia. The seating of 32 black delegates infuriated southern politicians. The selection of a black Baptist minister to open one session with a prayer outraged South Carolina Senator Ellison D. "Cotton Ed" Smith, who, accompanied by Mayor Burnet Maybank of Charleston and other delegates, marched off the floor, proclaiming that they refused to support "any political organization that looks upon the Negro and caters to him as a political and social equal." Smith declared he was "sick of the whole damn thing." Undaunted, the black minister simply observed that "Brother Smith needs more prayer." The next day when Congressman Mitchell of Illinois took to the floor, Smith repeated his walkout. The South Carolina delegation subsequently adopted a protest resolution denouncing the appearance of black men on the convention's program. Southern white protests, however, had no effect on the political decisions of black men and women. Heeding the advice of the NAACP, they voted their personal interests.

Despite the rise of black Democrats, southern congressmen succeeded in excluding many African Americans from key government programs. For example, they insisted on denying the benefits of the NLRA and the SSA to agricultural laborers and domestic servants. These white southerners could not, however, stop the tilt toward fairer admin-istration of programs or the revival of the push for equal rights, which had lain all but dormant since the end of Reconstruction.

18.4.5 The WPA and Black America

The WPA illustrates the changes that resulted because of the second New Deal and the movement of African Americans to the Democratic Party. The WPA, with Harry Hopkins as its head, had received $1.39 billion in federal funds. The WPA put thousands of men and women to work building new roads, hospitals, city halls, courthouses, and schools. Under the aegis of the WPA, American citizens built bridges, ports, and water systems. Larger-scale infrastructure projects included the Lincoln Tunnel under the Hudson River connecting New York and New Jersey, the Triborough Bridge system linking Manhattan to Long Island, and the Bonneville and Boulder dams. (Boulder Dam was later renamed the Hoover Dam by a Republican-controlled Congress in 1946.)

One of the most effective New Deal agencies, the WPA offered African Americans numerous opportunities for vocational training. Young men learned from experienced craftsmen. As this 1942 photo illustrates, the intricate lathe operations instruction prepared the trainee with skills that could be used in the defense industries.

WPA poster for the all-black production of *Macbeth*.

The WPA was operated far more fairly than did the first New Deal programs. The national government explicitly rejected racial discrimination and made sure local officials complied. Although far from perfect, by 1939 it had provided assistance to one million black families on a far more equitable basis. The same pattern prevailed in the WPA's four arts programs—the Federal Art Project, the Federal Music Project, the Federal Theater Project, and the Federal Writers' Project—which employed thousands of musicians, intellectuals, writers, and artists. A fifth program created in 1937, the Historical Records Survey, sent teams of writers, including Zora Neale Hurston, to collect folklore and to study ethnic groups. One team collected the life histories of 2,000 former slaves.

Between 1935 and 1943, the WPA helped artists display their talents and made their work widely available. Among the black artists hired to adorn government buildings, post offices, and public parks were Aaron Douglas, Charles Alston, Richmond Barthe, Sargent Johnson, Archibald Motley, Jr., and Augusta Savage. Savage was a sculptor who worked in clay, marble, and bronze. She established arts schools in New York City in the 1930s—the Savage School of Arts and Crafts, Savage Studios, and the Uptown Art Laboratory. In 1937, she became the first director of the Harlem Community Art Center. Her students included Jacob Lawrence, William Artis, Norman Lewis, and Elton Fax.

The Federal Theater Project established 16 black theater units. Among their most notable productions was a version of *Macbeth* set in Haiti with an all-black cast. White actor John Houseman and black actress Rose McClendon directed the Harlem Federal Theater Project. This project—more than the others—proved controversial due to the fear of communist influence and the leftist political views of some African-American writers and performers.

18.5 Misuses of Medical Science: The Tuskegee Study

Explain the purpose of the Tuskegee Study and evaluate its lasting impact on race relations and black health care status.

The 1930s marked the rising prominence of black scholars and intellectuals. Paradoxically, the decade also witnessed the worst manifestation of racism in American science. This shocking episode of racial mistreatment occurred in Macon County, Alabama, through medical experimentation on impoverished and vulnerable populations. There, in 1932, U.S. Public Health Service (USPHS) officials initiated several major studies of syphilis, a sexually transmitted disease that can cause paralysis, insanity, heart failure, and eventually death. For the subjects of its program—titled the Tuskegee Study of Untreated Syphilis in the Male Negro—the USPHS recruited 622 black men, all of them poor sharecroppers and the majority illiterate. Of these men, 431 had advanced cases of syphilis. The rest were free of the disease and served as controls for comparison.

Another experiment decades prior to the one in Tuskegee involved people in Guatemala. As historian Susan Reverby explained, "This experiment in the global, rather than the American South, differed from the Study in Alabama in two major ways: government doctors did infect people with syphilis and then did treat them with penicillin." In 1944 the Public Health Service deliberately injected gonorrhea in "volunteers" who were inmates at the Terre Haute Federal Penitentiary in Indiana but abandoned the study when it proved "difficult to get the men to exhibit infection."

The **Tuskegee Study** was called a treatment program, but it turned out to be an experiment, designed to chart the progression and development of a potentially fatal disease. To gain the men's trust, the government doctors centered their work at Tuskegee Institute and hired a black nurse, Eunice Rivers, who convinced the men they had "bad blood" and needed special treatment. Although penicillin, which can cure the disease, became available in the 1940s, the sharecroppers never received it. Instead, they were given ineffective placebos, which they were told would cure them.

Initially the Tuskegee Study was to last only 6 to 12 months, but it was repeatedly extended. The men received regular physical examinations, which included a painful lumbar puncture. This insertion of a needle into the spinal cord to obtain fluid for diagnosis often caused the men severe headaches, and in a few isolated cases it resulted in paralysis and even death. For almost 40 years, Tuskegee Study doctors observed the men, keeping careful records of their health and performing autopsies on those who died, but they never treated them for syphilis. So little understood was the Tuskegee Study that men not only remained in the program but believed they were fortunate to have the physical examinations, the hot lunches provided on examination days, and the burial allowance the government guaranteed their families. The medical community knew of the Tuskegee experiment, but the general public learned of it only in 1972 when a reporter broke the story. Black attorney Fred D. Gray of Alabama sued the U.S. government on behalf of the participants and their families, but before the case went to trial, the government made a $9 million settlement to the Tuskegee survivors and the descendants of those who had died.

Tuskegee Study
A medical study by the U.S. Public Health Service of the effects of syphilis on 622 black men. The study ran from 1932 to the 1970s, and the men were never given treatment when new therapeutics were discovered that could have saved the lives of many of them and members of their families.

From 1932 to 1972, the U.S. Public Health Service conducted an experiment on approximately 400 black Alabama sharecroppers to trace the evolution of untreated syphilis. The men were never informed that they had the disease, nor were they given penicillin when it became available. On May 16, 1997, President Bill Clinton on behalf of the U.S. government finally apologized for this cruel and clearly racist experiment on human subjects.

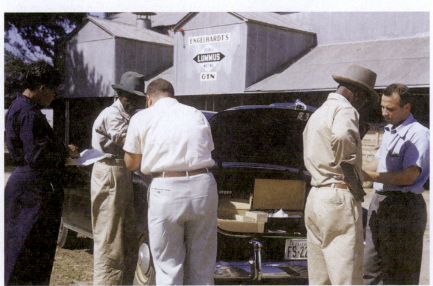

18.6 Organized Labor and Black America

Delineate the significant role that organized labor played in the radicalization of black Americans during the 1930s.

The relationship of African Americans to labor unions changed profoundly during the 1930s. Before this time, most local unions affiliated with the national AFL barred black people or restricted them to segregated locals. The railroad unions, which called themselves "brotherhoods," excluded black workers entirely. The New Deal, especially after 1935, did much to transform the labor movement. The NLRA and the militancy of workers provided the opportunity to organize the nation's great mass production industries. Still, leaders of the AFL were unwilling to incorporate into their unions the masses of unskilled workers, many of whom were African American or recent European immigrants. Frustrated by this situation, in 1935 the head of the United Mine Workers, John L. Lewis (1880–1969), and his followers formed the **Committee for Industrial Organization (CIO)** to take on the task.

> **Committee for Industrial Organization (CIO)**
>
> Labor organization that was committed to interracial and multiethnic organizing.

Unlike the AFL, the CIO was committed to interracial and multiethnic organizing and so enabled more African Americans to participate in the labor movement. Its leaders knew it was in organized labor's best interest to admit black men and women to membership. As one black union organizer said, "We colored folks can't organize without you and you white folks can't organize without us." But it took a massive change in outlook to achieve this unity. By 1940 the CIO had enlisted approximately 210,000 black members. Unions that valued and sustained interracial cooperation included the International Mine, Mill, and Smelter Workers; the Food, Tobacco, and Agricultural Workers Union; and the United Farm Equipment and Metal Workers.

A. Philip Randolph's Brotherhood of Sleeping Car Porters (BSCP) remained with the AFL, but it also benefited from New Deal legislation. In 1934 Congress had amended the Railway Labor Act in a way that helped the BSCP overcome the opposition of the Pullman Company. The law required that corporations bargain in good faith with unions if the unions could demonstrate through elections monitored by the National Mediation Board that they genuinely represented the corporations' employees. The Pullman Company resisted, but in 1937, long after an election certified the BSCP as the workers' representative, the company finally recognized the brotherhood. Then—and only then—did the AFL grant the BSCP full membership as an international union. After more than 12 years, A. Philip Randolph and thousands of black men won their struggles against a giant corporation and a powerful labor organization. These were no small victories.

Although most black people in unions were men, some unions also represented and helped improve the lives of black working women. For example, since the early nineteenth century there had been a rigid hierarchy among workers in the tobacco industry, one of the few areas of the economy outside agriculture or domestic service that employed many black women. Jobs were assigned on the basis of race and gender, with black women receiving the most difficult and tedious job, that of "stemmer." In 1939 stemmer Louise "Mama" Harris instigated a series of walkouts at the I. N. Vaughn Company in Richmond. The strikes, which CIO affiliates—including the white women of the International Ladies Garment Workers Union—supported, led to the formation of the Tobacco Workers Organizing Committee, another CIO affiliate. In 1943 black women union leaders and activists, including Theodosia Simpson and Miranda Smith, were involved in a strike against the R. J. Reynolds tobacco company to force it to the negotiating table. Smith later became southern regional director of the Food, Tobacco, Agricultural, and Allied Workers of America. It was the highest position a black woman held in the labor movement up to that time.

Voices

A. Philip Randolph Inspires a Young Black Activist

In 1928 young E. D. Nixon heard A. Philip Randolph speak, and it changed Nixon's life. He became president of the Montgomery branch of the Brotherhood of Sleeping Car Porters that year and remained in the post until 1964. During that period he played a leading role in mobilizing and organizing the Montgomery bus boycott ignited by Rosa Parks's arrest for refusing to relinquish her seat to a white male passenger. He recalls Randolph's speech in the following passage.

When I heard Randolph speak [in 1928], it was like a light. Most eloquent man I ever heard. He done more to bring me in the fight for civil rights than anybody. Before that time, I figure that a Negro would be kicked around and accept whatever the white man did. I never knew the Negro had a right to enjoy freedom like everyone else. When Randolph stood there and talked that day, it make a different man out of me. From that day on, I was determined that I was gonna fight for freedom until I was able to get some of it for myself.

1. What does Nixon's reaction to Randolph's speech say about the importance of leadership in the labor movement?

2. How did Randolph's speech influence Nixon's later involvement in the struggle for black civil rights?

SOURCE: Quoted in Studs Turkel, *Hard Times: An Oral History of the Great Depression* (1970; reprint, New York: New Press, pbk ed., 2000), 119.

18.7 The Communist Party and African Americans

Discuss the issues that were at the core of the *Scottsboro* case and the consequences of the U.S. Supreme Court decisions delivered in the case.

Throughout the 1930s the Communist Party intensified its support of African Americans' efforts to address unemployment and job discrimination and to seek social justice. The communists' militant antiracism and determination to be interracial attracted some African Americans. The party expelled members who exhibited racial prejudice and gave black men key leadership positions. James Ford, an African American, ran as the party's vice-presidential candidate in the election of 1932. Although few black men and women actually joined the Communist Party, some became increasingly sympathetic to left-wing ideas and prescriptions as the Depression wore on.

Many black workers were drawn to the Communist Party because it criticized the refusal of organized white labor to include them. The communists maintained that "the low standard of living of Negro workers is made use of by the capitalists to reduce the wages of the white workers." They chided "the mis-leaders of labor, the heads of the reformist and reactionary trade union organizations" for refusing to organize black workers. They insisted "this anti-Negro attitude of the reactionary labor leaders helps to split the ranks of labor, allows the employers to carry out their policy of 'divide and rule,' frustrates the efforts of the working class to emancipate itself from the yoke of capitalism, and dims the class-consciousness of the white workers as well as of the Negro workers." Indeed, much of the push for racial equality within the CIO emanated from those connected with the party.

18.7.1 The International Labor Defense and the "Scottsboro Boys"

The *Scottsboro* case brought the Communist Party to the attention of many African Americans. It began when nine black youths who had caught a ride on a freight train in Alabama were tried, convicted, and sentenced to death for allegedly raping two white women. Their ordeal started on the night of March 25, 1931, when a group of young white hobos accosted them. A fight broke out. The black youths threw the white youths off the train. The losers filed a complaint with the Scottsboro, Alabama, sheriff charging that black hoodlums had assaulted them. The sheriff ordered his deputies to round up every black person on the train. The sweep netted the nine young black men: Ozie Powell, Clarence Norris, Charlie Weems, Olen Montgomery, Willie Robertson, Haywood Patterson, Eugene Williams, Andy Wright, and Roy Wright. The police also discovered two young white women: 19-year-old Victoria Price and 17-year-old Ruby Bates.

Afraid of being arrested and perhaps ashamed of being hobos, Price and Bates falsely claimed that the nine black youths had sexually assaulted them. On the basis of that accusation, the **"Scottsboro Boys"** (ranging in age from 13 to 20) were given a hasty trial. They never had a chance. Their white court-appointed attorney came to court drunk each day. Three days after the trial started and 15 days after their arrest, the jurors found them all guilty. Eight received the death sentence, and the youngest was sentenced to life imprisonment, even though medical examinations of Price and Bates proved that neither had been raped.

While other organizations dawdled or refused to intervene, the Communist Party's International Labor Defense (ILD) rushed to help the "boys" by appealing the conviction and death sentence to the Supreme Court. The case produced two important decisions that reaffirmed black people's right to the basic protections that all other American citizens enjoyed. In *Powell v. Alabama* (1932), the Court ruled that the *Scottsboro* defendants had not been given adequate legal counsel and that the trial had taken place in a hostile and volatile atmosphere. Asserting that the youths' right to due process as set forth in the Fourteenth Amendment had been violated, the Court ordered a new trial. Alabama did as instructed, but the new trial resulted in another guilty verdict and sentences of death or life imprisonment. The ILD promptly appealed, and in *Norris v. Alabama* (1935) the Court decided that all Americans have the right to a trial by a jury of their peers. The systematic exclusion of African Americans from the *Scottsboro* juries, the Court held, denied the defendants equal protection under the law, which the Fourteenth Amendment guaranteed. Chief Justice Charles Evans Hughes pointed out that no black citizens had served on juries in the Alabama counties for decades, even though many were qualified to serve. The Court noted that the exclusion was blatant racial discrimination and called for yet another trial.

Despite these stunning defeats and increasing evidence that the "boys" had been falsely convicted, Alabama still pursued the case. Even when Ruby Bates publicly admitted the rape charge had been a hoax, white Alabamians ignored her. Finally, in 1937 Alabama dropped its charges against five of the nine men, and in the 1940s the state released those still in jail. Altogether, nine innocent black men had collectively served some three-quarters of a century in prison. Clarence Willie Norris, however, escaped and fled to Michigan, returning decades later to receive a ceremonious pardon from Governor George Wallace. When a reporter asked Norris how he felt, he declared, "I'm just glad to be free." The experience had taught him "to stand up for your rights, even if it kills you. That's all life consists of."

18.7.2 Debating Communist Leadership

Throughout the *Scottsboro* case, the NAACP tried unsuccessfully to wrest control from the Communist Party. Indeed, as the case evolved, tensions and competition between the Communist Party and the NAACP for leadership of black America

Scottsboro Boys

Nine young African-American men unjustly accused of raping two white women in Alabama in 1931. The Supreme Court overturned their convictions in 1937.

The "Scottsboro Boys," a case of southern justice gone awry, attracted international attention and fueled competition between the NAACP and the Communist Party. In this 1937 photograph the NAACP's Juanita E. Jackson Mitchell visits with the Scottsboro Boys, nine unemployed black young men accused of raping two white women mill workers on a Southern Railroad freight car on March 25, 1931. All were sentenced to death, with one exception. Eugene Williams's life was spared because he was only 13. Victoria Price and Ruby Bates recanted their stories, but it made no difference. The U.S. Supreme Court overturned the death convictions and sentences in two landmark cases, one of which established the right of the accused to competent legal counsel.

flared into open hostility. At first, the NAACP had hesitated to defend accused rapists, but it moved more decisively after the Communist Party had taken the lead.

The contest between the NAACP and the communists reveals the differences between the two groups. The party organized protest marches and demonstrations and used its press to denounce more cautious middle-class organizations. In Harlem, for example, the communists staged a 1931 protest march that attracted over 3,000 black men and women and ended with an address by Ada Wright, the mother of two of the defendants, who praised the ILD for its help. The NAACP countered with a carefully orchestrated campaign that questioned the sincerity and effectiveness of the communists and sought to repair its own reputation as a respectable and effective advocate for African Americans.

Black public opinion divided in its evaluation of the party. Some black men and women applauded the communists. Journalist Eugene Gordon wrote,

> Negro workers think of the countless times Communists have been beaten insensible for defending . . . Negro workers. . . . They see the ILD . . . supported by the Communist Party, rushing to the defense of the nine Negro youths at Scottsboro before other Negro organizations in the country condescended to glance superciliously in their direction. . . . Seeing and hearing all these things, the Negro worker in the United States would be a fool not to recognize the leadership that he has been waiting for since his freedom.

Historian Carter G. Woodson praised the Communist Party in the *New York Age*:

> I have talked with any number of Negroes who call themselves Communists, and I have never heard one express a desire to destroy anyone or anything but oppression. . . . Negroes who are charged with being Communists advocate the stoppage of peonage, equality in employment of labor. . . . If this makes a man "Red," the world's greatest reformers belong to this class, and we shall have to condemn our greatest statesmen, some of whom have attained the presidency of the United States.

But other African Americans ridiculed the party. George Schuyler, a columnist for the *Pittsburgh Courier*, used his razor-sharp wit to castigate the party and persuade black people that its claim to champion African Americans was a lie. Schuyler objected to the communists' "campaign of vilification . . . against the NAACP":

> No Ku Kluxer ever denounced the latter organization more vigorously and unfairly. The Communists know they are lying when they assert time and time again that the NAACP wants to see the boys convicted and is betraying the race. They have quite the same sort of grooved mentality as Ku Kluxers, Garveyites and other race fanatics, black and white. The course they tentatively pursue is held the only true one and whoever takes exception is denounced as an enemy of humanity, even though they may have to change that course in a few months.

Although most African Americans applauded the antiracist work that the Communist Party supported and performed, there was no chance they would defect from the traditional American political system, as W. E. B. Du Bois wrote in 1931:

> American Negroes do not propose to be the shock troops of the Communist Revolution, driven out in the front to death, cruelty and humiliation in order to win victories for white workers. . . . Negroes know perfectly well that whenever they try to lead revolution in America, the nation will unite as one fist to crush them and them alone.

The infighting between the Communist Party and other groups doomed a major attempt to unite all the disparate African-American protest groups into the **National Negro Congress (NNC)**. John P. Davis, a Washington-based economist, organized the NNC, modeling it on his experience as the executive secretary of the Joint Committee on National Recovery, a coalition of black groups that pressed for fairness in the early New Deal. The NNC was to be a federation of organizations on a national scale

National Negro Congress (NNC)

Organization founded in 1936 to unite African-American protest groups.

Profile

Angelo Herndon

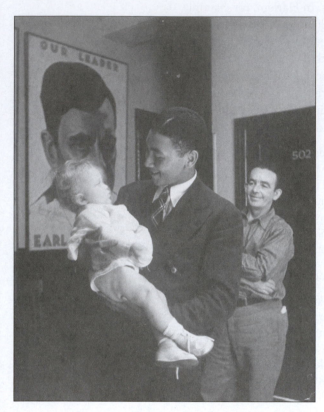

In the South, the Communist Party gravitated toward those areas where black and white laborers were grossly exploited. The party's efforts in Georgia, Alabama, and Mississippi produced black organizers such as Hosea Hudson, Nate Shaw, and Angelo Herndon, who became targets of white supremacists.

In 1932, young organizer Angelo Herndon was arrested, tried, and convicted in Atlanta for inciting insurrection. One of 13 children, Herndon was born May 6, 1913, in Ohio. Seeking better opportunities, Herndon, at age 13, escaped the poverty of his home region to work in the coal mines in Alabama. At 18 he was already a seasoned miner but disillusioned and angry at the exploitation of coal miners. He attended a Communist Party meeting and was impressed by its commitment to equality, both racial and social. He joined the party and poured enormous energy into organizing and recruiting members from among the mine workers and the unemployed. In 1934, Herndon explained why he joined the party:

> All my life I'd been sweated and stepped on and Jim-Crowed. I lay on my belly in the mines for a few dollars a week, and saw my pay stolen and slashed, and my buddies killed. I lived in the worst section of town, and rode behind the "Colored" signs of streetcars, as though there was something disgusting about me? I heard myself called "nigger" and "darky" and I had to say "Yes, sir" to every white man. . . . I had always detested it, but I had never known that anything could be done about it. And here, all of a sudden, I had found organizations . . . that weren't scared to come out for equality for the Negro people, and for the rights of workers. The Jim-Crow system, the wage-slave system, weren't everlasting after all! It was like all of a sudden turning a corner on a dirty, old street and finding yourself facing a broad, shining highway. . . . I felt then, and I know now, that the Communist program is the only program that the Southern workers—whites and Negroes both—can possibly accept in the long run. It's the only program that does justice to the southern worker's ideas that everybody ought to have an equal chance, and that every man has rights that must be respected.

The party sent Herndon to Atlanta, where he organized an interracial relief group and staged peaceful demonstrations against hunger. This proved his undoing. One week later, while picking up his mail at the post office, he was arrested on the charge that he had violated an old ordinance forbidding black and white people from mingling together. Herndon's trial and conviction made him the best-known African-American communist in the nation. The case underscored the fear that the specter of social equality across racial lines inspired in white southerners. The Communist Party assigned a young black attorney, Benjamin Davis, Jr., to represent Herndon. Davis challenged the constitutionality of the ordinance and of Atlanta's jury system, which excluded African Americans from service. His defense was unsuccessful, and the judge sentenced Herndon to 20 years on a chain gang. The severity of the sentence and the judge's racist sentiments sparked a nationwide movement to free Herndon as black organizations, labor unions, and religious groups joined with the Communist Party to fight for his immediate release. After four years of appeals, in 1937 the Supreme Court, in a 5-to-4 decision, declared Georgia's slave insurrection law unconstitutional and ordered the state to release him.

Profile

Ralph Waldo Ellison

Ralph Ellison, the noted author of the great novel *Invisible Man* (1952), a book published some two decades after his hoboing experience and that detailed the social and intellectual challenges faced by African Americans in the mid-twentieth century, recalled his harrowing experience as a young black "hobo" after the arrest of the "Scottsboro Boys" during the Great Depression.

By the 1930s, hoboing—boarding a train illegally—had been a common practice for decades. During the Depression, however, the number of hobos increased dramatically, as hard times drove thousands to "hit the rails" in search of work, adventure, or a chance to start over someplace new. Economic hardship, it seemed, was the driving force behind hoboing as a large number of migratory workers left home in an effort to better their own lives and the lives of their family members.

The situation was similar for Ellison, who as a young man boarded a freight train to travel to the Tuskegee Institute in order to take advantage of a scholarship he had been granted. With limited funds and no time to earn the cost of a full-fare ticket, he decided to try this form of travel, hopping aboard a train with a disparate group of people. He was desperate, knowing that a college education was one way to improve his life, and despite his youth and inexperience, was adventurous enough to wend his way across America to continue his studies. His impression of hoboing was romantic, with thoughts of the Rover Boys, popular characters in a young-adult series, and the thrill-seeking Huck Finn going through his mind as he prepared to leave his home.

The realities of hoboing were much starker, particularly for Ellison, a young black man journeying during a dangerous time in American racial history. Upon arriving in the freight yards of Decatur, Alabama, Ellison found himself in a line-up with another forty or fifty passengers—both black and white—with two armed, white detectives at the scene. Ellison realized that the town in which he was now standing was where the Scottsboro case, a case in which nine black teenagers were accused of raping two white women, was being tried, and the situation in terms of race relations was deteriorating quickly. Ellison knew that the racial environment of the town was fraught and that as a black man, he may be looked upon unfavorably; to him the Scottsboro trial was a "kangaroo proceeding" that he knew would end in swift and brutal punishment for the accused.

Ellison feared the worst, standing in the freight yard, so when the opportunity to flee presented itself, he joined a group of white boys who ran for cover, hiding among their ranks as they made their way away from the scene. He dove beneath a shed and waited there until dawn, grabbing a ride on the first train he saw heading south. But the night in the Decatur freight yard stayed with him even after he reached Tuskegee, his feelings of fear and helplessness lingering in his heart and mind.

---

supported by regional councils. Over 800 delegates representing 585 organizations attended its first meeting, held in Chicago in 1936. However, prominent black activists, leaders, and intellectuals were conspicuously absent, notably those associated with the NAACP. A. Philip Randolph was elected president, and Davis became the executive secretary. The group resolved not to be dominated by any one political faction and to build on the strength of all parts of the black community. Although handicapped by lack of funds, the NNC initially worked effectively at the local or community level. With branches in approximately 70 cities, the organization gained for its members increased employment opportunities, better housing, and adequate relief work. The NNC also prodded labor unions, in particular the CIO, to fight for better conditions and higher wages for black workers.

At the NNC's second meeting in Philadelphia in 1937, a skeptical Davis maintained that the Democratic Party would never allow black people to benefit fairly from the New Deal. Eventually the increasing importance of communists in the NNC alienated most other groups and reduced the organization's ability to speak for most black people. By 1940 it was greatly weakened. Randolph was voted out of office.

Conclusion

Transformative changes occurred during the early 1930s. Against the backdrop of the Great Migration and the New Deals, the NAACP came of age, black women found their voice, white left-wing leaders joined with black men and women in interracial alliances, organized labor bridged the race chasm, and black voters switched allegiance from the Republican to the Democratic Party. The first and second New Deals stimulated economic recovery and, more important, laid the basis for a strong national state and forged a political coalition that, beginning with World War II, would challenge the nation's racial caste system. The Tuskegee Syphilis experiment, however, will forever fuel black ambivalence. Memories of the Tuskegee experiment convinced many Americans to be wary and suspect the worst of federal government–sponsored health care projects.

Chapter Timeline

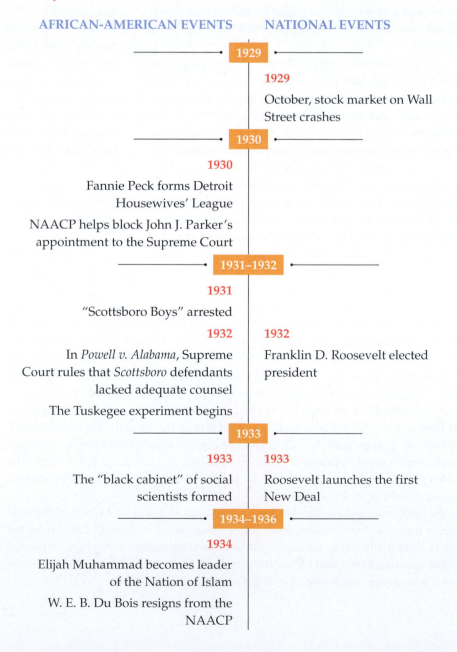

AFRICAN-AMERICAN EVENTS   **NATIONAL EVENTS**

1929

1929

October, stock market on Wall Street crashes

1930

1930

Fannie Peck forms Detroit Housewives' League

NAACP helps block John J. Parker's appointment to the Supreme Court

1931–1932

1931

"Scottsboro Boys" arrested

1932

In *Powell v. Alabama*, Supreme Court rules that *Scottsboro* defendants lacked adequate counsel

The Tuskegee experiment begins

1932

Franklin D. Roosevelt elected president

1933

1933

The "black cabinet" of social scientists formed

1933

Roosevelt launches the first New Deal

1934–1936

1934

Elijah Muhammad becomes leader of the Nation of Islam

W. E. B. Du Bois resigns from the NAACP

AFRICAN-AMERICAN EVENTS	NATIONAL EVENTS
1935	**1935**
Mary McLeod Bethune forms the National Council of Negro Women	The CIO is formed
Norris v. Alabama establishes right to trial by a jury of one's peers	Roosevelt's second New Deal— Social Security Act, National Labor Relations Act, and Works Progress Administration
Free Angelo Herndon Campaign begins	
National Negro Congress formed	
1936	**1936**
African Americans shift allegiance to the Democratic Party	Roosevelt reelected in a landslide
Mary McLeod Bethune named director of the Division of Negro Affairs	

1937

1937

William Hastie named first black federal judge

Bethune organizes conference on Problems of the Negro and Negro Youth

---

Review Questions

1. Why did African Americans abandon their long association with the Republican Party in favor of the Democratic Party?

2. How did black radicalism influence Roosevelt's New Deal policies and programs?

3. How did black people respond to and survive the Great Depression? How did the experiences of black women during the Depression reflect their race, class, and gender status?

4. How did the New Deal adversely affect black sharecroppers, tenants, and farmers? What were the political, social, and economic repercussions of the large-scale migration of African Americans out of the South during the 1930s?

5. What role did racism play in the Tuskegee experiment and the "Scottsboro Boys" case?

6. Why were W. E. B. Du Bois's editorials in the *Crisis* about segregation so divisive and explosive? How did black activists and scholars respond to the idea of voluntary self-segregation?

Retracing the Odyssey

Apollo Theater, New York City. When other venues were closed to African Americans, many talented men and women destined to become top performers in twentieth-century America launched their careers at the Apollo Theater. Since the 1930s, performers such as Duke Ellington, Count Basie, Charlie Parker, Bessie Smith, Billie Holiday, and Ella Fitzgerald have graced the Apollo stage. Renowned comedians such as Bill Cosby, Richard Pryor, and Redd Foxx honed their talents here, as well as numerous others.

The Mary McLeod Bethune Council House, Washington, D.C. Mary McLeod Bethune, born in 1875 in Mayesville, South Carolina, was one of the most politically engaged black women in the first half of the twentieth century. She was the president of Bethune-Cookman College in Daytona Beach, Florida, when President Franklin Delano Roosevelt appointed her director of Negro affairs of the National Youth Council. An ardent black clubwoman, Bethune is celebrated as the founder, in 1935, and first president of the National Council of Negro Women (NCNW). It remains a significant umbrella group for organizations of black women. The Bethune Museum and Archive Center was her home and headquarters of the NCNW from 1943 to 1966. It contains exhibits and sponsors programs that emphasize the contributions of African-American women to American society. The archive contains important manuscript collections and other research materials pertaining to the NCNW and to black women's history.

Charles H. Wright Museum of African American History, Detroit, Michigan. This is the largest African-American history museum in America. It sponsors a variety of educational programs throughout the year.

Recommended Reading

Edwin Black. *War Against the Weak: Eugenics and America's campaign to Create a Master Race*. Washington, D.C.: Dialog Press, 2003. A thoughtful discussion of America's connection to the eugenics movement and to German Nazism.

John Egerton. *Speak Now Against the Day: The Generation Before the Civil Rights Movement in the South.* New York: Alfred A. Knopf, 1994. An excellent survey of the period before the modern civil rights era, with chapters on the Depression in the South and black and white southerners' reactions to it.

Robin D. G. Kelley. *Hammer and Hoe: Alabama Communists During the Great Depression.* Chapel Hill: University of North Carolina Press, 1990. A splendid study of the radicalizing activism of steelworkers and farmers during the 1930s. Kelley shows why the communists appealed to black workers.

Koritha Mitchell. *Living with Lynching: African American Lynching Plays, Performance, and Citizenship, 1890–1930.* Urbana: University of Illinois Press, 2012. A uniquely original and brilliant analysis of lynching plays that facilitated the survival of African-American communities during a period of rampant mob violence.

Mark Naison. *Communists in Harlem During the Depression.* Urbana: University of Illinois Press, 1983. A well-researched and clear-sighted study of the Communist Party in Harlem and the National Negro Congress.

Susan M. Reverby. *Examining Tuskegee: The Infamous Syphilis Study and Its Legacy.* Chapel Hill: University of North Carolina Press, 2009. A comprehensive study and brilliant analysis of the African American men involved as patients, their families, and the health care professionals who participated in the famous government-financed study of untreated syphilis.

Samuel Kelton Roberts, Jr. *Infectious Fear: Politics, Disease, and the Health Effects of Segregation.* Durham, NC: University of North Carolina Press, 2003. An illuminating and important examination of the tuberculosis crisis that deepens understanding of the impact of racialized medicine on public health care.

Raymond Wolters. *Negroes and the Great Depression: The Problem of Economic Recovery.* Westport, CT: Greenwood, 1974. A solid survey that covers the Depression's impact on African Americans, the workings of the "black cabinet," and the effects of the New Deal agencies on black Americans.

Additional Bibliography

Politics and History

Adam Fairclough. *Better Day Coming: Blacks and Equality, 1890–2000.* New York: Viking, 2001.

Glenda Elizabeth Gilmore. *Defying Dixie: The Radical Roots of Civil Rights, 1919–1950.* New York: W. W. Norton, 2008.

Kenneth W. Goings. *"The NAACP Comes of Age": The Defeat of Judge John J. Parker.* Bloomington: Indiana University Press, 1990.

Matthew Pratt Guterl, *The Color of Race in America, 1900–1940* (Cambridge, MA: Harvard University Press, 2002)

Charles V. Hamilton. *Adam Clayton Powell, Jr., the Political Biography of an American Dilemma.* New York: Atheneum, 1991.

Darlene Clark Hine. *Black Victory: The Rise and Fall of the White Primary in Texas.* New edition with essays by Darlene Clark Hine, Steven F. Lawson, and Merline Pitre. Columbia: University of Missouri Press, 2003.

Christopher R. Reed. *The Chicago NAACP and the Rise of Black Professional Leadership, 1910–1966.* Bloomington: Indiana University Press, 1997.

_____. *The Depression Comes to the South Side: Protest and Politics in the Black Metropolis, 1930–1933*. Bloomington: Indiana University Press, 2011.

Patricia Sullivan. *Days of Hope: Race and Democracy in the New Deal Era*. Chapel Hill: University of North Carolina Press, 1996.

_____. *Lift Every Voice: The NAACP and the Making of the Civil Rights Movement*. New York: New Press, 2009.

Mark V. Tushnet. *The NAACP's Legal Strategy Against Segregated Education, 1925–1950*. Chapel Hill: University of North Carolina Press, 1987.

Nancy J. Weiss. *Farewell to the Party of Lincoln: Black Politics in the Age of FDR*. Princeton, NJ: Princeton University Press, 1983.

Labor

Lizabeth Cohen. *Making a New Deal: Industrial Workers in Chicago, 1919–1939*. New York: Cambridge University Press, 1990.

Olen Cole, Jr. *The African-American Experience in the Civilian Conservation Corps*. Gainesville: University Press of Florida, 1999.

Dennis C. Dickerson. *Out of the Crucible: Black Steelworkers in Western Pennsylvania, 1875–1980*. Albany: State University of New York Press, 1986.

August Meier and Elliott Rudwick. *Black Detroit and the Rise of the UAW*. New York: Oxford University Press, 1979.

Education

Badia Sahar Ahad. *Freud Upside Down: African American Literature and Psychoanalytic Culture*. Urbana: University of Illinois Press, 2010.

Derrick P. Alridge. *The Educational Thought of W.E.B. Du Bois: An Intellectual History*. New York: Teachers College Press, 2008.

James D. Anderson. *The Education of Blacks in the South, 1860–1935*. Chapel Hill: University of North Carolina Press, 1988.

Marcia Chatelain. *South Side Girls: Growing Up in the Great Migration*. Durham, NC: Duke University Press, 2015.

Pero Gaglo Dagbovie. *The Early Black History Movement, Carter G. Woodson and Lorenzo Johnston Greene*. Urbana: University of Illinois Press, 2007.

Richard Kluger. *Simple Justice: The History of* Brown v. Board of Education *and Black America's Struggle for Equality*. New York: Random House, 1976. New rev. ed., 2004.

Kenneth W. Mack. *Representing the Race: The Creation of the Civil Rights Lawyer*. Cambridge, MA: Harvard University Press, 2012.

Thomas J. Ward, Jr. *Black Physicians in the Jim Crow South*. Fayetteville: University of Arkansas Press, 2003.

Zachery R. Williams. *In Search of the Talented Tenth: Howard University Public Intellectuals and the Dilemmas of Race, 1926–1970*. Columbia: University of Missouri Press, 2009.

Francille Rusan Wilson. *The Segregated Scholars: Black Social Scientists and the Creation of Black Labor Studies, 1890–1950*. Charlottesville: University of Virginia Press, 2006.

Black Radicalism

Ramla M. Bandele. *Black Star: African American Activism in the International Political Economy*. Urbana: University of Illinois Press, 2008.

Dan Carter. *Scottsboro: A Tragedy of the American South*. Baton Rouge: Louisiana State University Press, 1969.

Vanessa Northington Gamble. *Making a Place for Ourselves: The Black Hospital Movement, 1920–1945*. New York: Oxford University Press, 1995.

Michael K. Honey. *Southern Labor and Black Civil Rights: Organizing Memphis Workers*. Urbana: University of Illinois Press, 1993.

Jacqueline Jones. *Labor of Love, Labor of Sorrow: Black Women, Work, and the Family from Slavery to the Present*. New York: Basic Books, 1985.

Lionel Kimble, Jr. *A New Deal for Bronzeville: Housing, Employment, and Civil Rights in Black Chicago, 1935–1955*. Carbondale: Southern Illinois University Press, 2015.

Nicholas Natanson. *The Black Image in the New Deal: The Politics of FSA Photography*. Knoxville: University of Tennessee Press, 1992.

Christopher R. Reed. *The Chicago NAACP and the Rise of Black Professional Leadership, 1910–1966*. Bloomington: Indiana University Press, 1997.

Meredith L. Roman. *Opposing Jim Crow: African Americans and the Soviet Indictment of U.S. Racism, 1928–1937*. Lincoln: University of Nebraska Press, 2012.

Daryl Michael Scott. *Contempt and Pity: Social Policy and the Image of the Damaged Black Psyche, 1880–1996*. Chapel Hill: University of North Carolina Press, 1997.

Mark Solomon. *The Cry Was Unity: Communists and African Americans, 1917–1936*. Jackson: University Press of Mississippi, 1998.

Richard W. Thomas. *Life for Us Is What We Make It: Building Black Community in Detroit, 1915–1945.* Bloomington: Indiana University Press, 1992.

Economics

Charles T. Banner-Haley. *To Do Good and to Do Well: Middle Class Blacks and the Depression, Philadelphia, 1929–1941.* New York: Garland, 1993.

Robert E. Weems, Jr. *Black Business in the Black Metropolis: The Chicago Metropolitan Assurance Company, 1924–1985.* Bloomington: Indiana University Press, 1996.

Biography and Autobiography

Felix L. Armfield. *Eugene Kinckle Jones: The National Urban League and Black Social Work, 1910–1940.* Urbana: University of Illinois Press, 2012.

Andrew Buni. *Robert L. Vann of the Pittsburgh Courier.* Pittsburgh, PA: University of Pittsburgh Press, 1974.

Cornelius L. Bynum. *A. Philip Randolph and the Struggle for Civil Rights.* Urbana: University of Illinois Press, 2010.

Henry Louis Gates, Jr., and Evelyn Brooks Higginbotham, eds. *African American Lives.* New York: Oxford University Press, 2004.

Joyce A. Hanson. *Mary McLeod Bethune and Black Women's Political Activism.* Columbia: University of Missouri Press, 2003.

Randal Maurice Jelks. *Benjamin Elijah Mays, Schoolmaster of the Movement: A Biography.* Chapel Hill: University of North Carolina Press, 2012.

Spencie Love. *One Blood: The Death and Resurrection of Charles R. Drew.* Chapel Hill: University of North Carolina Press, 1996.

Audrey Thomas McCluskey. *A Forgotten Sisterhood: Pioneering Black Women Educators and Activists in the Jim Crow South.* Lanham: Rowman and Littlefield, 2015.

Audrey Thomas McCluskey and Elaine M. Smith, ed. *Mary McLeod Bethune: Building a Better World, Essays and Selected Documents.* Bloomington: Indiana University Press, 1999.

Jacqueline A. McLeod. *Daughter of the Empire State: The Life of Judge Jane Bolin.* Urbana: University of Illinois Press, 2012.

Genna Rae McNeil. *Groundwork: Charles Hamilton Houston and the Struggle for Civil Rights.* Philadelphia: University of Pennsylvania Press, 1983.

Aldon Morris. *The Scholar Denied: W. E. B. Du Bois and the Birth of Modern Sociology.* Berkeley: University of California Press, 2015.

Jeffrey B. Perry, ed. *The Hubert Harrison Reader.* Middletown, CT: Wesleyan University Press, 2001.

Barbara Ransby. *Ella Baker and the Black Freedom Movement.* Chapel Hill: University of North Carolina Press, 2003.

John Herbert Roper, Sr. *The Magnificent Mays: A Biography of Benjamin Elijah Mays.* Columbia: University of South Carolina Press, 2012.

Mark V. Tushnet. *Making Civil Rights Law: Thurgood Marshall and the Supreme Court, 1935–1961.* New York: Alfred A. Knopf, 1994.

Gilbert Ware. *William Hastie: Grace Under Pressure.* New York: Oxford University Press, 1984.

Isabel Wilkerson. *The Warmth of Other Suns: The Epic Story of America's Great Migration.* New York: Random House, 2010.

Roy Wilkins with Tom Mathews. *Standing Fast: The Autobiography of Roy Wilkins.* New York: Da Capo Press, 1994.

Oscar R. Williams. *George S. Schuyler: Portrait of a Black Conservative.* Knoxville: University of Tennessee Press, 2007.

Black Internationalism

Carol Anderson. *Eyes Off the Prize: The United Nations and the African American Struggle for Human Rights, 1944–1955.* Cambridge, UK: Cambridge University Press, 2003.

Kate A. Baldwin. *Beyond the Color Line and the Iron Curtain: Reading Encounters Between Black and Red, 1922–1963.* Durham, NC: Duke University Press, 2002.

Douglas A. Blackmon. *Slavery by Another Name: The Re-enslavement of Black Americans from the Civil War to World War II.* New York: Doubleday, 2008.

Tina Campt. *Other Germans: Black Germans and the Politics of Race, Gender, and Memory in the Third Reich.* Ann Arbor: University of Michigan Press, 2003.

Joy Gleason Carew. *Blacks, Reds, and Russians: Sojourners in Search of the Soviet Promise.* New Brunswick, NJ: Rutgers University Press, 2008.

Carole Boyce Davies. *Left of Karl Marx: The Political Life of Black Communist Claudia Jones.* Durham, NC: Duke University Press, 2008.

Mary L. Dudziak. *Cold War Civil Rights: Race and the Image of American Democracy.* Princeton, NJ: Princeton University Press, 2006.

Brent Hayes Edwards. *The Practice of Diaspora: Literature, Translation, and the Rise of Black Internationalism.* Cambridge, MA: Harvard University Press, 2003.

Lashawn Harris. "Running with the Reds: African American Women and the Communist Party During the Great Depression," *Journal of African American History* 94, no. 1 (Winter 2009): 21–43.

Cheryl Higashida. *Black Internationalist Feminism: Women Writers of the Black Left, 1945–1995.* Urbana: University of Illinois Press, 2011.

Minkah Makalani. *In the Cause of Freedom: Radical Black Internationalism from Harlem to London, 1917–1939.* Chapel Hill: University of North Carolina Press, 2012.

Erik S. McDuffie. *Sojourning for Freedom: Black Women, American Communism, and the Making of Left Feminism.* Durham, NC: Duke University Press, 2011.

Susan Pennybacker. *From Scottsboro to Munich: Race and Political Culture in 1930.* Princeton, NJ: Princeton University Press, 2009.

Brenda Gayle Plummer. *Rising Wind: Black Americans and U.S. Foreign Affairs, 1935–1960.* Chapel Hill, NC: University of North Carolina Press, 1996.

Cedric J. Robinson. *Black Marxism: The Making of the Black Radical Tradition.* 1983; Reprint, Chapel Hill, NC: University of North Carolina Press, 2000.

Jonathan Rosenberg. *How Far the Promised Land: World Affairs and the African American Civil Rights Movement from the First World War to Vietnam.* Princeton, NJ: Princeton University Press, 2006.

Randi Storch. *Red Chicago: American Communism at its Grassroots, 1928–1935.* Urbana: University of Illinois Press, 2007.

Tyler Stovall. "The Color Line Behind the Lines: Racial Violence in France During the Great War." *American Historical Review* 103, no. 3 (June 1998): 737–69.

Penny Von Eschen. *Race Against Empire: Black Americans and Anticolonalism, 1937–1957.* Ithaca, NY: Cornell University Press, 1997.

Peter Wallerstein. *Tell the Court I Love My Wife: Race, Marriage, and Law: An American History.* New York: Palgrave Macmillan, 2002.

Victoria W. Wolcott. *Remaking Respectability: African American Women in Interwar Detroit.* Chapel Hill: University of North Carolina Press, 2001.

Jeff Woods. *Black Struggles, Red Scare: Segregation and Anti-Communism in the South, 1948–1968.* Baton Rouge: Louisiana State University Press, 2004.

Chapter 19

Meanings of Freedom: Black Culture and Society

1930–1950

Pitching great Leroy Paige warms up at New York's stadium in 1942.

 ## Learning Objectives

After reading this chapter, students should be able to:

19.1   Describe the ways in which local leaders and parents provided support for the cultural training and educational institutions for their communities.

19.2   Analyze the ways in which black artists used their diverse artistic talents and skills to support social justice struggles at home and abroad.

19.3 Distinguish the differences between the music genres or styles of big band, bebop, and swing.

19.4 Analyze the ways in which popular presentations of African Americans in popular culture may have reinforced negative stereotypes during the Great Depression era.

19.5 Describe the similarities and delineate the differences between key authors, artists, musicians, and performers who were prominent in the Black Chicago Renaissance.

19.6 Discuss the ways in which black graphic artists offered different ways to view or express the ways in which they reimagined themselves and their people.

19.7 Compare and contrast the nuanced differences and similarities in the works and lives of the twentieth century's most prominent African-American writers. Identify similar or shared themes in their novels.

19.8 Analyze the contributions African-American sports figures made to American culture and the barriers that they overcame in order to do so.

19.9 Identify some of the strongest characteristics of black religious culture and how the church was transformed into a haven for those engaged in resistance struggles.

He would not Africanize America, for America has too much to teach the world and Africa. He would not bleach his Negro soul in a flood of white Americanism, for he knows that Negro blood has a message for the world. He simply wished to make it possible for a man to be both a Negro and an American, without being cursed and spit upon by his fellows, without having the doors of opportunity closed roughly in his face. This, then, is the end of his striving: to be a co-worker in the kingdom of culture, to escape both death and isolation, to husband and use his best powers and his latent genius.

—*W. E. B. Du Bois, The Souls of Black Folk: Essay and Sketches*

W. E. B. Du Bois commented often on the gifts black people had given to America. Even before he wrote the passage that opens this chapter, Du Bois had proclaimed, "We are the first fruits of this new nation. . . . We are the people whose subtle sense of song has given America its only American music, its only American fairy tales, its only touch of pathos and humor amid its money-getting plutocracy." African-American "destiny is not a servile imitation of Anglo-Saxon culture, but a stalwart originality which shall unswervingly follow Negro ideals."

A key theme in black life from the 1930s to the early 1950s was the many strategies African Americans devised to protest second-class citizenship, resist negative racial stereotypes, and end white entrepreneurs' appropriation of black culture. At heart, black cultural workers and creative artists sought to shape the representation of black people in American society and to sustain a viable black culture for a rapidly urbanizing people. A central issue in this chapter is the extent to which black culture from the 1930s to the 1950s became a source of strength—cultural power—that helped African Americans define and assert themselves within American society.

Cultural power allowed African Americans to craft positive images of black people that challenged negative distortions and helped to build community. The new black cultural power had to fight the well-worn stereotypes of the dumb and lazy black man, the selfless mammy, and the promiscuous dark Venus. As we have seen throughout this book, black people were disfranchised and socially and economically marginalized. But in the arts, black people drove a small wedge into the wall of racial segregation and discrimination. In literature and the visual and performing arts, talented African Americans, such as singer and actor Paul Robeson, who starred in Shakespeare's *Othello* on Broadway in 1930, novelist Richard Wright, and expatriate singer and dancer Josephine Baker, compelled the attention of white Americans. The 1930s, 1940s, and 1950s—when most black people were suffering from the lingering effects of the Depression and the entrenched Jim Crow regime—were a fertile period in the history of black expressive culture.

19.1 Black Culture in a Midwestern City

Describe the ways in which local leaders and parents provided support for the cultural training and educational institutions for their communities.

Beginning in the 1930s, a second wave of black migrants made St. Louis the fifth largest city in the United States. Yet, because of segregation and discrimination, the city's black community developed institutions to nurture and advance its educational interests and cultural needs. St. Louis was known as a dynamic center where both popular and classical music flourished. A number of musicians who began their careers in classical music would evolve into significant contributors to dynamic popular genres including the blues and jazz. Black residents struggled to secure training in classical music and performance opportunities. The author of *The Weary Blues* (1926), Langston Hughes, an integral member of the Harlem Renaissance and one of the earliest writers of jazz poetry, embraced the proliferation of black culture in the Midwest, writing about various members of the artistic movement and the possibilities and excitement that life in a Midwestern city held for black people. He acknowledged several of the main players on the scene in his poetry, specifically W.C. Handy, Josephine Baker, and E. Simms Campbell.

With respect to the Midwestern rise of black culture, W.C. Handy put St. Louis on the map as a center of unique musical innovation. His song "The St. Louis Blues," became a favorite in black music culture. Other artists including Scott Joplin, Tom Turpin, Louis Armstrong, and singer and dance phenomenon Josephine Baker spread this new musical form to national and international audiences.

St. Louis, located in the heart of a region many considered remote from the cultural centers of New York's Harlem and Chicago's Bronzeville, actually nurtured a generation of outstanding jazz musicians. To be sure, the musicians who gave birth to ragtime and jazz also created space for themselves in classical music. Early black support for classical music emerged in the 1930s and 1940s in spite of the objection of some white St. Louis citizens. Schools, churches, labor, and media leaders in St. Louis created their own opportunities and venues for black children interested in classical music. The two largest black newspapers, the *St. Louis Argus* and the *St. Louis American*, publicized recitals and concerts. Black schools at the elementary and college levels supported classical music education. Most notable were Lincoln University in Jefferson City (founded in 1866 as a school created by and for black Civil War veterans and their families) and Sumner High School (founded in 1875 as the first secondary school for black people west of the Mississippi).

By the 1940s Lincoln University had educated a significant number of men and women who would perform in a variety of community institutions. Music instructors organized a range of cultural programs. Teachers at Sumner High School supervised student orchestras, bands, choirs, and glee clubs. Actually, many of the local music teachers possessed advanced degrees from prestigious institutions. Perhaps the most influential teacher was Kenneth Billups who was an arranger, composer, and founding director of the Legend Singers, a black professional chorus that appeared with the St. Louis Symphony and the Municipal Opera Company (MUNY) in productions of *Show Boat*, often dressed in demeaning slave costumes. Billups's response to criticism of black performers appearing in such shows was ambivalent. He was realistic about the compromises black artists made in racially restrictive environments:

> I've seen situations where I felt inwardly . . . I might have had to do some things; for example, let's take this Showboat thing at MUNY Opera. There is the need of a black chorus to go there, and I had the privilege of doing that with my Legend Singers, simply because one of the first requirements was to have a black chorus.

To counter the stifling racism, black churches—including Antioch Baptist, Central Baptist, and Berea Presbyterian—often sponsored religious programs highlighting the works of both black and white composers. Local 197 of the American Federation of Musicians and the St. Louis Music Association, which was the local branch of the National Association of Negro Musicians, promoted black performing organizations and training. Simultaneously community groups also provided scholarships and summer choirs for boys and girls.

19.2 The Black Culture Industry and American Racism

Analyze the ways in which black artists used their diverse artistic talents and skills to support social justice struggles at home and abroad.

Black American artists confronted discrimination and exploitation in the culture industry. Most artists could not finance both the production and the dissemination of their creative work. Thus they were often exploited by the leaders of record companies, publishers, and the owners of radio stations and film studios. Nevertheless, resilient black artists against the backdrop of the Great Depression and the World War II calamity shaped a consciousness that would generate an eruption of black consciousness in the 1950s.

Notably, the world-renowned musical genius Paul Robeson not only won acclaim as a great performing artist, but he became a leading black internationalist and an outspoken critic of colonialism and racism. Robeson befriended and supported African freedom fighters. Many creative artists and political leaders supported Kwame Nkrumah in Ghana, Jomo Kenyatta in Kenya, and Dr. Nnamdi Azikiwe of Nigeria. In 1945, the NAACP awarded Robeson its prestigious Spingarn Medal. The Federal Bureau of Investigation had been monitoring him for years by the time he made his infamous remarks at the end of the 1949 World Peace Conference in Paris. There, he called it "unthinkable" that African Americans would fight in a war against the Soviet Union, given the difference between how the American and Soviet societies treated blacks. The State Department repealed his passport and barred him from international travel. Record companies, television producers, and movie executives blackballed him. He refused to answer whether or not he was a Communist Party member, refused to name any members he knew, refused to retract his praise for the Soviet Union. Rather, he critiqued American racial injustice. Robeson never recovered his stature as a performer. In 1956, the House Committee on Un-American Activities summoned him to testify. He refused. The U.S. State Department revoked his passport because of his anticolonialism and his support for radical social and economic reform and African liberation.

Singer and actor Paul Robeson (1898–1976) as "Othello" in 1943. A man of astonishing magnetism and creative power, Paul Robeson became, in 1943, the first black actor to play "Othello" in the United States. He was fluent in many languages, produced over 300 recordings of spiritual and folk music gathered from around the world, and appeared in 11 motion pictures. An unflinching proponent of freedom from racism and want, Robeson received the NAACP's Spingarn Medal in 1945.

Often, the political content of black art provoked heated debates. Many black Americans insisted that music, the visual and performing arts, literature, and oratory serve both a political function and an aesthetic purpose. They expected black artists not only to create beauty but also to use their art to promote freedom across the black diaspora and to forge cultural and political linkages with all oppressed peoples. African-American artists and intellectuals joined with people throughout the African Diaspora to support Ethiopian resistance to Italian aggression in 1935. To be sure, the disparate reasons for white involvement in the marketing and use of black culture created tension among black artists. Although many white Americans had long appreciated black culture, some had also appropriated it for their own profit.

19.3 Black Music Culture: From Swing to Bebop

Distinguish the differences between the music genres or styles of big band, bebop, and swing.

The very creativity that white Americans valued, enjoyed, and often appropriated, ironically, reflected the artists' ability to project intellectual and emotional autonomy. Black artists had to juxtapose the requirements of earning a living with the need to remain true to their art. Musicians continuously had to refine, expand, and perfect their art not only for themselves and each other but also for a white-dominated marketplace. In many respects black music is synonymous with black culture; the experience of segregation or self-imposed separation often made possible the creation of new cultural expressions. Music encapsulates and reflects the core values and underlying tensions and anxieties in black communities. In black music we witness cultural producers developing strategies of resistance to white domination.

The Great Depression wrought havoc on the vibrant black culture industry of the 1920s. Record sales plummeted. In 1932 sales were only a sixth of those in 1927. Louis Armstrong had enjoyed a golden age of creativity during the 1920s. White-owned record companies had created separate black music labels and sold tens of thousands of records to southern migrants moving to the big cities. New bands sprouted up from Kansas City to Chicago; Memphis to Detroit; and Washington, D.C., to New York. On the West Coast, Los Angeles, San Francisco, and Seattle became centers for black music enthusiasts and an array of black performers. Territorial (traveling) bands took the music to the outposts of America. Big bands under Fletcher Henderson, Duke Ellington, Count Basie, and Cab Calloway played in white urban dance halls and ballrooms, many of which only admitted black people as staff.

Many black musicians felt they had to go to New York in order to establish a reputation. Still, after entertaining affluent white people or providing backup music for the Apollo Theater in Harlem, black musicians discarded their masks of docility and deference and made a different sound in their own space and on their own time in late-night jam sessions. In Harlem's small clubs, such as Monroe's Uptown House and Minton's Playhouse a few blocks from the Apollo, a new kind of jazz was born.

The big band swing style that became popular in the 1930s transformed white American culture. Swing emerged as white bands reduced the music of the more innovative black bandleaders to a broadly appealing formula based on a swinging 4/4 beat, well-blended saxophone sections, and pleasant vocals. The big swing bands of the 1930s played written, arranged music. Swing's popularity helped boost the careers of

Profile

Charlie Parker

Charlie Parker was one of the most innovative and influential of all American musicians. With his inspired saxophone playing, his technical mastery of his instrument, and his melodic, rhythmic, and harmonic innovations, he was an architect of modern jazz, or "bebop." His playing challenged his contemporaries, influenced generations of jazz musicians, and helped transform jazz from entertainment into one of America's most respected art forms. But Parker was also troubled by drug addiction, mental instability, and tumultuous relationships.

Charles Parker, Jr. was born on August 29, 1920, in Kansas City, Kansas. In 1927 his family moved across the state line to Kansas City, Missouri. He had little formal musical instruction. But Kansas City had a dynamic jazz scene. Pianist and composer Mary Lou Williams remembered the freewheeling atmosphere: "Now, at this time, which was still Prohibition . . . [m]ost of the night spots were run by politicians and hoodlums, and the town was wide open for drinking, gambling, and pretty much every form of vice. Naturally, work was plentiful for musicians though some of the employers were tough people." Young Parker became a fixture in the local clubs, where he also acquired a heroin habit that plagued him for the rest of his life.

In 1939, Parker left Kansas City for New York, then the jazz capital of the country. There Parker began to sit in, or "jam," at Harlem nightclubs. In 1942 he was back in Kansas City playing in Jay McShann's popular "territory band," which traveled from Lincoln, Nebraska, to New Orleans. During this time he acquired the nickname "Bird."

Parker left the McShann band in 1942 to join pianist Earl Hines's band in New York. In March and April 1943, all the following musicians were in the band with Parker: "Little" Benny Harris, Bennie Green, Wardell Gray, and vocalists Billy Eckstine and Sarah Vaughan. This collection of talent reflected a musical environment that fostered innovation. New ideas spread from musician to musician and in late-night jam sessions. It was from the close collaboration between Parker and Dizzy Gillespie in this period that bebop emerged.

Charlie Parker joined the first bebop big band, formed by Billy Eckstine in 1944. Eckstine's friend and valet, Bob Redcross, remembers a night that year when the band was at its best: "Everybody was on. [Art] Blakey was on; John [Gillespie] was on; Bird was on; Bidd [Johnson] was on; everybody. Man, they upset this place. They had people screaming and hollering."

In 1944 a recording of Parker's composition, "Red Cross," the first to be copyrighted in his name, was released on the Savoy label.

Parker and Gillespie first recorded together commercially in 1945. Gillespie formed his first bebop big band and took it on a tour of the South as part of the "Hepsations-1945" package tour. Also in 1945, Parker led an expanded group at the Spotlite club that included trumpeter Miles Davis, tenor saxophonist Dexter Gordon, bassist Leonard Gaskin, and drummer Stan Levey. During a disastrous trip to California, Parker had a nervous breakdown and spent months at Camarillo State Hospital.

In 1947, when Parker returned to New York, he formed his "classic" quintet, with trumpeter Miles Davis, drummer Max Roach, pianist Duke Jordan, and Tommy Potter on bass. The recordings this quintet produced, four sides on the Savoy label, are the foundation on which much of Parker's reputation rests.

In 1949, in a fitting tribute to Parker's genius by his contemporaries, a New York nightclub, Birdland, was named for him. Charlie Parker died in New York on March 12, 1955.

black and white bandleaders, but it also led to a creative slump that disheartened many younger black musicians. Tired of swing's predictability, they began improvising in the jazz clubs, sharpening their reflexes, ears, and minds.

In the 1940s at least seven musicians—Charlie Parker, Dizzy Gillespie, Thelonious Monk, Bud Powell, Kenny Clarke, Max Roach, and Ray Brown—were among the men most responsible for revolutionizing jazz, ushering in a new sound and dimension that became known, scornfully at first, as *bebop*. Bebop featured complex rhythms and harmonies and highlighted improvisation. Gillespie (1917–1993) said that Kansas City–born Charlie "Yardbird" and then just "Bird" Parker (1920–1955) created a unique style that made it possible for many different horns to blend in perfect pitch and sound like one.

White America resisted bebop. The nation was about to enter World War II and was too preoccupied to switch from the big band swing ballroom dancing music to bebop. Moreover, because jazzmen played in intimate clubs too small for big bands, they had more freedom from the expectations of white society. Bebop music was of such enduring quality, however, that it shaped American popular culture and style for two generations. Before long, bebop became the principal musical language of jazz musicians around the world.

Bebop was a way of life and had its own attendant styles whose nuances depended on class status and, perhaps, age. Gillespie helped create one side of bebop style in dress, language, and demeanor. He began to wear dark glasses on stage to reduce the glare after he had cataract surgery. He grew a goatee because shaving irritated his bottom lip. He wore pegged pants, jackets with wide lapels, and a beret when men were still wearing hats with brims. Other bebop musicians emulated and modified this attire. For example, they wore cashmere jackets without lapels. Beboppers also created their own slang, hip Black English that mingled colorful and obscene language. They also engaged in a freewheeling lifestyle that often included love across the color line. But there was a downside to bebop. Some musicians became drug addicts, engaged in parasitical relationships with women, and spent their money recklessly.

Black working-class young men adopted their own style of talking and hip dressing, reflected in their zoot suits and conked hair. Zoot suits featured high-waisted, baggy, pegged pants and long draped coats. A 16-year-old Malcolm Little (who later took the name Malcolm X) plunged into hipster culture when he moved to Boston. His first zoot suit was sky blue with a matching hat, gold watch chain, and monogrammed belt. To savor this new identity, he recalled, "I took three of those twenty-five cent sepia-toned, while-you-wait pictures of myself, posed the way 'hipsters' wearing their zoots would 'cool it'—hat dangled, knees drawn close together, feet wide apart, both index fingers jabbed toward the floor." He then mastered the lindy hop dance style and took to the floor of the Roseland Ballroom, where he shed his life as an unskilled wageworker and became freer and more empowered. He recalled the ballroom's patrons' escape from their dreary lives: "They'd jam pack that ballroom, the black girls in way out silk and satin dresses and shoes, their hair done in all kinds of styles, the men sharp in their zoot suits and crazy conks, and everybody grinning and greased and gassed."

Bebop was the dominant black music of the World War II decade. After the war, returning veterans preferred a slower-paced music, simple love songs, and melodies. This contributed to bebop's waning and led to more transformations. All artistic innovation extracts a high price. Bebop was no exception. Many of the most talented musicians—like Billie Holiday, discussed later in this chapter—paid that price in lives decimated by drugs, poverty, sickness, and broken relationships. Few black musicians received the respect, recognition, and financial rewards from white America that their creativity warranted. Ultimately, white Americans wanted the art but not the artists.

19.4 Popular Culture for the Masses: Comic Strips, Radio, and Movies

Analyze the ways in which popular presentations of African Americans in popular culture may have reinforced negative stereotypes during the Great Depression era.

The masses of African Americans participated in more accessible black popular culture outlets. Everyone needed relief from the bleakness and despair of the Depression years. Comic strips, radio programs, and movies were affordable forms of artistic creativity that allowed momentary escape. Newspapers were widely shared, and families gathered around the radio for nightly programs of comedy and music. For black city dwellers, the movies offered escape from poverty and want.

19.4.1 The Comics

African Americans quickly noted the difference between the fun that black people made of each other and the mockery white people made of them. These differences were reflected in tone, intent, and sympathetic versus derisive laughter. During the Depression, comic strips in newspapers and comic books featuring superheroes diverted millions of Americans. Comic strips in black newspapers entertained but also affirmed the values and ideals of black people. They portrayed humorous situations and tales of intrigue and action.

The *Philadelphia Independent*, a black paper, ran a serial in the 1930s called "The Jones Family." This strip, drawn by an editorial cartoonist named Branford, was an example of the dual function of entertaining and affirming. The strip centered on the young Jones boy's search for the "good life" of money, success, love, and a happy marriage. But at every turn he confronts a harsh reality. Unable to get a job because of the Depression, he becomes an outlaw and narrowly escapes jail. Constantly "on the run" from oppression, his only consolations are his family and his beautiful, ever-faithful girlfriend.

"The Jones Family" illuminates the gray areas that most African Americans, regardless of their class, faced when attempting to live rational, coherent lives in the northern cities. Although they cherished middle-class values, they often had to live with poverty, crime, and racial oppression. The black comic strips sought to provide entertaining, nonjudgmental prescriptions and blueprints for middle-class life, but to more cynical and alienated black people they seemed to be promoting unattainable values and lifestyles.

19.4.2 Radio and Jazz Musicians and Technological Change

Although there were individual exceptions, African-American jazz musicians embraced the commercial and technological developments that revolutionized the music industry in the 1920s. The phonograph allowed for wide distribution of the music they created, just as the recording studios served as incubators for their creative innovations. By the end of the 1920s, black musicians had embraced electrical recording, and in the 1930s they learned to appreciate microphone amplification—a product of radio technology— which allowed for the dominating rhythmic pulse of electric guitars and basses that would radically change black popular music. By the 1930s jazz musicians were making records that replicated live performances more closely than ever before. Radio and improved record-making helped spread black music and ensured its survival.

During the 1930s black musicians, including Duke Ellington, Fats Waller, and Art Tatum, starred in regular radio programs. Many black musicians acquired their first lucrative jobs in radio as full-time staff musicians. Some earned higher salaries

Profile
Duke Ellington

Arguably the most celebrated and best known, and most elegant, jazz musician in America and abroad, Duke Ellington, called his music "America's Music." During the course of a fifty-year career he composed over 3,000 songs and played over 20,000 performances. Edward Kennedy "Duke" Ellington was born on April 29, 1899, in Washington, D.C., to James Edward (a blueprint-maker who occasionally worked as a butler at the White House) and Daisy Ellington. (His father was with him at the White House in 1969 when President Richard Nixon presented to his son the Medal of Freedom, the nation's highest

civilian award. He died on May 24, 1974, in Washington, D.C.) He studied at the Pratt Institute in Brooklyn, New York, in 1927 and landed a job at the Cotton Club and remained there until 1932. By 1935 the Swing Era had arrived and coincided with the institutionalization of the mass media of records, radio, and motion pictures. It was the collaboration between Ellington and a Jewish music publisher, Irving Mills, who paid him to play his songs, that ignited his career. Mills devised a three-prong model that involved using electronic media, radio, to secure national exposure that would stimulate interest and build reputation. The second step involved working territorial tours at home. After completing the home tours the goal was to secure extended engagements abroad. This carefully structured three-prong career process was later applied to shape the career of Cab Calloway and other jazz performers. Bands cherished a recording label in order to enhance their reputation and increase booking prices.

A present-day jazz great, Winton Marsalis, described Ellington's music as being "beyond category." Among his most memorable songs are: "It Don't Mean a Thing If It Ain't Got That Swing," "Sophisticated Lady," and "Mood Indigo." He confided that the sources of his inspiration were the men in his orchestras, and "my race." He confided, "I try to catch the character and mood and feeling of my people." Ellington infused his extended jazz suites with resonance and purpose.

Today Duke Ellington is widely remembered as having been the most brilliant jazz composer in the twentieth century.

SOURCE: Thomas J. Hennessey, *From Jazz to Swing: African American Jazz Musicians and Their Music, 1890–1935* (Detroit, MI: Wayne State University, 1994), 122–39.

than writers, announcers, and white performers. Black musicians succeeded in the radio medium because they were heard and not visible. It was the mastery of their instruments that won audience approval. Perhaps most important, black radio staff musicians could communicate to larger audiences than those who played in clubs and on the traveling circuits. Thus, they enhanced the appeal of their music for a much wider audience.

19.4.3 Radio and Black Disc Jockeys

Chicago was a pioneering center both for recording and performing music. As black music became a commodity, influential black disc jockeys like Al Benson (Arthur B. Leaner was his real name) appeared on the radio and attracted a large following in "Bronzeville." Benson, a migrant from Mississippi, was as skilled a businessman as he was a cultural impresario. He attracted followers drawn by his "black everyman's style." By 1948, he was hosting shows on three radio stations. Readers of the *Defender* voted him the "Mayor of Bronzeville." A determined entrepreneur, Benson arranged "first play rights" with record producers and distributors, catapulting Chicago into a major launch site for new releases. Diverse artists, including bluesman Muddy Waters and gospel singer Mahalia Jackson, benefited from the airplay. Historian Adam Green concludes that because of the power and machinations of black disc jockeys, "black popular music would never again face the disastrous conditions of destitution and near-erasure it faced during the depression."

In the post-Depression and premodern civil rights era, black disc jockeys played the blues, gospel, and jazz and attracted listeners with their sharp banter and fast, smooth-talking style. The number of black disc jockeys rose from 16 in 1946 to over 500 by 1955. They used their radio shows not only to entertain and to sell records but also to promote the careers of black musicians. As awareness of the buying power of black consumers sank in, both white- and black-owned businesses eagerly sponsored black-appeal radio programs. Black radio stations thus became platforms for independent black music and were essential to the building of black community businesses. Black radio communicated the news, shared announcements, and molded urban black consciousness. Following Benson's lead, a young apprentice, Don Cornelius, would, decades later, launch a legendary music and dance show, *Soul Train*, on WCIU-TV (August 17, 1970) in Chicago. Cornelius explained how his start in radio inspired him: "It was with the advent of black radio that I thought black people would watch music television programs oriented toward themselves." *Soul Train* successfully combined images of blackness with technical proficiency and production control by black people in the white-dominated entertainment industry.

19.4.4 Radio and Race

During the Depression, black actors in radio and film were frequently marginalized, exploited, or excluded. Commercial radio delivered an audience of white consumers to white advertisers, and it denied black people jobs as announcers, journalists, or technicians. White entertainers schooled in blackface minstrelsy portrayed black radio characters. The major labor unions in the entertainment side of the radio industry restricted membership to white people. Still—with its offerings of vaudeville, big bands, drama, and comedy—radio provided relief from the miseries of the Depression to all Americans, black as well as white.

The most popular comedy radio program in the early 1930s—a precursor to the soap operas and sitcoms that were to become staples of radio and television programming—was *The Amos 'n' Andy Show*. The inauguration of this program was a significant moment in radio history. Two white performers, Charles Correll and Freeman Gosden, not only wrote and performed scripts laced with oxymorons and malapropisms but they also played the title roles. Skillful showmen, Correll and Gosden ingratiated themselves in Chicago's black community, appearing at parades and posing with black children. The *Chicago Defender* endorsed them, and they received standing ovations at the Regal Theater in Chicago's black South Side. Part of the amusement they generated derived from their mispronounced words, garbled grammar, and their show's minstrel ambience. Each episode highlighted an improbable situation involving the black cab driver (Amos) and his gullible overweight friend (Andy). Other characters included the scheming con artist Kingfish, his overbearing wife Sapphire, and his domineering mother-in-law, Mama. On radio, Gosden and Correll furnished voices for the members of Amos and Andy's fraternal lodge and for an array of other characters. The characters and their humor reinforced unflattering racial and gender stereotypes, but the show was not mean-spirited. Some of the characters conducted themselves with dignity, modeling such positive values as marital fidelity, strong families, hard work, and economic independence. An *Amos 'n' Andy* movie, *Check and Double Check*— released in 1930 when hard times made black entertainers grateful for any employment they could get—featured music by Duke Ellington's orchestra. The movie introduced Ellington to a wider audience of affluent white people and enhanced his reputation.

Black audiences recognized the minstrel stereotyping in *Amos 'n' Andy*, yet many of them still enjoyed the show. A vocal component of the ever more sophisticated and urbanized black population, however, complained that this show and other radio programs reinforced negative images—of black women as bossy Sapphires or Mammies and black men as childish clowns—in the nation's consciousness. Educator and activist Nannie Helen Burroughs considered the show demeaning. Robert L. Vann, editor of the *Pittsburgh Courier*, argued that it exploited African Americans for white commercial gain. Vann sponsored a petition to the Federal Communications Commission to ban the show, but his efforts were futile. By the 1940s, *The Amos 'n' Andy Show* was less popular. In the early 1950s, it had a brief life as a television series, this time with black actors. Alvin Childress, an experienced stage actor and director, became Amos, and Spencer Williams, Jr., who had written, directed, and starred in several independent all-black movies, played Andy. Tim Moore assumed the role of the Kingfish of the Mystic Knights of the Sea Lodge. Johnny Lee portrayed the shyster lawyer, Algonquin J. Calhoun.

The show never demonstrated how the characters' race affected their lives or the psychological or economic costs of racism. It taught white America to laugh at striving black men and women. The best-known and most successful African-American actor on network radio in the late 1930s was Eddie Anderson, who played Jack Benny's sidekick Rochester in NBC's *The Jack Benny Show*. Like the characters in *Amos 'n' Andy*, Rochester reinforced negative racial stereotypes. Anderson's rationalization of his role suggests his discomfort with it:

> I don't see why certain characters are called stereotypes. The Negro characters being presented are not labeling the Negro race any more than "Luigi" is labeling the Italian people as a whole. The same goes for "Beulah," who is not playing the part of thousands of Negroes, but only the part of one person, "Beulah." They're not saying here is the portrait of the Negro, but here is "Beulah."

Richard Durham (1917–1984) migrated to Chicago with his family in the 1920s. From 1948 to 1950 his unique radio series *Destination Freedom* educated the citizens of Bronzeville about the long black struggle for civil rights.

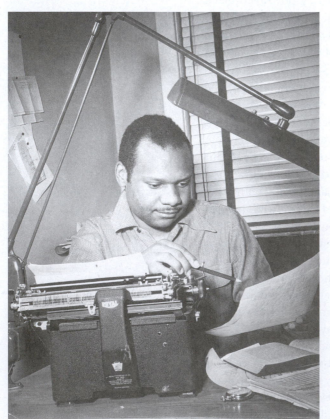

19.4.5 Radio and *Destination Freedom*

Between 1948 and 1950, black writers and actors in Chicago produced a unique local radio program about African-American politics, culture, and history for northern urban audiences (a form of "narrowcasting"). According to historian Barbara Diane Savage, this program, called *Destination Freedom*, "provide[d] a glimpse of the politically creative ways African Americans could use the medium of radio when they had freer rein over it. . . . This kind of broadcast was possible because of black migration and the formation of an urban market of working-class and middle-class African Americans." She concluded that *Destination Freedom*, conceived and written by black journalist and radio scriptwriter Richard Durham (a migrant born in Mississippi), was "by far the single most effective use of radio to teach black history and to make political arguments on behalf of the black quest for freedom." Durham stated his vision of this program with its positive depiction of black lives:

> Somewhere in this ocean of Negro life, with its cross-current and under-currents, lies the very soul of America. . . . It lies there because the real-life story of a single Negro in Alabama walking into a voting booth across a Ku Klux Klan line has more drama and world implications than all the stereotypes Hollywood or radio can turn out in a thousand years.

While Durham enjoyed enormous latitude in developing biographical profiles of black men and women, his power was not absolute. For example, he was not allowed to air a profile of Paul Robeson. In 1950, station WMAQ, despite the success of the program, discontinued it, fearful of the threat of rising anticommunist conservatism. Durham moved on to serve in the 1960s as editor of Elijah Muhammad's publication *Muhammad Speaks*, and helped Muhammad Ali write his 1977 biography, *The Greatest*.

19.4.6 A Black Filmmaker: Oscar Micheaux

One of the most enterprising black filmmakers, Oscar Micheaux (1884–1951), made films aimed primarily at the black public. White Hollywood directors and producers often ignored or insulted black people. Unlike the dominant Hollywood stereotypes, the black men and women in Micheaux's films were often educated, cultured, and prosperous. Micheaux endowed black Americans with cinematic voice and subjectivity. His films featured middle-class or identity issues such as "passing for white."

Micheaux produced more than 30 feature films between 1919 and 1948. In 1932, he released *The Exile*, the first sound motion picture to be made by, with, and for black Americans. The following year he produced *Veiled Aristocrats*, about passing for white among Chicago's black professional class. The characters in the film are considered "aristocrats" because they are descended from the white gentry of the Old South and Europe. They are "veiled" because of their color. The plot turns on the revelation that the wealthy "white" heroine is actually "colored," which enables her to marry the talented mulatto hero.

Micheaux tried to transform Hollywood without changing it, much as members of the black bourgeoisie struggled to be included in American society. His films captured the dilemma of black double-consciousness. As W. E. B. Du Bois put it, black people always experienced that "peculiar sensation," that "sense of always looking at one's self through the eyes of others, of measuring one's soul by the tape of a world that looks on in amused contempt and pity." Black culture existed within and was shaped by American culture, while simultaneously transforming it. To the degree that black Americans had been assimilated, white American culture was also their culture.

Oscar Micheaux (1884–1951) was born on a farm in Metropolis, Illinois. He became the greatest black filmmaker of his time. He wrote articles for the *Chicago Defender* and a thinly veiled autobiography, *The Conquest: The Story of a Negro Pioneer*, and made dozens of sophisticated films that captured the complexity of African-American life and culture.

19.4.7 Black Hollywood: Race and Gender

In the 1930s and 1940s—after the introduction of sound in motion pictures—black and white producers began to make what were known as **race films** for African-American audiences. To succeed commercially, African-American filmmakers had to disguise their dissent or appeal to an exclusively black audience. Except for these race films, white film executives, since the beginning of the film industry, had cast black men and women in roles designed to comfort, reassure, and entertain white audiences. Continuing this trend, African Americans in Hollywood movies of the 1930s were usually cast in servile roles and were often portrayed as buffoons. For example, the first black actor to receive major billing in American films, Stepin Fetchit (1902–1985, born Lincoln Theodore Monroe Perry), purportedly earned $2 million in 10 years playing a servile, dim-witted, slow-moving character.

Black performers appeared as servants in many other box-office successes during the Depression era. Among them were Gertrude Howard and Libby Taylor, who played servants to Mae West's characters in *I'm No Angel* (1933) and *Belle of the Nineties* (1934). In *Imitation of Life* (1934), Louise Beavers played a black servant whose light-skinned daughter, played by Fredi Washington, tried to pass for white. The black tap dancer and

race films

Movies often made by and for African-American audiences in the 1930s and 1940s.

stage performer Bill "Bojangles" Robinson was featured in four popular films—*The Little Colonel* (1935), *The Littlest Rebel* (1935), *Just Around the Corner* (1938), and *Rebecca of Sunnybrook Farm* (1938)—as a servant to white child star Shirley Temple.

The film that most firmly cemented the role of black Americans as servants in the American consciousness was *Gone with the Wind* (1939). Hattie McDaniel and Butterfly McQueen were the black "stars" in this epic adaptation of Margaret Mitchell's romantic salute to the Old South. McDaniel had played servant or "Mammy" roles throughout the 1930s. The image of Mammy, the headscarf-wearing, obese, dutiful black woman who preferred nurturing white families to caring for her own children, appealed to white America. But in *Gone with the Wind*, McDaniel gave the performance of a lifetime and in 1940 became the first African American to win an Oscar. Many in the black community criticized her for playing "female Tom" roles. McDaniel retorted she would rather play a maid and earn $700 a week than *be* one and earn $7 a week. In time, however, McDaniel and other black actors—dismayed by their relegation to demeaning roles—formed the **Fair Play Committee** to lobby the white-dominated movie industry for more substantial roles, to get rid of dialect speech, and to ban the term *nigger* from the screen. But in the *Beulah* radio show, which premiered in 1947, McDaniel again played a wise but subservient maid who provides the family that employs her with advice, guidance, and direction.

Fair Play Committee
Organization formed to promote black actors in the movie industry and improve the image of blacks in film.

Eventually, during and after World War II, Hollywood developed more sophisticated race-directed movies. Of particular significance was the positive, even romanticized, portrayal of black Americans in a movie the War Department financed to gain support among African Americans for the U.S. role in World War II. *The Negro Soldier*, directed by Frank Capra in 1944, played to vast audiences of enthusiastic black people. But even before *The Negro Soldier*, some motion pictures had depicted African Americans positively. Paul Robeson made two movies, *The Emperor Jones* (1933) and *Show Boat* (1936), in which he attempted to change how black men and women were represented on screen. He proclaimed in 1934, "In my music, my plays, my films I want to carry always this central idea: to be African. Multitudes of men have died for less worthy ideals; it is even more eminently worth living for." Robeson's films, however, were not box-office successes, and he left the United States for Europe. There his commitment to communism and leftist politics made him a target of the anticommunist hysteria that gripped the United States as the Cold War took hold in the late 1940s (see Chapter 20).

19.5 The Black Chicago Renaissance

Describe the similarities and delineate the differences between key authors, artists, musicians, and performers who were prominent in the Black Chicago Renaissance.

Black culture flourished during the 1930s and 1940s, decades otherwise noted for economic depression and global warfare. African-American musicians thrived in cities as far from Harlem as Kansas City (Missouri), Dallas, Denver, and Oklahoma City. They created a southwestern style of jazz with a blues inflection. Jazz pianist Mary Lou Williams (1910–1981) worked in Kansas City during the 1930s. She recalled, "I found Kansas City to be a heavenly city—music everywhere in the Negro section of town, and fifty or more cabarets rocking on Twelfth and Eighteenth Streets." The southwestern musical style rivaled the West Coast jazz scene (which often included black and Latino musicians) that radiated from Los Angeles to Portland, Seattle, San Francisco, and Oakland. It even reached as far as Honolulu and found patrons in such Asian cities as Yokohama in Japan, Shanghai and Hong Kong on the coast of China, and Manila in the Philippines.

In many respects, however, Black Chicago became the center of black culture innovation and expressivity during the 1930s and 1940s. In contrast to some of the artists of the "Harlem Renaissance," the leading writers in Chicago harbored no illusions that art would solve the problems caused by white supremacy and black subordination. The Chicago writers of the 1930s and 1940s emphasized the idea that black art had to combine aesthetics and function. It had to be art that served the cause of black freedom.

Arna Bontemps (1902–1973) was to the Black **Chicago Renaissance** what Alain Locke had been to the Harlem Renaissance. "The Depression," Bontemps asserted,

> put an end to the dream world of renaissance Harlem and scattered the band of poets and painters, sculptors, scholars and singers who had in six exciting years made a generation of Americans aware of unnoticed and hitherto unregarded creative talents among Negroes. . . . What they did not dream was that a second awakening, less gaudy but closer to realities, was already in prospect. . . . One way or the other, Harlem got its renaissance in the middle twenties, centering around the *Opportunity* contests and the Fifth Avenue Awards Dinners. . . . Ten years later Chicago reenacted it on WPA [Works Progress Administration] without finger bowls but with increased power.

Born in Louisiana, Bontemps migrated in 1935 from California to Chicago, where he met Richard Wright and joined the South Side Writers Group, which Wright founded in 1936. The group included poet Margaret Walker and playwright Theodore Ward. It offered criticism and moral support to black writers. Bontemps's association with the group influenced his own writing. After 1935 his novels and short stories reflected a restlessness and revolutionary spirit. In 1936 he published *Black Thunder* about the nineteenth-century slave conspiracy led by Gabriel, and in 1939 he published *Drums at Dusk* about the Haitian Revolution and Toussaint Louverture. Richard Wright's writings also celebrated resistance, but with more nuance. He published *Uncle Tom's Children* in 1938 and his masterpiece, *Native Son*, in 1940.

Among the artists who launched their careers on WPA funds were Margaret Walker and Willard Motley. Walker attracted attention when her collected poems, *For My People*, appeared in the Yale Series of Younger Poets. Willard Motley worked with a radio group while writing his novel *Knock on Any Door* (1947), which depicted the transformation of an Italian-American altar boy into a criminal headed for the electric chair. The novel invited comparisons with Wright's *Native Son*.

Before the 1930s, black intellectuals misjudged Chicago's potential to become a center of black culture. In the late 1920s, black social scientists Charles S. Johnson and E. Franklin Frazier expressed disdain for Black Chicago's artistic and intellectual prospects. Frazier proclaimed that "Chicago has no intelligentsia," and in 1923 Johnson asked rhetorically,

> Who can write of lilies and sunsets in the pungent shadows of the stockyards? . . . It is no dark secret why literary societies fail, [why] there are no art exhibits or libraries about, why periodicals presuming upon an I.Q. above the age of 12 are not read, why so little literature comes out of the city. No, the kingdom of the second ward [the black neighborhood] has no self-sustaining intelligentsia, and a miserably poor acquaintance with that of the world surrounding it.

Johnson did, however, admit one saving grace in Chicago's cultural wasteland: "It leads these colored United States in its musical aspirations with, perhaps, the best musical school in the race, as these go."

Johnson and Frazier were too harsh. Just as Chicago's industrial economy attracted working-class black people, it also nurtured artists who drew inspiration from and reflected this stratum of moving and striving, strolling and styling black people who wanted to transgress class and geographical lines. These working-class people aspired to enjoy the middle-class life of accomplishment and consumption. A critical pulse point on Chicago's South Side came to be known as Bronzeville. It measured and reflected

Chicago Renaissance
A cultural explosion featuring innovative artists whose work reimagined black identity in Chicago during the 1930s and 1940s.

Voices

Margaret Walker on Black Culture

In 1942 Margaret Walker (1915–1998) published For My People, *the most important collection of poetry written by a participant in the Black Chicago Renaissance before Gwendolyn Brooks's* A Street in Bronzeville *(1945). In a 1992 collection of her essays, Walker reflected on the meaning and significance of black culture:*

Black culture has two main streams: a sociological stream . . . and an artistic stream. . . . In this artistic stream black culture has five branches. These are language, religion, art, music, and literature. . . .

Black music is perhaps the most acceptable of our black culture. The modern world is willing to accept the unique character of African rhythms and the language of the drum. White America, in general, reluctantly admits that black American music is the American music and most indigenous to our culture. In every category or classification of music, moreover, Black America has achieved monumentally. With a broad base of folk music— spirituals and gospel music, seculars (blues, work songs, prison hollers)—individuals have risen in notable achievement in classical, popular, and various forms of jazz. From Black Patti to Marian Anderson and Leontyne Price, the great black American singer has gained worldwide eminence. Roland Hayes, William Warfield, Todd Duncan, the late Ellabelle Davis, Dorothy Maynor, and Mattiwilda Dobbs are notable black artists known the world over. Our blues singers like Bessie Smith, Ma Rainey, and B. B. King; folk singers like Leadbelly, and the greats like Louis Armstrong, Jimmie Lunceford, and Count Basie; great composers like Scott Joplin, Eubie Blake, Charlie Parker, and the incomparable Duke Ellington are significant contributors to the modern world and all represent the undeniable genius of the black American musician.

Individual achievement, while part of our general cultural picture, is not all. It is in language and religion that Black Americans as a group have made a significant contribution to the national fiber of American life and to the modern world.

As spiritual creatures we have shown through unmerited suffering that we have a sense of humanity that can enrich the moral fiber and contribute to a new world ethos. Our black culture is aware of human needs and human values. Handicapped as we have been by a racist system of dehumanizing slavery and segregation, our American history of nearly five hundred years reveals that our cultural and spiritual gifts brought from our African past are still intact. It is not only that we are singers and dancers, poets and prophets, great athletes and perceptive politicians—but we are also a body of charismatic and numinous people yet capable of cultic fire as seen in our black churches and still creative enough in intellect to signal the leap forward into a new and humanistic age. We are the authors of the new paradigm. . . .

How then has black culture been disseminated and kept alive? Black culture has survived in the black institutions of Black America. In the black family, the Black Church, the black school, the black press, the black nation, and the black world. This is where our black culture has survived and thrived. This is where it must continue to grow. The ground of common humanity is not yet a reality in the modern world but when it comes as it must in the twenty-first century, Black Africa and black humanity must be as always the foundation on which it stands and from which it logically proceeds. One world of international brotherhood does not negate the nationalism of black people. It only enforces and re-enforces our common humanity.

1. According to Walker, external factors either shaped and sustained or undermined the production of black culture. What are some of the central or recurring themes in black culture?

SOURCE: *On Being Female, Black, and Free/Essays by Margaret Walker, 1932–1992*, edited by Maryemma Graham. Jackson, University of Mississippi Press, 1997. Reprinted by permission.

the lives of ordinary working-class people. As Harlem had its 125th Street, Chicago had 35th and State Street and 47th and South Park (now Martin Luther King, Jr. Drive).

Chicago was heir to the Harlem Renaissance. In 1930 Langston Hughes published *Not Without Laughter*, the first major novel about the black experience in Chicago. Hughes moved to the city himself in 1941 and wrote for the *Chicago Defender*. The city epitomized urban industrial America. As the northern terminus of the Illinois Central Railroad, it had long attracted displaced agricultural workers from the southern cotton fields. By 1930 it had a black population of 233,903. The migrants arrived eager to absorb Chicago's hard-driving blues and jazz culture.

During the 1920s a discernible class structure among African Americans emerged in Chicago, fueled in part by the new migrants. These men and women expanded the consumer base and gave rise to a cadre of educated professionals and entrepreneurs who developed an appreciation for the arts. The *Black Metropolis*, as social scientists St. Clair Drake and Horace R. Cayton designated Chicago's South Side, became a black city within a city. Black businesses, such as banks and insurance companies, formed the financial foundation. Entrepreneur Walter L. Lee started Your Cab Company and put on the streets each day a half dozen chauffeur-uniformed drivers of vehicles. In the late 1940s, John Johnson would launch a publishing empire with such magazines as *Negro Digest*, *Jet*, and *Ebony*. These businesses depended less on white patronage than on black support. It was in their best interest to support the arts and provide venues for performances.

Music was the primary inspiration for the creativity of black cultural movements in America. Avant-garde developments in black music preceded black cultural activity in the visual arts, poetry, drama, dance, literature, film, and sports. Cultural creativity was a potent force for raising consciousness and stirring resentment against oppressive living conditions and economic exploitation in different locations in America.

Within the South Side of Chicago, black musical giants—such as trumpeter Louis Armstrong (1898–1971) and his wife, Lillian Hardin Armstrong (1898–1971), a well-known and respected classically trained pianist—nurtured a distinct jazz culture. "Lil" Armstrong was born in Memphis, Tennessee, and received formal music training at Fisk University, the Chicago College of Music (earning a teaching certificate in 1924), and the New York College of Music (graduating in 1929). She led her own band and arranged, composed, and sang. She played with great performers and befriended Louis Armstrong when he arrived in Chicago. They were married in 1924. Lil Armstrong eventually encouraged her husband to leave King Oliver's Creole Jazz Band and join Fletcher Henderson in New York. The Armstrongs were divorced in 1938. She continued her recording career with Decca Records under the name Lil Hardin.

In his autobiography, *Music Is My Mistress*, Duke Ellington remarked,

> Chicago always sounded like the most glamorous place in the world to me when I heard the guys in Frank Holliday's poolroom talking about their travels. . . . They told very romantic tales about nightlife on the South Side. By the time I got there in 1930, it glittered even more . . . the Loop, the cabarets . . . city life, suburban life, luxurious neighborhoods—and the apparently broken-down neighborhoods where there were more good times than any place in the city.

At this point, Ellington was recording some of his best jazz, such as *Mood Indigo* (1930) and *Ko-Ko* (1940). Ellington's stay in Chicago left a powerful impression on vocalist Joe Williams, who made a special effort to change his class schedule in high school just so he could return home to turn on the radio to listen to Duke Ellington's band program, "Red Hot and Low Down."

The seeds that blossomed into full-bodied jazz culture were planted across America at the turn of the century. The most famous musicians, however, all went to or passed through Chicago. As the Chicago Jazz Age came into its own, "Pretty Baby" became the city's theme song. It was written by Tony Jackson, whom Jelly Roll Morton (the self-proclaimed "inventor of jazz") called "maybe the best entertainer the world has ever seen." The South Side, specifically along State Street between 31st and 35th, was the beating heart of the city's Jazz Age. Although Chicago did not replace New York as the major location for the aspiring jazz musician, it was the place you went to prove you had what it took to make a name for yourself.

Archibald Motley (1891–1981) captures in *Barbeque* (1934) the exuberance and vitality of nightlife in Chicago's Bronzeville. Motley was a major artistic talent during Chicago's Black Renaissance of the 1930s and 1940s.

19.5.1 Gospel in Chicago: Thomas A. Dorsey

The term *gospel* designates the traditional religious music of the black church. It was nurtured and flourished in Chicago's Holiness, Sanctified, Pentecostal, Baptist, and Methodist churches, in storefronts and in large edifices. Gospel music became the backbone of urban and contemporary black religion and is deeply entrenched in worship. The use of instruments—tambourines, drums, pianos, horns, guitars, and Hammond organs—distinguishes gospel from earlier spiritual and black folk music. During the 1930s and 1940s, it developed its own idioms and performance techniques. There were always tensions between genres of black music, and gospel provoked its share of critics. Members of the older generation deemed it too secular and insufficiently spiritual.

The doctrines of black "folk churches" encouraged free expression, group participation, spontaneous testimonies, prayers, witnessing, and music. Singers and choirs rarely performed the same songs in the same way more than once. The performer paid attention to the quality of the sound and to the careful manipulation of timbre, range, and shading. The style of the delivery used the whole body in synchronized movement. The mechanics of the delivery were designed to intensify the performance, giving it added textual variation and melodic improvisation. Performers expanded a melody by a variety of technical devices, including repetition, shouts, slides, slurs, moans, and grunts. The supporting piano and organ frequently engaged in call-and-response interplay.

Gospel singer Pearl Williams-Jones makes clear the distinction between black church music and music of the other churches: "The traditional liturgical forms of plain chant, chorales, and anthems do not fulfill the needs of traditional black folk religious worship and rituals."

In Chicago, Thomas A. Dorsey (1899–1993)—one of the leading composers of the blues since the mid-1920s—was most responsible for developing black urban gospel. Dorsey synthesized elements of the blues with religious hymns to create a gospel blues. His gospel pieces, performed with a ragtime-derived, boogie-woogie piano accompaniment, radiated an urban religious spirit. In 1930 Dorsey gained attention when Willie Mae Ford Smith (1904–1994) performed his "If You See My Savior, Tell Him That You Saw Me" at the National Baptist Convention in Chicago. Two years later, in 1932, Dorsey's place in musical history was assured when Theodore Frye, with Dorsey at the piano, performed in the Ebenezer Baptist Church in Chicago his now-classic gospel song "Take My Hand, Precious Lord." The song had a profound impact on gospel performers and their audiences. Dorsey's abundant works provided a foundation for shout worship formed in the 1930s and succeeding decades in the urban Protestant churches that transplanted black southerners.

One of the greatest gospel singers, Chicago-based Mahalia Jackson (1911–1972), promoted Dorsey's songs all over the country on the church circuit and at religious conventions between 1939 and 1944. Jackson once said of the music, "Gospel songs are the songs of hope. When you sing them you are delivered of your burden." During the Depression and World War II, gospel became big business.

Profile

Langston Hughes

Langston Hughes identified with poor and working-class black people. He used his poetry, prose, and plays to make the dignity and beauty of black people visible and known.

Hughes once referred to himself as "a literary sharecropper." Admirers called him a range of names—for starters, "Poet Laureate of the Negro People." During his career he produced 15 volumes of poetry, two collections of short stories, one novel, two volumes of autobiography—*The Big Sea* (1940) and *I Wonder as I Wander* (1956)—and 15 plays, along with librettos, scripts, essays, songs, translations, anthologies, children's stories, biographies and histories for the young, and two decades of weekly newspaper columns. He recorded the humor, wisdom, dialects, moods, and music of black people. One of the best examples of his social poetry was "The Negro Speaks of Rivers":

> *I've known rivers:*
> *I've known rivers ancient as the world and older*
> *than the flow of human blood in human veins.*
> *My soul has grown deep like the rivers.*
> *I bathed in the Euphrates when dawns were young.*
> *I built my hut near the Congo and it lulled me to sleep.*
> *I looked upon the Nile and raised the pyramids*
> *above it.*
> *I heard the singing of the Mississippi when Abe*
> *Lincoln went down to New Orleans, and I've seen its*
> *muddy bosom turn all golden in the sunset.*

> *I've known rivers:*
> *Ancient, dusky rivers.*
> *My soul has grown deep like the rivers.*

Hughes was born in Joplin, Missouri, in 1902 and was raised by his maternal grandmother, Mary Langston. His father, James Hughes, emigrated to Mexico, and his mother, Carrie Langston, remarried. Hughes became fascinated by black urban folk culture, which the Great Migration had transplanted from the rural South. He joined his mother in Cleveland in 1916, attended an integrated high school, and began to publish. Hughes felt ambivalent about his parents, who left him adrift, emotionally and financially. He dropped out of Columbia University in 1922, lived in Harlem, and traveled to Europe and Africa.

With the publication of *The Weary Blues* in 1926, his career took off. The language of the blues enchanted Hughes—its warmth, stoicism, incongruous humor, ironic laughter mixed with tears, and the "pain that was swallowed in a smile." In 1943 he introduced in his *Chicago Defender* column the character Jesse B. Semple, a racially conscious barfly philosopher—unlettered but wise. The college-educated, somewhat uptight narrator of the series interrogates Semple about black life, from love of women and watermelon to the fortunes of rich gospel singers and the whereabouts of leaders who hide from the black people they lead. At one point Semple observed,

> Not only am I half dead right now from pneumonia, but everything else has happened to me! I've been cut, shot, stabbed, run over, hit by a car, and tromped by a horse. I have also been robbed, fooled, deceived, two-timed, double-crossed, dealt seconds, and mightily near blackmailed—but I'm still here! . . . I have been fired, laid off, and last week given an indefinite vacation, also Jim Crowed, segregated, barred out, insulted, eliminated, called black, yellow, and red, locked in, locked out, locked up, and also left holding the bag.

In 1932 Hughes visited Moscow, where he felt comfortable and appreciated. He was impressed by the absence of Jim Crow segregation and discrimination and ignored Stalin's oppression and murders. But Hughes never joined the Communist Party. He was an artist who championed black folk culture as authentic American culture.

SOURCE: Poem from *Collected Poems* by Langston Hughes. ©1994 by the Estate of Langston Hughes. Used by permission of Alfred A. Knopf, a division of Random House, Inc.

One of America's premier dance artists, the internationally acclaimed Katherine Dunham (1909–2006) performed in the Boboli Gardens in Florence, Italy, in 1950. A talented choreographer, anthropologist, and writer, Dunham founded one of the first black dance companies. She was an outspoken critic of Jim Crow segregation.

19.5.2 Chicago in Dance and Song: Katherine Dunham and Billie Holiday

The influence of the WPA in Chicago was especially reflected in dance. Dance has always been an integral part of African-American life, and the dances of black people have always been important in the American theater. The first performances by black dancers given within and taken seriously by the concert dance world occurred in the 1930s. The first "Negro Dance Recital in America" was performed in 1931 by the New Negro Art Theater Dance Company, cofounded by Edna Buy and Hemsley Winfield. In that same year, Katherine Dunham (1909–2006) founded the Negro Dance Group in Chicago, which survived thanks to WPA support. As Dunham later recalled, "Black dancers were not allowed to take classes in studios in the '30s. I started a school because there was no place for blacks to study dance. I was the first to open the way for black dancers and I was the first to form a black dance company."

Dunham was unique. Trained in anthropology, she studied African-based ritual dance in the Caribbean. In 1938 her troupe stunned an audience with the sexual vitality of its performance of one of her works. When the company, renamed the Katherine Dunham Dance Company, performed in February 1940, audiences and critics were awed. The *New York Times* declared,

With the arrival of Katherine Dunham on the scene the development of a substantial Negro dance Art begins to look decidedly bright. Her performance with her group at the Windsor Theater may very well become a historic occasion, for certainly never before in all efforts of recent years to establish the Negro dance as a serious medium has there been so convincing and authoritative approach. . . . The potential greatness of the Negro dance lies in its discovery of its own roots and the crucial nursing of them into growth and flower. . . . It is because she has showed herself to have both the objective quality of the student and the natural instinct of the artist that she has done such a truly important job.

What kept audiences returning to Dunham dance performances, however, was the dancer's bold sensuality. A reviewer of *Tropical Revue*, for example, wrote that it was "likely to send thermometers soaring to the bursting point. . . . Tempestuous and torrid, raffish and revealing." The *New York Sun* marveled, "Shoulders, midsections and posteriors went round and round. Particularly when the cynosure was Miss Dunham, the vista was full of pulchritude."

Dunham explained her motivation:

I felt a new dance form was needed for black people to be able to appear in any theater in the world and be accepted and exciting. One of the prerequisites of art is uniqueness. Rather than taking years to build a classical ballet company for blacks, I decided to create a dance with an authentic base for black people. Through my anthropological work, I studied primitive and folk dances and created the Dunham dance from them.

Dunham's success in New York led to film offers. The producers of the all-black musical extravaganza *Cabin in the Sky* hired the dance troupe and gave the featured role of Georgia Brown to Dunham. The role gave Dunham, as the *Times* dance critic wrote, the chance "to sizzle." But it also undermined her seriousness, allowing white audiences to view her as the stereotypical sultry black sexpot.

Profile

Billie Holiday and "Strange Fruit"

"Strange Fruit," which Billie Holiday first performed in 1939, became her signature piece. It was written by a white school-teacher who went by the name of Lewis Allan (his real name was Abel Meeropol). While the lyrics capture the brutality of lynching, Holiday's incomparable vocal style and delivery gave the song its political, emotional, and cultural power and made it the anti-lynching anthem:

> *Southern trees bear a strange fruit,*
> *Blood on the leaves and blood at the root,*
> *Black body swinging in the Southern breeze,*
> *Strange fruit hanging from the poplar trees.*
> *Pastoral scene of the gallant South,*
> *The bulging eyes and the twisted mouth,*
> *Scent of magnolia sweet and fresh,*
> *And the sudden smell of burning flesh!*
> *Here is a fruit for the crows to pluck*
> *For the rain to gather, for the wind to suck,*
> *For the sun to rot, for a tree to drop.*
> *Here is a strange and bitter crop.*

"Every time she sang that song," recalled Barney Josephson, a New York nightclub owner, "it was unforgetta-ble. . . . I made her do it as her last number. . . . When she sang 'Strange Fruit' she never moved. Her hands were down. She didn't even touch the mike. With the little light on her face. The tears never interfered with her voice, but the tears would come and just knock everybody in that house out."

Billie Holiday was born Eleanora Fagan in Philadelphia, Pennsylvania, on April 7, 1915, to teenagers Sadie Fagan and Clarence Holiday. She grew up in Baltimore and became argu-ably the greatest jazz singer ever recorded, a unique improviser and soloist. She set the standards to which future vocalists such as Sarah Vaughan, Carmen McRae, and Lena Horne would aspire. Much attention has focused on the tragic and destructive dimensions of her private life, but it is her musical talent that compels interest and admiration. Holiday used her talent to do more than entertain. She challenged and often disturbed her listeners. While frequently inaccurate, Holiday's autobiography, *Lady Sings the Blues* (1956), and the equally distorted 1972 movie starring Diana Ross emphasize her strug-gle against sexism and racism within the music world and soci-ety. Holiday appeared in two movies. In 1935 she performed in Duke Ellington's *Symphony in Black*, singing "Big City Blues." In 1946 she sang three songs in *New Orleans*, opposite her musical mentor Louis Armstrong. Saxophonist Lester Young, who began recording with Holiday in 1937, gave her the nick-name "Lady Day." By the late 1940s, Holiday's addiction to drugs was hurting her career. In 1947 she entered a clinic but could not stay clean. Following her discharge, the police arrested her and she served nine and a half months at the Fed-eral Reformatory for Women at Alderson, West Virginia. New York officials revoked her cabaret card and prohibited her from performing in nightclubs in the city. Still, she gave concerts in other cities and on international tours. A year before her death, Holiday recorded her most popular album, *Lady in Satin* (1958). She died in New York City on July 17, 1959. Thousands of friends and fans attended the funeral, a formal requiem high mass held at St. Paul the Apostle Church. She was buried in St. Raymond's Catholic Cemetery in the Bronx.

Nevertheless, the profits from the film funded the dancers' stage performances and Dunham's research. In 1943 Dunham moved to New York and opened the Katherine Dunham School of Arts and Research, which trained artists in dance, theater, literature, and world cultures.

Dunham protested racial segregation, even though it hurt her popularity. In the early 1940s she denounced discrimination. In 1944 in Louisville, Kentucky, Dunham announced after a performance, "We are glad we have made you happy. We hope you have enjoyed us. This is the last time I shall play Louisville because the management refuses to let people like us sit by people like you. Maybe after the war we shall have democracy and I can return." Dunham is important because she was a gifted and talented pioneer in dance whose choreography inspired future generations. She also underscored the responsibility that a black artist had to the black community to fight racism.

Billie Holiday (1915–1959), another great performer whose career took shape during the Depression, also used her art to challenge the oppression of black people. Holiday, popularly known as "Lady Day," began singing at age 15 and was discovered three years later by John Hammond, a Chicago jazz producer and promoter. In 1933 Hammond arranged for Holiday's first recording session, and in 1934 she made her debut at the Apollo Theater in Harlem. An incomparable singer known for subtle and artful improvisation, she left a wealth of recordings.

19.6 Black Visual Art

Discuss the ways in which black graphic artists offered different ways to view or express the ways in which they reimagined themselves and their people.

Chicago artists, such as Charles White, Elizabeth Catlett, and Eldzier Cortor, and Harlem's Jacob Lawrence celebrated working-class black people while implicitly criticizing the racial hierarchy of power and privilege. Their art belonged to the social realist school that flourished in the 1930s. Social realist art was intensely ideological. It strove to fuse propaganda—both left and right wing—to art to make it socially and politically relevant.

As the Depression worsened, black artists became even more determined to portray the crisis in capitalism. This involved depicting social and racial inequality. Charles White wrote that "paint is the only weapon I have with which to fight what I resent. If I could write I would write about it. If I could talk I would talk about it. Since I paint, I must paint about it."

Defense Worker, a painting by Dox Thrash, reflects these concerns. Completed in 1942, just after the United States had entered World War II, it shows a black worker looming over the horizon. The heroic proletarian imagery alludes to the dream of a racially integrated labor force, equal opportunity, and social reform in the wake of the New Deal and the demand for labor triggered by the war.

The Harmon Foundation sponsored five juried exhibitions (1926–1931, 1933) of the work of black artists. The William E. Harmon Awards for Distinguished Achievement among Negroes celebrated black artists in the hope they would serve as role models for others. William E. Harmon, a real-estate investor from Iowa, established the New York–based foundation in 1925. In the 1930s the WPA established art workshops and art centers in black urban communities such as Chicago (Southside Community Art Center), Cleveland (Karamu House Artist Association), Detroit (Heritage House), and Harlem (Harlem Art Workshop and the Harlem Community Art Center) to teach art to neighborhood young people and provide work for artists. Sculptor Augusta Savage, as the first director of the Harlem Community Art Center, presided over more than 1,500 students enrolled in day and evening classes in drawing, painting, sculpture, printmaking, and design. Among the teachers was Selma Burke (1900–1995), who sculpted the relief of Franklin D. Roosevelt that appears on the dime coin.

Federal Arts Project

New Deal agency formed to promote the creation of public art.

The **Federal Arts Project**, another New Deal agency, sponsored the creation of murals that illustrated American ideals in public buildings, such as post offices and schools. Murals by black artists celebrated the heritage, contributions to society, and struggles of African Americans. Aaron Douglas, a leading painter of such public art, spoke about his work and that of his colleagues in a 1936 essay, "The Negro in American Culture":

> One of our chief concerns has been to establish and maintain recognition of our essential humanity, in other words, complete social and political equality. This has been a difficult fight as we have been the constant object of attack by all manner of propaganda from nursery rhymes to false scientific racial theories. . . . In this struggle the rest of the proletariat almost invariably has been arrayed against us. . . . But the Negro artist, unlike the white artist, has never known the big house. He is essentially a product of the masses and can never take a position above or beyond their level.

Douglas and other black artists pressed the WPA to appoint more African Americans to its local boards and to hire them for more projects. The Harlem Artists Guild and the Arts and Crafts Guild in Chicago provided forums where black artists could foster the visual arts and support the social and political issues that affected black people.

19.7 Black Literature

Compare and contrast the nuanced differences and similarities in the works and lives of the twentieth century's most prominent African-American writers. Identify similar or shared themes in their novels.

Black literature, like black art, has been assessed in terms of what it reveals about the social, cultural, and political landscape at a given historical moment. The most distinguishing feature of black literature may be the way that black writers have attempted to create spaces of freedom in their work, to liberate place, a trait that also marks black religious culture and folk cultural practices, such as storytelling. Black literature, like all black cultural production, is valued both for aesthetic reasons on its own and for the way it represents the struggles of black people to attain freedom. Black writers in the 1930s and 1940s felt obliged to address questions of identity and to define and describe urban life to the dispossessed and impoverished black migrants who moved to the cities. They tried to delineate the dimensions of a shared American heritage by portraying the contributions that African Americans had made to American society. Finally, and perhaps most ambitiously, black writers explored the issue of the rights African Americans were entitled to as Americans and the demands they could and should make on the state and society.

Richard Wright (1908–1960) was the first black writer to commandeer serious attention in mainstream American literature. In *Native Son* (1940) and *Black Boy* (1945), Wright provided incisive critiques of American racism. He received support from the Federal Writers Project and in his early works he poignantly portrayed the pathos of black southern migrants to the urban industrial North.

19.7.1 Richard Wright's *Native Son*

In 1940 Richard Wright (1908–1960) published *Native Son*, the first of many important novels by Depression-generation black authors. Reviewers hailed it as "the new American tragedy." Its tale of the downfall of the young Bigger Thomas could be read as a warning about how economic hardship, segregation, and discrimination could lead young black men to lash out in violence and rage. Setting out for an interview for a job as a chauffeur, Bigger meets with his South Side Chicago neighborhood friends who want him to help them rob a grocery store. Bigger's fear of whites prevents him from going along. Instead, he picks a fight to camouflage his fear and avoid committing the crime. Bigger gets the chauffeur's job, which requires him to drive for the wealthy Dalton family. On his first assignment, he is supposed to drive young Mary Dalton to a university lecture. But she talks him into picking up her boyfriend, Jan—a communist—and taking them to a restaurant in the black neighborhood. Jan and Mary are oblivious to the patronizing way they treat Bigger. After dinner Bigger drives them around the city while they drink and make love in the back seat.

When Jan leaves, Bigger takes an intoxicated Mary home. Because Mary is too drunk to walk, Bigger carries her to her room and is putting her to bed when blind Mrs. Dalton comes to check on her daughter. Bigger panics and covers Mary's head with a pillow to keep her quiet. When Mrs. Dalton leaves, Bigger discovers he has smothered Mary. He burns her body in the basement furnace. Not fully grasping what he has done, Bigger writes a ransom note signed with a phony name to make it seem that Mary has been kidnapped. When Mary's remains are discovered, Bigger flees. Fearing she might betray him, Bigger then murders his girlfriend, Bessie. Bigger is captured, tried, and condemned. The remainder of the novel explores the hysteria and bigotry that envelop the case, the harsh criminal justice system, the insensitivity of the Communist Party—which seeks to exploit Bigger's plight—and the poverty and social ills that plagued Chicago's African-American communities during the Depression.

At the center of the drama is Wright's exploration of how Bigger comes to terms with his murder of Mary and Bessie. In conversations with Max, his communist lawyer, he realizes his irrational fear of white people had caused him to kill the two women and that he was a product of his experiences in the ghetto. At the end of the novel he says, "What I killed for I am."

Wright's novel thrust the impact of urbanization and racism on black men and women into the collective consciousness of the American people. One white critic declared, "Speaking from the black wrath of retribution, Wright insisted that history can be punishment. He told us the one thing even the most liberal whites preferred not to hear: that Negroes were far from patient or forgiving, that they were scarred by fear, that they hated every moment of their suppression even when seeming most acquiescent, and that often enough they hated us the decent and cultivated white men who from complicity or neglect shared in the responsibility of their plight."

In his closing arguments, the lawyer, Max, describes the psychological conditions that led Bigger to kill and warns of the destructive potential of suppressed black rage:

> The hate and fear which we have inspired in him, woven by our civilization into the very structure of his consciousness and into his blood and bones, into the hourly functioning of his personality, have become the justification of his existence. . . . Kill him and swell the tide of pent up lava that will some day break loose, not in a single, blundering crime, but in a wild cataract of emotion that will brook no control.

Native Son was an immediate success. It became a Book-of-the-Month Club selection and has sold millions of copies.

19.7.2 James Baldwin Challenges Wright

Wright's influence on American literature has been immense. He was the first African-American writer to enjoy an international reputation, and he showed that success and militancy were not mutually exclusive. A younger generation of black writers, however, especially James Baldwin (1924–1987), took issue with Wright. African Americans, they argued, need not be portrayed as hapless victims of racism. In his famous 1949 essay, "Everybody's Protest Novel," Baldwin argued that Bigger's tragedy was not that he was black, poor, and scared but that he had accepted "a theology that denies him life, that he admits the possibility of his being sub-human and feels constrained, therefore, to battle for his humanity according to those brutal criteria bequeathed him at his birth. . . . The failure of the protest novel lies in its rejection of life, the human being, the denial of his beauty, dread, power, in its insistence that it is his categorization alone which is real and which cannot be transcended." In turn, Wright accused Baldwin of trying to destroy his reputation and of betraying all African-American writers who wrote protest literature: "All literature is protest. You can't name a single novel that isn't protest."

Baldwin answered Wright in a second essay in 1951 titled "Many Thousand Gone." "Wright's work," Baldwin declared, "is most clearly committed to the social struggle . . . that artist is strangled who is forced to deal with human beings solely in social terms; and who has, moreover, as Wright had, the necessity thrust on him of being the representative of some thirteen million people. It is a false responsibility (since writers are not congressmen) and impossible, by its nature, of fulfillment."

The controversy ended the friendship between Wright and Baldwin, and Baldwin, whose work would soon include many powerful novels and essays, inherited the mantle of "best-known black American male writer"(see Chapter 22).

19.7.3 Ralph Ellison and *Invisible Man*

The most intricate novel about the black experience in America written during this era was Ralph Ellison's (1914–1994) *Invisible Man*, which won the National Book Award for fiction in 1952. Partially autobiographical, it traces the life of a young black man from his early years in a southern school (a thinly disguised Tuskegee Institute) through his migration to New York City. The novel explores class tensions within American society and the black community. It offers a balanced, incisive perspective on the interaction between white and black Americans.

Invisible Man was Ellison's only completed novel. He argued that the black tradition teaches one "to deflect racial provocation and to master and control pain. . . . It is a tradition which abhors as obscene any trading on one's own anguish for gain or sympathy. . . . It takes fortitude to be a man and no less to be an artist. Perhaps it takes even more if the black man would be an artist." He concluded, "It would seem to me, therefore, that the question of how the 'sociology of his existence' presses upon the Negro writer's work depends upon how much of his life the individual writer is able to transform into art."

Echoing Du Bois's classic characterization of the "twoness" of the African-American character, Ellison observed, "[Black people] are an American people who are geared to what is and who yet are driven by a sense of what it is possible for human life to be in this society."

19.8 African Americans in Sports

Analyze the contributions African-American sports figures made to American culture and the barriers that they overcame in order to do so.

It is in the arena of professional sports that black Americans have demonstrated what human life can achieve when unconstrained by racism. The experiences of black men and women in American sports are a microcosm of their lives in American society. The privileges whites enjoyed in sports in this era paralleled the disadvantages and exclusions that were a constant part of black life. In the 1930s two black athletes, Jesse Owens and Joe Louis, captured the world's attention and inspired African Americans with pride, hope, and pleasure.

19.8.1 Jesse Owens and Joe Louis

Jesse Owens (1913–1980) was born James Cleveland Owens in Oakville, Alabama. His family were sharecroppers who sought a better live and migrated to Cleveland. A teacher asked the nine-year-old his name and mistakenly thought that he said "J.C." From that point, he was called Jesse. A talented runner, Owens studied at Ohio State University and prepared for the 1936 Olympics held in Berlin, Germany. Many African-American leaders objected to participating in the games because they believed so doing helped legitimate the Nazi myth of Aryan racial superiority. Owen's victories made him the first Olympian to win four gold medals. The myth may have been crushed, but racism persisted. Owens recalled, "When I came back to my native country . . . I couldn't ride in the front of the bus . . . I had to go to the back door. I couldn't live where I wanted. I wasn't invited to shake hands with Hitler, but I wasn't invited to the White House to shake hands with the President either."

Joe Louis Barrow (1914–1981) was also a son of Alabama sharecroppers. His family migrated to Detroit when he was 12. Although his mother wanted him to be a violinist, Joe Louis—he dropped the name Barrow—had other interests. As a youth, he won a string of local boxing victories. In 1935 he faced former heavyweight champion Primo Carnera. A record crowd of 62,000 attended the fight in New York, which also had political overtones. Louis was fighting an Italian-American when Benito Mussolini, the fascist dictator of Italy, was about to invade Ethiopia. This was the oldest black independent nation in Africa, and many African Americans admired its ruler, Emperor Haile Selassie. Sports writers and police were amazed to observe everyone cheering when Louis beat Carnera in the sixth round. Louis won the world heavyweight title against James J. Braddock in 1937 and beat the German Max Schmeling in a symbolic victory over Nazism in 1938. Louis retained the world heavyweight title until 1949.

19.8.2 Breaking the Color Barrier in Baseball

Although African Americans were integrated in track and boxing, professional baseball remained segregated until after World War II. Despite the hardships of the Depression, however, virtually every major black community tried to field its own baseball team. The Negro National League, which had folded in 1932, was revived in 1934, and the Negro American League was formed in 1937. Many of the players in the Negro leagues, including the legendary Josh Gibson, Satchel Paige, Leon Day, and Cool Papa Bell, would have equaled or excelled their white counterparts in the major leagues. Except for Paige, they never had that chance.

In 1947, however, major league baseball, which had had no black players since the departure of Fleetwood Walker in 1887, became integrated again when Jackie Robinson (1919–1972) signed to play with the Brooklyn Dodgers. In 1945 Branch Rickey, the Dodgers' general manager, decided to sign a black ball player to improve the team's chances of winning the National League pennant and the World Series. After scouting the Negro leagues, he signed 26-year-old Jackie Robinson.

Robinson was the ideal choice, a superb athlete and a man of fortitude and determination. Born in Georgia and raised in southern California, he had been an All-American running back in football at UCLA and then had played baseball for the legendary Kansas City Monarchs of the Negro leagues. Robinson was also committed to black people and racial progress. He played the 1946 season for the Dodgers' minor league team in Montreal, where the Canadians welcomed him and his wife Rachel. But spring training in segregated Florida was difficult. Robinson broke the color barrier when he opened at first base for the Dodgers in April 1947. Taunted, ridiculed, and threatened by some spectators and players, he responded by playing spectacular baseball. He won the Rookie of the Year honors in 1947, and the Dodgers won the National League pennant. Robinson retired in 1957 but remained outspoken on racial issues until his death from diabetes in 1972.

In July 1947 Larry Doby became the first black player in the American League when he joined the Cleveland Indians. As other major league teams also signed black players, the once popular Negro leagues withered.

Jackie Robinson (1919–1972) broke baseball's color barrier when he joined the Brooklyn Dodgers in 1947. He silently endured considerable hostility and threats from angry white citizens.

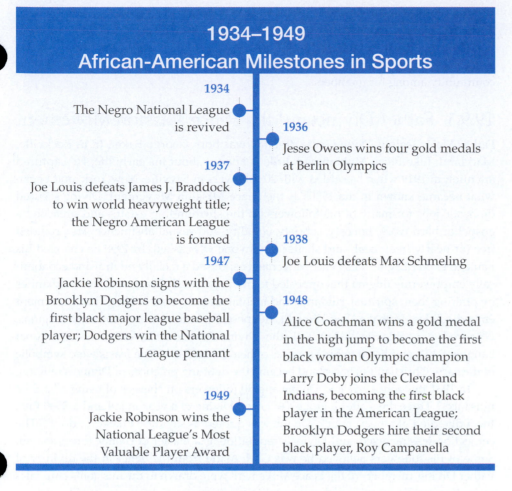

1934–1949
African-American Milestones in Sports

1934
The Negro National League is revived

1936
Jesse Owens wins four gold medals at Berlin Olympics

1937
Joe Louis defeats James J. Braddock to win world heavyweight title; the Negro American League is formed

1938
Joe Louis defeats Max Schmeling

1947
Jackie Robinson signs with the Brooklyn Dodgers to become the first black major league baseball player; Dodgers win the National League pennant

1948
Alice Coachman wins a gold medal in the high jump to become the first black woman Olympic champion

Larry Doby joins the Cleveland Indians, becoming the first black player in the American League; Brooklyn Dodgers hire their second black player, Roy Campanella

1949
Jackie Robinson wins the National League's Most Valuable Player Award

19.9 Black Religious Culture

Identify some of the strongest characteristics of black religious culture and how the church was transformed into a haven for those engaged in resistance struggles.

Just as black religion was the "invisible institution" that helped African Americans survive slavery, the black church was the visible institution that helped hundreds of thousands of migrants adjust to urban life while affirming a set of core values consisting of freedom, justice, equality, and an African heritage. There was, of course, no single "black church." The term is shorthand for a pluralistic collection of institutions, including most prominently seven independent, historic, and black-controlled denominations: the African Methodist Episcopal Church; the African Methodist Episcopal Zion Church; the Christian Methodist Episcopal Church; the National Baptist Convention, Incorporated; the National Baptist Convention of America, Unincorporated; the Progressive National Baptist Convention; and the Church of God in Christ. Together, these denominations account for more than 80 percent of African American Christians.

The black church helped workers transition from being southern agricultural laborers to becoming northern urban industrial workers. Yet the relationship between black religious tradition and the secular lives of church members changed in important ways. The blues and jazz performed in social spaces influenced the development of urban gospel music. Many of the nightclub musicians and singers received their training and held their first public performances in their churches. During the Depression, the black church helped black people survive by enabling them to pool their resources and by offering inspiration and spiritual consolation. Several alternative religious groups became prominent during the 1930s and 1940s and addressed specific needs growing out of the Depression and the traumatic experience of relocating to alien and often hostile northern cities. Father Divine's Peace Mission Movement combined secular concerns with sacred beliefs. He strengthened a sense of identity, affirmation, and community among his members.

19.9.1 Father Divine and the Peace Mission Movement

Peace Mission Movement

Religious movement led by Father Major Jealous Divine.

Father Major Jealous Divine (c. 1879–1965) was born George Baker, Jr. in Rockville, Maryland. Like Elijah Muhammad, little is known about his early life. He captured attention in 1919 when he settled with 20 followers in Sayville, New York, and began what became known in the 1930s as the **Peace Mission Movement**. Divine secured domestic jobs for many of his followers on the surrounding estates and preached a gospel of hard work, honesty, sobriety, equality, and sexual abstinence. He provided free (or nearly free) meals and shelter for anyone who asked. In 1930 he changed his name to Father Divine. His Peace Movement espoused a racially neutral and economically empowering dogma that appealed to poor and needy black and white urbanites by offering them spiritual guidance and mental and physical healing. The movement embodied ideas from the New Thought, Holiness, Perfectionist, and Adventist religions. Hundreds of people traveled to see Father Divine on weekends, feast at his communal banquet table, and listen to his promises of heaven on Earth. The feasts were symbolic of the early Christian Eucharist and became the defining practices of Divine's religion.

In 1931 the police arrested Divine and 80 followers on charges of being a "public nuisance." Three days after a judge sentenced Divine to a year in jail and a $500 fine, the judge died of a heart attack. Divine was quoted as saying, "I hated to do it." The conviction was reversed, and Divine's reputation as a master of cosmic forces soared. Some of his followers believed he was God. Aside from the belief in the divinity of Father Divine, members of the Peace Movement were drawn to the mission's emphasis on ending racial prejudice and economic inequalities.

In 1933 Divine moved his headquarters to Harlem, where his Peace Mission Movement prospered. He eventually purchased key real-estate and housing projects called "heavens." These acquisitions and other businesses in the Midwest enhanced Divine's ability to provide shelter, jobs, and incomes for his followers. He launched the journal *New Day* in 1937 to disseminate his teachings. Divine also protested social injustice and encouraged his followers to become politically engaged. Between 1936 and 1940, he lobbied for a federal antilynching law. At the time of Divine's death in 1965, the holdings of the Peace Mission were estimated to be worth $10 million. Father Divine's movement echoed the Protestant ethic: work hard, keep both your mind and body healthy, eat right, dress properly, keep good company, and avoid evil and vice.

Conclusion

The Depression caused intense hardship. Yet, against this reality, African Americans forged new urban identities. They had an unprecedented impact on American urban culture. Through the medium of radio, black Americans powerfully helped to change American popular entertainment and gave rise to a modern and progressive consciousness. They cultivated a new appreciation of belonging. Black people excelled in sports, arts, drama, and music. The Works Projects Administration (WPA) funded artists whose cultural productions were accessible, inclusive, and populist.

On the heels of the Harlem Renaissance, the Chicago Black Renaissance reflected the positive impact that the WPA had on the lives of hundreds of artists. A new generation of black jazz musicians transformed black music into an art form that won worldwide admiration and emulation. Black musicians weaned Americans from swing to bebop. Gospel music satisfied the needs of the black urban migrants to express their spiritual and communal feelings. Disc jockeys of black-appeal radio programs helped make black music commercially profitable.

These positive changes occurred against a backdrop of discrimination and segregation. Still, some African Americans found satisfying jobs in film and radio while many others were excluded or relegated to stereotypical roles. Many black women actresses including Hattie McDaniel and Louise Beavers paved the way for a dynamic generation of black actresses who would make movies and television appearances in the 1950s and 1960s. These actresses included Lena Horne, Eartha Kitt, Dorothy Dandridge, Ruby Dee, Josephine Baker, Diane Carroll, and Cicely Tyson.

Negative typecasting motivated innovative black filmmakers to develop alternative films and artistic institutions that allowed the development of a more balanced representation of black life and culture. However, such creative ventures seldom produced the profits that white entrepreneurs reaped from marketing black cultural productions to white consumers. The mass appeal and unparalleled success of entertainers such as Louis Armstrong and Duke Ellington should not obscure the fate of those artists who refused to entertain white America and instead sought to oppose racism and social injustice and economic exploitation.

Black counterculture artists had a lasting impact on America and facilitated the spread of black internationalism and anticolonialism. Black artists reflected a growing pride and a determination to resist complete assimilation into white culture. The comic strips, the Semple stories of Langston Hughes, the black press, the radio broadcast of *Destination Freedom*, and the black church preserved black people's dignity. Black culture prepared black people for the next level of struggle against the American Jim Crow regime and resistance to ideologies of white supremacy across the black diaspora.

Chapter Timeline

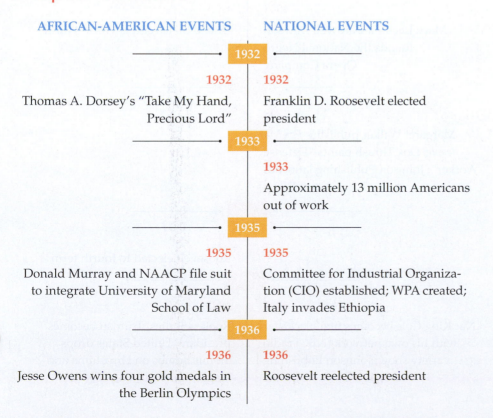

AFRICAN-AMERICAN EVENTS	NATIONAL EVENTS
1932	
1932	**1932**
Thomas A. Dorsey's "Take My Hand, Precious Lord"	Franklin D. Roosevelt elected president
1933	
	1933
	Approximately 13 million Americans out of work
1935	
1935	**1935**
Donald Murray and NAACP file suit to integrate University of Maryland School of Law	Committee for Industrial Organization (CIO) established; WPA created; Italy invades Ethiopia
1936	
1936	**1936**
Jesse Owens wins four gold medals in the Berlin Olympics	Roosevelt reelected president

AFRICAN-AMERICAN EVENTS   **NATIONAL EVENTS**

1937

1937

Joe Louis becomes heavyweight champion; Katherine Dunham receives Guggenheim Award to study dance in the Caribbean

1938

1938

CIO separates from the American Federation of Labor

1939

1939

Billie Holiday sings "Strange Fruit" for the first time; Marian Anderson performs at Lincoln Memorial after DAR bars her from Constitution Hall; "Bojangles" Robinson organizes the Black Actors' Guild

1939

World War II begins in Europe

1940

1940

Richard Wright publishes *Native Son*; Hattie McDaniel receives an Oscar for her role in *Gone with the Wind*

1940

Roosevelt elected to third term as president

1941

1941

Mary Lucinda Cardwell Dawson founds the National Negro Opera Company

1941

United States enters World War II

1942

1942

Margaret Walker publishes *For My People*; Dox Thrash paints "Defense Worker"; Johnson Publishing launches *Negro Digest*

1944

1944

Roosevelt elected to fourth term

1945

1945

Nat King Cole becomes first black star with his own network (NBC) radio variety show; Johnson Publishing launches *Ebony* magazine

1945

Roosevelt dies, Truman becomes president; United States drops atomic bombs on Hiroshima and Nagasaki; World War II ends

AFRICAN-AMERICAN EVENTS   NATIONAL EVENTS

1947

1947

Jackie Robinson and Larry Doby
become the first two black major
league baseball players

1948

1948   **1948**

Alice Coachman becomes the first   Truman elected president
black woman Olympic champion;
Richard Durham broadcasts
Destination Freedom

Review Questions

1. What impact did the Great Depression and the
Works Progress Administration have on the
development of black religious institutions and a
new black expressive culture?

2. What were some of the significant contributions that
Black artists, writers, and filmmakers had on the
development of urban popular culture in Chicago?

3. What were some of the differences between Big
Band and Bebop music?

4. Describe the roles that Black actors and
actresses were restricted to in early Hollywood
movies. Who were some of the major Hollywood
Black stars?

5. What were some of the unique cultural features of
the Black Chicago Renaissance?

6. Discuss the accomplishment of major
African-American athletes during the 1930s
and 1940s.

Retracing the Odyssey

Harold Washington Library Center, Chicago, Illinois.
Named in honor of Harold Washington, Chicago's first
African-American mayor, the 10-story library, art, and
computer reference center features the Harold Washington Archives and Collections (on the ninth floor),
the collection of the Chicago Blues Archive, and the
work of several African-American artists. Jacob Lawrence contributed a mural-sized mosaic titled "Events
in the Life of Harold Washington" on the north wall of
the library.

DuSable Museum of African American History, Chicago,
Illinois. Artist Margaret Goss Burroughs opened the
Ebony Museum in 1961 in her home in Chicago. She
moved it in 1973 to its present location at Washington
Park and renamed it the DuSable Museum of African-
American History. The DuSable Museum honors the
accomplishments of Jean Baptiste Pointe DuSable, a

Haitian-born immigrant who arrived in Chicago in
1779 and was the first non-Indian to settle in the area.
The museum houses an extensive collection of artifacts,
art, books, and civil rights documents and sponsors a
diverse array of cultural and educational programs and
exhibits.

Carter G. Woodson Regional Library, Chicago, Illinois.
This branch of the Chicago Public Library, named in
honor of the "Father of Black History," Carter G. Woodson, contains a wealth of photographs, books, documents, and manuscript collections concerning the artists
and authors, women's clubs, and social institutions that
detail the Black Chicago Renaissance. The Vivian Harsh
Collection of Afro-American History and Literature contains over 70,000 volumes by Langston Hughes, Richard Wright, Gwendolyn Brooks, and Arna Bontemps,
among others.

George Cleveland Hall Library, Chicago, Illinois. This branch of the Chicago Public Library was named in honor of the prominent black surgeon, civic leader, and activist Dr. George Cleveland Hall (1864–1930). Opening in 1932, Hall was the first Chicago Public Library to hire a Black branch manager, Vivian Gordon Harsh. In 2000, the branch became a landmark institution that served as a meeting venue for writers including Arna Bontemps, Gwendolyn Brooks, Lorraine Hansberry, Langston Hughes, Zora Neale Hurston, Claude McKay, and Richard Wright.

Recommended Reading

William Barlow. *Voice Over: The Making of Black Radio.* Philadelphia: Temple University Press, 1999. A lucid, informative cultural history of black radio and the personalities who made it a powerful instrument for disseminating black music, culture, language, and politics, and for constructing an African-American public sphere.

Pearl Bowser and Charles Musser. *Oscar Micheaux and His Circle: African American Filmmaking and Race Cinema of the Silent Era.* Bloomington: Indiana University Press, 2005. Informative new perspectives on a great filmmaker and the era in which he worked.

Scott DeVeaux. *BeBop: A Social and Musical History.* Berkeley: University of California Press, 1997. A perceptive study of the creative artistry and lives of the pivotal black professional musicians. Beginning in the jazz age and flourishing during the 1930s and 1940s, they made bebop commercially successful.

Erik S. Gellman. *Death Blow to Jim Crow: The National Negro Congress and the Rise of Militant Civil Rights.* Durham: University of North Carolina Press, 2012. Breaks new ground and deepens our understanding of the militant, radical, antiracism interracial reformers who founded one of the earliest civil rights movement's organizations.

Darlene Clark Hine and John McCluskey, Jr., eds. *The Black Chicago Renaissance.* Urbana: University of Illinois Press, 2012. A collection of original essays that focus on the lives and work of black creative, literary, visual, and performance artists in Black Chicago Renaissance during the 1930s to the 1950s. Essays focus on Charles White, Richard Wright, Horace Cayton, and Gwendolyn Brooks. It includes a lengthy history of Black Chicago visual artists with representative illustrations of their painting and sculptures.

Barbara Dianne Savage. *Broadcasting Freedom: Radio, War, and the Politics of Race, 1938–1948.* Chapel Hill: University of North Carolina Press, 1999. An illuminating and ingenious social history of African-American men and women who struggled to create a public venue to discuss racial consciousness and the desire for freedom during the 1940s.

Sonja D. Williams. *Word Warrior: Richard Durham, Radio, and Freedom.* Urbana: University of Illinois Press, 2015. An excellent, thoroughly researched, revealing, and important study of Durham's magnificent efforts to teach black history via radio and the opposition he encountered.

Additional Bibliography

Art

Michael D. Harris and Moyo Okediji. *Colored Pictures: Race and Visual Representation.* Chapel Hill: University of North Carolina Press, 2003.

Peter T. Nesbett and Michelle DuBois. *Over the Line: The Art and Life of Jacob Lawrence.* Seattle: University of Washington Press, 2002.

Sharon F. Patton. *African-American Art.* New York: Oxford University Press, 1998.

Richard J. Powell. *Black Art and Culture in the 20th Century.* New York: Thames and Hudson, 1997.

Tyler Stovall. *Paris Noir: African Americans in the City of Light.* Boston: Houghton Mifflin, 1996.

Maren Strange. *Bronzeville: Black Chicago in Picture, 1941–1943.* New York: New Press, 2003.

William E. Taylor and Harriet G. Warkel. *A Shared Heritage: Art by Four African Americans.* Bloomington: Indiana University Press, 1996.

Black Chicago Renaissance

Wallace Best. *Passionately Human, No Less Divine: Religion and Culture in Black Chicago, 1915–1932.* Princeton, NJ: Princeton University Press, 2005.

Robert Bone. "Richard Wright and the Chicago Renaissance." *Callaloo* 9, no. 3 (1986): 446–68.

Richard Courage and Robert A. Bone. *The Muse in Bronzeville: African American Creative Expression in*

Chicago, 1932–1950. New Brunswick, NJ: Rutgers University Press, 2011.

Adam Green. *Selling the Race: Culture, Community, and Black Chicago, 1940–1955.* Chicago: University of Chicago Press, 2007.

Lionel Kimble, Jr. *A New Deal for Bronzeville: Housing, Employment, and Civil Rights in Black Chicago.* Carbondale: Southern Illinois University Press, 2015.

Anne Meis Knupfer. *The Chicago Black Renaissance and Women's Activism.* Urbana: University of Illinois Press, 2006.

Richard J. Powell. *Archibald Motley: Jazz Age Modernist.* Durham, NC: Duke University Press, 2014.

Clovis E. Semmes. *The Regal Theatre and Black Culture.* New York: Palgrave, 2006.

Craig Werner. "Leon Forrest, the AACM and the Legacy of the Chicago Renaissance." *The Black Scholar* 23, no. 3/4 (1993): 10–23.

Culture

Christine Acham. *Revolution Televised: Prime Time and the Struggle for Black Power.* Minneapolis: University of Minnesota Press, 2004.

Gerald Early, ed. *"Ain't But a Place": An Anthology of African American Writings About St. Louis.* St. Louis: Missouri Historical Society Press, 1998.

Melvin Patrick Ely. *The Adventures of Amos 'n' Andy: A Social History of an American Phenomenon.* New York: Free Press, 1991.

Geneviève Fabre and Robert O'Meally, eds. *History and Memory in African-American Culture.* New York: Oxford University Press, 1994.

Kenneth W. Goings. *Mammy and Uncle Mose: Black Collectibles and American Stereotyping.* Bloomington: Indiana University Press, 1994.

Jacqueline Goldsby. *A Spectacular Secret: Lynching in American Life and Literature.* Chicago: University of Chicago Press, 2006.

John Edward Hasse. *Beyond Category: The Life and Genius of Duke Ellington.* New York: Simon and Schuster, 1993.

Darlene Clark Hine, Trica Danielle Keaton, and Stephen Small, eds. *Black Europe and the African Diaspora.* Urbana: University of Illinois Press, 2009.

Robin D. G. Kelley. *Race Rebels: Culture, Politics, and the Black Working Class.* New York: Free Press, 1994.

Tommy L. Lott. *The Invention of Race: Black Culture and the Politics of Representation.* Malden, MA: Blackwell, 1999.

Mel Watkins. *On the Real Side: Laughing, Lying, and Signifying.* New York: Simon and Schuster, 1994.

Robert E. Weems, Jr. *Desegregating the Dollar: African American Consumerism in the Twentieth Century.* New York: New York University Press, 1998.

Victoria Wolcott. *Remaking Respectability: African American Women in Interwar Detroit.* Chapel Hill: University of North Carolina Press, 2001.

Dance

Katherine Dunham. *A Touch of Innocence.* London: Cassell, 1959.

Bennetta Jules-Rosette. *Josephine Baker in Art and Life: The Icon and the Image.* Urbana: University of Illinois Press, 2007.

Anthea Kraut. "Between Primitivism and Diaspora: The Dance Performances of Josephine Baker, Zora Neale Hurston, and Katherine Dunham." *Theatre Journal* 55, no. 3 (October, 2003): 433–50.

Susan Manning. *Modern Dance, Negro Dance: Race in Motion.* Minneapolis: University of Minnesota Press, 2004.

Films

Donald Bogle. *Brown Sugar: Eighty Years of America's Black Female Superstars.* New York: Crown, 1980.

Thomas Cripps. *Making Movies Black: The Hollywood Message Movie From World War II to the Civil Rights Era.* New York: Oxford University Press, 1993.

Jane M. Gaines. *Fire and Desire: Mixed-Race Movies in the Silent Era.* Chicago: University of Chicago Press, 2001.

Jacqueline Najuma Stewart. *Migrating to the Movies: Cinema and Black Urban Modernity.* Berkeley: University of California Press, 2005.

Literature

Henry Louis Gates and Nellie Y. McKay, eds. *Norton Anthology of African American Literature.* New York: Norton, 1997.

Robert G. O'Meally. *The Craft of Ralph Ellison.* Cambridge, MA: Harvard University Press, 1980.

Arnold Rampersad. *The Life of Langston Hughes.* New York: Oxford University Press, 1986.

Margaret Walker. *Richard Wright, Daemonic Genius: A Portrait of the Man, a Critical Look at His Work.* New York: Morrow, 1988.

Richard Wright. *12 Million Black Voices*, Photos by Edward Rosskam. (1941). Reprint. New York: Basic Books, 2002.

Music and Radio

William Barlow. *Looking Up at Down: The Emergence of Blues Culture.* Philadelphia: Temple University Press, 1989.

Thomas Brothers, ed. *Louis Armstrong: In His Own Words.* New York: Oxford University Press, 1999.

John Chilton. *The Song of the Hawk: The Life and Recordings of Coleman Hawkins.* Ann Arbor: University of Michigan Press, 1990.

Linda Dahl. *Morning Glory: A Biography of Mary Lou Williams.* New York: Pantheon Books, 2000.

Miles Davis and Quincy Troupe. *Miles: The Autobiography.* New York: Simon & Schuster, 1989.

Duke Ellington. *Music Is My Mistress.* New York: Da Capo Press, 1973.

John Birks Gillespie and Wilmot Alfred Fraser. *To Be or Not . . . to Bop: Memoirs—Dizzy Gillespie with Al Fraser.* New York: Doubleday, 1979. New ed., University of Minnesota Press, 2009.

Farah Jasmine Griffin. *If You Can't Be Free, Be a Mystery: In Search of Billie Holiday.* New York: Oxford University Press, 2001.

Michael Harris. *The Rise of Gospel Blues: The Music of Thomas Andrew Dorsey in the Urban Church.* New York: Oxford University Press, 1992.

Allan Keiler. *Marian Anderson: A Singer's Journey.* New York: Scribner, 2000.

Robin D. G. Kelley. *Thelonious Monk: The Life and Times of an American Original.* New York: Free Press, 2009.

Jules Schwerin. *Got to Tell It: Mahalia Jackson, Queen of Gospel.* New York: Oxford University Press, 1992.

Alyn Shipton. *Groovin' High: The Life of Dizzy Gillespie.* New York: Oxford University Press, 1999.

Eileen Southern. *The Music of Black Americans: A History.* 2nd ed. New York: W.W. Norton, 1983.

Rosalyn M. Story. *And So I Sing: African-American Divas of Opera and Concert.* New York: Warner Books, 1990.

Quintard Taylor. *In Search of the Racial Frontier: African Americans in the American West, 1528–1900.* New York: W.W. Norton, 1998.

Terry Teachout. *Pops: A Life of Louis Armstrong.* New York: Houghton Mifflin Harcourt, 2009.

J. C. Thomas. *Chasin' the Trane: The Music and Mystique of John Coltrane.* Garden City, NY: Doubleday, 1975.

Dempsey J. Travis. *Autobiography of Black Jazz.* Chicago: Urban Research Press, 1983.

Sports

Arthur Ashe, with the assistance of Kip Branch, Ocania Chalk, and Francis Harris. *A Hard Road to Glory: A History of the African-American Athlete.* New York: Warner Books, 1988.

Richard Bak. *Joe Louis: The Great Black Hope.* New York: Da Capo Press, 1998.

Trudie Engel. *He Changed the Face of Baseball: The Larry Doby Story.* Bloomington, IN: Xlibris, 2014

Robert Peterson. *Only the Ball Was White: A History of Legendary Black Players and All-Black Professional Teams.* New York: McGraw-Hill, 1984.

Arnold Rampersad. *Jackie Robinson: A Biography.* New York: Alfred A. Knopf, 1997.

Jackie Robinson. *I Never Had It Made.* New York: G. P. Putnam's Sons, 1972.

Jeffrey T. Sammons. *Beyond the Ring: The Role of Boxing in American Society.* Urbana: University of Illinois Press, 1988.

Scott Simon. *Jackie Robinson and the Integration of Baseball.* New York: Wiley, 2002.

Religion

Claude Andrew Clegg III. *An Original Man: The Life and Times of Elijah Muhammad.* New York: St. Martin's Griffin, 1997.

C. Eric Lincoln and Lawrence H. Mamiya. *The Black Church in the African American Experience.* Durham, NC: Duke University Press, 1990.

Jill Watts. *God, Harlem U.S.A.: The Father Divine Story.* Berkeley: University of California Press, 1992.

Robert Weisbrot. *Father Divine and the Struggle for Racial Equality.* Urbana: University of Illinois Press, 1983.

Chapter 20

The World War II Era and the Seeds of a Revolution

1940–1950

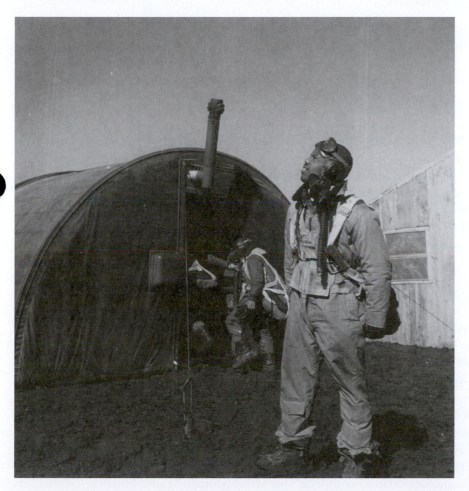

Racial segregation as practiced by the U.S. military reminded African Americans of their second-class status in America. The World War II crisis made impossible continued acquiescence to blatant inequalities. The black "Double V" campaign sought victory against racism on the home and fascism on the foreign fronts.

Learning Objectives

After reading this chapter, you should be able to:

20.1 Discuss the ways in which African Americans used the World War II crisis in order to protest against racial discrimination in America.

20.2 Analyze the strategies that African Americans devised in order to end segregation in military hospitals and to win integration in the nursing profession.

20.3 Enumerate the contributions of the Tuskegee Airmen to the Allied victory in World War II.

20.4 Explain the ways in which World War II made more visible the tensions and competition between white and black Americans over fair housing and equal opportunities for jobs.

20.5 Separate the positive from the negative impact that the Cold War had on African Americans, in both their political and cultural activism.

> **The treatment that the Negro soldier has received has been resented not only by the Negro soldier but by the Negro civilian population as well. In fact, any straight-thinking person with a sense of justice and right, without any respect to color or race, must realize the dangers inherent in the evil practices that have been permitted to exist in the Army. It is not a pleasant thought for Negroes to ponder that their tax money is being spent to help maintain an army that has little regard for the real principles of democracy.**
>
> —*David H. Bradford, the Louisville Courier Journal, September 2, 1941*

Events, both national and international, had a transformative impact on the fortunes and consciousness of African Americans during the 1940s. Indeed, the role of the United States in world affairs changed in many ways. The victory in World War II of the Allies—the Soviet Union, Great Britain, the United States, and dozens of other countries—over the Axis powers of Germany, Italy, and Japan marked America's emergence as the dominant global power. An expanded international role placed new constraints on the nation's domestic policies, particularly when, following the Axis surrender in 1945, suspicions between the United States and the Soviet Union developed into the Cold War. This period also witnessed the rise of black internationalism. Many African Americans forged close bonds with Africans who fought against European colonialism in Africa. The Cold War lasted until 1989 and led to a vast expansion in the size and power of the federal government, particularly its military. It also greatly influenced domestic politics and race relations in America.

In the 1940s international events replaced the Great Depression as the defining force in the lives of African Americans. In preparing for and fighting World War II, America finally emerged from the Depression and laid the basis for an era of unprecedented prosperity. Industrial and military mobilization resulted in the movement of millions of people, many of them African Americans who ignited a second Great Migration in their movement from southern farms into northern and western cities and states. This population shift substantially increased black voting strength in the North and West, which—combined with a moral recoil from the savage racial policies of the Nazis—drove the issue of black equality to the forefront of national politics. Moreover, hundreds of thousands of black men and women had learned new skills and acquired different ideas about race relations while serving in the armed forces. Upon returning home, African American men and women resolved to claim their citizenship rights. Clearly, events abroad and within the United States throughout the 1940s heightened black consciousness and inspired a more aggressive militancy among local leaders and especially among black citizens in every southern state. Black men who had served in the military during the War effort were frequently attacked when they returned home, especially when they wore military uniforms. This pattern was a repeat of the interracial violence that erupted at the end of World War I.

The Cold War affected African Americans and their struggle for freedom. The two sides of this global conflict avoided direct confrontation with each other. Instead, they sought to enlist Africans, Asians, and Latin Americans as proxies. American leaders, trying to convince these peoples of America's virtues as a democracy, were pressed to address the segregation and racial discrimination that remained firmly imbedded in American life. The U.S. Department of State sponsored worldwide tours of outstanding black jazz musicians to represent the positive dimensions of American culture. Still, the advocacy groups and black press that came of age during the 1930s and 1940s focused attention on fighting racism and demanded the full rights and responsibilities of citizenship for all people. The result was a powerful movement for civil rights that many liberal white Americans and, increasingly, key institutions in the national government supported. Rising opposition to European colonialism in Africa and the development of numerous African independence wars also inspired black American militancy and human rights activism.

These favorable developments, however, provoked strong resistance. Egged on by their politicians, white southerners defended segregation with all the power at their command. The emerging conflict with the Soviet Union prompted many white conservatives to charge that all those seeking to fight racial injustice were agents of the communist enemy. These contrary currents—on one hand, the push for an inclusive new democracy, and, on the other, the Cold War mentality—would indelibly stamp the emerging civil rights movement.

20.1 On the Eve of War, 1936–1941

Discuss the ways in which African Americans used the World War II crisis in order to protest against racial discrimination in America.

As the world economy had wallowed in the Great Depression, the international order collapsed in Europe and Asia. Germany under Adolf Hitler (1889–1945) and Italy under Benito Mussolini (1883–1945) created an alliance, known as the Axis, to control Europe. These fascist dictators advocated a political program based on extreme nationalism that suppressed internal opposition and used violence to gain their will abroad. Germany was the dominant partner in the Axis. Its National Socialist, or Nazi, Party in part blamed communists and foreign powers for the nation's economic depression and loss of power. However, even more than by anticommunism, Hitler was driven by virulent racism and his belief in Anglo-Saxon, or white Aryan, supremacy. Unlike racists in the United States, he blamed Jews for Germany's social and economic problems. The Nazis also despised black people and considered them inferior or subhuman beings. They discriminated against Germans with African ancestors and banned jazz as "nigger" music. Beginning in the mid-1930s, the Germans and Italians embarked on a series of aggressive confrontations and military campaigns that placed much of Central Europe under their power. In August 1939 Germany signed a nonaggression pact with the Soviet

Union, a prelude to its September 1 attack on Poland, which the Soviets joined a few weeks later. Poland's allies, Britain and France, reacted by declaring war on Germany, thus beginning World War II.

As Germany and Italy pursued their aggression in Europe, the empire of Japan sought to dominate East Asia. The Japanese considered themselves the foremost power in the Far East and wanted to drive out or supplant both the European states—mainly Britain, France, and the Netherlands—and the United States, which had extensive economic interests and colonial possessions there. (The United States controlled the Philippines, Hawaii, Guam, and other Pacific islands.) Japan's aggressive expansionist policies also led to conflict in the 1930s with the Soviet Union in Manchuria and to a long and bloody war with the Nationalist regime in China. The United States supported China and encouraged the Europeans to resist Japanese demands for economic and territorial concessions in their Asian colonies. Japan's alliance with Nazi Germany and fascist Italy further aggravated United States–Japanese relations, which deteriorated rapidly after the outbreak of World War II in Europe. These tensions led to war on December 7, 1941, when the Japanese bombed American warships at Pearl Harbor, Hawaii, and launched a massive offensive against British, Dutch, and American territory throughout the Pacific.

President Franklin D. Roosevelt watched the events in Europe and Asia during the 1930s with growing concern, but his ability to react was limited. Despite its large economy and large navy, America was not a preeminent military power at the time. Roosevelt had trouble convincing Congress to enlarge the army because a significant segment of the American population, the isolationists, believed the United States had been hoodwinked into fighting World War I and should avoid becoming entangled in another foreign war. During the late 1930s, the president had managed to overcome some of this opposition and had won the authority to increase the size of the nation's armed forces. By early 1940 the United States had instituted its first peacetime draft to provide men for the army and navy.

20.1.1 African Americans and the Emerging International Crisis

Many African Americans responded to the emerging world crisis with growing activism. When Italy invaded Ethiopia—which, along with Liberia and Haiti, was one of the world's three black-ruled nations—in 1935, black communities throughout the United States organized to send it aid. In New York, black nurses under the leadership of Salaria Kee raised money to purchase medical supplies, and black physician John West volunteered to treat wounded Ethiopians at a hospital supported by black American donations. Mass meetings to support the Ethiopians were held in New York City under the auspices of the Provisional Committee for the Defense of Ethiopia and the Ethiopian World Federation. Similar rallies occurred in other large cities while reporters from black newspapers, such as J. A. Rogers of the *Pittsburgh Courier*, brought the horror of this war home to their readers. Although American law forbade citizens to engage in active combat in Ethiopia, over 17,000 African Americans indicated a desire to help Emperor Haile Selassie (r. 1930–1974) resist the Italians. Despite fierce resistance, the Italians won the war in 1936, in part by using poison gas. The conflict alerted many African Americans to the dangers of fascism and fueled even greater interest in and identification with Africa. The flames of black internationalism became even hotter after World War II.

Civil war in Spain stimulated renewed activism among leftist African Americans. In 1936 a fascist-conservative movement led by General Francisco Franco (1892–1975), supported by Germany and Italy, started a civil war to overthrow the left-leaning Spanish Republic. About a hundred African Americans traveled to Spain in 1936–1937 to serve with the Abraham Lincoln Brigade, an integrated fighting force of 3,000 socialist and communist American volunteers. Among the African Americans were two women: Salaria Kee, who nursed the wounded on the battlefield, and Thyra Edwards, who worked for the Medical Bureau and North American Committee to Aid Spanish Democracy. Support of the Abraham Lincoln Brigade reflected a commitment by a few African Americans to the communists' vision of internationalism. Mobilization for war, however, would soon bring most black people and their organizations into the fight against fascism abroad and for equality and justice in the United States (the **"Double V" campaign**).

20.1.2 A. Philip Randolph and the March on Washington Movement

In 1939 and 1940, the American government, along with the governments of France and Britain, spent so much on arms that the U.S. economy was finally lifted out of the Depression. But the United States mobilized its economy for war and rebuilt its military in keeping with past practices of discrimination and exclusion. As unemployed white workers streamed into aircraft factories, shipyards, and other centers of war production, jobless African Americans were left waiting at the gate. Most aircraft manufacturers, for example, would hire black people only in janitorial positions no matter what their skills were. Many all-white American Federation of Labor (AFL) unions enforced closed-shop agreements that prevented their employers from hiring black workers who were not members of the labor organization. Indeed, many working-class whites were also excluded because of closed-shop agreements. Government-funded training programs regularly rejected black applicants, often reasoning that training them would be pointless given their poor prospects of finding skilled work. The United States Employment Service (USES) filled "whites-only" requests for defense workers. The military itself made it clear that although it would accept black men in their proportion to the population, about 11 percent at the time, it would put them in segregated units and assign them to service duties. The navy limited black servicemen to menial positions. The Marine Corps and the Army Air Corps refused to accept them altogether.

When a young African-American man wrote the *Pittsburgh Courier* and suggested a "Double V" campaign—victory over fascism abroad and victory over racism at home—the newspaper adopted his words as the battle cry for the entire race. Fighting this struggle in a nation at war would be difficult, but the effort led to the further development of black organizations and transformed the national and international worldviews of many African-American soldiers and civilians. Black internationalism was never a more prominent component of black people's consciousness than during the spirited "Double V" campaign in which African-American protest groups and newspapers criticized discrimination at home and fascism abroad. Two months before the 1940 presidential election, the NAACP, the Urban League, and other groups pressed President Roosevelt to act against discrimination in defense programs. The president listened to their protests, but aside from a few token gestures—appointing Howard University Law School Dean William Hastie as a "civilian aide on Negro affairs" in the Department of War and promoting Benjamin O. Davis, the senior black officer in the army, to brigadier general—he responded with little of substance. As a result, during late 1940 the NAACP and other groups staged mass protest rallies around the nation. With the election safely won, the president—anxious

Double V campaign
Slogan during World War II that stood for victory over fascism abroad and over racism at home for blacks.

Horace Pippin's (1888–1946) *Mr. Prejudice* (1943) hammers a wedge of racism through a giant V (the sign of victory). It is a powerful expression of black Americans' ongoing struggle against racial discrimination, segregation, and violence even within a nation at war against fascism and Nazism and the spread of communism.

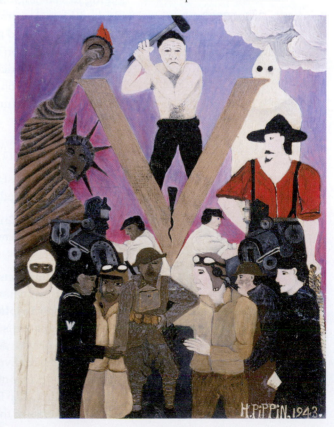

not to offend white southern politicians he needed to back his war program—refused even to meet with black leaders.

In January 1941 A. Philip Randolph, who was president of the Brotherhood of Sleeping Car Porters and who had been working with other groups to get Roosevelt's attention, called on black people to unify their protests and direct them at the national government. He suggested that 10,000 African Americans march on Washington under the slogan "We loyal Negro-American citizens demand the right to work and fight for our country." In the following months, Randolph helped create the **March on Washington Movement (MOWM)**, which soon became the largest African-American organization since Marcus Garvey's Universal Negro Improvement Association of the 1920s. The MOWM's demands included a presidential order forbidding companies with government contracts from engaging in racial discrimination, eliminating race-based exclusion from defense training courses, and requiring the USES to supply workers on a nonracial basis. Randolph also wanted an order to abolish segregation in the armed forces and the president's support for a law withdrawing the benefits of the National Labor Relations Act from unions that refused to grant membership to black Americans. Unlike the leaders of most other African-American protest groups of the time, Randolph prohibited white involvement and encouraged the black working class to participate.

Many African Americans who had never taken part in the activities of middle-class-dominated groups like the NAACP responded to Randolph's appeal. Soon he alarmed the president by raising the number expected to march to 50,000. Roosevelt, fearing the protest would undermine America's democratic rhetoric and provide grist for the German propaganda mills, dispatched First Lady Eleanor Roosevelt and New York City Mayor Fiorello La Guardia to dissuade Randolph from marching. Their pleas for patience fell on deaf ears, compelling Roosevelt and his top military officials to meet with Randolph and other black leaders. The president offered a set of superficial changes, but the African Americans stood firm in their demands and raised the stakes by increasing their estimate of the number of black marchers coming to Washington to 100,000. By the end of June 1941, the president capitulated and had his aides draft **Executive Order 8802**, prompting Randolph to call off the march. It was a grand moment. "To this day," NAACP leader Roy Wilkins wrote in his autobiography, "I don't know if he would have been able to turn out enough marchers to make his point stick . . . but, what a bluff it was. A tall, courtly black man with Shakespearean diction and the stare of an eagle had looked the patrician Roosevelt in the eye—and made him back down."

20.1.3 Executive Order 8802

On the surface, at least, the president's order marked a significant change in the government's stance. It stated in part,

> I do hereby affirm the policy of the United States that there shall be no discrimination in the employment of workers in the defense industry or government because of race, creed, color, or national origin.

The order instructed all agencies that trained workers to administer such programs without discrimination. To ensure full cooperation with these guidelines, Roosevelt created the **Fair Employment Practices Committee (FEPC)** with the power to investigate complaints of discrimination. The order said nothing about desegregation of the military, but private assurances were made that the barriers to entry in key services would be lowered. Eventually, more than a dozen African-American scientists participated in the development of radar and in research projects on several secret defense technologies at Camp Evans in New Jersey. Camp Evans was a U.S. Army Signal Corps base and was one of the principal U.S. sites associated with the development of radar.

March on Washington Movement (MOWM)

Movement created by A. Philip Randolph to pressure the federal government to end discrimination in the defense industry and government.

Executive Order 8802

Order issued by President Franklin D. Roosevelt in 1941 banning discrimination in employment in defense industries and the federal government.

Fair Employment Practices Committee (FEPC)

A committee created by Franklin Roosevelt to investigate complaints of discrimination.

Executive Order 8802, although it was the first major presidential action countering discrimination since Reconstruction, was no new Emancipation Proclamation. Black excitement with the order soon soured as many industries, particularly in the South, made only token hirings of African Americans. What the black community learned in this instance, and what it would witness repeatedly in the decades to come, was that merely articulating antidiscrimination principles and establishing commissions and committees did not eradicate inequalities. Moreover, the order did not mention union discrimination. Nonetheless, the threat of the March on Washington, the issuance of the executive order, and the creation of the FEPC marked the formal acknowledgment by the federal government that it bore some responsibility for protecting black and minority rights in employment. Black activists and their allies would have to continue their fight if the order was to have meaning. Randolph sought to lead them but would find it difficult to do so because of the opposition of key government agencies—notably the military—as well as the power of southern congressmen and a belief among white people that winning the war took precedence over racial issues.

20.2 Race and the U.S. Armed Forces

Analyze the strategies that African Americans devised in order to end segregation in military hospitals and to win integration in the nursing profession.

The demands of A. Philip Randolph and other black leaders and healthcare professionals to end segregation in the Armed Forces initially met stiffer resistance than their pleas for change in the civilian sector. Black men were expected to serve their country; however, at the beginning of the war, most were assigned to segregated service battalions, relegated to noncombat positions, kept out of the more prestigious branches of the service, and confronted by tremendous obstacles to becoming officers. This was particularly galling because military segregation was a symbol of the rampant discrimination black men and women encountered in their daily lives.

During the prewar mobilization period (1940–1941), black physicians and leaders of their organization, the National Medical Association, remembering the segregation they had experienced during World War I, queried the War Department about their status. In a new war, would black physicians be integrated into the medical corps or be required to practice in separate facilities set aside for sick and wounded black soldiers? In a 1940 speech, Dr. G. Hamilton Francis underscored the black doctors' concerns: "Our nation is again preparing to defend itself against aggression from without. Today, we are ready and willing to contribute all of our skill and energy and to wholeheartedly enlist our services as members of the medical profession, but we must be permitted to take our right places, as evidenced by our training, experience, and ability."

20.2.1 Institutional Racism in the American Military

Much of the armed forces' racial policy derived from negative attitudes and discriminatory practices common in American society. Reflecting this ingrained racism, a 1925 study by the American War College concluded that African Americans were physically unqualified for combat duty, were by nature subservient and mentally inferior, believed themselves to be inferior to

Fort Monmouth physicist Dr. Walter S. McAfee (1914–1995) is shown with President Dwight D. Eisenhower after a White House ceremony in 1956. He was awarded one of the first Secretary of the Army's Research Fellowships, which provided for his postdoctoral study at Harvard University and at laboratories in Europe and Australia.

white people, were susceptible to the influence of crowd psychology, could not control themselves in the face of danger, and lacked the initiative and resourcefulness of white people.

Based on this and later studies, the War Department laid out two key policies in 1941 for the use of black soldiers. Although they would be taken into the military at the same rate as white inductees, African Americans would be segregated and would serve primarily in noncombat units. Responding with disdain for those who criticized these policies, Undersecretary of War Robert Patterson wrote,

> The Army is not a sociological laboratory; to be effective it must be organized and trained according to principles which will insure success. Experiments to meet the wishes and demands of the champions of every race and creed for the solution of their problems are a danger to efficiency, discipline and morale and would result in ultimate defeat. Out of these fundamental thoughts have been evolved broad principles relating to the employment of all persons in the military service.

In creating these policies, the military ignored evidence of the fighting ability that African Americans had shown in previous wars, confirmed by the heroism of Doris "Dorie" Miller during the attack on Pearl Harbor. Miller was the son of Texas share-croppers and had enlisted in the navy in 1938. Like all black sailors in the navy at the time, he had been assigned to mess attendant duty. In other words, he was a cook and a waiter. When the Japanese air force attacked the naval base on December 7, 1941, the 22-year-old Miller was below decks on the battleship U.S.S. *West Virginia*. When his captain was wounded, Miller braved bullets to help move him to a more protected area of the deck. He then took charge of a machine gun, shooting down at least two and perhaps six enemy aircraft before running out of ammunition. Miller had never before fired the gun. On May 27, 1942, the navy cited him for "distinguished devotion to duty, extraordinary courage and disregard for his own personal safety" and awarded him a Navy Cross, the highest medal that the navy could bestow. It then sent Miller back to mess duty without a promotion.

This World War II War Department recruitment poster recognizes the heroism of Dorie Miller (1919–1943) at Pearl Harbor. His bravery, however, did not alter the navy's policy of restricting black sailors to the kitchen and boiler rooms of navy vessels.

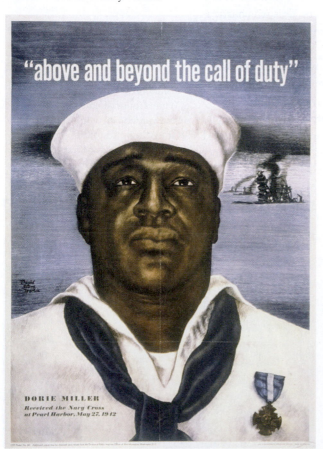

"above and beyond the call of duty"

DORIE MILLER
Received the Navy Cross at Pearl Harbor, May 27, 1942

20.2.2 The Costs of Military Discrimination

Although the War and Navy departments held to the fiction of "separate but equal" in their segregation programs, their policies gave black Americans inferior resources or excluded them entirely. Sick and injured black soldiers were treated in segregated wards in military hospitals. Black physicians could treat only black military personnel. At army camps black soldiers were usually placed in the least desirable spots and denied the use of officers' clubs, base stores, and base recreational facilities. Four-fifths of all training camps were located in the South, where black soldiers were harassed and discriminated against off base as well as on. Even on leave, black soldiers were not offered space in the many hotels the government leased and had to make do with the limited accommodations that had been available to black people before the war. For southern African Americans, even going home in uniform could be dangerous. For example, when Rieves Bell of Starkville, Mississippi, was visiting his family in 1943, three young white men cornered him on a street and attempted to strip off his uniform. Bell fought back and injured one of them with a knife. The army could not save him from the wrath of local civilian

Profile

Steven Robinson and the Montford Point Marines

These are among the very first African-American men to serve in the U.S. Marine Corps. Beginning in 1942 they trained at a separate facility at Montford Point near Camp Lejeune, North Carolina.

When 17-year-old Steven Robinson joined the military in May 1942, he was among the first African Americans to become a marine. From its founding in 1798 until World War II, the Marine Corps accepted only white men. Although President Roosevelt's Executive Order 8802 ended that racial exclusion, it did not outlaw segregation in the military.

With grim reluctance, the Marine Corps began to accept black men. The commandant of the corps, Major General Thomas Holcomb, disdained the prospect of black marines: "If it were a question of having a Marine Corps of 5,000 whites or 250,000 Negroes, I would rather have the whites." The corps would not allow black men to train with white recruits at Parris Island in South Carolina. Instead, it established a separate training facility for black men at Montford Point in North Carolina.

Robinson immediately encountered hostility as he traveled south for basic training. For the first time, he experienced segregated railroad coaches and stations. He inadvertently entered a white waiting room in Rocky Mount, North Carolina, and was curtly instructed to leave: "So I went out the door and as I went out the door, something [said], look, look back and I looked back, I looked over at the station, at the entrance to the station, and I saw a sign. It had to be three feet in width and maybe five feet in length and it says 'For White Only.'"

During basic training Robinson impressed white drill instructors and officers, and he was promoted to platoon sergeant before departing for the war in the Pacific. On the troop train to the West Coast, black marines were refused service when they tried to buy soda in Arizona. They saw German and Italian prisoners of war enjoying the company of American women in restaurants, bars, and clubs that excluded African Americans.

Doubting their fitness, the Marine Corps did not want black men in combat, and most of the Montford Point marines were assigned support roles in ammunition and depot companies. Nevertheless, the black marines participated in several major amphibious operations in the Pacific, including Iwo Jima.

Robinson and a contingent of black marines went ashore on Iwo Jima on February 19, 1945, and took part in some of the fiercest fighting of World War II. One of Robinson's close friends, Jimmy Wilkins, was mortally wounded: "Jimmy was on my right shoulder about two feet [away] when he got hit. And he was killed . . . everybody liked him in the platoon. I mean, he was just a likable seventeen-year-old young teenager. And I might add, a good Marine." Wilkins was also one of the marines who had not been able to buy a soda in Arizona.

Robinson and other marines were aware that they were fighting to defeat two enemies: "We were fighting the war against the bigotry at home and fighting the war against the bigotry overseas. And we were fighting the war to liberate people who had more liberty than we had."

Photographers and filmmakers generally avoided documenting the activities of the black marines, but Robinson and other black marines witnessed the famous flag raising on Iwo Jima's Mount Suribachi. Robinson would spend 106 days on Iwo Jima. More than 6,000 marines and 21,000 Japanese troops died on the small volcanic island before the Americans gained control.

Nearly 20,000 black men trained at Montford Point during and immediately after World War II. In 1949, as a result of President Harry Truman's Executive Order 9981, the Marine Corps began to integrate, and the separate training facility at Montford Point closed. Black marines would be trained and would fight alongside white marines in Korea, Vietnam, Afghanistan, and Iraq.

Taking advantage of the G.I. Bill of Rights after World War II, Steven Robinson graduated from the University of Pittsburgh and earned a law degree. He practiced law for more than 50 years in Warren, Ohio, where he was active in state and local politics. Robinson died in 2006.

authorities, who sentenced Bell to three and a half years in the notorious Parchman state penitentiary for the crime of self-defense.

Perhaps most galling was the fact that enemy prisoners of war were often accorded better treatment than African-American soldiers. Dempsey Travis of Chicago recalled his experiences at Camp Shenango, Pennsylvania: "I saw German prisoners free to move around the camp, unlike black soldiers who were restricted. The Germans walked right into the doggone places like any white American. We were wearin' the same uniform, but we were excluded." In 1944 black servicemen stationed at Fort Lawton in Washington State objected to living and working conditions that were inferior to those granted to Italian prisoners of war (POWs). Not only did the Italians receive lighter work assignments than the black Americans, but some Italian POWs were allowed to go to local bars that refused to admit African Americans. The resentment erupted into a riot on August 14, 1944, when black soldiers stoned the barracks housing the Italians. One prisoner was killed, and 24 others were injured. A court-martial convicted 23 black servicemen.

Because of the military's policies, most of the nearly one million African Americans who served during World War II did so in auxiliary units, notably in the transportation and engineering corps. Soldiers in the transportation corps, almost half of whom were black, loaded supplies and drove them in trucks to the front lines. Operating in the Red Ball Express or the later White Ball Express—the names for the trucking operations used to supply the American forces as they drove toward Germany in 1944 and 1945—African Americans braved enemy fire and delivered the fuel, ammunition, and other goods that made the fight possible. Black engineers built camps and ports, constructed and repaved roads, and performed many other tasks to support frontline troops. Black soldiers performed well in these tasks but were often subject to unfair military discipline. In Europe, many more black soldiers than white soldiers were executed even though African Americans made up only 10 percent of the total number of soldiers stationed there.

20.2.3 Port Chicago "Mutiny"

One of the most glaring examples of unfair treatment was the navy's handling of a "mutiny" at its Port Chicago base north of San Francisco. On July 17, 1944, in the worst home-front disaster of the war, an explosion at the base killed 320 sailors, of whom 202 were black ammunition loaders. In the following month, 328 of the surviving ammunition loaders were sent to fill another ship. When 258 of them refused to do so, they were arrested. Eventually the navy charged 50 men with mutiny, convicted them, and sentenced them to terms of imprisonment ranging from 8 to 15 years at Terminal Island in California. The NAACP's Thurgood Marshall filed a brief arguing that the men had been railroaded into prison because of their race, but to no avail.

20.2.4 Soldiers and Civilians Protest Military Discrimination

In military segregation, black American leaders identified a formidable but vulnerable target. Employing a variety of strategies, they mobilized the black civilian workforce, black women's groups, black college students, and an interracial coalition to resist this blatant inequality. They provoked a public dialogue with government and military officials at a pivotal moment when America's leaders most wanted to present a united democratic front to the world.

Examples of black protest abound. In 1942 the NAACP's journal the *Crisis* and the National Urban League's *Opportunity* published many editorials denouncing military segregation. Walter White traveled across the country and throughout the world visiting camps and making contacts with black soldiers and their white officers. He inundated the War Department and the president with letters citing examples of improper, hostile, and humiliating treatment of black servicemen by military personnel and in the white communities where bases were located. Frustration with continued military intransigence, however, forced William Hastie to resign as an adviser on Negro affairs on January 5, 1943.

Profile

William H. Hastie

William H. Hastie earned his L.L.B. in 1930 and his S.J.D. in 1935 at Harvard Law School. He taught at Howard University Law School, where he, along with Charles Hamilton Houston, trained the first generation of civil rights lawyers, the most illustrious of whom were Thurgood Marshall and Oliver Hill. In 1943, the NAACP presented Hastie with the Spingarn Medal. Appointed by President Harry Truman in 1949, Hastie became the first black American to serve as a federal judge. He sat on the Third Circuit Court of Appeals until 1971.

In January of 1943, William H. Hastie, who had been on leave from his post as dean of the Howard University Law School, resigned as civilian aide to Secretary of War Henry L. Stimson to protest the failure to outlaw discrimination in the military. Hastie had taken the position in 1940, but throughout his tenure he had experienced frustration and hostility in attempting to secure equal treatment for black men and women in uniform. In his letter of resignation, which was published in the *Chicago Defender*, he explained that the Army Air Forces' reactionary policies and discriminatory practices were the catalyst to his resignation.

In his resignation letter, Hastie noted the growing importance of the Army Air Forces and worried that discriminatory practices and policies established in the Army Air Force would spread to other branches of the army. Hastie's feelings were anchored in experience: When he took the office of civilian aide to Secretary Stimson, all questions of policy and any proposals that might affect African Americans in the Armed Forces were referred to his office for comment or approval before being enacted as policy. In December of 1940, Hastie was asked to comment on a plan at Tuskegee, a plan that included the development of a segregated training center for African-American airmen. Going into detail about his reservations, Hastie discovered that his views were completely disregarded and, subsequently, the Air Command did not forward any plan or project to him for comment. His role diminished, Hastie had to actively look for information so that he could volunteer his opinion about what he found.

The situation escalated two years later when in December of 1942, Hastie learned through War Department army press releases that the Air Command was looking at a similar plan to the one at Tuskegee, this time in Jefferson Barracks, Missouri. Here, the African-American officers would train in a segregated unit for ground duty with the Army Air Forces. Hastie once again found the proposal at odds with his own feelings about segregation in the armed forces and with what he knew to be true of the officer candidate-training program: that the program was the one significant area where the army was eliminating racial segregation. Although Hastie had written to the Air Command weeks earlier when news of the new program at Jefferson Barracks was breaking, the command gave no indication at the time of a plan for a segregated officer candidate school.

His role and office diminished and marginalized, Hastie became disillusioned. He wrote in his resignation that he believed the African-American soldier and any man in uniform for that matter must carry out his duties to the best of his ability, knowing that outside of the armed forces, countless Americans were working tirelessly to remove racial barriers and every practice that may have caused humiliation that was confronting the African-American serviceman. He implored African-American soldiers to be always the best soldier they could be. But his own treatment by the War Department and the failure of that Department to consult with him on discriminatory practices in the military led him to the unfortunate and tragic decision to resign from a post where he believed he could have made a difference.

20.2.5 Black Women in the Struggle to Desegregate the Military

The role of black women in the struggle to desegregate the military has often been overlooked, but their militancy contributed to the effort. A 1942 editorial in the *Crisis* suggested why:

> The colored woman has been a more potent factor in shaping Negro society than the white woman has been in shaping white society because the sexual caste system has been much more fluid and ill-defined than among whites. Colored women have worked with their men and helped build and maintain every institution we have. Without their economic aid and counsel we would have made little if any progress.

The most prominent example of black women's struggle is found in the history of the National Association of Colored Graduate Nurses. Mabel K. Staupers, its executive director, led an aggressive fight to eliminate quotas in the U.S. Army Nurse Corps. Although many black nurses volunteered during World War II, the navy refused to admit them, and the army allowed few to serve. To draw attention to the unfairness of quotas, Staupers met with First Lady Eleanor Roosevelt in November 1944 and described black nurses' troubled relationship with the armed forces. She told Mrs. Roosevelt that 82 black nurses were serving 150 patients at the all-black hospital at Fort Huachuca, Arizona, at a time when the army was complaining of a nursing shortage and debating the need to draft nurses. Staupers cited the practice of using black women to care for German POWs and asked if this was to be the special role of the black nurse in the war: "When our women hear of the great need for nurses in the Army and when they enter the service it is with the high hopes that they will be used to nurse sick and wounded soldiers who are fighting our country's enemies and not primarily to take care of these enemies."

Soldiers and sailors also resisted segregation and discrimination while in the service. They mounted well-organized efforts to desegregate officers' clubs. At Freeman Field, Indiana, for example, one hundred black officers refused to back down when their commanders threatened to arrest them for seeking to use the officers' club. In other bases, African-American soldiers responded with violence to violence, intimidation, and threats. Their actions, although quickly suppressed, prompted the army brass to reevaluate their belief in the military efficiency of discrimination.

20.2.6 The Beginning of Military Desegregation

In response to the militancy of black officers, civil rights leaders, and the press, the War Department made changes and began to reeducate soldiers, albeit in a limited fashion. The Advisory Committee on Negro Troop Policies was charged with coordinating the use of black troops and developing policy on social questions and personnel training. In 1943 the War Department also produced its own propaganda film—*The Negro Soldier*, directed by Frank Capra—to alleviate racial tensions. This patronizing film emphasized the contributions black soldiers had made in the nation's wars since the American Revolution and was designed to appeal to both black and white audiences.

The War Department also attempted to use propaganda to counter black protest groups and the claims of discrimination reported in the black press. The key to this effort was boxer Joe Louis, whom the army believed was "almost a god" to most black Americans. "The possibilities for using him," a secret internal report stated, "are almost unlimited, such as touring the army camps as special instructor on physical training; exhibition bouts, for use in radio or in movies; in a movie appearance a flashback

Profile

Mabel K. Staupers

Mabel K. Staupers was born in Barbados, in the British West Indies, on February 27, 1890, to Thomas Clarence and Pauline (Lobo) Doyle. Mother and daughter immigrated to New York in 1903. Mabel's father joined them later. In 1917 Mabel became a U.S. citizen. In short order, she married James Max Keaton, from whom she was later divorced, and received her R.N. diploma from Freedmen's Hospital School of Nursing in Washington, D.C. She worked as a private-duty nurse in Washington and New York City, where she helped to organize and served as the superintendent from 1920 to 1922 of the Booker T. Washington Sanatorium, an inpatient clinic for African Americans with tuberculosis. This was one of the few facilities in New York that permitted black physicians to treat their patients when they were hospitalized. Most other hospitals denied black medical professionals attending or staff privileges and positions. Staupers further honed her

organizing and leadership skills when she became executive secretary of the Harlem Committee of the New York Tuberculosis and Health Association from 1922 to 1934. In 1935 Staupers joined with Mary McLeod Bethune to found the National Council of Negro Women. In 1934 Staupers became the first executive director of the National Association of Colored Graduate Nurses (NACGN) and served until 1949, when she was named the organization's president. Under her stewardship the NACGN officially dissolved in 1951, after black nurses gained membership in the American Nursing Association.

Staupers's organizational and leadership talent was put to its greatest test during World War II. With verve and perfect timing, she mobilized wide-ranging support to end quotas that the military had established to limit the numbers of black nurses in the armed forces nurse corps. While the army initially indicated that it would accept 56 black nurses to work in the hospital units at Camp Livingston in Louisiana and Fort Bragg in North Carolina, the navy refused to accept any black women nurses. The matter came to a head when, in January 1945, President Franklin D. Roosevelt announced his support of legislation to draft nurses. Staupers was appalled that the government would entertain such a notion when hundreds of black women nurses were eager to serve. She led the struggle to end quotas and discrimination against black women nurses in the armed forces. Staupers published her account of this struggle in *No Time for Prejudice: A Story of the Integration of Negroes in Nursing in the United States* (New York: Macmillan, 1961). In recognition of her courageous struggle against racial discrimination, the NAACP awarded Staupers the Spingarn Medal in 1951. An array of honors followed. In 1967, New York Mayor John V. Lindsay gave her a citation that read, "To an immigrant who came to the United States and by Individual Effort through Education and Personal Achievement has become an Outstanding American Leader and Distinguished Citizen of America." She died of pneumonia at her home in Washington, D.C., in 1989.

could be shown of Louis knocking out Max Schmeling, the champion of the Germans." The same report also mentioned other prominent black men and women who had "great value in any propaganda programs. Other athletes like Ray Robinson, also track athletes, etc.; name bands like Cab Calloway, [Jimmy] Lunceford; stage, screen and concert stars like Ethel Waters, Bill Robinson, Eddie Anderson, Paul Robeson, etc." This propaganda did little to counter the prejudice and discrimination that most black Americans experienced in their daily lives.

Voices

Separate but Equal Training for Black Army Nurses?

In August 1944 Mabel Staupers received this reply from Under Secretary of War Robert Patterson in response to her query about a segregated training center the army had established at Fort Huachuca, Arizona, for black nurses:

AUGUST 7, 1944

Mrs. Mabel K. Staupers R.N., Executive Secretary, National Association of Colored Graduate Nurses, Inc., 1790 Broadway, New York 19, N.Y.

Dear Mrs. Staupers:

Thank you for your letter of July 19 with reference to the establishment of the first basic training center for Army Negro nurses at Fort Huachuca.

In establishing the first basic training center for Army Negro nurses at Fort Huachuca, the War Department desired that these nurses receive the best possible training and the most valuable experience for the type of service they would be required to render as Army nurses. It is the policy of the War Department to assign Negro nurses to those hospitals where there is a substantial number of Negro troops in relation to the personnel of the entire installation. The trainee at Fort Huachuca will therefore have the advantage of serving in a facility and under conditions parallel to those under which she will serve as an Army nurse.

You may be assured that the facilities for training afforded Negro nurses at Fort Huachuca will in no way be inferior to those of other similar establishments, and in their subsequent assignments these nurses will have full opportunity to render valuable service to the Army.

Sincerely yours,
(Signed) ROBERT P. PATTERSON
ROBERT P. PATTERSON,
Under Secretary of War

1. How does Patterson's letter reflect the military's position that "separate but equal" did not constitute discrimination against African Americans?
2. Why did Mabel Staupers and the National Association of Colored Graduate Nurses object to separate training facilities for black women?

SOURCE: War Department Files, File #2912, National Archives, Washington, D.C.

Racism remained strong throughout the war, but the persistent push of protest groups and the military's need for soldiers gradually loosened its grip. After the attack on Pearl Harbor, the services had to relax their restrictions on African Americans. The navy, previously the most resistant service, began to accept black men as sailors and noncommissioned officers. By 1943 it allowed African Americans into officer training schools. The Marine Corps, exclusively white throughout its history, began taking African Americans in 1942. Black officers were trained in integrated settings in all services except the Army Air Corps. The War Department even compelled recalcitrant commanding officers to recommend black servicemen for admission to the officer training schools, and soon over 2,000 a year graduated.

Many African Americans also saw combat, although under white officers. Several African-American artillery, tank destroyer, antiaircraft, and combat engineer battalions fought with distinction in Europe and Asia. Military prejudice seemed to be borne out by the poor showing of the all-black 92nd Combat Division in the Italian campaign in 1944–1945, but investigation revealed that its failure was the result of poor training and leadership by its white commander, General Edward M. Almond, who had no confidence in his men. After the Battle of the Bulge, a massive German counterattack in Belgium in December 1944, 2,500 black volunteers fought in integrated units. The army did not repeat the experiment during the rest of the war, but its success laid the groundwork for the eventual end of segregated units.

Although subject to many of the same kinds of discrimination as African-American men, African-American women also found expanded opportunities in the military. Approximately 4,000 black women served in the Women's Army Auxiliary Corps.

Mabel Staupers's efforts finally bore fruit in 1945. When the War Department claimed there was a shortage of nurses, Staupers mobilized nursing groups of all races to protest the discrimination against black nurses in the Army and Navy Nurse Corps. There was an immediate groundswell of public support to remove quotas. Buried beneath an avalanche of telegrams from an inflamed public, the War Department declared an end to quotas and exclusion. On January 10, 1945, the army opened its Nurse Corps to all applicants without regard to race. The navy followed suit on January 15. Within weeks, Phyllis Daley became the first black woman inducted into the Navy Nurse Corps. The Army Nurse Corps eventually accepted over 300 black nurses.

20.3 The Tuskegee Airmen

Enumerate the contributions of the Tuskegee Airmen to the Allied victory in World War II.

The most visible group of black soldiers served in the Army Air Force. In January 1941 the War Department announced the formation of an all-black pursuit squadron of fighter planes and the creation of a training program at Tuskegee Army Air Field, Alabama, for black pilots.

Unlike all other units in the army, the 99th Squadron and the 332nd Group, made up of the 100th, 301st, and 302nd Squadrons, had black officers. The 99th went to North Africa in April 1943 and flew its first combat mission against the Italian island of Pantelleria in the Mediterranean on June 2. Later the squadron participated in the air battle over Sicily and supported the invasion of Italy. The squadron regularly engaged German pilots in aerial combat. General Benjamin O. Davis, Jr., commanded the 332nd Group when it was deployed to Italy in January 1944. In July, the 99th was added to the 332nd, and the group participated in campaigns in Italy, France, Germany, and the Balkans.

The **Tuskegee Airmen** gained an impressive record. They flew over 15,500 sorties, completed 1,578 missions, and escorted 200 heavy bombers deep into Germany's Rhineland. They accumulated 150 Distinguished Flying Crosses, a Legion of Merit, a Silver Star, 14 Bronze Stars, and 744 Air Medals. Coleman Young (1919–1997), mayor of Detroit from 1973 to 1993, was a proud Tuskegee Airman and retained fond memories of his military service.

Tuskegee Airmen

All-black combat air unit during World War II.

20.3.1 Technology: The Tuskegee Planes

To fly and participate in combat, the Tuskegee Airmen and the black ground troops who looked after their planes had to overcome more than the racism that cast doubt on black soldiers' ability to fight. They also had to master the technology of complex machines. The 332nd Fighter Group flew more different kinds of fighter planes than any other group of pilots during World War II. They were initially equipped with P-40 Warhawks, then with P-39 Airacobras, later with P-47 Thunderbolts, and finally with the P-51 Mustang, the airplane with which they became most identified. Keeping these different kinds of planes in top form placed extreme pressure on the black mechanics who serviced them. The mechanics had to master the schematics of

Voices

A Tuskegee Airman Remembers

Virgil Richardson was a Tuskegee Airman. In an oral history told to historian Ben Vinson III, Patterson recalled both the excitement of being an airman and the racism the Tuskegee Airmen endured:

Between December of 1944 and March of 1945 we saw more action. After having muscled into France, the Allies were preparing to make their final thrust at Hitler. I remember when we flew escort for over 1,000 bombers on their way to Germany. It was an awesome sight, seeing bombers in every direction for a 150-mile stretch. Looking down into the sea we saw still more activity, throngs and throngs of ships. During these months our planes bombarded German factories and troop positions that were preparing to repel the Allied invasion. Thankfully, the Germans didn't have use of the French fleet, which had been scuttled. But the Germans did have friends amongst the French, which made the Allied job more difficult.

Part of our responsibilities included strafing radar installations along the coast of France. On one sortie, I was part of a mission of four planes led by a man named Ballard. My wingman was Jefferson. His wingman was a pilot named Daniels. As we came in towards the ground from an altitude of almost 15,000 feet, I suddenly looked back to find Jefferson and noticed that Daniels, who was flying in front of me, was going up in smoke. I pulled up and started following Ballard, who didn't look back. That's when I noticed that Jefferson was being shot down as well. Ballard and I went

in as close to the coast as we dared and fired furiously at our targets. One, two, three . . . fire! One, two, three . . . fire! That was the interval. I shot short bursts while flying above the ocean at nearly 500 miles an hour.

We lost a number of pilots that day. When I returned to base I learned that Faulkner, our squadron leader, who had been flying at 30,000 feet, turned over and went down. They radioed him, knowing that something must have gone wrong. He was probably unconscious because he didn't respond. A poor oxygen connection apparently caused him to pass out during flight. As for Daniels, I learned many years later that he had survived his ordeal and had become a POW. Ironically, once behind enemy lines, the Germans treated him with proper respect. He was an officer, not a *black* officer. It seemed interesting to me to see how black soldiers had to be in the clutches of the enemy before being bestowed some of the honor that they deserved.

---

1. What emotions did combat evoke in Richardson?
2. What do his comments about the German treatment of black POWs imply about racism in the U.S. military?
3. Do you think Richardson and the other Tuskegee Airmen wanted to be treated as officers or as black officers?

completely different engines and repair them. Despite the challenges this presented, the Tuskegee mechanics acquired the respect of the airmen and were recognized for their exceptional mechanical abilities during the war. They frequently worked round-the-clock, sleeping and eating in shifts in the airplane hangars.

Standardization was impossible because each type of plane was designed differently from the others. For example, while the P-39's engine was behind the pilot, the P-40's engine was in front of him. Virgil Richardson, one of the Tuskegee mechanics, talked about servicing the P-39: "First of all, you entered the cockpit through a door, as if you were getting into a car. The plane's motor was located behind the pilot, and there was a propeller shaft that came from the motor, under the pilot's seat, to the three-blade metal propeller. P-39s were equipped with a 37-millimeter cannon in the propeller hub. There were also two .50-caliber machine guns in each wing, and two more in the nose. That was substantial armament! The plane had wide, tricycle landing gear . . . [it] was a joy to fly, since there was no torque."

20.3.2 The Transformation of Black Soldiers

A new generation of African Americans became soldiers during World War II, and the experience gave many of them an enhanced sense of themselves and a commitment to the fight for black equality. They returned home with a broader perception of the world and a transformed consciousness. Unlike the black soldiers in World War I, a greater percentage of those drafted at the outset of World War II had attended high school, and more of them were either high school or college graduates. Some black soldiers brought so-called radical ideas with them as they were drafted and sent to segregated installations. The urban and northern black servicemen and women and many of the southern rural recruits had a strong sense of their own self-worth and dignity. In their study of Chicago, sociologists St. Clair Drake and Horace Cayton noted:

> At least half of the Negro soldiers—and Bronzeville's men fall into this class—
> were city people who had lived through a Depression in America's Black Ghet-
> toes, and who had been exposed to unions, the Communist movement, and
> to the moods of racial radicalism that occasionally swept American cities.
> Even the rural southern Negroes were different this time—for the thirty years
> between the First and Second World War has seen a great expansion of school
> facilities in the South and distribution of newspapers and radios.

The armed forces first exposed many African Americans to a world outside the segregated South and nurtured a budding international consciousness. Haywood Stephney of Clarksdale, Mississippi, recalled that when he first encountered segregation in the military he simply thought it was supposed to be that way: "Because you grow up in this situation you don't see but one side of the coin. Having not tasted the freedom or the liberty of being and doing like other folks then you didn't know what it was like over across the street. So we accepted it." Like many others, his experiences during the war quickly removed him from "total darkness" and raised fundamental questions about the nation's racial system.

Douglas Conner, another Mississippi veteran, captured the collective understanding of the social and political meaning of the war shared by the men in his unit, the 31st Quartermaster Battalion stationed in Okinawa: "The air people in Tuskegee, Dorie Miller, and the others gave the blacks a sense that they could succeed and compete in a world that had been saying that 'you're nothing.' " Conner insisted that "because of the world war, I think many people, especially blacks, got the idea that we're going back, but we're not going back to business as usual. Somehow we're going to change this nation so that there's more equality than there is now." The personal transformation that Conner and others experienced, combined with a number of international, national, and regional forces, laid the foundation for a modern freedom movement.

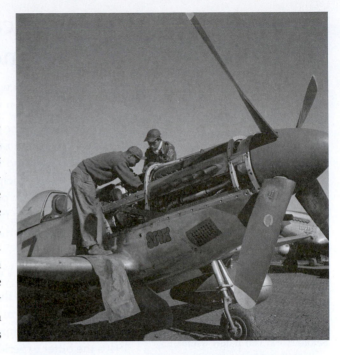

Tuskegee Airmen Marcellus G. Smith, Louisville, Kentucky, and Roscoe C. Brown, New York, New York, service their airplane in Ramitelli, Italy, March 1945.

The distinguished World War II record of the "Tuskegee Airmen," pilots who trained and fought in all-black fighter squadrons, confounded the expectations of white officers who doubted the black men had the ability or nerve to pilot fighter aircraft.

20.4 African Americans on the Home Front

Explain the ways in which World War II made more visible the tensions and competition between white and black Americans over housing and jobs.

Just as they did in the military, African Americans at home fought a dual war against the Axis powers and racism in the United States. Black workers and volunteers helped staff the factories and farms that produced goods for the fight while also purchasing war bonds and participating in other defense activities. The changes the war brought on also created new points of conflict while exacerbating preexisting problems and occasionally igniting full-scale riots. Throughout the war, protest groups and the black press fought employment discrimination and political exclusion.

20.4.1 Black Workers: From Farm to Factory

The war accelerated the migration of African Americans from rural areas to the cities. Even though the farm economy recovered during the war, high-paying defense jobs and other urban occupations tempted many black farmers to abandon the land. By the 1940s the bitter experiences of the previous decades had made it clear there was little future in the cotton fields. Boll weevils, competition from other cotton-growing parts of the world, and mechanization reduced the need for black labor. Indeed, by the end of the war in 1945, only 28 percent of black men worked on farms, down from 41 percent in 1940. More than 300,000 black men left agricultural labor between 1940 and 1944 alone.

The wartime need for workers, backed by pressure from the government, helped break down some barriers to employing African Americans in industry. During the war the number of black workers in nonfarm employment rose from 2,900,000 to 3,800,000, and thousands moved into previously whites-only jobs. African Americans found employment in the aircraft industry, and tens of thousands were employed in the nation's shipyards.

With so many of their men away at war, black women increasingly found work outside the laundry and domestic service that had previously been their lot. Nationally 600,000 black women—400,000 of them former domestic servants—shifted into industrial jobs. As one aircraft worker wryly put it, "Hitler was the one that got us out of the white folks' kitchen." Even those women who stayed in domestic work often saw their wages improve as the supply of competent workers dwindled.

The abundance of industrial jobs helped spur and direct the second phase of the Great Migration, in which some 1.5 million migrants—nearly 15 percent of the population—left the South, swelling the black communities in northern and western cities that had significant war industries. By 1950 the percentage of the nation's black population living in the South had fallen from 77 percent to 68 percent. The most dramatic rise in black population was in southern California. Because of its burgeoning aircraft industry and the success of civil rights groups and the federal government in limiting discrimination, Los Angeles saw its relatively small African-American community increase by more than 340,000 during the war.

Before World War II, few white women and still fewer black women worked in heavy industries, but with so many men in the armed forces, women were recruited for jobs in shipyards and airplane factories, like this aircraft worker. Between 1940 and 1944, the percentage of black women in the industrial workforce increased from 6.8 percent to 18 percent.

Many unions became more open to African-American workers as black men and women took jobs in industries. Between 1940 and 1945, black union membership rose from 200,000 to 1.25 million. Those unions connected to the Committee for Industrial Organization (CIO), particularly the United Automobile Workers, were the most open to black membership, whereas AFL affiliates were the most likely to treat African Americans as second-class members or to exclude them altogether. Some white unionized workers continued to oppose hiring black workers, even going on strike to prevent it, but the union leadership, the government, and employers often deflected their resistance. The growth in black membership did not end racism in unions, even in the CIO, but it did provide African Americans with a stronger foundation on which to protest discrimination in employment.

20.4.2 The FEPC during the War

After President Roosevelt issued the executive order banning job discrimination in defense industries with government contracts, thousands of impoverished black southerners rushed to cities in the Pacific Northwest, especially to Seattle. Wartime Seattle had offered jobs in its shipyards, in logging-truck manufacturing, and at the Boeing aircraft production plants. By 1945, Boeing employed over 1,200 black workers, approximately 3 percent of its labor force. African Americans also accounted for 7 percent of Seattle's shipyard workers. By 1948 black families in Seattle boasted a median income of $3,314, a mere 10 percent lower than the median for the nation's white families. However, the economic good fortune of black workers on the West Coast was not typical of the rest of the country.

In the Midwest and on the East Coast, many African Americans criticized industry's failure to end economic discrimination. In May 1943 President Roosevelt responded to the ineffectiveness of the FEPC. Executive Order 9346 established a new Committee on Fair Employment Practice, increased its budget, and placed its operation directly under the Executive Office of the President. Roosevelt appointed Malcolm Ross, a combative white liberal, to head the committee. Ross initiated nationwide hearings of cases concerning discrimination in the shipbuilding and railroad industries. These proceedings embarrassed some companies and increased compliance with the FEPC's orders. Resistance, however, was more common. In Mobile, Alabama, for example, the white employees of the Alabama Dry Dock and Shipbuilding Company opposed the FEPC's efforts to pressure the company to promote 12 of the 7,000 African Americans it employed in menial positions to racially mixed welding crews. The white workers went on a rampage, assaulting 50 African Americans. The FEPC thereupon withdrew its plan and acquiesced in the traditional Jim Crow arrangements for all work assignments. White workers retained their more lucrative positions. As a result of this kind of intransigence, the committee failed to redress most of the grievances of black workers. An effort to continue the committee after the war was defeated.

20.4.3 Anatomy of a Race Riot: Detroit, 1943

One of the bloodiest race riots in the nation's history took place in 1943 in Detroit, Michigan, where black and white workers were competing fiercely for jobs and housing. Relations between the two communities had been smoldering for months, with fighting in the plants and on the streets, against housing segregation and economic discrimination. The brutality of white police officials was an especially potent factor. Tensions were so palpable that weeks before the riot, the NAACP's Walter White had warned that the city could explode.

The immediate trigger for the riot was a squabble on June 20 between white and black bathers at the segregated city beaches on Belle Isle in the Detroit River. Within hours, 200 white sailors from a nearby base joined the white mob that attacked black men and women. A rumor that white citizens had killed a black woman and thrown her baby over a bridge spread across the city. Soon the riot was in full swing and spread quickly along Woodward Avenue, the city's major thoroughfare, into Paradise Valley, where some 35,000 southern black migrants had joined, by the spring of 1943, the city's already crowded black population. By Monday morning white men in search of more victims had overrun downtown Detroit. The mayor refused to acknowledge that the situation had gotten out of hand, but by Tuesday evening he could no longer deny the crisis.

Six thousand federal troops had to be dispatched to Detroit to restore order. When the violence ended, 34 people had been killed (25 black and nine white people) and more than 700 injured. Of the 25 black people who died, the Detroit police killed 17. However, the police did not kill any of the white men who assaulted African Americans or committed arson. Property damage was extensive, and one million man-hours were lost in war production.

In the aftermath, the city created the Mayor's Interracial Committee, the first permanent municipal body designed to promote civic harmony and fairness. Despite the efforts of labor and black leaders, many white people in Detroit, including Wayne County prosecutor William E. Dowling, blamed the black press and the NAACP for instigating the riot. Dowling and others accused the city's black citizens of pushing too hard for economic and political equality and insisted that they operated under communist influence. One report concluded that black leaders provoked the riot because they had compared "victory over the axis . . . [with] a corresponding overthrow in the country of those forces which . . . prevent true racial equality." In contrast, black leaders, radical trade unionists, and members of other ethnic organizations, especially Jewish groups, blamed "the KKK, the Christian Front, the Black Dragon Society, the National Workers League, the Knights of the White Camelia, the Southern Voters League, and similar organizations based on a policy of terror and . . . white supremacy."

20.4.4 The G.I. Bill of Rights and Black Veterans

In 1944, President Roosevelt signed the Servicemen's Readjustment Act (known as the "G.I. Bill of Rights"), legislation that would profoundly affect American life and society. It rewarded the sacrifices and accomplishments of black and white veterans in the war with college tuition allowances, stipends for books, and guaranteed loans of up to $2,000 (a substantial sum at the time) at low interest rates, with which to purchase homes or launch small businesses. Congress would eventually pay approximately $14.5 billion for the G.I. Bill's provisions.

By 1947, veterans accounted for half of all college students. The G.I. Bill made possible the upward mobility of a generation of American men who entered professions and trades and purchased homes that would become the basis of future wealth. Between 1950 and 1960, Americans built more than 13 million new homes—11 million of them were in the suburbs, where one-quarter of the entire population relocated after the war. The G.I. Bill fueled the boom in higher education, transportation, and the construction industries that undergirded the postwar prosperity America enjoyed.

While many black veterans benefited from the G.I. Bill of Rights, they never received their fair share of funds and assistance. Mississippi Congressman John E. Rankin sabotaged the transformative potential of the G.I. Bill by insisting that state and local veterans' administrators control the distribution of the benefits. The resulting racial disparities were predictable in southern states. In Mississippi, by the summer of 1947, local officials had approved over 3,000 Veterans Administration home loans, but only two went to African-American veterans. In northern urban areas, real estate agencies and banks practiced "redlining" and denied black men mortgages in desirable areas.

The denial of loans and the violence that often erupted when black families attempted to move into suburban areas curtailed upward and outward mobility. Roosevelt may have thought he was signing a color-blind law, but its execution proved otherwise.

20.4.5 Old and New Protest Groups on the Home Front

The NAACP grew tremendously during the war; by the war's end, it stood poised for even greater achievements. Under the editorial direction of Roy Wilkins, the circulation of the NAACP's journal, the *Crisis*, grew from 7,000 to 45,000. During the war, the *Crisis* was one of the most important sources for information about black men and women. The NAACP's membership increased from 50,000 in 1940 to 450,000 at the end of the war. Much of this growth occurred in the South, which by 1945 had more than 150,000 members. Supreme Court victories and especially close monitoring of the "Double V" campaign helped explain these huge increases.

Success, however, bred conflict and ambivalence. Leaders split over the value of integration versus self-segregation and questioned the benefit of relying so heavily on legal cases rather than paying more attention to the concerns and needs of working-class black men and women. Wilkins acknowledged the organization's uncertainty and indecisiveness:

> The war was a great watershed for the NAACP. We had become far more powerful, and now the challenge was to keep our momentum. Everyone knew the NAACP stood against discrimination and segregation, but what was our postwar program to be? Beyond discrimination and segregation, where would we stand on veterans, housing, labor-management relations, strikes, the Fair Employment Practices Commission, organizations at state levels, education? What would we do to advance the fight for the vote in the South? . . . We had a big membership . . . but we didn't know how to use them.

In 1944 southern white liberals joined with African Americans to establish the **Southern Regional Council (SRC)**. This interracial coalition, an important example of the local initiative of private citizens, was devoted to expanding democracy in a region better known for the political and economic oppression and exploitation of its black citizens. The SRC conducted research and focused attention on the political, social, and educational inequalities endemic to black life in the South. Although the events of the 1950s and 1960s would soon overtake its patient, gradualist program, the SRC challenged the facade of southern white supremacy.

In 1942 a far more strident group called the **Congress of Racial Equality (CORE)** was formed. It pursued different tactics from those of the NAACP, Urban League, and other existing civil rights groups. CORE began in Chicago when an interracial group of Christian pacifists gathered to find ways to make America live up to the ideals of equality and justice on which it based its war program. James Farmer and Bayard Rustin were key in getting the group off the ground. Unlike the NAACP, CORE was a decentralized, intensely democratic organization. CORE dedicated itself to the principles of nonviolent direct action as expounded by Indian leader Mohandas Gandhi. During the war this pacifist organization expanded to other cities and challenged segregation in the North with sit-ins and other protest tactics that the civil rights movement would later adopt in the South.

African Americans fought discrimination in many ways. Women were central to these efforts. Throughout the 1940s, in countless communities across the South and the Midwest, black women organized women's political councils and other groups to press for integration of public facilities—hospitals, swimming pools, theaters, and restaurants—and for the right to pursue collegiate and professional studies. Others were

Southern Regional Council (SRC)

Organization that conducted research and focused attention on social, political, and educational inequality in the South.

Congress of Racial Equality (CORE)

Protest group committed to nonviolent direct action.

galvanized by the war and took advantage of the limited social and political spaces afforded them to create lasting works in the arts, literature, and popular culture. Women whose names would become virtually synonymous with the modern civil rights movement in the 1950s and 1960s helped lay its foundation in the World War II era. For example, Ella Baker was accumulating contacts and sharpening her organization skills as she served as the NAACP field secretary. Rosa Parks began resisting segregation laws on Montgomery, Alabama, buses during the 1940s.

Black college students also began protesting segregation in public accommodations. The spark that ignited the Howard University campus civil rights movement came in January 1943. Three sophomore women—Ruth Powell from Massachusetts and Marianne Musgrave and Juanita Morrow from Ohio—sat at a lunch counter near the

Profile

Bayard Rustin

Bayard Rustin spent his life actively engaged in civil rights causes. He struggled against discrimination during the 1940s, was special assistant to Martin Luther King, Jr. in the 1950s, acted as a behind-the-scenes architect of the March on Washington in 1963, and was executive director of the A. Phillip Randolph Institute. Robert Maas captures his quiet dignity in this 1982 photograph.

Bayard Rustin, the preeminent strategist of nonviolent resistance, was born on March 17, 1910, in West Chester, Pennsylvania. Rustin worked behind the scenes to give shape and coherence to the modern civil rights movement. During his youth, he belonged to the Young Communist League; however, in the 1940s he, along with Pauli Murray and James Farmer, became staff members of the pacifist organization Fellowship of Reconciliation (FOR) and experimented with Gandhian techniques of nonviolent resistance to racial injustice. In 1942, Rustin and Farmer were active in founding the Congress of Racial Equality (CORE). A year later, Rustin refused to be drafted, rejecting even the traditional Quaker compromise of

alternative service in an army hospital. Convicted of violating the Selective Service Act, he served three years in a federal penitentiary in Kentucky.

While in prison, Rustin honed the philosophy that would guide his life. Rustin wrote,

> There are three ways in which one can deal with an injustice. (a) One can accept it without protest. (b) One can seek to avoid it. (c) One can resist the injustice nonviolently. To accept it is to perpetuate it. To avoid it is impossible. To resist by intelligent means, and with an attitude of mutual responsibility and respect, is much the better course.

On release from prison, Rustin became race relations secretary for FOR and participated in countless protest organizations. He organized a Free India Committee to press for the end of British rule in India and directed A. Philip Randolph's Committee Against Discrimination in the Armed Forces. He orchestrated CORE's 1947 Journey of Reconciliation (a precursor to the Freedom Rides of 1961), in which 16 black and white men traveled by bus through the Upper South to test new federal laws prohibiting segregated services in interstate transportation. Outside Chapel Hill, North Carolina, the group was assaulted and arrested. Rustin and three of his colleagues were sentenced to 30 days on a road gang, of which he served 22 days. In the late 1950s Rustin was an adviser to Martin Luther King, Jr. and one of the key figures in the civil rights movement of the 1950s and 1960s.

Rustin, who was gay, fought oppression all his life. After the ebb tide of the civil rights movement, he shifted to combating homophobia. He declared shortly before his death on August 24, 1987, that "the barometer of where one is on human rights questions is no longer the black community, it's the gay community. Because it is the community which is most easily mistreated."

campus and were refused service. They demanded to see the manager and vowed to wait until he came. Instead, two policemen arrived who instructed the waitress to serve them. When the check arrived, the trio learned they had been charged 25 cents each instead of the customary 10 cents. They placed 35 cents on the counter, turned to leave, and were arrested. Ruth Powell later reported that "the policeman who arrested us told us we were being taken in for investigation because he had no proof that we weren't 'subversive agents.' " In fact, no charges were lodged against the women. The purpose of their arrest had been to intimidate them, but the incident instead fanned the smoldering embers of resentment in the Howard University student body.

20.4.6 Post–World War II Racial Violence

After the German surrender in May 1945 and the Japanese surrender in August 1945, the United States began the transition to peace. The experiences of many black men who returned home after World War II mirrored the same racist violence that World War I black veterans had suffered. Many of the gains of black men and women were wiped away as the armed forces demobilized and the factories began reinstituting the discriminatory hiring systems that were in place before the conflict. Access to fair, decent, and affordable housing remained a sore issue, as did the inequalities in educational opportunities and the continuing scourge of police brutality. Thus, as the country tried to regain its prewar footing, it was clear that segregation and discrimination would face a huge challenge in the coming years and that the African-American community was ready, willing, and able to fight in ways undreamed of in earlier eras. However, in the immediate aftermath of World War II the level of hatred of returning black servicemen, especially in the South, underscored the intransigence of racial oppression.

Black men who served in U.S. military forces during World War II sometimes received violent receptions and little justice upon returning to their homes in the South. As the war concluded, many white southerners were determined—as they had been following World War I—to maintain white supremacy no matter the contributions of African American soldiers and sailors to the Allied victory over fascism in Europe and the Pacific.

Isaac Woodard was a 27-year-old sergeant in the U.S. Army who had been awarded a battle star and Good Conduct medal for his service in the South Pacific. Still in uniform following his discharge, he was on a Greyhound bus bound for his home of Winnsboro, South Carolina, in February 1946 when he got into a dispute with the bus driver. The driver summoned the police in Batesburg, South Carolina. Law enforcement officers detained Woodard, charged him with disorderly conduct, and proceeded to beat him. They placed him in the local jail where he was beaten again, permanently blinded, and denied medical care.

Released after two days, Woodard spent weeks recovering in a military hospital. Walter White, the Executive Secretary of the NAACP, learned of Woodard's beating and mounted a publicity campaign. White informed President Harry Truman, who was appalled. "My God! I had no idea . . . ." He ordered a Department of Justice investigation. Famed Hollywood director Orson Welles told a nationwide ABC radio audience about Woodward's treatment. There were protests and demonstrations, including a rally of 20,000 people at Lewisohn Stadium in Harlem co-chaired by heavyweight champion Joe Louis. Folk singer and composer Woody Guthrie sang "The Blinding of Isaac Woodard."

In South Carolina in federal court, Batesburg Police Chief Linwood Shull and several of his officers were charged with violating Isaac Woodard's civil rights. Shull admitted striking Woodard but insisted he had not blinded the veteran. It took a half an hour for an all-white and all-male jury to acquit Shull. Cheers rang out in the courtroom.

As Woodard gradually recovered from his injuries, white men in Columbia, Tennessee, attacked and partially destroyed the town's black neighborhood known as "the Bottom" or sometimes as "Mink Slide." In February 1946, Gladys Stephenson, accompanied by her son James who was in the U.S. Navy, stopped by a local appliance store to complain that her radio had not been properly repaired. The white clerk, Billy Fleming, thought that James failed to show him sufficient respect. He struck the young black man with his fist, unaware that Stephenson was on the welterweight boxing team in the Navy. Stephenson responded with several punches and sent Fleming sprawling through the plate glass window with a badly lacerated leg.

Both mother and son were charged with attempted murder and confined to the nearby jail. Outraged at the brazen assertiveness of two African Americans, a mob quickly gathered with the apparent intention of breaking the Stephensons out of jail and lynching them. Unable to locate them because they had been taken from the jail for their own protection, the armed white men invaded the black section of town. Black men, in the meantime, had themselves organized to protect their families and property. With the help of local police and the Tennessee Highway Patrol, the white mob prevailed and wreaked havoc and destruction on "the Bottom." Two black men were shot dead "trying to escape." Two dozen black men were arrested and jailed.

The NAACP dispatched attorneys Thurgood Marshall and Alexander Looby to Tennessee where they were assisted by a local white lawyer, Maurice Weaver. In the trials of the black men that following November, the three lawyers won "not guilty" verdicts for 24 of the men from juries consisting solely of white men. One black man was convicted on a lesser charge and released on bail. Disgusted with this version of justice, a group of white men pursued Marshall as he drove out of town with the apparent intention of another lynching. Marshall and Looby barely managed to escape.

In the summer of 1946, two black couples were unable to escape and were lynched near Moore's Ford Bridge about 60 miles east of Atlanta, Georgia. George W. Dorsey had spent five years in the U.S. Army in the South Pacific. He was married to Mae Murray Dorsey, then seven months pregnant. Dorothy Malcom, George Dorsey's sister, was married to Roger Malcom. Both couples had worked as sharecroppers on the farm of J. Loy Harrison.

The postwar violence did not end with President Harry Truman's executive order in December 1946, creating a committee to investigate civil rights that issued a report in 1947, "To Secure These Rights." Two years later four young African American men were accused of raping a young white woman near Groveland, Florida. Two black Army veterans—Walter Irvin and Samuel Shepard—stopped their car on a warm July night in 1949 to assist two white people whose 1940 Ford had broken down. Irvin and Shepard were each 22 years old. Willie Padgett was 23 years old and his wife, Norma Lee, was 17. Irvin and Padgett got into a fist fight after the four of them shared a bottle of whisky. The black man knocked the white man down. The next day Norma claimed the black men had raped her.

Incensed at the sexual assault, white men organized and invaded the black neighborhood near Groveland, sending its residents fleeing for their lives into the nearby woods and swamps. White law enforcement personnel, assisted by volunteers including members of the Ku Klux Klan, pursued likely suspects. Ernest Thomas, who was nowhere near the alleged rape, fled and was shot and killed by a posse about 200 miles from Groveland. Charles Greenlee, who was at the local train station, was apprehended and charged with rape. Walter Irvin and Samuel Shepard were taken into custody by Lake County Sheriff Willis McCall and savagely beaten until they confessed to raping Norma Padgett.

The NAACP dispatched attorneys Franklin Williams and Jack Greenberg to Florida where they were assisted by local attorney Alex Akerman in defending Greenlee, Irvin, and Shepard. They were convicted by an all-white jury. Irvin and Shepard were sentenced to death while Greenlee received a life sentence because he was 17 years old. The NAACP appealed to the U.S. Supreme Court, which overturned the convictions. Irvin and Shepard were scheduled to be tried again. On the trip from prison back to

Lake County and in the custody of Sheriff Willis McCall, both black men were shot by McCall because he said they tried to escape when they stopped on an isolated road. Shepard died but Irvin survived.

Defended in his second trial by NAACP attorney Thurgood Marshall, an all-white jury found Walter Irvin guilty. Marshall and the NAACP worked relentlessly and successfully to have Irvin's sentence commuted to life in prison. Later, Florida Governor Leroy Collins in 1955 commuted the sentence. Irvin was pardoned and released in 1968. Charles Greenlee was paroled from his life sentence in 1960.

20.5 The Cold War and International Politics

Separate the positive from the negative impact that the Cold War had on African Americans, in both their political and cultural activism.

As the defeat of the Axis powers neared in early 1945, the United Nations began planning for the peace. Within a short time, however, the opposing interests of the Soviet Union and the United States led to a long period of intense hostility that became known as the Cold War. This conflict soon led to a division of Europe into two spheres, with the Soviets dominating part of Germany and the nations to its east and a coalition of democratic capitalist regimes allied with the United States in the west. Thereafter, the overriding goal of the United States and its allies was the "containment" of communism. To this end, the **North Atlantic Treaty Organization (NATO)** was formed in 1949 to provide a military counterforce to Soviet power in Europe while American dollars helped rebuild Western Europe's war-shattered economy. The United States forged a similarly close relationship with Japan. Much of the rest of the world, however, became contested terrain during the Cold War.

As the nations of Asia and Africa gained independence from colonial domination over the ensuing decades, the United States struggled to keep them out of the Soviet orbit. It did so through foreign aid, direct military force, and, occasionally, through clandestine operations run by the Central Intelligence Agency. These interventions were matched by a rising diplomatic and propaganda effort to convince the emerging nations that the United States was a model to be emulated and an ally to be trusted.

The Cold War had an enormous influence on American society precisely when the powerful movement for African-American rights was beginning to emerge. The long conflict resulted in the rise of a large permanent military establishment in the United States. The reorganized American military enlisted millions of men and women by the early 1950s and claimed most of the national budget. The federal government also grew in power during the war and provided a check on the control that white southerners had exercised over race relations in their region for so long. American policymakers also became concerned about the nation's ability to win the allegiance of Africans and other nonwhite people in the emerging nations. Soviet propaganda could discredit American sincerity by pointing to the deplorable state of race relations within the United States. Hence, during the Cold War, external pressures reinforced domestic efforts to change American racial policy.

North Atlantic Treaty Organization (NATO)

Military alliance formed to counter the threat posed by the Soviet Union and its allies.

America's Cold War propaganda targeted all citizens, black and white. This anticommunism poster was one of the many designed to remind Americans of threats to their freedom and to fan the flames of patriotism.

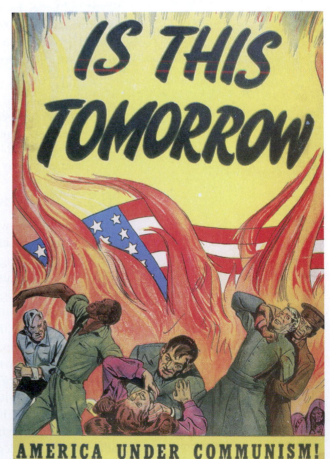

20.5.1 African Americans in World Affairs: W. E. B. Du Bois and Ralph Bunche

The Cold War gave new importance to the voices of African Americans in world affairs. Two men, W. E. B. Du Bois and Ralph Johnson Bunche (1904–1971), represented alternative strategies for responding to this opportunity. Du Bois was highly critical of American policy. For half a century, he had linked the fate of African Americans with that of Africans, and by 1945 was widely hailed as the "Father of Pan-Africanism." In that year he directed the Fifth Pan-African Congress, which met in Manchester, England. Africans who had been radicalized by World War II dominated the conference and encouraged it to denounce Western imperialism. Du Bois considered the United States a protector of the colonial system and opposed its stance in the Cold War. On returning from the Manchester congress, he declared,

> We American Negroes should know . . . until Africa is free, the descendants of Africa the world over cannot escape their chains. . . . The NAACP should therefore put in the forefront of its program the freedom of Africa in work and wage, education and health, and the complete abolition of the colonial system.

In contrast to Du Bois, scholar-diplomat Ralph Bunche opted to work within the American system. Bunche held a Harvard doctorate in government and international relations and had spent much of the 1930s studying the problems of African Americans. During World War II, the American government found his expertise on Africa of tremendous value, and Bunche became one of the key policymakers for the region. His analysis of events and changes in Africa and the Far East after World War II led to his appointment as adviser to the U.S. delegation at the San Francisco conference that drafted the United Nations (UN) Charter. In 1948 he served as acting mediator of the UN Special Committee on Palestine, and in 1949 he negotiated an armistice between Egypt and Israel. He received the Spingarn Medal of the NAACP in 1949, and in 1950 he became the first African American to receive the Nobel Peace Prize. Although Bunche worked in concert with national policymakers, he was committed to winning independence for African nations and freedom for his own people. As he wrote:

> Today, for all thinking people, the Negro is the shining symbol of the true significance of democracy. He has demonstrated what can be achieved with democratic liberties even when grudgingly and incompletely bestowed. But the most vital significance of the Negro . . . to American society . . . is the fact that democracy which is not extended to all of the nation's citizens is a democracy that is mortally wounded.

20.5.2 Anticommunism at Home

The rising tensions with the Soviet Union affected all aspects of domestic life in the United States. Conservatives used fears of communist subversion to attack anyone who advocated change in America. This included people who were or had been members of the Communist Party, union members, liberals, and those who had fought for African-American rights. The Truman administration (1945–1953) responded to fears of subversion by instituting government loyalty programs. Government employees were dismissed for the merest suspicion of disloyalty. Militant American anticommunism reached a feverish peak in the immediate postwar years and ignited an explosion of red-baiting hysteria that led to the rise of Wisconsin Republican Senator Joseph McCarthy (1909–1957) and the **House Un-American Activities Committee (HUAC)**. The relentless pursuit of "communist sympathizers" by McCarthy and HUAC ruined many lives. HUAC hounded people in the media and the entertainment industry. Even so prominent a figure as Du Bois was ripe for attack. On February 8, 1951, HUAC indicted him for allegedly serving as an "agent of a foreign principal" in his work with the Peace Information Center. In November a federal judge dismissed the

House Un-American Activities Committee (HUAC)

Congressional committee formed to investigate the activities of communists and "communist sympathizers" in America.

charges. The government had been unable to prove Du Bois was an agent of communism. Despite his past contributions, fear and personal malice prevented most African-American leaders from defending him.

20.5.3 Paul Robeson

Paul Robeson (1898–1976) was one of the most tragic victims of these anticommunist witch hunts. This fine scholar and star collegiate athlete, Columbia Law School graduate, consummate performer, and star of stage and screen had always advocated the rights of African Americans and workers. During the 1930s he worked closely with the Communist Party (although he was never a member), becoming one of the most famous defenders of the Soviet Union. Many leftists of the time became disaffected with the Soviet Union after its 1939 pact with Hitler and its brutal repressiveness became clear. Robeson, however, doggedly stuck to his belief in Soviet communism.

In the late 1940s, Robeson's pro-Soviet views and inflammatory statements aroused the ire of the U.S. government and its red hunters. A statement he made at the communist-dominated World Congress of the Defenders of Peace in Paris in 1949 provoked outrage. "It is unthinkable," Robeson said, "that American Negroes would go to war on behalf of those [the United States] who have oppressed us for generations against a country [the Soviet Union] which in one generation has raised our people to full human dignity of mankind." Later in 1949 crowds twice disrupted a Robeson concert in Peekskill, New York, the first time preventing the concert from being held, the second time terrorizing performers and audience members after the concert by throwing rocks at them.

Throughout the 1940s Robeson consistently linked the struggles of black America with the struggles of black Africa, brown India, yellow Asia, black Brazilians and Haitians, and workers throughout Latin America. Robeson also refused to sign an affidavit concerning past membership in the Communist Party. In response, the U.S. State Department revoked his passport in 1950 "because the Department considers that Paul Robeson's travel abroad at this time would be contrary to the best interest of the United States." Robeson provided his own explanation for the State Department's decision to revoke his passport. He elaborated, "I should not be allowed to travel because I have struggled for years for the independence of the colonial peoples of Africa." He declared that he was being punished for insisting on the "rights of my people who are still second-class citizens in this United States of America." His travel ban remained in effect until the Supreme Court declared it unconstitutional in 1958. He had combined his art and his politics to attack racial discrimination, segregation, and the ideology of white supremacy and black inferiority in America. During the Cold War the United States would tolerate no such dissent even by a world-acclaimed black artist.

20.5.4 Henry Wallace and the 1948 Presidential Election

Robeson's struggles illustrate how conservative attacks choked off left-wing involvement in the struggle for black equality. The attacks destroyed Robeson's brilliant singing career. The increasing importance of black votes to Democrats, however, meant that key elements of the African-American liberation struggle remained at the center of national politics. Nowhere was this more apparent than in the 1948 presidential election.

President Harry S. Truman was not expected to win this election because he faced a strong challenge from Thomas Dewey, the popular and well-financed Republican governor of New York. A challenge from his former secretary of commerce, Henry Wallace, who had been Roosevelt's vice president from 1941 to 1945, compounded Truman's problems.

Wallace ran on the ticket of the communist-backed Progressive Party, which sought to take the votes of liberals, leftists, and civil rights advocates disappointed by Truman's moderation. Wallace also supported a peaceful accommodation with the Soviet Union. To undercut Wallace's challenge, Truman began to press Congress to pass liberal programs.

Black votes in key northern states were central to Truman's strategy for victory. African Americans in these tightly contested areas could make the difference between victory and defeat, so Truman, to retain their allegiance, sought to demonstrate his administration's support of civil rights. In January 1948 he embraced the findings of his biracial Committee on Civil Rights and called for their enactment into law. The committee's report, "To Secure These Rights," was a blueprint for changing the racial caste system in the United States. It recommended passage of federal antilynching legislation, ending discrimination at the ballot box, abolishing the poll tax, desegregating the military, and many other measures.

The reaction of white southern politicians was swift and threatening, causing Truman to pause. But as the election neared, fear of black disaffection at the polls became so great that the Democratic convention passed a strong pro–civil rights plank. Many white southerners, led by South Carolina's Governor Strom Thurmond, bolted from the convention and formed their own States' Rights, or "Dixiecrat," Party. In the election, the Dixiecrats carried South Carolina, Alabama, Mississippi, and Louisiana. Wallace carried no state. Dewey carried 13 northern and midwestern states, but Truman won a plurality in the popular vote and a majority in the Electoral College. The failure of the bulwark of white supremacy to prevent the Democratic Party from advocating African-American rights, and Truman's victory, despite the defection of hard-line racists, represented a turning point in American politics.

20.5.5 Desegregating the Armed Forces

The importance of the black vote, the fight for the allegiance of the emerging nations, and the emerging civil rights movement hastened the desegregation of the military. In February 1948 a communist coup in Czechoslovakia raised the possibility of war between the United States and the Soviet Union and heightened concerns among military leaders about African Americans' willingness to serve yet again in a Jim Crow army. When Congress reinstated the draft in March 1948, A. Philip Randolph, who—in a replay of the March on Washington scenario—had formed the League for Non-Violent Civil Disobedience Against Military Segregation in 1947, warned the nation that black men and women were fed up with segregation and Jim Crow and would not take a Jim Crow draft lying down. Black New York Congressman Adam Clayton Powell, Jr., also supported this stance. There were not enough jails in America to hold the black men who would refuse to bear arms in a Jim Crow army, he declared. On June 24, 1948, the Soviet Union heightened tensions even further when it imposed a blockade on West Berlin.

On July 26, Truman, anticipating war between the superpowers and hoping to shore up his support among black voters for the approaching November elections, issued **Executive Order 9981**, which mandated "equality of treatment and opportunity for all persons in the armed services without regard to race, color, religion, or national origin." After Truman signed the order, Randolph and Grant Reynolds, a former minister and co-chair of the League for Nonviolent Civil Disobedience against Military Segregation, disbanded the organization and called off marches planned for Chicago and New York.

President Truman's Executive Order 9981 did have a positive impact on the struggles of African American women who desired to serve in auxiliary units and to win placement in diverse military facilities. To be sure, general discrimination persisted, but there were some breakthroughs. In April 1945, Captain Delia H. Raney, Army Nurse Corps, became the first African American nurse to head the nursing staff at the station

Executive Order 9981

Order issued by President Harry Truman in 1948 desegregating the armed forces.

hospital at Camp Beale, California. At least 800 black women of the 6888th Central Postal Directory Battalion set up facilities at Rouen, France, and invited hundreds of black soldiers to its open house on May 26, 1945. They were led by Major Charity Adams Earley. Meanwhile, Lt. Harriet Ida Pickens and Ens. Frances Wills became the first African American WAVES commissioned by the U.S. Navy. Janet Harmon Waterford Bragg was one of a few women pilots to secure admission into the Tuskegee Airmen pilot program. She had to overcome the refusal of the executive officer of the Women's Flying Training Detachment, who refused to admit her. Braggs went to Tuskegee, Alabama, and received commercial flight training from Charles Alfred "Chief" Anderson.

It was not until the 1950s and the outbreak of the Korean War, however, that Truman's order was fully implemented. The Korean War reflected the American Cold War policy of containment, which was intended to stop what American leaders believed to be a worldwide conspiracy orchestrated by Moscow to spread communism. In 1950 the North Koreans, allied with the Soviets, attacked the American-supported government in South Korea and launched a "hot war" in the midst of the Cold War. After the North Koreans invaded South Korea, the United States under UN auspices intervened. Heavy casualties early in the war depleted many white combat units. Thus, early in 1951, the army acted on Truman's executive order and authorized the formal integration of its units in Korea. By 1954 the army had disbanded its last all-black units, and the armed forces became one of the first sectors of American society to abandon segregation.

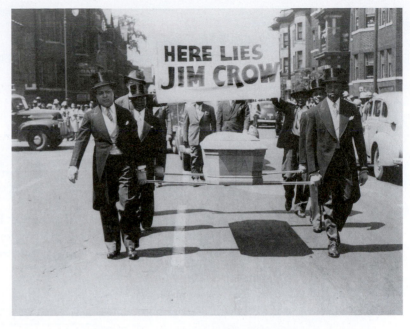

African-American civilians demonstrated firm resolve to end racial segregation at home while Americans fought to make the world safe for democracy. The NAACP Detroit branch's 1944 "Parade for Victory" featured pallbearers with caskets as they marched behind a sign that proclaimed "HERE LIES JIM CROW." It conveyed the sentiment, if not the reality. But Jim Crow's days were numbered.

Conclusion

The years between 1940 and 1954 were a dynamic period of black activism and witnessed a rising international consciousness among African Americans. In spite of white resistance, the black quest for racial justice in the military and on the home front became an integral part of the ongoing struggle for economic opportunity, political rights, and social justice. President Roosevelt's Executive Order 8802 was a significant victory for A. Philip Randolph's March on Washington Movement and for black workers, who were able to appeal racial discrimination in defense industries to the FEPC. The rise of fascism in Europe alarmed black and white Americans who correctly perceived ideologies based on racial tyranny and state dominance to be hostile to individual freedom and democracy. World War II profoundly transformed black servicemen and servicewomen. Yet, in very important ways, African Americans continued to suffer from white terrorism and judicial injustice in spite of the valor with which they fought for America.

The Cold War created a climate in America that was both hospitable and hostile to the African-American freedom movement. Radicals such as Paul Robeson and W. E. B. Du Bois found no place in this movement or in American society. Instead, more moderate organizations, such as the NAACP's Legal Defense and Educational Fund, pursued their goals within the ideological and legal constraints of the American political system and met with some success. The coming civil rights movement would, however, soon lead to a more varied, vibrant, and successful challenge to racism.

Chapter Timeline

AFRICAN-AMERICAN EVENTS	NATIONAL AND WORLD EVENTS

1936

1936

Abraham Lincoln Brigade goes to Spain to resist Franco

1938–1939

1939

June 27, 1939, the Civilian Pilot Training Act opens the way for the Tuskegee Airmen

1938

Germany annexes Austria and part of Czechoslovakia

1939

Germany invades Poland, beginning World War II

1940–1941

1941

Dorie Miller, hero of Pearl Harbor, receives Navy Cross

A. Philip Randolph organizes March on Washington Movement

1940

Benito Mussolini and Adolf Hitler form Axis

Germany conquers most of Western Europe

Selective Training and Service Act begins

Roosevelt wins third term

1941

Executive Order 8802 is issued; Japan attacks Pearl Harbor; America joins World War II

1942–1943

1942

Congress of Racial Equality (CORE) founded in Chicago

Charity Adams (Early) becomes first black commissioned officer in the Women's Army Auxiliary Corps

First black cadets graduate from flying school at Tuskegee, Alabama

1943

William H. Hastie resigns in protest from War Department

Race riots in Mobile, Detroit, and Harlem

The black 99th Pursuit Squadron flies its first combat mission

1942

100,000 Japanese Americans interred in camps

1943

Roosevelt signs G.I. Bill

AFRICAN-AMERICAN EVENTS   **NATIONAL AND WORLD EVENTS**

1944–1945

1944

Adam Clayton Powell, Jr. is elected to U.S. House of Representatives from Harlem

Supreme Court overthrows the white primary in *Smith v. Allwright*

1945

Mabel Staupers secures end to discrimination against black nurses in the military

Du Bois, Bethune, White, and Bunche attend UN founding in San Francisco

Paul Robeson receives NAACP Spingarn Medal

1944

D-Day, Allied invasion of German-occupied France, begins

Roosevelt wins fourth term

Servicemen's Readjustment Act provides funds for housing and education after the war

Battle of the Bulge, last major German counteroffensive

1945

United Nations founded

President Roosevelt dies; Truman becomes president

Germany surrenders

United States bombs Hiroshima and Nagasaki; Japan surrenders

1946–1947

1947

Journey of Reconciliation project begins, precursor to the 1961 Freedom Rides

1946

President Truman creates the Committee on Civil Rights

1948–1949

1948

Ada Lois Sipuel v. Board of Regents

Truman's Executive Order 9981 desegregates the military

1949

Riots disrupt Robeson concerts in Peekskill, New York

1948

Truman wins presidential election with support of black voters

Review Questions

1. How did World War II change the status of African Americans in the military? What were some of the consequences of so many black servicemen fighting in Europe against fascism and Nazism? How did the Tuskegee Airmen contribute to the Allied victory in Europe?

2. How did black women participate in the campaign to desegregate the U.S. military and in the Abraham Lincoln Brigade? How did Mabel Staupers win acceptance of black women into the military nurses corps?

3. What did the "Double V" campaign accomplish? How did African-American civilians support black servicemen? What institutional resources were African Americans able to marshal in their campaign against racism at home?

4. How did World War II affect black workers in America? What was the significance of A. Philip Randolph's March on Washington Movement, and how did President Roosevelt respond to it?

5. Why did the Cold War originate, and what was its significance for black activism? How did the World War II era promote the internationalization of African-American consciousness? How did the State Department attempt to downplay black dissent in America, and why?

6. Why did President Truman decide to desegregate the U.S. military?

7. Explain why black men who returned from World War II often encountered a great deal of anger and violence from white neighbors and unequal treatment before the courts.

Retracing the Odyssey

National Museum of the Tuskegee Airmen at Historic Fort Wayne (Detroit, Michigan). This museum documents the achievements of the combat aviators who served as a segregated unit of the U.S. armed forces in World War II. They received their training at the Army Air Corps base in Tuskegee, Alabama. During World War II these black aviators shot down enemy aircraft, bombed barges and enemy power stations, and successfully escorted American bombers on their missions across Europe.

Port Chicago Naval Magazine National Memorial, Concord Naval Weapons Station, California. The memorial contains artifacts and exhibits. Much of the base is now a wildlife preserve.

Recommended Reading

John D'Emilio. *Lost Prophet: The Life and Times of Bayard Rustin.* New York: Simon and Schuster, 2003. A first-rate, well-written, thoughtful biography of a key although often underappreciated leader in the long struggle for social justice for all Americans.

Mary L. Dudziak. *Cold War Civil Rights: Race and the Image of American Democracy.* Princeton, NJ: Princeton University Press, 2000. An excellent study of Cold War diplomacy and the centrality of race issues, as well as a splendid analysis of the Truman administration's commitment to civil rights.

Darlene Clark Hine. "Black Professional and Race Consciousness: Origins of the Civil Rights Movement, 1890–1950." *Journal of American History* 89, no. 4 (2003): 1279–94. A detailed discussion of the struggle of black physicians and nurses to end the racial segregation of medicine in the armed forces during World War II.

Paula F. Pfeffer. *A. Philip Randolph, Pioneer of the Civil Rights Movement.* Baton Rouge: Louisiana State University Press, 1990. A richly insightful biography of a pioneering labor leader and activist whose March on Washington Movement in 1941 was essential to the formation of the first Fair Employment Practices Committee and the integration of the armed services.

William R. Scott. *The Sons of Sheba's Race: African-Americans and the Italo-Ethiopian War, 1935–1941.* Bloomington: Indiana University Press, 1993. A detailed and illuminating account of African-American responses to the Italian invasion of Ethiopia and the growth of black internationalism.

Laura Wexler. *Fire in a Canebrake: The Last Mass Lynching in America.* New York: Scribner's, 2003. A riveting and sobering account of the lynching by a white mob of four victims on July 25, 1946, in Walton County, Georgia, at Moore's Ford Bridge. The book is a poignant study of the pernicious power of racism in the wake of the global holocaust of World War II.

Additional Bibliography

African Americans and the Military

Robert Allen. *Port Chicago Mutiny: The Story of the Largest Mass Mutiny in U.S. Naval History.* New York: Warner Books/Amistad Books, 1989.

Martin Binkin and Mark J. Eitelberg with Alvin J. Schexnider and Marvin M. Smith. *Blacks and the Military: Studies in Defense Policy.* Washington, DC: Bookings Institution, 1982.

Richard Dalfiume. *Desegregation of the U.S. Armed Forces: Fighting on Two Fronts, 1939–1953.* Columbia: University of Missouri Press, 1969.

Thomas E. Daniels. "Contributions of Black Americans to Electronic Research, Development, Production Distribution, and Training at Fort Monmouth, 1940–1982." www.campusevans.org.

Department of Defense. *A History of Army Communications and Electronics at Fort Monmouth, New Jersey, 1917–2007.* Wall Township, NJ: Fort Monmouth Historical Office, 2008.

Charles W. Dryden. *A-Train: Memoirs of a Tuskegee Airman.* Tuscaloosa: University of Alabama Press, 1997.

Charity Adams Earley. *One Woman's Army: A Black Officer Remembers the WAC.* College Station: Texas A&M University Press, 1989.

Darlene Clark Hine. *Black Women in White: Racial Conflict and Cooperation in the Nursing Profession, 1890–1950.* Bloomington: Indiana University Press, 1989.

Gilbert King. *Devil in the Grove: Thurgood Marshall, the Groveland Boys, and the Dawn of a New America.* New York: HarperPerennial, 2012.

Ulysses Lee. *The Employment of Negro Troops.* Washington, DC: Center of Military History, 1990.

Melton A. McLaurin. *The Marines of Montford Point: America's First Black Marines.* Chapel Hill: University of North Carolina Press, 2007.

Neil McMillen, ed. *Remaking Dixie: The Impact of World War II on the American South.* Jackson: University Press of Mississippi, 1997.

Mary Penick Motley. *The Invisible Soldier: The Experience of the Black Soldier, World War Two.* Detroit, MI: Wayne State University Press, 1975.

Alan M. Osur. *Blacks in the Army Air Forces During World War II: The Problem of Race Relations.* Washington, DC: Office of Air Force History, 1977.

Lou Potter. *Liberators: Fighting on Two Fronts in World War II.* New York: Harcourt Brace Jovanovich, 1992.

Stanley Sandler. *Segregated Skies: All-Black Combat Squadrons of WWII.* Washington, DC: Smithsonian Institution Press, 1992.

Howard Sitkoff. "Racial Militancy and Interracial Violence in the Second World War." *Journal of American History* 58, no. 3 (1971): 663–83.

Paul Stillwell, ed. *The Golden Thirteen: Recollections of the First Black Naval Officers.* Annapolis, MD: Naval Institute Press, 1993.

Ben Vinson III. *Flight: The Story of Virgil Richardson, a Tuskegee Airman in Mexico.* New York: Palgrave/Macmillan, 2004.

Black Urban Studies

Albert Broussard. *Black San Francisco: The Struggle for Racial Equality in the West, 1900–1954.* Lawrence: University Press of Kansas, 1993.

Dominic Capeci. *The Harlem Riot of 1943.* Philadephia: Temple University Press, 1977.

_____. *Race Relations in Wartime Detroit: The Sojourner Truth Housing Controversy of 1942.* Philadelphia: Temple University Press, 1984.

Dominic Capeci and Martha Wilkerson. *Layered Violence: The Detroit Rioters of 1943.* Jackson: University Press of Mississippi, 1991.

Lawrence B. DeGraaf. "Significant Steps on an Arduous Path: The Impact of World War II on Discrimination Against African Americans in the West." *Journal of the West* 35, no. 1 (1996): 24–33.

St. Clair Drake and Horace R. Cayton. *Black Metropolis: A Study of Negro Life in a Northern City.* New York: Harcourt Brace, 1945.

Richard W. Thomas. *Life for Us Is What We Make It: Building Black Community in Detroit, 1915–1945.* Bloomington: Indiana University Press, 1992.

Black Americans, Domestic Radicalism, and International Affairs

Beth Tompkins Bates. *Pullman Porters and the Rise of Protest Politics in Black America, 1925–1945.* Chapel Hill: University of North Carolina Press, 2001.

William C. Berman. *The Politics of Civil Rights in the Truman Administration.* Columbus: Ohio State University Press, 1970.

John Morton Blum. *V Was for Victory: Politics and American Culture During World War II.* New York: Harcourt Brace Jovanovich, 1996.

Gabrielle Simon Edgecomb, *From Swastika to Jim Crow: Refugee Scholars at Black Colleges.* Malabar, FL: Krieger, 1993.

Herbert Garfinkel. *When Negroes March: The March on Washington Movement in the Organizational Politics for FEPC.* New York: Atheneum, 1973.

Erik S. Gellman. *Death Blow to Jim Crow: The National Negro Congress and the Rise of Militant Civil Rights.* Chapel Hill: University of North Carolina Press, 2012.

Erik S. Gellman and Jarod Roll. *The Gospel of the Working Class: Labor's Southern Prophets in New Deal America.* Urbana: University of Illinois Press, 2011.

Joseph Harris. *African American Reactions to War in Ethiopia, 1936–1941.* Baton Rouge: Louisiana State University Press, 1994.

Gerald Horne. *Black and Red: W. E. B. Du Bois and the Afro-American Response to the Cold War.* Albany: State University of New York Press, 1986.

Andrew Edmund Kersten. *Race and War: The FEPC in the Midwest, 1941–46.* Urbana: University of Illinois Press, 2000.

George Lipsitz. *Rainbow at Midnight: Labor and Culture in the 1940s.* Urbana: University of Illinois Press, 1994.

Gail Williams O'Brien. *The Color of the Law: Race, Violence and Justice in the Post–World War II South.* Chapel Hill: University of North Carolina Press, 1999.

Brenda Gayle Plummer. *Rising Wind: Black Americans and U.S. Foreign Affairs, 1935–1960.* Chapel Hill: University of North Carolina Press, 1996.

Linda Reed. *Simple Decency and Common Sense: The Southern Conference Movement, 1938–1963.* Bloomington: Indiana University Press, 1991.

Joe William Trotter and Jared E. Day, eds. *Race and Renaissance: African Americans in Pittsburgh Since World War*. Pittsburgh, PA: University of Pittsburgh Press, 2010.

Patricia Scott Washburn. *A Question of Sedition: The Federal Government's Investigation of the Black Press During World War II*. New York: Oxford University Press, 1986.

Autobiography and Biography

Andrew Buni. *Robert Vann of the Pittsburgh Courier*. Pittsburgh, PA: University of Pittsburgh Press, 1974.

Martin Bauml Duberman. *Paul Robeson: A Biography*. New York: Ballantine Press, 1989.

Kenneth R. Janken. *Rayford W. Logan and the Dilemma of the African American Intellectual*. Amherst: University of Massachusetts Press, 1993.

Spencie Love. *One Blood: The Death and Resurrection of Charles Drew*. Chapel Hill: University of North Carolina Press, 1996.

Manning Marable. *W. E. B. Du Bois: Black Radical Democrat*. Boston: Twayne, 1986.

Constance Baker Motley. *Equal Justice Under Law: An Autobiography*. New York: Farrar, Straus and Giroux, 1998.

Pauli Murray. *Song in a Weary Throat: An American Pilgrimage*. New York: Harper & Row, 1987.

Bayard Rustin. *Troubles I've Seen*. New York: HarperCollins, 1996.

Brian Urquhart. *Ralph Bunche: An American Life*. New York: Norton, 1993.

Gilbert Ware. *William Hastie: Grace Under Pressure*. New York: Oxford University Press, 1984.

Roy Wilkins with Tom Mathews. *Standing Fast: The Autobiography of Roy Wilkins*. New York: Da Capo Press, 1994.

Connecting the Past

The Significance of the Desegregation of the U.S. Military

Howard P. Perry, the first African American to enlist in the Marine Corps.

Through their military service African Americans have played important roles in the construction and preservation of American democracy. Since their participation in the colonial militia and the Continental Army during the American Revolution, through the recent wars against Iraq and in Afghanistan in the twenty-first century, black Americans have viewed military service as a way to prove their loyalty and bravery, and to show their right to freedom and citizenship.

At the birth of the new nation in 1775–1776, black people composed one-fifth of the population. They fought mostly in integrated colonial militias and army regiments during the American Revolution, but it would take over two centuries and many more wars before military integration became permanent national policy. In the Civil War, the Spanish-American War, World War I, and World War II, black and white servicemen fought in racially segregated units in the Army and Navy. (The Marines did not allow black men to serve until 1942.) The desegregation of the military during the 1950s was thus, in many respects, a monumental and historic achievement. Throughout World War II black communities had waged a "Double V" campaign against Fascism and Nazism abroad and racial segregation and discrimination at home. President Harry Truman's Executive Order 9981, ordering the desegregation of the U.S. military in 1948, helped to set the stage for the emergence of the modern civil rights movement. Desegregation in the military preceded the end of legal segregation and Jim Crow in civilian life by more than a decade. Today, the U.S. military is one of the most racially neutral institutions in America.

The War for Independence (1775–1783) was, as scholars now attest, "the first mass slave rebellion in American history." Enslaved black men fought on both sides of the war. Some fought for the British, but even larger numbers joined the Patriot cause, believing that they would be freed as compensation for their service to the new nation. In 1775, Lord Dunmore, Virginia's last royal governor, promised to free any slave or indentured servant in exchange for their military service to the Crown. In response, George Washington, the Patriot commander, initially vacillated but soon allowed the enlistment of free black men in his army. In both the Battle of Bunker Hill and the Battle of Long Island in 1776, African-American soldiers from the northern states "served in twice the proportion of their numbers in the population." By 1781, at the decisive Battle of Yorktown, which ensured American independence, black troops were estimated to make up one-quarter of the Patriot Army. Despite their military service and contributions, however, the American Revolution would remain the unfinished revolution for African Americans.

Slavery endured and flourished until the 1860s when the election of President Abraham Lincoln, followed by the secession of South Carolina and 10 other southern states, ignited the Civil War. Free African Americans who supported the abolition of slavery pressured an initially reluctant Lincoln to make the destruction of slavery a military objective. When Lincoln issued the Emancipation Proclamation in 1863 and also allowed states to raise black militias, the Civil War became an opportunity for African Americans to fight for their own liberation.

During the Civil War, more than 185,000 African Americans fought in the Union Army and Navy. They provided the crucial margin of manpower that facilitated the North's victory. Approximately 29,000 African American men made up one-fourth of the entire naval enrollment. The recruitment and enlistment of African Americans into the Union Army was controversial, however. Frederick Douglass, the leading advocate of arming black men, reminded Lincoln that African Americans had fought well enough to help win American independence and insisted that they were eager and

more than qualified to fight for their people's freedom and to preserve that independence. On August 25, 1862, the War Department granted General Rufus Saxton, military governor of South Carolina's Sea Islands, the power to raise five regiments of black troops on the islands, albeit under the command of white officers.

The northern victory in the Civil War preserved the Union and ended slavery. But again, black military service failed to end military segregation and discrimination in the military academies at West Point and Annapolis. The closing decades of the nineteenth century simultaneously witnessed the rise of legal segregation and political disfranchisement and helped to fan the Great Migration from the South to northern cities. Still, black people's desire to serve in the military never wavered. Black public protest against military segregation and discrimination continued during World War I and reached a peak in World War II when a nation with a segregated military fought Germany and Japan, nations that embraced a master race ideology.

Black Americans seized the national crisis of World War II to make their demands for civil and human rights heard. In 1949, Wesley A. Brown became the first black midshipman to graduate from the U.S. Naval Academy (founded in 1845). Representative Adam Clayton Powell, Jr. of New York had interceded on his behalf. One of Brown's classmates was future President Jimmy Carter. The desegregation of the military, one of the most significant institutions in American public life, opened opportunities for black men and women. A generation later Colin Luther Powell, born in Harlem, New York, to Jamaican-American parents, reached the highest position in the military when he became the twelfth Chairman of the Joint Chiefs of Staff (1985–1989), after which he was named the Secretary of State in 2001 by President George W. Bush. Today, African Americans constitute almost 20 percent of service men and women in the U.S. armed forces.

Colin Powell (center), Chairman of the Joint Chiefs of Staff, with Former Vice President Richard Cheney and General Norman Schwarzkopf.

Part VI
The Black Revolution

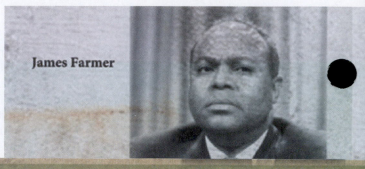

James Farmer

	1950–1965	1965–1975

RELIGION

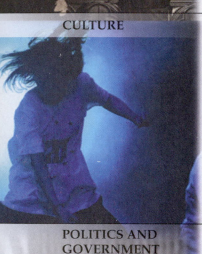

1954 Malcolm X becomes minister of Harlem's Temple 7
1963 Malcolm X founds the Muslim Mosque

CULTURE

1957 Althea Gibson, Tennis Champion wins Wimbledon and U.S. Nationals
1958 Alvin Ailey found, Alvin Ailey Dance Theatre
Ella Fitzgerald and William "Count" Basie win Grammy Awards
1959 Berry Gordy, Jr. forms Motown Records
Miles Davis records *Kind of Blue*
1960 Louis Armstrong's jazz band tours Africa
1963 James Baldwin, *The Fire Next Time*
Sidney Poitier, Best Actor Academy Award for *Lilies of the Field*
Marian Anderson and Dr. Ralph J. Bunche, receives Presidential Medal of Freedom
1965 Alex Haley publishes *The Autobiography of Malcolm X*
LeRoi Jones founds Black Arts Repertory Theater

1966 San Francisco State University sets up nation's first black studies program
1969 Robert Chrisman and Nathan Hare edits *The Black Scholar*
1970 Imamu Amiri Baraka founds the Congress of African Peoples
Charles Gordone, receives Pulitzer Prize in drama, *No Place to Be Somebody*
1974 National Council for Black Studies organi[...]
Clive Campbell "DJ Kool Herc" creates th[...] breakbeat technique, laid the foundation for rap music
1975 Arthur Ashe wins Wimbledon

POLITICS AND GOVERNMENT

1954 *Brown v. Board of Education*
1955 *Brown II* schools to desegregate with "all deliberate speed"
1957 Little Rock Nine
1964 Equal Employment Opportunity Commission established

1965 President Lyndon Johnson advocates "affirmative action"; signs Voting Rights Act of 1965
1966 Edward Brooke, U.S. Senator of Massachusetts
Black Panther Party founded
1967 Thurgood Marshall, Justice on U.S. Supreme Court
1968 *Kerner Commission Report* released
Shirley Chisholm elected to U.S. Congress
1972 Barbara Jordan and Andrew Young, Black Southerners elected to Congress
1973 Black Mayors: Tom Bradley, Los Angeles; Maynard H. Jackson, Jr., Atlanta; Coleman Young, Detroit
1975 Tuskegee Airman Daniel "Chappie" James, Jr. becomes a Four-Star General

SOCIETY AND ECONOMY

1955 Rosa Parks in Montgomery, Alabama
Emmett Till murdered
1957 Southern Christian Leadership Conference
Dorothy I. Height, President of the National Council of Negro Women, serves forty-one years
1960 SNCC founded
1961 Freedom Riders attacked in Alabama
1962 James Meredith enters University of Mississippi
1963 Medgar Evers assassinated
March on Washington
16th Street Baptist church bombed, Birmingham, Alabama, Addie Mae Collins, Denise McNair, Carole Robertson, and Cynthia Wesley killed
1964 Mississippi Freedom Summer Project
Martin Luther King, Jr. awarded Nobel Peace Prize

1965 Malcolm X assassinated
Watts riot
Selma March
1967 Riots in Detroit and Newark
1968 Martin Luther King, Jr. assassinated
1969 Chicago police assassinates Black Panthers Fred Hampton and Mark Clark
1970 Dr. Clifton R. Wharton, Jr., president Michigan State University
Jackson State College killings: Phillip Lafa[...] and James Earl Green
1971 Jesse Jackson founds PUSH
Congressional Black Caucus founded
1973 National Black Feminist Organization founded
Marion Wright Edelman heads the Children's Defense Fund

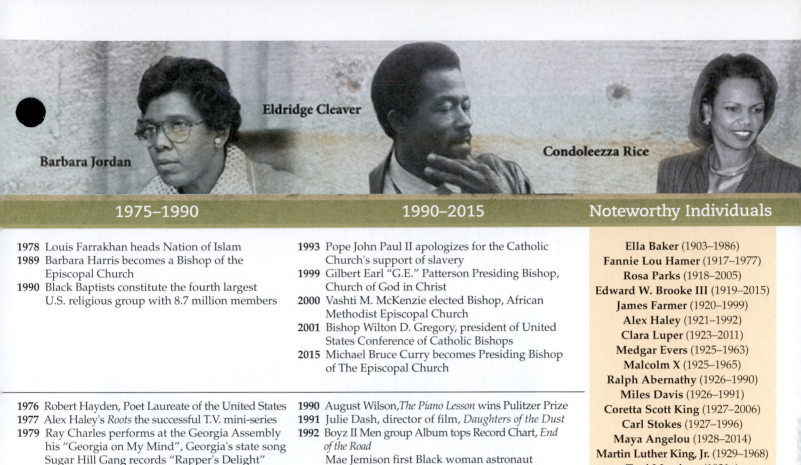

Barbara Jordan

Eldridge Cleaver

Condoleezza Rice

| 1975–1990 | 1990–2015 | Noteworthy Individuals |

1978 Louis Farrakhan heads Nation of Islam
1989 Barbara Harris becomes a Bishop of the Episcopal Church
1990 Black Baptists constitute the fourth largest U.S. religious group with 8.7 million members

1993 Pope John Paul II apologizes for the Catholic Church's support of slavery
1999 Gilbert Earl "G.E." Patterson Presiding Bishop, Church of God in Christ
2000 Vashti M. McKenzie elected Bishop, African Methodist Episcopal Church
2001 Bishop Wilton D. Gregory, president of United States Conference of Catholic Bishops
2015 Michael Bruce Curry becomes Presiding Bishop of The Episcopal Church

1976 Robert Hayden, Poet Laureate of the United States
1977 Alex Haley's *Roots* the successful T.V. mini-series
1979 Ray Charles performs at the Georgia Assembly his "Georgia on My Mind", Georgia's state song
Sugar Hill Gang records "Rapper's Delight"
1980 Toni C. Bambara's *Salt Eaters* American Book Award recipient
BET was founded by Robert L. Johnson
Rev. James Cleveland, first gospel artist to receive a star on Hollywood Walk of Fame
1982 Michael Jackson's *Thriller*, best-selling album
1983 Alice Walker, *The Color Purple*, wins Pulitzer Prize
Temple University, offers first Ph.D. degree in African-American Studies

1990 August Wilson,*The Piano Lesson* wins Pulitzer Prize
1991 Julie Dash, director of film, *Daughters of the Dust*
1992 Boyz II Men group Album tops Record Chart, *End of the Road*
Mae Jemison first Black woman astronaut
1993 Toni Morrison, Nobel Prize for Literature recipient
1997 Wynton Marsalis, Pulitzer Prize in Jazz "Blood on the Fields", an opera
2000 Charley Pride, Country Music Hall of Fame inductee
2001 Judith Jamison receives National Medal of Arts
2005 Shonda Rhimes create a top-ten T.V. series
2008 Tyler Perry, first and only black owner of major television and film studio, Tyler Perry Studios, Atlanta, GA

1977 Randall Robinson founds TransAfrica
Patricia Harris becomes the first black woman to serve in the Cabinet
1983 Harold Washington, Mayor of Chicago
1989 L. Douglas Wilder, Governor of Virginia
David Dinkins, Mayor of New York
1990 Sharon Pratt Kelley, Mayor of Washington, D.C.

1991 Clarence Thomas nominated to the Supreme Court
1992 Carol Moseley Braun, U.S. Senator (Illinois)
1993 Dr. Joycelyn Elders appointed Surgeon General
2001 Colin Powell, Secretary of State
2005 Condoleezza Rice, Secretary of State
2007 Deval Patrick, Governor of Massachusetts
2008 Barack Hussein Obama, President of the United States
2009 Michael S. Steele, Chairman of the Republican National Committee
Eric H. Holder, Jr., U.S. Attorney General
2010 Kamala Harris, California Attorney General
2012 President Obama wins second term
2015 Loretta E. Lynch, appointed U.S. Attorney General

1992 Los Angeles riot police officers acquitted Rodney King beating
1995 Million Man March, Washington, D.C.
1997 Million Woman March, Washington, D.C.
2005 Hurricane Katrina ravages the city of New Orleans
2006 Coretta Scott King dies

Ella Baker (1903–1986)
Fannie Lou Hamer (1917–1977)
Rosa Parks (1918–2005)
Edward W. Brooke III (1919–2015)
James Farmer (1920–1999)
Alex Haley (1921–1992)
Clara Luper (1923–2011)
Medgar Evers (1925–1963)
Malcolm X (1925–1965)
Ralph Abernathy (1926–1990)
Miles Davis (1926–1991)
Coretta Scott King (1927–2006)
Carl Stokes (1927–1996)
Maya Angelou (1928–2014)
Martin Luther King, Jr. (1929–1968)
Toni Morrison (1931–)
James Brown (1933–2006)
Myrlie Evers-Williams (1933–)
James Meredith (1933–)
Vernon Jordan (1935–)
Eldridge Cleaver (1935–1998)
Bobby Seale (1936–)
Barbara Jordan (1936–1996)
Colin Powell (1937–)
Maxine Waters (1938–)
Marian W. Edelman (1939–)
John Lewis (1940–)
Jesse Jackson (1941–)
Stokely Carmichael (1941–1998)
Muhammad Ali (1942–)
Molefi Kete Asante (1942–)
Aretha Franklin (1942–)
Huey Newton (1942–1989)
Angela Davis (1944–)
Alice Walker (1944–)
August Wilson (1945–2005)
Clarence Thomas (1948–)
Henry Louis Gates (1950–)
Cornell West (1953–)
Condoleezza Rice (1954–)
Oprah Winfrey (1954–)
Spike Lee (1957–)
Barack Obama (1962–)
Loretta E. Lynch (1959–)

Chapter 21

The Long Freedom Movement

1950–1970

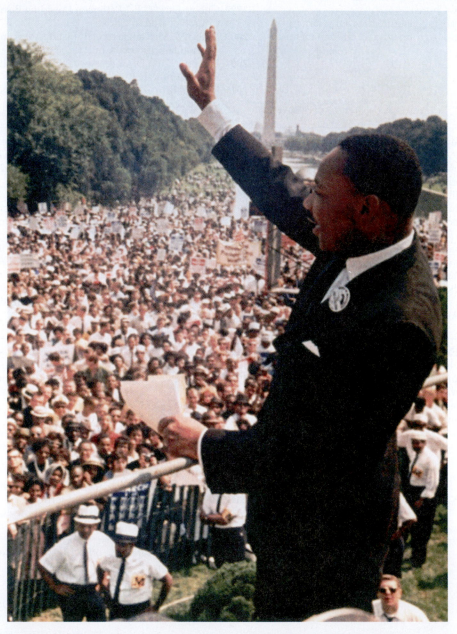

At the height of his moral authority, Martin Luther King, Jr. (1929–1968) delivers the memorable "I Have a Dream" speech at the 1963 March on Washington.

Learning Objectives

After reading this chapter, you should be able to:

21.1 Describe the backgrounds of key black men and women in the classic phase of the modern civil rights movement. Evaluate the effect that specific events had on the shape and contours of the 1950s phase of the modern civil rights movement and that laid the groundwork for the emergence of the Black Power movement.

21.2 Enumerate the events that inspired the NAACP to take up the case that resulted in the 1954 *Brown v. Board of Education* Supreme Court decision. Discuss why some may consider *Brown* to be one of the, if not *the*, most important cases in the twentieth century.

21.3 Identify the key components of white southerners' strategy of massive resistance and explain their impact on the modern civil rights movement.

21.4 Explain the evolution of the Montgomery Bus Boycott and how it affected race relations in Alabama.

21.5 Identify the major goals of the Civil Rights Act of 1957.

21.6 Explain the evolution of tactics used in the 1940s and those developed and practiced by the 1960s generation of student activists.

21.7 Discuss the individuals who were in the first wave of post–World War II leaders. Explain some of the differences in civil rights demands following the end of World War II and during the 1950s.

21.8 Analyze the impact of the federal government's intermittent support on the Long Freedom Movement.

Up to the mid-1950s, my people were afraid. They figured if they spoke out, they'd be pushed around on their job, or they would lose their job, so they kept silent. In my case, my paycheck came from Chicago, and they couldn't get me fired so easy. So when I saw the opportunity, I knew I could reach out and grab for it.

—E. D. Nixon, Pullman Car Porter and NAACP activist. Quoted from Nixon, in Donnie Williams with Wayne Greenhaw, The Thunder of Angels: The Montgomery Bus Boycott and the People Who Broke the Back of Jim Crow (Chicago: Lawrence Hill Books, 2006), 53

Between 1954 and 1965, the civil rights movement achieved a revolution, transforming the legal and social status of African Americans. Bold movements—beginning with the "Double V" Campaign during World War II and the NAACP's long legal struggle to overthrow the "separate but equal" doctrine—triumphed in the ***Brown v. Board of Education of Topeka*** decision in 1954. Black men and women protested against

Brown v. Board of Education of Topeka

Decision by the Supreme Court in 1954 that overturned the "separate but equal" doctrine.

segregation and discrimination through the Montgomery Bus Boycott of 1955–1956, and against white-only lunch counters and public transportation. Black protest culminated in massive grassroots campaigns throughout the South in 1963, 1964, and 1965—and changed the face of race relations in the United States. Despite fierce resistance, legally sanctioned segregation, racial discrimination, and disfranchisement fell before a mighty coalition of civil rights groups and their allies. Demonstrations and the pressures of the Cold War compelled high government officials to abandon their early caution. Although racism remained powerful in American life after 1965, and African Americans continued to suffer from severe economic disadvantages, the enlargement of freedom of opportunity and recognition of African Americans' full citizenship rights transformed America and radiated across the globe.

The heart of the story of the modern civil rights movement is the courage and tenacity people showed in their own communities in their determination to attack segregation and exclusion from the political process. Behind the charismatic leaders and the spectacles of the NAACP's Supreme Court victories and the marches and demonstrations captured so dramatically on television were the ordinary citizens who initiated protests, formulated strategies and tactics, and garnered other essential resources that made collective action work. The people's actions were made effective through their families, churches, voluntary associations, political organizations, women's clubs, labor unions, and colleges. The sacrifices and experience gained in the previous one hundred years of struggle had, by the mid-1950s, accumulated sufficiently to permit an all-out attack on white supremacy. The civil rights movement would be long and bloody, and it would not lead to the Promised Land, but it would change America.

21.1 The 1950s: Prejudice and Protest

Describe the backgrounds of key black men and women in the classic phase of the modern civil rights movement. Evaluate the effect that specific events had on the shape and contours of the 1950s phase of the modern civil rights movement and that laid the groundwork for the emergence of the Black Power movement.

For most white Americans, the 1950s were an era of unparalleled prosperity, consumer consumption, and a patriarchal business culture. Affluent white Americans fled to the suburbs; by 1960, 52 percent of Americans owned their own homes. The decade is remembered nostalgically as a time of large, stable nuclear families; wives and mothers who stayed at home; and communities untroubled by drugs, crime, and juvenile delinquency. It was a time of backyard barbecues and hula hoops, when nightly television shows like *Ozzie and Harriet* and *I Love Lucy* projected a vision of domestic tranquility.

For most black Americans, however, the 1950s were less blissful. American society remained rigidly segregated in housing and education. Despite the gains African Americans made during the World War II era, Jim Crow still reigned. Although the *Smith v. Allwright* Supreme Court decision in 1944, which declared the "white primary" unconstitutional, helped reenfranchise black voters in Florida, Tennessee, and Texas, Jim Crow restrictions and the threat of white violence kept millions of African Americans from voting in the Deep South. Likewise, although the 1948 *Shelley v. Kramer* Supreme Court decision—which outlawed the restricted residential covenants that had allowed homeowners to refuse to sell, rent, or lease their property to African Americans—was a significant victory, violence and extralegal practices still made housing integration a distant dream.

More important, most African Americans did not benefit from the economic boom of the 1950s that allowed so many white Americans to purchase homes in the suburbs. Moving into urban centers, where the number of factories and jobs were just beginning to decline, African Americans suffered a higher unemployment rate than any other segment of the population. White workers, fearing for their jobs, felt threatened by competition from unemployed black workers. As urban neighborhoods deteriorated, conditions ripened for a massive explosion.

21.2 The Road to *Brown*

Enumerate the events that inspired the NAACP to take up the case that resulted in the 1954 *Brown v. Board of Education* Supreme Court decision. Discuss why some may consider *Brown* to be one of the, if not *the*, most important cases in the twentieth century.

In 1954, with the Supreme Court's decision in *Brown v. Board of Education of Topeka, Kansas*, progress in the desegregation of American society moved into the civilian realm. The *Brown* decision undermined state-sanctioned segregation. The NAACP's legal program of the 1920s and 1930s was largely responsible for this victory. In 1940 the NAACP set up the Legal Defense and Educational Fund (NAACP-LDEF) to attack the legal foundations of race inequality in American education. Thereafter, the NAACP-LDEF fought segregation and discrimination in education, housing, employment, and politics. In the first years of its existence, attorneys for the fund won stunning victories, including a 1944 Supreme Court decision, *Smith v. Allwright*, declaring white primaries unconstitutional, and *Shelley v. Kramer* (1948), outlawing restrictive residential covenants. The life and career of one of the NAACP-LDEF lawyers, Constance Baker Motley, symbolizes the struggle that black professionals, both men and women, waged to overcome racial and gender exclusion as well as the union of disparate forces that planted and nurtured the seeds of the coming revolution. Motley is our guide on the road to *Brown*.

21.2.1 Constance Baker Motley and Black Lawyers in the South

Constance Baker Motley was born in 1921 to immigrant parents, Rachel Huggins and Willoughby Alva Baker, from Nevis, in the British West Indies. She grew up in a tightly knit West Indian community in New Haven, Connecticut. The members of New Haven's black community, including Baker's parents, worked as domestics or in service jobs for Yale University. Baker attended integrated schools and experienced episodic racism, including being refused admission to a local beach and a skating rink. In high school, Baker developed a strong racial consciousness: "My interest in civil rights [was] a very early interest which developed when I was in high school. The fact that I was a Black, a woman, and a member of a large, relatively poor family was also the base of this great ambition [to enter the legal profession]."

The most important event in her early life was the lecture that George Crawford, a 1903 Yale Law School graduate who worked in New Haven as an NAACP lawyer, gave at the local Dixwell Community Center. The talk concerned the Supreme Court decision in *State of Missouri ex rel. Gaines v. Canada*. Crawford explained that the University of Missouri's law school had denied Gaines admission but had offered to pay his tuition expenses to an out-of-state school. The NAACP Legal Committee under Charles H. Houston's leadership won a victory when the Supreme Court ruled that the state had violated the Fourteenth Amendment's mandate that state laws provide equal protection regardless of race. After *Gaines*, states had to furnish within their borders facilities for legal education for black people equal to those offered for white citizens.

Baker desperately wanted to go to law school, but her family could not even afford to send her to college. For a year and a half after graduation from high school in 1939, Baker earned $50 a month varnishing chairs for a building restoration project under the auspices of the National Youth Administration. In 1940, however, Baker came to the attention of Clarence Blakeslee, a local white philanthropist who offered to finance her education after hearing her speak at a meeting of black and white community residents. She attended Fisk University until 1942 and then transferred to New York University, where she graduated in 1943. She then became the second black woman ever to attend Columbia University Law School. In 1946 she married former New York University law student Joel Motley and went to work for the NAACP's LDEF.

Constance Baker Motley first met Thurgood Marshall in October 1945 when he hired her as a law clerk during her second year in law school. Marshall assigned her to work on the hundreds of army court-martial cases filed after World War II. Motley recalled, "From the first day I knew that this was where I wanted to be. I never bothered interviewing anywhere else. But for this fortuitous event, I do not think that I would have gotten very far as a lawyer. Women were simply not hired in those days."

In the late 1940s, the NAACP-LDEF's attack on inequality in graduate education provided the basis for a full-scale assault on segregation. No longer would the organization be satisfied only to push for fulfillment of the promise of "separate but equal" facilities. In 1948 the University of Oklahoma Law School denied Ada Lois Sipuel admission because she was black. The Supreme Court, signaling it was willing to take a more activist stance, ordered Oklahoma, in *Sipuel v. Board of Regents of the University of Oklahoma*, to "provide [a legal education] for [Sipuel] in conformity with the equal protection clause of the Fourteenth Amendment and provide it as soon as it does for applicants of any other group."

Another case, *Sweatt v. Painter*, which the Supreme Court decided in 1950, began when the University of Texas at Austin attempted to circumvent court orders to admit Heman Sweatt to its law school by creating a separate facility consisting of three basement rooms, a small library, and a few instructors who would lecture to him alone.

Constance Baker Motley endured many hardships and even assaults as she tried school desegregation cases in the South. Here she leaves the federal court in Birmingham after an unsuccessful attempt to force the University of Alabama to accept a black student.

1938–1954 United States Supreme Court Decisions: The Road to *Brown*

1938
Missouri ex rel. Gaines v. Canada

1948
Sipuel v. Oklahoma State Board of Regents

1950
McLaurin v. Oklahoma
Sweatt v. Painter

1954
Brown v. Board of Education of Topeka

The court ruled that the university had deprived Sweatt of intangibles such as "the essential ingredient of a legal education . . . the opportunity for students to discuss the law with their peers and others with whom they would be associated professionally in later life."

On the same day the justices ruled in *Sweatt*, they also declared illegal the University of Oklahoma's segregation of George W. McLaurin from white students attending the Graduate School of Education. The University of Oklahoma had admitted McLaurin but made him sit in the hallway at the classroom door, study in a private part of the balcony of the library, and eat in a sequestered part of the lunchroom. When he finally gained a seat in the classroom, it was marked "reserved for colored." In these precedent-setting cases, the Supreme Court signaled a readiness to reconsider the "separate but equal" doctrine of *Plessy* (1896) and to redefine the meaning of the "equal protection of the laws" clause of the Fourteenth Amendment. These cases were important stepping-stones on the road to *Brown*.

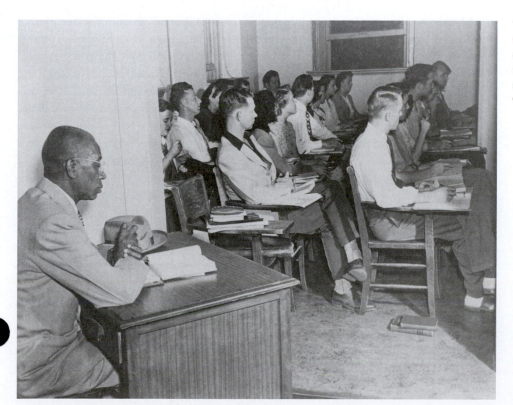

This student at the University of Oklahoma was not allowed to sit in a classroom with white students. It took two Supreme Court decisions to end such segregation at the University of Oklahoma.

21.2.2 *Brown* and the Coming Revolution

A year after the *Sweatt* and *McLaurin* decisions, black parents and their lawyers filed suits in Kansas, South Carolina, Virginia, Delaware, and the District of Columbia asking the courts to apply the qualitative test of the *Sweatt* case to elementary and secondary schools and to declare the "separate but equal" doctrine invalid in public education. Black lawyers in the South handling civil rights cases were frequently assaulted. On February 27, 1942, for example, a former deputy sheriff attacked NAACP attorney Leon A. Ransom in the hall of the Davidson County Courthouse in Nashville, Tennessee. The *Crisis* reported,

> The attack came when Ransom walked out into the hall from the courtroom where he was sitting with Z. Alexander Looby, local NAACP attorney, on a case involving the exclusion of Negroes from a jury. . . . When the scuffle began, Negroes who would have aided Ransom were held back by a former constable (white) named Hill, who drew his gun and shouted: "We are going to teach these northern Negroes not to come down here raising fancy court questions."

At Ransom's death in 1954, Thurgood Marshall eulogized,

> Negro Americans, whether they know it or not, owe a great debt of gratitude to Andy Ransom and men like him who battled in the courts down a span of years to bring us to the place we now occupy in the enjoyment of our constitutional rights as citizens, in helping to build up the NAACP legal program step by step, in the skill which he gave to individual cases and to the planning of strategy, Dr. Ransom left a legacy to the whole population.

It was no less difficult for a black woman lawyer to venture into the South in search of justice. Black attorney Derrick Bell, who also worked for the LDEF, said of Motley's work,

> Nothing in the Southern lawyers' background could have prepared them for Connie. To them Negro women were either mammies, maids, or mistresses. None of them had ever dealt with a Negro woman on a peer basis, much less on a level of intellectual equality, which in this case quickly became superiority.

Motley was keenly aware of her precarious situation. "Often a southern judge would refer to men attorneys as Mister, but would make a point of calling me 'Connie,' since traditionally Black women in the South were only called by their first name." Housing was another problem. Motley recalled that when in a southern town for a long trial, "I knew that it was going to be impossible to stay in a decent hotel." These lawyers had to depend on the good graces and courage of local people. Motley explained, "Usually in these situations a Black family would agree to put you up. But there was so much publicity involved with civil rights cases that no Black family dared have us—they were too afraid." While in Mississippi arguing a teachers' equalization of salaries case, Motley declared, "A Black doctor invited us to dinner, but that was about it. . . . I wonder how many lawyers have had the experience of preparing for trial in a flophouse. That was the only room I could get."

In the late 1940s, the black parents of children attending Scott's Branch School in Clarendon County, South Carolina, approached Roderick W. Elliott, the chairman of the school board, with a modest request. There were 6,531 black students and only 2,375 white students enrolled in the county's schools. Although the county had 30 buses to convey the white students to their schools, no buses were available to black schoolchildren. Some black students had to walk 18 miles round-trip each day. Once they arrived, they entered buildings heated by wood stoves and lit by kerosene lamps. For a drink of water or to go to the toilet they had to go outdoors.

With the encouragement of African Methodist Episcopal pastor and schoolteacher Rev. Joseph Armstrong DeLaine, the parents mustered the courage to petition the school board for buses. Elliott's reply was short: "We ain't got no money to buy a bus for your nigger children." In 1949 DeLaine went to the NAACP officials in Columbia, and Thurgood Marshall was there. On December 20, 1950, Harry Briggs, a navy veteran, and 24 other Clarendon County residents sued the school district. The case, *Briggs v. Elliott*, was the first legal challenge to elementary school segregation to originate in the South. Meanwhile, however, four other cases in different parts of the country were advancing through the federal courts. These would be combined into one case that would decide the fate of the *Plessy* doctrine of "separate but equal."

The years of preparation and hardship paid off. Motley worked with a dream team of black lawyers and academics, an inner circle of advisers that included Louis Redding from Wilmington, Delaware; James Nabrit from Washington, D.C.; Robert Ming from Chicago; psychologist Kenneth Clark from New York; and historian John Hope Franklin to prepare the case *Brown v. Board of Education of Topeka* and to argue it before the Supreme Court. Motley, Robert Carter, Jack Greenberg, and Marshall also sought assistance from Spottswood Robinson and Oliver Hill of Richmond, Virginia, and read papers prepared by historians C. Vann Woodward and Alfred Kelly about the original equalitarian intentions of the post–Civil War amendments and other legislation. In his argument, Marshall appealed to the Court to meet the *Plessy* doctrine head on and declare it erroneous:

> It [*Plessy*] stands mirrored today as a legal aberration, the faulty conception of an era dominated by provincialism, by intense emotionalism in race relations . . . and by the preaching of a doctrine of racial superiority that contradicted the basic concept upon which our society was founded. Twentieth century America, fighting racism at home and abroad, has rejected the race views of *Plessy v. Ferguson* because we have come to the realization that such views obviously tend to preserve not the strength but the weakness of our heritage.

By the time Marshall made this argument, black intellectuals, scholars, and activists and their progressive white allies had closed ranks to support integration. To suggest other alternatives as the goal for African Americans was to swim against the current.

During late 1953 and early 1954, Chief Justice Earl Warren persuaded the Court to support Marshall's position. On May 17, 1954, the Court ruled unanimously in favor of the NAACP lawyers and their clients that a classification based solely on race violated the Fourteenth Amendment. In a stirring passage Warren declared,

> We come then to the question presented: Does segregation of children in public schools solely on the basis of race, even though the physical facilities and other 'tangible' factors may be equal, deprive the children of the minority group of equal educational opportunities? We believe that it does. . . . To separate them from others of similar age and qualifications solely because of their race generates a feeling of inferiority as to the status in the community that may affect their hearts and minds in a way unlikely ever to be undone. . . . We conclude that in the field of public education the doctrine of "separate but equal" has no place. Separate educational facilities are inherently unequal.

The *Brown* decision would eventually lead to the dismantling of the entire structure of Jim Crow laws that regulated important aspects of black life in America: movement, work, marriage, education, housing, and even death and burial. The *Brown* decision, more than any other case, signaled the emerging primacy of equality as a guide to constitutional decisions.

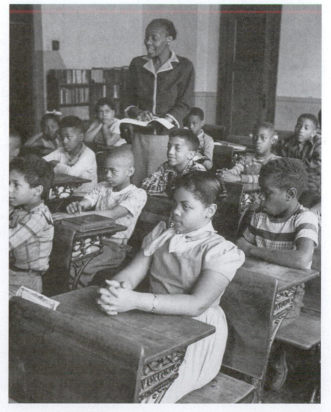

In 1950, when the all-white Sumner School in Topeka, Kansas, refused to admit Linda Brown (1943–), her father, Oliver Brown, filed a lawsuit and testified in court that his daughter had to travel an hour and 20 minutes to attend a black school. The Sumner School was only seven blocks away but practiced racial exclusion. Linda became the "named plaintiff" in the landmark U.S. Supreme Court case *Brown v. Board of Education* (1954), which declared unconstitutional laws mandating public school segregation.

This and subsequent decisions helped advance the rights of other minorities and women. As Motley reflected, "In the *Brown* case and in the decisions that followed, we blazed a trail for others by showing the competence of Black lawyers."

A year after the *Brown* decision, in May 1955, the Supreme Court issued a second ruling, commonly known as *Brown II*, which addressed the practical process of desegregation. The Court underscored that the states in the suits should begin prompt compliance with the 1954 ruling and that this should be done with "all deliberate speed." Many black Americans interpreted this to mean "immediately." White southerners hoped it meant a long time or never. Ominously, President Eisenhower seemed displeased with the Court's rulings and refused to put the moral authority of his office behind their enforcement.

Nevertheless, in 1955 and early 1956, desegregation proceeded without hindrance in Maryland, Kentucky, Delaware, Oklahoma, and Missouri. Alabama Governor Jim Folsom declared that his state would obey the courts. Other moderate white southern politicians counseled calm and worked to head off a full-scale conflict with the federal government.

21.3 Challenges to *Brown*

Identify the key components of white southerners' strategy of massive resistance and explain their impact on the modern civil rights movement.

White moderates, however, found themselves a shrinking minority. Extremists, determined to maintain white supremacy at any cost, prepared to resist the Court's decisions. The extremists' rhetoric bordered on hysteria but found a receptive audience among many.

21.3.1 White Resistance

Jerry Falwell, a young minister from Virginia, explained that black people were the descendants of Noah's son Ham and were destined to be servants because of a curse God had put on him. Falwell also claimed that Moscow had inspired the Supreme Court's decisions. In 1955 leading businessmen, white-collar professionals, and clergy began organizing, in virtually every southern city, White Citizens' Councils dedicated to preserving "the southern way of life" and the South's "sacred heritage of freedom." The councils used their economic and political power to intimidate African Americans who challenged segregation. They fired black people, evicted them, and refused them credit.

Many white politicians took up the banner of massive resistance. Mississippi Senator James O. Eastland had called the *Brown* decision a "monstrous crime." The Virginia legislature had closed all public schools in Prince Edward County to thwart integration. On March 12, 1956, 96 southern congressmen led by North Carolina's Senator Sam Ervin, Jr. and South Carolina's Senator Strom Thurmond issued "The Southern Manifesto," vowing to fight to preserve segregation and the southern way of life. The manifesto called the *Brown* decisions an "unwarranted exercise of power by the court, contrary to the Constitution." The only southern senators who refused to sign the manifesto were Albert Gore, Sr. of Tennessee and Lyndon B. Johnson of Texas.

The NAACP came under siege after the *Brown* decision as southern states tried to destroy it. By 1957 nine southern states had filed suit to eradicate the organization. Some states, alleging the NAACP was linked to a worldwide communist conspiracy, made membership illegal. Membership plummeted from 128,716 to 79,677, and the association lost 246 branches in the South.

Under these pressures, educational desegregation ground to a halt. By 1958, only 13 school systems had been desegregated. By 1960, two years later, the total had risen to only 17. Massive resistance successfully challenged the possibility of achieving change through court action alone. In two 2007 decisions, Justices Clarence Thomas and John Roberts, both of whom were appointed by Presidents George H. W. and George W. Bush, respectively, sought to end the practice of racial classification as a means to achieve racial diversity in public schools. They ruled in two cases involving school assignment plans developed by the boards of education in Seattle, Washington, and in Jefferson County, Kentucky, which included the city of Louisville. The Seattle school district classified children as white or nonwhite and used this system as the basis for allocating slots to attend the better, or oversubscribed, city high schools. On the other hand, the Jefferson County school district classified children as either black or as "other" and used that system to assign students to elementary schools and to inform decisions about transfer requests.

The Court ruled that both plans violated the Fourteenth Amendment, which guarantees equal protection of the laws. Chief Justice John Roberts, writing the majority opinion, declared, "The way to stop discrimination on the basis of race is to stop discriminating on the basis of race." In a separate opinion, Justice Clarence Thomas insisted, "Racial imbalance is not segregation," adding, "there is no danger of re-segregation."

Joining Roberts and Thomas were Justices Antonin Scalia and Samuel Alito. In his concurring opinion, Justice Anthony Kennedy left open the door for school districts to devise nonracial measures to achieve diversity while limiting the use of racial classification: "Such measures may include strategic site selection of new schools; drawing attendance zones with general recognition of neighborhood demographics; allocating resources for special programs; recruiting students and faculty in a targeted fashion; and tracking enrollments, performance, and other statistics by race."

In a spirited dissent, Justice Stephen Breyer called the majority decision a reversal of precedent and a fundamental weakening of *Brown*. Breyer argued that the majority opinion amounted to a retreat from the principle that allowed local school districts to exercise discretion about the best means to end racial segregation, curb resegregation due to segregated housing patterns, and overcome class division and racial exclusion. (Michigan Congressman John Conyers, chair of the House Judiciary Committee, called the ruling "shameful" and a "step backward" from *Brown*.)

The Court's decisions had affected hundreds of school districts across the country. School systems had to struggle to devise their own strategies to avoid or reduce racial concentration, to reverse the wide gaps between white and black students on state tests in reading and math, and to resist the resegregation of schools that had arisen from the growing patterns of housing segregation.

21.3.2 The Lynching of Emmett Till

In the wake of the 1954 *Brown* decision, white southerners' had violent reactions to black victories and assertiveness, as seen in the summer of 1955 in the lynching of 14-year-old Emmett Till of Chicago. This event helped galvanize the emerging civil rights movement. Till was visiting relatives in the small town of Money, Mississippi. Till was unaware how far white people would go to avenge any real or apparent breach of white supremacy's racial etiquette. What was actually said by Till to the white woman owner of the store he entered may never be known. It is fair to say that the general racially hostile atmosphere emboldened Bryant's husband and brother-in-law to kidnap and murder young Emmet Till. His body was subsequently found in the Tallahatchie River tied to a heavy cotton gin fan. Till had a bullet in his head and had been tortured before his murder. Despite overwhelming evidence and the testimony of Till's uncle and others, an all-white jury acquitted the two men who had lynched Till. In early 1956 the murderers sold their confession to *Look* magazine and gloated over their escape from justice.

The Till lynching helped to shape the consciousness of a generation of young African-American activists. Partly this was due to Till's mother, Mamie Bradley. Unwilling to let America turn away from this crime, she had her son's mangled body

In August 1955, 14-year-old Emmett Till was visiting relatives in Money, Mississippi, when he transgressed the line of racial etiquette by speaking to a white woman in a country store. He paid the ultimate price. The lynching of Emmett Till and the subsequent acquittal of his murderers reflected the low regard in which black life was held in the Jim Crow South and the extent to which whites were determined to maintain the racial status quo.

displayed in an open casket in Chicago. Thousands of mourners paid their respects, and many committed themselves to fighting the system that made this crime possible. Bradley also traveled around the nation speaking to groups on whom her grief had a profound impact. Myrlie Evers, who would later have a role in the movement, remembered how she felt: "I bled for Emmett Till's mother. I know when she came to Mississippi and appeared at the mass meetings how everyone poured out their hearts to her, went into their pockets when people had only two or three pennies, and gave."

21.4 New Forms of Protest: The Montgomery Bus Boycott

Explain the evolution of the Montgomery Bus Boycott and how it affected race relations in Alabama.

Strong local communities formed the core of the civil rights movement in the South, and the deeds of brave individuals often sparked them to action. The first and one of the most important expressions of this process occurred in Alabama's capital city. Blessed with well-organized educational, religious, and other institutions, Montgomery's African-American community of 45,000 was poised to make history.

21.4.1 The Roots of Revolution

The movement in Montgomery did not emerge out of the blue, although it must have seemed that way to many white southerners. It was the result of years of organization and planning by protest groups. In addition to its numerous churches, two black colleges, and other social organizations, Montgomery had a core of protest groups. One, the Women's Political Council (WPC), had been founded in 1946 by Mary Frances Fair Burks, chair of the Department of English at Alabama State College, after the all-white League of Women Voters had refused to allow black women to participate in its activities. The WPC had only 40 members, all middle-class, courageous, and competent leaders who were willing to stand up to powerful white people. The WPC was joined by a chapter of the NAACP led by E. D. Nixon, a Pullman train car porter and head of the Alabama chapter of the Brotherhood of Sleeping Car Porters. In 1943 Nixon had founded the Montgomery Voters League, which was dedicated to helping African Americans navigate Alabama's tortuous voter registration process. In the decade after 1945, these groups searched for a way to mobilize the black community to challenge white power.

The 1954 *Brown* decision seemed to provide a means to destroy segregation and discrimination in the city. Four days after it was announced, Jo Ann Robinson, a professor at Alabama State College, wrote to Montgomery's mayor on behalf of the WPC reiterating the complaints of the black community about conditions on the city's buses: "Please consider this plea, for even now plans are being made to ride less, or not at all, on our buses." The mayor ignored the warning, and the buses remained as segregated as before. All seemed quiet, but Montgomery's black lawyers and NAACP chapter began laying the groundwork for a test case challenging segregation of the city's bus lines.

On March 2, 1955, a 15-year-old Booker T. Washington High School student, Claudette Colvin, was arrested for refusing to give up her seat on a bus to a white woman. The WPC was

Claudette Colvin was a teenager when she refused to obey the transportation segregation laws in Montgomery.

Voices

Letter of the Montgomery Women's Political Council to Mayor W. A. Gayle

In this letter threatening a boycott of Montgomery's buses, the Women's Political Council politely asks not for the desegregation of the buses but only for new regulations that would prevent black riders from being forced to move to accommodate white riders.

May 21, 1954

Honorable Mayor W. A. Gayle
City Hall
Montgomery, Alabama

Dear Sir:

The Women's Political Council is very grateful to you and the City Commissioners for the hearing you allowed our representative during the month of March, 1954, when the "city-bus-fare-increase case" was being reviewed. There were several things the Council asked for:

1. A city law that would make it possible for Negroes to sit from back toward front, and whites from front toward back until all the seats were taken.

2. That Negroes would not be asked or forced to pay fare at front and go to the rear of the bus to enter.

3. That buses stop at every corner in residential sections occupied by Negroes as they do in communities where whites reside.

We are happy to report that buses have begun stopping at more corners now in some sections where Negroes live than previously. However, the same practices in seating and boarding the bus continue.

Mayor Gayle, three-fourths of the riders of these public conveyances are Negroes. If Negroes did not patronize them, they could not possibly operate.

More and more of our people are already arranging with neighbors and friends to ride to keep from being insulted and humiliated by bus drivers.

There has been talk from twenty-five or more local organizations of planning a city-wide boycott of buses. We, sir, do not feel that forceful measures are necessary in bargaining for a convenience which is right for all bus passengers. We, the Council, believe that when this matter has been put before you and the Commissioners, that agreeable terms can be met in a quiet and in a sensible manner to the satisfaction of all concerned.

Many of our Southern cities in neighboring states have practiced the policies we seek without incident whatsoever. Atlanta, Macon and Savannah in Georgia have done this for years. Even Mobile, in our own state, does this and all the passengers are satisfied.

Please consider this plea, and if possible, act favorably upon it, for even now plans are being made to ride less, or not at all, on our buses. We do not want this.

Respectfully yours,
The Women's Political Council
Jo Ann Robinson, President

---

1. Explain the objectives or goals that inspired the activism of the members of the Women's Political Council as revealed in the letter by Jo Ann Robinson.

2. Analyze the significance of black women's political organizations in the early stages of the modern civil rights movement.

SOURCE: Reprinted by permission of The University of Tennessee Press. From Jo Ann Gibson Robinson's *The Montgomery Bus Boycott and the Women Who Started It: The Memoir of Jo Ann Gibson Robinson*, edited, with a foreword, by David G. Garrow. Copyright © 1987 by The University of Tennessee Press.

---

ready to use this incident to initiate the threatened bus boycott. E. D. Nixon called 24-year-old Fred D. Gray, who agreed to represent Colvin in her challenge to Jim Crow segregation laws. Gray was one of only two black lawyers in Montgomery. The March 18, 1955, hearings resulted in a guilty verdict, and Claudette was placed on probation in the custody of her parents. Jo Ann Robinson recalled, "Claudette's agonized sobs penetrated the atmosphere of the courthouse. Many people brushed away their own tears." The Colvins were not members of the black social elite in Montgomery, and for various reasons community leaders decided against protesting Claudette's conviction for allegedly "assaulting" the police officers who had dragged her from the bus. They decided to wait for another opportunity to launch a protest movement. Fred Gray, however, decided to appeal Colvin's case.

21.4.2 Rosa Parks

On Thursday, December 1, 1955, Rosa Parks, a 43-year-old department store seamstress and civil rights activist, boarded a city bus and moved to the back where African Americans were required to sit. All seats were taken, so she sat in one toward the middle of the bus. When a white man boarded the bus, the driver ordered Parks to vacate her seat for him. There was nothing unusual in this, but on this fateful day, Parks refused to move. She had not planned to resist on that day, but, as she later said, she had "decided that I would have to know once and for all what rights I had as a human being and a citizen. . . . I was so involved with the attempt to bring about freedom from this kind of thing . . . I felt just resigned to give what I could to protest against the way I was being treated, and felt that all of our meetings, trying to negotiate, bring about petitions before the authorities . . . really hadn't done any good at all." At the time Parks was portrayed as simply tired, but she had been training for just this kind of challenge for years. When her moment came, she seized it; with this act of resistance, she launched the **Montgomery Bus Boycott** and inspired the modern civil rights struggle for freedom and equality.

The plans of the WPC and NAACP came into play after Parks's arrest for violating Montgomery's transportation laws. She was ordered to appear in court on the following Monday. Meanwhile, E. D. Nixon bailed her out of the city jail and began mobilizing the leadership of the black community behind her. Working in tandem with Nixon, Robinson wrote and circulated a flyer calling for a one-day boycott of the buses followed by a mass meeting of the community to discuss the matter. Robinson took the flyer to the Alabama State College campus, stayed up all night, and, with the help of a colleague, mimeographed 30,000 copies of it. The WPC had planned distribution routes months earlier, and the next day, Robinson and nearly 200 volunteers distributed bundles of flyers to beauty parlors and schools, to factories and grocery stores, and to taverns and barbershops throughout the black neighborhoods.

Montgomery Bus Boycott

Refusal from 1955 to 1957 of African Americans in Montgomery, Alabama, to ride the city's buses until the bus lines were desegregated.

21.4.3 Montgomery Improvement Association

On December 5, 1955, the black community did not ride the buses, and the movement had begun. Nixon and other community leaders, including Jo Ann Gibson Robinson, who would become its chief strategist, formed a new organization, the Montgomery Improvement Association (MIA), to coordinate the boycott. They selected a 26-year-old minister, Martin Luther King, Jr., as its president. That evening there was an overflowing mass meeting of the black community at the Holt Street Baptist Church to decide whether to continue the boycott. King, with barely an hour to prepare, defined the goals of the boycott and the civil rights movement that followed. In his dramatic voice, he connected the core values of America and of the Judeo-Christian tradition to the goals of African Americans nationwide as well as in Montgomery. Fred Gray and his fiancée were in the church and recalled the impact of King's speech:

> The high point of the meeting was the speech by Dr. Martin Luther King. This was the first time he had spoken to so many people. It was the first speech of his career as a civil rights leader, later to become an internationally known figure. Each of us listened to his words and waited for his next phrase. My fiancée Bernice was in the audience. She later described how King's inspiring speech ignited the crowd and was the motivating factor that was needed to make the protest successful. It was his message and his encouragement and his speech that gave those thousands of African Americans the courage, the enthusiasm and the desire to stay off the buses.

21.4.4 Martin Luther King, Jr.

King's speech electrified the meeting, which unanimously decided to boycott the buses until the MIA's demands were met. The speech also marked the beginning of King's role as a leader of the civil rights movement. King had been raised in a prominent ministerial

Profile

Rosa Louise McCauley Parks

Rosa Parks, in this 1956 photograph by Paul Richards, is venerated as the mother of the civil rights movement and has remained an important symbol of hope and courage.

Rosa Louise Mccauley Parks was born on February 4, 1913, to James and Leona (Edwards) McCauley, a carpenter and a schoolteacher, of Tuskegee, Alabama. Her father migrated north when his daughter was two years old. When she was 11, Rosa attended the Montgomery Industrial School for Girls while living with a widowed aunt. In 1932 Rosa married Raymond Parks, who worked in the Atlas Barber Shop in Montgomery. She worked as a department store seamstress. They were both active in the efforts to secure the release of the Scottsboro Boys. Rosa Parks enjoyed a full and busy life, serving as the secretary of the Montgomery branch of the NAACP (1943–1956) and as a member of the African Methodist Episcopal Church. In the late 1940s Rosa Parks worked to mobilize the black Montgomery community to protest white sexualized violence against black women. The assault on Gertrude Perkins, in the 1940s, and on many other black women by white men who were never punished made Parks even more determined in her activism. She participated in voter registration campaigns, and in 1954 she attended the Highlander Folk School, a training center for social change in Monteagle, Tennessee.

On December 1, 1955, when Rosa Parks refused to give up her seat on a Montgomery bus, little could she have anticipated that she would become a living symbol of the African-American quest for freedom, justice, and equality of opportunity. With great dignity and little fanfare, Parks chose to be arrested rather than to comply with the white bus driver's order to move to the back-of-the-bus section reserved for black people. Parks's behavior was a thoughtful reflection of her larger pattern of personal and public resistance. As word of Parks's arrest reverberated through Montgomery's black community, Jo Ann Robinson and members of the Women's Political Council (WPC) swung into action. On December 2, 1955, Robinson wrote and circulated, with assistance from students and club women, 30,000 copies of a flyer that declared, "Another Negro woman has been arrested and thrown in jail because she refused to get up out of her seat on the bus for a white person to sit down. It is the second time since the Claudette Colvin case that a Negro woman has been arrested for the same thing. This has to be stopped. Negroes have rights too, for if Negroes did not ride the buses, they could not operate." Robinson and the WPC asked the community to stay off the buses for a day to show their opposition to bus segregation and their solidarity with Rosa Parks.

The success of the one-day boycott aroused the community and motivated thousands to attend the first mass meeting at the Holt Street Baptist Church and to found, under the leadership of Rev. Martin Luther King, Jr., the Montgomery Improvement Association. A year later, on December 20, 1956, the Supreme Court ruled Alabama's state and local segregation laws unconstitutional. In retaliation, the department store fired Parks. The response was, perhaps, irrelevant.

In 1957 Parks, her husband, and her mother moved to Detroit, where her brother resided. For a quarter of a century, Rosa Parks worked as a special assistant to Congressman John Conyers. In 1979 the NAACP awarded Parks its Spingarn Medal. Detroit named a street, Rosa Parks Boulevard, in her honor. In keeping with a lifetime commitment to social justice and the pursuit of freedom, at the celebration of her 77th birthday in 1990 at the Kennedy Center in Washington, D.C., Parks implored the 3,000 revelers to "pray and work for the freedom of Nelson Mandela and all of our sisters and brothers in South Africa."

Rosa Parks lived a quiet life in Detroit until her death on October 24, 2005, at the age of 92. Her casket lay in state in the rotunda of the U.S. Capitol for two days, an honor usually reserved for presidents, as the nation paid its last respects to this extraordinary woman.

family with a long history of standing up for African-American rights. His grandfather had led a protest to force Atlanta to build its first high school for African Americans. King's father spoke out for African-American rights as pastor of the Ebenezer Baptist Church. At age 15, King had entered Morehouse College but did not embrace the ministry as his profession until he came under the influence of its president, Dr. Benjamin E. Mays. By age 25, King had been awarded a Ph.D. in theology from Boston University. He moved to Alabama with his wife, Coretta Scott King, to become pastor of the Dexter Avenue Baptist Church in Montgomery.

In addition to his verbal artistry, King had the ability to inspire moral courage and teach people how to maintain themselves under excruciating pressure. King merged the nonviolence advocated by the Indian nationalist leader Mohandas Gandhi with black Christian faith and church culture to create a unique ideology well suited for the civil rights struggle. King declared that the boycott would continue with or without its leaders because the conflict was not "between the white and the Negro" but "between justice and injustice." He told the Montgomery boycotters, "If we are arrested every day, if we are exploited every day, if we are trampled over every day, don't ever let anyone pull you so low as to hate them. . . . We must realize so many people are taught to hate us that they are not totally responsible for their hate." King's faith was tested. As the boycott proceeded, his home was bombed. Segregationists also bombed Nixon's home and those of two other black clergymen and MIA leaders, Ralph Abernathy and Fred Shuttlesworth, and assaulted other boycott participants.

21.4.5 Walking for Freedom

Although men occupied the top leadership positions in the boycott, women were the key to its effectiveness. The boycott lasted more than a year—381 days—and over its course nearly all the black women previously dependent on the buses to get to work refused to ride them. Some walked 12 miles a day. Others had the support of their white women employers, who provided transportation. And many helped organize a carpool of 200 vehicles that proved critical to sustaining the boycott. The community held mass meetings nightly in local churches. Robinson edited the MIA newsletter. Other women supported the boycott in dozens of ways. Some organized bake sales and made door-to-door solicitations to raise the $2,000 per week needed to keep the car pools going. The boycott took 65 percent of the bus company's business, forcing it to cut schedules, lay off drivers, and raise fares. White merchants also suffered. Impressive as it was, the boycott by itself could not end segregation on the buses. Black Montgomery needed a two-pronged strategy of mass local pressure and legal recourse through the courts. The legal backing of the federal government was necessary to end Jim Crow. Thus, NAACP lawyers and MIA's lawyer Fred Gray filed a suit in the names of Claudette Colvin, Mary Louise Smith, and three other women.

21.4.6 Friends in the North

The Montgomery movement was not without allies outside the South. Money poured into the MIA's coffers from concerned Americans. Many northern activists who had long been hoping black southerners would begin just this kind of resistance also swung into action to help. Indeed, black and white activists in many northern cities including New York and Chicago had launched challenges to overthrow housing segregation and promote open access to public beaches and amusement parks. Activist and civil rights groups joined with labor unionists to support issues of economic justice, fair employment, and an end to police corruption and brutality. Two people who were particularly important in the "Long Civil Rights" movement were Bayard Rustin and liberal Jewish lawyer Stanley Levison. Two and a half months into the boycott, Montgomery officials indicted King and 100 other leaders on charges of conspiracy to disrupt the bus system, and Bayard Rustin arrived in Montgomery.

He encouraged the leaders to follow Gandhian practice and submit freely to arrest. In a diary entry, Rustin wrote,

> Many of them did not wait for the police to come but walked to the police station and surrendered. Nixon was the first. He walked into the station and said, "You are looking for me? Here I am." This procedure had a startling effect on both the Negro and the white communities. White community leaders, politicians, and police were dumbfounded. Negroes were thrilled to see their leaders surrender without being hunted down. Soon hundreds of Negroes gathered outside the police station and applauded the leaders as they entered, one by one.

Rustin continued working behind the scenes as one of King's most trusted advisers on nonviolent principles and tactics. Stanley Levison and Ella Baker created a group called In Friendship, which raised money for the boycott. (For more on Ella Baker, see Chapter 18.)

Levison was a wealthy attorney committed to social justice. He had worked with the Communist Party, and Rustin had a long history of association with radical groups. Their influence soon attracted the attention of the FBI, which had long been obsessed with black leaders and organizations. King was not a communist, but FBI director J. Edgar Hoover hated him and other black leaders. Hoover called King "the most dangerous man in America," and he pressed his subordinates to prove King was a communist and that the civil rights movement was a Moscow-inspired conspiracy. The FBI began tapping King's telephone and hotel room phones and even threatened to expose his extramarital affairs if he did not commit suicide. By the early 1960s, the FBI had stopped warning King when it uncovered threats to his life.

21.4.7 Victory

As the bus boycott reached the one-year mark, it was obvious that the all-white city government would not budge, no matter how long the boycott lasted. Any white politician who hoped to remain in office had to defend segregation. King and the others who suffered through the ordeal grew discouraged, and in November 1956 their hopes seemed to fade when it became clear the state courts would declare the car pools illegal.

Salvation for the movement came from the cases local women (Claudette Colvin, Aurelia Browder, Susie McDonald, and Mary Louise Smith), Fred Gray, and the NAACP had taken to the federal courts. In keeping with the *Brown* precedent, on November 13, 1956, the Supreme Court in *Browder v. Gayle* ordered an end to Montgomery's bus segregation and overturned the convictions of Colvin and the other women. This decision, unlike the *Brown* decision, also expressly overturned the 1896 *Plessy v. Ferguson* decision because, like *Plessy*, it applied to transportation. Ironically, the ruling was handed down on the same day an Alabama court issued an injunction to end the MIA carpool. The bus company agreed not only to end segregation but also to hire African-American drivers and to treat all passengers with equal respect. The city's black community rejoiced. On December 21, 1956, black citizens of Montgomery boarded the buses and sat wherever they pleased. The victory at Montgomery set an example for future protests. It was the result of a highly organized black community led by committed and capable black leaders. These local efforts were bolstered by advice from and involvement of activists from outside the South. The attention of a sympathetic national press and the intervention from the federal courts strengthened black resolve to continue the struggle. But local victories could only go so far, particularly as white resistance intensified. In the three years following the boycott, and the Supreme Court decision, black southerners and their allies across the nation prepared for a broader movement. At the same time, federal officials outside the judiciary realized that no longer was it possible to ignore the white South's incipient rebellion without grave consequences for both the nation and their own power.

Profile

Clara Luper: Victory in Oklahoma

Clara Luper is revered and celebrated in Oklahoma. She was born Clara Mae Shepard on May 3, 1923. Her father Ezell Shepard was a brick worker and her mother, Isabel Shepard, worked as a maid. When her brother became ill, the local hospital denied him treatment and that became one of the defining memories shaping her consciousness. Luper's biographer, Brenda L. Perry, affectionately refers to her as the "Iron Orchid." According to Perry, in 1950 Luper, a 1944 graduate of Langston University, the only historically black college in Oklahoma, joined a group of students determined to desegregate the University of Oklahoma. In 1951 she became the first black graduate from the University of Oklahoma's graduate history program. Her activism as a student continued into her adult professional life as a teacher at Dunjee High School and as an adviser to the Oklahoma City NAACP's youth council. When the young people asked her how they could participate in the movement for first-class citizenship, Luper swung into action.

On August 19, 1958, Clara Luper led her two children and a group of approximately a dozen or so young African Americans, ranging in ages from 6 to 17, to Katz Drug Store in downtown Oklahoma City to protest against the segregation policies of the lunch counter. According to Perry, Lupur requested what would become a student mantra, "Thirteen Cokes, please." Of course they were refused service, but the routine persisted for weeks. Eventually Katz Drug Store gave in to the protesters. The owners agreed to provide service without regard to race throughout its 38 stores across Oklahoma, Missouri, Kansas, and Iowa.

One of Luper's activist students recalled her clear-voiced instructions for the sit-in:

> As we sit-in, we must remember the important dates in Black history. DATES! DATES! Important dates in Black History from the dark skies of the receding nights, a strong group of people survived. People who picked the brightest stars and with brave hands, courageous spirits and patriotic hearts wrote pages of history, adding a new unknown dimension to American History . . . .

Clara Luper later marched with Dr. Martin Luther King. In the Selma March in 1965 she was wounded when an officer's club smacked her in the knees. She revered Dr. King and wrote a play in his honor titled "Brother President: The Story of Dr. Martin Luther King, Jr." She was arrested 26 times. Luper served as the adviser to the Youth Council of the Oklahoma City Chapter of the NAACP for fifty years. She retired from teaching at Oklahoma City high schools in 1991. Retirement did not stop her from teaching. She is reported to have said, "My biggest job now is making white people understand that black history is white history. We cannot separate the two" (Peter Rothberg, "Remembering Clara Luper," *The Nation*, June 10, 2011).

Today, the citizens in Oklahoma City treasure and honor her memory. According to Perry, Clara Lupur "remains a symbolic force who constantly reminds us of the strength, courage, and often tough-love that is necessary for the advancement of humanity." She continued, Luper led "her fight against racial injustice at a crucial time in Oklahoma." One former student recalled, "I remember as a teen how influential she was in my life." Another student testified, "Miss Luper was my civics teacher in high school. She was a great teacher and a great person, and I learned a lot from her about justice and about bravery." The student concluded, "The world needs more people like her."[1]

---

[1]Clara Luper, *Behold the Walls* (Oklahoma City: Jim Wire, 1979).

21.5 No Easy Road to Freedom: The 1960s

● **Identify the major goals of the Civil Rights Act of 1957.**

By the end of the campaign in Montgomery, Martin Luther King, Jr. emerged as a moral leader of national stature. On the advice of Stanley Levison, Bayard Rustin, and Ella Baker, he helped to create a new organization, the **Southern Christian Leadership Conference (SCLC)**, and thus provide an institutional base for continuing the struggle.

21.5.1 Martin Luther King, Jr. and the SCLC

The SCLC was a federation of civil rights groups, community organizations, and churches that sought to coordinate the burgeoning local movements. King assumed leadership of the SCLC, crisscrossing the nation to build support and raise money. The organization also began training black activists, particularly on college campuses, in the tactics of nonviolent protest. Because the ballot was deemed the critical weapon needed to complete school desegregation and secure equal employment opportunity, adequate housing, and equal access to public accommodations, the SCLC focused on securing voting rights for black people. In the three years after the Montgomery Bus Boycott, the SCLC also aided black communities in challenging bus segregation in Tallahassee, Florida, and Atlanta.

The SCLC shared many of the NAACP's goals, but tensions arose between the two organizations. The NAACP's leadership doubted the effectiveness of the protest tactics the SCLC favored. They resented having to divert resources from work on important court cases to defend people arrested in protests and were troubled by the left-wing connections of King's advisers. The fortunes of the NAACP in the South, however, plummeted in the late 1950s as southern states persecuted its members. This left the field to the SCLC. The SCLC and the NAACP worked together, but the tensions over tactics were never far below the surface.

21.5.2 Civil Rights Act of 1957

Despite President Eisenhower's tepid response to *Brown*, Congress proved willing to take a modest step toward ending racial discrimination. Buttressing the Supreme Court's desegregation initiatives, it enacted the Civil Rights Act of 1957. To pass this legislation, liberals in the Senate had to end a filibuster by southern conservatives; clearly, the law, its symbolic importance notwithstanding, was weak. It created a commission to monitor violations of black civil rights and to propose remedies for infringements on black voting. It upgraded the Civil Rights Section into a division within the Justice Department and gave it the power to sue states and municipalities that discriminated on the basis of race. Although an important step on the long road toward black enfranchisement, this act disappointed black activists because it lacked enforcement power sufficient to counter white reaction. Moreover, most black leaders doubted that the Eisenhower administration would enforce the provisions.

21.5.3 The Little Rock Nine

President Dwight Eisenhower may have had little inclination to support the fight for black rights, but the defiance of Arkansas Governor Orville Faubus forced him to. At the beginning of the school year in 1957, Faubus posted 270 Arkansas national guardsmen outside Little Rock Central High School to prevent nine black youths from entering.

Southern Christian Leadership Conference (SCLC)

Organization spearheaded by Martin Luther King, Jr. to provide an institutional base for the civil rights movement.

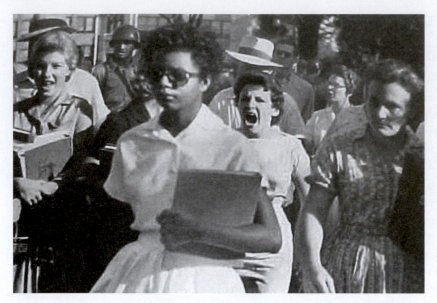

Elizabeth Eckerd, one of nine black students who sought to enroll at Little Rock Central High School in September 1957, endures the taunts of an angry white crowd as she tries to make her way to the school.

Faubus was determined to flout *Brown* and maintain school segregation. When a federal court order forced the governor to allow the children into the school, he simply withdrew the state guard and left the children to face a hate-filled mob.

To defend the sovereignty of the federal courts and the Constitution, Eisenhower had to act. He sent in 1,100 paratroopers from the 101st Airborne Division to Little Rock and put the Arkansas National Guard under federal authority. It was the first time since Reconstruction that troops had been sent to the South to protect the rights of African American citizens. The troops remained in Little Rock Central High School for the rest of the school year. Governor Faubus closed the Little Rock public schools in 1958–1959.

Eight of the nine black students withstood the abuse and curses of segregationists both inside and outside the facility and eventually desegregated the high school. Young African Americans throughout the South would show similar courage. President Eisenhower wrote to the parents and supporters of the students to express his willingness "to come down and address the student body if invited by the student leaders of the school." Although he received no such invitation, the President assured Daisy Bates, leader of the NAACP branch in Arkansas, that, "In the course of our country's progress toward equality of opportunity, you have shown dignity and courage in circumstances which would daunt citizens of little faith." In 1958, the first African American graduate of Little Rock Central High School, Earnest Green, continued his college studies at Michigan State where he received his Bachelor of Arts and Master's degrees in social science and sociology. Melba Pattillo Beals earned a Doctorate of Education degree from San Francisco State University, while Terrence J. Roberts earned a Ph.D. in Psychology from Southern Illinois University in 1977. For others the psychological wounds never healed. Thus, it was important that on November 9, 1999, President Bill Clinton conferred on the Little Rock Nine Congressional Gold Medals, in recognition of their courageous resistance to racial hatred and bigotry.

21.6 Black Youth Stand Up by Sitting Down

Explain the evolution of tactics used in the 1940s and those developed and practiced by the 1960s generation of student activists.

Beginning in 1960, motivated black college students adapted a strategy that the Congress of Racial Equality (CORE) had used in the 1940s—the "sit-in"—and emerged as the vanguard of the civil rights movement. Their distinctive and independent contributions to the black protest movement accelerated the pace of social change. Before long the movement would inspire more northern black and white students. Some high school students in southern cities, including the "Ribault Ten" who integrated Jean Ribault High School in Jacksonville, Florida, in 1966, had to stand up for freedom. As one of the students, Jean Downing, recalled: "Our high school experience was not a pleasant one . . . but someone had to integrate the high schools."

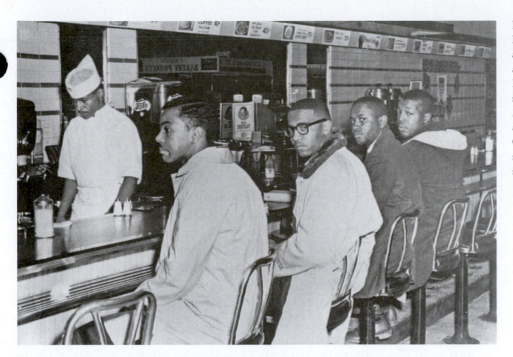

Four students—from the left, Joseph McNeil, Franklin McCain, Billy Smith, and Clarence Henderson—sit patiently at a Woolworth lunch counter on February 2, 1960, the second day of the sit-in in Greensboro, North Carolina. Although not the first sit-in protest against segregated facilities, the Greensboro action triggered a wave of sit-ins by black high school and college students across the South.

21.6.1 Sit-Ins: Greensboro, Nashville, Atlanta

On February 1, 1960, Joseph McNeil, Franklin McCain, David Richmond, and Ezell Blair, Jr., all freshmen at North Carolina Agricultural and Technical College, decided to desegregate local restaurants by sitting at the lunch counter of a Greensboro Woolworth five-and-dime store. Although black people were welcome to spend their money in the store, they could not eat at the lunch counter, making it a painful symbol of white supremacy. At 4:30 in the afternoon the students sat at the counter. They received no service that day but sat quietly doing their schoolwork until the store closed. The action of these four young men electrified their fellow students, and the next day many others joined them. Soon, black women students from Bennett College and a few white students from the University of North Carolina Women's College joined the protest, and by the fifth day hundreds of young, studious, neatly dressed African Americans crowded the downtown store demanding their rights.

Like the black people of Montgomery, the students in Greensboro acted with forethought and with the support of their community. They had long debated how they could best participate in the desegregation movement. All four of the black students had been members of NAACP college or youth groups and were aware of the currents of change flowing through the South. Although they began the sit-in on their own, it quickly gained the support of the black community. Many people in the North and West—both black and white—also joined the campaign by picketing local stores of the national chains that approved of segregation in the South. After facing the collective power of the black community and their allies for months, white businessmen and politicians gave in to the black community's demands.

The students at Greensboro were not alone in their desire to strike out at discrimination. Indeed, at Fisk University in Nashville, Tennessee, Diane Nash, John Lewis, Marion Barry, James Bevel, Curtis Murphy, Gloria Johnson, Bernard Lafayette, and Rodney Powell had begun organizing nonviolent workshops before the Greensboro sit-in. With youthful exuberance and idealism, they determined to follow the Rev. James Lawson's leadership and teaching on nonviolence and Christian brotherhood. Even better organized than their comrades in North Carolina, they had been training intensively for a sit-in campaign. Twelve days after the first sit-ins began, the Nashville group swung into action. Hundreds were arrested, and those who sat suffered insults, beatings, arrest, and torture while in jail. Nonetheless, by May 1960 they had compelled major restaurants to desegregate.

Atlanta, Martin Luther King, Jr.'s home base and the site of a large African-American community, spawned an even more dramatic movement. It began after Spelman College freshman Ruby Doris Smith persuaded her friends and classmates to launch sit-ins in the city. On March 15, 1960, two students at Atlanta University, Julian Bond and Lonnie King, executing a carefully orchestrated plan, deployed 200 sit-in students to 10 different eating places. They targeted government-owned property and public places, including bus and train stations and the state capitol, which should have been willing to serve all customers. At the Federal Building, Bond and his classmates attempted to eat in the municipal cafeteria and were arrested. After hours of incarceration they were released. In earlier years, a jail stint had been a mark of shame, but these students returned to the campus as heroes. The Atlanta sit-in students broadened their campaign demands to include desegregation of all public facilities, black voting rights, and equal access to educational and employment opportunities. On September 27, 1961, the Atlanta business and political elite gave in.

Just as in Greensboro, the students in Nashville, Atlanta, and other southern cities won the support of local people who had not been previously involved in organized resistance. By April 1960 more than 2,000 students from black high schools and colleges had been arrested in 78 southern towns and cities. Local people demonstrated their allegiance to them in numerous ways, but their most effective tactic was the economic boycott. When business began to suffer, white leaders proved willing to negotiate the racial status quo. By the summer, more than 30 southern cities had set up community organizations to respond to the complaints of black citizens.

21.6.2 The Student Nonviolent Coordinating Committee

Recognizing the significance of the region-wide student action and fearing it would soon melt away, SCLC's Ella Baker organized a conference for 150 students at her alma mater, Shaw University, in Raleigh, North Carolina. Baker, who managed operations in SCLC's Atlanta headquarters, chafed under the rigid male leadership of the organization. In contrast, she advocated decentralized leadership and celebrated participatory democracy. Her skepticism about SCLC struck a chord with the students.

Student Nonviolent Coordinating Committee (SNCC)

Civil rights organization founded by black college students in 1960 at the initiative of Ella Baker.

On April 15–17, 1960, delegates representing over 50 colleges and high schools from 37 communities in 13 states began discussing how to keep the movement going. Baker addressed the group in a speech titled "More Than a Hamburger" and became the midwife of a new organization named the **Student Nonviolent Coordinating Committee (SNCC)**. The newest addition to the roster of civil rights associations adhered to the ideology of nonviolence, but it also acknowledged the possible need for increased militancy and confrontation. More accommodating black leaders, even some of those in SCLC, objected to the students' use of direct confrontational tactics that disrupted race relations and community peace.

21.6.3 Freedom Rides

Freedom Rides

Effort in 1961 to desegregate interstate bus and rail travel.

The sit-in movement paved the way for the **"Freedom Rides"** of 1961. CORE's James Farmer and Bayard Rustin resolved that it was time for a reprise of their 1947 mission to ride interstate buses and trains in the Upper South. That early effort—a planned bus trip from Washington, D.C., to Kentucky—reached only as far as Chapel Hill, North

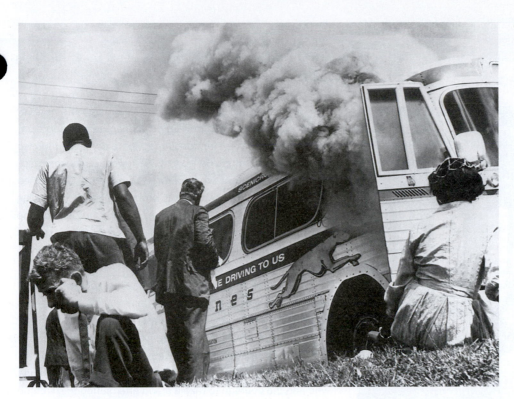

On May 14, in Anniston, Alabama, a white mob firebombed this Freedom Riders' bus and attacked passengers as they escaped the flames.

Carolina. There the group of interracial riders met violent resistance, were arrested, and were sentenced to 30 days on a road gang. This new journey tested the Justice Department's willingness to protect the rights of African Americans to use bus terminal facilities on a nonsegregated basis.

The Freedom Rides showed the world how far some white southerners would go to preserve segregation. The first ride ran into trouble on May 4, 1961, when John Lewis, one of the seven black riders, tried to enter the white waiting room of the Greyhound bus terminal in Rock Hill, South Carolina, and was beaten by local white people in full view of the police. The interracial group continued through Alabama toward Jackson, Mississippi, but white violence made escape from Alabama difficult. At Anniston, Alabama, a mob firebombed the bus and beat the escaping riders. Local African Americans, led by the Rev. Fred Shuttlesworth, took many of the shocked and injured riders to Birmingham.

With the police offering no protection, CORE abandoned the Freedom Rides, and most of the original riders left Alabama. But SNCC activists and students in Nashville refused to let the idea die. At least 20 civil rights workers went to Birmingham, where they vowed on May 20 to ride on to Montgomery. John Lewis remained with the group that arrived in Montgomery. Awaiting them was another angry mob of more than 1,000 white people and not a policeman in sight. This time Lewis was knocked unconscious, and all the riders had to be hospitalized. Even a presidential aide assigned to monitor the crisis was injured.

News services flashed around the world graphic images of the violence, and the federal government resolved to end the bloodletting. Attorney General Robert Kennedy sent 400 federal marshals to restore law and order. Martin Luther King, Jr. and Ralph Abernathy joined the conflict on May 21, as 1,200 men, women, and children met at Abernathy's church. The federal marshals averted further bloodshed by surrounding the building. Only then did Governor John Patterson order the National Guard and state troopers to protect the protesters. When the group arrived in Jackson, Mississippi, white authorities arrested them. By summer's end, more than 300 Freedom Riders had served time in Mississippi's notorious prisons.

Profile

Robert Parris Moses

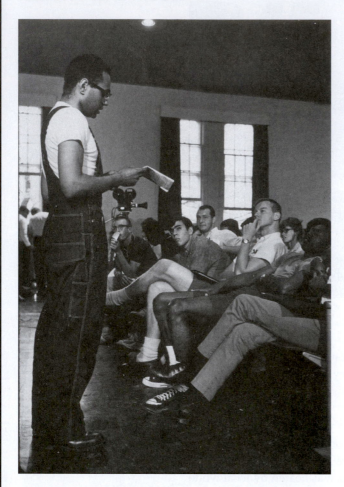

Robert "Bob" Moses instructs volunteers for the Freedom Summer campaign of 1964.

Bob Moses, one of the most dedicated and revered young civil rights activists, was a soft-spoken man possessed of a powerful intellect, iron courage, and a rare purity of moral conviction. Born in Harlem in 1935, Moses was an excellent student. He attended Hamilton College in New York State, and from his readings there in philosophy, including works on Buddhism and existentialism, he developed a sophisticated understanding of nonviolent protest, a topic he explored during his graduate studies in philosophy at Harvard.

When Moses learned of the sit-ins in 1960, he went south to participate. It was a fateful trip during which he met Amzie Moore, one of the World War II veterans who had returned home to make Mississippi safe for democracy. Moore was

the vice president of the state conference of the NAACP branches. The two men developed a deep-seated appreciation for each other's strengths, and Moore convinced Moses to work in Mississippi. By August 1961 Moses was an organizer for the Student Nonviolent Coordinating Committee (SNCC) in the small town of McComb, Mississippi. There his group registered black voters. In early 1962 he became the program director of the Council of Federated Organizations and remained in the center of the struggle in Mississippi for the next three years.

The violence of white people and the courage of local black people profoundly affected Moses. In McComb he was arrested, jailed, beaten, and threatened with death. One of the local black people who helped his group was murdered in cold blood by a state senator who was subsequently acquitted of the crime by an all-white jury. Moses respected anyone who had the courage to take a stand after suffering a lifetime of such abuse. He sought to give local people the tools to continue to control their lives long after movement organizers had left.

Although Moses refused to become a formal leader of the SNCC forces in Mississippi, the young civil rights worker set an example of nonviolent resistance and encouraged SNCC to avoid developing a hierarchical leadership. In late 1963 Moses became the driving force behind the Freedom Summer project and played a central role in persuading SNCC to accept white volunteers from the North. He also stood for principle rather than expediency when, at the 1964 Democratic Convention, he rejected the meager deal offered to the Mississippi Freedom Democratic Party (discussed later in the chapter).

In 1965 Moses began to drift away from the civil rights movement and toward opposition to the war in Vietnam. Exhausted from his ordeal in the South and seeking to avoid the draft, he emigrated first to Canada and then to the African nation of Tanzania. Moses returned after President Jimmy Carter offered amnesty to draft resisters in 1977 and began teaching math and science to inner-city black children. After receiving a MacArthur Foundation "genius grant," he developed the Algebra Project, which uses many of the empowerment strategies pioneered during the civil rights era to help children and their families gain the education they need in a computer-oriented economy.

21.7 A Sight to Be Seen: The Movement at High Tide

Discuss the individuals who were in the first wave of post–World War II leaders. Explain some of the differences in civil rights demands following the end of World War II and during the 1950s.

Between 1960 and 1963, the civil rights movement developed the techniques and organization that would finally bring America face-to-face with the conflict between its democratic ideals and the racism of its politics. Day after day the movement squared off against the die-hard resistance of the white South and created a situation that demanded that the president and Congress take action.

21.7.1 The Election of 1960

One of the persistent fears of white southerners was that black Americans, if armed with the ballot, would possess the balance of political power. The presidential election of 1960 proved this to be true. Initially, many African Americans favored the Republican nominee Richard Nixon, who had advocated strong civil rights legislation. Baseball star Jackie Robinson and many other well-known African Americans were Nixon supporters. It seemed as if the New Deal coalition had weakened and that black citizens would reverse their move into the Democratic Party. The Democratic nominee, Massachusetts Senator John F. Kennedy, in contrast, had done little to distinguish himself to black Americans in the struggles of the 1950s. As the campaign progressed, however, Kennedy made sympathetic statements in support of black protests. Meanwhile, Nixon attempted to strengthen his position with white southern voters and remained silent about civil rights issues, even though the Republican Party had a strong pro–civil rights record.

Shortly before the election, Martin Luther King, Jr. was sentenced to four months in prison for leading a nonviolent protest march in Atlanta. Kennedy telephoned Coretta Scott King to offer his support, while his brother Robert F. Kennedy used his influence to obtain King's release. These acts impressed African Americans and won their support. African-American voters in key northern cities provided the crucial margin that elected John F. Kennedy. In Illinois, for example, with black voters casting 250,000 ballots for Kennedy, the Democrats carried the state by only 9,000 votes.

21.7.2 The Kennedy Administration and the Civil Rights Movement

Early in his administration Kennedy grew concerned about the violence occasioned by the civil rights movement. As the Freedom Rides continued across the Deep South, the activists provoked confrontations and forced the federal government to intervene on their behalf. Kennedy's primary interest at this point was to prevent disorder from getting out of hand and to avoid compromising America's position with the developing nations. But he had little room to maneuver given the power of white southerners in his party and in Congress.

Despite these limitations, Kennedy did aid the cause of civil rights. He issued Executive Order 11063, which required government agencies to discontinue discriminatory policies and practices in federally supported housing, and he named Vice President Lyndon B. Johnson to chair the newly established Committee on Equal Employment Opportunity. Kennedy also nominated Thurgood Marshall to the Second Circuit Court of Appeals on September 23, 1961 (although opposition in the Senate blocked Marshall's confirmation until September 11, 1963). He named journalist Carl Rowan deputy assistant secretary of state. More than 40 African Americans took positions in the new administration, including Robert Weaver, director of the Housing and Home Finance Agency; Mercer Cook, ambassador to Norway; and George L. P. Weaver, assistant secretary of labor. Moreover, Kennedy's brother Robert put muscle into the Civil Rights Division of the Justice Department by hiring an impressive team of lawyers headed by Washington attorney Burke Marshall.

Like Eisenhower, when President Kennedy felt that intractable southern governors were challenging his authority, he acted decisively. On June 25, 1962, one year after James Meredith had filed a complaint of racial discrimination against the University of Mississippi, the U.S. Court of Appeals ruled that the university had to admit him. Governor Ross Barnett vowed to resist, but Kennedy sent 300 federal marshals to uphold the order. Thousands of students rioted at the campus. Two people died, 200 were arrested, and nearly half the marshals were injured. Kennedy did not back down. He federalized the Mississippi National Guard to ensure Meredith's admission. Although isolated and harassed throughout his time at the University of Mississippi, Meredith eventually graduated. Likewise, in June 1963, the Kennedy administration compelled Governor George Wallace to allow the desegregation of the University of Alabama.

21.7.3 Voter Registration Projects

On June 16, 1961, Robert Kennedy urged student leaders to redirect their energies to voter registration projects and to lessen their concentration on direct-action activities. He and Justice Department aides persuaded the students that the free exercise of the ballot would result in profound and significant social change. James Foreman, SNCC's executive director, followed Kennedy's lead. By October 1962 SNCC had joined forces with the NAACP, SCLC, and CORE in the Voter Education Project funded by major philanthropic foundations and administered by the Southern Regional Council. SNCC was responsible for Alabama and Mississippi. Drawing on the expertise of Robert Moses and working with a cadre of local leaders like Amzie Moore, head of the NAACP in Mississippi's Cleveland County, and Fannie Lou Hamer of Ruleville, SNCC opened voter registration schools. When the "graduates" attempted to register to vote, it unleashed a wave of white violence and murder across Mississippi.

21.7.4 The Albany Movement

In Albany, Georgia, the civil rights movement met sophisticated resistance and experienced its most profound defeat up to that time. The movement in Albany began in the summer of 1961 when SNCC members moved into the city to register voters. Local groups decided to form a coalition called the Albany Movement and elected William G. Anderson as its president. The movement's goal expanded from securing the vote to the total desegregation of the town.

In Laurie Pritchett, Albany's police chief, the movement faced an uncommonly sophisticated opponent. Pritchett studied the past tactics of SNCC and King and resolved not to confront the federal government directly and to avoid the violence that brought negative media attention. When students from a black college decided to desegregate the bus terminal, Pritchett arrested them after they entered the white waiting room and attempted to eat in the bus terminal dining room. Shrewdly, he charged the students with violating a city ordinance for failing to obey a law enforcement officer. The Albany Movement decided to invite King and SCLC to aid them and to overwhelm the police department by filling the jails with protesters. King answered the call. On December 16, 1961, he and more than 250 demonstrators were arrested, joining the 507 people already in jail. The plan was to stay in jail to, as Charles Sherrod explained, "break the system down from within. Our ability to suffer was somehow going to overcome their ability to hurt us." King vowed to remain in jail until the city desegregated. Sheriff Pritchett, however, made arrangements to

Profile

Fannie Lou Hamer

Fannie Lou Hamer, in words and deeds, refused to compromise with racial injustice. Representing the Mississippi Freedom Democratic Party, Hamer testified before the Credentials Committee of the Democratic National Convention in Atlantic City, August 22, 1964.

Fannie Lou Hamer (1917–1977) emerged from the ranks of "local people" in Mississippi to become one of the most powerful leaders and orators of the civil rights movement. Hamer, the youngest of 20 children, grew up in extreme poverty and had only a few years of education. She worked and lived as a timekeeper on a plantation in Ruleville,

Mississippi. When SNCC workers came to the community for a voting rights campaign, Hamer was one of the first to participate.

On August 1, 1962, Hamer attempted to register to vote in Indianola, Mississippi. In response, she was fired from her plantation job and evicted from her land. Still, she refused to capitulate and accepted full-time employment as a field secretary for the SNCC, where she worked on the Voter Education Project.

Despite her lack of education, Hamer was a spellbinding orator. Her televised testimony before the 1964 Democratic Convention won national support for the MFDP's challenge to the party regulars from Mississippi. The next year Hamer, who had run for the House of Representatives, challenged the seating of the Mississippi congressional delegation. Although unsuccessful, her action paved the way for the Voting Rights Act of 1965.

Although basic civil and voting rights had been won by 1965, most black people in the Mississippi Delta still lived in deep poverty. In 1968 Hamer sought to address this problem by setting up the nonprofit Freedom Farms Corporation as an agricultural cooperative. The mixed results of this last campaign, however, cannot diminish the profound changes that Fannie Lou Hamer was so instrumental in bringing about.

house almost 2,000 people in surrounding jail facilities and trained his deputies in the use of nonviolent techniques. Thus, Pritchett avoided confrontation, violence, and federal intervention.

On December 18, 1961, two days after King's arrest, the city and the Albany Movement announced a truce. King returned to Atlanta, and the city refused to implement the terms of the agreement. When King and Ralph Abernathy returned to Albany in July 1962 for sentencing on their December arrests, they chose 45 days in jail rather than admit guilt by paying a fine. The mass marches resumed, but again Pritchett thwarted King by releasing him from jail to avoid negative publicity. The city's attorney then secured a federal injunction to prevent King and the other leaders from demonstrating. Given his dependence on the federal government, King felt he could not violate the injunction, and he abandoned the protest. For King, the Albany Movement was a failure, his most glaring defeat, and one that called into question the future of the movement.

21.7.5 The Birmingham Confrontation

By early 1963 the movement appeared to be stalled. Black communities in much of the South were strong and well organized, but their efforts had achieved only modest changes. It was impossible to overcome the power of southern state and local governments without the intervention of the federal government, but national politicians, including President Kennedy, remained reluctant to act unless faced with open defiance by white people or with televised violence against peaceful protesters. King and other black leaders knew that if city governments throughout the South followed the model of Sheriff Pritchett in Albany, the civil rights movement might lose momentum. To rejuvenate the movement, SCLC decided to launch a massive new campaign during 1963, the year of the 100th anniversary of the Emancipation Proclamation.

Birmingham, Alabama, a large, tightly segregated industrial city, was chosen as the site for the action. The city was ripe for such a protest, in part because its black community suffered from police brutality and economic, educational, and social discrimination. The Ku Klux Klan terrorized people with impunity. The black community had, however, developed a strong phalanx of protest organizations called the Alabama Christian Movement for Human Rights (ACMHR) led by the Rev. Fred Shuttlesworth. The ACMHR and SCLC planned a campaign of boycotts, pickets, and demonstrations code-named "Project C for Confrontation." Their program would be far more extensive than any before, with demands to integrate public facilities, for guarantees of employment opportunities for black workers in downtown businesses, to desegregate the schools, to improve services in black neighborhoods, and to provide low-income housing. Organizers hoped to provoke the city's public safety commissioner Eugene T. "Bull" Connor, who, unlike Sheriff Pritchett, had a reputation for viciousness. Civil rights leaders believed Connor's conduct would horrify the nation and compel Kennedy to act.

Project C began on April 3 with student sit-ins. Days later, marches began, and Connor, following the lead of Pritchett, arrested all who participated but avoided overt violence. When the state courts prohibited further protests, King and Abernathy, among others, violated the ruling. They were arrested and jailed on Good Friday, April 12, 1963.

While in jail, King received a letter from eight local Christian and Jewish clergymen who objected to what they considered the "unwise and untimely" protest activities of black citizens. King had smuggled a pen into jail and on scraps of paper, including toilet paper and the margins of the Birmingham *News*, he wrote an eloquent treatise on the use of direct action. His "Letter From Birmingham City Jail" was widely published in newspapers and magazines. In it, King dismissed those who called for black people to wait. The letter resonated with black journalist Carl T. Rowan, who recalled, "My entire journalistic career had embraced a personal war against the gradualists, the whites of power who asked black Americans to wait." Wyatt Walker was empowered by the Birmingham campaign, declaring, "The most important thing that happened, was that people decided that they were not going to be afraid of white folks anymore." He concluded, "Dr. King's most lasting contribution is that he emancipated black people's psyche. We threw off the slave mentality. Going to jail had been the whip which kept black folks in line. Now going to jail was transformed into a badge of honor."

King's "Letter From A Birmingham City Jail" (1963) had a national impact. But the Birmingham movement lost momentum because many of the protesters either were in jail or could not risk new arrests. At this juncture James Bevel of SCLC proposed using schoolchildren to continue the protests. Many observers, and some of those in the movement, criticized this idea; King and other leaders, however, believed it was necessary to risk harm to children to ensure their freedom. Thus, on May 2 and 3, 1963, a "children's crusade" involving thousands of youths, some as young as six, marched. This tactic enraged "Bull" Connor and his officers. The police not only arrested the children but flailed away with nightsticks and set dogs on them. On Connor's order, firefighters aimed their hoses at the youngsters, ripping the clothes from their backs, cutting flesh, and tumbling children down the street. In the ensuing days, many of the children and their parents began to fight back, hurling bottles and rocks at their uniformed tormentors. As the violence escalated, white businessmen became concerned, and the city came to the bargaining table.

President Kennedy deployed Assistant Attorney General for Civil Rights Burke Marshall to negotiate a settlement. On May 10, 1963, white businessmen agreed to integrate downtown facilities and hire black men and women. The following night the KKK bombed the A. G. Gaston Motel, where SCLC had its headquarters, and the house that belonged to King's brother, the Rev. A. D. King. Black citizens in turn burned cars and buildings and attacked the police. Only intervention by King and other leaders prevented a riot. White moderates delivered on the promises, and the agreement stuck.

Although SCLC did not win every demand, Birmingham was a major triumph and a turning point in the movement. The summer of 1963 saw protests across the South, with nearly 800 marches, demonstrations, and sit-ins. Ten civil rights protesters were killed and 20,000 arrested as the white South desperately sought to stem the tide. On June 12, 1963, in one of the most tragic losses for the movement, white extremist Byron de la Beckwith gunned down Medgar Evers in the driveway of his home in Jackson, Mississippi. Evers had been the executive secretary of the NAACP's Mississippi organization and the center of a movement in Jackson. His cold-blooded murder dramatized the hatred some white southerners felt and the lengths to which they would go to prevent change.

21.8 A Hard Victory

Analyze the impact of the federal government's intermittent support on the Long Freedom Movement.

The sacrifices in Birmingham and the intensification of the movement throughout the South set the stage for Congress to pass legislation for a Second Reconstruction that would at last fulfill the promise of the first.

21.8.1 The March on Washington

The lingering image of Birmingham and the growing number of demonstrations throughout the South compelled action from President Kennedy. On June 11, 1963, he made his strongest statement about civil rights to the nation: "We face . . . a moral crisis as a country and a people. It cannot be met by repressive police action. It cannot be left to increased demonstrations in the streets. It cannot be quieted by token moves or talk. It is a time to act in the Congress, in your state and local legislative body, and above all, in all our daily lives. A great change is at hand, and our task, our obligation, is to make that revolution . . . peaceful and constructive for all." Kennedy proposed the strongest civil rights bill the country had yet seen; however, despite the public's heightened awareness of discrimination, he could not muster sufficient support in Congress to counter the southern bloc within his own party.

To demonstrate their support for Kennedy's civil rights legislation, a coalition of civil rights organizations—SCLC, NAACP, CORE, SNCC, and the National Urban League—and their leaders resurrected the idea of organizing a march on Washington that A. Philip Randolph had first proposed in 1941. In 1962 Randolph and Bayard Rustin had proposed a march to protest black unemployment. Their initial call received a tepid response; however, after Birmingham the major civil rights organizations reconsidered. Reflecting renewed hope, Randolph christened it a march for "Jobs and Freedom."

On August 28, 1963, nearly 250,000 marchers gathered before the Lincoln Memorial to support the civil rights bill and the movement at large. Throughout the day they sang freedom songs and listened to speeches from civil rights leaders. Finally, late in the afternoon, Martin Luther King, Jr. arose and, casting aside his prepared remarks, delivered an impassioned speech. Most powerfully, King spoke of his vision of the future.

Historian Harvard Sitkoff provides an insightful assessment of the power of King's March on Washington speech by underscoring both its masterful delivery and its declaration of the rights of black people. He declared,

King's message and majestic delivery made the day historic. At a time when most Americans did not perceive the injustice or the immorality of the nation's racism, King depicted it at its most searing to the millions who watched on television and to the many more millions who had heard it on the radio or would see it excerpted on the evening news. At a time when the sight of black kids and white kids going to the same school inflamed racist mobs, he demanded an end to all barriers separating the races. . . . King confronted white America with the undeniable justice of African-American demands and succeeded in associating black rights with accepted values. . . . No harmless dreamer, the preacher interpreted the vast social upheaval, slaying expectations of gradualism or of moderation if America failed to make good on its promises.

King's words did not still the angry opposition of white southerners. On September 15, 1963, only days after the March on Washington, white racists bombed the 16th St. Baptist Church in Birmingham and killed four girls attending Sunday school: Addie Mae Collins, Denise McNair, Carole Robertson, and Cynthia Wesley. Chris McNair, the father of the youngest victim, pleaded for calm out of the depth of his own pain: "We must not let this change us into something different than who we are. We must be human."

The event shook the nation and, combined with the reaction to Kennedy's assassination on November 22, 1963, set the stage for real change.

21.8.2 The Civil Rights Act of 1964

Kennedy's successor, Lyndon B. Johnson, lobbied hard to pass the landmark Civil Rights Act. Many in the civil rights movement feared that Johnson, a southerner, would back his region's defiance. Nonetheless, only four days after taking the oath of office, Johnson told the nation he planned to support the civil rights bill as a memorial for the slain president. A master politician, Johnson pushed the bill through Congress despite a marathon filibuster by its opponents.

1955–1968
Violence and the Civil Rights Movement

May 7, 1955
Rev. George Lee killed for leading voter registration drive, Belzoni, Mississippi

August 13, 1955
Lamar Smith murdered for organizing black voters, Brookhaven, Mississippi

August 28, 1955
Emmett Louis Till murdered for speaking to white woman, Money, Mississippi

October 22, 1955
John Earl Reese slain by night riders opposed to black school improvements, Mayflower, Texas

January 23, 1957
Willie Edwards, Jr. killed by Klan, Montgomery, Alabama

1955–1968
Violence and the Civil Rights Movement

September 24, 1957

President Eisenhower orders federal troops to enforce school desegregation, Little Rock, Arkansas

April 27, 1959

Mack Charles Parker taken from jail and lynched, Poplarville, Mississippi

May 14, 1961

Freedom Riders attacked in Alabama while testing compliance with bus desegregation laws

September 25, 1961

Voter registration worker Herbert Lee killed by a white legislator, Liberty, Mississippi

April 1, 1962

Civil rights groups launch voter registration drive

April 9, 1962

Roman Ducksworth, Jr. taken from bus and killed by police, Taylorsville, Mississippi

September 30, 1962

Riots erupt when James Meredith, a black student, enrolls at the University of Mississippi; Paul Guihard, European reporter, killed

April 23, 1963

William Lewis Moore slain during one-man march against segregation, Attalla, Alabama

May 3, 1963

Birmingham police attack marching children with dogs and fire hoses

June 12, 1963

Medgar Evers assassinated, Jackson, Mississippi

September 15, 1963

Schoolgirls Addie Mae Collins, Denise McNair, Carole Robertson, and Cynthia Wesley killed in the bombing of the 16th St. Baptist Church, Birmingham, Alabama

September 15, 1963

Virgil Lamar Ware killed during racist violence, Birmingham, Alabama

January 31, 1964

Louis Allen, witness to the murder of a civil rights worker, assassinated, Liberty, Mississippi

April 7, 1964

Rev. Bruce Klunder killed protesting construction of a segregated school, Cleveland, Ohio

1955–1968
Violence and the Civil Rights Movement

May 2, 1964

Henry Hezekiah Dee and Charles Eddie Moore killed by Klan, Meadville, Mississippi

June 21, 1964

Civil rights workers James Chaney, Andrew Goodman, and Michael Schwerner abducted and slain by Klan, Philadelphia, Mississippi

July 11, 1964

Lt. Col. Lemuel Penn killed by Klan, Colbert, Georgia

February 26, 1965

Jimmie Lee Jackson, civil rights marcher, killed by state trooper, Marion, Alabama

March 11, 1965

Selma to Montgomery march volunteer, Rev. James Reeb, beaten to death, Selma, Alabama

March 25, 1965

Viola Gregg Liuzzo killed by Klan while transporting marchers, Selma Highway, Alabama

June 2, 1965

Oneal Moore, black deputy, killed by night riders, Varnado, Louisiana

July 18, 1965

Willie Wallace Brewster killed by night riders, Anniston, Alabama

August 20, 1965

Jonathan Daniels, seminary student, killed by deputy, Hayneville, Alabama

January 3, 1966

Samuel Younge, Jr., student civil rights activist, killed in dispute over whites-only restroom, Tuskegee, Alabama

January 10, 1966

Vernon Dahmer, black community leader, killed in Klan bombing, Hattiesburg, Mississippi

June 10, 1966

Ben Chester White killed by Klan, Natchez, Mississippi

July 30, 1966

Clarence Triggs slain by night riders, Bogalusa, Louisiana

February 2, 1967

Wharlest Jackson, civil rights leader, killed when police fire on protesters, Jackson, Mississippi

February 8, 1968

Students Samuel Hammond, Jr., Delano Middleton, and Henry Smith killed when highway patrolmen fire on protesters, Orangeburg, South Carolina

April 4, 1968

Dr. Martin Luther King, Jr. assassinated, Memphis, Tennessee

The **Civil Rights Act of 1964** was the culmination of the civil rights movement to that time. The act banned discrimination in places of public accommodation, including restaurants, hotels, gas stations, and entertainment facilities, as well as schools, parks, playgrounds, libraries, and swimming pools. The desegregation of public accommodations irrevocably changed the face of American society. The issue of legally mandated racial separation was now settled. The act also banned discrimination by employers and labor unions on the basis of race, color, religion, national origin, and sex in regard to hiring, promoting, dismissing, or making job referrals. The act had strong provisions for enforcement. Most important, it allowed government agencies to withhold federal money from any program permitting or practicing discrimination. This provision had particular importance for the desegregation of schools and colleges across the country. The act also gave the attorney general the power to initiate proceedings against segregated facilities and schools on behalf of people who could not do so on their own. Finally, it created the Equal Employment Opportunity Commission to monitor discrimination in employment.

Civil Rights Act of 1964

Federal law banning discrimination in places of public accommodation.

21.8.3 Mississippi Freedom Summer

While Congress considered the Civil Rights Act, movement activists renewed their focus on voter registration in the Deep South. In the fall of 1963, many CORE and SNCC workers saw segregation crumbling; however, they knew that without the ballot, African Americans could never drive racist politicians from office, gain a fair hearing in court, reduce police and mob violence, or get equal services from state and local governments. CORE took responsibility for running registration campaigns in Louisiana, South Carolina, and Florida, while SNCC took on the two most repressive states, Alabama and Mississippi. Mississippi was widely known in the movement as the "toughest nut to crack"—the symbolic center of American racism and white violence. By the summer of 1964, national attention had shifted from Alabama to Mississippi, the site of a massive project known as "Freedom Summer."

The voter registration campaign in Mississippi began in late 1963 when Robert "Bob" Moses mobilized the Council of Federated Organizations (COFO), which had been established in 1962 to aid imprisoned Freedom Riders. Moses convinced the members of COFO (CORE, SNCC, SCLC, and the NAACP) to sponsor a mock Freedom Election in Mississippi. On Election Day, 80,000 disfranchised black people voted for COFO candidates. Impressed with the turnout, Moses and other COFO members believed a massive effort to register voters during the summer of 1964 might break the white monopoly on the ballot box.

COFO decided to invite northern white students to participate in the Mississippi project. These students, about 1,000 in all, were to be drawn primarily from the nation's most prestigious universities. This move contradicted the movement's emphasis on black empowerment, but COFO leaders calculated that the presence of elite white students in the Magnolia State would attract increased media attention and pressure the federal government to provide protection.

Shortly after the project began, three volunteers—two white New Yorkers, 24-year-old Michael Schwerner and 21-year-old Andrew Goodman, and a black Mississippian, 21-year-old James Chaney—disappeared. Unknown at the time, Cecil Price, deputy sheriff of Philadelphia, Mississippi, had arrested the three on a trumped-up speeding charge. That evening the young men were delivered to a deserted road where three carloads of Klansmen waited. Schwerner and Goodman were shot to death. Chaney was beaten with chains and then shot.

These events were not publicly known until Klan informers, enticed by a $30,000 reward, led investigators to the earthen dam in which Goodman, Schwerner, and Chaney had been buried. The disappearance of the three nonetheless focused

A missing persons poster displays the photographs of civil rights workers Andrew Goodman, James Earl Chaney, and Michael Henry Schwerner after they disappeared in 1964.

Mississippi Freedom Democratic Party (MFDP)

Interracial group set up to challenge Mississippi's all-white delegation to the Democratic National Convention in 1964.

national attention on white terrorism. During that summer, approximately 30 homes and 37 churches were bombed, 35 civil rights workers were shot at, 80 people were beaten, six were murdered, and more than 1,000 were arrested. In the face of this violence, uncertainty, and fear, many SNCC activists rejected Martin Luther King's commitment to nonviolence, the inclusion of white activists in the movement, and the wisdom of integration. Divisions over these issues increased tensions within the movement.

Despite the problems it encountered, the Freedom Summer organized dozens of Freedom Schools and community centers throughout Mississippi. Its efforts mobilized the state's black people to an extent not seen since the first Reconstruction. Many communities began to develop the rudiments of a political movement, one that would grow in coming years.

21.8.4 The Mississippi Freedom Democratic Party

Freedom Summer intersected with national politics at the Democratic Party National Convention in August 1964 in Atlantic City, New Jersey. White Mississippians routinely excluded African Americans from the political process, and Robert Moses encouraged COFO to set up the **Mississippi Freedom Democratic Party (MFDP)** to challenge the state's regular Democratic delegation at the convention. Under the leadership of veteran activists Fannie Lou Hamer, Victoria Gray, Annie Divine, and Aaron Henry, the MFDP held its first state convention on August 6. Approximately 80,000 citizens put their names on the rolls. The convention elected 64 delegates who traveled to the national convention to present their credentials.

The MFDP challenge caused difficulty for the Democratic Party. Many liberals wanted to seat the civil rights delegation, but President Johnson, who was running for reelection, did not want to alienate white southerners, fearing they would vote for Barry Goldwater, his Republican opponent. Liberal Democratic Senator Hubert H. Humphrey, from Minnesota, worked out a compromise calling for Mississippi regulars to be seated if they swore loyalty to the national party and agreed to cast their 44 votes accordingly. The compromise also created two "at-large" seats for MFDP members Aaron Henry and Ed King. The rest of the Freedom Democrats could attend the convention as nonvoting guests.

Martin Luther King, Jr., Bayard Rustin, and other black leaders counseled acceptance of this compromise. Johnson and the Democrats, they argued, had achieved much of the legislative program the movement favored, and if the party were returned to power, they could do much more. But most of the MFDP delegation, fed up with the violence of Mississippi and unwilling to settle for token representation, rejected the compromise. Many members of SNCC turned their backs on liberalism and cooperation with white people of any political persuasion.

21.8.5 Selma and the Voting Rights Act of 1965

The Civil Rights Act of 1964 contained provisions for helping black voters to register, but white resistance in the Deep South had rendered them ineffective. In Alabama, for example, at least 77 percent of black citizens were unable to vote. Their cause was taken up by businesswoman Amelia P. Boynton, owner of an employment and insurance agency in Selma; her husband; and a high school teacher, the Rev. Frederick Reese, who also led the Dallas County Voters League. These three, with others, fought for black enfranchisement and an end to discrimination. Their struggle would help pass the **Voting Rights Act of 1965**, which finally ended the systematic exclusion of African Americans from southern politics.

Selma's sheriff, James G. Clark, worked to block the voter registration activity sponsored by the Boyntons, Reese, and SNCC suffrage workers. By 1964 fewer than 400 of the 15,000 eligible African Americans had registered to vote in Dallas County. President Johnson refused requests to deploy federal marshals to the county to protect voter registration workers. Seeking reinforcements, the workers sent a call to Martin Luther King, Jr. and SCLC. King came and was arrested. In mid-February 1965, during a night march in neighboring Perry County, 26-year-old Jimmie Lee Jackson was shot as he tried to shield his mother from a beating by a state trooper. His death and the thrashing of several reporters attracted the national media.

SCLC announced plans for a mass march from Selma to Montgomery to begin on Sunday, March 7, 1965. At the forefront of 600 protesters were King; one of his aides, Hosea Williams; and SCNC's chairman, John Lewis. As the marchers approached the Edmund Pettus Bridge, state troopers and the county police tear-gassed and beat the retreating marchers while their horses trampled the fallen. Captured in graphic detail by television cameras, this battle became known as "Bloody Sunday." Seizing the moment, King and the activists rescheduled a pilgrimage for March 9. The SCLC leader soon found himself in a dilemma. A federal judge who was normally supportive of civil rights had issued an injunction against the march. Moreover, President Johnson and other key figures in the government urged King not to go through with it. King was reluctant to violate a federal injunction, and he knew he needed Johnson's support to win strong voting rights legislation. But the people of Selma and the hundreds of young SNCC workers would probably march even if King did not.

When the day of the march came, 1,500 protesters marched to the bridge singing "Ain't Gonna Let Nobody Turn Me 'Round" and other freedom songs. To their surprise, King crossed the Pettus Bridge, prayed briefly, and turned around. He had made a face-saving compromise with the federal authorities. SNCC workers felt betrayed, and King's leadership suffered. That evening local white people clubbed to death James Reeb, a white Unitarian minister from Boston. His martyrdom created a national outcry and prompted Johnson to act. On March 15 the president, in a televised address to Congress, announced he would submit voter registration legislation. He electrified civil rights activists when he invoked the movement's slogan in his Texas drawl, "We shall overcome."

The protests at Selma and the massive white resistance spurred Congress to pass the Voting Rights Act of 1965, which President Johnson signed on August 6. The act outlawed educational requirements for voting in states or counties where less than half the voting-age population had been registered on November 1, 1964, or where less than half had voted in the

Voting Rights Act of 1965
Federal law banning the methods that had systematically excluded African Americans from registering or voting in southern state elections.

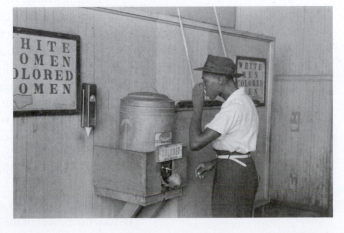

Young black man drinking from a segregated fountain.

Map 21-1 The Effect of the Voting Rights Act of 1965

The Voting Rights Act enabled millions of previously disfranchised African Americans in the South to vote.

Why was gaining the right to vote so important for southern African Americans?

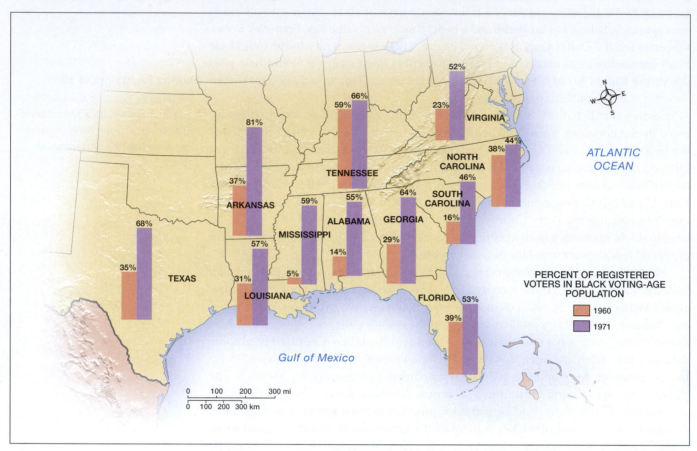

1964 presidential election. It also empowered the attorney general to have the Civil Rights Commission assign federal registrars to enroll voters. Attorney General Nicholas Katzenbach immediately deployed federal registrars in nine southern counties. Within months, they had registered approximately 80,000 new voters. In Mississippi, black registrants soared from 28,500 in 1964 to 251,000 in 1968 (see Map 21-1).

Gaining voting rights made a tremendous difference. Before passage of the 1965 Act, Fannie Lou Hamer had unsuccessfully challenged the seating of the Mississippi representatives before the U.S. House of Representatives. In 1968 she was selected as a delegate to the Democratic Party convention. To be sure, southern state legislators resisted the act. They instituted a dazzling array of disfranchisement devices such as gerrymandering, at-large elections, more appointive offices, and higher qualifications for candidates. While it may be tempting to declare that white supremacy as the core of southern politics was over, it was only on temporary life support. In the twenty-first century southern policies and United States Supreme Court decisions reinvigorated after the election of President Barack Obama converged in an even more determined effort to eviscerate a core component of the achievements of the civil rights movement. The new redistricting and gerrymandering efforts and a couple of U.S. Supreme Court decisions encouraged state- and local-level politicians to intensify efforts to further reduce the power of the black ballot. They embraced strategies and questionable legislation to make it difficult and more challenging for Black people to secure identifications and thus meet new requirements to cast a ballot.

Profile

Dorothy Irene Height

Dorothy Irene Height (March 24, 1912–April 20, 2010) was born in Richmond, Virginia, to a father, James Height, who was a building and painting contractor, and a mother, Fannie Burroughs, who was a nurse. They migrated to a small town, Rankin, Pennsylvania, where Height graduated from Rankin High School in 1929. A scholarship from the Elks helped her attend college. From the outset she demonstrated a gift for oratory that would facilitate her rise to become one of the great African-American leaders in the struggle for human rights and civic equality in the twentieth century.

Height's father had been active in Republican Party politics, but she refused to be defined by a political affiliation. On March 4, 2004, President George W. Bush presented her with the Congressional Gold Medal. Other presidents, from Harry S. Truman to Barack Obama, would seek her council or acknowledge her contributions to the struggle for civil rights. How did an African-American woman earn a living

As leader of two major black women organizations, the NCNW and the Delta Sigma Theta sorority, Dorothy Irene Height was one of the most influential women in twentieth-century America.

while devoting her life to social justice? The first requirement was an education, which she wasted little time acquiring and spared no effort to attain. Within four years, Height earned both a bachelor's and a master's degree in educational psychology at New York University, and thereafter she continued to take courses at Columbia University and the New York School of Social Work.

She launched her career as a caseworker for the Department of Social Services of New York City at the height of the Great Depression. She became active in New Deal youth programs and found employment with the Young Women's Christian Association (YWCA). In 1937, Mary McLeod Bethune, founder and president of the National Council of Negro Women (NCNW), met Height in New York and invited her to join the NCNW. They shared a long and rewarding friendship. Over four decades, Height combined working for the YWCA with volunteering for the NCNW. Thus, she conjoined her commitment to improving the lives of children with securing greater rights for women and resolving tensions and misunderstandings between black and white women. Height worked closely and tirelessly with Bethune to lobby for jobs for women, greater educational opportunities for women and men, and food drives for the poor. She spearheaded voter registration drives for black southerners and voter education for black northerners.

Height became the director of the YWCA's Center for Racial Justice in 1965 and remained an employee of the organization until she retired in 1977. Her position with the YWCA enabled her to travel across the globe to train women and observe firsthand the issues that affected them in societies from Haiti to India. In 2000, the YWCA established the Dorothy I. Height Racial Justice Award. The first recipient was President Bill Clinton.

From 1947 to 1956, Height was president of the Delta Sigma Theta sorority. In 1957, she succeeded Bethune as president of the NCNW, a position she held until 1998. She worked to turn Bethune's dream of a politically empowered, economically secure, well-educated black womanhood committed to social justice and the protection of children into a reality. As leader of two of the largest and most powerful organizations of black women in America, she nurtured generations of black women. These women would prove indispensable to the civil rights movement, as the life and agency of Jo Ann Gibson Robinson, president of the Women's Political Council in Montgomery, Alabama, demonstrated at the time of the Montgomery Bus Boycott in the 1950s.

But gender conventions proved difficult to alter within the black community, and try as she might, Height could not persuade the leaders of the 1963 March on Washington to allow her to speak. The only woman's voice heard on that historic day was that of gospel great Mahalia Jackson. Nevertheless, Height wielded enormous power in both white and black leadership circles in the remaining 50 years of her life. In the 1990s, she received a bank vault of recognitions and awards, including the NAACP's Spingarn Medal (1993), induction into the National Women's Hall of Fame (1993), and the Presidential Medal of Freedom (1994) from Bill Clinton.

Dorothy Height was renowned for her quiet dignity and unrelenting determination to speak out on behalf of African-American women, black families, and their communities. Through her mastery of advocacy politics and ability to mobilize educated and resourceful black women, she helped overturn racial second-class citizenship and much of the gender discrimination that forced women into subordinate positions in the American economy. She entered the fray, whether it was to expand educational opportunities, open ballot boxes, or end legal segregation. Her voice never waivered, and she used it with skill and to great effect. At her memorial service, President Barack Obama said of Height, "She deserves a place in our history books. She deserves a place of honor in America's memory." Virtually the entire nation took note of her passing.

Conclusion

The two *Brown* decisions ended the legal underpinning of segregation and discrimination and set in motion events that would irrevocably transform the political and social status of African Americans. White southerners resisted the changes *Brown* unleashed, and as their resistance gained momentum, violence against African Americans and their allies exploded. For decades the Supreme Court would hear cases and render decisions that would challenge the *Brown* decision and the continuing efforts to combat the lingering effects of structural racial discrimination.

To be sure, the successes of the modern civil rights movement depended on many factors. The federal government intervened at crucial moments to enact historic civil rights legislation, and to issue judgments on behalf of the imprisoned protesters and organizers. Crucial federal court decisions protected the rule of law as did strategic deployment of marshals and soldiers. Some black leaders pursued and advocated strategies to provoke confrontations and thus ensure federal intervention as they gained invaluable media coverage. Over the course of a tumultuous decade, freedom fighters of the civil rights movement stormed the legal barricades of segregation. The uncompromising struggle of African Americans, their myriad organizations, and strong-willed white allies pressured federal officials in the legislative, executive, and judicial branches of government to enact major civil rights legislation, issue executive orders, and deliver judicial decisions to dismantle segregation in the South.

The victories of this era were far reaching, but as they were achieved, new issues arose that would fracture the movement. Until recently, scholarship concerning the rise and evolution of the civil rights movement focused largely on the South. Impressive new research focuses on the long history of struggles for civil rights and economic justice that occurred during the Great Depression and World War II eras. To be sure, by the advent of the civil rights movement in the South, black residents in northern and western cities, thanks to federal legislation, enjoyed access to public facilities, schools, and jobs in a more diverse economic sector. The civil rights movement has largely been focused on the South because black northerners already had many of the rights granted by the federal legislation of the era. Nonetheless, in all regions, long after the victories of the civil rights movement, many black individuals and communities still suffered the negative impact of discrimination and segregation. The future dictated the need for different techniques and new ways of thinking.

Chapter Timeline

AFRICAN-AMERICAN EVENTS	NATIONAL EVENTS
1954–1958	
1954	**1954**
Supreme Court's *Brown v. Board of Education* decision declares separate but equal education unconstitutional	First White Citizens Council in Mississippi
1955	**1955**
Supreme Court's *Brown II* decision calls for school districts to desegregate immediately or "with all deliberate speed"	The American Federation of Labor and Congress of Industrial Organizations merge to form the AFL-CIO
	1956
The Interstate Commerce Commission outlaws segregated buses and waiting rooms for interstate passengers	Segregationists in Congress issue the "Southern Manifesto"
	Eisenhower wins second term as president

AFRICAN-AMERICAN EVENTS

Claudette Colvin arrested for refusing to relinquish her seat to a white woman on a bus in Montgomery

Emmett Till lynched

Rosa Parks arrested for refusing to give up her seat on a city bus, beginning the Montgomery Bus Boycott

1956

The Supreme Court, in *Gayle v. Browder*, bars segregation in intrastate travel

1957

Congress passes the Civil Rights Act of 1957

President Eisenhower enforces integration of Little Rock's Central High School with federal troops

Martin Luther King, Jr. and other religious leaders organize SCLC

1960–1965

1960

Black students sit in at a Woolworth lunch counter in Greensboro, North Carolina

SNCC founded

Black vote is critical to John F. Kennedy's election

1961

Freedom Riders attacked in Alabama and Mississippi

Kennedy names Thurgood Marshall to the Second Circuit Court of Appeals

Herbert Lee killed in Amite County, Mississippi

"Friendship Nine" students sit-in at segregated McCrory's Five and Dime, Rock Hill, SC, convicted of trespassing and sentenced to hard labor—"Jail no Bail" thereafter became the mantra of protesters

1962

COFO is formed

James Meredith desegregates the University of Mississippi with federal support

NATIONAL EVENTS

1960

John F. Kennedy elected president

1963

Kennedy is assassinated; Lyndon Johnson succeeds to the presidency

1964

Equal Employment Opportunity Commission established

1965

Johnson outlines the Great Society program to attack poverty

AFRICAN-AMERICAN EVENTS	NATIONAL EVENTS
The Albany Movement fails	
Voter Education Project launched	
1963	
Project C highlights racial injustices in Birmingham; King writes his celebrated "Letter From Birmingham Jail"	
Federal government compels Governor George C. Wallace to desegregate the University of Alabama	
Medgar Evers murdered	
W. E. B. Du Bois dies in Ghana, Africa, at age 95	
The March on Washington	
Martin Luther King, Jr. delivers his "I Have a Dream" speech	
Ku Klux Klan bombs the 16th Street Baptist Church in Birmingham, Alabama, killing four girls	
Malcolm X breaks with Elijah Muhammad and the Nation of Islam and founds his own movement, Muslim Mosque	
1964	
SNCC launches the Mississippi Freedom Summer Project to promote voter registration	
Twenty-Fourth Amendment to the Constitution outlaws the poll tax	
James E. Chaney, Michael Schwerner, and Andrew Goodman murdered in Mississippi	
Civil Rights Act of 1964 enacted	
The Mississippi Freedom Democratic Party denied seating at the Democratic National Convention	
Martin Luther King, Jr. wins the Nobel Peace Prize	
1965	
Civil rights marchers walk from Selma to Montgomery after violent confrontation in Selma	
Voting Rights Act of 1965 enacted	

Review Questions

1. What roles did "ordinary" or local people play in the civil rights movement? Explain how children were able to contribute to the civil rights movement's successes. How did children contribute to the struggle for social change?

2. Why did the federal government intervene in the civil rights movement? What were the major pieces of legislation enacted, and how did they dismantle legalized segregation?

3. What were the ideologies, objectives, and tactics adopted by the major civil rights organizations and their leaders?

4. Who were some of the individuals who have not been forgotten but are still engaged in the freedom struggle?

5. What were the major successes and failures of the freedom movement? What intergenerational tensions plagued the movement? How did the movement transform American politics and society?

Retracing the Odyssey

Brown v. Board of Education National Historic Site, Topeka, Kansas. The Sumner and Monroe Elementary Schools compose the *Brown v. Board of Education* National Historic Landmark. The 1954 *Brown v. Topeka Board of Education* decision written by U.S. Supreme Court Chief Justice Earl Warren removed the legal foundation on which the entire system of racial segregation and discrimination in the South was based and reaffirmed the ideal of the equal protection under the law clause in the Fourteenth Amendment to the U.S. Constitution. The *Brown* decision struck down the 1896 *Plessy v. Ferguson* doctrine of "separate but equal." *Brown* was the culmination of a long struggle waged by the NAACP's team of lawyers headed by Thurgood Marshall and dozens of ordinary citizens in local communities.

Birmingham Civil Rights Institute. Exhibits depict the history of the black freedom struggle. The museum chronicles the dramatic and often violent activities that occurred in Birmingham, Alabama, during the 1960s as black protests confronted massive white resistance.

The Lincoln Memorial, Washington, D.C. The Lincoln Memorial was built to celebrate President Abraham Lincoln and memorialize the Civil War (1861–1865) that preserved the Union. It possesses a particular relevance and meaning to African Americans. The Lincoln Memorial was the site of the August 1963 March on Washington, during which Martin Luther King delivered his powerful "I Have a Dream" speech.

The Martin Luther King, Jr., Center for Nonviolent Social Change, Atlanta, Georgia. Founded by Coretta Scott King in 1968 as a living memorial dedicated to the preservation and advancement of the work of her husband, the Martin Luther King, Jr., Center for Nonviolent Social Change features exhibits that detail the life and legacy of Martin Luther King, Jr. It contains a unique exhibit of his personal memorabilia. The King Library and Archives contains the world's largest existing collection of civil rights materials.

Recommended Reading

Taylor Branch. *Parting the Waters: America in the King Years, 1954–63.* New York: Simon and Schuster, 1988. Richly researched, lively study that places King at the center of American politics during a transformative decade.

Clayborne Carson. *In Struggle: SNCC and the Black Awakening of the 1960s.* Cambridge, MA: Harvard University Press, 1981. One of the best historical studies of SNCC and the contributions students made to the civil rights movement.

Vickie Crawford, Jacqueline Rouse, and Barbara Woods, eds. *Women in the Civil Rights Movement: Trailblazers and Torchbearers.* Brooklyn, NY: Carlson Publishing, 1990. An important anthology drawing attention to the women who contributed to the freedom struggle of the 1950s and 1960s.

Phillip Hoose. *Claudette Colvin: Twice Toward Justice.* New York: Farrar, Straus and Giroux, 2009. Essential reading. A splendidly documented book that corrects many erroneous assumptions about the courageous 15-year-old high school student who refused to give up her bus seat on March 2, 1955, in Montgomery, Alabama.

Richard Kluger. *Simple Justice: The History of "Brown v. Board of Education" and Black America's Struggle for Equality.* New York: Alfred A. Knopf, 1976. New ed., 2004. An excellent treatment of the historical events leading up to *Brown* and of the people whose lives were forever changed because of their resistance to Jim Crow segregation. The new edition includes an illuminating assessment of the 50 years since *Brown*.

Steven F. Lawson. *Running for Freedom: Civil Rights and Black Politics in America Since 1941.* 2nd ed. Philadelphia: Temple University Press, 2008. A succinct analysis of the politics, legislative measures, and individuals that figured in the successes and failures of the civil rights movement and recent political developments.

Danielle L. McGuire. *At the Dark End of the Street: Black Women, Rape, and Resistance—A New History of the Civil Rights Movement from Rosa Parks to the Rise of Black Power.* New York: Alfred A. Knopf, 2010. A revealing and important book that illuminates the organized resistance of black women to resist white male sexual aggression as part of the civil rights movement.

Aldon D. Morris. *The Origins of the Modern Civil Rights Movement: Black Communities Organizing for Change.* New York: Free Press, 1984. An insightful analysis of the mobilization and organizing strategies pursued by diverse communities for social change that paved the way for the modern civil rights movement.

Additional Bibliography

General Overviews of Civil Rights Movement and Organizations

Robert Fredrick Burk. *The Eisenhower Administration and Black Civil Rights.* Knoxville: University of Tennessee Press, 1984.

Stewart Burns. *Daybreak of Freedom: The Montgomery Bus Boycott.* Chapel Hill: University of North Carolina Press, 1997.

John Dittmer. *Local People: The Struggle for Civil Rights in Mississippi.* Urbana: University of Illinois Press, 1994.

Glenda Elizabeth Gilmore. *Defying Dixie: The Radical Roots of Civil Rights, 1919–1950.* New York: Alfred A. Knopf, 2008.

Risa L. GoluBoff. *The Lost Promise of Civil Rights.* Cambridge, MA: Harvard University Press, 2007.

Lance Hill. *The Deacons for Defense: Armed Resistance and the Civil Rights Movement.* Chapel Hill: University of North Carolina, 2004.

Michael J. Klarman. *From Jim Crow to Civil Rights: The Supreme Court and the Struggle for Racial Equality.* New York: Oxford University Press, 2003.

Nancy MacLean. *Freedom Is Not Enough: The Opening of the American Workplace.* Cambridge, MA: Harvard University Press, 2006.

Manning Marable. *Malcolm X: A Life of Reinvention.* New York: Viking, 2011.

Robert J. Norrell. *Reaping the Whirlwind: The Civil Rights Movement in Tuskegee.* New York: Alfred A. Knopf, 1985.

James T. Patterson. *Brown v. Board of Education: A Civil Rights Milestone and Its Troubled Legacy.* New York: Oxford University Press, 2000.

Charles M. Payne. *I've Got the Light of Freedom: The Organizing Tradition and the Mississippi Freedom Struggle.* Berkeley: University of California Press, 1995.

Belinda Robnett. *How Long? How Long?: African-American Women in the Struggle for Civil Rights.* New York: Oxford University Press, 1997.

Amilcar Shabazz. *Advancing Democracy: African Americans and the Struggle for Access and Equity in Higher Education in Texas.* Chapel Hill: University of North Carolina Press, 2004.

Tobin Miller Shearer. *Daily Demonstrators: The Civil Rights Movement in Mennonite Homes and Sanctuaries.* Baltimore: Johns Hopkins University Press, 2010.

Black Urban Politics/White Resistance

Elizabeth Jacoway and David R. Colburn. *Southern Businessmen and Desegregation.* Baton Rouge: Louisiana State University Press, 1982.

Hasan Kwame Jeffries. *Bloody Lowndes: Civil Rights and Black Power in Alabama's Black Belt.* New York: New York University Press, 2009.

Patrick D. Jones. *The Selma of the North: Civil Rights Insurgency in Milwaukee.* Cambridge, MA: Harvard University Press, 2009.

Lisa Levenstein. *A Movement Without Marches: African American Women and the Politics of Poverty in Postwar*

Philadelphia. Chapel Hill: University of North Carolina Press, 2009.

Doug McAdam. *Freedom Summer*. New York: Oxford University Press, 1988.

Neil R. McMillen. *The Citizen's Council: A History of Organized Resistance to the Second Reconstruction*. Urbana: University of Illinois Press, 1971.

Heather Ann Thompson. *Whose Detroit?: Politics, Labor, and Race in a Modern American City*. Ithaca, NY: Cornell University Press, 2001.

Autobiography and Biography

Daisy Bates. *The Long Shadow of Little Rock: A Memoir*. New York: David McKay Co., 1962.

Taylor Branch. *Pillar of Fire: America in the King Years, 1963–65*. New York: Simon and Schuster, 1998.

Eric R. Burner. *And Gently He Shall Lead Them: Robert Parris Moses and Civil Rights in Mississippi*. New York: New York University Press, 1994.

Katherine Mellen Charron. *Freedom's Teacher: The Life of Septima Clark*. Chapel Hill: University of North Carolina Press, 2009.

Robert S. Dallek. *Flawed Giant: Lyndon Johnson and His Times, 1961–1973*. New York: Oxford University Press, 1998.

Dennis C. Dickerson. *Militant Mediator: Whitney M. Young, Jr.* Lexington: University Press of Kentucky, 1998.

Charles W. Eagles. *The Price of Defiance: James Meredith and the Integration of Ole Miss*. Chapel Hill: University of North Carolina Press, 2009.

James Farmer. *Lay Bare the Heart: An Autobiography of the Civil Rights Movement*. New York: Arbor House, 1985.

Cynthia Griggs Fleming. *Soon We Will Not Cry: The Liberation of Ruby Doris Smith Robinson*. Lanham, MD: Rowman and Littlefield, 1998.

David J. Garrow. *Bearing the Cross: Martin Luther King, Jr., and the Southern Christian Leadership Conference*. New York: William Morrow, 1986.

Henry Hampton and Steve Fayer, eds. *The Voices of Freedom: An Oral History of the Civil Rights Movement From the 1950s Through the 1980s*. New York: Bantam Books, 1990.

Dorothy I. Height. *Open Wide the Freedom Gates: A Memoir*. New York: Public Affairs, 2003.

Chana Kai Lee. *For Freedom's Sake: The Life of Fannie Lou Hamer*. Urbana: University of Illinois Press, 1999.

Genna Rae McNeil. *Groundwork: Charles Hamilton Houston and the Struggle for Civil Rights*. Philadelphia: University of Pennsylvania Press, 1983.

Anne Moody. *Coming of Age in Mississippi*. New York: Dial Press, 1968.

Barbara Ransby. *Ella Baker and the Black Freedom Movement*. Chapel Hill: University of North Carolina Press, 2003.

Jo Ann Gibson Robinson, with David Garrow. *The Montgomery Bus Boycott and the Women Who Started It*. Knoxville: University of Tennessee Press, 1987.

Harvard Sitkoff. *King: Pilgrimage to the Mountaintop*. New York: Hill and Wang, 2008.

Timothy B. Tyson. *Radio Free Dixie: Robert F. Williams and the Roots of Black Power*. Chapel Hill: University of North Carolina Press, 1999.

Donnie Williams and Wayne Greenhaw. *The Thunder of Angels: The Montgomery Bus Boycott and the People Who Broke the Back of Jim Crow*. Chicago: Lawrence Hill Books, 2006.

Hoda M. Zaki. *Civil Rights and Politics at Hampton Institute: The Legacy of Alonzo G. Moron*. Urbana: University of Illinois Press, 2007.

Chapter 22

Black Nationalism, Black Power, and Black Arts

1965–1980

The raised arm with clinched fist symbolizes both black solidarity and the major shift from the passive resistance of the civil rights movement to the militant consciousness of the Black Power movement generation.

Learning Objectives

After reading this chapter, you should be able to:

22.1 Discuss the factors that fueled the rising tide of Black Nationalism in the mid to late 1960s.

22.2 Analyze the social, political, and economic conditions that existed in urban communities that ignited urban rebellions in the 1960s.

22.3 Identify the ways in which the Vietnam War adversely affected President Johnson's War on Poverty and his Great Society initiatives.

22.4 Examine the relationship or connections between the Black Power movement and the Black Arts movement of the 1960s.

22.5 Describe the specific policies and initiatives developed during the Nixon administration that adversely affected the civil rights of African Americans.

22.6 Enumerate some of the most significant accomplishments of the Black Power movement in the 1970s.

The future of the Negro is very largely in the hands of the Negro citizen and voter. . . . There is no attempt here to underestimate the forces of resistance, the ignorance, trickery, fear, threats, and physical assault that have been employed and will continue to be employed. . . . Let no man say that it is somehow unfair or unethical for Negro citizens to push politically for their rights as citizens. If it is legitimate to lobby and use political pressure to secure wider markets and fatter profits, what is so wrong with using political power to secure human rights? The answer is "nothing" and Negro Americans should proceed on that basis.

—Medgar W. Evers

When Lyndon B. Johnson became president in 1963 following John F. Kennedy's assassination, he brought to the position impressive political skills and a willingness to use them to help reconcile the racial, social, and economic disparities in American society. Johnson's escalation of America's involvement in Vietnam, however, undermined his domestic agenda. While Dr. Martin Luther King, Jr. intensified his push for jobs and justice for African Americans, a dynamic Nation of Islam minister, Malcolm X, and others questioned whether American racism could be overcome without violent struggle. A younger generation of freedom fighters lost faith in America's promise of justice and equal opportunity for all who played by the rules. Rather, some embraced the black radical tradition and a nationalist ideology of community empowerment and mobilization to end economic exploitation and disparities in social justice, educational opportunities, and employment. Some also armed for self-defense against police brutality.

At the same time, a white backlash against the gains of the civil rights movement convinced black leaders and scholars—such as Stokely Carmichael and Charles V. Hamilton—to pursue a Black Power agenda to mobilize black communities to exercise their recently regained voting rights. An emerging community-centered leadership embraced new strategies in the movement for civil rights. Some dismissed the interracialism of the civil rights movement and found fault with President Johnson's democratic liberalism. Although King was initially ambivalent about Black Power, it was clear that the winds had shifted direction. The new spirit of change embraced an array of community-level organizers and political figures, from Fannie Lou Hamer in Mississippi to Shirley Chisholm in New York, and organizations from the Deacons of Defense in New Orleans to the Black Panther Party in Oakland, California. The venerable race leader, A. Philip Randolph, however, was less charitable about the idea of Black Power in the black liberation struggle. He called it a "menace to peace and prosperity" and declared, "No Negro who is fighting for civil rights can support Black Power, which is opposed to civil rights and integration."

Between 1967 and 1980, the dynamics of the civil rights freedom struggle shifted from protest against segregation, disfranchisement, and discrimination to mobilization for the election of black officials to public office who would be responsible for meeting the needs and addressing the interests of their community constituents. African-American communities elected an unprecedented number of black politicians as mayors in dozens of America's larger cities. But while witnessing these electoral victories by black officials, the older civil rights movement coalitions fizzled and frayed. Assassins killed Malcolm X in 1965 and both Martin Luther King, Jr. and Robert Kennedy in 1968. Black community organizers and activists were also murdered, including Fred Hampton, deputy chairman of the Illinois Black Panther Party.

22.1 The Rise of Black Nationalism

Discuss the factors that fueled the rising tide of Black Nationalism in the mid to late 1960s.

President Lyndon Johnson easily defeated Republican Senator Barry Goldwater in the 1964 election. His victory, however, proved not to be a mandate for civil rights. In California, for example, voters gave Johnson a decisive win but simultaneously approved an amendment to the state constitution to repeal laws that prohibited housing discrimination. The passage of this law, which was subsequently struck down by the U.S. Supreme Court, reflected white ambivalence to integration. In general elections, white voters further demonstrated their opposition to civil rights. They elected several Republicans; one, a former movie actor, Ronald Reagan, became governor of California. In Alabama, the resentment of white voters was strong. It was not a coincidence that Alabama Governor George Wallace became a national political figure as he displayed virulent opposition to desegregation. Rewarded by favorable responses from many northern white voters in 1968, Wallace planned a full-scale presidential run in 1972. He was shot and left partially paralyzed by a would-be assassin.

As white Americans' support weakened for the goals of the civil rights movement, many black Americans searched for new leaders. Thus, many embraced the Black Radical Tradition. They advocated different strategies as white violence escalated. White groups terrorized the workers in the Council of Federated Organizations in Mississippi. Floyd McKissick of the Congress of Racial Equality (CORE) and Stokely Carmichael of the Student Nonviolent Coordinating Committee (SNCC) became disillusioned and doubted that Martin Luther King's moderation, nonviolence, and universalism would secure freedom, justice, and civil equality. Carmichael argued after the 1964 failure of the Mississippi Freedom Democratic Party that it was time to form an independent black political party. In 1965, after the Selma-to-Montgomery march, he helped to found the Lowndes County (Mississippi) Freedom Organization.

It became the first political organization in the civil rights movement to adopt the symbol of the Black Panther.

Black people in northern and western cities also lost patience with the slow pace of racial change. Long into the post-1965 era, African Americans confronted the "invisible" racism embedded in American economic, political, social, and educational institutions and challenged the opposition of white people to fair housing, environmental justice, and all policies that required a redistribution of power and resources. In this context, President Lyndon Johnson's "War on Poverty" may have been seen as an extension of the black freedom struggle. Nevertheless, many black churchmen castigated mainstream white religious groups for their complicity with racism. Some demanded reparations for slavery, and others agitated for substantive power or leadership roles within the governing structures of the National Council of Churches. Black theologians even developed a theology that critiqued racism within white religious groups and called for reparations. Black feminists developed an oppositional theology that called for greater gender equality in the leadership of black churches and vehemently denounced sexism in the larger society.

Black Power transformed black and white leaders of mainstream religious organizations. In 1946, the Federal Council of Churches, composed of Protestants, Catholics, and Jews, pledged to work for "a non-segregated church and a non-segregated society." Between 1963 and 1965, the National Council of Churches (NCC) gave financial and moral support to the civil rights movement. In 1963, the NCC founded its Commission on Religion and Race to support the black freedom movement. The Commission was a white-controlled and white-managed operation, however, three of its eight staff members were African Americans: Anna Hedgeman, J. Oscar Lee, and James Breeden. The NCC supported events such as the March on Washington and lobbied for passage of both the Civil Rights Act of 1964 and the Voting Rights Act of 1965.

In 1965, the NCC appointed Benjamin Payton as director of the Commission. Payton, a native of Orangeburg, South Carolina, had been educated at Harvard Divinity School and had earned a Ph.D. at Yale. He had taught at Howard University and was a member of the National Baptist Convention and the largest African-American denomination. Under his stewardship the Commission was incorporated into the Division of Christian Life and Mission and later became part of the NCC's Department of Social Justice that included five other special task forces.

Payton had his own views about how organized religion could address racial problems. He viewed the economic development of black people and their communities as the critical prerequisite to improving national racial relations. In his first address to the NCC, Payton emphasized the need for "a program of economic development to make civil rights real, in housing, employment, education and health care." In July 1966, he convened a small cadre of men that included Gayraud S. Wilmore, who served as the director of the United Presbyterian's Commission on Religion and Race. Out of this gathering emerged the National Commission of Black Churchmen, which became a key mainstream ecumenical church group advocating Black Power concepts and strategies for the rest of the 1960s. In May 1967, however, the NCC's Department of Social Justice lost some of its momentum and direction when Payton left to become president of Benedict College in Columbia, South Carolina.

The Black Power movement spurred the creation of black caucuses within predominantly white churches. In February 1968, James Lawson headed the Black Methodists for Church Renewal, a caucus within the United Methodist Church. In the same year, the Black Presbyterians United replaced the Presbyterian Interracial Council. The Episcopal Union of Black Clergy and Laity replaced the interracial Episcopal Society for Racial and Cultural Unity. By the early 1970s, there were nine such caucuses. Black Roman Catholics insisted that the church demonstrate more respect for African-American patterns of worship. All these black religious groups pressed for more black leaders within their denominations. Thus, the stage was set for James Forman's Black Manifesto.

In April 1969, James Forman, a former Chicago schoolteacher and renowned for his work with SNCC, addressed the National Black Economic Development Conference in Detroit, sponsored by the Interreligious Foundation for Community Organizations (which was supported by predominantly white churches). Forman demanded that white churches pay $500 million in reparations for their participation in and benefit from American slavery and racial exploitation. His sharply secular critique of American religion may have precipitated the withdrawal of some mainstream white religious groups from active participation in the civil rights movement. Forman's Black Power rhetoric and revolutionary ideology offended those groups whose members recoiled at the idea that black and other minority groups wanted to share real power within the white-dominated churches. Relations between black people and Jews steadily deteriorated as countercharges circulated of "Jewish racism" and "black anti-Semitism." To be sure, there were some black religious groups, such as the Nation of Islam, that did not seek or desire white participation or support in their affairs.

22.1.1 The Nation of Islam

Nation of Islam (NOI)

A religious group composed of African-American Muslims currently headed by Minister Louis Farrakhan.

The **Nation of Islam** emerged in 1929, the year Timothy Drew died. Drew, who took the name Nobel Drew Ali, was founder of the Moorish Science Temple of America, which flourished in Chicago, Detroit, and other cities in the 1920s. After his death, a modified version of the Moorish Science Temple emerged in 1930 in Detroit. It was led by a mysterious door-to-door peddler of silks and other items that supposedly originated in Africa, Nobel Drew Ali, also known variously as Wallace D. Fard, Master Farad Muhammad, or Wali Farad. He wrote two instruction manuals, *The Secret Ritual of the Nation of Islam* and *Teaching for the Lost-Found Nation of Islam in a Mathematical Way*. He taught that black people were the true Muslims. He attracted many poor residents in Depression-era Detroit. In addition to the beliefs of Nobel Drew Ali, Fard's Nation of Islam also taught a mixture of Koranic principles, the Christian Bible, his own beliefs, and those of nationalist leader of the Universal Negro Improvement Association, Marcus Garvey.

In 1934, after establishing a Temple of Islam, Fard disappeared, and one of his disciples, Elijah Poole (1897–1975), renamed Elijah Muhammad by Fard, became leader of the Detroit temple and then of a second temple in Chicago. The Nation attracted the attention of federal authorities during World War II when its members refused to serve in the military. Muhammad was arrested in May 1942 on charges of inciting his followers to resist the draft and was imprisoned until 1946. After his release he settled in Chicago and began to expand his movement.

The Nation of Islam taught that black people were the Earth's original human inhabitants who had lived, according to Elijah Muhammad, in the Nile Valley. Approximately 6,000 years ago, a magician named Yakub produced white people. They proved so troublesome that they were banished to Europe, where they began to spread evil. Their worst crime was their enslavement of black people. Elijah Muhammad taught that white supremacy was ending and black people would rediscover their authentic history and culture. To prepare for the coming millennium, he instructed members to adhere to a code of behavior that included abstaining from many traditionally southern foods, especially pork. Members subscribed to a family-centered culture in which women's role was to produce and rear the next generation. The Nation also demanded part of the South for a black national state. One of the most charismatic young ministers in the Nation of Islam in the early 1960s was Malcolm X (1925–1965), whose father had been a follower of Marcus Garvey.

Malcolm X delineated the critical elements or characteristics of the Black Radical Tradition in three speeches delivered in Detroit between 1963 and 1965. He also advocated unity among black people all over the world and espoused Black Nationalism. Black Studies professor Manning Marable defined Black Nationalism:

> Black Nationalism is a political and social tradition that includes certain characteristics. First, Black Nationalism advocated black cultural pride and the integrity of the group, which implicitly rejects racial integration. Second, it identifies with the cultures of Africa and advocates either immigrating there or maintaining extensive contacts with Africans. (Of course, black nationalists also advocate interaction between African Americans, African Caribbeans, and Africans on the continent of Africa itself.) Third, Black Nationalism works toward the construction of all-black social institutions such as self-help agencies, schools, and religious organizations and support for group economic advancement, such as black cooperatives, "Buy Black" campaigns, and efforts to promote capital formation within the African-American community. Finally, Black Nationalism advances . . . and supports the development of all-black political organizations and protest formations.

Malcolm X, the son of a Baptist preacher, was born Malcolm Little in Omaha, Nebraska, but grew up in Lansing, Michigan. Klan terrorists burned his family's home, and his father was murdered in 1938 when Malcolm was 13. His mother was subsequently committed to a mental institution, and welfare agencies separated the children. Malcolm was sent to a juvenile detention home, quit school after the eighth grade, and moved to Boston to live with his sister. There he became involved in the street life of gambling, drugs, and burglary. He was arrested and sentenced to a 10-year prison term in 1946. During the six-and-a-half years he spent in prison, he embraced the teachings of Elijah Muhammad of the Nation of Islam, renounced his "slave name," and called himself Malcolm X. In 1954, he became minister of Harlem's Temple Number 7.

Articulate, charismatic, and courageous, Malcolm rejected both the tenets of nonviolence and racial integration. His words and thoughts resonated with many black residents in northern urban communities. In 1961, Malcolm began publishing *Muhammad Speaks*, the official newspaper of the Nation. In *The Autobiography of Malcolm X*, published in 1965 by writer Alex Haley of *Roots* fame, Malcolm declared,

> Few white people realize that many black people today dislike and avoid spending any more time than they must around white people. This "integration" image, as it is popularly interpreted, has millions of vain, self-exalted white people convinced that black people want to sleep in bed with them—and that's a lie! Oh you can't tell the average white man that the Negro man's prime desire isn't to have a white woman—another lie!

Malcolm X attracted the attention of an increasingly disillusioned component of the black population. He dismissed the goal of racial integration and considered King's message of redemption through brotherly love misguided. Malcolm X's voice and critique of capitalism and white supremacy resonated with those who had experienced white violence. "The day of nonviolent resistance is over," Malcolm insisted. He declared that "Revolutions are never based upon love-your-enemy, and pray-for-those-who-spitefully-use-you. And revolutions are never waged by singing 'We Shall Overcome.' Revolutions are based on bloodshed."

Malcolm X (1925–1965) was eloquent, passionate, a courageously outspoken champion of black people, and a critic of American racism. Today he is an iconic figure memorialized in poems, songs, films, books, and operas.

22.1.2 Malcolm X's New Departure

Malcolm X's popularity created tensions between himself and the leadership of the Nation of Islam. He grew disillusioned when he learned of Elijah Muhammad's multiple wives. Elijah Muhammad in turn grew jealous of Malcolm's success. When Malcolm described the Kennedy assassination as a case of "the chickens coming home to roost" (meaning Kennedy was a victim of the same kind of violence that afflicted black people), Elijah Muhammad, who had ordered him to remain silent, suspended him for this infraction. Malcolm reacted to the suspension by breaking with the Nation of Islam. He founded his own organization, the Muslim Mosque, Inc. That same year he went on a pilgrimage to Mecca. He changed his name to El-Hajj Malik El-Shabazz, founded the Organization for Afro-American Unity (after the Organization of African Unity), repudiated the Nation of Islam's doctrine that all white people are evil, and began lecturing on the connection between the civil rights struggle in the South and the struggle against European colonialism in Africa. On February 14, 1965, assassins associated with the Nation of Islam killed him as he addressed an audience in Harlem.

Malcolm's militant advocacy of self-defense, of "overturning systems" that deprived African Americans of basic human rights, recalled a long tradition of black radicalism in America dating back to Frederick Douglass and Henry Highland Garnet in the years before the Civil War. The modern Black Power movement moved radicalism forward by emphasizing the importance of community-based leaders and urged ordinary people to mobilize and secure their best interests through participating in electoral politics.

22.1.3 Stokely Carmichael and Black Power

In 1966 Stokely Carmichael, a native of Trinidad but raised in New York City and educated at Howard University, became chairman of SNCC. Later he abandoned the ideal of interracial collaboration and moved SNCC toward a stronger embrace of Black Nationalism. SNCC's few white staffers, including Bob Zellner, who had been with the organization since its inception, left to pursue other activism.

About this time, James Meredith began a one-man "March Against Fear" from Memphis, Tennessee, to Jackson, Mississippi, to encourage black southerners to register and vote. On this march, a white gunman wounded him. SNCC and Carmichael joined with other organizations to complete the march. Carmichael now began to popularize the slogan "Black Power," which later became SNCC's rallying cry. "The only way we gonna stop them white men from whippin' us," he announced to a cheering crowd, "is to take over. We been saying freedom for six years and we ain't got nothin'. What we gonna start saying is Black Power." Carmichael and SNCC members spent the spring and summer of 1965 in Lowndes County, Alabama, where Carmichael suggested that African Americans should found their own political party.

Inspired by the organizing philosophy of Ella Baker, Carmichael believed in the right of ordinary citizens to elect their own leaders and devise strategies to achieve the goals they wanted. They renamed this political party the Lowndes County Freedom Party after the November 1966 elections and selected a snarling black panther as the party logo. Ruth Howard, a SNCC field secretary, described the significance of this logo: "The Black Panther is an animal that when it is pressured it moves back until it is cornered, then it comes out fighting for life or death." Carmichael was specific about what Black Power meant to black southerners:

> A man needs a black panther on his side when he and his family must endure . . . loss of job, eviction, starvation, and sometimes death, for political activity. . . .
>
> In Lowndes County [Alabama], for example, black power will mean that if a Negro is elected sheriff, he can end police brutality. If a black man is elected tax assessor, he can collect and channel funds for the building of better roads

and schools serving black people—thus advancing the move from political power into the economic arena. . . . Politically, black power means what it has always meant to SNCC: the coming-together of black people to elect representatives and to force those representatives to speak to their needs. It does not mean merely putting black faces into office.

When critics attacked Black Power as reverse racism, Carmichael rejoined that it promoted positive self-identity, racial pride, and independent political and economic power.

As black people became more disillusioned about the slow pace of social change, some questioned whether white people belonged in their organizations. In 1968, CORE followed SNCC's example and ejected its white members, with a resulting loss of financial resources.

In May 1967 Hubert G. Brown became head of SNCC. "H. Rap" Brown, as he became known, raised the militancy of the Black Power movement's rhetoric, calling white people "honkies" and the police "pigs." In August 1967 Brown told enthusiastic listeners in the black neighborhood of Cambridge, Maryland, that "black folks built America, and if America don't come around, we're going to burn America down." When a fire erupted a few hours later in a dilapidated school in the heart of the city's black community, white firemen refused to fight it. Police charged Brown with inciting a riot and committing arson, but he posted bail and fled. Later he was arrested on other charges.

Stokely Carmichael (1941–1998) changed his name to Kwame Turé, a combination of the names of two major African leaders, Kwame Nkrumah and Ahmed Sékou Touré. After he settled in Guinea in 1969, he founded the All-African People's Revolutionary Party.

22.1.4 The Black Panther Party

The most enduring expression of the new black militant political activism was the Black Panther Party for Self-Defense created by Huey P. Newton and Bobby Seale in Oakland, California, in October 1966. Newton and Seale took the name of the party from the black panther symbol of the **Lowndes County Freedom Organization (LCFO)**. The Black Panthers combined Black Nationalist ideology with Marxist-Leninist doctrines. Working with white radicals, the Black Panthers hoped to transform the party into a revolutionary vanguard dedicated to ending police brutality. For a few months Stokely Carmichael, who had become estranged from SNCC, was named the party's prime minister. However, Carmichael soon shifted his interest to pan-Africanism. He moved to Guinea in West Africa and changed his name to Kwame Turé. Eldridge Cleaver, the Panthers' minister of education, helped formulate the party's ideology.

Lowndes County Freedom Organization (LCFO)

Political organization founded in 1965.

Cleaver began writing the autobiographical essays that appeared as *Soul on Ice* in 1968, the year the party dropped "Self-Defense" from its name. Black people, Cleaver maintained, were victims of colonization. Integrationism could not meet their needs. Instead, like other colonized peoples, they had to be liberated. "To achieve these ends," he wrote, "we believe that political and military machinery that does not exist now and has never existed must be created. We need functional machinery that is able to deal with these two interrelated sets of political dynamics which, strictly speaking, make up

"You can jail a revolutionary, but you can't jail a revolution!" Fred Hampton, Chairman of the Illinois chapter of the Black Panther Party, spoke at a rally outside the Federal Building in Chicago on October 29, 1969, protesting the trial of eight people accused of conspiracy to start a riot at the 1968 Democratic National Convention.

Black Panther Party founders Huey P. Newton and Bobby Seale. The Panthers advocated a radical economic, social, and educational agenda that made it the target of a determined campaign of suppression and elimination by the police and the FBI.

the total political situation on the North American continent." Cleaver and other Panther leaders were arrested after a shootout with Oakland police in 1968. Cleaver escaped and fled into exile in Algeria and Cuba. Upon returning to the United States in 1975, he abandoned his radicalism and became involved with the Republican Party and fundamentalist Christianity.

22.1.5 The FBI's COINTELPRO and Police Repression

The Panthers, imposing in appearance when dressed in black leather jackets, berets, and "Afro" haircuts, alarmed white policemen, especially as they armed themselves for self-defense and patrolled their own neighborhoods to monitor the police. A series of bloody confrontations in Oakland, California, distracted attention from the Panthers' broader political objectives and community service projects. In Oakland and Chicago, the Panthers arranged free breakfast for young schoolchildren. They created healthcare programs, thus proving essential services for poor people in their neighborhoods. They worked to instill racial pride, lectured and wrote about black history, launched some of the earliest drug education programs, and created a newspaper that generated income while providing news about events and anticolonial struggles around the world. These multilayered activities won community support and admiration. The Panthers adopted and lived by the slogan "Power to the People."

The Black Panther Party leaders clearly envisioned themselves as being part of an international liberation movement. They spoke of the black community as an internal colony. The Panthers did not advocate separatism. Actually, they encouraged interracial coalition-building. The Panthers developed ties with Students for a Democratic Society and with the white Peace and Freedom Party of socialists and activists.

FBI director J. Edgar Hoover hated the Black Panther Party even more than he disliked Martin Luther King, Jr. and Malcolm X. Hoover infiltrated, harassed, destabilized, and endeavored to destroy all Black Nationalist groups and their leaders. The FBI cooperated with local law enforcement officials deliberately to ridicule, undermine, and discredit leaders and members of the Black Panther Party. In August 1967 Hoover distributed a memorandum that detailed the FBI's counterintelligence program against Black Nationalist groups. The purpose, according to the memo, of this new "counterintelligence (COINTELPRO) endeavor is to expose, disrupt, misdirect, discredit, or otherwise neutralize the activities of black nationalist, hate-type organizations and groupings, their leadership, spokesmen, membership, and supporters, and to counter their propensity for violence and civil disorder." Undercover federal agents infiltrated the Panthers and provoked violence and criminal acts. This is not to say that Black Panthers were all saints. Huey P. Newton had a long criminal record. He was imprisoned for murder in 1968 but was acquitted and released, only to be charged with murder and assault again in 1974. After fleeing to Cuba to avoid trial, he returned in 1977 and was again acquitted. He was killed at age 42 in a drug dispute in Oakland in 1989. Still, the FBI and its counterintelligence agents provoked much of the mayhem and violence that became associated with the Panthers. Certainly, COINTELPRO helped shape negative public opinion of Black

Voices

The Black Panther Party Platform

Huey Newton and Bobby Seale's Ten-Point Program reflected their determination to move from the pursuit of civil rights to a radical restructuring of American society along socialist lines, with work and rewards equally shared.

October 1966

Black Panther Party Platform and Program: What We Want, What We Believe

1. We want freedom. We want power to determine the destiny of our Black Community . . .

2. We want full employment for our people . . .

3. We want an end to the robbery of the capitalists of our Black Community . . .

4. We want decent housing fit for shelter of human beings . . .

5. We want education for our people that exposes the true nature of this decadent American society. We want education that teaches us our true history and our role in present-day society . . .

6. We want all Black men to be exempt from military service . . .

7. We want an immediate end to POLICE BRUTALITY and MURDER of Black people . . .

8. We want freedom for all Black men held in federal, state, county and city prisons and jails . . .

9. We want all Black people when brought to trial to be tried in court by a jury of their peer group or people from their Black communities, as defined by the Constitution of the United States . . .

10. We want land, bread, housing, education, clothing, justice, and peace. And as our major political objective, a United Nations supervised plebiscite to be held throughout the Black colony in which only Black colonial subjects will be allowed to participate, for the purpose of determining the will of Black people as to their national destiny.

---

1. Compare and contrast the Ten-Point Program to the Bill of Rights in the U.S. Constitution. Analyze the differences.

2. Describe the Panthers' strategies to achieve black liberation. Explain their emphasis on the need to study history. Discuss the reasons for the conflict and tension between the Panthers' program and those of the older, more established civil rights organizations.

SOURCE: Clayborne Carson et al., eds., *Eyes on the Prize Civil Rights Reader: Documents, Speeches, and Firsthand Accounts from the Black Freedom Struggle, 1954–1990* (New York: Viking Penguin, 1991), 346–47. Reprinted by permission.

Nationalism. Federal and local law enforcement officials killed an estimated 28 Panthers in Oakland, Seattle, and Los Angeles, and imprisoned 750 others. In perhaps the most brazen act of murder, police in Chicago killed Chairman of the Illinois Black Panther Party Fred Hampton and Mark Clark in their sleep in a predawn raid on the Illinois Panther headquarters on December 4, 1969. The police fired hundreds of rounds, while only two shots were fired back from within the apartment.

22.1.6 Prisoners' Rights

Despite such repression, black militancy survived in many forms, including the prisoners' rights movement. One of the Panthers' most unique social programs focused on the conditions of black prisoners. By 1970 a substantial percentage of the inmates in U.S. prisons were African American. In New York State, black Americans were around 70 percent of the prison population. Black activists argued that many African Americans were in jail for political reasons and suffered from unfair sentences and endured deplorable conditions because of racism and social class bias.

Angela Davis, a philosophy professor at the University of California at Los Angeles, became the first black woman on the FBI's Ten Most Wanted list because of her involvement in prisoners' rights. In 1969, UCLA's board of regents refused to renew her contract, citing her lack of a Ph.D., but in fact they objected to her membership in the Communist Party. During the late 1960s, she had worked on behalf of the Soledad Brothers, three prisoners—George Jackson, John Clutchette, and Fleeta Drumgo—accused of murdering a white guard at Soledad Prison. On August 7, 1970, George Jackson's younger

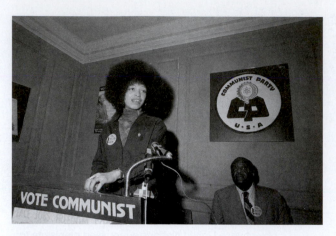

Although the iconic "Afro" is gone, today Angela Davis continues her forceful advocacy for the rights of prisoners. She serves on the advisory board of the Prison Activist Resource Center and teaches in the Department of the History of Consciousness at the University of California, Santa Cruz.

brother, 17-year-old Jonathan Jackson, staged a one-man raid on the San Rafael courthouse in Marin County, California, to try to seize hostages to exchange for the Soledad Brothers. In the ensuing shootout, he was killed along with two prisoners and a judge. Angela Davis, accused of supplying the weapons for the raid, was charged with murder, kidnapping, and conspiracy. She escaped and lived as a fugitive, but she was eventually captured and spent over a year in jail. After a long ordeal and a national "Free Angela" campaign, a jury acquitted Davis. On August 21, 1971, George Jackson was shot and killed at San Quentin Prison by guards who claimed he was trying to escape.

Across the country, prisoners at Attica, a maximum-security prison in northern New York State, began a fast in memory of George Jackson that erupted into a full-scale rebellion. On September 9, 1971, 1,200 inmates seized control of half of Attica and took hostages. Four days later, state police and prison guards suppressed the uprising. Tom Wicker, a columnist for the *New York Times*, filed this report:

> A task force consisting of 211 state troopers and corrections officers retook Attica using tear gas, rifles, and shotguns. After the shooting was over, ten hostages and twenty-nine inmates lay dead or dying. At least 450 rounds of ammunition had been discharged. Four hostages and eighty-five inmates suffered gunshot wounds that they survived. After initial reports that several hostages had died at the hands of knife-wielding inmates, pathologists' reports revealed that hostages and inmates all died from gunshot wounds. No guns were found in the possession of inmates.

A state commission, assembled in October 1971 to reconstruct the events at Attica, concluded, "With the exception of Indian massacres in the late nineteenth-century, the State Police assault which ended the four-day prison uprising was the bloodiest one-day encounter between Americans since the Civil War."

22.2 Black Urban Rebellions in the 1960s

Analyze the social, political, and economic conditions that existed in urban communities that ignited urban rebellions in the 1960s.

The militant nationalism and growing embrace of black radicalism reflected growing alienation and anger in America's impoverished inner cities. In 1965, 29.1 percent of black households, compared with only 7.8 percent of white households, lived below the poverty line. Almost 50 percent of nonwhite families lived in substandard housing compared with 18 percent of white families. Despite a drop in the number of Americans living in poverty from 38.0 million in 1959 to 32.7 million in 1965, the percentage of impoverished black people increased from 27.5 percent to 31 percent. In 1965 the black unemployment rate was 8.5 percent, almost twice the white unemployment rate of 4.3. For black teenagers the unemployment rate was 23 percent compared with 10.8 percent for white teenagers. As psychologist Kenneth Clark declared in 1967, "The masses of Negroes are now starkly aware of the fact that recent civil rights victories benefited a very small percentage of middle-class Negroes while their predicament remained the same or worsened."

The passage of civil rights laws and voting rights legislation did not resolve or erase glaring social, educational, and economic disparities between black and white citizens. This created a fertile environment for the rise in inner-city alienation. As jobs moved to suburbs to which inner-city residents could neither travel nor relocate, black neighborhoods became poorer. School dropout rates reached epidemic proportions, crime and drug use increased, and fragile family structures weakened. These conditions led militant leaders like the Panthers to liken their neighborhoods to exploited colonies kept poor by repressive white political and economic institutions. Few white Americans understood the depths of the black despair that erupted into violence each summer between 1965 and 1969. The Watts rebellion of 1965 illuminated the conditions that residents could no longer tolerate.

22.2.1 Watts

In the summer of 1965, a section of Los Angeles called Watts exploded. Watts was 98 percent black. Its residents suffered from severe overcrowding, high unemployment, inaccessible healthcare facilities, inadequate public transportation, rising crime rates, and growing rates of drug addiction. Almost 30 percent of Watts' black males were unemployed. The poverty, combined with anger at the often-brutal behavior of Los Angeles' police force in Watts, proved to be an incendiary combination. On August 11, 1965, a policeman pulled over a young black man to check him for drunk driving. The man was arrested, but not before a crowd gathered. The policeman called for reinforcements, and when they arrived, the crowd pelted them with stones, bottles, and other objects. Within hours, Watts was in a total riot.

Governor Pat Brown, a Democrat, sent in the National Guard to restore order, but by the sixth day of the conflagration, Watts had been reduced to rubble and ashes. One reporter commented that Watts looked like Germany at the end of World War II. Thirty-four people had been killed, more than 900 injured, and 4,000 arrested. Total property damage was more than $35 million, equivalent to hundreds of millions of dollars today. The Watts rebellion was the beginning of four summers of uprisings that would engulf cities in the North and Midwest. There were riots in the summer of 1966, but worse ones erupted in Newark and Detroit in 1967.

22.2.2 Newark

Newark, New Jersey, had more than 400,000 inhabitants in 1967. As was true in many other urban areas, white flight to the suburbs in the 1950s and 1960s had made Newark a majority black city; nonetheless, it operated on an inadequate tax base and under white political control. The city could not meet its inhabitants' social needs. The school system had deteriorated as unemployment increased. In 1967 Newark had the highest unemployment rate among black men in the nation. As tensions flared and police brutality escalated, white officials paid little attention to black people's complaints. On July 12, after a black cab driver in police custody was beaten, protesters gathered at the police station near the Hayes Homes housing project. When a firebomb hit the wall of the station house, the police charged, clubbing the crowd. This triggered one of the most destructive civic rebellions of the period. During four days of rioting, the police and National Guard killed 25 black people—most of them innocent bystanders, including two children. A white policeman and fireman were also killed. Widespread looting and arson caused millions of dollars in property damage.

22.2.3 Detroit

When Detroit erupted a few days after Newark, it caught everyone by surprise, except its inner-city residents. Detroit had seemed like a model of prosperity and interracial accord. Some of the country's most dynamic popular music flowed from Detroit's Motown recording company. Owned by the astute Berry Gordy, Motown was a classic up-by-the-bootstraps success story. Gordy, his wife Raynoma, and their extended family had, by 1967, produced such stars as Diana Ross and Mary Wells. "Before Motown," said Wells, "there were three careers available to a black girl in Detroit—babies, the factories or daywork."

In 1967, blacks in Detroit expressed their anger and disillusionment about a constellation of social injustices and economic woes.

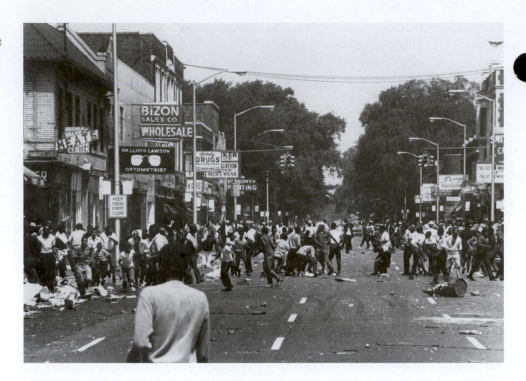

But success like Gordy's was rare among the black migrants and their children, who poured into Detroit during and after World War II. The parents held their disappointment in check, but the children, particularly young men aged between the ages of 17 and 35, sought an outlet for their anger and alienation. Some joined the Nation of Islam. Others embraced the Panthers or formed even more radical organizations calling for an all-black nation.

On the night of Saturday, July 23, police raided an after-hours drinking establishment in the black community where more than 80 people were celebrating the return of two veterans from Vietnam. The raid triggered five days of rioting. John Conyers, the black representative for Michigan's First Congressional District, knew many of the people in the area and tried to get them to disperse, but they refused: "People were letting feelings out that had never been let out before, that had been bottled up. It really wasn't that they were that mad about an after-hours place being raided and some people being beat up as a result of the closing down of that place. It was the whole desperate situation of being black in Detroit."

Of the 59 urban rebellions that occurred in 1967, Detroit's was the deadliest. Forty-three black people died, most of them shot by members of the National Guard, which had been sent in by Republican Governor George Romney. But even the National Guard, combined with 200 state police and 600 Detroit police, could not restore order. President Johnson had to order 4,700 troops of the elite 82nd and 101st Airborne units to Detroit. Republicans criticized Johnson's move as designed to embarrass Romney, who was a contender for the Republican presidential nomination in 1968. Johnson vehemently denied the charge. Others argued that Johnson's social welfare policies had raised expectations beyond the country's ability or desire to fulfill them and had subsidized the rioters.

22.2.4 The Kerner Commission

On July 29, 1967, after the Newark and Detroit riots, President Johnson established the National Advisory Commission on Civil Disorders, headed by Illinois Governor Otto Kerner. The commission included two black members, Republican Senator Edward W. Brooke of Massachusetts (elected in 1966 and the first black senator since

Reconstruction) and Roy Wilkins, executive director of the NAACP. Explaining why he had set up the commission, Johnson declared,

> The only genuine, long-range solution for what has happened lies in an attack—mounted at every level—upon the conditions that breed despair and violence. All of us know what those conditions are: ignorance, discrimination, slums, poverty, disease, not enough jobs. We should attack these conditions—not because we are frightened by conflict, but because we are fired by conscience. We should attack them because there is simply no other way to achieve a decent and orderly society in America.

In its final report, released in 1968, the Kerner Commission indicted white racism as the underlying cause of the riots and warned that America was "moving towards two societies, one white, and one black— separate and unequal. . . . Negroes firmly believe that police brutality and harassment occur repeatedly in Negro neighborhoods. This belief is unquestionably one of the major reasons for intense Negro resentment against the police. . . . Physical abuse is only one source of aggravation in the ghetto. In nearly every city surveyed, the Commission heard complaints of harassment of interracial couples, dispersal of social street gatherings and the stopping of Negroes on foot or in cars without objective basis." The report called for massive government aid to the cities, including funds for public housing, better and more integrated schools, two million new jobs, and funding for a "national system of income supplementation." None of its major proposals was enacted.

22.2.5 Difficulties in Creating the Great Society

The urban rebellions of the late 1960s undercut support for the broadest attack the federal government had yet waged on the problems of poor Americans, what President Johnson in his election campaign in 1964 had called "the Great Society." Much of the legislation Johnson pushed through Congress in 1964 and 1965—Medicare, for example, which provided medical care for the elderly and disabled under the Social Security system, or federal aid to education from elementary through graduate school—remained popular. But the most ambitious Great Society programs—what Johnson called "an unconditional war on poverty"—were controversial and tested the limits of American reform.

Lyndon Johnson was a savvy politician. He had to be to rise from Stonewall, Texas, to the pinnacle of power. But he never lost a deep sympathy for the disadvantaged and the powerless. Entering Congress in 1937, he had been an enthusiastic New Dealer. Elected to the Senate in 1948, he had refused to sign the Southern Manifesto (see Chapter 21) and, as majority leader, had overcome southern filibusters to pass the 1957 and 1960 Civil Rights Acts. As president, he pushed the 1964 Civil Rights Act and the 1965 Voting Rights Act through Congress.

Johnson's concern for the disadvantaged showed itself in the cornerstone of his War on Poverty, the **Economic Opportunity Act of 1964**. This act created an Office of Economic Opportunity that administered programs like Head Start to help disadvantaged preschoolers, Upward Bound to prepare impoverished teenagers for college, and Volunteers in Service to America (or VISTA) to serve as a domestic peace corps to help the poor and undereducated across the country. These programs included community-governing boards on which black men and women gained representation, learning such essential political skills as bargaining and organizing.

The War on Poverty was the first government-sponsored effort to involve poor African Americans directly in designing and implementing programs to serve low-income communities. For example, in the New Careers program, residents of poor neighborhoods found jobs as community organizers, daycare workers, and teacher aides. The program provided meaningful work, access to education, and critical resources to poor people so that they would become leaders in their own communities and run for office. The **Community Action Programs (CAPs)** insisted on "maximum feasible participation" by the poor. The Education Act increased federal funding to

Economic Opportunity Act of 1964

Federal law creating the Office of Economic Opportunity and a number of programs aimed at poor communities.

Community Action Programs (CAPs)

Antipoverty programs involving "maximum feasible participation" by the poor themselves.

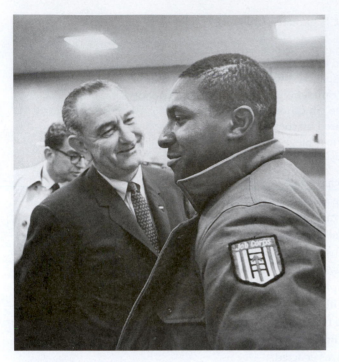

One of the most prominent programs of President Johnson's War on Poverty was the Job Corps, which provided occupational training for poor Americans. In this photo, Johnson speaks with James Trueville at a Job Corps center in Camp Catoctin, Maryland.

colleges and universities and provided low-interest student loans.

Johnson faced opposition to CAPs and other Great Society programs. Local politicians, fearing the federal government was subsidizing their opponents and undercutting their power, were especially threatened by programs that empowered the previously disfranchised and dispossessed. Others, reflecting persistent white stereotypes of African Americans, complained that Johnson was rewarding lawlessness and laziness with handouts to the undeserving poor. The black residents of America's inner cities, for their part, had their expectations raised by the promises of the Great Society, only to be frustrated by white backlash and minimal gains. They felt as betrayed by its programs as Johnson's white critics felt robbed by them.

No one will ever know whether Johnson could have won his War on Poverty had he been given the resources to do so. As it turned out, the nation's resources were increasingly diverted into his other war, the war in Vietnam. Statistics tell the story. Government spending, including spending for domestic programs, increased dramatically under Johnson. But most of the money spent on domestic programs during Johnson's presidency, $44.3 billion, went to Social Security benefits, which now included Medicare. Appropriations for the War on Poverty came to only $10 billion. The war in Vietnam, in contrast, consumed $140 billion.

22.3 Johnson and King: The War in Vietnam

Identify the ways in which the Vietnam War adversely affected President Johnson's War on Poverty and his Great Society initiatives.

Vietnam was a French colony from the 1860s until the Japanese seized it during World War II. After the war the Vietnamese communists, led by Ho Chi Minh, declared independence, but the French, with massive U.S. financial aid, fought to reassert their control until they were finally defeated in 1954. In retrospect, it is easy to argue that American policymakers should have been more impressed by the French failure to defeat the communists in Vietnam. But in 1954, with the French pulling out, the Americans arranged a temporary division of the country into a communist-controlled North Vietnam and a U.S.-supported South Vietnam (which, however, contained many communist guerrillas, whom the Americans called "Viet Cong"). The United States ignored the possibility that as guarantor of South Vietnam, it would replace the French as targets for those Vietnamese who were determined to end foreign domination and unify their country.

For nine years, under Presidents Eisenhower and Kennedy, American aid and advisers propped up the corrupt and incompetent South Vietnamese government in Saigon. By the time Johnson became president, only the dramatic escalation of American involvement—the bombing of North Vietnam and the introduction of large numbers of American troops into combat in South Vietnam—could keep the South Vietnamese government in power. Johnson himself doubted the advisability of a wholesale American commitment and did not want a foreign war to distract the public's attention or divert resources from the Great Society programs about which he cared so much. "I knew from the start," Johnson claimed later, that I was bound to be crucified either way I moved. If I left the woman I really loved—the Great Society—in order to get involved with that bitch of a war on the other side of the world, then I would lose everything at home. All my programs. All my hopes to feed the hungry and shelter the homeless. All my dreams to provide education and medical care to the browns and the blacks and the lame and the poor. But if I left that war and let the Communists take over South Vietnam, then I would be seen as a coward and my nation would be seen as an appeaser and we would both find it impossible to accomplish anything for anybody anywhere on the entire globe.

And so, half aware he was entering a quagmire but determined to slug through it, Johnson intervened in Vietnam—gradually, massively, and inexorably.

After the North Vietnamese allegedly attacked U.S. destroyers in the Gulf of Tonkin in August 1964, Johnson pushed a resolution through Congress that gave him authority to escalate American involvement in Vietnam. In the spring of 1965, he authorized the bombing of selected North Vietnamese targets, but that failed to stop the North Vietnamese from reinforcing their forces in the south. The American military presence in South Vietnam then grew rapidly. By the end of 1966, more than 385,000 U.S. troops were stationed there and by 1968 more than 500,000.

Troopers of the 327th Infantry, 101st Air Cavalry Division patrol the Laotian border during "Operation Plain," August 1968.

22.3.1 Black Americans and the Vietnam War

In the mid-1960s, black Americans made up 10 percent of the armed forces. This percentage increased during the Vietnam War. (In 1969, for example, 18.1 percent of active duty soldiers were black.) Black overrepresentation among the U.S. troops in Vietnam resulted, in large part, from draft deferments for college and graduate students who were predominantly white and middle class (such as George W. Bush and Dick Cheney). Black men and women entered the military for many reasons, in addition to the draft. One was patriotism. Another was that the military offered educational and vocational opportunities that the children of the working black poor could not otherwise obtain. Still another was Project 100,000.

22.3.2 Project 100,000

In 1966 the Defense Department launched **Project 100,000** to reduce the military's high rejection rate. The project enabled recruitment officers to accept applicants whom they otherwise would have rejected because of criminal records or lack of skills. It supplied more than 340,000 new recruits for Vietnam, 136,000 of whom were African Americans. As some have argued, this imbalance made the Vietnam War a white man's war but a black man's fight. Although the recruits were promised training and "rehabilitation," they saw more combat duty than regular recruits.

Project 100,000

Military project with the goal of reducing the number of African Americans rejected by the military.

22.3.3 Johnson: Vietnam Destroys the Great Society

By the end of 1967, the nation seemed to be heading toward total racial polarization. In their rage against economic exploitation and police brutality, some inner-city black people had destroyed their own neighborhoods. Frightened white people, unable to comprehend black anger, rallied behind those who promised to restore order by any means. The two men who, only a few years before, had seemed the most effective

Voices

"Homosexuals Are Not Enemies of the People" Black Panther Party Founder, Huey P. Newton

During the past few years, strong movements have developed among women and among homosexuals seeking their liberation. There has been some uncertainty about how to relate to these movements. I say "whatever your insecurities are" because as we very well know, sometimes our first instinct is to want to hit a homosexual in the mouth, and want a woman to be quiet.

We must gain security in ourselves and therefore have respect and feelings for all oppressed people. We must not use the racist attitude that the White racists use against our people because they are Black and poor. Many times the poorest White person is the most racist because he is afraid that he might lose something, or discover something that he does not have.

Remember, we have not established a revolutionary value system; we are only in the process of establishing it. We have not said much about the homosexual at all, but we must relate to the homosexual movement because it is a real thing. And I know through reading, and through my life experience and observations, that homosexuals are not given freedom and liberty by anyone in the society. They might be the most oppressed people in the society.

. . . . We know that homosexuality is a fact that exists, and we must understand it in its purest form: that is, a person should have the freedom to use his body in whatever way he wants. There is nothing to say that a homosexual cannot also be a revolutionary. Quite the contrary, maybe a homosexual could be the most revolutionary.

When we have revolutionary conferences, rallies, and demonstrations, there should be full participation of the gay liberation movement and the women's liberation movement . . . Friends are allowed to make mistakes. The enemy is not allowed to make mistakes because his whole existence is a mistake, and we suffer from it. But the women's liberation front and gay liberation front are our friends, they are our potential allies, and *we need as many allies as possible*. . . . Homosexuals are not enemies of the people.

We should try to form a working coalition with the gay liberation and women's liberation groups. We must always handle social forces in the most appropriate manner.

---

1. Why does Huey P. Newton advocate for liberation solidarity?

2. Distinguish the differences and similarities between the 1970s and modern day liberation struggles.

advocates of racial reconciliation—Lyndon Johnson and Martin Luther King, Jr.—were both trying to regain the initiative. Each, tragically, alienated the other.

By 1967 Johnson's situation was untenable. He had escalated the war in Vietnam without convincing many Americans it was worth fighting. Misleading claims about the progress of the war had forfeited public trust and opened what journalists called "the credibility gap." Johnson hoped that, with more bombing and more troops, the Vietnamese communists would give up, but he knew that if Congress had to choose between spending on the war and spending on domestic programs, it would choose the war. After Johnson asked for a tax increase, his Great Society programs met increasing resistance. When, for example, he proposed a special program to exterminate the rats that infested inner-city neighborhoods, congressional opponents turned it into a joke, calling it a "civil rats bill" and proposing to enlist an army of cats.

An even more dramatic example of the ugly mood on Capitol Hill was the House of Representatives' expulsion in 1967 of the most prominent African-American politician in the United States, Adam Clayton Powell, Jr. Pastor of the Abyssinian Baptist Church in Harlem and a longtime civic activist, Powell had first been elected to represent his Harlem district in 1944 and became the foremost champion of civil rights in the House.

Because of his seniority he became chairman of the Education and Labor Committee in 1961 and had been instrumental in passing Johnson's education and antipoverty legislation.

Powell gave ammunition to his enemies. He mismanaged the committee's budget, took numerous trips abroad at government expense, and was exiled from his district when threatened with arrest there because of his refusal to pay a slander judgment against him. Yet the sentiment behind his ouster owed much to the dislike he inspired as a champion of minorities and the poor and as a flamboyant black man. The Supreme Court, overruling the House, upheld his right to his seat, and although he lost his chairmanship, Harlem voters kept him in office until his death in 1972.

Despite opposition in Congress, Johnson did not give up on the Great Society. He knew he could initiate no major programs while the Vietnam War lasted, but he continued to push measures, including a law to prohibit discrimination in housing. He also named the architect of the NAACP's attack on segregation, Thurgood Marshall, to the Supreme Court in 1967.

Vietnam trapped Johnson. As the hundreds of thousands of people who demonstrated against the war reminded him, Vietnam was incontestably "Lyndon Johnson's war." It was not, he would have replied, the war he had wanted to fight— that was the war against poverty and discrimination—but he was committed to seeing it through. He believed his and the nation's honor were at stake. Even though objective commentators considered the conflict a stalemate, optimistic reports in 1967, from military commanders and intelligence agents, convinced the president he might yet prevail.

Then, on January 30, 1968, at the start of the Vietnamese New Year (called Tet), communist insurgents attacked 36 of the 44 provincial capitals in South Vietnam as well as its national capital, Saigon, where they penetrated the grounds of the American embassy. Although American and South Vietnamese forces recaptured all the territory that was lost and inflicted massive casualties on the enemy, the Tet Offensive was a major psychological blow for the American public, deepening the suspicion that the administration had not been telling the truth about the war. Washington was forced to reconsider its strategy.

On March 31, 1968, President Johnson told the nation he would halt the bombing of North Vietnam to encourage the start of peace negotiations, which began in Paris in May. Then, as if an afterthought, he added that he would not seek renomination as president. Worn out by Vietnam, frustrated in his efforts to achieve the Great Society, the target of bitter criticism, and dispirited by a poor showing in the New Hampshire primary, Lyndon Johnson ended his public career rather than engaging in a potentially bruising renomination battle.

Adam Clayton Powell, Jr. (1908–1972). Beginning in 1954, Powell's Harlem constituency elected him to 11 successive terms in the U.S. House of Representatives. His brilliant leadership of the Education and Labor Committee proved crucial to the successful passage of social reform legislation in the 1960s.

22.3.4 King: Searching for a New Strategy

Like Johnson, Martin Luther King, Jr. was attacked on many fronts. Many white people considered him a dangerous radical. Black militants considered him an ineffectual moderate. His first response to the urban rebellions in 1965 and 1966 had been to move his campaign to the North to demonstrate the national range of the civil rights movement. In 1966 King and the SCLC set up operations in Chicago at the invitation of the Chicago Freedom Movement. King was confident he would receive the support of the city's white liberals and the black community. James Bevel, King's Chicago lieutenant, declared,

"We are going to create a new city. . . . Nobody will stop us." His optimism proved unwarranted.

Chicago's powerful, wily Mayor Richard Daley viewed King suspiciously from the outset, but he treated him with respect and cautioned the police not to use violence against King's civil rights demonstrators. Because King's movement depended on provoking confrontation, not much happened until King attempted to march into the white ethnic enclave of Marquette Park and the all-white suburb of Cicero.

The ensuing violence attracted the nation's television cameras. Chicago's white liberals joined with King and Daley in negotiating the Summit Agreement on housing, which amounted to a hasty retreat by King in the face of virulent white rage and black militancy. The Chicago strategy was a dismal failure.

But Chicago reinforced two important lessons for King. First, racial discrimination was more than a southern problem: in Chicago he witnessed an intensity of hatred and hostility that surpassed even that of Birmingham. Second, racial discrimination was inextricably intertwined with the country's economic structure. And so he began to think more critically about the need not only to eradicate poverty but to end systemic economic inequality. "What good is it to be allowed to eat in a restaurant," he remarked, "if you can't afford a hamburger?" In the fall of 1967, he announced plans for his most ambitious and militant project, an integrated, non-violent **"Poor People's Campaign"** the following spring. According to the plan, tens of thousands of the nation's dispossessed would descend on Washington to focus attention on the disadvantaged in American society. Among other things, King and his aides wanted a federally guaranteed income policy.

Poor People's Campaign

Project supported by Martin Luther King involving the march of tens of thousands of poor people on Washington.

22.3.5 King on the Vietnam War

While planning the Poor People's Campaign, King began to attack the war in Vietnam. He rejected what he considered the hypocrisy of the federal government's determination to send black and white men to Vietnam "to slaughter, men, women, and children" while failing to protect black American civil rights protesters in places like Albany, Birmingham, and Selma. His statements that the president was more concerned about winning in Vietnam than winning the "war against poverty" in America turned Johnson against him and further alienated King from many of Johnson's black supporters, including the more traditional civil rights leaders who supported the war. At the same time, the young militants in SNCC, who had already condemned the war, did not rush to embrace him. But King persisted, and by 1968 he had become one of the war's most trenchant critics.

22.3.6 The Assassination of Dr. Martin Luther King, Jr.

Dr. Martin Luther King's search for a new strategy led him to a closer involvement with labor issues. In February 1968, while attempting to gain union recognition for municipal workers in Memphis, 1,300 members of a virtually all-black sanitation workers local went on strike and, together with the local black community, boycotted downtown merchants. But Mayor Henry Loeb refused to negotiate. On March 18, 1968, responding to a call from James Lawson, a longtime civil rights activist and the minister of Centenary Methodist Church in Memphis, Dr. King went to Memphis to address the striking sanitation workers.

The occasion was marked by violence. Nevertheless, King returned to Memphis on April 3 and delivered his last and perhaps most prophetic speech about seeing the Promised Land. The next day James Earl Ray murdered King as he stood on the balcony of the Lorraine Motel in Memphis. His assassination unleashed a torrent of civic rage in black communities. More than 125 cities experienced uprisings.

Profile

Muhammad Ali

Muhammad Ali declared himself "The Greatest," and for many African Americans he was the epitome of the uncompromised and proud black man.

Boxing is a brutal sport. During the 1960s and 1970s, Cassius Clay showed that boxing was also an art, that it could be beautiful, and that the boxer could become a symbol of racial pride, endearing wit, and even love. Born Cassius Marcellus Clay in 1942 in Louisville, Kentucky, Clay won a gold medal in Rome in 1960 as a member of the U.S. Olympic boxing team.

Clay turned the boxing world on its head with audacious assertions of his own greatness as a boxer and beauty as a black man. His defeats of Floyd Patterson and Sonny Liston confirmed the first claim. On February 25, 1964, Clay pounded Liston to become the world heavyweight champion. The next day he announced that he had joined the Nation of Islam and had taken a new name, Muhammad Ali. Explaining his timing of the announcement, he said, "When I joined the Nation in 1961, I figured I'd be pressured if I revealed it, so I kept it quiet for about three years. . . . But after beating Sonny Liston, I was getting more recognition and more power. I revealed it after that fight."

Ali was a master at "playing the dozens," a boasting style that angered his opponents and annoyed white reporters covering his bouts. In 1967, however, it was his refusal to be drafted into the military that incurred the wrath of the boxing establishment and white America. Ali argued that his religion was opposed to military service just as it was against civil rights activism and integration. He was the new black man who refused to accept the white man's rules about how to behave. He embodied the assertive black consciousness that invaded social and cultural life in the 1960s and 1970s.

But most black people also adored Ali for other reasons, recalled basketball player Kareem Abdul-Jabbar, who in 1971 discarded the name Lew Alcindor:

When Ali announced his refusal to accept the draft, I thought it was a very brave stand. . . . A meeting to help Ali was called by black athletes back in 1967. We let black people around the country know that we supported Ali. I think by that time Black Americans understood that their presence in Vietnam was highly disproportionate to their percentage of the American population and that the front-line casualties were being absorbed by Black Americans in much greater numbers than they should have.

A federal court found Ali guilty of draft evasion, but he was released on bail pending his appeal. Ali immediately became a popular antiwar speaker. In June 1970 the Supreme Court overturned his conviction on the grounds that the FBI had illegally wiretapped his telephone.

Actor Harry Belafonte described Ali in admiring terms:

He brought America to its most wonderful and its most naked moment. "I will not play in your game of war. I will not kill in your behalf. What you ask is immoral, unjust, and I stand here to attest to that fact. Now do with me what you will," he said. I mean he was, in many ways, as inspiring as Dr. King, as inspiring as Malcolm. Cassius was a black, young American. Out of the womb of oppression he was our phoenix, he was the spirit of our young. He was our manhood. . . . He was the vitality of what we hoped would emerge . . . the perfect machine, the wit, the incredible athlete, the facile, articulate, sharp mind on issues, the great sense of humor, which was out of our tradition.

In 1974 Ali fought George Foreman to regain his world heavyweight boxing title. Four years later he lost the title to Leon Spinks. He regained it, retired, and then attempted a comeback that ended with his October 2, 1980, loss to Larry Holmes. He was elected to the Boxing Hall of Fame in 1987. In 1996 he lit the Olympic Flame to open the summer games in Atlanta. Muhammad Ali died on June 3, 2016. World leaders attended the funeral, and tens of thousands lined the funeral procession in his home town, Louisville, Kentucky. He was an inspiration to all, not only due to boxing championships, but because of his unflinching commitment to the struggle for peace, social justice, and freedom for all.

By April 11, 46 people were dead, 35,000 were injured, and more than 20,000 had been arrested.

In what seemed to many a belated gesture of racial reconciliation, within days of King's assassination, Congress passed the **Civil Rights Act of 1968**. Proposed by Johnson two years before, the act outlawed discrimination in the sale and rental of housing and gave the Justice Department authority to bring suits against such discrimination.

King's assassination also boosted support for the SCLC's faltering Poor People's Campaign. The campaign began in May when more than 2,000 demonstrators settled into a shantytown they called Resurrection City in Washington, D.C. For more than a month, they marched daily to federal offices and took part in a mass demonstration on June 19. On June 24, police evicted them and the campaign ended, leaving an uncertain legacy.

Civil Rights Act of 1968

Federal law banning discrimination in housing.

22.4 The Black Arts Movement and Black Consciousness

Analyze the relationship or connections between the Black Power movement and the Black Arts movement of the 1960s.

The years between 1967 and 1975 witnessed some of the most intense political and cultural discussions in the history of the black freedom struggle. Black Power stimulated debate about both the future of black politics in the post–civil rights era and the role of black art and artists in the quest for black liberation. Creative people revisited the long-standing issue of whether black art is political or aesthetic. For a decade, discussion about black culture and identity focused on the relationship between art, the artist, and the political movement within the black community. This period became known as the "**Black Arts movement.**" Among the outstanding poets who helped shape the revolutionary movement, introducing new forms of black writing and delivering outspoken attacks on "the white aesthetic" while stressing black beauty and pride, were Sonia Sanchez, Nikki Giovanni, and Don L. Lee (Haki Madhubuti). One of the best examples of Giovanni's militant poems is "The True Import of Present Dialogue, Black vs. Negro," which appeared in her first collection, a self-published volume titled *Black Feeling, Black Talk* (1967). In a shocking opening line, she asked, "nigger/Can you kill/Can you kill/Can a nigger kill/Can a nigger kill a honkie." The poem continues, "Can you kill the nigger/in you/Can you kill your nigger mind/And free your Black hands to/strangle." Sanchez also captured the era's violence and turbulence. In 1970 she published a major collection of poetry, *We a BaddDDD People*. Of equal significance in the development and evolution of this creative flowering was playwright and poet LeRoi Jones.

The formal beginning of the movement was the founding in 1965 of the Black Arts Repertory Theater by Jones, who changed his name to Imamu Amiri Baraka in 1967. Jones was the bridge that linked the political and cultural aspects of Black Power. He had been associated with the white avant-garde poets in New York in the 1950s and early 1960s, but he began to change in 1965 from an integrationist to a black cultural nationalist.

The guiding ethos of the Black Arts movement was the determination of black artists to produce black art for black people and thereby to accomplish black liberation. Baraka declared, "The Black man must seek a Black politics, an ordering of the world that is beneficial to his culture, to his interiorization and judgment of the world. The Black Artist . . . is desperately needed to change the

Black Arts movement

Artistic movement that sought to promote black art by black artists for black people.

Imamu Amiri Baraka means "spiritual leader, prince, blessed" in Swahili and is the chosen name of LeRoi Jones. The celebrated "father of the Black Arts movement" remained prolific, influential, and controversial after five decades of creative engagement in America's "culture war."

images his people identify with, by asserting Black feeling, Black mind, and Black judgment." In 1968 he coedited with Larry Neal the anthology *Black Fire*, which revealed the extent to which black writers and thinkers had rejected integration in favor of a new black consciousness and nationalist political engagement.

Larry Neal, who was part of the Revolutionary Action movement, defined this important dimension of the freedom struggle:

> The black arts movement is radically opposed to any concept of the artist that alienates him from his community. Black Art is the aesthetic and spiritual sister of the black power concept. As such, it envisions an art that speaks directly to the needs and aspirations of Black Americans. In order to perform this task, the black arts movement proposes a radical reordering of the western cultural aesthetic. It proposes a separate symbolism, mythology, critique, and iconography. The black arts and the black power concept both relate broadly to the Afro-American's desire for self-determination and nationhood. Both concepts are nationalistic. One is concerned with the relationship between art and politics; the other with the art of politics.

The Black Arts movement was criticized because of its celebration of black maleness, its racial exclusivity, and its homophobia. It was never a unified movement in the sense that all black artists spoke in one voice. There was creative dissent and competing visions of freedom. In 1970 Maya Angelou published an autobiographical novel, *I Know Why the Caged Bird Sings*, which unveiled her experience with sexual abuse and the silencing of black women within black communities. Other black women writers would create a black women's literary renaissance in the 1970s. Still, prominent integrationist writers agreed with some of the Black Arts movement's tenets and were converted to its principles.

The works of Langston Hughes, Lorraine Hansberry, Gwendolyn Brooks, and James Baldwin linked the black cultural renaissances of the 1930s, 1940s, and 1950s to the Black Arts movement. Brooks, for example, stressed the commitment of artists to community and the importance of the relationship between the artist and her audience. She had supported community-based arts programs, and it seemed natural that she should "convert" to a Black Nationalist perspective during the 1960s and join forces with younger artists.

But the most popular black writer of the era was James Baldwin. Baldwin was an integrationist. In his work he had resisted the simple inversion of racial hierarchies that characterized parts of the Black Power and Black Arts movements. He wrote, "I think all theories are suspect, that the finest principles may have to be modified, or may even be pulverized by the demands of life, and that one must find therefore, one's own moral center and move through the world hoping that this center will guide one aright." Yet in many ways, Baldwin was as alienated and angry as some of the artists identified with Black Arts.

In *The Fire Next Time* (1963), Baldwin concluded with a phrase that echoed years later through discussions of the rebellions in Watts, Newark, and Detroit: "If we do not now dare everything, the fulfillment of that prophecy, recreated from the bible in song by a slave, is upon us: 'God gave Noah the rainbow sign, No more water, the fire next time!'"

Baldwin was also unflinching about white racism and had a major impact on public discourse. At one point he told his white readers, "There appears to be a vast amount of confusion on this point, but I do not know many Negroes who are eager to be 'accepted' by white people, still less to be loved by them; they, the blacks, simply don't wish to be beaten over the head by the whites every instant of our brief passage on this planet." And in *No Name in the Street*, Baldwin declared, "I agree with the Black Panther position concerning black prisoners: not one of them has ever had a fair trial, for not one of them has ever been tried by a jury of his peers." He explained, "White middle-class America is always the jury, and they know absolutely nothing about the lives of the people on whom they sit in judgment: and this fact is not altered, on the contrary it is rendered more implacable by the presence of one or two black faces in the jury box."

22.4.1 Poetry and Theater

The Black Arts movement had its most significant impact in poetry and theater. The movement had three geographical centers: Harlem, Chicago and Detroit, and San Francisco.

The Chicago-based *Negro Digest/Black World*, edited by Hoyt Fuller and published by John Johnson, promoted the new generation of creative artists. Fuller, a well-connected intellectual with an exhaustive command of black literature, became editor of the monthly magazine in 1961. In 1970 he changed the magazine's name to *Black World* to signal the rejection of "Negro" and the adoption of "black" to designate people of African descent. The new name identified African Americans with both the African Diaspora and Africa itself.

In Detroit, Naomi Long Madgett's Lotus Press and Dudley Randall's Broadside Press republished the previous generation of black poets, notably Gwendolyn Brooks, Margaret Walker, and Sterling Brown. In Chicago, poet and literary critic Don L. Lee, who changed his name to Haki Madhubuti, launched Third World Press, which published many of the Black Arts poets and writers.

The Chicago–Detroit publishing nexus promoted new poets like Nikki Giovanni, Etheridge Knight, and Sonia Sanchez. These and other poets produced some of the most accomplished and experimental work of the Black Arts movement. It resonated with the sounds of the African-American vernacular, combining the rhythmic cadences of sermons with popular music and black "street speech" into a spirited new form of poetry that was free, conversational, and militantly cool.

Theater was another prominent genre of the Black Arts movement. Playwright Ed Bullins edited a special issue of the journal *Drama Review* in the summer of 1968 that featured essays and plays by most of the major activists in Black Arts, including Sonia Sanchez, Ron Milner, and Woodie King, Jr. This volume became the textbook of Black Arts. In his plays, Bullins, who was greatly influenced by Baraka, portrayed ordinary black life and explored the inner forces that prevented black people from realizing their own liberation and potential. He showed how racism had deformed the black experience and consciousness. Across the country, local black communities formed their own theater groups, including Val Gray Ward's Kuumba Workshop in Chicago and Baraka's Spirit House Theater in New Jersey. These groups hosted seminars, guest appearances, fashion shows, art exhibits, dance recitals, parades, and media parties.

On the West Coast, in 1969, Robert Chrisman and Nathan Hare launched *The Black Scholar*, the first serious journal to promote black studies. Chrisman compared the Black Arts movement with the Harlem Renaissance of the 1920s: "More so than the Harlem Renaissance, in which Black artists were always on the leash of white patrons and publishing houses, the Black Arts movement did it for itself. Black people going out nationally, in mass, saying we are an independent Black people and this is what we produce."

22.4.2 Music

The cultural nationalists in the Black Arts movement championed modern jazz musicians as icons of the quest for black freedom. Baraka argued that jazz and other black music were the language that black people developed to give uncensored accounts of their experiences. He and other cultural nationalists believed music could promote black

Profile

Lorraine Hansberry

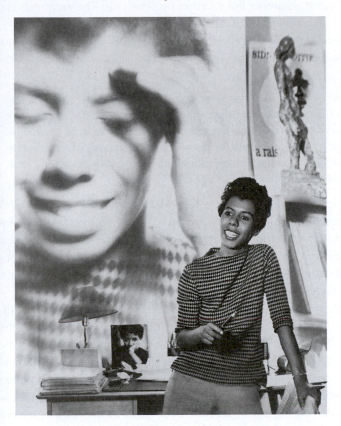

Playwright Lorraine Hansberry was, arguably, the artist/activist who spoke most powerfully to three generations of African Americans. Her play *A Raisin in the Sun* has inspired audiences and readers from the 1950s through the civil rights movement to the hip-hop era. Hansberry grew up on the South Side of Chicago and attended the University of Wisconsin, the Art Institute of Chicago, and Roosevelt College (now University) before settling in New York City.

Before achieving national acclaim for *Raisin*, Hansberry worked for Paul Robeson's Harlem newspaper, *Freedom*. In a 1955 essay for the paper, "Life Challenges Negro Youth," she declared, "From the time he is born, the Negro child is surrounded by a society organized to convince him that he belongs to a people whose past is so worthless and shameful that it amounts to no past at all. . . . In a land where the Grace Kelly-Marilyn Monroe monotype 'ideal' is imposed on the national culture, racist logic insists that anything directly opposite—no matter how lovely—is naturally ugly."

In 1953 Hansberry married Robert Nemiroff, but they separated soon after when she told him that she was a lesbian. She and Nemiroff remained close friends and collaborators, however, and the larger world never knew about her sexual identity. Like Bayard Rustin, Hansberry was acutely aware of the homophobia in American society. She disclosed her private life only to a few trusted friends.

In 1965 Hansberry died of pancreatic cancer. Six hundred people attended her funeral, including Malcolm X, James Forman, Nina Simone, Sammy Davis, Jr., Ossie Davis, and Ruby Dee. Martin Luther King, Jr. and James Baldwin sent messages. Paul Robeson delivered a eulogy.

A Raisin in the Sun premiered on Broadway in 1959 to rave reviews. Hansberry explained, "I wrote it between my 26th and 27th birthday. One night, after seeing a play I won't mention, I suddenly became disgusted with a whole body of material about Negroes. Card board characters. Cute dialect bits. Or hip-swinging musicals from exotic scores. . . . Even the most sympathetic novel for the Negro . . . happens to have been built around the most offensive character in American literature—who is Uncle Tom." In *Raisin*, Hansberry captured the tribulations of the Younger family's attempt to move from their crowded apartment in Chicago's Bronzeville to a house in the suburbs and what they hope will be a better life. It is a story of upward mobility running up against American racism. Walter Lee Younger wants to use the money from his father's insurance policy to open a liquor store. His mother wants to buy a house for the extended family. His sister wants the money to help pay her tuition to medical school. Their mother prevails and holds the family together even when a friend swindles Walter Lee out of most of the money, and racist neighbors make it clear that the Youngers are not welcome. At the end of the play, the Youngers move into the new home as a united family even though their future there is uncertain.

In her book, *To Be Young, Gifted and Black*, Lorraine Hansberry revealed the depth of her commitment to, and thoughts about, a range of tactics that African Americans must consider deploying in the struggle for freedom. She declared, "I think, then, that Negroes must concern themselves with every means of struggle: legal, illegal, passive, active, violent and non-violent. That they must harass, debate, petition, give money to court struggles, sit-in, lie-down, strike, boycott, sing hymns, pray on steps, and shoot from their windows when the racists come cruising through their communities. The acceptance of our present condition is the only form of extremism which discredits us before our children."

In 2004, hip-hop impresario Sean (P. Diddy) Combs revived *Raisin* on Broadway and played the role of Walter Lee that Sidney Poitier had played in the original production. Such was the excitement generated by a play still powerfully resonant 45 years after its premier that the producers recouped their $2.6 million investment within two months. Lorraine Hansberry's writings remain a potent source of inspiration for artists to deploy their creative talents in the struggle for liberation from the biases and fears that oppress and dehumanize people because of their race, class, gender, and sexual identity.

identity and encourage the pride that was vital for political struggle. The jazzmen's music was often dense and austere, but it could also be powerfully primitive and dazzlingly complex. Above all, the music appeared to challenge Western conceptions of harmony, rhythm, melody, and tone. In jazz you have to improvise, to create your own form of expression by using whatever information inspires you. The emphasis is not on an original score but on individual articulation.

Cultural nationalists perceived jazz to be a self-consciously engaged, economically independent, politically useful art form. Novelist Ralph Ellison put it most succinctly:

> True jazz is an art of individual assertion within and against the group. Each true jazz moment (as distinct from the uninspired commercial performance) springs from a contest in which each artist challenges all the rest; each solo flight, or improvisation, represents (like the successive canvases of a painter) a definition of his identity: as individual, as member of the collectivity and as a link in the chain of tradition.

This outlook explains why Miles Davis's legendary album *Kind of Blue* (1959), one of the most progressive jazz albums ever produced, also became one of the most popular. Davis showed that art could be accessible without sacrificing excellence and rigor. Davis, in the words of one admirer, was able to "dance underwater and not get wet." For black cultural nationalists, Davis projected an image of uncompromising and uncompromised black identity.

Among other celebrated jazz musicians were Archie Shepp, Ornette Coleman, Pharoah Sanders, Eric Dolphy, Thelonious Monk, and John Coltrane. Playwright Ronald Milner described Coltrane as "a man who through his saxophone before your eyes and ears completely annihilates every single western influence." Coltrane also played the deep—and deeply political—blues of "Alabama," written in response to the Birmingham church bombings.

Jazz, however, tended to appeal to intellectuals. Most black people preferred rhythm and blues, gospel, and soul. During the height of the black consciousness movement, black popular musicians gave performances to raise funds and assert racial pride. Aretha Franklin and Ray Charles, for example, allowed SNCC workers to attend their concerts for free. Just as the freedom songs had done, the soul music of the Black Power era helped unify black people.

No history of the era would be complete without mentioning the performances of the "Godfather of Soul," James Brown; the "Queen of Soul," Aretha Franklin, best known for her powerful rendition of the song "Respect"; and the financial contributions of Berry Gordy of Motown. James Brown's "Say It Loud, I'm Black and I'm Proud" became an anthem for the era. Brown linked commercial marketing to social commentary, confronting American racism with racial pride and righteous indignation. He confessed, "I may not do as much as some other individuals who have made it big," but, "you can bet your life that I'm doing the best I can. . . . I owe it to the black community to help provide scholarships, to help children stay in school, to help equip playgrounds and recreation centers, and to keep kids off the streets." Brown was "totally committed to Black Power, the kind that is achieved not through the muzzle of a rifle but through education and economic leverage."

Berry Gordy contributed to black freedom struggles both artistically and financially. To support King's Chicago movement, Gordy arranged for Stevie Wonder to give a benefit concert at Soldier Field in Chicago. He contributed to black candidates, the NAACP and its Legal Defense and Educational Fund, and the Urban League.

With Gordy's encouragement, his performers flirted just enough with black radicalism to gain a patina of militancy. During the late 1960s and early 1970s, the musical and lyrical innovations of the Temptations, Stevie Wonder, and Marvin Gaye reflected Motown's politicization. In an address to one of the sessions launching Jesse Jackson's People United to Save Humanity (PUSH) in 1971, Gordy declared, "I have been fortunate to be able to provide opportunities for young people. . . . Opportunities are supposed to knock once in a lifetime, but too often we have to knock for an opportunity. The first obligation we (as black businessmen) have is to ourselves and our own employees, the second is to create opportunities for others." Musician Curtis Mayfield explained simply, "Our purpose is to educate as well as to entertain. Painless preaching is as good a term as any for what we do."

22.4.3 The Black Student Movement: A Second Phase

The most dramatic expression of militant assertiveness after 1968 occurred among black college students. The Black Power generation of students was committed to transforming society and institutions of higher education by agitating for curricula reform and the establishment of Black Studies programs and departments. Some observers describe the period of activism between 1968 and 1975 as the "second phase" of the black students' movement.

22.4.4 The Orangeburg Massacre

In this view, students at southern black colleges launched the first phase in the early 1960s. It began with the sit-ins in Greensboro, North Carolina, and the Freedom Rides and culminated in the Mississippi Freedom Summer of 1964. By 1968, however, many of the student organizations that had grown out of the civil rights movement were invested in mobilizing local communities to overthrow the remaining vestiges of overt discrimination and segregation. The massacre of black students at South Carolina State College in Orangeburg on February 8, 1968, was an appalling demonstration of state violence and a failure of the justice system. Students attending the historically black institution had protested a local bowling alley's whites-only admission policy. When the tension and protests escalated, state officials deployed the highway patrol and National Guard. On the evening of February 8, the students assembled at the front of the campus and taunted the officers. Some threw rocks, bricks, and bottles. One officer was hit by a piece of lumber. Later, without warning, nine highway patrolmen opened fire on the students with shotguns. The officers killed three young men and wounded 28. Most of them were shot in the back. All the officers involved were later acquitted, but a young black activist and SNCC leader, Cleveland Sellers, was convicted of rioting and served nearly a year in prison. He was pardoned in 1993. On February 8, 2001, South Carolina Governor James Hodges apologized to a group of survivors who had assembled in Orangeburg. Since 2008, Dr. Cleveland Sellers has served as president of the traditionally black institution, Voorhees College, in Denmark, South Carolina.

South Carolina State College Massacre, 1968, Orangeburg, South Carolina. The three young men killed in the Orangeburg Massacre were Henry Smith and Samuel Hammond, both age 18, and 17-year-old high school student Delano Middleton. See *Scarred Justice* (2008), a powerful and illuminating PBS documentary film by Judy Richardson.

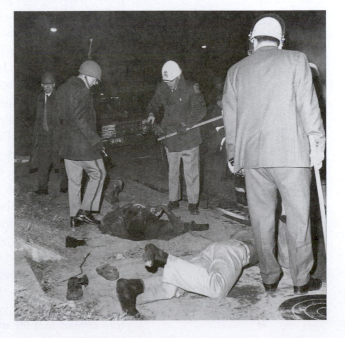

22.4.5 Black Studies

Long before African-American students attending newly integrated white colleges and universities began the movement that resulted in the establishment of black studies and the recruitment and hiring of black faculty, scholars at the historically black higher education institutions had taught courses in African history and culture. Howard University Professor William Leo Hansberry (an uncle of Lorraine Hansberry) was one of the most forceful early proponents of research and teaching an accurate history of Africa. His work, along with that of linguist Lorenzo Dow Turner at Fisk University and sociologist St. Clair Drake at Roosevelt University, would become essential to the development of courses and curriculum in Black Studies departments and programs formed in response to student demands in the late 1960s.

The movement for black studies and the transformation of college curriculums owed some of its inspiration to the Black Power and Black Arts movements. The black studies revolution on campus began with the enrollment of large numbers of black students in predominantly white institutions across the country. These students demanded courses in black history, culture, literature, and art as alternatives to the "Eurocentric" bias of the average university curriculum. Many black students also formed all-black organizations, such as the Black Allied Students' Association at New York University and the Black Organization of Students at Rutgers University.

Black students understood that education was essential to empowerment. In 1967 black students accounted for only 2 percent of the total enrollment at predominantly white colleges and universities. This meant that only 95,000 African Americans were among the approximately five million full-time undergraduates at these schools. Rutgers University in New Jersey provides a case study. Out of 24,000 baccalaureate degrees it awarded between 1952 and 1967, only about 200 went to African Americans. Federal legislation—especially the Civil Rights Act of 1964 and the Higher Education Act of 1965—outlawed discrimination or segregation in higher education, and by instituting an array of financial aid programs, it spurred colleges and universities to recruit black students. Where there had been about 100 black undergraduates at Rutgers in 1965, there were more than 400 by 1968, nearly 3 percent of the undergraduate enrollment.

On the national level, the overall status of black people in education reflected the accomplishments of the classic phase of the civil rights movement, but the Black Power generation was determined to make its own mark on the struggle. In 1960 only 227,000 black Americans attended the nation's colleges (including those at predominantly black institutions). By 1970, enrollments had increased by 100 percent, and in 1977, 1.1 million black students attended America's universities. This was an almost 500 percent increase over 1960. This generation of students was politically diverse, but they shared the sense of being strangers in a white-controlled environment. Many found the campuses hostile, alien places and discovered little there with which they could identify. They resolved to change this.

At San Francisco State College, Nathan Hare, formerly a professor at Howard University, and black students demanded not only curriculum changes but also changes to the structural transformation of the college. In the 1966–1967 academic year, the Black Student Union orchestrated a strike that involved thousands of students of diverse ethnic and racial backgrounds. The students chose to strike rather than take over buildings so that they could circulate on the campus, increasing their support and maintaining their momentum. Among their demands were the creation of an autonomous degree-granting Black Studies Department and the admission of more black students. The college ultimately created the first Black Studies Department in 1968, with Hare as its head.

Black students also took over administration buildings at other institutions such as Northwestern University, demanding not only that the schools offer more Black Studies courses and programs and hire more black faculty but also insisting that classrooms and facilities be made available to local black communities. The upheavals that shut down Columbia University in 1968 began when black student members of the Students Afro-American Society and Students for a Democratic Society demonstrated to block construction of a university gymnasium in nearby Morningside Park. The demonstrators argued that the gym would impinge on one of the few parks in Harlem and that the Harlem community vehemently objected to it.

In 1968 Yale University's Black Student Alliance sponsored a symposium to discuss the need, status, and function of Afro-American studies. Conference organizer Armstead Robinson saw it as an attempt to create a viable program of Afro-American studies. In December 1968 the faculty voted to make Yale one of the first major universities in the country to institute a degree-granting African-American studies program. In 1969 Harvard University created an Afro-American Studies Department, and other schools soon followed. In 1969 the Institute of the Black World in Atlanta conducted a project to define the methods and purpose of black studies and then sponsored a black studies directors' seminar. Ron Karenga wrote what remains a major textbook for the new field, *Introduction to Black Studies*. By 1973 some 200 Black Studies programs existed in the United States. By the late 1980s, several of the programs—such as those at Cornell, Yale, and the University of California, Los Angeles—offered master's degrees in African-American studies. In 1988 Temple University in Philadelphia, under the leadership of Dr. Molefi Kete Asante, became the first university to offer a Ph.D. in African-American studies. In 2002, Michigan State University became the sixth to offer the doctorate in the discipline. In 2006 Northwestern University welcomed its first group of five students into the new graduate program in African-American studies. By 2012 there were at least a dozen doctoral programs in African and African-American studies.

While there is no universally accepted definition of black studies, the discipline has continued to evolve. James E. Turner, founder of Africana studies at Cornell, viewed black studies as a collective, interdisciplinary, scholarly approach to the experiences of people of African descent throughout the African Diaspora and the world. History, in black studies, constituted the foundation for analyzing common patterns of life and thought that reflected the social and material conditions of black people. Africana studies or black studies theoreticians have generally agreed on four goals for this new field: (1) it should develop solutions to the problems facing black people in the African Diaspora; (2) it should provide an analysis of black culture and life that challenges and replaces preexisting Eurocentric models; (3) it should promote social change and educational reform throughout the academy; and (4) it should institutionalize the study of black people as a field with its own theories, methods, ideologies, symbols, language, and culture. In short, the first generation of advocates envisioned black studies as a revolutionary, historically grounded, educational reform movement that sought to make the study of African descendants—their culture, problems, belief systems, internationalism, radical traditions, and spirituality—a serious scholarly endeavor with practical implications for improving black people's lives.

22.5 The Presidential Election of 1968 and Richard Nixon

Describe the specific policies and initiatives developed during the Nixon administration that adversely affected the civil rights of African Americans.

In the presidential campaign of 1968, the Democrats provided the excitement but lost the election. In late 1967 Senator Eugene McCarthy of Minnesota entered the race as the antiwar alternative to Lyndon Johnson; Senator Robert Kennedy of New York entered the race in mid-March, after most of the convention delegates had been pledged to Johnson. When Johnson withdrew, these delegates aligned with Humphrey. Whether Kennedy could have gained the nomination will never be known. In the second traumatic assassination of 1968, Robert Kennedy was killed on June 6 in Los Angeles.

A combustible mixture of grief, anger, bitterness, and antiwar sentiment became the fuel for a Chicago explosion. It was the most tumultuous political convention in modern American history, with Chicago policemen clubbing, gassing, and arresting antiwar demonstrators. In November, Republican Richard Nixon narrowly defeated Humphrey.

Of all modern presidents, Richard Nixon is probably the hardest to pin down with neat ideological labels. By the standards of the early twenty-first century, much of his record seems progressive. He created the Environmental Protection Agency, endorsed an equal rights amendment to the Constitution that would have prohibited gender discrimination, and signed more regulatory legislation than any other president. His naming of Daniel Patrick Moynihan, one of Johnson's experts on social policy, to be his domestic policy adviser illustrates his willingness to innovate in policies affecting African Americans. But Nixon also pursued a "southern strategy" that realigned the Republican Party with the white southern backlash to civil rights and weakened the New Deal coalition.

22.5.1 The "Moynihan Report"

Moynihan Report

Report attributing many of the problems of poor black communities to the breakdown of the "lower-class" black family.

Moynihan first attracted national attention as assistant secretary of labor in the Johnson administration when a confidential memorandum he wrote—loosely organized and full of sweeping generalizations—was leaked to the press. It would later be published as "The Negro Family: The Case for National Action" and is popularly known as the "**Moynihan Report**." Moynihan's guiding assumption was that civil rights legislation, necessary as it was, would not address the problems of the inner city. There, he argued, the breakdown of the "lower-class" black family had led to the "pathology" of juvenile delinquency, illegitimacy, drug addiction, and poor performance in school. He attributed the vulnerability of the black family to "three centuries of almost unimaginable treatment" by white society: exploitation under slavery, the strain of urbanization, and persistent unemployment.

These forces, he argued, weakened the role of black men and resulted in a disproportionate number of dysfunctional female-headed families. In the report's most-often repeated passage, Moynihan declared that the black community had been forced into "a matriarchal structure, [which] because it is so out of line with the rest of American society, seriously retards the progress of the group as a whole, and imposes a crushing burden on the Negro male. . . . Obviously, not every instance of social pathology afflicting the Negro community can be traced to the weakness of family structure . . . [but] once or twice removed, it will be found to be the principal source of most of the aberrant, inadequate, or anti-social behavior that did not establish, but now serves to perpetuate the cycle of poverty and deprivation."

Although based on the work of black scholars, such as E. Franklin Frazier, Moynihan's condemnation of "matriarchy" drew fire. Black social scientists, such as Joyce Ladner, Andrew Billingsley, and feminist sociologist Carol Stack countered that the structure of the black family reflected a functional adaptation that black people had made to survive in a hostile and racist American society. Historians Herbert Gutman and John Blassingame argued that Moynihan underestimated the prevalence of two-parent black families in the past. Although many of the criticisms of the report were deserved, they diverted attention from its positive thrust. Moynihan wanted to eliminate poverty and unemployment in the black community, and he recommended vigorous enforcement of the civil rights laws to achieve equality of opportunity. Moynihan was one of the first policymakers to appreciate how white resentment of the CAPs and the expansion of the welfare rolls would make both programs politically unfeasible.

Family Assistance Plan (FAP)

Plan giving financial assistance to families with no wage earner.

Intrigued with Moynihan's independence, Nixon told him to develop a plan to assist poor families. Under the **Family Assistance Plan (FAP)** that Nixon unveiled in the summer of 1969, each family of four with no wage earner would receive an annual payment of $1,600 plus $800 in food stamps. With its across-the-board guarantee of income, the plan eliminated an oppressive welfare bureaucracy and reduced the invidious comparison between "welfare recipients" and everyone else.

Had it passed, FAP would have promoted two-parent families by removing the prohibition against assistance to dependent children whose fathers were alive, well, and living at home. It would also have encouraged work by requiring able-bodied recipients to accept jobs or vocational training and by providing benefits to those accepting low-paying jobs. Although the House approved the plan, the Senate—under pressure from conservatives who objected to any government programs for the poor and from welfare-rights advocates who complained the payments were too low—killed it. Arguably, at least until President Clinton's abortive healthcare plan in the 1990s, Nixon's FAP was the most significant failed initiative in the history of American social policy.

22.5.2 Busing

Yet, however flexible he might have been on many issues, Nixon was acutely aware that he moved in a changed political environment and particularly in a far more conservative Republican Party. In 1968 it was an influx of southern segregationists whom Barry Goldwater had attracted to the Republican Party in 1964 who Nixon had to appease. For example, South Carolina's Senator Strom Thurmond and his allies demanded that Nixon slow down court-ordered school desegregation in the South.

The Nixon administration crafted a southern strategy and embarked on a collision course with civil rights organizations such as the NAACP, which supported busing to achieve school integration. Thus, the major battle over civil rights in the early 1970s was over the federal courts' willingness to implement desegregation goals by busing students across district lines. Nixon, in 1971, advised federal officials to stop pressing to desegregate schools through "forced busing." He argued that such efforts were ultimately "counterproductive, and not in the interest of better race relations."

Educational segregation in the North reflected residential segregation. In Boston, the site of some of the most acrimonious busing protests, schools in black neighborhoods received less funding than their white counterparts. Buildings were derelict, overcrowded, and deficient in supplies and equipment, even desks. In 1974 U.S. Judge W. Arthur Garrity ruled in favor of black parents who had filed a class-action suit against the Boston School Committee. The ruling found the committee guilty of violating the equal protection clause of the Fourteenth Amendment. To achieve racial balance in the Boston schools, the judge ordered the busing of several thousand students between mostly white South Boston, Hyde Park, and Dorchester and mostly black Roxbury.

White people who opposed busing organized demonstrations and boycotts to prevent their children from being bused into black communities, as well as to prevent black children from being bused into white schools. During the first week of busing, white students and their mothers clashed with police officers outside South Boston High School. Hostilities continued for weeks despite the arrests of dozens of people and the closing of bars and liquor stores. Sporadic violence persisted for another two years in Boston.

22.5.3 Nixon and the War

Meanwhile, the war in Vietnam seemed to drag on endlessly, with the peace negotiations that had begun in Paris in May 1968 making no apparent progress. Nixon realized that what most Americans disliked about the war was that it was killing their sons and husbands. So in 1969 he began to phase out direct U.S. involvement in the war. This "Vietnamization," he claimed, was made possible by the growing ability of the South Vietnamese to fight for themselves. What Nixon did not say was that the morale of American soldiers was plunging rapidly. Drug abuse among troops was widespread; some soldiers had killed their officers, and some of those incidents had racial overtones. Along with his domestic record, Nixon's promise to "wind down the war" assured his reelection. In 1972 he defeated South Dakota Senator George McGovern in a landslide.

Few in the Nixon administration, however, took South Vietnam's military capability seriously, and Nixon, just as much as Johnson, was unwilling to "lose" Vietnam. Between 1969 and 1971, Nixon stepped up the war. Even as American soldiers were being sent home, he escalated the air war. In Cambodia in 1969–1970, for example, the United States dropped more bombs than it had on all of Asia in World War II.

But each time Nixon escalated the war—in 1970 with a joint American–South Vietnamese invasion of Cambodia, in 1971 with American air support for an invasion of Laos, and in 1972 with the bombing of North Vietnam and the mining of its harbors—opposition to it grew. Antiwar demonstrations kept Nixon off balance and may have deterred him from further escalation.

The most dramatic protests came after the invasion of Cambodia in April 1970, which triggered antiwar demonstrations on many campuses. In one such protest, on May 4, Ohio National Guardsmen shot and killed four white students at Kent State University. The response of students across the country was electric: the first nationwide student strike in American history. Ten days later in Mississippi, the shooting and killing of two black students at Jackson State University attracted much less attention from either white students or the media. Finally, in 1973, the United States and North Vietnam signed a peace agreement. Congress then prohibited the reintroduction of American troops or the resumption of bombing, and in 1974 it began cutting off military aid to South Vietnam. The result was predictable: In 1975 the communists launched another offensive, and South Vietnam collapsed.

Nixon became president in 1969 with popular mandates to restore law and order. The disorder that irritated the American public included many things: the inner-city riots, the antiwar demonstrations and campus protests, and the rise in crime. Responding to this mood, Nixon pushed legislation through Congress that gave local law enforcement officials expanded power to use wiretaps and enter premises without advance warning.

But Nixon's personality—a combination of paranoia and ruthlessness—pushed him beyond what the public would tolerate and even beyond the law itself. He confused criminals with principled protesters and political opponents and decided to punish them all. He created an extralegal ring of burglars, operating out of the White House, to gather incriminating information about his opponents. In June 1972 these burglars were caught breaking into Democratic National Committee headquarters in the Watergate apartment complex in Washington. Full details emerged in a Senate investigation in 1973–1974, and on August 9, 1974, threatened with impeachment, Nixon resigned. His downfall, however, left no one of his stature or with his flexible attitude toward public policy to resist the takeover of the Republican Party by more dogmatic conservatives. One early intimation of this was the difficulty Nixon's successor, Gerald Ford, had in securing the 1976 Republican presidential nomination against the right's new hero, former California Governor Ronald Reagan.

22.6 The Rise of Black Elected Officials

Enumerate some of the most significant accomplishments of the Black Power movement in the 1970s.

In the Black Power movement that followed the civil rights movement, a new generation of black leaders gained prominence. They were determined to mobilize the newly enfranchised black electorate to win political office. After the Voting Rights Act of 1965, Vernon Jordan, director of the Voter Education Project, coordinated registration drives across the South. As he explained, "Too many of these people have been alienated from the political process for too long a time . . . and so we have to . . . teach them what a local government is, how it operates, and try to relate their votes to the things they want."

By 1974 there were 1,593 black elected officials outside the South; by 1980 there were 2,455. Although black people in northern cities had been able to vote for a century and had been slowly developing political muscle and winning representation in state legislatures and on city councils, they had not been able to command an equal voice in city governance. The rise of Black Power and the Voting Rights Act, however, signaled a new departure. People now eagerly engaged in the electoral process to achieve the political influence to which their numbers entitled them. In 1967 in Cleveland, where the black population had skyrocketed after World War II, Carl Stokes became the first black mayor of a major American city (see Table 22-1), winning with the support of

Table 22-1 Black Power Politics: The Election of Black Mayors, 1967–1990

Cities	Names	Years in Office
Atlanta, Georgia	Maynard H. Jackson	(1974–82); (1990–94)
	Andrew J. Young	(1982–90)
Chicago, Illinois	Harold L. Washington	(1983–90)
Cleveland, Ohio	Carl B. Stokes	(1967–72)
Compton, California	Doris A. Davis	(1973–77)
Detroit, Michigan	Coleman A. Young	(1973–93)
Gary, Indiana	Richard G. Hatcher	(1967–87)
Los Angeles, California	Thomas J. Bradley	(1973–93)
Memphis, Tennessee	Willie W. Herenton	(1991–2009)
Newark, New Jersey	Kenneth A. Gibson	(1970–86)
New Orleans, Louisiana	Ernest N. Morial	(1978–86)
New York, New York	David N. Dinkins	(1990–94)
Raleigh, North Carolina	Clarence E. Lightner	(1973–75)
Roanoke, Virginia	Noel C. Taylor	(1975–92)
Washington, D.C.	Walter E. Washington	(1974–79)
	Marion S. Barry, Jr.	(1980–90); (1994–98)

African-American mayors of metropolitan cities with populations over 50,000.

white business leaders and the solid backing of the black community. In the same year prosecutor Richard G. Hatcher became mayor of Gary, Indiana, where the black population had also increased greatly after the war. Hatcher won by a mere 1,389 votes, garnering 96 percent of the black vote and 14 percent of the white vote.

22.6.1 The Gary Convention and the Black Political Agenda

These victories made possible one of the most significant events of postwar black political history, the Gary National Black Political Convention of 1972. The co-chairs of the convention were Detroit Congressman Charles Diggs, Hatcher, and writer Amiri Baraka. Political scientist Ronald Walters, who helped plan the convention, recalled that various ideological factions had to be placated to make it work: "The most important thing about 1972 was the fact that it was an election year, so it provided the environment for the politics taking place. So you had two groups of people who saw this as an opportunity to make some very important statements. One of these, of course, was the black nationalist movement led by Amiri Baraka, Maulana Karenga, and others at that time." The nationalists interpreted "Black Power" to mean that black people should control their own communities and create separate cultural institutions distinct from those of white society. These views clashed with those of the black elected officials represented by Stokes and Hatcher. According to Walters, "It was this body of people who really were contending for the national leadership of the black community in the early seventies. And in the seventies this new group of black elected officials joined the civil rights leaders and became a new leadership class, but there was sort of a conflict in outlook between them and the more indigenous, social, grass roots-oriented nationalist movement."

Hatcher observed that "people had come to Gary from communities all over the United States where they were politically impotent, but . . . they went back home and rolled up their sleeves and dived into the political arena." Approximately 8,000 people gathered to develop an agenda for black empowerment. The discussions about bloc voting, the efficacy of coalitions, and the feasibility of a third party inspired scores of individual African Americans to run for local office. The convention was not homogeneous, however, and no unified black consensus emerged.

Discussions over strategies to secure common interests revealed deep-seated internal divisions that allowed ancillary issues to provoke even more impassioned disagreement. Coleman Young and other Michigan delegates walked out to protest a proposal for African Americans to reject "discriminatory" unions and form their own. Others walked out over a resolution condemning Israel for its "expansionist policy" toward the Palestinians. Others argued that "forced racial integration of schools" through busing insulted black students and would cost black teachers their jobs.

Nonetheless, the Gary convention signaled a shift in the political focus of the black community toward electoral politics and away from mass demonstrations and protests. Unity continued to elude subsequent conventions, however, and delegates at the last National Black Convention at Little Rock, Arkansas, in 1974 abandoned the idea of a black political party. Deep ideological differences and institutional cleavages precluded coalitions and cooperation between black nationalists and the rising numbers of black elected officials. These same differences prevented some nationalists and elected officials from taking seriously the 1972 Democratic Party presidential bid of New York Congresswoman Shirley Chisholm.

22.6.2 Shirley Chisholm: "I Am the People's Politician"

Shirley Anita St. Hill was born on November 20, 1924, in Brooklyn, New York, to Charles St. Hill, a factory laborer from Guyana, and Ruby Seale St. Hill, a seamstress from Barbados. She earned a B.A. from Brooklyn College in sociology in 1946 and worked as a nursery school teacher and then as director of two daycare centers. In 1949 she married Conrad Q. Chisholm, a private investigator. From 1964 to 1968 she served in the New York State Assembly. In 1968 Chisholm defeated James Farmer, former leader of CORE, to become the first African-American woman to serve in Congress. In 1970 she published her first autobiography, *Unbought and Unbossed*. A second autobiography, *The Good Fight* (1973), described her 1972 campaign for the Democratic presidential nomination—during which she received little support from white women's organizations or from black men. Chisholm retired from politics in 1983. In the late 1960s and early 1970s, she remained an outspoken critic of the Vietnam War and a fierce proponent of the war on poverty.

Shirley Chisholm was outspoken against the Vietnam War and a fierce advocate of women's rights.

22.6.3 Black People Gain Local Offices

Despite the demise of the National Black Convention movement, African Americans registered impressive gains in electoral politics. Statistics indicate the success of black politicians. When the leaders first convened the Gary convention, there were 13 African-American members of Congress. By 2010 there were 42. In 1972 there were 2,427 black elected officials, among them Texas state senator Barbara Jordan. By 2001 there were 9,101.

An amendment to the Voting Rights Act in 1975 enabled minorities to challenge at-large voting practices that diluted the impact of bloc voting. This helped increase the number of black elected officials. Districts were redrawn with race as the predominant factor. On November 5, 1985, state senator L. Douglas Wilder was elected lieutenant governor in Virginia, making him the first African-American lieutenant governor in a southern state since Reconstruction. In 1989 he was elected governor, making him the first black governor of any state since Reconstruction.

Voices

Shirley Chisholm's Speech to the U.S. House of Representatives

Excerpts from "The Business of America Is War, and It Is Time for a Change," March 16, 1969

"Secretary of Defense Melvin Laird came to Capitol Hill. . . . His mission was to sell the antiballistic-missile insanity to the Senate. . . . Mr. Laird talked of being prepared to spend at least two more years in Vietnam. Two more years, two more years of hunger for Americans, of death for our best young men, of children here at home suffering the lifelong handicap of not having a good education when they are young.

Two more years of high taxes, collected to feed the cancerous growth of a Defense Department budget that now consumes two-thirds of our federal income. Two more years of too little being done to fight our greatest enemies, poverty, prejudice and neglect, here in our own country. Two more years of fantastic waste in the Defense Department and of penny pinching on social programs. Our country cannot survive two more years, or four, of these kinds of policies. It must stop—this year—now. . . .

We Americans have come to feel that it is our mission to make the world free. We believe that we are the good guys, everywhere—in Vietnam, in Latin America, wherever we go. We believe we are the good guys at home, too. When the Kerner Commission told white America what black America had always known, that prejudice and hatred built the nation's slums, maintain them and profit by them, white America would not believe it. But it is true. Unless we start to fight and defeat the enemies of poverty and racism in our own country and make our talk of equality and opportunity ring true, we are exposed as hypocrites in the eyes of the world when we talk about making other people free.

We are now spending eighty billion dollars a year on defense—that is two-thirds of every tax dollar. At this time, gentlemen, the business of America is war, and it is time for a change."

1. What reasons does Chisholm give for her opposition to the war in Vietnam?

2. What connections does she make to separate the difference between supporting the war on poverty and racism in the United States and the Vietnam War?

SOURCE: Warren J. Halliburton, ed., *Historic Speeches of African Americans* (New York: Franklin Watts, 1993). 141–43.

Between 1971 and 1975, the number of African-American mayors rose from 8 to 135, leading to the founding of the National Conference of Black Mayors in 1974. In 1973 Coleman Young in Detroit and Thomas Bradley in Los Angeles became the first African-American mayors of cities of more than a million citizens. Bradley won in Los Angeles even though black people made up only 15 percent of the city's electorate. Ten years later, in 1983, Chicago swore in its first black mayor, Harold Washington. The era of the black elected official had arrived.

22.6.4 Economic Downturn

The 1970s were a decade of recessions and economic instability. Many black people experienced this economic downturn as a depression. During the 1970s, as the gap between the incomes of the upper 20 percent of African Americans and their white counterparts narrowed, the gap between black men and women at the bottom of the economic ladder and their white counterparts expanded. Poor black people were losing ground. In 1969 approximately 10 percent of white men and 25 percent of black men earned less than $10,000 (in 1984 constant dollars). In 1984 about 40 percent of black men between the ages of 25 and 55 earned less than $10,000 compared with 20 percent of comparable white men. Put a different way, between 1970 and 1986, the proportion of black families with incomes of less than $10,000 grew from 26.8 to 30.2 percent. Still, there were some improvements. The black middle class grew. In 1970, 4.7 percent of black families had incomes of more than $50,000. By 1986 the number had almost doubled to 8.8 percent. But, in general, the relative economic status of black workers did not improve.

22.6.5 Black Americans and the Carter Presidency

In 1976 the United States celebrated its bicentennial. Flags flew and fire hydrants were painted red, white, and blue. Tall ships sailed into New York Harbor from around the world, and there were more parades than anyone could count. For African Americans, it was an important year, but for another reason. For the first time since 1964, the man most of them voted for was elected president—Jimmy Carter, a former governor of Georgia. Ninety percent of African-American voters favored the soft-spoken, religious Democrat over President Gerald Ford. As in 1960, their votes were crucial. Without them, Carter could not have even carried his native South.

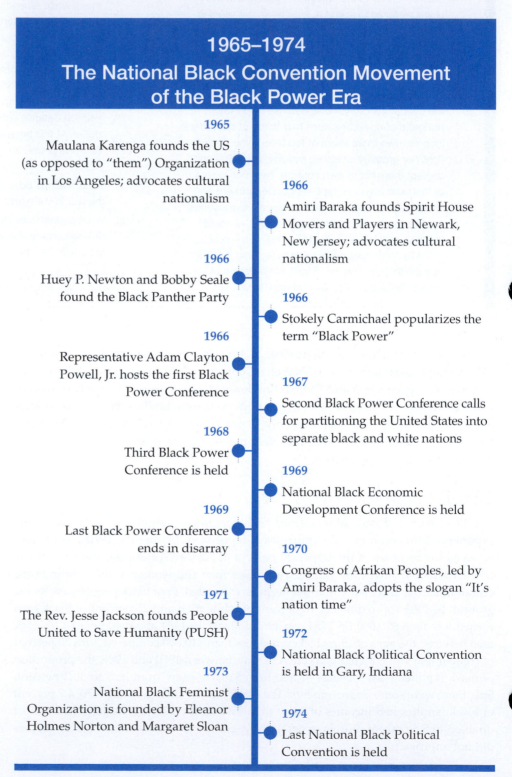

1965–1974
The National Black Convention Movement of the Black Power Era

1965
Maulana Karenga founds the US (as opposed to "them") Organization in Los Angeles; advocates cultural nationalism

1966
Amiri Baraka founds Spirit House Movers and Players in Newark, New Jersey; advocates cultural nationalism

1966
Huey P. Newton and Bobby Seale found the Black Panther Party

1966
Stokely Carmichael popularizes the term "Black Power"

1966
Representative Adam Clayton Powell, Jr. hosts the first Black Power Conference

1967
Second Black Power Conference calls for partitioning the United States into separate black and white nations

1968
Third Black Power Conference is held

1969
National Black Economic Development Conference is held

1969
Last Black Power Conference ends in disarray

1970
Congress of Afrikan Peoples, led by Amiri Baraka, adopts the slogan "It's nation time"

1971
The Rev. Jesse Jackson founds People United to Save Humanity (PUSH)

1972
National Black Political Convention is held in Gary, Indiana

1973
National Black Feminist Organization is founded by Eleanor Holmes Norton and Margaret Sloan

1974
Last National Black Political Convention is held

22.6.6 Black Appointees

Carter acknowledged his debt to the black electorate by appointing African Americans to highly visible posts. He named Patricia Harris secretary of housing and urban development, making her the first black woman to serve in the cabinet. Carter appointed Andrew Young, former congressman from Georgia and a longtime political ally, ambassador to the United Nations. (Young was forced to resign in 1979.) Clifford Alexander, Jr. became the secretary of the army. Eleanor Holmes Norton became the first woman to chair the Equal Employment Opportunity Commission (EEOC). Ernest Green, who had been one of the nine students to desegregate Little Rock's Central High School, was appointed assistant secretary of labor. Wade McCree was appointed solicitor general in the Justice Department. Drew Days III became assistant attorney general for civil rights. Historian and former University of Colorado chancellor Mary Frances Berry was appointed assistant secretary for education. Carter also named Louis Martin his special assistant, making him the first African American in a position of influence on a White House staff.

22.6.7 Carter's Domestic Policies

There are many ways to judge the significance of the Carter presidency to African Americans. Carter's black appointments were practically and symbolically important. Never had so many black men and women occupied positions that had direct and immediate impact on the day-to-day operations of the federal government. Carter also helped cement gains for civil rights. When Congress passed legislation to stop busing for schoolchildren as a means of integrating the schools, Carter vetoed it. He tried to improve fair employment practices by strengthening the powers of the EEOC. His Justice Department chose cases to prosecute under the Fair Housing Act that involved widespread discrimination, to make the greatest possible impact.

Yet most African Americans found Carter's overall record unsatisfactory. He failed to help Democrats in Congress pass either full-employment or universal healthcare bills. Under his watch Congress cut social welfare programs to balance the budget, and the cuts included school lunch programs and student financial aid.

A sluggish economy diminished Carter's popularity, but it was the Iran hostage crisis in 1979 that doomed his chances for reelection. For many black people, Carter had become a disappointment, who had done little to bring about greater social justice and economic advancement. Republicans' nomination of the conservative Ronald Reagan, however, left black voters no alternative to Carter. In the election of 1980, 90 percent of black voters again supported Carter, but could not prevent his defeat.

Conclusion

The Black Power and Black Arts movements continued the struggle for freedom in northern and western cities and states where housing discrimination, high unemployment, and unrelenting police brutality sparked rebellions that resulted in many deaths and widespread destruction in Los Angeles, Newark, Detroit, and other cities. Although African Americans did not create a third party, they were able to elect an impressive number of black mayors and send the first two black women to the United States House of Representatives. Thus, one of the Black Power era's most enduring political legacies was the rise of black elected officials and the perfection of coalition-building.

Clearly the most triumphant dimension of the Black Studies movement was the revolutionary change in academic knowledge and in the expansion of opportunities for black students and professors. Black student militancy resulted in structural changes in the academy with the establishment of Black Studies departments and cultural centers.

The legacies of the Black Panther Party, including its social service experiments in providing free breakfasts to schoolchildren in impoverished communities and operating free healthcare clinics for residents, have yet to be fully appreciated and were often overshadowed by the relentless vilification of party leaders and members by white police authorities and media. Throughout the late 1960s and 1970s, the Black Arts movement opened up new venues for cultivations of black unity and an empowering positive black identity.

The legislative successes of the civil rights movement, the Civil Rights Act of 1964, the Voting Rights Act of 1965, and affirmative action were important steps in the long journey toward an egalitarian society. To varying degrees, Presidents Johnson, Nixon, and Carter attempted to address the needs of the poor. Their efforts produced mixed results, hampered by the disastrous war in Vietnam and massive white backlash against school busing and government-mandated desegregation. In the 1980s, Republicans reaped the benefits of the Democratic Party's disarray, and the plight of the black poor worsened.

Chapter Timeline

AFRICAN-AMERICAN EVENTS	NATIONAL EVENTS
1965–1966	
1965	**1965**
Malcolm X assassinated	President Johnson authorizes the bombing of North Vietnam
Watts riot	
Voting Rights Act of 1965 enacted	**1966**
1966	National Organization for Women (NOW) formed
Black Panther Party formed	
Stokely Carmichael coins the slogan "Black Power"	
Martin Luther King's Chicago campaign begins	
Edward Brooke of Massachusetts elected the first black U.S. senator since Reconstruction	
Robert C. Weaver becomes first black cabinet officer	
Strike at San Francisco State University results in first Black Studies program	
1967–1968	
1967	**1968**
Uprisings in Newark, Detroit, and other cities	North Vietnam launches Tet Offensive
Muhammad Ali refuses to be drafted	United States and North Vietnam begin peace talks
Thurgood Marshall confirmed as first black Supreme Court justice	Johnson declines to run for another term
Adam Clayton Powell, Jr. denied his seat in Congress	Robert Kennedy assassinated
	Richard M. Nixon elected president
	Secret bombing of Cambodia

AFRICAN-AMERICAN EVENTS	NATIONAL EVENTS

1968

Kerner Commission Report

Poor People's Campaign in Washington, D.C.

Orangeburg Massacre, three students killed protesting racial segregation

Martin Luther King, Jr. assassinated

Shirley Chisholm elected to the U.S. House of Representatives

Carl Stokes elected mayor of Cleveland and Richard Hatcher elected mayor of Gary, Indiana

1969–1970

1969

Harvard establishes an Afro-American studies program

Maulana Karenga writes *Introduction to Black Studies*

Black Panther leaders Fred Hampton and Mark Clark killed in Chicago police raid

1970

Jackson State killings

Angela Davis placed on the FBI's Ten Most Wanted list

1970

U.S. incursion into Cambodia

Kent State killings

1971–1972

1971

Jesse Jackson founds PUSH

Busing to achieve integration begins

1972

First National Black Political Convention held in Gary, Indiana

Shirley Chisholm makes a bid for the Democratic presidential nomination

Angela Davis acquitted

1972

Watergate break-in

Nixon reelected president

1973–1974

1973

Thomas Bradley elected mayor of Los Angeles

Coleman Young elected mayor of Detroit

1974

National Council for Black Studies formed

1974

Watergate hearings

Nixon resigns

AFRICAN-AMERICAN EVENTS   NATIONAL EVENTS

1975–1977

1975	1975
Antibusing protests in Boston	South Vietnam falls
1977	1976
Andrew Young named ambassador to the United Nations	Jimmy Carter elected president

Review Questions

1. What were the conditions that provoked African-American rebellions in Watts, Newark, and Detroit in 1965–1967? What did these rebellions suggest about the value of the classic phase of the civil rights movement?

2. How did the visions and ideals, successes and failures of Martin Luther King, Jr. compare with those of Lyndon B. Johnson? Discuss the conflicts between them. Why were these men at odds with each other?

3. What role did African Americans play in the Vietnam War?

4. In what ways can the presidency of Richard Nixon can be considered progressive? Which reforms initiated by President Johnson were supported by President Nixon after he took office? What was "the southern strategy"?

5. What were the major ideological concerns of the artists of the Black Arts movement? To what extent did James Baldwin and Amiri Baraka have similar views about art, consciousness, aesthetics, and politics?

6. What reasons prevented African Americans from forming a third political party during the 1970s? Why were so many African Americans elected to political positions in state and federal governments?

7. Why were African Americans disappointed with the presidency of Jimmy Carter?

Retracing the Odyssey

Motown Museum, Detroit, Michigan. Birthplace of Berry Gordy's Motown Record Corporation, founded in 1957. The "Motown sound" exemplified the music of such performers as the Jackson Five, Gladys Knight and the Pips, Marvin Gaye, and Stevie Wonder. A sign hangs on the front of the structure, "Hitsville U.S.A.," acknowledging the importance of this state historic site. The museum is composed of two adjoining houses filled with memorabilia of gold record awards, album covers, costumes, and musical instruments. Visitors are able to view in Studio A the original control booth where hits by the Temptations, Supremes, and other artists were recorded.

DuSable Museum of African-American History, Chicago. In 1961 artist Margaret Goss Burroughs opened, in her home, the Ebony Museum, which moved in 1973 to its present location at Washington Park. It is now one of the nation's major museums of black history, life, and culture. It houses an extensive collection of artifacts, art, books, and civil rights documents and sponsors a diverse array of cultural and educational programs. The DuSable Museum is named in honor of Jean Baptiste Pointe DuSable, a Haitian-born immigrant who arrived in Chicago in 1779 and was the first non-Indian to settle in the area.

Southern Poverty Law Center Civil Rights Memorial, Montgomery, Alabama. The Civil Rights Memorial captures the history of the freedom struggle while ensuring that we do not forget the costs so many paid in the ongoing struggle against racism and social inequality.

The Martin Luther King, Jr., National Historic Site, Atlanta, Georgia. The district is composed of Martin Luther King's birthplace and gravesite. The Ebenezer Baptist Church, where three generations of King men served as pastors, along with an informative National Park Service Visitors Center, provides a detailed overview of King's life. Also in the district is the Martin Luther King, Jr., Center for Non-Violent Social Change, which contains King's personal papers and the records of the Southern Christian Leadership Conference in addition to an oral history collection.

The Vietnam Veterans Memorial, Washington, D.C. The memorial contains all of the names of Americans who lost their lives in the Vietnam War.

Recommended Reading

Martha Biondi. *The Black Revolution on Campus.* Berkeley: University of California Press, 2012. Essential reading for a comprehensive understanding of the Black Studies movement.

Stokely Carmichael and Charles V. Hamilton. *Black Power: The Politics of Liberation in America.* New York: Vintage Books, 1967. One of the most important books of the era of Black Power.

Robert Dallek. *Flawed Giant: Lyndon Johnson and His Times, 1961–1973.* New York: Oxford University Press, 1998. A definitive biography of Lyndon Johnson with fresh insights, grounded in exhaustive research.

Henry Hampton and Steve Fayer, eds. *Voices of Freedom: An Oral History of the Civil Rights Movement from the 1950s Through the 1980s.* New York: Bantam Books, 1990. Contains the recollections of the key participants in the critical battles and movements of the three decades that transformed race relations in America.

Michael D. Harris. *Colored Pictures: Race and Visual Representation.* Chapel Hill: University of North Carolina Press, 2003. A splendid study of how race has been represented and visualized, with insightful analyses of arts movements and informative discussions of black painters.

Lance Hill. *The Deacons for Defense: Armed Resistance and the Civil Rights Movement.* Chapel Hill: University of North Carolina Press, 2004. An excellent contribution to Black Power studies. This is a well-researched and detailed analysis of an important, but often overlooked, organization of armed for self-defense black working-class activist leaders.

Hasan Kwame Jeffries. *Bloody Lowndes: Civil Rights and Black Power in Alabama's Black Belt.* New York: New York University Press, 2009. An essential and important study. It is a thorough, illuminating, and persuasively argued study of the Lowndes County Freedom Organization.

Jama Lazerow and Yohuru Williams, editors. *In Search of the Black Panther Party: New Perspectives on Revolutionary Movement.* Durham, NC: Duke University Press, 2006. A valuable collection of essays providing an overview of the critical intellectual shifts in our understanding of the Black Panther Party.

Alondra Nelson. *Body and Soul: The Black Panther Party and the Fight Against Medical Discrimination.* Minneapolis: University of Minnesota Press, 2011. A remarkable, well-researched, insightful study of the healthcare advocacy work of the Black Panther Party. A valuable addition to black studies scholarship.

Wallace Terry. *Bloods: An Oral History of the Vietnam War by Black Veterans.* New York: Ballantine Books, 1984. One of the best sources for firsthand accounts of the Vietnam War as experienced by black soldiers.

Craig Hansen Werner. *Playing the Changes: From Afro-Modernism to the Jazz Impulse.* Urbana: University of Illinois Press, 1994. An insightful study of the gospel, blues, and jazz impulse among key black writers, including James Baldwin and Leon Forrest, during the post–civil rights movement era.

Additional Bibliography

The Black Panther Party

Curtis J. Austin. *Up Against the Wall: Violence in the Making and Unmaking of the Black Panther Party.* Fayetteville: University of Arkansas Press, 2006.

Joshua Bloom and Waldo Martin, Jr. *Black Against Empire: The History and Politics of the Black Panther Party.* Berkeley: University of California Press, 2013.

Lucas Burke and Judson Jeffries. *The Portland Black Panthers: Empowering Albina and Remaking a City.* Seattle: University of Washington Press, 2016.

Philip S. Foner, ed. *The Black Panther Speaks.* Philadelphia: Lippincott, 1970.

Toni Morrison, ed. *To Die for the People: The Writings of Huey P. Newton.* New York: Writers and Readers Publishing, 1995.

Kenneth O'Reilly. *Racial Matters: The FBI's Secret File on Black America, 1960–1972.* New York: Free Press, 1989.

Ibram H. Rogers. *The Black Campus Movement: Black Students and the Racial Reconstitution of Higher Education, 1965–1972.* New York: Palgrave/Macmillan, 2012.

Robert Scheer, ed. *Eldridge Cleaver: Post-Prison Writings and Speeches.* New York: Random House, 1969.

Jacobi Williams. *From the Bullet to the Ballot: The Illinois Chapter of the Black Panther Party and Racial Coalition Politics in Chicago.* Chapel Hill: University of North Carolina Press, 2013.

Black Nationalism, Black Power, and Black Politics

Robert L. Allen. *Black Awakening in Capitalist America*. Trenton, NJ: Africa World Press, 1990.

Elaine Brown. *A Taste of Power: A Black Woman's Story*. New York: Pantheon, 1992.

Robert Carr. *Black Nationalism in the New World: Reading the African-American and West Indian Experience*. Durham, NC: Duke University Press, 2002.

Zoe A. Colley. *Ain't Scared of Your Jail: Arrest, Imprisonment, and the Civil Rights Movement*. Gainesville: University of Florida Press, 2012.

James H. Cone. *Martin & Malcolm & America: A Dream or a Nightmare*. Maryknoll, NY: Orbis, 1991.

Theodore Cross. *The Black Power Imperative: Racial Inequality and the Politics of Nonviolence*. New York: Faulkner Books, 1984.

Sidney Fine. *Violence in the Model City: The Cavanagh Administration, Race Relations and the Detroit Riot of 1967*. Ann Arbor: University of Michigan Press, 1989.

James F. Finley, Jr. *Church People in the Struggle: The National Council of Churches and the Black Freedom Movement, 1950–1970*. New York: Oxford University Press, 1993.

Wesley C. Hogan. *Many Minds, One Heart: SNCC'S Dream for a New America*. Chapel Hill: University of North Carolina Press, 2007.

Richard Iton. *In Search of the Black Fantastic: Politics and Popular Culture in the Post-Civil Rights Era (Transgressing Boundaries Series: Studies in Black Politics and Black Communities)*. New York: Oxford University Press, 2008.

Peniel E. Joseph. *Waiting 'til the Midnight Hour: A Narrative History of Black Power in America*. New York: Henry Holt, 2006.

B. I. Kaufman. *The Presidency of James Earl Carter, Jr.* Lawrence: University Press of Kansas, 1993.

Steven Lawson. *In Pursuit of Power: Southern Blacks and Electoral Politics, 1965–1982*. New York: Columbia University Press, 1985.

Manning Marable. "On Malcolm X: His Message & Meaning." *Open Magazine Pamphlet Series*. Westfield, NJ, November 1992.

Manning Marable. *Malcolm X: A Life of Reinvention*. New York: Viking Press, 2011.

Gordan A. Martin, Jr. *Count Them One by One: Black Mississippians Fighting for the Right to Vote*. Jackson: University of Mississippi Press, 2010.

John T. McCartney. *Black Power Ideologies: An Essay in African-American Thought*. Philadelphia: Temple University Press, 1992.

J. Todd Moye. *Let the People Decide: Black Freedom and White Resistance in Sunflower County*. Chapel Hill: University of North Carolina Press, 2004.

Larry G. Murphy. *Down by the Riverside: Readings in African American Religion*. New York: New York University Press, 2000.

William E. Nelson, Jr., and Philip J. Meranto. *Electing Black Mayors: Political Action in the Black Community*. Columbus: Ohio State University Press, 1977.

Robert A. Pratt. *The Color of Their Skin: Education and Race in Richmond, Virginia, 1954–89*. Charlottesville: University Press of Virginia, 1992.

James R. Ralph, Jr. *Northern Protest: Martin Luther King, Jr., Chicago, and the Civil Rights Movement*. Cambridge, MA: Harvard University Press, 1993.

Wilbur C. Rich. *Coleman Young and Detroit Politics*. Detroit, MI: Wayne State University Press, 1989.

Bobby Seale. *Seize the Time*. New York: Random House, 1970.

Cleveland Sellers, with Robert Terrell. *The River of No Return: The Autobiography of a Black Militant and the Life and Death of SNCC*. New York: William Morrow, 1987.

Stephen G. N. Tuck. *Beyond Atlanta: The Struggle for Racial Equality in Georgia, 1940–1980*. Athens: University of Georgia Press, 2001.

James Melvin Washington. *Frustrated Fellowship: The Black Baptist Quest for Social Power*. Macon, GA: Mercer University Press, 1986.

Michael Vinson Williams. *Medgar Evers: Mississippi Martyr*. Fayetteville: University of Arkansas Press, 2011.

Gayraud S. Wilmore. *Black Religion and Black Radicalism*. New York: Anchor Press, 1973.

Black Studies and Black Students

Talmadge Anderson, ed. *Black Studies: Theory, Method, and Cultural Perspectives*. Pullman: Washington State University Press, 1990.

Jack Bass and Jack Nelson. *The Orangeburg Massacre*. 1970. New ed. Mason, GA: Mercer University Press, 2003.

William H. Exum. *Paradoxes of Protest: Black Student Activism in a White University*. Philadelphia: Temple University Press, 1985.

Richard P. McCormick. *The Black Student Protest Movement at Rutgers*. New Brunswick, NJ: Rutgers University Press, 1990.

Albert L. Samuels. *Is Separate Unequal?: Black Colleges and the Challenge to Desegregation*. Lawrence: University Press of Kansas, 2004.

Jack Shuler. *Blood and Bone: Truth and Reconciliation in a Southern Town*. Columbia: University of South Carolina Press, 2012.

Derrick E. White. *The Challenge of Blackness: The Institute of the Black World and Political Activism in the 1970s.* Gainesville: University of Florida Press, 2011.

Class, Race, and Gender

Michelle Alexander. *The New Jim Crow: Mass Incarceration in the Age of Colorblindness.* New York: The New Press, 2010.

Jack M. Bloom. *Class, Race, and the Civil Rights Movement.* Bloomington: Indiana University Press, 1987.

Martin Gilens. *Why Americans Hate Welfare: Race, Media, and the Politics of Antipoverty Policy.* Chicago: University of Chicago Press, 1999.

Cheryl Higashia. *Black Internationalist Feminism: Women Writers of the Black Left, 1945–1995.* Urbana: University of Illinois Press, 2011.

Faith S. Holsaert, Martha Prescod Norman Noonan, Judy Richardson, Betty Garman Robinson, Jean Smith Young, Dorothy M. Zellner, eds. *Hands on the Freedom Plow: Personal Accounts by Women in SNCC.* Urbana: University of Illinois Press, 2010.

Bart Landry. *The New Black Middle Class.* Berkeley: University of California Press, 1987.

Mary Pattillo. *Black Picket Fences: Privilege and Peril Among the Black Middle Class.* Chicago: University of Chicago Press, 1999.

Shirley Sherrod with Catherine Whitney. *The Courage to Hope: How I Stood Up to the Politics of Fear.* New York: Atria Books, 2012.

Kimberly Springer. *Living for the Revolution: Black Feminist Organizations, 1968–1980.* Durham, NC: Duke University Press, 2005.

Heather Ann Thompson. *Whose Detroit?: Politics, Labor, and Race in a Modern American City.* Ithaca, NY: Cornell University Press, 2001.

Black Arts and Black Consciousness Movements

James Baldwin. *Notes of a Native Son.* New York: Dial Press, 1955.

_____. *Nobody Knows My Name.* New York: Dial Press, 1961.

_____. *The Fire Next Time.* New York: Dial Press, 1963.

_____. *No Name in the Street.* New York: Dial Press, 1972.

Imamu Amiri Baraka. *Dutchman and the Slave: Two Plays by LeRoi Jones.* New York: William Morrow, 1964.

Samuel A. Hay. *African American Theater: An Historical and Critical Analysis.* Cambridge, MA: Cambridge University Press, 1994.

LeRoi Jones and Larry Neal, eds. *Black Fire: An Anthology of Afro-American Writing.* New York: William Morrow, 1968.

Robin D. G. Kelley. *Thelonious Monk: The Life and Times of an American Original.* New York: Free Press, 2010.

Larry Neal. *Visions of a Liberated Future: Black Arts Movement Writings.* New York: Thunder's Mouth Press, 1989.

Suzanne E. Smith. *Dancing in the Streets: Motown and the Cultural Politics of Detroit.* Cambridge, MA: Harvard University Press, 2000.

Brian Ward. *Just My Soul Responding: Rhythm and Blues, Black Consciousness, and Race Relations.* Berkeley: University of California Press, 1998.

Autobiography and Biography

Imamu Amiri Baraka. *The Autobiography of LeRoi Jones.* New York: Freundlich Books, 1984.

John Carlos and Dave Zirvin; Foreword by Cornel West. *The John Carlos Story: The Sports Moment That Changed the World.* Chicago: Haymarket Books, 2011.

Stokely Carmichael, with Ekwume Michael Thewell. *Ready for Revolution: The Life and Struggles of Stokely Carmichael (Kwame Ture).* New York: Scribner, 2003.

Shirley Chisholm. *Unbought and Unbossed.* Boston: Houghton Mifflin, 1970.

_____. *The Good Fight.* New York: Harper & Row, 1973.

James Farmer. *Lay Bare the Heart: An Autobiography of the Civil Rights Movement.* New York: Arbor House, 1985.

Marshall Frady. *Jesse: The Life and Pilgrimage of Jesse Jackson.* New York: Random House, 1996.

Jimmie Lewis Franklin. *Back to Birmingham: Richard Arrington, Jr., and His Times.* Tuscaloosa: University of Alabama Press, 1989.

Elliott J. Gorn, ed. *Muhammad Ali: The People's Champ.* Urbana: University of Illinois Press, 1995.

Charles V. Hamilton. *Adam Clayton Powell, Jr.: The Political Biography of an American Dilemma.* New York: Atheneum, 1991.

Samuel A. Hay. *Ed Bullins: A Literary Biography.* Detroit, MI: Wayne State University Press, 1997.

Wil Haygood. *King of the Cats: The Life and Times of Adam Clayton Powell, Jr.* Boston: Houghton Mifflin, 1993.

David Remnick. *King of the World: Muhammad Ali and the Rise of an American Hero.* New York: Random House, 1998.

Mary Beth Rogers. *Barbara Jordan: American Hero.* New York: Bantam Books, 1998.

Kathleen Rout. *Eldridge Cleaver.* Boston: Twayne, 1991.

Bobby Seale. *Seize the Time.* New York: Random House, 1970.

Nancy J. Weiss. *Whitney M. Young, Jr., and the Struggle for Civil Rights.* Princeton, NJ: Princeton University Press, 1989.

Chapter 23

Black Politics and President Barack Obama

1980–2016

President Barack Obama enjoys a respite from battles with Republican congressmen over universal health care to play football with the family dog, Bo (May 12, 2009).

 Learning Objectives

After reading this chapter, you should be able to:

23.1   Discuss the evolution of Jesse Jackson's rise to prominence within the Democratic Party.

23.2   Analyze the strategies devised by Presidents Reagan and Bush to dismantle the "Great Society" and to diminish social welfare programs.

23.3   Identify some of the key roles that black conservatives played in the Republican Party from the 1990s to the present.

23.4 Distinguish some of the major differences between the "old" and the "new" civil rights.

23.5 Identify the focal points of black activism during the Reagan and Bush presidencies.

23.6 Explain how general white perceptions of young black men affected trends in criminal justice during the closing decade of the twentieth century and the opening decades of the twenty-first century.

23.7 Analyze the reasons why African Americans remained supportive of Bill Clinton's presidency and sustained loyalty to the Democratic Party.

23.8 Evaluate the significance of the events of 9/11, the wars in Iraq and Afghanistan, Hurricane Katrina, and the election of President Barack Obama on black political consciousness.

23.9 Discuss the ways in which the reelection of President Obama represented a triumph of black politics.

23.10 Explain the emergence of the Black Lives Matter movement and its significance.

If there is anyone out there who still doubts that America is a place where all things are possible, who still wonders if the dream of our founders is alive in our time, who still questions the power of our democracy, tonight is your answer. . . . This is our time, to put our people back to work and open doors of opportunity for our kids; to restore prosperity and promote the cause of peace; to reclaim the American dream and reaffirm that fundamental truth, that, out of many, we are one; that while we breathe, we hope. And where we are met with cynicism and doubts and those who tell us that we can't, we will respond with that timeless creed that sums up the spirit of a people: Yes, we can.

—*Barack Obama, from his victory speech on November 4, 2008, Chicago, Illinois*

The evolution of black politics from the passage of the Voting Rights Act of 1965 to the election in 2008 and reelection in 2012 of the first African American president of the United States, Barack Obama, was the culmination of decades of struggle for social justice, economic fairness, and political empowerment. In the 1970s African Americans began to elect significant numbers of elected officials on local and state levels. Especially noteworthy was the election of numerous black mayors and state legislators. Clearly black voting in the aftermath of the civil rights movement consolidated in support of the Democratic Party. Black voters pushed for policies to strengthen their communities. The excitement generated by Jesse Jackson's two attempts to win the Democratic Party's nomination for president in 1984 and 1988 and the efforts to mobilize black communities had an impact on local, state, and national politics.

An equally important development in black politics was the rise to prominence of a significant, highly visible number of black conservatives within the Republican Party; in a completely unexpected way, the presidential election of 2008 represented the triumph of black politics. No one could have predicted the election of a relatively unknown African-American senator from Illinois, Barack Hussein Obama, would become the nation's first African-American president of the United States and that, moreover, he would win in 2012 a second term.

While more than 90 percent of black voters supported President Obama's re-election in 2012, black progressives debated whether he had significantly improved the lives of black people. A few questioned and debated why limited progress was made on issues including chronic economic distress and relentless political assaults (such as the adoption by over 30 states of legislation that operated to restrict black voting).

Among many issues of concern during President Obama's second term revolved around the large number of police killings of black men and boys and the prominence of environmental racism, most notably the Toxic Water Crisis in Flint, Michigan, that endangered the health of thousands of poor black residents and their children.

23.1 Jesse Jackson and the Rainbow Coalition

Discuss the evolution of Jesse Jackson's rise to prominence within the Democratic Party.

In 1983, Jesse Jackson announced his campaign for the presidency of the United States. The first African American to seek the presidential nomination of a major political party had been Congresswoman Shirley Chisholm in 1972. Chisholm had little money and only a small organization. Neither her male competitors nor the press took her seriously. Her campaign, nonetheless, helped raise the visibility of African-American voters. Although Chisholm won more than 150 votes on the first ballot at the Democratic National Convention, in the male-dominated world of presidential politics, a black man was considered a more credible contender.

Jackson's preparation for political battle was not the traditional climb from one elective office to another. Rather, he arose through the ranks of the civil rights movement, working alongside Martin Luther King, Jr. in the Southern Christian Leadership Conference and heading Operation Breadbasket, an organization that mobilized Chicago's black poor. After King's death, Jackson had founded People United to Save (later Serve) Humanity (PUSH). This Chicago-based organization induced major corporations with large markets in the black community to adopt affirmative action programs. PUSH/Excel, which focused on education, succeeded in raising students' test scores, and the Carter administration gave it a large grant. In 1983, angered by Ronald Reagan's social welfare and civil rights rollbacks, Jackson and PUSH began a drive to register black voters. Jackson's charismatic style engendered enthusiasm, especially as the Democrats searched for a presidential candidate who could challenge Reagan in 1984.

On November 4, 1983, Jackson declared his candidacy for the Democratic nomination and honed an effective style of grassroots mobilization. He began by appealing to what he would call a "rainbow coalition" of people who felt politically marginalized and underrepresented. The **Rainbow Coalition** was composed of diverse groups, including black people, white workers, liberals, Latinos, feminists, students, and environmentalists. Jackson developed a comprehensive economic policy focusing on tax reform, deficit reduction, and employment. The centerpiece of his plan was "Rebuilding America," a program to coordinate government, business, and labor in a national industrial policy. The Jackson platform was well within the tradition of American liberal reform but far more progressive than anything his competitors proposed. In January 1984, Jackson gained credentials in international affairs when he traveled to Syria to plead for the release of U.S. Air Force pilot Robert Goodman, who had been held captive there for a year after being shot down in Syrian-controlled airspace. Jackson returned to America in triumph with the freed pilot.

Rainbow Coalition

Political coalition of African Americans, workers, liberals, feminists, gay people, environmentalists, and others formed by Jesse Jackson in the 1980s.

Jackson eventually garnered almost one-fourth of the votes in the Democratic primaries and caucuses and one-eighth of the delegates to the convention. His speech to the convention cemented his position as a voice for progressive change and a spiritual heir to both Martin Luther King, Jr. and Robert Kennedy. Walter Mondale, Jimmy Carter's vice president, who won the nomination, broke new ground when he made Congresswoman Geraldine Ferraro his running mate and the first woman on a major party's presidential ticket. But many Jackson supporters had hoped Mondale would pick Jackson.

In November 1984, black voters overwhelmingly favored the Democratic ticket, but Reagan nonetheless won by a landslide. Mondale carried only his home state of Minnesota and the largely black District of Columbia. Clearly, most white Americans backed Reagan's conservative policies. Undeterred by defeat, Jackson worked to build his Rainbow Coalition, reaching out to a variety of constituencies, including the unemployed, militant trade unionists, small farmers, and gay, lesbian, bisexual, and transgender communities. Perhaps most important, Jackson's campaign registered enough new voters to help Democrats retain control of the House of Representatives in 1984 and regain a majority in the Senate in the 1986 midterm elections.

By the time Jackson announced he would again run for president in October 1987, he had become a serious contender. He won 15 presidential primaries and caucuses and garnered seven million votes, one-third of all those cast. His Rainbow Coalition, however, never materialized. His victories in the primaries were based on mobilizing his black supporters. Almost all of his white support tended to come from college towns. Jackson's campaign strategies, nevertheless, were a precursor to those devised by the strategists for Barack Obama in 2008.

Despite Jackson's voter registration drives and the hopes of the black community, Reagan's vice president, George H. W. Bush, triumphed in the 1988 election. Bush's call for "a kinder, gentler America" was belied by the most memorable feature of his campaign, a polarizing television ad that featured Willie Horton, a black convict who had raped a white woman while on furlough from a Massachusetts prison as part of a program approved both by Bush's opponent Governor Michael Dukakis and his Republican predecessor as governor. Jackson and other black leaders attacked the ad as a blatant appeal to white racism, but it helped elect Bush.

Black support for the Democrats solidified as a resurgent, more conservative, increasingly southern-dominated Republican Party fought to roll back the progress that civil rights leaders and activists had won in the 1950s and 1960s. Republican resurgence was aided by the cultivation of a small but prominent cadre of black neoconservatives. The overwhelming mass of black voters, however, remained bound to the Democratic Party and helped elect William Jefferson Clinton president both in 1992 and in 1996. Clinton used political appointments and symbolism to maintain black allegiance even as he pursued some policies that black people rejected. Even though Republican George W. Bush would appoint several African-American conservatives to his cabinets between 2001 and 2008, most black people remained solidly committed to the Democratic Party.

23.1.1 Black Voters Embrace President Bill Clinton

African Americans anticipated that the Clinton victory in 1992 represented the solidification of the Rainbow Coalition of progressive forces that Jesse Jackson had championed. Clinton was

In 1988 Rev. Jesse Jackson addressed the Democratic National Convention. He made two unsuccessful bids for the White House (1984 and 1988) but remained a powerful force in the Democratic Party because of his success in registering and mobilizing voters and building coalitions.

undoubtedly a friend to African Americans, but many of their hopes were only partly fulfilled. Yet as Donna Brazile—who had worked in Jesse Jackson's campaign and who, in 2000, would manage Al Gore's doomed race for the White House—asserted, the Clinton 1990s appeared to be a new era of black power. In retrospect, given what occurred under President George W. Bush, this may have been true. The conservative triumph in the 2000 and 2004 elections caused many African-American leaders to reassess black political strategies. The NAACP and other social justice and civil rights organizations crafted a broad national and international political agenda during the 2004 presidential race. A new generation of black politicians, such as Barack Obama of Illinois and Governor Deval Patrick of Massachusetts, addressed the economic, healthcare, education, and security concerns of black and white America in a healing new centrist voice. The 2008 victory that catapulted Barack Obama into the White House represented the triumph of "Rainbow Coalition" building. The radical right Tea Party faction of the Republican Party won enough local elections to regain control of the House of Representatives and pursue a strategy of obstruction that derailed many of the initiatives that the Obama administration advocated to address the country's fiscal crisis.

The third phase of black politics helped to elect Barack Obama to the presidency and preserved a Democratic Party majority in the U.S. Senate. In both his 2008 and 2012 election campaigns, Obama won in no small part because he successfully mobilized black and Latino voters. Obama represented a new type of black leader, one who, as some argued, was "post-black" or "post-race," who represented a shift from "color-blind politics" or "pluralism" to a politics of "hybridity." Both of his presidential campaigns were supported by a majority of racial minority, women, and gay voters.

23.1.2 The Present Status of Black Politics

In 2007 Senator Barack Obama of Illinois launched his campaign to become the Democratic presidential candidate, challenging Americans to embrace audacity and hope in the face of mounting despair and economic anguish. The closing decades of the twentieth century were characterized by sharp divisions between white and black Americans and between the Democratic and Republican parties, and by growing economic disparities between working-class and middle-class Americans and the rich. The conservative right used these years to create political organizations that supported school prayer, attacked women's reproductive rights and their right to choose, and denied the civil rights claims of gays, lesbians, and bisexual and transgendered Americans.

Throughout the 1980s white conservatives had nurtured and mobilized their base of disillusioned southerners, alienated northerners, and wealthy elites to reverse liberal-progressive policies such as affirmative action and reforms epitomized by the Voting Rights Act of 1965. African Americans, throughout the presidencies of Ronald Reagan and George H. W. Bush (1981–1993), witnessed a consolidation of Republican Party power. Black American leaders and community activists developed and adhered to a liberal-progressive agenda that emphasized jobs, universal healthcare, and access to better education, environmental justice, and freedom of opportunity. African Americans did not develop a race-conscious third party movement. Instead, black voters overwhelmingly put their hopes in the Democratic Party.

To be sure, the access to greater opportunities in education and employment helped to fuel growing divisions within black America. Not all black Americans benefited equally from the gains of the civil rights movement. Fractures along class lines within the black community became more visible. While the ranks of the urban black poor swelled, the growing black middle and upper class embraced electoral politics to win a greater share in America's educational, social, and political institutions.

By 2000, a white conservative backlash, combined with inadequate housing, lack of health insurance, resource-starved schools, and reduced funding for welfare and job training programs, dampened the expectations and damaged the health and dignity of many poorer black people. Neither Democrats nor Republicans supported massive urban development and jobs programs for black citizens comparable to the Marshall Plan that had helped rebuild Europe after World War II. In sum, as scholar Nikhil Pal Singh noted, "Despite the growth of a black middle class [during the prosperous 1990s], three decades after the passage of the Civil Rights Act the median net worth of whites—which includes inherited assets as well as income—is a staggering twelve times that of blacks." To be sure, the 2008–2010 recession delivered a major blow to black people in every income bracket, although those in service professions and holding low-skilled jobs fared far worse. The high unemployment of black female-headed households and the so-called welfare-reform policies pursued during the Clinton presidency especially devastated families and communities.

23.2 Ronald Reagan and the Conservative Reaction

Analyze the strategies devised by Presidents Reagan and Bush to dismantle the "Great Society" and to diminish social welfare programs.

Just as African Americans began mobilizing their communities for full participation in the country's political life in the late 1970s, American politics took a hard turn to the right. This shift had a devastating impact on African Americans, particularly the poor. With the 1980 election of Ronald Reagan (1911–2004) to the presidency, the executive branch sought to curtail civil rights. It reduced welfare programs and staffed key agencies and the federal judiciary with opponents of affirmative action. An overwhelmingly white Republican Party became increasingly entrenched in the South and ended the Democratic Party's long dominance. The political landscape of the 1980s and 1990s was thus marked by a hardening of ideological conflict between liberal and progressive Democrats on one side and conservative, indeed radical, Republicans on the other.

Ronald Reagan's defeat of Jimmy Carter paved the way for the dominance of the New Right. Reagan possessed charm and the ability to communicate with the American people. His election, however, was the result of more than just personal charisma. Powerful conservative political organizations found a home in the Republican Party. These groups were opposed to equal rights for women, especially their reproductive rights. They sought to overturn Supreme Court decisions protecting the rights of the accused and prohibiting compulsory prayer from the public schools. Many white southerners opposed labor unions, and they joined forces with white northerners who objected to school busing, affirmative action programs, and the tax burden they associated with welfare and entitlement policies.

23.2.1 The King Holiday

Many African Americans invested symbolic importance in making Martin Luther King, Jr.'s birthday a national holiday, elevating him to the stature of George Washington and Abraham Lincoln, both of whom are honored with a holiday. At first Reagan resisted the idea, but he eventually gave in to pressure from African Americans and their white allies. On January 20, 1985, the United States officially observed Martin Luther King, Jr. Day for the first time. In 2011 President Barack Obama unveiled the Martin Luther King, Jr. statue, the first African-American monument on the Washington National Mall.

23.2.2 Dismantling the Great Society

One of the New Right's chief goals was to dismantle the social welfare programs created during and after the New Deal and Johnson's Great Society. From 1981 to 1992, Reagan and George H. W. Bush halved federal grants to cities. As the federal government slashed funds for redeveloping inner cities and constructing public housing between 1980 and 1992, the percentage of city budgets derived from funds from the federal government declined from 14.3 percent to 5 percent. As a result, inner-city neighborhoods where 56 percent of poor residents were African Americans became more unstable. Reagan advanced a trickle-down theory of economics. He believed that if the wealthiest Americans got richer, their increased prosperity and the spending associated with it would percolate through the middle and working classes to benefit the poor. Unemployment statistics soon challenged this theory. By December 1982, the unemployment rate had risen to 10.8 percent, and the rate for African Americans was twice that of white Americans. The annual income of the highest-paid 1 percent of the nation, meanwhile, increased from $312,206 to $548,970 by 1988 (the equivalent of over $1,190,000 a year in 2012).

Reagan and Bush often cloaked their intent to undermine rights-oriented policies by appointing black conservatives to key positions. Reagan chose William Bell, for example, to replace Eleanor Holmes Norton as chair of the Equal Employment Opportunity Commission (EEOC). Bell had few qualifications for the post, and civil rights organizations protested his appointment. Reagan simply replaced Bell the following year with yet another black conservative, Clarence Thomas, who opposed affirmative action. Thomas reduced the commission's staff and allowed the backlog of affirmative action cases to grow to 46,000 and the processing time for a case to increase to 10 months.

Reagan tried to change the direction of the U.S. Commission on Civil Rights (CCR), but in this case he met with resistance. Since its creation in 1957, the commission had been a civil rights watchdog, with no real enforcement powers but with some influence on public opinion. Soon after Reagan took office, the CCR began to issue reports critical of his civil rights policies. Reagan responded by appointing commissioners sympathetic to his perspective. He replaced the commission's chair, Arthur S. Flemming, who was white, with a black Republican, Clarence Pendleton, former executive director of the San Diego Urban League. The vice chair, however, was Mary Frances Berry, a respected civil rights activist and historian whom Carter had appointed and who frequently clashed with the new president. In 1984 Reagan tried to remove Berry from the CCR, but she sued to retain her position. When she won, she became known as "the woman the president could not fire." Nevertheless, the CCR soon declined to insignificance.

23.3 Black Conservatives

Identify some of the key roles that black conservatives played in the Republican Party from the 1990s to the present.

William Bell, Clarence Thomas, and Clarence Pendleton were members of a vocal cadre of black, middle-class, conservative intellectuals, professionals, and politicians who came to prominence during the Reagan years. To augment their influence, the Republican Party nurtured a small, well-educated, articulate cadre of black men and women intellectuals that included Thomas Sowell, Walter Williams, Shelby Steele, Armstrong Williams, Ward Connerly, and, until he broke with them in the late 1990s, Glenn Loury. There was a critical difference, however, between elite black Republican and black Democratic politicians: black Republicans rarely exercised meaningful power within their party. They were expected to embrace the values and support the goals of the white party leaders. In contrast, black Democratic politicians could and often did make their influence felt. Moreover, black Democrats represented a large and essential constituency within the party. Following Obama's victory in 2008, the Republican Party elected black conservative Michael Steele as chair of the Republican National Committee to create an illusion of racial inclusion within the party. Steele was replaced in 2011 by an even more conservative white chairman who was more closely aligned with the Tea Party insurgents.

23.3.1 The Thomas–Hill Controversy

The role of black conservatives was highlighted when, in 1991, President George H. W. Bush nominated Clarence Thomas to the Supreme Court. Thomas was born in 1948 in rural Georgia. He graduated from Holy Cross College in Massachusetts and Yale Law School. The symbolism of Thomas, who opposed the expansion of civil rights, replacing Thurgood Marshall, the greatest civil rights lawyer of the twentieth century, could not have been more dramatic.

As a justice on the U.S. Supreme Court, Clarence Thomas has staunchly adhered to conservative values in all of his opinions.

Thomas's nomination precipitated a public display of gender conflict within the black community. While Marshall had been one of the Court's great liberals and a staunch defender of civil rights, Thomas was a black conservative whose record on civil rights did not endear him either to white liberals or many within the black community. His credentials for the Court were questioned. He had served only 15 months as an appellate court judge. Nevertheless, the black community was loath to openly contest his nomination or to challenge the cynical tokenism of the Bush administration. Some civil rights organizations expressed reservations about the Thomas nomination. The Urban League shrewdly declared, "We welcome the appointment of an African-American jurist to fill the vacant seat left by Justice [Thurgood] Marshall. Obviously, Judge Thomas is no Justice Marshall. But if he were, this administration would not have appointed him. We are hopeful that Judge Thomas's background of poverty and minority status will lead him to greater identification with those in America who today are victimized by poverty and discrimination. And [we] expect the Senate, in the confirmation hearings, to explore whether he is indeed likely to do so."

The anticipated easy confirmation process derailed when black law professor Anita Hill appeared before the Senate Judiciary Committee, which heard testimony on Thomas's confirmation. Hill accused Thomas of sexually harassing her when she worked for him at the EEOC.

Both Anita Hill and Clarence Thomas were conservative Republicans, and both had earned law degrees at Yale. Hill did not volunteer to testify about Thomas's sexual harassment. She had answered questions put to her in a

Anita Hill, a law professor at the University of Oklahoma, testified before the U.S. Senate Judiciary Committee confirmation hearings that Supreme Court nominee Clarence Thomas had sexually harassed her. Thomas was confirmed in spite of these sexual harassment charges.

Voices

Black Women in Defense of Themselves

Days after Anita Hill appeared before the Senate Judiciary Committee, a group of black women led by Elsa Barkley Brown, Barbara Ransby, and Deborah King raised more than $50,000 to print this statement in the New York Times, *"In Defense of Ourselves." Appearing on November 17, 1991, it was signed by 1,603 black women. Five black newspapers—the* San Francisco Sun Reporter, *the* Los Angeles Sentinel, *the* New York City Sun, *the* Atlanta Inquirer, *and the* Chicago Defender— *also published the declaration.*

As women of African descent, we are deeply troubled by the recent nomination, confirmation and seating of Clarence Thomas as an Associate Justice of the U.S. Supreme Court. We know that the presence of Clarence Thomas on the Court will be continually used to divert attention away from the historic struggles for social justice through suggestions that the presence of a Black man on the Supreme Court constitutes an assurance that the rights of African Americans will be protected. Clarence Thomas's public record is ample evidence that this will not be true. Further, the consolidation of a conservative majority on the Supreme Court endangers the working class people and the elderly. The seating of Clarence Thomas is an affront not only to African American women and men, but to all people concerned with social justice.

We are particularly outraged by the racist and sexist treatment of Professor Anita Hill, an African American woman who was maligned and castigated for daring to speak publicly of her own experience of sexual abuse. The malicious defamation of Professor Hill insulted all women of African descent and sent a dangerous message to all women who might contemplate a sexual harassment complaint.

We speak here because we recognize that the media are now portraying the Black community as prepared to tolerate the dismantling of affirmative action and the evil of sexual harassment in order to have any Black man on the Supreme Court. We want to make clear that the media have ignored and distorted many African American voices. We will not be silenced.

Many have erroneously portrayed the allegations against Clarence Thomas as an issue of either gender or race. As women of African descent, we understand sexual harassment as both. We further understand that Clarence Thomas outrageously manipulated the legacy of lynching in order to shelter himself from Anita Hill's allegations. To deflect attention away from the reality of sexual abuse in African American women's lives, he trivialized and misrepresented this painful part of African American people's history. This country, which has a long legacy of racism and sexism, has never taken the sexual abuse of Black women seriously. Throughout U.S. history Black women have been sexually stereotyped as immoral, insatiable, perverse, the initiators in all sexual contacts—abusive or otherwise. The common assumption in legal proceedings as well as in the larger society has been that Black women cannot be raped or otherwise sexually abused. As Anita Hill's experience demonstrates, Black women who speak of these matters are not likely to be believed. In 1991, we cannot tolerate this type of dismissal of any one Black woman's experience or this attack upon our collective character without protest, outrage, and resistance.

As women of African descent, we express our vehement opposition to the policies represented by the placement of Clarence Thomas on the Supreme Court. The Bush administration, having obstructed the passage of civil rights legislation, impeded the extension of unemployment compensation, cut student aid and dismantled social welfare programs, has continually demonstrated that it is not operating in our best interests. Nor is this appointee. We pledge ourselves to continue to speak out in defense of one another, in defense of the African American community and against those who are hostile to social justice no matter what color they are. No one will speak for us but ourselves.

---

1. Discuss the rationale offered by African-American women signers of this letter.

2. Analyze the reasons why black women offered to explain the necessity of opposing Thomas's confirmation to the U.S. Supreme Court. Explain why many women were unsympathetic to Thomas's claim that he had been a victim of a "high-tech" lynching.

SOURCE: African American Women in Defense of Ourselves by Elsa Barkley Brown, Barbara Ransby and Deborah King, *New York Times*, November 17, 1991, 53. Reprinted by permission.

confidential investigation. When her answers were leaked to the press, she agreed to appear before the committee. Some senators questioned her character and integrity. Thomas charged that he was a victim of a "high-tech lynching" in the media and that Hill's accusations were false. Although many in the black community supported Thomas, progressive feminists, white liberals, and some black people supported Hill. Activist black women were incensed by the treatment that Hill received from the Senate and were determined to voice their opposition to Thomas's political views. Despite the opposition, Thomas won confirmation to the Court by a narrow 52 to 48 majority. On the Court, Justice Thomas remains an archconservative who unwaveringly votes with the conservative majority. He adamantly opposes affirmative action.

23.4 Debating the "Old" and the "New" Civil Rights

Distinguish some of the major differences between the "old" and the "new" civil rights.

The Reagan and Bush administrations distinguished between what might be called the "old civil rights law," which they claimed to support, and the "new civil rights law," which they opposed. Developed between the *Brown* decision in 1954 and the Voting Rights Act of 1965, the old civil rights law prohibited intentional discrimination, be it legal segregation in the schools, informal discrimination in the workplace, or racial restrictions on voting. The new civil rights law was concerned with discriminatory outcomes, as measured by statistical disparities, rather than with discriminatory intent. If, for example, black children overall are disproportionately in all-black schools; if the workforce in a given firm, compared with the community in which it is located, is disproportionately white (or male); or if elected officials in a multiracial state or municipality are disproportionately white, discrimination is assumed.

The remedies for such historic discrimination, collectively labeled **affirmative action**, tend to be statistical in nature. They include increasing the number of minority pupils, minority employees, or minority elected officials (by redrawing the districts from which they were elected) to correspond to the percentage of the relevant minority population. In employment (and in admissions to colleges and universities), the methods used in reaching these goals became known as affirmative action "guidelines." Sometimes guidelines were imposed by court order. More often, they were the result of voluntary efforts by legislatures, government agencies, businesses, and colleges and universities to comply with civil rights laws and court rulings.

affirmative action

Civil rights policy or program that seeks to redress the effects of past discrimination due to race or gender by giving preference to women and minorities in education and employment.

23.4.1 Affirmative Action

Few civil rights policies in the twentieth century proved more controversial than affirmative action. Many white Americans argued that it ran contrary to the concept of achievement founded on merit and amounted to reverse racial or sexual discrimination. Ironically, because the 1964 Civil Rights Act had made gender discrimination in employment illegal, white women were among the major beneficiaries of affirmative action. But its chief advocates have been African Americans who viewed it as a remedy for centuries of discrimination. The debate over affirmative action not only led to racial polarization, it divided the black community.

The majority of African Americans defend affirmative action as a policy designed to open doors to opportunities in employment and education that had been firmly closed during the long era of Jim Crow segregation and discrimination.

President Lyndon Johnson had first used the term "affirmative action" in a 1965 executive order that required federal contractors to "take affirmative action" to guarantee that job seekers and employees "are treated without regard to their race, color, religion, sex, or national origin." In 1969 Arthur A. Fletcher, a black assistant secretary of labor in the Nixon administration, developed the "Philadelphia Plan," in which firms with federal construction contracts were obligated to set and meet hiring goals for African Americans or be penalized. The plan became a model for subsequent "set-aside" programs that reserved some contracts for minority-owned businesses or that favored hiring women and minorities. Setting goals and timetables to achieve full compliance with federal civil rights requirements appealed to large corporations and accounted for the early success of affirmative action initiatives.

23.4.2 The Backlash

Although it produced more litigation, affirmative action in employment proved less controversial than affirmative action in college and university admissions. State higher-education institutions occupied the center of the controversy both because they were narrowly bound by the Fourteenth Amendment's prohibitions against racial discrimination and because they, far more than elite private institutions, were the gateways to upward mobility for many Americans, white and black, Asians, and Latino/as. Nevertheless, both to aid disadvantaged minorities and increase racial and cultural diversity on campus, admissions offices were forced to employ different admission criteria. Conservatives called these criteria "racial preferences" that promoted unfairness and white resentment.

The case of *Regents of the University of California v. Bakke* reflected the white backlash to affirmative action. The medical school at the University of California, as a form of affirmative action, had set aside 16 of its 100 places in each entering class for disadvantaged and minority students. They were considered for admission in a separate system. A white student named Alan Bakke sued the University for discrimination after it rejected his application. In 1976 the California Supreme Court ruled he should be admitted, but the university appealed to the U.S. Supreme Court, which also ruled in Bakke's favor in 1978. Of the nine justices, five agreed that the university violated Bakke's rights. However, other related legal issues were involved, and the Court split without a majority on nearly all of them. Only one justice declared that affirmative action cases should be judged on the same strict level of scrutiny applied to "invidious" (intentionally harmful) discrimination. All the other justices stated that race-conscious remedies could be used in some circumstances to correct discrimination.

California was at the center of the affirmative action storm because of its multiracial population. In 1995 Republican Governor Pete Wilson ended affirmative action in state employment. In 1996 California voters approved Proposition 209, the so-called California Civil Rights Initiative, which banned all state agencies from implementing affirmative action programs. Ward Connerly, a conservative black entrepreneur, led the campaign for the proposition. Born in 1939 in rural Louisiana, he had earned a B.A. from Sacramento State College and had received over $140,000 from state contracts set aside for minority businesses. Nonetheless, Connerly maintained that affirmative action exacerbated negative stereotyping of African Americans and had failed to address problems of poverty, unemployment, and inadequate education that beset the truly disadvantaged. Instead, it had merely helped those least in need of assistance, especially middle-class white women. Finally, Connerly accepted the broader argument that affirmative action assaulted the concept of individual merit and violated core American values of equality and opportunity.

Fifty-four percent of California voters agreed with Connerly, and the Supreme Court upheld the proposition. Its effect and that of similar laws or court rulings around the nation is now known. The number of African Americans and other protected minorities admitted to the University of California system dropped, and the numbers at Berkeley, the University of California's most prestigious campus, fell precipitously. In both California and Texas, which abandoned affirmative action in its university system after a court challenge, administrators have attempted to ensure a diverse student body by offering admission to their top schools to all students in the top ranks of their high school class.

On June 23, 2003, the Supreme Court, in two separate decisions, handed the University of Michigan both a victory, when it upheld the law school's practice of using race as a criterion in admissions procedures to create a diverse student body, and a defeat, when it banned the university from awarding points based on race as a criterion for admitting undergraduates. In the first case, *Grutter v. Bollinger*, a 5–4 decision declared that the law school could use race to achieve diversity, thus endorsing the *Bakke* decision written by Justice Powell. Justice Sandra Day O'Connor's majority opinion declared that the equal protection clause of the Fourteenth Amendment did not prohibit the law school's narrowly tailored use of race in admissions decisions. She was persuaded that the law school acted out of a compelling interest to obtain the educational benefits that accrued from a diverse student population and meaningful integration. However, writing for the majority in the second case, *Gratz v. Bollinger*, Chief Justice Rehnquist appeared to contradict O'Connor's opinion. Rehnquist maintained that in admitting undergraduates the university crossed the line of what was permissible by giving points to black applicants: "The university's policy, which automatically distributed 20 points, or one-fifth of the points needed to guarantee admission, to every single 'underrepresented minority' applicant solely because of race, is not narrowly tailored to achieve the interest in educational diversity that respondents claim justifies their program."

1979–2009
Supreme Court Cases on Affirmative Action in Employment

1979

United Steelworkers v. Weber upheld preferential treatment in hiring and training by private firms

1982

American Tobacco Co. v. Patterson upheld seniority plans in place before 1964 unless discriminatory intent could be shown

1986

Local 93 of International Association of Firefighters v. City of Cleveland upheld the promotion of minorities ahead of white applicants with higher test scores and greater seniority

1987

U.S. v. Paradise upheld a judicial order imposing racial quotas in hiring and promotions of Alabama state troopers

1989

Martin v. Wilks ruled that employees may challenge an affirmative action plan after it has gone into effect. Congress overruled this decision in the Civil Rights Act of 1991

1990

Metro Broadcasting v. FCC upheld the affirmative action plan increasing minority broadcasting owners, returning to *Fullilove*

2003

Grutter v. Bollinger upheld the University of Michigan Law School's use of racial preferences in admissions to achieve a more diverse student body

1980

Fullilove v. Klutznick upheld government programs that reserved places for minorities

1986

Wygant v. Jackson Board of Education rejected a school board's plan for laying off white teachers while retaining less senior black teachers, but it also rejected the Reagan administration position that affirmative action be limited to actual victims of discrimination, thus broadly upholding affirmative action

1986

Local 28 of Sheet Metal Workers v. EEOC upheld the order that unions meet minority quotas for membership

1987

Johnson v. Transportation Agency of Santa Clara County upheld a plan that promoted women over men

1989

Richmond v. J. A. Croson Co. ruled that the Fourteenth Amendment prohibited set-asides for minority contractors, thus going against the spirit of *Weber* and the letter of *Fullilove v. Klutznick* and implying that all such plans face "strict scrutiny (intense examination)"

1995

Adarand Constructors v. Pena struck down a congressional statute requiring 10 percent of federal highway money to go to minority contractors and broadly asserted that any such programs using racial classifications were constitutionally suspect

2009

Ricci v. DeStefano limited the New Haven, Connecticut, fire department from using race instead of merit exams to promote firemen

23.5 Black Political Activism at the End of the Twentieth Century

Identify the focal points of black activism during the Reagan and Bush presidencies.

The increased participation of black men and women in the upper echelons of the Democratic Party reflected the success of black electoral politics and the internal mobilization of black communities. While in 1964 the nation had only 103 black elected officials, by 1994 there were nearly 8,500. By 2010, 43 African Americans were serving in Congress. In 1988 Representative William H. Gray of Pennsylvania became the first African American to reach the top ranks of congressional leadership, first as chair of the House Democratic caucus and then in 1989 as majority whip of the House of Representatives. In February 1989, Ronald H. Brown became the first African American to lead a major national political party when he was elected chairman of the Democratic Party. That same year, David Dinkins was elected the first black mayor of New York City. In 1990 Sharon Pratt Dixon (Kelly) was elected mayor of Washington, D.C., becoming the first woman and the first District of Columbia native to serve in that position. By the mid-1990s, black men and women held the mayor's office in 400 towns and cities. Clearly, the days of black political powerlessness had ended—or had they?

By the 1990s African Americans had become an indispensable base of the Democratic Party. Reflecting the importance of African-American voters to the party, congressional Democrats passed equal rights legislation to solidify gains that blacks had won. The Civil Rights Restoration Act of 1988 authorized withholding federal funds from an entire institution if any program within it discriminated against women, racial minorities, the aged, or the disabled. The Fair Housing Act of 1988 stipulated that either an individual or the Department of Housing and Urban Development could bring a complaint of housing discrimination and authorize administrative judges to investigate housing complaints, issue injunctions and fines, and award punitive damages. These laws and the Civil Rights Act of 1991 were a response to Supreme Court decisions that narrowed the scope of earlier civil rights legislation.

23.5.1 Reparations

While party politics attracted attention, many African Americans focused on specific issues, including reparations for slavery and the spread of HIV/AIDS in the United States and Africa. In 1969 James Foreman, in his "Black Manifesto," called on America's churches and synagogues to collect $500 million as "a beginning of the reparations due us as a people who have been exploited and degraded, brutalized, killed, and persecuted." Although Foreman's call was widely publicized, churches made no serious effort to respond to his demand. Four years later, Boris Bittker, a Yale Law School professor, argued in *The Case for Black Reparations* that slavery and the persistence of government-sanctioned racial discrimination justified a program to compensate black Americans. Since 1993 black Democratic Congressman John Conyers from Detroit has introduced a bill in every session of Congress—not to pay reparations but to establish a federal commission to investigate slavery and the legacy of racial discrimination. The bill never came to the floor of the House for a vote.

In 2000 the issue of reparations for slavery received widespread attention when Randall Robinson, founder and president of TransAfrica, published *The Debt: What America Owes to Blacks*. Robinson reasoned that because Jews and Japanese Americans had been compensated for the indignities and horrors they experienced in World War II, African Americans were also due financial indemnification for slavery, "246 years of an enterprise murderous both of a people and their culture." Robinson maintained that many African Americans still bear the scars of slavery in terms of poor housing, inadequate health care, and insufficient educational opportunities. He insisted that reparations would remedy the effect of such inequalities. Temple University professor and Afrocentrist Molefi Asante proposed that, instead of "a one-time cash payout," the American government should make long-term commitments for "educational, health care, land or property grants, and a combination of such grants." He elaborated, "What I have argued for is the establishment of some type of organization that would evaluate how reparations would be determined and distributed: the National Commission of African Americans (NCAA) would be the overarching national organization to serve as the clearinghouse for reparations."

Some black writers and journalists rejected arguments that reparations were a realistic resolution of the nation's slave and racist legacy. Two black journalists, William Raspberry and Juan Williams, objected to the very idea of reparations. Instead, Raspberry favored more investment in education for African Americans, "not because of debts owed to or incurred by our ancestors, but because America needs its citizens to be educated and productive." Williams declared, "The suffering of long-dead ancestors is not a claim check for a bag full of cash. I don't want any money that belongs to any slave. That is obscene. The struggle of African-Americans for civil rights is not about selling out for a check." The debate over reparations is far from settled. In the early decades of the twenty-first century many advocates of reparations argued that African Americans unjustly imprisoned for crimes they did not commit should be compensated by the government.

23.5.2 TransAfrica and Black Internationalism

Black activism persisted on the international as well as the national front. Much of this effort focused on ending the oppressive conditions of apartheid—the complete social, political, and economic isolation and subjection of black people—in South Africa and its glorification of white racial supremacy.

Randall Robinson, a native of Richmond, Virginia, and a graduate of Harvard Law School who had worked for Michigan Congressman Charles Diggs, sought to link African-American liberation struggles with those that Africans in South Africa and elsewhere waged. In 1977 he founded TransAfrica to lobby for black political prisoners in South Africa, chief among them Nelson Mandela. In 1984 Mary Francis Berry, Eleanor Holmes Norton, and others joined Robinson for a series of sit-ins at the South African embassy in Washington, D.C., during which hundreds were arrested.

The antiapartheid movement became a major priority for African-American activists. They enlisted the sympathy and help of white Americans on college campuses and pressured universities into divesting their investments in South Africa. Similar pressures were put on corporations, especially those vulnerable to consumer boycotts. In 1986 the Black Congressional Caucus persuaded its colleagues to enact a trade embargo against South Africa and to sustain it over President Reagan's veto.

In 1990, bowing to international pressure, black activism, and a souring domestic economy, South African President F.W. de Klerk removed the ban on the African National Congress, the key opposition party, and ended the 28-year incarceration of Nelson Mandela. Soon thereafter, South Africa became a multiracial democracy, and Mandela was elected its president.

Nelson Mandela's release from prison was celebrated around the globe as the event that signaled the final days of South Africa's system of racial apartheid.

23.6 The Rise in Black Incarceration

Explain how general white perceptions of young black men affected trends in criminal justice during the closing decade of the twentieth century and the opening decades of the twenty-first century.

The general white perception of black men as criminals increased following Bush's election. Even during the Democratic Party's resurgence in the 1990s, the perceptions of black youths as criminals acquired potent political currency, resulting in the mass incarceration of young black men and an increase in police brutality and racial profiling. After the disputed 2000 presidential election, the black community became even more aware of the adverse consequences of mass incarceration because so many states deny the right to vote to convicted and incarcerated felons. Approximately, 1.8 million of the 5.9 million felons and former felons in the United States were black. Researchers concluded that "If not for disfranchisement . . . the 2000 presidential election would have been reversed, if former felons in a single state (Florida) had had the right to vote." Moreover, black people, especially black men, are incarcerated in astonishingly high numbers. (For the statistics on black incarceration, see Table 24-2 in Chapter 24.)

Reformers continued to focus attention on the brutal conditions within U.S. prisons. In 1994 Supreme Court Justice Clarence Thomas argued, in voting to dismiss claims that prisons failed to protect inmates, that "prisons are necessarily dangerous places, they house society's most antisocial and violent people in close proximity with one another. Regrettably, some level of brutality and sexual aggression among [prisoners] is inevitable no matter what the guards do . . . unless all prisoners are locked in their cells twenty-four hours a day and sedated."

23.6.1 Policing the Black Community

In March 1991 Los Angeles police pulled Rodney Glen King from his car after a high-speed chase and beat him with nightsticks. A bystander captured the incident on videotape, which television newscasts broadcast repeatedly, fueling long-simmering anger over police brutality among African Americans in Los Angeles. When a jury of 11 white Americans and one Hispanic American acquitted the four

The videotaped beating of Rodney King by Los Angeles police—shown repeatedly on national television—bolstered charges by African Americans in Los Angeles that they were frequent victims of police brutality. Despite the graphic evidence, the officers were acquitted of using excessive force.

police officers involved in the incident of all but one of the charges brought against them, south-central Los Angeles erupted in protest. The verdict highlighted the gulf between the perceptions of white and black Americans about the police and the criminal justice system. Where the mostly white jury had seen the police maintaining law and order, black Americans saw police repression and racism. Altogether, 52 people were killed in the outbreak that followed the verdict. Arsonists and looters devastated much of the community. Thousands of people were injured, 4,000 were arrested, and an estimated half-billion-dollars' worth of property was damaged or destroyed. The four officers were later retried in federal court on charges of violating King's civil rights. This time juries found two of them guilty and acquitted the other two. Meanwhile, a jury in King's civil suit ordered Los Angeles to pay him $3.8 million in damages.

The Rodney King police beating resonated with black men across the country. Earl Ofari Hutchinson suggested why:

> Black professionals or business owners still tell harrowing tales of being spread-eagle over the hoods of their expensive BMW's or Porsches while the police ran makes on them and tore their cars apart searching for drugs. In polls taken after the Rodney King beating, blacks were virtually unanimous in saying that they believed any black person could have been on the ground that night being pulverized by the police. These were eternal reminders to the "new" black bourgeoisie that they could escape the hood, but many Americans still considered them hoods.

23.6.2 Black Men and Police Brutality: Where Is the Justice?

Several high-profile cases focused public attention on the relation of black communities to white police authorities from the 1980s into the 2000s. Police repression was and remains a long-festering cause of tension and hostility. It had been behind many of the riots of the 1960s. On November 16, 1992, two Detroit police officers were charged with the murder of Malice Green, a 35-year-old black resident of the city. In 1997 a Haitian immigrant, Abner Louima, was beaten and sodomized while in custody at a Brooklyn police station. In 1999 New York police shot Amadou Diallo, a West African immigrant, 41 times when they mistook his reaching for a wallet for going for a gun. A jury in Albany, New York, acquitted the four police officials charged in the Diallo killing. In 2000, Patrick Dorismond (another Haitian immigrant) was shot and killed in New York after he got into an argument with undercover police officers after he refused to buy drugs from them. In 2006 New York police officers killed unarmed 23-year-old Sean Bell, who was on his way to marry the mother of his two children. Apparently Bell was caught in the middle of an undercover sting operation. Police fired at least 50 bullets into his car. In each instance, an enraged black community protested the police profiling as another instance of bias toward black men and one that targeted all minorities for illegal detention. At a protest rally over Bell's shooting, Rev. Al Sharpton declared, "We cannot allow this to continue to happen. We've got to understand that all of us were in that car."

23.6.3 Human Rights in America

In October 1998 the human rights group Amnesty International, known for condemning human rights abuses in countries with repressive governments, reported on police brutality in the United States. The report covered local and state police, the FBI, the Immigration and Naturalization Service, and the prison system. Its contents came as no surprise to most black Americans or, indeed, to any resident of America's poor urban neighborhoods. The report detailed violations of the UN Code of Conduct for Law

Enforcement Officials and the UN Basic Principles on the Use of Force and Firearms. Among the violations cited were the following:

- The shooting of unarmed suspects fleeing a minor crime scene
- Excessive force used on mentally ill or disturbed people
- Multiple shootings of a suspect, sometimes after the suspect was apprehended or disabled
- The beating of unresisting suspects
- The misuse of batons, chemical sprays, and electroshock weapons

These violations all involved the misuse of force during arrests, traffic stops, searches, and so forth. The report also cited sexual abuse of prisoners and the denial of food and water to them. The report noted that while most victims of American law enforcement abuse were members of racial and ethnic minorities, most police officers were white.

It is too easy to interpret these findings as showing that American police officers, as a group, are racists who oppress people they do not like. In fact, the issue of police brutality is not nearly so simple. Police officers are under tremendous pressure and live dangerous lives, in part because guns are so widely available in America. No one can be expected to have perfect judgment about using force, and the cumulative effect of years of dealing with violence can destroy a person's sense of perspective and moral equilibrium.

Neither is the problem of crime by black Americans a simple one. No one disputes the fact that levels of crime in black communities are high. The murder rate, for example, for African Americans in 2009 was seven times that of whites, and black victims accounted for 46.9 percent of all those murdered, even though African Americans made up only 12 percent of the population. Police argue defensively that over 90 percent of those who murder, rape, and assault black people are black themselves. The murder rate for young black men between the ages of 14 and 17 tripled between 1976 and 1993. Since the late 1990s the overall rate has fallen. Still, the security of too many African Americans remains imperiled.

Crime devastates black neighborhoods. High crime rates raise the costs of business, driving jobs and investment dollars out of the areas that most need them. Fear of violence leads many in the inner cities to barricade themselves inside their homes. Crime has transformed once vibrant neighborhoods into virtual ghost towns where only the sound of gunfire disturbs the silence of the streets. Filmmaker Spike Lee was shocked in 1994 when he returned to the Brooklyn neighborhood in which he had grown up to shoot his film *Crooklyn*. He found the streets had become so unsafe that the local children he used as extras had to be taught how to play the games he had played growing up in the 1970s because they had never been allowed to play outside. "Nowadays," Lee reflected, "these kids, they'll shoot you dead in a second and not even think about it. The two big problems are crack and how accessible guns are. And also, you're talking about what Reagan did during his eight years. If I was a parent, I'd be terrified anytime my children left my sight. When I was growing up, I just had to be home by dark." Spike Lee continued to deploy his artistic filmmaking talent to underscore the scourge of violence in a controversial 2015 film, Chi-Rac, focused on South Side Chicago.

Being disproportionately the victims of crime, most African Americans looked to the nation's police departments for protection. Encouraged by their growing political power, black community leaders sought, not always successfully, to make the police both responsive to crime and to be fair in enforcing the laws. As a means for changing the behavior of law enforcement officials, black leaders advocated the appointment of black police chiefs and the creation of more diverse representation within police departments.

23.7 Black Politics, 1992–2001: The Clinton Presidency

Analyze the reasons why African Americans remained supportive of Bill Clinton's presidency and sustained loyalty to the Democratic Party.

During his first campaign for the presidency in 1992, black Americans welcomed Arkansas Governor Bill Clinton into their churches, schools, and homes. Black citizens and the civil rights leadership embraced Clinton's candidacy against incumbent Republican George H. W. Bush, who had done little to win their loyalty. White Americans, too, were dissatisfied with the Bush presidency. Although he enjoyed high approval ratings in early 1991 following American military success in evicting Iraq from Kuwait in the first Gulf War, by early 1992 his popularity had slumped in the face of an economic downturn. Still, at first, few operatives believed Clinton would unseat Bush.

Shrewdly, however, Clinton positioned himself as a centrist within the mainstream of American politics. This required him to at least appear to place some distance between himself and the liberal-progressive arm of the Democratic Party represented by Jesse Jackson and the Rainbow Coalition. Undeterred by charges of womanizing, draft evasion, and marijuana smoking, Clinton attacked Bush's record and promised to make government more responsive to the needs of Americans. The strategy worked. Clinton won in November 1992 with just 43 percent of the popular vote to Bush's 38 percent and third-party candidate H. Ross Perot's 19 percent. However, Clinton garnered 78 percent of the black vote and 39 percent of the white vote in key states including New Jersey, Michigan, New York, Illinois, and California. The election was not a clear mandate. Although Democrats maintained control of Congress, they gained no seats in the Senate and lost seats in the House. Republicans used the ambiguous outcome to launch a relentless campaign to undermine Clinton's presidency.

Most black people, however, considered Clinton the best president on race issues since Lyndon Johnson. Writer Toni Morrison called Clinton the first "black president," and in some circles he was called "the first woman president" because of his support for equal rights for women, both black and white. Clinton appointed women, including many black women, to 37 percent of the 500 upper-level positions in the White House and federal bureaucracy. During the campaign, he visited the riot-torn ruins of south-central Los Angeles, played the saxophone on *The Arsenio Hall Show*, and worshiped in black churches, where he was warmly received. In Clinton, black Americans had a

President William Jefferson Clinton is seen here with members of the Little Rock Nine, who, as teenagers, defied hostile mobs to desegregate Central High School in Little Rock, Arkansas, in 1957. African Americans claimed Clinton as the first "black president," given his comfort around black people and the number of African Americans he considered friends.

HONORING OUR AMERICAN HISTORY

friend. Indeed, he named his black friends to his transition team: attorney Vernon Jordan (as co-chair), Barbara Jordan, William Gray III, and Marian Wright Edelman, founding president of the Children's Defense Fund. Clinton also created a cabinet that mirrored the diversity of the American population, in some cases—such as Hazel O'Leary as secretary of the Department of Energy, Alexis Herman as secretary of Labor, and Ron Brown as secretary of Commerce—he appointed black people to posts that had nothing to do with race. Clinton also gave to Washington, D.C.'s, delegate to Congress, Eleanor Holmes Norton, the prerogative, normally reserved to U.S. senators, of selecting U.S. district court judges, U.S. marshals, and the U.S. attorney for the District of Columbia. Moreover, not only did Clinton appoint many African-American officials and judges, he was the first American president to visit sub-Saharan Africa.

23.7.1 "It's the Economy, Stupid!"

In 1996 Clinton became the first Democratic president to win a second term since Franklin Roosevelt. Throughout his two terms in office, Clinton focused attention on the economy, a strategy that won grudging support from moderate Republicans. His objective was to strengthen the economy, since a stronger economy would improve economic opportunities for black Americans. In a significant departure from the policies of his predecessors, Clinton increased the taxes of higher-income Americans and pushed for an expansion of the earned income tax credit. His college student-aid program increased federal loan benefits. When Clinton left office in 2001, the country had the lowest poverty rate in 20 years.

Clinton's economic programs were supported by the Congressional Black Caucus (CBC). In 1993 CBC chairman Representative Kweisi Mfume of Maryland and the highest-ranking black congressman, Representative John Lewis of Georgia, delivered the caucus vote that saved Clinton's $500 billion economic budget (the Omnibus Budget Reconciliation Act of 1993) in both the House and the Senate. In return, black congressmen gained financial support for inner cities, poor families, children, and the elderly. For example, Representative Mfume credited the CBC for saving both the $2.5 billion allocation for food stamps that the Senate sought to eliminate and $3.5 billion in funding for empowerment zones in cities and rural areas.

Unemployment plummeted from 7.2 percent when Clinton took office to 4.0 percent when he left it. American businesses created 10 million new jobs, and many black people who feared they would never gain a foothold in the economy found work, some for the first time. Reduced federal spending and the 1993 tax increase helped cut the annual federal deficit in half.

23.7.2 Welfare Reform, Mass Incarceration, and the Black Family

Prior to his reelection in August 1996, and to the chagrin of his African-American political base, Clinton opportunistically signed the Personal Responsibility and Work Opportunity Reconciliation Act, a welfare reform bill. African Americans and many white political progressives were disappointed. The legislation combined Clinton's own ideas with those espoused in the Republicans' "Contract with America" blueprint for conservative changes. In 1994, the Republicans used this platform to secure control of both houses of Congress. The main target of the Personal Responsibility Act was Aid to Families of Dependent Children (AFDC), a program created in 1935 as part of the Social Security Act to prevent children from suffering due to the poverty of their parents. Critics claimed AFDC stipends discouraged poor mothers from finding work, that it was responsible for the breakdown of the family among the nation's poor, and that it did little to reduce poverty. They insisted the states did not have enough flexibility in administering welfare. The conservative welfare "reform" measure ended guarantees of federal aid to poor children, turning control of such programs over to the states along with allocations of block grants. The Welfare Reform Act denied benefits to legal immigrants, mandated drastic reductions in food stamp appropriations, and limited families to five years of benefits. It also required most adult welfare recipients to find employment within two years.

There were no good reasons to believe the welfare reform bill would accomplish its sponsors' objectives. Most of the people who would be "encouraged to find work" by having their benefits reduced or cut entirely were among the least employable people in the labor force. A study of individuals terminated from general assistance in Michigan, for example, revealed that as many as two-thirds remained unemployed. As for the bill's effect on families, it is true that most women on welfare had their first children when they were unmarried teenagers, but little evidence indicated that cutting welfare prevented teenage pregnancies. There was, however, evidence that the reforms that targeted improving the collection of child support payments for divorced mothers did reduce welfare costs far more effectively and humanely. Clinton's support of the welfare act was consistent with his centrist ideology. Furthermore, it immunized him from Republican attacks while leaving black support intact. Clinton endorsed policies that had a negative impact on African Americans and seemed, at least symbolically, to reassure white moderates. He signed a crime bill that allowed local communities to hire more police officers and build more prisons. He supported the implementation of a "three-strike" policy of stiffer penalties for those who had at least two prior criminal convictions. The actions that ushered in the era of welfare reform and black mass incarceration had devastating consequences on the black family. Writer Ta-Nehisi Coates, in an October 2015 *Atlantic* essay, "The Black Family in the Age of Mass Incarceration," noted, "The United States now accounts for less than 5 percent of the world's inhabitants—and about 25 percent of its incarcerated inhabitants." He continued, "from the mid-1970s to the mid-'80s, America's incarceration rates doubled. From the mid-'80s to the mid-'90s, it doubled again. Then it went still higher"(pp. 60–84). By the turn of the century African-American drug offenders made up more than twice the number of inmates than white Americans in state prisons. Coates concluded, "By the close of the 20th century, prison was a more common experience for young black men than college graduation or military service." Black families became even more fractured as the number of men in prison escalated.

Another issue of grave concern for black families centered on access to quality healthcare. President Clinton failed, in the teeth of intense Republican opposition, to enact comprehensive health care legislation. With little political alternative, having abandoned a third-party political strategy, black support for Clinton remained strong. Clinton won a second term, easily trumping his Republican opponent, Kansas senator Robert Dole. The preliminary results of the new welfare reform strictures indicated that, within a couple of years, half of those who had taken jobs had returned to lives of unemployment, poverty, and quiet desperation. As the economy took a downturn at the end of Clinton's second term, conditions for poor mothers and children deteriorated steadily. The debate over welfare policy receded to the back burner during the 2000 election campaign and disappeared completely after George W. Bush entered the White House.

23.7.3 Black Politics in the Clinton Era

Congressional Republicans and radical conservatives hated Clinton's presidency, and many of them hated Clinton himself. They vowed to take back the White House. Republicans raised huge sums of money and organized local constituencies, especially in the South. The Democrats seemed demoralized and did little to mobilize their base, especially in the black community. Their passivity had predictable results. Many African Americans did not vote in the congressional elections in 1994, and the Democrats lost control of Congress. For the first time in 40 years, the Republicans could implement their conservative agenda, which included rolling back environmental protection policies, reducing taxes for the rich, cutting benefits for the elderly, increasing military spending, establishing the primacy of Christianity over other religions, and advancing white supremacy.

Belatedly awake to the peril of black political alienation, younger Democratic leaders began to fight back. In 1994 Jesse Jackson, Jr. won a seat in Congress from Chicago, and held it until his resignation in 2012. Jackson outlined a comprehensive social democratic agenda for black America that included full employment, health care, high-quality public education, decent and affordable housing, a safe and sustainable environment, the right to vote, and equality of sexes before the law. Progressive Democrats understood that race was no longer a matter of just black and white people. Many other groups and movements were emerging, including Asian/Pacific Island-Americans, Arab-Americans, and Native Americans. Immigrants, especially migrant workers from Mexico, were forming labor organizations to fight for immigrant rights and social justice. But Democrats were now in the congressional minority, and party leaders seemed loath to knit together these diverse constituencies into viable grassroots organizations and to foster solidarity projects and efforts crucial to social change, such as affordable housing, higher-minimum-wage laws, universal healthcare coverage, and driver's licenses for immigrants.

While Democrats unraveled, Republicans drew strength from the appointment of Kenneth Starr as an independent counsel to investigate allegations surrounding Bill and Hillary Clinton's investment in an Arkansas land development deal known as Whitewater. As the investigations escalated, Clinton became caught up in a sex scandal. He denied sexual involvement with a White House intern, Monica Lewinsky. On December 19, 1998, the Republican majority in the House narrowly voted to impeach Clinton for perjury and obstruction of justice for tampering with witnesses to conceal his relationship with Lewinsky. The Senate, however, refused to convict him, and he remained in office. In the midst of the turmoil, Clinton derived solace from the unwavering support of black people, the CBC, and his friends, including Vernon Jordan and Jesse Jackson.

23.7.4 The Contested 2000 Election

The election of 2000 revealed fault lines of culture and geography and the changing demographics of race, class, and gender. A gender gap of about 11 percent reflected the fact that men strongly supported Republican candidates and women favored Democratic candidates. The middle of the country and the South voted for Republican Texas governor George W. Bush. Democratic candidate Vice President Albert Gore, Jr. carried the states of the upper Midwest, the Northeast, and the Pacific coast. Gays and lesbians voted 70 percent for Gore, whereas those who identified themselves as conservative Christians voted 80 percent for Bush. The campaign focused largely on economic issues—social security, taxes, healthcare, and education.

Black community leaders and organizations worked hard to register voters and increase turnout for the 2000 election. The NAACP, for example, spent $9 million on Operation Big Vote. Organizers even registered more than 11,000 inmates in county jails in the South.

23.7.5 *Bush v. Gore*

In a hotly contested election, the outcome hung on one state: Florida. In the end, the Supreme Court, in a five-to-four ruling (*Bush v. Gore*), decided the issue by halting the recount of ballots in Florida. The Court's majority based its ruling on the Fourteenth Amendment's prohibition of states denying citizens equal protection of the law. The Court insisted the recount had to be stopped because the Florida Supreme Court, which had authorized it, had failed to provide uniform standards for determining the intent of the voters. Bush was declared the winner in Florida by fewer than 600 votes, which gave him a four-vote majority in the Electoral College.

Bill Clinton called *Bush v. Gore* "an appalling decision" and compared its impact on African Americans to the infamous *Dred Scott* and *Plessy v. Ferguson* decisions of the nineteenth century. Indeed, African Americans reported serious discrimination and interference with their voting in Florida. A lawsuit in Jacksonville, Florida, claimed that many votes were thrown out as "undervotes" or "overvotes," especially in the four districts with the highest concentration of African Americans in the state. According to the lawsuit, 26,000 ballots were not counted in Duval County, and more than 9,000 of those were cast in largely African-American precincts where Gore had captured more than 90 percent of the vote. Indeed, the U.S. Civil Rights Commission found that tens of thousands of African Americans were disfranchised in Florida. In a draft report, it declared, "African American voting districts were disproportionately hindered by antiquated and error-prone equipment like the punch card ballot system." This meant that more black and low-income voters, who tended to vote Democratic, had their ballots invalidated.

The chair of the commission, Mary Frances Berry, wrote in 2001 in the *Journal of American History*,

> The United States Supreme Court helped undermine the pursuit of equal opportunity by African Americans for most of our history. . . . *Bush v. Gore* was so striking, in part, because the 5–4 majority has been assiduous about deference to state courts and states' rights in general. What the Court has done is to remind us that judges have social and political views that are reflected in their decisions. Each side has used the equal protection clause of the Fourteenth Amendment to convey its policy preferences. But, unlike the majority, in cases involving African American voting and the outcome of the 2000 election, the justices in dissent have remained consistent.

23.8 Republican Triumph

Evaluate the significance of the events of 9/11, the wars in Iraq and Afghanistan, Hurricane Katrina, and the election of President Barack Obama on black political consciousness.

In the 2000 elections, Republicans retained narrow majorities in Congress. The U.S. Supreme Court's ruling in *Bush v. Gore* thus not only put George W. Bush in the White House but also meant that for the first time since 1954, the Republican Party gained control of the presidency and both houses of Congress.

23.8.1 George W. Bush's Black Cabinet

President Bush was aware that few African Americans had voted for him. But this did not prevent him from appointing well-educated, articulate, and accomplished black men and women to key posts. Such appointments tended to mute black criticism and placate white swing voters who disdained racial exclusion. Bush named General Colin L. Powell to be secretary of state. Powell, the son of Jamaican immigrants, had served as chairman of the Joint Chiefs of Staff (1989–1993), the highest military position in the Department of Defense. During his tenure he oversaw Operation Desert Storm, the victorious 1991 Persian Gulf War. Secretary Powell not only assisted in the formulation of foreign policy but also "represented the race." In a speech at Howard University, he expressed pride in his complex role of representing America's universalism on the global stage: "It's just terrific to be able to walk into a room somewhere in Africa, Russia, Asia, and Europe, and you know they're looking at you. You know how they be. They're looking at you and they recognize your position and who you are, and they also recognize that you're black. And it's always a source of inspiration and joy to see people look at me and through me see my country and see what promise my country offers to all people to come to these shores for a better life." Bush also appointed Condoleezza Rice to be his national security adviser. Rice was the first African American and the first woman to hold this post. During the 2000 election, Rice had formed a strong personal bond with Bush, and this relationship became the foundation of her power in his administration.

In the 2000 campaign, Bush had vowed to reform public education. This was an issue of vital importance to both black and white families. Black parents were especially alarmed over the de facto resegregation of black children in urban schools. Thus, many were heartened when Bush selected black Texan Rod Paige as the secretary of education.

Paige introduced the No Child Left Behind Act, an education reform that Bush ardently embraced. This legislation, signed into law in 2002, required all schools to test students at regular intervals in reading, math, and science. States also had to publish the test results and sanction schools whose students failed to do well on the tests. Implicitly, the measure rejected integration as a primary social policy objective and retreated from mandatory busing while promoting parents' freedom to enroll their children in the schools of their choice through voucher programs.

Some African Americans, such as Anthony Williams, the mayor of Washington, D.C., supported the voucher program, arguing that competition with strong schools would force weaker schools to improve their performance. However, Reginald Weaver, the black president of the National Educational Association, argued that the voucher program ignored the needs of most students in poor schools. The No Child Left Behind Act, he said, "gives $13 million to 2,000 kids who are going to voucher school, and $13 million to 27,000 kids to a charter school, and then $13 million to 167,000 other kids. . . . I think it is political, not educational." No Child Left Behind was soon mired in controversy. Critics, including many conservatives, blasted it for setting unrealistic goals and for not including sufficient federal funding to help schools meet the higher standards. In 2007 Congress increased funding under the act, but No Child Left Behind remains controversial, and many critics would still like to see it repealed or substantially modified.

Rod Paige was selected by President George W. Bush to be secretary of the Department of Education. Paige spearheaded a program in which employees of the department volunteered to mentor students in select schools in the District of Columbia. In this 2003 photo, Paige answers questions from students during a visit to the Skinner Magnet Center in Omaha, Nebraska.

23.8.2 September 11, 2001

Americans were stunned on September 11, 2001, when terrorists seized four commercial airliners and crashed them into New York's World Trade Center, the Pentagon in Washington, and rural Pennsylvania. Hundreds of African Americans were among the more than 3,000 people who died that day.

If the debate over reparations dramatized the separate pasts that black and white Americans have experienced, then September 11, 2001, reminded them of their common future. But the sense of national unity did not last. Less than two years later, as the United States prepared to invade Iraq, activist and scholar Manning Marable wrote of the lessons he had learned from the 9/11 tragedy: "No political ideology, no crusade, no belief in a virtuous cause, can justify the moral bankruptcy of terror. Yet, because of the military actions of our own government, any claims to moral superiority have now disintegrated, in the minds of much of the black and brown world."

23.8.3 War

Americans expected President Bush to devise an effective strategy against the Taliban regime in Afghanistan and to destroy Osama bin Laden and the al-Qaeda network, which was responsible for 9/11. The president pledged retribution, and the war in Afghanistan began on October 7, 2001. The Taliban were easily overthrown, but bin Laden and the Taliban leader, Mullah Omar, escaped.

Still, the Bush administration called its Afghan foray a success even though the Taliban launched a new guerrilla war and much of Afghanistan remained in the control of warlords and insurgents. Critics, such as Richard A. Clarke, the former chief counterterrorism adviser to Presidents Clinton and George W. Bush, argued that the Bush administration's real target after 9/11 was not Afghanistan and al-Qaeda but Saddam Hussein's Iraq. Clarke charged that Bush and National Security Adviser Condoleezza Rice had failed to heed the reports of a planned terrorist attack before September 11, 2001. Al-Qaeda, which claimed responsibility for the bombing of U.S. embassies in Kenya and Tanzania in 1998 and for an attack on the USS *Cole* in Yemen in 2000, should have been the national security priority. Rice denied these charges, but early in 2002 the administration began to shift the nation's attention from Afghanistan to Iraq.

The prospect of war in Iraq aroused mass protests at home and vociferous opposition abroad and at the United Nations, which refused to back the United States despite strenuous lobbying led by Secretary of State Colin Powell. In a speech before the UN Security Council in February 2003, Powell argued, based on what turned out to be misleading and possibly distorted intelligence reports, that Saddam not only had weapons of mass destruction but also had ties to international terrorist networks, including al-Qaeda. The Security Council was not convinced and voted against the invasion, but the United States invaded Iraq anyway on March 19, 2003. Only Britain gave it significant support.

As in Afghanistan, victory in Iraq appeared to come quickly, and Bush declared the mission there accomplished when Baghdad was occupied after a few weeks of fighting. However, it proved much easier to overthrow Saddam than to pacify Iraq. The country quickly descended into chaos. Insurgents attacked American occupation forces and those Iraqis who cooperated with them. Critics blasted the administration for failing to develop a coherent peace plan. The war, they charged, had actually strengthened terrorism, while the failure to secure UN support or to find weapons of mass destruction or establish ties between Saddam and al-Qaeda had damaged America's credibility and weakened the fabric of international cooperation.

23.8.4 Black Politics in the Bush Era

Massachusetts Senator John F. Kerry won the Democratic Party's nomination for president in 2004. The war in Iraq dominated other issues, including gay marriage and abortion rights. Kerry selected Senator John Edwards from North Carolina to be his running mate against incumbents George W. Bush and Dick Cheney. While these men campaigned, African Americans registered an important but subtle shift in their status within the Democratic Party as it became clear that they would play a key role in determining the outcome of the election.

The process of political transformation begun in the 1960s peaked in the 2004 presidential primaries. In these contests, African Americans emerged as the most reliable Democratic base and made their views heard and their power acknowledged. They wanted Americans to understand that little divided blacks and whites when it came to regaining the White House from the Republicans. In so doing, African-American leaders skillfully moved away from being considered spokespersons for a small special interest group. In 2004 they demanded acknowledgment of their central role as Democratic standard-bearers. Two of the nine contenders for the Democratic nomination were African Americans: Carol Moseley Braun, former U.S. senator from Illinois, and Rev. Al Sharpton of New York. Braun and Sharpton participated in all of the primary debates before throwing their support to Kerry.

In the spirit of presenting a united front, Braun, Sharpton, and Jesse Jackson addressed the delegates at the Democratic National Convention in Boston. The black star of the convention, however, was the little-known 42-year-old state senator from Illinois, Barack Obama, who was running for the U.S. Senate. Obama's keynote speech, claiming that good and efficient government would improve the life chances of all Americans, catapulted him into the limelight.

23.8.5 Bush's Second Term

On November 4, 2004, Americans reelected George W. Bush by a three-million-vote margin. After the election Colin Powell resigned. In repayment for her loyalty and experience in international affairs, President Bush appointed Condoleezza Rice to replace Powell as secretary of state. However, Bush's popularity soon began to plummet. Scandals rocked the administration. But it was Bush's mishandling of the Iraq War and the fumbling and inadequate federal response in 2005 to the devastation wrought by Hurricane Katrina to parts of the Gulf Coast and the city of New Orleans that defined his second term. In the 2006 midterm elections, the Democrats regained control of Congress. Nancy Pelosi became the first woman Speaker of the House, and several African Americans became chairs of House committees. Democrats also captured most of the state governorships. Deval Patrick of Massachusetts became the second African American to be elected governor in history.

23.8.6 The Iraq War

At the outset of his second term, Bush insisted again that America was on the right course in Iraq and that victory would soon be achieved there. Events soon proved him wrong. As the death toll in Iraq mounted—more than 3,500 U.S. troops and tens of thousands of Iraqis had been killed by the summer of 2007—most Americans lost faith in the administration's handling of the conflict, which had become a bloody civil war among Iraq's sectarian and ethnic groups. Civic life in Iraq all but collapsed amid daily suicide bombings, attacks on U.S. troops, kidnappings, murders, and other acts of terrorism. Corruption was rampant. Millions of Iraqis had become refugees. International opinion turned solidly against America.

By 2007, in response to Bush's low poll numbers and the unpopularity of the war, eight Democrats had launched campaigns for their party's presidential nomination. The prospective candidates included a woman, Senator Hillary Rodham Clinton of New York; an African American, Senator Barack Obama of Illinois; and a Hispanic-American, Governor Bill Richardson of New Mexico. This was the most diverse roster of presidential candidates of any party in American history.

23.8.7 Hurricane Katrina and the Destruction of Black New Orleans

Although Hurricane Katrina also hit the Mississippi and Alabama coasts hard, New Orleans suffered the worst effects. Federal funding for flood control in New Orleans, which is almost completely surrounded by water and part of which lies below sea level, had been reduced by 44 percent since 2001 when Bush took office. State and federal emergency services were so reduced and disorganized that they offered almost no protection from natural disasters. The plan to evacuate New Orleans if a major hurricane threatened the city ignored the fact that most of its poor residents, who were predominantly black, lacked the means to flee. Moreover, one-third (35 percent) of the Louisiana National Guard, needed to furnish aid and keep order in a disaster, were in Iraq.

What suddenly became apparent to the nation and the world after Katrina struck was that most of the people trapped in New Orleans—abandoned, rendered homeless, starving, and destitute—were poor African Americans. New Orleans had been a black-majority city almost since its founding by the French in 1718. Although most black residents of New Orleans had always been poor, the city also had a thriving black professional middle class, private black colleges and universities (Dillard University, Xavier University), and black businesses. Over the course of three centuries, the city's black community had produced a rich culture, famous for its food, music, literature, and artistic heritage. More than 1,500 lives were lost in the city as a result of the Hurricane Katrina. Homes, schools, and entire neighborhoods were damaged, in some cases, beyond repair.

Katrina moved ashore on Monday, August 29, 2005, and caused the highest storm surge in U.S. history. It punctured the levees that protected New Orleans in 53 places and inundated 80 percent of the city under 20 feet of water. Most of New Orleans's more affluent residents had escaped before the hurricane hit, leaving behind an estimated 100,000 people to weather the storm. With nowhere else to go and no means with which to get there, thousands of black people made their way to the Louisiana Superdome and the Convention Center, where they found wretched conditions—inadequate food, water, electricity, and poor sanitation.

Many African-American residents in New Orleans found themselves stranded literally and figuratively when the levees broke in the wake of Hurricane Katrina and the federal and state governments failed to provide prompt and sufficient relief and rescue efforts.

The aftermath was as bad as the hurricane itself. President George W. Bush cut short his vacation and flew over the wrecked city, but he did not visit New Orleans until September 2. By that time it was apparent to the citizens that Michael Brown, the director of the Federal Emergency Management Agency (FEMA), was not well suited for the job before him. Still, President Bush insisted that Brown was doing "a heck of a job." Actually, FEMA's response and Brown's performance were ineffectual. Brown was forced to resign on September 12. Hip-hop rapper Kanye West departed from the script of a nationally televised program organized to raise relief funds for the displaced Hurricane victims, declaring that "George Bush does not care about black people."

In the face of government ineptitude, individuals and groups relied on their own resources and agency to bring relief to those trapped in New Orleans. Local community organizations mobilized to promote recovery, rebuilding, and renewal. Media stars and celebrities including Oprah Winfrey, Tyler Perry, and Brad Pitt pledged funds to rebuild homes;

Jesse Jackson led a caravan to transport hundreds of homeless residents back to safety in Chicago. Eleven thousand homeless residents were bused 350 miles away to shelter at the Houston Astrodome. Churches and international relief organizations such as the Red Cross sent supplies, money, and clothes. The need was great for thousands of citizens that had lost jobs, homes, and loved ones. Universities across the country welcomed students and faculty from historically black institutions in New Orleans, including Dillard University. Indeed, many professional organizations launched book drives to help rebuild libraries and sponsored volunteers to help reconstruct lives. All of the aid helped, but the recovery was slow. Even recovery could not erase the memory of the government's failed response. By 2015 impressive progress had been made on many fronts. The main streets and businesses in the downtown and tourist areas of New Orleans had been rebuilt. The tourist economy rebounded. To be sure, many black and poor people never returned. Thus, there remain sections and pockets in black communities in need of money, services, and infrastructural and economic development. Too many schools, hospitals, and social service centers are still waiting restoration in many black neighborhoods and communities.

23.9 Barack Obama, President of the United States, 2008–2016

Discuss the ways in which the reelection of President Obama represented a triumph of black politics.

Barack Obama accepted the nomination of the Democratic Party as its presidential candidate on August 28, 2008, in Denver, Colorado. In his acceptance speech, he promised if elected to usher in a new era: "We meet at one of those defining moments—a moment when our nation is at war, our economy is in turmoil, and the American promise has been threatened once more."

23.9.1 Obama versus McCain

The 2008 presidential election campaign was unlike any other in recent American history. The differences between the one-term Illinois Senator Barack Obama and the multitermed Arizona Senator John McCain quickly became apparent. Obama used his matchless oratorical skills to call for change and inspire hope for a better future. He attacked George W. Bush's failed economic, educational, and social policies relentlessly. He also attacked the administration's rush to war in Iraq, its support for tax cuts for the wealthy, and a series of questionable cabinet appointments and scandals. Obama reminded voters that he had had the good judgment to oppose the Iraq War from the outset. He shrewdly selected Delaware senator Joseph Biden as his vice-presidential running mate. Biden's 36 years in the Senate and foreign policy expertise made him a formidable candidate in his own right.

To be sure, on occasion both Obama and McCain deployed similar language about change and hope. Both spoke about the need for Americans to bridge their differences, pledged to work to perfect our union, and promised to inaugurate new politics of civility. McCain declared himself a "maverick" who had often opposed Republican policies during his Senate career. He also touted his experience and military background, especially his five years as a prisoner of war in North Vietnam. McCain insisted that he was ready to be commander-in-chief on day one if elected president. In contrast, the Republicans cited Obama's lack of experience and emphasized his "celebrity" to suggest that he was all fluff and little substance. Moreover, McCain predicted that Obama would raise the taxes of middle-class workers and indulge in wasteful spending.

McCain stunned the nation and delighted his supporters by selecting Sarah Palin, the first-term governor of Alaska, as his running mate. McCain believed she would attract white women who were disillusioned by Obama's victory over Hillary Clinton in the Democratic primaries. Palin was the first woman to share a Republican Party presidential ticket. A mother of five children, Palin's opposition to abortion rights, conservative rhetoric, and anti-Washington stand on government spending for pork-barrel projects (although as a mayor and governor she had accepted hundreds of millions of dollars in federal funds for Alaska) enthralled the Republicans' Evangelical Protestant base and energized McCain's campaign. However, Palin failed to win broad support from women, and interviews with journalists quickly revealed her ignorance of political, economic, and foreign affairs and raised doubts about her ability to be president should McCain die in office.

The turning point in the campaign occurred when the nation suffered the worst financial crisis since the Great Depression. McCain suspended his campaign to rush to Washington to help pass a huge federal government rescue plan for Wall Street banks. He tried to assure Americans that the "fundamentals of the economy are strong," though every indicator suggested the opposite. McCain appeared erratic, impulsive, and out of touch. By contrast, Obama seemed calm, steady, reasonable, reliable, and capable. Obama won the three televised debates between the candidates.

More than 120 million Americans voted on November 4, 2008. Approximately 67 million voted for Barack Obama, giving him one of the largest winning percentages in American history. The Electoral College registered the extent of the Obama victory. He won 367 electoral votes to McCain's 173. Obama redrew the old electoral blue states/red states map by carrying states in every region of the country, including Virginia and Indiana (which no Democratic presidential candidate had won since 1964) and North Carolina, which the Democrats had not carried since Jimmy Carter won it in 1976 (see Map 23-1). He received an unprecedented 95 percent of the African-American vote.

Map 23-1 Election of 2008

This map captures the magnitude of Obama's presidential election triumph. It redraws the decades-long alignment of Republican red states and Democratic blue states. In the 2008 election, Americans moved closer to realizing the dream of one nation.

Which southern states most notably voted for Obama?

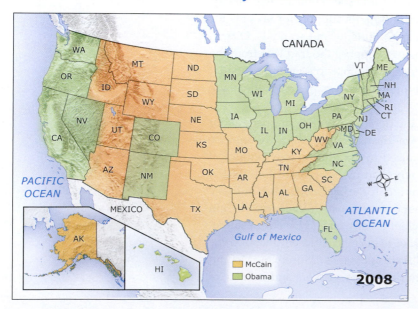

For many Americans, Obama's victory signaled that "race" or "blackness" was no longer an insuperable barrier to the highest political office. His election heralded the dawn of a new day, the beginning of a new chapter in the United States and in the African-American odyssey. On election night, Obama stood in Grant Park in Chicago and told the world, "If there is anyone out there who still doubts that America is a place where all things are possible, who still wonders if the dream of our founders is alive in our time, who still questions the power of our democracy, tonight is your answer." Echoing Abraham Lincoln, Obama captured the moment:

> In this country, we rise or fall as one nation, as one people. Let's resist the temptation to fall back on the same partisanship and pettiness and immaturity that have poisoned our politics for so long. Let's remember that it was a man from this state who first carried the banner of the Republican Party to the White House, a party founded on the values of self-reliance and individual liberty and national unity.
>
> These are values that we all share. And while the Democratic Party has won

a great victory tonight, we do so with a measure of humility and determination to heal the divides that have held back our progress. As Lincoln said to a nation far more divided than ours, we are not enemies but friends. Though passion may have strained, it must not break our bonds of affection.

And to those Americans whose support I have yet to earn, I may not have won your vote tonight, but I hear your voices. I need your help and I will be your president, too.

On January 20, 2009, before a global televised audience of billions and before the two million who gathered on the National Mall in Washington, Barack Obama placed his hand on the bible that Abraham Lincoln had used and took the oath of office to become the first black president of the United States of America.

23.9.2 Obama versus Romney

In the 2008 campaign, Obama was helped by the support of his wife Michelle, who became an exceptionally popular and revered first lady. She was an even stronger and more powerful asset in his reelection bid. Again, black social and political icons from Oprah Winfrey and Tyler Perry to Colin Powell ardently supported both of Obama's election bids. Political supporters touted the fact that he had saved the American automobile industry. Others emphasized the national Affordable Health Care Act, the support for rebuilding America's infrastructure, the granting of citizenship to children of illegal immigrants, and his repudiation of the military's antigay policy, referred to as "Don't Ask, Don't Tell." Obama raised hundreds of millions of dollars in his second campaign. He used a considerable amount of this money early in the campaign to define the Republican Party candidate Mitt Romney as being hopelessly out of touch with the everyday realities of the lives of most Americans. Romney cemented this depiction in remarks (caught on tape) in which he dismissed 47 percent of Americans as being hopelessly dependent on government handouts and people who refused to take responsibility for their own lives.

In both the 2008 and 2012 bids, Obama's calm and steadfast demeanor, his eloquent and passionate oratory (at times resonant of the best of black preaching), and his manifest intelligence enabled him to capture the imagination, spirit, and yearning for change in an America weary of war and government incompetence, indifference, and economic insecurity. Prior to the November 2012 election, the fury of Hurricane Sandy wreaked havoc on the lives and property of millions of citizens in New York, New Jersey, Connecticut, and Maryland. Through it all, President Obama remained vigilant, supportive, and on the ground with residents and political leaders including New Jersey Governor Chris Christie, a Republican. The images of Obama being an active and caring president determined to alleviate suffering and to restore lives were powerful reminders of how much capable and compassionate leadership matters.

On November 6, 2012—after a bitterly contested, long, and costly campaign—the American public voted to retain Barack Obama as president of the United States. One of the most important occurrences during 2012 was the great lengths Republican politicians on both the state and national level went to in order to enact voter identification laws to suppress the black vote and reduce black electoral clout. The voter suppression movement had the opposite effect, however; through unrelenting mobilization, black voters turned out in a higher percentage than any other demographic group to return Obama and his family to the White House. This resilience and determination to keep their hands on the freedom plow bodes well for the future of black politics in America, and by extension across the diaspora. At the dawn of "the Obama Era," African, African-American Studies, and History Professor Paul Tiyambe Zeleza anticipated the emergence of "a more global and nationalistic world," a world that is "impatient with the old injustices and hungry for development, democracy, and self-determination."

Profile

Barack Obama

Twice-elected (2008 and 2012) President Barack Obama secured enactment of the Patient Protection and Affordable Care Act and ended the War in Iraq.

Barack Obama was born in Honolulu on August 4, 1961. His personal history captures the complexity of identity in contemporary America. Obama's father was an immigrant from Kenya who married a white American from Kansas. When his father abandoned the family to complete his studies at Harvard, two-year-old Barack and his mother moved in with her family. In 1967, Obama and his mother relocated with her second husband to Indonesia, where Obama attended both a Roman Catholic and a Muslim school. Obama and his mother later returned to Hawaii, where he lived with his maternal grandparents and completed high school in 1979.

After high school, Obama entered Occidental College in Los Angeles before graduating from New York's Columbia University in 1983. His father, whom he had seen only once in the interim, died in an automobile accident in Kenya before his graduation. After a couple of years in the corporate world, Obama became a community organizer in Chicago, working to start a job placement and training center. His experiences as a community organizer taught him "that meaningful change always begins at the grassroots, and that engaged citizens working together can accomplish extraordinary things." He decided to pursue a law degree "to learn power's currency in all its intricacy and detail."

In 1991 Obama graduated from Harvard Law School, where he was the first African-American editor of the *Law Review*. He returned to Chicago and married Michelle Robinson, a native of Chicago's South Side who had also graduated from Harvard Law School. They have two daughters, Malia and Sasha.

In 1996, Obama was elected to the Illinois State Senate, where he voted to ban racial profiling and supported increased funding for child healthcare. He also helped pass a law requiring police to videotape interrogations of suspects in all capital crime cases.

In 2004, as a candidate for the U.S. Senate, Obama electrified the Democratic National Convention with an impassioned keynote speech. He declared, to thunderous applause, "The pundits like to slice-and-dice our country into Red States and Blue States. . . . But I've got news for them . . . We worship an awesome God in the Blue States, and we don't like federal agents poking around our libraries in Red States. We coach Little League in the Blue States and have gay friends in the Red States. . . . We are one people." A national political star was born.

In the Senate election, Obama coasted to an easy victory over his Republican opponent, black conservative Alan Keyes. Obama's victory made him the second African-American man to serve in the U.S. Senate in the twentieth century and the second black U.S. senator in Illinois history. The freshman senator wasted no time before opposing the Iraq War. Indeed, Obama had been a consistent critic of the war since the Bush administration first proposed it in 2002.

After months of speculation, in February 2007 Obama announced his candidacy to become the presidential nominee of the Democratic Party. He was a formidable campaigner, raising enormous amounts of money and attracting enthusiastic support from a wide spectrum of Americans. He addressed many of the key issues—the war in Iraq, healthcare, and public education—that were equally as important to African Americans as they were to others. Yet some African Americans were ambivalent about his candidacy. When asked to explain this, Obama said, "It's interesting that the people who are most hesitant about this oftentimes are African Americans because they feel protective of me. They're either concerned about the attacks I'd be subjected to or they are skeptical oftentimes that America is prepared to elect a black president."

2009–2012
First-Term Accomplishments of President Obama

January 2009

Lily Ledbetter Fair Pay Act: This act made it illegal for employers to pay unequal wages to men and women who perform the same work

2009

The Resurgence of the American Automotive Industry: This government financial intervention prevented the death of the automobile industry and saved tens of thousands of American jobs. Thanks to this legislation, Chrysler and GM rebounded from near bankruptcy

May 2009–2010

President Obama appointed Sonia Sotomayor and Elena Kagan to the U.S. Supreme Court: These appointments brought the number of female justices on the U.S. Supreme Court to three, a historic high

March 2010

Patient Protection and Affordable Care Act: This act established universal healthcare

December 2010

The Don't Ask, Don't Tell Repeal Act of 2010: This legislation allowed LBGT military personnel to serve openly in the United States Armed Services

May 2011

"Osama bin Laden is dead!": The president made this announcement after he had ordered Navy Seals to kill a secluded bin Laden, who was the architect of the September 11, 2001, terrorist attack on America

July 2011

President Obama supported the Respect for Marriage Act, which was introduced by Senator Dianne Feinstein and Congressman Jerrold Nadler. This legislation upheld the principle that the federal government should not deny gay and lesbian couples the same rights and legal protections as straight couples

December 2011

The President withdrew troops from Iraq and ended America's long-standing war in Iraq

May 2012

President Obama announced plans for complete withdrawal from the Afghanistan War in 2014 through a systematic reduction of U.S. Armed Forces

June 2012

The President supported the DREAM Act (Development, Relief, and Education for Alien Minors), explaining, "It makes no sense to be using our enforcement resources against young people who have known no other country but this one, and who have shown their desire to study and serve"

President Obama, against opposition of Republican Party Leaders who were determined to make him a one-term president, accomplished an impressive array of transformational policies

SOURCE: The White House.

Profile

Michelle LaVaughn Robinson Obama

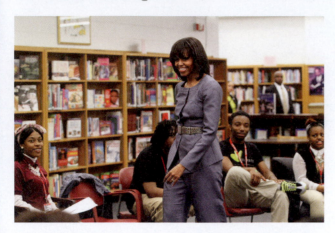

First Lady Michelle Obama made health, education, safety of children, and military families a top priority on her "Mom-in-Chief" agenda.

The First Lady of the United States, Michelle LaVaughn Robinson, was born in Chicago in 1964 to working-class parents. An honor student, she graduated from Chicago's first magnet school for the academically gifted, Whitney Young High School, in 1981 and from Princeton University with a major in sociology and a minor in African-American studies in 1985. In 1988 Michelle earned her law degree at Harvard. In June 1989 she began dating Barack Obama. They married in 1992 and have two daughters, Malia Ann and Natasha (Sasha).

While information about her ancestry is sketchy, her paternal grandparents, Fraser and LaVaughn Robinson, Jr., were part of the Great Migration generation that left the South for northern cities, in this case from South Carolina and Mississippi, respectively. Michelle Obama noted the linked fate of black and white Americans: "Somewhere there was a slave owner—or a white family—in my great grandfather's time that gave him a

place, a home that helped him build a life—that again led to me. So who were those people? I would argue they're just as much a part of my history as my great-grandfather."

After three years working in corporate law, in 1991 Michelle became an assistant commissioner of planning and development and a member of Chicago Mayor Richard M. Daley's staff. In early 1993, she became the founding executive director of the Chicago Office of Public Allies, a nonprofit organization that trained young adults for public service. In 2002, she became executive director of community affairs for the University of Chicago Hospitals. In 2007 she took a leave of absence to work on her husband's campaign for the presidency.

For 21 months, she played an invaluable role in humanizing, normalizing, and explaining her husband to a sometimes skeptical public that often questioned his ethnicity, citizenship, religion, experience, and vision and challenged her pride in her country.

Michelle Obama, the nation's first black First Lady, indicated that her primary responsibility was to ensure that their daughters grew up as normally as life in the White House allowed. In her official capacity, Michelle focused on the needs of military families, women's efforts to balance work and family, and on improving public education and nutrition in part to reduce childhood obesity. One of her first initiatives was to plant a White House vegetable garden—and simultaneously to serve as a role model for young, marginalized, and disadvantaged Americans.

Michelle, the youngest First Lady since Jacqueline Kennedy in 1961, became an important agent of change in American society's perception of black women and a strong role model for all girls and women across the globe. She represents millions of women juggling the demands of career, work, and family.

23.9.3 Factors Affecting the Elections of 2008 and 2012

Many factors contributed to Obama's improbable presidential victories both in 2008 and in 2012. The most important were his skilled, dedicated, and cohesive staff and a mastery of computer technology. His use of the Internet gave him a decisive advantage over McCain in 2008, and again in 2012 over former Massachusetts Governor Mitt Romney. In both the 2008 and 2012 elections, Obama's campaign staff executed a masterful ground game strategy that increased minority voter turnout. It was the higher black voting rate that, when combined with Hispanic votes and those of Asian Americans, proved decisive in 2012. Obama appealed to millions of new voters in both elections while the white vote continued to decline (see Map 23-2). In 2012, Obama won 80 percent of the nonwhite vote (including 93 percent of black voters, 73 percent of Asian American voters, and 71 percent of Hispanic voters).

Obama's presidential campaigns were the most technologically and computer-savvy in history. His background as a community organizer, his support of new immigration

Map 23-2 Election of 2012

This map captures the extent of Obama's presidential election triumph. It underscores the realignments of Republican red states and Democratic blue states.

Which states returned to the Republican fold according to the election map?

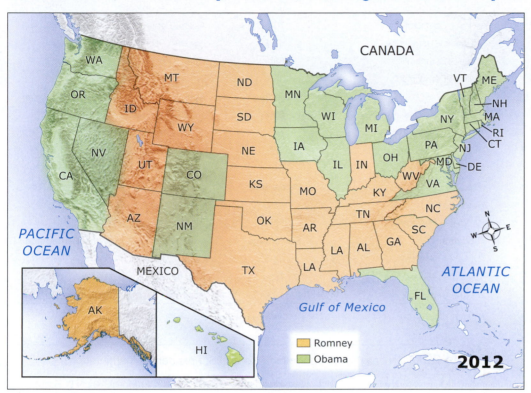

CANADA

WA

OR

MT

ID

WY

NV

UT

CA

AZ

NM

ND

SD

NE

CO

KS

OK

TX

MN

IA

MO

AR

LA

WI

IL

IN

KY

TN

MS

MI

OH

WV

VA

NC

SC

AL

GA

FL

VT

NY

PA

MD

NJ

DE

ME

NH

MA

RI

CT

PACIFIC
OCEAN

MEXICO

ATLANTIC
OCEAN

Gulf of Mexico

AK

HI

☐ Romney
☐ Obama

2012

policies (especially the DREAM Act), and his embrace of the rights of same-sex couples to marry expanded his support in key demographic groups. His grassroots movement of volunteers on local and national levels and the use of celebrity supporters including hip-hop mogul Jay-Z appealed to younger voters while performer Bruce Springsteen attracted white working-class support. The Republican Party's cavalier attitude toward women's concerns, especially the negative remarks by Tea Party candidates challenging women's rights to make their own reproductive decisions, alienated white women voters who turned out in record numbers to support Democratic candidates. In the presidential reelection campaign, white women also voted overwhelmingly for Barack Obama (see Table 23-1).

Black Americans had participated in U.S. presidential inaugurations since 1953 and 1957 when opera singers Dorothy Maynor and Marion Anderson respectively performed the national anthem for Dwight D. Eisenhower's sequential terms in office. (Table 23-2 illuminates the extent of black involvement and presence at presidential inaugurations across the decades.) In 2012 hip hop star Beyonce performed the Star-Spangled Banner to the enormous delight of a people, many of whom doubted that a black man would ever become president of the United States of America. The inclusion of so many black Americans in the inauguration ceremonies of President Barack Obama conveyed the meanings of hope and change.

23.9.4 The Consequential Presidency of Barack Obama

In the 2012 presidential election the Democratic Party failed to maintain control of the House of Representatives. Republican Party leaders were confident that there would be little of consequence to note during President Obama's second term. It may be fair to say that Barrack Obama's two terms have been enormously

Table 23-1 2012 Election Results: Voting Demographics

Total Popular Vote—Obama		65,455,010	**51.0% wins**
Total Popular Vote—Romney		60,771,703	**47.0%**

Ethnicity	Percentage	Ethnicity	Percentage
Black—Democratic	93%	Black—Republican	6%
Asian—Democratic	73%	Asian—Republican	26%
Hispanic—Democratic	71%	Hispanic—Republican	27%
Other—Democratic	58%	Other—Republican	38%
White—Democratic	39%	White—Republican	59%

Age	Percentage	Age	Percentage
18–29—Democratic	60%	18–29—Republican	37%
30–44—Democratic	52%	30–44—Republican	45%
45–64—Democratic	47%	45–64—Republican	51%
65–100—Democratic	44%	65–100—Republican	56%

Gender	Percentage	Gender	Percentage
Men—Democratic	45%	Men—Republican	52%
Women—Democratic	55%	Women—Republican	44%

Location	Percentage	Location	Percentage
Urban—Democratic	62%	Urban—Republican	36%
Suburban—Democratic	48%	Suburban—Republican	50%
Rural—Democratic	39%	Rural—Republican	59%

SOURCE: Based on CNN, *Huffington Post*, and Mail Online. © Darlene Clark Hine.

Table 23-2 African-American Participants in U.S. Presidential Inaugurations

1953	Dorothy Maynor	The Star-Spangled Banner	President Dwight D. Eisenhower
1957	Marian Anderson	The Star-Spangled Banner	President Dwight D. Eisenhower
1961	Marian Anderson	The Star-Spangled Banner	President John F. Kennedy
1965	Leontyne Price	America, the Beautiful	President Lyndon B. Johnson
1969	Bishop Charles Ewbank Tucker	Invocation	President Richard M. Nixon
1973	Rev. Dr. E. V. Hill Ethel Ennis	Invocation The Star-Spangled Banner	President Richard M. Nixon
1977	Atlanta University, Morehouse College, Morris Brown College, Spelman College, Dr. Wendell P. Whalum, Conductor	"Battle Hymn of Republic"	President James E. Carter
1985	Jessye Norman	"Simple Gifts"	President Ronald W. Reagan
1989	Staff Sergeant Alvy Powell	The Star-Spangled Banner & God Bless America	President George H. W. Bush
1993	Dr. Maya Angelou Philander Smith Collegiate Choir directed by Stephen L. Hayes	Poem: "On the Pulse of the Morning" "City on the Hill"	President William J. Clinton
1997	Satina Jackson Jessye Norman Rev. Gardner C. Taylor	The Star-Spangled Banner Medley of Freedom songs Benediction	President William J. Clinton
2001	Pastor Kirbyjon H. Caldwell	Benediction	President George W. Bush
2005	Denyce Graves Pastor Kirbyjon H. Caldwell	The American Anthem Benediction	President George W. Bush
2009	Aretha Franklin Elizabeth Alexander Rev. Dr. Joseph E. Lowery	My Country 'Tis of Thee Poem: "Praise Song for the Day" Benediction	President Barack H. Obama
2013	Myrlie Evers-Williams Beyoncé	Invocation The Star-Spangled Banner	President Barack H. Obama

SOURCE: Compiled by Marshanda Smith. © Darlene Clark Hine.

consequential. Historians will undoubtedly have much to debate in the ensuing years as to whether President Obama was the most consequential U.S. president since Abraham Lincoln.

To be sure, a full assessment of the successes of President Obama's two terms will take years. Meanwhile, it is possible to highlight some of the most important—that is, consequential—accomplishments. Two United States Supreme Court decisions buttressed two of President Obama's major domestic policies.

The much beleaguered Affordable Health Care Act survived and proved to be enormously popular with the American people. Only Republican leaders in Congress would attempt over 50 times to repeal the law. In 2015 the United States Supreme Court in the *King* v. *Burwell* decision voted to preserve the subsidy provisions of the Affordable Health Care Act. The first United States Supreme Court case, *NFIB* v. *Sckeles*, decided in 2012 by a 5–4 majority, had held that the ACA law did not limit insurance subsidies only to patients who were enrolled in state health insurance exchanges. This decision prevented the exclusion or elimination of patients in the states where government-sponsored exchanges existed. The matter is now settled. The Affordable Care Act made health care insurance available to over 11 million Americans by the end of open enrollment in 2015. To date, at least 16.4 million people have gained insurance in the five years that the Affordable Care Act has been in operation. President Obama advocated raises in minimum wages and helped to improve the economic status of millions of low-wage workers. In support of another much-needed reform in our criminal justice system, President Obama ordered a review by the Sentencing Commission of mandatory minimum sentences.

A second U. S. Supreme Court decision validated and affirmed President Obama's support of same-sex marriage rights. The Court's decision in *Obergefell* v. *Hodges* sustained the Cultural Revolution waged in support of equal rights for same-sex couples. The decision overturned the 1986 ruling in *Bowers* v. *Hardwick* that had permitted states to make same-sex intercourse a criminal offense. The five justices in support of equal rights for same-sex relationships were Anthony Kennedy, Ruth Bader Ginsberg, Stephen Breyer, Sonia Sotomayor, and Elena Kagen. The opposition included Chief Justice John Roberts, Samuel Alito, Antonin Scalia, and Clarence Thomas.

President Obama achieved two major foreign policy successes. One occurred when he normalized relations with Cuba. In December 2014 President Obama announced plans to resume full diplomatic relations with Cuba and thus to end over 50 years of separation and hostility. On April 11, 2015, at the Summit of the Americas in Panama, President Obama met with Cuban President Raul Castro. He declared, "The United States will not be impressed by the past. . . . The Cold War has been over for a long time." On July 20, 2015, the Cuban flag was positioned above Cuba's embassy in Washington. On August 14, 2015, with Secretary of State John Kerry present, America's flag was raised above the U.S. embassy in Havana.

One of the most significant foreign policy successes was the U.S.-brokered Iran Treaty. Along with five other nations, Iran agreed to allow the U.S. and its allies to regulate and inspect its nuclear program. Obama faced stiff opposition from the Republican-led Congress and from Israeli Prime Minister Benjamin Netanyahu. President Obama prevailed, and in so doing severely reduced the threat of nuclear war.

23.9.5 Twenty-Three Mass Shootings

President Obama's list of accomplishments were significant and numerous. However, the first seven years of his presidency also witnessed an escalation in the number of tragic mass murders and shootings that took the lives of hundreds of innocent children, college students, participants in political meetings, movie theater patrons, and citizens in healthcare facilities and community centers. President Obama spoke eloquently and with great feeling and pain about the need to reduce the number of firearms made too easily accessible to those with mental illnesses. Again and again he implored Congress to enact more vigorous gun-control legislation and to pass laws mandating background checks of those who purchased guns at gun shows and from dealers without licenses. His pleas went unheeded and the numbers of deaths continued to escalate. The gun lobby opposition became more determined. President Obama considered this to be one of the most painful failures of his presidency. From a Tucson shopping center on January 8, 2011, that wounded Arizona's Congresswoman Gabrielle Giffords to the Sandy Hook Elementary School, in Newtown, Connecticut, on December 12, 2012, to Emanuel African Methodist Episcopal Church in North Charleston, South Carolina, the numbers of deaths increased. Speaking from the White House on June 17, 2015, following the killings in Charleston, a shaken President Obama declared, "I've had to make statements like this too many times. Communities like this have had to endure tragedies like this too many times. We don't have all the facts, but we do know that, once again, innocent people were killed in part because someone who wanted to inflict harm had no trouble getting their hands on a gun."

A moment that captured President Obama's profound mixture of grief, pain, frustration, and steely resolve occurred when he delivered an eulogy on June 26, 2015, at the funeral services of South Carolina minister Clementa Pinckney, one of nine African Americans killed in the AME church massacre. In earlier comments after mass shootings the President expressed the need for gun-control or background-check legislation. This time he focused attention on the consequences of too-easy access to guns combined with festering racial hatred: "As a nation, out of this terrible tragedy, God has visited grace upon us, for he has allowed us to see where we've been blind to the way past injustices continue to shape the present. Perhaps we see that now." It was President Obama's singing of the spiritual "Amazing Grace" in combination with his remarks that helped to bring down the Confederate battle flag from the South Carolina state house grounds, a most egregious and painful symbol of white racial antipathy for too many generations of African Americans.

23.10 Black Lives Matter

Explain the emergence of the Black Lives Matter movement and its significance.

> **Prince Jones was a one of one, and they had destroyed his body, scorched his shoulders and arms, ripped open his back, mangled lung, kidney, and liver. . . . When the assembled members bowed their heads in prayer, I was divided from them because I believe that the void would not answer back.**
>
> —*Ta-Nehisi Coates (Between the World and Me, 2015, p. 79)*

An unprecedented series of homicides surged through many low-income black and Hispanic communities in the second decade of the twenty-first century. Police officers shot and killed a number of unarmed black men and boys across the country. To be sure, much of the violence in black neighborhoods stemmed from the easy availability of firearms and the turf wars that erupted among rival gangs that peddled drugs. Too often, innocent men, women, and children were caught in the crossfire. MacArthur Prize–winning author Ta-Nehisi Coates's meditation on the shooting death of a close friend and former Howard University student is poignant and disturbing. His powerful book is well placed in company with James Baldwin's *The Fire Next Time* (1963) for its sober critique of the continued existence of the policies and practices that result in the deaths of black people.

In January 2013 Hadiya Pendleton, a 15-year-old student and drum majorette at King College Prep, was killed in an exchange of gunfire by competing gangs in

Chicago. A few days earlier, she and her classmates had performed at President Obama's second inauguration. As alarming and tragic as these deaths are, ironically, the total number of gun-related violence is declining. In 1993, 18,253 people died in firearm homicides. By 2011, that number dropped to 11,101. This does not erase the fact that more than 60,000 people have been killed in gun-related violence since 2007.

What attracted the most recent national and international attention was the series of incidents in which law-enforcement personnel shot and killed unarmed black males. Trayvon Martin, a 17-year-old high school student, was accosted by a neighborhood watch volunteer, George Zimmerman, in Sanford, Florida, in February 2012. Following a scuffle, Martin was shot and killed. A jury subsequently found Zimmerman not guilty of second-degree murder.

Supporters of the Black Lives Matter movement participated in the 30th annual Kingdom Day Parade in South Los Angeles, California, on January 19, 2015, to commemorate Martin Luther King Jr. Day.

In July 2014 New York City police officers stopped Eric Garner for allegedly selling untaxed "loosie" cigarettes. Officer Daniel Pantaleo grabbed Garner around the neck in a chokehold and wrestled him to the ground. Garner pleaded 11 times, "I can't breathe." He stopped breathing. No one administered CPR. Rather, police officials agreed to an out-of-court settlement of $5.9 million to Garner's widow.

Less than a month after Garner's death, Michael Brown, an 18-year-old resident of Ferguson, Missouri, was stopped along with his friend Dorian Johnson by officer Darren Wilson who had received a report that two black men had stolen cigarillos from a convenience store. Following a struggle between Brown and Wilson, the policeman shot at the unarmed Brown 12 times, hitting him six times. Wilson resigned from the police department. A grand jury, however, failed to indict him. The U.S. Department of Justice also investigated Brown's death. In the end, no charges were filed against Wilson.

Twelve-year-old Tamir Rice, carrying a pellet gun in a city park, was shot and killed by Cleveland police officer Timothy Loehmann in November 2014. After several investigations that lasted nearly a year, a grand jury declined to indict the officer. A local prosecutor agreed with the decision.

In Baltimore in April 2015, 25-year-old Freddie Gray died of spinal cord injuries while in the custody of police officers. Six officers were charged in connection with Gray's death. The first of those officers brought to trial was William G. Porter, an African American. His trial resulted in a hung jury and mistrial in December 2015. He will be tried again.

Opal Tometi, Alicia Garza, and Patrisse Cullors, founders of the Black Lives Matter movement, march in Cleveland, Ohio, July 2015, protesting the police killings of black boys and men.

Walter Scott, a 50-year-old black man and Coast Guard veteran, was stopped in April 2015 in North Charleston, South Carolina, by Officer Michael Slager for having a broken taillight on his automobile. When Scott fled, Slager shot and killed him. Michael Slager was released on bail in January 2016, and he still awaits trial.

Months before Scott's death in October 2014, 17-year-old Laquan McDonald was shot 16 times by Chicago police officer Jason Van Dyke. But it was not until a video of the shooting was released to the media more than a year later that a storm of protests erupted. Van Dyke was charged with murder and released on bail. Until the video was released police officials contended McDonald lunged at officers with a knife.

But the video showed no aggressive moves by McDonald toward Van Dyke. Before the video was made public, Chicago's city council approved a settlement of $5 million with McDonald's family.

Advances in technology have been crucial in recent years in alerting the public to the behavior and actions of police officers. The cases of Eric Garner, Tamir Rice, Michael Brown, Walter Scott, and Laquan McDonald were recorded on video. Before the video was made public, the officers involved in the shootings of Brown, Scott, and McDonald maintained that their lives were in jeopardy, and that they had acted in self-defense. But the availability of cell-phone video, dashboard cameras on police vehicles, and body cameras worn by policemen have provided graphic evidence of what happens in civilian–police confrontations that previously did not exist. New technology has also enabled people to communicate almost instantly through Twitter, Instagram, and text messaging. People no longer rely as extensively on radio, television, and newspapers when a major incident occurs. The technology permits people and groups to organize demonstrations and marches quickly to protest what happened.

"Black Lives Matter" emerged as a movement following Michael Brown's death. The founders, Alicia Garza, Opal Tometi, and Patrisse Cullors, along with followers demanded that police officers involved in shootings be treated by the same standard used to judge others. The badge should not be a license to kill. "I can't breathe" became a rallying cry after Eric Garner died. Professional athletes including LeBron James and college players including the Notre Dame women's basketball team wore warm-up jerseys emblazoned with "I Can't Breathe." Tens of thousands of protestors across the gamut of identities—unburdened by differences in color, ethnicity, gender, class, sexuality, political affiliation, region, and/or occupation—participated in wide-ranging improvised and spontaneous disruptive protests as they demanded police reforms. Indeed, protesters and demonstrators called into question the destructive policies and outdated practices of mass incarceration and the lengthy sentences meted out for minor infractions that resulted in the warehousing of a million black men and tens of thousands of black women across the decades since the late twentieth century up to the present moment.

Conclusion

Jesse Jackson, whose Rainbow Coalition reflected a quest for unity amid diversity, asked at the 1988 Democratic convention, "Shall we expand, be inclusive, find unity and power; or suffer division and impotence?" The Hurricane Katrina disaster in 2005 reminded the black community of how precarious life remained for those trapped in poverty. The 2007 Democratic primary campaign illustrated the political strength of black Americans and the extent to which the Democratic Party had embraced its diverse constituency. African Americans remained committed to a progressive political agenda that emphasized universal healthcare, quality education, urban economic development, job training, and safe environments, and called for an end to racial profiling and police brutality. Black activists and white allies called for an end to the prison-industrial complex that shattered families and communities and left disfranchised those men and women who had paid their debt and still could not vote like other citizens. The election of President Barrack Obama marked another stage in the black odyssey toward freedom and the transformation of American society. Witnesses to his inauguration on January 20, 2009, to become the 44th president of the United States, also noted that black politics had come of age.

Few black Americans anticipated the depth of animosity and viral hatred that circulated within the Republican Party and among those whites who supported the rise of the Tea Party. Many Republican politicians vowed to make Barack Obama a "one-term president." They vigorously pursued an obstructionist stance and tried to block every progressive measure that Obama supported or advocated. The election campaign of 2012 became a referendum on the policies President Obama pursued in his first term. The success of the 2012 campaign, his 51 to 47 percent victory over his opponent Mitt Romney, underscored the triumph of coalition politics and the importance of grassroots community organizing and mobilization strategies in the twenty-first century.

It is little wonder given the Republicans' obstructionist stance that President Obama took advantage of every available opportunity to put the spotlight on African Americans who had overcome barriers even more daunting than those posed against him. One occasion stands out. World War II Veteran Emma Didlake had to wait a long time to receive an expression of gratitude for the sacrifice and service that she had rendered to her country. On July 17, 2015, President Obama welcomed to the White House the oldest known World War II veteran, 110-year-old Emma Didlake of Detroit. Veteran Didlake had helped to integrate the armed services during World War II. About the Detroit resident and her service, President Obama declared, "We are so grateful that she is here today, and it's a great reminder of not only the sacrifices that a greater generation made on our behalf but also the kind of trailblazing women veterans made, African American veterans who helped to integrate our Armed Services." He concluded, "We are very, very proud of them so that's why we've got to make sure we do right by them." In spite of the obstructionists, President Barack Obama did right by America.

Chapter Timeline

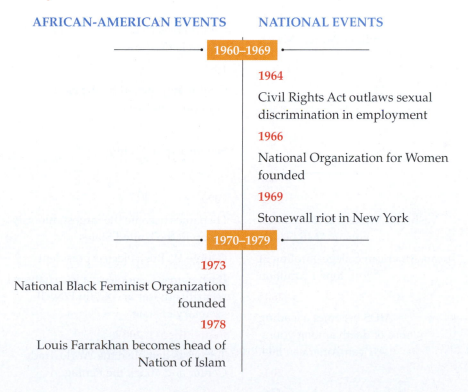

AFRICAN-AMERICAN EVENTS   NATIONAL EVENTS

1960–1969

1964
Civil Rights Act outlaws sexual discrimination in employment

1966
National Organization for Women founded

1969
Stonewall riot in New York

1970–1979

1973
National Black Feminist Organization founded

1978
Louis Farrakhan becomes head of Nation of Islam

AFRICAN-AMERICAN EVENTS	NATIONAL EVENTS
1980–1989	
1982	**1980**
Alice Walker and Charles Fuller win Pulitzer Prizes in fiction and drama	Ronald Reagan elected president
	1981
1984	Recession settles in; Economic Recovery Tax Act passed
Russell Simmons forms Def Jam Records	**1984**
	President Reagan reelected
1987	**1988**
August Wilson wins Pulitzer Prize for drama	George H. W. Bush elected president
1988	
N.W.A.'s *Straight Outta Compton* marks the rise of gangsta rap	
1990–1999	
1990	**1990–1999**
Anna Deavere Smith and August Wilson win Pulitzer Prizes for poetry and drama	1.4 million Caribbean and African immigrants move to the United States
	1991
1993	Operation Desert Storm against Iraq
Toni Morrison becomes the first black woman to win the Nobel Prize for literature	**1992**
	Bill Clinton elected president
1995	**1994**
Million Man March	Republicans gain control of Congress
1997	**1996**
Million Woman March	Clinton reelected; Clinton signs welfare reform legislation
	1998
	Clinton impeached by the House of Representatives
	1999
	Senate acquits Clinton
2000–2015	
2000	**2000**
Vashti M. McKenzie elected first woman AME bishop	Hispanics become the largest minority group in the United States
African-American college enrollment tops 1.5 million	George W. Bush elected president
	Bush names Condoleezza Rice national security adviser and Colin Powell secretary of state
2001	
AIDS becomes a leading cause of death among young African-American men	**September 11, 2001**
	Terrorists demolish the World Trade Center and attack the Pentagon
2002	**2004**
Wilton Gregory heads U.S. Catholic bishops	George W. Bush reelected president

AFRICAN-AMERICAN EVENTS	NATIONAL EVENTS
2004	**2005**
Carol Moseley Braun and Al Sharpton run for president	Hurricane Katrina devastates New Orleans
Barack Obama elected to U.S. Senate	**2013**
Condoleezza Rice appointed secretary of state	In a 5–4 decision authored by Chief Justice John Roberts, the U.S. Supreme Court struck down as unconstitutional a key provision of the Voting Rights Act of 1965 that determines which jurisdictions have to preclear any voting changes with the federal government. The decision in *Shelby County v. Holder* effectively ended the use of Section 5 of the Voting Rights Act, which requires any changes to voting rules in covered states and jurisdictions to be approved by the U.S. Justice Department before they can go into effect.
2009	
Barack Obama inaugurated as the 44th President of the United States	
President Obama receives the Nobel Peace Prize	
Annette Gordon-Reed wins Pulitzer Prize in history	
2015	
Loretta Lynch appointed Attorney General of the United States	**2014**
	Black Lives Matter founded to protest the killings of young and unarmed black boys and men and women and girls by police authorities.
	2015
	In a historic 5–4 decision, in *Obergefell v. Hodges*, the Court struck down state bans on same-sex marriage, thereby granting the constitutional right to marry to LGBT Americans throughout the country.

Review Questions

1. To what extent did the Reagan and Bush presidencies nullify and dismantle Great Society legislation? Describe the African American response to the Republican conservative reaction.

2. What was the significance of Jesse Jackson's campaigns for the Democratic presidential nomination? Why did African Americans become so important for the Democratic Party?

3. How did the welfare reform legislation passed under Clinton and George W. Bush's No Child Left Behind Act affect African Americans?

4. Why did affirmative action become so controversial in the 1990s? How did affirmative action in the workplace differ from affirmative action in education?

5. How did the Rodney King case illuminate the differences between how black and white Americans saw the police and the justice system?

6. How did the Hurricane Katrina disaster expose the fault lines of race, class, and gender in American society?

7. Explain the strategy Barack Obama devised to defeat John McCain in 2008. Discuss the significance of Obama's election to African Americans.

Retracing the Odyssey

The *Amistad* Research Center, Tilton Hall, Tulane University, New Orleans. The *Amistad* Center contains manuscripts and art that illuminate the history and culture of diverse ethnic groups and race relations in the United States. Approximately 90 percent of its holdings document the history and records of African Americans'

community organizations and struggles. The center also houses records related to religious denominations—Protestant, Catholic, and Jewish. Its art gallery frequently exhibits the work of early black artists such as Aaron Douglas.

Recommended Reading

Martha Biondi. "The Rise of the Reparations Movement." *Radical History Review* 87 (Fall 2003): 5–18. A superb brief historical overview of the black reparations movement from the Civil War to the present era.

Ta-Nehisi Coates. *Between the World and Me.* New York: Spiegel & Grau, 2015. Coates is one of America's most important writers on the subject of race today. His profoundly moving meditation earns him a rightful place in the company of Richard Wright, Ralph Ellison, James Baldwin, and Albert Murray. His book and articles are essential readings.

Ta-Nehisi Coates. "The Black Family in the Age of Mass Incarceration." *The Atlantic*, October 2015, pp. 60–84.

Cathy J. Cohen. *The Boundaries of Blackness: AIDS and the Breakdown of Black Politics.* Chicago: University of Chicago Press, 1999. A political scientist's sophisticated

and provocative exploration into the social, political, and cultural impact of the AIDS epidemic on the African-American community.

Charles P. Henry, Robert L. Allen, and Robert Chrisman, eds. *The Obama Phenomenon: Towards a Multiracial Democracy.* Urbana: University of Illinois Press, 2011. An excellent anthology of thought-provoking essays covering a range of topics on Obama's first election, public policy, and culture.

Deborah Gray White. *Too Heavy a Load: Black Women in Defense of Themselves, 1894–1994.* New York: W.W. Norton, 1998. A brilliant study by a black historian of black women and the community organizations they founded to fight for the ballot, equal opportunities, and an end to sexism and misogyny in black life.

Additional Bibliography

Culture and Race Studies

Michelle Alexander. *The New Jim Crow: Mass Incarceration in the Age of Colorblindness.* New York: New Press, 2010.

Robin D. G. Kelley. *Race Rebels: Culture, Politics, and the Black Working Class.* New York: Free Press, 1994.

Jacob Levenson. *The Secret Epidemic: The Story of AIDS and Black America.* New York: Pantheon, 2004.

Manning Marable. *The Great Wells of Democracy: The Meaning of Race in American Life.* New York: Basic Books, 2002.

Terry McMillan. *Five for Five: The Films of Spike Lee.* New York: Stewart, Tabori & Chang, 1991.

Mary Pattillo, David Weiman, and Bruce Western, eds. *Imprisoning America: The Social Effects of Mass Incarceration.* New York: Russell Sage Foundation, 2004.

Nikhil Pal Singh. *Black Is a Country: Race and the Unfinished Struggle for Democracy.* Cambridge, MA: Harvard University Press, 2004.

Paul Tiyambe Zeleza. *Barack Obama and African Diasporas: Dialogues and Dissensions.* Athens: Ohio University Press, 2009.

Black Politics and Economics

Barry Bluestone and Bennett Harrison. *The Deindustrialization of America: Plant Closings, Community Abandonment, and the Dismantling of Basic Industry.* New York: Basic Books, 1982.

Donna Brazile. *Cooking with Grease: Stirring the Pot in American Politics.* New York: Simon and Schuster, 2004.

Roy L. Brooks, ed. *When Sorry Isn't Enough: The Controversy Over Apologies and Reparations for Human Injustice.* New York: New York University Press, 1999.

Michael K. Brown. *Race, Money, and the American Welfare State.* Ithaca, NY: Cornell University Press, 1999.

Martin Carnoy. *Faded Dreams: The Politics and Economics of Race in America.* Cambridge, UK: Cambridge University Press, 1994.

Dalton Conley. *Being Black, Living in the Red: Race, Wealth, and Social Policy in America.* Berkeley: University of California Press, 1999.

Robert Dallek. *Ronald Reagan: The Politics of Symbolism.* Cambridge, MA: Harvard University Press, 1984.

W. Avon Drake and Robert D. Holsworth. *Affirmative Action and the Stalled Quest for Black Progress.* Urbana: University of Illinois Press, 1996.

Robert Gooding-Williams, ed. *Reading Rodney King: Reading Urban Uprising.* New York: Routledge, 1993.

Lani Guinier. *Tyranny of the Majority: Fundamental Fairness and Representative Democracy.* New York: Free Press, 1995.

Andrew Hacker. *Two Nations: Black and White, Separate, Hostile, Unequal.* Rev. ed. New York: Ballantine Books, 1995.

Fredrick C. Harris. *The Price of the Ticket: Barack Obama and the Rise and Decline of Black Politics.* New York: Oxford University Press, 2012.

Melissa Victoria Harris-Lacewell. *Barbershops, Bibles, and BET: Everyday Talk and Black Political Thought.* Princeton, NJ: Princeton University Press, 2004.

Charles P. Henry. *Jesse Jackson: The Search for Common Ground.* Oakland, CA: Black Scholar Press, 1991.

Anita Faye Hill and Emma Coleman Jordan, eds. *Race, Gender, and Power in America: The Legacy of the Hill–Thomas Hearings.* New York: Oxford University Press, 1995.

James Jennings. *Welfare Reform and the Revitalization of Inner City Neighborhoods.* East Lansing: Michigan State University Press, 2003.

Randall Kennedy. *The Persistence of the Color Line: Racial Politics and the Obama Presidency.* New York: Pantheon Books, 2011.

Roland S. Martin. *The First: President Barack Obama's Road to the White House as Originally Reported by Roland S. Martin.* Chicago: Third World Press, 2010.

Douglas S. Massey and Nancy A. Denton. *American Apartheid: Segregation and the Making of the Underclass.* Cambridge, MA: Harvard University Press, 1993.

Adolph Reed, Jr. *The Jesse Jackson Phenomenon: The Crisis of Purpose in Afro-American Politics.* New Haven, CT: Yale University Press, 1986.

Andrea Y. Simpson. *The Tie That Binds: Identity and Political Attitudes in the Post–Civil Rights Generation.* New York: New York University Press, 1998.

Special Issue on Affirmative Action. *Western Journal of Black Studies* 27, no. 1 (Spring 2003).

Thomas J. Sugrue. *Not Even Past: Barack Obama and the Burden of Race.* Princeton, NJ: Princeton University Press, 2010.

The Election Issue. *Souls: A Critical Journal of Black Politics, Culture, and Society* 14, no. 1–2 (January–June 2012).

Ronald W. Walters. *Freedom Is Not Enough: Black Voters, Black Candidates, and American Presidential Politics.* Lanham, MD: Rowman and Littlefield, 2005.

William Julius Wilson. *The Bridge Over the Racial Divide: Rising Inequality and Coalition Politics.* Berkeley: University of California Press, 1999.

Liberation Studies

Derrick Bell. *Faces at the Bottom of the Well: The Permanence of Racism.* New York: Basic Books, 1992.

Dan Berger. *Captive Nation: Black Prison Organizing in the Civil Rights Era.* Chapel Hill: University of North Carolina Press, 2014.

Michael C. Dawson. *Behind the Mule: Race and Class in African-American Politics.* Princeton, NJ: Princeton University Press, 1994.

W. Marvin Dulaney. *Black Police in America.* Bloomington: Indiana University Press, 1996.

David H. Ikard and Martell Lee Teasley. *Nation of Cowards: Black Activism in Barack Obama's Post-Racial America.* Bloomington: Indiana University Press, 2012.

Brenda Gayle Plummer, ed. *Window on Freedom: Race, Civil Rights, and Foreign Affairs, 1945–1988.* Chapel Hill: University of North Carolina Press, 2003.

Randall Robinson. *The Debt: What America Owes to Blacks.* New York: Plume, 2000.

Ytasha L. Womack. Foreword by Derek T. Dingle. *Post Black: How a New Generation Is Redefining African American Identity.* Chicago: Chicago Press Review, 2010.

Black Conservatives

Herman Cain. *This Is Herman Cain!: My Journey to the White House.* New York: Threshold Editions, 2011.

Michael L. Ondaatie. *Black Conservative Intellectuals in Modern America.* Philadelphia: University of Pennsylvania Press, 2009.

Joe Soss, Richard C. Fording, and Sanford F. Schram. *Disciplining the Poor: Neoliberal Paternalism and the Persistent Power of Race.* Chicago: University of Chicago Press, 2011.

Thomas Sowell. *Preferential Policies: An International Perspective*. New York: William Morrow, 1990.

Shelby Steele. *A Dream Deferred: The Second Betrayal of Black Freedom in America*. New York: HarperCollins, 1998.

_____. *A Bound Man: Why We Are Excited About Obama and Why He Can't Win*. New York: Free Press, 2008.

Clarence Thomas. *My Grandfather's Son: A Memoir*. New York: HarperCollins, 2007.

Autobiography and Biography

Marshall Frady. *Jesse: The Life and Pilgrimage of Jesse Jackson*. New York: Random House, 1996.

John Hope Franklin. *Mirror to America: The Autobiography of John Hope Franklin*. New York: Farrar, Straus and Giroux, 2005.

David Maraniss. *Obama, the Story*. New York: Simon and Schuster, 2012.

Barack Obama. *Dreams From My Father: A Story of Race and Inheritance*. 1995. Reprint, New York: Three Rivers Press, 2004.

Rev. Al Sharpton, with Karen Hunter. *Al on America*. New York: Kensington, 2002.

Peter Slevin and Robin Miles. *Michelle Obama: A Life*. New York: Random House, 2015.

Rachel L. Swarns. *American Tapestry: The Story of the Black, White, and Multiracial Ancestors of Michelle Obama*. New York: Amistad, 2012.

Richard Wolfe. *Renegade: The Making of a President*. New York: Crown, 2009.

Chapter 24

African Americans End the Twentieth Century and Enter into the Twenty-First Century

1980–2016

Co-heading the "Heart of the City" tour, "hip-hop royalty" Mary J. Blige and Jay-Z brought the house down in Detroit in 2008.

Learning Objectives

After reading this chapter, you should be able to:

24.1 Analyze the economic disparities that explain the gulf between the wealth of white Americans and that of African Americans.

24.2 Discuss the factors that have institutionalized poverty among African Americans.

24.3 Describe the achievements African Americans made in the areas of music, literature, and film from the 1980s through the twenty-first century.

24.4 Discuss the factors that made it possible for rap music to achieve international popularity.

24.5 Analyze the variety of approaches that constitute Afrocentricity.

24.6 Identify some of the strengths and tensions that persist within today's black church.

24.7 Explain Louis Farrakhan's views about the status and challenges black men confront in present-day America.

24.8 Explore the many dimensions of black identity, culture, and status in the twenty-first century.

It is a peculiar sensation, this double consciousness, this sense of always looking at one's self through the eyes of others, of measuring one's soul by the tape of a world that looks on in amused contempt and pity. One ever feels his two-ness,—an American, a Negro; two warring ideals in one dark body, whose dogged strength alone keeps it from being torn asunder.

—*W. E. B. Du Bois, The Souls of Black Folk (1901)*

In *The Souls of Black Folk*, W. E. B. Du Bois dreamed of a nation in which black people could be both African and American, embracing their own rich cultural heritage and sharing it with America while becoming full-fledged citizens. This merging of the "two-ness" of the African and American "souls" did not happen in Du Bois's lifetime, but at his death in 1963, the civil rights movement was poised on the edge of its greatest successes. Had Du Bois lived to the dawn of the twenty-first century, he would have been both pleased by the progress made toward fulfilling his dream and saddened by the extent to which the ideals of that dream remain beyond the reach of so many African Americans.

What Du Bois could not have imagined was the globalization of hip-hop, a black youth-generated culture movement that transformed the world into a "hip-hop planet." Hip-hop became the latest of a long series of cultural movements improvised by marginalized but creative black young people determined to refashion empowering images of themselves and to critique the impoverished material conditions of their lives in urban America. They used a wide array of artistic forms to tell the stories of their lives in the early twenty-first century.

In the 2000s, many African Americans advanced to the top ranks of government, the military, sports, entertainment, business, the professions, and academia. The African "soul" that Du Bois urged black Americans to take pride in moved from the shadowy edges of American culture to its heart, and black Americans were honored for their contributions to the nation's music, language, and fine arts.

As a result of the legislative successes of the modern civil rights movement, laws now prohibit racial segregation, disfranchisement, and job discrimination. In their wake, millions of black men and women escaped the deep poverty to which nearly all African Americans had been confined when Du Bois wrote *Souls*. Like other Americans, many more black people now complete high school and college and live healthier and longer lives, although white Americans still, on average, earn more and live longer.

Undoubtedly, Du Bois would be appalled by the extreme poverty, poor education, substance addiction, sub-standard housing, environmental racism, and violent crime that still plague both inner-city and rural black populations. But he might not be surprised by the deep racism and ugly stereotyping that continue to define the journey of black people in America, notwithstanding the election of Barack Obama to the presidency of the United States in 2008 and his reelection in 2012. By the end of his second term, it appeared as if the lives of black boys and men were in a greater jeopardy.

A "two-ness" dilemma persists a century after Du Bois wrote about "double consciousness," and contemporary scholars, authors, and public intellectuals ponder questions about "post-black" and "post-racial" identities. Such debates are complicated both by the successes African Americans have achieved in recent decades and by demographic and global political changes. Tensions have always festered between a racially defined identity and the many other ways in which African Americans define themselves. Differences of class, color, ethnicity, belief, and region have divided Americans for centuries. Today, other factors further complicate identities, including sexual preference, religious affiliation, immigration status, and political philosophy. Reconciling all these self-understandings within a larger racial identity remains one of the major challenges of the continuing African-American odyssey.

24.1 Progress and Poverty: Income, Education, and Health

Analyze the economic disparities that explain the gulf between the wealth of white Americans and that of African Americans.

After the triumphs of the civil rights era, many African Americans made great strides in overcoming the economic and educational disadvantages that had plagued their ancestors. Partly as a result of this progress, they are living longer, healthier lives. Yet the disparities between the levels of wealth, schooling, and health status of African Americans and the white majority, although narrowed, have persisted. The persistence of black poverty and the social problems associated with it erupted into a major controversy in black communities in 2004 when Bill Cosby used the 50th anniversary of the *Brown v. Board of Education* decision to criticize what he termed "irresponsible black poor parents and their delinquent children." Cosby called for greater "personal responsibility" from middle-class black people who, he argued, should put themselves and their children forward as role models for poor African Americans who isolate themselves from the American mainstream and imitate the black inner-city street cultures. Many black commentators objected to this attack and accused Cosby of "airing the black community's dirty laundry."

24.1.1 High-Achieving African Americans

The decades after 1970 witnessed a consolidation of black economic, civic, and political progress and the expansion of a black middle and upper class of professionals, media celebrities, and business entrepreneurs. The success of the black upper class was exemplified by the prominence of highly visible African Americans such as media mogul Oprah Winfrey, Bill Clinton's secretary of commerce Ronald Brown, chairman

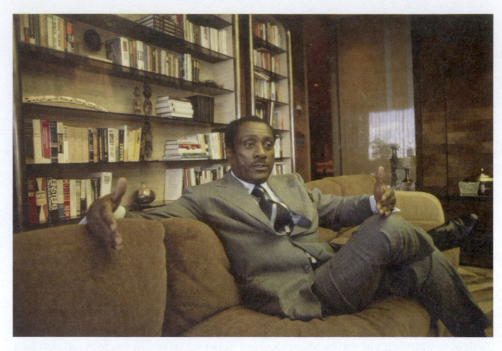

The late *Ebony* and *Jet* publisher John Johnson.

of the Joint Chiefs of Staff and later secretary of state Colin Powell and his immediate successor as secretary of state, Condoleezza Rice, and Harvard University professor Henry Louis Gates. To be sure, the ultra-rich remained rare in the black community, but their ranks grew. Winfrey, Cosby, Michael Jackson, Michael Jordan, Jay-Z, and Beyoncé acquired fortunes as entertainers or athletes. Others among the fortunate few included businessman Robert L. Johnson, founder of Black Entertainment Television (BET), who became the first African American to own a professional basketball team, the Charlotte, North Carolina, Bobcats; the late John H. Johnson, publisher of *Ebony* and *Jet* magazines; Berry Gordy, founder of Motown Records; and Russell Simmons, a recording and fashion entrepreneur.

The career of Reginald Lewis illustrated the possibilities open to black people in other industries. Armed with a degree from Harvard Law School, he purchased the McCall Pattern Company in 1984. In 1987 he bought Beatrice Foods, an international packaged-goods company, for $2.5 billion. At the time it was the largest leveraged buyout in U.S. history, and Lewis became the wealthiest African American. Before his death in 1993, Lewis gave back to his community by donating millions of dollars to Howard University and the NAACP.

24.1.2 African Americans' Quest for Economic Security

The achievements of the most successful African Americans were impressive, but the increase in job opportunities, income, and wealth for a broad cross section of working African Americans was more significant. Before the 1960s most black men worked in the lower rungs of agriculture, construction, transportation, and manufacturing. Black women predominantly worked in domestic and food service jobs. Few black men or women had a chance to move into higher-paid and more prestigious skilled or managerial positions in the corporate world.

Antidiscrimination laws and affirmative action programs allowed millions of black people to climb up the rungs of career ladders. In 1940, for example, only 5.2 percent of black men and 6.4 percent of black women worked in white-collar occupations. Fifty years later, those figures increased to 35.3 percent for black men and 62.3 percent for black women. Many black people moved into jobs in government, education, and banking, and into professions including engineering, law, and medicine. They would continue to build upon the legacy of the first generation of black science, technology, engineering, and mathematics professionals and scientists.

24.1.3 Black Americans in Science, Technology, Engineering, and Mathematics

Interest in science, technology, engineering, and mathematics (STEM) expanded exponentially in the twenty-first century. Long before the millennium, however, an impressive cohort or vanguard of African Americans had achieved success and distinction in STEM fields. Marjorie Lee Browne was the first of three black women to earn Ph.D. degrees in mathematics. Euphemia Haynes and Evelyn Boyd Granville were the others. Born in Memphis, Tennessee, in 1914, Browne's fascination with math was nurtured and inspired by her father, who worked as a railway postal man and cultivated a lifelong interest in numbers and mathematics. An infant when her mother died, Browne earned a bachelor's degree at Howard University in 1935. She taught school for a time before earning, in 1949, a Ph.D. in mathematics at the University of Michigan. Her dissertation was titled, "Studies of One Parameter Subgroups of Certain Topological and Matrix Groups." Browne taught mathematics at North Carolina Central University in Durham for 30 years. In 1960 Brown helped to establish one of the first computer laboratories on any U.S. campus, with the aid of a $60,000 grant from IBM. Professor Browne died in 1979.

Born in 1921 in Queens, New York, Maria Daly's father, like Browne's, was also a postal clerk. He nurtured an abiding interest in science in spite of the fact that he had, due to lack of funds, dropped out of Cornell University. His daughter absorbed her father's interest in science, and was able to graduate from Queen's College in Flushing, New York, and proceeded to earn a Ph.D. degree in chemistry at Columbia University. In 1947 Daly became the first African-American woman with a doctorate in chemistry. With the assistance of a grant from the American Cancer Society, Daly worked for seven years at the Rockefeller Institute, where she investigated the way in which the human body builds proteins. She later joined the Albert Einstein College of Medicine at Yeshiva University in New York City and studied metabolism of arterial walls. Daly's research helped to demonstrate the link between smoking and heart disease. She died in 2003.

Between the 1980s and 1990s, Alexa Canady became a prominent pediatric neurosurgeon. Born in Lansing, Michigan, in 1950, she attended the University of Michigan as an undergraduate and in 1975 she earned a medical degree there. Dr. Canady had planned to specialize in internal medicine but was drawn to children who were challenged with spinal problems, brain tumors, and trauma. Dr. Canady served as chief of neurosurgery at the Children's Hospital of Michigan from 1987 to 2001. Even after retiring to Florida, she continued to treat children as a part-time neurosurgeon.

Born in Decatur, Alabama, in 1956 and raised in Chicago, in 1991 Mae Jemison became the first African-American woman to venture into space as an astronaut aboard the space shuttle *Endeavour* in 1991. She developed an early interest in science and attended Stanford University where she majored in chemistry. Following receipt of a medical degree at Cornell University, Jemison spent two years as a Peace Corps volunteer and physician in Sierra Leone and in Liberia. Initially rejected by NASA, her persistence and determination to join the space program bore fruit. It is only fitting that Jemison would appear, in 1993, in an episode of *Star Trek*. Not confining herself solely to science and space, Dr. Jemison has nourished a long-standing passion for modern dance.

Middle-class black family income increased dramatically. In 1940 only 1 percent of black families, compared with 12 percent of white families, had incomes at least twice

Profile

Mark Dean

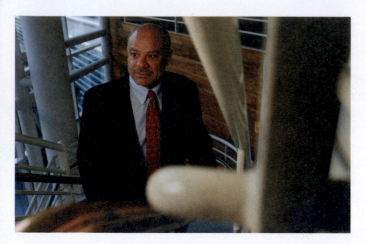

In the 1980s and 1990s, a period of urban deindustrialization, working-class black people experienced the highest rate of unemployment in America. To be sure, because of affirmative action policies, more African Americans found employment in skilled positions and in professional occupations. Unlike their white counterparts, however, black unemployed workers at the lower rungs of the job ladder often could not find jobs in the emerging fields such as aerospace technology, electronics, and computer technology that replaced the older industries such as steel.

Despite their small numbers in the computer industry, a few African Americans stood out, none more so than Mark Dean. Dean was born in Jefferson City, Tennessee, in 1957, a year in which African Americans were fighting to end segregation in higher education and state-supported professional schools across the South. Dean's entry into the higher education system was made possible by the civil rights movement,

equal opportunity legislation, and affirmative action. He earned a B.S. degree in electrical engineering from the University of Tennessee in 1979, an M.S. degree in electrical engineering from Florida Atlantic University in 1982, and a Ph.D. from Stanford University in 1992.

Before affirmative action, a scientific career such as Dean's would have been hard to imagine in black communities. The 1980s and 1990s witnessed the rise of microcomputers and personal computers. Many businesses were required to hire black employees to obtain government contracts. In 1980 IBM hired Dean. Today he has approximately 40 patents and holds three of the nine patents for IBM's original PC. Dean's work as an IBM chief engineer focused on personal computers. His inventions changed the way Americans conduct business and manage their lives. In 1995, Dr. Dean was appointed an IBM Fellow, the company's highest technical honor.

Dean, along with colleague Dennis Moeller, developed the Industry Standard Architecture systems bus that allowed add-on devices such as disk drives, keyboards, and printers to be connected to the motherboard of a personal computer. For this innovation, Dean, Moeller, and Robert H. Dennard were inducted into the National Inventors Hall of Fame in 1997. In the same year, Dean was named director of the Austin Research Laboratory and director of Advanced Technology Development for the IBM Enterprise Server Group. Dean's team made important breakthroughs including the testing of the first gigahertz CMOS microprocessor. He also led the team that developed the Blue Gene supercomputer. Dean is a member of the American Academy of Arts and Sciences and the National Academy of Engineering.

---

as high as the government's poverty line. By 1998, 50 percent of black families did, compared with 73 percent of white families. The disparity of income between similar families also decreased. In 1960 two-parent black families earned 61 percent as much as two-parent white families, but by 1998 they earned 87 percent as much. This figure was even more impressive because a larger proportion of black people than white people lived in the low-wage South. The economic boom of the Clinton presidency, from 1993 to 2001, was particularly beneficial to black people. Although the median income of black families remains well below that of white families, it increased substantially (see Figure 24-1).

During the 1990s while many African-American families narrowed the income gap, their average wealth remained far behind that of white families. This was due partly to the long heritage of poverty during which most black people accumulated little property or other wealth to pass on to their children. It was also closely tied to differences in the proportions of black and white people who owned their own homes because for most American families, their house is their primary asset. Because of low incomes and systematic discrimination, only 35 percent of African-American

Figure 24-1 Median Income of Black, Ethnic, and White Households, 1967–2011

families owned their homes in 1950. By 2005, thanks to rising incomes, laws that barred discrimination in housing, and government programs, 46.8 percent of African Americans owned their own homes (the figure for white ownership was 70.7 percent). However, the economic recession that began in 2008 devastated black communities. Unethical bank lending practices along with an array of bad decisions left millions of African-American home owners vulnerable to foreclosures. They had been awarded loans they could not afford to repay, especially when interest rates rose. The economic downturn dramatically increased the unemployment rates among African Americans to percentages unseen since the Great Depression of the 1930s. Almost 16 percent of African Americans were unemployed at the end of 2012 compared to around 7.9 percent of white Americans.

24.2 The Persistence of Black Poverty

Discuss the factors that have institutionalized poverty among African Americans.

Although many African Americans enjoyed greater absolute and relative increases in income by the turn of the millennium, too many remained mired in poverty. The poverty rate (in 2010 this meant an annual income below $22,050 for a family of four) for black people had dipped to a low of 22.7 percent during the Clinton boom but rose to 24.5 percent during George W. Bush's presidency and continued to outpace all other groups under President Barack Obama. Equally as alarming, more poor black people remain trapped in inner-city neighborhoods plagued by gang warfare, crime, substance abuse, HIV/AIDS, mass incarceration, and murder.

In the urban impoverished communities where so many of the young live, they are cut off from meaningful participation in the social and economic life of the nation and experience fewer educational and other opportunities that might allow them to escape from poverty. More than twice as many 18- and 19-year-old African Americans as 18- and 19-year-old white Americans are either not in school or not working. Another large concentration of black poverty is found in depressed rural areas, especially in the South, where mechanization and declining commodity prices for crops such as cotton, soybeans, and corn have long limited African-American opportunities. Despite cherished myths about rural life, these areas see many of the same social problems as the inner cities. Approximately 40 percent of black rural residents lack high school diplomas as opposed to 20 percent of white rural residents.

The high rate of poverty in the black community disproportionately affects children. In 2010, nearly 50 percent of all African Americans under age 18 lived in families with only one parent, generally with their mother (see Table 24-1). This pattern has continued up to 2015 and most black children lived in families at or near the poverty level. Many, if not most, single-parent families headed by females suffer from low incomes, meager public assistance, poor housing, and inferior schools. These conditions handicap children for the rest of their lives, perpetuating poverty from generation to generation. Given their proportion among African-American youth, this is an ominous sign for the future. Marian Wright Edelman, founder of the Children's Defense Fund, captured the plight of the black young when she wrote, "An unlevel playing field from birth contributes to many poor black children getting pulled into a cradle-to-prison-to-death pipeline that we must dismantle if the clock of racial and social progress is to not turn backwards."

24.2.1 Deindustrialization and Black Oakland

Poverty persists among urban African Americans in part because of the national economic restructuring that has occurred since the 1960s. Deindustrialization, relentless advances in labor-saving technology, and the growth of low-wage offshore production wiped out many jobs that African Americans with limited education and few skills once held. The history of Oakland, California, illustrates this process. In the 1940s and 1950s, Oakland attracted a large black population that was employed in everything from canning food to assembling automobiles. Thousands of black laborers unloaded ships at the ports or worked in the vast yards and repair facilities of the railroads. By the 1960s, however, manufacturing in Oakland was already in flight to lower-wage areas in the United States or overseas; in addition, the port was mechanized, which reduced both the need for longshoremen and the cost of importing foreign goods. Highways, often built through the heart of black business districts, replaced much of Oakland's rail traffic while displacing residents and weakening neighborhoods.

By 2000, Oakland had become a predominantly residential city through which goods made around the globe would flow but in which relatively little was produced or sold. This shift created wealth for some and provided jobs for many middle-class African Americans, but it left many of the once thriving black districts in the city without legitimate work. This paved the way for the rise of drug-related crime that plagued parts of the city. The economic boom of the late 1990s did improve the lot of many

Table 24-1 Black Children Under Age 18 and Their Living Arrangements, 1960–2015 (Numbers in Thousands)

| Year | Children under 18 Years Old, Total | Two Parents | Living with One Parent | | | No Parents | |
			Total	Mother Only	Father Only	Other Relatives	Nonrelatives
1960	8,650	5,795	1,896	1,723	173	826	132
1970	9,422	5,508	2,996	2,783	213	822	97
1980	9,375	3,956	4,297	4,117	180	999	123
1990	10,018	3,781	5,484	5,132	353	655	98
2000	11,412	4,286	6,080	5,596	484	879	167
2010	11,272	4,424	6,006	5,601	405	740	103
2015	11,091	4,287	6,719	5,477	466	727	131

The increase in the number of children under age 18 living with their mothers only demonstrates the change in the composition of the African-American households in the post–civil rights era. In 2015, most (over 45 percent) black children under age 18 lived with their mothers only. In 1960 only approximately 30 percent of black children lived with their mothers only, while 70 percent lived in two-parent households.

SOURCE: U.S. Census Bureau, Living Arrangements of Black Children Under 18 Years Old: 1960 to Present, Table CH-3. *www.census.gov/hhes/families/data/children.html.*

inner-city residents, with consequent drops in the rate of crime and poverty in Oakland and elsewhere, but the staying power of this renewal was weakened in the face of the severe recession that began in 2008 and persisted through the end of President Barack Obama's first term (see Map 24-1).

24.2.2 Racial Incarceration

The growth in crime in inner-city communities throughout the 1980s and 1990s combined with a national shift toward aggressive policing and harsher sentencing vastly increased the imprisonment rates of African-American boys and men. Incarceration became an

Map 24-1 Black Unemployment by State: 2011 Annual Averages

The average unemployment rate for African Americans in 2011 was 15.8%, compared to 7.9% for Whites, and 11.5% for Hispanics. African Americans remained unemployed longer than Whites and Hispanics in 2011, with a median duration of unemployment of 27.0 weeks (compared to 19.7 weeks for Whites and 18.5 weeks for Hispanics).

There have been some encouraging signs for African Americans. The unemployment rate for Blacks has been trending down since summer 2011. In January 2012, the unemployment rate for Blacks was 13.6 percent, down 3.1 percentage points from the peak of 16.7 percent in August 2011. Rising employment gains in private sector health care jobs since the end of the recession helped to reduce unemployment rates. Recently African Americans have benefitted from the slowing pace of job losses in state and local government.

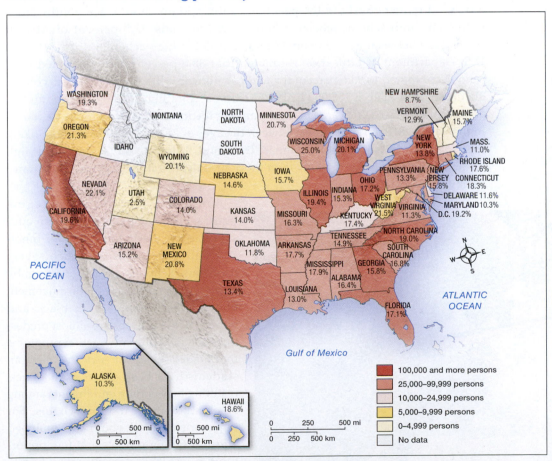

SOURCE: Bureau of Labor Statistics, Current Population Survey, 2011 annual average data. Retrieved from http://www.dol.gov/_sec/media/reports/BlackLaborForce/BlackLaborForce.pdf

* Due to small sample sizes, unemployment rates are not available for: Idaho, North Dakota, South Dakota, and Montana.

Table 24-2 Rates of Black Incarceration*

Age	Males				Females			
	Total	White	Black	Hispanic	Total	White	Black	Hispanic
20–29	**14,610**	1,542	9,302	3,766	**877**	222	396	259
30–39	**19,403**	2,140	12,534	4,729	**1,105**	301	493	311
40–49	**14,749**	1,757	9,457	3,535	**826**	209	416	201
50–59	**8,840**	1,033	5,509	2,298	**393**	84	200	109
60–64	**2,197**	252	1,265	680	**77**	15	37	25

*Imprisonment rate of sentenced prisoners held in state or federal prison, by age, gender, and race per 100,000.

This table reflects the disproportionately larger number of young black males held in prisons and jails compared to white males. The largest number of black women in prison is between 30 and 39 years of age. The largest number of black men is between 30 and 39 years of age.

SOURCE: U.S. Department of Justice, Bureau of Justice Statistics. *Prisoners in 2014*, Revised September 2015. Table 10. www.bjs.gov/content/pub/pdf/p14.pdf.

increasingly common experience for poor young black males, compounding the barriers to advancement they already faced. From 1954 to 2005, the black prison population increased by almost 900 percent, from 98,000 to 910,000. As Table 24-2 shows, while the absolute numbers of both black and white prisoners have begun to fall, African Americans still, in 2014, make up 37 percent of the nation's prisoners even though only about 12 percent of Americans are black.

24.2.3 Black Education a Half-Century after *Brown*

Education is the key factor that distinguishes the African Americans who achieve economic success from those who do not. Black rates of school completion have advanced tremendously in the past half century. Many more black youths graduate from high school than ever before. In 1960 only 37.7 percent of African Americans between ages 25 and 29 had completed high school, but by 2007 the U.S. Department of Education estimated that 88.8 percent had completed high school, compared to 93.6 percent for white Americans. Black enrollment in college also rose from a mere 136,000 in 1960 to almost 2 million in 2009. These rates of achievement placed African Americans among the most educated groups of people in the world. African Americans between the ages of 25 and 34 are now more likely than young adults in Canada, France, Italy, and Britain to have completed high school, and they are more likely than those in Italy, Britain, Germany, and France to have completed college.

Today African-American students pursue education in diverse fields. The Irwin S. Chanin School of Architecture at Cooper Union for the Advancement of Science and Art in New York City offers one path to a brighter future.

Yet, despite these encouraging figures, black people who want an education, particularly those in poor inner-city and rural areas, still face severe problems. Schools starved of funds by regressive tax policies and the movement of wealthier people—both black and white—to the suburbs are almost predestined to fail. Affirmative action programs that made a place for African-American students have been cut in many states, resulting in declining enrollments among black students at the top schools. For impoverished black youth, the combined effect of failing schools and few opportunities results in dropout rates sharply higher than those for more affluent African Americans.

24.2.4 The Black Health Gap

As in income and education, African Americans have made significant progress toward living longer, healthier lives, but they still suffer greater incidence of disease and mortality for most major illnesses. In 1970, the first year for which we have statistics, life expectancy was 60 years for black men and 68.3 years for black women. By 2009 it had risen to 69.5 and 76.5 years, respectively. Improvements in the quality of care accessible to black people are partly responsible for these increases, but higher infant mortality rates and greater numbers of deaths from diseases kept them well below the 75.7-year lifespan for white men and 80.8 years for white women.

Cancer and HIV/AIDS infections remain among the greatest threats to black health. African-American men are more likely than white men to develop cancer and die from the disease within five years of diagnosis. Black women have a lower incidence of cancer than do white women, but those black women who do get cancer die at a higher rate from it than white women. Cancer is a complicated disease caused by a variety of factors. Some of the higher rate of its incidence among African Americans is related to risky behaviors common to all impoverished people: smoking, heavy drinking, obesity, and ignorance of healthcare. A lack of access to insurance or quality healthcare compounds the impact of these behaviors. Many African Americans also mistrust the healthcare system, while medical workers tend to treat black cancer patients less aggressively than white patients.

African Americans are more likely to have HIV/AIDS than any other group in the United States, as Table 24-3 shows. According to Tavis Smiley's edited volume, *The Covenant with Black America*, published in 2006, "African Americans . . . account for 56 percent annually of new HIV infections. A quarter of these infections are among people under 25 years of age." Among American women, 63 percent of newly diagnosed HIV/AIDS cases are black. Although HIV/AIDS first spread in the United States primarily among gay men, and unprotected sex between men is still the primary form of transmission, only about one-third of African Americans contract the disease in this manner. Most acquire HIV/AIDS through intravenous drug use and unprotected heterosexual sex.

Although African Americans have had high rates of HIV infection from the beginning of the epidemic in the early 1980s, consciousness of this health crisis for black people only began to rise in the 1990s. At first many black leaders declared that the disease affected only gay white men and thus was not a crisis for black communities. This began to change when Los Angeles Lakers' star Earvin "Magic" Johnson told the world he had HIV in 1991. The deaths from AIDS of tennis star Arthur Ashe in 1993 and rapper Eric "Eazy-E" Wright in 1995 also shocked the black community into action.

Identity issues that concerned sexual orientation, feminine and masculine sexual roles, and male/female relationships acquired a new urgency when reports in 2003 and 2012 indicated that African-American women registered more new cases of HIV/ AIDS than any other sector of the population. Clearly, heterosexual African-American

Table 24-3 Unadjusted Numbers of Diagnosed Cases of Human Immunodeficiency Virus (HIV)/Acquired Immunodeficiency Syndrome (AIDS), per 100,000 in the United States, by Race and Year

Ethnicity	2010	2011	2012	2013	2014
Black	20,897	20,064	19,581	19,252	19,540
White	12,135	11,738	11,752	11,581	12,025
Hispanic	9,291	9,230	9,372	9,386	10,201

SOURCES: Centers for Disease Control and Prevention. *HIV Surveillance Report, 2014*; Vol. 26. *www.cdc.gov/hiv/pdf/library/reports/ surveillance/cdc-hiv-surveillance-report-us.pdf*. Published November 2015, Table 1a, p. 18.

women sought testing to a greater extent than black men. While women received treatment and understanding, their male partners remained in denial and avoided programs that could prolong their lives. While denying they were gay or bisexual, self-described straight men were having sex with both men and women and were spreading the virus that causes HIV/AIDS to their unsuspecting female partners. Articles in the *New York Times* and in magazines with large black readerships such as *Essence* ignited new conversations about black male sexuality. Books also contributed to public dialogue. E. Lynn Harris had done much to expose "down-low" behavior in his best-selling novels. In an interview to promote his book *On the Down Low: A Journey into the Lives of "Straight" Black Men Who Sleep with Men*, HIV activist and educator J. L. King declared,

> Many bisexual men choose not to reveal their sexual orientation because they dread the negative fallout that such a disclosure would likely cause. Homophobia is real. We all witness the harsh words and ridicule to which the gay/lesbian community is subjected. Also, there's tremendous normative pressure to keep closeted about any behavior that exists outside the prevailing social and religious norms. Being judged and ostracized isn't something most folks would sign up for, especially not a DL man whose sense of self is intricately linked to his ability to express masculinity and fulfill the traditional gender expectation assigned to men.

The future health of the black community demands open conversation and creative measures to address the HIV/AIDS crisis. That such conversations are now occurring is due in no small measure to the work of gay rights activists and to the support provided to the gay community by President Barack Obama and Vice President Joe Biden, who in spring 2012 announced their support for marriage equality, that is, the right of members of the LBGT communities to marry.

24.3 African Americans at the Center of Art and Culture

Describe the achievements African Americans made in the areas of music, literature, and film from the 1980s through the twenty-first century.

Cultural triumphs are consistently among the most positive developments for black Americans. Beginning in the 1980s, cultural renaissances emerged in virtually every American community that had a substantial African-American presence. Black-consciousness institutions proliferated and flourished. They included black history and culture museums, festivals, expositions, publishing houses, bookstores and boutiques, freedom schools, concerts, theaters, and dance troupes. In 1996 *Publishers Weekly* reported that bookstores specializing in African-American books had increased to more than 200 from only a dozen a few years earlier. By 1994 there were dozens of African-American publishing companies. In 1998 the National Literary Hall of Fame for Writers of African Descent opened at Chicago State University. Black painters used outdoor murals to celebrate the black experience. But with the rise of e-books and giant retailers like Amazon, nearly all of the black-owned bookstores had ceased operation by the second decade of the twenty-first century.

During the last days of the civil rights movement, attention shifted to another group of culture workers. Black playwrights were in the vanguard of a cultural explosion that helped revitalize American theater. August Wilson had begun writing overtly political plays in the 1960s and 1970s but focused on broader themes of race and personality as his work matured. His first great success came in 1984 with the Broadway production of *Ma Rainey's Black Bottom*, which explored racism in the music industry. He won praise for his use of the rhythmic and symbolic power of black speech. He had four other plays on Broadway, two of which won Pulitzer Prizes—*Fences* in 1987 and *The Piano Lesson* in 1990. Charles Fuller also made race the center of his plays, attacking stereotypes and exploring the complexity of racial identity in modern America. His best-known play is the 1982 *A Soldier's Tale*, which also won a Pulitzer Prize. It was made into a motion picture titled *A Soldier's Story*, which was nominated for two Academy Awards. George C. Wolfe was a playwright, director, and producer whose achievements helped demolish racial barriers in the theater. His plays, such as *The Colored Museum* and *Jelly's Last Jam*, won critical acclaim, and he received a Tony Award in 1994 as best director for *Angels in America*. His talent and energy were credited with returning the New York Shakespeare Festival to its former glory when he was its director from 1993 to 2004. Anna Deavere Smith pioneered new forms of theater with her powerful one-woman plays. Her first major success was *Fires in the Mirror*, about tensions between blacks and Jews in Brooklyn's Crown Heights neighborhood. This was followed by *Twilight: Los Angeles, 1992*, a portrayal of the Rodney King riots (see Chapter 23). Smith's achievements in drama and teaching were rewarded with a MacArthur Genius Grant in 1996.

The new cultural renaissance differed from the Black Arts movement of the 1960s and 1970s. The contemporary flowering was more inclusive and more appreciative of women artists. It also included the work of openly gay and lesbian artists, such as documentary filmmaker Marion Riggs, choreographer Bill T. Jones, and novelist E. Lynn Harris. Whereas poets and dramatists dominated earlier movements, novelists took center stage in the 1980s. Much of the new work in all fields appealed as much to white audiences as to black, providing insights into the lives of people of African heritage in a predominantly Eurocentric society.

A new wave of African-American women novelists emerged as early as 1977 when Toni Morrison's *Song of Solomon* became a Book-of-the-Month-Club selection, the first by a black author since Richard Wright's *Native Son* in 1940. Then Barbara Chase-Riboud made waves with *Sally Hemings* (1979), a fictional account of a real-life woman who was both a slave to and a mistress of President Thomas Jefferson. In 1980 Toni Cade Bambara won the American Book Award for *The Salt Eaters*. At least as significant as these individual books was the founding in 1981 of a new publishing house, Kitchen Table: Women of Color Press. Then, in 1982, Alice Walker won the Pulitzer Prize and the American Book Award for *The Color Purple*, which was later made into a movie by director Steven Spielberg, with Whoopi Goldberg in the starring role. In 1987 Rita Dove won the Pulitzer Prize for poetry. In 1993 she became America's poet laureate, and in the same year Toni Morrison became the first African American to win the Nobel Prize for Literature. President Bill Clinton invited Maya Angelou to read one of her poems at his first inauguration. In 2009 President Obama invited Elizabeth Alexander to read a poem at his inauguration.

Critics were not the only ones interested in these works. In 1992 three African-American women novelists—Morrison, Walker, and Terry McMillan—made the *New York Times* best-seller list simultaneously. In 2001 the works of four African Americans made the *Times* best-seller list and revealed the growing appreciation of black literature, biography, and history across the racial spectrum. In 2009 and 2012, several African Americans, including Annette Gordon-Reed, won the Pulitzer Prize. Gordon Reed took the honor for her study *The Hemingses of Monticello: An American Family*. Other black writers and historians whose work has attracted mainstream attention and acclaim include Isabel Wilkerson, Manning Marable, and in 2012 Ayana Mathis for her first novel, *The Twelve Tribes of Hattie*. In the 2000s,

Toni Morrison accepting the Nobel Prize. One of the most acclaimed writers in the history of U.S. literature, Toni Morrison's (b. 1931, in Lorrain, Ohio, as Chloe Ardelia Wofford) novels are, as a Nobel Prize press release put it, "characterized by visionary force and poetic import, [that] gives life to an essential aspect of American reality." Princeton University literary scholar Valerie Smith described Morrison's work as "always steeped in the realities of the political, social, economic, and historical constraints of African American culture." In 1996 Morrison received the National Book Foundation Medal for Distinguished Contribution to American Letters.

Profile

Michael Jackson

Michael J. Jackson was one of the greatest entertainers of the twentieth century. More than any figure of his generation, Jackson helped to make black popular music a global phenomenon. He was born in 1958 in Gary, Indiana, the seventh of nine children of Joseph and Katherine Jackson. His father was a steelworker who molded his sons into a musical group known as the Jackson Five. In 1968, Berry Gordy of Motown Records signed the group, who recorded chart-topping singles including "ABC," "I Want You Back," and "I'll Be There." Michael's voice and showmanship, charisma, and physical attractiveness made him the standout. Jackson attracted legions of fans. At a time when the black family was being maligned and described as "matriarchal" and "broken," the Jacksons represented wholesomeness and a potent blend of patriarchy and talent. Michael became the most beloved black child star of the twentieth century.

In 1976, Michael and his brothers left Motown Records to sign with Epic Records and fired his overbearing father/manager. The following year, Michael joined an all-black cast of *The Wiz*, starring former Supremes lead singer Diana Ross. While working on *The Wiz*, the gifted young star impressed legendary producer and composer Quincy Jones. The two collaborated on Michael's 1979 solo album *Off the Wall*; their subsequent collaboration made musical history and transformed American popular culture. The album *Thriller* (1982) became a phenomenal success. It featured #1 hits like "Billie Jean," the first black video to be shown on MTV, and opened the door for the wider dissemination of and greater appreciation for the music of African-American entertainers.

In 1983, Michael performed on the Motown 25th Anniversary Special and introduced millions of television viewers to his signature dance, The Moonwalk, in which he appeared to defy gravity and walk backward yet land on his toes. This iconic dance and his sequined glove cemented his global celebrity. The young Michael was as shrewd a businessman as he was a mesmerizing performer. In 1985, he purchased the ATV Music Publishing catalog, which contained 251 Beatles songs including "Yesterday" and "Let It Be," for $47.5 million. Today, the catalog is worth 10 times more than Michael's purchase price. Michael gave enormous amounts to charities, especially those devoted to improving the lives of children.

In the 1990s Michael underwent a series of surgeries that altered his features and skin color. The media speculated that he was trying to become a symbol of the universal white male or escape his blackness. But during an interview with Oprah Winfrey in 1993, Michael said that neither was true and that he suffered from a skin disorder that destroyed his pigmentation (a condition known as vitiligo).

There was a downside to his global celebrity. His behavior became increasingly scrutinized and criticized in the world's media. Charges of molestation of underage boys invited outrage and culminated in a sensational trial in California in 2005 in which Michael was acquitted. He left the country and all but ceased to perform. His finances became precarious. In 2008 Michael returned to the United States to restore his reputation and fortune in a planned 50-city world tour. It was not to happen. Because of an apparent drug overdose administered by his personal physician, Michael Jackson died on June 25, 2009. The loss of his creative genius shocked the world. The "King of Pop" was dead, and billions mourned his passing.

First, Martin Luther King, Jr. led the struggle that ended Jim Crow racial segregation. Then, Malcolm X inspired a generation to embrace a positive, empowering racial consciousness. When both King and Malcolm X were assassinated, Michael Jackson emerged and shattered cultural barriers between the races. The political, social, and cultural transformations that occurred in the last half of the twentieth century were facilitated and inspired by the visionary and creative work of, among others, these heroic African-American men. Each in his own way represented and underscored the humanity of black people as they prepared white America for the 2008 election of Barack Obama as president of the United States.

African-American performers earned recognition for their work on stage and in film that previous generations would have deemed unthinkable. In 2005, Oprah Winfrey spearheaded a new Broadway production of *The Color Purple*, and more than one million people saw the play in New York before it reopened in Chicago in 2007. Also in 2007, Forest Whitaker won the Academy Award for best actor for his depiction of Uganda's dictator Idi Amin in *The Last King of Scotland*, and Jennifer Hudson won the Academy Award for best supporting actress in *Dreamgirls*, which was loosely based on the rise of the Motown singing group The Supremes. Two years earlier Jamie Foxx had won an Oscar for best actor for his role in *Ray*, a film about singer Ray Charles, and Morgan Freeman won best supporting actor for his role in *Million Dollar Baby*. Playwright Tyler Perry turned his popular plays about the pistol-packing but wise female-in-drag character Madea into box office gold. Tyler Perry's *Madea Goes to Jail* earned $41,030,947 in its opening week in 2009. His media empire continued to expand as did his personal philanthropy and support of President Obama's reelection campaign in 2012. Following the reelection of Obama, Miriam Petty and Northwestern University's Block Museum hosted the first major scholarly conference and roundtable on a college campus to discuss Tyler Perry's films and plays and the ubiquitous Madea character.

24.4 The Hip-Hop Nation

Discuss the factors that made it possible for rap music to achieve international popularity.

Rap was the most commercially successful genre of black music to emerge in the late twentieth century. It became emblematic of the post–civil rights and Black Power movement generations of African Americans, known collectively as the hip-hop nation. There are many varieties of rap music. At its least complex, rap is a form of rhythmic speaking in rhyme. Hip-hop refers to the backup music for rap that is often composed of excerpts or "samples" from other songs.

24.4.1 Origins of a New Music: A Generation Defines Itself

The rap musical style arose in 1973 in New York City's South Bronx. Its original purpose was to promote musical and dance competitions among the area's inner-city youths, who had few outlets for their creative energies. Rap pioneer Kool Herc (aka Clive Campbell) began using simple raps to cover a mix of beats played from two turntables. At the same time, Afrika Bambaataa developed a political version of rap by merging the ideology of the Nation of Islam with the Black Panthers' cultural nationalism. Bambaataa's Zulu Nation promoted competition in break dancing, rapping, and graffiti art and helped spread rap among poor black and Latino neighborhoods.

The first commercial rap hit, "Rapper's Delight" by the Sugar Hill Gang, came out in 1979 and popularized the term **hip-hop**. This was followed by the rise to stardom of Grandmaster Flash and the Furious Five, which grew out of 1970s funk but added rap vocals and the technique of "scratching"—moving a record back and forth under a needle to produce a rhythmic, jarring sound and manipulating turntable speeds. Much of this music was made primarily for entertainment in the clubs, but some rappers, following the early lead of spoken-word artists and poets Amiri Baraka, Gil Scott-Heron, and The Last Poets, offered a political critique of American society wrapped in taunting humor.

For African-American youths, whom the world had seemingly left behind and ignored, hip-hop became the most important cultural happening of their lives. It was a creative force in which a dispossessed generation discussed the things that mattered most to them, their lives in cities burdened by racial poverty, heightened violence, and

hip-hop

The backup music for rap. It is also the term for the youth culture that developed with the rise of rap music.

failed schools. In the Reagan years (1981–1989), few middle-class Americans acknowledged the millions left behind in urban decay. Conditions in inner cities worsened during this period, as crack cocaine flooded neighborhoods and gang warfare erupted over drug turfs. The "keeping it real" lyrics of hip-hop artists helped forge a sense of community and common destiny among a trapped generation. As James McBride wrote in *National Geographic* in 2007, hip-hop "is a music dipped in the boiling cauldron of race and class."

24.4.2 Rap Music Goes Mainstream

Ironically, white indifference allowed the first hip-hop entrepreneurs to take control of the production, dissemination, and profits connected with this new music. Russell Simmons saw the potential of rap street music in the mid-1970s and recognized that the mainstream entertainment industry was not aware of it. He became a concert promoter, encouraging early rap groups to stay close to the dress styles and language of the inner-city African-American community. In 1984 he and a partner formed Def Jam Records. Their bands, such as Run-DMC and Public Enemy, became enormously popular, and many of their albums sold millions of copies. Simmons expanded his business to include marketing hip-hop clothing under the label "Phat Farm" and promoting poetry and comedy acts. In 2000 he sold his share of Def Jam for over $100 million. Like Simmons, P. Diddy (aka Sean "Puff Daddy" Combs) found success by working within the mainstream recording industry. Raised in a suburban neighborhood, P. Diddy dropped out of Howard University in 1990 to work for Uptown Records. In 1993 he formed his own company, Bad Boy Records, which was an immediate success.

Commercial success brought new groups to the fore, and the genre expanded. Rap bands such as Run-DMC, which dominated the charts in the mid-1980s, brought the sound to MTV and to a larger public, which soon included white suburban teens. Hip-hop culture quickly spread beyond New York to other African-American urban centers, and each developed a distinctive and often more graphic variant of the original. With the music came changes in clothing style, such as baggy, loose-fitting jeans, that trend-hungry fashion designers quickly adopted.

White suburban youths had always been the wealthiest consumers of hip-hop music and its cultural artifacts. By 2000, hip-hop had become a global cultural force and the source of astonishing profits for men such as Simmons and Combs—and for white-owned business and music companies. The recurrence of the tension between black creativity and white profits fueled new debate. As cultural studies analyst Gregg Tate put it, "Our music, our fashion, our hairstyles, our dances, our anatomical traits, our bodies, our souls continue to be considered ever ripe for the picking and the biting by the same crafty devils who brought you the African slave trade and the Middle Passage."

24.4.3 Gangsta Rap

gangsta rap

A genre of rap music characterized by violent and sexist lyrics.

The southern California group N.W.A. (Niggaz wit Attitudes) was one of the most successful new rap bands in the late 1980s. Their 1988 album *Straight Outta Compton* went triple platinum and heralded the rise of **gangsta rap**. Its song "Gangsta Gangsta" shocked many with its sexist and violent lyrics. Particularly troubling, however, was the persistent objectification of women in hard-core rap music and films. In 2015, the Oscar-nominated movie *Straight Outta Compton* broke box office records. The music and the movie underscored the tension between young black men and police authorities in black communities. However, many rap bands explicitly rejected hard core obscenity and violence. Queen Latifah, for example, avoided denigrating other African Americans as she promoted a message of empowerment for black women and men. In 2015, Queen Latifah produced and starred in *Bessie*, an illuminating HBO film about the queen of the blues, Bessie Smith.

Hip-hop migrated beyond the United States and became a global cultural force, a "hip-hop planet." It influenced music worldwide, particularly across the African

Diaspora. France, for example, has a thriving rap music scene. Most of its artists, whose music focuses on ethnic and racial discrimination and social criticism, are of Arab, African, or Spanish descent. Africa, the Caribbean, and Latin America also developed rap that builds on indigenous African music. The ability of rap to combine with other musical forms to create compelling hybrids, together with the global penetration of American popular culture, ensure that hip-hop will continue to thrive and evolve. In the words of *National Geographic*'s James McBride, "Hip-hop remains . . . a cry of 'I am' from the youth of the world."

24.5 African-American Intellectuals

Analyze the variety of approaches that constitute Afrocentricity.

The civil rights and Black Power movements forced predominantly white academic and cultural institutions to open their doors to African Americans. With a beachhead established, black scholars gained a prominence as public intellectuals to a degree unknown in earlier eras. These individuals go beyond their roles as academics to participate in public debate on major issues. In the past, most public intellectuals were white males. Some African Americans, like the formidable W. E. B. Du Bois and novelists Richard Wright, James Baldwin, and Ralph Ellison, were exceptions. The voices of black intellectuals were seldom heard in the mainstream before the 1960s. In the recent past five decades, however, many of the most prominent public intellectuals to emerge were African American. Among them are Cornel West, Henry Louis Gates, Jr., Melissa Harris-Perry, Johnnetta B. Cole, Beverly Guy-Sheftall, William Julius Wilson, Robin D. G. Kelley, Michael Eric Dyson, Earl Lewis, Mary Frances Berry, Joe Trotter, Christopher R. Reed, Deborah Gray White, Mark Anthony Neal, Thavolia Glymph, Lester Spence, Ta-Nehisi Coates, and Jamil Smith. Their views range across the ideological gamut, but they all strive to define black identity in the United States and explore the role of race in its social, economic, and political life. Their emergence and the acclaim accorded to them mark the end of America's long refusal to acknowledge the transformative cultural achievements and intellectual accomplishments of African Americans.

Many African-American scholars were connected to the Black Studies programs founded in the late 1960s and early 1970s. Initially marginalized and few in number, programs now exist in nearly every major university. They have become institutionalized—even prized—by institutions that once resisted them. Doctoral degrees in Black Studies are now offered at Northwestern University, Temple University, the University of Massachusetts at Amherst, Harvard, Yale, Michigan State University, the University of California, Berkeley, and Cornell University.

As befits a vibrant intellectual movement, there are several main approaches to understanding the path of African Americans through U.S. history into contemporary society. Three broad approaches are Afrocentrist: (1) what might be loosely termed an "intersectional" or "inclusionist" approach that has gained prominence more recently as an approach that emphasizes class, sexuality, and gender; (2) comparative race studies; and (3) diaspora studies.

In the 1980s and 1990s, a philosophy of culture referred to as **Afrocentricity** captured wide attention. Afrocentricity had been prominent in the political movement that created black studies, but Temple University professor Molefi Kete Asante

Afrocentricity

A philosophy of culture that celebrates Africa's role in history and stresses the enduring African roots and identity of black America.

Molefi Kete Asante changed his name from Arthur Lee Smith in 1973 to better reflect his African heritage. He served as Professor and Chair of the Department of African American Studies at Temple University from 1984 to 1996. About Afrocentricism, Asante elaborated, "It's a very simple idea. African people for 500 years have lived on the intellectual terms of Europeans. The African perspective has finally come to dinner."

gave it a presence and a personality. In the 1980s Asante published three books—*Afrocentricity*; *Kemet, Afrocentricity and Knowledge*; and *The Afrocentric Idea*—in which he argued that an African-centered perspective was needed to reorient African Americans from the Eurocentric periphery to the center of their own history. Many black educators embraced Afrocentricity as a way to celebrate and reclaim a positive African identity and to unite the peoples of the African Diaspora. Afrocentrists rejected the idea of America as a melting pot. Assimilation, they argued, meant rejecting their African cultural heritage. At the heart of this position is an indictment of American ideas and institutions for their complicity in the long oppression of black people. Molefi Asante explained Afrocentricity as the idea that "African people and interests must be viewed as actors and agents in human history, rather than as marginal to the European histori-cal experience—which has been institutionalized as universal."

Long before the emergence of Black Studies, William Leo Hansberry had advocated throughout his career for the centrality of the study of African history. He is considered to be the father of African Studies. Hansberry believed that programs should include courses in African History and should be required of all students interested in learning about African American life, culture, and history. Hansberry attended Atlanta Univer-sity where he was encouraged by W. E. B. DuBois to transfer to Harvard University. He earned a B.A. degree in 1921 and an M.A. degree in 1932. He was W. E. B. Du Bois's research associate for a time. In 1922, he pioneered the study of African history in American universities. He taught African history for 42 years at Howard University and in African countries. Hansberry mentored Nnamdi Azikiwe the first president of the Federal Republic of Nigeria. In 1963 in honor of Hansberry's work, Nigeria named one of its academic centers after him, the Hansberry College of African Studies, and named him its first director. After Hansberry's death, his protégé, Joseph E. Harris, edited his two volumes: *Pillars in Ethiopian History* (Washington, D.C.: Howard Univer-sity Press, 1974) and *Africa and Africans as Seen by Classical Writers* (Washington, D.C.: Howard University Press, 1977).

24.5.1 African-American Studies Come of Age

Under the leadership of Henry Louis Gates, Jr., Harvard University, in 1991, attracted several leading scholars to African-American studies. Gates declared: "We're eager to demonstrate that Afro-American studies is an academic department. It is not a place for ethnic cheerleading; it is not a place for a 12-step recovery program to restore your sense of identity. It is a place where one studies an academic discipline in a fashion as rigorous as the study of mathematics or physics, English or history." Apart from intel-lectual rigor, what held the department together was a belief that race is a malleable category of identity to be analyzed critically and that effective scholarship in the field does not depend on the scholar's racial profile.

As with American intellectual life as a whole, the emergence of scholarship that questioned prevailing gender assumptions also influenced African-American studies. Just as the Black Studies movement challenged racial ideology, women's studies forced a reconsideration of deeply held gender beliefs while raising historical and social science questions that went unasked in an earlier era. African-American scholars in "womanism" studies, a term Alice Walker popularized to describe the intellectual projects of women of color, pay particular attention to how gender interacted with racial and class hierarchies to shape the historical experiences and contemporary lives of black women. Early journals such as *SAGE* and organizations including the Associa-tion of Black Women Historians, founded by Rosalyn Terborg-Penn and Eleanor Smith, advanced scholarship in black women's studies. Gradually, their scholarly, literary, historical, and polemical works attracted general readers and secured a place in women's studies curricula. As more black women enrolled in college, courses like "Black Women Writers" and "Black Women's History" became part of black studies curricula.

The field of black women's history has grown rapidly: Scholarly monographs, reference works, anthologies, conferences, and exhibitions have all been devoted to the contribution black women have made to the political struggles and artistic accomplishments of African Americans. In 2007, the journal *Black Women, Gender & Families*, edited by Jennifer Hamer, began as an official organ of the National Council of Black Studies. In 2008 the Organization of American Historians announced the establishment of the Darlene Clark Hine Award for the best book published annually in African-American women's and gender history. Black woman historian Wanda Hendricks spearheaded the fundraising effort to make concrete the legitimization of black women's history. The scholarship in African American Studies and History continues to flourish. One of the recent books best to engage the research by African-American studies scholars is Pero Gaglo Dagbovie's *What Is African American History?*

In the 2010s scholars fleshed out definitions and projects illuminating the Black Diaspora framework. Building on the work of Philip Curtin, Colin Palmer, Michael Gomez, Thomas C. Holt, and David Barry Gaspar, scholars have studied the Atlantic slave-labor economy and compared the centuries-old African-descended communities of the New World with those of more recent African immigrants to Europe. This analysis places African-American history in the context of a global story of movement, citizenship, anticolonialism, and antiracism struggles and the quest for belonging.

In 2011 and 2012, leaders of African American Studies Departments and programs organized major, well-attended symposia. Yale University's Department of African American Studies coordinated a state-of-the-art conference, "African American Studies: Past, Present and Future." A few months later, Northwestern University's Department of African American Studies brought together students and faculty from the 12 doctoral African American Studies departments and arranged previews of the work of the new generation: "A Beautiful Struggle: Transformative Black Studies in Shifting Political Landscapes—A Summit of Doctoral Programs." The College of Charleston's Avery Center for African American History and Culture hosted the first major Black Power conference, which attracted and featured many of the outstanding young scholars writing a new historiography of Black Power and black studies. In 2012, the Association for the Study of African American Life and History (founded by Carter G. Woodson in 1915) signaled the recognition and acceptance of black women's history by making "Black Women in American Culture and History" the theme of the annual convention, while the Association of Black Women Historians published a special issue of *Truth* that chronicled the organization's history from 1979 through 2012 and celebrated the work of a generation of black women historians. In 2014 and 2015 President Barack Obama presented National Humanities Medals, respectively, to historians Darlene Clark Hine and Evelyn Brooks Higginbotham. The medals attested to the merits of scholarship in Black Women's History.

24.6 Black Religion at the Dawn of the Millennium

Identify some of the strengths and tensions that persist within today's black church.

Religion remains at the heart of the African-American experience. Black churches, claiming over 25 million members, remain by far the largest black-controlled institutions in the nation. Houses of worship ranging from storefront operations with a few dozen congregants to "megachurches" with thousands of members are the sinew that binds together nearly every African-American community. The major denominations remain those with roots in the nineteenth century. Among the largest are the African American National Baptist Convention of America, Inc.; the Progressive National

Baptist Convention, Inc.; the African Methodist Episcopal (AME) Church; the National Missionary Baptist Convention of America; the Churches of Christ; and the AME Zion Church. Immigration from the Caribbean and Africa has increased African-American membership in some predominantly white denominations. For example, black worshipers make up more than 9 percent of the Catholic Church and over 10 percent of the Episcopal Church. Many African-American Catholics and Episcopalians attend predominantly black churches, so there is still truth in Martin Luther King's observation that "11:00 A.M. Sunday morning is the most segregated hour in America," but progress has been made.

African-American men and women have become leaders within predominantly white denominations since the 1960s. Harold R. Perry was consecrated a bishop in the Roman Catholic Church in 1966, and Wilton Gregory became the first African American to head the United States Conference of Catholic Bishops in 2002. Recognizing the importance of Africans and African Americans to the future of the church, in 1993 Pope John Paul II apologized for the Catholic Church's support of slavery. In 1970 African-American John M. Burgess became the first black bishop to head an Episcopal diocese in America. His leadership in Massachusetts was followed by John T. Walker in Washington, D.C., in 1977. African Americans made similar gains in other denominations as churches worked to rid themselves of racist practices.

Despite this continuity with the past and the successes of black religious leaders, African-American religious life has changed in the past several decades. Most African Americans remain Protestants, but demographic and social changes have challenged the mainline denominations. One difficulty is the movement of middle-class parishioners from the close-knit urban communities that once supported churches with people from many different walks of life. Greater levels of education and different life experiences combine with geographical distance to create large suburban megachurches with a distinct character and worship practice. Often Pentecostal, these churches' theology emphasizes the individual's relationship to God. Their ministers speak to the tensions and anxiety of people with stressful lives and careers or with problems such as substance abuse or difficult relationships. They also provide community services for their parishioners.

Perhaps the best-known minister of this new African-American religious tradition is Bishop T. D. Jakes. Starting in 1980 with a 10-member storefront church in Charleston, West Virginia, he built The Potter's House, an enormous ministry with a more than 30,000-member interracial congregation and a 5,000-seat church in Dallas, Texas. Jakes has written best-selling books and produced motion pictures such as *Woman, Thou Art Loosed*, which focused on using religion to heal the psychological wounds of modern society and troubled relationships. He distributes his message through seminars, television broadcasts, and the Internet.

24.6.1 Black Christians on the Front Line

Faced with the problems of the black community and with a changing population, African-American Christians in both traditional and nontraditional religious institutions have developed outreach programs to create supportive communities for the embattled and the vulnerable. Some of the new megachurches are in or near black inner-city communities and remain committed to local action. For example, the Salem Baptist Church in Chicago has over 17,000 members, many of whom patrol neighborhoods to discourage prostitutes and drug dealers. Rev. James T. Meeks led a campaign for an antiliquor referendum to combat the ravages of alcoholism in the community. Many black communities have similar ministries, often with radio and television broadcasts of services.

Rev. Eugene Rivers has developed a different approach from that of the megachurches. Along with former students at Harvard University, he founded the small Azusa Christian Community in a crime-plagued neighborhood in Boston. An evangelical Christian, Rivers believes "the church is the last best hope that black people have." He turned a former crack house into a Christian settlement named the Ella J. Baker House. Its primary goal is to keep children from killing one another. He and fellow black clergy formed the 10-Point Coalition and entered into a partnership with the police. The collaboration helped eliminate juvenile murders for two and a half years. Rivers advocates a pragmatic black nationalism aimed at developing a rich, viable black civil society centered on the church.

24.6.2 Tensions in the Black Church

Tensions have arisen within many black churches over their socially conservative message, patriarchal structure, staid ritual, and lack of social engagement. Gender and sexuality are two key sources of this tension. Along with other conservative Christians, the black church has long advocated the subordination of women to men. Although most black churchgoers are women, men overwhelmingly dominate church leadership. A few men and women have always challenged patriarchal assumptions in the churches, only in recent decades has the chorus grown too loud to ignore. As theologian, sociologist, and ordained Baptist minister Cheryl Townsend Gilkes puts it, "The cultural maxim 'If it wasn't for the women, you wouldn't have a church,' rises up against male attempts to exclude, ignore, trivialize, or marginalize women in a number of capacities." Some younger African-American women have left the church because of this marginalization. Others, like Gilkes, have stayed to challenge sexism in individual churches and the denominations.

The AME Church has been at the forefront of this reform. Although the AME has ordained women since 1898, the number of women ministers has only recently become significant. Now 3,000 of the AME's 8,000 ministers are female; in 2000 the church elected Vashti M. McKenzie bishop of its Southern African district. She took the post after a 10-year stint as pastor of Baltimore's Payne Memorial Church, where she increased membership from 300 to 1,700. Upon her election, Bishop McKenzie announced, "The stained glass ceiling has been pierced and broken!" She also connected her achievement

With the support of the Delta Sigma Theta sorority, family, and the Baltimore, Maryland, church community, Vashti Murphy McKenzie broke through "the stained glass ceiling" (her words) to become the first woman in the history of the AME Church to be appointed a bishop. She is a graduate of the University of Maryland, earned a master of divinity from Harvard University's Divinity School, and earned a doctorate in ministry at the United Theological Seminary in Dayton, Ohio.

to the past efforts of other women. "I stand here tonight," she told the AME convention, "on the shoulders of the unordained women who serve without affirmation or appointment. I don't stand here alone, but there is a cloud of witnesses who sacrificed, died and gave their best." Women's achievements in the churches have not come without conflict, and this promises to be at the center of black religious life in the twenty-first century.

Black churches also face conflicts over sexuality. Their theology has traditionally limited legitimate sexual activity to monogamous, heterosexual marriages. Baptist minister and Georgetown University professor Michael Eric Dyson lists the challenges for black Christians over sexuality: "The guilt and shame that result from unresolved conflicts about the virtues of black sexuality. . . . The role of eroticism in a healthy black Christian sexuality. The revulsion to and exploitation of homosexuals. The rise of AIDS in black communities. The sexual and physical abuse of black women and children by black male church members. The resistance to myths of super black sexuality." Of all of these challenges, those surrounding the HIV/AIDS crisis are most pressing but also the most difficult to address, given the church's traditional refusal to do more than denounce, or remain silent about, nontraditional sexualities.

24.6.3 Black Muslims

Although still a relatively small phenomenon among African Americans, Islam has been gaining converts. The Nation of Islam is the best known of the many African-American Muslim groups, but its 20,000 to 40,000 members make up only a small percentage of the estimated 1.5 million black American Muslims. After the death of founder Elijah Muhammad in 1975, his son Warith Deen Muhammad led the Nation of Islam. He eventually left to found the Muslim American Society, the largest group of African-American Muslims, with perhaps 500,000 members. The clarity and discipline of the Muslim faith and the solidarity African-American Muslims feel with Muslims around the world have attracted an estimated 18,000 converts per year in the United States.

With growing immigration from Islamic countries, African-American Muslims have become more closely connected to the larger trends in Islam. This is evident in the rise of more orthodox Islamic beliefs among American blacks. The attacks on the World Trade Center and the Pentagon on September 11, 2001, and the wars in Iraq and Afghanistan, two Muslim countries, have left many African-American Muslims conflicted. On the one hand, most denounce the attacks and the ideology that led to them. Imam Abdul Malik Mohammed, for example, declared, "While the Muslim World has had the Koran and they have recited the Koran and the Koran has dwelled in their hearts . . . I contend that, in view of circumstances that we have witnessed for many years, Mohammed the Prophet is not known to them." On the other hand, many African Americans are troubled by what they perceive to be an indiscriminate anti-Muslim feeling in the United States and are concerned the nation's War on Terror might become a holy war against Islam at home and abroad.

24.7 Louis Farrakhan and the Nation of Islam

Explain Louis Farrakhan's views about the status and challenges black men confront in present-day America.

Beginning in the 1980s, the Nation of Islam's minister Louis Farrakhan became a potent source of racial division in the United States. Farrakhan was the son of immigrants from the West Indies. As a young man, he attended a black teachers' college in Winston-Salem, North Carolina, but dropped out to become a Calypso singer known as "The Charmer." In 1955, while performing in Chicago, he heard Elijah Muhammad preach. This marked a turning point in his life. After Malcolm X's rupture with Elijah Muhammad and his murder in February 1965, Farrakhan became minister of Harlem Mosque No. 7 and Muhammad's national representative. Farrakhan opposed Warith Muhammad's move to a more orthodox Islam and by 1978 became leader of the Nation. In 1982 he purchased a building to publish the Nation's newspaper, the *Final Call*, and in 1985 he bought and moved into Elijah Muhammad's mansion in Chicago. Under Farrakhan's direction, the Nation developed media ventures, restaurants, clothing stores, and companies to provide security for apartment buildings, distribute soap and cosmetics, and manufacture pharmaceuticals. Farrakhan recruited among poor and marginalized urban African Americans and black prisoners. The national move to the right during the Reagan era complemented the reconstituted Nation's conservative social ideas, which harked back to those that Booker T. Washington advanced in the late nineteenth century. Like Elijah Muhammad, Farrakhan downplayed the struggle for political rights:

> God wants us to build a new world order: A new world order based on peace, justice and equality. Where do we start? . . . Physical separation is greatly feared [by whites], and it is not now desired by the masses of black people, but America is not willing to give us eight or ten states, or even one state. Let's be reasonable. . . . If we cannot go back to Africa, and America will not give us a separate territory . . . we should use the blessings that we have received from our sojourn in America to do for ourselves what we have been asking the whites in this nation to do for us.

Until 1984 most white Americans were barely aware of Farrakhan's existence. In that year, however, he broke the Nation of Islam's long-standing abstention from politics to support Jesse Jackson's bid for the Democratic presidential nomination and ignited a firestorm of controversy. When Jews took offense at Jackson's off-the-record reference to New York as "Hymietown" during a conversation with African-American reporters, Farrakhan, whose Fruit of Islam organization provided security for Jackson's campaign, defended him and made matters worse. On the *CBS Evening News*, Farrakhan warned, "I say to the Jewish people, who may not like our brother. It is not Jesse Jackson you are attacking. . . . When you attack him, you are attacking the millions who are lining up with him. You're attacking all of us. . . . Why dislike us? Why attack our champion? Why hurl stones at him? It's our champion. If you harm this brother, what do you think we should do about it?"

Always controversial, Louis Farrakhan and the Nation of Islam achieved the greatest feat in the history of black mass mobilization, the Million Man March. The actual numbers of black men who heeded his call on October 16, 1995, to attend the Million Man March may forever be in dispute. The figures range from 400,000 to 1.2 million.

Farrakhan's verbal assaults against Jews, whom he called a principal enemy of African Americans, attracted support from ultra-right-wing anti-Semitic forces and condemnation from Jewish Americans and the Anti-Defamation League. Dredging up anti-Semitic shibboleths reminiscent of Hitler's Germany, Farrakhan blamed Jews for many of the ills plaguing African Americans. Jewish Americans, many of whom had been among the principal allies of African Americans during the civil rights movement, called on African-American organizations and leaders to repudiate Farrakhan and his rhetoric of "Jewish domination and control."

24.7.1 Millennium Marches

In the 1990s Farrakhan reached out to a broader group of African Americans. He called a Million Man March in Washington, D.C. Farrakhan framed this march as a "Holy Day of Atonement and Reconciliation . . . to reconcile our spiritual inner beings and to redirect our focus to developing our communities, strengthening our families, working to uphold and protect our civil and human rights, and empowering ourselves through the Spirit of God, more effective use of our dollars, and through the power of the vote."

The estimated 400,000-strong crowd at the October 16, 1995, march made it a symbolic success and generated positive coverage even in the mainstream media. It inspired many black men to become more engaged with their communities and to speak out against oppression. On this occasion, the Nation's conservative philosophy of religion, self-respect, family values, community responsibility, and bootstrap capitalism found a responsive audience. Even though many marchers did not support the Nation's program, the peaceful solidarity of the gathering gave them hope.

Some of the goodwill dissipated, however, when, three months after the march, Farrakhan embarked on a "World Friendship Tour" to Africa and the Middle East. To the consternation of many, he met with the leader of the brutal military regime in Nigeria, General Sani Abacha. At home, Farrakhan's intemperate rhetoric made news, but he failed to forge a coherent strategy to resolve African Americans' continuing social problems.

Several black intellectuals objected to Farrakhan's conservative ideas, none more effectively than political scientist Adolph Reed, who said that Farrakhan "weds a radical oppositional style to a program that proposed private and individual responses to social problems; he endorses moral repressiveness; he asserts racial essentialism; he affirms male authority; and he lauds bootstrap capitalism. . . . His focus on self-help and moral revitalization is profoundly reactionary and meshes perfectly with the victim-blaming orthodoxy of the Reagan/Bush era."

The Million Man March inspired women to organize their own march. Initiated by two Philadelphia women—Phile Chionesu, a small-business owner, and Asia Coney, a public housing activist—an estimated 300,000 black women gathered in Philadelphia on October 25, 1997, to listen to speeches by California congresswoman and president of the Congressional Black Caucus Maxine Waters, rapper Sister Souljah, and South African activist Winnie Mandela. The march was a celebration, a call to unity, and a forum for black women to denounce domestic violence and inadequate access to quality healthcare and educational opportunities. The march got less media attention than the Million Man March, perhaps because the organizers were relatively unknown. The march nonetheless symbolized the struggle of black women to be seen and heard in American society and to counter negative stereotypes and derogatory images of black womanhood. Like the Million Man March, there was little in the way of specific policy demands, but the women marchers did gain a feeling of solidarity. As Detroit real estate agent Gloria Graves put it, "I thought that it was very important that we as black women come together in prayer and unity and the belief that we can bring back the family unit that has been lost. I wanted to meet other strong black women who had the same agenda and be united. It has been just great."

24.8 Complicating Black Identity in the Twenty-First Century

Explore the many dimensions of black identity, culture, and status in the twenty-first century.

The 2000 Census counted 281,421,906 Americans, a 13.2 percent increase from 1990. African Americans numbered 34.7 million, or about 12 percent of the total. For the first time in U.S. history, they were no longer the largest minority group: the 35.3 million Americans who identified themselves as Hispanic slightly outnumbered them.

As in the past, most black Americans (54 percent) live in the South; about 19 percent live in the Midwest, 18 percent in the Northeast, and 10 percent in the West. New York City had the largest black population of any urban area at 2.3 million, followed by Chicago at 1.1 million. Detroit, Philadelphia, and Houston were all in the 500,000 to 1 million range. A look beyond these raw numbers, however, reveals important information about the evolving nature of African-American identity in an increasingly multiethnic nation.

For the first time, the 2000 Census allowed respondents to choose more than one racial designation for themselves. Since the first census in 1790, the politics of race have shaped such classifications. Before the Civil War, an accurate count of slaves was important because they counted for three-fifths of a person in determining the representation of states in the House of Representatives. Throughout the nineteenth century, fears about miscegenation led census takers to identify individuals as black, white, or mixed race. With the rise of segregation in the late nineteenth and early twentieth centuries, the "one-drop" rule—the belief that any black ancestry, no matter how slight, made a person black—hardened, and the census takers' list of questions dropped the classification of "mulatto." During the early civil rights movement, the American Civil Liberties Union and other groups attempted to remove racial classifications altogether from the census data, reasoning that the only purpose of such distinctions was to disadvantage black people.

The civil rights laws of the 1960s changed the purpose of gathering data by racial classification. Reliable statistics on racial characteristics of people were now necessary to combat discrimination. With the rise of affirmative action programs, identifying oneself as an African American could be beneficial. The Black Power movement led many to embrace their identity as African Americans and reject the assimilation implied by abandoning racial categories.

In 1977 the Office of Management and Budget addressed the government's need for standard racial categories with its Statistical Policy Directive 15. This set up the familiar racial classifications: white, black, Asian and Pacific Islander, and Native American. "Hispanic" was chosen to denote an ethnicity and could be selected in addition to one of the four racial categories. Because there is no scientific backing for any biological racial distinctions, these categories are bureaucratic approximations of socially relevant distinctions designed to serve administrative needs. They were not necessarily meant to reflect the complex identities of many individuals included in them. For example, "Asian and Pacific Islander" encompasses people from nations with vastly different histories and cultures. The white category includes people descended from Arabs and Turks as well as Europeans. In terms of ethnicity, people now called Hispanic had formerly thought of themselves in terms of national identities, such as Mexican American, Cuban American, and so on, and overlapped with the "black" category for Dominicans and other African-descended people from the former Spanish Caribbean colonies. Over the quarter century after their adoption, these categories became incorporated into identities and social understandings and influenced business and government programs.

Two groups sought to change the categories. The first group saw an end to racial categories as the true legacy of the civil rights movement. These advocates point to the rhetoric of Martin Luther King, Jr. and the language of the Civil Rights Act of 1964, which forbade any discrimination on the basis of race, as evidence of the need to eliminate racial classifications by the government. Some adherents of this view want to abolish the notion of race altogether. They want a color-blind society that they believe will not arrive until a person's race ceases to affect access to education, government programs, or employment. Others who advocate this position, however, are ideological conservatives who want to limit the power of the federal government to redress inequality. They have bankrolled state referendums and court cases to end racial classifications and see this as a way to roll back the gains of the civil rights era.

Those who are biracial also oppose the old classification scheme. Racial mixing is nothing new in America. Many black women slaves were compelled to bear children to their white masters. There have also been consensual sexual relationships and marriages between African Americans and other ethnic and racial groups. The number of such unions and their social acceptance have grown precipitously since the civil rights movement destroyed many of the old racial barriers and the Supreme Court struck down the last **anti-miscegenation** laws in *Loving v. Virginia* in 1967. There are now more than 1.5 million mixed-race marriages in the United States and many children growing up in these households. Mixed-race marriages are much more common among younger generations and seem likely to increase rapidly.

There is a sharp debate over biracial and multiracial identities in the African-American community. One of the most significant concerns is that fundamental changes in the classification system will undermine the projects they were designed to advance. As poverty researcher John A. Powell put it, "Without racial statistics, we will not know how distributions of resources affect racial and ethnic groups. Without them, racism, which is still very much a part of our society, will be that much more difficult to eradicate, and that much more likely to remain a societal norm." The programs that use these statistics include the Equal Employment Opportunity Act, the Civil Rights Act of 1964, the Voting Rights Act of 1965, the Public Health Act, the Job Partnership Training Act, the Equal Credit Opportunity Act, the Fair Housing Act, and many others. Some argue that offering mixed-race people the option of not being black might undermine the racial solidarity that has been the basis for black advances. As historian Ibrahim K. Sundiata puts it, "The disaggregation of Blacks would drive a wedge into the community that would only increase the isolation of its most disadvantaged members."

Although only 1.8 million Americans opted for the biracial designation in the 2000 Census, the existence of the designation raises questions about the nature of racial identity. Clearly racism exists, and black Americans experienced centuries of discrimination that distinguishes them from other groups. But many who would have been considered black under the traditional American system of racial classification no longer think of themselves in the same way and may be increasingly able to assert a multiple identity. Immigration to the United States from Latin America, Asia, and Africa is also undermining what had once been a largely biracial dynamic.

anti-miscegenation

Laws that denied men and women of different racial identities the right to marry and that imposed the punishment of imprisonment for having sex across the color line during the era of legal segregation.

24.8.1 Immigration and African Americans

Because of immigration restrictions and the general oppression of people of African descent in America, few blacks, either from the Western Hemisphere or from Africa, immigrated to the United States before the past few decades. Changes in immigration laws, particularly the landmark 1965 Hart-Cellar Act, which abandoned the racially exclusive restrictions of the past, helped open the door. Military, economic, health, and environmental crises that have roiled Africa and the Caribbean since the 1960s have pushed substantial numbers from these regions through the door. These new black

Americans often do not fit their identity neatly into the traditional African-American category.

The number of black immigrants from the West Indies increased dramatically after the 1960s. In the 1950s, only 123,000 Caribbean people immigrated, but during the 1990s nearly one million did so. The Caribbean islands were one of the main areas of importation of African slaves. The islands' sugar production was the economic engine of the Spanish, French, Dutch, and British New World empires into the nineteenth century. These empires all abandoned slavery by the late 1800s, and the retreat of British colonialism from the Caribbean in the twentieth century left many micro-nations largely populated by people of African descent whose cultures have remained more influenced by Africa than was true of black people in the United

In 2003 the New York Haitian-American community celebrated the 200th anniversary of the Haitian Revolution. This Haitian flag–waving group of celebrants congregate on the Eastern Parkway in Brooklyn.

States. Hence, African cultural practices fused with those of the British in Jamaica, the French in Haiti, and the Spanish in Santo Domingo and Cuba. Although a racial hierarchy is not unknown in these societies, racial identity is less important than class and merit-based achievement. Upon immigration, mostly to New York, Florida, and other parts of the East Coast, Caribbean immigrants soon learn the importance of race in the United States, but they have also carved out a separate identity from other African Americans. First-generation West Indians tend to have more economic success than native African Americans, in part because employers often favor them. The second generation has often had a more difficult time as discrimination and poor schools take their toll.

Voluntary immigrants from Africa once were few, and before 1980 they were mainly European colonials or North Africans from nations such as Egypt. In the 1950s only 14,000 Africans came to the United States, but during the 1990s over 350,000 arrived. Most of these new immigrants were men and tended to be well educated. Part of their reason for coming to the United States was the destabilization of many African nations and oppression by autocratic regimes.

24.8.2 Black Feminism

The feminist and gay rights movements have challenged traditional ideas of racial identity in recent decades. Both arose as part of the broader "rights revolution" that began with the civil rights movement, but each highlights different aspects of a person's identity—gender or sexuality—in addition to race.

A new wave of feminism in the 1960s and 1970s transformed gender relations. This movement arose, in part, out of the successes of the African-American civil rights struggle. The 1964 Civil Rights Act outlawed sexual as well as racial discrimination in employment. Although this had not been a goal of the civil rights movement at that time and its inclusion was meant, in part, to lessen the prospect that Congress would enact the law, it helped open discussions of gender oppression that had lain dormant for decades. Many white women activists in the Student Nonviolent Coordinating Committee and other civil rights groups became leaders in the emerging feminist movement, often using the same strategies and tactics that had worked to fight racism.

Second-wave feminism achieved many changes. The National Organization for Women, founded in 1966, fought to end job discrimination against women, expand access to safe and effective birth control, legalize abortion, and secure government support for childcare. One of the movement's most important early successes was Title IX of the Educational Amendments Act of 1972, which required colleges and universities to ensure equal access for women. Another was the Supreme Court's decision legalizing abortion in 1973 in *Roe v. Wade*. Beyond these victories, the feminist movement opened up choices for women in nearly every aspect of their lives that traditional gender roles had precluded. It also engendered a backlash as conservative men and women fought passage of the Equal Rights Amendment to the Constitution, access to abortion and legalized abortion itself, and sex education in schools.

Black women shaped modern feminism from the start. The core of black feminist thinking is a dual critique of the women's and black liberation ideology. Black women scholars argued that a critique of patriarchy had to include race and class. Whereas white leaders of the women's movement were silent on race, many male leaders in the African-American freedom movement were all too forthright about gender. As Black Panther leader Elaine Brown put it, "A woman in the Black Power movement was considered at best irrelevant. A woman asserting herself was a pariah." Many believed that racial oppression was the primary evil and that feminism either was a distraction or, by encouraging women to be strong and self-reliant, undermined black men's efforts to overcome the emasculating effects of white male power. Black feminists such as Frances Beale countered that racism and sexism had oppressed black women: "It is true that our husbands, fathers, brothers and sons have been emasculated, lynched, and brutalized. They have suffered from the cruelest assault on mankind that the world has ever known. However, it is a gross distortion of fact that black women have oppressed black men."

Responding to sexism in the Black Power movement, many black women writers and activists sought to make the struggle against sexism as important as that against racism. Between 1973 and 1975, the National Black Feminist Organization (NBFO) articulated many of the concerns specific to black women, from anger with black men for dating and marrying white women; to internal conflict over skin color, hair texture, and facial features; to sexual violence and harassment against black women; to differences in the economic mobility of white and black women. Black feminists also attacked the myth of black matriarchy and stereotypical portrayals of black women in popular culture. Although the NBFO was short lived, it broke the silence black liberation movements had imposed on black women. Black feminists also helped other women talk openly about domestic violence, rape, and sexual harassment in employment. University of California, Los Angeles, law professor Kimberlé Crenshaw summed up their message: "When feminism does not explicitly oppose racism, and when antiracism does not incorporate opposition to patriarchy, race and gender politics often end up being antagonistic to each other and both interests lose."

24.8.3 Gay and Lesbian African Americans

The success of the civil rights movement encouraged gay, lesbian, bisexual, and transgender (LGBT) black Americans to fight openly against the discrimination they had faced for centuries. Their movement was small and quiet until 1969, when gay men at the Stonewall Inn, a bar in New York's Greenwich Village, resisted a police raid. The multiracial crowd's refusal to continue submitting to the kind of police harassment that gays had long been subjected to in the United States sparked an explosion of activism. By the 1980s, many states and cities had decriminalized homosexual behavior and forbade discrimination in employment on the basis of sexuality. Although tensions arose between lesbians and gay men, they worked together to pursue the full range of civil rights heterosexuals enjoy despite persistent opposition from conservative groups.

LGBT African Americans have struggled against their marginality within the larger gay rights movement and homophobia in their own communities. Like the women's movement, the early gay and lesbian rights movement tended to be predominantly white and middle class. Although not explicitly racist, it tended to see racial issues as secondary to or separate from the goal of ending discrimination based on sexual preference.

Despite hostility toward the LGBT rights movement by some African Americans, many black leaders, such as Jesse Jackson, Eleanor Holmes Norton, and John Lewis, and civil rights organizations, such as the NAACP, embraced its agenda. Many black activists in social justice struggles accepted the analogy between the struggles against repression with regard to sexual preference as analogous to that which sought to end race-based discrimination and second-class citizenship. The debate between black feminists and gay rights activists, who argued that gender and class identities must be taken into account in political and scholarly analysis, and nationalists, who focus on

Voices

"Our National Virtues": U.S. Attorney General Loretta E. Lynch on LBGTQ Rights

The North Carolina General Assembly passed House Bill 2 in special session on March 23, 2016. The bill sought to strike down an anti-discrimination provision in a recently-passed Charlotte, North Carolina, ordinance, as well as to require transgender people in public agencies to use the bathrooms consistent with their sex as noted at birth, rather than the bathrooms that fit their gender identity. . . . [The] U.S. Civil Rights Division notified state officials that House Bill 2 violated federal civil rights laws. [T]he state of North Carolina and its governor chose to respond by suing the Department of Justice.

Attorney Loretta Lynch responded: Today, we are filing a federal civil rights lawsuit against the state of North Carolina, Governor Pat McCrory, the North Carolina Department of Public Safety and the University of North Carolina. We are seeking a court order declaring House Bill 2's restroom restriction impermissibly discriminatory, as well as a statewide bar on its enforcement. . . . This action is about a great deal more than just bathrooms. This is about the dignity and respect we accord our fellow citizens and the laws that we, as a people and as a country, have enacted to protect them—indeed, to protect all of us.

This is not the first time that we have seen discriminatory responses to historic moments of progress for our nation. We saw it in the Jim Crow laws that followed the Emancipation Proclamation. We saw it in fierce and widespread resistance to *Brown v. Board of Education*. And we saw it in the proliferation of state bans on same-sex unions intended to stifle any hope that gay and lesbian Americans might one day be afforded the right to marry. That right, of course, is now recognized as a guarantee embedded in our Constitution, and in the wake of that historic triumph, we have seen bill after bill

in state after state taking aim at the LGBT community. Some of these responses reflect a recognizably human fear of the unknown, and a discomfort with the uncertainty of change. But this is not a time to act out of fear. This is a time to summon our national virtues of inclusivity, diversity, compassion and open-mindedness. . . .

Let me also speak directly to the transgender community itself. Some of you have lived freely for decades. Others of you are still wondering how you can possibly live the lives you were born to lead. But no matter how isolated or scared you may feel today, the Department of Justice and the entire Obama Administration wants you to know that we see you; we stand with you; and we will do everything we can to protect you going forward. Please know that history is on your side. This country was founded on a promise of equal rights for all, and we have always managed to move closer to that promise, little by little, one day at a time. It may not be easy—but we'll get there together.

---

1. Why did the North Carolina Assembly enact legislation that favored sex at birth as noted on the birth certificate and not the lived gender identity?

2. In what ways does U.S. Attorney General Loretta Lynch's reassurance to the transgender community reflect the continuation of the Civil Rights Movement of the 1960s? What are "our national virtues"?

SOURCE: "Attorney General Loretta E. Lynch Delivers Remarks at Press Conference Announcing Complaint Against the State of North Carolina to Stop Discrimination Against Transgender Individuals." Washington, DC, United States ~ Monday, May 9, 2016, https://www.justice.gov/opa/speech/attorney-general-loretta-e-lynch-delivers-remarks-press-conference-announcing-complaint black identity as primary, continues to influence African-American life in the twenty-first century. As Coretta Scott King put it in a 2002 speech to the National Gay and Lesbian Task Force, "I believe very strongly that all forms of bigotry and discrimination are equally wrong and should be opposed by right-thinking Americans everywhere. Freedom from discrimination based on sexual orientation is surely a fundamental human right in any great democracy, as much as freedom from racial, religious, gender, or ethnic discrimination." In 2008 California voters approved a referendum overturning a decision of the California Supreme Court that had legalized same-sex marriage in the state. To the dismay of the gay community, African Americans were instrumental in passing this referendum, which restricted marriage to unions between a man and a woman. However, as the great singer Sam Cook put it, a change was coming. In 2011 President Barack Obama announced his support of same-sex marriage. Over a dozen states adopted supportive legislation guaranteeing the rights of members of the LGBT community. Resistance and protests erupted in many white communities. In 2015, the U.S. Supreme Court's decision in *Obergefell v. Hodges* struck down all of the state laws that declared same-sex marriages illegal. The Supreme Court's decision guaranteed LBGT Americans throughout the country the constitutional right to marry.

Conclusion

The closing of the twentieth century saw remarkable progress for some African Americans, even as a significant component of the community remained mired in poverty. African Americans still experienced the burden of racism that was so familiar to W. E. B. Du Bois at the nadir of the nineteenth century. Black people confronted those challenges by engaging in collective political action and maintaining predominantly black churches, colleges, and social action groups. The black soul that Du Bois thought had so much to give America now flows freely through its art, language, scholarship, and popular culture, and especially in the hip-hop national and international culture movement. At the same time, increasing diversity in the ways that African Americans live their lives has led to differences in how individuals understand their identities. Some long for the possibility of asserting those identities in ways not limited by race, sexuality, gender, and class. The tension between racial, ethnic, class, gender, and sexual identities, however, is likely to persist and will profoundly shape the course of the African-American odyssey in the twenty-first century.

Chapter Timeline

AFRICAN-AMERICAN EVENTS   **NATIONAL EVENTS**

1978

1978
Supreme Court decides *Regents of the University of California v. Bakke*

1980–1983

1980
Ronald Reagan elected president

1981
Recession settles in; Economic Recovery Tax Act passed

AFRICAN-AMERICAN EVENTS   **NATIONAL EVENTS**

1984

1984   **1984**

Jesse Jackson creates Rainbow Coali- Reagan reelected
tion and seeks Democratic nomination
for president

1986–1987

1987

August Wilson wins Pulitzer Prize for
his play *Fences*

1988–1989

1988   **1988**

Jesse Jackson's second run for the   George H. W. Bush elected president
Democratic nomination for president

Fair Housing Act passed

1989

Ron Brown elected chairman of the
Democratic Party

1990–1991

1991   **1991**

Clarence Thomas wins Senate confir-   Operation Desert Storm against Iraq
mation to the Supreme Court

John Singleton's *Boyz N the Hood* wins
box-office success

Rodney King is beaten by four white
Los Angeles policemen

1992–1993

1992   **1992**

Los Angeles riots after King's police   William Jefferson Clinton elected
assailants are acquitted   president

Carol Moseley Braun of Illinois is the
first black woman elected to the Senate

1993

Clinton names Ron Brown and Hazel
O'Leary to cabinet

1994–1995

1994   **1994**

Jesse Jackson, Jr. elected to Congress Midterm elections give Republicans
                                       control of Congress

1996

                                       1996

                                       Clinton reelected, signs welfare reform
                                       legislation

AFRICAN-AMERICAN EVENTS   **NATIONAL EVENTS**

1998–1999

1998

Clinton impeached

1999

Senate acquits Clinton

2000–2001

2000

Donna Brazile manages the presidential campaign of Al Gore

2000

George W. Bush becomes president

2001

Bush names Condoleezza Rice national security adviser and Colin Powell secretary of state

September 11, 2001

Terrorists demolish the World Trade Center in New York City and attack the Pentagon

October 2001

United States invades Afghanistan

2002–2003

2003

Supreme Court upholds use of racial preferences in admission to University of Michigan Law School

2002

No Child Left Behind Act

2003

United States invades Iraq

2004–2005

2004

Carol Moseley Braun and Al Sharpton run for president

Barack Obama elected to Senate

Condoleezza Rice appointed secretary of state

2004

George W. Bush reelected president

2005

Hurricane Katrina devastates New Orleans

2006–2015

2006

James Brown dies; Deval Patrick elected governor of Massachusetts

2009

Barack Obama inaugurated as 44th president of the United States

Obama receives the Nobel Peace Prize

Eric Holder, Jr. becomes first African American attorney general

Michael Jackson dies

2008

New York Governor Eliot Spitzer resigns and is replaced by David Paterson

Michael Steele elected chairman of Republican Party National Committee

Roland W. Burris replaces Barack Obama as senator

AFRICAN-AMERICAN EVENTS   **NATIONAL EVENTS**

2006–2015

2010

Lena Horne dies

2012

Don Cornelius dies; Whitney
Houston dies

2014

Ruby Dee dies; Maya Angelou dies

2015

Riley "B.B" King dies; Edward
Brooke III dies; Andraé Crouch dies;
Marva Collins dies; Julian Bond dies;
Amelia Boynton Robinson dies

2009

Edward M. Kennedy dies

Barack Obama secures passage of an
Affordable Healthcare Act

Sonia Sotomayor becomes first Latin
American to be appointed to the
United States Supreme Court

Review Questions

1. What social, economic, and material gains did African Americans make after the civil rights era? Why did some black Americans do better than others during this period? How are tensions surrounding class stratification manifested within the black community?

2. Why do white Americans tend to live longer than black Americans? How has the black community dealt with the problems of HIV/AIDS?

3. Who were some of the most important African-American writers, performers, and social critics in the late twentieth century? What is hip-hop, and what is meant by the term the "hip-hop planet"? What is the relationship between rap music and hip-hop?

4. What are the goals of the Afrocentricity movement? Why is it controversial?

5. Why has the church remained so important to African Americans? How are women's roles changing in the black church?

6. Were the Millenium Marches a success? Why has Louis Farrakhan been so controversial?

7. How has immigration from the Caribbean and Africa affected black America? What factors gave rise to black feminism? What problems do black gays and lesbians face in the black community?

Retracing the Odyssey

Harpo Studios, Chicago, Illinois. Harpo Studios is a state-of-the-art film production facility created by Oprah Winfrey. It is also the first multimedia complex owned and operated by an African American woman.

Rock and Roll Hall of Fame and Museum, Cleveland, Ohio. Among the museum's permanent collection of the 500 songs that most influenced the development of rock and roll are ones by early blues singers: Otis Redding, Chuck Berry, James Brown, Sam Cooke, Ray Charles, Marvin Gaye, Aretha Franklin, and B.B. King. There is a splendid exhibit on the Jackson Five and on Michael Jackson.

Recommended Reading

Patricia Hill Collins. *Black Feminist Thought: Knowledge, Consciousness, and the Politics of Empowerment*. Boston: Unwin Hyman, 1990. A classic text on black feminist theory and practice by one of black studies' foremost sociologists.

Kent B. Germany. *New Orleans After the Promises: Poverty, Citizenship, and the Search for the Great Society*. Athens: University of Georgia Press, 2007. A well-researched, thoughtful historical study of the successes and failures of the Great Society programs of the 1960s and 1970s that prefigured the Hurricane Katrina disaster in New Orleans in 2005.

Melissa V. Harris-Perry. *Sister Citizen: Shame, Stereotypes, and Black Women in America. For Colored Girls Who've Considered Politics When Being Strong Isn't Enough.* New Haven, CT: Yale University Press, 2011. A brilliant and important study of black women's complicated lives and political struggles.

Richard Iton. *In Search of the Black Fantastic: Politics and Popular Culture in the Post–Civil Rights Era.* New York: Oxford University Press, 2008. A sophisticated and profound study of race, as well as popular culture's impact on American politics. Especially insightful is the chapter on black responses to welfare reform efforts in the 1990s.

Jay-Z. *Decoded.* New York: Spiegel & Grau, 2011. A compelling autobiography by one of hip-hop's most accomplished impresarios. Jay-Z's story is an illuminating merger of art, economics, and politics.

Robin D. G. Kelley. *Yo' Mama's DisFunktional!: Fighting the Culture Wars in Urban America.* Boston: Beacon Press, 1998. Powerful essays about America's culture wars and an excellent critique of scholarship about black working-class culture by an elegant and profound scholar.

Tavis Smiley. *The Covenant with Black America.* Chicago: Third World Press, 2006. A valuable source on the status of African Americans at the dawn of the twenty-first century. It contains useful suggestions for individual and community empowerment programs and strategies.

Additional Bibliography

Black Culture Studies

H. Samy Alim and Geneva Smitherman. *Articulate While Black: Barack Obama, Language, and Race in the U.S.* Foreword by Michael Eric Dyson. New York: Oxford University Press, 2012.

Anthony Bogues. *Black Heretics, Black Prophets: Radical Political Intellectuals.* New York: Doubleday, 2003.

March Christian. "Black Studies in the 21st Century: Longevity Has Its Place." *Journal of Black Studies* 36, no. 5 (May 2006): 698–719.

Jennifer Delton. *Racial Integration in Corporate America, 1940–1990.* New York: Cambridge University Press, 2009.

Melissa Victoria Harris-Lacewell. *Barbershops, Bibles, and BET: Everyday Talk and Black Political Thought.* Princeton, NJ: Princeton University Press, 2004.

Cheryl L. Keyes. *Rap Music and Street Consciousness.* Urbana: University of Illinois Press, 2002.

J. L. King. *On the Down Low: A Journey into the Land of "Straight" Black Men Who Sleep with Men.* New York: Broadway Books, 2004.

Shayne Lee and Phillip Luke Sinitiere. *Holy Mavericks: Evangelical Innovators and the Spiritual Marketplace.* New York: New York University Press, 2009.

Terry McMillan. *Five for Five: The Films of Spike Lee.* New York: Stewart, Tabori & Chang, 1991.

Marcyliena Morgan. *The Real Hip Hop: Battling for Knowledge, Power, and Respect in the LA Underground.* Durham, NC: Duke University Press, 2009.

Mark Anthony Neal. *New Black Man.* New York: Routledge, 2006.

Imani Perry. *Prophets of the Hood: Politics and Poetics in Hip Hop.* Durham, NC: Duke University Press, 2004.

Kevin Powell. *Who's Gonna Take the Weight?: Manhood, Race, and Power in America.* New York: Three Rivers Press, 2003.

Riché Richardson. *Black Masculinity and the U.S. South: From Uncle Tom to Gangsta.* Athens: University of Georgia Press, 2007.

Tricia Rose. *Black Noise: Rap Music and Black Culture in Contemporary America.* Hanover, NH: Wesleyan University Press, 1994.

Barbara Dianne Savage. *Your Spirits Walk Beside Us: The Politics of Black Religion.* Cambridge, MA: Harvard University Press, 2008.

T. Denean Sharpley-Whiting. *Pimps Up, Ho's Down: Hip Hop's Hold on Young Black Women.* New York: New York University Press, 2007.

Greg Tate. *Flyboy in the Buttermilk.* New York: Fire-Side, 1992.

Deborah Willis. *Reflections in Black: A History of Black Photographers, 1840 to the Present.* New York: W.W. Norton, 2000.

Rhonda Y. Williams. *The Politics of Public Housing: Black Women's Struggles Against Urban Inequality.* New York: Oxford University Press, 2004.

Identity Studies

Molefi Kete Asante. *The Afrocentric Idea.* Philadelphia: Temple University Press, 1987.

Sherwin K. Bryant, Rachel Sarah O'Toole, and Ben Vinson III. *Africans to Spanish America: Expanding the Diaspora.* Urbana: University of Illinois Press, 2011.

Dawne Y. Curry, Eric D. Duke, and Marshanda A. Smith, eds. *Extending the Diaspora: New Histories of Black People.* Urbana: University of Illinois Press, 2009.

F. James Davis. *Who Is Black?: One Nation's Definition.* University Park: Pennsylvania State University Press, 1991.

Darlene Clark Hine, Trica Danielle Keaton, and Stephen Small, eds. *Black Europe and the African Diaspora.* Urbana: University of Illinois Press, 2009.

E. Patrick Johnson. *Appropriating Blackness: Performance and the Politics of Authenticity.* Durham, NC: Duke University Press, 2003.

E. Patrick Johnson. *Sweet Tea: Black Gay Men of the South, An Oral History.* Durham, NC: Duke University Press, 2009.

Trica Danielle Keaton, T. Denean Sharpley-Whiting, and Tyler Stovall, eds. *Black France/France Noire: The History and Politics of Blackness.* Durham, NC: Duke University Press, 2012.

Tsehloane Keto. *Vision, Identity and Time: The Afrocentric Paradigm and the Study of the Past.* Dubuque, IA: Kendall/Hunt, 1995.

Dwight A. McBride. *Why I Hate Abercrombie & Fitch: Essays on Race and Sexuality.* New York: New York University Press, 2005.

Nitasha Tamar Sharma. *Hip Hop Desis: South Asian Americans, Blackness and Global Race Consciousness.* Durham, NC: Duke University Press 2010.

Lisa B. Thompson. *Beyond the Black Lady: Sexuality and the New African American Middle Class.* Urbana: University of Illinois Press, 2009.

Clarence Walker. *You Can't Go Home Again.* New York: Oxford University Press, 2001.

Cornel West. *Race Matters.* Boston: Beacon Press, 1993.

Erin N. Winkler. *Learning Race Learning Place: Shaping Racial Identities and Ideas in African American Childhoods.* New Brunswick, NJ: Rutgers University Press, 2012.

Race, Gender, and Class

Lois Benjamin. *The Black Elite: Facing the Color Line in the Twilight of the Twentieth Century.* Chicago: Nelson Hall, 1991.

Cassandra Jackson. *Violence, Visual Culture, and the Black Male Body.* New York: Routledge, 2011.

Christopher Jencks. *Rethinking Social Policy: Race, Poverty, and the Underclass.* Cambridge, MA: Harvard University Press, 1992.

Clarence Lang. *Grassroots at the Gateway: Class Politics and Black Freedom Struggle in St. Louis, 1936–75.* Ann Arbor: University of Michigan Press, 2009.

Shayne Lee. *Erotic Revolutionaries: Black Women, Sexuality, and Popular Culture.* Lanham, MD: Hamilton Books, 2010.

Haki R. Madhubuti. *Black Men—Obsolete, Single, Dangerous? Afrikan American Families in Transition: Essays in Discovery, Solution, and Hope.* Chicago: Third World Press, 1990.

Ayana Mathis. *The Twelve Tribes of Hattie: A Novel.* New York: Alfred A. Knopf, 2012.

Harriette Pipes McAdoo, ed. *Black Families.* 4th ed. London: Sage, 2007.

Jody Miller. *Getting Played: African American Girls, Urban Inequality, and Gendered Violence.* New York: New York University Press, 2008.

Leith Mullings. *On Our Own Terms: Race, Class, and Gender in the Lives of African American Women.* New York: Routledge, 1997.

Steven Shulman, ed. *The Impact of Immigration on African Americans.* New Brunswick, NJ: Transaction, 2004.

Marshanda Smith, Rose Thevenin, and Ida Jones, eds. *Truth.* www.abwh.org/images/pdf/TruthNewsletter2012.pdf.

Celeste Watkins-Hayes. *The New Welfare Bureaucrats: Entanglement of Race, Class, and Policy Reform.* Chicago: University of Chicago Press, 2009.

Autobiography and Biography

Amy Alexander, ed. *The Farrakhan Factor: African--American Writers on Leadership, Nationhood and Minister Louis Farrakhan.* New York: Grove Press, 1998.

E. Lynn Harris. *What Becomes of the Broken Hearted?* New York: Doubleday, 2003.

Nelson Mandela. *Conversations with Myself.* Foreword by President Barack Obama. New York: Farrar, Straus and Giroux, 2010

Joan Morgan. *When Chickenheads Come Home to Roost: My Life as a Hip-Hop Feminist.* New York: Simon and Schuster, 1999.

Charlotte Pierce-Baker. *Surviving the Silence: Black Women's Stories of Rape.* New York: W.W. Norton, 1998.

Randall Robinson. *Defending the Spirit: A Black Life in America.* New York: NAL/Dutton, 1998.

Connecting the Past

The Significance of Black Culture

John Coltrane (1926–1967) was one of the most profound and remarkable jazz musicians in the twentieth century, a master of the tenor and soprano saxophone to be revered for his instrumental improvisation. His most celebrated album, *A Love Supreme*, was released in 1965.

In an address celebrating black history week in 1935, Kirkland W. Green, Dean of Arts and Sciences at South Carolina State College, declared, "The Negro has traveled through four hundred years of American history amidst thorns of torture, ridicule, scorn, degradation, and shame. These thorns have torn his flesh and wounded his soul. Bathed in blood and tears, he prayed and sang for the coming of a new day when he would come into his own, in possession of his birthright, freedom, recognition of a man's chance—the right to live his best self to fulfill his God given mission. Millions waited for this day and died."

Across the centuries, African Americans created and forged significant black culture movements at pivotal turning points in their long odyssey from slavery to full citizenship. In the twentieth century there were black renaissances in 1920s Harlem and in Chicago from the 1930s through the 1950s against the backdrop of the Great Depression and World War II. Across the United States in the first half of the twentieth century, the cultural achievements of talented black writers and performers made black people feel at home and proud in their new urban environments created by the Great

Migration from the rural South to northern and western cities. The southern rural, agricultural-based Negro evolved first into "The New Negro," then into the "black metropolitan," and finally into empowered members of an "industrial working class" who became activists for social change through their membership in labor unions. At each stage in this evolution or transformation, black cultural workers, artists, writers, and performers forged new weapons that enabled black people to achieve a sense of belonging both to their own community and to the nation as a whole. It also enabled them to shake off the demeaning and dehumanizing stereotype of blackness that centuries of oppression had forced on them.

Indeed, the U.S. government, especially the State Department in the early years of the Cold War against Soviet Communism, recognized this and tried to harness the power and appeal of black culture to win allies in third-world countries. The State Department sponsored international tours and cultural programs by representative black entertainers and spokespersons, including musicians such as Louis Armstrong, Count Basie, and Ella Fitzgerald; painters and writers; actors and dancers like Katherine Dunham; and sportsmen, from Joe Louis to Jackie Robinson, to testify that America was not the most racist country on Earth as depicted in communist propaganda.

In the 1960s and 1970s, the Black Arts movement flourished in New York, Chicago, Detroit, Los Angeles, and Washington, D.C. It was the creative and artistic counterpart to the civil rights and Black Power movements. Black musicians produced two strands of art during these decades when the rhythm and blues and soul music of artists like James Brown, Stevie Wonder, and Aretha Franklin flourished alongside the innovative jazz of giants like Miles Davis and John Coltrane.

More recently, the hip-hop cultural movement expressed the hopes and needs of a generation that felt it had received little benefits from the civil rights and Black Power movements. Globalization and deindustrialization, which destroyed the jobs that previous generations of black people had depended on, meant that too many black boys and girls of the millennial generation lived in communities with rising rates of poverty and heightened measures of social distress. Because their songs, poetry, body piercings, clothes, body language, movies, paintings, and even humor depicted an alternate reality that few adults could fathom or appreciate, they were repudiated for their use of profanity, sexist language, and seeming glorification of violence.

In each cultural movement of the twentieth and early twenty-first centuries, African-American artists and cultural workers rescued black consciousness from despair and oppression and gave birth to new identities and political awareness. Black cultural innovations reflected resilience and rebirth even when the future seemed most bleak, and the institutional,

Spike Lee, director and activist, directing one of his ground-breaking films.

racist, and ethnic barriers seemed too high to be overcome. Thus, the poems, novels, essays, paintings, and sculpture, and the new styles of music and dance, the changing religious practices and theology, the oratory, and the employment of old and new technology and media emerged just in time to nurture the seeds of progressive black political activism and generate community mobilization, coalition politics, and the creation of empowering communal and individual identities.

At each stage, black culture movements not only helped destroy demeaning racial stereotypes. They also transformed the black community. In the 1990s, the hip-hop movement showcased fundamental human and citizenship rights whose appeal went far beyond the borders of the United States. Hip-hop was enthusiastically adopted by a youth generation across the globe that was battling post-colonial domination, oppressive governments, and economic exploitation, and in the United States had to endure mass incarceration, educational failure, substance addiction, deportation, bullying, and sexual abuse. In other words, hip-hop gave a voice to the disinherited and dispossessed youth not only in the African Diaspora, but in Asia, Latin America, the Caribbean, and Europe. But hip-hop was also, at its birth, just plain fun.

Culture is intimately connected with political awareness. The black cultural movements of the twentieth and early twenty-first centuries merged the "double consciousness" that W. E. B. Du Bois talked about in *The Souls of Black Folk* into "better and truer" black selves. Black cultural productions have continually provided new "intellectual equipment" that black people have used to examine, showcase, and discuss the realities and experiences of their lives and dreams. In this way, the lives and art of African-American culture workers have inspired oppressed people around the world.

Black culture has sometimes been dismissed as superficial and inconsequential. Yet the innovative, dynamic, and resonant productions of black artists, musicians, and performers have been in the vanguard of those movements whose appeal cuts across borders and smashes the negative social and political barriers that divide Americans along the fault lines of race, class, gender, and sexuality. The writers, musicians, and artists of the Harlem and Chicago Renaissances humanized black people, raised individual and group pride, and helped expand and preserve democracy for all Americans. They built bridges that connected the resolve of black people in disparate communities, nationally and internationally, to resist and reject dehumanization. Black culture workers from those Renaissances to the creators of the hip-hop movement were not only entertainers and artists. They also strengthened opposition to racial oppression, economic exploitation, political powerlessness, and social injustice. The complex, compelling, and inclusive nature of black culture is one of the great African-American achievements. It deserves to be studied with the same seriousness that we bring to the study of black migration; the struggles for political, social, and economic rights; and the history of sports.

Epilogue

Since the first Africans were brought to America's shores in the seventeenth century, black people have been a constant and distinct presence in America. They have constituted a separate ethnic, racial, and cultural group. During the prolonged course of the Atlantic slave trade, approximately 400,000 Africans were sold into servitude in what became the United States. By the outbreak of the Civil War in 1861 there were nearly four million African Americans in the United States. Today black people number over 46 million and make up over 13 percent of the nation's population. Initially most white Americans regarded African Americans merely as an enslaved labor force used to produce cash crops, and not as a people who could enjoy an equal role in the political and social affairs in the country.

Therefore people of African descent developed ambivalent relationships with the white majority in America. Never fully accepted and never fully rejected, black people relied largely on themselves as they created their own institutions and communities. In 1852 Martin Delany declared, "We are a nation within a nation." A half century later, W. E. B. Du Bois observed that the black man wanted to retain his African identity *and* be an American as well. "He would not Africanize America, for America has too much to teach the world and Africa. He would not bleach his Negro soul in a flood of white Americanism, for he knows that Negro blood has a message for the world. He simply wishes to make it possible for a man to be both a Negro and an American, without being cursed and spit upon by his fellows, without having the doors of Opportunity closed roughly in his face."

Sometimes in desperation or disgust, some black people have been willing to abandon America or reject assimilation. The slaves who engaged in South Carolina's 1739 Stono rebellion attempted to reach Spanish Florida. From the 1790s to the start of the Civil War, visions of nationhood in Africa attracted a minority of African Americans. During the 1920s, Marcus Garvey and the Universal Negro Improvement Association glorified Africa while seeking black autonomy in the United States. By the 1950s, Elijah Muhammad, Malcolm X, and the Nation of Islam emphasized a separate black destiny.

Yet in spite of the horrors of slavery, the indignity of Jim Crow, and the violence and discrimination inflicted, most African Americans did not reject America. African slaves brought religious practices and beliefs to America and when allowed they embraced and modified Christianity to help them adjust to their circumstances. Their descendants continued to find solace in their spiritual beliefs.

Black Americans have embraced American principles of brotherhood, justice, fairness, and equality before the law. The nation within a nation has never been homogeneous. There have been persistent class, gender, and color divisions. There have been tensions and ideological conflicts among black leaders and organizations. Some leaders, such as Booker T. Washington, have emphasized self-reliance and economic advancement, while others, including W. E. B. Du Bois and leaders of the NAACP, have advocated full inclusion in American society.

African Americans have been far more than victims, than an exploited labor force, or the subjects of segregation and stereotypes. They have contributed enormously to the development and character of American society and culture. As slaves, they provided billions of hours of unrequited labor to the American economy. Black people established churches, schools, and colleges that continue to thrive. They have demonstrated a willingness to fight and die for their country. African Americans have long made innovative contributions to art, music, literature, science and technology, athletics, and politics—and they continue to do so

In the twenty-first century, the long odyssey of people of African descent continues. African Americans remain "a nation within a nation." They continue to face injustice and discrimination. But the election of Barack Obama in 2008, and his reelection in 2012, represent a remarkable milestone. Michelle Obama gives her husband's presidency a deeper meaning, as America's first black first lady. Undoubtedly black people will continue to help mold and shape American civilization.

The Declaration of Independence

When in the course of human events it becomes necessary for one people to dissolve the political bands which have connected them with another and to assume, among the powers of the earth, the separate and equal station to which the laws of nature and of nature's God entitle them, a decent respect to the opinions of mankind requires that they should declare the causes which impel them to the separation.

We hold these truths to be self-evident, that all men are created equal; that they are endowed by their Creator with certain unalienable rights; that among these are life, liberty, and the pursuit of happiness. That, to secure these rights, governments are instituted among men, deriving their just powers from the consent of the governed; that, whenever any form of government becomes destructive of these ends, it is the right of the people to alter or to abolish it, and to institute a new government, laying its foundation on such principles, and organizing its powers in such form, as to them shall seem most likely to effect their safety and happiness. Prudence, indeed, will dictate that governments long established should not be changed for light and transient causes; and, accordingly, all experience hath shown that mankind are more disposed to suffer, while evils are sufferable, than to right themselves by abolishing the forms to which they are accustomed. But when a long train of abuses and usurpations, pursuing invariably the same object, evinces a design to reduce them under absolute despotism, it is their right, it is their duty, to throw off such government and to provide new guards for their future security. Such has been the patient sufferance of these colonies, and such is now the necessity which constrains them to alter their former systems of government. The history of the present King of Great Britain is a history of repeated injuries and usurpations, all having, in direct object, the establishment of an absolute tyranny over these States. To prove this, let facts be submitted to a candid world:

He has refused his assent to laws the most wholesome and necessary for the public good.

He has forbidden his governors to pass laws of immediate and pressing importance, unless suspended in their operation till his assent should be obtained; and, when so suspended, he has utterly neglected to attend to them.

He has refused to pass other laws for the accommodation of large districts of people, unless those people would relinquish the right of representation in the legislature, a right inestimable to them and formidable to tyrants only.

He has called together legislative bodies at places unusual, uncomfortable, and distant from the depository of their public records, for the sole purpose of fatiguing them into compliance with his measures.

He has dissolved representative houses, repeatedly for opposing, with manly firmness, his invasions on the rights of the people.

He has refused, for a long time after such dissolutions, to cause others to be elected; whereby the legislative powers, incapable of annihilation, have returned to the people at large for their exercise; the state remaining, in the meantime, exposed to all the danger of invasion from without and convulsions within.

He has endeavored to prevent the population of these States; for that purpose, obstructing the laws for naturalization of foreigners, refusing to pass others to encourage their migration hither, and raising the conditions of new appropriations of lands.

He has obstructed the administration of justice by refusing his assent to laws for establishing judiciary powers.

He has made judges dependent on his will alone for the tenure of their offices and the amount and payment of their salaries.

He has erected a multitude of new offices and sent hither swarms of officers to harass our people and eat out their substance.

He has kept among us, in time of peace, standing armies, without the consent of our legislatures.

He has affected to render the military independent of, and superior to, the civil power.

He has combined with others to subject us to a jurisdiction foreign to our Constitution and unacknowledged by our laws, giving his assent to their acts of pretended legislation—

For quartering large bodies of armed troops among us;

For protecting them, by mock trial, from punishment for any murders which they should commit on the inhabitants of these States;

For cutting off our trade with all parts of the world;

For imposing taxes on us without our consent;

For depriving us, in many cases, of the benefits of trial by jury;

For transporting us beyond seas to be tried for pretended offences;

For abolishing the free system of English laws in a neighboring province, establishing therein an arbitrary government, and enlarging its boundaries, so as to render it at once an example and fit instrument for introducing the same absolute rule into these colonies;

For taking away our charters, abolishing our most valuable laws, and altering, fundamentally, the powers of our governments.

For suspending our own legislatures and declaring themselves invested with power to legislate for us in all cases whatsoever.

He has abdicated government here by declaring us out of his protection and waging war against us.

He has plundered our seas, ravaged our coasts, burnt our towns, and destroyed the lives of our people.

He is, at this time, transporting large armies of foreign mercenaries to complete the works of death, desolation, and tyranny already begun with circumstances of cruelty and perfidy scarcely paralleled in the most barbarous ages, and totally unworthy the head of a civilized nation.

He has constrained our fellow citizens, taken captive on the high seas, to bear arms against their country, to become the executioners of their friends and brethren, or to fall themselves by their hands.

He has excited domestic insurrections amongst us and has endeavored to bring on the inhabitants of our frontiers, the merciless Indian savages, whose known rule of warfare is an undistinguished destruction of all ages, sexes, and conditions.

In every stage of these oppressions, we have petitioned for redress in the most humble terms; our repeated petitions have been answered only by repeated injury. A prince whose character is thus marked by every act which may define a tyrant is unfit to be the ruler of a free people.

Nor have we been wanting in attention to our British brethren. We have warned them, from time to time, of attempts made by their legislature to extend an unwarrantable jurisdiction over us. We have reminded them of the circumstances of our emigration and settlement here. We have appealed to their native justice and magnanimity, and we have conjured them, by the ties of our common kindred, to disavow these usurpations, which would inevitably interrupt our connections and correspondence. They, too, have been deaf to the voice of justice and consanguinity. We must, therefore, acquiesce in the necessity which denounces our separation, and hold them, as we hold the rest of mankind, enemies in war, in peace, friends.

We, therefore, the representatives of the United States of America, in general Congress assembled, appealing to the Supreme Judge of the world for the rectitude of our intentions, do, in the name and by the authority of the good people of these colonies, solemnly publish and declare, that these united colonies are, and of right ought to be, free and independent states: that they are absolved from all allegiance to the British Crown, and that all political connection between them and the state of Great Britain is, and ought to be, totally dissolved; and that, as free and independent states, they have full power to levy war, conclude peace, contract alliances, establish commerce, and to do all other acts and things which independent states may of right do. And, for the support of this declaration, with a firm reliance on the protection of Divine Providence, we mutually pledge to each other our lives, our fortunes, and our sacred honor.

Proposed Clause on the Slave Trade Omitted from the Final Draft of the Declaration

He has waged cruel war against human nature itself, violating its most sacred rights of life and liberty in the person of a distant people who never offended him; captivating and carrying them into slavery in another hemisphere, or to incur miserable death in their transportation thither. This piratical warfare, the opprobrium of infidel powers, is the warfare of the Christian king of Great Britain. Determined to keep open a market where men should be bought and sold, he has prostituted his negative for suppressing every legislative attempt to prohibit or restrain this execrable commerce.

SOURCE: Thomas Jefferson's Original Rough Draft of the Declaration of Independence, Written in June 1776. Library of Congress.

The Constitution of the United States of America

(with clauses pertaining to the status of African Americans highlighted)

We the people of the United States, in order to form a more perfect union, establish justice, insure domestic tranquility, provide for the common defense, promote the general welfare, and secure the blessings of liberty to ourselves and our posterity, do ordain and establish this Constitution for the United States of America.

Article I

Section 1

All legislative powers herein granted shall be vested in a Congress of the United States, which shall consist of a Senate and House of Representatives.

Section 2

1. The House of Representatives shall be composed of members chosen every second year by the people of the several States, and the electors in each State shall have the qualifications requisite for electors of the most numerous branch of the State legislature.

2. No person shall be a representative who shall not have attained to the age of twenty-five years, and been seven years a citizen of the United States, and who shall not, when elected, be an inhabitant of that State in which he shall be chosen.

3. Representatives and direct taxes[1] shall be apportioned among the several States which may be included within this Union, according to their respective numbers, which shall be determined by adding to the whole number of free persons, including those bound to service for a term of years, and excluding Indians not taxed, three fifths of all other persons.[2]

    The actual enumeration shall be made within three years after the first meeting of the Congress of the United States, and within every subsequent term of ten years, in such manner as they shall by law direct. The number of representatives shall not exceed one for every thirty thousand, but each State shall have at least one representative; and until such enumeration shall be made, the State of New Hampshire shall be entitled to choose three, Massachusetts eight, Rhode Island and Providence Plantations one, Connecticut five, New York six, New Jersey four, Pennsylvania eight, Delaware one, Maryland six, Virginia ten, North Carolina five, South Carolina five, and Georgia three.

4. When vacancies happen in the representation from any State, the executive authority thereof shall issue writs of election to fill such vacancies.

5. The House of Representatives shall choose their speaker and other officers; and shall have the sole power of impeachment.

Section 3

1. The Senate of the United States shall be composed of two senators from each State, chosen by the legislature thereof,[3] for six years; and each senator shall have one vote.

2. Immediately after they shall be assembled in consequence of the first election, they shall be divided as equally as may be into three classes. The seats of the senators of the first class shall be vacated at the expiration of the second year, of the second class at the expiration of the fourth year, and of the third class at the expiration of the sixth year, so that one third may be chosen every second year; and if vacancies happen by resignation, or otherwise, during the recess of the legislature of any State, the executive thereof may make temporary appointments until the next meeting of the legislature, which shall then fill such vacancies.[4]

3. No person shall be a senator who shall not have attained to the age of thirty years, and been nine years a citizen of the United States, and who shall not, when elected, be an inhabitant of that State for which he shall be chosen.

4. The Vice President of the United States shall be President of the Senate, but shall have no vote, unless they be equally divided.

5. The Senate shall choose their other officers, and also a president pro tempore, in the absence of the Vice President, or when he shall exercise the office of the President of the United States.

6. The Senate shall have the sole power to try all impeachments. When sitting for that purpose, they shall be on

---

[1] See the Sixteenth Amendment.
[2] See the Fourteenth Amendment.
[3] See the Seventeenth Amendment.
[4] See the Seventeenth Amendment.

oath or affirmation. When the president of the United States is tried, the chief justice shall preside: and no person shall be convicted without the concurrence of two thirds of the members present.

7. Judgment in cases of impeachment shall not extend further than to removal from office, and disqualification to hold and enjoy any office of honor, trust or profit under the United States: but the party convicted shall nevertheless be liable and subject to indictment, trial, judgment and punishment, according to law.

Section 4

1. The times, places, and manner of holding elections for senators and representatives, shall be prescribed in each State by the legislature thereof; but the Congress may at any time by law make or alter such regulations, except as to the places of choosing senators.

2. The Congress shall assemble at least once in every year, and such meeting shall be on the first Monday in December, unless they shall by law appoint a different day.

Section 5

1. Each House shall be the judge of the elections, returns and qualifications of its own members, and a majority of each shall constitute a quorum to do business; but a smaller number may adjourn from day to day, and may be authorized to compel the attendance of absent members, in such manner, and under such penalties as each House may provide.

2. Each House may determine the rules of its proceedings, punish its members for disorderly behavior, and, with the concurrence of two thirds, expel a member.

3. Each House shall keep a journal of its proceedings, and from time to time publish the same, excepting such parts as may in their judgment require secrecy; and the yeas and nays of the members of either house on any question shall, at the desire of one fifth of those present, be entered on the journal.

4. Neither House, during the session of Congress, shall, without the consent of the other, adjourn for more than three days, nor to any other place than that in which the two Houses shall be sitting.

Section 6

1. The senators and representatives shall receive a compensation for their services, to be ascertained by law, and paid out of the Treasury of the United States. They shall in all cases, except treason, felony, and breach of the peace, be privileged from arrest during their attendance at the session of their respective Houses, and in going to and returning from the same; and for

any speech or debate in either House, they shall not be questioned in any other place.

2. No senator or representative shall, during the time for which he was elected, be appointed to any civil office under the authority of the United States, which shall have been created, or the emoluments whereof shall have been increased, during such time; and no person holding any office under the United States shall be a member of either House during his continuance in office.

Section 7

1. All bills for raising revenue shall originate in the House of Representatives; but the Senate may purpose or concur with amendments as on other bills.

2. Every bill which shall have passed the House of Representatives and the Senate, shall, before it become a law, be presented to the President of the United States; if he approves he shall sign it, but if not he shall return it, with his objections, to that House in which it shall have originated, who shall enter the objections at large on their journal, and proceed to reconsider it. If after such reconsideration two thirds of that House shall agree to pass the bill, it shall be sent, together with the objections, to the other House, by which it shall likewise be reconsidered, and if approved by two thirds of that House, it shall become a law. But in all such cases the votes of both Houses shall be determined by yeas and nays, and the names of the persons voting for and against the bill shall be entered on the journal of each House respectively. If any bill shall not be returned by the President within ten days (Sundays excepted) after it shall have been presented to him, the same shall be a law, in like manner as if he had signed it, unless the Congress by their adjournment prevent its return, in which case it shall not be a law.

3. Every order, resolution, or vote to which the concurrence of the Senate and the House of Representatives may be necessary (except on a question of adjournment) shall be presented to the President of the United States; and before the same shall take effect, shall be approved by him, or being disapproved by him, shall be repassed by two thirds of the Senate and House of Representatives, according to the rules and limitations prescribed in the case of a bill.

Section 8. The Congress shall have the power

1. To lay and collect taxes, duties, imports, and excises, to pay the debts and provide for the common defense and general welfare of the United States; but all duties, imports, and excises shall be uniform throughout the United States.

2. To borrow money on the credit of the United States;

3. To regulate commerce with foreign nations, and among the several States, and with the Indian tribes;

4. To establish a uniform rule of naturalization, and uniform laws on the subject of bankruptcies throughout the United States;

5. To coin money, regulate the value thereof, and of foreign coin, and fix the standard of weights and measures;

6. To provide for the punishment of counterfeiting the securities and current coin of the United States;

7. To establish post offices and post roads;

8. To promote the progress of science and useful arts, by securing for limited times to authors and inventors the exclusive right to their respective writings and discoveries;

9. To constitute tribunals inferior to the Supreme Court;

10. To define and punish piracies and felonies committed on the high seas, and offenses against the law of nations;

11. To declare war, grant letters of marque and reprisal, and make rules concerning captures on land and water;

12. To raise and support armies, but no appropriation of money to that use shall be for a longer term than two years;

13. To provide and maintain a navy;

14. To make rules for the government and regulation of the land and naval forces;

15. To provide for calling forth the militia to execute the laws of the Union, suppress insurrections and repel invasions;

16. To provide for organizing, arming, and disciplining the militia, and for governing such part of them as may be employed in the service of the United States, reserving to the States respectively, the appointment of the officers, and the authority of training the militia according to the discipline prescribed by Congress;

17. To exercise exclusive legislation in all cases whatsoever, over such district (not exceeding ten miles square) as may, by cession of particular States, and the acceptance of Congress, become the seat of the government of the United States, and to exercise like authority over all places purchased by the consent of the legislature of the State in which the same shall be, for the erection of forts, magazines, arsenals, dockyards, and other needful buildings; and

18. To make all laws which shall be necessary and proper for carrying into execution the foregoing powers, and all other powers vested by this Constitution in the government of the United States, or any department or officer thereof.

Section 9

1. The migration or importation of such persons as any of the States now existing shall think proper to admit, shall not be prohibited by the Congress prior to the year one thousand eight hundred and eight, but a tax or duty may be imposed on such importation, not exceeding ten dollars for each person.

2. The privilege of the writ of habeas corpus shall not be suspended, unless when in cases of rebellion or invasion the public safety may require it.

3. No bill of attainder or ex post facto law shall be passed.

4. No capitation, or other direct, tax shall be laid, unless in proportion to the census or enumeration herein-before directed to be taken.[5]

5. No tax or duty shall be laid on articles exported from any State.

6. No preference shall be given by any regulation of commerce or revenue to the ports of one State over those of another: nor shall vessels bound to, or from, one State be obliged to enter, clear, or pay duties in another.

7. No money shall be drawn from the treasury, but in consequence of appropriations made by law; and a regular statement and account of the receipts and expenditures of all public money shall be published from time to time.

8. No title of nobility shall be granted by the United States: and no person holding any office of profit or trust under them, shall, without the consent of the Congress, accept of any present, emolument, office, or title, of any kind whatever, from any king, prince, or foreign State.

Section 10

1. No State shall enter into any treaty, alliance, or confederation; grant letters of marque and reprisal; coin money; emit bills of credit; make any thing but gold and silver coin a tender in payment of debts; pass any bill of attainder, ex post facto law, or law impairing the obligation of contracts, or grant any title of nobility.

2. No State shall, without the consent of the Congress, lay any imposts or duties on imports or exports, except what may be absolutely necessary for executing its inspection laws: and the net produce of all duties and imposts laid by any State on imports or exports, shall be for the use of the treasury of the United States; and all such laws shall be subject to the revision and control of the Congress.

3. No State shall, without the consent of the Congress, lay any duty of tonnage, keep troops, or ships of war in time of peace, enter into any agreement or compact

[5] See the Sixteenth Amendment.

with another State, or with a foreign power, or engage in war, unless actually invaded, or in such imminent danger as will not admit of delay.

Article II
Section 1

1. The executive power shall be vested in a President of the United States of America. He shall hold his office during the term of four years, and, together with the Vice President, chosen for the same term, be elected, as follows:

2. Each State shall appoint, in such manner as the legislature thereof may direct, a number of electors, equal to the whole number of senators and representatives to which the State may be entitled in the Congress: but no senator or representative, or person holding any office of trust or profit under the United States, shall be appointed an elector.

    The electors shall meet in their respective States, and vote by ballot for two persons, of whom one at least shall not be an inhabitant of the same State with themselves. And they shall make a list of all the persons voted for, and of the number of votes for each; which list they shall sign and certify, and transmit sealed to the seat of the government of the United States, directed to the president of the Senate. The president of the Senate shall, in the presence of the Senate and House of Representatives, open all the certificates, and the votes shall then be counted. The person having the greatest number of votes shall be the President, if such number be a majority of the whole number of electors appointed; and if there be more than one who have such majority, and have an equal number of votes, then the House of Representatives shall immediately choose by ballot one of them for President; and if no person have a majority, then from the five highest on the list the said House shall in like manner choose the President. But in choosing the President, the votes shall be taken by States, the representation from each State having one vote; a quorum for this purpose shall consist of a member or members from two thirds of the States, and a majority of all the States shall be necessary to a choice. In every case after the choice of the President, the person having the greatest number of votes of the electors shall be the Vice President. But if there should remain two or more who have equal votes, the Senate shall choose from them by ballot the Vice President.[6]

3. The Congress may determine the time of choosing the electors, and the day on which they shall give their votes; which day shall be the same throughout the United States.

4. No person except a natural born citizen, or a citizen of the United States, at the time of the adoption of this Constitution, shall be eligible to the office of President; neither shall any person be eligible to the office who shall not have attained to the age of thirty-five years, and been fourteen years a resident within the United States.

5. In case of the removal of the President from office, or of his death, resignation, or inability to discharge the powers and duties of the said office, the same shall devolve on the Vice President, and the Congress may by law provide for the case of removal, death, resignation or inability, both of the President and Vice President, declaring what officer shall then act as President, and such officer shall act accordingly until the disability be removed, or a President shall be elected.

6. The President shall, at stated times, receive for his services a compensation which shall neither be increased nor diminished during the period for which he shall have been elected, and he shall not receive within that period any other emolument from the United States, or any of them.

7. Before he enter on the execution of his office, he shall take the following oath or affirmation:—"I do solemnly swear (or affirm) that I will faithfully execute the office of president of the United States, and will to the best of my ability, preserve, protect and defend the Constitution of the United States."

Section 2

1. The President shall be commander in chief of the army and navy of the United States, and of the militia of the several States, when called into the actual service of the United States; he may require the opinion in writing, of the principal officer in each of the executive departments, upon any subject relating to the duties of their respective offices, and he shall have power to grant reprieves and pardons for offenses against the United States, except in cases of impeachment.

2. He shall have power, by and with the advice and consent of the Senate, to make treaties, provided two thirds of the senators present concur; and he shall nominate, and by and with the advice and consent of the Senate, shall appoint ambassadors, other public ministers and consuls, judges of the Supreme Court, and all other officers of the United States, whose appointments are not herein otherwise provided for, and which shall be established by law; but the Congress may by law vest the appointment of such inferior officers, as they think proper, in the President alone, in the courts of laws, or in the heads of departments.

---

[6] See the Twelfth Amendment.

3. The President shall have power to fill up all vacancies that may happen during the recess of the Senate, by granting commissions which shall expire at the end of their next session.

Section 3

He shall from time to time give to the Congress information of the state of the Union, and recommend to their consideration such measures as he shall judge necessary and expedient; he may, on extraordinary occasions, convene both houses, or either of them, and in case of disagreement between them with respect to the time of adjournment, he may adjourn them to such time as he shall think proper; he shall receive ambassadors and other public ministers; he shall take care that the laws be faithfully executed, and shall commission all the officers of the United States.

Section 4

The President, Vice President, and all civil officers of the United States, shall be removed from office on impeachment for, and conviction of, treason, bribery, or other high crimes and misdemeanors.

Article III

Section 1

The judicial power of the United States shall be vested in one Supreme Court, and in such inferior courts as the Congress may from time to time ordain and establish. The judges, both of the Supreme and inferior courts, shall hold their offices during good behavior, and shall, at stated times, receive for their services, a compensation, which shall not be diminished during their continuance in office.

Section 2

1. The judicial power shall extend to all cases, in law and equity, arising under this Constitution, the laws of the United States, and treaties made, or which shall be made, under their authority;—to all cases of admiralty and maritime jurisdiction;—to controversies to which the United States shall be a party;[7]—to controversies between two or more States;—between a State and citizens of another State;—between citizens of different States;—between citizens of the same State claiming lands under grants of different States, and between a State, or the citizens thereof, and foreign States, citizens or subjects.

2. In all cases affecting ambassadors, other public ministers and consuls, and those in which a State shall be party, the Supreme Court shall have original jurisdiction. In all the other cases before mentioned, the Supreme Court shall have appellate jurisdiction, both as to law and fact, with such exceptions, and under such regulations as the Congress shall make.

3. The trial of all crimes, except in cases of impeachment, shall be by jury; and such trial shall be held in the State where the said crimes shall have been committed; but when not committed within any State, the trial shall be such place or places as the Congress may by law have directed.

Section 3

1. Treason against the United States shall consist only in levying war against them, or in adhering to their enemies, giving them aid and comfort. No person shall be convicted of treason unless on the testimony of two witnesses to the same overt act, or on confession in open court.

2. The Congress shall have power to declare the punishment of treason, but no attainder of treason shall work corruption of blood, or forfeiture except during the life of the person attained.

Article IV

Section 1

Full faith and credit shall be given in each State to the public acts, records, and judicial proceedings of every other State. And the Congress may by general laws prescribe the manner in which such acts, records and proceedings shall be proved, and the effect thereof.

Section 2

1. The citizens of each State shall be entitled to all privileges and immunities of citizens in the several States.[8]

2. A person charged in any State with treason, felony, or other crime, who shall flee from justice, and be found in another State, shall on demand of the executive authority of the State from which he fled, be delivered up to be removed to the State having jurisdiction of the crime.

3. No person held to service or labor in one State under the laws thereof, escaping into another, shall, in consequence of any law or regulation therein, be discharged from such service or labor, but shall be delivered up on claim of the party to whom such service or labor may be due.[9]

Section 3

1. New States may be admitted by the Congress into this Union; but no new State shall be formed or erected within the jurisdiction of any other State, nor any State be formed by the junction of two or more States, or parts of States, without the consent of the legislatures of the States concerned as well as of the Congress.

[7] See the Eleventh Amendment.

[8] See the Fourteenth Amendment, Sec. 1.

[9] See the Thirteenth Amendment.

2. The Congress shall have power to dispose of and make all needful rules and regulations respecting the territory or other property belonging to the United States; and nothing in this Constitution shall be so construed as to prejudice any claims of the United States, or of any particular State.

Section 4

The United States shall guarantee to every State in this Union a republican form of government, and shall protect each of them against invasion; and on application of the legislature, or of the executive (when the legislature cannot be convened) against domestic violence.

Article V

The Congress, whenever two thirds of both Houses shall deem it necessary, shall propose amendments to this Constitution, or, on the application of the legislatures of two thirds of the several States, shall call a convention for proposing amendments, which in either case shall be valid to all intents and purposes, as part of this Constitution, when ratified by the legislatures of three fourths of the several States, or by conventions in three fourths thereof, as the one or the other mode of ratification may be proposed by the Congress; Provided that no amendment which may be made prior to the year one thousand eight hundred and eight shall in any manner affect the first and fourth clauses in the ninth section of the first article; and that no State, without its consent, shall be deprived of its equal suffrage in the Senate.

Article VI

1. All debts contracted and engagements entered into, before the adoption of this Constitution, shall be as valid against the United States under this Constitution, as under the Confederation.[10]

2. This Constitution, and the laws of the United States which shall be made in pursuance thereof; and all treaties made, or which shall be made, under the authority of the United States, shall be the supreme law of the land; and the judges in every State shall be bound thereby, any thing in the Constitution or laws of any State to the contrary notwithstanding.

3. The senators and representatives before mentioned, and the members of the several State legislatures, and all executive and judicial officers, both of the United States and of the several States, shall be bound by oath or affirmation to support this Constitution; but no religious test shall ever be required as a qualification to any office or public trust under the United States.

[10] See the Fourteenth Amendment, Sec. 4.

Article VII

The ratification of the conventions of nine States shall be sufficient for the establishment of this Constitution between the States so ratifying the same.

Done in Convention by the unanimous consent of the States present the seventeenth day of September in the year of our Lord one thousand seven hundred and eighty-seven, and of the independence of the United States of America the twelfth. In witness whereof we have hereunto subscribed our names.

Articles in addition to, and amendment of, the Constitution of the United States of America, proposed by Congress, and ratified by the legislatures of the several States, pursuant to the fifth article of the original Constitution.

Amendment I [First Ten Amendments Ratified December 15, 1791]

Congress shall make no law respecting an establishment of religion, or prohibiting the free exercise thereof; or abridging the freedom of speech, or of the press; or the right of the people peaceably to assemble, and to petition the government for a redress of grievances.

Amendment II

A well regulated militia, being necessary to the security of a free State, the right of the people to keep and bear arms, shall not be infringed.

Amendment III

No soldier shall, in time of peace be quartered in any house, without the consent of the owner, nor in time of war, but in a manner to be prescribed by law.

Amendment IV

The right of the people to be secure in their persons, houses, papers, and effects, against unreasonable searches and seizures, shall not be violated, and no warrants shall issue, but upon probable cause, supported by oath or affirmation, and particularly describing the place to be searched, and the persons or things to be seized.

Amendment V

No person shall be held to answer for a capital or otherwise infamous crime, unless on a presentment or indictment of a grand jury, except in cases arising in the land or naval forces, or in the militia, when in actual service in time of war or public danger; nor shall any person be subject for the same offense to be twice put in jeopardy of life or limb; nor shall be compelled in any criminal case to be a witness against himself, nor be deprived of life, liberty, or property, without due process of law; nor shall private property be taken for public use, without just compensation.

Amendment VI

In all criminal prosecutions, the accused shall enjoy the right to a speedy and public trial, by an impartial jury of the State and district wherein the crime shall have been committed, which district shall have been previously ascertained by law, and to be informed of the nature and cause of the accusation; to be confronted with the witnesses against him; to have compulsory process for obtaining witnesses in his favor, and to have the assistance of counsel for his defense.

Amendment VII

In suits at common law, where the value in controversy shall exceed twenty dollars, the right of trial by jury shall be preserved, and no fact tried by a jury shall be otherwise reexamined in any court of the United States, than according to the rules of the common law.

Amendment VIII

Excessive bail shall not be required, nor excessive fines imposed, nor cruel and unusual punishments inflicted.

Amendment IX

The enumeration in the Constitution of certain rights shall not be construed to deny or disparage others retained by the people.

Amendment X

The powers not delegated to the United States by the Constitution, nor prohibited by it to the States, are reserved to the States respectively, or to the people.

Amendment XI [January 8, 1798]

The judicial power of the United States shall not be construed to extend to any suit in law or equity, commended or prosecuted against one of the United States by citizens of another State, or by citizens or subjects of any foreign State.

Amendment XII [September 25, 1804]

The electors shall meet in their respective States, and vote by ballot for President and Vice President, one of whom, at least, shall not be an inhabitant of the same State with themselves; they shall name in their ballots the person voted for as President, and in distinct ballots the person voted for as Vice President, and they shall make distinct lists of all persons voted for as President and of all persons voted for as Vice President, and of the number of votes for each, which lists they shall sign and certify, and transmit sealed to the seat of the government of the United States, directed to the President of the Senate;—The President of the Senate shall, in the presence of the Senate and House of Representatives, open all the certificates and the votes shall then be counted;—The person having the greatest number of votes for President, shall be the President, if such number be a majority of the whole number of electors appointed; and if no person have such majority, then from the persons having the highest numbers not exceeding three on the list of those voted for as President, the House of Representatives shall choose immediately, by ballot, the President. But in choosing the President, the votes shall be taken by States, the representation from each State having one vote; a quorum for this purpose shall consist of a member or members from two thirds of the States, and a majority of all the States shall be necessary to a choice. And if the House of Representatives shall not choose a President whenever the right of choice shall devolve upon them, before the fourth day of March next following, then the Vice President shall act as President, as in the case of the death or other constitutional disability of the President. The person having the greatest number of votes as Vice President shall be the Vice President, if such number be a majority of the whole number of electors appointed, and if no person have a majority, then from the two highest numbers on the list, the Senate shall choose the Vice President; a quorum for the purpose shall consist of two thirds of the whole number of Senators, and a majority of the whole number shall be necessary to a choice. But no person constitutionally ineligible to the office of President shall be eligible to that of Vice President of the United States.

Amendment XIII [December 18, 1865]

Section 1

Neither slavery nor involuntary servitude, except as punishment for crime whereof the party shall have been duly convicted, shall exist within the United States, or any place subject to their jurisdiction.

Section 2

Congress shall have power to enforce this article by appropriate legislation.

Amendment XIV [July 28, 1868]

Section 1

All persons born or naturalized in the United States, and subject to the jurisdiction thereof, are citizens of the United States and of the State wherein they reside. No State shall make or enforce any law which shall abridge the privileges or immunities of citizens of the United States; nor shall any State deprive any person of life, liberty, or property, without due process of law; nor deny to any person within its jurisdiction the equal protection of the laws.

Section 2

Representatives shall be apportioned among the several States according to their respective numbers, counting the whole number of persons in each State, excluding Indians not taxed. But when the right to vote at any election for the choice of electors for President and Vice President of the United States, representatives in Congress, the executive and judicial officers of a State, or the members of the legislature thereof, is denied to any of the male inhabitants of such State, being twenty-one years of age, and citizens of the United States, or in any way abridged, except for participating in rebellion, or other crime, the basis of representation there shall be reduced in the proportion which the number of such male citizens shall bear to the whole number of male citizens twenty-one years of age in such State.

Section 3

No person shall be a senator or representative in Congress, or elector of President and Vice President, or hold any office, civil or military, under the United States, or under any State, who having previously taken an oath, as a member of Congress, or as an officer of the United States, or as a member of any State legislature, or as an executive or judicial officer of any State, to support the Constitution of the United States, shall have engaged in insurrection or rebellion against the same, or given aid or comfort to the enemies thereof. But Congress may by a vote of two thirds of each House, remove such disability.

Section 4

The validity of the public debt of the United States, authorized by law, including debts incurred for payment of pensions and bounties for services in suppressing insurrection or rebellion; shall not be questioned. But neither the United States nor any State shall assume or pay any debt or obligation incurred in aid of insurrection or rebellion against the United States, or any claim for the loss or emancipation of any slave; but all such debts, obligations, and claims shall be held illegal and void.

Section 5

The Congress shall have the power to enforce, by appropriate legislation, the provisions of this article.

Amendment XV [March 30, 1870]

Section 1

The right of citizens of the United States to vote shall not be denied or abridged by the United States or by any State on account of race, color, or previous condition of servitude.

Section 2

The Congress shall have power to enforce this article by appropriate legislation.

Amendment XVI [February 25, 1913]

The Congress shall have power to lay and collect taxes on incomes, from whatever source derived, without apportionment among the several States, and without regard to any census or enumeration.

Amendment XVII [May 31, 1913]

The Senate of the United States shall be composed of two senators from each State, elected by the people thereof, for six years; and each senator shall have one vote. The electors in each State shall have the qualifications requisite for electors of the most numerous branch of the State legislature.

When vacancies happen in the representation of any State in the Senate, the executive authority of such State shall issue writs of election to fill such vacancies: Provided, That the legislature of any State may empower the executive thereof to make temporary appointments until the people fill the vacancies by election as the legislature may direct.

This amendment shall not be so construed as to affect the election or term of any senator chosen before it becomes valid as part of the Constitution.

Amendment XVIII[11] [January 29, 1919]

After one year from the ratification of this article, the manufacture, sale, or transportation of intoxicating liquors within, the importation thereof into, or the exportation thereof from the United States and all territory subject to the jurisdiction thereof for beverage purposes is thereby prohibited.

The Congress and the several States shall have concurrent power to enforce this article by appropriate legislation.

This article shall be inoperative unless it shall have been ratified as an amendment to the Constitution by the legislatures of the several States, as provided in the Constitution, within seven years from the date of the submission hereof to the States by Congress.

Amendment XIX [August 26, 1920]

The right of citizens of the United States to vote shall not be denied or abridged by the United States or by any State on account of sex.

Congress shall have the power to enforce this article by appropriate legislation.

Amendment XX [January 23, 1933]

Section 1

The terms of the President and Vice President shall end at noon on the 20th day of January and the terms of Senators

---

[11] Repealed by the Twenty-first Amendment.

and Representatives at noon on the 3d day of January, of the years in which such terms would have ended if this article had not been ratified; and the terms of their successors shall then begin.

Section 2

The Congress shall assemble at least once in every year, and such meeting shall begin at noon on the 3d day of January, unless they shall by law appoint a different day.

Section 3

If, at the time fixed for the beginning of the term of president, the President-elect shall have died, the Vice President-elect shall become President. If a President shall not have been chosen before the time fixed for the beginning of his term, or if the President-elect shall have failed to qualify, then the Vice President-elect shall act as president until a President shall have qualified; and the Congress may by law provide for the case wherein neither a President-elect nor a Vice President-elect shall have qualified, declaring who shall then act as President, or the manner in which one who is to act shall be selected, and such person shall act accordingly until a President or Vice President shall have qualified.

Section 4

The Congress may by law provide for the case of the death of any of the persons from whom, the House of Representatives may choose a President whenever the right of choice shall have devolved upon them, and for the case of the death of any of the persons from whom the Senate may choose a Vice President whenever the right of choice shall have devolved upon them.

Section 5

Sections 1 and 2 shall take effect on the 15th day of October following the ratification of this article.

Section 6

This article shall be inoperative unless it shall have been ratified as an amendment to the Constitution by the legislatures of three-fourths of the several States within seven years from the date of its submission.

Amendment XXI [December 5, 1933]

Section 1

The Eighteenth Article of amendment to the Constitution of the United States is hereby repealed.

Section 2

The transportation or importation into any State, Territory, or possession of the United States for delivery or use therein of intoxicating liquors in violation of the laws thereof, is hereby prohibited.

Section 3

This article shall be inoperative unless it shall have been ratified as an amendment to the Constitution by conventions in the several States, as provided in the Consitution, within seven years from the date of the submission thereof to the States by the Congress.

Amendment XXII [March 1, 1951]

No person shall be elected to the office of the President more than twice, and no person who has held the office of President, or acted as President, for more than two years of a term to which some other person was elected President shall be elected to the office of the President more than once.

But this article shall not apply to any person holding the office of President when this article was proposed by the Congress, and shall not prevent any person who may be holding the office of President, or acting as President, during the term within which this article becomes operative from holding the office of President or acting as President during the remainder of such term.

This article shall be inoperative unless it shall have been ratified as an amendment to the Constitution by the legislatures of three-fourths of the several States within seven years from the date of its submission to the States by the Congress.

Amendment XXIII [March 29, 1961]

Section 1

The District constituting the seat of Government of the United States shall appoint in such manner as the Congress may direct:

A number of electors of President and Vice President equal to the whole number of Senators and Representatives in Congress to which the District would be entitled if it were a State, but in no event more than the least populous State; they shall be in addition to those appointed by the States, but they shall be considered, for the purposes of the election of President and Vice President, to be electors appointed by a State; and they shall meet in the District and perform such duties as provided by the twelfth article of amendment.

Section 2

The Congress shall have power to enforce this article by appropriate legislation.

Amendment XXIV [January 23, 1964]

Section 1

The right of citizens of the United States to vote in any primary or other election for President or Vice President, for electors for President or Vice President, or for Senator or Representative in Congress, shall not be denied or abridged by the United States or any State by reason of failure to pay any poll tax or other tax.

Section 2

The Congress shall have power to enforce this article by appropriate legislation.

Amendment XXV [February 10, 1967]

Section 1

In case of the removal of the President from office or of his death or resignation, the Vice President shall become President.

Section 2

Whenever there is a vacancy in the office of the Vice President, the President shall nominate a Vice President who shall take office upon confirmation by a majority of both Houses of Congress.

Section 3

Whenever the President transmits to the President pro tempore of the Senate and the Speaker of the House of Representatives his written declaration that he is unable to discharge the powers and duties of his office, and until he transmits to them a written declaration to the contrary, such powers and duties shall be discharged by the Vice President as Acting President.

Section 4

Whenever the Vice President and a majority of either the principal officers of the executive departments or of such other body as Congress may by law provide, transmit to the President pro tempore of the Senate and the Speaker of the House of Representatives their written declaration that the President is unable to discharge the powers and duties of his office, the Vice President shall immediately assume the powers and duties of the office as Acting President.

Thereafter, when the President transmits to the President pro tempore of the Senate and the Speaker of the House of Representatives his written declaration that no inability

exists, he shall resume the powers and duties of his office unless the Vice President and a majority of either the principal officers of the executive departments or of such other body as Congress may by law provide, transmit within four days to the President pro tempore of the Senate and the Speaker of the House of Representatives their written declaration that the President is unable to discharge the powers and duties of his office. Thereupon Congress shall decide the issue, assembling within forty-eight hours for that purpose if not in session. If the Congress, within twenty-one days after receipt of the latter written declaration, or, if Congress is not in session, within twenty-one days after Congress is required to assemble, determines by two-thirds vote of both houses that the President is unable to discharge the powers and duties of his office, the Vice President shall continue to discharge the same as Acting President; otherwise, the President shall resume the powers and duties of his office.

Amendment XXVI [June 30, 1971]

Section 1

The right of citizens of the United States who are eighteen years of age or older to vote shall not be denied or abridged by the United States or by any State on account of age.

Section 2

The Congress shall have power to enforce this article by appropriate legislation.

Amendment XXVII[12] [May 7, 1992]

No law, varying the compensation for services of the Senators and Representatives, shall take effect until an election of Representatives shall have intervened.

---

[12] James Madison proposed this amendment in 1789 together with the ten amendments that were adopted as the Bill of Rights, but it failed to win ratification at the time. Congress, however, had set no deadline for its ratification, and over the years—particularly in the 1980s and 1990s—many states voted to add it to the Constitution. With the ratification of Michigan in 1992 it passed the threshold of the states required for adoption, but because the process took more than 200 years, its validity remains in doubt.

SOURCE: U.S. Constitution.

The Emancipation Proclamation

By the President of the United States of America:

Whereas, on the twenty-second day of September, in the year of our Lord one thousand eight hundred and sixty-two, a proclamation was issued by the President of the United States, containing, among other things, the following, to wit:

> That on the first day of January, in the year of our Lord one thousand eight hundred and sixty-three, all persons held as slaves within any State or designated part of a State, the people whereof shall then be in rebellion against the United States, shall be then, thenceforward, and forever free; and the Executive Government of the United States, including the military and naval authority thereof, will recognize and maintain the freedom of such persons, and will do no act or acts to repress such persons, or any of them, in any efforts they may make for their actual freedom.

> That the Executive will, on the first day of January aforesaid, by proclamation, designate the States and parts of States, if any, in which the people thereof, respectively, shall then be in rebellion against the United States; and the fact that any State, or the people thereof, shall on that day be, in good faith, represented in the Congress of the United States by members chosen thereto at elections wherein a majority of the qualified voters of such State shall have participated, shall, in the absence of strong countervailing testimony, be deemed conclusive evidence that such State, and the people thereof, are not then in rebellion against the United States.

Now, therefore I, Abraham Lincoln, President of the United States, by virtue of the power in me vested as Commander-in-Chief, of the Army and Navy of the United States in time of actual armed rebellion against the authority and government of the United States, and as a fit and necessary war measure for suppressing said rebellion, do, on this first day of January, in the year of our Lord one thousand eight hundred and sixty-three, and in accordance with my purpose so to do publicly proclaimed for the full period of one hundred days, from the day first above mentioned, order and designate as the States and parts of States wherein the people thereof respectively, are this day in rebellion against the United States, the following, to wit:

Arkansas, Texas, Louisiana, (except the Parishes of St. Bernard, Plaquemines, Jefferson, St. John, St. Charles, St. James Ascension, Assumption, Terrebonne, Lafourche, St. Mary, St. Martin, and Orleans, including the City of New Orleans), Mississippi, Alabama, Florida, Georgia, South Carolina, North Carolina, and Virginia, (except the forty-eight counties designated as West Virginia, and also the counties of Berkley, Accomac, Northampton, Elizabeth City, York, Princess Ann, and Norfolk, including the cities of Norfolk and Portsmouth), and which excepted parts, are for the present, left precisely as if this proclamation were not issued.

And by virtue of the power, and for the purpose aforesaid, I do order and declare that all persons held as slaves within said designated States, and parts of States, are, and henceforward shall be free; and that the Executive government of the United States, including the military and naval authorities thereof, will recognize and maintain the freedom of said persons.

And I hereby enjoin upon the people so declared to be free to abstain from all violence, unless in necessary self-defense; and I recommend to them that, in all cases when allowed, they labor faithfully for reasonable wages.

And I further declare and make known, that such persons of suitable condition, will be received into the armed service of the United States to garrison forts, positions, stations, and other places, and to man vessels of all sorts in said service.

And upon this act, sincerely believed to be an act of justice, warranted by the Constitution, upon military necessity, I invoke the considerate judgment of mankind, and the gracious favor of Almighty God.

In witness whereof, I have hereunto set my hand and caused the seal of the United States to be affixed. Done at the City of Washington, this first day of January, in the year of our Lord one thousand eight hundred and sixty-three, and of the Independence of the United States of America the eighty-seventh.

By the President: Abraham Lincoln
William H. Seward, Secretary of State

SOURCE: The Emancipation Proclamation, By the President: Abraham Lincoln, January 1, 1863. U.S National Archives & Records Administration.

Key Provisions of the Civil Rights Act of 1964

An Act

To enforce the constitutional right to vote, to confer jurisdiction upon the district courts of the United States to provide injunctive relief against discrimination in public accommodations, to authorize the Attorney General to institute suits to protect constitutional rights in public facilities and public education, to extend the Commission on Civil Rights, to prevent discrimination in federally assisted programs, to establish a Commission on Equal Employment Opportunity, and for other purposes.

Be it enacted by the Senate and House of Representatives of the United States of America in Congress assembled, that this Act may be cited as the "Civil Rights Act of 1964."

Title I—Voting Rights

Section 101 . . . (2) No person acting under color of law shall—

a. In determining whether any individual is qualified under State law or laws to vote in any Federal election, apply any standard, practice, or procedure different from the standards, practices, or procedures applied under such law or laws to other individuals within the same county, parish, or similar political subdivision who have been found by State officials to be qualified to vote;

b. deny the right of any individual to vote in any Federal election because of an error or omission on any record or paper relating to any application, registration, or other act requisite to voting, if such error or omission is not material in determining whether such individual is qualified under State law to vote in such election;

c. employ any literacy test as a qualification for voting in any Federal election unless (i) such test is administered to each individual and is conducted wholly in writing, and (ii) a certified copy of the test and of the answers given by the individual is furnished to him within twenty-five days of the submission of his request made within the period of time during which records and papers are required to be retained and preserved pursuant to title III of the Civil Rights Act of 1960 (42 U.S.C. 1974–74e; 74 Stat. 88): Provided, however, That the Attorney General may enter into agreements with appropriate State or local authorities that preparation, conduct, and maintenance of such tests in accordance with the provisions of applicable State or local law, including such special provisions as are necessary in the preparation, conduct, and maintenance of such tests for persons who are blind or otherwise physically handicapped, meet the purposes of this subparagraph and constitute compliance therewith.

Title II—Injunctive Relief Against Discrimination in Places of Public Accommodation

Section 201

a. All persons shall be entitled to the full and equal enjoyment of the goods, services, facilities, and privileges, advantages and accommodations of any place of public accommodation, as defined in this section, without discrimination or segregation on the ground of race, color, religion, or national origin.

b. Each of the following establishments which serves the public is a place of public accommodation within the meaning of this title if its operations affect commerce, or if discrimination or segregation by it is supported by State action:

1. any inn, hotel, motel, or other establishment which provides lodging to transient guests, other than an establishment located within a building which contains not more than five rooms for rent or hire and which is actually occupied by the proprietor of such establishment as his residence;

2. any restaurant, cafeteria, lunchroom, lunch counter, soda fountain, or other facility principally engaged in selling food for consumption on the premises, including, but not limited to, any such facility located on the premises of any retail establishment; or any gasoline station;

3. any motion picture house, theater, concert hall, sports arena, stadium or other place of exhibition or entertainment;

4. any establishment (A)(i) which is physically located within the premises of any establishment otherwise covered by this subsection, or (ii) within the premises of which is physically located any such covered establishment, and (B) which holds itself out as serving patrons of such covered establishment. . . .

c. Discrimination or segregation by an establishment is supported by State action within the meaning of this title if such discrimination or segregation

1. is carried on under color of any law, statute, ordinance, or regulation; or

2. is carried on under color of any custom or usage required or enforced by officials of the State or political subdivision thereof; or

3. is required by action of the State or political subdivision thereof. . . .

Section 202

All persons shall be entitled to be free, at any establishment or place, from discrimination or segregation of any kind on the ground of race, color, religion, or national origin, if such discrimination or segregation is or purports to be required by any law, statute, ordinance, regulation, rule, or order of a State or any agency or political subdivision thereof.

Section 203

No person shall (a) withhold, deny, or attempt to withhold or deny, or deprive or attempt to deprive, any person of any right or privilege secured by section 201 or 202, or (b) intimidate, threaten, or coerce, or attempt to intimidate, threaten, or coerce any person with the purpose of interfering with any right or privilege secured by section 201 or 202, or (c) punish or attempt to punish any person for exercising or attempting to exercise any right or privilege secured by section 201 or 202.

Section 204

a. Whenever any person has engaged or there are reasonable grounds to believe that any person is about to engage in any act or practice prohibited by section 203, a civil action for preventive relief, including an application for a permanent or temporary injunction, restraining order, or other order, may be instituted by the person aggrieved and, upon timely application, the court may, in its discretion, permit the Attorney General to intervene in such civil action if he certifies that the case is of general public importance. Upon application by the complainant and in such circumstances as the court may deem just, the court may appoint an attorney for such complainant and may authorize the commencement of the civil action without the payment of fees, costs, or security. . . .

Section 206

a. Whenever the Attorney General has reasonable cause to believe that any person or group of persons is engaged in a pattern or practice of resistance to the full enjoyment of any of the rights secured by this title, and that the pattern or practice is of such a nature and is intended to deny the full exercise of the rights herein described, the Attorney General may bring a civil action in the appropriate district court of the United States by filing with it a complaint

1. signed by him (or in his absence the Acting Attorney General),

2. setting forth facts pertaining to such pattern or practice, and

3. requesting such preventive relief, including an application for a permanent or temporary injunction, restraining order or other order against the person or persons responsible for such pattern or practice, as he deems necessary to insure the full enjoyment of the rights herein described. . . .

Title III—Desegregation of Public Facilities

Section 301

a. Whenever the Attorney General receives a complaint in writing signed by an individual to the effect that he is being deprived of or threatened with the loss of his right to the equal protection of the laws, on account of his race, color, religion, or national origin, by being denied equal utilization of any public facility which is owned, operated, or managed by or on behalf of any State or subdivision thereof, other than a public school or public college as defined in section 401 of title IV hereof, and the Attorney General believes the complaint is meritorious and certifies that the signer or signers of such complaint are unable, in his judgment, to initiate and maintain appropriate legal proceedings for relief and that the institution of an action will materially further the orderly progress of desegregation in public facilities, the Attorney General is authorized to institute for or in the name of the United States a civil action in any appropriate district court of the United States against such parties and for such relief as may be appropriate. And such court shall have and shall exercise jurisdiction of proceedings instituted pursuant to this section. The Attorney General may implead as defendants such additional parties as are or become necessary to the grant of effective relief hereunder. . . .

Title IV—Desegregation of Public Education

Section 401

As used in this title—. . . .

"Desegregation" means the assignment of students to public schools and within such schools without regard to their race, color, religion, or national origin, but "desegregation" shall not mean the assignment of students to public schools in order to overcome racial imbalance. . . .

Survey and Report of Educational Opportunities

Section 402

The Commissioner shall conduct a survey and make a report to the President and the Congress, within two years of the enactment of this title, concerning the lack of availability of equal educational opportunities for individuals by reason of race, color, religion, or national origin in public educational institutions at all levels in the United States, its territories and possessions, and the District of Columbia. . . .

Title V—Commission on Civil Rights. . . .

Duties of the Commission

Section 104

a. The Commission shall—

1. investigate allegations in writing under oath or affirmation that certain citizens of the United States are being deprived of their right to vote and have that vote counted by reason of their color, race, religion, or national origin; which writing, under oath or affirmation, shall set forth the facts upon which such belief or beliefs are based;

2. study and collect information concerning legal developments constituting a denial of equal protection of the laws under the Constitution because of race, color, religion or national origin or in the administration of justice;

3. appraise the laws and policies of the Federal Government with respect to denials of equal protection of the laws under the Constitution because of race, color, religion or national origin or in the administration of justice;

4. serve as a national clearinghouse for information in respect to denials of equal protection of the laws because of race, color, religion or national origin, including but not limited to the fields of voting, education, housing, employment, the use of public facilities, and transportation, or in the administration of justice;

5. investigate allegations, made in writing and under oath or affirmation, that citizens of the United States are unlawfully being accorded or denied the right to vote, or to have their votes properly counted, in any election of presidential electors, Members of the United States Senate, or of the House of Representatives, as a result

of any patterns or practice of fraud or discrimination in the conduct of such election; . . . .

Title VI—Nondiscrimination in Federally Assisted Programs

Section 601

No person in the United States shall, on the ground of race, color, or national origin, be excluded from participation in, be denied the benefits of, or be subjected to discrimination under any program or activity receiving Federal financial assistance.

Section 602

Each Federal department and agency which is empowered to extend Federal financial assistance to any program or activity, by way of grant, loan, or contract other than a contract of insurance or guaranty, is authorized and directed to effectuate the provisions of section 601 with respect to such program or activity by issuing rules, regulations, or orders of general applicability which shall be consistent with achievement of the objectives of the statute authorizing the financial assistance in connection with which the action is taken. No such rule, regulation, or order shall become effective unless and until approved by the President. Compliance with any requirement adopted pursuant to this section may be effected

1. by the termination of or refusal to grant or to continue assistance under such program or activity to any recipient as to whom there has been an express finding on the record, after opportunity for hearing, of a failure to comply with such requirement, but such termination or refusal shall be limited to the particular political entity, or part thereof, or other recipient as to whom such a finding has been made and, shall be limited in its effect to the particular program, or part thereof, in which such non-compliance has been so found, or

2. by any other means authorized by law:

Provided, however, that no such action shall be taken until the department or agency concerned has advised the appropriate person or persons of the failure to comply with the requirement and has determined that compliance cannot be secured by voluntary means. In the case of any action terminating, or refusing to grant or continue, assistance because of failure to comply with a requirement imposed pursuant to this section, the head of the federal department or agency shall file with the committees of the House and Senate having legislative jurisdiction over the program or activity involved a full written report of the circumstances and the grounds for such action. No such action shall become effective until thirty days have elapsed after the filing of such report. . . .

Title VII—Equal Employment Opportunity. . . .

Discrimination Because of Race, Color, Religion, Sex, or National Origin

Section 703

a. it shall be an unlawful employment practice for an employer—

   1. to fail or refuse to hire or to discharge any individual, or otherwise to discriminate against any individual with respect to his compensation, terms, conditions, or privileges of employment, because of such individual's race, color, religion, sex, or national origin; or

   2. to limit, segregate, or classify his employees in any way which would deprive or tend to deprive any individual of employment opportunities or otherwise adversely affect his status as an employee, because of such individual's race, color, religion, sex, or national origin.

b. it shall be an unlawful employment practice for an employment agency to fail or refuse to refer for employment, or otherwise to discriminate against, any individual because of his race, color, religion, sex, or national origin, or to classify or refer for employment any individual on the basis of his race, color, religion, sex, or national origin.

c. it shall be an unlawful employment practice for a labor organization—

   1. to exclude or to expel from its membership, or otherwise to discriminate against, any individual because of his race, color, religion, sex, or national origin;

   2. to limit, segregate, or classify its membership, or to classify or fail or refuse to refer for employment any individual, in any way which would deprive or tend to deprive any individual of employment opportunities, or would limit such employment opportunities or otherwise adversely affect his status as an employee or as an applicant for employment, because of such individual's race, color, religion, sex, or national origin; or

   3. to cause or attempt to cause an employer to discriminate against an individual in violation of this section.

d. It shall be an unlawful employment practice for any employer, labor organization, or joint labor-management committee controlling apprenticeship or other training or retraining, including on-the-job training programs to discriminate against any individual because of his race, color, religion, sex, or national origin in admission to, or employment in, any program established to provide apprenticeship or other training. . . .

Other Unlawful Employment Practices

Section 704

a. It shall be an unlawful employment practice for an employer to discriminate against any of his employees or applicants for employment, for an employment agency to discriminate against any individual, or for a labor organization to discriminate against any member thereof or applicant for membership, because he has opposed any practice made an unlawful employment practice by this title, or because he has made a charge, testified, assisted, or participated in any manner in an investigation, proceeding, or hearing under this title.

b. It shall be an unlawful employment practice for an employer, labor organization, or employment agency to print or publish or cause to be printed or published any notice or advertisement relating to employment by such an employer or membership in or any classification or referral for employment by such a labor organization, or relating to any classification or referral for employment by such an employment agency, indicating any preference, limitation, specification, or discrimination, based on race, color, religion, sex, or national origin, except that such a notice or advertisement may indicate a preference, limitation, specification, or discrimination based on religion, sex, or national origin when religion, sex, or national origin is a bona fide occupational qualification for employment.

Equal Employment Opportunity Commission

Section 705

a. There is hereby created a Commission to be known as the Equal Employment Opportunity Commission, which shall be composed of five members, not more than three of whom shall be members of the same political party, who shall be appointed by the President by and with the advice and consent of the Senate. One of the original members shall be appointed for a term of one year, one for a term of two years, one for a term of three years, one for a term of four years, and one for a term of five years, beginning from the date of enactment of this title, but their successors shall be appointed for terms of five years each, except that any individual chosen to fill a vacancy shall be appointed only for the unexpired term of the member whom he shall succeed. The President shall designate one member to serve as Chairman of the Commission, and one member to serve as Vice Chairman. The Chairman shall be responsible on behalf of the Commission for the administrative operations of the Commission, and shall appoint, in accordance with the civil service laws, such officers, agents, attorneys, and employees as it deems necessary to assist it in the performance of its functions and to fix their compensation in accordance with Classification Act of 1949, as amended. . . .

Title VIII—Registration and Voting Statistics

Section 801

The Secretary of Commerce shall promptly conduct a survey to compile registration and voting statistics in such geographic areas as may be recommended by the Commission on Civil Rights. Such a survey and compilation shall, to the extent recommended by the Commission on Civil Rights, only include a count of persons of voting age by race, color, and national origin, and determination of the extent to which such persons are registered to vote, and have voted in any statewide primary or general election in which the Members of the United States House of Representatives are nominated or elected, since January 1, 1960. Such information shall also be collected and compiled in connection with the Nineteenth Decennial Census, and at such other times as the Congress may prescribe. The provisions of section 9 and chapter 7 of title 13, United States Code, shall apply to any survey, collection, or compilation of registration and voting statistics carried out under this title: Provided, however, that no person shall be compelled to disclose his race, color, national origin, or questioned about his political party affiliation, how he voted, or the reasons therefore, nor shall any penalty be imposed for his failure or refusal to make such disclosure. Every person interrogated orally, by written survey or questionnaire or by any other means with respect to such information shall be fully advised with respect to his right to fail or refuse to furnish such information.

Lyndon B. Johnson July 2, 1964

SOURCE: Bills and Statutes, United States Statutes at Large, U.S. Government Printing Office. 88th Congress, 2nd Session, 1964.

Key Provisions of the Voting Rights Act of 1965

An Act

To enforce the fifteenth amendment to the Constitution of the United States, and for other purposes.

Be it enacted by the Senate and House of Representatives of the United States of America in Congress assembled, That this Act shall be known as the "Voting Rights Act of 1965."

Section 2

No voting qualification or prerequisite to voting, or standard, practice, or procedure shall be imposed or applied by any State or political subdivision to deny or abridge the right of any citizen of the United States to vote on account of race or color.

Section 3

a. Whenever the Attorney General institutes a proceeding under any statute to enforce the guarantees of the fifteenth amendment in any State or political subdivision the court shall authorize the appointment of Federal examiners by the United States Civil Service Commission in accordance with section 6 to serve for such period of time and for such political subdivisions as the court shall determine is appropriate to enforce the guarantees of the fifteenth amendment

(1) as part of any interlocutory order if the court determines that the appointment of such examiners is necessary to enforce such guarantees or (2) as part of any final judgment if the court finds that violations of the fifteenth amendment justifying equitable relief have occurred in such State or subdivision: Provided, That the court need not authorize the appointment of examiners if any incidents of denial or abridgment of the right to vote on account of race or color (1) have been few in number and have been promptly and effectively corrected by State or local action, (2) the continuing effect of such incidents has been eliminated, and (3) there is no reasonable probability of their recurrence in the future.

b. If in a proceeding instituted by the Attorney General under any statute to enforce the guarantees of the fifteenth amendment in any State or political subdivision the court finds that a test or device has been used for the purpose or with the effect of denying or abridging the right of any citizen of the United States to vote on account of race or color, it shall suspend the use of tests and devices in such State or political subdivisions as the court shall determine is appropriate and for such period as it deems necessary. . . .

Section 4

a. To assure that the right of citizens of the United States to vote is not denied or abridged on account of race or color, no citizen shall be denied the right to vote in any Federal, State, or local election because of his failure to comply with any test or device in any State with respect to which the determinations have been made under subsection (b). . . .

b. The provisions of subsection (a) shall apply in any State or in any political subdivision of a state which (1) the Attorney General determines maintained on November 1, 1964, any test or device, and with respect to which (2) the Director of the Census determines that less than 50 per centum of the persons of voting age residing therein were registered on November 1, 1964, or that less than 50 per centum of such persons voted in the presidential election of November 1964. . . .

c. The phrase "test or device" shall mean any requirement that a person as a prerequisite for voting or registration of voting (1) demonstrate the ability to read, write, understand, or interpret any matter, (2) demonstrate any educational achievement or his knowledge of any particular subject, (3) possess good moral character, or (4) prove his qualifications by the voucher of registered voters or members of any other class. . . .

Section 6

Whenever (a) a court has authorized the appointment of examiners pursuant to the provisions of section 3 (a), or (b) unless a declaratory judgment has been rendered under section 4 (a), the Attorney General certifies with respect to any political subdivision named in, or included within the scope of, determinations made under section 4 (b) that (1) he has received complaints in writing from twenty or more residents of such political subdivision alleging that they have been denied the right to vote under color of law on account of race or color, and that he believes such complaints to be meritorious, or (2) that in his judgment (considering, among other factors, whether the ratio of nonwhite persons to white persons registered to vote within such subdivision appears to him to be reasonably attributable to violations of the fifteenth amendment or whether substantial evidence exists that bona fide efforts are being made within such subdivision to comply with the fifteenth amendment), the appointment of examiners is otherwise necessary to enforce the guarantees of the fifteenth amendment, the Civil Service Commission shall appoint as many examiners for such subdivision as it may deem appropriate to prepare and maintain lists of persons eligible to vote in Federal, State, and local elections. . . . Examiners and hearing officers shall have the power to administer oaths. . . .

Lyndon B. Johnson August 6, 1965

Executive Order 13050 President's Advisory Board on Race

By the authority vested in me as President by the Constitution and the laws of the United States of America, including the Federal Advisory Committee Act, as amended (5 U.S.C. App.), and in order to establish a President's Advisory Board on Race, it is hereby ordered as follows:

Section 1 Establishment

a. There is established the President's Advisory Board on Race. The Advisory Board shall comprise 7 members from outside the Federal Government to be appointed by the President. Members shall each have substantial experience and expertise in the areas to be considered by the Advisory Board. Members shall be representative of the diverse perspectives in the areas to be considered by the Advisory Board.

b. The President shall designate a Chairperson from among the members of the Advisory Board.

Section 2 Functions

a. The Advisory Board shall advise the President on matters involving race and racial reconciliation, including ways in which the President can:

1. Promote a constructive national dialogue to confront and work through challenging issues that surround race;

2. Increase the Nation's understanding of our recent history of race relations and the course our Nation is charting on issues of race relations and racial diversity;

3. Bridge racial divides by encouraging leaders in communities throughout the Nation to develop and implement innovative approaches to calming racial tensions;

4. Identify, develop, and implement solutions to problems in areas in which race has a substantial impact, such as education, economic opportunity, housing, health care, and the administration of justice.

b. The Advisory Board also shall advise on such other matters as from time to time the President may refer to the Board.

c. In carrying out its functions, the Advisory Board shall coordinate with the staff of the President's Initiative on Race.

Section 3 Administration

a. To the extent permitted by law and subject to the availability of appropriations, the Department of Justice shall provide the financial and administrative support for the Advisory Board.

b. The heads of executive agencies shall, to the extent permitted by law, provide to the Advisory Board such information as it may require for the purpose of carrying out its functions.

c. The Chairperson may, from time to time, invite experts to submit information to the Advisory Board and may form subcommittees or working groups within the Advisory Board to review specific matters.

d. Members of the Advisory Board shall serve without compensation but shall be allowed travel expenses, including per diem in lieu of subsistence, as authorized by law for persons serving intermittently in the Government service (5 U.S.C. 5701–5707).

Section 4 General

a. Notwithstanding any other Executive order, the functions of the President under the Federal Advisory Committee Act, as amended, except that of reporting to the Congress, that are applicable to the Advisory Board shall be performed by the Attorney General, or his or her designee, in accordance with guidelines that have been issued by the Administrator of General Services.

b. The Advisory Board shall terminate on September 30, 1998 unless extended by the President prior to such date.

William J. Clinton June 13, 1997

SOURCE: Eighty-ninth Congress of the United States of America, Public Law 89-110, August 6, 1965. William J. Clinton. Code of Federal Regulations (annual edition) - January 1, 1998 Edition. U.S. Government Printing Office.

Glossary Key Terms and Concepts

54th Massachusetts Regiment This all-black volunteer infantry regiment was recruited in the northern states for service with Union military forces in the Civil War. It was made up almost entirely of black men who had been free. It was commanded by white officers.

Acculturating Change in individuals who are introduced to a new culture.

Affirmative action Civil rights policy or program that seeks to redress the effects of past discrimination due to race or gender by giving preference to women and minorities in education and employment.

African Methodist Episcopal (AME) Church Founded in Philadelphia in 1816, this was the first black church and eventually became the largest independent black church.

Afrocentrists Scholars who view history from an African perspective.

Afrocentricity A philosophy of culture that celebrates Africa's role in history and stresses the enduring African roots and identity of black America.

Age of Revolution A period in Atlantic history that began with the American Revolution in 1776 and ended with the defeat of Napoleonic France in 1815.

Agricultural Adjustment Act (AAA) A federal program that provided subsidies to farmers to grow less to help stabilize prices.

American and Foreign Anti-Slavery Society (AFASS; 1840–1855) An organization of church-oriented abolitionists.

American Anti-Slavery Society (AASS; 1833–1870) The umbrella organization for immediate abolitionists during the 1830s and the main Garrisonian organization after 1840.

American Colonization Society (ACS; 1816–1912) An organization founded in Washington, D.C., by prominent slaveholders. It claimed to encourage the ultimate abolition of slavery by sending free African Americans to its West African colony of Liberia.

American Convention for Promoting the Abolition of Slavery and Improving the Condition of the African Race (1794–1838) A loose coalition of state and local societies, dominated by the Pennsylvania Abolition Society, dedicated to gradual abolition.

American Missionary Association This religious organization sent teachers and clergymen throughout the South following the Civil War to tend to the spiritual and educational needs of former slaves. It was instrumental in establishing dozens of schools, including Fisk, Hampton, and Avery.

Amistad A Spanish schooner on which West African Joseph Cinque led a successful slave revolt in 1839.

Animistic The belief that inanimate objects have spiritual attributes.

Anti-miscegenation Laws that denied men and women of different racial identities to marry and that imposed the punishment of imprisonment for having sex across the color line during the era of legal segregation.

Appalachian Mountains A large mountain chain in eastern North America that stretches from Newfoundland in the north to central Alabama in the south.

Asiento The monopoly over the slave trade from Africa to Spain's American colonies.

Assimilation The process by which people of different backgrounds become similar to each other in culture and language.

Barbados An island nation in the Lesser Antilles located to the southeast of Puerto Rico.

Battery Wagner This defensive fortification guarded Fort Sumter near the entrance to Charleston Harbor in South Carolina. It was the scene in July 1863 of a major Union assault by the 54th Massachusetts Regiment, a black unit. The assault failed, but the bravery and valor of the black troops earned them fame and glory.

Benevolent Empire Network of reform associations affiliated with Protestant churches in the early nineteenth century dedicated to the restoration of moral order.

Berbers A people native to North Africa and the Sahara Desert.

Black Arts movement Artistic movement that sought to promote black art by black artists for black people.

Black cabinet Informal group of highly placed African-American advisers to President Franklin D. Roosevelt.

Black codes Laws that were passed in each of the former Confederate states following the Civil War that applied only to black people. While conceding such rights as the right to marry, to contract a debt, or to own property, the codes severely restricted the rights and opportunities of former slaves in terms of labor and mobility.

Black Committee An organization of prominent black men in the North who assisted in recruiting African Americans to fight for the Union in the Civil War.

Black English A variety of American English that is influenced by West African grammar, vocabulary, and pronunciation.

Black laws Laws passed in states of the Old Northwest during the early nineteenth century banning or restricting black settlement and limiting the rights of black residents.

Black Manifesto In 1969, James Forman demanded, in a position paper, that white religious denominations and churches that had benefited from racial slavery and exploitation pay $500 million dollars in reparations to black Americans.

Black nationalist African Americans who hold the belief that they must seek their racial destiny by establishing separate institutions and, perhaps, migrating as a group to a location (often Africa) outside the United States.

Black Panther Party Black militant organization set up in 1966 by Huey P. Newton and Bobby Seale.

Black Power A nationalist ideology popularized by Stokely Carmichael that advocated black control of community resources and social institutions and the election of political representatives who would speak to the needs and interests of black people.

Border ruffians Proslavery advocates and vigilantes from Missouri who crossed the border into Kansas in 1855–1857 to support slavery in Kansas by threatening and attacking antislavery settlers.

Brooks-Sumner Affair South Carolina congressman Preston Brooks attacked and severely beat Massachusetts senator Charles Sumner on the floor of the U.S. Senate after Sumner had denounced the proslavery position of Brooks's uncle, South Carolina Senator Andrew Butler.

Brotherhood of Sleeping Car Porters (BSCP) Black men and women who worked on Pullman passenger coaches on the nation's railroads organized this labor union in 1925, with A. Philip Randolph as its leader.

Brown v. Board of Education of Topeka Decision by the Supreme Court in 1954 that overturned the "separate but equal" doctrine.

Brownsville Affair In 1906, a shooting in Brownsville, Texas, was blamed on black soldiers from the 25th Infantry Regiment. President Theodore Roosevelt summarily dismissed 167 black men from the U.S. Army. Later investigations exonerated the men.

Buffalo soldiers Named by the Plains Indians for the four regiments of black soldiers that served with the U.S. Army on the western frontier from the 1870s to the 1890s.

Call-and-response An African-American singing style rooted in Africa. A solo call tells a story to which a group responds, often with repeated lyrics.

Carpetbagger The derogatory term used during Reconstruction to describe northerners who came South following the Civil War to take advantage of political and economic opportunities. They were labeled "carpetbaggers" because they ostensibly carried all of their possessions in a solitary carpetbag.

Cash crop A crop grown for sale rather than subsistence.

Chattel or Chattel slavery A type of slavery in which enslaved people were treated legally as property.

Chicago Renaissance A cultural explosion featuring innovative artists whose work re-imagined black identity in Chicago during the 1930s and 1940s.

Church of England A Protestant church established in the sixteenth century as the English national or Anglican church with the English monarch as its head. After the American Revolution, its American branch became the Episcopal Church.

Civil Rights Act This act nullified the black codes and made African Americans citizens with the basic rights of life, liberty, and due process. It was passed over President Andrew Johnson's veto. Its main features were subsequently embedded in the Fourteenth Amendment to the Constitution.

Civil Rights Act of 1875 This federal legislation outlawed racial discrimination in public accommodations such as hotels and restaurants, and in transportation, including railroad coaches and steamboats. The Supreme Court invalidated it in 1883.

Civil Rights Act of 1964 Federal law banning discrimination in places of public accommodation.

Civil Rights Act of 1968 Federal law banning discrimination in housing.

Coffle A file of slaves chained together that was typical of the domestic slave trade.

Colfax Massacre At least 105 African Americans were murdered on Easter Sunday in 1873 in Colfax, Louisiana, in the single worst episode of racial violence during Reconstruction.

Colored American Published in New York from 1837 to 1842, the leading African-American newspaper of its time.

Colored Farmers' Alliance A large organization of black southern farmers in the 1880s and 1890s that had as many as one million members who agitated for improved conditions and income for black landowners, renters, and sharecroppers.

Committee for Industrial Organization (CIO) Labor organization that was committed to interracial and multiethnic organizing.

Communist Party Political party formed to promote communism.

Community Action Programs (CAPs) Antipoverty programs involving "maximum feasible participation" by the poor themselves.

Compensated emancipation Emancipation accompanied by the monetary compensation of former slave owners.

Compromise of 1850 An attempt by the U.S. Congress to settle divisive issues between the North and South, including slavery expansion, apprehension in the North of fugitive slaves, and slavery in the District of Columbia.

Compromise of 1877 This informal arrangement between national Democrats and Republicans settled the disputed presidential election of 1876 by permitting Republican Rutherford B. Hayes to become president while allowing Democrats to complete redemption by taking political control of Louisiana, Florida, and South Carolina.

Confederacy Association of slave states that left the Union in 1861.

Congress of Racial Equality (CORE) Protest group committed to nonviolent direct action.

Conscription law The 1862 Confederate law defining who was required to provide military service.

Continental Army The army created by the Continental Congress in June 1775 to fight British troops. George Washington was its commander in chief.

Continental Congress A representative assembly that first met in October 1775 and served as the de facto central government of the United States during the Revolutionary War.

Contraband Slaves who escaped to the Union or were captured by Union troops early in the Civil War; these slaves were considered enemy property.

Convict lease system Southern states and communities leased prisoners to privately operated mines, railroads, and timber companies. These businesses forced the prisoners, who were usually black men, to work in brutal, unhealthy, and dangerous conditions. Many convicts died of abuse and disease.

Cotton gin A simple machine invented by Eli Whitney in 1793 to separate cotton seeds from cotton fiber. It greatly speeded this task and encouraged the westward expansion of cotton growing in the United States.

Creoles Persons of African and/or European descent born in the Americas.

Crop lien Black and white farmers purchased goods on credit from local merchants. The merchant demanded collateral in the form of a lien on the crop, typically cotton. If the farmer failed to repay the loan, the merchant had the legal right to seize the crop.

Deindustrialization Beginning in the late 1960s major manufacturing companies and industries moved the production of their goods and products off shore and relocated to countries with lower wage standards and little protection against labor exploitation. While companies maximized profits, the closing of plants and loss of jobs at home had a devastating impact on black workers whose high unemployment rates continued to soar into the new millennium.

Disfranchisement White southern Democrats devised a variety of techniques in the late nineteenth and early twentieth centuries to prevent black people from voting. Those techniques included literacy tests, poll taxes, and the grandfather clause as well as intimidation and violence.

Divination A form of magic aimed at telling the future by interpreting a variety of signs.

Domestic slave trade A trade dating from the first decade of the nineteenth century in American-born slaves purchased primarily in the border South and sent overland or by sea to the cotton growing regions of the Old Southwest.

"Double V" campaign Slogan during World War II that stood for victory over fascism abroad and over racism at home for blacks.

Dred Scott v. Sandford The 1857 U.S. Supreme Court case that ruled against Missouri slave Dred Scott by declaring that black people were not citizens, possessed no constitutional rights, and were considered to be property.

Economic Opportunity Act of 1964 Federal law creating the Office of Economic Opportunity and a number of programs aimed at poor communities.

Ellenton Riot Between 30 and 100 African Americans were killed by marauding white men in September 1876 in Aiken County, South Carolina, after an alleged assault by a black man on an elderly white woman.

Emancipation Proclamation Issued by President Abraham Lincoln on January 1, 1863, the Emancipation Proclamation freed slaves in areas of the Confederate states not under Union control.

Enforcement Acts   Also known as the Force Acts, these measures were passed by Congress in the early 1870s to undermine the Ku Klux Klan and other terrorist organizations by authorizing the president to use military force and to suspend the writ of *habeas corpus*.

Executive Order 8802   Order issued by President Franklin D. Roosevelt in 1941 banning discrimination in employment in defense industries and the federal government.

Executive Order 9346   Order establishing a new Committee on Fair Employment Practices, with greater resources and direct oversight by the Executive Office of the president.

Executive Order 9981   Order issued by President Harry Truman in 1948 desegregating the armed forces.

Exodusters   Black migrants who left the South during and after Reconstruction and settled in Kansas, often in all-black towns.

Factories   Headquarters for a European company that traded for slaves or engaged in other commercial enterprises on the West African coast.

Fair Employment Practices Committee (FEPC)   A committee created by Franklin Roosevelt to investigate complaints of discrimination.

Fair Play Committee   Organization formed to promote black actors in the movie industry and improve the image of blacks in film.

Family Assistance Plan (FAP)   Plan giving financial assistance to families with no wage earner.

Federal Arts Project   New Deal agency formed to promote the creation of public art.

Federal Elections Bill   A measure, also known as the Force bill, to protect the voting rights of black men in the South by providing federal supervision of elections. It passed in the House of Representatives but failed in the Senate.

Fetish   A natural object or an artifact believed to have magical power. A charm.

Fifteenth Amendment   This constitutional amendment stipulated that the right to vote could not be denied on account of race, color, or because a person had been a slave.

First Confiscation Act   This 1861 Act stated that any slaves used by their masters to benefit the Confederacy would be freed.

First South Carolina Volunteers   This black military unit consisted of former slaves recruited in the South Carolina and Georgia low country in 1862 and 1863 for service with Union military forces in the Civil War.

Fort Pillow   This fort on the east bank of the Mississippi River north of Memphis, Tennessee, was the scene of a massacre of black Union troops as well as some white soldiers and officers by Confederate cavalry in April 1864.

Forty-Niners   The men and women who rushed to California in 1849 after gold had been discovered there.

Fourteenth Amendment   This amendment ratified during Reconstruction made any person born in the United States a citizen of the United States and of the state in which they lived.

Free labor   Mid-nineteenth-century Americans who were free and worked for income or compensation to advance themselves, as opposed to slave labor, which was work done with no financial compensation by people who were not free.

Free papers   Proof of freedom that free black people had to carry at all times in the southern states prior to emancipation. The papers, issued by state governments, identified an individual by name, age, sex, color, height, and so forth.

Free-Soil Party   An almost entirely northern political coalition from 1848 to 1853 opposed to the expansion of slavery into western territories. It included former supporters of the Whig, Democratic, and Liberty parties.

Freedmen's Bureau   Congress established the Bureau of Refugees, Freedmen, and Abandoned Lands in February 1865 to assist black and white southerners left destitute by the Civil War.

Freedmen's Savings Bank   A private financial institution chartered by Congress in 1865. Many black people and organizations deposited funds in the bank, which went bankrupt in 1874.

Freedom Rides   Effort in 1961 to desegregate interstate bus and rail travel.

Freedom suits   Legal cases in which slaves sued their master or master's heirs for freedom.

French and Indian War   A war between Great Britain and its American Indian allies and France and its American Indian allies, fought between 1754 and 1763 for control of the eastern portion of North America.

Fugitive Slave Act of 1793   An act of Congress permitting masters to recapture escaped slaves who had reached the free states and, with the authorization of local courts, return with the slave or slaves to their home state.

Fugitive Slave Law of 1850   Part of the Compromise of 1850. It required law enforcement officials as well as civilians to assist in capturing runaway slaves.

Fur trade   A North American colonial industry involving American Indians trapping fur-bearing animals (chiefly beavers) and exchanging their pelts for European products.

Gang system   A mode of organizing labor that had West African antecedents. In this system, American slaves worked in groups under the direction of a slave driver.

Gangsta rap   A genre of rap music characterized by violent and sexist lyrics.

Gary Convention   Meeting of black leaders and organizations in Gary, Indiana, to develop an agenda for black empowerment.

General Order 11   Order threatening retaliation for the mistreatment of black soldiers by Confederate forces.

Grandfather clause   A method southern states used to disfranchise black men. It stipulated that only men whose grandfathers were eligible to vote were themselves eligible to vote. The U.S. Supreme Court invalidated the grandfather clause in 1915.

Great Dismal Swamp   A heavily forested area on the Virginia–North Carolina border that served as a refuge for fugitive slaves during the eighteenth and nineteenth centuries.

Griot   A West African self-employed poet and oral historian.

Guinea Coast   The southward-facing coast of West Africa, from which many of the people caught up in the Atlantic slave trade departed for the Americas.

Habeas corpus   A court order that a person arrested or detained by law enforcement officers must be brought to court and charged with a crime and not held indefinitely.

Hamburg Massacre   White Democrats attacked black Republicans in July 1876 in the village of Hamburg, South Carolina. Five black men were murdered as the Democrats began a violent effort to redeem the state.

Harlem Renaissance   As New York City became a destination for black migrants before, during, and after World War I, most of them settled in Harlem—a large neighborhood in the northern portion of Manhattan Island—which by the 1920s became a center of African-American cultural activities including literature, art, and music.

Hierarchical   Refers to a social system based on class rank.

Hieroglyphics   A writing system based on pictures or symbols.

Hip-hop   The backup music for rap. It is also the term for the youth culture that developed with the rise of rap music.

Hired their own time   Refers to a practice in which a master allowed slaves to work for wages paid by someone other than the master himself.

Hominids   The biological family to which humans belong.

House of Burgesses   A representative body established at Jamestown, Virginia, in 1619.

House Un-American Activities Committee (HUAC)   Congressional committee formed to investigate the activities of communists and "communist sympathizers" in America.

Humanism   The belief that human achievement and interests are more important than theological issues.

Hunting-and-gathering societies   Small societies dependent on hunting animals and collecting wild plants rather than on agriculture.

Ideology   A body of ideas that presents a coherent view of human society and politics.

Immediatism   Refers to an antislavery movement that began in the United States during the late 1820s which demanded that slavery be abolished immediately rather than gradually.

Import duties   Taxes on goods brought into a country or colony.

Impressment   During the Civil War, Southern states and the Confederate government required slave owners to provide slaves to work on such public projects as fortifications, roads, and wharves. The owners (not the slaves) were usually compensated for the work.

Incest taboos   Customary rules against sexual relations and marriage within family and kinship groups.

Indentured servant   An individual who sells or loses his or her freedom for a specified number of years.

Indigo   A bluish-violet dye produced from the indigo plant.

Industrial Revolution   An economic change that began in England during the early eighteenth century and spread to Continental Europe and the United States. Industry rather than agriculture became the dominant form of enterprise.

Jim Crow   Jump Jim Crow was a nineteenth-century dance ridiculing black people that was transformed by the twentieth century into a term meaning racial discrimination and segregation; also a term used to describe railroad cars set aside for black people.

John Brown's raid   Brown's raid on Harpers Ferry, Virginia, in October 1859 failed to lead to a major slave insurrection, but it inflamed the controversy over slavery in the North and South.

Joint-stock companies   Primitive corporations that carried out British and Dutch colonization in the Americas during the seventeenth century.

Kansas-Nebraska Act   Legislation introduced by Democratic Senator Stephen Douglas in 1854 to organize the Kansas and Nebraska territories. It provided for "popular sovereignty," whereby settlers would decide whether slavery would be legal or illegal.

"Know-Nothing Party"   The nickname applied to members of the American Party, which opposed immigration in the 1850s.

Ku Klux Klan   A secret society founded by former Confederates in Pulaski, Tennessee, in 1866. It transformed itself into a terrorist organization during Reconstruction to drive black and white Republicans from political power in southern states.

Liberty Party (1840–1848)   The first antislavery political party. Most of its supporters joined the Free Soil Party in 1848, although its radical New York wing maintained a Liberty organization into the 1850s.

Lien   When black and white farmers purchased goods on credit from local merchants. The merchant demanded collateral in the form of a lien on the crop, typically cotton. If the farmer failed to repay the loan, the merchant had a legal right to seize the crop.

Lincoln-Douglas debates   Abraham Lincoln and Stephen Douglas debated seven times in the 1858 U.S. Senate race in Illinois. They spent most of their time arguing over slavery, its expansion, the *Dred Scott* decision, and the character of African Americans. Douglas won the election.

Lineage   A type of clan, typical of West Africa, in which members claim descent from a single ancestor.

Low country   The coastal regions of South Carolina and Georgia.

Lowndes County Freedom Organization (LCFO)   Political organization founded in 1965.

Loyalists   Those Americans who, during the Revolutionary War, wished to remain within the British Empire.

Lyceum   A public lecture hall.

Lynching   Killing by a mob without the benefit of a trial or conviction.

Manifest Destiny   Doctrine, first expressed in 1845, that the expansion of white Americans across the continent was inevitable and ordained by God.

Manumission   The act of freeing a slave by the slave's master.

March on Washington Movement (MOWM)   Movement created by A. Philip Randolph to pressure the federal government to end discrimination in the defense industry and government.

Market revolution   The process between 1800 and 1860 by which an American economy based on subsistence farming, production by skilled artisans, and local markets changed into an economy marked by commercial farming, factory production, and national markets.

Martinique   An island in the eastern Caribbean Sea that was a French sugar-producing colony from the seventeenth into the nineteenth century.

Matrilineal   Descent traced through the female line.

Mercenaries   German troops hired to fight on the British side.

Middle Passage   The voyage of slave ships (slavers) across the Atlantic Ocean from Africa to the Americas.

Militia Act of 1862   The 1862 Act authorizing Lincoln to enlist black soldiers.

Mississippi Freedom Democratic Party (MFDP)   Interracial group set up to challenge Mississippi's all-white delegation to the Democratic National Convention in 1964.

Missouri Compromise, 1820   A congressional attempt to settle the issue of slavery expansion in the United States by permitting Missouri to enter the Union as a slave state, admitting Maine as a free state, and banning slavery in the rest of the Louisiana Purchase north of the 36° 30' line of latitude.

Montgomery Bus Boycott   Refusal from 1955 to 1957 of African Americans in Montgomery, Alabama, to ride the city's buses until the bus lines were desegregated.

Moral suasion   A tactic endorsed by the American Anti-Slavery Society during the 1830s. It appealed to slaveholders and others to support immediate emancipation on the basis of Christian principles.

Moynihan Report   Report attributing many of the problems of poor black communities to the breakdown of the "lower-class" black family.

Nation of Islam (NOI)   A religious group composed of African-American Muslims currently headed by Minister Louis Farrakhan.

National Industrial Recovery Act (NIRA)   Federal law intended to promote the revival of manufacturing by allowing for cooperation among industries.

National Negro Congress (NNC)   Organization founded in 1936 to unite African-American protest groups.

Negro National League   A professional baseball league for black players and teams organized in 1912.

New Deal   Set of policies proposed by the Roosevelt administration in response to the Great Depression.

New York City draft riot   In early July 1863, in opposition to the forthcoming military draft, rioting erupted in New York City. Many of the victims were black men, women, and children.

North Atlantic Treaty Organization (NATO)   Military alliance formed to counter the threat posed by the Soviet Union and its allies.

North Star   A weekly newspaper published and edited by Frederick Douglass from 1847 to 1851. *Frederick Douglass' Paper* (1851–1860) succeeded it.

Northwest Ordinance   Based on earlier legislation drafted by Thomas Jefferson, it organized the Northwest Territory, providing for orderly land sales, public education, government, the creation of five to seven states out of the territory, and the prohibition of slavery within the territory.

Nuclear family   A family unit consisting solely of one set of parents and their children.

Nullification Crisis   Occurred between 1832 and 1833; arose when the South Carolina legislature declared the United States tariff "null and void" within the state's borders.

Orangeburg Massacre   On February 8, 1968, three students were killed and 28 were injured on the campus of South Carolina State College when Highway Patrolmen opened fire. Students had been protesting the persistence of segregation in the community.

Pamphlet   A short published essay.

Pan-Africanism   A movement of people of African descent from sub-Saharan Africa in the early twentieth century that emphasized their identity, shared experiences, and the need to liberate Africa from its European colonizers.

Patriarchal   A society ruled by a senior man.

Patrilineal   Descent through the male line.

Patriots   Those Americans who, during the Revolutionary War, favored independence.

Peace Mission Movement   Religious movement led by Father Major Jealous Divine.

Peonage   The system that forbade southern farmers, usually sharecroppers and renters, who accumulated debts to leave the land until the debt was repaid—often an impossible task.

Philadelphia Female Anti-Slavery Society   A biracial abolitionist organization (1833–1870) aligned with the American Anti-Slavery Society. White Quaker women dominated the society, but it included a significant number of black women.

Pidgin   A simplified mixture of two or more languages used to communicate between people who speak different languages.

Planter elite   Those who owned the largest tobacco plantations.

Plessy v. Ferguson   In 1896 in an 8-to-1 decision, the U.S. Supreme Court ruled that segregation did not violate the equal protection clause of the Fourteenth Amendment. The "separate but equal" doctrine remained the supreme law of the land until the 1954 *Brown v. Board of Education* decision overturned *Plessy*.

Polygynous family   A family unit consisting of a man, his wives, and their children.

Polytheistic   Many gods.

Poor People's Campaign   Project supported by Martin Luther King, involving the march of tens of thousands of poor people on Washington.

Popular sovereignty   A proposal in which the residents of a territory (such as Kansas) would vote to legalize or prohibit slavery in that territory.

Populist Party   Also known as the Peoples' Party, the Populists supported inflation; the free and unlimited coinage of silver and gold; government ownership of railroads, telephone, and telegraph companies; and an eight-hour workday. They won state and congressional elections but lost the presidential contests in 1892 and 1896.

Port Royal Experiment   An effort by northern white missionaries, educators, and businessmen in the Sea Islands near Beaufort, South Carolina, to transform former slaves into educated, reliable, and industrious wage earners. Most of the freedmen did not acquire the land they worked.

Preliminary Emancipation Proclamation   Proclamation issued on September 22, 1862, declaring that slaves residing in states still in rebellion on January 1, 1863, would be freed.

Prince Hall Masons   A black Masonic order formed in 1791 in Boston under the leadership of Prince Hall. He became its first grand master and promoted its expansion to other cities.

Privateers   Merchant vessels armed and authorized to a government to raid enemy shipping.

Project 100,000   Military project with the goal of reducing the number of African Americans rejected by the military.

Race films   Movies often made by and for African-American audiences in the 1930s and 1940s.

Radical Republicans   Members of the Republican Party during Reconstruction who vigorously supported the rights of African Americans to vote, hold political office, and have the same legal and economic opportunities as white people.

Rain forest   A dense growth of tall trees characteristic of hot, wet regions.

Rainbow Coalition   Political coalition of African Americans, workers, liberals, feminists, gay people, environmentalists, and others formed by Jesse Jackson in the 1980s.

Reconstruction   The 12 years (1865–1877) following the Civil War during which the former Confederate states were restored to the Union and former slaves became citizens and gained the right to vote and hold political office. It was also a time of violence and terrorism as many southern white people resisted the change in the status of African Americans.

Reconstruction Acts   Led by Radical Republicans, Congress divided the South into five military districts. Each former Confederate state (except Tennessee) was to frame a new state constitution and establish a new state government. The first Reconstruction Act provided for universal manhood suffrage, which granted the right to vote to all adult males, including black men.

Red Scare   The widespread fear among many Americans in the years immediately after World War I from about 1918 to about 1924 that Russia's 1917 Bolshevik Revolution might result in communists attempting to take over the U.S. government.

Redemption   The term used for the process, often violent, by which white conservative Democrats regained political control of a southern state from black and white Republicans during Reconstruction.

Rochester Convention   African-American leaders assembled in Rochester, New York, in 1853 to discuss slavery, abolition, the recently passed Fugitive Slave Law, and their prospects for life in America.

Savanna   A flat, nearly treeless grassland typical of large portions of West Africa.

Scalawag   The derogatory term used during Reconstruction to identify a native white southerner who supported black and white Republicans. They were considered traitors to their people and the Democratic Party.

Scottsboro Boys   Nine young African-American men unjustly accused of raping two white women in Alabama in 1931. The Supreme Court overturned their convictions in 1937.

Seasoning   The process by which newly arrived Africans were broken in to slavery in the Americas.

Second Confiscation Act   The 1862 act freeing all slaves of rebel owners.

Second Great Awakening   A series of religious revivals in the first half of the nineteenth century characterized by great emotionalism in large public meetings.

Secret societies   Social organizations that have secret ceremonies that only their members know about and can participate in.

Secularism   The belief that the present public welfare should predominate over religion in civil affairs.

Segregation   The separation of people based on their race in the use of such public facilities as hotels, restaurants, restrooms, drinking fountains, parks, and auditoriums. In many instances, segregation meant the exclusion of black people.

Semitic   Refers to languages, such as Arabic and Hebrew, native to southwest Asia.

Sharecropping   The system following the Civil War in which former slaves worked land owned by white people and "paid" for the use of the land and for tools, seeds, fertilizer, and mules by sharing the crop—usually cotton—with the owner.

Shotgun policy   In Mississippi in 1875, white men resorted to violence and intimidation against black and white Republicans to regain political control of the state for conservative Democrats.

Slave codes   Sometimes known as "black codes," a series of laws passed to define slaves as property and specify the legal powers of masters over slaves.

Slave power   A key concept in abolitionist and northern antislavery propaganda that depicted southern slaveholders as the driving force in a political conspiracy to promote slavery at the expense of white liberties.

Slaver   A ship used to transport slaves from Africa to the Americas.

Social Darwinism   Derived from Charles Darwin's theory of evolution, Herbert Spencer and William Graham Sumner asserted that life in modern society was competitive and only those individuals who were mentally, emotionally, and physically strong would prevail.

Sons of Liberty   A secret American organization formed in the Northeast during the summer of 1765 and committed to forcible opposition to the Stamp Act.

Southern Christian Leadership Conference (SCLC)   Organization spearheaded by Martin Luther King, Jr. to provide an institutional base for the civil rights movement.

Southern Homestead Act   Congress passed this measure in 1866 that set aside over three million acres of land for former slaves and loyal white southerners to farm following the Civil War. Most of the land was not fertile or suitable for agriculture, and the act largely failed.

Southern Regional Council (SRC)   Organization that conducted research and focused attention on social, political, and educational inequality in the South.

Spanish Armada   A fleet that unsuccessfully attempted to carry out an invasion of England in 1588.

Special Field Order #15   General William Tecumseh Sherman issued this military directive in January 1865. It set aside lands along the coast from Charleston, South Carolina, to Jacksonville, Florida, for former slaves. President Andrew Johnson revoked the order six months later.

Spirit possession   A belief rooted in West African religions that spirits may possess human souls.

Student Nonviolent Coordinating Committee (SNCC)   Civil rights organization founded by black college students in 1960 at the initiative of Ella Baker.

Syracuse Convention   A meeting of black leaders in Syracuse, New York, to discuss the future of African Americans following the abolition of slavery. They insisted that black people had earned and deserved the same political and legal rights as white Americans.

Talented Tenth   Term coined by W. E. B. Du Bois for the educated black elite of the late nineteenth and early twentieth centuries. The upper 10 percent was supposed to assume responsibility for the leadership and advancement of the remaining 90 percent of African Americans.

Ten-Point Program   The Black Panther Party under the leadership of Huey Newton and Bobby Seale devised a ten-point platform to help black people achieve liberation including demands for exemption from military service, freedom for all political prisoners, and an end to police brutality. It also asserted black people's rights to decent housing, jobs, and an empowering education.

Term slavery   A type of slavery prevalent in the Chesapeake from the late 1700s to the Civil War in which slaves were able to purchase their freedom from their masters by earning money over a number of years.

Terra-cotta   A hard, waterproof, ceramic clay.

Thirteenth Amendment   This amendment to the U.S. Constitution outlawed slavery and involuntary servitude.

Three-Fifths Clause   A clause in the U.S. Constitution providing that a slave be counted as three-fifths of a free person in determining a state's representation in Congress and the electoral college and three-fifths of a free person in regard to per capita taxes levied by Congress on the states.

Tuskegee Airmen   All-black combat air unit during World War II.

Tuskegee Machine   As the president of Tuskegee Institute, Booker T. Washington developed an extensive network of contacts that gave him extraordinary influence with white political leaders and philanthropists as well as with black businesspeople, journalists, and college presidents.

Tuskegee Study   A medical study by the U.S. Public Health Service of the effects of syphilis on 622 black men. The study ran from 1932 to the 1970s, and the men were never given treatment when new therapeutics were discovered that could have saved the lives of many of them and members of their families.

Uncle Tom's Cabin   This antislavery novel by Harriet Beecher Stowe was a best seller in the 1850s and it helped inflame the controversy over slavery.

Underground railroad   Refers to several loosely organized, semi-secret biracial networks that helped slaves escape from the border South to the North and Canada. The earliest networks appeared during the first decade of the nineteenth century; others operated into the Civil War years.

Union League   A social and fraternal organization that stirred political interest and support among black and white Republicans in the South during Reconstruction.

Universal Negro Improvement Association (UNIA)   Established in 1914 in Jamaica by Marcus Garvey, it fostered racial pride, African heritage, Christian faith, and economic uplift.

Voting Rights Act of 1965   Federal law banning the methods that had systematically excluded African Americans from registering or voting in southern elections.

White Primary law   The white primary law was a Texas law banning African-American participation in the Democratic primary.

Wilmot Proviso   A measure initially introduced in Congress in 1845 to prohibit slavery in any lands acquired from Mexico. It did not pass.

Presidents and Vice Presidents of the United States*

President	Vice President
1. George Washington (1789)	John Adams (1789)
2. John Adams (1797)	Thomas Jefferson (1797)
3. Thomas Jefferson (1801)	Aaron Burr (1801)
	George Clinton (1805)
4. James Madison (1809)	George Clinton (1809)
	Elbridge Gerry (1813)
5. James Monroe (1817)	Daniel D. Tompkins (1817)
6. John Quincy Adams (1825)	John C. Calhoun (1825)
7. Andrew Jackson (1829)	John C. Calhoun (1829)
	Martin Van Buren (1833)
8. Martin Van Buren (1837)	Richard M. Johnson (1837)
9. William H. Harrison (1841)	John Tyler (1841)
10. John Tyler (1841)	
11. James K. Polk (1845)	George M. Dallas (1845)
12. Zachary Taylor (1849)	Millard Fillmore (1849)
13. Millard Fillmore (1850)	
14. Franklin Pierce (1853)	William R. King (1853)
15. James Buchanan (1857)	John C. Breckinridge (1857)
16. Abraham Lincoln (1861)	Hannibal Hamlin (1861)
	Andrew Johnson (1865)
17. Andrew Johnson (1865)	
18. Ulysses S. Grant (1869)	Schuyler Colfax (1869)
	Henry Wilson (1873)
19. Rutherford B. Hayes (1877)	William A. Wheeler (1877)
20. James A. Garfield (1881)	Chester A. Arthur (1881)
21. Chester A. Arthur (1881)	
22. Grover Cleveland (1885)	Thomas A. Hendricks (1885)
23. Benjamin Harrison (1889)	Levi P. Morton (1889)

President	Vice President
24. Grover Cleveland (1893)	Adlai E. Stevenson (1893)
25. William McKinley (1897)	Garret A. Hobart (1897)
	Theodore Roosevelt (1901)
26. Theodore Roosevelt (1901)	Charles Fairbanks (1905)
27. William H. Taft (1909)	James S. Sherman (1909)
28. Woodrow Wilson (1913)	Thomas R. Marshall (1913)
29. Warren G. Harding (1921)	Calvin Coolidge (1921)
30. Calvin Coolidge (1923)	Charles G. Dawes (1925)
31. Herbert C. Hoover (1929)	Charles Curtis (1929)
32. Franklin D. Roosevelt (1933)	John Nance Garner (1933)
	Henry A. Wallace (1941)
	Harry S Truman (1945)
33. Harry S Truman (1945)	Alben W. Barkley (1949)
34. Dwight D. Eisenhower (1953)	Richard M. Nixon (1953)
35. John F. Kennedy (1961)	Lyndon B. Johnson (1961)
36. Lyndon B. Johnson (1963)	Hubert H. Humphrey (1965)
37. Richard M. Nixon (1969)	Spiro T. Agnew (1969)
	Gerald R. Ford (1973)
38. Gerald R. Ford (1974)	Nelson A. Rockefeller (1974)
39. James E. Carter, Jr. (1977)	Walter F. Mondale (1977)
40. Ronald W. Reagan (1981)	George H. Bush (1981)
41. George H. Bush (1989)	James D. Quayle III (1989)
42. William J. Clinton (1993)	Albert Gore (1993)
43. George W. Bush (2001)	Richard B. Cheney (2001)
44. Barack H. Obama (2009)	Joseph R. Biden (2009)

* Year of inauguration

Historically Black Four-Year Colleges and Universities

Institution and Location	Year Founded	Land-Grant, Public, Private, or Church-Affiliated Denomination
Alabama A&M University, Normal, Alabama	1875	Land-grant
Alabama State University, Montgomery, Alabama	1867	Public
Albany State University, Albany, Georgia	1903	Public
Alcorn State University, Lorman, Mississippi	1871	Land-grant
Allen University, Columbia, South Carolina	1870	AME
Arkansas Baptist College, Little Rock, Arkansas	1884	Baptist
Barber-Scotia College, Concord, North Carolina	1904	Presbyterian
Benedict College, Columbia, South Carolina	1870	Baptist
Bennett College, Greensboro, North Carolina	1873	United Methodist
Bethune-Cookman College, Daytona Beach, Florida	1904	United Methodist
Bluefield State College, Bluefield, West Virginia	1895	Public
Bowie State University, Bowie, Maryland	1865	Public
Central State University, Wilberforce, Ohio	1887	Public
Cheyney University, Cheyney, Pennsylvania	1837	Public
Claflin College, Orangeburg, South Carolina	1869	United Methodist
Clark Atlanta University, Atlanta, Georgia	1988	United Methodist
Concordia College, Selma, Alabama	1922	Lutheran
Coppin State University, Baltimore, Maryland	1900	Public
Delaware State University, Dover, Delaware	1891	Land-grant
Dillard University, New Orleans, Louisiana	1930	Congregational/United Methodist
Edward Waters College, Jacksonville, Florida	1866	AME
Elizabeth City State University, Elizabeth City, North Carolina	1891	Public
Fayetteville State University, Fayetteville, North Carolina	1867	Public
Fisk University, Nashville, Tennessee	1866	United Church of Christ
Florida A&M University, Tallahassee, Florida	1887	Land-grant
Florida Memorial College, Miami, Florida	1879	Baptist
Fort Valley State College, Fort Valley, Georgia	1895	Land-grant
Grambling State University, Grambling, Louisiana	1901	Public
Hampton University, Hampton, Virginia	1868	Private
Harris-Stowe State College, St. Louis, Missouri	1857	Public
Howard University, Washington, DC	1867	Public
Huston-Tillotson University, Austin, Texas	1952	United Church of Christ/United Methodist
Jackson State University, Jackson, Mississippi	1877	Public
Jarvis Christian College, Hawkins, Texas	1913	Disciple of Christ Christian Church
Johnson C. Smith University, Charlotte, North Carolina	1867	Presbyterian
Kentucky State University, Frankfort, Kentucky	1886	Land-grant
Lane College, Jackson, Tennessee	1882	Christian Methodist Episcopal
Langston University, Langston, Oklahoma	1897	Land-grant

Institution and Location	Year Founded	Land-Grant, Public, Private, or Church-Affiliated Denomination
LeMoyne-Owen College, Memphis, Tennessee	1870	United Church of Christ
Lincoln University, Jefferson City, Missouri	1866	Land-grant
Lincoln University, Lincoln, Pennsylvania	1854	Public
Livingstone College, Salisbury, North Carolina	1879	AME
Miles College, Birmingham, Alabama	1908	Christian Methodist Episcopal
Mississippi Valley State University, Itta Bena, Mississippi	1946	Public
Morehouse College, Atlanta, Georgia	1867	Baptist
Morgan State University, Baltimore, Maryland	1867	Public
Morris Brown College, Atlanta, Georgia	1881	AME
Morris College, Sumter, South Carolina	1908	Baptist
Norfolk State University, Norfolk, Virginia	1935	Public
North Carolina A&T State University, Greensboro, North Carolina	1892	Land-grant
North Carolina Central University, Durham, North Carolina	1909	Public
Oakwood College, Huntsville, Alabama	1896	Seventh-Day Adventist
Paine College, Augusta, Georgia	1882	United Methodist
Paul Quinn College, Dallas, Texas	1872	AME
Philander Smith College, Little Rock, Arkansas	1877	United Methodist
Prairie View A&M University, Prairie View, Texas	1878	Land-grant
Rust College, Holly Springs, Mississippi	1866	United Methodist
Saint Augustine's College, Raleigh, North Carolina	1867	Episcopal
Savannah State University, Savannah, Georgia	1890	Public
Selma University, Selma, Alabama	1878	Baptist
Shaw University, Raleigh, North Carolina	1865	Baptist
Sojourner-Douglass College, Baltimore, Maryland	1980	Private
South Carolina State University, Orangeburg, South Carolina	1896	Land-grant
Southern University and A&M College, Baton Rouge, Louisiana	1880	Land-grant
Southern University at New Orleans, New Orleans, Louisiana	1956	Public
Southwestern Christian College, Terrell, Texas	1949	Church of Christ
Spelman College, Atlanta, Georgia	1876	Presbyterian
Stillman College, Tuscaloosa, Alabama	1876	Presbyterian
Talladega College, Talladega, Alabama	1867	United Church of Christ
Tennessee State University, Nashville, Tennessee	1912	Land-grant
Texas College, Tyler, Texas	1894	Christian Methodist Episcopal
Texas Southern University, Houston, Texas	1947	Public
Tougaloo College, Tougaloo, Mississippi	1869	United Church of Christ/United Missionary Society
Tuskegee University, Tuskegee, Alabama	1881	Private
University of Arkansas at Pine Bluff, Pine Bluff, Arkansas	1873	Land-grant
University of the District of Columbia, Washington, D.C.	1977	Public
University of Maryland Eastern Shore, Princess Anne, Maryland	1886	Land-grant
University of the Virgin Islands, St. Thomas, United States Virgin Islands	1962	Public
Virginia State University, Petersburg, Virginia	1882	Land-grant

Institution and Location	Year Founded	Land-Grant, Public, Private, or Church-Affiliated Denomination
Virginia Union University, Richmond, Virginia	1865	Baptist
Voorhees College, Denmark, South Carolina	1897	Episcopal
West Virginia State College, Institute, West Virginia	1891	Public
Wilberforce University, Wilberforce, Ohio	1856	AME
Wiley College, Marshall, Texas	1873	United Methodist
Winston-Salem State University, Winston-Salem, North Carolina	1892	Public
Xavier University of New Orleans, New Orleans, Louisiana	1925	Roman Catholic

Photo and Text Credits

Photo, 611; Library of Congress Prints and Photographs Division [LC-USW3-022991-C], 616; Everett Collection Historical/Alamy Stock Photo, 617.

Part VI: Three Lions/Getty Images, 618; Ezra Shaw/Getty Images, 618; Library of Congress Prints and Photographs Division [LC-USZ62-60139], 618; Doug Mills/AP Images, 618; Library of Congress Prints and Photographs Division [LC-DIG-ppmsc-01266], 618; Library of Congress Prints and Photographs Division [LC-U9- 32512-12], 619; Library of Congress Prints and Photographs Division [LC-DIG-ppmsc-01265], 619; ITAR-TASS Photo Agency/Alamy Stock Photo, 619.

Chapter 21: AP Images, 620; Excerpted from *The Thunder of Angels* by Donnie Williams with Wayne Greenhaw. Copyright © 2006 by Donnie Williams with Wayne Greenhaw. Used with permission of Lawrence Hill Books, 621; Bettmann/Corbis, 624; Everett Collection Historical/Alamy Stock Photo, 625; Carl Iwasaki/The LIFE Images Collection/Getty Images, 627; Everett Collection, 629; From *Claudette Colvin: Twice Towards Justice* © 2009 by Phillip Hoose. Reprinted by permission of Farrar, Straus and Giroux, LLC. All Rights Reserved. 630; Don Cravens/The LIFE Images Collection/Getty Images, 633; Estate of Bayard Rustin, 635; AP Images, 636; St Petersburg Times/ZUMAPRESS/Newscom, 638; John G. Moebes/Corbis, 639; Bettmann/Corbis, 641; 1964 Steve Schapiro/Black Star/Newscom, 642; Bettmann/Corbis, 645; MPI/Getty Images, 652; Library of Congress Prints and Photographs Division [LC-DIG-fsa-8a26761], 653; Express Newspapers/Getty Images, 655.

Chapter 22: Bettmann/Corbis, 662; Republished with permission of Perseus Books Group, from *The Autobiography of Medgar Evers: A Hero's Life and Legacy Revealed Through His Writings, Letters, and Speeches* by Myrlie Evers-Williams and Manning Marable (2006); permission conveyed through Copyright Clearance Center, Inc., 663; "By Any Means Necessary: The Life and Legacy of Malcolm X" by Manning Marable. Speech given at Metro State College, Denver, Colorado, February 21, 1992. Reprinted by permission from Leith Mullings, 667; Library of Congress Prints and Photographs Division [LC-USZ62-119478], 667; Bettmann/Corbis, 669; STF/AP Images, 670; San Francisco Examiner/AP Images, 670; Bettmann/Corbis, 672; Keystone-France/Gamma-Keystone Getty Images, 674; Pictorial Parade/Getty Images, 676; Everett Collection Inc/Alamy Stock Photo, 677; National Archives and Records Administration, 679; Monty Fresco/Daily Mail/Rex/Alamy Stock Photo, 681; Henry Hampton Collection, Washington University Libraries, 681; *The True Import of Present Dialogue, Black vs. Negro*, Nikki Giovanni. Used by permission, 682; Everett Collection Inc/Alamy Stock Photo, 682; David Attie/Getty Images, 685; Lorraine Hansberry, "Life Challenges Negro Youth," *Freedom*, March 1955, p. 7. Used by permission, 685; AP Images, 687; Library of Congress Prints and Photographs Division [LC-DIG-ppmsc-01264], 694.

Chapter 23: White House Photo/Alamy Stock Photo, 704; Paul Conklin/PhotoEdit, Inc., 707; Mike Theiler/Reuters/Corbis, 711; Leighton Mark/Bettmann/Corbis, 711; Najlah Feanny/Corbis, 714; Peter Turnley/Corbis, 718; "Rodney King Beating Video" Copyright © 1991 George Holliday. All Rights Reserved, 719; Reprinted by permission from Earl Ofari Hutchinson, 720; TIM SLOAN/Getty Images, 722; Nati Harnik/AP Images, 727; Marko Georgiev/Getty Images, 730; Everett Collection Inc/Alamy Stock Photo, 734; Nancy Stone/Pool/Getty Images, 736; Joseph Sohm/Visions of America, LLC/Alamy Stock Photo, 741; Ben Baker/Redux Pictures, 741.

Chapter 24: ZUMA Press, Inc./Alamy Stock Photo, 749; Steven L. Raymer/National Geographic/Getty Images, 752; Michael Macor/San Francisco Chronicle/Corbis, 754; Viviane Moos/Corbis, 758; AP Images, 761; Rusty Kennedy/AP Images, 762; Dr. Molefi Kete Asante, 765; Al Behrman/AP Images, 769; Scott Olson/Getty Images, 771; David Grossman/The Image Works, 775; Herb Snitzer/Getty Images, 784; Address speech by Kirkland W. Green in *Black History Week* in 1935. Vol. 13 - No. 6, March 1935. Used with permission from South Carolina State University, 784; Jeff Vespa/Contour/Getty Images, 785.

Index